REEDS

PRACTICAL
Boat
BRITAIN'S BEST-S

SMALL
ALM

2014

EDITORS

Rob Buttress & Perrin Towler

THE UNITED KINGDOM AND IRELAND
PLUS DENMARK TO THE GIRONDE

PLEASE SEE IMPORTANT SAFETY NOTE ON PAGE 2

REEDS
PRACTICAL Boat Owner
BRITAIN'S BEST-SELLING SAILING MAGAZINE

SMALL CRAFT ALMANAC
2014

Editors: Rob Buttress & Perrin Towler

The Editors would like to thank the many official bodies who have kindly provided essential information in the preparation of this Almanac. They include the UK Hydrographic Office, Trinity House, Northern Lighthouse Board, Irish Lights, HM Nautical Almanac Office, HM Stationery Office, HM Customs, Meteorological Office and the Maritime and Coastguard Agency.

Information from the Admiralty List of Lights, Admiralty Tide Tables and the Admiralty List of Radio Signals is reproduced with the permission of the UK Hydrographic Office and the Controller of HMSO. Extracts from the following are published by permission of the Controller of HM Stationery Office: International Code of Signals, 1969; Meteorological Office Weather Services for Shipping. Phases of the Moon and Sun/Moon rising and setting times are included by permission of HM Nautical Almanac Office. UK and Foreign tidal predictions are supplied by the UK Hydrographic Office, Taunton TA1 2DN. Acknowledgment is also made to the following authorities for permission to use tidal predictions stated: Danish Safety Administration, Farvandsvæsnet: Esbjerg. SHOM, France: Dunkerque, Dieppe, Le Havre, Cherbourg, St Malo, Brest, Pointe de Grave, Authorisation (No 103/2013). Rijkswaterstaat, The Netherlands: Vlissingen, and Hoek van Holland. BSH, Hamburg and Rostock: Helgoland, Wilhelmshaven and Cuxhaven (BSH 11123/2008-07). Vlaamse Hydrografie, Belgium: Zeebrugge. **Warning**: The UK Hydrographic Office has not verified the reproduced data and does not accept any liability for the accuracy of reproduction or any modifications made thereafter.

Corrections Any necessary corrections will be published on the website www.reedsalmanacs.co.uk. Data in this almanac is corrected up to Edition 25/2013 of the *Admiralty Notices to Mariners.*

IMPORTANT SAFETY NOTE AND LEGAL DISCLAIMER

This Almanac is intended as a navigational aid only and to assist with basic planning for your passage. The information, charts, maps and diagrams in this Almanac should not be relied on for navigational purposes and should always be used in conjunction with current official hydrographic data. Whilst every care has been taken in its compilation, this Almanac may contain inaccuracies and is no substitute for the relevant official hydrographic charts and data, which should always be consulted in advance of, and while, navigating in the relevant area. Before setting out you should also check local conditions with the harbourmaster or other appropriate office responsible for your intended area of navigation.

Before using any waypoint or coordinate listed in this Almanac it must first be plotted on an appropriate official hydrographic chart to check its usefulness, accuracy and appropriateness for the prevailing weather and tidal conditions.

To the extent that the editors or publishers become aware that corrections are required, these will be published on the website www.reedsalmanacs.co.uk. Readers should therefore regularly check the website for any such corrections. Data in this Almanac is corrected up to Edition 25/2013 of the Admiralty Notices to Mariners.

The publishers, editors and their agents accept no responsibility for any errors or omissions, or for any accident, loss or damage (including without limitation any indirect, consequential, special or exemplary damages) arising from the use or misuse of, or reliance upon, the information contained in this Almanac.

The decision to use and rely on any of the data in this Almanac is entirely at the discretion of, and is the sole responsibility of, the Skipper or other individual in control of the vessel in connection with which it is being used or relied upon.

Correspondence Letters on general matters should be addressed to info@reedsalmanacs.co.uk, or on nautical issues to editor.britishisles@reedsalmanacs.co.uk (British Isles excluding Channel Islands) editor.continental@reedsalmanacs. co.uk (Denmark to Gironde, including Channel Islands).

Practical Boat Owner is published monthly by IPC Magazines Ltd, Blue Fin Building, 110 Southwark Street, London SE1 0SU. For subscription enquiries and overseas orders call +44 (0)844 848 0848 or visit www.pbo.co.uk/subs.

The mark 'Reeds' is a registered trade mark of A & C Black Publishers Ltd, a wholly owned subsidiary of Bloomsbury Publishing Plc.

Almanac manager: Chris Stevens
Cartography & production: Chris Stevens

Adlard Coles Nautical
50 Bedford Square, London WC1B 3DP
Tel: +44 (0)207 631 5600
www.reedsalmanacs.co.uk

Foreword

Welcome to the PBO Small Craft Almanac 2014. If you spend your time afloat in UK waters, perhaps venturing across the Irish Sea or to France, Germany, Belgium, Denmark or the Netherlands, this should be the first book on your boat's bookshelf.

You'll find all the tidal information you need packed into this handy volume, complete with tidal curves, but the wealth of information doesn't end there. With cruising boaters in mind, we've added waypoints and pilotage information for major marks, hazards and port entrances, plus a detailed tidal atlas for the cruising areas covered by the almanac and tips on how to negotiate tricky tidal gates.

Contact details for harbour authorities and information on how to obtain and interpret weather forecasts, not forgetting at-a-glance checklists for safety procedures and first aid, make this almanac a must-have for any boat owner.

Together with the editors at Reeds, all of us at *Practical Boat Owner* wish you fair winds and sunny skies for the 2014 season.

David Pugh
Editor
Practical Boat Owner
Britain's biggest-selling yachting magazine

Contents

ABBREVIATIONS

AC, ACA	Admiralty chart, chart agent
AC	Shore power (electrical)
ACN	Adlard Coles Nautical
Al	Alternating lt
ALL	Admiralty list of lights
ALRS	Admiralty list of radio signals
ASD	Admiralty sailing directions (Pilot)
ATT	Admiralty tide tables
ATT	Atterisage (landfall/SWM) buoy
Bcn, Bn	Beacon
Bkwtr	Breakwater
BST	British summer time (DST)
CD	Chart datum
Cf	Compare, cross-refer to
CG	Coastguard
Ch	Channel (VHF)
chan.	Channel (navigational)
COG	Course over the ground
CROSS	Centre régional opérationnel de surveillance et sauvetage (MRCC)
CRS	Coast radio station(s)
DF	Direction finding
Dia	Diaphone (fog signal)
Dir Lt	Directional light
DSC	Digital selective calling
DST	Daylight saving time
DZ	Danger zone (buoy)
E	East
ECM	East cardinal mark (buoy/beacon)
ED	Existence doubtful, European datum
EPIRB	Emergency pos'n indicating radio bn
F	Fixed light. Beaufort wind force
FFL	Fixed and flashing lt
Fl	Flashing light
FM	Frequency modulation
FV	Fishing vessel
G	Green. Gravel
GMDSS	Global maritime distress & safety system
H, Hrs, h	Hour(s)
H24	Continuous
HAT	Highest astronomical tide
Hbr	Harbour
Hd	Head, headland
HF	High frequency
HJ	Day service, sunrise to sunset
HO	Office hours, Hydrographic office
ht	Height
HW	High water
HX	No fixed hours
Hz	Hertz
IALA	Int'l association of lt ho authorities
IDM	Isolated danger mark (buoy/bcn)
IMO	Int'l maritime organisation
Inmarsat	Int'l maritime satellite system
IPTS	Int'l port traffic signals
Is, I	Island, Islet
Iso	Isophase light
ITZ	Inshore traffic zone
Kn	Knot(s)
Lanby	Large automatic navigational buoy
Lat	Latitude
LB	Lifeboat
Ldg	Leading (lt)
LF	Low frequency
Long	Longitude
LT	Local time
Lt(s)	Light(s)
Lt F	Light float
Lt Ho	Lighthouse
Lt V	Light vessel
LW	Low water
M	Sea mile(s)
m	Metre(s)
MCA	Maritime & Coastguard Agency
Météo	Météorologie/weather
MF	Medium frequency
MHWN	Mean HW neaps
MHWS	Mean HW springs
MHz	Megahertz
MLWN	Mean LW neaps
MLWS	Mean LW springs
MMSI	Maritime mobile service identity
Mo	Morse
MRCC	Maritime rescue co-ordination centre
MRSC	Maritime rescue sub-centre (not in UK)
MSI	Maritime safety information
N	North
NCM	North cardinal mark (buoy/bcn)
Oc	Occulting light
PHM	Port-hand mark (buoy/bcn)
Pt(e), (a)	Point(e), Punta
Q	Quick flashing
R	Red. River
Ra	Coast radar station
Racon	Radar transponder beacon
RG	Emergency RDF station
R/T	Radiotelephony
S	South
s	second(s) of time
SAR	Search and rescue
SCM	South cardinal mark (buoy/bcn)
SHM	Starboard-hand mark (buoy/bcn)
Sig Stn	Signal station
SMS	Short message service (texting)
SNSM	Société nationale de sauvetage en mer (French LB service)
SOG	Speed over the ground
SOLAS	Safety of life at sea (Convention)
SPM	Special mark (buoy/bcn)
SRR	SAR Region
SSB	Single sideband (radio)
Stn	Station
SWM	Safe water mark, landfall buoy
Tfc	Traffic
TSS	Traffic separation scheme
UQ	Ultra quick flashing lt
UT	Universal time
VHF	Very high frequency
VNF	Voie navigable de France (canals)
VQ	Very quick flashing lt
VTS	Vessel traffic service
W	West, White
WCM	West cardinal mark (buoy/bcn)
WGS	World geodetic system (datum)
WIP	Work in progress
WPT	Waypoint
Y	Yellow, orange, amber

GENERAL VOCABULARY. See also weather vocabulary on page 105

ENGLISH	GERMAN	FRENCH	DUTCH
ASHORE			
Ashore	An Land	A terre	Aan land
Airport	Flughafen	Aéroport	Vliegveld
Bank	Bank	Banque	Bank
Boathoist	Bootskran	Travelift	Botenlift
Boatyard	Bootswerft	Chantier naval	Jachtwerf
Bureau de change	Wechselstelle	Bureau de change	Geldwisselkantoor
Bus	Bus	Autobus	Bus
Chandlery	Yachtausrüster	Shipchandler	Scheepswinkel
Chemist	Apotheke	Pharmacie	Apotheek
Dentist	Zahnarzt	Dentiste	Tandarts
Doctor	Arzt	Médecin	Dokter
Engineer	Motorenservice	Ingénieur/mécanique	Ingenieur
Ferry	Fähre	Ferry/transbordeur	Veer/Pont
Garage	Autowerkstatt	Station service	Garage
Harbour	Hafen	Port	Haven
Hospital	Krankenhaus	Hôpital	Ziekenhuis
Mast crane	Mastenkran	Grue	Masten kraan
Post office	Postamt	Bureau de poste/PTT	Postkantoor
Railway station	Bahnhof	Gare de chemin de fer	Station
Sailmaker	Segelmacher	Voilier	Zeilmaker
Shops	Geschäfte	Boutiques	Winkels
Slip	Slip	Cale	Helling
Supermarket	Supermarkt	Supermarché	Supermarkt
Taxi	Taxi	Taxi	Taxi
Village	Ort	Village	Dorp
Yacht club	Yachtclub	Club nautique	Jacht club
NAVIGATION			
Abeam	Querab	A côté	Naast
Ahead	Voraus	Avant	Voor
Astern	Achteraus	Arrière	Achter
Bearing	Peilung	Cap	Peiling
Buoy	Tonne	Bouée	Boei
Binoculars	Fernglas	Jumelles	Verrekijker
Channel	Kanal	Chenal	Kanaal
Chart	Seekarte	Carte	Zeekaart
Compass	Kompass	Compas	Kompas
Compass course	Kompass Kurs	Cap du compas	Kompas koers
Current	Strömung	Courant	Stroom
Dead reckoning	Koppelnavigation	Estime	Gegist bestek
Degree	Grad	Degré	Graden
Deviation	Deviation	Déviation	Deviatie
Distance	Entfernung	Distance	Afstand
Downstream	Flußabwärts	En aval	Stroom afwaards
East	Ost	Est	Oost
Ebb	Ebbe	Jusant	Eb
Echosounder	Echolot	Sondeur	Dieptemeter
Estimated position	Gegißte Position	Point estimé	Gegiste positie
Fathom	Faden	Une brasse	Vadem
Feet	Fuß	Pieds	Voet
Flood	Flut	Flot	Vloed
Handbearing compass	Handpeilkompass	Compas de relèvement	Handpeil kompas

ENGLISH	GERMAN	FRENCH	DUTCH
Harbour guide	Hafenhandbuch	Guide du port	Havengids
High water	Hochwasser	Peine mer	Hoog water
Latitude	Geographische Breite	Latitude	Breedte
Leading lights	Feuer in Linie	Alignement	Geleide lichten
Leeway	Abdrift	Dérive	Drift
Lighthouse	Leuchtturm	Phare	Vuurtoren
List of lights	Leuchtfeuer Verzeichnis	Liste des feux	Lichtenlijst
Log	Logge	Loch	Log
Longitude	Geographische Länge	Longitude	Lengte
Low water	Niedrigwasser	Basse mer	Laag water
Metre	Meter	Mètre	Meter
Minute	Minute	Minute	Minuut
Nautical almanac	Nautischer Almanach	Almanach nautique	Almanak
Nautical mile	Seemeile	Mille nautique	Zeemijl
Neap tide	Nipptide	Morte-eau	Dood tij
North	Nord	Nord	Noord
Pilot	Lotse	Pilote	Loods/Gids
Pilotage book	Handbuch	Instructions nautiques	Vaarwijzer
RDF	Funkpeiler	Radio gonio richtingzoeker	Radio
Radar	Radar	Radar	Radar
Radio receiver	Radio, Empfänger	Réceptor radio	Radio ontvanger
Radio transmitter	Sender	Emetteur radio	Radio zender
River outlet	Flußmündung	Embouchure	Riviermond
South	Süd	Sud	Zuid
Spring tide	Springtide	Vive-eau springvloed	Springtij/
Tide	Tide, Gezeit	Marée	Getijde
Tide tables	Tidenkalender	Annuaire des marées	Getijdetafel
True course	Wahrer Kurs	Vrai cap	Ware Koers
Upstream	Flußaufwärts	En amont	Stroom opwaards
VHF	UKW	VHF	Marifoon
Variation	Mißweisung	Variation	Variatie
Waypoint	Wegpunkt	Point de rapport punt	Waypoint/Route
West	West	Ouest	West

OFFICIALDOM

Certificate of registry	Schiffszertifikat	Acte de franchisation	Zeebrief
Check in	Einklarieren	Enregistrement	Check-in
Customs	Zoll	Douanes	Douane
Declare	Verzollen	Déclarer	Aangeven
Harbour master	Hafenmeister	Capitaine du port	Havenmeester
Insurance	Versicherung	Assurance	Verzekering
Insurance certificate	Versicherungspolice	Certificat d'assurance	Verzekeringsbewijs
Passport	Paß	Passeport	Paspoort
Police	Polizei	Police	Politie
Pratique	Verkehrserlaubnis	Pratique	Verlof tot ontscheping
Prohibited area	Sperrgebiet	Zone interdite	Verboden gebied
Register	Register	Liste de passagers	Register
Ship's log	Logbuch	Livre de bord	Logboek
Ship's papers	Schiffspapiere	Papiers de bateau	Scheepspapieren
Surveyor	Gutachter	Expert maritime	Opzichter

Chapter 1 – Navigation

PASSAGE PLANNING AND SOLAS V

All passages by any vessel that goes to sea *must* be planned. 'Going to sea' is defined as proceeding beyond sheltered waters. Even in very familiar waters every passage, however short, should be properly planned. Before you set sail you need to determine where you are going, how to get there and what factors may influence the plan.

Full passage planning requirements may be found in Chapter V of the International Convention for Safety of Life at Sea (SOLAS), but more digestible guidance for small craft is in the MCA's Pleasure Craft Information Pack at: **www.dft.gov.uk/mca/ pleasure_craft_information_packdec07-2.pdf.**

Although the passage plan does not have to be recorded on paper, in the event of legal action a written plan is clear proof that the required planning has been completed; it can also be referred to during the passage. A suggested passage planning form is overleaf. When completed this would constitute, with due consideration of the points below, a reasonable passage plan. The blank form may be photocopied and modified to suit individual needs.

Although spot checks on small craft are unlikely, the MCA could, following an accident or incident, take action under the Merchant Shipping Act if it could be proved that the skipper did not have a reasonable passage plan.

Passage planning considerations

All passage plans should at least consider the following:

• **Weather.** Before setting out check the weather forecast and know how to get regular updates during the passage.

• **Tides.** Check tidal predictions and determine if there are any limiting depths at your port of departure, during the passage and at the port of arrival (and at alternative ports, if applicable). Tidal streams will almost certainly affect the plan.

• **Vessel.** Confirm she is suitable for the intended trip, is properly equipped, and has sufficient fuel, water and food on board.

• **Crew.** Take into account your crew's experience, expertise and stamina. Cold, tiredness and seasickness can be debilitating – and skippers are not immune.

• **Navigation.** Make sure you are aware of all navigational dangers by consulting up to date charts, pilot books and this Almanac. Never *rely* on GPS for fixing your position.

• **Contingency plan.** Consider bolt holes which can be entered *safely* in an emergency, if the weather deteriorates or mutiny threatens.

• **Information ashore.** Make sure someone ashore knows your plans, when they should become concerned and what action to take if necessary. Be sure to join the Coastguard Voluntary Identification Scheme (Form CG66).

"The winds and waves are always on the side of the ablest navigators." (Edward Gibbon)

Passage planning form

The following notes amplify some of the items on the form:

• The height of tide affects the depth, and tidal streams may hinder sensible progress – off headlands or in narrow passages, for example. On longer passages, which cross main tidal streams, determine the net effect of the streams and calculate a course to steer – more efficient than trying to maintain a track.

• Note which harbours and marinas have restricted times of access due to bars, sills or locks. These may affect your ETA and, probably, your ETD.

• Prepare a detailed pilotage plan for entry/exit of any unfamiliar harbour; a sketch is invaluable.

• Squinting into the setting sun can make pilotage very difficult. At night, light from a full moon can help enormously.

• Know when you expect to see lights at night – a good check on progress. See table of dipping/rising lights.

• Look up and note relevant VHF channels and/or phone numbers for ports of departure and arrival.

PASSAGE PLANNING FORM

DATE:........................ FROM: .... TO: .... DIST: ....M

ALTERNATIVE DESTINATION(S): ....

WEATHER FORECAST: ....

FORECASTS AVAILABLE DURING PASSAGE: ....

....

TIDES

DATE:....................................	DATE:....................................	DATE:....................................
PLACE:...................................	PLACE:...................................	PLACE:...................................
HW	HW	HW ....
LW	LW	LW ....
HW	HW	HW ....
LW	LW	LW ....

COEFFICIENT: ....

HEIGHT OF TIDE AT: ....

.... hrs ....m .... hrs ....m .... hrs ....m

DEPTH CONSTRAINTS: ....

TIDAL STREAMS AT: ....

TURNS .... AT .... TOTAL SET (FM .... TO ....): ....° .... M

TURNS .... AT .... TOTAL SET (FM .... TO ....): ....° .... M

NET TIDAL STREAM FOR PASSAGE: ....° .... M

ESTIMATED TIME: ....hrs ETD: .... ETA: ....

SUN/MOON   SUNRISE: .... SUNSET: ....

MOONRISE: .... MOONSET: .... PHASE: ....

WAYPOINTS	NO	NAME	TRACK/DISTANCE (TO NEXT WAYPOINT)
	....	....	.... / ....
	....	....	.... / ....
	....	....	.... / ....
	....	....	.... / ....
	....	....	.... / ....

DANGERS   CLEARING BEARINGS/RANGES/DEPTHS

....

....

LIGHTS/MARKS EXPECTED ....

....

....

COMMUNICATIONS   PORT/MARINA .... VHF .... ☎ ....

PORT/MARINA .... VHF .... ☎ ....

NOTES (CHARTS PREPARED & PAGE NUMBERS OF RELEVANT PILOTS/ALMANACS/ETC): ....

....

....

FRANCE/CI \ ENGLAND	Longships	Falmouth	Fowey	Plymouth bkwtr	Salcombe	Dartmouth	Torbay	Weymouth	Poole Hbr Ent	Needles Lt Ho	Nab Tower	Littlehampton	Shoreham	Brighton	Newhaven	Eastbourne	Folkestone	Dover
Le Conquet	114	118	134	142	139	152	158	181	199	203	236	256	260	264	269	281	313	318
L'Aberwrac'h	101	103	114	120	122	133	142	171	191	197	197	236	246	247	248	258	297	301
Roscoff	110	97	101	97	91	100	107	130	144	149	165	184	193	197	200	211	246	252
Trébeurden	118	105	107	100	95	103	110	128	148	148	168	186	197	201	206	218	257	262
Tréguier	131	114	112	102	93	99	104	116	132	136	153	170	182	187	192	211	252	253
Lézardrieux	139	124	119	107	97	102	105	117	129	133	150	167	179	184	189	208	249	250
St Q.-Portrieux	151	134	128	120	109	114	115	128	133	136	151	174	180	185	188	200	238	242
St Malo	172	152	145	132	118	121	124	125	130	133	148	170	176	182	185	195	235	240
St Helier	156	133	124	110	95	97	100	103	108	110	125	145	155	160	163	175	211	218
St Peter Port	140	113	105	89	75	71	73	81	87	90	105	126	135	139	142	155	190	196
Braye (Alderney)	149	129	107	90	74	72	71	63	68	71	86	108	115	120	123	135	173	178
Cherbourg	173	144	130	111	98	94	93	67	64	63	72	89	99	102	107	120	153	158
St Vaast	194	165	151	134	119	117	119	86	78	72	69	84	91	94	97	104	140	147
Ouistreham	231	203	190	173	158	155	159	121	111	100	88	93	94	94	93	96	132	133
Deauville	238	210	198	181	164	163	160	127	114	103	89	90	89	87	87	89	124	126
Le Havre	239	210	197	180	164	162	165	125	112	98	84	84	83	82	82	83	119	120
Fécamp	246	218	206	188	173	169	165	127	111	98	81	72	69	66	63	63	98	98
Dieppe	273	243	231	214	200	194	191	151	133	121	97	86	76	72	67	62	78	80
Boulogne	294	264	247	231	216	204	202	161	143	132	101	86	77	73	65	54	28	28
Calais	307	276	261	244	229	218	214	174	155	143	114	99	91	86	78	64	29	24

NAVIGATION

NOTES

1. This Table applies to Areas 1–3, and 14–16, each of which also contains its own internal Distance Table. Approximate distances in nautical miles are by the most direct route, while avoiding dangers and allowing for Traffic Separation Schemes.

2. For ports within the Solent, add the appropriate distances given in Area 2 to those shown above under either Needles Lighthouse or Nab Tower.

AREA 1 *South West England - Isles of Scilly to Anvil Point*

SELECTED LIGHTS, BUOYS & WAYPOINTS | Positions are referenced to WGS84

ISLES OF SCILLY TO LAND'S END

Bishop Rock ☆ Fl (2) 15s 44m **20M**; part obsc 204°-211°, obsc 211°-233° and 236°-259°; Gy ○ twr with helo platform; *Racon T, 18M, 254°-215°*; 49°52'·37N 06°26'·74W. Round Rk ⌇ 49°53'·10N 06°25'·19W. Old Wreck ⌇ VQ; 49°54'·26N 06°22'·81W.

ST AGNES and ST MARY'S

Peninnis Hd ⚓ Fl 20s 36m 9M; 231°-117° but part obsc 048°-083° within 5M; W ○ twr on B frame, B cupola; 49°54'·28N 06°18'·21W.

Spanish Ledge ⌇ Q (3) 10s; *Bell*; 49°53'·94N 06°18'·86W.
Bartholomew Ledges ⌇ QR 12m; 49°54'·37N 06°19'·89W.
N Bartholomew ⌇ Fl R 5s; 49°54'·49N 06°19'·99W.
Bacon Ledge ⌇ Fl (4) R 5s; 49°55'·22N 06°19'·26W.
Ldg lts 097·3°: Front, Iso RW (vert) 2s; W △, 49°55'·12N 06°18'·50W. Rear, Oc WR (vert) 10s; Or X on W bcn.
St Mary's Pool pier ⚓ Fl WRG 2s 5m 4M; 070°-R-100°-W-130°-G-070°; 49°55'·11N 06°19'·00W.
Crow Rock ⌇ Fl (2) 10s; 49°56'·26N 06°18'·49W.
Hats ⌇ VQ (6) + L Fl 10s; 49°56'·21N 06°17'·14W.

AROUND TRESCO, BRYHER and ST MARTIN'S

Tresco Flats, Hulman ⌇ Fl G 4s, 49°56'·29N 06°20'·30W.
Little Rag Ledge ⌇ Fl (2) R 5s, 49°56'·44N 06°20'·43W.
Bryher, Bar Quay ⌇ Q (3) 10s, 49°57'·37N 06°20'·84W.
Spencers Ledge ⌇ Q (6) + L Fl 15s; 49°54'·78N 06°22'·06W.
Steeple Rock ⌇ Q (9) 15s; 49°55'·46N 06°24'·24W.
Round Island ☆ Fl 10s 55m **18M**, also shown in reduced vis; 021°-288°; W ○ twr; *Horn (4) 60s*; 49°58'·74N 06°19'·39W.
St Martin's, Higher Town quay ⚓ Fl R 5s, 49°57'·45N 06°16'·84W.

SCILLY TO LAND'S END

Seven Stones Lt V ⚓ Fl (3) 30s 12m **15M**; R hull; *Horn (3) 60s*; *Racon O, 15M*; 50°03'·63N 06°04'·32W.
Wolf Rock ☆ Fl 15s 34m **16M**; H24; *Horn 30s*; *Racon T, 10M*; 49°56'·72N 05°48'·57W.
Longships ☆ Fl (2) WR 10s 35m **W15M**, R11M; 189°-R-327°-W- 189°; also shown in reduced vis; Gy ○ twr with helicopter platform; *Horn 10s*; 50°04'·01N 05°44'·81W.
Carn Base ⌇ Q (9) 15s; 50°01'·48N 05°46'·18W.
Runnel Stone ⌇ Q (6) + L Fl 15s; *Whis*; 50°01'·18N 05°40'·36W.

LAND'S END TO PLYMOUTH

Tater-du ☆ Fl (3) 15s 34m **20M**; 241°-072°; W ○ twr. FR 31m 13M, 060°-072° over Runnel Stone; 50°03'·14N 05°34'·67W.

NEWLYN

Low Lee ⌇ Q (3) 10s; 50°05'·56N 05°31'·38W.
S Pier ⚓ Fl 5s 10m 9M; W ○ twr; 253°-336°; 50°06'·18N 05°32'·57W.
N Pier ⚓ FWG 4m 2M; 238°-G-248°, W over hbr; 50°06'·18N 05°32'·62W.

PENZANCE

S Pier ☆ Fl WR 5s 11m **W17M**, R12M; 159°-R (unintens)-224°-R-268°-W-344·5°-R-shore; 50°07'·06N 05°31'·68W.
Mountamopus ⌇ Q (6) + L Fl 15s; 50°04'·62N 05°26'·25W.

Lizard ☆ Fl 3s 70m **26M**; 250°-120°, partly visible 235°-250°; W 8-sided twr; *Horn 30s*; 49°57'·61N 05°12'·13W.
Manacle ⌇ Q (3) 10s; *Bell*; 50°02'·81N 05°01'·91W.

FALMOUTH

St Anthony Head ☆ Iso WR 15s 22m, **W16M**, R14M, H24; 295°-W-004°-R (over Manacles)-022°-W-172°; W 8-sided twr; *Horn 30s*; 50°08'·46N 05°00'·96W.
Black Rock Fl (2) 10s 3M; B IDM bcn twr; 50°08'·72N 05°02'·00W.
Black Rock ⌇ Fl R 2·5s; 50°08'·68N 05°01'·74W.
Castle ⚓ Fl G 2·5s; 50°08'·99N 05°01'·62W.
St Mawes ⌇ Q (6) + L Fl 15s; 50°09'·10N 05°01'·42W.
The Governor ⌇ VQ (3) 5s; 50°09'·15N 05°02'·40W.
West Narrows ⌇ Fl (2) R 10s; 50°09'·39N 05°02'·07W.
East Narrows ⚓ Fl (2) G 10s; 50°09'·43N 05°01'·90W.
The Vilt ⚓ Fl (4) G 15s; 50°09'·99N 05°02'·28W.
Northbank ⌇ Fl R 4s; 50°10'·34N 05°02'·26W.
St Just ⌇ QR; 50°10'·44N 05°01'·72W.
Mylor appr chan ⚓ Fl G 6s; 50°10'·79N 05°02'·70W.
⌇ Fl R 5s.
Messack ⚓ Fl G 15s; 50°11'·31N 05°02'·22W.
Carrick ⚓ Fl (2) G 10s; 50°11'·59N 05°02'·74W.
Pill ⚓ Fl (3) G 15s; 50°12'·05N 05°02'·40W.
Turnerware Bar ⚓ Fl G 5s; 50°12'·40N 05°02'·15W.
Inner Harbour
N Arm ⚓ QR 5m 3M; 50°09'·42N 05°03'·20W.
Visitors Yacht Haven ⚓ 2 FR (vert); 50°09'·27N 05°03'·91W.
Falmouth Marina ⌇ VQ (3) 5s; 50°09'·91N 05°04'·99W.

DODMAN POINT and MEVAGISSEY

Naval gunnery targets SSE of Dodman Point:
'A' ⌇ Fl Y 10s; 50°08'·53N 04°46'·37W.
'B' ⌇ Fl Y 5s; 50°10'·30N 04°45'·00W.
'C' ⌇ Fl Y 2s; 50°10'·40N 04°47'·51W.

Gwineas ⌇ Q (3) 10s; *Bell*; 50°14'·48N 04°45'·40W.
Mevagissey, Victoria Pier ⚓ Fl (2) 10s 9m 12M; *Dia 30s*; 50°16'·15N 04°46'·92W.

FOWEY

Cannis Rock ⌇ Q (6) + L Fl 15s; *Bell*; 50°18'·38N 04°39'·95W.
Fowey ⚓ L Fl WR 5s 28m W11M, R9M; 284°-R-295°-W-028°-R-054°; W 8-sided twr, R lantern; 50°19'·63N 04°38'·83W.
St Catherine's Pt ⚓ Fl R 2·5s 15m 2M; 150°-295°; 50°19'·69N 04°38'·66W.
Lamp Rock ⌇ Fl G 5s 3m 2M; vis 357°-214°; 50°19'·70N 04°38'·41W. Whitehouse Pt ⚓ Iso WRG 3s 11m W11M, R/G8M; 017°-G-022°- W-032°-R-037°; R col; 50°19'·98N 04°38'·28W.

POLPERRO, LOOE, EDDYSTONE and WHITSAND BAY

Udder Rock ⚓ VQ (6) + L Fl 10s; *Bell;* 50°18'·93N 04°33'·85W.

POLPERRO, W pier ⚡ FW 4m 4M; FR when hbr closed in bad weather; 50°19'·86N 04°30'·96W.

Spy House Pt ⚡ Iso WR 6s 30m 7M; W288°-060°, R060°-288°; 50°19'·81N 04°30'·69W.

LOOE, Ranneys ⚓ Q (6) + L Fl 15s; 50°19'·85N 04°26'·37W.

Mid Main ⚓ Q (3) 10s 2M; 50°20'·56N 04°26'·94W.

Banjo Pier ☆ Oc WR 3s 8m **W15M**, R12M; 207°-R267°-W-313°-R-332°; 50°21'·06N 04°27'·06W.

White Rock ⚡ Fl R 3s 5m 2M; 50°21'·03N 04°27'·09W.

Eddystone ☆ Fl (2) 10s 41m **17M**. Same twr, Iso R 10s 28m 8M; vis 110°-133° over Hand Deeps; Gy twr, helicopter platform; *Horn 30s; Racon T, 10M;* 50°10'·84N 04°15'·94W.

Hand Deeps ⚓ Q (9) 15s; 50°12'·68N 04°21'·10W.

PLYMOUTH

PLYMOUTH SOUND, WESTERN CHANNEL

Draystone ⚓ Fl (2) R 5s; 50°18'·85N 04°11'·07W.

Knap ▲ Fl G 5s; 50°19'·56N 04°10'·02W.

Plymouth bkwtr W head, ⚡ Fl WR 10s 19m W12M, R9M; 262°-W-208°-R-262°; W ○ twr. Same twr, Iso 4s 12m 10M; vis 033°-037°; *Horn 15s;* 50°20'·07N 04°09'·52W.

Maker ⚡ Fl (2) WRG 10s 29m, W11M, R/G6M; 270°-G330°-W-004°-R-050°; W twr, R stripe; 50°20'·51N 04°10'·87W.

Queens Ground ⚓ Fl (2) R 10s; 50°20'·29N 04°10'·08W.

New Ground ⚓ Fl R 2s; 50°20'·47N 04°09'·43W.

Melampus ⚓ Fl R 4s; 50°21'·15N 04°08'·72W.

PLYMOUTH SOUND, EASTERN CHANNEL

Wembury Pt ⚡ Oc Y 10s 45m; occas; 50°19'·01N 04°06'·63W.

West Tinker ⚓ VQ (9) 10s; 50°19'·25N 04°08'·64W.

East Tinker ⚓ Q (3) 10s; 50°19'·20N 04°08'·30W.

Whidbey ⚓ Oc (2) WRG 10s 29m, W8M, R/G6M, H24; 000°-G-137·5°-W-139·5°-R-159°; Or and W col; 50°19'·53N 04°07'·27W.

The Breakwater, E head ⚓ L Fl WR 10s 9m W8M, R6M; 190°-R-353°-W-001°-R-018°-W-190°; 50°20'·01N 04°08'·24W.

Staddon Pt ⚓ Oc WRG 10s 15m W8M, R/G5M; H24. 348°-G-038°-W-050°-R-090°; W structure, R bands; 50°20'·17N 04°07'·54W.

Withyhedge Dir ⚡ 070° (for W Chan): WRG 13m W13M, R/G5M; H24; 060°-FG-065°-Al WG (W phase increasing with brg) -069°-FW-071°-Al WR (R phase increasing with brg)-075°-F R-080°; W ▽, orange stripe on col. Same col, Fl (2) Bu 5s; vis 120°-160°; 50°20'·75N 04°07'·44W.

SMEATON PASS (W of Mount Batten and S of The Hoe)

Ldg lts 349°. Front, Mallard Shoal ⚓ Q WRG 5m W10M, R/G3M; W △, Or bands; 233°-G-043°- R-067°- G-087°-W-099°-R-108° (ldg sector); 50°21'·60N 04°08'·33W. Rear, 396m from front, Hoe ⚓ Oc G 1·3s 11m 3M, 310°-040°; W ▽, Or bands; 50°21'·81N 04°08'·39W.

S Mallard ⚓ VQ (6) + L Fl 10s; 50°21'·51N 04°08'·30W.

W Mallard ▲ QG; 50°21'·57N 04°08'·36W.

S Winter ⚓ Q (6) + L Fl 15s; 50°21'·40N 04°08'·55W.

NE Winter ⚓ QR; 50°21'·54N 04°08'·50W.

NW Winter ⚓ VQ (9) 10s; 50°21'·55N 04°08'·70W.

ENTRANCE TO THE CATTEWATER

QAB (Queen Anne's Battery) ldg lts ⚡ 048·5°. Front, FR; Or/W bcn; 50°21'·84N 04°07'·84W. Rear, Oc R 8s 14m 3M; 139m NE.

Fishers Nose ⚡ Fl (3) R 10s 6m 4M; 50°21'·80N 04°08'·01W.

Also F Bu ≠ 026·5° with F Bu 50°22'·00N 04°07'·86W, for Cobbler Chan.

DRAKE CHANNEL, THE BRIDGE and THE NARROWS

Asia ⚓ Fl (2) R 5s; 50°21'·47N 04°08'·85W.

St Nicholas ⚓ QR; 50°21'·55N 04°09'·20W.

N Drakes Is ⚓ Fl R 4s; 50°21'·52N 04°09'·38W.

E Vanguard ▲ QG; 50°21'·47N 04°09'·70W.

W Vanguard ▲ Fl G 3s; 50°21'·49N 04°09'·98W.

Devils Point ⚓ QG 5m 3M; Fl 5s in fog; 50°21'·59N 04°10'·04W. Battery ⚓ Fl R 2s; 50°21'·52N 04°10'·21W.

The Bridge Channel

No 1, ⚓ QG 4m; 50°21'·03N 04°09'·53W. No 2, ⚓ QR 4m.

No 3, ⚓ Fl (3) G 10s 4m. No 4, ⚓ Fl (4) R 10s 4m; 50°21'·09N 04°09'·63W.

Mount Wise, Dir ⚡ 343°: WRG 7m, W13M, R/G5M; H24. 331°-FG-338°-Al WG-342° (W phase increasing with brg)-FW-344°-Al WR-348° (R phase increasing with bearing)-FR-351°. In fog, 341·5°-FW-344·5°; 50°21'·96N 04°10'·33W.

Ocean Court Dir Q WRG 15m, W11M, R/G3M; 010°-G-080°-W-090°-R-100°; 50°21'·85N 04°10'·11W.

PLYMOUTH TO START POINT

RIVER YEALM Sand bar ⚓ Fl R 5s; 50°18'·59N 04°04'·12W.

SALCOMBE

Sandhill Pt Dir ⚡ 000°: Fl WRG 2s 27m W/R/G 8M; 337·5°-G-357·5°-W-002·5°-R-012·5°; R/W ◊ on W mast, rear daymark; 50°13'·77N 03°46'·67W. Front daymark, Pound Stone R/W ⚓.

Bass Rk ⚓ Fl R 5s; 50°13'·47N 03°46'·71W.

Wolf Rk ▲ Fl G 5s; 50°13'·53N 03°46'·58W.

Blackstone Rk ⚓; 50°13'·61N 03°46'·51W.

Ldg lts 042·5°, front Fl 1·8s, rear Fl 4·8s 5/45m 8M. Front 50°14'·53N 03°45'·31W.

Start Pt ☆ Fl (3) 10s 62m **25M**; 184°-068°. Same twr: FR 55m 9M; 210°-255° over Skerries Bank; *Horn 60s;* 50°13'·34N 03°38'·54W.

START POINT TO PORTLAND BILL

DARTMOUTH

Kingswear Dir ⚡ 328°: Iso WRG 3s 9m 8M; 318°-G-325°-W-331°-R-340°; W ○ twr; 50°20'·82N 03°34'·09W.

Mewstone ⚓ VQ (6) + L Fl 10s; 50°19'·92N 03°31'·89W.

West Rock ⚓ Q (6) + L Fl 15s; 50°19'·86N 03°32'·47W.

Homestone ⚓ QR; 50°19'·61N 03°33'·55W.

Castle Ledge ▲ Fl G 5s; 50°19'·99N 03°33'·11W.

Checkstone ⚓ Fl (2) R 5s; 50°20'·45N 03°33'·81W.

Dir ⚡ 104·5°: FW 5m 9M; vis 102°-107°; 50°20'·65N 03°33'·80W.

BRIXHAM

Berry Head ☆ Fl (2) 15s 58m **19M**; vis 100°-023°; W twr;

50°23'·98N 03°29'·01W. R lts on radio mast 5·7M NW, inland of Paignton.

Victoria bkwtr ⚓ Oc R 15s 9m 6M; W twr; 50°24'·33N 03°30'·78W.

No. 1 ⬤ Fl G; 50°24'·30N 03°30'·89W.

No. 2 ⬤ Fl R; 50°24'·32N 03°30'·83W.

PAIGNTON and TORQUAY

⬤ Q G (May-Sep); 50°27'·42N 03°31'·80W, 85m off Haldon Pier.

Haldon Pier (E) ⚓ QG 9m 6M; 50°27'·43N 03°31'·73W.

Princess Pier (W) ⚓ QR 9m 6M; 50°27'·46N 03°31'·73W.

TEIGNMOUTH

Outfall ⬤ Fl Y 5s; 50°31'·97N 03°27'·77W, 288°/1·3M to hbr ent.

Bar ⬤ Fl G 2s; 50°32'·44N 03°29'·25W.

Trng wall, middle ⚓ Oc R 6s 4m 3M; 50°32'·33N 03°29'·93W.

The Point ⚓ Oc G 6s 3M & FG (vert); 50°32'·42N 03°30'·05W.

RIVER EXE to SIDMOUTH and AXMOUTH

Exe ⬤ Mo(A) 10s; 50°35'·92N 03°23'·75W.

No. 1 ⬤ 50°36'·07N 03°23'·78W.

No. 2 ⬤ 50°36'·03N 03°23'·91W.

Ldg lts 305°. Front, Iso 2s 6m 7M; 50°36'·99N 03°25'·34W. Rear, Q 12m 7M; 57m from front. No. 10 ⬤ Fl R 3s; 50°36'·73N 03°24'·77W.

No. 12 Warren Pt ⬤ 50°36'·91N 03°25'·41W.

Sidmouth ⚓ Fl R 5s 5m 2M; 50°40'·48N 03°14'·43W.

Axmouth jetty ⚓ Fl G 4s 7m 2M; 50°42'·12N 03°03'·29W.

LYME REGIS

Outfall ⚓ Q (6) + L Fl 15s; 50°43'·17N 02°55'·66W.

Ldg lts 284°: Front, Victoria Pier ⚓ Oc WR 8s 6m, W9M, R7M; 284°-R-104°-W-284°; Bu col; 50°43'·19N 02°56'·17W. Rear, FG 8m 9M.

WEST BAY (BRIDPORT)

W pier root, Dir ⚓ 336°: F WRG 5m 4M; 165°-G-331°-W-341°-R-165°; 50°42'·62N 02°45'·89W.

W pier outer limit ⚓ Iso R 2s 5m 4M; 50°42'·51N 02°45'·83W.

E pier outer limit ⚓ Iso G 2s 5m 4M; 50°42'·53N 02°45'·80W.

PORTLAND BILL TO ANVIL POINT

Portland Bill lt ho ☆ Fl (4) 20s 43m **25M.** vis 221°-244° (gradual change from 1 Fl to 4 Fl); 244°-117° (shows 4 Fl); 117°-141° (gradual change from 4 Fl to 1 Fl). W ○ twr; *Dia 30s;* 50°30'·85N 02°27'·39W. Same twr, FR 19m 13M; 271°-291° over Shambles.

W Shambles ⚓ Q (9) 15s; *Bell;* 50°29'·78N 02°24'·41W.

E Shambles ⚓ Q (3) 10s; *Bell;* 50°30'·78N 02°20'·08W.

PORTLAND HARBOUR

Outer Bkwtr Fort Head (N end) ⚓ QR 14m 5M; 013°-268°; 50°35'·11N 02°24'·87W.

NE Bkwtr (A Hd) ⚓ Fl 2·5s 22m 10M; 50°35'·16N 02°25'·07W.

NE Bkwtr (B Hd) ⚓ Oc R 15s 11m 5M; 50°35'·65N 02°25'·88W.

N Arm (C Hd) ⚓ Oc G 10s 11m 5M; 50°35'·78N 02°25'·95W.

WEYMOUTH

Ldg lts 239·6°: both FR 5/7m 7M; Front 50°36'·46N 02°26'·87W, S Pier hd ⚓ Q 10m 9M; 50°36'·58N 02°26'·49W. IPTS 190m SW.

LULWORTH RANGE TO ANVIL POINT

Targets off St Alban's Hd: DZ 'A' ⬤, Fl Y 2s, 50°33'·34N 02°06'·52W.

DZ 'B' ⬤, Fl Y 10s, 50°32'·11N 02°05'·92W.

DZ 'C' ⬤, Fl Y 5s, 50°32'·76N 02°04'·56W.

Anvil Pt ⚓ Fl 10s 45m 9M; vis 237°-076° (H24); W ○ twr and dwelling; 50°35'·51N 01°57'·60W. Measured mile close west.

		1	2	3	4	5	6	7	8	9	10	11	12	13	14	15	16	17
1	Longships	**1**																
2	Scilly (Crow Rock)	22	**2**															
3	Penzance	15	35	**3**														
4	Lizard Point	23	42	16	**4**													
5	Falmouth	39	60	32	16	**5**												
6	Mevagissey	52	69	46	28	17	**6**											
7	Fowey	57	76	49	34	22	7	**7**										
8	Looe	63	80	57	39	29	16	11	**8**									
9	Plymouth (bkwtr)	70	92	64	49	39	25	22	11	**9**								
10	River Yealm (ent)	72	94	66	51	41	27	24	13	4	**10**							
11	Salcombe	81	102	74	59	50	40	36	29	22	19	**11**						
12	Start Point	86	103	80	63	55	45	40	33	24	21	7	**12**					
13	Dartmouth	95	116	88	72	63	54	48	42	35	32	14	9	**13**				
14	Torbay	101	118	96	78	70	62	55	50	39	36	24	15	11	**14**			
15	Exmouth	113	131	107	90	82	73	67	61	51	48	33	27	24	12	**15**		
16	Lyme Regis	126	144	120	104	96	86	81	74	63	60	48	41	35	30	21	**16**	
17	Portland Bill	135	151	128	112	104	93	89	81	73	70	55	49	45	42	36	22	**17**

DISTANCE TABLES
Approx distances in nautical miles are by the most direct route allowing for dangers and TSS.

AREA 2 *South Central England – Anvil Point to Selsey Bill*

SELECTED LIGHTS, BUOYS & WAYPOINTS | Positions are referenced to WGS84

SWANAGE TO ISLE OF WIGHT

SWANAGE
Pier Hd ⚡ 2 FR (vert) 6m 3M; 50°36'·56N 01°56'·95W.
Peveril Ledge ⚓ QR; 50°36'·41N 01°56'·10W.

POOLE BAR and SWASH CHANNEL
Poole Bar (No. 1) ⚓ QG; *Bell*; 50°39·29N 01°55'·14W.
(Historic wreck) ⚓ Fl Y 5s; 50°39'·70N 01°54'·86W.
South Hook (No. 11) ⚓ 50°39'·70N 01°55'·20W.
No. 2 ⚓ Fl R 2s; 50°39'·23N 01°55'·24W.
No. 3 ⚓ Fl G 3s; 50°39'·76N 01°55'·49W.
No. 4 ⚓ Fl R 2s; 50°39'·72N 01°55'·60W.
Training Bank ⚓ 2 FR (vert); 50°39'·82N 01°55'·86W.
No. 6 ⚓ Fl R 4s; 50°40'·14N 01°55'·91W.
No. 5 ⚓ Fl G 5s; 50°40'·19N 01°55'·81W.
Hook Sands (No. 7) ⚓ Fl G 3s; 50°40'·50N 01°56'·16W.
Channel (No. 8) ⚓ Fl R 2s; 50°40'·45N 01°56'·27W.
No. 10 ⚓ Fl R 4s; 50°40'·84N 01°56'·86W.
Swash (No. 9) ⚓ Q (9) 15s; 50°40'·88N 01°56'·70W.

EAST LOOE CHANNEL
East Hook ⚓ 50°40'·58W 01°55'·23W.
East Looe 1 ⚓ Fl G 5s; 50°41'·09N 01°55'·82W.
East Looe 2 ⚓ Fl R 4s; 50°41'·07N 01°55'·83W.
East Looe 3 (Limit 10 knots) ⚓ Fl G 3s; 50°41'·11N 01°56'·16W.
East Looe 4 (Limit 10 knots) ⚓ Fl R 2s; 50°41'·09N 01°56'·17W.
North Hook ⚓ Fl (2) R 5s; 50°41'·01N 01°56'·44W.

BROWNSEA ROADS
No. 12 ⚓ Q R; 50°40'·94N 01°57'·17W.
No.14 ⚓ Fl R 2s; 50°41'·03N 01°57'·32W.
N Haven ⚓ Q (9) 15s 5m; 50°41'·15N 01°57'·17W.
Brownsea ⚓ Q (3) 10s; 50°41'·14N 01°57'·39W.
Brownsea Island Dir lt 299°F WRG; 296·5°-G-297·8°-AltWG-298·8°-W-299·2°-AltWR-300·2°-R-301·5°; 50°41'·16N 01°57'·67W (only shown for commercial vessels); 2FR(vert); 301·5°-296·5° (H24).

MIDDLE SHIP CHANNEL
Bell (No. 15) ⚓ Q (6) + L Fl 15s; 50°41'·36N 01°57'·12W.
No. 16 ⚓ VQ R; 50°41'·43N 01°57'·25W.
No. 17 ⚓ Fl G 3s; 50°41'·68N 01°57'·02W.
Aunt Betty (No. 22) ⚓ Q (3)10s; 50°41'·97N 01°57'·25W.
Diver (No. 25) ⚓ Q (9) 15s; 50°42'·29N 01°58'·32W.

NORTH CHANNEL
Salterns Marina Outer Bkwtr Hd ⚡ 2 FR (vert) 2M; Tfc sigs; 50°42'·23N 01°57'·10W.
Parkstone YC platform ⚡ Q 8m 1M; hut on dolphin; 50°42'·37N 01°58'·08W.
Stakes (No. 29) ⚓ Q (6) + L Fl 15s; 50°42'·43N 01°59'·00W.

POOLE BAY
Bournemouth Rocks ⚓ 50°42'·32N 01°53'·40W.
Lightwave ⚓ 50°41'·50N 01°51'·68W.
Christchurch Ledge ⚓ 50°41'·57N 01°41'·55W (Apr-Oct).
⚓ (x2) Fl (5) Y 20s; 50°37'·98N 01°43'·02W; (265° 2·6M from Needles F'wy)

WESTERN APPROACHES TO THE SOLENT

NEEDLES CHANNEL
Needles Fairway ⚓ L Fl 10s; *Whis*; 50°38'·24N 01°38'·98W.
SW Shingles ⚓ Fl R 2·5s; 50°39'·29N 01°37'·52W.
Bridge ⚓ VQ (9) 10s; *Racon (T) 10M*; 50°39'·63N 01°36'·88W.
Needles 50°39'·73N 01°35'·50W; Oc (2) WRG 20s 24m **W17M**, R14M, R13M G14M; ○ Twr, R band and lantern; vis: shore-R-300°-W-083°-R (unintens)-212°-W-217°-G-224° (H24). *Horn (2) 30s.*

Shingles Elbow ⚓ Fl (2) R 5s; 50°40'·37N 01°36'·05W.
Mid Shingles ⚓ Fl (3) R 10s; 50°41'·21N 01°34'·66W.
Warden ⚓ Fl G 2·5s; *Bell*; 50°41'·48N 01°33'·55W.
NE Shingles ⚓ Q (3) 10s; 50°41'·96N 01°33'·41W.

Hurst Point ☆ 50°42'·48N 01°33'·03W; FL (4) WR 15s 23m W13M, R11M; W ○ Twr; vis:080°-W(unintens)-104°, 234°-W-244°-R-250°- W-053°. Same structure, Iso WRG 4s 19m **W21M, R18M, G17M**; vis: 038·8°-G-040·8°-W-041·8°-R- 043·8°; By day W7M, R5M, G5M.

NORTH CHANNEL
North Head ⚓ Fl (3) G 10s; 50°42'·69N 01°35'·52W.

THE WESTERN SOLENT

Note: Numerous yellow yacht racing buoys are laid throughout the Solent (seasonal, Mar-Dec). Most, but not all, are lit Fl Y 4s.

SOLENT MARKS
Sconce ⚓ Q; *Bell*; 50°42'·53N 01°31'·43W.
Black Rock ⚓ Fl G 5s; 50°42'·57N 01°30'·59W.
Lymington Bank ⚓ Fl (2) R 5s; *Bell*; 50°43'·10N 01°30'·85W.
Solent Bank ⚓ Fl (3) R 10s; 50°44'·23N 01°27'·37W.
Hamstead Ledge ⚓ Fl (2) G 5s; 50°43'·87N 01°26'18W.
Newtown River ⚓ Q (9) 15s; 50°43'·75N 01°24'·96W.
W Lepe ⚓ Fl R 5s; 50°45'·24N 01°24'·09W.
Salt Mead ⚓ Fl (3) G 10s; 50°44'·51N 01°23'·04W.
Gurnard Ledge ⚓ Fl (4) G 15s; 50°45'·51N 01°20'·59W.
E Lepe ⚓ Fl (2) R 5s; *Bell*; 50°45'·93N 01°21'·07W.
Lepe Spit ⚓ Q (6) + L Fl 15s; 50°46'·78N 01°20'·64W.
Gurnard ⚓ Q; 50°46'·22N 01°18'·84W.

YARMOUTH
East Fairway ⚓ Fl R 2s; 50°42'·62N 01°29'·95W.
Poole Belle ⚓ Fl Y 5s; 50°42'·54N 01°30'·17W.
Pier Head, centre, ⚡ 2 FR (vert) 2M; G col. High intensity FW (occas); 50°42'·51N 01°29'·97W.
Ldg Lts 187·6° Front FG 5m 2M; 50°42'·36N 01°30'·06 W. Rear, 63m from front, FG 9m 2M; both W ◇.

LYMINGTON
Jack in the Basket ⚓ Fl R 2s 9m; 50°44'·27N 01°30'·57W.
Ldg Lts 319·5°, Or posts. Front, FR 12m 8M; 50°45'·19N 01°31'·65W. vis: 309·5°-329·5°. Rear, FR 17m 8M.
Cross Boom No. 2 ⚓ Fl R 2s 4m 3M; R☐ on pile; 50°44'·36N 01°30'·58W.
No. 1 ⚓ Fl G 2s 2m 3M; G △ on pile; 50°44'·41N 01°30'·48W.

Lymington Yacht Haven Idg Its 244°. Front FY 4m; R △; 50°45'·09N 01°31'·53W. Rear, 22m from front, FY 6m; R ▽.

BEAULIEU RIVER

Millennium Dir lt 334°. ⚡ Oc WRG 4s 13m W4M, R3M, G3M; vis: 318°-G-330°-W-337°-R-348°; 50°47'·12N 01°21'·90W.
Beaulieu Spit, E end ⚓ Fl R 5s 3M; R dolphin, W band; 50°46'·85N 01°21'·76W.
No. 1 ⚓ 50°46'·91N 01°21'·70W.
No 2 ⚓ 50°46'·92N 01°21'·78W.

COWES

South Bramble ⚓ Fl G 2·5s; 50°46'·98N 01°17'·72W.
Prince Consort ⚓ VQ; 50°46'·42N 01°17'·55W.
Prince Consort Shoal ⚓ Fl (4) Y 10s; 50°46'·29N 01°17'·71W.
Shrape Bn ⚓ LFl R 10S 3m 3M; 50°46'·09N 01°16'·90W.
No. 1 ⚓ Fl G 3s; 50°46'·07N 01°18'·03W.
No. 2 ⚓ Q R; 50°46'·07N 01°17'·87W.
E. Cowes Bkwtr Hd ⚡ 2F R; 50°45'·88N 01°17'·52W.

CENTRAL SOLENT AND SOUTHAMPTON WATER

Note: Numerous yellow yacht racing buoys are laid throughout the Solent (seasonal, Mar-Dec). Most, but not all, are lit Fl Y 4s.

SOLENT MARKS

Lepe Spit ⚓ Q (6) + L Fl 15s; 50°46'·78N 01°20'·64W.
NE Gurnard ⚓ Fl (3) R 10s; 50°47'·06N 01°19'·42W.
W Bramble ⚓ VQ (9) 10s; *Bell*; **Racon (T) 3M**; 50°47'·20N 01°18'·65W.
Thorn Knoll ⚓ Fl G 5s; 50°47'·50N 01°18'·44W.
Bourne Gap ⚓ Fl R 3s; 50°47'·83N 01°18'·34W.
West Knoll ⚓ Fl Y 2·5s; 50°47'·43N 01°17'·84W.
North Thorn ⚓ QG; 50°47'·91N 01°17'·84W.
Stanswood Outfall ⚓ Iso R 10s 6m 5M; 4 FR Lts; 50°48'·26N 01°18'·82W.

CALSHOT REACH

East Knoll ⚓ 50°47'·96N 01°16'·83W.
CALSHOT SPIT ⚓ Fl 5s 5m 10M; R hull, Lt Twr amidships; *Horn (2) 60s*; 50°48'·35N 01°17'·64W.
Calshot ⚓ VQ; *Bell*; 50°48'·44N 01°17'·03W.
Castle Point ⚓ IQ R 10s; 50°48'·71N 01°17'·67W.
Reach ⚓ Fl (3) G 10s; 50°49'·05N 01°17'·65W .
Black Jack ⚓ Fl (2) R 4s; 50°49'·13N 01°18'·09W.
Hook ⚓ QG; *Horn (1) 15s*; 50°49'·52N 01°18'·30W.
Coronation ⚓ Fl Y 5s; 50°49'·55N 01°17'·62W.
Bald Head ⚓ Fl G 2·5s; 50°49'·80N 01°18'·06W.

RIVER HAMBLE

Hamble Pt ⚓ Q (6) + L Fl 15s; 50°50'·15N 01°18'·66W.
Hamble Common Dir lt 351·7°, Oc (2) WRG 12s 5m W4M; R4M; G4M; vis: 348·7°-G-350·7°-W-352·7°-R-354·7°; 50°51'·00N 01°18'·84W.
Sailing Club Dir lt 028·9° ⚡ Iso WRG 6s 5m W4M, R4M, G4M: vis: 025·9°-G-027·9°-W-029·9°-031·9°; 50°51'·10N 01°18'·34W.

SOUTHAMPTON WATER

Fawley Marine Terminal. SE end ⚡ 2 FR (vert) 9m 10M; 50°50'·06N 01°19'·42W.
Greenland ⚓ Iso G 2s; 50°51'·11N 01°20'·38W.
Cadland ⚓ Fl R 3s; 50°51'·02N 01°20'·54W.

Lains Lake ⚓ Fl (2) R 4s; 50°51'·59N 01°21'·65W.
Hound ⚓ Fl (3) G 10s; 50°51'·68N 01°21'·52W.
Netley ⚓ Fl G 3s; 50°52'·03N 01°21'·81W.
Deans Elbow ⚓ Oc R 4s; 50°52'·16N 01°22'·76W.
NW Netley ⚓ Fl G 7s; 50°52'·31N 01°22'·73W.
Weston Shelf ⚓ Fl (3) G 15s; 50°52'·71N 01°23'·26W.

HYTHE

Hythe Pier Hd ⚡ 2 FR (vert) 12m 5M; 50°52'·49N 01°23'·61W.
Hythe Marina Ent ⚓ Q (3) 10s; 50°52'·63N 01°23'·88W.
Hythe Knock ⚓ Fl R 3s; 50°52'·83N 01°23'·81W.

SOUTHAMPTON and RIVER ITCHEN

Swinging Ground No. 1 ⚓ Oc G 4s; 50°53'·00N 01°23'·44W.
E side. No. 1 ⚓ QG; 50°53'·15N 01°23'·40W.
No. 2 ⚓ Fl G 5s 2M; 50°53'·29N 01°23'·38W.
No. 3 ⚓ Fl G 7s; 50°53'·48N 01°23'·28W.
No. 4 ⚓ QG 4m 2M; 50°53'·62N 01°23'·16W.

SOUTHAMPTON and RIVER TEST

Queen Elizabeth II Terminal, S end ⚡ 4 FG (vert) 16m 3M; 50°53'·00N 01°23'·71W.
Gymp ⚓ QR; 50°53'·17N 01°24'·30W.
Town Quay Ldg Lts 329°, both F 12/22m 3/2M.
Gymp Elbow ⚓ Oc R 4s; 50°53'·50N 01°24'·68W.
Dibden Bay ⚓ Q; 50°53'·70N 01°24'·92W.

THE EASTERN SOLENT

Note: Numerous yellow yacht racing buoys are laid throughout the Solent (seasonal, Mar-Dec). Most, but not all, are lit Fl Y 4s.

SOLENT MARKS

West Ryde Middle ⚓ Q (9) 15s; 50°46'·48N 01°15'·79W.
Norris ⚓ Fl (3) R 10s; 50°45'·97N 01°15'·51W.
North Ryde Middle ⚓ Fl (4) R 20s; 50°46'·61N 01°14'·31W.
South Ryde Middle ⚓ Fl G 5s; 50°46'·13N 01°14'·16W.
Peel Bank ⚓ Fl (2) R 5s; 50°45'·49N 01°13'·35W.
SE Ryde Middle ⚓ VQ (6)+L Fl 10s; 50°45'·93N 01°12'·10W.
NE Ryde Middle ⚓ Fl (2) R 10s; 50°46'·21N 01°11'·88W.
Mother Bank ⚓ Fl R 3s; 50°45'·49N 01°11'·21W.
Browndown ⚓ Fl G 15s; 50°46'·57N 01°10'·95W.
Fort Gilkicker ⚡ Oc G 10s 7M; 50°46'·43N 01°08'·47W.
N Sturbridge ⚓ VQ; 50°45'·33N 01°08'·23W.
Ryde Sands ⚓ Fl R 10s; 50°44'·54N 01°07'·19W.
Ryde Sands ⚓ L Fl R 12s; 50°44'·16N 01°05'·99W.
No Man's Land Fort; 50°44'·40N 01°05'·70W.
No Man's ⚓ Iso R 2s; 50°44'·44N 01°05'·60W.
Horse Sand Fort ⚡ Iso G 2s 21m 8M; 50°45'·01N 01°04'·34W.
Saddle ⚓ VQ (3) G 10s; 50°45'·20N 01°04'·98W.

NORTH CHANNEL and HILLHEAD

Calshot ⚓ VQ; *Bell (1) 30s*; 50°48'·44N 01°17'·03W.
Hillhead ⚓ Fl R 2·5s; 50°48'·07N 01°16'·00W.
E Bramble ⚓ VQ (3) 5s; 50°47'·23N 01°13'·64W.

WOOTTON CREEK

Wootton Beacon ⚓ Q 1M; (NB); 50°44'·53N 01°12'·13W.
Dir lt. Oc WRG 10s vis: 220·8°-G-224·3°-W-225·8°-R-230·8°; 50°44'·03N 01°12'·86W.

RYDE

Ryde Pier ⚓, NW corner, N and E corner marked by 2 FR (vert). In fog FY from N corner, vis: 045°-165°, 200°-320°; 50°44'·34N 01°09'·72W.

Leisure Hbr E side ⚓ 2 FR (vert) 7m 1M. FY 6m shown when depth of water in Hbr greater than 1m; 2 FY 6m when depth exceeds 1·5m; 50°43'·99N 01°09'·29W.

PORTSMOUTH APPROACHES

Horse Sand ▲ Fl G 2·5s; 50°45'·53N 01°05'·27W.

Outer Spit ⚓ Q (6) + L Fl 15s; 50°45'·58N 01°05'·50W.

Mary Rose ⚬ Fl Y 5s; 50°45'·80N 01°06'·20W.

Boyne ▲ Fl G 5s; 50°46'·15N 01°05'·26W.

Spit Refuge ⚓ Fl R 5s; 50°46'·15N 01°05'·46W.

Spit Sand Fort ⚓ Fl R 5s; 18m 7M. 50°46'·24N 01°05'·94W.

Castle (NB)▲ Fl (2) G 6s; 50°46'·45N 01°05'·38W.

Southsea Castle N corner ⚓ Iso 2s 16m 11M, W stone Twr, B band; vis: 337°-071°; 50°46'·69N 01°05'·33W.

Southsea Castle Dir lt 001·5° WRG 11m W13M, R5M, G5M; same structure; vis: 351·5°-FG-357·5°-Al WG (W phase incr with brg), 000°-FW-003°-AlWR(R phase incr with brg), 005·5°-FR-011·5°; 50°46'·69N 01°05'·33W.

Ridge ⚓ Fl (2) R 6s; 50°46'·44N 01°05'·65W.

No. 1 Bar (NB) ▲ Fl (3) G 10s; 50°46'·77N 01°05'·81W.

No. 2 ⚓ Fl (3) R 10s; 50°46'·69N 01°05'·97W.

No. 3 ▲ QG; 50°47'·08N 01°06'·24W.

No. 4 ⚓ QR; 50°47'·01N 01°06'·36W.

BC Outer ⚓ Oc R 15s; 50°47'·32N 01°06'·68W.

PORTSMOUTH HARBOUR

Fort Blockhouse ⚓ Dir lt 320°; WRG 6m W13M, R5M, G5M; vis: 310°- Oc G-316°-Al WG(W phase incr with brg), 318·5°-Oc-321·5°- Al WR (R phase incr with brg), 324°-Oc R-330°. 2 FR (vert) 20m E; 50°47'·37N 01°06'·74W.

Ballast ⚓ Fl R 2·5s; 50°47'·62N 01°06'·83W.

Hbr Ent Dir lt (NB) (Fuel Jetty) ⚓ WRG 2m 1M; vis: 322·5°-Iso G 2s -330°-Al WG-332·5°-Iso 2s(main chan) -335°-Al WR-337·5°-Iso R 2s-345° (Small Boat Chan) H24; 50°47'·85N 01°06'·98W.

EASTERN APPROACHES to THE SOLENT

Outer Nab 1 ⚓ VQ (9) 10s; 50°38'·18N 00°56'·88W.

Outer Nab 2 ⚓ VQ (3) 5s; 50°38'·43N 00°57'·70W.

Nab Tower ⚓ 50°40'·08N 00°57'·15W; Fl (2) 5s 28m 5M.

N 2 ⚓ Fl Y 2·5s. 6M; 50°41'·03N 00°56'·74W.

N 1 ⚓ Fl Y (4)10s; 50°41'·26N 00°56'·52W.

N 4 ⚓ Fl Y 7·5s; 50°41'·50N 00°57'·02W.

N 3 ⚓ Fl (3) Y 15s; 50°41'·63N 00°56'·74W.

N 5 ⚓ Fl Y 5s; 50°41'·99N 00°56'·97W.

N 7 ⚓ Fl Y 2·5s; 50°42'·35N 00°57'·20W.

New Grounds ⚓ VQ (3) 5s; 50°41'·84N 00°58'·49W.

Nab End ⚓ Fl R 5s; Whis; 50°42'·63N 00°59'·49W.

Dean Tail ▲ Fl G 5s; 50°42'·99N 00°59'·17W.

Dean Tail S ⚓ Q (6) + L Fl 10s; 50°43'·04N 00°59'·57W.

Dean Tail N ⚓ Q; 50°43'·13N 00°59'·57W.

Horse Tail ▲ Fl (2) G 10s; 50°43'·23N 01°00'·23W.

Nab East ⚓ Fl (2) R 10s; 50°42'·86N 01°00'·80W.

Dean Elbow ▲ Fl (3) G 15s; 50°43'·69N 01°01'·88W.

St Helens ⚓ Fl (3) R 15s; 50°43'·36N 01°02'·41W.

Horse Elbow ▲QG; 50°44'·26N 01°03'·88W.

Cambrian Wreck ⚓ 50°44'·43N 01°03'·43W.

Warner ⚓ QR; Whis; 50°43'·87N 01°03'·99W.

BEMBRIDGE

St Helen's Fort ☆ (IOW) Fl (3) 10s 16m 8M; large ○ stone structure; 50°42'·30N 01°05'·05W.

Bembridge Tide Gauge ⚓ Fl Y 2s 1M; 50°42'·46N 01°05'·02W.

SOUTH EAST COAST of the ISLE OF WIGHT

St Catherine's Point ☆ 50°34'·54N 01°17'·87W; Fl 5s 41m 25M; vis: 257°-117°; FR 35m 13M (same Twr) vis: 099°-116°.

Ventnor Haven W Bwtr ⚓ 2 FR (vert) 3M; 50°35'·50N 01°12'·30W.

Sandown Pier Hd ⚓ 2 FR (vert) 7m 2M; 50°39'·05N 01°09'·18W.

W Princessa ⚓ Q (9) 15s; 50°40'·16N 01°03'·65W.

Bembridge Ledge ⚓ Q (3) 10s; 50°41'·15N 01°02'·81W

#		1	2	3	4	5	6	7	8	9	10	11	12	13	14	15	16	17	18
1	Portland Bill	1																	
2	Weymouth	8	2																
3	Swanage	23	22	3															
4	Poole Hbr ent	28	26	6	4														
5	Needles Lt Ho	35	34	14	14	5													
6	Lymington	42	40	21	21	7	6												
7	Yarmouth (IOW)	40	39	19	19	6	2	7											
8	Beaulieu River ent	46	45	25	25	12	7	7	8										
9	Cowes	49	46	28	28	15	15	9	5	9									
10	Southampton	55	54	34	34	24	15	15	9	9	10								
11	R. Hamble (ent)	53	51	32	32	19	12	12	6	6	4	11							
12	Portsmouth	58	57	37	37	24	18	18	11	15	18	15	12						
13	Langstone Hbr	61	59	40	40	25	22	24	15	12	16	13	5	13					
14	Chichester Bar	63	62	42	42	29	29	24	17	15	20	17	8	5	14				
15	Bembridge	59	58	38	38	24	15	19	12	10	19	14	6	6	8	15			
16	Nab Tower	60	63	39	39	30	25	25	18	16	21	18	10	7	6	6	16		
17	St Catherine's Pt	45	44	25	25	14	15	18	27	25	30	27	19	20	19	17	15	17	
18	Littlehampton	79	79	60	61	46	44	45	38	36	45	42	31	28	25	28	22	35	18

DISTANCE TABLES

Approx distances in nautical miles are by the most direct route allowing for dangers and TSS.

NAVIGATION

17

LANGSTONE and APPROACHES

Eastney Pt Fraser Trials Range ⚡ FR, Oc (2) Y 10s, and FY Lts (occas) when firing taking place; 50°47'·19N 01°02'·22W.

Winner *↓*; 50°45'·10N 01°00'·10W.

Roway Wk ↓ Fl (2) 5s; 50°46'·11N 01°02'·28W.

Langstone Fairway ↓ L Fl 10s; 50°46'·32N 01°01'·36W.

Eastney Pt Outfall ⚡ QR 2m 2M; 50°47'·23N 01°01'·68W.

East Milton ⚓ Fl (4) R 10s; 50°48'·16N 01°01'·76W.

NW Sinah ▲ Fl G 5s; 50°48'·14N 01°01'·58W.

CHICHESTER ENTRANCE

West Pole (tripod) ♟ Fl R 5s 14m 7M; 50°45'·45N 00°56'·59W.

Bar ↓ Fl(2) R 10s 10m 4M; 50°46'·02N 00°56'·38W.

Eastoke ⚓ QR; 50°46'·68N 00°56'·11W.

West Winner ↓ QG; Tide gauge. 50°46'·88N 00°55'·98W.

EMSWORTH CHANNEL

Fishery ↓ Q (6) + L Fl 15s; 50°47'·38N 00°56'·07W.

NW Pilsey ▲ Fl G 5s; 50°47'·50N 00°56'·20W.

Verner ↓ Fl R 10s; 50°48'·20N 00°56'·63W.

Marker Pt ↓ Fl (2) G 10s 8m; 50°48'·91N 00°56'·72W.

Emsworth ↓ Q (6) + L Fl 15s; tide gauge; 50°49'·66N 00°56'·76W.

THORNEY CHANNEL

Camber ↓ Q (6) + L Fl 15s; 50°47'·87N 00°54'·06W.

Pilsey ↓ Fl (2) R 10s ; 50°47'·98N 00°54'·24W.

Thorney ↓ Fl G 5s; 50°48'·20N 00°54'·28W.

CHICHESTER CHANNEL

NW Winner ▲ Fl G 10s; 50°47'·19N 00°55'·92W.

N Winner ▲ Fl (2) G 10s; 50°47'·31N 00°55'·83W.

Mid Winner ▲ Fl (3) G 10s; 50°47'·38N 00°55'·69W.

Stocker ⚓ Fl (3) R 10s; 50°47'·45N 00°55'·52W.

Copyhold ⚓ Fl (4) R 10s; 50°47'·50N 00°54'·93W.

East Head Spit ▲ Fl (4) G 10s; 50°47'·45N 00°54'·82W.

Snowhill ▲ Fl G 5s; 50°47'·52N 00°54'·34W.

Sandhead ⚓ Fl R 10s; 50°47'·67N 00°54'·25W.

Chalkdock ↓ Fl (2) G 10s; 50°48'·49N 00°53'·30W.

AREA 3 *South East England – Selsey Bill to North Foreland*

SELECTED LIGHTS, BUOYS & WAYPOINTS

| Positions are referenced to WGS84 |

OWERS TO BEACHY HEAD

SELSEY BILL and THE OWERS

S Pullar ↓ VQ (6) + L Fl 10s; 50°38'·84N 00°49'·29W.

Pullar ↓ Q (9) 15s; 50°40'·47N 00°50'·09W.

Boulder ▲ Fl G 2·5s; 50°41'·56N 00°49'·09W.

Street ⚓ QR; 50°41'·69N 00°48'·89W.

Owers ↓ Q (6) + L Fl 15s; *Bell*; **Racon (O) 10M**; 50°38'·59N 00°41'·09W.

E Borough Hd ↓ Q (3) 10s *Bell*; 50°41'·54N 00°39'·09W.

LITTLEHAMPTON

West Pier Hd ↓ QR 7m 6M; 50°47'·88N 00°32'·46W.

Training Wall Hd ↓ QG 10m 2M; 50°47'·87N 00°32'·38W.

Ldg Lts 346°. Front, E Pier Hd ↓ FG 6m 7M; B col. Rear, 64m from front, Oc WY 7·5s 9m10M; W twr; vis: 290°-W-356°-Y-042°; 50°48'·09N 00°32'·51W.

Outfall ⚓ Fl Y 5s; 50°46'·27N 00°30'·53W.

Littlehampton ⚡ Fl (5) Y 20s 9m 5M; 50°46'·19N 00°29'·54W.

WORTHING and SHOREHAM

Met Mast ⚡ Mo(U)16m 10M; 50°41'·29N 00°20'·59W; Aero FR (103m), *Horn Mo(U) 15s*.

Outfall ↓ Fl R 2·5s 3m; 50°48'·38N 00°20'·34W.

Express ↓ Fl Y 5s; (Apr-Oct); 50°47'·28N 00°17'·09W.

W Bkwtr Head ⚡ Fl R 5s 7m 7M; 50°49'·49N 00°14'·89W.

Ldg Lts 355°. Middle Pier Front, Oc 5s 8m 10M; W watch-house, R base; tidal Lts, tfc sigs; *Horn 20s*. **Rear**, 192m from front, Fl 10s 13m **15M**; Gy twr vis: 283°-103°; 50°49'·75N 00°14'·88W.

Outfall ↓ Fl Y 5s; 50°49'·47N 00°14'·39W.

Shoreham Outfall ↓ Q (6) + L Fl 15s; 50°48'·88N 00°13'·72W.

BRIGHTON and BRIGHTON MARINA

Black Rk Ledge ↓ Fl Y 4s; 50°48'·07N 00°06'·46W.

W Bkwtr Hd ⚡ QR 10m 7M; W ○ structure, R bands; *Horn (2) 30s*; 50°48'·50N 00°06'·38W.

E Bkwtr Hd ⚡ QG 8m 7M and Fl (4) WR 20s 16m W10M, R8M; W pillar, G bands; vis: 260°-R-295°-W-100°; 50°48'·47N 00°06'·37W.

Saltdean Outfall ⚓ Fl Y 5s; 50°46'·72N 00°02'·13W.

NEWHAVEN

Bkwtr Head ⚡ Oc (2) 10s 17m 12M; 50°46'·56N 00°03'·50E.

E Pier Hd ⚡ Iso G 10s 12m 6M; W twr; 50°46'·81N 00°03'·59E.

OFFSHORE MARKS

CS 1 ↓ Fl Y 2·5s; *Whis*; 50°33'·69N 00°03'·92W.

GREENWICH ⌒ 50°24'·54N 00°00'·10E; Fl 5s 12m **15M**; Riding light FW; R hull; **Racon (M) 10M**; *Horn 30s* .

CS 2 ↓ Fl Y 5s; 50°39'·14N 00°32'·60E.

CS 3 ↓ Fl Y 10s; 50°52'·04N 01°02'·18E.

BEACHY HEAD TO DUNGENESS

Beachy Head ⚡ 50°44'·03N 00°14'·49E; Fl (2) 20s 31m 8M; W round twr, R band and lantern; vis: 248°-101°; (H24).

Royal Sovereign ⚡ Fl 20s 28m 12M; W ○ twr, R band on W cabin on col; *Horn (2) 30s*; 50°43'·45N 00°26'·09E.

Royal Sovereign ⚓ QR; 50°44'·23N 00°25'·84E.

EASTBOURNE and SOVEREIGN HARBOUR

SH ↓ Fl Y 10s; 50°47'·40N 00°20'·71E.

Martello Tower ⚡ Fl (3) 15s 12m 7M.; 50°47'·24N 00°19'·83E.

Dir lt 258°Fl WRG 5s 4m 1M; vis: 252·5°-G-256·5°-W-259·5°-R-262·5°; 50°47'·28N 00°19'·71E.

S Bkwtr Hd ⚡ Fl (4) R 12s 3m 6M; 50°47'·30N 00°20'·03E.

St Leonard's Outfall ⚓ Fl Y 5s; 50°49'·31N 00°31'·95E.

HASTINGS

Ldg Lts 356·3°. Front, FR 14m 4M; 50°51'·29N 00°35'·38E. Rear, West Hill, 357m from front, FR 55m 4M; W twr.

RYE

Rye Fairway, L Fl 10s; 50°54'·04N 00°48'·04E.

W Groyne Hd No. 2 ⚓ Fl R 5s 7m 6M; 50°55'·58N 00°46'·55E.
E Arm Hd No. 1 ⚓ Q (9) 15s 7m 5M; G △; *Horn 7s*; 50°55'·73N 00°46'·46E.
Dungeness Outfall ⚓ Q (6) + L Fl 15s; 50°54'·45N 00°58'·21E.
Dungeness ☆ 50°54'·81N 00°58'·56E; Fl 10s 40m **21M**; B ○ twr, W bands and lantern, floodlit; Part obsc 078°-shore; (H24). F RG 37m 10M (same twr); vis: 057°-R-073°-G-078°-196°-R-216°; *Horn (3) 60s*; FR Lts shown between 2·4M and 5·2M WNW when firing taking place. QR on radio mast 1·2M NW.

DUNGENESS TO NORTH FORELAND

FOLKESTONE
Hythe Flats Outfall ⚓ Fl Y 5s; 51°02'·52N 01°05'·32E.
Breakwater Head ☆ Fl (2) 10s 14m **22M**; 51°04'·56N 01°11'·69E.

DOVER
Admiralty Pier Extension Head ⚓ 51°06'·69N 01°19'·66E; Fl 7·5s 21m **20M**; W twr; vis: 096°-090°, obsc in The Downs by S Foreland inshore of 226°; *Horn 10s*; Int Port Tfc sigs.
S Bkwtr W Hd ☆ 51°06'·78N 01°19'·80E;Oc R 30s 21m **18M**; W twr.
Knuckle ☆ 51°07'·04N 01°20'·49E; Fl (4) WR 10s 15m **W15M**, R13M; W twr; vis: 059°-R-239°-W-059°.
N Head ⚓ Fl R 2·5s 11m 5M; 51°07'·20N 01°20'·61E.
Eastern Arm Hd ⚓ Fl G 5s 12m 5M; *Horn (2) 30s*; Int port tfc sigs; 51°07'·31N 01°20'·59E.

DOVER STRAIT
Bullock Bank ⚓ VQ; 50°46'·94N 01°07'·60E.
Ridens SE ⚓ VQ (3) 5s; 50°43'·47N 01°18'·87E.
Colbart SW ⚓ VQ (6) + L Fl 10s; 50°48'·86N 01°16'·30E.
South Varne ⚓ Q (6) + L Fl 15s; 50°55'·64N 01°17'·30E.
Mid Varne ⚓ VQ(9)10s; 50°58'·94N 01°19'·88E.
East Varne ⚓ VQ(3)5s; 50°58'·22N 01°20'·90E.
Colbart N ⚓ VQ; 50°57'·45N 01°23'·29E.

VARNE ⚓ 51°01'·29N 01°23'·90E; Fl R 5s 12m **15M**; *Racon (T) 10M*; 992351038; *Horn 30s*.

CS 4 ⚓ Fl (4) Y 15s; 51°08'·62N 01°33'·92E.
MPC ⚓ Fl Y 2·5s; *Racon (O) 10M*; 51°06'·12N 01°38'·20E.

SW Goodwin ⚓ Q (6) + L Fl 15s; 51°08'·50N 01°28'·88E.
S Goodwin ⚓ Fl (4) R 15s; 51°10'·60N 01°32'·26E.
SE Goodwin ⚓ Fl (3) R 10s; 51°12'·99N 01°34'·45E.

E GOODWIN ⚓ 51°13'·26N 01°36'·37E; Fl 15s 12m **23M**; R hull with lt twr amidships; *Racon (T) 10M*; 992351035; *Horn 30s*.

E Goodwin ⚓ Q (3) 10s; 51°15'·67N 01°35'·69E.
NE Goodwin ⚓ Q (3) 10s; *Racon (M) 10M*. 51°20'·31N 01°34'·16E.

DEAL and THE DOWNS
Trinity Bay VQ (9) 10s; 51°11'·60N 01°29'·00E.
Deal Bank ⚓ QR; 51°12'·92N 01°25'·57E.
Goodwin Fork ⚓ Q (6) + L Fl 15s; *Bell*; 51°14'·38N 01°26'·70E.
Downs ⚓ Fl (2) R 5s; *Bell*; 51°14'·50N 01°26'·22E.

GULL STREAM
W Goodwin ⚓ Fl G 5s; 51°15'·61N 01°27'·38E.
S Brake ⚓ Fl (3) R 10s; 51°15'·77N 01°26'·82E.
NW Goodwin ⚓ Q (9) 15s; 51°16'·73N 01°28'·60E.
Brake ⚓ Fl (4) R 15s; 51°16'·98N 01°28'·19E.
N Goodwin ⚓ Fl G 2·5s; 51°18'·12N 01°30'·35E.
Gull Stream ⚓ QR; 51°18'·26N 01°29'·69E.
Gull ⚓ VQ (3) 5s; 51°19'·57N 01°31'·30E.
Goodwin Knoll ⚓ Fl (2) G 5s; 51°19'·57N 01°32'·20E.

RAMSGATE CHANNEL
B2 ⚓ Fl (2) G 5s; 51°18'·26N 01°23'·93E.
W Quern ⚓Q (9) 15s; 51°18'·98N 01°25'·39E.

RAMSGATE
RA ⚓ Q(6) + L Fl 15s; 51°19'·60N 01°30'·13E.
E Brake ⚓ Fl R 5s; 51°19'·47N 01°29'·20E.
No. 1 ⚓QG; 51°19'·56N 01°27'·29E.
No. 2 ⚓ Fl (4) R 10s; 51°19'·46N 01°27'·28E.
No. 3 ⚓ Fl G 2·5s; 51°19'·56N 01°26'·61E.
No. 4 ⚓ QR; 51°19'·46N 01°26'·60E.
N Quern ⚓ Q; 51°19'·41N 01°26'·11E.
No. 5 ⚓ Q (6) + L Fl 15s; 51°19'·56N 01°25'·91E.
No. 6 ⚓ Fl (2) R 5s; 51°19'·46N 01°25'·91E.
South Bkwtr Hd ⚓ VQ R 10m 5M; 51°19'·46N 01°25'·41E.
N Bkwtr Hd ⚓ QG 10m 5M; 51°19'·56N 01°25'·47E.
Western Marine terminal Dir lt 270° ⚓, Oc WRG 10s 10m 5M; B △, Or stripe; vis: 259°-G-269°-W- 271°-R-281°;

1	Nab Tower	**1**														
2	Boulder Lt Buoy	5	**2**													
3	Owers Lt Buoy	10	6	**3**												
4	Littlehampton	19	13	12	**4**											
5	Shoreham	32	24	21	13	**5**										
6	Brighton	35	28	24	17	5	**6**									
7	Newhaven	40	34	29	24	12	7	**7**								
8	Beachy Head Lt	46	41	36	30	20	14	8	**8**							
9	Eastbourne	51	45	40	34	24	19	12	7	**9**						
10	Rye	72	67	62	56	46	41	34	25	23	**10**					
11	Dungeness Lt	76	71	66	60	50	44	38	30	26	9	**11**				
12	Folkestone	92	84	81	76	65	60	53	43	40	23	13	**12**			
13	Dover	97	89	86	81	70	65	58	48	45	28	18	5	**13**		
14	Ramsgate	112	104	101	96	85	80	73	63	60	43	33	20	15	**14**	
15	N Foreland Lt	115	107	104	99	88	83	76	66	63	46	36	23	18	3	**15**
16	Sheerness	146	139	135	132	119	114	107	97	96	79	67	54	49	34	31	**16**
17	London Bridge	188	184	177	177	161	156	149	139	141	124	109	96	91	76	73	45	**17**

DISTANCE TABLES
Approx distances in nautical miles are by the most direct route allowing for dangers and TSS.

51°19'·51N 01°24'·85E. Rear 493m from front Oc 5s 17m 5M; B ▽, Or stripe; vis: 263°-278°.

BROADSTAIRS and NORTH FORELAND
Broadstairs Knoll ~ Fl R 2·5s; 51°20'·88N 01°29'·48E.
Pier SE End ⚡ 2 FR (vert) 7m 4M; 51°21'·50N 01°26'·74E.
Elbow ⚓ Q; 51°23'·23N 01°31'·59E.

North Foreland ☆ 51°22'·49N 01°26'·70E; Fl (5) WR 20s 57m **W19M, R16M, R15M**; W 8-sided twr; vis: shore-W-150°-R(**16M**)-181°-R(**15M**)-200°-W-011°; H24.

OFFSHORE MARKS
SANDETTIE ⚓ 51°09'·36N 01°47'·12E; Fl 5s 12m **15M**; R hull with lt twr amidships; *Racon; 992351029*; *Horn 30s.*

F1 ⚓ Fl (4) Y 15s; 51°11'·21N 01°44'·91E.
South Falls ⚓ Q (6) + L Fl 15s; 51°13'·84N 01°43'·93E.
Sandettie W ⚓ Fl (3) G 12s; 51°15'·09N 01°54'·47E.
Mid Falls ⚓ Fl (3) R 10s; 51°18'·63N 01°46'·99E.
Inter Bank ⚓ Fl Y 5s; *Bell; Racon (M) 10M*; 51°16'·47N 01°52'·23E.
F2 ⚓ Fl (4) Y 15s; 51°20'·41N 01°56'·19E.

AREA 4 *East England – North Foreland to Berwick-upon-Tweed*

SELECTED LIGHTS, BUOYS & WAYPOINTS

Positions are referenced to WGS84

THAMES ESTUARY – SOUTHERN
(Direction of buoyage generally East to West)

APPROACHES to THAMES ESTUARY
Foxtrot 3 ⊂⊃ 51°24'·20N 02°00'·40E; Fl 10s 12m **15M**; *Racon (T) 10M*; *Horn 10s.*
Falls Hd ⚓ Q; 51°28'·23N 01°49'·89E.
Drill Stone ⚓ Q (3) 10s; 51°25'·88N 01°42'·89E.
Thanet N ⚓ VQ 15s; 51°28'·28N 01°38'·06E.
NE Spit ⚓ VQ (3); *Racon (T) 10M*; 5s; 51°27'·93N 01°29'·89E.
East Margate ~ Fl R 2·5s; 51°27'·03N 01°26'·40E.
Elbow ⚓ Q; 51°23'·23N 01°31'·59E.
Foreness Pt Outfall ⚓ Fl R 5s; 51°24'·61N 01°26'·02E.
Longnose ⚓ 51°24'·15N 01°26'·08E.
Longnose Spit ⚓ Fl R 2·5s 5m 2M; 51°23'·93N 01°25'·68E.

MARGATE and GORE CHANNEL
SE Margate ⚓ Q (3) 10s; 51°24'·05N 01°20'·40E.
S Margate ⚓ Fl G 2·5s; 51°23'·83N 01°16'·65E.
Copperas ⚓ QG; 51°23'·81N 01°11'·18E.
Reculver ~ QR; 51°23'·63N 01°12'·56E.

HERNE BAY
Beltinge Bay Bn ⚓ Fl Y 5s; 51°22'·73N 01°08'·63E.
Landing Stage ⚓ Q 18m 4M, (isolated); 51°22'·91N 01°06'·89E.
N Pier Hd ⚡ 2 FR (vert); 51°22'·43N 01°07'·27E.

WHITSTABLE
Whitstable Street ⚓ ; 51°24'·00N 01°01'·54E. (See The Swale.)
Oyster ~ Fl (2) R 10s; 51°22'·14N 01°01'·16E.
W Quay Dn ⚡ Fl G 5s 2m.

THE SWALE
Whitstable Street ⚓ Fl R 2s; 51°24'·00N 01°01'·54E.
Columbine ⚓ Fl G 2s; 51°24'·26N 01°01'·34E.
Columbine Spit ⚓ Fl (3) G 10s; 51°23'·86N 01°00'·03E.
Ham Gat ⚓ Q G; 51°23'·08N 00°58'·32E.
Pollard Spit ~ Q R; 51°22'·98N 00°58'·57E.
Sand End ⚓ Fl G 5s; 51°21'·43N 00°55'·90E.
Receptive Point ⚓ Fl G 10s; 51°20'·86N 00°54'·41E.
Queenborough Spit ⚓ Q (3) 10s; 51°25'·81N 00°43'·93E.
South Oaze ~ Fl R 2s; 51°21'·34N 00°56'·01E.

QUEENS CHANNEL and FOUR FATHOMS CHANNEL
E Margate ~ Fl R 2·5s; 51°27'·03N 01°26'·40E.
Spaniard ⚓ Q (3) 10s; 51°26'·23N 01°04'·00E.
Spile ⚓ Fl G 2·5s; 51°26'·43N 00°55'·70E.

PRINCES CHANNEL
Tongue Sand E ⚓ VQ (3) 5s; 51°29'·48N 01°22'·21E.
Tongue Sand N ⚓ Q; 51°29'·68N 01°22'·03E.
Princes Outer ⚓ VQ (6) + L Fl 10s; 51°28'·89N 01°20'·43E.
Princes North ⚓ Q G; 51°29'·25N 01°18'·35E.
Princes South ~ Q R; 51°28'·74N 01°18'·26E.
Princes No.1 ⚓ Fl (4) G 15s; 51°29'·23N 01°16'·02E.
Princes No.2 ~ Fl (2) R 5s; 51°28'·81N 01°13'·08E.
Princes No.3 ⚓ Fl (2) G 5s; 51°29'·33N 01°13'·10E.
Princes No.4 ~ Fl (3) R 10s; 51°28'·83N 01°09'·90E.
Princes No.5 ⚓ Fl (3) G 10s; 51°29'·39N 01°10'·00E.
Princes Mid ⚓ Fl Y 5s; 51°29'·19N 01°09'·00E.
Shivering Sand Twr N ⚓ Q; 51°30'·01N 01°04'·76E.
Shivering Sand Twr S ⚓ Q (6) + L Fl 15s; *Bell;* 51°29'·75N 01°04'·83E.
Princes No.8 ~ Fl (2) R 5s; 51°29'·14N 01°03'·00E.
Princes Inner ⚓ Fl Y 2·5s; 51°29'·59N 01°03'·47E.

FOULGER'S GAT and KNOB CHANNEL
The N Edinburgh Channel is not buoyed. Fisherman's Gat is a commercial ship channel; Foulger's Gat, suitable for leisure craft, is marked at each end with SWMs.
Long Sand Inner ⚓ Mo 'A' 15s; 51°38'·80N 01°25'·60E.
Long Sand Outer ⚓ L Fl 10s; 51°35'·90N 01°26'·00E.
SE Knob ⚓ Fl G 5s; 51°30'·89N 01°06'·41E.
Knob ⚓ Iso 5s; *Whis;* 51°30'·69N 01°04'·28E.

OAZE DEEP
Oaze Deep ⚓ Fl (2) G 5s; 51°30'·03N 01°00'·70E.
Red Sand Trs N ~ Fl (3) R 10s; *Bell;* 51°28'·73N 00°59'·32E.
N Oaze ~ QR; 51°30'·03N 00°57'·65E.
Oaze ⚓ Fl (4) Y 10s; 51°29'·06N 00°56'·93E.
W Oaze ⚓ Iso 5s; 51°29'·06N 00°55'·43E.
Oaze Bank ⚓ Q G 5s; 51°29'·36N 00°56'·95E.
Cant ⚓ (unlit); 51°27'·77N 00°53'·36E.
East Cant ~ QR; 51°28'·53N 00°55'·60E.

MEDWAY, SHEERNESS
Medway ⚓ Mo (A) 6s; 51°28'·83N 00°52'·81E.
No. 1 ⚓ Fl G 2·5s; 51°28'·55N 00°50'·50E.
No. 2 ⚓ Q; 51°28'·33N 00°50'·52E.
No. 7 ⚓ Fl G 10s; 51°27'·91N 00°47'·52E.
No. 9 ⚓ Fl G 5s; 51°27'·74N 00°46'·61E.
No. 11 ⚓ Fl (3) G 10s; 51°27'·51N 00°45'·80E.
Grain Hard ⚓ Fl G 5s; 51°26'·98N 00°44'·17E.
Isle of Grain ⚡ Q 20m 13M; R & W ◇ on R twr; 51°26'·70N 00°43'·38E.
Queenborough Spit ⚓ Q (3) 10s; 51°25'·81N 00°43'·93E.

RIVER THAMES

SEA REACH, NORE and YANTLET
No. 1 ⚓ Fl Y 2·5s; *Racon (T) 10M*; 51°29'·45N 00°52'·57E.
No. 2 ⚓ Iso 5s; 51°29'·40N 00°49'·75E.
No. 3 ⚓ Oc 10s; 51°29'·33N 00°46'·54E.
No. 4 ⚓ Fl Y 2·5s; 51°29'·61N 00°44'·18E.
No. 5 ⚓ Iso 5s; 51°29'·95N 00°41'·44E.
No. 6 ⚓ Iso 2s; 51°30'·03N 00°39'·83E.
No. 7 ⚓ Fl Y 2·5s; *Racon (T) 10M*; 51°30'·10N 00°37'·04E.
Nore Swatch ⚓ Fl (4) R 15s; 51°28'·28N 00°45'·55E.
Mid Swatch ⚓ Fl G 5s; 51°28'·68N 00°44'·16E.
W Nore Sand ⚓ Fl (3) R 10s; 51°29'·41N 00°40'·85E.
East Blyth ⚓ Fl (2) R 10s; 51°29'·72N 00°37'·80E.
Mid Blyth ⚓ Q; 51°30'·08N 00°32'·38E.

LEIGH-ON-SEA and SOUTHEND-ON-SEA
Leigh ⚓ ; 51°31'·07N 00°42'·56E.
Southend Pier E End ⚓ 2 FG (vert) 7m; *Horn Mo (N) 30s, Bell (1)*
SE Leigh ⚓ Q (6) + L Fl 15s; 51°29'·42N 00°47'·07E.

GRAVESEND
Shornmead ⚓ Fl (2) WR 10s 12m 11/7M , W11M, W7M, R11M; vis 070°-W-084°-R(Intens)-089°-W(Intens)-094°-W-250°; 51°26'·92N 00°26'·24E.
Northfleet Upper ☆ Oc WRG 10s 30m **W16M**, R12M, G12M; vis:126°-R-149°-W-159°-G-268°-W-279°; 51°26'·93N 00°20'·06E.

THAMES TIDAL BARRIER
Span B (51°29'·73N 00°02'·23E) is used for small craft/yachts Eastbound and Span G (51°29'·91N 00°02'·21E) is used for small craft/yachts Westbound. Spans B, C, D, E, F & G are navigable. Spans C to F are for larger vessels. All spans display a F GR ⚡. A **Green** ➝ indicates span open for navigation. A **Red X** indicates span closed to navigation. In low visibility fixed lights are shown either side of those spans which are displaying a **Green** ➝.

THAMES ESTUARY – NORTHERN

KENTISH KNOCK
Kentish Knock ⚓ Q (3) 10s; 51°38'·08N 01°40·43E.
S Knock ⚓ Q (6) + L Fl 15s; *Bell*; 51°34'·13N 01°34'·29E.

KNOCK JOHN CHANNEL
No. 7 ⚓ Fl (4) G 15s; 51°32'·03N 01°06'·40E.
No. 5 ⚓ Fl (3) G 10s; 51°32'·49N 01°07'·75E.
No. 4 ⚓ QR 10s; 51°32'·33N 01°07'·90E.
No. 2 ⚓ Fl (3) R 10s; 51°33'·11N 01°09'·85E.
No. 3 ⚓ Q (6) + L Fl 15s; 51°33'·23N 01°09'·70E.
No. 1 ⚓ Fl G 5s; 51°33'·75N 01°10'·72E.
Knock John ⚓ Fl (2) R 5s; 51°33'·61N 01°11'·37E.

BLACK DEEP
No. 12 ⚓ Fl (4) R 15s; 51°33'·83N 01°13'·50E.
No. 11 ⚓ Fl (3) G 10s; 51°34'·33N 01°13'·40E.
No. 10 ⚓ Fl (3) R 10s; 51°34'·74N 01°15'·60E.
No. 9 ⚓ Q (6) + L Fl 15s; 51°35'·13N 01°15'·09E.
No. 8 ⚓ Q (9) 15s; 51°36'·36N 01°20'·43E.
No. 7 ⚓ QG. 51°37'·08N 01°17'·69E.
No. 6 ⚓ Fl R 2·5s; 51°38'·53N 01°24'·41E.
No. 5 ⚓ VQ (3) 5s; 51°39'·53N 01°23'·00E.
No. 4 ⚓ Fl (2) R 5s; 51°41'·42N 01°28'·49E.
Long Sand Bcn ⚓ ; 51°41'·48N 01°29'·49E.
No. 3 ⚓ Fl (3) G 15s; 51°42'·39N 01°26'·66E.

No. 1 ⚓ Fl G 5s, 51°44'·03N 01°28'·09E.
No. 2 ⚓ Fl (4) R 15s; 51°45'·63N 01°32'·20E.
Sunk Head Tower ⚓ Q; *Whis*; 51°46'·63N 01°30'·51E.
Black Deep ⚓ QR; 51°48'·10N 01°36'·60E.
Trinity ⚓ Q (6) + L Fl 15s; 51°49'·03N 01°36'·39E.
Long Sand Head ⚓ VQ; *Whis*; 51°47'·90N 01°39'·42E.

FISHERMANS GAT
Outer Fisherman ⚓ Q (3) 10s; 51°34'·02N 01°25'·10E.
Fisherman No. 1 ⚓ Fl G 2·5s (sync); 51°34'·50N 01°23'·52E.
Fisherman No. 2 ⚓ Fl R 2·5s (sync); 51°34'·30N 01°23'·50E.
Fisherman No. 3 ⚓ Fl G 5s; 51°34'·78N 01°22'·65E.
Fisherman No. 4 ⚓ Fl (2) R 5s; 51°34'·77N 01°22'·08E.
Fisherman No. 5 ⚓ Fl (2) G 5s; 51°35'·25N 01°21'·84E.
Fisherman No. 6 ⚓ Fl (3) R 10s; 51°35'·08N 01°21'·56E.
Inner Fisherman ⚓ Q R; 51°36'·10N 01°19'·97E.

BARROW DEEP
SW Barrow ⚓ Q(6) + L Fl 15s; *Bell*; 51°32'·29N 01°00'·31E.
Barrow No. 14 ⚓ Fl R 2·5s; 51°31'·83N 01°00'·43E.
Barrow No. 13 ⚓ Fl (2) G 5s; 51°32'·82N 01°03'·07E.
Barrow No. 12 ⚓ Fl (2) R 5s; 51°32'·77N 01°04'·13E.
Barrow No.11 ⚓ Fl (3) G 10s; 51°34'·08N 01°06'·70E.
Barrow No. 9 ⚓ VQ (3) 5s; 51°35'·34N 01°10'·30E.
Barrow No. 8 ⚓ Fl (2) R 5s; 51°35'·03N 01°11'·40E.
Barrow No. 6 ⚓ Fl (4) R 15s; 51°37'·30N 01°14'·69E.
Barrow No. 5 ⚓ Fl G 10s; 51°40'·03N 01°16'·20E.
Barrow No. 4 ⚓ VQ (9) 10s; 51°39'·88N 01°17'·48E.
Barrow No. 3 ⚓ Q (3) 10s; *Racon (M)10M*; 51°42'·02N 01°20'·24E.
Barrow No. 2 ⚓ Fl (2) R 5s; 51°41'·98N 01°22'·89E.

WEST SWIN and MIDDLE DEEP
Blacktail (W) ⚓ ; 51°31'·46N 00°55'·19E.
Maplin ⚓ Q G (sync with W Swin); *Bell*; 51°33'·66N 01°01'·40E.
W Swin ⚓ Q R (sync with Maplin); 51°33'·40N 01°01'·97E.
Maplin Edge ⚓ Fl G 2.5s; 51°35'·33N 01°03'·64E.
Maplin Bank ⚓ Fl (3) R 10s; 51°35'·50N 01°04'·70E.

EAST SWIN and KING'S CHANNEL
NE Maplin ⚓ Fl G 5s; *Bell*; 51°37'·43N 01°04'·90E.
W Hook Middle ⚓ 51°39'·18N 01°07'·97E.
S Whitaker ⚓ Fl (2) G 10s; 51°40'·17N 01°09'·11E.
N Middle ⚓ Q; 51°41'·35N 01°12'·61E.
W Sunk ⚓ Q (9) 15s; 51°44'·33N 01°25'·80E.
Gunfleet Spit ⚓ Q (6) + L Fl 15s; *Bell*; 51°45'·33N 01°21'·70E.

WHITAKER CHANNEL and RIVER CROUCH
Whitaker ⚓ Q (3) 10s; *Bell*; 51°41'·43N 01°10'·51E.
Inner Whitaker ⚓ VQ (6) + L Fl 10s; 51°40'·76N 01°08'·40E.
Swin Spitway ⚓ Iso 10s; *Bell*; 51°41'·95N 01°08'·35E.
Whitaker 1 ⚓ FlG 5s (sync Whit 2), 51° 40'.69N 01° 06'.67E.
Whitaker 2 ⚓ FlR 5s (sync Whit 1), 51° 40'.41N 01° 06'.78E.
Whitaker 3 ⚓ Fl(2) G 5s (sync Whit 4) 51° 40'.41N 01° 04'.74E.
Whitaker 4 ⚓ Fl(2) R 5s (sync Whit 3) 51° 40'.16N 01° 04'.91E.
Whitaker 5 ⚓ Fl(3) G 10s (sync Whit 6) 51° 40'.03N 01° 03'.22E.
Whitaker 6 ⚓ Fl(3) R 10s(sync Whit 5) 51° 39'.77N 01° 03'.43E.
Whitaker 7 ⚓ Fl(4) G 10s(sync Whit 8) 51° 39'.54N 01° 02'.00E.
Whitaker 8 ⚓ Fl(4) R 10s(sync Whit 7), 51° 39'.35N 01° 02'.00E.
Swallowtail 1 ⚓ Fl Y 5s, 51° 41'.38N 01° 08'.20E.
Swallowtail 2 ⚓ Fl Y 10s, 51° 41'.19N 01° 06'.28E.

21

Swallowtail 3 ℺ Fl Y 15s, 51° 40.84N 01° 04.39E.
Swallowtail 4 ℺ (2) Y 10s, 51° 40'.52N 01° 03'.47E.
Buxey Edge ▲ Fl G 10s, 51° 40'.65N 01° 03'.48E.
Swallowtail ↓ VQ (9) 10s, 51° 40'.04N 01° 02'.65E.
Sunken Buxey ↓ VQ; 51°39'·59N 01°00'·77E.
Buxey No. 1 ↓ VQ (6) + L Fl 10s; 51°39'·18N 01°01'·13E.
Buxey No. 2 ↓ Q; 51°39'·08N 01°00'·23E.
Outer Crouch 1 ▲ Fl G 5s (sync Cro 2) 51° 38'.71N 00° 59'.00E.
Outer Crouch 2 ℺ Fl R 5s (sync Cro 1) 51° 38'.62N 00° 59'.20E.
Outer Crouch 3 ▲ Fl G 10s (sync Cro 4) 51° 38'.10N 00° 57'.83E.
Outer Crouch 4 ℺ Fl R 10s (sync Cro 3) 51° 37'.95N 00° 58'.00E.
Crouch ↓ Q.Fl, 51° 37.650N 00° 56.582E.
Inner Crouch ↓ L Fl 10s, 51° 37'.19N 00° 55'.09E.
Branklet (RGR) **Pref Chan to Stbd,** Comp grp Fl (R) 2+1 10s, 51° 36'.99N 00° 52'.10E.

GOLDMER GAT and WALLET
NE Gunfleet ↓ Q (3) 10s; 51°49'·93N 01°27'·79E.
Wallet No. 2 ℺ Fl R 5s; 51°48'·88N 01°22'·99E.
Wallet No. 4 ℺ Fl (4) R 10s; 51°46'·53N 01°17'·23E.
Wallet Spitway ℺ L Fl 10s; *Bell;* 51°42'·86N 01°07'·30E.
Knoll ↓ Q; 51°43'·88N 01°05'·07E.
Eagle ▲ QG; 51°44'·13N 01°03'·82E.
N Eagle ↓ Q; 51°44'·71N 01°04'·32E.
NW Knoll ℺ Fl (2) R 5s; 51°44'·35N 01°02'·17E.
Colne Bar ▲ Fl (2) G 5s; 51°44'·61N 01°02'·57E.
Bench Head ▲ Fl (3) G 10s; 51°44'·69N 01°01'·10E.

RIVER BLACKWATER
The Nass ↓ VQ (3) 5s 6m 2M; 51°45'·83N 00°54'·83E.
Thirslet ▲ Fl (3) G 10s; 51°43'·73N 00°50'·39E.
No. 1 ▲ ; 51°43'·44N 00°48'·02E.

RIVER COLNE and BRIGHTLINGSEA
Inner Bench Head No. 2 ℺ Fl (2) R 5s; 51°45'·96N 01°01'·74E.
Colne Pt No. 1 ▲ Fl G 3s; 51°46'·01N 01°01'·92E.
No. 8 ℺ Fl R 3s; 51°46'·90N 01°01'·30E.
No. 9 ▲ Fl G 3s; 51°47'·36N 01°01'·07E.
Ldg lts 041°. Front, FR 7m 4M; W □, R stripe on post; vis: 020°-080°; 51°48'·39N 01°01'·20E. Rear, 50m from front, FR 10m 4M; W □, R stripe on post. FR lts are shown on 7 masts between 1·5M and 3M NW when firing occurs.

WALTON BACKWATERS
Pye End ℺ L Fl 10s; 51°55'·03N 01°17'·90E.
No. 2 ℺ Fl (2) 5s; 51°54'·62N 01°16'·80E.
Crab Knoll No. 3 ▲ Fl G 5s; 51°54'·41N 01°16'·41E.

HARWICH APPROACHES
(Direction of buoyage is North to South)

MEDUSA CHANNEL
Medusa ▲ Fl G 5s; 51°51'·23N 01°20'·35E.
Stone Banks ℺ FlR 5s; 51°53'·19N 01°19'·23E.
Pennyhole △ ; 51°53'·55N 01°18'·00E (Mar–Sep).

CORK SAND and ROUGH SHOALS
S Cork ↓ Q (6) + L Fl 15s; 51°51'·33N 01°24'·09E.
SE Roughs Tower ↓ Q (3) 10s; 51°53'·64N 01°28'·94E.
NW Roughs Tower ↓ VQ (9) 10s; 51°53'·81N 01°28'·77E.
Cork Sand ↓ Fl (3) R 10s; 51°55'·51N 01°25'·42E.

HARWICH CHANNEL
Sunk Inner ⊐ Iso 3s 11m 12M, **Racon T**; *Horn 30s;* 51°51'·03N 01°34'·89E.
S Threshold ↓ Fl (4) Y 10s; 51°52'·20N 01°33'·14E.
S Shipwash ↓↓ 2 By(s) Q (6) + L Fl 15s; 51°52'·71N 01°33'·97E.
Outer Tidal Bn ↓ Mo (U) 15s 2m 3M; 51°52'·85N 01°32'·34E.
E Fort Massac ↓ VQ (3) 5s; 51°53'·36N 01°32'·79E.
W Fort Massac ↓ VQ (9) 10s; 51°53'·36N 01°32'·49E.
Walker ↓ Q (9)15s; 51°53'·79N 01°33'·90E.
N Threshold ↓ Fl Y 5s; 51°54'·49N 01°33'·47E.
SW Shipwash ↓ Fl Y 2·5s; 51°54'·75N 01°34'·21E.
Haven ↓ Mo (A) 5s; 51°55'·76N 01°32'·56E.
W Shipwash ℺ Fl (2) R 10s; 51°57'·13N 01°35'·89E.
NW Shipwash ℺ Fl R 5s; 51°58'·98N 01°37'·01E.
Harwich App (HA) ↓ Iso 5s; 51°56'·75N 01°30'·66E.
Cross ↓ Fl (3) Y 10s; 51°56'·23N 01°30'·48E.
Harwich Chan No. 1 ℺ Fl Y 2·5s; **Racon (T) 10M**; 51°56'·13N 01°27'·06E.
Harwich Chan No. 3 ℺ Fl (3) Y 10s; 51°56'·04N 01°25'·54E.
Harwich Chan No. 5 ℺ Fl (5) Y 10s; 51°55'·96N 01°24'·01E.
Harwich Chan No. 7 ℺ Fl (3) Y 10s; 51°55'·87N 01°22'·49E.
S Bawdsey ↓ Q (6) + L Fl 15s; *Whis;* 51°57'·23N 01°30'·19E.
Washington ▲ QG; 51°56'·52N 01°26'·59E.
Felixstowe Ledge ▲ Fl (3) G 10s; 51°56'·30N 01°23'·72E.
Wadgate Ledge ↓ Fl (4) G 15s; 51°56'·16N 01°21'·99E.
Platters ↓ Q (6) + L Fl 15s; 51°55'·64N 01°20'·97E.
Rolling Ground ▲ QG; 51°55'·55N 01°19'·75E.
Beach End ▲ Fl (2) G 5s; 51°55'·62N 01°19'·21E.
Cork Sand Yacht Bn ↓ VQ 2M; 51°55'·21N 01°25'·20E.
Rough ↓ VQ; 51°55'·19N 01°31'·00E.
Pitching Ground ℺ Fl (4) R 15s; 51°55'·43N 01°21'·05E.
Inner Ridge ℺ QR; 51°55'·38N 01°20'·20E.
Deane ℺ L Fl R 6s; 51°55'·36N 01°19'·28E.
Landguard ↓ Q; 51°55'·45N 01°18'·84E.

RIVERS STOUR AND ORWELL
RIVER STOUR and HARWICH
Shotley Spit ↓ Q (6) + L Fl 15s; 51°57'·21N 01°17'·69E.
Shotley Marina Lock E side Dir lt 339·5° 3m 1M (uses Moiré pattern); Or structure; 51°57'·46N 01°16'·60E.
Guard ℺ Fl R 5s; *Bell;* 51°57'·07N 01°17'·86E.

RIVER ORWELL and IPSWICH
Suffolk Yacht Harbour. Ldg lts Front Iso Y 1M; 51°59'·73N 01°16'·09E. Rear Oc Y 4s 1M.

HARWICH TO ORFORD NESS
FELIXSTOWE, R DEBEN and WOODBRIDGE HAVEN
Woodbridge Haven ℺ Mo(A)15s; 51°58'·20N 01°23'·85E.
Deben ⌀ ; 51°59'·30N 01°23'·53E.

RIVERS ORE and ALDE
Orford Haven ℺ L Fl 10s; *Bell.* 52°01'·62N 01°28'·00E.

OFFSHORE MARKS
S Galloper ↓ Q (6) L Fl 15s; **Racon (T) 10M**; 51°43'·98N 01°56'·43E.
N Galloper ↓ Q; 51°49'·84N 01°59'·99E.
S Inner Gabbard ↓ Q (6) + L Fl 15s. 51°49'·92N 01°51'·89E.
N Inner Gabbard ↓ Q; 51°59'·20N 01°56'·00E.
Outer Gabbard ↓ Q (3) 10s; **Racon (O) 10M;** 51°57'·83N 02°04'·19E.
NHR-SE ▲ Fl G 5s; 51°45'·39N 02°39'·89E.

SHIPWASH and BAWDSEY BANK

E Shipwash ⚓ VQ (3) 5s; 51°57'·08N 01°37'·89E.
NW Shipwash ⚓ Fl R 5s; 51°58'·98N 01°37'·01E.
N Shipwash ⚓ Q 7M; *Racon (M) 10M*; *Whis*; 52°01'·73N 01°38'·27E.
S Bawdsey ⚓ Q (6) + L Fl 15s; *Whis*; 51°57'·23N 01°30'·22E.
Mid Bawdsey ⚓ Fl (3) G 10s; 51°58'·88N 01°33'·59E.
NE Bawdsey ⚓ Fl G 10s; 52°01'·73N 01°36'·09E.

CUTLER and WHITING BANKS

Cutler ⚓ QG; 51°58'·51N 01°27'·48E.
SW Whiting ⚓ Q (6) + L Fl 10s; 52°00'·96N 01°30'·69E.
Whiting Hook ⚓ Fl R 10s; 52°02'·98N 01°31'·82E.
NE Whiting ⚓ Q (3) 10s; 52°03'·61N 01°33'·32E.

ORFORD NESS TO WINTERTON

(Direction of buoyage is South to North)
Orford Ness Lt Ho (dis) 52°05'·04N 01°34'·45E; W ○ twr, R bands.
Aldeburgh Ridge ⚓ QR; 52°06'·49N 01°36'·95E.

SOUTHWOLD

Southwold ☆ 52°19'·63N 01°40'·89E; Fl 10s 37m **W24M**; vis 204°-W-032·5°, 992351019.

LOWESTOFT and APPR VIA STANFORD CHANNEL

E Barnard ⚓ Q (3) 10s; 52°25'·14N 01°46'·38E.
Newcome Sand ⚓ QR; 52°26'·28N 01°46'·97E.
S Holm ⚓ VQ (6) + L Fl 10s; 52°27'·05N 01°47'·15E.
Stanford ⚓ Fl R 2·5s; 52°27'·35N 01°46'·67E.
SW Holm ⚓ Fl (2) G 5s; 52°27'·87N 01°46'·99E.
Kirkley ⚓ Oc WRG 10s 17m, W8M, R6M, G6M, vis: 210°-G-224°-W-229°-R-313°; 52°27'·71N 01°44'·54E.
Outer Hbr S Pier Hd ⚓ Oc R 5s 12m 6M; *Horn (4) 60s*; Tfc sigs; 52°28'·29N 01°45'·36E.
N Newcome ⚓ Fl (4) R 15s; 52°28'·39N 01°46'·37E.
Lowestoft ☆ 52°29'·22N 01°45'·35; Fl 15s 37m **23M**; W twr; part obscd 347°- shore.

LOWESTOFT NORTH ROAD and CORTON ROAD

Lowestoft Ness SE ⚓ Q (6) + L Fl 15s; 52°28'·84N 01°46'·25E.
Lowestoft Ness N ⚓ VQ (3) 5s; *Bell*; 52°28'·89N 01°46'·23E.
W Holm ⚓ Fl (3) G 10s; 52°29'·80N 01°47'·09E.
NW Holm ⚓ Fl (4) G 15s; 52°31'·93N 01°46'·70E.

GREAT YARMOUTH APPROACH via HOLM CHANNEL

E Newcome ⚓ Fl (2) R 5s; 52°28'·51N 01°49'·21E.
Holm Approach ⚓ Q (3) 10s; 52°30'·88N 01°50'·22E.
Holm Sand ⚓ Q (9) 15s; 52°33'·18N 01°46'·54E.
S Corton ⚓ Q (6) + L Fl 15s; *Bell*; 52°32'·94N 01°49'·12E.
NE Holm ⚓ Fl R 2·5s; 52°32'·69N 01°48'·48E.
Mid Corton ⚓ Fl G 2·5s; 52°33'·62N 01°48'·01E.
N Holm ⚓ Q. 52°33'·93N 01°47'·23E.

GREAT YARMOUTH and GORLESTON

W Corton ⚓ Fl (3) G 10s; 52°34'·12N 01°47'·50E.
Gorleston South Pier Hd ⚓ Fl R 3s 11m 11M; vis: 235°-340°; 52°34'·33N 01°44'·28E.
N Pier Hd ⚓ QG 8m 6M; vis: 176°-078°; *Horn(3) 60s*; 52°34'·38N 01°44'·38E.

GREAT YARMOUTH TO THE WASH

(Direction of buoyage ⚐ South to North)

YARMOUTH and CAISTER ROADS/COCKLE GATEWAY

SW Scroby ⚓ Fl G 2·5s; 52°35'·13N 01°46'·69E.

Scroby Elbow ⚓ Fl (2) G 5s; *Bell*; 52°36'·55N 01°46'·26E.
Yarmouth Outfall ⚓ Q R; 52°37'·58N 01°45'·70E.
Mid Caister ⚓ Fl (2) R 5s; *Bell*; 52°38'·99N 01°45'·66E.
NW Scroby ⚓ Fl (3) G 10s; 52°40'·36N 01°46'·31E.
N Caister ⚓ Fl (3) R 10s; 52°40'·77N 01°45'·65E.
Hemsby ⚓ Fl R 2·5s; 52°41'·80N 01°46'·00E.
N Scroby ⚓ VQ; 52°41'·39N 01°46'·47E.
Cockle ⚓ VQ (3) 5s; *Bell*; 52°44'·03N 01°43'·59E.

OFFSHORE ROUTE

Cross Sand ⚓ L Fl 10s 6m 5M; *Racon (T) 10M*; 52°37'·03N 01°59'·14E.
E Cross Sand ⚓ Fl (4) R 15s; 52°38'·55N 01°53'·55E.
NE Cross Sand ⚓ VQ (3) 5s; 52°44'·22N 01° 53'·80E.
Smith's Knoll ⚓ Q (6) + L Fl 15s 7M; *Racon (T) 10M*; 52°43'·52N 02°17'·89E.
S Winterton Ridge ⚓ Q (6)+L Fl 15s; 52°47'·21N 02°03'·44E.
E Hammond Knoll ⚓ Q (3) 10s; 52°52'·32N 01°58'·64E.
Hammond Knoll ⚓ Q (9) 15s; 52°49'·68N 01°57'·54E.
Newarp ⚓ L Fl 10s 7M; *Racon (O) 10M*; 52°48'·37N 01°55'·69E.
S Haisbro ⚓ Q (6) + L Fl 15s; *Bell*; 52°50'·82N 01°48'·29E.
Mid Haisbro ⚓ Fl (2) G 5s; 52°54'·22N 01°41'·59E.
N Haisbro ⚓ Q; *Racon (T) 10M*; 53°00'·22N 01°32'·29E.
Happisburgh ☆ Fl (3) 30s 41m 14M; 52°49'·21N 01°32'·18E.

(Direction of buoyage ⚐ East to West)

CROMER

Cromer ☆ 52°55'·45N 01°19'·01E; Fl 5s 84m **21M**; W 8-sided twr; vis: 102°-307° H24; *Racon (O) 25M*.
Tayjack Wk ⚓ Fl R 2·5s; 52°57'·61N 01°15'·37E.
E Sheringham ⚓ Q (3) 10s; 53°02'·21N 01°14'·84E.
W Sheringham ⚓ Q (9) 15s; 53°02'·95N 01°06'·72E.

BLAKENEY

Blakeney Fairway (SWM) ⚓ 52°59'·31N 00°57'·83E (approx).
Blakeney Overfalls ⚓ Fl (2) R 5s; *Bell*; 53°03'·01N 01°01'·37E.

WELLS-NEXT-THE-SEA/BRANCASTER STAITHE

Wells WCM ⚓ Q(9) 15s; 52°59'·64N 00°51'·00E.
Bridgirdle ⚓ Fl R 2·5s; 53°01'·73N 00°43'·95E.

APPROACHES TO THE WASH

S Race ⚓ Q (6) + L Fl 15s; *Bell*; 53°07'·81N 00°57'·34E.
E Docking ⚓ Fl R 2·5s; 53°09'·82N 00°50'·39E.
N Race ⚓ Fl G 5s; *Bell*; 53°14'·98N 00°43'·87E.
N Docking ⚓ Q; 53°14'·82N 00°41'·49E.
Scott Patch ⚓ VQ (3) 5s; 53°11'·12N 00°36'·39E.
S Inner Dowsing ⚓ Q (6) + L Fl 15s; *Bell*; 53°12'·12N 00°33'·69E.
Boygrift Tower ⚓ Fl (2) 10s 12m 5M; 53°17'·63N 00°19'·24E.
Burnham Flats ⚓ Q (9) 15s; *Bell*; 53°07'·53N 00°34'·89E.

THE WASH

West Ridge ⚓ Q (9) 15s; 53°19'·06N 00°44'·47E.
N Well ⚓ L Fl 10s; *Bell*; *Racon (T) 10M*; 53°03'·02N 00°27'·90E.
Roaring Middle L Fl 10s 7m 8M; 52°58'·64N 00°21'·08E.

CORK HOLE/KING'S LYNN

Sunk ⚓ Q (9) 15s; 52°56'·29N 00°23'·40E.
Seal Sand ⚓ Q; *Bell*; 52°56'·00N 00°20'·00E.

WISBECH CHANNEL/RIVER NENE

Beacons are moved as required.

Masts on W side of River Nene to Wisbech carry FG Lts and those on E side QR or FR Lts.

FREEMAN CHANNEL

Boston Roads ⚓ L Fl 10s; 52°57'·67N 00°16'·03E.
Boston No. 1 ▲ Fl G 3s; 52°57'·88N 00°15'·16E.
Alpha ⬗ Fl R 3s; 52°57'·65N 00°14'·99E.
No. 3 ▲ Fl G 6s; 52°58'·08N 00°14'·07E.
No. 5 ▲ Fl G 3s; 52°58'·51N 00°12'·72E.
Freeman Inner ⌕ Q (9) 15s; 52°58'·59N 00°11'·36E.
Delta ⬗ Fl R 6s; 52°58'·38N 00°11'·25E.

BOSTON LOWER ROAD

Boston No. 7 ▲ Fl G 3s; 52°58'·62N 00°10'·00E.
Boston No. 9 ▲ Fl G 3s; 52°57'·58N 00°08'·36E.
Black Buoy ⬗ Fl (2) R 6s; 52°56'·82N 00°07'·74E.
Tabs Head ⌕ Q WG 4m 1M; R □ on W mast; vis: W shore - 251°- G - shore; 52°56'·00N 00°04'·91E.

BOSTON, NEW CUT AND RIVER WITHAM

Ent N side, Dollypeg ⌕ QG 4m 1M; B △ on Bn; 52°56'·13N 00°05'·03E.

New Cut ⌕ Fl G 3s; △ on pile; 52°55'·98N 00°04'·67E.
New Cut Ldg Lts 240°. Front, No. 1, F 5m 5M; 52°55'·85N 00°04'·40E. Rear, 90m from front, F 8m 5M.

WELLAND CUT/RIVER WELLAND

SE side ⚡ Iso R 2s; NW side Iso G 2s. Lts QR (to port) and QG (to stbd) mark the chan upstream; 52°55'·72E 00°04'·68E.

(Direction of buoyage ⬖ North to South)

BOSTON DEEP/WAINFLEET ROADS

Scullridge ▲ ; 52°59'·76N 00°13'·86E.
Friskney ▲ ; 53°00'·59N 00°16'·76E.
Long Sand ▲ ; 53°01'·27N 00°18'·30E.
Pompey ▲ ; 53°02'·19N 00°19'·26E.
Swatchway ▲ ; 53°03'·81N 00°19'·70E.
Off Ingoldmells Point ⚡ Fl Y 5s 22m 5M; Mast; *Mo (U) 30s;* 53°12'·49N 00°25'·85E.

THE WASH TO THE RIVER HUMBER

(Direction of buoyage ⬖ South to North)

Dudgeon ⌕ Q (9) 15s 7M; *Racon (O) 10M;* 53°16'·62N 01°16'·90E.
E Dudgeon ⌕ Q (3) 10s; 53°19'·72N 00°58'·69E.
Mid Outer Dowsing ▲ Fl (3) G 10s; 53°24'·82N 01°07'·79E.
N Outer Dowsing ⌕ Q; 53°33'·52N 00°59'·59E; *Racon (T) 10M.*

B.1D Platform Dowsing ⌗ 53°33'·68N 00°52'·63E; Fl (2) 10s 28m **22M**; Morse (U) R 15s 28m 3M; *Horn (2) 60s.*

RIVER HUMBER APPROACHES

W Ridge ⌕ Q (9) 15s; 53°19'·04N 00°44'·50E.
Inner Dowsing ⌕ Q (3) 10s 7M, *Racon (T) 10M; Horn 60s;* 53°19'·10N 00°34'·80E.
Protector ⬗ Fl R 2·5s; 53°24'·84N 00°25'·12E.
DZ No. 4 ⬗ Fl Y 5s; 53°27'·15N 00°19'·06E.
DZ No. 3 ⬗ Fl Y 2·5s 53°29'·30N 00°19'·21E.
Rosse Spit ⬗ Fl (2) R 5s 53°30'·56N 00°16'·60E.
Haile Sand No. 2 ⬗ Fl (3) R 10s; 53°32'·42N 00°13'·18E.

Humber lt float L Fl G 10s 5M; *Racon (T) 7M;* 53°38'·70N 00°21'·24E.
Humber Gateway Met Mast ⌗ Mo(U) 15s 12m 10M; 53°38'·24N 00°15'·73E; *Horn Mo(U) 30s;* Y framework mast.
N Binks ▲ Fl G 4s; 53°36'·01N 00°18'·28E.
S Binks ▲ Fl G 2s 53°34'·74N 00°16'·55E.

SPURN Q (3) 10s 10m 8M; *Racon (M) 5M;* 53°33'·56N 00°14'·20E.
SE CHEQUER VQ (6)+L Fl 10s 6m 6M; 53°33'·38N 00°12'·55E.
Chequer No. 3 ⌕ Q (6) + L Fl 15s; 53°33'·07N 00°10'·63E.
No 2B ⬗ Fl R 4s; 53°32'·33N 00°09'·10E.
Tetney ⬖ 2 VQ Y (vert); *Horn Mo (A)60s;* QY on 290m floating hose; 53°32'·35N 00°06'·76E.

RIVER HUMBER/GRIMSBY/HULL

Binks No. 3A ▲ Fl G 4s; 53°33'·92N 00°07'·43E.
Spurn Pt ⌕ Fl G 3s 11m 5M; 53°34'·37N 00°06'·47E.
BULL ⌕ VQ 8m 6M; 53°33'·54N 00°05'·70E.
Bull Sand ⬗ Q R ; 53°34'·45N 00°03'·69E.
North Fort ⌕ Q; 53°33'·80N 00°04'·19E.
South Fort ⌕ Q (6) + L Fl 15s; 53°33'·65N 00°03'·96E.
Haile Sand Fort ⚡ Fl R 5s 21m 3M; 53°32'·07N 00°01'·99E.
Haile Chan No. 4 ⬗ Fl R 4s; 53°33'·64N 00°02'·84E.
Middle No. 7 VQ (6) + L Fl 10s; 53°35'·80N 00°01'·50E.

Grimsby Royal Dock ent E side ⚡ Fl (2) R 6s 10m 8M; Dn; 53°35'·08N 00°04'·04W.
Killingholme Lts in line 292°. Front, Iso R 2s 10m 14M. 53°38'·78N 00°12'·96W. Rear, 215m from front, F WRG 22m 3M; vis: 289·5°-G-290·5°-G/W-291·5°-W-292·5°-R/W-293·5° -R-294·5° (H24).

RIVER HUMBER TO WHITBY

Canada & Giorgios Wreck ⌕ VQ (3) 5s; 53°42'·37N 00°07'·16E.

BRIDLINGTON

SW Smithic ⌕ Q (9) 15s; 54°02'·41N 00°09'·21W.
N Pier Hd ⚡ Fl 2s 12m 9M; *Horn 60s;* (Tidal Lts) Fl R or Fl G; 54°04'·77N 00°11'·19W.
N Smithic ⌕ VQ; *Bell;* 54°06'·22N 00°03'·90W.

Flamborough Hd ☆ 54°06'·98N 00°04'·96W; Fl (4) 15s 65m **24M**; W ○ twr; *Horn (2) 90s.*

FILEY/SCARBOROUGH/WHITBY

Filey Brigg ⌕ Q (3) 10s; *Bell;* 54°12'·74N 00°14'·60W.

Scarborough E Pier Hd ⚡ QG 8m 3M; 54°16'·88N 00°23'·36W.
Scarborough Pier ⚡ Iso 5s 17m 9M; W ○ twr; vis: 219°-039° (tide sigs); *Dia 60s;* 54°16'·91N 00°23'·40W.
Whitby ⌕ Q; *Bell;* 54°30'·33N 00°36'·58W.

Whitby High ☆ 54°28'·67N 00°34'·10W; Fl WR 5s 73m **18M**,R16M; W 8-sided twr & dwellings; vis:128°-R-143°-W- 319°.

Whitby E Pier ⚡ Fl(2) R 4s 16m 5M; 54°29'·57N 00°36'·71W; Masonry Twr.

Whitby E Pier Ext Hd ⚡ Q R 12m 5M; 54°29'·65N 00°36'·74W.

Whitby W Pier ⚡ Fl(2) G 4s 24m 5M; 54°29'·57N 00°36'·78W; Masonry Twr.

Whitby W Pier Ext Hd ⚡ Q G 12m 5M; 54°29'·65N 00°36'·80W.

WHITBY TO THE RIVER TYNE

RUNSWICK/REDCAR

Salt Scar ⚓ 54°38'·12N 01°00'·12W VQ; *Bell*.
Luff Way Ldg Lts 197°. Front, on Esplanade, FR 8m 7M; vis: 182°-212°; 54°37'·10N 01°03'·71W. Rear, 115m from front, FR 12m 7M; vis: 182°-212°.
High Stone. Lade Way Ldg Lts 247°. Front, Oc R 2·5s 9m 7M; 54°37'·15N 01°03'·92W. Rear, 43m from front, Oc R 2·5s 11m 7M; vis: 232°-262°.

TEES APPROACHES/HARTLEPOOL

Tees Fairway ⚓Iso 4s 8m 8M; *Racon (B) unknown range*; *Horn (1) 5s*; 54°40'·94N 01°06'·48W.

Bkwtr Hd S Gare ☆ 54°38'·85N 01°08'·25W; Fl WR 12s 16m **W20M, R17M**; W ○ twr; vis: 020°-W-240°-R-357°; Sig Stn.

Ldg Lts 210·1° Front, FR 18m 13M; 54°37'·22N 01°10'·20W. **Rear**, 560m from front, FR 20m **16M**.

Longscar ⚓ Q (3) 10s; *Bell*; 54°40'·86N 01°09'·89W.
The Heugh ☆ 54°41'·79N 01°10'·56W; Fl (2) 10s 19m **19M**; W twr.

Hartlepool Marina Lock Dir Lt 308° Dir Fl WRG2s 6m 3M; vis: 305·5°-G-307°-W-309°-R-310·5°; 54°41'·45N 01°11'·92W.

SEAHAM/SUNDERLAND

Seaham N Pier Hd ⚡ Fl G 10s 12m 5M; W col, B bands; 54°50'·26N 01°19'·26W.

Sunderland Roker Pier Hd ☆ 54°55'·28N 01°21'·15W; Fl 5s 25m **23M**; W □ twr, 3 R bands and cupola: vis: 211°-357°; *Siren 20s*.

Old N Pier Hd ⚡ QG 12m 8M; metal column; 54°55'·13N 01°21'·61W.

DZ ⚓ 54°57'·04N 01°18'·90W and ⚓ 54°58'·61N 01°19'·90W; both Fl Y 2·5s.

TYNE ENTRANCE/NORTH SHIELDS

Ent North Pier Hd ☆ 55°00'·88N 01°24'·18W; Fl (3) 10s 26m **26M**; Gy □ twr, W lantern; *Horn 10s*.
Herd Groyne Hd Dir Ldg Lt 249°, Oc 10s 14m **19M**; vis: 246·5°-W-251·5°; R pile structure, R&W lantern. Same structure Oc RG 10s 13m, 11M; vis: 224°-G-246·5°, 251·5°-R-277°; sync with Dir lt FR (unintens) 080°-224°. *Bell (1) 5s*; 55°00'·49N 01°25'·44W.

RIVER TYNE TO BERWICK-UPON-TWEED

CULLERCOATS and BLYTH

Cullercoats Ldg Lts 256°. Front, FR 27m 3M; 55°02'·06N 01°25'·91W. Rear, 38m from front, FR 35m 3M.
Blyth Ldg Lts 324°. Front ⚓, F Bu 11m 10M; 55°07'·42N 01°29'·82W. Rear ⚓, 180m from front, F Bu 17m 10M. Both Or ⚓ on twr.
Blyth E Pier Hd ☆ 55°06'·98N 01°29'·21W; Fl (4) 10s 19m **21M**, W twr; same structure FR 13m 13M, vis:152°-249°; Horn (3) 30s.
Met Mast ⚡; Mo(U)15s 17m 10M; 55°08'·78N 01°25'·25W; Aero 3 FR (107m), *Horn 30s*.

COQUET ISLAND, AMBLE and WARKWORTH

Coquet ☆ 55°20'·03N 01°32'·39W; Fl (3) WR 20s 25m **W19M, R15M**; W □ twr, turreted parapet, lower half Gy; vis: 330°-R-140°-W-163°-R-180°-W-330°; sector boundaries are indeterminate and may appear as Alt WR; *Horn 30s*.
Amble N Pier Head ⚡ Fl G 6s 12m 6M; 55°20'·39N 01°34'·25W.

SEAHOUSES, BAMBURGH and FARNE ISLANDS

N Sunderland ⚓ Fl R 2·5s; 55°34'·62N 01°37'·12W.
Bamburgh Black Rocks Point ☆ 55°36'·99N 01°43'·45W; Oc(2) WRG 8s 12m **W14M**, R11M, G11M; W bldg; vis: 122°-G-165°-W- 175°-R-191°-W- 238°-R- 275°-W- 289°-G-300°.
Inner Farne ⚡ Fl (2) WR 15s 27m W10M, R7M; W ○ twr; vis: 119°- R - 280° - W -119°; 55°36'·92N 01°39'·35W.
Longstone ☆ **W side** 55°38'·63N 01°36'·66W; Fl 20s 23m **24M**; R twr, W band.
Swedman ▲ Fl G 2·5s; 55°37'·65N 01°41'·63W.

HOLY ISLAND

Ridge ⚓ Q (3) 10s; 55°39'·70N 01°45'·97W.
Plough Rock ⚓ Q (9) 15s; 55°40'·24N 01°46'·00W.
Old Law E Bn ⚡ (Guile Pt) Oc WRG 6s 9m 4M; vis: 180·5°-G-258·5°-W-261·5°-R-300°, 55°39'·49N 01°47'·59W; stone obelisk.
Heugh ⚡ Oc WRG 6s 24m 5M; vis: 135°-G-308°-W-311-R-shore; 55°40'·09N 01°47'·99W.
Plough Seat ⚓ QR; 55°40'·37N 01°44'·97W.
Goldstone ⚓ QG; 55°40'·25N 01°43'·64W.

BERWICK-UPON-TWEED

Bkwtr Hd ⚡ Fl 5s 15m 6M; vis: 201°-009°, (obscured 155°-201°); W ○ twr, R cupola and base; FG (same twr) 8m 1M; vis 009°-G-155°; 55°45'·88N 01°59'·06W.

1	Ramsgate	1		11	31	61	78	91	107	126	189	205	205	232	Berwick-upon-Tweed	11
2	Sheerness	34	2		10	27	42	65	81	102	157	176	185	203	Amble	10
3	Gravesend	56	22	3		9	16	36	51	70	138	149	156	180	Sunderland	9
4	London Bridge	76	45	23	4		8	24	39	58	122	137	140	169	Hartlepool	8
5	Burnham-on-Crouch	44	34	54	77	5		7	16	35	88	114	121	143	Whitby	7
6	Brightlingsea	41	28	48	71	21	6		6	20	81	98	105	130	Scarborough	6
7	Harwich	40	50	66	93	31	20	7		5	58	83	87	114	Bridlington	5
8	River Deben (ent)	45	55	75	98	36	25	6	8		4	79	75	113	Hull	4
9	Southwold	62	72	92	115	53	42	25	23	9		3	34	83	Boston	3
10	Lowestoft	72	82	102	125	63	52	35	33	10	10		2	85	King's Lynn	2
11	Great Yarmouth	79	87	105	132	70	59	42	40	18	7	11		1	Great Yarmouth	1

AREA 5 *E Scotland – Berwick-upon-Tweed to C Wrath & N Isles*

SELECTED LIGHTS, BUOYS & WAYPOINTS

Positions are referenced to WGS84

BERWICK-UPON-TWEED TO BASS ROCK

BURNMOUTH
Ldg lts 241°. Front, FR 29m 4M; 55°50'·53N 02°04'·25W.
Rear, 45m from front, FR 35m 4M. Both on W posts (unclear by day).

EYEMOUTH
Blind Buss ⚓ Q; 55°52'·80N 02°05'·25E.
Ldg Lts 174°. Front, W Bkwtr Hd ⚡, FG 9m 6M; 55°52'·47N 02°05'·29W. Rear, elbow 55m from front, FG 10m 6M.

ST ABBS to DUNBAR and BASS ROCK
St Abbs Hd ☆ 55°54'·96N 02°08'·29W; Fl 10s 68m **26M**; W twr; *Racon (T) 18M*.
Barns Ness Tower (Lt ho disused 36m); 55°59'·22N 02°26'·76W.
Bayswell Hill Ldg Lts 198°. Front, Oc G 6s 15m 3M; W △ on Or col; 188°·G(intens)-208°; 56°00'·25N 02°31'·21W. Rear, Oc G 6s 22m 3M; ▽ on Or col; synch with front, 188°-G(intens)-208°.
Bass Rock, S side, ⚡ Fl (3) 20s 46m 10M; W twr; vis: 241°-107°; 56°04'·61N 02°38'·48W.

FIRTH OF FORTH AND SOUTH SHORE

(Direction of buoyage East to West)

NORTH BERWICK
Outfall ⚓ Fl Y; 56°04'·29N 02°40'·89W.
Fidra ☆ 56°04'·39N 02°47'·13W; Fl (4) 30s 34m **15M**; W twr; obsc by Bass Rock, Craig Leith and Lamb Island.

PORT SETON, COCKENZIE, FISHERROW and S CHANNEL
Port Seton, E Pier Hd ⚡ Iso WR 4s 10m W9M, R6M; vis: shore - R - 105°- W - 225°- R - shore; *Bell (occas)*; 55°58'·40N 02°57'·23W.
Fisherrow E Pier Hd ⚡ Oc 6s 5m 6M; 55°56'·79N 03°04'·11W.
Narrow Deep ⚑ Fl (2) R 10s; 56°01'·46N 03°04'·59W.
Herwit ⚓ Fl (3) G 10s; 56°01'·05N 03°06'·52W.
North Craig ⚓ Q (3) 10s 56°01'·02N 03°03'·52W.
Craigh Waugh ⚓ Fl (2) 10s; 56°00'·26N 03°04'·47W.
Diffuser Hds (Outer) ⚓ 55°59'·81N 03°07'·84W.

LEITH and GRANTON
Leith Approach ⚑ Fl R 3s; 55°59'·95N 03°11'·51W.
East Bkwtr Hd ⚡ Iso R 4s 7m 9M; 55°59'·48N 03°10'·94W.
GrantonE Pier Head ⚡ Fl R 2s 5m 6M; 55°59'·28N 03°13'·27W.

NORTH CHANNEL and MIDDLE BANK
Inchkeith Fairway ⚑ Iso 2s; *Racon (T) 5M*; 56°03'·49N 03°00'·10W.
No. 1 ⚓ Fl G 9s; 56°03'·22N 03°03'·71W.
No. 2 ⚑ Fl R 9s; 56°02'·90N 03°03'·72W.
No. 3 ⚓ Fl G 6s; 56°03'·22N 03°06'·10W.
No. 4 ⚑ Fl R 6s; 56°02'·89N 03°06'·11W.
No. 5 ⚓ Fl G 3s; 56°03'·18N 03°07'·88W.
No. 6 ⚑ Fl R 3s; 56°03'·05N 03°08'·44W.
No. 8 ⚑ Fl R 9s 56°02'·95N 03°09'·62W.

Inchkeith ⚡ 56°02'·01N 03°08'·17W; Fl 15s 67m 14M; stone twr.
Pallas Rock ⚓ VQ (9) 10s 56°01'·50N 03°09'·30W.
East Gunnet ⚓ Q (3) 10s; 56°01'·41N 03°10'·38W.
West Gunnet ⚓ Q (9) 15s 56°01'·34N 03°11'·06W.
No. 7 ⚓ QG; *Racon (T) 5M*; 56°02'·80N 03°10'·97W.
No. 9 ⚓ Fl G 6s; 56°02'·32N 03°13'·48W.
No. 10 ⚑ Fl R 6s; 56°02'·07N 03°13'·32W.
No. 11 ⚓ Fl G 3s 56°02'·08N 03°15'·26W.
No. 12 ⚑ Fl R 3s; 56°01'·78N 03°15'·15W.
No. 13 ⚓ Fl G 9s; 56°01'·77N 03°16'·94W.
No. 14 ⚑ Fl R 9s; 56°01'·52N 03°16'·82W.
Oxcars ⚡ Fl (2) WR 7s 16m W13M, R12M; W twr, R band; vis: 072°-W-087°- R-196°-W-313°-R-072°; 56°01'·36N 03°16'·84W.
Inchcolm E Pt ⚡ Fl (3) 15s 20m 10M; Gy twr; part obsc by land 075°-145·5°; 56°01'·72N 03°17'·83W.
No. 15 ⚓ Fl G 6s; 56°01'·39N 03°18'·95W.

MORTIMER'S DEEP
Hawkcraig Point Ldg Lts 292°. Front, Iso 5s 12m 14M; W twr; vis: 282°-302°; 56°03'·03N 03°17'·07W. Rear, 96m from front, Iso 5s 16m 14M; W twr; vis: 282°-302°.
Inchcolm S Lts in line 066°. Front, 84m from rear, Q 7m 7M; W twr; vis: 062·5°-082·5°; 56°01'·78N 03°18'·28W. Common Rear, Iso 5s 11m 7M; W twr; vis: 062·5°-082·5°; 56°01'·80N 03°18'·13W. N Lts in line 076·7°. Front, 80m from rear, Q 7m 7M; W twr; vis: 062·5°-082·5°.

APPROACHES TO FORTH BRIDGES
No. 17 ⚓ Fl G 3s; 56°01'·23N 03°19'·84W.
No. 16 ⚑ Fl R 3s; 56°00'·87N 03°19'·60W.
No. 19 ⚓ Fl G 9s; 56°00'·71N 03°22'·47W.
Beamer Rk W ⚡ Fl 3s 5m 9M; W post; vis: 050°-230°; 56°00'·30N 03°24'·79W.
Beamer Rk E ⚡ Fl 3s 5m 9M; W post; vis: 230°-050°; 56°00'·27N 03°24'·72W.

PORT EDGAR
W Bkwtr Hd ⚡ Fl R 4s 4m 8M; 55°59'·86N 03°24'·78W. W blockhouse.

FIRTH OF FORTH – NORTH SHORE (INWARD)

BURNTISLAND
W Pier Outer Hd ⚡ Fl (2) R 6s 7m; W twr; 56°03'·22N 03°14'·26W.
E Pier Outer Hd ⚡ Fl (2) G 6s 7m 5M; 56°03'·24N 03°14'·17W.

ABERDOUR, BRAEFOOT BAY and INCHCOLM
Hawkcraig Pt ⚡ (see **MORTIMER'S DEEP** above).
Braefoot Bay Terminal, W Jetty. Ldg Lts 247·3°. **Front**, Fl 3s 6m **15M**; W △ on E dolphin; vis: 237·2°-257·2°; 56°02'·16N 03°18'·71W; 4 dolphins with 2 FG (vert). **Rear**, 88m from front, Fl 3s 12m **15M**; W ▽ on appr gangway; vis: 237·2°-257·2°; synch with front.

INVERKEITHING BAY
St David's ⚓ Fl G 5s 3m 7M; Or ☐, on pile; 56°01'·37N 03°22'·29W.
Channel ⚓ QG; 56°01'·43N 03°23'·02W.

ROSYTH

Main Chan Dir lt 323·5°. Bn 'A' Oc WRG 7m 4M; R☐on W post with R bands; vis: 318°-G-321°-321°-W-326°-R-328° (H24); 56°01'·19N 03°25'·61W.

Dir lt 115°, Bn 'C' Oc WRG 6s 7m 4M; W ▽ on W Bn; vis: 110°-R -113° W -116·5° - G -120°; 56°00'·61N 03°24'·25W.

S Arm Jetty Hd ⚓ L Fl (2) WR 12s 5m W9M; R6M; vis: 010°-W-280°-R-010°; 56°01'·09N 03°26'·58W.

RIVER FORTH

ROSYTH to GRANGEMOUTH

Dhu Craig ⚓ Fl G 5s; 56°00'·74N 03°27'·23W.
Blackness ⚓ QR; 56°01'·06N 03°30'·30W.
Tancred Bank ⚓ Fl (2) R 10s; 56°01'·58N 03°31'·91W.
Dods Bank ⚓ Fl R 3s; 56°02'·03N 03°34'·07W.
Bo'ness ⚓ Fl R 10s; 56°02'·23N 03°35'·38W.
Torry ⚓ Fl G 10s 5m 7M; G ○ structure; 56°02'·46N 03°35'·28W.
Bo'ness Bcns ⚓ 2 QR 3m 2M; 56°01'·85N 03°36'·22W.
Bo'ness Hbr ⚓; 56°01'·26N 03°36'·46W.

GRANGEMOUTH

Grangemouth App No. 1 ⚓ Fl (3) 10s 4m 6M;56°02'·12N 03°38'·10W.
Hen & Chickens ⚓ Fl (3) G 10s; 56°02'·35N 03°38'·08W.

FIRTH OF FORTH – NORTH SHORE (OUTWARD)

KIRKCALDY and METHIL

Kirkaldy E. Pier Hd ⚓ Fl WG 10s 12m 8M; vis: 156°-G-336°-W-156°; 56°06'·78N 03°08'·90W.
Methil Outer Pier Hd ⚓ Oc G 6s 8m 5M; W twr; vis: 280°-100°; 56°10'·76N 03°00'·48W.

ELIE and ST MONANS

Elie Ness ☆ 56°11'·04N 02°48'·77W; Fl 6s 15m **17M**; W twr.
St Monans Bkwtr Hd ⚓ Oc WRG 6s 5m W7M, R4M, G4M; vis: 282°-G-355°-W-026°-R-038°; 56°12'·20N 02°45'·94W.

PITTENWEEM and ANSTRUTHER EASTER

Pittenweem, Ldg Lts 037° Middle Pier Hd. Front, FR 4m 5M. Rear, FR 8m 5M. Both Gy Cols, Or stripes; 56°12'·69N 02°43'·69W.
Pittenweem, E Bkwtr Hd ⚓ Fl (2) RG 5s 9m R9M, G6M; vis: 265°-R-345°-G-055°; Horn 90s (occas); 56°12'·63N 02°43'·74W.
Anstruther, Ldg Lts 019°. Front FG 7m 4M; 56°13'·28N 02°41'·76W. Rear, 38m from front, FG 11m 4M, (both W masts).

MAY I, CRAIL, ST ANDREWS and FIFE NESS to MONTROSE

Isle of May ☆ 56°11'·12N 02°33'·46W(Summit); Fl (2) 15s 73m **22M**; ☐ twr on stone dwelling.
Crail, Ldg Lts 295°. Front, FR 24m 6M (not lit when hbr closed); 56°15'·46N 02°37'·84W. Rear, 30m from front, FR 30m 6M.
Fife Ness ☆ 56°16'·74N 02°35'·19W; Iso WR 10s 12m **W21M, R20M**; W bldg; vis: 143°-W-197°-R-217°-W-023°.
N Carr ⚓ Q (3) 10s 3m 5M; 56°18'·05N 02°32'·94W.
St Andrews ⚓ 56°20'·38N 02°47'·07W; Dir lt 277·7; Iso WRG 2s 17m 9M; vis: 272°-G-276°-AlWG-277°-W-278°-AlWR-279°-R-283°.
St Andrews N Bkwtr Bn ⚓ Fl G 3M 56°20'·36N 02°46'·77W.
Bell Rk ☆ 56°26'·08N 02°23'·21W; Fl 5s 28m 18M; Racon (M) 18M.

RIVER TAY, TAYPORT, DUNDEE and PERTH

Tay Fairway ⚓ L Fl 10s; Bell; 56°28'·30N 02°36'·60W.
Middle ⚓ Fl G 3s; 56°28'·08N 02°38'·24W.
Middle ⚓ Fl (2) R 6s 56°27'·65N 02°38'·23W.
Abertay N ⚓ Q (3) 10s; Racon (T) 8M; 56°27'·39N 02°40'·36W.
Abertay S (Elbow) ⚓ Fl R 6s 56°27'·13N 02°39'·83W.
Tayport High Lt ☆ 56°27'·17N 02°53'·96W; Dir lt 269°; Iso WRG 3s 24m **W22M, R17M, G16M**; W twr vis: 267°-G-268°-W-270°-R-271°.

ARBROATH

Ldg lts 299·2°. Front , FR 7m 5M; W col; 56°33'·29N 02°35'·16W. Rear, 50m from front, FR 13m 5M; W col.

MONTROSE

Scurdie Ness ☆ 56°42'·10N 02°26'·24W; Fl (3) 20s 38m **23M**; W twr; Racon (T) 14-16M.
Outer Ldg Lts 271·5°; Front, FR 11m 5M; W twin pillars, R bands; 56°42'·21N 02°27'·41W; Rear, 272m from front, FR 18m 5M; W twr, R cupola.
Inner Ldg Lts 265°; Front FG 21m 5M; Rear FG 33m 5M.

MONTROSE TO RATTRAY HEAD

JOHNSHAVEN and GOURDON HARBOUR

Johnshaven, Ldg Lts 316°. Front, FR 5m; 56°47'·62N 02°20'·26W. Rear, 85m from front, FG 20m; shows R when unsafe to ent hbr. Gourdon Hbr, Ldg Lts 358°. Front, FR 5m 5M; W twr; shows G when unsafe to enter; Siren (2) 60s (occas); 56°49'·69N 02°17'·24W. Rear, 120m from front, FR 30m 5M; W twr.
Todhead Lighthouse (disused), white tower, 13m.

STONEHAVEN to GIRDLE NESS

Outer Pier Hd ⚓ Iso WRG 4s 7m 5M; vis: 214°-G-246°-W-268°-R-280°; 56°57'·59N 02°12'·00W.
Girdle Ness ☆ Fl (2) 20s 56m **22M**; obsc by Greg Ness when brg more than about 020°; Racon (G) 25M; 57°08'·34N 02°02'·91W.

ABERDEEN

Fairway ⚓ Mo (A) 5s; Racon (T) 7M; 57°09'·31N 02°01'·95W.
Aberdeen Harbour Ent ⚓ 57°08'·38N 02°04'·48W; Dir lt 235·7° Fl WRG 1s 7m 9M; metal post; vis: 235·2°-QG-236·2°-AlQGW-236·7°-QW-237·7°-AlQRW-238·2°-QR-239·2°.
S Bkwtr Hd ⚓ Fl (3) R 8s 23m 7M; 57°08'·69N 02°03'·34W.
N Pier Hd ⚓ Iso G 4s 11m 10M; W twr; 57°08'·74N 02°03'·69W.
In fog FY 10m (same twr) vis: 136°-336°; Bell (3) 12s.

BUCHAN NESS TO INVERNESS

PETERHEAD and RATTRAY HEAD

Buchan Ness ☆ Fl 5s 40m **18M**; W twr, R bands; Racon (O) 14-16M; 57°28'·23N 01°46'·51W.
Kirktown Ldg lts 314°. Front, Oc R 6s 14m 10M; Or △ on lattice mast; 57°30'·22N 01°47'·21W. Rear, Oc R 6s 21m 10M (sync with front); Or ▽ on lattice mast.
S Bkwtr Hd ⚓ Fl (2) R 12s 24m 7M; 57°29'·79N 01°46'·54W.
N Bkwtr Hd ⚓ Iso RG 6s 19m 11M; W tripod; vis: 171°-R-236°-G-171°; Horn 30s; 57°29'·84N 01°46'·32W.
Rattray Hd ☆ 57°36'·61N 01°49'·03W Fl (3) 30s 28m **18M**; W twr; Racon (M) 15M; Horn (2) 45s.

FRASERBURGH

Fraserburgh Ldg lt 291°; Iso R 2s 12m 9M; 57°41'·57N 02°00'·13W. Rear, 75m from front, Iso R 2s 17m 9M.

Fraserburgh, Balaclava Bkwtr Head ⚡ Fl (2) G 8s 26m 6M; dome on W twr; vis: 178°-326°; 57°41'·51N 01°59'·70W.

Kinnaird Hd ☆ 57°41'·87N 02°00'·26W Fl 5s 25m **22M**; vis: 092°-297°.

MACDUFF, BANFF and WHITEHILLS

Macduff Pier Hd ⚡ Fl (2) WRG 6s 12m W9M, R7M; W twr; vis: shore-G-115°-W-174°-R-210°; 57°40'·25N 02°30'·02W.

Macduff Ldg Lts 127°, Front FR 44m 3M; 57°40'·12N 02°29'·75W. Rear, 60m from front, FR 55m 3M; both Or △ on mast.

Banff Ldg Lts 295°, Front Fl R 4s; 57°40·30N 02°31·36W. Rear, QR; both vis: 210°-345°.

Whitehills Pier Hd ⚡ 57°40'·80N 02°34'·88W Fl WR 3s 7m W9M, R6M; W twr; vis: 132°-R-212°-W-245°.

PORTSOY and FINDOCHTY

Portsoy Pier Ldg Lts 173°, Front Fl G 4s 20m 3M; post; 57°41'·09N 02°41'·40W; Rear Q G 22m 3M; R △ on BW post.

Findochty Middle Pier Ldg Lts 166°, Front FR 6m 3M; 57°41'·90N 02°54'·20W. Rear FR 10m 3M.

BUCKIE

West Muck ⚡ QR 5m 7M; tripod; 57°41'·06N 02°58'·01W.

N Pier 60m from Hd ☆ 57°40'·9N 02°57'·5W Oc R 10s 15m **15M** W twr.

LOSSIEMOUTH, HOPEMAN and BURGHEAD

Lossiemouth S Pier Hd ⚡ Fl R 6s 11m 5M; 57°43'·42N 03°16'·69W.

Halliman Skerries ⚡ Q; *Racon M,* 57°44'·33N 03°18'·57W.

Hopeman Ldg Lts 081°, Front,FR 3m; 57°42'·71N 03°26'·18W. Rear, 10m from front, FR 4m.

Burghead N Bkwtr Hd ⚡ Oc 8s 7m 5M; 57°42'·09N 03°30'·03W.

FINDHORN, NAIRN and INVERNESS FIRTH

Findhorn Landfall ⚡ LF 10s 57°40'·34N 03°38'·77W.

Nairn E Pier Hd ⚡ Oc WRG 4s 6m 5M; 8-sided twr; vis: shore-G-100°-W-207°-R-shore; 57°35'·62N 03°51'·65W.

Riff Bank E ⚡ Fl Y 10s 3m 5M 57°38'·38N 03°58'·18W.

SOUTH CHANNEL

Riff Bank S ⚡ Q (6) + L Fl 15s; 57°36'·73N 04°00'·97W.

Chanonry ⚡ 57°34'·45N 04°05'·56W Oc 6s 12m 12M; W twr; vis: 148°-073°.

Munlochy ⚡ L Fl 10s; 57°32'·91N 04°07'·65W .

Petty Bank ⚡ Fl R 5s 57°31'·58N 04°08'·98W.

Meikle Mee ⚡ Fl G 3s 57°30'·26N 04°12'·02W.

Longman Pt ⚡ Fl WR 2s 7m W5M, R4M; vis: 078°-W-258°-R-078°; 57°29'·99N 04°13'·31W.

Craigton Point ⚡ Fl WRG 4s 6m W11M, R7M, G7M; vis: 312° - W - 048° - R - 064° - W - 085° G - shore; 57°30'·05N 04°14'·09W.

Bridge Centre, Or △; *Racon (K) 6M*; 57°29'·97N 04°13'·79W.

INVERNESS and CALEDONIAN CANAL

R. Ness Outer ⚡ QR 3m 4M; 57°29'·83N 04°13'·93W.

Carnarc Pt ⚡ Fl G 2s 8m 4M; G lattice twr; 57°29'·72N 04°14'·25W.

Clachnaharry, S Tr'ng Wall Hd ⚡ Iso G 4s 5m 2M; tfc sigs; 57°29'·43N 04°15'·86W.

CROMARTY FIRTH and INVERGORDON

Fairway ⚡ L Fl 10s; *Racon (M) 5M*; 57°39'·96N 03°54'·19W.

Cromarty Bank ⚡ Fl (2) G 10s; 57°40'·66N 03°56'·78W.

Buss Bank ⚡ Fl R 3s 57°40'·97N 03°59'·54W.

Cromarty - The Ness (Lt ho disused W tr 13m); 57°40'·98N 04°02'·20W

Nigg Oil Terminal Pier Hd ⚡ Oc G 5s 31m 5M; Gy twr; floodlit; 57°41'·54N 04°02'·60W.

DORNOCH FIRTH to LYBSTER

Tarbat Ness ☆ 57°51'·88N 03°46'·76W Fl (4) 30s 53m **24M**; W twr, R bands; *Racon (T) 14-16M.*

Lybster, S Pier Hd ⚡ Oc R 6s 10m 3M; 58°17'·79N 03°17'·41W.

Clyth Ness Lt Ho (unlit); W twr, R band; 58°18'·64N 03°12'·74W.

WICK

S Pier Hd ⚡ Fl WRG 3s 12m W12M, R9M, G9M; W 8-sided twr; vis: 253°-G-270°-W-286°-R-329°; *Bell (2) 10s* (occas).

Dir lt 288·5° F WRG 9m W10M, R7M, G7M; col, N end of bridge; vis: 283·5°-G-287·2°-W-289·7°-R-293·5°; 58°26'·54N 03°05'·34W

Noss Hd ☆ 58°28'·71N 03°03'·09W Fl WR 20s 53m **W25M, R21M**; W twr; vis: shore-R-191°-W-shore.

Duncansby Hd ☆ 58°38'·65N 03°01'·58W Fl 12s 67m **22M**; W twr; *Racon (T).*

Muckle Skerry ☆ 58°41'·41N 02°55'·49W Fl (3) 30s 52m **23M**; W twr.

Lother Rock ⚡ Fl 2s 13m 6M; *Racon (M) 10M*; 58°43'·79N 02°58'·69W.

Swona ⚡ Fl 8s 17m 9M; vis: 261°-210°; 58°44'·25N 03°04'·24W.

Swona N Hd ⚡ Fl (3) 10s 16m 10M; 58°45'·11N 03°03'·10W.

Stroma ☆, Swilkie Point 58°41'·75N 03°07'·01W Fl (2) 20s 32m **26M**; W twr.

Dunnet Hd ☆ 58°40'·28N 03°22'·60W Fl (4) 30s 105m **23M**.

THURSO, SCRABSTER and CAPE WRATH

Thurso Ldg Lts 195°. Front, FG 5m 4M; Gy post; 58°35'·96N 03°30'·76W. Rear, FG 6m 4M; Gy mast.

Scrabster Q. E. Pier Hd ⚡ Fl (2) 4s 8m 8M 58°36'·66N 03°32'·31W.

Strathy Pt Lt Ho (disused) W twr on W dwelling; 58°36'·04N 04°01'·12W.

Sule Skerry ☆ 59°05'·09N 04°24'·38W Fl (2) 15s 34m **21M**; W twr; *Racon (T)*.
North Rona ☆ 59°07'·27N 05°48'·91W Fl (3) 20s 114m **22M**.
Sula Sgeir ⚡ Fl 15s 74m 11M; ☐ structure; 59°05'·61N 06°09'·57W.
Loch Eriboll, White Hd ⚡ Fl WR10s 18m W13M, R12M; W twr and bldg; vis: 030°-W-172°-R-191°-W-212°; 58°31'·01N 04°38'·90W.
Cape Wrath ☆ 58°37'·54N 04°59'·94W Fl (4) 30s 122m **22M**; W twr.

ORKNEY ISLANDS

Tor Ness ☆ 58°46'·78N 03°17'·86W Fl 5s 21m **17M**; W twr.
Cantick Hd (S Walls, SE end) ⚡ 58°47'·23N 03°07'·88W Fl 20s 35m 13M; W twr.

SCAPA FLOW and APPROACHES

Long Hope, S Ness Pier Hd ⚡ Fl WRG 3s 6m W7M, R5M, G5M; vis: 082°-G- 242°-W- 252°-R-082°; 58°48'·05N 03°12'·35W.
Hoxa Head ⚡ Fl WR 3s 15m W9M, R6M; W twr; vis: 026°-W-163°-R-201°-W-215°; 58°49'·31N 03°02'·09W.
Nevi Skerry ⚡ Fl (2) 6s 7m 6M; 58°50'·67N 03°02'·70W.
Rose Ness ⚡ 58°52'·33N 02°49'·97W Fl 6s 24m 8M; W twr.
Barrel of Butter ⚡ Fl (2) 10s 6m 7M; 58 53'·40N 03°07'·62W.
Cava ⚡ Fl WR 3s 11m W10M, R8M; W ○ twr; vis: 351°-W-143°-196°-W-251°-R-271°-R-298°; 58°53'·21N 03°10'·70W.
Houton Bay Ldg Lts 316°. Front ⚡ Fl G 3s 8m. Rear ⚡, 200m from front, FG 16m; vis: 312°- 320°; 58°54'·97N 03°11'·56W.

CLESTRAN SOUND and HOY SOUND

Graemsay Is Hoy Sound ☆ Ldg Lts 104°. Front Low, 58°56'·42N 03°18'·60W Iso 3s 17m 12M; W twr; vis: 070°-255°. **High Rear**, 1·2M from front, Oc WR 8s 35m **W20M, R16M**; W twr; vis: 097°-R-112°-W-163°-W-178°-W-332°; obsc on Ldg line within 0·5M.
Skerry of Ness ⚡ Fl WG 4s 7m W7M, G4M; vis: shore -W-090°- G-shore; 58°56'·95N 03°17'·83W.

STROMNESS

Ldg Lts 317°. Front, FR 29m 11M; post on W twr; 58°57'·61N 03°18'·15W. Rear, 55m from front, FR 39m 11M; vis: 307°-327°; H24.

AUSKERRY

Copinsay ☆ 58°53'·77N 02°40'·35W Fl (5) 30s 79m **21M**; W twr.
Auskerry ☆ 59°01'·51N 02°34'·34W Fl 20s 34m **20M**; W twr.
Helliar Holm, S end ⚡ Fl WRG 10s 18m W14M, R11M, G11M; W twr; vis: 256°-G-276°-W-292°-R-098°-W-116°-G-154°; 59°01'·13N 02°54'·09W.
Balfour Pier Shapinsay ⚡ Fl (2) WRG 5s 5m W3M, R2M, G2M; vis: 270°-G-010°-W-020°-R-090°; 59°01'·86N 02°54'·49W.

KIRKWALL

Thieves Holm, ⚡ Q R 8M; 59°01'·09N 02°56'·21W.
Pier N end ☆ 58°59'·29N 02°57'·72W Iso WRG 5s 8m **W15M**, R13M, G13M; W twr; vis: 153°-G-183°-W-192°-R-210°.

WIDE FIRTH

Linga Skerry ⚡ Q (3) 10s; 59°02'·39N 02°57'·56W.
Boray Skerries ⚡ Q (6) + L Fl 15s; 59°03'·65N 02°57'·66W.
Skertours ⚡ Q; 59°04'·11N 02°56'·72W.
Galt Skerry ⚡ Q; 59°05'·21N 02°54'·20W.
Brough of Birsay ☆ 59°08'·19N 03°20'·41W Fl (3) 25s 52m **18M**.
Papa Stronsay NE end, The Ness ⚡ Fl(4)20s 8m 9M; W twr; 59°09'·34N 02°34'·93W.

SANDAY ISLAND and NORTH RONALDSAY

Quiabow ⬥ Fl (2) G 12s; 59°09'·82N 02°36'·30W.
Start Pt ☆ 59°16'·69N 02°22'·71W Fl (2) 20s 24m **18M**.
Kettletoft Pier Hd ⚡ Fl WRG 3s 7m W7M, R5M, G5M; vis: 351°-W- 011°-R-180°-G-351°; 59°13'·80N 02°35'·86W.
N Ronaldsay ☆ NE end, 59°23'·34N 02°22'·91W Fl 10s 43m **24M**; R twr, W bands; *Racon (T) 14-17M*.

EDAY and EGILSAY

Calf Sound ⚡ Fl (3) WRG 10s 6m W8M, R6M, G6M; W twr; vis: shore-R-215°-W-222°-G-301°-W-305°; 59°14'·21N 02°45'·82W.
Backaland Pier ⚡ 59°09'·43N 02°44'·88W Fl R 3s 5m 4M; vis: 192°-250°.
Egilsay Graand ⚡ Q (6) + L Fl 15s; 59°06'·86N 02°54'·42W.

WESTRAY and PIEROWALL

Noup Head ☆ 59°19'·86N 03°04'·23W Fl 30s 79m **20M**; W twr; vis: about 335°-282° but partially obsc 240°-275°.
Pierowall E Pier Head ⚡ Fl WRG 3s 7m W11M, R7M, G7M; vis: 254°-G-276°-W-291°-R-308°-G-215°; 59°19'·35N 02°58'·53W.
Papa Westray, Moclett Bay Pier Head ⚡ Fl WRG 5s 7m W5M, R3M, G3M; vis: 306°-G-341°-W-040°-R-074°; 59°19'·60N 02°53'·52W.

SHETLAND ISLES

FAIR ISLE

Skadan South ☆, 59°30'·84N 01°39'·16W Fl (4) 30s 32m **22M**; W twr; vis: 260°-146°, obsc inshore 260°-282°.
Skroo ☆ N end 59°33'·13N 01°36'·58W Fl (2) 30s 80m **22M**; W twr; vis: 086·7°-358°.

MAINLAND, SOUTH

Sumburgh Head ☆ 59°51'·21N 01°16'·58W Fl (3) 30s 91m **23M**.
Mousa, Perie Bard ⚡ Fl 3s 20m 10M; 59°59'·84N 01°09'·51W.

BRESSAY and LERWICK

Bressay, Kirkabister Ness ⚡ 60°07'·20N 01°07'·31W; Fl (2) 20s 18m 10M. Adjacent Lt Ho disused.
Maryfield Ferry Terminal ⚡ Oc WRG 6s 5m 5M; vis: W008°-R013°-G-111°-008°; 60°09'·43N 01°07'·45W.
North Ness ⚡ Iso WG 4s 4m 5M; vis: shore-W-158°-G-216°-W-301°; 60°09'·57N 01°08'·77W
Loofa Baa ⚡ Q (6) + L Fl 15s 4m 5M; 60°09'·72N 01°08'·79W.
Soldian Rock ⚡ Q (6) + L Fl 15s 60°12'·51N 01°04'·73W.
N ent Dir lt 215°, Oc WRG 6s 27m 8M; Y △, Or stripe; vis: 211°-R-214°-W-216°-G-221°; 60°10'·47N 01°09'·53W.
Rova Hd ⚡ 60°11'·46N 01°08'·60W Fl (3) WRG 18s 12m W12M, R9M, G9M; W twr; vis: 090°-R-182°-W-191°-G-

213°-R-241°-W-261·5°-G-009°-R-040°. Same structure and synchronised: Fl (3) WRG 18s 14m **W16M**, R13M, G13M; vis: 176·5°-R-182°-W-191°-G-196·5°.

Dales Voe ⚲ Fl (2) WRG 8s 5m W4M, R3M, G3M; vis: 220°-G-227°-W-233°-R-240°; 60°11'·79N 01°11'·23W.

Hoo Stack ⚲ Fl (4) WRG 12s 40m W7M, R5M, G5M; W pylon; vis: 169°-R-180°-W-184°-G-193°-W-169°. Same structure, Dir lt 182°. Fl (4) WRG 12s 33m W9M, R6M, G6M; vis: 177°- R-180°-W-184°-W-187°; synch with upper lt; 60°14'·96N 01°05'·38W.

Mull (Moul) of Eswick ⚲ Fl WRG 3s 50m W9M, R6M, G6M; W twr; vis: 028°-R-200°-W-207°-G-018°-W-028°; 60°15'·74N 01°05'·90W.

Inner Voder ⚰ Q (9) 15s; 60°16'·43N 01°05'·18W.

WHALSAY and SKERRIES

Symbister Ness ⚲ Fl (2) WG 12s 11m W8M, G6M; W twr; vis: shore-W-203°-G-shore; 60°20'·43N 01°02'·29W.

Suther Ness ⚲ Fl WRG 3s 10m W10M, R8M, G7M; vis: shore -W-038°-R-173°-W-206°-G-shore; 60°22'·12N 01°00'·20W.

Bound Skerry ☆ 60°25'·47N 00°43'·72W Fl 20s 44m **20M**; W twr.

South Mouth. Ldg Lts 014°. Front, FY3m 2M; 60°25'·33N 00°45'·01W. Rear, FY 12m 2M.

Muckle Skerry ⚲ Fl (2) WRG 10s 15m W7M, R5M, G5M; W twr; vis: 046°-W-192°-R-272°-W-348°-W-353°-R-046°; 60°26'·41N 00°51'·84W.

YELL SOUND

S ent, Lunna Holm ⚲ Fl (3) WRG 15s 19m W10M,R7M,G7M; W ◯twr; vis: shore-R-090°-W-094°-G-209°-W-275°-R-shore; 60°27'·34N 01°02'·52W.

Firths Voe ☆, N shore 60°27'·21N 01°10'·63W Oc WRG 8s 9m **W15M**, R10M, G10M; W twr; vis: 189°-W-194°-G-257°-W-261°-R-339°-W-066°.

Linga Is. Dir lt 150° ⚲ Q (4) WRG 8s 10m W9M, R9M, G9M; vis: 145°-R-148°-W-152°-G-155°. Q (4) WRG 8s 10m W7M, R4M, G4M; same structure; vis: 052°-R-146°, 154°-G-196°-W-312°; synch; 60°26'·80N 01°09'·13W.

The Rumble Bn ⚲ R Bn; Fl 10s 8m 4M; *Racon (O)*; 60°28'·16N 01°07'·26W.

Yell, Ulsta Ferry Term. Bkwtr Hd ⚲ Oc RG 4s 7m R5M, G5M; vis: shore-G-354°, 044°-R-shore. Same structure; Oc WRG 4s 5m W8M, R5M, G5M; vis: shore-G-008°-W-036°-R-shore; 60°29'·74N 01°09'·52W.

Toft Ferry Terminal ☆,Dir lt 241° (H24); Dir Oc WRG 10s 8m **W16M**, R10M, G10M; vis: 236° -G-240°-W-242°-R-246°; by day W2M, R1M, G1M. 60°27'·96N 01°12'·34W.

Ness of Sound, W side ⚲ Fl (3) WRG 12s 18m W9M, R6M, G6M; vis: shore-G-345°-W-350°-R-160°-W-165°-G-shore; 60°31'·34N 01°11'·28W.

Brother Is. Dir lt 329°, Fl (4) WRG 8s 16m W10M, R7M, G7M; vis: 323·5°-G-328°-W-330°-R-333·5°; 60°30'·95N 01°14'·11W.

Mio Ness ⚲ Q (2) WR 10s 12m W7M, R4M; W ◯ twr; vis: 282° - W - 238° - R - 282°; 60°29'·66N 01°13'·68W.

Tinga Skerry ⚲ Q(2)G 10s 9m 5M. W ◯ twr; 60°30'·48N 01°14'·86W.

YELL SOUND, NORTH ENTRANCE

Bagi Stack ⚲ Fl (4) 20s 45m 10M; 60°43'·53N 01°07'·54W.

Gruney Is ⚲ Fl WR 5s 53m W8M, R6M; W twr; vis: 064°-R-180°-W-012°; *Racon (T) 14M*; 60°39'·15N 01°18'·17W.

Pt of Fethaland ☆ 60°38'·05N 01°18'·70W Fl (3) WR 15s 65m **W24M, R20M**; vis 080°-R-103°-W-160°-206°-W-340°.

Muckle Holm ⚲ Fl (4) 10s 32m 10M 60°34'·83N 01°16'·01W.

Little Holm ⚲ Iso 4s 12m 6M; W twr; 60°33'·42N 01°15'·88W.

Outer Skerry ⚲ Fl 6s 12m 8M; 60°33'·04N 01°18'·32W.

Quey Firth ⚲ Oc WRG 6s 22m W12M, R8M, G8M; W twr; vis: shore (through S & W)-W-290°-G-327°-W-334°-W-shore; 60°31'·43N 01°19'·58W.

Lamba, S side ⚲Fl WRG 3s 30m W8M, R5M, G5M; W twr; vis: shore-G-288°-W-293°-R-327°-W-044°-R-140°-W-shore. Dir lt 290·5° Fl WRG 3s 24m W10M, R7M, G7M; vis: 285·5°-G-288°-W-293°-W-295·5°; 60°30'·73N 01°17'·84W.

SULLOM VOE

Gluss Is ☆ Ldg Lts 194·7° (H24). **Front**, 60°29'·77N 01°19'·44W F 39m **19M**; ☐ on Gy twr; **Rear**, 0·75M from front, F 69m **19M**; ☐ on Gy twr; both Lts 9M by day.

Little Roe ⚲ Fl (3) WR 10s 16m W5M, R4M; W structure, Or band; vis: 036°-R-095·5°-W-036°; 60°29'·99N 01°16'·46W.

Skaw Taing ⚲ Ldg Lts 150·5°. Front, Oc WRG 5s 21m W8M, R5M, G5M; Or and W structure; vis: 049°-W-078°-G-147°-W-154°-R-169°-W-288°; 60°29'·10N 01°16'·86W. Rear, 195m from front, Oc 5s 35m 8M; vis: W145°-156°.

Ness of Bardister ⚲ Oc WRG 8s 20m W9M, R6M, G6M; Or &W structure; vis: 180·5°- W-240°- R-310·5°- W-314·5°-G-030·5°; 60°28'·19N 01°19'·63W.

Fugla Ness. Lts in line 212·3°. Rear, 60°27'·25N 01°19'·74W Iso 4s 45m 14M. Common front 60°27'·45N 01°19'·57W Iso 4s 27m 14M; synch with rear Lts. Lts in line 203°. Rear, 60°27'·26N 01°19'·81W Iso 4s 45m 14M.

Sella Ness ☆ Dir lt 133·5°; 60°26'·76N 01°16'·66W Oc WRG 10s 19m **W16M**, R3M, G3M; vis: 123·5° -G- 130·5°-Al WG (white phase increasing with brg)-132·5°-W-134·5°-Al WR(R phase inc with brg)-136·5°-R-143·5°; H24. By day Oc WRG 10s 19m W2M, R1M,G1M as above.

EAST YELL, UNST and BALTA SOUND

Whitehill ⚲ Fl WR 3s 24m W9M, R6M; W clad metal frame twr; vis: 147°-W-163°-R-211°-W-352°-R-003°; 60°34'·80N 01°00'·22W. Fetlar. Hamars Ness ⚲ Iso G 6s 5m 3M; 60°37'·78N 00°55'·73W.

Balta Sound ⚲Fl WR 10s 17m 10M, R7M; vis: 249°-W-008°-R-058°-W-154°; 60°44'·43N 00°47'·68W.

Holme of Skaw ⚲ Fl 5s 8m 8M; white metal framework twr; 60°49'·87N 00°46'·30W.

Muckle Flugga ☆ 60°51'·32N 00°53'·13W Fl (2) 20s 66m **22M**.

Yell. Cullivoe Bkwtr Hd ⚲ Fl (2) WRG 10s 3m 4M; vis: 080°-G- 294°-W-355°-R-080°; 60°41'·86N 00°59'·70W.

Unst. Head of Mula ⚲ Fl WRG 5s 48m W10M, G7M, R7M; metal framework twr; vis: 292°-G-357°-W-002°-R-157°-W-161·5; 60°40'·76N 00°57'·58W.

MAINLAND, WEST

Esha Ness ✪ 60°29'·34N 01°37'·65W Fl 12s 61m **25M**.

Ness of Hillswick ⚓ Fl (4) WR 15s 34m W9M, R6M; vis: 217°-W-093°-R-114°; 60°27'·21N 01°29'·80W.

Muckle Roe, Swarbacks Minn ⚓ Fl WR 3s 30m W9M, R6M; vis: 314°-W-041°-R-075°-W-137°; 60°20'·98N 01°27'·07W.

W Burra Firth Outer ⚓ Oc WRG 8s 27m W9M, R7M, G7M; vis: 136°-G-142°-W-150°-R-156°. H24; 60°17'·79N 01°33'·56W.

W Burra Firth Inner ✪ 60°17'·78N 01°32'·17W F WRG 9m **W15M**, R9M, G9M; vis: 095°-G-098°-W-102°-105°; H24.

Ve Skerries ⚓ Fl (2) 20s 17m 11M; W twr; *Racon (T) 15M*; 60°22'·36N 01°48'·78W.

Papa Stour Housa Voe Dir lt 228° ⚓ F WRG 2m W9M, R7M, G7M; vis: 219°- G-226°- W-230°-R-239°; 60°19'·58N 01°40'·47W.

Rams Head ⚓ Fl WRG 8s 16m W9M, R6M; G6M; W house; vis: 265°-G-355°-W-012°-R-090°-W-136°, obsc by Vaila I when brg more than 030°; 60°11'·96N 01°33'·47W.

North Havra ⚓ Fl(3) WRG 12s 24m W11M, R8M, G8M; W twr; vis: 001°-G-053·5°-W-060·5°-R-182°, 274°- G-334°-W-337·5°-R -001°; 60°09'·85N 01°20'·31W.

SCALLOWAY

Bullia Skerry ⚓ Fl 5s 5m 5M; steel pillar & platform 60°06'·55N 01°21'·57W.

Point of the Pund ⚓ Fl WRG 5s 20m W7M, R5M, G5M; W twr; vis: 350°-R-090°-G-111°-R-135°-W-140°-G-177°, 267°-W-350°; 60°07'·99N 01°18'·31W.

Whaleback Skerry ⚓ Q; 60°07'·95N 01°18'·90W.

Blacks Ness Pier SW corner ⚓ Oc WRG 10s 10m W11M, G8M, R8M; vis: 052°-G-063·5°-W-065·5°-R-077°; 60°08'·02N 01°16'·59W.

Fugla Ness ⚓ Fl (2) WRG 10s 20m W10M, R7M, G7M; W twr; vis: 014°-G-032°-W-082°-R-134°-W-shore; 60°06'·38N 01°20'·85W.

FOULA

South Ness ✪ 60°06'·75N 02°03'·86W Fl WR (3) 15s 36m **W18M** R14M; W twr; vis: 221°-W-255°-R-277°-W-123°-obscured-221°.

Left-hand distance table

#	Place	1	2	3	4	5	6	7	8	9	10	11
1	Berwick-upon-Tweed	**1**										
2	Eyemouth	10	**2**									
3	Dunbar	26	17	**3**								
4	Port Edgar	58	50	34	**4**							
5	Methil	45	36	20	20	**5**						
6	Fife Ness	38	29	17	34	16	**6**					
7	Dundee	58	49	37	54	36	20	**7**				
8	Montrose	59	51	43	61	43	27	27	**8**			
9	Stonehaven	72	66	60	78	60	44	45	20	**9**		
10	Aberdeen	82	78	73	90	72	56	57	32	13	**10**	
11	Peterhead	105	98	93	108	94	78	80	54	35	25	**11**

Right-hand distance table

Place	#										
Cape Wrath	**11**	155	79	47	76	104	144	126	120	125	145
Lerwick	**10**	95	124	120	148	190	170	162	156	160	
Kirkwall	**9**	50	46	74	114	104	90	95	115		
Scrabster	**8**	31	59	99	89	75	80	100			
Wick	**7**	29	69	58	44	50	72				
Helmsdale	**6**	43	32	26	44	74					
Inverness	**5**	13	34	59	90						
Nairn	**4**	23	48	79							
Lossiemouth	**3**	25	56								
Banff/Macduff	**2**	33									
Peterhead	**1**										

AREA 6 *NW Scotland – C Wrath to Oban including The Western Isles*

SELECTED LIGHTS, BUOYS & WAYPOINTS

> Positions are referenced to WGS84

CAPE WRATH TO LOCH TORRIDON

Cape Wrath ✪ 58°37'·54N 04°59'·99W Fl (4) 30s 122m **22M**; W twr.

LOCH INCHARD and LOCH LAXFORD

Kinlochbervie Dir lt 327° ✪. 58°27'·49N 05°03'·08W WRG 15m **16M**; vis: 326°-FG-326·5°-Al GW-326·75°-FW-327·25°-Al RW-327·5°-FR-328°.

Creag Mhòr Dir lt 147°; Iso WRG 2s 16m 4M; vis: 136·5°-R -146·5°-W-147·5°-G-157·5°; 58°26'·99N 05°02'·45W.

Stoer Head ✪ 58°14'·43N 05°24'·07W Fl 15s 59m **24M**; W twr.

LOCH INVER, SUMMER ISLES and ULLAPOOL

Soyea I ⚓ Fl (2) 10s 34m 6M; 58°08'·56N 05°19'·67W.

Glas Leac ⚓ Fl WRG 3s 7m 5M; vis: 071°- W-078°-R-090°-G-103°- W-111°, 243°-W-247°-G-071°; 58°08'·68N 05°16'·36W.

Rubha Cadail ⚓ Fl WRG 6s 11m W9M, R6M, G6M; W twr; vis: 311°-G-320°-W-325°-R-103°-W-111°-G-118°-W-127°-R-157°-W-199°; 57°55'·51N 05°13'·40W.

Ullapool Pt ⚓ Iso R 4s 8m 6M; W twr; vis: 258°-108°; 57°53'·59N 05°09'·93W.

Cailleach Head ⚓ Fl (2) 12s 60m 9M; W twr; vis: 015°-236°; 57°55'·81N 05°24'·23W.

LOCH EWE and LOCH GAIRLOCH

Fairway ⚓ L Fl 10s; 57°51'·98N 05°40'·09W.

Rubha Reidh ✪ 57°51'·52N 05°48'·72W Fl (4) 15s 37m **24M**.

Glas Eilean ⚓ Fl WRG 6s 9m W6M, R4M; vis: 080°-W-102°-R-296°-W-333°-G-080°; 57°42'·79N 05°42'·42W.

OUTER HEBRIDES – EAST SIDE

LEWIS

Butt of Lewis ✪ 58°30'·89N 06°15'·84W Fl 5s 52m **25M**; R twr; vis: 056°-320°.

Tiumpan Head ✪ 58°15'·66N 06°08'·29W Fl (2) 15s 55m **25M**; W twr.

Broad Bay Tong ⚓ Ldg Lts 320°, Oc R 8s 8m 4M; 58°14'·48N 06°19'·98W. Rear, 70m from front, Oc R 8s 9m 4M.

STORNOWAY

Arnish Point ⚓ Fl WR 10s 17m W9M, R7M; W ○ twr; vis: 088°-W-198°-R-302°-W-013°; 58°11'·50N 06°22'·16W.

Sandwick Bay, NW side ⚓ Oc WRG 6s 10m 9M; vis: 334°-G-341°-W-347°-R-354°; 58°12'·20N 06°22'·11W.

No. 1 Pier SW corner ⚓ Q WRG 5m 11M; vis: shore-G-335°-W-352°-R-shore; 58°12'·36N 06°23'·43W.

Creed Estuary ⚓ Iso WRG 10s 24m 5M; vis: 277°-G-282°-W-290°-R-295°; 58°12'·03N 06°23'·47W.

No. 3 Pier ⚓ Q (2) G 10s 7m 2M 58°12'·31N 06°23'·28W.

Glumaig Hbr ⚓ Iso WRG 3s 8m 3M; 58°11'·27N 06°22'·9W; grey framework twr; vis: 150°-G-174°-W-180°-R-205°.

LOCH ERISORT, LOCH SHELL and EAST LOCH TARBERT

Shiants ▲ QG; 57°54'·57N 06°25'·70W.

Sgeir Inoe ▲ Fl G 6s; *Racon (M) 5M*; 57°50'·93N 06°33'·93W.

Eilean Glas (Scalpay) ☆ 57°51'·41N 06°38'·55W Fl (3) 20s 43m **23M**; W twr, R bands; *Racon (T) 16-18M*.

Sgeir Graidach ⚓ Q (6) + L Fl 15s; 57°50'·36N 06°41'·37W.

Sgeir Ghlas ⚓ Iso WRG 4s 9m W9M, R6M, G6M; W ○ twr; vis: 282°-G-319°-W-329°-R-153°-W-164°-G-171°; 57°52'·36N 06°45'·24W.

Tarbert ⚓ Dir Iso WRG 4s 9m 4M; vis : 290°-Iso G-297°-Al WG-300°-Iso W-303°-Al WR-306°-Iso R306°-313°; 57°53'·82N 06°47'·93W.

SOUND OF HARRIS, LEVERBURGH and BERNERAY

No.1 ▲ QG; 57°41'·20N 07°02'·67W.

No. 3 ▲ Fl G 5s; 57°41'·86N 07°03'·44W.

No. 4 ▲ Fl R 5s; 57°41'·76N 07°03'·63W.

Suilven ⚓ Fl (3)R 10s; 57°41'·68N 07°04'·36W.

Cabbage ⚓ Fl (2) R 6s; *Racon (T) 5M (3cm)*; 57°42'·13N 07°03'·96W.

Leverburgh Ldg Lts 014·7°. Front, Q 10m 4M 57°46'·23N 07°02'·04W. Rear, Oc 3s 12m 4M.

Jane's Tower ⚓ Q (2) G 5s 6m 4M; vis: obscured 273°-318°; 57°45'·76N 07°02'·12W.

Leverburgh Reef ⚓ Fl R 2s 4m 57°45'·97N 07°01'·86W.

Leverburgh Pier Ldg Lts 063°. Front, Iso Bu 4s 8s 6m 4M; 57°46'·00N 07°01'·61W, metal col. Rear, Iso Bu 4s 8s 7m 4M.

NORTH UIST

Fairway ⚓ L Fl 10s; 57°40'·23N 07°01'·39W.

Vallay Island ⚓ Fl WRG 3s 4m 8M; vis: 206°-W-085°-G-140°-W-145°-R-206°; 57°39'·69N 07°26'·42W.

Griminish Hbr Ldg Lts 183°. Front, QG 6m 4M; 57°26'·75W. Rear, 110m from front, QG 7m 4M.

LOCH MADDY and GRIMSAY

Weaver's Pt ⚓ 57°36'·49N 07°06'·00W Fl 3s 24m 7M; W hut.

Glas Eilean Mòr ⚓ 57°35'·95N 07°06'·70W Fl (2) G 4s 8m 5M.

Vallaquie I Dir lt 207·5°/ 255·5° ⚓ 57°35'·50N 07°09'·40W; W pillar; vis: Fl (3) WRG 8s 11m W5M, R5M, G5M; shore - G -205°-W-210°-R-240°;

Fl (3) WRG 8s 11m W8M, R8M, G8M; 249°-G-254°-W-257°-R-262°.

Lochmaddy Ldg Lts 298°. Front, Ro-Ro Pier 2 FG (vert) 8m 4M. Rear, 110m from front, Oc G 8s 10m 4M; vis: 284°-304°; 57°35'·76N 07°09'·36W.

Grimsay No. 1 ⚓ Fl (2) R 8s; 57°28'·26N 07°11'·82W.

SOUTH UIST and LOCH CARNAN

Landfall ⚓ L Fl 10s; 57°22'·27N 07°11'·52W.

Ldg Lts 222°. Front Fl R 2s 7m 5M; W ◇ on post; 57°22'·00N 07°16'·34W. Rear, 58m from front, Iso R 10s 11m 5M; W ◇ on post.

Ushenish ☆ (S Uist) 57°17'·89N 07°11'·58W Fl WR 20s 54m **W19M, R15M**; W twr; vis: 193°-W-356°-R-018°.

LOCH BOISDALE

MacKenzie Rk ⚓ Fl (3) R 15s 3m 4M; 57°08'·24N 07°13'·71W.

Calvay E End ⚓ Fl (2) WRG 10s 16m W7M, R7M, G7M; twr; vis: 111°-G-190°-R-202°-W-286°-R-111°; 57°08'·53N 07°15'·38W.

Gasay I ⚓ Fl WR 5s 10m W7M, R7M; W twr; vis: 120°-W-284°-R-120°; 57°08'·93N 07°17'·39W.

Loch Boisdale Dir lt ⚓ 292·5°; WRG 4s 4m 5M; vis: 287·5°-IsoG-290·5°-AlWG-292°-IsoW-293°-AlW-294·5°-IsoR-298·5°; 57°09'·19N 07°18'·24W.

LUDAIG and ERISKAY

Ludaig Bwtr ⚓ 2 FR (vert) 6m 3M; 57°06'·17N 07°19'·49W.

Acairseid Mhor Ldg Lts 285°. Front, Oc R 6s 9m 4M; 57°03'·89N 07°17'·25W. Rear, 24m from front, Oc R 6s 10m 4M.

BARRA, CASTLEBAY and VATERSAY SOUND

Drover Rocks ⚓ Q (6) + L Fl 15s; 57°04'·08N 07°23'·54W.

Binch Rock ⚓ Q (6) + L Fl 15s; 57°01'·60N 07°17'·12W.

Curachan ⚓ Q (3) 10s; 56°58'·56N 07°20'·51W.

Ardveenish ⚓ Oc WRG 6m 9/6M; vis: 300°-G-304°-W-306°-R-310°; 57°00'·21N 07°24'·43W.

Bo Vich Chuan ⚓ Q(6) + L Fl 15s; *Racon (M) 5M*; 56°56'·15N 07°23'·31W.

Channel Rk ⚓ Fl WR 6s 4m W6M, R4M; vis: 121·5°-W-277°-R-121·5°; 56°56'·24N 07°28'·94W.

Sgeir a Scape ▲ Fl (2) G 8s; 56°56'·25N 07°27'·21W.

Rubha Glas. Ldg Lts 295°. Front ⚓ FBu 9m 6M; Or △ on W twr; 56°56'·77N 07°30'·64W. Rear ⚓, 457m from front, FBu 15m 6M; Or ▽ on W twr; vis: 15° and 8° respectively either side of ldg line.

Barra Hd ☆ 56°47'·12N 07°39'·21W Fl 15s 208m **18M**; W twr; obsc by islands to NE.

OUTER HEBRIDES – WEST SIDE

Flannan I ☆, Eilean Mór Fl (2) 30s 101m **20M**; W twr; 58°17'·29N 07°35'·29W, obsc in places by ls to W of Eilean Mór.

Rockall ⚓ Fl 15s 19m 8M (unreliable); 57°35'·76N 13°41'·27W.

Gasker Lt ⚓ Fl (3) 10s 38m 10M; 57°59'·05N 07°17'·20W.

Whale Rock ⚓ Q (3) 10s 5m 5M; *Racon (T)*; 57°54'·40N 07°59·91W.

Haskeir I ☆ 57°41'·98N 07°41·36W Fl 20s 44m **23M**; W twr; *Racon (M) 17–15M*.

Monach Isles ☆ Fl (2) 15s 47m **18M**; R brick twr; 57°31'·55N 07°41'·68W.

EAST LOCH ROAG

Aird Laimishader Carloway ⚓ Fl 6s 63m 8M; W hut; obsc on some brgs; 58°17'·06N 06°49'·50W.

Ardvanich Pt ⚓ Fl G 3s 4m 2M; 58°13'·48N 06°47'·68W.

Tidal Rk ⚓ Fl R 3s 2m 2M (sync with Ardvanich Pt above); 58°13'·45N 06°47'·57W.

Grèinam ⚓ Fl WR 6s 8m W8M, R7M; W Bn; vis: R143°-169°, W169°-143°; 58°13'·30N 06°46'·16W.

NORTH UIST and SOUTH UIST

Vallay I ⚓ Fl WRG 3s 8M; vis: 206°-W-085°-G-140°-W-145°-R-206°; 57°39'·70N 07°26'·34W.

Falconet twr ⚓ FR 25m 8M (3M by day); shown 1hr before firing, changes to Iso R 2s 15 min before firing until completion; 57°22'·04N 07°23'·58W.

ST KILDA

Ldg Lts 270°. Front, Oc 5s 26m 3M; 57°48'·32N 08°34'·31W. Rear, 100m from front, Oc 5s 38m 3M; sync.

LOCH TORRIDON TO MALLAIG

LITTLE MINCH and W SKYE

Eugenie Rock ⚓ Q 6 + LF 15s; 57°46'·47N 06°27'·28W.

Eilean Trodday ⚓ Fl (2) WRG 10s 52m W12M, R9M, G9M; W Bn; vis: W062°-R088°-130°-W-322°-G-062°; 57°43'·64N 06°17'·89W.

Uig, Edward Pier Hd ⚓ 57°35'·09N 06°22'·29W Iso WRG 4s 9m W7M, R4M, G4M; vis: 180-W-006°-G-050°-W-073°-R-180°.

Waternish Pt ⚓ Fl 20s 21m 8M; W twr; 57°36'·48N 06°37'·99W.

Loch Dunvegan, Uiginish Pt ⚓ Fl WRG 3s 16m W7M,R5M,G5M; W lattice twr; vis: 041°-G-132°-W-145°-R-148°-W-253°-R- 263°-W-273°-G-306°, (>148° obsc by Fiadhairt Pt); 57°26'·84N 06°36'·53W.

Neist Point ☆ 57°25'·41N 06°47'·30W Fl 5s 43m **16M**; W twr.

Loch Harport, Ardtreck Pt ⚓ 57°20'·38N 06°25'·80W Fl 6s 18m 9M; small W twr.

RONA, LOCH A'BHRAIGE and INNER SOUND

Na Gamhnachain ⚓ Q; 57°35'·89N 05°57'·71W.

Rona NE Point ☆ 57°34'·68N 05°57'·56W Fl 12s 69m **19M**; W twr; vis: 050°-358°.

Loch A'Bhraige, Sgeir Shuas ⚓ Fl R 2s 6m 3M; vis: 070°-199°; 57°35'·02N 05°58'·61W.

Ldg Lts 136·5°. Front, ⚓ Q WRG 3m W4M, R3M; vis: 135°-W- 138°-R- 318°-G-135°; 57°34'·41N 05°58'·09W. Rear, ⚓ Iso 6s 28m 5M.

Ru Na Lachan ⚓ Oc WR 8s 21m 10M; twr; vis: 337°-W-022°- R-117°-W-162°; 57°29'·02N 05°52'·15W.

SOUND OF RAASAY, PORTREE and CROWLIN ISLANDS

Sgeir Mhór ⚓ Fl G 5s; 57°24'·57N 06°10'·53W.

Eilean Beag ⚓ Fl 6s 32m 6M; W Bn; 57°21'·21N 05°51'·42W.

RAASAY and LOCH SLIGACHAN

Suisnish ⚓ 2 FG (vert) 8m 2M; 57°19'·87N 06°03'·91W.

Eyre Point ⚓ Fl WR 3s 6m W9M, R6M; W twr; vis: 215°-W-266°-R- 288°-W-063°; 57°20'·01N 06°01'·29W.

KYLEAKIN and KYLE OF LOCH ALSH

Carragh Rk ⚓ Fl (2) G 12s; *Racon (T) 5M*; 57°17'·18N 05°45'·36W.

Bow Rk ⚓ Fl (2) R 12s; 57°16'·71N 05°45'·85W.

Fork Rks ⚓ Fl G 6s; 57°16'·85N 05°44'·93W.

Black Eye Rk ⚓ Fl R 6s; 57°16'·72N 05°45'·31W.

Eileanan Dubha East ⚓ Fl (2) 10s 9m 8M; vis: obscured 104°-146°; 57°16'·56N 05°42'·32W.

8 Metre Rock ⚓ Fl G 6s 5m 4M; 57°16'·60N 05°42'·69W.

String Rock ⚓ Fl R 6s; 57°16'·50N 05°42'·89W.

Sgeir-na-Caillich ⚓ Fl (2) R 6s 3m 4M; 57°15'·59N 05°38'·90W.

SOUND OF SLEAT

Kyle Rhea ⚓ Fl WRG 3s 7m W8M, R5M, G5M; W Bn; vis: shore-R-219°-W-228°-G-338°-W-346°-R-shore; 57°14'·22N 05°39'·93W.

Sandaig I, NW point ⚓ Fl 6s 13m 8M; W twr; 57°10'·05N 05°42'·29W.

Ornsay, SE end ⚓ 57°08'·60N 05°46'·85W Oc 8s 18m 12M; W twr; vis: 157°-030°.

Pt. of Sleat ⚓ Fl 3s 20m9M; W twr; 57°01'·08N 06°01'·08W.

MALLAIG and LOCH NEVIS ENTRANCE

Sgeir Dhearg ⚓ QG; 57°00'·74N 05°49'·50W.

Northern Pier E end ⚓ Iso WRG 4s 6m W9M, R6M, G6M; Gy twr; vis: 181°-G-185°-W-197°-R-201°. Fl G 3s 14m 6M; same structure; 57°00'·47N 05°49'·50W.

Sgeir Dhearg ⚓ 57°00'·63N 05°49'·61W Fl (2) WG 8s 6m 5M; Gy Bn; vis: 190°-G-055°-W-190°.

SMALL ISLES AND WEST OF MULL

CANNA and RUM

Canna, E end Sanday Is ⚓ Fl 10s 32m 9M; W twr; vis: 152°-061°; 57°02'·82N 06°28'·02W.

Loch Scresort ⚓ Q; 57°00'·79N 06°14'·61W.

HYSKEIR, EIGG, MUCK and ARISAIG

Humla ⚓ Fl G 6s 3m 4M 57°00'·46N 06°37'·39W.

Hyskeir ☆ 56°58'·14N 06°40'·87W Fl (3) 30s 41m **24M**; W twr. *Racon (T) 14-17M*.

SE point Eigg (Eilean Chathastail) ⚓ Fl 6s 24m 8M; W twr; vis: 181°-shore; 56°52'·25N 06°07'·28W.

Eigg, Sgeir nam Bagh (Ferry Terminal) ⚓ Dir 245°; Fl WRG 3s 9m W14, R11, G11; H24; steel pole; vis: 242·5°-G-244°-W-246°-R-247·5°. 2FR(vert) on same structure; 56°52'·80N 06°07'·60W.

Isle of Muck (Port Mor) ⚓ Dir Fl WRG 3s 7m W14, R11, G11, by day W1, R1, G1; steel twr; vis: 319·5°-G-321°-W-323°-R-324·5°; 56°49'·96N 06°13'·64W.

Bogha Ruadh ⚓ Fl G 5s 4m 3M; 56°49'·56N 06°13'·05W.

Bo Faskadale ⚓ Fl (3) G 18s; 56°48'·18N 06°06'·37W.

Ardnamurchan ☆ 56°43'·63N 06°13'·58W Fl (2) 20s 55m **24M**; Gy twr; vis: 002°-217°.

Cairns of Coll, Suil Ghorm ⚓ Fl 12s 23m 10M; W twr; 56°42'·26N 06°26'·75W.

TIREE, COLL and ARINAGOUR

Loch Eatharna, Pier Head ⚓ Dir 325°; Oc WRG 7s 6m 2M; vis: 316°-G-322°-W-328°-R-334°; 56°36'·86N 06°31'·29W.

Loch Eatharna, Bogha Mór ⚓ Fl G 6s; 56°36'·65N 06°30'·90W.

Roan Bogha ⚓ Q (6) + L Fl 15s 3m 5M; 56°32'·23N 06°40'·18W.

Placaid Bogha ⚓ Fl G 4s; 56°33'·22N 06°44'·06W.

Scarinish ⚓, S side of ent 56°30'·02N 06°48'·26W Fl 3s 11m 12M; W ☐ twr; vis: 210°-030°.

Cairn na Burgh More (Treshnish Is), Fl (3) 15s 36m 8M; solar panels on framework tr; 56°31'·05N 06°22'·95W.

Gott Bay Ldg Lts 286·5°. Front FR 8m; 56°30'·61N 06°47'·82W. Rear 30m from front FR 11m.

Skerryvore ☆ Fl 10s 46m **23M**; Gy twr; *Racon (M) 18M*. 56°19'·36N 07°06'·88W

LOCH NA KEAL and LOCH NA LÀTHAICH
Sgeir a Charraigein ⚓ Q(6) + LFl 15s; 56°28'·29N 06°07'·71W.
Eileanan na Liathanaich, SE end ⚓ Fl WR 6s 12m W8M, R6M; vis: R088°- W108°-088°; 56°20'·56N 06°16'·38W.

DUBH ARTACH
Dubh Artach ☆ 56°07'·94N 06°38'·08W Fl (2) 30s 44m **20M**; Gy twr, R band.

SOUND OF MULL

LOCH SUNART, TOBERMORY and LOCH ALINE
Ardmore Pt ⚓ Fl (2) 10s 18m 13M; 56°39'·37N 06°07'·70W.
New Rks ▲ Fl G 6s 56°39'·05N 06°03'·30W.
Rubha nan Gall ☆ 56°38'·33N 06°04'·00W Fl 3s 17m **15M**; W twr.
Eileanan Glasa (Dearg Sgeir) ⚓ Fl WR 6s 7m 8M; W ○ twr.
Fiunary Spit ▲ 56°32'·66N 05°53'·17W Fl G 6s.
Loch Aline, ⚓ Dir 357°; Oc WRG 6s 2m 4M; vis: 353°-G-356°-W-358°-R-002°; Or concrete plinth; 56°32'·38N 05°46'·47W.
Ardtornish Pt ⚓ Fl (2) WRG 10s 8m W8M, R6M, G6M; W twr; vis: G shore- 301°-W-308°-R-342°-W-057°-R-095°-W-108°-G-shore; 56°31'·09N 05°45'·21W.
Craignure Ldg Lts 240·9°. Front, FR 10m; 56°28'·26N 05°42'·28W. Rear, 150m from front, FR 12m; vis: 225·8°-255·8°.

MULL TO CALEDONIAN CANAL AND OBAN
Lismore ☆, SW end 56°27'·34N 05°36'·45W Fl 10s 31m **17M**; W twr; vis: 237°-208°.
Lady's Rk ⚓ Fl 6s 12m 5M; 56°26'·92N 05°37'·05W.
Duart Pt ⚓ Fl (3) WR 18s 14m W5M, R3M; vis: 162°-W-261°-R- 275°-W-353°-R-shore; 56°26'·84N 05°38'·77W.

LOCH LINNHE
Corran Shoal ⚓ QR 56°43'·69N 05°14'·39W.
Ent W side, Corran Pt ⚓ Iso WRG 4s 12m W10M, R7M, G7M; vis: shore-R-195°-W-215°-G-020-W-030°-R-shore;56°43'·25N 05°14'·54W.
Corran Narrows NE ⚓Fl 5s 4m 4M; W twr; vis: S shore-214°; 56°43'·62N 05°13'·90W .
Clovullin Spit ⚓ Fl (2) R 15s; 56°42'·29N 05°15'·56W.
Cuil-cheanna Spit ▲ Fl G 6s; 56°41'·17N 05°15'·72W.

FORT WILLIAM and CALEDONIAN CANAL
Corpach, Caledonian Canal Lock ent ⚓ Iso WRG 4s 6m

5M; W twr; vis: G287°- W310°- R335°-030°; 56°50'·52N 05°07'·44W.

LYNN OF LORN
Sgeir Bhuidhe Appin ⚓ Fl (2) WR 7s 8m W9M R6M; W Bn; vis: W013·5°- R184°-220°; 56°33'·63N 05°24'·65W.
Appin Point ▲ Fl G 6s; 56°32'·69N 05°25'·97W.
Dearg Sgeir, off Aird's Point ⚓ Fl WRG 2s 2m W3M, R1M, G1M; vis: 196°-R-246°-W-258°-G-041°-W-058°-R-093°-W-139°; 56°32'·20N 05°25'·22W.
Rubha nam Faoileann (Eriska) ⚓ QG 2m 2M; G col; vis 128°-329°; 56°32'·20N 05°24'·11W.
Branra Rk ⚓ Fl(2) 10s 4m 5M; metal frame on white twr; 56°32'·02N 05°26'·60W.

DUNSTAFFNAGE BAY/OBAN
N spit of Kerrera ⚓ Fl R 3s 9m 5M; W col, R bands; 56°25'·49N 05°29'·56W.
Dunollie ⚓ Fl (2) WRG 6s 6m W8M, R6M, G6M; vis: 351°-G- 020°- W-047°-R-120°-W-138°-G-143°; 56°25'·37N 05°29'·05W.
Corran Ledge ⚓ VQ (9) 10s; 56°25'·19N 05°29'·11W.

OBAN TO LOCH CRAIGNISH
Heather Is ⚓ Fl R 2·5s 11m 2M; 56°24'·41N 05°30'·24W.
Sgeirean Dubha ⚓ Fl (2) 12s 7m 5M; W ○ twr; 56°22'·27N 05°32'·27W.
Bogha Nuadh ⚓ Q (6) + LFl 15s; 56°21'·69N 05°37'·88W.
Bogha Ghair ⚓ Q (3) 10s; 56°16'·50N 05°40'·44W.
Bono Rock ⚓ Q (9) 15s; 56°16'·21N 05°41'·22W.
Fladda ⚓ Fl (2) WRG 9s 13m W11M, R9M, G9M; W twr; vis: 169°-R-186°-W-337°-G-344°-W-356°-R-026°; 56°14'·89N 05°40'·83W.
Dubh Sgeir (Luing) ⚓ Fl WRG 6s 9m W6M, R4M. G4M; W twr; vis: W000°- R010°- W025°- G199°-000°; *Racon (M)* **5M**; 56°14'·76N 05°40'·20W.
The Garvellachs, Eileach an Naoimh, SW end ⚓ Fl 6s 21m 9M; W Bn; vis: 240°-215°; 56°13'·04N 05°49'·06W.

LOCH MELFORT and CRAOBH HAVEN
Melfort Pier ⚓ Dir FR 6m 3M; (Apr -Nov); 56°16'·14N 05°30'·19W.
▲ 56°12'·88N 05°33'·59W.
Craobh Marina Bkwtr Hd ⚓ Iso WRG 5s 10m, W5M, R3M, G3M; vis:114°-G-162°-W-183°-R-200°; 56°12'·78N 05°33'·52W.

		1	2	3	4	5	6	7	8	9	10	11	12	13	14	15	16	17
1	Cape Wrath	**1**																
2	Ullapool	54	**2**															
3	Stornoway	53	45	**3**														
4	East Loch Tarbert	75	56	33	**4**													
5	Portree	83	57	53	42	**5**												
6	Kyle of Lochalsh	91	63	62	63	21	**6**											
7	Mallaig	112	82	83	84	42	21	**7**										
8	Eigg	123	98	97	75	54	35	14	**8**									
9	Castlebay (Barra)	133	105	92	69	97	76	59	46	**9**								
10	Tobermory	144	114	115	87	74	53	32	20	53	**10**							
11	Loch Aline	157	127	128	100	87	66	45	33	66	13	**11**						
12	Fort William	198	161	162	134	121	98	75	63	96	43	34	**12**					
13	Oban	169	138	139	111	100	77	56	44	77	24	13	29	**13**				
14	Loch Melfort	184	154	155	117	114	93	69	61	92	40	27	45	18	**14**			
15	Craobh Haven	184	155	155	117	114	92	70	60	93	40	27	50	21	5	**15**		
16	Crinan	187	157	158	129	112	95	74	63	97	42	30	54	25	14	9	**16**	
17	Mull of Kintyre	232	203	189	175	159	143	121	105	120	89	87	98	72	62	57	51	**17**

DISTANCE TABLES
Approx distances in nautical miles are by the most direct route allowing for dangers and TSS.

SELECTED LIGHTS, BUOYS & WAYPOINTS

Positions are referenced to WGS84

COLONSAY TO ISLAY

COLONSAY
Scalasaig, Rubha Dubh ✠ Fl (2) WR 10s 8m W8M, R6M; W bldg; vis: shore-R- 230°-W-337°-R-354°; 56°04'·01N 06°10'·90W.

SOUND OF ISLAY
Rhubh' a Mháil (Ruvaal) ✠ 55°56'·18N 06°07'·46W Fl (3) 15s 45m **19M**; W twr.
Carragh an t'Struith ✠ Fl 3s 8m 9M; W twr; vis: 354°-180°; 55°52'·30N 06°05'·78W.
Carraig Mòr ✠ Fl (2) WR 6s 7m W8M, R6M; W twr; vis: shore-R- 175°-W-347°-R-shore; 55°50'·42N 06°06'·13W.
McArthur's Hd ✠ Fl (2) WR 10s 39m W13M, R10M; W twr; W in Sound of Islay from NE coast,159°-R-244°-W-E coast of Islay; 55°45'·84N 06°02'·90W.

PORT ELLEN and LOCH INDAAL
Carraig Fhada ✠ Fl WRG 3s 20m W8M, R6M, G6M; W ☐ twr; vis: W shore- 248°-G-311°-W-340°-R-shore; 55°37'·22N 06°12'·71W.
Otter Gander ✦ VQ (3) 5s; 55°36'·60N 06°12'·34W.
Rubh'an Dùin ✠ Fl (2) WR 7s 15m W11M, R8M; W twr; vis: shore-R-218°-W-249°-R-350°-W-shore; 55°44'·70N 06°22'·28 W.
Orsay Is, **Rhinns of Islay** ✠ 55°40'·40N 06°30'·84W Fl 5s 46m **24M**; W twr; vis: 256°-184°.

JURA TO MULL OF KINTYRE

SOUND OF JURA, CRAIGHOUSE, L SWEEN and GIGHA
Na Cùiltean ✠ Fl 10s 9m 9M; 55°48'·64N 05°54'·90W.
Gamhna Gigha ✠ Fl (2) 6s 7m 5M; 55°43'·78N 05°41'·08W.

WEST LOCH TARBERT
Dunskeig Bay ✠ Q (2) 10s 11m 8M; 55°45'·22N 05°35'·00W.
Eileen Tráighe (off S side) ⌡ Fl (2) R 5s 5m 3M; R post; 55°45'·37N 05°35'·75W.

MULL OF KINTYRE
Mull of Kintyre ✠ 55°18'·64N 05°48'·25W Fl (2) 20s 91m **24M**; W twr on W bldg; vis: 347°-178°.

CRINAN CANAL and ARDRISHAIG
Crinan, E of lock ent ✠ Fl WG 3s 8m 4M; W twr, R band; vis: shore-W-146°-G-shore; 56°05'·48N 05°33'·37W.
Ardrishaig Bkwtr Hd ✠ L Fl WRG 6s 9m 4M; vis: 287°-G-339°-W- 350°-R-035°; 56°00'·76N 05°26'·59W.

LOCH FYNE TO SANDA ISLAND

EAST LOCH TARBERT
Eilean na Beithe ✠ Fl WRG 3s 7m 5M; vis: G036°- W065°-R078°-106°; 55°52'·68N 05°19'·62W.

KILBRANNAN SOUND, CRANNAICH and CARRADALE BAY
Port Crannaich Bkwtr Hd ✠ Fl R 10s 5m 6M; vis: 099°-279°; 55°35'·60N 05°27'·84W.

CAMPBELTOWN LOCH to SANDA ISLAND
Davaar N Pt ✠ 55°25'·69N 05°32'·42W Fl (2) 10s 37m **23M**; W twr; vis: 073°-330°.

Sanda Island ✠ 55°16'·50N 05°35'·01W Fl 10s 50m **15M**; W twr; vis: 242°-121°.
Patersons Rock ⌐ Fl (3) R 18s; 55°16'·90N 05°32'·48W.

KYLES OF BUTE TO RIVER CLYDE

KYLES OF BUTE and CALADH
Ardlamont Point No. 47 ⌐ W Fl R 4s; 55°49'·59N 05°11'·76.
Ardmaleish Point No. 41 ⌡ Q (3) 10s; 55°53'·02N 05°04'·70W.
Bogany Point No. 36 ⌐ Fl R 4s; 55°50'·78N 05°01'·41W.

FIRTH OF CLYDE
Toward Pt ✠ 55°51'·73N 04°58'·79W Fl 10s 21m **22M**; W twr.
No. 34 ⌡ Q (3) 10s; 55°51'·44N 04°59'·11W.
Skelmorlie ⌡ Iso 5s; 55°51'·65N 04°56'·34W.

WEMYSS and INVERKIP
Cowal ⌡ L Fl 10s; 55°56'·00N 04°54'·83W.
The Gantocks ⌡ Fl R 6s 12m 6M; ○ twr; 55°56'·45N 04°55'·08W.

DUNOON
Cloch Point ✠ Fl 3s 24m 8M; W ○ twr, B band, W dwellings; 55°56'·55N 04°52'·74W.

LOCH LONG and LOCH GOIL
Loch Long ⌡ Oc 6s; 55°59'·15N 04°52'·42W.
Baron's Pt No. 3 ✠ Oc (2) Y 10s 5m 3M; 55°59'·18N 04°51'·12W.
Ravenrock Pt ✠ Fl 4s 12m 10M; W twr on W col. Dir lt 204°, WRG 9m (same twr); vis: 201·5°-F R-203°-Al WR(W phase incr with brg)-203·5°-FW-204·5°-Al WG(G phase incr with brg)-205°-FG-206·5°; 56°02'·14N 04°54'·39W.
Port Dornaige ✠ Fl 6s 8m 11M; W col; vis: 026°-206°; 56°03·75N 04°53'·65W.
Rubha Ardnahein ✠ Fl R 5s 3m 3M; vis: 132°-312°; 56°06'·15N 04°53'·60W.
The Perch, Ldg Lts 318° Front, F WRG 3m 5M; vis: 311°-G-317°-W- 320°-R-322°. Same structure, Fl R 3s 3m 3M; vis: 187°-322°; 56°06'·90N 04°54'·31W. Rear, 700m from front, F 7m 5M; vis: 312°-322·5°.
Cnap Pt ✠ Ldg Lts 031°. Front, Q 8m 10M; W col; 56°07'·40N 04°49'·97W. Rear, 87m from front F 13m; R line on W twr.

GOUROCK
Ashton ⌡ Iso 5s; 55°58'·10N 04°50'·65W.
Rosneath Patch ⌡ Fl (2) 10s 5m 10M; 55°58'·52N 04°47'·45W.

ROSNEATH, RHU NARROWS and GARELOCH
Ldg Lts 356°. **Front, No. 7N** ⌡ 56°00'·05N 04°45'·36W Dir lt 356°. WRG 5m **W16M**, R13M, G13M; vis: 353°-Al WG- 355°- FW-357°-Al WR-000°-FR-002°.
Dir lt 115° WRG 5m **W16M**, R13M, G13M; vis: 111°-Al WG-114°-FW- 116°-Al WR-119°-FR-121°. Passing lt Oc G 6s 6m 3M; G △ on G pile . Rear, Ardencaple Castle Centre ✠ 56°00'·54N 04°45'·43W 2 FG (vert) 26m 12M; twr on Castle NW corner; vis: 335°-020°.

No. 8N Lt Bn ⚓ 55°59'·09N 04°44'·21W Dir lt 080° WRG 4m; **W16M**, R13M,G13M;vis: 075°-FG-077·5°-Al WG-079·5°-FW-080·5°-AltWR-082·5°-FR-085°. **Dir lt 138°** WRG 4m **W16M**, R13M, G13M; vis: 132°-FG-134°-Al WG-FW137°-139°-Al WR-142°. Passing lt Fl Y 3s 6m 3M.

Gareloch No. 1 Lt Bn ⚓ VQ (4) Y 5s 9m; Y 'X' on Y structure; 55°59'·12N 04°43'·89W.

No. 3N Lt Bn ⚓ 56°00'·07N 04°46'·72W Dir lt 149° WRG 9m **W16M**, R13M, G13M F & Al; vis: 144°-FG-145°-Al WG-148°-FW-150°-Al WR-153°-FR-154°. Passing lt Oc R 8s 9m 3M.

Rosneath DG Jetty ⚓ 2 FR (vert) 5M; W col; vis: 150°-330°; 56°00'·39N 04°47'·51W.

Rhu Pt ⚓ Q (3) WRG 6s 9m W10M, R7M, G7M; vis: 270°-G-000°-W-114°-R-188°; 56°00'·95N 04°47'·19W.

Dir lt 318° WRG **W16M**, R13M,G13M; vis: 315°-Al WG-317°-F-319°-Al WR-321°-FR-325°.

Limekiln No. 2N Lt Bn ⚓ 56°00'·67N 04°47'·64W Dir lt 295° WRG 5m **W16M**, R13M, G13M F & Al; R □ on R Bn; vis: 291°-Al WG- 294°-FW- 296°-Al WR-299°-FR-301°.

Mambeg Dir lt 331°, Q (4) WRG 8s 10m 14M; vis: 328·5°-G-330°-W- 332°-R-333°; H24; 56°03'·74N 04°50'·47W.

GREENOCK and PORT GLASGOW

Anchorage Lts in line 196°. Front, FG 7m 12M; Y col; 55°57'·62N 04°46'·58W. Rear, 32m from front, FG 9m 12M. Y col.

Lts in line 194·5°. Front, FG 18m; 55°57'·45N 04°45'·91W. Rear, 360m from front, FG 33m.

Steamboat Quay, W end ⚓ FG 12m 12M; B&W chequered col; vis 210°-290°; 55°56'·25N 04°41'·44W. From here to Glasgow Lts on S bank are Fl G and Lts on N bank are Fl R.

CLYDE TO MULL OF GALLOWAY

LARGS and FAIRLIE

Approach ⚓ L Fl 10s; 55°46'·40N 04°51'·85W.

Fairlie Patch ⚓ Fl G 1·5s; 55°45'·38N 04°52'·34W.

MILLPORT and GREAT CUMBRAE

Ldg Lts 333°. Pier Head front, 55°45'·04N 04°55'·85W FR 7m 5M. Rear, 137m from front, FR 9m 5M.

Mountstuart ⚓ L Fl 10s; 55°48'·00N 04°57'·57W.

Runnaneun Pt (Rubha'n Eun) ⚓ Fl R 6s 8m 12M; W twr; 55°43'·79N 05°00'·23W.

Little Cumbrae Is, Cumbrae Elbow ⚓ Fl 6s 28m 14M; W twr; vis: 334°-193°; 55°43'·22N 04°58'·06W.

ARDROSSAN

Approach Dir lt 055°, WRG 15m W14M, R11M, G11M; vis: 050°-F G-051·2°-Alt WG(W phase inc with Brg)- 053·8°-FW-056·2°-AltWR(R phase inc with brg)-058·8°-FR-060°; 55°38'·66N 04°49'·22W. Same structure FR 13m 6M; vis: 325°-145°.

Lt ho Pier Hd ⚓ Iso WG 4s 11m 9M; W twr; vis: 035°-W-317°-G-035°; 55°38'·47N 04°49'·57W.

IRVINE

Ldg Lts 051°. Front, FG 10m 5M; 55°36'·40N 04°41'·57W. Rear, 101m from front, FR 15m 5M; G masts, both vis: 019°-120°.

TROON

Troon Approach ⚓ Fl G 4s; 55°33'·06N 04°41'·34W.

W Pier Hd ⚓ Fl (2) WG 5s 11m 9M; W twr; vis: 036°-G-090°-W-036°; 55°33'·07N 04°41'·02W.

Lady I ⚓ Fl 2s 19m 11M; W Tr R vert stripes; *Racon (T) 13-11M*; 55°31'·63N 04°44'·05W.

ARRAN, RANZA, LAMLASH and BRODICK

Pillar Rk Pt ☆ (Holy Island), 55°31'·04N 05°03'·67W Fl (2) 20s 38m **25M**; W □ twr.

Holy Is SW end ⚓ Fl G 3s 14m 6M; W twr; vis: 282°-147°; 55°30'·73N 05°04'·21W.

Pladda ☆ 55°25'·50N 05°07'·12W Fl (3) 30s 40m **17M**; W twr.

AYR and AILSA CRAIG

S Pier Hd ⚓ Q 7m 7M; R twr; vis: 012°-161°. Also FG 5m 5M; vis: 012°-082°; 55°28'·17N 04°38'·74W.

Ldg Lts 098°. Front, FR 10m 5M; Tfc sigs; 55°28'·15N 04°38'·38W. Rear, 130m from front Oc R 10s 18m 9M.

Maidens Hbr, E side ⚓ Fl G 5s 4m 3M; 55°20'·24N 04°49'·20W.

Maidens Hbr, W side ⚓ Fl R 3s 4m 2M; 55°20'·23N 04°49'·19W.

Turnberry Point ☆, near castle ruins 55°19'·56N 04°50'·71W Fl 15s 29m **24M**; W twr.

Ailsa Craig ☆ 55°15'·12N 05°06'·52W Fl 4s 18m **17M**; W twr; vis: 145°-028°.

GIRVAN

S Pier Hd ⚓2 FG (vert) 8m 4M; W twr; 55°14'·72N 04°51'·90W.

LOCH RYAN and STRANRAER

Milleur Point ⚓ Q; 55°01'·28N 05°05'·66W.

Fairway ⚓ Iso 4s; 54°59'·77N 05°03'·82W.

Forbes Shoal ⚓ QR; 54°59'·47N 05°02'·96W.

Loch Ryan W ⚓QG;54°59'·23N 05°03'·24W .

1	Loch Craignish	1												
2	Crinan	5	2											
3	Ardrishaig	14	9	3										
6	East Loch Tarbert	24	19	10	4									
5	Campbeltown	55	50	39	31	5								
6	Lamlash	48	43	34	25	24	6							
7	Largs	48	43	34	24	39	17	7						
8	Kip Marina	53	48	39	28	50	25	10	8					
9	Greenock	59	54	45	36	53	31	16	6	9				
10	Rhu (Helensburgh)	62	57	48	37	59	33	19	9	4	10			
11	Troon	54	49	40	33	33	16	20	29	34	38	11		
12	Girvan	67	62	53	43	29	20	33	46	49	51	21	12	
13	Stranraer	89	84	75	65	34	39	56	69	65	74	44	23	13
14	Kirkcudbright	136	131	122	114	88	92	110	116	124	125	97	94	71	14

DISTANCE TABLES

Approx distances in nautical miles are by the most direct route allowing for dangers and TSS.

Cairn Pt ⚡ Fl (2) R 10s 14m 12M; W twr; 54°58'·46N 05°01'·85W.
Cairnryan ⚡ Fl R 5s 5m 5M; 54°57'·77N 05°00'·99W.
Stranraer No.1 ⚓ Oc G 6s; 54°56'·67N 05°01'·32W.
No. 3 ⚓ QG; 54°55'·87N 05°01'·60W.
No. 5 ⚓ Fl G 3s; 54°55'·08N 05°01'·86W.
E Pier Hd ⚡ 2 FR (vert) 9m; 54°54'·61N 05°01'·60W.
Corsewall Point ☆ 55°00'·41N 05°09'·58W Fl (5) 30s 34m **22M**; W twr; vis: 027°-257°.
Black Head Old Lighthouse (disused); W tower, 22m; 54°51'·70N 05°08'·80W.

PORTPATRICK
Ldg Lts 050·5°. Front, FG (occas); 54°50'·50N 05°07'·02W. Rear, 68m from front, FG 8m (occas).
Crammag Hd ☆ 54°39'·90N 04°57'·92W Fl 10s 35m **18M**; W twr.
Mull of Galloway ☆, SE end 54°38'·08N 04°51'·45W Fl 20s 99m **28M**; W twr; vis: 182°-105°.

MULL OF GALLOWAY and WIGTOWN BAY
Port William Ldg Lts 105°. Front, Pier Hd Fl G 3s 7m 3M; 54°45'·66N 04°35'·28W. Rear, 130m from front, FG 10m 2M.
Isle of Whithorn ⚡ Fl WR 3s 20m 6/4M; vis: 310°-W-005°-R-040°; 54°41'·79N 04°21'·54W.
Whithorn Ldg Lts 335°. Front, Oc R 8s 7m 7M; Or ♦; 54°42'·01N 04°22'·05W. Rear, 35m from front, Oc R 8s 9m 7M; Or ♦, synch.
Little Ross ⚡ Fl 5s 50m 12M; W twr; obsc in Wigtown B when brg more than 103°; 54°45'·93N 04°05'·10W.

KIRKCUDBRIGHT BAY and KIPPFORD
Little Ross NNE end of Is ⚡ Fl (2) 5s 21m 5M; Stone bcn; 54°46'·06N 04°05'·02W.
Hestan I, E end ⚡ Fl (2) 10s 42m 9M; 54°49'·95N 03°48'·53W.

AREA 8 *NW England, Isle of Man & N Wales – Solway Firth to Bardsey I*

SELECTED LIGHTS, BUOYS & WAYPOINTS

Positions are referenced to WGS84

SOLWAY FIRTH TO BARROW-IN-FURNESS

SILLOTH and MARYPORT
Lees Scar ⚡ Fl G 5s 11m 4M; W piles; 54°51'·78N 03°24'·79W.
Groyne Hd ⚡ 2 FG (vert) 4m 4M; Fl Bu tfc signals close by; 54°52'·14N 03°23'·93W.
Maryport S Pier Hd ⚡.Fl 1·5s 10m 6M; 54°43'·07N 03°30'·64W.

WORKINGTON and HARRINGTON
N Workington ⚓ Q; 54°40'·10N 03°38'·18W.
S Workington ⚓ VQ (6) + L Fl 10s; 54°37'·01N 03°38'·58W.
South Pier ⚡ Fl 5s 11m 5M; R bldg; 54°39'·12N 03°34'·67W.
Ldg Lts 131·8°. Front, FR 10m 3M; 54°38'·92N 03°34'·19W. Rear, 134m from front, FR 12m 3M.

WHITEHAVEN
W Pier Hd ⚡ Fl G 5s 16m 8M; W ○ twr; 54°33'·17N 03°35'·92W.
N Pier Hd ⚡ Fl R 5s 8m 10M; W ○ twr; 54°33'·17N 03°35'·75W.
Saint Bees Hd ☆ 54°30'·81N 03°38'·23W Fl (2) 20s 102m **18M**; W○ twr; obsc shore-340°.

RAVENGLASS
Blockhouse ⚡ FG; (Eskdale Range); 54°20'·16N 03°25'·34W.
Selker ▲ Fl (3) G 10s; *Bell;* 54°16'·14N 03°29'·58W.

BARROW-IN-FURNESS
Lightning Knoll ◓ L Fl 10s; 53°59'·83N 03°14'·28W.
Halfway Shoal ⚓ QR 19m 10s; R&W chequer Bn; 54°01'·46N 03°11'·88W.
Isle of Walney ☆ 54°02'·92N 03°10'·64W Fl 15s 21m **23M**; stone twr; obsc 122°-127° within 3M of shore.
Walney Chan Ldg Lts 040·7°. No.1 Front ⚓, Q 7m 10M; B Pile; 54°03'·19N 03°09'·22W. No. 2 Rear ⚓, 0·61m from front, Iso 2s 13m 10M; Pile.
Rampside Sands Ldg Lts 005·1°. No. 3 Front ⚓, Q 9m 10M; W ○ twr; 54°04'·41N 03°09'·79W. No. 4 Rear ⚓, 0·77M from front, Iso 2s 14m 6M; R col, W face.

ISLE OF MAN

Whitestone Bank ⚓ Q (9) 15s; 54°24'·58N 04°20'·41W.
Point of Ayre ☆ 54°24'·94N 04°22'·13W Fl (4) 20s 32m **19M**; W twr, two R bands, *Racon (M) 13-15M*.
Low Lt Ho (unlit), RW twr, B base, 54°25'·03N 04°21'·86W.

PEEL
Peel Bkwtr Hd ⚡ Oc 7s 11m 6M; W twr; 54°13'·67N 04°41'·69W.

PORT ERIN and PORT ST MARY
Ldg Lts 099·1°. Front, 54°05'·23N 04°45'·57W FR 10m 5M; W twr, R band. Rear, 39m from front, FR 19m 5M; W col, R band.
Calf of Man Lighthouse (disused), white 8-sided tower.
Chicken Rk ⚡ Fl 5s 38m **21M**; *Racon (C)* 54°02'·27N 04°50'·32W.
Alfred Pier Hd ⚡ Oc R 10s 8m 6M; 54°04'·33N 04°43'·82W.

CASTLETOWN and DERBY HAVEN
Dreswick Pt ⚡ Fl (2) 30s 23m 12M; W twr; 54°03'·29N 04°37'·45W.
New Pier Hd ⚡ Oc R 15s 8m 5M; 54°04'·33N 04°38'·97W.
Derby Haven, Bkwtr SW end ⚡Iso G 2s 5m 5M; W twr, G band; 54°04'·58N 04°37'·06W.

DOUGLAS
Douglas Head ☆ 54°08'·60N 04°27'·95W Fl 10s 32m **24M**; W twr; obsc brg more than 037°. FR Lts on radio masts 1 and 3M West.
No. 1 ▲ Q (3) G 5s; 54°09'·04N 04°27'·68W.
Princess Alexandra Pier Hd ⚡ Fl R 5s 16m 8M; R mast; *Whis (2) 40s;* 54°08'·84N 04°27'·85W.
Ldg Lts 229·3°, Front ⚓, Oc Bu 10s 9m 5M; W △ R border on mast; 54°08'·72N 04°28'·25W. Rear ⚓, 62m from front, Oc Bu 10s 12m 5M; W ▽ on R border; synch with front.

Victoria Pier Hd ⚓ Iso G 10s 10m 3M; W col; vis: 225°-327°; Intnl Port Tfc Signals; 54°08'·84N 04°28'·08W.
Conister Rk Refuge ⚓ Q 3M; vis: 234°-312°; 54°09'·03N 04°28'·12W.

LAXEY to RAMSEY

Laxey Pier Hd ⚓ Oc R 3s 7m 5M; W twr, R band; obsc when brg less than 318°; 54°13'·50N 04°23'·43W.
Maughold Head ☆ 54°17'·72N 04°18'·58W Fl (3) 30s 65m **21M**.
Bahama ⚓ VQ (6) + L Fl 10s; 54°20'·01N 04°08'·57W.
Queens Pier Dn ⚓ Fl R 5s; 54°19'·28N 04°21'·95W.
King William Bank ⚓ Q (3) 10s; 54°26'·01N 04°00'·08W.

BARROW TO RIVERS MERSEY AND DEE

MORECAMBE

Lightning Knoll ⚓ L Fl 10s; 53°59'·84N 03°14'·28W.
Morecambe ⚓ Q (9) 15s; 53°52'·00N 03°22'·00W.
Lune Deep ⚓ Q (6) + L Fl 15s; *Racon (T)*; 53°56'·07N 03°12·90W.
Lts in line about 090°. Front, FR 10m 2M; G mast; 54°04'·41N 02°52'·63W. Rear, 140m from front, FR 14m 2M; G mast.

HEYSHAM

SW Quay Ldg Lts 102·2°. Front ⚓, both F Bu 11/14m 2M; Or & B ◆ on masts; 54°01'·91N 02°55'·22W.

RIVER LUNE, GLASSON DOCK and FLEETWOOD

R Lune ⚓ Q (9) 15s; 53°58'·63N 03°00'·03W.
Fairway No. 1(Fleetwood) ⚓ 53°57'·67N 03°02'·03W Q; *Bell*.
Fleetwood Esplanade Ldg Lts 156°. Front, Iso G 2s 14m 9M; 53°55'·71N 03°00'·56W. Rear, 320m from front, Iso G 4s 28m 9M. Both vis on Ldg line only. (H24) (chan liable to change).

RIVER RIBBLE

Gut ⚓ L Fl 10s; 53°41'·74N 03°08'·98W.
Perches show Fl R on N side, and Fl G on S side of chan.
S side, 14¼M Perch ⚓ Fl G 5s 6m 3M; 53°42'·75N 03°04'·90W.
Jordan's Spit ⚓ Q (9) 15s; 53°35'·76N 03°19'·28W.
FT ⚓ Q; 53°34'·56N 03°13'·20W.

RIVER MERSEY and LIVERPOOL

Bar ⚓ Fl.5s 12M; *Racon (T) 10M*; 53°32'·01N 03°20'·98W.
Q1 ⚓ VQ; 53°31'·00N 03°16'·72W.
Q2 ⚓ VQ R; 53°31'·47N 03°14'·95W.

Q3 ⚓ Fl G 3s; 53°30'·95N 03°15'·10W.
Formby ⚓ Iso 4s; 53°31'·13N 03°13'·48W.
C4 ⚓ Fl R 3s; 53°31'·82N 03°08'·51W.
Crosby ⚓ Oc 5s; 53°30'·72N 03°06'·29W.
C14 ⚓ Fl R 3s; R hull; 53°29'·91N 03°05'·34W.
Brazil ⚓ QG; 53°26'·85N 03°02'·23W.

RIVER DEE, MOSTYN and CONNAH'S QUAY

HE1 ⚓ Q (9) 15s; 53°26'·33N 03°18'·08W.
HE2 ⚓ Fl G 2·5s; 53°24'·90N 03°12'·88W.
West Hoyle Spit (Earwig) Dir Lt 090. ⚓ 53°21'·21N 03°24'·07W; Iso WRG 2s W10M, R7M, G7M (day W3M, R2M, G2M).
vis: 087·5°-G-089·5°-W-090·5°-R-092·5°; occasional.
Mostyn Dir Lt ⚓ 177·5°. 53°19'·23N 03°16'·38W Iso WRG 2s 11m W 10M R,G 7M, by day W 3M R,G 2M; vis: 175°-G-177°-W-178°-R-180°; H24.

WALES – NORTH COAST AND INNER PASSAGE

South Hoyle Outer ⚓ Fl R 2·5s; 53°21'·47N 03°24'·70W.
Prestatyn ⚓ QG; 53°21'·51N 03°28'·51W.
Inner Passage ⚓ Fl R 5s; 53°21'·91N 03°31'·95W.
Mid Patch Spit ⚓ QR; 53°22'·25N 03°32'·67W.
North Hoyle Wind Farm (30 turbines, see 9.10.5) centred on 53°25'·00N 03°27'·00W. NW, NE, SW, SE extremities (F.R Lts) Fl Y 2.5s 5M Horn Mo (U) 30s.
Mast ⚓ Mo (U) 15s 12m 10M & 2FR (vert); Horn Mo (U) 30s; Mast (80); 53°28'·84N 03°30'·50W.
W Constable ⚓ Q (9) 15s; *Racon (M) 10M*; 53°23'·14N 03°49'·26W.
N Constable ⚓ VQ; 53°23'·76N 03°41'·42W.

RHYL, LLANDUDNO and CONWY

River Clwyd Outfall ⚓ 53°19'·59N 03°30'·63W.
Llandudno Pier Hd ⚓ 2 FG (vert) 8m 4M; 53°19'·90N 03°49'·51W.
Great Ormes Hd Lt Ho, (unlit); 53°20'·56N 03°52'·17W.
Conwy Fairway ⚓ L Fl 10s; 53°17'·95N 03°55'·58W.
C1 ⚓ Fl G 10s; 53°17'·83N 03°54'·58W.
C2 ⚓ Fl (2) R 10s; 53°17'·94N 03°54'·52W.
River Conwy ent. ⚓ L Fl G 15s 5m 2M; 53°18'·03N 03°50'·86W.

ANGLESEY

Point Lynas ☆ 53°24'·98N 04°17'·35W Oc 10s 39m **18M**; W castellated twr; vis: 109°-315°; H24.

AMLWCH to HOLYHEAD BAY

Main Bkwtr ⚓ Fl G 15s 11m 3M; W mast; vis: 141°-271°; 53°25'·02N 04°19'·91W.

		1	2	3	4	5	6	7	8	9	10	11	12	13	14	15	16	17
1.	Portpatrick	**1**																
2.	Mull of Galloway	16	**2**															
3.	Kirkcudbright	48	32	**3**														
4.	Maryport	65	49	26	**4**													
5.	Workington	63	47	25	6	**5**												
6.	Ravenglass	70	54	40	30	23	**6**											
7.	Point of Ayre	38	22	28	37	31	34	**7**										
8.	Peel	41	26	46	55	49	52	18	**8**									
9.	Douglas	60	42	46	50	44	39	19	30	**9**								
10.	Glasson Dock	101	85	74	66	60	37	64	85	63	**10**							
11.	Fleetwood	95	79	68	59	53	30	58	80	57	10	**11**						
12.	Liverpool	118	102	97	89	83	60	80	86	70	52	46	**12**					
13.	Conwy	111	95	95	92	86	58	72	72	59	62	56	46	**13**				
14.	Beaumaris	109	93	94	95	89	72	71	73	58	66	60	49	12	**14**			
15.	Caernarfon	117	103	104	105	99	82	81	73	68	76	70	59	22	10	**15**		
16.	Holyhead	93	81	94	96	90	69	68	62	50	79	73	68	36	32	26	**16**	
17.	Fishguard	171	158	175	175	169	160	153	140	134	153	147	136	100	88	78	89	**17**

DISTANCE TABLES

Approx distances in nautical miles are by the most direct route allowing for dangers and TSS.

Furlong ⚓ Fl G 2·5s; 53°25'·41N 04°30'·47W.
Archdeacon Rock ⚑ Q; 53°26'·71N 04°30'·87W.
Victoria Bank ⚑ VQ; 53°25'·61N 04°31'·37W.
Coal Rk ⚑ Q (6) + L Fl 15s; 53°25'·91N 04°32'·79W.
Ethel Rk ⚑ VQ; 53°26'·64N 04°33'·67W.
The Skerries ☆ 53°25'·27N 04°36'·55W Fl (2) 15s 36m **20M**; W ○ twr, R band; *Racon (T) 25M*. Iso R 4s 26m 10M; same twr; vis: 233°-252°; *Horn (2) 60s*. H24 in periods of reduced visibility.
Langdon ⚑ Q (9) 15s; 53°22'·74N 04°38'·74W.
Bolivar ⚓ FL G 2·5s; 53°21'·51N 04°35'·33W.
Wk ⚓ Fl (2) R 10s; 53°20'·43N 04°36'·60W.

HOLYHEAD to SOUTH STACK
Bkwtr Head ⚔ Fl (3) G 10s 21m 14M; W ☐ twr, B band; Fl Y vis: 174°-226°; *Siren 20s*; 53°19'·86N 04°37'·16W.
Spit ⚓ Fl G 3s; 53°19'·79N 04°37'·15W.
South Stack ☆ 53°18'·41N 04°41'·98W Fl 10s 60m **24M**; (H24); W ○ twr; obsc to N by N Stack and part obsc in Penrhos bay; *Horn 30s*. Fog Det lt vis: 145°-325°.

MENAI STRAIT TO BARDSEY ISLAND
Ten Feet Bank ⚓ QR; 53°19'·47N 04°02'·82W.
Dinmor ⚓ QG; 53°19'·34N 04°03'·32W.
Trwyn-Du ⚔ Fl 5s 19m 12M; W ○ castellated twr, B bands; vis: 101°-023°; *Bell (1) 30s*, sounded continuously;

53°18'·77N 04°02'·44W. FR on radio mast 2M SW.

APPROACHES to BEAUMARIS and BANGOR (Direction of buoyage ↗ NE to SW)
Perch Rock ⚑ Fl R 5s; 53°18'·73N 04°02'·09W.

PORT DINORWIC and CAERNARFON
Port Dinorwic Pier Hd ⚔ 53°11'·18N 04°12'·64W F WR 5m 2M; vis: 225°-R- 357°-W-225°.
(Direction of buoyage ↗ SW to NE)
Caernarfon N Pier Hd ⚔ 2 FG (vert) 5m 2M; 53°08'·72N 04°16'·56W.
Abermenai Point ⚔ Fl WR 3·5s 6m 3M; W mast; vis: 065°-R-245°-W-065°; 53°07'·62N 04°19'·72W.
C1 ⚓ Fl G 5s; 53°06'·85N 04°24'·35W.
C2 ⚓ Fl R 10s; 53°06'·95N 04°24'·46W.
Caernarfon Bar ⚑ L Fl 10s; 53°06'·45N 04°25'·00W.
Llanddwyn I ⚔Fl WR 2·5s 12m W7M, R4M; W twr; vis: 280°-R- 015°-W-120°; 53°08'·05N 04°24'·79W.

PORTH DINLLÄEN
CG Stn ⚔ FR when firing 10M N; 52°56'·82N 04°33'·89W.
Careg y Chwislen ⚑ 52°56'·99N 04°33'·51W.
Bardsey I ☆ 52°44'·97N 04°48'·02W Fl (5) 15s 39m **26M**; W ☐ twr, R bands; obsc by Bardsey Is 198°-250° and in Tremadoc B when brg < 260°.

AREA 9 *S Wales & SW England – Cardigan Bay to St Ives*
SELECTED LIGHTS, BUOYS & WAYPOINTS

| Positions are referenced to WGS84 |

CARDIGAN BAY (SEE ALSO AREA 8)
Bardsey I ☆ 52°45'·00N 04°47'·98W Fl (5) 15s 39m **26M**; W ☐ twr, R bands; obsc by Bardsey I 198°-250° and in Tremadoc B when brg less than 260°.
St Tudwal's ⚔ Fl WR 15s 46m W14, R10M; vis: 349°-W-169°-R- 221°-W-243°-R-259°-W-293°-R-349°; obsc by East I 211°-231°; 52°47'·92N 04°28'·30W.

PWLLHELI and PORTHMADOG
Pwllheli App ⚑ Iso 2s; 52°53'·02N 04°23'·07W.
Porthmadog Fairway ⚓ L Fl 10s; 52°53'·01N 04°11'·10W.

BARMOUTH and ABERDOVEY
Diffuser ⚑ Fl Y 5s; 52°43'·19N 04°05'·38W.
Barmouth Outer ⚑ L Fl 10s; 52°42'·62N 04°04'·83W.
Aberdovey Outer ⚓ Iso 4s; 52°32'·00N 04°05'·56W.
Cynfelyn Patches, Patches ⚑ Q (9) 15s; 52°25'·83N 04°16'·41W.

ABERYSTWYTH, ABERAERON and NEW QUAY
Aberystwyth S Bkwtr Hd ⚔ Fl (2) WG 10s 12m 10M; vis: 030°-G- 053°-W-210°; 52°24'·40N 04°05'·52W.
Ldg Lts 133°. Front, FR 4m 5M; 52°24'·37N 04°05'·39W.
Rear, 52m from front, FR 7m 6M.
Aberaeron N Pier ⚔ Fl (4) WRG 15s 10m 6M; vis: 050°-G-104°-W-178°-R-232°; 52°14'·61N 04°15'·87W.
Carreg Ina ⚑ Q; 52°13'·25N 04°20'·75W.
New Quay Pier Hd ⚔ Fl WG 3s 12m W8M, G5M; G △; vis: 135°-W- 252°-G-295°; 52°12'·95N 04°21'·35W.

CARDIGAN and FISHGUARD
Cardigan Channel ⚑ Fl (2) 5s; 52°06'·44N 04°41'·43W.

Cardigan Cliff Base Bn 1 ⚔ Fl R 4s 3M; 52°07'·05N 04°41'·39W.
Cardigan Cliff Base Bn 2 ⚔ Fl R 2s 3M; 52°06'·91N 04°41'·34W.
Fishguard N Bkwtr Hd ⚔ Fl G 4·5s 18m 13M; *Bell (1) 8s*; 52°00'·76N 04°58'·23W.
Strumble Head ☆ 52°01'·79N 05°04'·43W Fl (4) 15s 45m **26M**; vis: 038°-257°; (H24).

BISHOPS and SMALLS
South Bishop ☆ 51°51'·14N 05°24'·74W Fl 5s 44m **16M**; W ○ twr; *Horn (3) 45s; Racon (O)10M*; (H24).
The Smalls ☆ 51°43'·27N 05°40'·19W Fl (3) 15s 36m **18M**; *Racon (T)*; *Horn (2) 60s*. Same twr, Iso R 4s 33m 13M; vis: 253°-285° over Hats & Barrels Rk; both Lts shown H24 in periods of reduced visibility.
Skokholm I ⚔, 51°41'·64N 05°17'·22W Fl WR 10s 54m W8M, R8M; vis: 301°-W-154°-R-301°; partially obsc 226°-258°.

WALES – SOUTH COAST – BRISTOL CHANNEL
MILFORD HAVEN
St Ann's Head ☆ 51°40'·87N 05°10'·42W Fl WR 5s 48m **W18M, R17M**, R14M; W 8-sided twr; vis: 233°-W-247°-R-285°-R(intens)- 314°-R-332°-W131°, partially obscured 124°-129°; *Horn (2) 60s*.
W Blockhouse Point ⚑ Ldg Lts 022·5°. Front, F 54m 13M; B stripe on W twr; vis: 004·5°-040·5°; intens on lead. By day 10M; vis: 004·5°-040·5°; *Racon (Q)*; 51°41'·31N 05°09'·56W.
Watwick Point Common Rear ☆, 0·5M from front, F 80m **15M**; vis: 013·5°-031·5°. By day 10M; vis: 013·5°-031·5°; *Racon (Y)*.

W Blockhouse Point ↳ Q WR 21m W9M, R7M; R lantern on W base: vis: 220°-W-250°-R-020°-W-036°-R-049°; 51°41'·31N 05°09'·56W.

Dale Fort ⚡ Fl (2) WR 5s 20m W5M, R3M; vis: 222°-R-276°-W-019°; 51°42'·16N 05°09'·01W.

Gt Castle Hd ↳ F WRG 27m W5M, R3M, G3M; vis: 243°-R-281°-G- 299°-W-029°; also Dir WRG (040°) 038·25°-G-039°-Al WG-039·5°-W- 040·5°-AlWR-041°-R-041·75°; 51°42'·67N 05°07'·07W (**not** used in conjunction with the following front light) Ldg Lts 039·7° **Front**, Oc 4s 27m **15M**; vis: 031·2°-048·2°. **Rear**, 890m from front. 05°06'·60W Oc 8s 53m **15M** (by day 10M) vis: 031·2°-048·2°.

St Ann's ↺ Fl R 2·5s; 51°40'·25N 05°10'·51W.

Mid Channel Rks ↯ Q (9) 15s; 51°40'·18N 05°10'·14W.

Sheep ▲ QG; 51°40'·06N 05°08'·31W.

Millbay ↺ Fl (2) R 5s; 51°41'·05N 05°09'·45W.

W Chapel ▲ Fl G 10s; 51°40'·98N 05°08'·67W.

E Chapel ↺ Fl R 5s; 51°40'·87N 05°08'·15W.

Rat ▲ Fl G 5s; 51°40'·80N 05°07'·86W.

Angle ↯ VQ; 51°41'·63N 05°08'·27W.

Thorn Rock ↯ Q (9) 15s; 51°41'·53N 05°07'·76W.

Turbot Bank ↯ VQ (9) 10s; 51°37'·41N 05°10'·08W.

ODAS Fl(5) Y 20s; 51°36'·70N 05°08'·70W

St Gowan ↯ Q (6) + L Fl 15s, *Racon (T) 10M*; 51°31'·93N 04°59'·77W.

TENBY to SWANSEA BAY

Caldey I ⚡ Fl (3) WR 20s 65m W13M, R9M; vis: R173°-W212°- R088°-102°; 51°37'·90N 04°41'·08W.

Woolhouse ↯ Q (6) + L Fl 15s; 51°39'·35N 04°39'·69W.

Burry Port Inlet ⚡ 51°40'·62N 04°15'·06W Fl 5s 7m **15M**.

W. Helwick (W HWK) ↯ (9) 15s; *Racon (T) 10M*; 51°31'·40N 04°23'·65W Q.

E. Helwick ↯ VQ (3) 5s; *Bell*; 51°31'·80N 04°12'·68W.

SWANSEA BAY and SWANSEA

Ledge ↯ VQ (6) + L Fl 10s; 51°29'·93N 03°58'·77W.

Mixon ↺ Fl (2) R 5s; *Bell*; 51°33'·12N 03°58'·78W.

Outer Spoil Gnd ↺ Fl Y 2·5s; 51°32'·11N 03°55'·73W.

Grounds ↯ VQ (3) 5s; 51°32'·81N 03°53'·47W.

Mumbles ☆ 51°34'·01N 03°58'·27W Fl (4) 20s 35m **15M**; W twr; *Horn (3) 60s.*

SW Inner Green Grounds ↯ Q (6) + L Fl 15s; *Bell*; 51°34'·06N 03°57'·03W.

Swansea Lts in line 020°. Front: E Breakwater head, Oc G 4s 5m 2M & 2FG(vert) 10m 6M; 51°36'·38N 03°55'·62W. Rear, 3·1ca from front: FG 6M.

SWANSEA BAY, RIVER NEATH and PORT TALBOT

Neath App Chan ▲ Fl G 5s; 51°35'·71N 03°52'·83W.

Cabenda ↯ VQ (6) + L Fl 10s; *Racon (Q)*; 51°33'·36N 03°52'·23W.

Ldg Lts 059·8° (occas). Front, Oc R 3s 12m 6M; 51°34'·92N 03°48'·10W. Rear, 400m from front, Oc R 6s 32m 6M.

BRISTOL CHANNEL – NORTH SHORE (E PART)

W Scar ↯ Q (9) 15s, *Bell*, *Racon (T) 10M*; 51°28'·31N 03°55'·57W.

South Scar (S SCAR) ↯ Q (6) + L Fl 15s; 51°27'·61N 03°51'·58W.

Hugo ↺ Q R; 51°28'·57N 03°47'·98W.

E. Scarweather ↯ Q (3) 10s; *Bell*; 51°27'·98N 03°46'·76W.

PORTHCAWL

Fairy ↯ Q (9) 15s; *Bell*; 51°27'·86N 03°42'·07W.

Porthcawl Bkwtr Hd ⚡ 51°28'·39N 03°41'·98W F WRG 10m W6M, R4M, G4M; vis: 302°-G-036°-W-082°-R-122°.

W Nash ↯ VQ (9) 10s ; *Bell*; 51°25'·99N 03°45'·95W.

Nash ☆ 51°24'·03N 03°33'·06W Fl (2) WR 15s 56m **W21M, R16M**; vis: 280°-R-290°-W-100°-R-120°-W-128°.

Breaksea ↯ L Fl 10s; *Racon (T) 10M*; 51°19'·88N 03°19'·08W.

BARRY

W Bkwtr Hd ⚡ Fl 2·5s 12m 10M; 51°23'·46N 03°15'·52W.

N. One Fathom ↯ Q; 51°20'·94N 03°12'·17W.

Mackenzie ↺ QR; 51°21'·75N 03°08'·24W.

CARDIFF and PENARTH ROADS

Lavernock Outfall ↺ Fl Y 5s; 51°23'·95N 03°09'·50W.

Ranie ↺ Fl (2) R 5s; 51°24'·23N 03°09'·39W.

S Cardiff ↯ Q (6) + L Fl 15s; *Bell*; 51°24'·18N 03°08'·57W.

Mid Cardiff ▲ Fl (3) G 10s; 51°25'·60N 03°08'·09W.

Cardiff Spit ↺ QR; 51°24'·57N 03°07'·12W.

N Cardiff ▲ QG; 51°26'·52N 03°07'·19W.

Wrach Chan Dir lt 348·5°. Oc WRG 10s 5m; W3M, R3M, G3M; vis: 344·5°-G-347°-W-350°-R-352°; H24; 51°27'·16N 03°09'·75W.

Outer Wrach ↯ Q (9) 15s; 51°26'·20N 03°09'·46W.

FLATHOLM to THE BRIDGE

Flat Holm ☆, SE Pt 51°22'·54N 03°07'·14W Fl (3) WR 10s 50m **W15M**, R12M; W ○ twr; vis: 106°-R-140°-W-151°-R-203°-W-106°; (H24).

Monkstone ⚡ Fl 5s 13m 12M; R column on W ○ twr; 51°24'·89N 03°06'·01W.

Tail Patch ▲ QG; 51°23'·53N 03°03'·65W.

Hope ↯ Q (3) 10s; 51°24'·84N 03°02'·68W.

NW Elbow ↯ VQ (9) 10s; *Bell*; 51°26'·28N 02°59'·93W.

EW Grounds ↯ L Fl 10s 7M; *Whis*; *Racon (T) 7M*; 51°27'·12N 02°59'·95W.

NEWPORT DEEP, RIVER USK and NEWPORT

Newport Deep ▲ Fl (3) G 10s; *Bell*;51°29'·36N 02°59'·12W.

East Usk ☆ 51°32'·40N 02°58'·01W; Fl (2) WRG 10s 11m W11M,R10M, G10M; vis: 284°-W-290° -obscured shore-324°-R- 017°-W-037°-G-115°-W-120°. Also Oc WRG 10s 10m W11M, R9M, G9M; vis: 013°-G-017°-W- 019°-R-023°. Julians Pill Ldg Lts 062°. Front, FG 5m 4M; 51°33'·30N 02°57'·94W. Rear, 61m from front, FG 8m 4M.

BRISTOL CHANNEL – SOUTH SHORE (E PART)
BRISTOL DEEP

N Elbow ▲ QG; *Bell*; 51°26'·97N 02°58'·65W.

S Mid Grounds ↯ VQ (6) + L Fl 10s; 51°27'·62N 02°58'·68W.

E Mid Grounds ↺ Fl R 5s; 51°27'·75N 02°54'·98W.

Clevedon ↯ VQ; 51°27'·39N 02°54'·93W.

Welsh Hook ↯ Q (6) + L Fl 15s; 51°28'·53N 02°51'·86W.

Avon ▲ Fl G 2·5s; 51°27'·92N 02°51'·73W.

Black Nore Pt Lt Ho; W ○ twr on frame; 51°29'·09N 02°48'·05W.

Newcome ↺ 51°30'·01N 02°46'·71W Fl (3) R 10s.

Denny Shoal ↯ VQ (6) + L Fl 10s; 51°30'·15N 02°45'·45W.

Cockburn ↺ 51°30'·45N 02°44'·10W Fl R 2·5s.

W Dock Middle ▲ 51°29.95'·01N 02°44'·20W Q G.

W Dock Outer ▲ 51°30'·00N 02°44'·85W Fl G 5s.

Firefly ↺ Fl (2) G 5s; 51°29'·96N 02°45'·35W.

Portishead Point ☆ 51°29'·68N 02°46'·42W Q (3) 10s 9m **16M**; B twr, W base: vis: 060°-262°; *Horn 20s*.

PORTISHEAD

Pier Hd ⚡ Iso G 2s 5m 3M; 51°29'·69N 02°45'·27W.

Seabank. Lts in line 086·8°. Front, IQ 13m 5M; vis: 070·3°-103·3°;

by day 1M vis: 076·8°-096·8°; 51°30'·07N 02°43'·80W. Dir WG 6m 5M; vis: 085·8°-FG-086·7°-AltWG-086·9°-FW-089·7°. Rear, 500m from front, IQ 16m 5M; vis: 070·3°-103·3°; by day 1M, vis: 076·8°-096·8°.
Knuckle Lts in line 099·6°, Oc G 5s 6m 6M; 51°29'·94N 02°43'·67W. Rear, 165m from front, FG 13m 6M; vis: 044°-134°.

AVONMOUTH
Royal Edward Dock N Pier Hd ≰ Fl 4s 15m 10M; vis: 060°-228·5°; 51°30'·49N 02°43'·09W.
King Road Ldg Lts 072·4°. N Pier Hd ≰ Front, Oc R 5s 5m 9M; W obelisk, R bands; vis: 062°-082°; 51°30'·49N 02°43'·09W. Rear ≰, 546m from front, QR 15m 10M; vis: 066°-078°.

RIVER AVON, CUMBERLAND BASIN and AVON BRIDGE
S Pier Hd ≰ Oc RG 30s 9m 10M and FBu 4m 1M; vis: 294°-R-036°-G-194°; 51°30'·37N 02°43'·10W. Bell(1) 10s.
Ldg Lts 127·2°. Front ⚓, Iso R 2s 6m 3M, vis: 010°-160°; 51°30'·10N 02°42'·59W. Rear⚓, Iso R 2s10m 3M; vis: 048°-138°.

BRISTOL CHANNEL (SOUTH SHORE)
WESTON-SUPER-MARE
Pier Hd ≰ 2 FG (vert) 6m; 51°20'·88N 02°59'·26W.
E Culver ⚓ Q (3) 10s; 51°18'·00N 03°15'·44W.
W Culver ⚓ VQ (9) 10s; 51°17'·47N 03°19'·00W.
Gore ⚓ Iso 5s; Bell; 51°13'·94N 03°09'·79W.

BURNHAM-ON-SEA and RIVER PARRETT
Ent ≰ Fl 7·5s 7m 12M; vis: 074°-164°; 51°14'·89N 03°00'·36W;
Dir lt 076°. F WRG 4m W12M, R10M, G10M; vis: 071°-G-075°-W-077°- R-081°.
DZ No. 1 ⚓ Fl Y 2·5s; 51°15'·28N 03°09'·49W.
DZ No. 2 ⚓ Fl Y 10s; 51°13'·77N 03°19'·86W.
DZ No. 3 ⚓ Fl Y 5s; 51°16'·34N 03°14'·98W.

WATCHET, MINEHEAD and PORLOCK WEIR
Watchet W Bkwtr Hd ≰ Oc G 3s 9m 9M; 51°11'·03N 03°19'·74W.
Watchet E Pier ≰ 2 FR (vert) 3M; 51°11'·01N 03°19'·72W.
Minehead Bkwtr Hd ≰ Fl (2) G 5s 4M; vis: 127°-262°; 51°12'·81N 03°28'·36W.
Lynmouth Foreland ☆ 51°14'·73N 03°47'·21W Fl (4) 15s 67m 18M; W ○ twr; vis: 083°-275°; (H24).

LYNMOUTH and WATERMOUTH
River Training Arm ≰ 2 FR (vert) 6m 5M; 51°13'·90N 03°49'·83W.
Harbour Arm ≰ 2 FG (vert) 6m 5M; 51°13'·92N 03°49'·84W.

Sand Ridge ⚓ Q G; 51°15'·01N 03°49'·77W.
Copperas Rock ⚓ Fl G 2·5s; 51°13'·78N 04°00'·60W.
Watermouth ≰ Oc WRG 5s 1m 3M; W △; vis: 149·5°-G-151·5°-W- 154·5°-R-156·5°; 51°12'·93N 04°04'·60W.

ILFRACOMBE to BAGGY POINT
Ldg Lts 188°. Front, Oc 10s 8m 3M; 51°12'·53N 04°06'·65W.
Rear, Oc 10s 6m 3M.
Horseshoe ⚓ Q; 51°15'·02N 04°12'·96W.
Bull Point ☆ 51°11'·94N 04°12'·09W Fl (3) 10s 54m 20M; W ○ twr, obscd shore-056°. Same twr; FR 48m 12M; vis: 058°-096°.
Morte Stone ⚓ Fl G 5s; 51°11'·30N 04°14'·95W.
Baggy Leap ⚓ Fl (2) G 10s; 51°08'·92N 04°16'·97W.

BIDEFORD, RIVERS TAW and TORRIDGE
Bideford Fairway ⚓ L Fl 10s; Bell; 51°05'·25N 04°16'·25W.
Bideford Bar ⚓ Q G; 51°04'·89N 04°14'·62W.
Instow ☆ Ldg Lts 118°. Front, 51°03'·62N 04°10'·66W Oc 6s 22m 15M; vis: 103·5°-132°. Rear, 427m from front, Oc 10s 38m 15M; vis: 103°-132·5°; (H24).
Crow Pt ≰ Fl WR 2. 5s 8m W6M R5M; vis: 225°-R-232°-W-237°-R-358°-W- 015°-R-045°; 51°03'·96N 04°11'·39W.

LUNDY
Near North Point ☆ 51°12'·10N 04°40'·65W Fl 15s 48m 17M; vis: 009°-285°.
South East Point ☆ 51°09'·72N 04°39'·37W Fl 5s 53m 15M; vis: 170°-073°.
Hartland Point ≰ 51°01'·3N 04°31'·6W Fl (6) 15s 30m 8M; adjacent to Hartland Point Light House (disused).

NORTH CORNWALL
BUDE, PADSTOW and NEWQUAY
Compass Point twr 50°49'·71N 04°33'·42W.
Stepper Point (Padstow) ≰ L Fl 10s 12m 4M; 50°34'·12N 04°56'·72W.
Trevose Head ☆ 50°32'·94N 05°02'·13W Fl 7·5s 62m 21M.
North Pier Hd (Newquay) ≰ 2 FG (vert) 5m 2M; 50°25'·07N 05°05'·19W.

HAYLE and ST IVES
The Stones ⚓ Q; 50°15'·64N 05°25'·51W.
Godrevy I ≰ Fl WR 10s 28m 8M; metal post; vis: 022°-W-101°-R-145°-W-272°; 50°14'·56N 05°24'·01W; adjacent to Godrevy Light House (disused).
Hayle App ⚓ QR; 50°12'·26N 05°26'·30W.
St Ives App ⚓ 50°12'·85N 05°28'·42W
Pendeen ☆ 50°09'·90N 05°40'·32W Fl (4) 15s 59m 16M; vis: 042°-240°; in bay between Gurnard Hd and Pendeen it shows to coast; Horn 20s.

1	Aberystwyth	1		12	64	66	122	164	192	224	254	286	299	318	361		Kilrush	12
2	Fishguard	40	2		11	13	69	111	139	171	201	233	246	265	308		Dingle	11
3	Milford Haven	84	48	3		10	56	102	131	165	188	227	242	252	295		Valentia	10
4	Tenby	107	71	28	4		9	42	70	102	132	164	177	196	239		Baltimore	9
5	Swansea	130	94	55	36	5		8	35	69	95	135	150	168	202		Kinsale	8
6	Cardiff	161	125	86	66	46	6		7	34	65	100	115	133	172		Youghal	7
7	Sharpness	192	156	117	106	75	33	7		6	32	69	84	102	139		Dunmore East	6
8	Avonmouth	175	139	100	89	58	20	18	8		5	34	47	66	108		Rosslare	5
9	Burnham-on-Sea	169	133	94	70	48	53	50	33	9		4	15	36	75		Arklow	4
10	Ilfracombe	128	92	53	35	25	44	74	57	45	10		3	21	63		Wicklow	3
11	Padstow	142	106	70	70	76	97	127	110	98	55	11		2	48		Dun Laoghaire	2
12	Longships	169	133	105	110	120	139	169	152	140	95	50	12		1		Carlingford Lough	1

AREA 10 *Ireland – Clockwise from Lambay Island*

SELECTED LIGHTS, BUOYS & WAYPOINTS

| Positions are referenced to WGS84 |

LAMBAY ISLAND TO TUSKAR ROCK

MALAHIDE and LAMBAY ISLAND
Taylor Rks 𝖎 Q; 53°30'·21N 06°01'·87W.
Burren Rocks 𝖎 Fl G 5s; 53°29'·35N 06°02'·35W.
Malahide approach ⌖ L Fl 10s; 53°27'·12N 06°06'·87W.

HOWTH
Rowan Rocks 𝖎 Q (3) 10s; 53°23'·88N 06°03'·27W.
Howth ▲ 53°23.727'N 006°03.593'W; 992501250.
E Pier Hd ⚡ Fl (2) WR 7·5s 13m W12M, R9M; W twr; vis: W256°- R295°-256°; 53°23'·64N 06°04'·02W.
Baily ☆ 53°21'·69N 06°03'·16W Fl 15s 41m **18M**; twr. Fog Det Lt VQ; 992501010.
Rosbeg E 𝖎 Q (3) 10s; 53°21'·02N 06°03'·45W.
Rosbeg S 𝖎 Q (6) + L Fl 15s; 53°20'·22N 06°04'·17W.

PORT OF DUBLIN
Dublin Bay 𝖎 Mo (A) 10s; *Racon (M)*; 53°19'·92N 06°04'·64W.
No. 1 ▲ Fl (3) G 5s; 53°20'·30N 06°05'·56W.
No. 3 ▲ IQ G; 53°20'·57N 06°06'·76W.
No. 4 ⌑ IQ R; 53°20'·48N 06°06'·93W.
No. 5 ▲ Fl G 2s; 53°20'·64N 06°08'·60W.
No. 6 ⌑ Fl R 2s; 53°20'·56N 06°08'·75W.
Great S Wall Hd Poolbeg ⚡ Fl R 4s 20m 10M *(sync with N.Bull)*; R ○ twr; 53°20'·52N 06°09'·08W.
N Bull ⚡ Fl G 4s 15m, 10M; G ○ twr; 53°20'·70N 06°08'·98W.
N Bank ☆ 53°20'·69N 06°10'·59W Oc G 8s 10m **16M**; G □ twr.

DUN LAOGHAIRE
E Bkwtr Hd ⚡ Fl (2) R 8s 16m **17M**; granite twr, R lantern 7M; 53°18'·14N 06°07'·62W. Fog Det Lt VQ.
Outfall ⌑ Fl Y 5s; 53°18'·41N 06°08'·35W.
Muglins ⚡ Fl R 5s 14m 11M; 53°16'·52N 06°04'·58W.

OFFSHORE MARKS
Bennett Bank 𝖎 Q(6)+ L Fl 15s; 53°20'·17N 05°55'·11W; 992501012.
Kish Bank ☆ 53°18'·65N 05°55'·42W Fl (2) 20s 29m **21M** (H24); W twr, R band; *Racon (T) 15M*; 992501017.
N Kish 𝖎 VQ; 53°18'·56N 05°56'·44W.
E Kish ⌑ Fl (2) R 10s; 53°14'·35N 05°53'·56W.
N Burford 𝖎 Q 53°20.51'N 006° 01.49'W; 992501016.
S Burford 𝖎 VQ(6)+L Fl 10s; 53°18.06'N 006° 01.30'W; 992501018.
E Codling ⌑ Fl (4) R 10s; 53°08'·54N 05°46'·07W; 992501024.
W Codling ▲ Fl G 10s; 53°06'·97N 05°54'·51W.
S Codling 𝖎 VQ (6) + L Fl 10s; 53°04'·74N 05°49'·76W.
Codling 𝖎 Q(3) 10s; 53°03.020'N 005°40.815'W; *Racon (G) 10M*, 992501028.
Breaches Shoal ⌑ Fl (2) R 6s; 53°05'·67N 05°59'·81W.
North India 𝖎 Q; 53°03'·12N 05°53'·46W.
South India 𝖎 Q (6) + L Fl 15s; 53°00'·36N 05°53'·31W.

WICKLOW to ARKLOW
Wicklow ⌑ Fl (4) Y 10s; 52°59'·54N 06°01'·29W.
E Pier Hd ⚡ Fl WR 5s 11m 6M; W twr, R base and cupola; vis: 136°-R-293°-W-136°; 52°58'·99N 06°02'·07W.
W Packet Quay Hd ⚡ Fl WG 10s 5m 6M; vis: 076°-G-256°-W-076°; 52°58'·88N 06°02'·08W.

Wicklow Hd ☆ 52°57'·95N 05°59'·89W Fl (3) 15s 37m **23M**; W twr.
Horseshoe ⌑ Fl R 3s; 52°56'·84N 05°58'·47W; 992501032.
N Arklow 𝖎 Q; 52°53'·86N 05°55'·21W; 992501034.
Arklow Bank Wind Farm from 52°48'·47N 05°56'·57W to 52°46'·47N 05°57'·11W, N and S Turbines Fl Y 5s14m 10M. No 7 Turbine 992501302. Other turbines Fl Y 5s.

ARKLOW to WEXFORD

S Pier Hd ⚡ Fl WR 6s 11m 13M; twr; vis: R shore- W223°-R350°-shore; 52°47'·61N 06°08'·22W.
Roadstone Bkwtr Hd ⚡ QY; 52°46'·65N 06°08'·23W.
S Arklow 𝖎 Q (6) + LFl 15s; *Racon (O) 10M*; 52°40'·20N 05°58'·89W; 992501040.
No. 2 Glassgorman ⌑ Fl (4) R 10s; 52°45'·35N 06°05'·34W.
No. 1 Glassgorman ⌑ Fl (2) R 6s; 52°37'·69N 06°07'·34W.
N Blackwater 𝖎 Q; 52°32'·22N 06°09'·51W.
No. 6 Rusk ⌑ Fl R 3s; 52°32'·65N 06°10'·41W.
No. 4 Rusk ⌑ Fl (2) R 5s; 52°31'·07N 06°10'·86W.
No. 2 Rusk ⌑ Fl (2) R 5s; 52°28'·64N 06°12'·61W.
No. 1 Rusk ▲ Fl (2) G 5s; 52°28'·54N 06°11'·80W.
W Blackwater ▲ Fl G 6s; 52°25'·87N 06°13'·56W.
SE Blackwater 𝖎 Q (3) 10s, 52°25'·62N 06°08'·42W; *Racon (M) 10M*; 992501050.
S Blackwater 𝖎 Q (6) + L Fl 15s; 52°22'·76N 06°12'·87W.
North Long 𝖎 Q; 52°21'·44N 06°17'·04W.
West Long ▲ QG; 52°18'·18N 06°17'·96W.
Lucifer 𝖎 VQ (3) 5s; 52°17'·02N 06°12'·67W; 992501054.

ROSSLARE

S Long ▲ Fl (2) G 6s (sync with Splaugh); 52°14'·74N 06°15'·80W.
Splaugh ⌑ Fl (2) R 6s (sync with S Long); 52°14'·37N 06°16'·76W; 992501062.
South Holdens ▲ Fl G 3s; 52°15'·14N 06°17'·24W. (sync Calmines).
Calmines ⌑ Fl R 3s; 52°15'·01N 06°17'·77W. (sync S Holdens).
W Holdens ▲ Fl (3) G 10s; 52°15'·77N 06°18'·74W.
Rosslare Pier Hd ⚡ Oc WRG 5s 15m W13M, R10M, G10M; R twr; vis:098°-G-188°-W-208°-R-246°-G-283°-W-286°-R-320°; 52°15'·43N 06°20'·29W.
Ballygeary ⚡ Oc WR 1·7s 7m 4M vis: shore-R-152°-W-200°- W(unintens)-205°; 52°15'·25N 06°20'·48W .

TUSKAR ROCK TO OLD HEAD OF KINSALE

Tuskar ☆ 52°12'·17N 06°12'·44W Q (2) 7·5s 33m **24M**; W twr; *Racon (T) 18M*; 992501065.
S Rock 𝖎 Q (6)+L Fl 15s; 52°10'·80N 06°12'·84W; 992501068.
Fundale ⌑ Fl (2) R 10s; 52°11'·04N 06°19'·78W.
Barrels 𝖎 Q (3) 10s; 52°08'·32N 06°22'·05W; 992501070.

KILMORE

Kilmore Quay SWM 𝖎 Iso 10s; (Apr-Sep); 52°09'·20N 06°35'·30W.
Kilmore Bkwtr Hd ⚡ Q RG 7m 5M; vis: 269°-R-354°-G-003°-R-077°; 52°10'·20N 06°35'·15W.
Ldg lts 007·9°, Front 52°10'·37N 06°35'·08W Oc 4s 3m 6M. Rear, 100m from front, Oc 4s 6m 6M; sync with front.
Bore Rks 𝖎 Q (3) 10s; 52°06.07'N 006°31.87'W; 992501072.
Coningbeg 𝖎 Q(6)+LFl 15s; 52°03'·20N 06°38'·57W; *Racon (T) 7M*; 992501074.
Red Bank W ; 52°04.499'N 006°41.652'W; 992501076.

'M5' ODAS 35 ⌐ 51°41'·40N 06°42'·24W; Fl (5) Y 20s.

WATERFORD
Hook Hd ☆ 52°07'·42N 06°55'·77W Fl 3s 46m **23M**; W twr, two B bands; *Racon (K) 10M*. Fog Det Lt VQ. 992501079.
Waterford ⚓ Fl R 3s. Fl (3) R 10s; 52°08'·95N 06°57'·00W.
Duncannon Dir lt ⚓ F WRG 13m 10M, white tower on fort, 359·5°-FG-001·2°-Alt GW-001·7°-FW-002·4°-Alt WR-002·9°-FR-004·5°; 52°13'·23N 06°56'·25W; Oc WR 4s 13m W 9M R 7M on same tower, 119°-R-149°-W-172°.
Passage Pt ⚓ Fl WR 5s 7m W6M, R5M; R pile structure; vis: W shore- R127°-302°; 52°14'·26N 06°57'·77W.
Cheek Pt ⚓ Q WR 6m 5M; W mast; vis: W007°-R289°-007°; 52°16'·12N 06°59'·38W.
Sheagh ⚓ Fl R 3s 29m 3M; Gy twr; vis: 090°-318°; 52°16'·29N 06°59'·34W.
Snowhill Point Ldg lts 255°. Front, Fl WR 2·5s 5m 3M; vis: W222°- R020°- W057°-107°; 52°16'·39N 07°00'·91W. Rear, Flour Mill, 750m from front, Q 12m 5M.
Queen's Chan Ldg lts 098°. Front, QR 8m 5M; B twr, W band; vis: 030°-210°;52°15'·32N 07°02'·38W. Rear, 550m from front, Q 15m 5M; W mast.
Beacon Quay ⚓ Fl G 3s 9m; vis: 255°-086°; 52°15'·50N 07°04'·21W.
Cove ⚓ Fl WRG 6s 6m 2M; W twr; vis: R111°- G161°- W234°-111°; 52°15'·05N 07°05'·16W.
Smelting Ho Pt ⚓ Q 8m 3M; W mast; 52°15'·15N 07°05'·27W.
Ballycar ⚓ Fl RG 3s 5m; vis: G127°- R212°-284°; 52°15'·06N 07°05'·51W.

DUNMORE EAST
East Pier Head ☆ 52°08'·93N 06°59'·34W Fl WR 8s 13m **W17M**, R13M; Gy twr, vis: W225°- R310°-004°.
W Wharf ⚓ Fl G 2s 6m 4M; vis: 165°-246°; 52°08'·97N 06°59'·45W.

DUNGARVAN
Ballinacourty Pt ⚓ Fl (2) WRG 10s 16m W10M, R8M, G8M; W twr; vis: G245°- W274°- R302°- W325°-117°; 52°04'·69N 07°33'·18W.
Helvick ⚓ Q (3) 10s; 52°03'·61N 07°32'·25W.
Mine Head ⚓ 51°59'·56N 07°35'·23W Fl (4) 30s 87m 12M; W twr, B band; vis: 228°-052°.

YOUGHAL
Bar Rocks ⚓ Q (6) + L Fl 15s; 51°54'·85N 07°50'·05W.
Blackball Ledge ⚓ 51°55'·34N 07°48'·53W Q (3) 10s.
W side of ent ☆ 51°56'·57N 07°50'·53W Fl WR 2·5s 24m **W17M**, R13M; W twr; vis: W183°- R273°- W295°- R307°- W351°-003°.

BALLYCOTTON
Ballycotton ☆ 51°49'·52N 07° 59'·17W Fl WR 10s 59m **W21M, R17M**; B twr, within W walls, B lantern; vis: 238°-W-048°-R-238°; Fog Det Lt VQ. 992501093.
The Smiths ⌐ Fl (3) R 10s; 51°48'·62N 08°00'·71W.
Power ⚓ Q (6) + L Fl 15s; 51°45'·59N 08°06'·67W.

CORK
Cork ⚓ L Fl 10s; 51°42'·92N 08°15'·60W; *Racon (T) 7M*; 992501100.
Daunt Rock ⌐ Fl (2) R 6s; 51°43'·52N 08°17'·65W.
Fort Davis Ldg lts 354·1°. Front, 51°48'·82N 08°15'·80W Dir WRG 17M; FG351·5°-AlWG352·25°-FW353°-AlWR355°-FR355·75°-356·5°. Rear, Dognose Quay, 203m from front, Oc 5s 37m 10M; Or 3, synch with front.

Roche's Pt ☆ 51°47'·60N 08°15'·30W Fl WR 3s 30m **W20M, R16M**; vis: shore-R-292°-W-016°-R-033°, 033°- W (unintens)-159°-R-shore.
Outer Hbr Rk E2 ⌐ Fl R 2·5s; 51°47'·52N 08°15'·67W.
Chicago Knoll E1 ▲ Fl G 5s; 51°47'·66N 08°15'·54W.
W1 ▲ Fl G 10s; 51°47'·69N 08°16'·05W.
W2 ⌐ Fl R 10s; 51°47'·69N 08°16'·34W.
White Bay Ldg lts 034·6°. Front, Oc R 5s 11m 5M; W hut; 51°48'·53N 08°15'·22W. Rear, 113m from front, Oc R 5s 21m 5M; W hut; synch with front.
Spit Bank Pile ⚓ Iso WR 4s 10m W10M, R7M; W house on R piles; vis: R087°- W196°- R221°- 358°; 51°50'·72N 08°16'·45W.

KINSALE and OYSTER HAVEN
Bulman ⚓ Q (6) + L Fl 15s; 51°40'·14N 08°29'·74W.
Charlesfort ⚓ Fl WRG 5s 18m W9M, R6M, G7M; vis: G348°-W358°- R004°-168°; H24; 51°41'·75N 08°29'·84W.

OLD HEAD OF KINSALE TO MIZEN HEAD

Old Head of Kinsale ☆, S point 51°36'·29N 08°32'·02W Fl (2) 10s 72m **20M**; B twr, two W bands; 992501107.

COURTMACSHERRY
Barrel Rock ⌐ 51°37'·01N 08°37'·30W.
Black Tom ▲ Fl G 5s; 51°36'·41N 08°37'·95W.
Wood Pt (Land Pt) ⚓ Fl (2) WR 5s 15m 5M; vis: W315°-R332°-315°; 51°38'·16N 08°41'·00W.
Galley Head ☆ summit 51°31'·80N 08°57'·21W Fl (5) 20s 53m **23M**; W twr; vis: 256°-065°.

GLANDORE and CASTLETOWNSHEND
Reen Point ⚓ Fl WRG 10s 9m W5M, R3M, G3M; W twr; vis: shore-G-338°-W-001°-R-shore; 51°30'·98N 09°10'·50W.
Kowloon Bridge ⚓ Q (6) + L Fl 15s; 51°27'·58N 09°13'·75W.

BALTIMORE and FASTNET
Barrack Pt ⚓ Fl (2) WR 6s 40m W6M, R3M; vis: R168°-W294°-038°; 51°28'·33N 09°23'·65W.
Loo Rock ▲ Fl G 3s; 51°28'·43N 09°23'·45W.
Fastnet ☆, W end 51°23'·35N 09°36'·19W Fl 5s 49m **27M**; Gy twr, *Racon (G) 18M*. Fog Det Lt VQ; 992501123.

SCHULL and LONG ISLAND CHANNEL
Amelia ▲; 51°29.979'N 009°31.461'W; 992501120.
Copper Point ⚓ Fl (3) 10s 16m 8M.
Ldg lts 346° Front, Oc 5s 5m 11M, W mast; 51°31'·68N 09°32'·43W. Rear, 91m from front, Oc 5s 8m11M; W mast.

CROOKHAVEN
Rock Is Pt ⚓ L Fl WR 8s 20m W13M, R11M; W twr; vis: W over Long Is B to 281°-R-340°; inside harbour 281°-R-348°-towards N shore; 51°28'·59N 09°42'·27W; 992501124.

MIZEN HEAD TO DINGLE BAY

Mizen Head ⚓ 51°26'·96N 09°49'·19W Iso 4s 55m 12M; vis: 313°-133°.
Sheep's Hd ☆ 51°32'·59N 09°50'·92W Fl (3) WR 15s 83m **W18M R15M**; W bldg; vis: 011·3°-R-016·6°-W-212·5°-(unint)W-222·2°; 992501129.

BANTRY BAY, CASTLETOWN BEARHAVEN, WHIDDY ISLE, BANTRY and GLENGARIFF
Roancarrigmore ⚓ 51°39'·18N 09°44'·82W Fl WR 5s 13m W11M, R9M, R(unintens)5M ; s/steel twr; vis: 312°-W-

43

050°-R-122°-R (unintens)- 207°-obsc-246°-R-312°. Old Lt ho W twr, B band; 992501130.

Ardnakinna Pt ☆ 51°37'·10N 09°55'·09W Fl (2) WR 10s 62m **W17M**, R14M; W ○ twr; vis: 319°-R- 348°-W- 066°-R-shore; 992501131.

Castletown (Dinish Is) Dir lt 023·25° ⚓ Oc WRG 5s 7m W15M, R12M, G12M; W hut, R stripe; vis: 019·5°-G-023°-W-023·5°-R-027°; 51°38'·78N 09°54'·32W; 992501125.

Castletown Ldg lts 008°. Front, Oc Bu 6s 4m 6M; W col, R stripe; vis: 005°-013°; 51°39'·16N 09°54'·40W. Rear, 80m from front, Oc Bu 6s 7m 6M; W with R stripe; vis: 005°-013°.

Bull Rock ☆ 51°35'·52N 10°18'·07W Fl 15s 91m **18M**; W twr 992501131.

KENMARE RIVER, DARRYNANE and BALLYCROVANE

Darrynane Ldg lts 034°. Front, Oc 3s 10m 4M; 51°45'·90N 10°09'·20W. Rear, Oc 3s 16m 4M.

Skelligs Rock ⚓ 51°46'·11N 10°32'·52W Fl (3) 15s 53m 12M; W twr; vis: 262°-115°; part obsc within 6M 110°-115°; 992501137.

VALENTIA and PORTMAGEE

Fort (Cromwell) Point ☆ 51°56'·02N 10°19'·28W Fl WR 2s 16m **W17M, R15M**; W twr; vis: 304°-R-351°,102°-W-304°; obsc from seaward by Doulus Head when brg more than 180°.

Dir lt 141° ⚓ Oc WRG 4s 25m W11M, R8M, G8M (by day: W3M, R2M, G2M); W twr, R stripe; vis:136°-G-140°-W-142°-R-146°; 51°55'·51N 10°18'·42W.

DINGLE BAY TO LOOP HEAD

DINGLE BAY, VENTRY and DINGLE

Ldg lts 182° Oc 3s. Front 52°07'·41N 10°16'·59W, rear 100m behind.

Inishtearaght ☆, W end Blasket Islands 52°04'·54N 10°39'·67W Fl (2) 20s 84m **19M**; W twr; vis: 318°-221°; *Racon (O);* 992501143.

BRANDON BAY, TRALEE BAY and FENIT HARBOUR

Little Samphire Is ☆ 52°16'·26N 09°52'·91W Fl WRG 5s 17m **W16M**, R13M; G13M; Bu ○ twr; vis: 262°-R-275°, 280-R-090°-G-140°-W-152°-R-172°.

Great Samphire I ⚓ QR 15m 3M; vis: 242°-097°; 52°16'·15N 09°51'·81W.

Fenit Hbr Pier Hd ⚓ 2 FR (vert) 12m 3M; vis: 148°-058°; 52°16'·24N 09°51'·55W.

SHANNON ESTUARY

Ballybunnion ⚓ VQ; *Racon (M) 6M*; 52°32'·52N 09°46'·93W; 992501146.

Kilstiffin ⚓ Fl R 3s; 52°33'·80N 09°43'·83W; 992501148.

Kilcredaun ⚓ Q R (sync); 52°34'·42N 09°41'·16W.

Tail of Beal ⚓ Q G (sync); 52°34'·37N 09°40'·71W; 992501150.

Kilcredaun Head ⚓, W twr; 52°34'·78N 09°42'·58W.

Carrigaholt ⚓ Fl (2) R 6s (sync); 52°34'·90N 09°40'·47W.

Beal Spit ⚓ Fl (2) G 6s (sync); 52°34'·80N 09°39'·94W.

Beal Bar ⚓ Fl G 3s (sync); 52°35'·18N 09°39'·05W.

Doonaha ⚓ Fl R 3s (sync); 52°35'·54N 09°39'·01W.

Letter Point ⚓ Fl R 7s; 52°35'·44N 09°35'·89W.

Asdee ⚓ Fl R 5s; 52°35'·09N 09°34'·55W.

Rineanna ⚓ QR; 52°35'·59N 09°31'·24W.

North Carraig ⚓ Q; 52°35'·60N 09°29'·76W.

Scattery Is, Rineanna Pt ⚓ Fl (2) 8s 15m 10M; W twr; vis: 208°-092°; 52°36'·35N 09°31'·07W.

KILRUSH

Marina Ent Chan Ldg lts 355°. Front, Oc 3s; 52°37'·99N 09°30'·27W. Rear, 75m from front, Oc 3s.

Tarbert Is N Point ⚓ Q WR 4s 18m W14M, R10M; W ○ twr; vis: W069°- R277°- W287°-339°; 52°35'·52N 09°21'·83W.

Tarbert (Ballyhoolahan Pt) Ldg lts 128·2° ⚓. Front,Iso 3s 13m 3M; △ on W twr; vis: 123·2°-133·2°; 52°34'·35N 09°18'·80W. Rear, 400m from front, Iso 5s 18m 3M; G stripe on W Bn.

Garraunbaun Pt ⚓ Fl (3) WR 10s 16m W8M, R5M; W □ col, vis: R shore - W072°- R242°- shore; 52°35'·62N 09°13'·94W.

Rinealon Pt ⚓ Fl 2·5s 4m 7M; B col, W bands; vis: 234°-088°; 52°37'·12N 09°09'·82W.

FOYNES

W Chan Ldg lts 107·9° (may be moved for changes in chan). Front, Oc 4s 34m 12M; 52°36'·91N 09°06'·59W . Rear, Oc 4s 39m 12M.

RIVER SHANNON

Beeves Rock ⚓ Fl WR 5s 12m W12M, R9M; vis: 064·5°-W-091°-R- 238°-W-265°-W(unintens)-064·5°; 52°39'·01N 09°01'·35W .

North Channel Ldg lts 093°. Front, Tradree Rock Fl R 2s 6m 5M; W Trs; vis: 246°-110°; 52°41'·00N 08°49'·87W. Rear 0·65M from front, Iso 6s 14m 5M; W twr, R bands; vis: 327°-190°.

N side, Ldg lts 061°. Front, 52°40'·72N 08°45'·27W, Crawford Rock 490m from rear, Fl R 3s 6m 5M. Crawford No. 2, Common Rear, Iso 6s 10m 5M; 52°40'·85N 08°44'·88W.

Ldg lts 302·1°, Flagstaff Rock, 670m from rear, Fl R 7s 7m 5M; 52°40'·66N 08°44'·40W.

Ldg lts 106·5°. Meelick Rk, Front Iso R 4s 6m 5M; 52°40'·24N 08°42'·32W. Meelick No. 2, rear 275m from front Iso R 4s 9m 5M; both W beacons.

LOOP HEAD

Loop Head ☆ 52°33'·67N 09°55'·94W Fl (4) 20s 84m **23M**; vis: 280°-218°; 992501161.

Mal Bay s Fl(5) Y 20s 52°46.00'N 009°34.74'W; *AIS.*

LISCANNOR BAY TO SLYNE HEAD

GALWAY BAY and INISHMORE

Eeragh, Rock Is ☆ 53°08'·91N 09°51'·40W Fl 15s 35m **18M**; W twr, two B bands; vis: 297°-262°.

Straw Is ☆ 53°07'·06N 09°37'·84W Fl (2) 5s 11m **15M**; W twr.

Killeany Ldg lts 192°. Front, Oc 5s 6m 3M; W col on W □ base; vis: 142°-197°, 53°06'·25N 09°39'·74W. Rear, 43m from front, Oc 5s 8m 2M; W col on W □ base; vis: 142°-197°.

Inishmaan, Ldg lts 199°, Oc 6s 8M; 53°06'·08N 09°34'·77W.

Killeaney ⚓ Fl G 3s; 53°07.33'N 009°38.37'W; 992501166.

Inisheer ☆ 53°02'·78N 09°31'·58W Iso WR 12s 34m **W20M, R16M**; vis: 225°-W(partially vis >7M)-231°, 231°-W-245°-R-269°-W-115°; *Racon (K) 13M;* 992501165.

Finnis ⚓ Q (3) 10s; 53°02'·82N 09°29'·14W, 992501164.

Black Hd ⚓ Fl WR 5s 20m W11M, R8M, W □ twr; vis: 045°- R268°-276°; 53°09'·25N 09°15'·83W.

GALWAY

Margaretta Shoal ⚓ Fl G 3s; *Whis;* 53°13'·68N 09°05'·99W. 992501170.

Leverets ⚓ Q WRG 9m 10M; B ☐ twr, W bands; vis: 015°-G-058°-W-065°-R-103°-G-143·5°-W-146·5°-R-015°; 53°15'·33N 09°01'·90W.

Rinmore ⚓ Iso WRG 4s 7m 5M; W ☐twr; vis: 359°-G-008°-W-018°-R-027°; 53°16'·12N 09°01'·97W.

Appr Chan Dir lt 325°, WRG 7m 3M; vis: 322·25°-FG-323·75°-AlFG-324·75°-FW-325·25°-AlRW-326·25°-FR-331·25°-FlR-332·25°; 53°16'·12N 09°02'·83W.

GALWAY to SLYNE HEAD

Barna Quay Hd ⚓ Fl 2 WRG 5s 6m W8M, R5M, G5M; vis:250°-G-344·5°-W-355·5°-R-090°; 53°14'·93N 09°08'·90W.

Spiddle Pier Hd ⚓ Fl WRG 3·5s 11m W8M, R8M, G8M; Y col; vis: 265°-G-308°-W-024°-R-066°; 53°14'·42N 09°18'·54W.

Cashla Bay Ent, W side ⚓ Fl (3) WR 10s 8m W6M, R3M; W col on concrete twr; vis: 216°-W-000°-R-069°; 53°14'·23N 09°35'·20W.

Lion Pt Dir lt 010°, Iso WRG 5s 6m (H24) G6M, W8M, R6M,(night), G2M, W3M, R2M(day); vis: 005°-G- 008·5°-W-011·5°-R-015°; 53°15'·83N 09°33'·98W.

Rossaveel Pier Ldg lts 116°. Front, 53°16'·02N 09°33'·38W Oc 3s 7m 3M; W mast. Rear, 90m from front, Oc 3s 8m 3M.

Kiggaul Bay ⚓ Fl WRG 3s 5m W5M, R3M, G3M; vis: 310°-G-329°-W-349°-R-059°; 53°14'·03N 09°43'·02W.

Croaghnakeela Is ⚓ Fl 3·7s 7m 5M; W col; vis: 034°-045°, 218°-286°, 311°-325°; 53°19'·40N 09°58'·21W.

Inishnee ⚓ Fl (2) WRG 10s 9m W5M, R3M, G3M; W col on W ☐ base; vis: 314°-G-017°-W-030°-R-080°-W-194°; 53°22'·75N 09°54'·53W.

Slyne Head, North twr, Illaunamid ☆ 53°23'·99N 10°14'·05W Fl (2) 15s 35m 19M; B twr; 992501175.

SLYNE HEAD TO EAGLE ISLAND

CLIFDEN BAY and INISHBOFIN

Carrickrana Rocks Bn, large W Bn; 53°29'·24N 10°09'·48W.

Cleggan Point ⚓ Fl (3) WRG 15s 20m W6M, R3M, G3M; W col on W hut; vis: shore-G-091°-W-124°-R-221°; 53°34'·48N 10°07'·69W.

Inishlyon Lyon Head ⚓ Fl WR 7·5s 13m W7M, R4M; W post; vis: 036°-W-058°-R-184°-W-325°-R-036°; 53°36'·74N 10°09'·56W.

Gun Rock ⚓ Fl (2) 6s 8m 4M; W col; vis: 296°-253°; 53°36'·59N 10°13'·23W.

Inishbofin Dir lt 021°, Oc WRG 6s 10m 11M; W pole; vis: 015·75°-G-020·75°-W-021·25°-R-026·25°; 53°36'·78N 10°13'·16W.

CLEW BAY and WESTPORT

Roonagh Quay Ldg lts 144°. Front 53°45'·75N 09°54'·23W. Rear, 54m from front, both Iso Bu 10s 9/15m.

Inishgort ⚓ L Fl 10s 10M; 53°49.594'N 009°40.259'W; 992501179.

Cloughcormick ⚓ Q (9) 15s; 53°50'·56N 09°43'·20W.

Achillbeg I, S Point ☆ 53°51'·51N 09°56'·84W Fl WR 5s 56m W16M, R18M, R11M; W ○ twr on ☐ building; vis: 262°-R-281°-W-342°-R-060°-W-092°-R(intens)-099°-W-118°; 992501181.

ACHILL SOUND

Ldg lts 330°, 53°52'·50N 09°56'·91W Whitestone Point. Front and rear both Oc 4s 5/6m; W ◇, B stripe.

Achill I Ldg lts 310°, Purteen, Oc 8s 5m; 53°57'·83N 10°05'·93W (PA). Rear, 46m from front Oc 8s 6m.

BLACKSOD BAY

Blacksod ⚓ Q (3) 10s; 54°05'·89N 10°03'·01W.

Blacksod Pier Root ⚓ Fl (2) WR 7·5s 13m W12M, R9M; W twr on bldg; vis: 189°-R-210°-W-018°; 54°05'·92N 10°03'·63W; 992501186.

Carrigeenmore ⚓ VQ(3) 5s 3M; 54°06'·56N 10°03'·4W.

Black Rock ☆ 54°04'·06N 10°19'·23W Fl WR 12s 86m **W20M, R16M**; W twr; vis: 276°-W-212°-R-276°; 992501183.

Eagle Is, W end ☆ 54°17'·02N 10°05'·56W Fl (3) 15s 67m **19M**; W twr; 992501189.

EAGLE ISLAND TO RATHLIN O'BIRNE

BROAD HAVEN BAY

Rinroe Pt ⚓ Fl (2) 10s 5m 3M; 54°17'·83N 09°50'·59W.

Gubacashel Point ⚓ Iso WR 4s 27m **W17M**, R12M; 110°-R-133°-W-355°-R-021° W twr; 54°16'·06N 09°53'·33W.

KILLALA

Inishcrone Pier Root ⚓ Fl WRG 1·5s 8m 2M; vis: 098°-W-116°-G- 136°-R-187°; 54°13'·21N 09°05'·79W.

Ldg lts 230°. Rinnaun Point. Front No. 1, Oc 10s 7m 5M; ☐ twr; 54°13'·21N 09°05'·79W. Rear, 150m from front, No. 2 Oc 10s 12m 5M; ☐ twr.

Inch Is Dir lt 215°, Fl WRG 2s 6m 3M; ☐ twr; vis: 205°-G-213°-W- 217°-R-225°; 54°13'·29N 09°12'·30W.

Ldg lts 196°. Kilrne. Front, 54°12'·63N 09°12'·33W Oc 4s 5m 2M; ☐ twr. Rear,120m from front, Oc 4s 10m 2M; ☐ twr.

Ldg lts 236°. Pier. Front, Iso 2s 5m 2M; W ◇ on twr; 54°13'·02N 09°12'·84W. Rear, 200m from front, Iso 2s 7m 2M; W ◇ on pole.

SLIGO

Black Rock ⚓ Fl WR 5s 24m 10/8M; vis: 130°-W-107°-R-130° (R sector covers Wheat and Seal rks); W twr, B band; 54°18'·45N 08°37'·06W.

Lower Rosses, (N of Cullaun Bwee) ⚓ Fl (2) WRG 10s 8m 10M; W hut on piles; vis: 061°-G-066°-W-070°-R-075°; shown H24; 54°19'·73N 08°34'·41W.

Ldg lts 125° Fl (3) 6s 7M (sync). Front, Metal Man; 54°18'·24N 08°34'·55W, 3m. Rear, Oyster Is, 365m from front, 13m; H24. Wheat Rock ⚓ Q (6) + LFl 15s; 54°18'·84N 08°39'·10W.

DONEGAL BAY and KILLYBEGS

St John's Pt ⚓ Fl 6s 30m 14M; W twr; 54°34'·16N 08°27'·66W; 992501197.

Bullockmore ⚓ Q (9) 15s; 54°33'·98N 08°30'·14W; 992501198.

Rotten I ☆ 54°36'·97N 08°26'·41W Fl WR 4s 20m **W15M**, R11M; W twr; vis: W255°- R008°- W039°-208°.

New Landing Dir lt 338°, Oc WRG 8s 17m; vis: 328°-G-334°-Al WG-336°-W-340°-Al WR-342°-R-348°; 54°38'·14N 08°26'·38W.

Killybegs Outer ⚓ VQ (6) + L Fl 10s; 54°37'·92N 08°29'·15W.

RATHLIN O'BIRNE TO BLOODY FORELAND

S of ARAN and RUTLAND S CHANNEL

Rathlin O'Birne ⚓ Fl WR 15s 35m W12M, R10M; W twr; vis: 195°-R-307°-W-195°; *Racon (O) 13M*, vis 284°-203°. 54°39'·82N 08°49'·95W; 992501203.

Dawros Head ☆ L Fl 10s 39m 4M; 54°49'·63N 08°33'·64W.

Wyon Point ⚓ Fl (2) WRG 10s 8m W6M, R3M; W ☐twr; vis: shore-G-021°-W-042°-R-121°-W-150°-R-shore; 54°56'·51N 08°27'·54W.

BURTONPORT
Ldg lts 068·1°. Front , FG 17m 1M; Gy Bn, W band; 54°58'·95N 08°26'·40W. Rear, 355m from front, FG 23m 1M; Gy Bn, Y band.

N SOUND OF ARAN and RUTLAND N CHANNEL
Rutland I Ldg lts 137·6°. Front, 54°58'·97N 08°27'·68W Oc 6s 8m 1M; W Bn, B band. Rear, 330m from front, Oc 6s 14m 1M.
Inishcoo Ldg lts 119·3°. Front, Iso 6s 6m 1M; W Bn, B band; 54°59'·43N 08°29'·63W. Rear, 248m from front, Iso 6s 11m 1M.
Ldg lts 186°. Front, Oc 8s 8m 3M; B Bn, W band; 54°58'·94N 08°29'·27W. Rear, 395m from front, Oc 8s 17m 3M; B Bn.
Aranmore, Rinrawros Pt ☆ 55°00'·90N 08°33'·67W Fl (2) 20s 71m **27M**; W twr; obsc by land about 234°-007° and about 013°. Auxiliary lt Fl R 3s 61m 13M, same twr; vis: 203°-234°; <u>992501205</u>.

OWEY SOUND to INISHSIRRER
Cruit Is. Owey Sound Ldg lts 068·3°. Oc 10s. Front, 55°03'·06N 08°25'·85W. Rear, 107m from front.
Rinnalea Point ⚡ 55°02'·59N 08°23'·72W Fl 7·5s 19m 9M; ☐ twr; vis: 132°-167°.
Gola Is Ldg lts 171·2°. Oc 3s 2M (sync). Front, 9m; W Bn, B band; 55°05'·11N 08°21'·07W. Rear, 86m from front, 13m; B Bn, W band.
Glassagh. Ldg lts 137·4°. Front, Oc 8s 12m 3M; 55°06'·83N 08°18'·97W. Rear, 46m from front, Oc 8s 17m 3M; synch.
Inishsirrer, NW end ⚡ Fl 3·7s 20m 4M; W ☐ twr vis: 083°-263°; 55°07'·40N 08°20'·93W.

BLOODY FORELAND TO INISHTRAHULL

BLOODY FORELAND to SHEEPHAVEN
Bloody Foreland ⚡ Fl WG 7·5s 14m W6M, G4M; vis: 062°-W-232°-G-062°; 55°09'·51N 08°17'·03W.
Tory Island ☆ 55°16'·36N 08°14'·96W Fl (4) 30s 40m **18M**; B twr, W band; vis: 302°-277°; *Racon (M) 12-23M*; <u>992501211</u>.
West Town Ldg lts 001° ⚡ Iso 2s 9m 7M △ on Y structure R stripe; 55°15'·79N 08°13'·50W. Rear Iso 2s 11m 7M ▽ ditto (sync).
Ballyness Hbr. Ldg lts 119·5°. Front, Iso 4s 25m 1M; 55°09'·06N 08°06'·98W. Rear, 61m from front, Iso 4s 26m 1M.
Portnablahy Ldg lts 125·3°. Front Oc 6s 7m 2M; B col, W bands; 55°10'·79N 07°55'·65W. Rear, 81m from front, Oc 6s 12m 2M; B col, W bands.

MULROY BAY
Limeburner ⚓ Q Fl; 55°18'·54N 07°48'·40W; <u>992501214</u>.
Ravedy Is ⚡ Fl 3s 9m 3M; vis 177°-357°; 55°15'·14N 07°46'·90W

LOUGH SWILLY, BUNCRANA and RATHMULLAN
Fanad Head ☆ 55°16'·57N 07°37'·92W Fl (5) WR 20s 39m **W18M**, R14M; W twr; vis 100°-R-110°-W-313°-R-345°-W-100°; <u>992501215</u>.
Swillymore ⚓ Fl G 3s; 55°15'·12N 07°35'·79W; <u>992501216</u>.
Dunree ⚡ Fl (2) WR 5s 46m W12M, R9M; vis: 320°-R-328°-W-183°-R-196°; 55°11'·89N 07°33'·25W.
Buncrana Pier near Hd ⚡ Iso WR 4s 11m W13M, R10M; R twr, W band; vis: R shore- over Inch spit, 052°-W-139°-R-shore over White Strand Rock; 55°07'·60N 07°27'·88W.
Rathmullan Pier Hd ⚡ Fl G 3s 5M; vis: 206°-345°; 55°05'·70N 07°31'·66W.

Inishtrahull ☆ 55°25'·89N 07°14'·63W Fl (3) 15s 59m **19M**; W twr; obscd 256°-261° within 3M; *Racon (T) 24M 060°-310°*. Fog Det Lt VQ; <u>992501229</u>.

INISHTRAHULL TO RATHLIN ISLAND

LOUGH FOYLE
Foyle ⚓ L Fl 10s; 55°15'·32N 06°52'·60W; <u>992501230</u>.
Tuns ⚓ Fl R 3s; 55°14'·00N 06°53'·46W; <u>992501232</u>.
Inishowen Dunagree ☆ 55°13'·60N 06°55'·70W Fl (2) WRG 10s 28m **W18M**, R14M, G14M; W twr, 2 B bands; vis: 197°-G-211°-W-249°-R-000°. Fog Det lt VQ 16m vis: 270°.
Greencastle S Bkwtr Dir lt 042·5°. Fl (2) WRG 3s 4m W11M, R9M, G9M; vis 307°-G- 040°-W-045°-R-055°; 55°12'·17N 06°59'·13W.
McKinney's ⚓ Fl R 5s; 55°10'·9N 07°00'·5W.
Moville ⚡ Fl WR 2·5s 11m 4M; W house on G piles vis: 240°-W-064°-R-240°; 55°10'·98N 07°02'·13W.

RIVER BANN, COLERAINE and PORTRUSH
River Bann Ldg lts 165°. Front, Oc 5s 6m 2M; W twr; 55°09'·96N 06°46'·23W. Rear, 245m from front, Oc 5s 14m 2M; W ☐ twr.
W Mole ⚡ Fl G 5s 4m 2M; vis: 170°-000°; 55°10'·25N 06°46'·45W.
Portstewart Point ⚡ Oc R 10s 21m 5M; R ☐ hut; vis: 040°-220°; 55°11'·33N 06°43'·26W.
N Pier Hd ⚡ Fl R 3s 6m 3M; vis: 220°-160°; 55°12'·34N 06°39'·58W.
Skerries ⚓ Fl R 5s; 53°13'·90N 06°36'·90W; <u>992351096</u>.

RATHLIN ISLAND
Rathlin W 0·5M NE of Bull Pt ⚡ 55°18'·05N 06°16'·82W Fl R 5s 62m **22M**; W twr, lantern at base; vis: 015°-225°; H24. Fog Det Lt VQ; <u>992351000</u>.
Drake Wreck ⚓ 55°17'·00N 06°12'·48W Q (6) + L Fl 15s.
Manor House ⚡ Oc WRG 4s 5M; vis: 020°-G-023°-W-026°-R-029°; 55°17'·52N 06°11'·73W.
Rue Pt ⚡ Fl(2) 5s 16m 14M; W twr B bands; 55°15'·53N 06°11'·47W.
Altacarry Head ☆ 55°18'·11N 06°10'·31W Fl (4) 20s 74m **26M**; W twr, B band; vis: 110°-006° and 036°-058°; *Racon (G) 15-27M*; <u>992320707</u>.

FAIR HEAD TO LAMBAY ISLAND

RED BAY, CARNLOUGH and LARNE
Red Bay Pier ⚡ Fl 3s 10m 5M; 55°03'·93N 06°03'·21W.
Carnlough Hbr N Pier ⚡ Fl G 3s 4m 5M; 54°59'·59N 05°59'·29W.
East Maiden ☆ Fl (3) 15s 29m **23M**; W twr, B band; *Racon (M) 11-21M*. Auxiliary lt Fl R 5s 15m 8M; 54°55'·75N 05°43'·71W; same twr; vis:142°-182° over Russel and Highland Rks; <u>992351110</u>.
N Hunter Rock ⚓ Q; 54°53'·04N 05°45'·13W.
S Hunter Rock ⚓ VQ(6) + LFl 10s; 54°52'·69N 05°45'·22W; <u>992351007</u>.
Larne No. 1 ⚓ QG; 54°51'·68N 05°47'·67W; *AIS*.
Chaine Twr ☆ Iso WR 5s 23m **W16M**, R12M; Gy twr; vis: 232°-W-240°-R-000° (shore); 54°51'·27N 05°47'·90W.
Larne Ldg lts 184°, No. 11 Front, 54°49'·60N 05°47'·81W Oc 4s 6m 12M; W 2 with R stripe on R pile structure; vis: 179°-189°. No. 12 Rear, 610m from front, Oc 4s 14m 12M; W 2 with R stripe on R ☐ twr; synch with front, vis: 5° either side of Ldg line.

CARRICKFERGUS
Black Hd ☆ 54°46'·02N 05°41'·34W Fl 3s 45m **27M**; W 8-sided twr; 992351002.
Cloghan Jetty ◣ 54°44'·10N 05°41'·58W QG. Marina Ent Appr ⚓ Dir Oc WRG 3s 5m 3M; vis: G308°- W317·5°- R322·5°-332°; 54°42'·58N 05°48'·78W.

BELFAST LOUGH and BANGOR
Mew Is ☆ NE end 54°41'·91N 05°30'·79W Fl (4) 30s 37m **24M**; B twr, W band; *Racon (O) 14M*. Fog Det Lt VQ; 992351109.
Belfast Fairway ⚓ Iso 4s; 54°42'·32N 05°42'·30W; *Racon (G); AIS*.
Kilroot ◣ Fl QG (sync); 54°42'·85N 05°42'·85W.
Helen's Bay ⚓ QR (sync); 54°41'·86N 05°42'·85W.
No 1 ◣ Fl G 2s (sync); 54°41'·67N 05°46'·51W.
No 2 ⚓ Fl R 2s (sync); 54°41'·55N 05°46'·43W.

DONAGHADEE, BALLYWATER and PORTAVOGIE
Donaghadee ☆, S Pier Hd 54°38'·71N 05°31'·86W Iso WR 4s 17m **W18M**, R14M; twr; vis: shore-W-326°-R-shore; 002320792.
Ballywalter, Bkwtr Hd Fl WRG 3s 4m 9M; vis: 240°-G-267°- W-277°-R-314°; 54°32'·68N 05°28'·83W.
Skulmartin ⚓ L Fl 10s; 54°31'·82N 05°24'·80W; 992351022.
Portavogie Bkwtr Hd ⚓ Iso WRG 5s 9m W10M, R8M, G8M; ☐ twr; vis: shore-G-258°-W-275°-R-348°; 54°27'·44N 05°26'·14W.
Plough Rock ⚓ 54°27'·40N 05°25'·12W Fl R 3s.
South Rock ⚓ Fl (3) R 30s 7M 54°24'·49N 05°22'·02W; 992351004.

STRANGFORD LOUGH
Strangford ⚓ L Fl 10s; 54°18'·63N 05°28'·69W; 992351028.
Bar Pladdy ⚓ Q (6) + L Fl 15s; 54°19'·34N 05°30'·51W.
Dogtail Pt Ldg lts 341°. Front, Fl 4s 2m 5M; 54°20'·79N 05°31'·84W.Rear, Gowlands Rk, 0·8M fm front, LFl 8s 6m 5M.
Swan Is ⚓ Q (3) 5m; BYB brick twr; 54°22'·38N 05°33'·16W.
Strangford East Ldg lts 256°. Front, Oc WRG 5s 6m W9M, R6M, G6M: vis: 190°-R-244°-G-252°-W- 260°-R-294°; 54°22'·29N 05°33'·27W. Rear, 46m from front, Oc R 5s 10m 6M; vis: 250°-264°.
Portaferry Pier Hd ⚓ Oc WR 10s 9m W9M, R6M; Or mast; vis: W335°- R005°- W017°-128°; 54°22'·82N 05°33'·03W.

ARDGLASS
Inner Pier Hd ⚓ Iso WRG 4s 10m W8M, R7M, G5M; twr; vis: shore-G-308°-W-314°-R-shore; 54°15'·79N 05°36'·33W.

DUNDRUM BAY
St John's Point ☆ 54°13'·61N 05°39'·61W Q (2) 7·5s 37m **25M**; B twr, Y bands. **Auxiliary Light** ☆ Fl WR 3s 14m **W15M**, R11M, same twr, vis: 064°-W-078°-R-shore; Fog Det lt VQ 14m vis: 270°; 992351005.
DZ East ⚓ Fl (2) Y 10s; 54°12'·05N 05°45'·30W.
DZ West ⚓ Fl Y 5s; 54°11'·84N 05°50'·82W.

ANNALONG
E Bkwtr Hd ⚓ Oc WRG 5s 8m 9M; twr; vis: 204°-G-249°- W-309°-R-024°; 54°06'·51N 05°53'·73W.

KILKEEL
Pier Hd ⚓ Fl WR 2s 8m 8M; vis: R296°-W313°-017°; 54°03'·46N 05°59'·30W.

CARLINGFORD LOUGH and NEWRY RIVER
Hellyhunter ⚓ Q(6) + LFl 15s; 54°00'·35N 06°02'·10W; 992351009.
Haulbowline ⚓ 54°01'·19N 06°04'·74W Fl (3) 10s 32m 10M; Grey twr; 992501235.
Ldg lts 310·4° Front, Oc 3s 7m 11M; R △ on twr; vis: 295°-325°; 54°01'·80N 06°05'·43W; 992501237. Rear, 457m from front, Oc 3s 12m 11M; R ▽ on twr; vis: 295°-325°; both H24.
Newry River Ldg lts 310·4°. Front, 54°06'·37N 06°16'·51W. Rear, 274m from front. Both Iso 4s 5/15m 2M; stone cols.

DUNDALK
Imogene ⚓ Fl (2) R 10s; 53°57'·41N 06°07'·02W.
Pile Light ⚓ 53°58'·56N 06°17'·71W Fl WR 15s 10m 10M; W Ho.
Dunany ⚓ Fl R 3s; 53°53'·56N 06°09'·47W.

SKERRIES BAY
Skerries Pier Hd ⚓ Oc R 6s 7m 7M; W col; vis: 103°-R-154°; 53°35'·09N 06°06'·49W

DROGHEDA to LAMBAY ISLAND
Port Approach Dir lt 53°43'·30N 06°14'·73W WRG 10m **W19M, R15M**, G15M; vis: 268°-FG-269°-Al WG-269·5°- FW-270·5°-Al WR-271°-FR-272°; H24.
Balbriggan ⚓ Fl (3) WRG 10s 12m W13M, R10M, G10M; W twr; vis: 159°-G-193°-W-288°-R-305°; 53°36'·76N 06°10'·80W.
Rockabill ☆ 53°35'·81N 06°00'·30W Fl WR 12s 45m **W17M, R13M**; W twr, B band; vis: 178°-W-329°-R-178°; 992501246.
Skerries Bay Pier Hd ⚓ Oc R 6s 7m 7M; W col; vis: 103°- 154°; 53°35'·09N 06°06'·49W.

1	Strangford Lough	**1**														
2	Bangor	34	**2**													
3	Carrickfergus	39	6	**3**												
4	Larne	45	16	16	**4**											
5	Carnlough	50	25	26	11	**5**										
6	Portrush	87	58	60	48	35	**6**									
7	Lough Foyle	92	72	73	55	47	11	**7**								
8	L Swilly (Fahan)	138	109	104	96	81	48	42	**8**							
9	Burtonport	153	130	130	116	108	74	68	49	**9**						
10	Killybegs	204	175	171	163	148	115	109	93	43	**10**					
11	Sligo	218	189	179	177	156	123	117	107	51	30	**11**				
12	Eagle Island	234	205	198	193	175	147	136	123	72	62	59	**12**			
13	Westport	295	266	249	240	226	193	187	168	120	108	100	57	**13**		
14	Galway	338	309	307	297	284	253	245	227	178	166	163	104	94	**14**	
15	Kilrush	364	335	332	323	309	276	270	251	203	191	183	142	119	76	**15**

DISTANCE TABLES
Approx distances in nautical miles are by the most direct route allowing for dangers and TSS.

47

AREA 11 *West Denmark – Skagen to Rømø*
SELECTED LIGHTS, BUOYS & WAYPOINTS

Positions are referenced to WGS84

SKAGEN TO THYBORØN

SKAGEN

Skagen W ☆ Fl (3) WR 10s 31m **W17M/R12M**; 053°-W-248°-R-323°; W ○ twr; 57°44'·94N 10°35·70E.

Skagen ☆ Fl 4s 44m **23M**; Gy ○ twr; *Racon G, 20M*; 57°44'·14N 10°37'·81E.

Skagen No 1A ⌀ L Fl 10s; *Racon N*; 57°43'·46N 10°53'·55E. (Route T)

Skagen No. 2 ⌀ L Fl 10s; 57°37'·61N 11°05'·51E. (Route T)

Skagens Rev ⌀ Q; 57°45'·97N 10°43'·74E.

⌀ Q (3) 10s; 57°43'·87N 10°42'·31E.

Skagen Harbour

Ldg Its 334·5°, both Iso R 4s 13/22m 8M. Front, 57°43'·06N 10°35'·45E; mast. Rear, 57°43'·19N 10°35'·34E; twr.

E bkwtr ⚡ Fl G 3s 8m 5M; G twr; *Horn (2) 30s*; 57°42'·88N 10°35'·66E.

W bkwtr ⚡ Fl R 3s 8m 5M; R twr; 57°42'·84N 10°35'·60E.

HIRTSHALS

Hirtshals ☆ F Fl 30s 57m **F 18M; Fl 25M**; W ○ twr, approx 1M SSW of hbr ent; 57°35'·10N 09°56'·55E.

Ldg Its 166°, both 156°-176°. Front, Iso R 2s 10m 11M; R △ on twr; 57°35'·69N 09°57'·64E; marina ent is close N of this lt. Rear, Iso R 4s 18m 11M; R ▽ on twr; 330m from front.

Approach chan ▲ Fl (3) G 10s; 57°36'·18N 09°56·94E.

⚲ Fl R 3s; 57°36'·44N 09°57'·67E.

⚲ Fl (5) Y 20s; 57°36'·43N 09°57'·72E.

▲ Fl G 5s; 57°36'·11N 09°57'·14E.

Outer W mole ⚡ Fl G 3s 14m 6M; G mast; *Horn 15s*; 57°35'·97N 09°57'·37E.

W mole spur ⚡ Fl G 5s 9m 4M; G mast; 57°35'·77N 09°57'·51E.

E mole ⚡ Fl R 5s 9m 6M; G mast; 57°35'·85N 09°57'·61E.

LØKKEN

Lee bkwtr ⚡ Fl 5s 5m 5M; 57°22'·39N 09°42'·11E.

TRANUM STRAND (Firing ranges)

Tranum No. 1 ☆ Al Fl WR 4s 19m W7M, R7M; twr; by day Q 4M; shown when firing in progress; 57°12'·43N 09°30'·34E.

Tranum No. 2 ☆ light as per No.1; 57°10'·57N 09°26'·22E.

LILD STRAND

Bragerne ▲ Fl G 5s; 57°10'·67N 08°56'·35E.

Ldg Its 138°, three ⚡: F 12/22m 7/8M; 127°-149°; 3 masts. Front 57°09'·22N 08°57'·75E.

HANSTHOLM

Hanstholm ☆ Fl (3) 20s 65m **26M**; shown by day in poor vis; W 8-sided twr; 57°06'·77N 08°35'·92E, approx 1M S of the hbr ent.

Hanstholm ⌀ LFl 10s; 57°08'·06N 08°34'·87E.

Ldg Its 142·6°, both Iso 2s 37/45m 13M; synch; 127·6°-157·6°; R △ on mast. Front, 57°07'·12N 08°36'·15E. Rear, 170m from front, R ▽ on mast.

Note: The 4 outer/inner mole heads are floodlit.

W outer mole ⚡ Fl G 3s 11m 9M; G pillar; 57°07'·56N 08°35'·45E. E outer mole ⚡ Fl R 3s 11m 9M; R pillar; 57°07'·61N 08°35'·57E.

Roshage ⚡ Fl 5s 7m 5M; 57°07'·75N 08°37'·25E (1M E of hbr).

NØRRE VORUPØR

Mole ⚡ Fl G 5s 6m 5M; 56°57'·75N 08°21'·679E.

Ldg Its, both Iso R 4s 20/30m 9M, indicate safest landing place for FVs; vis 22·5° either side of ldg line; synch. Front 57°57'·46N 08°22'·10E. Rear, 80m from front.

Lodbjerg ☆ Fl (2) 20s 48m **23M**; ○ twr; 56°49'·40N 08°15'·76E.

THYBORØN

Landfall ⌀ L Fl 10s; *Racon T, 10m*; 56°42'·54N 08°08'·69E.

Agger Tange ldg Its 082°: Front, Iso WRG 4s 8m W11M, R/G8M; 074·5°-G-079·5°-W-084·5°-R-089·5°; R △ on bcn; 56°42'·97N 08°14'·14E. Rear, Iso 4s 17m 11M; 075°-089°; synch; R ▽ on Gy twr; 804m from front.

Off Havmolen ⚲ 56°43'·25N 08°12'·52E.

Approach ☆ Fl (3) 10s 24m 12M; intens 023·5°-203·5°; also lit by day in poor vis; lattice twr; 56°42'·49N 08°12'·91E (S side of ent).

Langholm ldg Its 120°, both Iso 2s 7/13m 11M; synch; 113°-127°. Front, R △ on R hut, 56°42'·45N 08°14'·54E. Rear, R ▽ on Gy twr.

Thyborøn Havn ⚡ Oc (2) WRG 12s 6m W11M, R/G8M; 122·5°-G-146·5°- W-150°- R-211·3°-G-337·5°- W-340°-R-344°; W twr R band; 56°42'·35N 08°13'·39E (680m N of ent to Yderhavn and Basins).

1	Skagen	**1**																
2	Hirtshals	33	**2**															
3	Hanstholm	85	52	**3**														
4	Thyborln	114	84	32	**4**													
5	Torsminde	141	108	56	24	**5**												
6	Hvide Sande	162	179	77	45	24	**6**											
7	Esbjerg	200	174	122	90	76	54	**7**										
8	Fanl	210	177	125	93	79	57	3	**8**									
9	Rlml	233	200	148	116	94	73	30	33	**9**								
10	H rnum	248	215	163	131	108	86	70	73	29	**10**							
11	Husum	275	247	195	163	152	131	95	98	68	45	**11**						
12	Kiel/Holtenau	261	233	281	249	232	208	180	183	189	126	129	**12**					
13	Bremerhaven	306	285	233	201	185	163	127	129	107	83	82	123	**13**				
14	Wilhelmshaven	414	296	242	310	184	162	125	128	106	82	82	123	45	**14**			
15	Helgoland	259	238	186	154	141	119	83	85	63	39	47	104	44	43	**15**		
16	Cuxhaven	304	284	232	200	162	138	110	113	85	56	66	70	58	56	38	**16**	
17	Wangerooge	283	262	210	178	168	147	109	112	94	68	52	108	38	27	24	42	**17**
18	Hamburg	338	317	265	233	216	192	163	167	139	99	113	90	81	110	88	54	61	**18**

DISTANCE TABLES
Approx distances in nautical miles are by the most direct route allowing for dangers and TSS.

Yderhavn, N mole ⚡ Fl G 3s 6m 4M; G pedestal; 56°42'·02N 08°13'·52E.

S mole ⚡ Fl R 3s 6m 4M; R pedestal; 56°41'·97N 08°13'·53E.

LIMFJORD TO 08°42'E

Sælhundeholm Løb, into Nissum Bredning ('Broad').
No. 1 ▲ Fl (2) G 5s; 56°41'·14N 08°14'·17E.
No. 3 ▲ Fl G 3s; 56°40'·75N 08°13'·79E.
No. 7 ▲ Fl G 3s; 56°40'·31N 08°13'·52E.
No. 11 ◢ Fl G 3s; 56°39'·83N 08°13'·59E.
No. 16 ◿ Fl R 3s; 56°38'·51N 08°13'·89E.
No. 18 ◿ Fl (2) R 5s; 56°38'·20N 08°14'·34E.
No. 21 ▲ Fl G 3s; 56°38'·98N 08°14'·71E.
No. 26 ◿ Fl R 3s; 56°38'·71N 08°15'·38E.
No. 29 ▲ Fl G 3s; 56°38'·40N 08°15'·94E.
◿ Q; 56°38'·06N 08°16'·70E.

APPROACHES TO LEMVIG (Marina and Havn)
Toftum Dir ⚡ 120°, Iso WRG 4s 24m, W12M, R/G 8M; 110°-G-120°-W-137°-R-144°; hut; 56°33'·09N 08°18'·33E.
Rønnen ▲ Fl G 3s; 56°36'·71N 08°21'·74E.
Rønnen ◢ L Fl 10s; 56°35'·58N 08°21'·62E.
Søgard Mark ldg lts 243·5°: both FR 20/30m 5M; vis 90° either side of ldg line. Front, ◢ R △ on W bcn; 56°34'·39N 08°17'·29E. Rear, R ▽ on W post; 235m from front.
Chan ▲ 56°33'·27N 08°18'·31E.
Ldg lts, W of hbr 177·7°, both FR 8/20m 5M; 153°-203°. Front ◢ R △ on twr; 56°33'·04N 08°18'·16E. Rear, R ▽ on W post; 184m from front.
Vinkel Hage marina, N mole ⚡ FG 3m 5M; 56°33'·09N 08°18'·33E.
S mole, FR 3m 4M. Marina is 9ca N of the Havn on the W side.
Ostre Havn ⚓ 56°33'·17N 08°18'·40E. Havn ent, FG/FR 4m 5M.

THISTED HAVN (Marina)
Outer W mole ⚡ Fl R 3s 4m 2M; 56°57'·10N 08°41'·90E.
Outer E mole ⚡ Fl G 3s 4m 2M; 56°57'·10N 08°41'·95E.
Thisted Bredning ⚡ Aero 3 Fl R 1·5s (vert; 45m apart) 183m 10M; TV mast; 56°58'·52N 08°41'·15E, 1·55M NNW of hbr ent.

THYBORØN TO BLÅVANDS HUK

Bovbjerg ☆ Fl (2) 15s 62m 16M; 56°30'·79N 08°07'·18E.
Wave recorder buoy ◿ Fl (5) Y 20s; 56°28'·49N 08°03'·35E.

THORSMINDE HAVN
(All Lat/Longs for this harbour are approximate)
Lt ho ⚡ F 30m 13M; Gy twr; 56°22'·34N 08°06'·99E.
Groyne, N ⚡ Fl 5s 8m 5M; Gy hut; 56°22'·46N 08°06'·82E.
N mole ⚡ Iso R 2s 9m 4M; R hut; 56°22'·36N 08°06'·62E.
S mole ⚡ Iso G 2s 9m 4M; G hut; 56°22'·26N 08°06'·92E.
West hbr, W mole ⚡ FG 5m 2M; Gy post; 56°22'·36N 08°07'·12E.
E mole ⚡ FR 5m 2M; Gy post; 56°22'·26N 08°07'·18E.
NW dolphin ⚡ FG 5m 4M; Gy post; 56°22'·26N 08°07'·22E.
SE dolphin ⚡ FG 5m 4M; Gy post; 56°22'·26N 08°07'·26E.
Lock, E side ⚡ Iso 4s 12m 4M; Gy mast; 020°-160°; 56°22'·36N 08°07'·22E.
Road bridge ⚡ Iso 4s 5m 4M; 200°-340°; 56°22'·36N 08°07'·26E.

HVIDE SANDE
Lyngvig ☆ Fl 20s 53m **17M** (may have Y tint); W ○ twr; 56°02'·99N 08°06'·22E.
N outer bkwtr ⚡ Fl R 3s 7m 8M; R hut; 55°59'·94N 08°06'·55E.
N mole ⚡ Fl R 5s 10m 6·5M; R floodlit edifice; 55°59'·98N 08°06'· 84E.
S mole ⚡ Fl G 5s 10m 6M; 55°59'·96N 08°06'·98E.
Lt ho ⚡ F 27m 14M; Gy twr; 56°00'·00N 08°07'·35E.
Nordhavn, E pier ⚡ FG 4m 4M; 56°00'·16N 08°07'·42E.
W pier ⚡ 2 FR 3m 2M; W posts; 060°-035°; 56°00'·07N 08°07'·12E.
Sydhavn, W pier ⚡ FG 4m 2M; 56°00'·06N 08°07'·52E.
E Pier ⚡ FR 4m 2M; Gy post; 56°00'·06N 08°07'·53E.
Lock entrance ldg lts 293·5°: both FR 11/14m 2M; 201·6°-021·6°. Front, R ◿ on Gy tr, 56°00'·0N 08°07'·8E. Rear, R ▽ on Gy twr, 72m from front.
Fjordhavn ldg lts 246·6° (both vis 7·5° either side of ldg line): Front, Iso G 2s 4m 4M; Or △ on mast; 56°00'·5N 08°07'·9E. Rear, Iso G 4s 6m 4M, Or ▽ on mast, 128m from front.

HORNS REV (marks westward from coast)
Oskbøl firing range. Two lights (4M apart), both AlFl WR 4s 35m **16M**, R13M, (by day Q 10M), are shown when firing is in progress: North ☆ 55°37'·3N 08°07'·1E. South ☆ 55°33'·6N 08°04'·7E.
Range safety buoys: ◿ Fl Y 5s; 55°42'·32N 08°06'·92E.◿ Fl Y 3s; 55°38'·63N 07°50'·91E.◿ Fl Y 3s; 55°37'·35N 07°56'·98E.◿ 55°36'·02N 08°02'·49E.
Blåvands Huk ☆ Fl (3) 20s 55m **23M**; W □ twr; 55°33'·46N 08°04'·95E.
Horns Rev is encircled by:
Tuxen ◿ Q; 55°34'·22N 07°41'·92E on the N side.
Vyl ◢ Q (6) + L Fl 15s; 55°26'·22N 07°49'·99E on the S side.
No. 2 ◢ L Fl 10s; 55°28'·74N 07°36'·49E on the SW side.
Horns Rev W ◢ Q (9) 15s; 55°34'·47N 07°26'·05E, off the W end.
Slugen Channel (crosses Horns Rev ESE/WNW)
▲ L Fl G 10s; 55°33'·99N 07°49'·38E.
▲ Fl G 3s; 55°32'·26N 07°53'·65E.
◿ Fl (2) R 5s; 55°31'·46N 07°52'·88E.
▲ Fl (2) G 5s; 55°30'·52N 07°59'·20E.
◿ Fl (3) R 10s; 55°29'·42N 08°02'·56E.
Søren Bovbjergs Dyb (unlit N/S side channel off Slugen Chan)
◢ 55°33'·57N 07°55'·55E.
◿ 55°32'·80N 07°55'·30E.
◢ 55°32'·19N 07°56'·29E.
◢ 55°31'·24N 07°57'·46E.
Wind farm in □ 2·7M x 2·5M, centred on 55°29'·22N 07°50'·21E: 80 turbines all R lts, the 12 perimeter turbines are lit Fl (3) Y 10s.
NE turbine, *Racon (U)*; 55°30'·28N 07°52'·63E & transformer platform, 2 Mo (U) 15s 9m 5M, 55°30'·52N 07°52'·53E.
SW turbine, *Racon (U)*; 55°28'·11N 07°48'·26E.
Horns Rev II wind farm in U2M x 6M, centred on 55°36'·08N 07°34'·78E: 91 turbines all R lts, the 12 perimeter turbines are lit Fl (3) Y 10s.
2 Met masts, both 70m, ⚡ 2 Mo (U) 15s 12m 5M and Aero QR: 151B (55°29'·21N 07°54'·72E) and 151C (55°29'·24N 07°58'·52E).

BLÅVANDS HUK TO RØMØ
APPROACHES TO ESBJERG
Grådyb ⚓ L Fl 10s; *Racon G, 10M*; 55°24'·63N 08°11'·59E.
Sædding Strand 053·8° triple ldg lts: valid up to Nos 7/8 buoys; H24: **Front** Iso 2s 13m **21M**; 052°-056°; R bldg; 55°29'·74N 08°23'·87E.
Middle Iso 4s 26m **21M**; 051°-057°; R twr, W bands; 55°29'·94N 08°24'·33E, 630m from front.
Rear F 37m **18M**; 052°-056°; R twr; 55°30'·18N 08°24'·92E, 0·75M from front.
No. 1 ⚓ Q; 55°25'·49N 08°13'·89E.
No. 2 ⚓ Fl (3) R 10s; 55°25'·62N 08°13'·73E.
No. 3 ▲ Fl G 3s; 55°25'·93N 08°14'·84E.
No. 4 ⚓ Fl R 3s; 55°26'·02N 08°14'·72E.
Tide Gauge ⚡ Fl (5) Y 20s 8m 4M; 55°26'·05N 08°15'·93E.
No. 5 ▲ Fl G 5s; 55°26'·32N 08°15'·83E.
No. 6 ⚓ Fl R 5s; 55°26'·44N 08°15'·70E.
No. 7 ⚓ Q; 55°26'·76N 08°16'·91E.
No. 8 ⚓ Fl (2) R 5s; 55°26'·89N 08°16'·81E.
Ldg lts 067°, valid up to Nos 9/10 buoys. Both FG 10/25m **16M**, H24. Front, Gy tripod; rear, Gy twr, 55°28'·76N 08°24'·70E.
No. 9 ▲ Fl (2) G 10s; 55°27'·04N 08°18'·21E.
No.10 ⚓ Fl (2) R 10s; 55°27'·20N 08°18'·04E.
Ldg lts 049°, valid up to No 16 buoy/Jerg. Both FR 16/27m **16M**, H24. Front, W twr; rear, Gy twr, 55°29'·92N 08°23'·75E.
No. 11 ▲ Fl G 3s; 55°27'·71N 08°19'·59E.
No. 12 ⚓ Fl R 3s; 55°27'·88N 08°19'·39E.
No. 13 ▲ Fl G 5s; 55°28'·40N 08°20'·99E.
No. 14 ⚓ Fl R 5s; 55°28'·57N 08°20'·73E.
Jerg ⚡ Fl G 3s 7m 5M; G twr, Y base; 55°28'·88N 08°22'·00E.
No. 16 ⚓ Q (6) + L Fl 15s; 55°29'·04N 08°21'·80E.
No. 15A ▲ Fl (2) G 5s; 55°29'·01N 08°22'·47E.
No 18 ⚓ Fl (2) R 5s; 55°29'·19N 08°22'·71E.
Fovrfelt N ⚡ Oc (2) WRG 6s 7m W6M, R/G4M; 066·5°-G-073°-W-077°-R-085·5°; 327°-G-331°- W-333·5°-R-342°; Y twr; 55°29'·29N 08°23'·79E.
Fovrfelt ⚡ Fl (2) R 10s 11m 6M; R twr; 55°29'·03N 08°23'·75E.
No 15B ▲ Fl (2) G 10s; 55°28'·83N 08°23'·65E.

ESBJERG HAVN
Strandby, shelter mole, NW corner ⚡ Oc WRG 5s 6m W13M, R/G9M; 101·7°-G-105·5°-W-109·5°-R-111·7°; W bldg, R band; 55°28'·76N 08°24'·63E.
Industrifiskerihavn, W mole ⚡ Fl R 5s 6m 4M; R structure; 55°28'·57N 08°24'·89E.
E mole ⚡ Fl G 5s 7m 4M; G structure; 55°28'·52N 08°25'·03E.
Nordsøkai ↓ Q (9) 15s 5m; Y twr, B band; 55°28'·45N 08°25'·04E.
Konsumfiskerihavn, W mole ⚡ FlR 3s 6m; 203°-119°; R twr; 55°28'·31N 08°25'·33E. Yacht hbr in SSE part of Basin II.
E mole ⚡ Fl G 3s 6m; 023°-256°; G tr; 55°28·31N 08°25·40E.
Trafikhavn, NW corner, ⚡ Oc (2) WRG 12s 6m W11M, R/G8M; 118°-G-124·5°-W-129°-R-131°; W bldg, R band; 55°28·22N 08°25·43E.
N mole ⚡ FR 8m 5M; 232°-135°; R bldg; 55°28'·13N 08°25'·46E.
S mole ⚡ FG 8m 4M; 045°-276°; G bldg; 55°28'·08N 08°25'·51E.

No. 22 ⚓ Fl (2) R 5s; 55°27'·62N 08°25'·50E.
Sønderhavn (industrial) W mole ⚡ FR 9m 4M; 55°27'·49N 08°26'·12E. E mole ⚡ FG 9m 4M; 55°27'·43N 08°26'·31E.
Aero ⚡ 3 x Fl 1·5s (vert, 82m apart) 251m 12M, H24; on chimney; 55°27'·27N 08°27'·32E (1200m ESE of Sønderhavn ent).

FANØ
Slunden outer ldg lts 242°, both Iso 2s 5/8m 3M; 227°-257°. Front, twr; 55°27'·20N 08°24'·53E. Rear, twr, 106m from front.
E shore, reciprocal ldg lts 062°, both FR 10/13m 3M; 047°-077°. Front, twr; 55°27'·65N 08°26'·01E. Rear, twr, 140m from front.
No. 1 ⚡ Fl (2) G l0s 5m 2M; G pile; 55°27'·45N 08°25'·28E.
No. 2 ⚡ Fl (2+1) Y 5s 5m 2M; Y pile; 55°27'·42N 08°25'·32E.
No. 3 ⚡ Fl G 3s 5m 2M; G pile; 55°27'·39N 08°25'·07E.
No. 4 ⚡ Fl R 3s 5m 2M; R pile; 55°27'·35N 08°25'·10E.
Nordby ldg lts 214°, both FR 7/9m 4M; 123·7°-303·7°. Front, W mast;55°26'·94N 08°24'·44E. Rear, Gy twr, 84m from front.-Kremer Sand ⚡ FG 5m 3M; G dolphin; 55°27'·3N 08°24'·9E.
Næs Søjord ⚡ FR 5m 3M; R pile; 55°27'·27N 08°24'·86E.
Nordby marina 55°26'·65N 08°24'·53E.

KNUDEDYB
G ⚓ 55°20'·50N 08°24'·28E.
K ⚓ 55°18'·92N 08°20'·06E.
No. 2 ⚑ 55°18'·82N 08°21'·33E.
No. 4 ⚑ 55°18'·81N 08°22'·21E.
No. 6 ⚑ 55°18'·38N 08°24'·63E.
No. 10 ⚑ 55°18'·68N 08°28'·50E.
Knoben ⚑ 55°18'·71N 08°30'·60E.

JUVRE DYB
No. 4 ⚑ 55°13'·76N 08°24'·73E.
No. 6 ⚑ 55°13'·41N 08°26'·60E.
No. 8 ⚑ 55°12'·69N 08°26'·83E.
No. 10 ⚑ 55°12'·55N 08°28'·72E.
Rejsby Stjært ⚓ 55°13'·15N 08°30'·55E.

OUTER APPROACH (Lister Tief) TO RØMØ
See also Area 15 for details of lights on Sylt.
Rode Klit Sand ⚓ Q (9) 15s, 55°11'·11N 08°04'·88E, (130°/9M to Lister Tief ⚓).
Lister Tief ⚓ Iso 8s, *Whis*; 55°05'·32N 08°16'·80E.
No. 1 ⚓ 55°05'·48N 08°18'·50E.
No. 3 ⚓ Fl G 4s; 55°05'·36E 08°20'·14E.
No. 2 ⚓ Fl (3) R 10s; 55°04'·23N 08°22'·32E.
No. 9 ⚓ Fl (2) G 9s; 55°03'·76N 08°23'·05E.
Lister Landtief No 5 ▲ 55°03'·68N 08°24'·73E.
No. 4 ⚓ FL (2) R 5s; 55°03'·84N 08°25'·29E.
G1 ⚓ Fl Y 4s; 55°03'·27N 08°28'·32E.

RØMØ DYB and HAVN
No. 1 ▲ Fl (2) G 10s; 55°03'·23N 08°30'·30E.
No. 10 ⚡ Fl (2) R 10s 5m 3M; R pole; 55°03'·50N 08°31'·10E.
No. 14 ⚡ Fl R 3s 6m 2M; R pole; 55°03'·85N 08°32'·55E.
No. 20 ⚡ Fl R 5s 5m 2M; R pole; 55°04'·79N 08°34'·13E.
No. 9 ▲ 55°04'·79N 08°34'·63E.
No. 11 ▲ 55°05'·17N 08°34'·69E.

Rømø Hbr:
S mole ⚡ Fl R 3s 7m 2M; Gy twr; 55°05'·19N 08°34'·31E.
N mole ⚡ Fl G 3s 7m 2M; Gy twr; 55°05'·23N 08°34'·30E.
Inner S mole ⚡ FR 4m 1M; 55°05'·2N 08°34'·2E.

AREA 12 *Germany (North Sea coast) – List to Emden*

SELECTED LIGHTS, BUOYS & WAYPOINTS

Positions are referenced to WGS84

DANISH BORDER TO BÜSUM

SYLT
Lister Tief ⌡ Iso 8s; *Whis;* 55°05'·33N 08°16'·79E.
List West (Ellenbogen) ⚡ Oc WRG 6s 19m W14M, R11M, G10M; 040°-R-133°-W-227°-R-266·4°-W-268°-G-285°-W-310°-W(unintens)-040°; W twr, R lantern; 55°03'·15N 08°24'·00E.
List Hafen, S mole ⚡ FR 5m 4M; 218°-353°; R mast; 55°01'·01N 08°26'·51E.
Hörnum ☆ Fl (2) 9s 48m **20M**; 54°45'·23N 08°17'·47E.
Vortrapptief ⌡ Iso 4s; 54°34'·88N 08°12'·97E, toward Hörnum.
S mole ⚡ FR 7m 4M; 54°45'·57N 08°17'·97E.

AMRUM ISLAND
Rütergat ⌡ Iso 8s; 54°30'·08N 08°12'·32E.
Amrum ☆ Fl 7·5s 63m **23M**; R twr, W bands; 54°37'·84N 08°21'·23E.
Wriakhorn Cross ⚡ L Fl (2) WR 15s 26m W9M, R7M; 297·5°-W-319·5°-R-330°-W-005·5°-R-034°; 54°37'·62N 08°21'·22E.

FÖHR ISLAND
Nieblum Dir lt showing over Rütergat. ☆ Oc (2) WRG 10s 11m **W19M, R/G15M**; 028°-G-031°-W-032·5°-R-035·5°; R twr, W band; 54°41'·10N 08°29'·20E.
Ohlörn ⚡ Oc (4) WR 15s 10m 13/10M, 208°-W-237·5°-R-298°- W-353°- R-080°; R twr, Gy lantern; 54°40'·85N 08°34'·00E (SE Föhr).
Wyk Hbr outer ent, FR 54°41'·55N 08°34'·69E; and FG.

DAGEBÜLL
Dagebüll Iso WRG 8s 23m **W18M, R/G15M**; 042°-G-043°-W-044·5°- R-047°; 54°43'·82N 08°41'·43E. FW lts on ent moles.

LANGENESS ISLAND
Nordmarsch ⚡ L Fl (3) WR 20s 13m W14M, R11M; 268°-W-279°-R-306°-W-045°-R-070°-W-218°; dark brown twr; 54°37'·58N 08°31'·85E.

SCHLÜTTSIEL
No. 2/SA 26 ⌡ 54°36'·84N 08°38'·95E. Hbr ent ▲ 54°40'·89N 08°45'·10E.

RIVER HEVER
Hever ⌡ Iso 4s; *Whis;* 54°20'·41N 08°18'·82E.
Westerheversand ☆ Oc (3) WRG 15s 41m **W21M, R17M, G16M**; 012·2°-W-069°-G-079·5°-W-080·5° (ldg sector for Hever)-R-107°-W-233°-R-248°; R twr, W bands; 54°22'·37N 08°38'·36E.
Norderhever No. 1 ⌡ Fl (2+1) R 15s; 54°22'·46N 08°30'·83E.

PELLWORM ISLAND
Pellworm ☆ Oc WRG 5s 38m **20M, R 16M, G 15M**; 037·5°-G-040°-W-042·5°-R-045°; R twr, W band; 54°29'·78N 08°39'·98E.

NORDSTRAND
Suderhafen, S mole ⌡ 54°28'·07N 08°55'·62E.

HUSUM
⌡ Fl G 4s, 54°28'·80N 08°58'·60E, start of access chan. Ldg lts 090°, both Iso G 8s 7/9m 3M.

RIVER EIDER
Eider ⌡ Iso 4s; 54°15'·71N 08°28'·00E.
St Peter ☆ L Fl (2) WR 15s 23m **W15M**, R12M; 271°-R-280·5°-W-035°-R-055°-W-068°-R-091°-W-120°; 54°17'·24N 08°39'·10E.
Eiderdamm lock, N mole, W end ⚡ Oc (2) R 12s 8m 5M; W twr.

BÜSUM
Süderpiep ⌡ Iso 8s; *Whis;* 54°05'·82N 08°25'·70E.
Büsum ☆ Iso WR 6s 22m **W19M**, R12M; 248°-W-317°-R-024°-W-148°; 54°07'·60N 08°51'·48E.
E mole ⚡ Oc (3) G 12s 10m 4M; vis 260°-168°; G twr; 54°07'·19N 08°51'·65E.

GERMAN BIGHT TO RIVER ELBE

GB Light V ⌫ Iso 8s 12m **17M**; R hull marked G-B; *Horn Mo (R) 30s;* **Racon T, 8M;** 54°10'·80N 07°27'·60E.

HELGOLAND
Helgoland ☆ Fl 5s 82m **28M**; brown ☐ twr, B lantern, W balcony; 54°10'·91N 07°52'·93E.
Vorhafen. Ostmole, S elbow ⚡ Oc WG 6s 5m W6M, G3M; 203°-W-250°-G-109°; G post; fog det lt; 54°10'·31N 07°53'·94E.

RIVER ELBE (LOWER)

APPROACHES
Nordergründe N ⌡ VQ; 53°57'·06N 08°00'·12E.
Elbe ⌡ Iso 10s; **Racon T, 8M;** 53°59'·95N 08°06'·49E.
No.1 ⌡ QG; 53°59'·21N 08°13'·20E.
No.25 ⌡ QG; 53°56'·62N 08°38'·25E.
Neuwerk ☆, S side, L Fl (3) WRG 20s 38m **W16M**, R12M, G11M; 165·3°-G-215·3°-W-238·8°-R-321°; 343°-R-100°; 53°54'·92N 08°29'·73E.

CUXHAVEN
No. 31 ⌡ Fl G 4s; 53°53'·93N 08°41'·21E.
Yacht hbr ent, F WR and F WG lts; 53°52'·43N 08°42'·49E.

OTTERNDORF
No. 43 ⌡ Oc (2) G 9s; 53°50'·23N 08°52'·24E.
Otterndorf 3 ▲ Fl (3) G 12s; 53°50'·22N 08°53'·94E.

BRUNSBÜTTEL
No. 57a ⌡ Fl G 4s; 53°52'·62N 09°07'·93E, 030°/ 8 cables to lock.
Alter Vorhafen ent, mole 1 ⚡ F WG 14m W10M, G6M; 266·3°-W-273·9°-G-088·8°, floodlit; 53°53'·27N 09°08'·59E.

RIVER ELBE (BRUNSBÜTTEL TO HAMBURG)
Some of the more accessible yacht hbrs are listed below, but not the many ldg lts and dir lts which define the main river fairway.

FREIBURG
Reede 1 ⌫ Oc (2) Y 9s; 53°50'·41N 09°19'·45E, off ent.

STÖRLOCH
Stör ldg lts 093·8°, both Fl 3s 7/12m 6M; synch. Front, 53°49'·29N 09°23'·91E; △ on R ○ twr. Rear, 200m east; ▽ on white mast.

51

GLÜCKSTADT

Glückstadt ldg lts 131·8°, both Iso 8s 15/30m **19/21M**; intens on ldg line; W twrs, R bands. **Front** ☆, 53°48'·31N 09°24'·24E. **Rear** ☆, 0·68M from front.

Rhinplatte Nord ⚡ Oc WRG 6s 11m W6M, R4M, G3M; 122°-G-144°-W-150°-R-177°- W-122°; 53°48'·09N 09°23'·36E.

N mole ⚡ Dir Oc WRG 6s 9m W9M R7M, G6M; 330°-R-343°-W-346°-G-008°; 123°-G-145°-W-150°-R-170°; W twr with gallery; 53°47'·12N 09°24'·53E.

N pier hd ⚡ FR 5m 5M; 53°47'·10N 09°24'·50E. (S mole hd, FG).

KRUCKAU

S mole Oc WRG 6s 8m, W6M, R4M, G3M; 116·3°-W-120·7° (ldg sector)-R-225°-G-315°-R-331·9°-W-335·4° (ldg sector)-335·4°-G-116·3°; B dolphin; 53°42'·85N 09°30'·72E.

PINNAU

Ldg lts 112·7°, both Iso 4s8/13m 6M. Front, 53°40'·08N 09°34'·02E.

STADE

Stadersand ⚡ Iso 8s 20m 14M; 53°37'·69N 09°31'·64E (at ent).

HAMBURG YACHT HARBOUR, WEDEL

Both entrances show FR & FG, May to Oct; 53°34'·25N 09°40'·77E.

CITY SPORTHAFEN

Brandenburger Hafen Ent ⚡ Iso Or 2s; 53°32'·52N 09°58'·81E.

WESER ESTUARY

ALTE WESER

Schlüsseltonne ⚓ Iso 8s; 53°56'·25N 07°54'·76E.

Alte Weser ☆ F WRG 33m **W23M, R19M, G18M**; 288°-W-352°-R-003°-W-017° (ldg sector for Alte Weser)- G-045°-W-074°-G-118°- W-123° (ldg sector for Alte Weser)- R-140°-G-175°-W-183°-R-196°-W-238°; R ◯ twr, 2 W bands, B base; Fog det lt; *Horn Mo (AL) 60s;* 53°51'·79N 08°07'·65E.

16/A15 ⬡ Fl (2+1) R 15s; 53°49'·66N 08°06'·44E (junction with Neuwe Weser).

NEUE WESER

Tegeler Plate, N end ☆ Oc (3) WRG 12s 21m **W21M, R17M, G16M**; 329°-W-340°-R-014°-W-100°-G-116°- W-119° (ldg sector for Neue Weser)-R-123°-G-144°-W-147° (ldg sector for Alte Weser)-R-264°; R ◯ twr, gallery, W lantern, R roof; Fog det lt; 53°47'·87N 08°11'·45E.

BREMERHAVEN

No. 61 ⚓ QG; 53°32'·26N 08°33'·93E (Km 66·0).

Vorhafen N pier ⚡ FR 15m 5M; 245°-166°; F in fog; 53°32'·15N 08°34'·50E.

RIVER JADE

1b/Jade 1: Oc G 4s; 53°52'·40N 07°44'·00E.

Mellumplate ☆ FW 28m **24M**; 116·1°-116·4° (ldg sector for outer part of Wangerooger Fahrwasser); R ☐ twr, W band; 53°46'·28N 08°05'·51E.

No.19 ⚓ QG; 53°47'·10N 08°01'·83E.

No. 31/P-Reede/W Siel 1 ⚓ Oc (3) G 12s; 53°41'·59N 08°04'·51E.

HOOKSIEL

No. 37/Hooksiel 1 ⚓ IQ G 13s; 53°39'·37N 08°06'·58E.

Vorhafen ent ⚡ L Fl R 6s 9m 3M; 53°38'·63N 08°05'·25E.

WILHELMSHAVEN

Fluthafen N mole ⚡ F WG 9m,W6M, G3M; 216°-W-280°-G-010°-W-020°-G-130°; G twr; 53°30'·86N 08°09'·32E.

EAST FRISIAN ISLANDS

NORTH EDGE OF INSHORE TRAFFIC ZONE

TG9/Weser 2 ⚓ Fl (2+1) G 15s; 53°55'·0N 07°44'·60E.

TG13 ⚓ Oc (3) G 12s; 53°50'·85N 07°15'·43E.

TG7 ⚓ Fl (2) G 9s; 53°47'·24N 06°49'·65E.

TG1 ⚓ Oc (3) G 12s; 53°44'·90N 06°33'·20E.

WANGEROOGE

Harle ⚓ Iso 8s; 53°49'·26N 07°48'·92E.

Wangerooge, W end ☆ Fl R 5s 60m **23M**; R ◯ twr, 2 W bands; 53°47'·40N 07°51'·37E.

Dir lt 145·5°, Dir WRG 24m W22M G18M R17M; 119·4°-G-138·8°-W-152·2°-R-159·9°.

Buhne H ⚓ VQ (9) 10s; 53°46'·86N 07°49'·65E.

D4⚓ ; 53°46'·25N 07°51'·89E, off hbr ent.

SPIEKEROOG

Otzumer Balje ⚓ Iso 4s; 53°47'·98N 07°37'·12E (often moved).

Spiekeroog ⚡ FR 6m 4M; 197°-114°; R mast; 53°45'·0N 07°41'·3E.

LANGEOOG

Accumer Ee ⚓ Iso 8s; 53°46·92N 07°25·92E (frequently moved).

W mole head ⚡ Oc WRG 6s 8m W7M, R5M, G4M; 064°-G-070°-W-074°-R-330°-G-335°-R-064°; R basket on R mast; *Horn Mo (L) 30s* (0730-1800LT); 53°43'·42N 07°30'·13E.

BALTRUM

Groyne hd ⚡ Oc WRG 6s 6m; W6M, R4M, G3M; 074·5°-G-090°-W-095°-R-074·5°; 53°43'·3N 07°21'·7E.

		1	2	3	4	5	6	7	8	9	10	11	12	13	14	15	16	17	18
1	Esbjerg	**1**																	
2	H rnum Lt (Sylt)	47	**2**																
3	Husum	95	48	**3**															
4	Hamburg	163	112	113	**4**														
5	Kiel/Holtenau	179	128	129	90	**5**													
6	Brunsb ttel	126	75	76	37	53	**6**												
7	Cuxhaven	110	63	66	54	70	17	**7**											
8	Bremerhaven	127	80	82	81	131	78	58	**8**										
9	Wilhelmshaven	125	78	82	110	123	70	56	45	**9**									
10	Hooksiel	116	69	73	101	117	64	47	36	9	**10**								
11	Helgoland	83	38	47	88	104	51	38	44	43	35	**11**							
12	Wangerooge	109	60	52	61	108	55	42	38	27	19	24	**12**						
13	Langeoog	119	72	77	114	130	77	60	47	43	34	35	21	**13**					
14	Norderney	123	77	85	81	137	84	69	62	53	44	44	29	18	**14**				
15	Emden	165	129	137	174	190	137	120	115	106	97	85	80	63	47	**15**			
16	Borkum	133	97	105	104	163	110	95	88	80	71	67	55	46	31	32	**16**		
17	Delfzijl	155	119	127	159	173	120	105	100	89	83	81	65	56	41	10	22	**17**	
18	Den Helder	187	192	198	229	245	192	175	180	159	150	153	148	130	115	125	95	115	**18**

DISTANCE TABLES

Approx distances in nautical miles are by the most direct route allowing for dangers and TSS.

NORDERNEY

Norderney ☆ Fl (3) 12s 59m **23M**; unintens 067°-077° and 270°-280°; R 8-sided twr; 53°42'·54N 07°13'·79E.
Dovetief ↯ Iso 4s; 53°45'·47N 07°12'·70E.
Schluchter ↯Iso 8s; 53°44'·48N 07°02'·27E.
W mole head ⚡ Oc (2) R 9s 13m 4M; 53°41'·9N 07°09'·9E.

JUIST

Juist-N ↯ VQ; 53°43'·82N 06°55'·42E.
Training wall, S end ⚡ Oc (2) R 9s 7m 3M; 53°39'·65N 06°59'·81E.

MAINLAND HARBOURS: RIVER JADE TO R EMS

HARLESIEL

Carolinensieler Balje, Leitdamm ⚡ L Fl 8s 7m 6M; G mast; 53°44'·13N 07°50'·10E.
Ldg lts 138°, both Iso 6s 12/18m 9M, intens on ldg line; Front 53°40'·70N 07°34'·50E. Rear 167m from front.
N mole head ⚡ Iso R 4s 6m 7M; 53°42'·58N 07°48'·64E.

NEUHARLINGERSIEL

Training wall head ⚡ Oc 6s 6m 5M; 53°43'·22N 07°42'·30E.

BENSERSIEL

E training wall head ⚡ Oc WRG 6s 6m W5M, R3M, G2M; 110°-G-119°-W-121°-R-110°; R post & platform; 53°41'·80N 07°32'·84E.

DORNUMER-ACCUMERSIEL

W bkwtr head, approx 53°41'·04N 07°29'·30E.

NESSMERSIEL

N mole head ⚡ Oc 4s 6m 5M; G mast; 53°41'·9N 07°21'·7E.

NORDDEICH

W trng wall head ⚡ FG 8m 4M, 021°-327°; G framework twr; 53°38'·62N 07°09'·0E.

GREETSIEL

Meßstation lt bcn, Fl Y 4s 15m 3M; 53°32'·94N 07°02'·18E.

RIVER EMS

APPROACHES

GW/EMS ⬚ Iso 8s 12m **17M**; *Horn Mo (R) 30s (H24)*; *Racon T, 8M;* 54°09'·96N 06°20'·72E.
Borkumriff ↯ Oc 4s; *Racon T, 8M;* 53°47'·44N 06°22'·05E.
Osterems ↯ Iso 4s; 53°41'·91N 06°36'·17E.
Riffgat ↯ Iso 8s; 53°38'·96N 06°27'·10E.
Westerems ↯ Iso 4s; *Racon T, 8M;* 53°36'·93N 06°19'·39E.
H1 ↯ 53°34'·91N 06°17'·97E.

BORKUM

Borkum Grosser ☆ Fl (2) 12s 63m **24M**; brown ○ twr; 53°35'·32N 06°39'·64E. Same twr, ⚡ F WRG 46m **W19M**, **R/G15M;** 107·4°-G-109°-W-111·2°- R-112·6°.
Fischerbalje ⚡ Oc (2) 16s 15m 3M; 260°-W-123°. Fog det lt; R/W ○ twr on tripod; 53°33'·18N 06°42'·90E.
Schutzhafen, E mole hd ⚡ FG10m 4M; 53°33'·48N 06°45'·02E. W mole hd, FR 8m 4M.

RIVER EMS (LOWER)

No. 27 ↯ Fl G 4s; 53°30'·24N 06°47'·52E.
No. 35 ↯ Fl G 4s; 53°27'·03N 06°52'·80E.
No. 37 ↯ QG; 53°26'·01N 06°54'·85E.
No. 41 ↯ Fl (2) G 9s; 53°24'·25N 06°56'·68E.
No. 49 ↯ Oc (2) G 9s; 53°19'·95N 06°59'·71E.

KNOCK

Knock ⚡ F WRG 28m W12M,R9M, G8M; 270°-W-299°-R-008·3°-G-023°-W-026·8°-R-039°-W-073°-R-119°-W-154°; fog det lt; Gy twr, white conical radar antenna; 53°20'·32N 07°01'·40E.

EMDEN

No. 59 ↯ Oc (2) G 9s; 53°19'·41N 07°03'·86E.
No. 65 ↯ Fl (2) G 9s; 53°19'·82N 07°06'·56E.
Outer hbr, W pier ⚡ FR 10m 4M; R 8-sided twr; *Horn Mo (ED) 30s;* 53°20'·06N 07°10'·49E.
E pier ⚡ FG 7m 5M; G mast on pedestal; 53°20'·05N 07°10'·84E.

AREA 13 *Netherlands & Belgium – Delfzijl to Nieuwpoort*

SELECTED LIGHTS, BUOYS & WAYPOINTS

Positions are referenced to WGS84

TSS OFF NORTHERN NETHERLANDS

TERSCHELLING-GERMAN BIGHT TSS
TG1/Ems ↯ IQ G 13s; 53°43'·33N 06°22'·24E.
TE5 ↯ Fl (3) G 10s; 53°37'·79N 05°53'·69E.
TE1 ↯ Fl (3) G 10s; 53°29'·58N 05°11'·31E.

OFF VLIELAND TSS
VL-CENTER ⬚ Fl 5s 12M; *Racon C, 12–15M;* 53°26'·93N 04°39'·88E. VL7 ↯ L Fl G 10s; 53°26'·40N 04°57'·60E.
VL1 ↯ Fl (2) G 10s; 53°10'·96N 04°35'·31E.

DELFZIJL TO HARLINGEN

DELFZIJL
PS3/BW26 ⚡ Fl (2+1) G 12s; 53°19'·25N 07°00'·32E.
W mole ⚡ FG; 53°19'·01N 07°00'·27E.
Ldg lts 203° both Iso 4s. Front, 53°18'·63N 07°00'·17E.

SCHIERMONNIKOOG AND LAUWERSOOG
WG (Westgat) ◌ Iso 8s; *Racon N;* 53°32'·00N 05°58'·54E.
WRG ↯ Q; 53°32'·87N 06°03'·24E.
AM ↯ VQ; 53°30'·95N 05°44'·72E.
Schiermonnikoog ☆ Fl (4) 20s 43m **28M**; dark R ○ twr. Same twr: F WR 29m **W15M**, R12M; 210°-W-221°-R-230°. 53°29'·20N 06°08'·79E.
Lauwersoog W mole ⚡ FG; *Horn (2) 30s;* 53°24'·68N 06°12'·00E.

ZEEGAT VAN AMELAND

BR ↯ Q; 53°30'·66N 05°33'·52E.
TS ↯ VQ; 53°28'·15N 05°21'·53E.
WA ⚓ 53°28'·35N 05°28'·64E. (Westgat buoys are all unlit)
Ameland, W end ☆ Fl (3) 15s 57m **30M**; 53°26'·89N 05°37'·42E.

NES

VA2-R1 ↯ VQ(6) + L Fl 10s; 53°25'·71N 05°45'·88E.
Reegeul R3 ⚡ Iso G 4s; 53°25'·80N 05°45'·93E.
R7 ⚡ QG; 53°25'·91N 05°46'·21E.

HET VLIE (ZEEGAT VAN TERSCHELLING)
ZS (Zuider Stortemelk) ⬤ Iso 4s; *Racon T*; 53°19'·58N 04°55'·77E.

ZS1 ▲ VQ G; 53°19'·22N 04°57'·58E.

ZS5 ▲ L Fl G 8s; 53°18'·53N 05°01'·10E.

ZS11-VS2 ⬥ Q (9) 15s; 53°18'·66N 05°05'·95E.

NOORD MEEP/SLENK TO WEST TERSCHELLING
WM3 ▲ Iso G 2s; 53°17'·45N 05°12'·28E.

NM 4-S 21 ⬥ VQ (3) 5s; 53°19'·02N 05°15'·47E.

SG 15-S 2 ⬥ Q (9) 15s; 53°20'·44N 05°11'·70E.

Brandaris Twr ☆ Fl 5s 54m **29M**; Y ☐ twr partly obscured by dunes; 53°21'·62N 05°12'·86E.

W Terschelling W hbr mole ⚓ FR 5m 5M; R post, W bands; *Horn 15s*; 53°21'·26N 05°13'·09E. E pier hd ⚓ FG 4m 4M.

VLIELAND
VS3 (Vliesloot) ▲ VQ G; 53°18'·27N 05°06'·25E.

VS14 ⬤ Iso R 4s; 53°17'·58N 05°05'62E.

VS16-VB1 ⬥ Fl (2+1) R 10s; 53°17'·62N 05°05'·19E.

E/W mole hds ⚓ FG and ⚓ FR; 53°17'·68N 05°05'·51E.

Ldg lts 282° ⚓ Iso 4s 10/16m 1M, synch; 53°17'·75N 05°04'·47W (100m apart); mainly for the ferry terminal at E Vlieland.

E Vlieland (Vuurduin) ☆ Iso 4s 54m **20M**; 53°17'·75N 05°03'·49E.

APPROACHES TO HARLINGEN (selected marks):
VLIESTROOM buoys are frequently moved.

VL1 ▲ QG; 53°18'·99N 05°08'·82E. VL 2 ⬤ QR; 53°19'·40N 05°09'·19E.

VL 11 ▲ Iso G 8s; 53°16'·42N 05°09'·70E.

BLAUWE SLENK
BS1-IN2 ⬥ VQ (3) 5s; 53°15'·41N 05°09'·41E.

BS13 ▲ QG; 53°13'·31N 05°17'·13E. BS19 ▲ VQ G; 53°11'·90N 05°18'·28E.

BS23 ▲ L Fl G 8s; 53°11'·42N 05°19'·60E.

POLLENDAM
Ldg lts 112°, both Iso 6s 8/19m 13M (H24); B masts, W bands. Front, 53°10'·52N 05°24'·19E. Use only between P2 and P6. P2 ⬦; 53°11'·47N 05°20'·38E on the training wall. P4, Iso R 8s; P6, Iso R 4s; P8, Iso R 8s; and P10, Iso R 2s. Yachts should keep outboard of P1 thru 7 SHM buoys. P1 ▲ Iso G 2s; 53°11'·39N 05°20'·32E. P7 ▲ VQ G; 53°10'·68N 05°23'·45E.

HARLINGEN
S mole hd ⚓ FG 9m; *Horn (3) 30s*; 53°10'·56N 05°24'·18E. N mole hd ⚓ FR 9m 4M; R/W pedestal; 53°10'·59N 05°24'·32E.

TEXEL AND THE WADDENZEE

APPROACHES TO EIERLANDSCHE GAT
Eierland ☆ Fl (2) 10s 52m **29M**; R ◯ twr; 53°10'·93N 04°51'·31E.

TX ⬥ Q(9) 15s; 53°06'·81N 04°41'·19E.

MOLENGAT (from the N)
MG-A, ⬦ (starboard marker); 53°02'·54N 04°41'·88E.

MG-B, Y buoy; 53°02'·00N 04°42'·11E

MG-D, Y buoy; 53°00'·90N 04°42'·04E;

MG-G, Y buoy; 52°59'·30N 04°42'·56E;

MG-H, ⬦ (starboard marker); 52°58'·91N 04°43'·10E.

OUDESCHILD
T12 ⬤ Iso R 8s; 53°02'·23N 04°51'·52E.

Oudeschild Dir ⚓ Oc 6s; intens 291°; 53°02'·40N 04°50'·94E; leads 291° into hbr between N mole head FG 6m; and S mole head ⚓ FR 6m; 53°02'·33N 04°51'·17E.

APPROACHES TO KORNWERDERZAND SEALOCK

DOOVE BALG (From Texelstroom eastward)
T23 ▲ VQ G; 53°03'·60N 04°55'·85E, 066°/3M from Oudeschild.

T29 ▲ 53°03'·25N 05°00'·05E.

D1 ⬤ Iso G 4s; 53°02'·18N 05°03'·42E.

D21 ⬤ Iso G 8s; 53°03'·55N 05°15'·71E.

BO2-WG1 ⬥ Q (6) + L Fl 10s; 53°05'·00N 05°17'·91E.

KORNWERDERZAND SEALOCK
W mole ⚓ FG 9m 7M; *Horn Mo(N) 30s*; 53°04'·78N 05°20'·03E.

E mole ⚓ FR 9m 7M; 53°04'·70N 05°20'·08E.

W mole elbow ⚓ Iso G 6s 6m 7M; 53°04'·61N 05°19'·90E.

APPROACHES TO DEN OEVER SEALOCK

MALZWIN and VISJAGERSGAATJE CHANS TO DEN OEVER
MH4-M1 ⬥ VQ (9) 10s; 52°58'·14N 04°47'·49E, close N Den Helder.

M15 ▲ QG; 52°59'·39N 04°55'·48E (hence use DYC 1811.3).

VG1-W2 ▲ Fl (2+1) G 10s; 52°59'·00N 04°56'·85E.

O9 ▲ Iso G 8s; 52°56'·63N 05°02'·38E.

DEN OEVER SEALOCK
Ldg lts 131°, both Oc 10s 6m 7M; 127°-137°. Front, 52°56'·32N 05°02'·98E. Rear, 280m from front.

E end of swing bridge, ⚓ Iso WRG 5s 14m 10/7M; 226°-G-231°-W-235°-R-290°-G-327°-W-335°-R-345°; 52°56'·12N 05°02'·52E.

ZEEGAT VAN TEXEL AND DEN HELDER

OFFSHORE MARKS W and SW OF DEN HELDER
NH (Noorderhaaks) ⬥ VQ; 53°00'·24N 04°35'·37E.

MR ⬥ Q (9) 15s; 52°56'·77N 04°33'·82E.

ZH (Zuiderhaaks) ⬥ VQ (6) + L Fl 10s; 52°54'·65N 04°34'·72E.

Vinca G wreck ⬥ Q (9) 15s; *Racon D*; 52°45'·93N 04°12'·31E.

SCHULPENGAT (from the SSW)
Schulpengat Dir ☆ 026·5°, Dir WRG, Al WR, Al WG, **W22M R/G18M**, church spire; 025.1°-FG-025.6°-AlWG-026.3°-FW-026.7°-Al WR-027.4°-F R-027.9°; shown H24.

Schilbolsnol ☆ F WRG 27m **W15M**, R12M, G11M; 338°-W-002°-G-035°-W(ldg sector for Schulpengat)-038°-R-051°-W-068°; post; 53°00'·50N 04°45'·70E (on Texel).

SG ⬥ Mo (A) 8s; *Racon Z*; 52°52'·90N 04°37'·90E.

S1 ▲ Iso G 4s; 52°53'·53N 04°38'·82E.

S7 ▲ QG; 52°56'·25N 04°40'·92E. S6A ⬤ QR; 52°56'·52N 04°40'·51E.

S10 ⬤ Iso R 8s; 52°57'·59N 04°41'·57E. S14-MG17 ⬥, see Molengat.

S11 ▲ Iso G 8s; 52°57'·55N 04°43'·25E.

Huisduinen ⚓ F WR 26m W14M, R11M; 070°-W-113°-R-158°-W-208°; ☐ twr; 52°57'·14N 04°43'·30E (abeam S10 PHM buoy).

Kijkduin ☆ Fl (4) 20s 56m **30M**; vis 360°, except where obsc'd by dunes on Texel; brown twr; 52°57'·33N 04°43'·58E (mainland).

MARSDIEP and DEN HELDER

T1 ▲ Fl (3) G 10s; 52°57'·99N 04°44'·62E.
T3 ▲ Iso G 8s; 52°58'·07N 04°46'·42E.
Den Helder ldg lts 191°, both Oc G 5s 16/25m 3M, synch. Front, vis 183·5°-198·5°; B ▽ on bldg; 52°57'·37N 04°47'·08E.
Marinehaven, W bkwtr head ⚓ QG 11m 8M; *Horn 20s;* 52°57'·95N 04°47'·07E (Harssens Island).
W side, ⚓ Fl G 5s 9m 4M (H24); 180°-067°; 52°57'·78N 04°47'·08E.
Yacht hbr (KMYC), ent ⚓ FR & FG; 165m SW of ⚓ Fl G 5s, above.
E side, MH6 ⚓ Iso R 4s; 52°57'·99N 04°47'·41E.
Ent E side, ⚓ QR 9m 4M (H24); 52°57'·77N 04°47'·37E.

DEN HELDER TO AMSTERDAM

Zanddijk Grote Kaap ⚓ Oc WRG 10s 30m W11M, R8M, G8M; 041°-G-088°-W-094°-R-131°; brown twr; 52°52'·86N 04°42'·88E.
Petten ⚓ VQ (9) 10s; 52°47'·33N 04°36'·78E (Power stn outfall).
Egmond-aan-Zee ☆ Iso WR 10s 36m **W18M**, R14M; 010°-W-175°-R-188°; W ◯ twr; 52°36'·99N 04°37'·16E.
Wind farm approx 6·4M W of Egmond-aan-Zee is marked by: a Meteomast, Mo (U) 15s 11m 10M; 52°36'·36N 04°23'·41E; and by L Fl Y 15s; Horn Mo (U) 30s on 5 of the peripheral wind turbines.

IJMUIDEN

Baloeran ⚓ Q (9) 15s; 52°29'·21N 04°32'·00E.
IJmuiden ⚓ Mo (A) 8s; *Racon Y, 10M;* 52°28'·45N 04°23'·92E.
Ldg lts 100·5° (FW 5M by day; 090·5°-110·5°). **Front** ☆ F WR 30m **W16M**, R13M; 050°-W-122°-R-145°-W-160°; (Tidal and traffic sigs); dark R ◯ twrs; 52°27'·70N 04°34'·47E. **Rear** ☆ Fl 5s 52m **29M**; 019°-199° (FW 5M by day; 090·5°-110·5°); 560m from front.
S bkwtr hd ⚓ FG 14m 10M (in fog Fl 3s); *Horn (2) 30s;* W twr, G bands; 52°27'·82N 04°31'·93E.
N bkwtr hd ⚓ FR 15m 10M; 52°28'·05N 04°32'·55E.
IJM 1 ▲ Iso G 4s; 52°27'·75N 04°33'·59E.
S outer chan ⚓ Iso G 6s, 52°27'·75N 04°33'·81E. ⚓ Iso R 6s, 52°27'·84N 04°34'·39E (Forteiland). Kleine Sluis 52°27'·84N 04°35'·43E.

AMSTERDAM

IJ8 ⚓ Iso R 8s (for Sixhaven marina); 52°22'·86N 04°54'·37E.
Oranjesluizen, N lock 52°22'·93N 04°57'·60E (for IJsselmeer).

AMSTERDAM TO ROTTERDAM

Noordwijk-aan-Zee ☆ Oc (3) 20s 32m **18M**; W ☐ twr; 52°14'·88N 04°26'·02E.

SCHEVENINGEN

Lighthouse ☆ Fl (2) 10s 48m **29M**; 014°-244°; brown twr; 52°06'·23N 04°16'·13E, 5ca E of hbr ent.
Ldg lts 156°, both Iso 4s 18/22m 14M, H24; synch; Gy masts. Front 52°05'·87N 04°15'·54E; rear 489m from front. Intens at night.

SCH ⚓ Iso 4s; 52°07'·76N 04°14'·12E.
KNS ⚓ Q (9)15s; 52°06'·41N 04°15'·32E.
W mole ⚓ FG 12m 9M; G twr, W bands; 52°06'·23N 04°15'·16E.
E mole ⚓, FR 12m 9M; R twr, W bands; 52°06'·24N 04°15'·37E.
Inner ldg lts 131°: both Iso G 4s synch; Gy posts. Front 52°05'·81N 04°15'·89E. Rear, 34m from front.

NOORD HINDER N & S TSS and JUNCTION

NHR-N ⚓ L Fl 8s; *Racon K, 10M;* 52°10'·91N 03°04'·76E.
Noord Hinder ⚓ Fl (2) 10s; *Horn (2) 30s; Racon T, 12-15M;* 52°00'·10N 02° 51'·11E.
NHR-S ⚓ Fl Y 10s; 51°51'·37N 02°28'·72E.
NHR-SE ▲ Fl G 5s; 51°45'·42N 02°39'·96E.
Birkenfels ⚓ Q (9) 15s; 51°38'·98N 02°31'·75E.
Twin ⚓ Fl (3) Y 9s; 51°32'·00N 02°22'·59E.
Garden City ⚓ Q (9) 15s; 51°29'·20N 02°17'·54E.

APPROACHES TO HOEK VAN HOLLAND

Europlatform ⚓ Mo (U) 15s; W structure, R bands; helicopter platform; *Horn Mo(U) 30s;* 51°59'·89N 03°16'·46E.
Goeree ☆ Fl (4) 20s 32m **28M**; R/W chequered twr on platform; helicopter platform; *Horn (4) 30s; Racon T, 12-15M;* 51°55'·42N 03°40'·03E.
Maasvlakte ☆ Fl (5) 20s 67m **28M**; H24; 340°-267°; W twr, B bands; 51°58'·20N 04°00'·84E, 1·5M SSW of Maas ent.
Maas Center ⚓ Iso 4s; *Racon M, 10M;* 52°00'·92N 03°48'·79E.
MO ⚓ Mo (A) 8s; 52°01'·10N 03°58'·19E.
MN3 ▲ Fl (3) G 10s; 52°07'·04N 04°00'·00E.
MN1 ▲ Fl G 5s; 52°02'·23N 04°01'·91E.

HOEK VAN HOLLAND

Maasmond ldg lts 112° (for deep draught vessels): both Iso 4s 30/46m **21M**; 101°-123°, synch; W twr, B bands. **Front**, 51°58'·88N 04°04'·88E (NW end of Splitsingsdam). **Rear**, 0·6M from front.
Indusbank N ⚓ VQ; 52°02'·89N 04°03'·57E.
MVN ⚓ VQ; 51°59'·61N 04°00'·23E.
MV ⚓ Q (9) 15s; 51°58'·40N 03°56'·58E.
Maas 1 ▲ L Fl G 5s; 51°59'·35N 04°01'·68E.
Nieuwe Waterweg ldg lts 107°: both Iso R 6s 29/43m **18M**; 099.5°-114.5°; R twr, W bands. Front, 51°58'·55N 04°07'·52E. Rear, 450m from front.
Noorderdam Head ⚓ FR 25m 10M (In fog Al Fl WR 6s; 278°-255°); R twr, W bands; 51°59'·67N 04°02'·80E.
Nieuwe Zuiderdam ⚓ FG 25m 10M, 330°-307°; (In fog Al Fl WG 6s); G twr, W bands; 51°59'·14N 04°02'·49E.

ROTTERDAM

Maassluis ⚓ FG 6m; 51°54'·94N 04°14'·81E; and FR.
Vlaardingen ⚓ FG; 51°53'·99N 04°20'·95E; and FR.
Spuihaven, W ent ⚓ FR; 51°53'·98N 04°23'·97E.
Veerhaven, E ent ⚓ FG; 51°54'·42N 04°28'·75E; and FR.
City marina ent, 51°54'·64N 04°29'·76E.

APPROACHES TO HARINGVLIET

Buitenbank , Iso 4s; 51°51'·16N 03°25'·71E.
Hinder ⚓ Q (9) 15s; 51°54'·55N 03°55'·42E.
SH ⚓ VQ (9) 10s; 51°49'·49N 03°45'·79E.

Westhoofd ☆ Fl (3) 15s 55m **30M**; R ☐ tr; 51°48'·79N 03°51'·85E.

Ooster ⚓ Q (9) 15s; 51°47'·90N 03°41'·27E.

SLIJKGAT

SG ⚓ Iso 4s; 51°51'·95N 03°51'·42E.

SG 2 ⚓ Iso R 4s; 51°51'·71N 03°53'·45E.

SG 5 ⚓ Iso G 4s; 51°50'·00N 03°55'·56E.

SG 11 ⚓ Iso G 4s; 51°50'·81N 03°58'·52E.

P1 ⚓ Iso G 4s; 51°51'·30N 04°01'·12E.

P3 ⚓ Iso G 8s; 51°51'·12N 04°01'·45E.

P9 ⚓ Iso G 8s; 51°49'·98N 04°02'·15E.

STELLENDAM

N mole ⚓ FG; *Horn (2) 15s;* 51°49'·88N 04°02'·03E.

Buitenhaven ⚓ Oc 6s; 51°49'·73N 04°01'·75E.

APPROACHES TO OOSTERSCHELDE

OUTER APPROACHES

Schouwenbank ⚓ Mo (A) 8s; *Racon O, 10M;* 51°44'·94N 03°14'·32E.

Middelbank ⚓ Iso 8s; 51°40'·86N 03°18'·20E.

MW ⚓ Q (9) 15s; 51°44'·55N 03°24'·04E (Schouwendiep).

MD 3 ⚓ Fl G 5s; 51°42'·70N 03°26'·98E.

SW Thornton ⚓ Iso 8s; 51°30'·98N 02°50'·90E.

Rabsbank ⚓ Iso 4s; 51°38'·25N 03°09'·93E.

Westpit ⚓ Iso 8s; 51°33'·65N 03°09'·92E.

ZSB ⚓ VQ (9) 10s; 51°36'·57N 03°15'·62E.

OG1 ⚓ QG; 51°36'·14N 03°20'·08E.

WESTGAT, OUDE ROOMPOT and ROOMPOTSLUIS

West Schouwen ☆ Fl (2+1)15s 57m **30M**; Gy twr, R diagonals on upper part; 51°42'·52N 03°41'·50E, 5·8M N of Roompotsluis.

OG-WG ⚓ VQ (9) 10s; 51°37'·18N 03°23'·82E.

WG1 ⚓ Iso G 8s; 51°38'·00N 03°26'·24E.

WG4 ⚓ L Fl R 8s; 51°38'·62N 03°28'·78E.

WG7 ⚓ Iso G 4s 51°39'·40N 03°32'·67E.

WG-GB (Geul van de Banjaard) ⚓ 51°39'·72N 03°32'·69E.

OR1 ⚓ 51°39'·15N 03°33'·59E.

OR5 ⚓ Iso G 8s; 51°38'·71N 03°35'·53E.

OR11 ⚓ Iso G 4s; 51°36'·98N 03°38'·40E.

OR12 ⚓ Iso R 4s; 51°37'·27N 03°39'·25E.

OR-R ⚓ VQ (3) 5s; 51°36'·41N 03°38'·96E.

Roompotsluis ldg lts 073·5°, both Oc G 5s; synch. Front, 51°37'·33N 03°40'·75E. Rear, 280m from front.
N bkwtr ⚓ FR 7m; 51°37'·31N 03°40'·09E.

WESTKAPELLE TO VLISSINGEN

OOSTGAT

Ldg lts 149·5°: Front, Noorderhoofd Oc WRG 10s 20m; W13M, R/G10M; 353°-R-008°-G-029°-W-169°; R ○ twr, W band; 51°32'·40N 03°26'·21E, 0·73M from rear (Westkapelle).

Westkapelle ☆, rear, Fl 3s 50m **28M**; obsc'd by land on certain brgs; ☐ twr, R top; 51°31'·75N 03°26'·83E.

Kaloo ⚓ Iso 8s; 51°35'·55N 03°23'·24E. Chan is well buoyed/lit.

OG5 ⚓ Iso G 8s; 51°33'·95N 03°25'·92E.

OG-GR ⚓ VQ (3) 5s; 51°32'·74N 03°24'·71E.

Molenhoofd ⚓ Oc WRG 6s 10m; 306°-R-329°-W-349°-R-008°-G-034·5°-W-036·5°-G-144°-W-169°-R-198°; W mast R bands; 51°31'·58N 03°26'·05E.

Zoutelande FR 21m 12M; 321°-352°; R ☐ twr; 51°30'·28N 03°28'·41E.

Kaapduinen, ldg lts 130°: both Oc 5s 25/34m 13M; synch; Y ☐ twrs, R bands. Front, 115°-145°; 51°28'·47N 03°30'·99E. Rear, 107·5°-152·5°; 220m from front.

Fort de Nolle ⚓ Oc WRG 9s 11m W6M, R/G4M; 293°-R-309°-W-324·5°-G-336·5°-R-014°-G-064°-R-099·5°-W-110·5°-G-117°-R-130°; W col, R bands; 51°26'·94N 03°33'·12E.

Ldg lts 117°: Front, Leugenaar, Oc R 5s 6m 7M; intens 108°-126°; W&R pile; 51°26'·43N 03°34'·14E.

Rear, Sardijngeul Oc WRG 5s 8m W12M, R9M, G8M; synch; 245°-R-272°-G-282.5°-W-123°-R-147°; R △, W bands on R & W mast; 550m from front; 51°26'·30N 03°34'·56E.

OFFSHORE: W HINDER TSS TO SCHEUR CHAN

West Hinder ☆ Fl (4) 30s 23m 13M; *Horn Mo (U) 30s; Racon W;* 51°23'·30N 02°26'·27E.

WH Zuid ⚓ Q (6) + L Fl 15s; 51°22'·78N 02°26'·25E.

Oost-Dyck ⚓ Q; 51°21'·38N 02°31'·12E.

Bergues N ⚓ Q; 51°19'·96N 02°24'·53E.

Oost-Dyck West ⚓ Q (9) 15s; 51°17'·15N 02°26'·32E.

Oostdyck radar twr; ⚓ Mo (U) 15s 15m 12M on 4 corners; *Horn Mo (U) 30s; Racon O.* R twr, 3 W bands, with adjacent red twr/helipad; 51°16'·49N 02°26'·85E.

AN ⚓ Fl (4) R 20s; 51°23'·45N 02°36'·92E.

AZ ⚓ Fl (3) G 10s; 51°21'·15N 02°36'·92E.

KB2 ⚓ VQ; 51°21'·04N 02°42'·22E.

KB ⚓ Q; *Racon K;* 51°21'·03N 02°42'·83E.

MBN ⚓ Q; 51°20'·82N 02°46'·29E.

Akkaert-SW ⚓ Q (9) 15s; 51°22'·28N 02°46'·34E.

VG ⚓ Q ; 51°23'·38N 02°46'·21E, Vaargeul 1.

VG1 ⚓ VQ G; 51°25'·03N 02°49'·04E.

VG2 ⚓ Q (6) + L Fl R 15s; *Racon V;* 51°25'·96N 02°48'·16E.

VG3 ⚓ QG; 51°25'·05N 02°52'·92E.

VG5 ⚓ Fl G 5s; 51°24'·63N 02°57'·92E.

VG7 ⚓ Q ; 51°24'·53N 02°59'·92E.

Goote Bank ⚓ Q (3) 10s; 51°26'·95N 02°52'·72E.

A1 ⚓ Iso 8s; 51°22'·36N 02°53'·33E.

A1bis ⚓ L Fl 10s; 51°21'·68N 02°58'·02E.

WESTERSCHELDE APPROACHES

SCHEUR CHANNEL

S1 ⚓ Fl G 5s; 51°23'·14N 03°00'·12E.

S3 ⚓ Q; 51°24'·30N 03°02'·92E.

MOW 0 ⊙ Fl (5) Y 20s; *Racon S, 10M;* 51°23'·67N 03°02'·75E.

S5 ⚓ Fl G 5s; 51°23'·70N 03°06'·30E.

S7 ⚓ Fl G 5s; 51°23'·98N 03°10'·42E.

S9 ⚓ QG; 51°24'·42N 03°14'·99E.

S12 ⚓ Fl (4) R 10s; 51°24'·67N 03°18'·22E.

S-W ⚓ Q; 51°24'·13N 03°18'·22E, here Wielingen chan merges.

S14 ⚓ Fl R 5s; 51°24'·58N 03°19'·67E.

WIELINGEN CHANNEL

BVH ⚓ Q (6) + L Fl R 15s; 51°23'·15N 03°12'·04E.

MOW3 tide gauge ⚓ Fl (5) Y 20s; *Racon H, 10M;* 51°23'·38N 03°11'·92E.

W ⚓ Fl (3) G 15s; 51°23'·27N 03°14'·92E.

W1 ⚓ Fl G 5s; 51°23'·48N 03°18'·22E.

Fort Maisonneuve ⚓ VQ (9) 10s; wreck; 51°24'·20N 03°21'·50E.

W3 ⚓ Iso G 8s; 51°23'·96N 03°21'·49E.

W5 ⚓ Iso G 4s; 51°24'·31N 03°24'·50E.

W7 ⚓ Iso G 8s; 51°24'·60N 03°27'·27E.

W9 ▲ Iso G 4s; 51°24'·96N 03°30'·43E.

Nieuwe Sluis ⚲ Oc WRG 10s 26m W14M, R11M, G10M; 055°-R-089°-W-093°-G-105°-R-134°-W-136·5°-G-156·5°-W-236·5°-G-243°-W-254°-R-292°-W-055°; B 8-sided twr, W bands; 51°24'·41N 03°31'·29E.

Songa ▲ QG; 51°25'·26N 03°33'·66E.

W10 ⚬ QR; 51°25'·85N 03°33'·28E.

VLISSINGEN

Koopmanshaven, W mole root, ⚲ Iso WRG 3s 15m W12M, R10M, G9M; 253°-R-277°-W-284°-R-297°- W-306·5°-G-013°-W-024°-G-033°-W-035°-G-039°-W-055°-G-084·5°-R-092°-G-111°-W-114°; R pylon; 51°26'·37N 03°34'·52E.

Sardijngeul Oc WRG 5s; 51°26'·30N 03°34'·56E: see OOSTGAT last 3 lines. E mole head, ⚲ FG 7m; W mast; 51°26'·32N 03°34'·67E.

Buitenhaven ent, W side ⚲ FR 10m 5M; also Iso WRG 4s: W073°-324°, G324°-352°, W352°-017°, G017°-042°, W042°-056°, R056°-073°; W post, R bands; tfc sigs; 51°26'·38N 03°36'·06E.

Buitenhaven ent, E side ⚲ FG 7m 4M; 51°26'·41N 03°36'·38E.

Schone Waardin ⚲ Oc WRG 9s 10m W13M, R10M, G9M; 235°-R-271°-W-288°-G-335°-R-341°-G-026°-W-079°-R-091°; R mast, W bands; 51°26'·54N 03°37'·91E (1M E of Buitenhaven ent).

BRESKENS

ARV-VH ⚐ Q; 51°24'·71N 03°33'·89E.

VH2 (Vaarwaterlangs Hoofdplaat) ⚐ 51°24'·34N 03°33'·90E.

Yacht hbr, W mole ⚲ FG 7m; in fog FY; Gy post; 51°24'·03N 03°34'·06E. E mole ⚲ FR 6m; Gy mast; 51°23'·95N 03°34'·09E.

WESTERSCHELDE: TERNEUZEN TO PAAL

TERNEUZEN

Nieuw Neuzenpolder ldg lts 125°, both Oc 5s 6/16m 9/13M; intens 117°-133°; synch. Front, W col, B bands; 51°20'·97N 03°47'·24E. Rear, B & W twr; 365m from front.

Oost Buitenhaven E mole ⚲ FR 5M; 51°20'·56N 03°49'·19E.

Former ferry hbr (W part) & marinas (E part), W mole head ⚲ FG, Gy mast; 51°20'·57N 03°49'·64E. E mole, FR.

W mole ⚲ Oc WRG 5s 15m W9M, R7M, G6M; 090°-R-115°-W-120°-G-130°-W-245°-G-249°-W-279°-R-004°; B & W post; 51°20'·54N 03°49'·58E, close SW of ⚲ FG.

HANSWEERT

W mole ⚲ Oc WRG 10s 9m W9M, R7M, G6M; (in fog FY); 288°-R-311°-G-320°-W-332·5°-G-348·5°-W-042·5°-R-061·5°-W-078°-G-099°-W-114·5°-R-127·5°-W-288°; R twr, W bands; 51°26'·41N 04°00'·53E.

BELGIUM: ZANDVLIET TO ANTWERPEN

ZANDVLIET

Dir ⚲ 118·3°,WRG 20m W4M, R/ G3M; 116·63°-Oc G-117·17°- FG-117·58°-Alt GW-118·63°-F-118·63°-Alt RW-119·18°-FR-119·58°- Oc R-120·13°; 51°20'·61N 04°16'·47E, near Zandvliet locks.

ANTWERPEN

No 107 ▲ Iso G 8s, 51°14'·12N 04°23'·80E (Kattendijksluis for Willemdok ④).

Royerssluis, ldg lts 091°, both FR. Ent FR/FG.

No. 109 ▲ Iso G 8s; 51°13'·88N 04°23'·87E, (off Linkeroever ④).

Linkeroever marina ⚓ F WR 9m W3M, R2M; shore-W-283°- R-shore; B ⊙, R lantern; 51°13'·91N 04°23'·70E. Marina ent, FR/FG.

COASTAL MARKS

SWW ⚐ Fl (4) R 20s; 51°21'·95N 03°00'·94E; Wandelaar.

WBN ▲ QG; 51°21'·50N 03°02'·59E; Wandelaar.

Oostende Bank N ⚐ Q; 51°21'·20N 02°52'·93E.

Wenduine Bank E ⚐ QR; 51°18'·83N 03°01'·64E.

Wenduine Bank W ⚐ Q (9) 15s; 51°17'·23N 02°52'·76E.

Nautica Ena wreck ⚐ Q; 51°18'·08N 02°52'·79E.

Oostendebank E ⚐ Fl R 20s; 51°17'·35N 02°51'·91E.

Oostendebank W ⚐ Q (9)15s; 51°16'·20N 02°44'·74E.

LST 420 ⚐ Q (9)15s; 51°15'·45N 02°40'·67E.

MBN ⚐ Q; 51°20'·82N 02°46'·29E.

Middelkerke Bank ▲ Fl G 5s; 51°18'·19N 02°42'·75E.

Middelkerke Bank S ⚐ Q (9) R 15s; 51°14'·73N 02°41'·89E.

D1 ⚐ Q (3) 10s; 51°13'·95N 02°38'·59E.

BT Ratel ⚐ Fl (4) R 15s; 51°11'·63N 02°27'·92E; Buiten Ratel.

ZEEBRUGGE TO THE FRENCH BORDER

ZEEBRUGGE

AW ⚐ Iso 8s; 51°22'·41N 03°07'·05E.

Ldg lts 136°, both Oc 5s 22/45m 8M; 131°-141°; H24, synch; W cols, R bands. Front, 51°20'·71N 03°13'·11E. Rear, 890m SE.

SZ ⚐ Q (3) 10s; 51°23'·30N 03°08'·65E (Scheur Channel).

Z ▲ QG; 51°22'·48N 03°09'·95E.

WZ ⚐ Q (9) 15s; 51°22'·57N 03°10'·72E.

W outer mole ⚲ Oc G 7s 31m 7M; G vert strip lts visible from seaward; 057°-267°; Horn (3) 30s; IPTS; 51°21'·74N 03°11'·17E.

E outer mole ⚲ Oc R 7s 31m 7M; R vert strip lts visible from seaward; 087°-281°; Bell 25s; 51°21'·78N 03°11'·86E.

Ldg lts 154°: Front, Oc WR 6s 20m 3M, 135°-W-160°-R-169°; W pylon, R bands; 51°20'·33N 03°12'·89E. Rear, Oc 6s 38m 3M, H24, synch; 520m from front.

Leopold II mole ✪ Oc WR 15s 22m, **W20M, R18M**; 068°-W-145°-R-212°-W-296°; IPTS; Horn (3+1) 90s; 51°20'·85N 03°12'·17E.

Entrance to Marina and FV hbr 51°19'·88N 03°11'·85E.

BLANKENBERGE

Promenade pier Fl (3) Y 20s, 8m 4M; 51°19'·28N 03°08'·18E.

Lt ho ✪ Fl (2) 8s 30m **20M**; 065°-245°; W twr, B top; 51°18'·75N 03°06'·85E.

Ldg lts 134°, both FR 5/9m 3/10M; R cross (X) topmarks on masts; front 51°18'·70N 03°08'·82E; rear 81m from front.

E pier ⚲ FR 12m 11M; 290°-245°; W ○ twr; Bell (2) 15s; 51°18'·91N 03°06'·55E.

W pier ⚲ FG 14m 11M; intens 065°-290°, unintens 290°-335°; W ○ twr; 51°18'·89N 03°06'·42E.

OBST 4 – OBST 14 are eleven ⚐s Q approx 3ca offshore, marking Spoil Ground between Blankenberge and Oostende.

OOSTENDE

Oostendebank East ⚐ Fl (4) R 20s; 51°17'·35N 02°51'·91E.

Wenduinebank West ⚐ Q (9) 15s; 51°17'·23N 02°52'·76E.

Buitenstroombank ⚐ Q; 51°15'·17N 02°51'·71E.

Binnenstroombank ⚐ Q (3) 10s; 51°14'·47N 02°53'·65E.

Ldg lts 143°: both Iso 4s (triple vert) 36/46m 4M, 068°-218°; X on metal mast, R/W bands. Front, 51°13'·80N 02°55'·89E.

Oostende lt ho ☆ Fl (3) 10s 65m **27M**; obsc 069·5°-071°; Gy twr, 2 sinusoidal Bu bands; 51°14'·18N 02°55'·84E.
WIP until 2013 is marked by 1 NCM buoy Q; 2 SPM buoys QY; and 3 PHM buoys QR. IPTS is shown from sig mast 51°14'·25N 02°55'·44E, plus QY when chan closed for ferry.
Inner W pier ⚡ FG 12m 10M, 057°-327°; *Bell 4s*; W ○ twr 51°14'·31N 02°55'·03E.

NIEUWPOORT
Zuidstroombank ◌ Fl R 5s; 51°12'·28N 02°47'·37E.
Weststroombank ◌ Fl (4) R 20s; 51°11'·34N 02°43'·03E.
Wreck 4 ⚓ Q (6) + L Fl 15s; 51°10'·90N 02°405'·03E.
Nieuwpoort Bank ⚓ Q (9) 15s; 51°10'·16N 02°36'·09E.
Oostduinkerke ⚓ Q; 51°09'·15N 02°39'·44E.
Lt ho ☆ Fl (2) R 14s 28m **16M**; R/W twr; 51°09'·27N 02°43'·79E.

E pier ⚡ FR 10m 10M; vis 025°-250° & 307°-347°; W ○ twr; 51°09'·41N 02°43'·08E.
W pier ⚡ FG 10m 9M; vis 025°-250° & 284°-324°; W ○ twr; 51°09'·35N 02°43'·00E.
⚡ QG 51°08'·65N 02°44'·31E marks the Y-junction where the channel forks stbd for KYCN and port for WSKLM and VVW-N.

WESTDIEP and PASSE DE ZUYDCOOTE
Den Oever wreck 2 ⚓ Q; 51°08'·11N 02°37'·43E.
Wreck 1 ⚓ Q; 51°08'·32N 02°35'·03E (adjacent to ◌ next line).
Wave recorder ◌ Fl (5) Y 20s; 51°08'·25N 02°34'·98E.
Trapegeer ▲ Fl G 10s; 51°08'·41N 02°34'·36E.
E12 ⚓ VQ (6) + L Fl 10s; 51°07'·89N 02°30'·68E.
French waters, for continuity (see also Area 17):
CME ⚓ Q (3) 10s; 51°07'·30N 02°30'·00E.
E11 ⚓ Fl G 4s; 51°06'·90N 02°30'·90E.
E10 ⚓ Fl (2) R 6s; 51°06'·30N 02°30'·47E.
E9 ⚓ Fl (2) G 6s; 51°05'·64N 02°29'·68E.
E8 ⚓ Fl (3) R 12s; 51°05'·16N 02°28'·67E.

		1															
1	Delfzijl	1															
2	Terschelling	85	2														
3	Harlingen	102	19	3													
4	Den Oever	110	34	21	4												
5	Den Helder	115	39	30	11	5											
6	Amsterdam	159	83	81	62	51	6										
7	IJmuiden	146	70	68	49	38	13	7									
8	Scheveningen	171	95	93	74	63	38	25	8								
9	Rotterdam	205	129	127	108	97	72	59	34	9							
10	Hook of Holland	185	109	107	88	77	52	39	14	20	10						
11	Stellendam	201	125	123	104	93	68	55	30	36	16	11					
12	Roompotsluis	233	157	155	136	125	100	87	50	68	48	32	12				
13	Vlissingen	228	152	150	131	120	99	86	61	67	47	45	24	13			
14	Zeebrugge	239	163	161	142	131	106	93	68	74	54	50	28	16	14		
15	Blankenberge	244	168	166	147	136	111	98	73	79	59	55	33	21	5	15	
16	Oostende	239	163	161	142	131	110	106	81	87	67	72	40	29	13	9	16
17	Nieuwpoort	262	186	184	165	154	129	116	91	97	77	83	51	39	23	18	9	17

DISTANCE TABLES
Approx distances in nautical miles are by the most direct route allowing for dangers and TSS.

AREA 14 *North France – Dunkerque to Cap de la Hague*

SELECTED LIGHTS, BUOYS & WAYPOINTS

Positions are referenced to WGS84

OFFSHORE MARKS: W Hinder to Dover Strait
Fairy South ⚓ VQ (6) + L Fl 10s; 51°21'·20N 02°17'·31E.
Fairy West ⚓ VQ (9) 10s 6M; 51°23'·86N 02°09'·30E.
Hinder 1 ⚓ Fl (2) 6s; 51°20'·80N 02°10'·93E.
Bergues ⚓ Fl G 4s 7m 4M; 51°17'·14N 02°18'·63E.
Bergues S ⚓ Q (6) + L Fl 15s; 51°15'·09N 02°19'·42E.
Ruytingen E ⚓ VQ; 51°14'·55N 02°17'·93E.
Ruytingen N ⚓ VQ 4M; 51°13'·16N 02°10'·28E.
Ruytingen SE ⚓ VQ (3) 15s; 51°09'·20N 02°08'·94E.
Ruytingen NW ⚓ Fl G 4s 3M; 51°09'·11N 01°57'·30E.
Ruytingen W ⚓ VQ 4M; 51°06'·93N 01°50'·45E.
Ruytingen SW ⚓ Fl (3) G 12s 3M; 51°05'·00N 01°46'·84E.
Sandettié N ⚓ VQ 6M; 51°18'·47N 02°04'·81E.
Sandettié E ⚓ Fl R 4s 7m 3M; 51°14'·88N 02°02'·65E.

DUNKERQUE TO BOULOGNE

PASSE DE ZUYDCOOTE
E12 ⚓ VQ (6) + L Fl 10s; 51°07'·89N 02°30'·68E (Belgium).
CME ⚓ Q (3) 10s; 51°07'·30N 02°30'·00E.
E11 ⚓ Fl G 4s; 51°06'·90N 02°30'·90E.
E10 ⚓ Fl (2) R 6s; 51°06'·30N 02°30'·47E.
E9 ⚓ Fl (2) G 6s; 51°05'·64N 02°29'·68E.
E8 ⚓ Fl (3) R 12s; 51°05'·16N 02°28'·68E. (E7 does not exist)

PASSE DE L'EST
E6 ⚓ QR; 51°04'·90N 02°27'·00E.
E4 ⚓ Fl R 4s; 51°04'·49N 02°24'·54E.
E1 ⚓ Fl (2) G 6s; 51°04'·06N 02°23'·10E.
E2 ⚓ Fl (2) R 6s; 51°04'·35N 02°22'·31E.
⚓ Q (6) + L Fl 15s; 51°04'·28N 02°21'·73E.

DUNKERQUE PORT EST
E jetty ☆ Fl (2) R 6s 12m 10M; R □, W pylon; 51°03'·59N 02°21'·20E.
W jetty ☆ Fl (2) G 6s 35m 11M; W twr, brown top; 51°03'·63N 02°20'·95E.
Ldg lts 137·5°, front Q7m11M 51°02'·98N 02°22'·05E, rear, Q10m11M, 114m from front, both W cols, R tops, synched.
Inner W jetty ⚓ Q 11m 9M; 51°03'·33N 02°21'·43E.
Dunkerque lt ho ☆ Fl (2) 10s 59m **26M**; 51°02'·93N 02°21'·86E.

DUNKERQUE INTERMEDIATE CHANNEL
DW30 ⚓ QR; 51°04'·14N 02°20'·16E.
DW29 ⚓ QG; 51°03'·83N 02°20'·25E. .
DW16 ⚓ Fl (2) R 6s; 51°03'·31N 02°08'·98E.
DKB ⚓ VQ (9) 10s; 51°02'·95N 02°09'·26E.

DW12 Fl (3) R 12s; 51°03'·19N 02°05'·57E.
DW11 Fl (3) G 12s; 51°02'·88N 02°05'·77E. (DW10-7 omitted)

GRAVELINES
W jetty Fl (2) WG 6s 9m W/G4M; 085°-W-224°-G-085°; Y ○ twr, G top; 51°00'·94N 02°05'·49E.

PASSE DE L'OUEST
DW6 VQ R; 51°02'·60N 02°01'·01E.
DW5 QG; 51°02'·20N 02°00'·92E.
DKA L Fl 10s; 51°02'·55N 01°56'·96E.
RCE (Ridens de Calais East) Iso G 4s; 51°02'·44N 01°53'·24E.
Dyck Fl 3s; *Racon B*; 51°02'·99N 01°51'·79E.
RCA (Ridens de Calais Approach) Q; 51°00'·90N 01°48'·72E.

CALAIS
E jetty Fl (2) R 6s 12m **17M**; (in fog two Fl (2) 6s (vert) on request); Gy twr, R top; *Horn (2) 40s*; 50°58'·39N 01°50'·45E.
W jetty Iso G 3s 12m 9M; (in fog Fl 5s on request); W twr, G top; *Bell 5s*; 50°58'·24N 01°50'·40E.
Calais Fl (4) 15s 59m **22M**; vis 073°-260°; W 8-sided twr, B top; 50°57'·68N 01°51'·21E (440m E of marina entry gate).

CALAIS, WESTERN APPROACH
CA4 Fl (2)R 6s; 50°58'·38N 01°48'·65E.
CA6 Fl (3) R 12s; 50°58'·63N 01°49'·92E.
Les Quénocs VQ; 50°56'·85N 01°41'·12E.
CA1 Fl G 4s; 50°57'·64N 01°46'·14E (0·5M NNW of Sangatte).
Sangatte Oc WG 4s 13m W8M, G5M; 065°-G-089°-W-152°-G-245°; W pylon, B top; 50°57'·19N 01°46'·50E.
Abbeville wreck VQ (9) 10s; 50°56'·08N 01°37'·58E.
Cap Gris-Nez Fl 5s 72m **29M**; 005°-232°; W twr, B top; 50°52'·09N 01°34'·96E.

OFFSHORE MARKS: DOVER STRAIT TSS, French side
Colbart N Q 6M; 50°57'·46N 01°23'·29E.
Colbart SW VQ (6) + L Fl 10s 8m; 50°48'·87N 01°16'·32E.
ZC2 (Zone Cotière) Fl (2+1) Y 15s 5M; 50°53'·54N 01°30'·89E.
ZC1 Fl (4) Y 15s 4MN; 50°44'·99N 01°27'·21E.
Ridens SE VQ (3) 5s 6M; 50°43'·48N 01°18'·87E.
Bassurelle Fl (4) R 15s 6M; *Racon B, 5-8M*; 50°32'·74N 00°57'·69E.
Vergoyer N VQ 5M; *Racon C, 5-8M*; 50°39'·67N 01°22'·21E;
Vergoyer NW Fl (2) 6s 4M; 50°37'·16N 01°17'·85E.
Vergoyer E VQ (3) 5s 6M; 50°35'·76N 01°19'·70E.
Vergoyer W Fl G 4s 4M; 50°34'·66N 01°13'·57E.
Vergoyer SW VQ (9) 10s 6M; 50°27'·01N 01°00'·03E.

BOULOGNE TO DIEPPE
BOULOGNE
Bassure de Baas VQ; 50°48'·53N 01°33'·05E.
Approches Boulogne VQ (6) + L Fl 10s 8m 6M; 50°45'·31N 01°31'·07E.
Digue N (detached) Fl (2) R 6s 10m 7M; 50°44'·71N 01°34'·18E.
Digue S (Carnot) Fl (2+1) 15s 25m **19M**; W twr, G top; 50°44'·44N 01°34'·05E.
Clearing brg 122·4° : Front, FG in a neon ▽ 4m 5M; 50°43'·71N 01°35'·66E. Rear, FR 44m 11M; intens 113°-133°; 560m from front.

Inner NE jetty FR 11m 7M; 50°43'·91N 01°35'·24E.
Inner SW jetty FG 17m 5M; W col, G top; *Horn 30s*; 50°43'·90N 01°35'·11E.
Cap d'Alprech Fl (3) 15s 62m **23M**; 50°41'·91N 01°33'·75E, 2·5M S of hbr ent.

LE TOUQUET/ÉTAPLES
Pointe de Lornel VQ (9) 10s 6m 3M; 50°33'·24N 01°35'·12E.
Mérida wreck 50°32'·85N 01°33'·44E.
Camiers lt ho Oc (2) WRG 6s 17m W10M, R/G7M; 015°-G-090°-W-105°-R-141°; R pylon; 50°32'·86N 01°36'·28E.
Canche Est groyne Fl R 4s 8m; 50°32'·57N 01°35'·66E.
Le Touquet Fl (2) 10s 54m **25M**; Or twr, brown band, W&G top; 50°31'·43N 01°35'·52E.
Pointe du Haut-Blanc Fl 5s 44m **23M**; W twr, R bands, G top; 50°23'·90N 01°33'·67E (Berck).

BAIE DE LA SOMME
ATSO Mo (A) 12s; 50°14'·00N 01°28'·08E (shifts frequently).
Pte du Hourdel Oc (3) WG 12s 19m, W12M, G9M; 053°-W-248°-G-323°; tidal sigs; *Horn (3) 30s*; W twr, G top; 50°12'·90N 01°33'·98E.
Cayeux-sur-Mer Fl R 5s 32m **22M**; W twr, R top; 50°11'·65N 01°30'·72E.
Le Crotoy Oc (2) R 6s 19m 8M; 285°-135°; W pylon; 50°12'·91N 01°37'·40E. Marina Fl R & Fl G 2s 4m 2M; 50°12'·98N 01°38'·20E.

ST VALÉRY-SUR-SOMME
Trng wall head, Fl G 2.5s 2m 1M; 50°12'·25N 01°35'·85E,.
Embankment head Iso G 4s 9m 9M; 347°-222°; W pylon, G top; 50°12'·25N 01°36'·02E.
La Ferté môle Fl R 4s 9m 9M; 000°-250°; W pylon, R top; 50°11'·18N 01°38'·14E (ent to marina inlet).

LE TRÉPORT
Ault Oc (3) WR 12s 95m **W15M**, R11M; 040°-W-175°-R-220°; W twr, R top; 50°06'·28N 01°27'·23E (4M NE of Le Tréport).
W jetty Fl (2) G 10s 15m **20M**; W twr, G top; *Horn (2) 30s*; 50°03'·88N 01°22'·14E.

DIEPPE
W jetty Iso G 4s 11m 8M; W twr, G top; *Horn 30s*; 49°56'·27N 01°04'·97E.
Quai de la Marne QR 12m 3M; 49°55'·93N 01°05'·20E, E quay.
Pointe d'Ailly Fl (3) 20s 95m **31M**; W □ twr, G top; *Horn (3) 60s*; 49°54'·96N 00°57'·50E.

DIEPPE TO LE HAVRE
SAINT VALÉRY-EN-CAUX
W jetty Fl (2) G 6s 13m 11M; W twr, G top; 49°52'·40N 00°42'·54E. Paluel power station Q; 49°52'·22N 00°38'·03E.

FÉCAMP
N jetty Fl (2) 10s 15m **16M**; Gy twr, R top; 49°45'·94N 00°21'·80E.

PORT D'ANTIFER
Cap d'Antifer Fl 20s 128m **29M**; 021°-222°; Gy 8-sided twr, G top, on 90m cliffs; 49°41'·01N 00°09'·93E.
A17 Iso G 4s; 49°41'·53N 00°01·75E.

A18 ⚓ QR; 49°42'·02N 00°02'·18E. Cross the chan W of A17/18.

Ldg lts 127·5°, both Dir Oc 4s 113/135m **22M**; 127°-128°; by day F **33M** 126·5°-128·5° occas. **Front** ☆, 49°38'·32N 00°09'·12E.

LE HAVRE, APPROACH CHANNEL

Cap de la Hève ☆ Fl 5s 123m **24M**; 225°-196°; W 8-sided twr, R top; 49°30'·74N 00°04'·16E.

LHA ⌑ Mo (A) 12s 10m 6M; R&W; *Racon, 8-10M* (a series of 8 dots, or 8 groups of dots; distance between each dot or group represents 0·3M); 49°31'·38N 00°09'·86W. Reserve lt Mo (A).

Ldg lts 106·8°, both Dir F 36/78m **25M** (H24); intens 106°-108° ; Gy twrs, G tops. Front, 49°28'·91N 00°06'·50E; rear, 0·73M from front.

LH3 ⚓ QG; 49°30'·84N 00°04'·02W. (LH1 & 2 buoys do not exist).

LH4 ⚓ QR; 49°31'·11N 00°03'·90W.

FVs and yachts <19.8m LOA may cross the appr chan west of LH 7/8 buoys, keeping clear of all other shipping, even if under sail:

LH7 ⚓ Iso G 4s; 49°30'·25N 00°00'·82W.

LH8 ⚓ Fl (2) R 6s; 49°30'·44N 00°00'·70W.

Note the W-E longitude change. (LH9 buoy does not exist).

LH13 ⚓ Fl G 4s; 49°29'·32N 00°03'·62E (Ent to Port 2000).

LH14 ⚓ Fl R 4s; 49°29'·67N 00°03'·43E; 1m shoal depth close W.

LH16 ⚓ Fl (2) R 6s; 49°29'·45N 00°04'·28E.

LH 2000 ⚓ VQ (9) 10s; 49°29'·14N 00°04'·78E (Ent to Port 2000).

LE HAVRE

Digue N ☆ Fl R 5s 15m **21M**; IPTS; W ○ twr, R top; *Horn 15s;* 49°29'·19N 00°05'·44E.

Digue S ⚡ VQ (3) G 2s 15m 11M; W twr, G top; 49°29'·05N 00°05'·38E.

Marina ent, W spur ⚡ Fl (2) R 6s 3M; 49°29'·22N 00°05'·53E.

THE SEINE ESTUARY UP TO HONFLEUR

CHENAL DE ROUEN

Nord du Mouillage ⚓ Fl (4) Y 15s; 49°28'·80N 00°00'·22E.

No. 2 ⚓ QR; *Racon T;* 49°27'·70N 00°00'·60E.

No. 4 ⚓ Fl R 2·5s; 49°27'·19N 00°01'·97E. Yachts keep N of chan.

Amfard SW ⚓ QR; 49°26'·30N 00°04'·82E.

No. 10 ⚓ Fl R 4s; 49°26'·10N 00°06'·39E.

Digue du Ratier ⚓ VQ 10m 4M; 49°25'·94N 00°06'·59E.

Falaise des Fonds ☆ Fl (3) WRG 12s 15m, **W17M**, R/G13M; 040°-G-080°-R-084°-G-100°- W-109°-R-162°-G-260°; W twr, G top; 49°25'·47N 00°12'·85E.

No. 20 ⚓ QR; 49°25'·85N 00°13'·71E. (Cross here to Honfleur)

HONFLEUR

Digue Ouest ⚡ QG 10m 6M; 49°25'·67N 00°13'·83E.

Digue Est ⚡ Q 9m 8M; *Horn (5) 40s;* 49°25'·67N 00°13'·95E.

Inner E jetty, Oc (2) R 6s 12m 6M; W twr, R top; 49°25'·38N 00°14'·12E.

No. 22 ⚓ QR; 49°25'·85N 00°15'·38E.

TROUVILLE TO COURSEULLES

CHENAL DE ROUEN TO DEAUVILLE and TROUVILLE

Ratelets ⚓ Q (9) 15s; 49°25'·29N 00°01'·71E.

Semoy ⚓ VQ (3) 5s; 49°24'·15N 00°02'·35E, close to 148° ldg line.

Trouville SW ⚓ VQ (9) 10s; 49°22'·54N 00°02'·56E.

DEAUVILLE and TROUVILLE

Ldg lts 148°, both Oc R 4s 11/17m 12/10M: Front, East inner jetty (*estacade*); 330°-150°; W twr, R top; 49°22'·03N 00°04'·48E.

Rear, Pte de la Cahotte; synch; 120°-170°; 49°21'·93N 00°04'·58E.

W trng wall ⚡ Fl WG 4s 10m W9M, G6M; 005°-W-176°-G-005°; B pylon, G top; 49°22'·37N 00°04'·11E. Also 4 unlit SHM bcns.

E trng wall ⚡ Fl (4) WR 12s 8m W7M, R4M; 131°-W-175°-R-131°; W pylon, R top; 49°22'·22N 00°04'·33E. Also 3 unlit PHM bcns.

W outer bkwtr ⚡ Iso G 4s 9m 5M; 49°22'·11N 00°04'·33E.

West inner jetty (*estacade*) ⚡ QG 11m 9M; 49°22'·03N 00°04'·43E.

DIVES-SUR-MER *Note the E-W longitude change.*

DI ⚓ Iso 4s; 49°19'·17N 00°05'·86W.

No. 1 ⚓ VQ G; 49°18'·50N 00°05'·67W. Buoys are moved to mark chan.

No. 2 ⚓ VQ R; 49°18'·51N 00°05'·56W.

No. 3 ⚓ QG 7m 4M; W pylon, G top; 49°18'·30N 00°05'·55W.

No. 5 ⚓ Fl G 4s 8m 4M; W pylon, G top; 49°18'·09N 00°05'·50W.

Bcns 3 & 5, if damaged, may be temporarily replaced by buoys.

No. 7 ⚓ Fl G 4s; 49°17'·65N 00°05'·31W.

OUISTREHAM and CAEN

Merville ⚓ VQ; 49°19'·65N 00°13'·39W; spoil ground buoy.

Ouistreham ⚓ VQ (3) 5s; wreck buoy; 49°20'·42N 00°14'·81W.

Ldg lts 185°, both Dir Oc (3+1) R 12s 10/30m **17M**; intens 183·5°-186·5°, synch. **Front** ☆, E jetty, W mast, R top; 49°16'·99N 00°14'·81W. **Rear** ☆, 610m from front, tripod, R top.

No. 1 ⚓ QG; 49°19'·19N 00°14'·67W.

No. 2 ⚓ QR; 49°19'·17N 00°14'·43W.

Barnabé ⚡ QG 7m 5M; W pylon, G top; 49°18'·02N 00°14'·76W.

St-Médard ⚡ QR 7m 5M; 49°18'·02N 00°14'·62W.

Riva ⚡ Fl G 4s 9m 3M; W pylon, G top; 49°17'·73N 00°14'·79W.

Quilbé ⚡ Fl R 4s 9m 3M; W pylon, R top; 49°17'·72N 00°14'·67W.

Ouistreham lt ho ☆ Oc WR 4s 37m **W17M**, R13M; 115°-R-151°-W-115°; W twr, R top; 49°16'·79N 00°14'·87W.

COURSEULLES-SUR-MER

Courseulles ⚓ Iso 4s; 49°21'·28N 00°27'·68W.

W jetty ⚡ Iso WG 4s 7m; W9M, G6M; 135°-W-235°-G-135°; brown pylon on dolphin, G top; 49°20'·41N 00°27'·37W.

E jetty ⚡ Oc (2) R 6s 9m 7M; 49°20'·26N 00°27'·39W.

COURSEULLES TO ST VAAST

Ver ☆ Fl (3)15s 42m **26M**; obsc'd by cliffs of St Aubin when brg >275°; conspic lt ho, W twr, Gy top; 49°20'·41N 00°31'·13W.

ARROMANCHES

Ent buoys: ⚓ 49°21'·35N 00°37'·26W; ⚓ 49°21'·25N 00°37'·30W.

Bombardons ⚓ wreck buoys; 49°21'·66N 00°38'·97W.

PORT-EN-BESSIN
Ldg lts 204°, both Oc (3) 12s 25/42m 10/11M; synch. Front, 069°-339°, W pylon, G top; 49°20'·96N 00°45'·53W. Rear; 114°-294°, W and Gy ho; 93m from front.
E mole ⚓ Oc R 4s 14m 7M, R pylon; 49°21'·12N 00°45'·38W.
W mole ⚓ Fl WG 4s 14m, W10M, G7M; G065°-114·5°, W114·5°-065°; G pylon; 49°21'·17N 00°45'·43W.

COASTAL MARKS
Omaha Beach, 1M off : ∮ 49°22'·66N 00°50'·28W; ∮ 49°23'·17N 00°51'·93W; ∮ 49°23'·66N 00°53'·74W.
Broadsword ⚓ Q (3) 10s, wreck buoy; 49°25'·34N 00°52'·96W.
Est du Cardonnet ⚓ VQ (3) 5s; 49°26'·83N 01°01'·10W.

GRANDCAMP
Les Roches de Grandcamp: No. 1 ∮ 49°24'·72N 01°01'·75W; No. 3 ∮ 49°24'·92N 01°03'·70W; No. 5 ∮ 49°24'·78N 01°04'·98W.
Ldg lts 146°, both Dir Q 9/12m **15M**, 144·5°-147·5°. **Front** ☆, 49°23'·42N 01°02'·90W. **Rear** ☆,102m from front.
Jetée Est ⚓ Oc (2) R 6s 9m 9M; *Horn Mo(N) 30s;* 49°23'·53N 01°02'·96W.
Jetée Ouest ⚓ Fl G 4s 9m 6M; 49°23'·47N 01°02'·96W.

ISIGNY-SUR-MER
IS, small B/Y ⚓, no topmark (∮ on AC 2135); 49°24'·28N 01°06'·37W.
No 1 ⚓, Fl R 4s; 49°23'·60N 01°07·27W
Dir lts 173°, both Dir Q WRG 7m 9M; 49°19'·57N 01°06·78W.
Training wall heads ⚓ 49°21'·42N 01°07'·24W; ⚓ 49°21'·40N 01°07'·14W, off Pte du Grouin.

CARENTAN
C-I ⚓ Iso 4s; 49°25'·44N 01°07'·08W; 210°/1·76M to Nos 1 & 2 buoys.
No. 1 ⚓ Fl G 2·5s; 49°23'·93N 01°08'·52W.
No. 2 ⚓ Fl R 2·5s; 49°23'·88N 01°08'·37W.
Trng wall ⚓ Fl (4) G 15s; G △ on G bcn;49°21'·96N 01°09'·95W.
Trng wall ⚓ Fl (4) R 15s; R □ on R bcn;49°21'·93N 01°09'·878W.
Ldg lts 209·5°. **Front** ☆ Dir Oc (3) R 12s 6m **18M**; intens 208·2°-210·7°; W mast, R top; 49°20'·47N 01°11'·17W. Rear, Dir Oc (3) 12s 14m 10M; vis 120°-005°; W gantry, G top; 723m from front.

ÎLES SAINT-MARCOUF
Iles St-Marcouf ⚓ VQ (3) 5s 18m 8M; □ Gy twr, G top; 49°29'·86N 01°08'·81W.
Ouest-Saint-Marcouf ⚓ Q (9) 15s; 49°29'·73N 01°11'·97W.
Saint Floxel ∮ 49°30'·64N 01°13'·94W.
Quineville ⚓ Q (9) 10s, wreck buoy; 49°31'·79N 01°12'·38W.

ST VAAST TO POINTE DE BARFLEUR

ST VAAST-LA-HOUGUE
Ldg lts 267°: Front, La Hougue Oc 4s 9m 10M; W pylon, G top; 49°34'·25N 01°16'·37W. Rear, Morsalines Oc (4) WRG 12s 90m, W11M, R/G8M; 171°-W-316°-G-321°-R-342°-W-355°; W 8-sided twr, G top; 49°34'·16N 01°19'·10W, 1·8M from front.
Le Manquet ∮ 49°34'·26N 01°15'·56W.
Le Bout du Roc ∮ 49°34'·68N 01°15'·27W.
La Dent ∮ 49°34'·57N 01°14'·20W.
Le Gavendest ⚓ Q (6) + L Fl 15s; 49°34'·36N 01°13'·89W.
Jetty ⚓ Dir Oc (2) WRG 6s 12m W10M, R/G7M; 219°-R-237°-G-310°-W-350°-R-040°; W 8-sided twr, R top; *Siren Mo(N) 30s;* 49°35'·17N 01°15'·41W.
Pte de Saire ⚓ Oc (2+1) 10s 11m 10M; squat W twr, G top; 49°36'·36N 01°13'·78W.

BARFLEUR
Ldg lts 219·5°, both Oc (3) 12s 7/13m 10M; synch. Front, W □ twr;49°40'·18N 01°15'·61W. Rear, 085°-355°; Gy and W □ twr, G top; 288m from front.
La Grotte ⚓ 49°41'·06N 01°14'·86W.
Roche-à-l'Anglais ⚓ 49°40'·78N 01°14'·93W.
La Vimberge ⚓ 49°40'·54N 01°15'·25W.
W jetty ⚓ Fl G 4s 8m 6M; 49°40'·32N 01°15'·57W.
E jetty ⚓ Oc R 4s 5m 6M; 49°40'·31N 01°15'·47W.
La Jamette ∮ 49°41'·87N 01°15'·59W.
Pte de Barfleur ☆ Fl (2) 10s 72m **25M**; obsc when brg less than 088°; Gy twr, B top; 49°41'·78N 01°15'·96W.

POINTE DE BARFLEUR TO CAP DE LA HAGUE

Les Équets ⚓ Q 8m 3M; 49°43'·62N 01°18'·36W.
Basse du Rénier ⚓ VQ 8m 4M; 49°44'·84N 01°22'·09W.
Les Trois Pierres ∮ 49°42'·90N 01°21'·80W.
Anse de Vicq, 158° ldg lts; both Iso R 4s 8/14m 6M; front 49°42'·20N 01°23'·95W.
La Pierre Noire ⚓ Q (9) 15s 8m 4M;49°43'·54N 01°29'·07W.

PORT DU LÉVI
Cap Lévi ☆ Fl R 5s 36m **22M**; Gy □ twr; 49°41'·75N 01°28'·38W.
Port Lévi ⚓ Oc (2) WRG 6s 7m 7M; 055°-G-083°-W-105°-R-163°; W & Gy hut, W lantern; 49°41'·24N 01°28'·34W.

PORT DU BECQUET
Ldg lts 186·5°, both intens 183°-190°; synch. Front, Oc (2+1) 12s 8m 10M; W 8-sided twr; 49°39'·22N 01°32'·85W. Rear, Oc (2+1) R 12s 13m 7M. W 8-sided twr, R top; 49m from front.

CHERBOURG, EASTERN ENTRANCES
Passe Collignon ⚓ Fl (2) R 6s 5m 4M; 49°39'·59N 01°34'·24W.
Passe de l'Est, Jetée des Flamands ldg lts 189°, both Q 9/16m 13M. Front, 49°39'·33N 01°35'·94W . Rear, 516m from front.
Roches du Nord-Ouest ⚓ Fl R 2·5s; 49°40'·64N 01°35'·28W.
La Truite ⚓ Fl (4) R 15s; 49°40'·33N 01°35'·49W.
Fort d'Île Pelée ⚓ Oc (2) WR 6s 19m; W10M, R7M; 055°-W-120°-R-055°; W & R pedestal; 49°40'·21N 01°35'·08W.
Fort de l'Est ⚓ 49°40'·28N 01°35'·92W, Iso G 4s 19m 9M.
Fort Central ⚓ VQ (6) + L Fl 10s 5m 4M; 322°-032°; 49°40'·40N 01°37'·04W.

CHERBOURG, PASSE DE L'OUEST
CH1 ⊙; V-AIS; 49°43'·24N 01°42'·09W.
Passe de l'Ouest outer ldg lts 141·2°. **Front,** Dir Q (2 horiz, 63m apart) 5m **17M**; intens 137·3°-143·3° & 139·2°-145·2°; W △ on bcn; 49°39'·55N 01°37'·95W. **Rear,** Dir Q 35m **19M**; intens 140°-142·5°; W △ on Gy pylon.
Fort de l'Ouest ☆ Fl (3) WR 15s 19m **W24M, R20M**; 122°-W-355°-R-122°; Gy twr, R top; 49°40'·45N 01°38'·87W.
Fort de l'Ouest ⚓ Fl R 4s; 49°40'·39N 01°38'·89W.
⚓ Q (6) + L Fl 15s; 49°40'·34N 01°38'·65W.

Digue de Querqueville ⚓ Fl (2) G 6s 8m 6M; W col, G top; 49°40'·30N 01°39'·80W.

Inner ldg lts 124·3°; both intens 114·3°-134·3°: Front, Digue du Homet head, QG 10m 6M; 49°39'·48N 01°36'·96W. Rear, Dir Iso G 4s 16m 13M; W col, B bands, 397m from front. La Ténarde ⚓ VQ 8m 4M; 49°39'·74N 01°37'·75W.

CHERBOURG, PETITE RADE and MARINA

Entrance, W side, Digue du Homet ⚓ QG 10m 8M; intens 114·3°-134·3°; W pylon, G top; 49°39'·48N 01°36'·96W.
E side, ⚓ Q R, off Jetée des Flamands; 49°39'·44N 01°36'·60W.
Marina ent, E side, ⚓ Fl (3) R 12s 6m 6M; W col, R lantern; 49°38'·91N 01°37'·08W.
W mole ⚓ Fl (3) G 12s 7m 6M; G pylon; 49°38'·87N 01°37'·15W.

1. Dunkerque-Est	**1**																	
2. Calais	28	**2**																
3. **Boulogne**	49	21	**3**															
4. St Valéry-sur-Somme	86	58	37	**4**														
5. Le Tréport	90	62	41	16	**5**													
6. **Dieppe**	100	74	53	30	15	**6**												
7. St Valéry-en-Caux	109	81	62	42	28	16	**7**											
8. **Fécamp**	121	93	76	57	44	32	17	**8**										
9. **Le Havre**	148	121	103	84	71	61	47	27	**9**									
10. **Honfleur**	157	129	108	92	80	67	51	35	13	**10**								
11. **Deauville/Trouville**	152	125	108	91	79	61	53	34	9	13	**11**							
12. Dives-sur-Mer	155	129	110	94	83	66	55	38	16	19	9	**12**						
13. **Ouistreham**	160	138	115	97	85	73	59	41	20	24	15	9	**13**					
14. Courseulles	162	136	115	100	87	75	60	44	24	30	23	18	14	**14**				
15. Grandcamp	177	150	130	118	104	94	80	62	47	52	45	41	37	27	**15**			
16. Carentan	187	159	139	126	112	100	85	69	56	61	55	50	45	36	13	**16**		
17. **St Vaast**	179	151	131	120	107	96	80	65	54	61	54	50	46	35	16	20	**17**	
18. Barfleur	175	147	128	118	105	94	78	64	49	57	53	48	39	21	26	10	**18**	
19. **Cherbourg**	188	160	142	131	120	108	94	80	71	77	73	69	66	57	40	44	28	21	**19**

E quay ⚓ Fl (4) R 15s 3m 3M; R bcn; 49°38'·79N 01°37'·12W.
Wavescreen pontoon, N end ⚓ Fl (4) G 15s 4m 2M; W post, G top.

CHERBOURG TO CAP DE LA HAGUE

Raz de Bannes ⚓ 49°41'·32N 01°44'·53W.
Omonville Dir lt 257°: Iso WRG 4s13m; W10M, R/G7M; 180°-G-252°-W-262°-R-287°; W pylon, G top; 49°42'·24N 01°50'·15W.
L'Étonnard ⚓ 49°42'·33N 01°49'·84W.
Basse Bréfort ⚓ VQ 8m 4M; 49°43'·90N 01°51'·15W.
Jobourg Nuclear plant chimney, R lts; 49°40'·80N 01°52'·91W.
La Plate ⚓ Fl (2+1) WR 10s 11m; W9M, R6M; 115°-W-272°-R-115°; Y 8-sided twr, with B top; 49°43'·97N 01°55'·74W.
Cap de la Hague (Gros du Raz) ☆ Fl 5s 48m **23M**; Gy twr, W top; *Horn 30s*; 49°43'·31N 01° 57'·26W.
La Foraine ⚓ VQ (9) 10s, 12m 6M; 49°42'·90N 01°58'·31W.

> **DISTANCE TABLES**
> Approx distances in nautical miles are by the most direct route allowing for dangers and TSS.

AREA 15 *N Central France (Cap de la Hague to St Quay) & Channel Is*

SELECTED LIGHTS, BUOYS & WAYPOINTS

> Positions are referenced to WGS84

CAP DE LA HAGUE TO ST MALO

GOURY

La Foraine ⚓ VQ (9) 10s 12m 6M v 49°42'·90 N 01°58'·32W.
Ldg lts 065·2°: Front, QR 5m 7M; R □ in W □ on pier, 49°42'·89N 01°56'·70W. Rear, 116m from front, Q 11m 7M; intens 056·2°-074·2°; W pylon on hut.
Hervieu ⚓ 49°42'·77N 01°56'·92W.

DIELETTE

W bkwtr Dir lt 140°, Iso WRG 4s 12m W10M, R/G7M; 070°-G-135°-W-145°-R-180°; W twr, G top ;49°33'·18N 01°51'·81W.
E bkwtr ⚓ Fl R 4s 6m 2M; 49°33'·21N 01°51'·78W.
Inner N jetty, Fl (2) R 6s. Inner S jetty, Fl (2) G 6s; both 6m 1M.
Banc des Dious ⚓ Q (9) 15s; 49°32'·58N 01°54'·02W.

CARTERET

Cap de Carteret ☆ Fl (2+1) 15s 81m **26M**; Gy twr, G top; 49°22'·40N 01°48'·41W.
W bkwtr ⚓ Oc R 4s 7m 7M; W post, R top; 49°22'·07N 01°47'·32W.
E training wall ⚓ Fl G 2·5s 4m 2M; W post, G top; 49°22'·17N 01°47'·30W.

Channel bend ⚓ Fl (2) R 6s 5m 1M; R pylon; 49°22'·58N 01°47'·23W. Inside the bend: ⚓ Fl (2) G 6s 5m 1M; G pylon; 49°22'·55N 01°47'·20W.
Marina entry sill: ⚓ Fl (3) R 12s and Fl (3) G 12s; R & G pylons.

PORTBAIL

PB ⚓ 49°18'·37N 01°44'·75W.
Ldg lts 042°: Front, Q 14m 10M; W pylon, R top, 49°19'·75N 01°42'·50W. Rear, 870m from front, Oc 4s 20m 10M; stubby ch spire.
⚓ 49°19'·32N 01°43'·16W.
⚓ 49°19'·20N 01°43'·00W.
Training wall head ⚓ Q (2) R 5s 5m 1M; W mast, W top; 49°19'·43N 01°42'·99W.

REGNÉVILLE

La Catheue ⚓ Q (6) + L Fl 15s, 48°57'·67N 01°42'·23W.
Le Ronquet ⚓ Fl (2) WR 6s, W6M, R4M; 100°-R-293°-W-100°; 49°00'·11N 01°38'·07W.
Pte d'Agon ⚓ Oc (2) WR 6s 12m, W10M, R7M; 063°-R-110°-W-063°; W twr, R top, W dwelling; 49°00'·18N 01°34'·63W.
Dir lt 028°, Oc WRG 4s 9m, W12M, R/G9M; 024°-G-027°-W-029°-R-033°; house; 49°00'·63N 01°33'·36W.

PASSAGE DE LA DÉROUTE

Les Trois-Grunes ⚓ Q (9) 15s, 49°21'·84N 01°55'·21W.
Écrévière ⚓ Q (6) + L Fl 15s; *Bell;* 49°15'·27N 01°52'·16W.
Basse Jourdan ⚓ Q (3) 10s; 49°06'·85N 01°43'·96W.
Le Boeuf ⚓ 49°06'·56N 01°47'·17W.
Les Boeuftins ⚓ 49°07'·03N 01°45'·96W.
La Basse du Sénéquet ⚓ 49°05'·96N 01°41'·11W.
Le Sénéquet ⚓ Fl (3) WR 12s 18m W13M, R10M; 083·5°-R-116·5°-W-083·5°; W twr; 49°05'·48N 01°39'·73W.
Les Nattes ⚓ 49°03'·46N 01°41'·81W.
International F ⚓ 49°02'·16N 01°42'·98W.
International E ⚓ 49°02'·08N 01°47'·21W.
Basse le Marié ⚓ Q (9) 15s; 49°01'·79N 01°48'·57W.
NE Minquiers ⚓ VQ (3) 5s; *Bell;* 49°00'·85N 01°55'·30W.
Les Ardentes ⚓ Q (3) 10s; 48°57'·89N 01°51'·53W.
SE Minquiers ⚓ Q (3) 10s; *Bell;* 48°53'·42N 02°00'·09W.
S Minquiers ⚓ Q (6) + L Fl 15s; 48°53'·09N 02°10'·10W.

ÎLES CHAUSEY

La Pointue ⚓ 48°54'·44N 01°50'·92W.
L'Enseigne, W twr, B top; 48°53'·67N 01°50'·37W.
L'Etat, B ⚓, 48°54'·67N 01°46'·21W.
Anvers wreck ⚓ 48°53'·91N 01°41'·07W.
Le Founet ⚓ Q (3) 10s; 48°53'·25N 01°42'·34W.
Le Pignon ⚓ Fl (2) WR 6s 10m, W9M, R6M; 005°-R-150°-W-005°; B twr, W band; 48°53'·49N 01°43'·36 W.
La Haute Foraine ⚓ 48°52'·89N 01°43'·66W.
Grande Île ☆ Fl 5s 39m **23M;** Gy ☐ twr, G top; *Horn 30s;* 48°52'·19N 01°49'·34W.
Channel ⚓ Fl G 2s; 48°52'·07N 01°49'·08W.
La Crabière Est ⚓ Dir Oc(3)WRG 12s 5m, W9M, R/G6M;079°-W-291°-G-329°-W-335°-R-079°; B beacon, Y top; 48°52'·46N 01°49'·39W.
La Cancalaise ⚓ 48°51'·90N 01°51'·11W.

GRANVILLE

Le Videcoq ⚓ VQ (9) 10s; 48°49'·66N 01°42'·06W.
La Fourchie ⚓ 48°50'·15N 01°37'·00W.
Pointe du Roc ☆ Fl (4) 15s 49m **23M;** 48°50'·06N 01°36'·78W.
Le Loup ⚓ Fl (2) 6s 8m 11M; 48°49'·57N 01°36'·24W.
Avant Port, E jetty ⚓ Fl G 2·5s 11m 4M; 48°49'·93N 01°36'·19W.
W jetty ⚓ Fl R 2·5s 12m 4M; 48°49'·86N 01°36'·23W.
Marina S bkwtr ⚓ Fl (2) R 6s 12m 5M; W post, R top; *Horn (2) 40s;* 48°49'·89N 01°35'·90W.
N bkwtr ⚓ Fl (2) G 6s 4m 5M; 48°49'·93N 01°35'·90W.
Sill, E & W sides: Oc (2) G 6s & Oc (2) R 6s, G & R topped pylons.

CANCALE

La Fille ⚓ 48°44'·16N 01°48'·46W.
Pierre-de-Herpin ☆ Oc (2) 6s 20m 13M; W twr, B top and base; 48°43'·77N 01°48'·92W.
Ruet ⚓ *Bell;* 48°43'·44N 01°50'·11W.
Grande Bunouze ⚓ 48°43'·17N 01°50'·95W.
Barbe Brûlée ⚓ 48°42'·11N 01°50'·57W.
Jetty hd ⚓ Oc (3) G 12s 9m 3M; W pylon B top; 48°40'·10N 01°51'·11W.

ST MALO AND RIVER RANCE

CHENAL DE LA BIGNE

Basse Rochefort (aka Basse aux Chiens) ⚓ 48°42'·69N 01°57'·31W.
La Petite Bigne ⚓ 48°41'·66N 01°58'·72W.
La Crolante ⚓; 48°41'·01N 01°59'·51W, off Pte de la Varde.

Les Létruns ⚓; *Bell;* 48°40'·71N 02°00'·61W.
Roches-aux-Anglais ⚓ Fl G 4s; 48°39'·65N 02°02'·27W.
Les Crapauds-du-Bey ⚓ Fl R 4s; 48°39'·37N 02°02'·57W.

CHENAL DES PETITS POINTUS

Dinard ch spire (74m) brg 203° to right of Le Petit Bé rks.
La Saint-Servantine ⚓ Fl G 2·5s; *Bell;* 48°41'·93N 02°00'·94W.
Les Petits Pointus ⚓ 48°41'·30N 02°00'·86W.

CHENAL DE LA GRANDE CONCHÉE

Villa Brisemoulin 181·5°, on with LH edge of Le Petit Bé rks.
La Plate ⚓ Q WRG 11m, W10M, R/G7M; 140°-W-203°-R-210°-W-225°-G-140°; 48°40'·78N 02°01'·91W.
Le Bouton ⚓ 48°40'·59N 02°01'·85W.

CHENAL DU BUNEL

Dinard water twr lt 158·2° on with St Énogat lts.
St Énogat ldg lts 158·2°; both Iso 4s 3/85m 6/8M, synch. Front 48°38'·29N 02°04'·11W, vis 126°-236°. Rear, 1.4M from front, on water twr; vis 143°-210°.
Bunel ⚓ Q (9) 15s; 48°40'·84N 02°05'·38W.

CHENAL DE LA PETITE PORTE

Outer ldg lts 129·7°: **Front, Le Grand Jardin** ☆ Fl (2) R 10s 24m **15M,** 48°40'·20N 02°04'·97W. Rear, **La Balue** ☆ FG 20m **22M;** 3·1M from front; intens 128°-129·5°; Gy ☐ twr; 48°38'·16N 02°01'·30W.
Vieux-Banc E ⚓ Q; 48°42'·38N 02°09'·12W.
Vieux-Banc W ⚓ VQ (9) 10s; 48°41'·84N 02°10'·20W.
St Malo Atterrisage (Fairway) ⚓ Iso 4s; 48°41'·39N 02°07'·28W.
Les Courtis ⚓ Fl G 4s 14m 7M; 48°40'·46N 02°05'·80W.
Nearing Le Grand Jardin, jink stbd briefly onto Ch du Bunel 152·8° ldg lts to pick up:
Inner ldg lts 128·6°, both Dir FG 20/69m **22/25M;** H24. Front, **Les Bas Sablons** ☆, intens 127·2°-130·2°; W ☐ twr, B top; 48°38'·16N 02°01'·30W. Rear, **La Balue** ☆, 0·9M from front; intens 128·5°; Gy ☐ twr; 48°37'·60N 02°00'·24W.
Basse du Nord No. 5 ⚓ 48°39'·98N 02°05'·04W.
Les Pierres-Garnier No. 8 ⚓ 48°39'·98N 02°04'·41W.
Les Patouillets ⚓ Fl (3) G 12s, 48°39'·68N 02°04'·30W.
Clef d'Aval No. 10 ⚓ 48°39'·72N 02°03'·91W.
Basse du Buron No. 12 ⚓ Fl (4) R 15s, 48°39'·42N 02°03'·51W.
Le Buron ⚓ Fl (4) G 15s 15m 7M; G twr, 48°39'·32N 02°03'·66W.
Les Grelots ⚓ VQ (6) + L Fl 10s, 48°39'·16N 02°03'·03W.

CHENAL DE LA GRANDE PORTE

Banchenou ⚓ VQ, 48°40'·44N 02°11'·48W.
Outer ldg lts 089·1°: **Front, Le Grand Jardin** ☆ Fl (2) R 10s 24m **15M,** 48°40'·20N 02°04'·97W.
Rear, **Rochebonne** ☆ Dir FR 40m **24M;** intens 088·2°-089·7°; Gy ☐ twr, R top, 4·2M from front; 48°40'·26N 01°58'·71W.
Buharats W No. 2 ⚓ Fl R 2·5s; 48°40'·22N 02°07'·50W.
Buharats E No. 4 ⚓ *Bell;* 48°40'·24N 02°07'·20W.
Bas du Boujaron No. 1 ⚓ Fl (2) G 6s, 48°40'·17N 02°05'·97W.
Le Sou ⚓ Q (3) 5s; 48°40'·11N 02°05'·30W.
Continue on inner 128·6° ldg line: see Chenal de la Petite Porte.

RADE DE ST MALO

Plateau Rance Nord ⚓ VQ, 48°38'·64N 02°02'·35W.
Plateau Rance Sud ⚓ Q (6) + L Fl 15s, 48°38'·43N 02°02'·28W.
Crapaud de la Cité ⚓ QG, 48°38'·34N 02°02'·01W.

ST MALO

Môle des Noires hd ⚡ VQ R 11m 6M; W twr, R top; *Horn (2) 20s*; 48°38'·52N 02°01'·91W.

Écluse du Naye ldg lts 070·4°, both FR 7/23m 3/7M. Front, 48°38'·58N 02°01'·48W. Rear, 030°-120°.

Ferry jetty hd, ⚡ VQ G 6M; 48°38'·44N 02°01'·82W (also on 128·6° ldg line).

Ferry jetty, ⚡ Fl R 4s 3m 1M; 260°-080°; 48°38'·44N 02°01'·76W.

Bas-Sablons marina, mole head ⚡ Fl G 4s 7m 5M; Gy mast; 48°38'·42N 02°01'·70W.

LA RANCE BARRAGE

La Jument ⚓ Fl G 4s 6m 4M; G twr, 48°37'·44N 02°01'·76W.

ZI 12 ⚓ Fl R 4s, 48°37'·47N 02°01'·62W.

NE dolphin ⚡ Fl (2) R 6s 6m 5M; 040°-200°, 48°37'·09N 02°01'·71W.

Barrage lock, NW wall ⚡ Fl (2) G 6s 6m 5M,191°-291°; G pylon, 48°37'·06N 02°01'·73W.

Barrage lock, SW wall, ⚡ Fl (3) G 12s, 48°37'·00N 02°01'·70W.

SE dolphin ⚡ Fl (3) R 12s, 48°36'·97N 02°01'·66W.

ZI 24 ⚓ Fl (2) R 6s, 48°36'·63N 02°01'·33W.

ST MALO TO ST QUAY-PORTRIEUX

ST BRIAC

R. Frémur mouth. Dir lt 125° Iso WRG 4s 10m, W13M, R/G 11M; 121·5°-G-124·5°-W-125·5°-R-129·5°; W mast on hut, 48°37'·07N 02°08'·20W.

ST CAST

Les Bourdinots ⚓ 48°39'·01N 02°13'·48W.

St Cast môle ⚡ Iso WG 4s 12m, W9M, G6M; 180°-G-206°-W-217°-G-235°-W-245°-G-340°; G & W structure; 48°38'·41N 02°14'·61W.

Laplace ⚓, 48°39'·73N 2°16'·45W; wreck 6m, 5ca SE of Pte de la Latte.

Cap Fréhel ☆ Fl (2) 10s 85m **29M**; Gy □ twr, G lantern; 48°41'·05N 02°19'·13W. Reserve lt range **15M**.

CHENAL and PORT D'ERQUY

Les Justières ⚓ Q (6) + L Fl 15s; 48°40'·56N 02°26'·48W.

Basses du Courant ⚓ VQ (6) + L Fl 10s; 48°39'·21N 02°29'·16W.

L'Evette ⚓ 48°38'·51N 02°31'·45W.

S môle ⚡ Fl (2) WRG 6s 11m W10M, R/G7M; 055°-R-081°-W-094°-G-111°-W-120°-R-134°; W twr; 48°38'·06N 02°28'·68W.

Inner jetty ⚡ Fl (3) R 12s 10m 3M; R/W twr; 48°38'·09N 02°28'·39W.

DAHOUET

Petit Bignon ⚓ 48°36'·82N 02°35'·06W.

Le Dahouet ⚓ 48°35'·15N 02°35'·43W.

La Petite Muette ⚓ Fl WRG 4s 10m W9M, R/G6M; 055°-G-114°-W-146°-R-196°; W twr, G band; 48°34'·82N 02°34'·29W.

Entry chan, Fl (2) G 6s 5m 1M; 156°-286°; 48°34'·71N 02°34'·19W.

BAIE DE ST BRIEUC

Grand Léjon ☆ Fl (5) WR 20s 17m **W18M**, R14M; 015°-R-058°-W-283°-R-350°-W-015°; R twr, W bands; 48°44'·91N 02°39'·87W.

Petit Léjon ⚓ ; 48°41'·80N 02°37'·55W.

Les Landas ⚓ Q, 48°41'·43N 02°31'·29W.

Le Rohein ⚓ Q (9) WRG 15s 13m, W8M, R/G5M; 072°-R-105°-W-180°-G-193°-W-237°-G-282°-W-301°-G-330°-W-072°; Y twr, B band; 48°38'·80N 02°37'·77W.

SAINT-BRIEUC LE LÉGUÉ

Tra-Hillion ⚓ 48°33'·38N 02°38'·50W.

Le Légué ⚓ Mo (A)10s; 48°34'·32N 02°41'·15W.

No. 1 ⚓ Fl G 2·5s; 48°32'·42N 02°42'·51W.

No. 2 ⚓ Fl R 2·5s; 48°32'·37N 02°42'·40W.

No. 3 ⚓ Fl (2) G 6s; 48°32'·27N 02°42'·78W.

No. 4 ⚓ Fl (2) R 6s; 48°32'·23N 02°42'·70W.

No. 5 ⚓ Fl (3) G 12s; 48°32'·18N 02°42'·92W.

No. 6 ⚓ Fl (3) R 12s; 48°32'·14N 02°42'·90W.

NE jetty ⚡ VQ R 4M; 48°32'·12N 02°42'·88W.

Pte à l'Aigle jetty ⚡ VQ G 13m 8M; 160°-070°; W twr, G top; 48°32'·12N 02°43'·11W.

No. 7 ⚓ Fl (4) G 15s; 48°32'·11N 02°43'·08W.

No. 8 ⚓ Fl R 2·5s; 48°32'·01N 02°43'·16W.

No. 9 ⚓ Fl (2) G 6s; 48°31'·96N 02°43'·29W.

No. 10 ⚓ Fl (2) R 6s; 48°31'·91N 02°43'·31W.

Custom House jetty ⚡ Iso G 4s 6m 2M; W cols, G top; 48°31'·90N 02°43'·43W.

No. 11 ⚓ Fl (3) G 12s; 48°31'·90N 02°43'·43W.

No. 13 ⚓ Fl (4) G 15s; 48°31'·76N 02°43'·56W.

No. 14 ⚓ Fl (4) G 15s; 48°31'·70N 02°43'·61W.

BINIC

N môle ⚡ Oc (3) 12s 12m 11M; unintens 020°-110°; W twr, G lantern; 48°36'·07N 02°48'·92W.

ST QUAY-PORTRIEUX

Les Hors ⚓ 48°39'·60N 02°44'·04W.

Caffa ⚓ Q (3) 10s; 48°37'·82N 02°43'·08W.

La Longue ⚓ 48°37'·88N 02°44'·68W.

La Roselière ⚓ VQ (6) + L Fl 10s; 48°37'·31N 02°46'·19W.

Herflux ⚓ Dir ⚡ 130°, Fl (2) WRG 6s 10m, W 8M, R/G 6M; 115°-G-125°-W-135°-R-145°; 48°39'·07N 02°47'·95W.

Île Harbour (Roches de Saint-Quay) ⚡ Fl WRG 4s 16m, W9M, R/G 6M; 011°-R-133°-G-270°-R-306°-G-358°-W-011°; W twr & dwelling, R top; 48°39'·99N 02°48'·49W.

Madeux ⚓ 48°40'·41N 02°48'·81W.

Grandes Moulières de St Quay ⚓ 48°39'·76N 02°49'·91W.

Moulières de Portrieux ⚓ 48°39'·26N 02°49'·21W.

Les Noirs ⚓ 48°39'·09N 02°48·46W.

Marina, **NE mole elbow**, Dir lt 318·2°: Iso WRG 4s 16m **W15M**, R/G11M; W159°-179°, G179°-316°, W316°-320·5°, R320·5° -159°; Reserve lt ranges 11/8M; 48°38'·99N 02°49'·09W.

NE môle hd ⚡ Fl (3) G 12s 10m 2M; 48°38'·84N 02°48'·91W.

S môle hd ⚡ Fl (3) R 12s 10m 2M; 48°38'·83N 02°49'·03W.

Old hbr ent: N side, Fl G 2.5s 11m 2M; 48°38'·71N 02°49'·36W.

S side, Fl R 2.5s 8m 2M; 48°38'·67N 02°49'·35W.

MID-CHANNEL MARKS

CHANNEL LT VESSEL ⚓ Fl 15s 12m **15M**; R hull with lt twr amidships; *Horn (20s)*; **Racon O, 15M**; 49°54'·46N 02°53'·74W.

E Channel ⚓ Fl Y 5s 6M; **Racon T, 10M**; 49°58'·67N 02°29'·01W.

COTENTIN PENINSULA (NW COAST)

La Plate ⚓ Fl (2+1) WR 10s 11m; W9M, R6M; 115°-W-272°-R-115°; Y 8-sided twr, with B top; 49°43'·98N 01°55'·76W.

Cap de la Hague (Gros du Raz) ☆ Fl 5s 48m **23M**; Gy twr, W top; *Horn 30s*; 49°43'·31N 01° 57'·27W.

La Foraine ⚓ VQ (9) 10s 12m 6M; 49°42'·90 N 01°58'·32W.

Cap de Carteret ☆ Fl (2+1) 15s 81m **26M**; Gy twr, G top; 49°22'·41N 01°48'·41W.

THE CASQUETS AND ALDERNEY

Casquets ☆ Fl (5) 30s 37m **18M**, H24; W twr, 2 R bands; NW'most of three; *Racon T, 25M;* 49°43'·32N 02°22'·63W.

Ortac rock, unlit; 49°43'·40N 02°17'·44W.

Pierre au Vraic, unmarked rk 1·2m ☀; 49°41'·61N 02°16'·94W.

Quenard Pt (Alderney) ⚓ Fl (4) 15s 37m 12M; 085°-027°; W ○ twr, B band; 49°43'·75N 02°09'·86W.

Château à L'Étoc Pt ⚓ Iso WR 4s 20m W10M, R7M; 071·1°-R- 111·1°-W-151·1°; 49°43'·94N 02°10'·63W.

BRAYE

Ldg bns 142° (to clear the submerged Adm'ty bkwtr). Front, W ⚓, 49°43'·90N 02°10'·97W. Rear, BW ⚓; 720m from front.

Ldg lts 215°: both Q 8/17m 9/12M, synch; 210°-220°; orange △s. Front, old pier elbow, 49°43'·40N 02°11'·91W. Rear, 215°/335m.

Admiralty bkwtr head ⚓ L Fl 10s 7m 5M; 49°43'·82N 02°11'·67W.

FairwayNo. 1 ▲ QG; 49°43'·72N 02°11'·72W.

No. 2 ◂ QR; 49°43'·60N 02°11'·75W.

Inner fairway ▲ Q (2) G 5s; 49°43'·58N 02°11'·98W.

Braye quay ⚓ 2 FR (vert) 8m 5M; 49°43'·53N 02°12'·00W.

Little Crabby hbr ent ⚓ FG & FR 5m 2M; 49°43'·45N 02°12'·12W.

GUERNSEY, NORTHERN APPROACHES

LITTLE RUSSEL CHANNEL

Grande Amfroque, two unlit bcn twrs: larger, BW-banded; smaller, white; 49°30'·57N 02°24'·62W.

Tautenay ⚓ Q (3) WR 6s 7m W7M, R6M; 050°-W-215°-R-050°; B & W striped bcn 49°30'·11N 02°26'·84W.

Platte Fougère ☆ Fl WR 10s 15m **16M**; 155°-W-085°-R-155°; W 8-sided twr, B band; *Horn 45s; Racon P;* 49°30'·83N 02°29'·14W.

Corbette d'Amont ⚓ Y bcn twr, topmark; 49°29'·64N 02°29'·38W.

Roustel ⚓ Q 8m 7M; BW chequered base, W framework col; 49°29'·23N 02°28'·79W.

Rousse, Y bcn twr, topmark ⌘; 49°28'·98N 02°28'·36W.

Platte ⚓, Fl WR 3s 6m, W7M, R5M; 024°-R-219°-W-024°; G conical twr; 49°29'·08N 02°29'·57W.

Vivian bcn twr, BW bands, 49°28'·45N 02°30'·66W.

Brehon ⚓ Iso 4s 19m 9M; bcn on ○ twr, 49°28'·28N 02°29'·28W.

Demie Flieroque, Y bcn twr, topmark F; 49°28'·13N 02°31'·38W.

BIG RUSSEL

Noire Pute ⚓ Fl (2) WR 15s 8m 6M; 220°-W-040°-R-220°; on 2m high rock; 49°28'·21N 02°25'·02W; unreliable.

Fourquies ⚓ Q; 49°27'·34N 02°26'·47W.

Lower Heads ⚓ Q (6) + L Fl 15s; *Bell;* 49°25'·85N 02°28'·55W.

GUERNSEY, HERM AND SARK

BEAUCETTE MARINA

Petite Canupe ⚓ Q (6) + L Fl 15s; 49°30'·20N 02°29'·14W.

Ldg lts 277°: Both FR. Front, W □, R stripe; 49°30'·19N 02°30'·23W. Rear, R □, W stripe; 185m from front.

Appr chan buoys: SWM L Fl 10s 49°30'·15N 02°29'·66W. SHM Fl G 5s, PHM Fl R 5s & Fl (3) R 5s. NCM perch Q 49°30'·165N 02°30'·06W. SHM perch Q (3) G 5s at ent; 49°30'·18N 02°30'·24W.

ST SAMPSON

Ldg lts 286°: Front, FR 3m 5M; 230°-340°; tfc sigs; 49°28'·90N 02°30'·74W. Rear, FG 13m; clock twr, 390m from front.

N Pier ⚓ FG 3m 5M; 230°-340°; 49°28'·92N 02°30'·71W.

Crocq pier ⚓ FR 11m 5M; 250°-340°; 49°28'·98N 02°31'·00W.

ST PETER PORT

Outer ldg lts 220°: **Front**, Castle bkwtr, Al WR 10s 14m **16M**; 187°-007°; dark ○ twr, W on NE side; *Horn 15s;* 49°27'·31N 02°31'·45W.

Rear 220° ldg lt, Belvedere, Oc 10s 61m 14M; 179°-269°; intens 217°-223°; W □ on W twr; 980m from front. The lts are synchronised so that the rear lt is on when the front is W, and the off when the front is R.

Queen Elizabeth II marina, 270° Dir Oc ⚓ WRG 3s 5m 6M; 258°-G-268°-W-272°-R-282°; 49°27'·73N 02°31'·87W.

Reffée ⚓ Q (6) + L Fl 15s; 49°27'·74N 02°31'·27W.

Appr buoys: outer pair ▲ QG; 49°27'·83N 02°31'·54W. ◂ QR; 49°27'·71N 02°31'·52W. Inner pair: ▲ QG; 49°27'·76N 02°31'·74W. ◂ QR; 49°27'·72N 02°31'·74W.

The Pool ldg lts 265° (*not* into moorings): Front, Victoria marina, S Pier ⚓ Oc R 5s 10m 14M; 49°27'·32N 02°32'·03W. Rear, ⚓ Iso R 2s 22m 3M; 260°-270°; on Creasey's bldg, 160m from front.

White Rock pier ⚓ Oc G 5s 11m 14M; intens 174°-354°; ○ twr; tfc sigs; 49°27'·38N 02°31'·59W.

S Fairway ▲ QG; 49°27'·30N 02°31'·76W; pontoon W of buoy.

◂ Fl R; 49°27'·28N 02°31'·74W. 49°27'·27N 02°31'·80W. 49°27'·27N 02°31'·86W.

HAVELET BAY

Oyster Rock ⚓ Y bcn, topmark 'O'; 49°27'·09N 02°31'·46W.

Oyster Rock ▲ QG; 49°27'·04N 02°31'·47W.

Moulinet ◂ QR; 49°26'·97N 02°31'·54W.

Moulinet ⚓ Y bcn, topmark 'M'; 49°26'·95N 02°31'·58W.

GUERNSEY, SOUTH-EAST and SOUTH COASTS

Anfré, Y bcn, topmark 'A'; 49°26'·45N 02°31'·48W.

Longue Pierre, Y bcn, topmark 'LP'; 49°25'·36N 02°31'·48W.

St Martin's Pt ⚓ Fl (3) WR 10s 15m 14M; 185°-R-191°-W-011°-R-061·5°; flat-topped, W bldg. *Horn (3) 30s;* 49°25'·30N 02°31'·70W.

GUERNSEY, NORTH-WEST COAST

Les Hanois ☆ Fl (2) 13s 33m **20M**; 294°-237°; Gy ○ twr, B lantern, helicopter platform; *Horn (2) 60s.* 49°26'·10N 02°42'·15W.

4 FR on mast 1·3M ESE of Les Hanois lt ho.

Portelet Hbr, bkwtr bcn, 49°26'·16N 02°39'·84W.

Cobo Bay, Grosse Rock, B bcn 11m; 49°29'·02N 02°36'·19W.

Grand Havre, Rousse Point bkwtr, B bcn; 49°29'·92N 02°33'·05W.

HERM

Corbette de la Mare, Wh disc (W side) and R disc (E side) on Y pole, 49°28'·48N 02°28'·72W.

Petit Creux ⚓ QR; red 'C' on red pole; 49°28'·09N 02°28'·72W.

Alligande ⚓ Fl (3) G 5s; B pole, Or 'A'; 49°27'·86N 02°28'·78W.

Épec ⚓ Fl G 3s; black 'E' on G mast; 49°27'·98N 02°27'·89W.

Vermerette ⚓ Fl (2) Y 5s; Or 'V' on bcn; 49°28'·12N 02°27'·75W.

Gate Rock (Percée Pass) ⚓ Q (9) 15s; 49°27'·88N 02°27'·54W.

Hbr ldg lts 078°: White drums. ⚓ 2F occas; 49°28'·25N 02°27'·11W.

Hbr pier, N end ⚓ 2 FG; G □ on G bcn; 49°28'·21N 02°27'·26W.

SARK

Courbée du Nez ⚓ Fl (4) WR 15s 14m 8M; 057°-W-230°-R-057°; W structure on rock; 49°27'·09N 02°22'·17W.

Point Robert ☆ Fl 15s 65m **20M**; vis 138°-353°; W 8-sided twr; *Horn (2) 30s;* 49°26'·19N 02°20'·75W.

Founiais ⚓, topmark 'F'; 49°26'·02N 02°20'·36W.

Blanchard ⚓ Q (3) 10s; *Bell;* 49°25'·36N 02°17'·42W.

Pilcher monument (070° appr brg); 49°25'·71N 02°22'·44W.

JERSEY, WEST AND SOUTH COASTS

Desormes ⚓ Q (9) 15s; 49°18'·94N 02°17'·98W.

Grosnez Point ☆ Fl (2) WR 15s 50m **W19M, R17M**; 081°-W-188°-R-241°; W hut; 49°15'·50N 02°14'·80W.

L a Rocco twr (conspic) 15m; 49°11'·90N 02°14'·05W.

La Frouquie ⚓ (seasonal); 49°11'·30N 02°15'·38W.

La Corbière ☆ Iso WR 10s 36m **W18M, R16M**; shore-W-294°-R-328°-W-148°-R-shore; W ○ twr; *Horn Mo (C) 60s;* 49°10'·79N 02°15'·01W.

Pt Corbière ⚓ FR; R □, W stripe; 49°10'·87N 02°14'·38W.

WESTERN PASSAGE

Ldg lts 082°. Front, La Gréve d'Azette Oc 5s 23m 14M; 034°-129°; 49°10'·16N 02°05'·09W. Rear, Mont Ubé, Oc R 5s 46m 12M; 250°-095°; 1M from front.

Passage Rock ⚓ VQ; 49°09'·54N 02°12'·26W.

Les Fours ⚓ Q; 49°09'·59N 02°10'·16W.

Noirmont Pt ⚓ Fl (4) 12s 18m 10M; B twr, W band; 49°09'·91N 02°10'·08W.

Pignonet ⚓ 49°09'·88N 02°09'·70W.

Ruaudière Rock ⚓ Fl G 3s; *Bell;* 49°09'·74N 02°08'·62W.

ST AUBIN'S BAY and HARBOUR

Les Grunes du Port ⚓ 49°10'·02N 02°09'·14W.

Diamond Rock ⚓ Fl (2) R 6s; 49°10'·12N 02°08'·64W.

Castle pier ⚓ Fl R 4s 8m 1M; 49°11'·13N 02°09'·634W.

North pier, Dir lt 254° ⚓ F WRG 5m, 248°-G-253°-W-255°-R-260°; 49°11'·22N 02°10'·03W. Same col, Iso R 4s 12m 10M.

Beach Rock ⚓ 49°11'·29N 02°08'·42W, (Apr-Oct).

Rocquemin ⚓ 49°10'·64N 02°07'·95W.

Baleine ⚓ 49°10'·41N 02°08'·23W.

ST HELIER

Elizabeth marina, west appr: Dir ⚓ 106°: F WRG 4m 1M; 096°-G-104°-W-108°-R-119°; R dayglo □, B stripe; 49°10'·76N 02°07'·12W.

La Vrachiére ⚓ 49°10'·90N 02°07'·59W, Fl (2) 5s 1M.

Fort Charles North ⚓ 49°10'·81N 02°07'·50W.

Marina ent ⚓ Oc G & Oc R, both 4s 2M; 49°10'·83N 02°07'·13W.

Red & Green Passage, ldg lts 022·7° on dayglo R dolphins: Front, Elizabeth E berth Dn ⚓ Oc G 5s 10m 11M; 49°10'·63N 02°06'·94W. Rear, Albert Pier root ⚓ Oc R 5s 18m 12M; synch; 230m SSW.

East Rock ⚓ QG; 49°09'·96N 02°07'·28W.

Dog's Nest Rk ⚓ Fl Y 3s 3M; Y cross on bcn; 49°09'·99N 02°06'·95W.

Oyster Rocks, R/W bcn, topmark 'O'; 49°10'·10N 02°07'·49W.

Platte Rock ⚓ Fl R 1·5s 6m 5M; R col; 49°10'·16N 02°07'·34W.

Small Road No. 2 ⚓ QR; 49°10'·39N 02°07'·24W.

No. 4 ⚓ QR; 49°10'·53N 02°07'·12W.

Elizabeth marina, S appr: E1 ⚓ Fl G 3s; 49°10'·59N 02°07'·09W.

E2 ⚓ Fl R 2s; 49°10'·58N 02°07'·13W.

E5 ⚓ Fl G 5s; 49°10'·70N 02°07'·17W.

E6 ⚓ Fl R 2s; 49°10'·69N 02°07'·21W.

Fort Charles East ⚓ Q (3) 5s 2m 1M; 49°10'·74N 02°07'·26W.

La Collette basin ⚓ QR; 49°10'·54N 02°06'·91W. ⚓ 49°10'·52N 02°06'·90W.

St Helier Hbr, ldg lts 078°, both FG on W cols. Front, 49°10'·62N 02°06'·66W. Rear, 80m from front.

Victoria pier hd, Port control twr; IPTS; 49°10'·57N 02°06'·88W.

JERSEY, SOUTH-EAST AND EAST COASTS

Hinguette ⚓ QR; 49°09'·33N 02°07'·32W.

Hettich ⚓ Fl Y 5s; 49°08'·10N 02°09'·00W.

South Pier Marine ⚓ Fl Y 5s; 49°09'·10N 02°06'·30W.

Demie de Pas ⚓ Mo (D) WR 12s 11m, W14M, R10M; 130°-R-303°-W-130°; *Horn (3) 60s; Racon T, 10M*; B bn twr, Y top; 49°09'·01N 02°06'·15W. Icho Tower (conspic, 14m) 49°08'·89N 02°02'·90W.

Canger Rock ⚓ Q (9) 15s; 49°07'·35N 02°00'·38W.

La Conchière ⚓ Q (6) + L Fl 15s 2M; 49°08'·22N 02°00'·17W.

Frouquier Aubert ⚓ Q (6) + L Fl 15s; 49°06'·08N 01°58'·84W.

Violet ⚓ L Fl 10s; 49°07'·81N 01°57'·14W.

Petite Anquette; SCM ⚓; 49°08'·47N 01°56'·29W.

Grande Anquette ⚓ VQ(9) 10s; 49°08'·32N 01°55'·20W.

Le Cochon ⚓ 49°09'·77N 01°58'·80W.

La Noire ⚓ 49°10'·13N 01°59'·23W. Le Giffard ⚓ 49°10'·59N 01°59'·00W.

GOREY

Pier Hd Dir lt 298°, ⚓ WRG, 6m 8M; 293·5°-G-296·5°-W-299·5°-R-302·5°; ⚓ Oc RG 5s 8m 12M; 304°-R-353°-G-304°; W twr on pierhead; 49°11'·80N 02°01'·34W.

Horn Rock ⚓, topmark 'H'; 49°10'·96N 01°59'·85W.

Les Burons, RW bcn, topmark 'B'; 49°11'·33N 02°00'·81W.

Fairway ⚓ QG; 49°11'·50N 02°00'·34W.

Écureuil Rock ⚓ 49°11'·67N 02°00'·78W.

Equerrière Rk, bcn 'fishtail' topmark; 49°11'·80N 02°00'·67W.

Les Arch ⚓, BW bcn, 'A' topmark; 49°12'·02N 02°00'·60W.

ST CATHERINE BAY

St Catherine Bay, Le Fara ⚓ Q (3) 10s 3M; 49°12'·85N 02°00'·48W.

Archirondel Tower (conspic, 16m) 49°12'·72N 02°01'·42W.

Verclut bkwtr ⚡ Fl 1·5s 18m 13M; 49°13'·34N 02°00'·64W. In line 315° with unlit turret, 49°13'·96N 02°01'·57W, on La Coupe Pt.

JERSEY, NORTH COAST

Rozel Bay Dir lt 245°, F WRG 11m 5M; 240°-G-244°-W-246°-R-250°; W col; 49°14'·21N 02°02'·76W.
Bonne Nuit Bay ldg lts 223°: both FG 7/34m 6M. Front, Pier 49°15'·10N 02°07'·17W. Rear, 170m from front.
Demie Rock ▲ 49°15'·56N 02°07'·36W.
Sorel Point ☆ L Fl WR 7·5s 50m **15M**; 095°-W-112°-R-173°-W-230°-R-269°-W-273°; W ○ twr, only 3m high; 49°15'·60N 02°09'·54W.

OFFLYING ISLANDS

LES ÉCREHOU

Écrevière ⚓ Q (6) + L Fl 15s; 49°15'·26N 01°52'·15W.
Mâitre Ile ⚓ 49°17'·08N 01°55'·60W.

PLATEAU DES MINQUIERS

N Minquiers ⚓ Q; 49°01'·64N 02°00'·58W.

NE Minquiers ⚓ VQ (3) 5s; *Bell;* 49°00'·85N 01°55'·30W.
SE Minquiers ⚓ Q (3) 10s; *Bell;* 48°53'·42N 02°00'·09W.
S Minquiers ⚓ Q (6) + L Fl 15s; 48°53'·09N 02°10'·10W.
SW Minquiers ⚓ Q (9) 15s 5M; *Whis;* 48°54'·35N 02°19'·41W.
NW Minquiers ⚓ Q 5M; *Whis;* 48°59'·63N 02°20'·59W.
Refuge ⚓; B/W bcn; 49°00'·13N 02°10'·16W.
Demie de Vascelin ▲ 49°00'·81N 02°05'·17W.
Grand Vascelin, BW bcn ⚓ 48°59'·97N 02°07'·26W.
Maitresse Ile, Puffin B&W bcn twr ⚓ 48°58'·33N 02°03'·65W.
Le Coq Reef, ⚓ Q (3) 10s 6m 3M; 48°57'·88N 02°01'·29W.

FRENCH MARKS NORTH OF ILE DE BRÉHAT

Roches Douvres ☆ Fl 5s 60m **24M**; pink twr on dwelling with G roof; 49°06'·30N 02°48'·87W (16M NNE of Ile de Bréhat).
Barnouic ⚓ VQ (3) 5s 15m 7M; 49°01'·64N 02°48'·41W.
Roche Gautier ⚓ VQ (9) 10s; 49°02'·013N 02°54'·36W.
Les Héaux de Bréhat ☆ Fl (4) WRG 15s 48m, **W15M**, R/G11M; 227°-R-247°-W-270°-G-302°-W-227°; Gy twr; 48°54'·50N 03°05'·18W (4·7M WNW of Ile de Bréhat).

DISTANCE TABLES
Approx distances in nautical miles are by the most direct route allowing for dangers and TSS.

		1																
1	Cherbourg	1																
2	Omonville	10	2															
3	Braye (Alderney)	25	15	3														
4	St Peter Port	44	34	23	4													
5	Creux (Sark)	37	29	22	10	5												
6	St Helier	64	51	46	29	24	6											
7	Carteret	41	29	28	31	23	26	7										
8	Portbail	49	33	32	35	27	25	5	8									
9	Iles Chausey	69	61	58	48	43	25	33	30	9								
10	Granville	75	67	66	55	50	30	38	35	9	10							
11	Dinan	102	91	85	66	64	50	62	59	29	35	11						
12	St Malo	90	79	73	54	52	38	50	47	17	23	12	12					
13	Dahouet	88	80	72	54	52	41	60	59	37	45	41	29	13				
14	Le Légué/St Brieuc	96	86	76	57	56	46	69	69	41	49	45	33	8	14			
15	Binic	95	84	75	56	55	46	70	70	43	51	45	33	10	8	15		
16	St Quay-Portrieux	88	80	73	56	51	46	64	64	47	54	47	35	11	7	4	16	
17	Lézardrieux	88	80	68	48	38	47	68	71	53	54	61	49	33	32	30	21	17

AREA 16 *N & S Brittany – Paimpol to Lesconil*

SELECTED LIGHTS, BUOYS & WAYPOINTS

Positions are referenced to WGS84

OFFSHORE MARKS

Roches Douvres ☆ Fl 5s 60m **24M**; pink twr on dwelling with G roof; 49°06'·30N 02°48'·87W.
Barnouic ⚓ VQ (3) 5s 15m 7M; 49°01'·63N 02°48'·41W.
Roche Gautier ⚓ VQ (9) 10s; 49°02'·013N 02°54'·36W.

PAIMPOL TO ÎLE DE BRÉHAT

PAIMPOL

Les Calemarguiers ⚓ 48°46'·98N 02°54'·84W.
L'Ost Pic ⚡ Fl(4)WR 15s 20m, W9M, R6M; 105°-W-116°-R-221°-W-253°-R-291°-W-329°; obsc by islets near Bréhat when brg < 162°; W twr/turret, R top; 48°46'·75N 02°56'·42W.
Les Charpentiers ⚓ 48°47'·89N 02°56'·01W.
Pte de Porz-Don ☆ Oc (2) WR 6s 13m **W15M**, R11M; 269°-W-272°-R-279°; W house; 48°47'·48N 03°01'·55W.
El Bras ⚓ Fl G 2·5s; 48°47'·21N 03°01'·50W.
⚓ Fl R 2·5s; 48°47'·17N 03°01'·49W.
Ldg lts 262·2°, both QR 5/12m 7/10M. Front, Kernoa jetty; W & R hut; 48°47'·09N 03°02'·44W. Rear, Dir QR, intens 260·2°-264·2°; W pylon, R top; 360m from front. ⚡ QG 48°47'·12N 03°02'·47W.

CHENAL DU FERLAS (277°-257°-271°)

Lel Ar Serive ⚓ 48°49'·98N 02°58'·76W.
Loguivy Dir lt 257°: Q WRG 12m 10/8M; 254°-G-257°-W-257·7°- R-260·7°; Gy twr; 48°49'·37N 03°03'·67W.
Les Piliers ⚓ 48°49'·77N 02°59'·99W.
Kermouster Dir ⚡ 271°: Fl WRG 2s 16m, W 10M, R/G 8M; 267°-G-270°-W-272°-R-274°; W col; 48°49'·55N 03°05'·19W (R. Trieux).

ÎLE DE BRÉHAT

Le Paon ⚡ Oc WRG 4s 22m W11M, R/G8M; 033°-W-078°-G-181°-W-196°- R-307°-W-316°-R-348°; Y twr; 48°51'·92N 02°59'·15W.
Roche Guarine ⚓ 48°51'·63N 02°57'·63W, Chenal de Bréhat.
Rosédo ☆ Fl 5s 29m **20M**; W twr; vis 006°-340° (334°); 48°51'·45N 03°00'·29W.
La Chambre ⚓ 48°50'·16N 02°59'·58W.
Men-Joliguet ⚓ Fl (2) WRG 4s 6m W11M, R/G8M; 255°-R-279°-W-283°-G-175°; 48°50'·12N 03°00'·20W.

LÉZARDRIEUX TO TRÉGUIER

LE TRIEUX RIVER to LÉZARDRIEUX
Nord Horaine ⚓ 48°54'·54N 02°55'·23W.

La Horaine ⚓ Fl (3) 12s 13m 7M; Gy 8-sided twr on B hut; 48°53'·50N 02°55'·22W.

Men-Marc'h ⌱ 48°53'·17N 02°51'·82W.

Ldg lts 224·8°: Front, **La Croix** ☆ Q 15m **18M**; intens 215°-235°; two Gy ○ twrs joined, W on NE side, R tops; 48°50'·23N 03°03'·25W. Rear **Bodic** ☆ Dir Q 55m **22M**; intens 221°-229°; W ho with G gable; 2·1M from front.

Les Sirlots ⚓ *Whis;* 48°52'·95N 02°59'·58W.

Men-Grenn ⌱ Q (9) 15s 7m 7M; 48°51'·22N 03°03'·89W.

Coatmer ldg lts 218·7°. Front, Q RG 16m R/G7M; 200°-R-250°-G-053°; W gable; 48°48'·26N 03°05'·75W. Rear, QR 50m 7M; vis 197°-242°; W gable; 660m from front.

Les Perdrix ⚓ Fl (2) WG 6s 5m, W6M, G3M; 165°-G-197°-W-202·5°-G-040°; G twr; 48°47'·74N 03°05'·79W.

CHENAL DE LA MOISIE (339·4°); PASSE DE LA GAINE (241·5°)

La Vieille du Tréou ⌱ 48°52'·00N 03°01'·09W.

An Ogejou Bihan ⌱ 48°53'·37N 03°01'·91W.

La Moisie ⌱ 48°53'·83N 03°02'·22W.

Les Héaux de Bréhat ☆ Fl (4) WRG 15s 48m, **W15M**, R/G11M; 227°-R-247°-W-270°-G-302°-W-227°; Gy ○ twr; 48°54'·50N 03°05'·17W.

Basse des Héaux ⌱ 48°54'·07N 03°05'·28W.

Pont de la Gaine ⌱ 48°53'·12N 03°07'·40W.

JAUDY RIVER TO TRÉGUIER

La Jument des Héaux ⌱ VQ; 48°55'·36N 03°08'·04W.

Grande Passe ldg lts 137°. Front, Port de la Chaine, Oc 4s 12m 11M; 042°-232°; W house; 48°51'·55N 03°07'·89W. Rear, **St Antoine** ☆ Dir Oc R 4s 34m **15M**; intens 134°-140°; R & W house; 0·75M from front. (Both marks are hard to see by day.)

Basse Crublent ⌱ QR; *Whis;* 48°54'·29N 03°11'·16W.

Le Corbeau ⌱ Fl R 4s; 48°53'·35N 03°10'·26W.

Pierre à l'Anglais ⌱ Fl G 4s; 48°53'·21N 03°10'·46W.

Petit Pen ar Guézec ⌱ Fl (2) G 6s; 48°52'·52N 03°09'·44W.

La Corne ⚓ Fl (3) WRG 12s 14m W8M, R/G6M; 052°-W-059°-R-173°-G-213°-W-220°-R-052°; W twr, R base; 48°51'·35N 03°10'·62W.

TRÉGUIER TO TRÉBEURDEN

PORT BLANC

Le Voleur Dir ⚓ 150°: Fl WRG 4s 17m, W14M, R/G 11M; 140°-G-148°-W-152°-R-160°; W twr; 48°50'·20N 03°18'·52W.

Basse Guazer ⌱ ; 48°51'·58N 03°20'·96W.

PERROS-GUIREC

Passe de l'Est, ldg lts 224·8°. Front, Le Colombier ⚓ Dir Q 28m 14M; intens 214·5°-234·5°; W house; 48°47'·87N 03°26'·66W. Rear, **Kerprigent** ☆, Dir Q 79m **21M**; intens 221°-228°; W twr, 1·5M from front.

Pierre du Chenal ⌱ 48°49'·29N 03°24'·67W.

Passe de l'Ouest. Kerjean ☆ Dir lt 143·6°, Oc (2+1) WRG 12s 78m, **W15M**, R/G12M; 133·7°-G-143·2°-W-144·8°-R-154·3°; W twr, B top; 48°47'·79N 03°23'·39W.

Les Couillons de Tomé ⌱ 48°50'·88N 03°25'·68W.

La Horaine ⌱ 48°49'·89N 03°27'·26W.

Roche Bernard ⌱ Fl WG 1M; 48°49'·43N 03°25'·46W.

Gommonénou ⌱ VQ R 1M; 48°48'·27N 03°25'·83W.

Jetée du Linkin ⚓ Fl (2) G 6s 4m 6M; W pile, G top; 48°48'·20N 03°26'·31W.

PLOUMANAC'H

Mean-Ruz ⚓ Oc WR 4s 26m W12M, R9M; 226°-W-242°-R-226°; obsc by Pte de Trégastel when brg <080°; partly

obsc by Les Sept-Îles 156°-207° and partly by Île Tomé 264°-278°; pink ☐ twr; 48°50'·25N 03°29'·00W.

LES SEPT ÎLES

Île-aux-Moines ☆ Fl (3) 20s 59m **24M**; obsc by Îliot Rouzic and E end of Île Bono 237°-241°, and in Baie de Lannion when brg <039°; Gy twr and dwelling; 48°52'·72N 03°29'·40W.

Les Dervinis ⌱ 48°52'·35N 03°27'·32W.

TRÉGASTEL-PLAGE

Île Dhu ⌱ 48°50'·37N 03°31'·24W.

Les Triagoz ⚓ Fl (2) WR 6s 31m W14M, R11M; 010°-W-339°-R-010°; obsc in places 258°-268° by Les Sept-Îles; Gy ☐ twr, R lantern; 48°52'·28N 03°38'·80W.

Bar-ar-Gall ⌱ VQ (9) 10s; 48°49'·79N 03°36'·22W.

Le Crapaud ⌱ Q (9) 15s; 48°46'·67N 03°40'·59W.

TRÉBEURDEN

Pte de Lan Kerellec ⚓ Iso WRG 4s; W8M, R/G5M; 058°-G-064°-W-069°-R-130°; Gy twr; 48°46'·74N 03°35'·06W.

Ar Gouredec ⌱ VQ (6) + L Fl 10s; 48°46'·41N 03°36'·59W.

An Ervennou ⌱ Fl (2) R 6s; 48°46'·48N 03°35'·96W.

NW bkwtr ⚓ Fl G 2·5s 8m 2M; IPTS; 48°46'·33N 03°35'·21W.

TRÉBEURDEN TO MORLAIX

LÉGUER RIVER

Beg-Léguer ⚓ Oc (4) WRG 12s 60m W12M, R/G9M; 007°-G-084°-W-098°-R-129°; west face of W house, R lantern; 48°44'·31N 03°32'·91W.

Kinierbel ⚓; *Bell;* 48°44'·15N 03°35'·18W.

LOCQUÉMEAU

Ldg lts 121°: Front, ⚓ QR 21m 7M; 068°-228°; W pylon, R top; 48°43'·41N 03°34'·44W. Rear, ⚓ QR 39m 7M; 016°-232°; W gabled house; 484m from front.

Locquémeau ⚓ *Whis;* 48°43'·86N 03°35'·93W.

LOCQUIREC

Gouliat ⌱ 48°42'·57N 03°38'·97W.

PRIMEL-TRÉGASTEL

Méloine ⌱ 48°45'·56N 03°50'·68W.

Ldg lts 152°, both ⚓ QR 35/56m 7M. Front, 134°-168°; W ☐, R stripe, on pylon; 48°42'·45N 03°49'·19W. Rear, R vert stripe on W wall; 172m from front.

W bkwtr ⚓ Fl G 4s 6m 7M; 48°42'·77N 03°49'·52W.

BAIE DE MORLAIX

Chenal de Tréguier ldg lts 190·5°: Front, ⚓ Île Noire Oc (2) WRG 6s 15m, W11M, R/G8M; 051°-G-135°-R-211°-W-051°; obsc in places; W ☐ twr, R top; 48°40'·35N 03°52'·54W. Common Rear, **La Lande** ☆ Fl 5s 85m **23M**; obsc by Pte Annelouesten when brg >204°; W ☐ twr, B top; 48°38'·20N 03°53'·14W.

La Pierre Noire ⌱ 48°42'·56N 03°52'·20W.

La Chambre ⌱ 48°40'·74N 03°52'·51W.

Grande Chenal ldg lts 176·4°: Front, **Île Louet** ☆ Oc (3) WG 12s 17m **W15M**, G10M; 305°-W (except where obsc by islands)-244°-G-305°; W ☐ twr, B top; 48°40'·41N 03°53'·34W. Common Rear, **La Lande** as above.

Pot de Fer ⌱ *Bell;* 48°44'·23N 03°54'·02W.

Stolvezen ⌱ 48°42'·64N 03°53'·41W.

Ricard ⌱ 48°41'·54N 03°53'·51W.

Vieille ⌱ 48°42'·60N 03°54'·11W. (Chenal Ouest de Ricard 188·8°)

La Noire ⌱ 48°41'·65N 03°54'·06W.

Corbeau ⌱ 48°40'·63N 03°53'·33W.

MORLAIX RIVER

Barre de-Flot No. 1 ⚓ 48°40'·18N 03°52'·95W.
No. 2 ⚓ Fl R 2s; 48°39'·88N 03°52'·53W.
No. 3 ⚓ Fl G 2s; 48°39'·25N 03°52'·32W.
No. 4 ⚓ Fl R 2s; 48°38'·62N 03°51'·62W.
No. 5 ⚓ Fl G 2s; 48°38'·04N 03°51'·34W.
No. 7 ⚓ 48°37'·68N 03°51'·03W.

PENZÉ RIVER

Cordonnier ⚓ 48°42'·93N 03°56'·59W.
Guerhéon ⚓ 48°42'·73N 03°57'·18W.
Trousken ⚓ 48°42'·26N 03°56'·54W.
Pte Fourche ⚓ 48°42'·14N 03°56'·76W.
Ar Tourtu ⚓ 48°41'·99N 03°56'·57W.
An Nehou (Caspari) ⚓ 48°41'·56N 03°56'·45W.
Le Figuier ⚓ 48°40'·46N 03°56'·16W.

ROSCOFF TO ÎLE VIERGE

BLOSCON/ROSCOFF

Astan ⚓ VQ (3) 5s 9m 6M; 48°44'·91N 03°57'·66W.
Le Menk ⚓ Q (9) WR 15s 6m W5M, R3M; 160°-W-188°-R-160°; 48°43'·28N 03°56'·71W.
Basse de Bloscon ⚓ VQ; 48°43'·71N 03°57'·55W.
Bloscon pier ⚓ Fl WG 4s 9m W10M, G7M (in fog Fl 2s); 200°-W-210°-G-200°; W twr, G top; 48°43'·21N 03°57'·69W.
⚓ Fl (2) R 6s, 48°43'·11N 03°57'·92W.
Ar Pourven ⚓ Q; 48°43'·04N 03°57'·70W.
Ar-Chaden ⚓ Q (6) + L Fl WR 15s 14m, W8M, R6M; 262°-R-289·5°-W-293°-R-326°- W-110°; YB twr; 48°43'·94N 03°58'·26W.
Men-Guen-Bras ⚓ Q WRG 14m, W9M, R/G6M; 068°-W-073°-R-197°-W-257°-G-068°; BY twr; 48°43'·76N 03°58'·07W.
Roscoff ldg lts 209°: Front, N môle ⚓ Oc (3) G 12s 7m 7M; synch; 078°-318°; W col, G top; 48°43'·59N 03°58'·67W.
Rear ☆ Oc (3) 12s 24m **15M**; 062°-242°; Gy ☐ twr, W on NE side; 430m from front.

CANAL DE L'ÎLE DE BATZ

Roc'h Zu ⚓ 48°43'·88N 03°58'·59W.
Jetty hd (LW landing) ⚓ Q 5m 1M; BY col; 48°43'·92N 03°58'·97W.
Run Oan ⚓ 48°44'·10N 03°59'·30W.
Perroch ⚓ 48°44'·10N 03°59'·71W.
Tec'hit Bihan ⚓ 48°44'·02N 04°00'·88W.
La Croix ⚓ 48°44'·19N 04°01'·30W.
L'Oignon ⚓ 48°44'·04N 04°01'·35W.
Basse Plate ⚓ 48°44'·25N 04°02'·53W.

ÎLE DE BATZ

Île aux Moutons ⚓ VQ (6)+ L Fl 10s 3m 7M; 48°44'·25N 04°00'·52W; landing stage, S end and ent to hbr.
Malvoch ⚓ 48°44'·26N 04°00'·67W, W side of ent.
Lt ho ☆ Fl (4) 25s 69m **23M**; Gy twr; 48°44'·71N 04°01'·62W.
Same twr, auxiliary lt, FR 65m 7M; 024°-059°.

MOGUÉRIEC

Ldg lts 162°: Front ⚓ Iso WG 4s 9m W11M, G6M; 158°-W-166°-G-158°; W twr, G top; jetty 48°41'·34N 04°04'·47W.
Rear ⚓ Iso G 4s 22m 7M, synch; 142°-182°; W col, G top; 440m from front.

PONTUSVAL

Pointe de Pontusval ⚓ 48°41'·42N 04°19'·32W.
Ar Peich ⚓ 48°40'·90N 04°19'·16W.
Pte de Beg-Pol ⚓ Oc (3) WR 12s 16m W10M, R7M; Shore-W-056°-R-096°-W-shore; W twr, B top, W dwelling;

48°40'·67N 04°20'·76W. QY and FR lts on towers 2·4M S.
Aman-ar-Ross ⚓ Q 7M; 48°41'·88N 04°27'·03W.
Lizen Ven Ouest ⚓ VQ (9) 10s 5M; 48°40'·53N 04°33'·63W.
Île-Vierge ☆ Fl 5s 77m **27M**; 337°-325°; Gy twr; *Horn 60s*; 48°38'·33N 04°34'·05W.

ÎLE VIERGE TO L'ABER-ILDUT

L'ABER WRAC'H

Libenter ⚓ Q (9) 15s 6M; 48°37'·45N 04°38'·46W.
Outer ldg lts 100·1°: Front, Île Wrac'h ☆ QR 20m 7M; W ☐ twr, Or top; 48°36'·88N 04°34'·56W. Rear, Lanvaon ☆ Q 55m 12M; intens 090°-110°; W ☐ twr, Or △ on top; 1·63M from front.
Grand Pot de Beurre ⚓ 48°37'·21N 04°36'·48W.
Petit Pot de Beurre ⚓ 48°37'·12N 04°36'·23W.
Basse de la Croix ⚓ Fl G 2·5s; 48°36'·92N 04°35'·99W.
Breac'h Ver ⚓ Fl (2) G 6s 6m 3M; △ on twr; 48°36'·63N 04°35'·38W.
Dir ⚓ 128°, Oc (2) WRG 6s 5m W13M, R/G11M; 125·7°-G-127·2°-W-128·7°-R-130·2°; 48°35'·89N 04°33'·82W, root of W bkwtr .
Marina ent: QG 3m 2M; vis 186°-167° (341°); 48°35'·97N 04°33'·64W. QR 3m 2M; vis 244°-226° (342°).

L'ABER BENOÎT

Petite Fourche ⚓ 48°36'·99N 04°38'·75W.
Rusven Est ⚓ 48°36'·30N 04°38'·63W.
Rusven Ouest ⚓ *Bell;* 48°36'·07N 04°39'·43W.
Basse du Chenal ⚓ 48°35'·81N 04°38'·53W.
Poul Orvil ⚓ 48°35'·52N 04°38'·29W.
La Jument ⚓ 48°35'·10N 04°37'·41W.
Ar Gazel ⚓ 48°34'·90N 04°37'·27W.
Le Chien ⚓ 48°34'·67N 04°36'·88W.

ROCHES DE PORTSALL

Le Relec ⚓ 48°35'·99N 04°40'·84W.
Corn-Carhai ⚓ Fl (3) 12s 19m 9M; W 8-sided twr, B top; 48°35'·19N 04°43'·94W.
Grande Basse de Portsall ⚓ VQ (9) 10s 9m 4M; 48°36'·70N 04°46'·13W.
Basse Paupian ⚓ 48°35'·31N 04°46'·27W.
Bosven Aval ⚓ 48°33'·82N 04°44'·27W.
Men ar Pic ⚓ 48°33'·65N 04°44'·03W.
Portsall ⚓ Oc (4) WRG 12s 9m W13M, R/G10M; 058°-G-084°-W-088°-R-058°; W col, R top; 48°33'·84N 04°42'·26W.

ARGENTON to L'ABER-ILDUT

Le Taureau ⚓ 48°31'·46N 04°47'·34W.
Argenton, Île Dolvez, front ldg bcn 086° ⚓ 48°31'·25N 04°46'·23W.
Le Four ☆ Fl (5) 15s 28m **22M**; Gy ○ twr; 48°31'·38N 04°48'·32W.
L'Aber-Ildut ☆ Dir Oc (2) WR 6s 12m **W25M, R20M**; 081°-W-085°-R-087°; W bldg; 48°28'·26N 04°45'·56W.

CHENAL DU FOUR AND CHENAL DE LA HELLE

Ldg lts 158·5°. Front, **Kermorvan** ☆ Fl 5s 20m **22M**; obsc'd by Pte de St Mathieu when brg <341°; W ☐ twr; *Horn 60s*; 48°21'·72N 04°47'·40W.
Rear, **Pte de St Mathieu** ☆ Fl 15s 56m **29M**; W twr, R top; 48°19'·79N 04°46'·26W. Same twr: Dir F 54m **28M**; intens 157·5°-159·5°.
☆ Q WRG 26m, W14M, R/G11M; 085°-G-107°-W-116°-R-134°; W twr 54 m WNW of previous entry; 48°19'·80N 04°46'·30W.

Plâtresses N ▲ Fl G 2·5s; 48°26'·46N 04°50'·71W.
Valbelle ⚓ Fl (2) R 6s 8m 5M; 48°26'·42N 04°50'·03W.
Plâtresses SE ▲ Fl (2) G 6s; 48°25'·96N 04°50'·52W.
Saint Paul ⚓ Oc (2) R 6s; 48°24'·82N 04°49'·16W.
Pte de Corsen ☆ Dir Q WRG 33m W12M, R/G8M; 008°-R-012°-W-015° (ldg sector)- G-021°; W hut; 48°24'·89N 04°47'·61W.

CHENAL DE LA HELLE

Ldg Its 137·9°: Front, **Kermorvan** ☆ see above. Rear, **Lochrist** ☆ Dir Oc (3) 12s 49m **22M**; intens 135°-140°; W 8-sided twr, R top; 48°20'·55N 04°45'·82W.
Luronne ↓; 48°26'·61N 04°53'·78W.
Ldg Its 293·5° astern (to join Ch du Four S of St Paul ⚓): Front, Le Faix ⚓ VQ 16m 8M; 48°25'·73N 04°53'·91W. Rear, **Le Stiff** ☆ (below at Ouessant); 6·9M from front.
Ldg line 142·5°, optional day only (to join Ch du Four SE of St Pierre ▲): Front, **Kermorvan** ☆ see above. Rear, two W gables (Les Pignons de Kéraval, 48m) 48°20'·10N 04°45'·55W.
Pourceaux ⚓ Q; 48°24'·00N 04°51'·31W.
Saint-Pierre ▲ 48°23'·09N 04°49'·09W.
Rouget ▲ Fl G 4s; 48°22'·04N 04°48'·88W (Ch du Four).
Grande Vinotière ⚓ L Fl R 10s 15m 5M; R 8-sided twr; 48°21'·93N 04°48'·42W.
Le Conquet, Môle Ste Barbe ☆ Oc G 4s 5m 6M; 48°21'·58N 04°46'·98W.
Les Renards ↓ 48°21'·00N 04°47'·48W.
Tournant et Lochrist ⚓ 48°20'·64N 04°48'·12W, Fl (2) R 6s.
Ar Christian Braz ▲ 48°20'·68N 04°50'·14W, E of Ile de Béniguet.
Ldg line 325°: Front, Grand Courleau ▲; rear, La Faix (above).
Ldg Its 007°: Front, **Kermorvan** ☆ above. Rear, **Trézien** ☆ Dir Oc (2) 6s 84m **20M**; intens 003°-011°; Gy twr, W on S side; 48°25'·41N 04°46'·74W.
Les Vieux-Moines ⚓ Fl R 4s 16m 5M; 280°-133°; R 8-sided twr; 48°19'·33N 04°46'·63W, 5ca SSW of Pte de St Mathieu.
La Fourmi ▲ 48°19'·25N 04°47'·97W.

OUESSANT AND ÎLE MOLÉNE

OFF USHANT TSS

Ouessant NE ⊙; V-AIS; 48°59'·51N 05°24'·00W.
Ouessant SW ⊙; V-AIS; 48°30'·00N 05°45'·00W.

ÎLE D'OUESSANT

Le Stiff ☆ Fl (2) R 20s 85m **24M**; two adjoining W twrs; 48°28'·47N 05°03'·41W. Radar twr, conspic, 340m NE, ☆ Q (day); ☆ FR (night).
Port du Stiff, E môle ☆ Dir Q WRG 11m W10M, R/G7M; 251°-G-254°-W-264°-R-267°; W twr, G top; 48°28'·12N 05°03'·25W.
Baie du Stiff: Gorle Vihan ▲ 48°28'·32N 05°02'·60W.
Men-Korn ▲ VQ (3) WR 5s 21m 8M; 145°-W-040°-R-145°; BYB twr; 48°27'·96N 05°01'·32W.
Men ar Froud ▲ 48°26'·62N 05°03'·67W.
La Jument ☆ Fl (3) R 15s 36m **22M**; 241°-199°; *Horn (3) 60s*; Gy 8-sided twr, R top; 48°25'·33N 05°08'·03W.
Nividic ☆ VQ (9) 10s 28m 10M; 290°-225°; Gy 8-sided twr, helicopter platform; 48°26'·74N 05°09'·06W.
Créac'h ☆ Fl (2) 10s 70m **32M**; obsc 247°-255°; *Horn (2) 120s*; W twr, B bands; 48°27'·55N 05°07'·76W.

ÎLE MOLÈNE and ARCHIPELAGO

Kéréon ☆ Oc (2+1) WR 24s 38m **W17M**, R7M; 019°-W-248°-R-019°; Gy twr; 48°26'·30N 05°01'·55W; unreliable.

Les Trois-Pierres ☆ Iso WRG 4s 15m W9M, R/G6M; 070°-G-147°-W-185°-R-191°-G-197°-W-213°-R-070°; W col; 48°24'·70N 04°56'·84W.
Molène, Old môle Dir ☆ 191°, Fl (3) WRG 12s 6m W9M, R/G7M; 183°-G-190°-W-192°-R-203°; 48°23'·85N 04°57'·29W.
Same structure: Chenal des Laz , Dir ☆ 261°: Fl (2) WRG 6s 9m W9M, R/G7M ; 252·5°-G-259·5°-W-262·5°-R-269·5°.
Pierres-Vertes ⚓ VQ (9) 10s 9m 5M; 48°22'·19N 05°04'·76W.
Pierres Noires ↓; 48°18'·47N 04°58'·15W.
Les Pierres Noires ☆ Fl R 5s 27m **19M**; W twr, R top; 48°18'·67N 04°54'·88W.

BREST AND APPROACHES

Basse Royale ⚓ Q (6) + L Fl 15s; 48°17'·45N 04°49'·61W.
Vandrée ⚓ VQ (9) 10s; *Whis*; 48°15'·21N 04°48'·24W.
Goëmant ↓ ; 48°15'·12N 04°46'·34W.
La Parquette ⚓ Fl RG 4s 17m R6M, G6M; 244°-R-285°-G-244°; W 8-sided twr, B diagonal stripes; 48°15'·90N 04°44'·29W.
Coq Iroise ↓ 48°19'·07N 04°43'·99W.
Charles Martel ⚓ Fl (4) R 15s; 48°18'·95N 04°41'·92W.
Trépied ▲ 48°16'·73N 04°41'·50W.
Swansea Vale ⚓ Fl (2) 6s; *Whis*; 48°18'·27N 04°38'·85W.

GOULET DE BREST

Le Chat ⊥ 48°20'·29N 04°41'·72W (Anse de Bertheaume).
Le Trez Hir ⊥ 48°20'·78N 04°41'·96W.
Pte du Petit-Minou ☆ Fl (2) WR 6s 32m **W19M, R15M**; Shore-R-252°-W-260°-R-307°-W(unintens)-015°-W-065·5°; 036·5°-R(intens)-039·5°; 70·5°-W-shore; Gy twr, R top; 48°20'·19N 04°36'·86W.
Ldg Its 068°, both Dir Q 30/54m **23/22M**. Front, Pte du **Petit-Minou**, intens 067·3°-068·8°. Rear, Pte du Portzic ☆, Aux Dir Q 54m **22M**; intens 065°-071° (see below).
Fillettes ⚓ VQ (9) 10s; 48°19'·75N 04°35'·66W.
Kerviniou ⚓ Fl R 2·5s; 48°19'·77N 04°35'·25W.
Basse Goudron ⚓ Fl (2) R 6s; 48°20'·03N 04°34'·86W.
Mengam ⚓ Fl (3) WR 12s 10m W11M, R8M; 034°-R-054°-W-034°; R twr, B bands; 48°20'·32N 04°34'·56W.
Pte du Portzic ☆ Oc (2) WR 12s 56m **W19M, R15M**; 219°-R-259°-W-338°-R-000°-W-065·5° (vis 041°-069° when west of Goulet)-W-219°; Gy twr; 48°21'·49N 04°32'·05W. Same lt ho, Aux Dir Q, rear 068° ldg lt. Aux ☆ Dir Q (6) + L Fl 15s 54m **23M**; intens 045°-050°.

BREST

Pénopèle ⚓ Fl R 2·5s; 48°21'·45N 04°30'·53W.
S jetty ☆ QR 10m 7M; 094°-048°; W/R twr; 48°22'·10N 04°29'·46W.
E jetty ☆ QG 10m 7M; W/G twr; 48°22'·15N 04°29'·22W.
Ldg Its 344°: Front ☆ Dir Q WRG 24m W9M, R/G6M; 334°-G-342°-W-346°-R-024°; 48°22'·79N 04°29'·63W. Rear ☆ Dir Q 32m 9M; intens 342°-346°; 115m from front.
Le Château Marina, S Jetty hd, ☆ Fl G 2·5s 8m 4M; 48°22'·66N 04°29'·49W.
Le Château Marina, N Jetty hd, ☆ Fl R 2·5s 8m 4M; 48°22'·67N 04°29'·45W.
Port de Commerce, E ent: N jetty ☆ Oc (2) G 6s 8m 7M; W/G pylon; 48°22'·60N 04°28'·53W. S jetty ☆ Oc (2) R 6s 8m 5M; W pylon, R top; 48°22'·69N 04°28'·48W.
R2 ⚓ Fl (2) R 6s; 48°22'·01N 04°28'·75W.
R1 ⚓ Fl G 6s; 48°21'·83N 04°28'·29W.

R4 ⚓ Fl (3) R 12s; 48°22′·22N 04°28′·06W.
R3 ⚓ Q (6) + L Fl 15s; 48°22′·48N 04°27′·36W.

LE MOULIN BLANC MARINA

Moulin Blanc ⚓ Fl (2) R 6s; 48°22′·79N 04°25′·99W.
MBA ⚓ Q(3) 10s 3m 2M; pontoon elbow; 48°23′·54N 04°25′·74W.

CAMARET

N môle ⚡ Iso WG 4s 7m W12M, G9M; 135°-W-182°-G-027°; W pylon, G top; 48°16′·85N 04°35′·31W.
Port Vauban wavebreak, S end, ⚡ Fl (2) G 6s 2m 2M; 48°16′·74N 04° 35′·33W.
S môle ⚡ Fl (2) R 6s 9m 5M; R pylon; 48°16′·63N 04°35′·33W.

POINTE DU TOULINGUET TO RAZ DE SEIN

Pte du Toulinguet ☆ Oc (3) WR 12s 49m **W15M**, R11M; Shore-W-028°-R-090°-W-shore; W ☐ twr; 48°16′·81N 04°37′·72W.
La Louve ⚓ 48°16′·76N 04°38′·03W.
Mendufa ⚓ 48°16′·05N 04°39′·43W.
Basse du Lis ⚓ Q (6) + L Fl 15s 9m 6M; 48°12′·99N 04°44′·53W.
Le Chevreau ⚓ 48°13′·30N 04°36′·98W.
Le Bouc ⚓ Q (9) 15s; 48°11′·51N 04°37′·37W.
Basse Vieille ⚓ Fl (2) 6s 8m 7M; 48°08′·22N 04°35′·75W.

MORGAT

Pointe de Morgat ☆ Oc (4) WRG 12s 77m **W15M**, R11M, G10M; Shore-W-281°-G-301°-W-021°-R-043°; W ☐ twr, R top, W dwelling; 48°13′·17N 04°29′·80W. ⚓ Fl R 4s; 48°13′·60N 04°29′·55W.

DOUARNENEZ to RAZ DE SEIN

Île Tristan ⚡ Fl (3) WR 12s 35m, W6M, R6M; Shore-W-138°-R-153°-W-shore; Gy twr, W band, B top; 48°06′·14N 04°20′·24W.
Pointe du Millier ☆ Oc (2) WRG 6s 34m **W16M**, R12M, G11M; 080°-G-087°-W-113°-R-120°-W-129°-G-148°-W-251°-R-258°; W house; 48°05′·92N 04°27′·93W.
Basse Jaune ⚓ 48°04′·70N 04°42′·45W.

RAZ DE SEIN

Tévennec ⚡ Q WR 28m W9M R6M; 090°-W-345°-R-090°; W☐twr and dwelling; 48°04′·28N 04°47′·73W. Same twr, Dir ⚡ Fl 4s 24m 12M; intens 324°-332° (through Raz de Sein).
La Vieille ☆ Oc (2+1) WRG 12s 33m **W18M**, R13M, G14M; 290°-W-298°-R-325°-W-355°-G-017°-W-035°-G-105°-W-123°-R-158°-W-205°; Gy ☐ twr; 48°02′·44N 04°45′·40W.
La Plate ⚓ VQ (9) 10s 19m 8M; 48°02′·37N 04°45′·58W.
Le Chat ⚓ Fl (2) WRG 6s 27m, W9M, R/ G6M; 096°-G-215°-W-230°-R-271°-G-286°-R-096°; YB twr; 48°01′·43N 04°48′·86W.

CHAUSSÉE DE SEIN and ÎLE DE SEIN

Cornoc-An-Ar-Braden ⚓ Fl G 4s; 48°03′·23N 04°50′·84W.
Men-Brial ⚡ Oc (2) WRG 6s 16m, W12M, R9M, G7M; 149°-G-186°-W-192°-R-221°-W-227°-G-254°; G&W twr; 48°02′·28N 04°50′·97W.
Île de Sein Fl (4) 25s 49m **29M**; W twr, B top; 48°02′·62N 04°52′·02W. Same twr, Dir Q WRG, W8M, R/G 6M; 267°-G-269°-W-271°-R-275°.
Ar-Men Fl (3) 20s 29m **23M**; W twr, B top; 48°03′·01N 04°59′·87W.
Chaussée de Sein ⚓ VQ (9) 10s 9m 6M; *Whis*; **Racon O (3cm), 10M**; 48°03′·74N 05°07′·75W.

AUDIERNE

Pointe de Lervily ⚡ FlWR 4s 20m W14M, R11M; 236°-W-269°-R-294°-W-087°-R-109°; W twr, R top; 48°00′·04N 04°33′·94W.
Gamelle W ⚓ VQ (9) 10s; 47°59′·46N 04°32′·85W.
Jetée de Ste-Évette ⚡ Fl (2) R 6s 2m 7M; R lantern; 090°-000° (270°); 48°00′·31N 04°33′·07W.
Passe de l'Est ldg lts 331°: Front, Jetée de Raoulic ⚡ Fl (3) RG 12s 11m, R/G6M; 085°-R-034°-G-085°-R-085°; 48°00′·55N 04°32′·46W.
Kergadec ⚡ 006°: Dir Q WRG 43m W12M, R/G9M; 000°-G-005·3°-W-006·7°-R-017°; W 8-sided twr, R top; 48°00′·96N 04°32′·78W.
Gamelle E ⚓; 47°59′·46N 04°32′·05W.

POINTE DE PENMARC'H

Eckmühl ☆ Fl 5s 60m **23M**; Gy 8-sided twr; 47°47′·89N 04°22′·36W.
Men-Hir ⚡ Fl (2) WG 6s 19m, W7M, G4M; G135°-315°, W315°-135°; W twr, B band; 47°47′·74N 04°23′·99W.
Cap Caval ⚓ Q (9) 15s; 47°46′·47N 04°22′·68W.
Locarec ⚡ Iso WRG 4s 11m, W9M, R/G6M; 063°-G-068°-R-271°-W-285°-R-298°-G-340°-R-063°; iron col on rk; 47°47′·29N 04°20′·31W.

LE GUILVINEC

Névez ⚓ Fl G 2·5s; 47°45′·84N 04°20′·08W.
Ldg lts (triple Q) 053°, all synch: **Front**, ⚡ Q 7m 8M; 233°-066°; W pylon; Môle de Léchiagat, spur; 47°47′·43N 04°17′·07W. Middle, ⚡ Q WG 12m W14M, G11M; 006°-W-293°-G-006°; synch; R ☐ on R col; Rocher Le Faoutés, 210m from front. Rear, ⚡ Q 26m 8M, 051·5°-054·5°, R ☐ on W twr; 0·58M from front.
Spineg ⚓ Q (6) + L Fl 15s; 47°45′·19N 04°18′·90W.

LESCONIL

Karek Greis ⚓ Q (3) 10s; 47°46′·03N 04°11′·36W.
Men-ar-Groas ⚡ Fl (3) WRG 12s 14m, W10M, R/G7M; 268°-G-313°-W-333°-R-050°; W lt ho, G top; 47°47′·79N 04°12′·68W.

DISTANCE TABLES

Approx distances in nautical miles are by the most direct route allowing for dangers and TSS.

1	Lézardrieux	**1**		12	16	18	24	42	43	45	72	97	100	105	124	Pornic	**12**
2	Tréguier	22	**2**		11	12	24	39	40	41	66	87	90	95	113	St Nazaire	**11**
3	Perros-Guirec	28	21	**3**		10	13	30	30	34	55	78	80	85	106	La Baule/Pornichet	**10**
4	Trébeurden	40	32	17	**4**		9	18	22	27	48	73	75	79	100	Le Croisic	**9**
5	Morlaix	60	46	36	23	**5**		8	28	36	57	78	80	84	105	Arzal/Camöel	**8**
6	Roscoff	54	41	28	17	12	**6**		7	16	37	58	60	64	85	Crouesty	**7**
7	L'Aberwrac'h	84	72	60	49	48	32	**7**		6	26	47	48	54	74	Le Palais (Belle Ile)	**6**
8	Le Conquet	106	99	83	72	68	55	29	**8**		5	32	33	38	61	Lorient	**5**
9	Brest (marina)	114	107	92	83	79	67	42	18	**9**		4	4	12	37	Concarneau	**4**
10	Morgat	126	118	103	92	88	75	49	20	24	**10**		3	12	36	Port-la-Forêt	**3**
11	Douarnenez	131	123	108	97	93	80	54	25	29	11	**11**		2	30	Loctudy	**2**
12	Audierne	135	128	113	102	98	86	55	30	34	27	30	**12**		1	Audierne	**1**

AREA 17 *South Biscay – River Loire to Bordeaux*

SELECTED LIGHTS, BUOYS & WAYPOINTS

Positions are referenced to WGS84

LOCTUDY TO CONCARNEAU

Rostolou ⚓ 47°46'·64N 04°07'·29W.
Boulanger ⚓ VQ (6) + L Fl 10s;47°47'·38N 04°09'·13W.
Chenal de Bénodet ⚓ 47°48'·53N 04°07'·04W.
Bilien ⚓ VQ (3) 5s; 47°49'·10N 04°08'·09W.

LOCTUDY

Pte de Langoz ☆ Fl (4) WRG 12s 12m, **W15M**, R/G11M;
115°-R-257°-G-284°-W-295°-R-318°-W-328°-R-025°; W
twr, R top; 47°49'·88N 04°09'·55W.
Karek-Saoz ⚓ Fl R 2·5s 3m 1M; R twr; 47°50'·02N
04°09'·38W.
Men Audierne ⚓ 47°50'·34N 04°08'·94W.
No. 2 (Karek-Croisic) ⚓ Fl (2) R 6s; 47°50'·19N 04°09'·49W.
No. 1 ⚓ Fl (2) G 6s; 47°50'·22N 04°09'·73W.
No. 3 ⚓ Fl (3) G 12s; 47°50'·22N 04°09'·99W.
Groyne head ⚓ Q 3m 10M; 47°50'·21N 04°10'·34W.
Le Blas ⚓ Fl (4) G 15s 5m 1M; truncated col; 47°50'·28N
04°10'·23W.

BENODET

Ldg lts 345·5°: Front, Pte du Coq ⚓ Dir Oc (3) G 12s 11m
10M; intens 345°-347°; W ○ twr, G stripe; 47°52'·31N
04°06'·70W. Pyramide ⚓ Oc (3) 12s 48m 14M; 338°-016°,
synch; W twr, G top; common rear, 348m from front.
Lts in line 000·5°: Front, Pte de Combrit ⚓ Oc (2) WR
6s 19m, W12M, R9M; 325°-W-017°-R-325°; W □ twr, Gy
corners 47°51'·86N 04°06'·78W. Common rear, Pyramide;
see above.
Rousse ⚓ 47°51'·55N 04°06'·47W. La Potée ⚓ 47°51'·78N
04°06'·55W.
Pte du Toulgoët ⚓ Fl R 2·5s 2m 1M; 47°52'·30N 04°06'·86W.
Le Taro ⚓ 47°50'·51N 04°04'·83W.
La Voleuse ⚓ Q (6) + L Fl 15s; 47°48'·76N 04°02'·49W.

ILE AUX MOUTONS and LES POURCEAUX

Île-aux-Moutons ☆ Iso WRG 2s 18m, **W15M**, R/G11M;
035°-W-050°-G-063°-W-081°-R-141°-W-292°-R-035°; W □
twr and dwelling; 47°46'·48N 04°01'·66W.
Rouge de Glénan ⚓ VQ (9) 10s 8m 8M; 47°45'·48N
04°03'·95W.
Grand Pourceaux ⚓ Q; 47°45'·98N 04°00'·80W.

ÎLES DE GLÉNAN

Penfret ☆ Fl R 5s 36m **21M**; W □ twr, R top; 47°43'·26N
03°57'·18W. Same twr: auxiliary ⚓ Dir Q 34m 12M; 295°-
315°.
La Pie ⚓ Fl (2) 6s 9m 3M; 47°43'·75N 03°59'·76W.
Pte de la Baleine ⚓ VQ (3) 5s 2M; 47°43'·26N
03°59'·20W.
Les Bluiniers ⚓ 47°43'·35N 04°03'·81W.
Offlying marks, anticlockwise from the west:
Basse Pérennès ⚓ Q (9) 15s 8m 5M; 47°41'·06N 04°06'·14W.
Jument de Glénan ⚓ Q (6) + L Fl 15s 10m 4M; 47°38'·76N
04°01'·41W.
Laoennou ⚓ 47°39'·65N 03°54'·70W.
Jaune de Glénan ⚓ Fl (3) 10s; 47°42'·56N 03°49'·83W.

PORT-LA-FORÊT

Linuen ⚓ Q (3) 10s; 47°50'·76N 03°57'·31W.
Laouen Pod ⚓ 47°51'·23N 03°58'·00W.
Cap Coz mole ⚓ Fl (2) WRG 6s 5m, W7M, R/G5M; Shore-R-

335°-G-340°-W-346°-R-shore; 47°53'·49N 03°58'·28W.
Le Scoré ⚓ 47°52'·75N 03°57'·56W.
Les Ormeaux ⚓ 47°53'·27N 03°58'·34W.
Entry channel ⚓ Fl G 2·5s; 47°53'·39N 03°58'·12W.
⚓ Fl R 2·5s; 47°53'·39N 03°58'·22W.
Kerleven mole ⚓ Fl G 4s 8m 6M; 47°53'·60N 03°58'·37W.

CONCARNEAU

Ldg lts 028·5°: Front, La Croix ⚓ Q 14m 13M; 006·5°-
093°; R&W twr; 47°52'·16N 03°55'·08W. **Rear, Beuzec** ☆
Dir Q 87m **23M**; synch, intens 026·5°-030·5°; spire, 1·34M
from front.
⚓ QR; 47°51'·40N 03°55'·75W.
Le Cochon ⚓ Fl (3) WRG 12s 5m W9M, R/G6M; 230°-
R-352°-W-048°-G-207°-Obsc'd-230°; G twr; 47°51'·47N
03°55'·55W.
Basse du Chenal ⚓ Fl R 4s; 47°51'·54N 03°55'·66W.
Men Fall ⚓ Fl (2) G 6s; 47°51'·76N 03°55'·28W.
Kersos ⚓ 47°51'·80N 03°54'·93W (Anse de Kersos).
Lanriec ⚓ QG 13m 8M; 063°-078°; G window on W gable
end; 47°52'·01N 03°54'·64W.
La Medée ⚓ Fl (3) R 12s 9m 4M; 47°52'·07N 03°54'·80W.
Ville-Close ⚓ Q WR, W9M, R6M; 209°-R-354°-W-007°-R-
018°; R turret; 47°52'·27N 03°54'·76W.
No. 1 ⚓ Fl (4) G 15s 4m 5M; G turret; 47°52'·16N
03°54'·72W.
Marina wavescreen ⚓ Fl (4) R 15s 3m 1M; 47°52'·23N
03°54'·79W. No. 2 ⚓ Fl R 4s 4m 5M; G turret; 47°52'·31N
03°54'·71W.
Ville-Close (NE end) ⚓ Fl (2) R 6s; R twr; 47°52'·37N
03°54'·68W.
Ent to FV basin ⚓ Fl (2) G 6s; G twr; 47°52'·36N
03°54'·63W.

Pouldohan ⚓ Fl G 4s 6m 8M; 053°-065°; W □ twr, G top;
47°50'·97N 03°53'·69W.
Roché Tudy ⚓ 47°50'·52N 03°54'·49W.

CONCARNEAU TO ÎLE DE GROIX

PTE DE TRÉVIGNON TO PORT MANEC'H

Les Soldats ⚓ VQ (9) 10s; 47°47'·86N 03°53'·42W.
Trévignon mole ⚓ Fl G 4s 5m 8M; 47°47'·70N
03°51'·30W.
Trévignon bkwtr root ⚓ Oc (3) WRG 12s 11m, W14M, R/
G11M; 004°-W-051°-G-085°-W-092°-R-127°; 322°-R-351°;
W □ twr, G top; 47°47'·59N 03°51'·32W.
Men Du ⚓ 47°46'·41N 03°50'·50W.
Men an Tréas ⚓ 47°45'·77N 03°49'·66W.

PORT MANEC'H (Aven and Bélon rivers)

Port Manech ⚓ Oc (4) WRG 12s 38m, W10M, R/G7M; obscd
by Pte de Beg-Morg when brg <299°; 050°-W (unintens)-
140°-W-296°-G-303°-W-311°-R (over Les Verrès)-328°-W-
050°; W & R twr; 47°47'·99N 03°44'·34W.
Les Verrès ⚓ 47°46'·65N 03°42'·71W.

BRIGNEAU

Brigneau ⚓ 47°46'·11N 03°40'·10W.
W mole, ⚓ Oc (2) WRG 6s 7m, W12M, R/G9M; R col, W
top; 280°-G-329°-W-339°-R-034°; 47°46'·86N 03°40'·18W.
In line 331° with W □ daymark behind, Hard to see, rear
beacon unlit.

MERRIEN
☆ Dir QR 26m 7M; 004°-009°; W ☐ twr, R top; 47°47'·04N 03°38'·97W.
Ent, W side ☖. E side ⚓ 47°46'·45N 03°38'·89W.

DOËLAN
Ldg lts 013·8°: Front ☆ Oc (3) WG 12s 20m, W13M, G10M; W shore-305°, G305°-314°, W314°-shore; W lt ho, G band and top; 47°46'·32N 03°36'·51W. Rear ☆ Oc (3)R 12s 27m 9M; W lt ho, R band & top; 326m from front.

LE POULDU
Ent ☖ 47°45'·74N 03°32'·25W.
Grand Cochon ⚓ 47°43'·03N 03°30'·81W.
Pte de Kerroc'h ☆ Oc (2) WRG 6s 22m W11M, R/G8M; 096·5°-R-112°·5-G-132°-R-302°-W-096·5°; W twr, R top; 47°41'·97N 03°27'·66W.

ÎLE DE GROIX
Pen Men ☆ Fl (4) 25s 60m **29M**; 309°-275°; W ☐ twr, B top; 47°38'·84N 03°30'·56W.
Speerbrecker, ⚓ 47°39'·10N 03°26'·33W.
Port Tudy, N môle ☆ Iso G 4s 12m 6M; W twr, G top; 47°38'·72N 03°26'·74W.
E môle ☆ Fl (2) R 6s 11m 6M; 112°-226°; W twr R top; 47°38'·68N 03°26'·78W.
Basse Melité ⚓ 47°38'·84N 03°25'·54W.
Pte de la Croix ☆ Oc WR 4s 16m, W12M, R9M; 169°-W-336°-R-345°-W-353°; W pedestal, R lantern; 47°38'·05N 03°25'·02W.
Edouard de Cougy ⚓ 47°37'·93N 03°23'·90W.
Pointe des Chats ☆ Fl R 5s 16m **19M**; W ☐ twr and dwelling; 47°37'·24N 03°25'·30W.
Les Chats ⚓ Q (6) + L Fl 15s; 47°35'·70N 03°23'·57W.

LORIENT AND RIVER ÉTEL

LORIENT, PASSE DE L'OUEST
Passe de l'Ouest ldg lts 057°: both Dir Q 11/22m 13/**18M**. Front, Les Sœurs; intens 042·5°-058·5°, 058·5°-042·5°, 4M range only; R twr, W bands; 47°42'·13N 03°21'·84W. Rear **Port Louis** ☆, 740m from front (see below).
Banc des Truies ⚓ Q (9) 15s; 47°40'·76N 03°24'·48W.
Loménèr, Anse de Stole, Dir ☆ 357·2°: Q WRG 13m, W10M, R/G8M; 349·2°-G-355·2°-W-359·2°-R-005·2°; W twr, R top; 47°42'·30N 03°25'·54W.
A2 ⚓ Fl R 2·5s; 47°40'·94N 03°24'·98W.
Les Trois Pierres ⚓ Q RG 11m R/G6M; 060°-G-196°-R-002°; B twr, W bands; 47°41'·53N 03°22'·47W.
A8 ⚓ Fl R 2·5s; 47°41'·90N 03°22'·52W.

PASSE DU SUD
Bastresses Sud ⚓ QG; 47°40'·77N 03°22'·09W.
Les Errants ⚓ Fl (2) R 6s; 47°41'·10N 03°22'·38W.
Bastresses Nord ⚓ Fl (2) G 6s; 47°41'·11N 03°22'·20W.
Locmalo ⚓ Fl (3) G 12s; 47°41'·67N 03°22'·13W.

SOUTH OF PORT LOUIS
La Paix ☖; 47°41'·97N 03°21'·84W.
Île aux Souris ☆ Dir Q WG 6m, W3M, G2M; 041·5°-W-043·5°-G-041·5°; G twr; 47°42'·15N 03°21'·52W.
⚓ Fl G 2·5s; 47°42'·13N 03°21'·21W.
Ban-Gâvres FV/yacht hbr, W jetty ☆ Fl (2) G 6s 3M; 47°42'·06N 03°21'·11W. E jetty ☆ Fl (2) R 6s 3M; 47°42'·06N 03°21'·06W.

ENTRANCE CHANNEL
Ldg lts 016·5°, both Dir QG 8/14m 13M; intens 014·5°-017·5°; synch; W twrs, G tops. Front ☆, 47°43'·47N

03°21'·63W (Île St Michel). Rear ☆, 306m from front.
La Citadelle ⚓ Oc G 4s 6m 6M; 012°-192°; 47°42'·59N 03°21'·94W.
Secondary yacht chan, ⚑ RGR, 47°42'·49N 03°22'·12W.
La Petite Jument ⚓ Oc R 4s 5m 6M; 182°-024°; R twr; 47°42'·58N 03°22'·07W.
Le Cochon ⚓ Fl R 4s 5m 5M; RGR twr; 03°22'·00W.
No. 1 ⚓ 47°42'·80N 03°21'·84W.

PORT LOUIS (Port de la Pointe)
D 1 ⚓ 47°42'·76N 03°21'·52W.
Jetty ☆ Fl G 2·5s 7m 6M; W twr, G top; 47°42'·71N 03°21'·37W.
Anse du Driasker Stage Head Fl R 2·5s 2M, metal mast.

KERNEVEL
Kéroman ldg lts 350°, both Dir Oc (2) R 6s 25/31m **15M**; synch; intens 349°-351°: **Front** ☆, 47°43'·60N 03°22'·02W, R ho, W bands. **Rear** ☆ R&W topmark on Gy pylon, R top; 91m from front.
Banc du Turc ⚓ Fl G 2·5s; 47°43'·33N 03°21'·85W.
Kernével marina, entrance: ☆ QR 1M; 47°43'·39N 03°22'·10W.
Ldg lts 217°, both Dir QR 10/18m **15M**; intens 215°-219°; synch: **Front, Kernével** ☆ R&W twr; 47°43'·02N 03°22'·32W. **Rear** ☆ W ☐ twr, R top; 290m from front.
⚓ Q (3) 10s; marks wreck; 47°43'·49N 03°22'·05W.

NORTHERN PART OF LORIENT HARBOUR
Grand Bassin (FV hbr), E side of ent, ☆ Fl RG 4s 7m 6M; 000°-G-235°-R-000°; W twr, G top; 47°43'·63N 03°21'·87W.
Ste Catherine marina ent ☆ QG 5m 3M; 47°43'·52N 03°21'·12W.
N side of marina ent ☆ QR 2m 2M 47°43'·53N 03°21'·10W.
Pengarne ⚓ Fl G 2·5s 3m 3M; W twr; 47°43'·88N 03°21'·23W.
No. 9 ⚓ Fl (2) G 6s; 47°43'·95N 03°21'·16W.
No. 11 ⚓ Fl (3) G 12s; 47°44'·04N 03°21'·01W.
Pen-Mané marina, bkwtr elbow ☆ Fl (2) G 6s 4M; 47°44'·11N 03°20'·86W.
Blavet River, No. 1 ⚓ Fl (2+1)G 10s; 47°44'·20N 03°20'·78W.
No. 2 ⚓ Fl R 2·5s; 47°44'·26N 03°20'·74W.
Pointe de l'Espérance, Dir ☆ 037°, Q WRG 8m W10M, R/G8M; 034·2°-G-036·7°-W-037·2°-R-047·2°; W twr, G top; 47°44'·51N 03°20'·66W.
Ro-Ro jetty ☆ QR 7m 2M; 47°44'·42N 03°20'·96W.
No. 8 ⚓ Fl R 2·5s; 47°44'·56N 03°20'·98W, ent to Lorient marina.

RIVIÈRE D'ÉTEL
Roheu ☖ 47°38'·54N 03°14'·70W.
Épi de Plouhinec ☆ Fl R 2·5s 7m 2M; 47°38'·59N 03°12'·86W.
W side ent ☆ Oc (2) WRG 6s 13m W9M, R/G6M; 022°-W-064°-R-123°-W-330°-G-022°; R twr; 47°38'·69N 03°12'·83W.
Conspic R/W radio mast (CROSS Étel), 47°39'·73N 03°12'·11W.
Les Pierres Noires ☖ 47°35'·53N 03°13'·29W.

BELLE ÎLE AND QUIBERON BAY (W OF 2° 50'W)

PLATEAU DES BIRVIDEAUX (6M NNW of Belle Île)
⚓ Fl (2) 6s 24m 10M; BRB twr; 47°29'·15N 03°17'·46W.

BELLE ÎLE

Pte des Poulains ☆ Fl 5s 34m **23M**; 023°-291°; W ☐ twr and dwelling; 47°23'·31N 03°15'·11W.
Les Poulains ⚲ 47°23'·44N 03°16'·68W.
N Poulains ⚲ 47°23'·68N 03°14'·88W.
Sauzon, NW jetty ⚲ Fl G 4s 8m 8M; 47°22'·49N 03°13'·04W.
SE jetty ⚲ Fl R 4s 8m 8M; 315°-272°; W twr, R top; 47°22'·45N 03°13'·00W. Inner hbr, W jetty ⚲, QG 9m 5M; 194°-045°; W twr, G top; 47°22'·37N 03°13'·13W.
Le Palais, N jetty ⚲ QG 11m 7M; obsc 298°-170° by Ptes de Kerdonis and Taillefer; W twr, G top; 47°20'·84N 03°09'·04W.
No 1 ◢ Fl (2) G 6s; 47°20'·82N 03°08'·96W;
No 2 ⚲ Fl R 4s; 47°20'·71N 03°08'·89W;
No 4 ⚲Fl (2) R 6s; 47°20'·78N 03°09'·01W.
S jetty ⚲ QR 11m 7M; obsc'd 298°-170° (see N jetty); W twr, R lantern; 47°20'·82N 03°09'·07W.
Pointe de Kerdonis ☆ Fl (3) R 15s 35m **15M**; obsc'd 025°-129° by Pointes d'Arzic and de Taillefer; W ☐ twr, R top and W dwelling; 47°18'·60N 03°03'·58W.
Les Galères ⚲ 47°18'·77N 03°02'·76W.
SW coast of Belle Île: La Truie ⚲ 47°17'·11N 03°11'·79W.
Goulphar ☆ Fl (2) 10s 87m **27M**; Gy twr; 47°18'·65N 03°13'·63W.

PORT MARIA (Quiberon ferry port)

Light ho ⚲ Q WRG 28m W14M, R/ G10M; 246°-W-252°-W-297°-G-340°-W-017°-R-051°-W-081°-G-098°-W-143°; W twr, G lantern; 47°28'·78N 03°07'·45W.
Le Pouilloux ⚲ 47°27'·88N 03°08'·01W.
Ldg lts 006·5°, both Dir QG 5/13m **16/17M**; intens 005°-008°; W twrs, B bands: **Front**, 47°28'·63N 03°07'·18W. **Rear**, 230m north.
Les Deux Frères ⚲ Fl R 2·5s; 175°-047°;47°28'·34N 03°07'·29W.
S bkwtr ⚲ Oc (2) R 6s 9m 7M; W twr, R top; 47°28'·54N 03°07'·31W.

CHAUSSÉE and PASSAGE DE LA TEIGNOUSE

Le Four ⚲ 47°27'·78N 03°06'·54W.
Les Trois Pierres ⚲ 47°27'·46N 03°05'·24W.
Roc er Vy ⚲ 47°27'·70N 03°04'·40W; Chenal en Toull Bras.
Roc er Vy ⚲ 47°27'·86N 03°04'·35W.
Basse Cariou ⚲ 47°26'·94N 03°06'·38W.
Basse du Chenal ⚲ 47°26'·66N 03°05'·77W.
Goué Vaz S ⚲ Q (6) + L Fl 15s; 47°25'·76N 03°04'·93W.
La Teignouse ☆ Fl WR 4s 20m **W15M**, R11M; 033°-039°-R-033°; W ⚪ twr, R top; 47°27'·44N 03°02'·75W.
Basse du Milieu ⚲ Fl (2) G 6s 9m 2M; 47°25'·91N 03°04'·12W.
Goué Vaz E ⚲ Fl (3) R 12s; 47°26'·23N 03°04'·28W.
NE Teignouse ⚲ Fl (3) G 12s; 47°26'·55N 03°01'·87W.
Basse Nouvelle ⚲ Fl R 2·5s; 47°26'·98N 03°01'·99W.

CHAUSSÉE and PASSAGE DU BÉNIGUET

Les Esclassiers ⚲ 47°25'·68N 03°03'·05W.
Le Grand Coin ⚲ 47°24'·45N 03°00'·26W.
Bonen Bras ⚲ 47°24'·26N 02°59'·88W.

ÎLE DE HOUAT

Le Rouleau ⚲ 47°23'·67N 03°00'·31W.
Port St-Gildas N môle ⚲ Fl (2) WG 6s 8m W9M, G6M; 168°-W-198°-G-210°-W-240°-G-168°; W twr, G top; 47°23'·57N 02°57'·34W.

Mussel beds, 1 -1.5M NNE of above ⚲ and in its G sector (198°-210°), marked by 2 ⚲ at S end, and ⚲ VQ (3) 5s & ⚲ VQ at N end.
Bcns SE and S of Houat: Men Groise ⚲ 47°22'·77N 02°55'·00W.
Er Spernec Bras ⚲ 47°22'·09N 02°55'·23W.
Men er Houteliguet ⚲ 47°22'·54N 02°56'·38W.

ÎLE DE HOËDIC

Les Sœurs ⚲ 47°21'·14N 02°54'·74W.
La Chèvre ⚲ 47°21'·08N 02°52'·55W.
Port de l'Argol bkwtr ⚲ Fl WG 4s 10m W9M, G6M; 143°-W-163°-G-183°-W-194°-G-143°; W twr, G top; 47°20'·66N 02°52'·48W.
Er Gurranic'h ⚲ 47°20'·51N 02°50'·44W.
Cohfournik ⚲ 47°19'·49N 02°49'·69W.
Grands Cardinaux ⚲ Fl (4) 15s 28m 13M; R and W twr; 47°19'·27N 02°50'·10W, 2·1M SE of Argol.
Le Chariot ⚲ 47°18'·87N 02°52'·95W.
Er Palaire ⚲ 47°20'·16N 02°55'·01W.

PORT HALIGUEN

Banc de Quiberon S ⚲ Q (6) + L Fl 15s; 47°28'·04N 03°02'·34W.
Banc de Quiberon N ⚲ 47°29'·65N 03°02'·58W.
E bkwtr hd ⚲ Oc (2) WR 6s 10m, W11M, R8M; 233°-W-240·5°-R-299°-W-306°-R-233°; W twr, R top; 47°29'·36N 03°05'·94W.
Port Haliguen ⚲ 47°29'·38N 03°05'·55W; marks 1·7m patch.
NW bkwtr hd ⚲ Fl G 2·5s 9m 6M; 47°29'·34N 03°06'·02W.
Bugalet wreck ⚲ 47°31'·19N 03°05'·45W.
Men er Roué ⚲ 47°32'·25N 03°06'·06W.

LA TRINITÉ-SUR-MER

Rivière de Crac'h Dir lt 347° Q WRG 11m W10M, R/G7M; 321°-G-345°-W-013·5°-R-080°; W twr, G top; 47°34'·09N 03°00'·37W.
Buissons de Méaban ⚲ 47°31'·66N 02°58'·49W.
Le Petit Buisson ⚲ 47°32'·14N 02°58'·57W.
Roche Révision ⚲ 47°32'·63N 02°59'·36W.
Petit Trého ⚲ Fl R 2·5s; 47°33'·47N 03°00'·71W.
R. de Crac'h Dir ⚲ 347°: Oc WRG 4s 9m W13M, R/G 11M; 345°-G-346°-W-348°-R-349°; W twr; 47°35'·03N 03°00'·98W.
S pier ⚲ Q WR 6s 6m, W9M, R6M; 090°-R-293·5°-W-300·5°-R-329°; W twr, R top; 47°35'·09N 03°01'·50W.
Marina wavebreak/pier ⚲ Iso R 4s 8m 5M; 47°35'·28N 03°01'·46W.

GOLFE DU MORBIHAN

Méaban ⚲ 47°30'·77N 02°56'·23W.
Outer ldg marks 001°: Front, Petit Vezid ⚲ ; W obelisk; 47°34'·17N 02°55'·23W. Rear, Baden ch spire (83m), 47°37'·20N 02°55'·14W.
Pointe de Port-Navalo ☆ Oc (3) WRG 12s 32m, **W15M**, R/ G11M; 155°-W-220°; 317°-G-359°-W-015°-R-105°; W twr and dwelling; 47°32'·87N 02°55'·11W.
Ldg marks 359°: Front, Grégan ⚲ Q (6) + L Fl 15s 3m 8M; 47°33'·91N 02°55'·05W. Rear, Baden ch spire (5 lines above).

Auray river: Catis ◢ 47°36'·14N 02°57'·23W.
César ⚲ 47°38'·36N 02°58'·22W.
No. 13 ⚲ 47°39'·48N 02°58'·64W (last bcn before 14m bridge).

Morbihan: Grand Mouton ⚓ QG; 47°33'·71N 02°54'·85W.
Gavrinis ⚓ 47°34'·21N 02°54'·05W.
Jument ⚓ 47°34'·29N 02°53'·43W.
Creizic S ↯ 47°34'·63N 02°52'·84W.
Creizic N ↯ 47°34'·93N 02°52'·20W.
Les Rechauds, two ⚓ 47°36'·18N 02°51'·30W.
Truie d'Arradon ⚓ 47°36'·58N 02°50'·27W.
Logoden ⚓ 47°36'·70N 02°49'·91W.
Drenec ⚓ 47°36'·84N 02°48'·39W.
Bœdic ↯ 47°36'·85N 02°47'·59W.
Roguédas ⚓ Fl G 2·5s 4m 4M; G twr; 47°37'·12N 02°47'·28W.

CROUESTY

Ldg lts 058°, both Dir Q 10/27m 8M; intens 056·5°-059·5°: Front ⚓ R panel, W stripe; 47°32'·53N 02°53'·95W. Rear ⚓, W twr; 315m from front.
No. 1 ⚓ QG; 47°32'·26N 02°54'·76W.
No. 2 ⚓ 47°32'·26N 02°54'·76W.
N jetty ⚓ Fl R 4s 9m 7M; R&W □ twr; 47°32'·47N 02°54'·14W.
S jetty ⚓ Fl G 4s 9m 7M; G&W □ twr; 47°32'·45N 02°54'·10W.

PLATEAU DU GRAND MONT

Chimère ↯ 47°28'·83N 02°53'·98W.
L'Epieu ↯ 47°29'·51N 02°52'·91W.
St Gildas ↯ 47°29'·78N 02°52'·87W.
Grand Mont ↯ 47°28'·98N 02°51'·12W.

QUIBERON BAY (E OF 2° 50'W) TO PTE DU CROISIC

PLATEAU DE SAINT JACQUES
Le Bauzec ⚓ 47°28'·89N 02°49'·40W.
St Jacques ↯ 47°28'·17N 02°47'·52W.
Port St Jacques, jetty ⚓ Oc (2) R 6s 5m 6M; W 8-sided twr, R top; 47°29'·24N 02°47'·41W.

PLATEAU DE LA RECHERCHE
Recherche ⚓ Q (9) 15s; 47°25'·56N 02°50'·39W.
Locmariaquer ↯ 47°25'·82N 02°47'·36W.

PÉNERF
⚓ Fl (5) Y 20s; 47°27'·58N 02°39'·56W.
Penvins ↯ 47°28'·93N 02°40'·09W. Borenis ↯ 47°29'·21N 02°38'·35W.
Tour des Anglais ⌂ W bcn; 47°30'·21N 02°37'·94W; appr brg 031·4°.
Pignon ⚓ Fl (3) WR 12s 6m W9M, R6M; 028·5°-R-167°-W-175°-R-349·5°-W-028·5°; R twr; 47°30'·03N 02°38'·89W.

VILAINE RIVER
Pte de Penlan ☆ Oc (2) WRG 6s 26m, **W15M**, R/G11M; 292·5°-R-025°-G-052°-W-060°-R-138°-G-180°; W sector defines Passe de la Grande Accroche; W twr, R bands; 47°30'·97N 02°30'·11W.
Bertrand ⚓ Iso WG 4s 6m, W9M, G6M; 040°-W-054°-G-227°-W-234°-G-040°; G twr; 47°31'·06N 02°30'·72W.
Basse de Kervoyal ⚓ Dir Q WR W8M, R5M; 269°-W-271°-R-269°; W sector leads to/from Nos 1 & 2 buoys; 47°30'·37N 02°32'·62W.
No. 1 ⚓ Fl G 2·5s; 47°30'·32N 02°28'·73W.
No. 2 ⚓ Fl R 2·5s; 47°30'·41N 02°28'·71W.
Pointe du Scal ⚓ QG 8m 4M; 47°29'·67N 02°26'·87W.

ÎLE DUMET
Fort ⚓ Fl (3) WRG 15s 14m, W7M, R/G4M; 090°-G-272°-W-285°-R-335°-W-090°; W col, G top; 47°24'·69N 02°37'·21W.

Basse-Est Île Dumet ⚓ Q (3) 10s; 47°25'·20N 02°34'·93W.
Île Dumet ↯ Q; 47°25'·90N 02°36'·05W.

MESQUER
Laronesse ⚓ 47°25'·96N 02°29'·50W.
Basse Normande ↯ 47°25'·47N 02°29'·80W.
Jetty ⚓ Oc WRG 4s 7m W10M, R/G7M; 067°-W-072°-R-102°-W-118°-R-293°-W-325°-G-067°; W col & bldg; 47°25'·31N 02°28'·05W.

PIRIAC-SUR-MER
Grand Norven ⚓ Q; 47°23'·55N 02°32'·89W.
Inner mole ⚓ Oc (2) WRG 6s 8m, W10M, R/G7M; 066°-R-148°-G-194°-W-201°-R-221°; W col; 47°22'·93N 02°32'·71W. *Siren 120s (occas), 35m SW.* E bkwtr ⚓ Fl R 4s 4m 5M; W pylon, R top; 47°23'·00N 02°32'·67W.
Les Bayonnelles ⚓ Q (9) 15s; 47°22'·56N 02°35'·23W.

LA TURBALLE
Ldg lts 006·5°, both Dir Iso R 4s 11/19m 3M; intens 004°-009°: Front, 47°20'·70N 02°30'·87W. Rear, 275m N of the front lt.
Ouest Jetée de Garlahy ⚓ Fl (4) WR 12s 13m, W10M, R7M; 060°-R-315°-W-060°; W pylon, R top; 47°20'·70N 02°30'·93W.
Digue Tourlandroux ⚓ Fl G 4s 4m 2M; G post, E side of access chan; 47°20'·75N 02°30'·88W.

LE CROISIC
Basse Hergo ⚓ Fl G 2·5s 5m 3M; 47°18'·62N 02°31'·69W.
Jetée du Tréhic ⚓ Iso WG 4s 12m W14M, G11M; 042°-G-093°-W-137°-G-345°; Gy twr, G top; 47°18'·49N 02°31'·42W. F Bu fog det lt, 100m SE.
Outer ldg lts 155·5°, both Dir Q 10/14m 13M; intens 154°-158°: Front ☆ 47°17'·96N 02°30'·99W . Rear ☆, 116m from front.
Middle ldg lts 174°, both QG 5/8m 11M; 170·5°-177·5°: Front 47°18'·06N 02°31'·07W. Rear, 48m from front.
Le Grand Mabon ⚓ Fl (3) R 12s 6m 2M; 47°18'·05N 02°31'·03W.
Inner ldg lts 134·7°, both QR 6/10m 8M; intens 132·5°-143·5°; synch.
Basse Castouillet ⚓ Q (9) 15s; 47°18'·12N 02°34'·37W.
Basse Lovre ↯ 47°15'·87N 02°29'·58W, Chenal du Nord.

PLATEAU DU FOUR/BANC DE GUÉRANDE
Bonen du Four ⚓ Q; 47°18'·53N 02°39'·29W.
Le Four ☆ Fl 5s 23m **18M**; W twr, B diagonal stripes; 47°17'·87N 02°38'·05W.
Ouest Basse Capella ⚓ Q (9) 15s; *Whis;* 47°15'·66N 02°42'·78W.
Goué-Vas-du-Four ⚓ Q (6) + L Fl 15s; 47°14'·91N 02°38'·20W.
Sud Banc Guérande ⚓ VQ (6) +·L Fl 10s; 47°08'·80N 02°42'·81W.

POINTE DU CROISIC TO POINTE DE ST GILDAS

PLATEAU DE LA BANCHE
NW Banche ⚓ Q 8m 4M; 47°12'·86N 02°31'·02W.
W Banche ⚓ VQ (9) 10s; 47°11'·64N 02°32'·41W.
La Banche ☆ Fl (2) WR 6s 22m **W15M**, R11M; 266°-R-280°-W-266°; B twr, W bands; 47°10'·62N 02°28'·08W.
SE Banche ↯ 47°10'·40N 02°26'·10W.

PLATEAU DE LA LAMBARDE

NW Lambarde ↓ 47°10'·84N 02°22'·93W.
SE Lambarde ↓ Q (6) + L Fl 15s; 47°10'·04N 02°20·80W.

BAIE DU POULIGUEN (or Baie de la Baule)

Penchateau ↓ Fl R 2·5s; 47°15'·24N 02°24'·35W.
Les Guérandaises ↓ Fl G 2·5s; 47°15'·03N 02°24'·29W.
↓ 47°15'·24N 02°23'·50W.
Les Evens ↓ 47°14'·32N 02°22'·55W.
Les Troves ↓ 47°14'·23N 02°22'·41W.
NNW Pierre Percée ↓ 47°13'·63N 02°20'·63W.
La Vieille ↓ 47°14'·03N 02°19'·51W.
Sud de la Vieille ↓ 47°13'·75N 02°19'·54W.
Le Caillou ↓ 47°13'·65N 02°19'·18W.
Le Petit Charpentier ↓ 47°13'·34N 02°18'·95W.
Le Grand Charpentier ☆ Q WRG 22m, W14M, R/G10M; 020°-G-054°-W-062°-R-092°-W-111°-R-310°-W-020°; Gy lt ho, G lantern; 47°12'·83N 02°19'·13W.

LE POULIGUEN

Basse Martineau ↓ 47°15'·54N 02°24'·34W.
Petits Impairs ↓ Fl (2) G 6s 6m 2M; 47°15'·99N 02°24'·61W.
SW jetty ↓ QR 13m 9M; 171°-081°; W col; 47°16'·39N 02°25'·39W.

PORNICHET (La Baule)

S bkwtr ☆ Iso WRG 4s 11m, W10M, R/G7M; 303°-G-081°-W-084°-R-180°; W twr, G top; 47°15'·49N 02°21'·14W.
Ent,W side ☆ QG 3m 1M; B perch, G top; 47°15'·51N 02°21'·12W.
E side ☆ QR 4m 1M; B perch, R top; 47°15'·50N 02°21'·10W.

ST NAZAIRE APPROACH (Chenal du Sud)

S-N1 ↓ L Fl 10s 8m 5M; *Racon Z (3cm), 3–8M;* 47°00'·07N 02°39'·84W.
S-N2 ↓ Iso 4s 8m 5M; 47°02'·08N 02°33'·47W.
Les Chevaux ↓ Fl G 2·5s; 47°03'·53N 02°26'·37W.
Thérèsia ↓ Fl R 2·5s; 47°04'·84N 02°27'·27W.
La Couronnée ↓ Fl (2) G 6s; *Racon T, 3–5M;* 47°07'·60N 02°20'·05W.
Lancastria ↓ Fl (2) R 6s; 47°08'·88N 02°20'·37W.

PASSE DES CHARPENTIERS

Portcé ☆ ldg lts 025·5°, both Dir Q 6/36m **22/24M: Front,** intens 024·7°-026·2°; synch; W col; 47°14'·57N 02°15'·44W. **Rear** ☆ (H24); intens 024°-027°; W □ twr, W stripe; 0·75M from front.
Wreck (Y) ↓ Fl (3) R 12s; 47°09'·87N 02°19'·46W.
No. 1 ↓ VQ G; 47°09'·94N 02°18'·40W.
No. 2 ↓ VQ R; 47°10'·06N 02°18'·72W.
No. 6 ↓ Fl (3) R 12s; 47°12'·05N 02°17'·31W.
No. 5 ↓ Fl (4) G 15s; 47°12'·65N 02°16'·57W.
No. 8 ↓ Fl (4) R 15s; 47°12'·75N 02°16'·86W.
No. 7 ↓ VQ G; 47°13'·30N 02°16'·11W.
No. 10 ↓ VQ R; 47°13'·62N 02°16'·16W. (Buoys 9 - 18 not listed).
Pointe d'Aiguillon ☆ Oc (3) WR 12s 27m, W13M, R10M; 207°-R-233°-W-293°; 297°-W-300°-R-327°-W-023°; 027°-R-089°; W lt ho, conspic; 47°14'·54N 02°15'·79W.
Ville-ès-Martin jetty ☆ Fl (2) 6s 10m 10M; W twr, R top; 47°15'·33N 02°13'·65W.
Morées ↓ Fl (3) WR 12s 12m, W6M, R4M; W058°-224°, R300°-058°; G twr; 47°15'·00N 02°13'·02W.

SAINT NAZAIRE

W jetty ☆ Oc (4) R 12s 11m 8M; W twr, R top; 47°15'·97N 02°12'·25W.
E jetty ☆ Oc (4) G 12s 11m 11M; W twr, G top; 47°15'·99N 02°12'·14W. (Ent for big ships locking into Bassin St Nazaire)
No. 20 ↓ QR; 47°16'·19N 02°11'·37W.
Sud Basse Nazaire ↓ Q (6) + L Fl 15s; 47°16'·21N 02°11'·51W.
Basse Nazaire ↓ Fl G 2·5s; 47°16'·24N 02°11'·63W.
SE Old mole ↓ Fl R 2·5s; 47°16'·24N 02°11'·73W.
Old Môle ☆ Q (3) 10s 18m 11M; 153·5°-063·5°; W twr, R top; weather signals; 47°16'·27N 02°11'·82W.
↓ Fl (2) R 6s 5m 1M; R dolphin ; 47°16'·37N 02°11'·80W.
Entrée Est ☆ Fl (3) R 12s 9m 9M; R pylon; 47°16'·47N 02°11'·85W.
Ldg lts 280° (into E lock) 2 VQ Vi; front 47°16'·49N 02°11'·92W.

EAST SIDE OF RIVER, SOUTH TO PTE DE ST GILDAS

Le Pointeau, Digue S ☆ Fl WG 4s 4m, W10M, G7M; 050°-G-074°-W-149°-G-345°-W-050°; G&W ○ hut; 47°14'·02N 02°10'·96W.
Port de Comberge La Truie ↓ 47°12'·06N 00°13'·36W.
S jetty ☆ Oc WG 4s 7m W9M, G6M; 123°-W-140°-G-123°; W twr, G top; 47°10'·70N 02°09'·90W.
Port de la Gravette La Gravette ↓ 47°09'·81N 02°13'·06W.
Bkwtr hd ☆ Fl (3) WG 12s 7m, W8M, G5M; 183°-W-188°-G-124°-W-138°-G-183°; W structure, G top; 47°09'·64N 02°12'·70W.
Anse du Boucau bkwtr ☆ Fl (2) G 6s 3M; 47°08'·41N 02°14'·80W.
Pte de Saint Gildas ☆ Q WRG 20m, W14M, R/G10M; 264°-R-308°-G-078°-W-088°-R-174°-W-180°-G-264°; col on W house, G top; 47°08'·02N 02°14'·74W.
Nord Couronnée ↓ Q; 47°07'·34N 02°17'·78W.

RIVER LOIRE TO NANTES

Well buoyed/lit to Île de Bois, thence G lts, S side; R lts N side.
No. 21 ↓ VQ G; 47°16'·96N 02°10'·25W.
Suspension bridge, mid-span ☆ Iso 4s 55m, vis up/down stream; 47°17'·10N 02°10'·24W; between 2 conspic R/W twrs.
MA ↓ Fl (2) G 6s; 47°17'·50N 02°09'·22W.
MB ↓ Fl (3) G 12s; 47°17'·95N 02°07'·53W.
Fernais-25 ↓ Fl (4) G 15s; 47°18'·10N 02°06'·60W.
Paimboeuf, môle root ☆ Oc (3) WG 12s 9m, W10M, G7M; Shore-G-123°-W-shore; W twr, G top; 47°17'·42N 02°01'·95W.
Île de Bois (upstream) Fl (2) G 6s; 47°12'·79N 01°48'·27W.
Ldg lts 064° Rear Dir VQ R; 47°12'·00N 01°34'·35W, Y-junction with Bras de la Madeleine.

POINTE DE SAINT GILDAS TO FROMENTINE

Pte de Saint Gildas ☆ Q WRG 20m, W14M, R/G10M; 264°-R-308°-G-078°-W-088°-R-174°-W-180°-G-264°; 47°08'·02N 02°14'·75W. Notre Dame ↓ VQ (9) 10s 7m 3M; 47°05'·42N 02°08'·26W.

PORNIC

Approaches ⚓ Fl G 4s; 47°06'·39N 02°06'·60W; ⚓ Fl R 4s; 47°06'·40N 02°06'·64W

Marina ent, S side ⚓ Fl (2) R 6s 4m 2M; 47°06'·47N 02°06'·67W.

Pte de Noëveillard ⚓ Oc (4) WRG 12s 22m W13M, R/G9M; Shore-G-051°-W-079°-R-shore; W ☐ twr, G top, W dwelling; 47°06'·62N 02°06'·92W.

ÎLE DE NOIRMOUTIER anti-clockwise from the East

Pte des Dames ☆ Oc (3) WRG 12s 34m, **W19M, R/G15M**; 016·5°-G-057°-R-124°-G-165°-W-191°-R191°-267°-W-357°-R-016·5°; W ☐ twr; 47°00'·67N 02°13'·26W. La Chaise ⚓ 47°01'·21N 02°12'·64W.

L'Herbaudière, ldg lts 187·5°, both Q 5/21m 7M, Gy masts. Front, 47°01'·59N 02°17'·84W. Rear, 310m from front. Martroger ⚓, Q WRG 11m W9M, R/G6M; 033°-G-055°-W-060°-R-095°-G-124°-W-153°-R-201°-W-240°-R-033°; 47°02'·61N 02°17'·11W.

W jetty ⚓ Oc (2+1) WG 12s 9m W10M, G7M; 187·5°-W-190°-G-187·5°; W col and hut, G top; 47°01'·63N 02°17'·84W.

E jetty ⚓ Fl (2) R 6s 8m 4M; 47°01'·61N 02°17'·81W.

Île du Pilier ☆ Fl (3) 20s 33m **29M**; Gy twr; 47°02'·55N 02°21'·60W. Same twr, auxiliary ⚓ QR 10m 11M, 321°-034°.

Passe de la Grise ⚓ Q (6) + L Fl 15s; 47°01'·66N 02°19'·97W.

Les Boeufs ⚓ VQ (9) 10s; 46°55'·04N 02°27'·99W.

Réaumur ⚓ Q (9) 15s; 46°57'·46N 02°24'·22W.

Le Bavard ⚓ VQ (6) + L Fl 10s; 46°56'·79N 02°23'·34W.

Pte du Devin (Morin) ⚓ Oc (4) WRG 12s 10m W11M, R/G8M; 314°-G-028°-W-035°-R-134°; W col & hut, G top; 46°59'·15N 02°17'·60W.

GOULET DE FROMENTINE

Fromentine ⚓ L Fl (3) 10s 3m 6M; 46°53'·10N 02°11'·40W (buoyed chan).

Milieu ⚓ Fl (4) R 15 s 6m 5M; 46°53'·59N 02°09'·63W.

Pte de Notre Dame-de-Monts ⚓ Dir Oc (2) WRG 6s 21m, W13M, R/G10M; 000°-G-043°-W-063°-R-073°-W-094°-G-113°-W-116°-R-175°-G-196°-R-230°; W twr, B top; 46°53'·33N 02°08'·54W.

ÎLE D'YEU TO BOURGENAY

ÎLE D'YEU

Petite Foule (main lt) ☆ Fl 5s 56m **24M**; W ☐ twr, G lantern; 46°43'·04N 02°22'·91W.

Les Chiens Perrins ⚓ Q (9) WG 15s 16m W7M, G4M; 330°-G-350°-W-200°; 46°43'·60N 02°24'·58W.

Pont d'Yeu ⚓ 46°45'·81N 02°13'·81W.

La Sablaire ⚓ Q (6) + L Fl 15s; 46°43'·62N 02°19'·49W.

Port Joinville ldg lts 219°, both QR 11/16m 6M, 169°-269°: Front, Quai du Canada 46°43'·61N 02°20'·94W. Rear, 85m from front.

NW jetty ⚓ Oc (3) WG 12s 7m, W11M, G8M; Shore-G-150°-W-232°-G-279°-W-285°-G-shore; W 8-sided twr, G top; 46°43'·77N 02°20'·82W. La Galiote ⚓ 46°43'·73N 02°20'·71W.

Pte des Corbeaux ☆ Fl (2+1) R 15s 25m **20M**; 083°-143° obsc by Île de Yeu; W ☐ twr, R top; 46°41'·41N 02°17'·08W.

Port de la Meule ⚓ Oc WRG 4s 9m, W9M, R/G6M; 007·5°-G-018°-W-027·5°-R-041·5°; Gy twr, R top; 46°41'·62N 02°20'·72W.

SAINT GILLES-CROIX-DE-VIE

Pte de Grosse Terre ☆ Fl (4) WR 12s 25m, **W18M, R15M**; 290°-R-339°-W-125°-R-145°; W truncated twr; 46°41'·54N 01°57'·92W.

Ldg lts 043·7°, both Q 7/28m **15M**; 033·5°-053·5°; synch; W ☐ twrs, R tops: Front, 46°41'·86N 01°56'·75W. Rear, 260m NE.

Pilours ⚓ Q (6) + L Fl 15s; *Bell;* 46°40'·99N 01°58'·09W.

Jetée de la Garenne ⚓ Fl G 4s 8m 6M; 46°41'·46N 01°57'·25W.

Jetée de Boisvinet ⚓ Fl R 4s 8m 6M; 46°41'·62N 01°57'·16W.

LES SABLES D'OLONNE

Les Barges ⚓ Fl (2) R 10s 25m 13M; Gy twr; 46°29'·70N 01°50'·50W.

Petite Barge ⚓ Q (6) + L Fl 15s 3M; *Whis;* 46°28'·90N 01°50'·61W.

L'Armandèche ☆ Fl (2+1) 15s 42m **24M**; 295°-130°; W 6-sided twr, R top; 46°29'·39N 01°48'·29W.

Nouch Sud ⚓ Q (6) + L Fl 15s; 46°28'·55N 01°47'·41W.

Nouch Nord ⚓ 46°28'·88N 01°47'·36W.

SW Pass, ldg lts 032·5°, both Iso 4s 12/33m **16M**, H24: **Front** ☆, 46°29'·42N 01°46'·37W; mast. **Rear** ☆, **La Potence,** W ☐ twr.

SE Pass, ldg lts 320°: Front, E jetty ⚓ QG 11m 8M; W twr, G top; 46°29'·44N 01°47'·51W. Rear, Tour d'Arundel ⚓ Q 33m 13M, synch; large Gy ☐ twr; 46°29'·63N 01°47'·74W.

Jetée St Nicolas (W jetty) ⚓ QR 1·2s 16m 8M; 143°-094°; W twr, R top; 46°29'·23N 01°47'·52W.

BOURGENAY

Ldg lts 040°, both QG 9/19m 7M. Front, 020°-060°; on S bkwtr; 46°26'·34N 01°40'·62W. Rear, 010°-070°; 162m from front.

Landfall ⚓ L Fl 10s; 46°25'·26N 01°41'·93W.

Ent ⚓ Fl R 4s 8m 9M & ⚓ Iso G 4s 6m 5M; 46°26'·29N 01°40'·75W.

PLATEAU DE ROCHEBONNE (Shoal 32M offshore)

NW ⚓ Q (9) 15s; *Whis;* 46°12'·92N 02°31'·58W.

NE ⚓ Iso G 4s; 46°12'·73N 02°24'·83W.

SE ⚓ Q (3) 10s; *Bell;* 46°09'·20N 02°21'·13W.

SW ⚓ Fl (2) R 6s; 46°10'·11N 02°27'·04W.

PERTUIS BRETON

JARD-SUR-MER and LA TRANCHE-SUR-MER

Ldg marks 036°, two unlit W bcns; 46°24'·47N 01°34'·16W.

Pte du Grouin du Cou ☆ Fl WRG 5s 29m, **W20M, R/G16M**; 034°-R-061°-W-117°-G-138°-W-034°; W 8-sided twr, B top; 46°20'·67N 01°27'·83W.

La Tranche pier ⚓ Fl (2) R 6s 6m 6M; R col; 46°20'·55N 01°25'·63W.

Mussel farm, No entry, marked by: ⚓ Q, 46°17'·17N 01°22'·19W.

⚓ Q (3) 10s, 46°15'·73N 01°18'·42W. ⚓ Q (6) + L Fl 15s, 46°15'·16N 01°19'·98W. ⚓ Q (9) 15s, 46°16'·28N 01°22'·88W.

L'AIGUILLON and LA FAUTE-SUR-MER

Le Lay ⚓ Q (6) + L Fl 15s; 46°16'·10N 01°16'·53W.

No. 1 ⚓ 46°16'·65N 01°16'·25W. Many mussel beds.

ANSE DE L'AIGUILLON (for La Sèvre Niortaise & Marans)
ATT de L'Aiguillon ⚓ L Fl 10s; 46°15'·33N 01°11'·50W.
Inner fairway ⚓ 46°17'·19N 01°09'·65W.
Port du Pavé ⚡ Fl G 4s 9m 7M; W col, G top; 46°18'·15N 01°08'·01W.

ÎLE DE RÉ

Les Baleineaux ⚡ VQ 23m 7M; pink twr, R top; 46°15'·81N 01°35'·22W.
Les Baleines ☆ Fl (4) 15s 53m **27M**; conspic Gy 8-sided twr, R lantern; 46°14'·64N 01°33'·69W.

ARS-EN-RÉ

Dir ⚡ 268° Oc WRG 4s, W10M, R/G 7M; 275·5°-G-267·5°-W-268·5°-R-274·5°; W hut with W☐topmark; 46°14'·05N 01°28'·60W.
Les Islattes ⚓ Q 13m 3M; NCM bcn twr 46°14'·03N 01°23'·32W.
Bûcheron No 1 ⚑ Fl G 2·5s; 46°14'·21N 01°25'·98W.
Bûcheron No 3 ⚑ Fl (2) G 6s; 46°14'·14N 01°26'·94W.
Le Fier d'Ars, inner ldg lts 232·5°, both Q 5/13m 9/11M:
Front ⚡ R/W frame on W col; 46°12'·75N 01°30'·59W.
Rear ⚡ 142°-322°; B vert rectangle on W mast, 370m from front.

ST MARTIN DE RÉ

Lt ho, E of ent ⚡ Oc (2) WR 6s 18m W10M, R7M; Shore-W-245°-R-281°-W-shore; W twr, R top; 46°12'·44N 01°21'·89W.
W mole ⚡ Fl G 2·5s 10m 5M; obsc'd by Pte du Grouin when brg <124°; W post, G top; 46°12'·49N 01°21'·91W.

LA FLOTTE

N bkwtr ⚡ Fl WG 4s 10m W12M, G9M; 130°-G-205°-W-220°-G-257°; W ○ twr, G top; 46°11'·33N 01°19'·30W.
Dir lt 212·5°, Moiré effect, is next to the main lt twr.
ÎLE DE RÉ (South coast, from the W, inc bridge)
Chanchardon ⚡ Fl WR 4s 15m W11M, R8M; 118°-R-290°-W-118°; B 8-sided twr, W base; 46°09'·71N 01°28'·41W.
Chauveau ☆ Oc (3) WR 12s 27m **W15M**, R11M; 057°-W-094°-R-104°-W-342°-R-057°; W ○ twr, R top; 46°08'·03N 01°16'·42W.
Bridge span (30m cl'nce) for SE-bound vessels, ⚡ Iso 4s 34m 8M; 46°10'·18N 01°14'·75W . Span (30m cl'nce) for NW-bound vessels, ⚡ Iso 4s 34m 8M; 46°10'·26N 01°14'·52W.
La Pallice, W mole, ⚡ Fl G 4s 5m 6M; 46°09'·78N 01°14'·45W. S end, ⚓ Q (6) + L Fl 15s 6m 9M; 46°09'·36N 01°14'·52W.

LA ROCHELLE AND LA CHARENTE TO ROCHEFORT

LA ROCHELLE

PA ⚓ Iso 4s 8m 7M; *Whis*; 46°05'·62N 01°42'·45W.
Chauveau ⚓ VQ (6) + L Fl 10s; 46°06'·56N 01°16'·06W.
Roche du Sud ⚓ Q (9) 15s; 46°06'·37N 01°15'·22W.
La Rochelle ldg lts 059°, both Dir Q 15/25m 13/14M; synch; by day Fl 4s. Front; intens 056°-062°; R ○ twr, W bands; 46°09'·35N 01°09'·16W. Rear, 044°-074°, obsc'd 061°-065°; W 8-sided twr, G top, 235m from front.
Lavardin ⚓ Fl (2) 6s 14m 7M; BRB IDM twr; 46°08'·09N 01°14'·52W.
Les Minimes ⚓ Q (9) 15s; 46°08'·01N 01°11'·60W.

Pte des Minimes ⚡ Fl (3) WG 12s 8m; W8M, G5M; 059°-W-213°; 313°-G-059°; 8-sided twr on piles; 46°08'·27N 01°10'·76W.
Chan buoy ⚑ QG; 46°08'·53N 01°10'·87W; marking hbr limit.
Tour Richelieu ⚓ Fl R 4s 10m 9M; R twr; 46°08'·90N 01°10'·34W.
Port des Minimes, W bkwtr ⚡ Fl (2) G 6s 9m 7M; 46°08'·82N 01°10'·15W.

LA CHARENTE

Fort Boyard twr ⚡ Q (9) 15s; 45°59'·96N 01°12'·85W.
Ldg lts 115°, both Dir QR 8/21m **19/20M**; intens 113°-117°; W ☐ twr, R top: **Front** ☆, 45°57'·96N 01°04'·38W.
Rear, Soumard ☆, 600m from front. Same twr: ⚡ QR 21m 8M; vis 322°-067°.
Île d'Aix ☆ Fl WR 5s 24m **W24M, R20M**; 103°-R-118°-W-103°; two conspic W ○ twrs, R top; 46°00'·60N 01°10'·67W.
Pte Ste Catherine, jetty hd ⚓ Q (6) + L Fl 15s 5m 4M; 45°59'·05N 01°07'·85W. Les Palles ⚓ Q; 45°59'·54N 01°09'·56W.
Fouras, Port Sud bkwtr ⚡ Fl WR 4s 6m 9/6M; 115°-R-177°-W-115°; 45°58'·97N 01°05'·72W. Rear 75m from front.

ROCHEFORT

Night passage by yachts is not advised.
⚡ Fl (2) G 6s; bcn 45°55'·21N 00°56'·98W, 1·4M S of Rochefort.

ÎLE D'OLÉRON

Pte de Chassiron ☆ Fl 10s 50m, **28M**; conspic W twr, B bands; 46°02'·80N 01°24'·62W, NW tip of island.
Antioche ⚓ Q 20m 11M; 46°03'·94N 01°23'·71W.

ST DENIS

Dir ⚡ 205°, Iso WRG 4s 14m, W11M, R/G8M; 190°-G-204°-W-206°-R-220°; 46°01'·61N 01°21'·92W.
E jetty ⚡ Fl (2) WG 6s 6m, W9M, G6M; 205°-G-277°-W-292°-G-165°; ☐ hut; 46°02'·10N 01°22'·06W.

PORT DU DOUHET and PASSAGE DE L'OUEST

Seaweed farm ⚓ VQ; 46°00'·65N 01°17'·38W.
N ent ⚓ 46°00'·10N 01°19'·20W.
Fishfarm ⚓ Q; 46°00'·24N 01°15'·34W. ⚓ Q (3) 10s; 45°59'·84N 01°14'·79W.

BOYARDVILLE

Mole ⚡ Fl (2) R 6s 8m 5M; obsc'd by Pte des Saumonards when brg <150°; W twr, R top; 45°58'·24N 01°13'·83W.

COUREAU D'OLÉRON and LE CHÂTEAU D'OLÉRON

Juliar ⚓ Q (3) WG 10s 12m, W11M; G8M; 147°-W-336°-G-147°; 45°54'·11N 01°09'·48W.
Chateau d'Oléron, ldg lts 318·5°, both QR 11/24m 7M; synch. Front, 191°-087°; R line on W twr; 45°53'·03N 01°11'·45W. Rear, W twr, R top; 240m from front.

LA SEUDRE RIVER

Pte du Mus de Loup ⚡ Oc G 4s 8m 6M; 118°-147°; 45°47'·70N 01°08'·60W.
Pertuis de Maumusson. Depths & buoys subject to change.
ATT Maumusson ⚓ L Fl 10s; 45°46'·16N 01°17'·92W.
La Barre ⚑ 45°46'·79N 01°15'·97W.
Tabouret ⬟ 45°46'·93N 01°16'·15W.
Mattes ⚑ 45°46'·93N 01°15'·29W.
Gatseau ⬟ 45°47'·36N 01°14'·70W.

LA COTINIÈRE (SW side of island)
Ent ldg lts 339°, both ☆ Dir Oc (2) 6s 6/14m 13/12M; synch: Front, 329°-349°; W twr, R top; 45°54'·72N 01°19'·79W. Rear, intens 329°-349°; W twr, R bands; 425m from front on W bkwtr.
W bkwtr head, Fl R 4s 10m; 45°54'·63N 01°19'·70W.

GIRONDE APPROACHES AND TO BORDEAUX

GRANDE PASSE DE L'OUEST
Pte de la Coubre ☆ Fl (2) 10s 64m **28M**; W twr, R top; 45°41'·78N 01°13'·99W. Same twr, F RG 42m10M; 030°-R-043°-G-060°-R-110°.
BXA ⚓ Iso 4s 8m 7M; *Racon B*; 45°37'·53N 01°28'·69W.
Ldg lts 081·5°. **Front** ☆, Dir Iso 4s 21m **20M**; intens 080·5°-082·5°; W pylon on dolphin; 45°39'·56N 01°08'·78W, 1·1M from rear. Same structure, Q (2) 5s 10m 3M.
La Palmyre, common rear ☆ Dir Q 57m **27M**; intens 080·7°-082·2°; W radar twr; 45°39'·71N 01°07'·25W.
Same twr, Dir FR 57m **17M**; intens 325·5°-328·5°.
No. 1 ⚓ QG; 45°38'·03N 01°22'·69W
No. 6 ⚓ VQ (6) + L Fl 10s; 45°38'·28N 01°18'·68W.
No. 7a ⚓ Fl G 4s; 45°38'·96N 01°14'·85W.
No. 9 ⚓ Q; 45°39'·43N 01°12'·79W.
No. 11 ⚓ Iso G 4s; 45°39'·06N 01°10'·60W.
No. 11A ⚓ Fl G 2·5s; 45°38'·37N 01°07'·90W.
No. 13 ⚓ Fl (2) G 6s; 45°37'·33N 01°06'·41W.
No. 13A ⚓ Fl (3) G 12s; 45°35'·68N 01°04'·19W.
No. 13B ⚓ QG; 45°34'·67N 01°02'·98W.
Ldg lts 327° (down-river): Front, Terre-Nègre ☆, Oc (3) WRG 12s 39m W14M, R/G11M; 304°-R-319°-W-327°-G-000°-W-004°-G-097°-W-104°-R-116°; W twr, R top on W side; 45°38'·77N 01°06'·39W, 1·1M from rear (La Palmyre above).
Cordouan ☆ Oc (2+1) WRG 12s 60m, **W19M, R16M, G15M**; 014°-W-126°-G-178·5°-W-250°-W (unintens) -267°-R (unintens)-294·5°-R-014°; obsc'd in estuary when brg >285°; W twr, Gy band; 45°35'·18N 01°10'·40W.

PASSE SUD (or DE GRAVE)
Ldg lts 063°: **Front, St Nicolas** ☆ Dir QG 22m **16M**; intens 061·5°-064·5°; W ☐ twr; 45°33'·73N 01°05'·01W.
Rear, Pte de Grave ☆ Oc WRG 4s 26m, **W17M, R/G13M**; 033°-W(unintens)-054°-W-233·5°-R-303°-W-312°-G-330°-W-341°- W(unintens)-025°; W ☐ twr, B corners and top, 0·84M from front.

G ⚓ 45°30'·33N 01°15'·55W. G3 ⚓ 45°32'·79N 01°07'·72W. Ldg lts 041°, both Dir QR 33/61m **18M. Front, Le Chay** ☆ 45°37'·31N 01°02'·43W. **Rear, St Pierre** ☆, 0·97M from front.
G4 ⚓ 45°34'·70N 01°05'·80W. G6 ⚓ 45°34'·88N 01°04'·80W.

ROYAN
R1 ⚓ Iso G 4s; 45°36'·56N 01°01'·96W.
S jetty ☆ Fl (2) R 10s 11m 12M; 199°-116°; 45°37'·00N 01°01'·81W.
Hbr ent, W jetty ☆ Fl (3) R 12s 8m 6M; 45°37'·12N 01°01'·53W.

PORT BLOC and PORT-MÉDOC
Pte de Grave, jetty ⚓ Q 6m 2M; 45°34'·42N 01°03'·68W.
Port Bloc, ent N side ☆ Fl G 4s 9m 3M; 45°34'·14N 01°03'·74W.
Port-Médoc, N bkwtr head ☆ QG 4M; 45°33'·40N 01°03'·39W.

MESCHERS, MORTAGNE, PORT MAUBERT, PAUILLAC and BLAYE
Meschers ldg lts 349·5°: 2 FW (privately maintained). Front 45°33'·20N 00°56'·62W, on E bkwtr head. Rear, 130m from front.
Mortagne ent ⚓ VQ (9) 10s; 45°28'·24N 00°49'·02W.
Port Maubert, ldg lts 024·5°, both QR 5/9m 5M; 45°25'·56N 00°45'·47W.
Pauillac, No. 43 ⚓ Fl (2) G 6s; 45°12'·44N 00°44'·27W.
NE elbow ☆ Fl G 4s 7m 5M; 45°11'·95N 00°44'·59W.
Ent E side ☆ QG 7m 4M; 45°11'·83N 00°44'·59W.
Blaye, No. S9 ▲ 45°09'·35N 00°40'·27W; 1·8M N of Blaye.
N quay ☆ Q (3) R 5s 6m 3M; 45°07'·49N 00°39'·99W.
D6 ⚓ Fl (2) R 6s; 45°06'·91N 00°39'·93W, 0.6M S of Blaye.
Bec d'Ambés ⚓ QG 5m 5M; 45°02'·53N 00°36'·47W (here Rivers Dordogne and Garonne flow into River Gironde).

BORDEAUX
Pont d'Aquitaine ☆ 4 F Vi; 44°52'·82N 00°32'·28W.
No 73 ⚓ Iso G 4s; 44°52'·72N 00°32'·24W.
Lormont Iso R 4s, S end of ◐ pontoon; 44°52'·62N 00°32'·12W.
Lock ent to Bassins Nos 1 and 2, 44°51'·72N 00°33'·07W.
Pont de Pierre, 44°50'·30N 00°33'·78W, Km 0.

		1	2	3	4	5	6	7	8	9	10	11	12	13	14	15	16
1	Port Joinville	1															
2	St Gilles-C-de-Vie	18	2														
3	Sables d'Olonne	31	16	3													
4	Bourgenay	40	25	9	4												
5	St Martin (I de Ré)	55	44	27	20	5											
6	La Rochelle	66	51	36	29	12	6										
7	Rochefort	84	75	61	54	36	26	7									
8	R La Seudre	89	71	58	52	33	24	30	8								
9	Port St Denis	59	48	33	30	21	13	26	22	9							
10	Port Bloc/Royan	97	85	71	60	56	52	68	27	42	10						
11	Bordeaux	152	140	126	115	111	107	123	82	97	55	11					
12	Cap Ferret	138	130	113	110	102	98	114	75	88	68	123	12				
13	Capbreton	192	186	169	166	165	156	172	131	145	124	179	58	13			
14	Anglet/Bayonne	200	195	181	178	177	168	184	143	157	132	187	70	12	14		
15	Santander	212	210	204	204	206	202	218	184	192	180	235	133	106	103	15	
16	Cabo Finisterre	377	395	393	394	406	407	423	399	397	401	456	376	370	373	274	16

DISTANCE TABLES
Approx distances in nautical miles are by the most direct route allowing for dangers and TSS.

Times are UT - add 1 hour in non-shaded months to convert to Summer Time

SUN RISE/SET LATITUDE 56°N – 2014

	Rise Set JANUARY	Rise Set FEBRUARY	Rise Set MARCH	Rise Set APRIL	Rise Set MAY	Rise Set JUNE
1	0831 1536	0755 1633	0652 1734	0531 1838	0416 1939	0322 2034
4	0830 1540	0749 1639	0644 1740	0523 1844	0410 1945	0319 2038
7	0828 1544	0743 1646	0637 1747	0515 1850	0403 1951	0317 2042
10	0826 1549	0737 1653	0629 1753	0508 1856	0357 1957	0315 2044
13	0823 1554	0730 1659	0621 1759	0500 1902	0351 2003	0314 2047
16	0820 1600	0723 1706	0613 1805	0452 1909	0346 2008	0313 2049
19	0816 1606	0716 1712	0605 1811	0445 1915	0340 2014	0313 2050
22	0812 1612	0709 1719	0557 1818	0438 1921	0335 2019	0313 2051
25	0807 1618	0702 1725	0549 1824	0430 1927	0331 2024	0314 2051
28	0802 1624	0654 1732	0542 1830	0423 1933	0327 2029	0316 2050
31	0757 1631		0534 1836		0323 2033	

	JULY	AUGUST	SEPTEMBER	OCTOBER	NOVEMBER	DECEMBER
1	0318 2049	0404 2008	0504 1855	0603 1736	0707 1620	0807 1531
4	0321 2047	0409 2002	0510 1847	0609 1728	0713 1613	0811 1529
7	0324 2045	0415 1955	0516 1839	0615 1720	0719 1607	0816 1527
10	0328 2042	0421 1949	0521 1831	0621 1712	0726 1601	0820 1526
13	0332 2039	0427 1942	0527 1823	0627 1705	0732 1556	0823 1525
16	0336 2035	0433 1935	0533 1815	0633 1657	0738 1551	0826 1525
19	0341 2031	0438 1927	0539 1807	0639 1650	0744 1546	0828 1526
22	0346 2026	0444 1920	0545 1759	0645 1643	0750 1541	0830 1527
25	0351 2021	0450 1913	0551 1751	0652 1636	0756 1537	0831 1529
28	0356 2016	0456 1905	0557 1744	0658 1629	0801 1534	0832 1532
31	0402 2010	0502 1857		0705 1622		0831 1535

SUN RISE/SET LATITUDE 48°N – 2014

	Rise Set JANUARY	Rise Set FEBRUARY	Rise Set MARCH	Rise Set APRIL	Rise Set MAY	Rise Set JUNE
1	0750 1617	0728 1700	0641 1744	0539 1830	0442 1913	0405 1951
4	0750 1620	0724 1705	0636 1749	0533 1834	0437 1917	0403 1954
7	0749 1624	0719 1709	0630 1753	0527 1839	0433 1921	0402 1956
10	0748 1628	0715 1714	0624 1758	0521 1843	0428 1925	0401 1958
13	0746 1631	0710 1719	0618 1802	0515 1847	0424 1929	0400 2000
16	0744 1636	0705 1724	0612 1807	0509 1851	0420 1933	0400 2002
19	0742 1640	0700 1729	0605 1811	0503 1856	0417 1937	0400 2003
22	0739 1644	0654 1733	0559 1815	0458 1900	0413 1941	0401 2003
25	0736 1649	0649 1738	0553 1820	0453 1904	0410 1944	0402 2004
28	0733 1653	0643 1743	0547 1824	0447 1909	0408 1947	0403 2004
31	0729 1658		0541 1828		0406 1950	

	JULY	AUGUST	SEPTEMBER	OCTOBER	NOVEMBER	DECEMBER
1	0404 2003	0436 1936	0518 1841	0559 1740	0645 1642	0728 1609
4	0406 2002	0440 1932	0522 1835	0603 1734	0649 1637	0732 1608
7	0409 2001	0444 1927	0526 1829	0607 1728	0654 1633	0735 1607
10	0411 1959	0448 1922	0530 1823	0612 1722	0658 1629	0739 1607
13	0414 1957	0452 1917	0534 1817	0616 1716	0703 1625	0741 1607
16	0417 1955	0456 1912	0538 1811	0620 1710	0708 1621	0744 1607
19	0420 1952	0500 1906	0542 1804	0625 1704	0712 1618	0746 1608
22	0424 1949	0504 1901	0546 1758	0629 1659	0716 1615	0747 1610
25	0427 1945	0508 1855	0551 1752	0634 1654	0721 1613	0749 1611
28	0431 1941	0512 1849	0555 1746	0638 1648	0725 1611	0749 1614
31	0435 1937	0516 1843		0643 1644		0750 1616

Times are UT - add 1 hour in non-shaded months to convert to Summer Time

SUN RISE/SET LATITUDE 40°N – 2014

	Rise Set JANUARY		Rise Set FEBRUARY		Rise Set MARCH		Rise Set APRIL		Rise Set MAY		Rise Set JUNE	
1	0722	1645	0709	1719	0634	1752	0544	1824	0500	1855	0433	1923
4	0722	1648	0706	1723	0629	1755	0540	1827	0457	1858	0432	1925
7	0722	1651	0703	1726	0625	1758	0535	1830	0453	1901	0431	1927
10	0722	1654	0659	1730	0620	1801	0530	1833	0450	1903	0431	1928
13	0721	1657	0656	1733	0615	1805	0526	1836	0447	1906	0431	1930
16	0720	1700	0652	1737	0610	1808	0521	1839	0444	1909	0431	1931
19	0718	1704	0648	1740	0605	1811	0517	1842	0441	1912	0431	1932
22	0717	1707	0644	1744	0601	1814	0512	1845	0439	1915	0432	1932
25	0714	1711	0640	1747	0556	1817	0508	1848	0437	1917	0432	1933
28	0712	1714	0635	1751	0551	1820	0504	1851	0435	1920	0433	1933
31	0710	1718			0546	1823			0434	1922		

	Rise Set JULY		AUGUST		SEPTEMBER		OCTOBER		NOVEMBER		DECEMBER	
1	0435	1933	0458	1914	0528	1832	0556	1743	0629	1658	0702	1635
4	0436	1932	0501	1911	0530	1827	0559	1738	0632	1654	0705	1635
7	0438	1931	0504	1907	0533	1822	0602	1733	0636	1651	0708	1635
10	0440	1930	0507	1903	0536	1817	0605	1728	0639	1648	0711	1635
13	0442	1929	0509	1900	0539	1812	0608	1724	0643	1646	0713	1635
16	0444	1927	0512	1856	0542	1807	0611	1719	0646	1643	0715	1636
19	0447	1925	0515	1851	0545	1802	0614	1715	0649	1641	0717	1637
22	0449	1923	0518	1847	0547	1757	0618	1711	0653	1639	0719	1638
25	0452	1921	0521	1843	0550	1753	0621	1707	0656	1638	0720	1640
28	0455	1918	0524	1838	0553	1748	0624	1703	0659	1636	0721	1642
31	0457	1915	0527	1833			0628	1659			0722	1644

MOON RISE/SET LATITUDE 56°N – 2014

	Rise Set JANUARY		Rise Set FEBRUARY		Rise Set MARCH		Rise Set APRIL		Rise Set MAY		Rise Set JUNE	
1	0755	1618	0807	1925	0630	1816	0607	2110	0543	2210	0702	2253
4	0942	2033	0915	2329	0741	2220	0750	****	0814	****	1016	****
7	1048	****	1038	0152	0914	0041	1027	0149	1125	0115	1341	0040
10	1202	0257	1249	0439	1139	0316	1340	0312	1450	0216	1722	0149
13	1401	0556	1552	0620	1447	0447	1709	0412	1831	0321	2044	0356
16	1656	0750	1916	0724	1814	0549	2051	0521	2200	0514	2243	0738
19	2017	0858	2249	0822	2151	0652	****	0723	****	0837	2355	1145
22	2347	0954	0113	0950	0013	0835	0134	1049	0103	1238	0042	1535
25	0215	1111	0416	1241	0256	1142	0257	1450	0211	1632	0218	1849
28	0538	1349	0604	1650	0430	1547	0407	1847	0339	1959	0451	2055
31	0740	1758			0541	1953			0602	2221		

	Rise Set JULY		AUGUST		SEPTEMBER		OCTOBER		NOVEMBER		DECEMBER	
1	0803	2209	1021	2133	1247	2130	1339	2204	1404	****	1322	0126
4	1124	2306	1351	2252	1545	****	1534	0032	1517	0342	1444	0520
7	1458	****	1706	0022	1736	0256	1652	0444	1647	0740	1654	0835
10	1826	0140	1910	0403	1853	0716	1817	0849	1908	1044	1957	1033
13	2043	0511	2028	0823	2021	1114	2026	1205	2214	1231	2315	1142
16	2201	0926	2148	1222	2235	1414	2324	1402	0025	1337	0129	1241
19	2314	1324	2348	1531	0032	1601	0134	1512	0349	1437	0501	1402
22	0020	1643	0138	1730	0346	1708	0457	1612	0723	1607	0814	1636
25	0245	1857	0450	1842	0710	1808	0828	1733	1023	1854	1014	2030
28	0553	2016	0811	1940	1038	1932	1136	1958	1210	2246	1130	****
31	0912	2113	1138	2054			1336	2338			1247	0308

Times are UT - add 1 hour in non-shaded months to convert to Summer Time

MOON RISE/SET LATITUDE 48°N – 2014

	Rise Set JANUARY	Rise Set FEBRUARY	Rise Set MARCH	Rise Set APRIL	Rise Set MAY	Rise Set JUNE
1	0722 1650	0756 1932	0623 1819	0625 2047	0614 2137	0731 2227
4	0928 2043	0927 2313	0756 2201	0822 2349	0845 2353	1028 2353
7	1057 ****	1107 0124	0945 0010	1057 0119	1141 0057	1334 0043
10	1229 0232	1323 0404	1210 0243	1354 0257	1447 0216	1656 0211
13	1436 0521	1613 0557	1505 0428	1703 0415	1808 0340	2010 0431
16	1721 0723	1918 0718	1812 0547	2025 0543	2126 0548	2226 0801
19	2023 0848	2231 0836	2129 0710	2333 0757	2349 0903	2359 1145
22	2334 1003	0044 1021	**** 0908	0108 1113	0055 1243	0059 1514
25	0148 1140	0343 1313	0226 1211	0252 1453	0224 1615	0250 1815
28	0503 1423	0550 1701	0420 1554	0422 1828	0409 1927	0522 2028
31	0722 1813		0552 1937		0635 2151	

	JULY	AUGUST	SEPTEMBER	OCTOBER	NOVEMBER	DECEMBER
1	0818 2157	1013 2143	1218 2200	1306 2236	1351 ****	1328 0124
4	1121 2312	1325 2319	1513 ****	1516 0054	1526 0337	1508 0457
7	1435 0009	1632 0056	1721 0315	1656 0443	1713 0714	1727 0802
10	1752 0214	1852 0425	1901 0711	1841 0827	1940 1012	2020 1009
13	2022 0536	2033 0822	2048 1049	2059 1132	2233 1210	2320 1135
16	2202 0929	2212 1159	2308 1341	2347 1338	0033 1332	0122 1251
19	2335 1305	**** 1458	0058 1538	0146 1504	0338 1450	0434 1429
22	0050 1610	0207 1705	0356 1702	0450 1622	0654 1637	0741 1709
25	0316 1828	0503 1832	0701 1819	0803 1800	0951 1925	0956 2046
28	0610 2002	0806 1948	1011 2000	1103 2030	1155 2258	1133 ****
31	0911 2117	1115 2120		1316 2355		1309 0247

MOON RISE/SET LATITUDE 40°N – 2014

	Rise Set JANUARY	Rise Set FEBRUARY	Rise Set MARCH	Rise Set APRIL	Rise Set MAY	Rise Set JUNE
1	0658 1713	0749 1937	0618 1822	0638 2031	0636 2114	0751 2209
4	0918 2051	0936 2301	0807 2147	0845 2326	0907 2333	1038 2347
7	1103 ****	1128 0104	1007 ****	1117 0058	1152 0044	1330 0045
10	1248 0214	1346 0341	1233 0221	1403 0245	1444 0215	1637 0226
13	1500 0457	1628 0541	1517 0414	1659 0416	1751 0354	1946 0455
16	1739 0705	1920 0715	1811 0546	2007 0558	2102 0612	2213 0817
19	2028 0842	2219 0846	2114 0722	2310 0821	2333 0921	**** 1145
22	2324 1010	0023 1043	**** 0931	0050 1130	0050 1246	0111 1458
25	0130 1200	0320 1336	0205 1231	0247 1454	0233 1603	0312 1752
28	0438 1447	0540 1710	0412 1559	0433 1814	0430 1904	0543 2008
31	0709 1824		0601 1926		0657 2130	

	JULY	AUGUST	SEPTEMBER	OCTOBER	NOVEMBER	DECEMBER
1	0829 2149	1008 2150	1158 2221	1244 2258	1342 0007	1332 0123
4	1118 2317	1307 2339	1451 0006	1504 0110	1531 0334	1526 0441
7	1418 0022	1609 0119	1711 0329	1659 0443	1733 0656	1750 0739
10	1728 0237	1839 0441	1907 0708	1858 0811	2002 0949	2036 0952
13	2006 0555	2036 0821	2107 1031	2121 1110	2248 1154	2323 1129
16	2203 0932	2229 1143	2330 1319	**** 1321	0039 1328	0116 1258
19	2350 1251	**** 1435	0116 1522	0154 1458	0331 1500	0416 1448
22	0112 1548	0228 1646	0402 1657	0445 1629	0634 1658	0718 1731
25	0338 1808	0513 1825	0654 1828	0745 1819	0929 1947	0943 2057
28	0623 1952	0802 1954	0952 2020	1041 2053	1144 2307	1135 ****
31	0911 2120	1058 2138		1302 ****		1325 0233

SPEED, TIME AND DISTANCE (NAUTICAL MILES)

Speed in knots

Time in minutes	1	2	3	4	5	6	7	8	9	10	15	20
1	0.0	0.0	0.1	0.1	0.1	0.1	0.1	0.1	0.2	0.2	0.3	0.3
2	0.0	0.1	0.1	0.1	0.2	0.2	0.2	0.3	0.3	0.3	0.5	0.7
3	0.1	0.1	0.2	0.2	0.3	0.3	0.4	0.4	0.5	0.5	0.8	1.0
4	0.1	0.1	0.2	0.3	0.3	0.4	0.5	0.5	0.6	0.7	1.0	1.3
5	0.1	0.2	0.3	0.3	0.4	0.5	0.6	0.7	0.8	0.8	1.3	1.7
6	0.1	0.2	0.3	0.4	0.5	0.6	0.7	0.8	0.9	1.0	1.5	2.0
7	0.1	0.2	0.4	0.5	0.6	0.7	0.8	0.9	1.1	1.2	1.8	2.3
8	0.1	0.3	0.4	0.5	0.7	0.8	0.9	1.1	1.2	1.3	2.0	2.7
9	0.2	0.3	0.5	0.6	0.8	0.9	1.1	1.2	1.4	1.5	2.3	3.0
10	0.2	0.3	0.5	0.7	0.8	1.0	1.2	1.3	1.5	1.7	2.5	3.3
11	0.2	0.4	0.6	0.7	0.9	1.1	1.3	1.5	1.7	1.8	2.8	3.7
12	0.2	0.4	0.6	0.8	1.0	1.2	1.4	1.6	1.8	2.0	3.0	4.0
13	0.2	0.4	0.7	0.9	1.1	1.3	1.5	1.7	2.0	2.2	3.3	4.3
14	0.2	0.5	0.7	0.9	1.2	1.4	1.6	1.9	2.1	2.3	3.5	4.7
15	0.3	0.5	0.8	1.0	1.3	1.5	1.8	2.0	2.3	2.5	3.8	5.0
16	0.3	0.5	0.8	1.1	1.3	1.6	1.9	2.1	2.4	2.7	4.0	5.3
17	0.3	0.6	0.9	1.1	1.4	1.7	2.0	2.3	2.6	2.8	4.3	5.7
18	0.3	0.6	0.9	1.2	1.5	1.8	2.1	2.4	2.7	3.0	4.5	6.0
19	0.3	0.6	1.0	1.3	1.6	1.9	2.2	2.5	2.9	3.2	4.8	6.3
20	0.3	0.7	1.0	1.3	1.7	2.0	2.3	2.7	3.0	3.3	5.0	6.7
21	0.4	0.7	1.1	1.4	1.8	2.1	2.5	2.8	3.2	3.5	5.3	7.0
22	0.4	0.7	1.1	1.5	1.8	2.2	2.6	2.9	3.3	3.7	5.5	7.3
23	0.4	0.8	1.2	1.5	1.9	2.3	2.7	3.1	3.5	3.8	5.8	7.7
24	0.4	0.8	1.2	1.6	2.0	2.4	2.8	3.2	3.6	4.0	6.0	8.0
25	0.4	0.8	1.3	1.7	2.1	2.5	2.9	3.3	3.8	4.2	6.3	8.3
30	0.5	1.0	1.5	2.0	2.5	3.0	3.5	4.0	4.5	5.0	7.5	10.0
35	0.6	1.2	1.8	2.3	2.9	3.5	4.1	4.7	5.3	5.8	8.8	11.7
40	0.7	1.3	2.0	2.7	3.3	4.0	4.7	5.3	6.0	6.7	10.0	13.3
45	0.8	1.5	2.3	3.0	3.8	4.5	5.3	6.0	6.8	7.5	11.3	15.0
50	0.8	1.7	2.5	3.3	4.2	5.0	5.8	6.7	7.5	8.3	12.5	16.7

DISTANCE (NAUTICAL MILES) OFF RISING/DIPPING LIGHTS

Height of eye in feet

Height of light in metres	2	3	4	5	6	7	8	9	10	20	30	40	50
2	4.6	4.9	5.2	5.5	5.7	6.0	6.2	6.4	6.6	8.1	9.2	10.2	11.0
3	5.2	5.6	5.9	6.2	6.4	6.6	6.8	7.0	7.2	8.7	9.9	10.8	11.7
4	5.8	6.1	6.4	6.7	6.9	7.2	7.4	7.6	7.8	9.3	10.4	11.4	12.2
5	6.3	6.6	6.9	7.2	7.4	7.7	7.9	8.1	8.3	9.8	10.9	11.9	12.7
6	6.7	7.1	7.4	7.6	7.9	8.1	8.3	8.5	8.7	10.2	11.3	12.3	13.2
7	7.1	7.5	7.8	8.0	8.3	8.5	8.7	8.9	9.1	10.6	11.8	12.7	13.6
8	7.5	7.8	8.2	8.4	8.7	8.9	9.1	9.3	9.5	11.0	12.1	13.1	14.0
9	7.8	8.2	8.5	8.8	9.0	9.2	9.5	9.7	9.8	11.3	12.5	13.5	14.3
10	8.2	8.5	8.8	9.1	9.4	9.6	9.8	10.0	10.2	11.7	12.8	13.8	14.6
11	8.5	8.9	9.2	9.4	9.7	9.9	10.1	10.3	10.5	12.0	13.1	14.1	15.0
12	8.8	9.2	9.5	9.7	10.0	10.2	10.4	10.6	10.8	12.3	13.4	14.4	15.3
13	9.1	9.5	9.8	10.0	10.3	10.5	10.7	10.9	11.1	12.6	13.7	14.7	15.6
14	9.4	9.7	10.0	10.3	10.6	10.8	11.0	11.2	11.4	12.9	14.0	15.0	15.8
15	9.6	10.0	10.3	10.6	10.8	11.1	11.3	11.5	11.6	13.1	14.3	15.3	16.1
16	9.9	10.3	10.6	10.8	11.1	11.3	11.5	11.7	11.9	13.4	14.6	15.5	16.4
17	10.2	10.5	10.8	11.1	11.3	11.6	11.8	12.0	12.2	13.7	14.8	15.8	16.6
18	10.4	10.8	11.1	11.4	11.6	11.8	12.0	12.2	12.4	13.9	15.1	16.0	16.9
19	10.7	11.0	11.3	11.6	11.8	12.1	12.3	12.5	12.7	14.2	15.3	16.3	17.1
20	10.9	11.3	11.6	11.8	12.1	12.3	12.5	12.7	12.9	14.4	15.5	16.5	17.3
25	12.0	12.3	12.6	12.9	13.2	13.4	13.6	13.8	14.0	15.5	16.6	17.6	18.4
30	13.0	13.3	13.6	13.9	14.1	14.4	14.6	14.8	15.0	16.5	17.6	18.6	19.4
40	14.7	15.1	15.4	15.7	15.9	16.1	16.3	16.5	16.7	18.2	19.4	20.3	21.2
50	16.3	16.6	16.9	17.2	17.4	17.7	17.9	18.1	18.3	19.8	20.9	21.9	22.7
60	17.7	18.0	18.3	18.6	18.8	19.1	19.3	19.5	19.7	21.2	22.3	23.3	24.1

CONVERSION TABLE

Sq inches to sq millimetres *multiply by* **645.20**	**Sq millimetres to sq inches** *multiply by* **0.0016**
Inches to millimetres *multiply by* **25.40**	**Millimetres to inches** *multiply by* **0.0394**
Sq feet to square metres *multiply by* **0.093**	**Sq metres to sq feet** *multiply by* **10.7640**
Inches to centimetres *multiply by* **2.54**	**Centimetres to inches** *multiply by* **0.3937**
Feet to metres *multiply by* **0.305**	**Metres to feet** *multiply by* **3.2810**
Nautical miles to kilometres *multiply by* **1.852**	**Kilometres to nautical miles** *multiply by* **0.5400**
Statute miles to kilometres *multiply by* **1.609**	**Kilometres to statute miles** *multiply by* **0.6214**
Statute miles to nautical miles *multiply by* **0.8684**	**Nautical miles to statute miles** *multiply by* **1.1515**
HP to metric HP *multiply by* **1.014**	**Metric HP to HP** *multiply by* **0.9862**
Pounds per sq inch to **kg per sq centimetre** *multiply by* **0.0703**	**Kg per sq centimetre** **to pounds per sq inch** *multiply by* **14.2200**
HP to kilowatts *multiply by* **0.746**	**Kilowatts to HP** *multiply by* **1.341**
Cu inches to cu centimetres *multiply by* **16.39**	**Cu centimetres to cu inches** *multiply by* **0.0610**
Imperial gallons to litres *multiply by* **4.540**	**Litres to imperial gallons** *multiply by* **0.2200**
Pints to litres *multiply by* **0.5680**	**Litres to pints** *multiply by* **1.7600**
Pounds to kilogrammes *multiply by* **0.4536**	**Kilogrammes to pounds** *multiply by* **2.2050**

LIGHT CHARACTERISTICS

CLASS OF LIGHT	International abbreviations	National abbreviations	Illustration Period shown ⊢————⊣
FIXED		F	
OCCULTING *(total duration of light longer than dark)*			
Single-occulting		Oc Occ	
Group-occulting	eg	Oc(2)	Gp Occ(2)
Composite group-occulting	eg	Oc(2+3)	Gp Occ(2+3)
ISOPHASE *(light and dark equal)*		Iso	
FLASHING *(total duration of light shorter than dark)*			
Single-flashing		Fl	
Long-flashing *(flash 2s or longer)*		L Fl	
Group-flashing	eg	Fl(3)	Gp Fl(3)
Composite group-flashing	eg	Fl(2+1)	Gp Fl(2+1)
QUICK *(50 to 79, usually either 50 or 60, flashes per min.)*			
Continuous quick		Q	Qk Fl
Group quick	eg	Q(3)	Qk Fl(3)
Interrupted quick		IQ	Int Qk Fl
VERY QUICK *(80 to 159, usually either 100 or 120, flashes per min.)*			
Continuous very quick		VQ	V Qk Fl
Group very quick	eg	VQ(3)	V Qk Fl(3)
Interrupted very quick		IVQ	Int V Qk Fl
ULTRA QUICK *(160 or more, usually 240 to 300, flashes per min.)*			
Continuous ultra quick		UQ	
Interrupted ultra quick		IUQ	
MORSE CODE	eg	Mo(K)	
FIXED AND FLASHING		F Fl	
ALTERNATING	eg	Al. WR	Alt. WR

COLOUR	International abbreviations	NOMINAL RANGE in miles	International abbreviations
White	W (may be omitted)	Light with single range	eg 15M
Red	R	Light with two different ranges	eg 15/10M
Green	G	Light with three or more ranges	eg 15-7M
Blue	Bu	**PERIOD** is given in seconds	eg 90s
Violet	Vi	**DISPOSITION** horizontally disposed	(hor)
Yellow	Y	**VERTICALLY DISPOSED**	(vert)
Orange	Y	**SYNCHRONISED** with (an)other light(s)	(sync)
Amber	Y	**ELEVATION** is given in metres (m) or feet (ft) above MHWS	

Chapter 2 – Weather

Beaufort scale

Force	Wind speed (knots)	(km/h)	(m/sec)	Description	State of sea	Probable wave ht(m)
0	0–1	0–2	0–0·5	Calm	Like a mirror	0
1	1–3	2–6	0·5–1·5	Light airs	Ripples like scales are formed	0
2	4–6	7–11	2–3	Light breeze	Small wavelets, still short but more pronounced, not breaking	0·1
3	7–10	13–19	4–5	Gentle breeze	Large wavelets, crests begin to break; a few white horses	0·4
4	11–16	20–30	6–8	Moderate breeze	Small waves growing longer; fairly frequent white horses	1
5	17–21	31–39	8–11	Fresh breeze	Moderate waves, taking more pronounced form; many white horses, perhaps some spray	2
6	22–27	41–50	11–14	Strong breeze	Large waves forming; white foam crests more extensive; probably some spray	3
7	28–33	52–61	14–17	Near gale	Sea heaps up; white foam from breaking waves begins to blow in streaks	4
8	34–40	63–74	17–21	Gale	Moderately high waves of greater length; edge of crests break into spindrift; foam blown in well-marked streaks	5·5

Terminology used in forecasts
Pressure systems' speed of movement

Slowly	< 15 knots
Steadily	15–25 knots
Rather quickly	25–35 knots
Rapidly	35–45 knots
Very rapidly	> 45 knots

Visibility

Good	> 5 miles
Moderate	2–5 miles
Poor	1000 metres–2 miles
Fog	< 1000 metres

Barometric pressure tendency

Rising/falling slowly: Change of 0·1 to 1·5 hPa/mb in the preceding 3 hours.
Rising/falling: Change of 1·6 to 3·5 hPa/mb in the preceding 3 hours.
Rising/falling quickly: Change of 3·6 to 6 hPa/mb in the preceding 3 hours.
Rising/falling very rapidly: Change of > 6 hPa/mb in the preceding 3 hours.
Now rising/falling: Pressure has been falling (rising) or steady in the preceding 3 hours, but was definitely rising (falling) at the time of observation.

Gale warnings

A *Gale* warning means that winds of at least F8 (34-40kn) or gusts up to 43-51kn are expected somewhere within the area, but not necessarily over the whole area

Severe Gale means winds of at least F9 (41-47kn) or gusts reaching 52-60kn

Storm means winds of F10 (48-55kn) or gusts of 61-68kn

Violent Storm means winds of F11 (56-63kn) or gusts of 69+ kn

Hurricane Force means winds of F12 (64+ kn)

Gale warnings remain in force until amended or cancelled. If a gale persists for >24 hours the warning is re-issued.

Timing of gale warnings from time of issue

Imminent	<6 hrs
Soon	6–12 hrs
Later	>12 hrs

Strong wind warnings

Issued, if possible 6 hrs in advance, when winds F6 or more are expected up to 5M offshore; valid for 12 hrs.

MAP OF UK SHIPPING FORECAST AREAS

SHIPPING FORECAST RECORD TIME/DAY/DATE ....

GENERAL SYNOPSIS   At 0048, 0520, 1201, 1754 UT/BST

System	Present position	Movement	Forecast position	At

Gales	SEA AREA FORECAST	Wind (At first)	(Later)	Weather	Visibility
	VIKING				
	NORTH UTSIRE				
	SOUTH UTSIRE				
	FORTIES				
	CROMARTY				
	FORTH				
	TYNE				
	DOGGER				
	FISHER				
	GERMAN BIGHT				
	HUMBER				
	THAMES				
	DOVER				
	WIGHT				
	PORTLAND				
	PLYMOUTH				
	BISCAY				
	TRAFALGAR (0048)				
	FITZROY				
	SOLE				
	LUNDY				
	FASTNET				
	IRISH SEA				
	SHANNON				
	ROCKALL				
	MALIN				
	HEBRIDES				
	BAILEY				
	FAIR ISLE				
	FAEROES				
	S E ICELAND				

COASTAL REPORTS at .... UT BST	Wind Direction	Force	Weather	Visibility	Pressure	Change
Tiree auto (T)						
Stornoway (St)						
Lerwick (L)						
Fife Ness (F)						
Bridlington (Br)						
Sandettié auto (S)						

COASTAL REPORTS	Wind Direction	Force	Weather	Visibility	Pressure	Change
Greenwich auto (G)						
Jersey (J)						
Channel auto (C)						
Scilly auto (Sc)						
Valentia (V)						
Ronaldsway (R)						
Malin Head (M)						

WEATHER

SOURCES OF WEATHER INFORMATION IN THE UK

BBC Radio 4 Shipping forecasts
are broadcast at:

0048 LT[1]	LW, MW, FM
0520 LT[1]	LW, MW, FM
1201 LT	LW only
1754 LT	LW, FM (Sat/Sun)

[1] Includes weather reports from coastal stations

Frequencies

LW		198 kHz
MW	Tyneside	603 kHz
	London & N Ireland	720 kHz
	Redruth	756 kHz
	Plymouth & Enniskillen	774 kHz
	Aberdeen	1449 kHz
	Carlisle	1485 kHz
FM	England	92·4–94·6 MHz
	Scotland	91·3–96·1 MHz
		103·5–104·9 MHz
	Wales	92·8–96·1 MHz
		103·5–104·9 MHz
	N Ireland	93·2–96·0 MHz
		103·5–104·6 MHz
	Channel Islands	94·8 MHz

The Shipping forecast contains:
Time of issue; summary of gale warnings in force at that time; a general synopsis of weather systems and their expected development and movement over the next 24 hours; sea area forecasts for the same 24 hours, including wind direction/force, weather and visibility in each; and an outlook for the following 24 hours.

Gale warnings for all affected areas are broadcast at the earliest break in Radio 4 programmes after receipt, as well as after the next news bulletin.

Shipping forecasts cover large sea areas, and rarely include the detailed variations that may occur near land. The inshore waters forecast can be more helpful on coastal passages.

Weather reports from coastal stations follow the 0048 and 0520 shipping forecasts. They include wind direction and force, present weather, visibility, and sea-level pressure and tendency, if available. The stations are shown on the previous page.

BBC Radio 4 Inshore waters forecast
A forecast for inshore waters (up to 12M offshore) in 17 areas around the UK and N Ireland, valid for 24 hrs, is broadcast after the 0048 and 0520 coastal station reports.

It includes forecasts of wind direction and force, weather, visibility, sea state and an outlook for a further 24 hrs. It ends with a national inshore outlook for the next 3 days. The 17 inshore areas are defined by the following well-known places and headlands, clockwise around the UK: Cape Wrath, Orkney, Rattray Hd, Berwick-upon-Tweed, Whitby, Gibraltar Point, N Foreland, Selsey Bill, Lyme Regis, Land's End, St David's Head, Great Ormes Head, Isle of Man, Mull of Galloway, Carlingford Lough, Lough Foyle, Mull of Kintyre, Ardnamurchan Pt and Shetland.

Strong wind warnings are issued by the Met Office whenever winds of Force 6 or more are expected over coastal waters up to 5M offshore.

Reports of actual weather. The 0048 broadcast includes a set of coastal station reports. These include: Boulmer, *Bridlington*, Sheerness, St Catherine's Point*, *Scilly**, Milford Haven, Aberporth, Valley, Liverpool (Crosby), *Ronaldsway*, Larne, Machrihanish*, Greenock, *Stornoway*, *Lerwick*, Wick*, Aberdeen and Leuchars. Asterisk* denotes an automatic station. Stations in italics also feature in the 0520 coastal reports.

BBC general (land) forecasts
Land area forecasts may include an outlook up to 48 hours beyond the shipping forecast, plus more details of frontal systems and weather along the coasts. The most comprehensive land area forecasts are broadcast by Radio 4 on the frequencies above.

Land area forecasts – Wind strength
Wind descriptions used in land forecasts, with their Beaufort scale equivalents, are:

Calm	0	Fresh	5
Light	1–3	Strong	6–7
Moderate	4	Gale	8

Land area forecasts – Visibility
The following visibility definitions are used in land forecasts:

Mist	2000m–1000m
Fog	<1000m
Dense fog	< 50m

NAVTEX

Navtex is the prime method of disseminating MSI, with typical coverage out to 270 miles offshore. A dedicated aerial, receiver and LCD screen (or integrated printer) are required but receipt is free and no contract is required. The user selects which stations and categories are recorded for automatic display or printing.

Two frequencies are used: 518 kHz and *490 kHz*. 518 kHz messages are in English (occas. in the national language as well), with excellent coverage of Europe. Interference between stations is avoided by time sharing and by limiting the range of transmitters to about 300M. Navtex information applies only to the geographic area for which each station is responsible.

490 kHz (for clarity shown in italics throughout this chapter) is used abroad for transmissions in the national language. In the UK it is used for inshore waters forecasts in English. Identification letters for 490 kHz stations differ from 518 kHz stations.

Weather information accounts for about 75% of all messages and Navtex is particularly valuable when out of range of other sources, otherwise occupied or if there is a language problem.

Messages

Each message is prefixed by a four-character group:

The first character is the code letter of the transmitting station (eg **E** for Niton).

The second character is the message category, see below.

The third and fourth are message serial numbers, running from 01 to 99 and then re-starting at 01.

The serial number 00 denotes urgent messages which are always printed.

Messages which are corrupt or have already been printed are rejected. Weather messages, and certain other message types, are dated and timed.

Message categories

A*	Navigational warnings
B*	Meteorological warnings
C	Ice reports
D*	SAR info and piracy warnings
E	Weather forecasts
F	Pilot service
H	Loran-C
J	Satellite navigation
K	Other electronic navaids
L	Subfacts and Gunfacts (UK)
V	Amplifies Navwarnings initially sent under A; plus weekly oil/gas rig moves.
W-Y	Special service, trials
Z	No messages on hand at scheduled time

Missing category letters are unallocated.

*The receiver cannot reject these categories.

Navtex stations/areas – UK & W Europe

Navtex Stations

(M) Jeloya (518 kHz)
(L) Rogaland (518 kHz)

(O) Portpatrick (518 kHz)
(C) Portpatrick (490 kHz)

(Q) Malin Head (518 kHz)
(A) Malin Head (490 kHz)

(G) Cullercoats (518 kHz)
(U) Cullercoats (490 kHz)

(P) Netherlands CG (518 kHz)

(W) Valentia (518 kHz)

(B) Oostende (490 kHz)
(T) Oostende (518 kHz)
(V) Oostende (518 kHz)

NAVAREA I (UK)

(E) Niton (518 kHz)
(K) Niton (518 kHz)
(I) Niton (490 kHz)
(T) Niton (490 kHz)

NAVAREA II (France)

(A) Corsen (518 kHz)
(E) Corsen (490 kHz)

(W) La Garde (518 kHz)
(S) La Garde (490 kHz)

(D) La Coruña (518 kHz)
(W) La Coruña (490 kHz)

NAVAREA III (Spain)

(R) Monsanto (518 kHz)
(G) Monsanto (490 kHz)

(T) Cagliari (518 kHz)
(X) Valencia (518 kHz)
(M) Valencia (490 kHz)

(G) Tarifa (518 kHz)
(T) Tarifa (490 kHz)

UK 518 kHz stations

The times (UT) of weather messages are in bold; the times of an extended outlook (a further 2 or 3 days beyond the shipping forecast period) are in italics.

G – Cullercoats	*0100*	0500	**0900**	1300	1700	**2100**
Fair Isle clockwise to Thames, excluding N & S Utsire, Fisher and German Bight.						
O – Portpatrick	*0220*	**0620**	1020	1420	**1820**	2220
Lundy clockwise to SE Iceland.						
E – Niton	*0040*	0440	**0840**	1240	1640	**2040**
Thames clockwise to Fastnet, excluding Trafalgar.						

UK 490 kHz stations (in yellow) provide forecasts for UK inshore waters, a national 3 day outlook for inshore waters and, at times in bold, reports of actual weather at some or all of the places listed below. To receive these reports select message category 'V' on the receiver. Times (UT) are listed in chronological order. Reports include some or all of: Sea level pressure (hPa/mb), wind direction and speed (kn), weather, visibility (M), air and sea temperatures (°C), dewpoint temperature (°C) and mean wave height (m).

A – Malin Head   0000   0400   0800   **1200**   **1600**   2000
Lough Foyle to Carlingford Lough, Mull of Galloway to Cape Wrath, the Minch.
Note times of forecasts and actuals not known at time of going to press.

C – Portpatrick Land's End to Shetland   0020   0420   0820   **1220**   **1620**   2020
N Rona, Stornoway, S Uist, Lusa (Skye), Tiree, Macrihanish, Belfast, Malin Hd, Belmullet, St Bees Hd, Ronaldsway, Crosby, Valley, Aberporth, Roches Pt, Valentia, St Mawgan.

I – Niton The Wash to St David's Head   0120   0520   **0920**   1320   1720   **2120**
Sandettie Lt V, Greenwich Lt V, Solent, Hurn airport, Guernsey airport, Jersey airport, Portland, Channel Lt V, Plymouth, Culdrose, Seven Stones Lt V, St Mawgan & Roches Pt.

U – Cullercoats Cape Wrath to N Foreland   0320   0720   **1120**   **1520**   1920   **2320**
Sandettie Lt V, Manston, Shoeburyness, Weybourne, Donna Nook, Boulmer, Leuchars, Aberdeen, Lossiemouth, Wick, Kirkwall, Lerwick, Foula, K7 Met buoy, Sule Skerry.

Navtex coverage abroad: Selected Navtex stations in Metareas I and II, with identity codes and transmission times, are listed below. Times of weather messages are shown in **bold**. Gale warnings are usually transmitted 4 hourly.

METAREA I (Co-ordinator – UK) / **Transmission times (UT)**

B – Oostende, *Belgium (mostly Dutch)*	*0010*	*0410*	*0810*	*1210*	*1610*	*2010*
K – Niton (Note 1)	0140	0540	0940	1340	1740	2140
L – Pinneberg, *Hamburg*	*0150*	*0550*	*0950*	*1350*	*1750*	*2150*
P – Netherlands CG, Den Helder	**0230**	0630	1030	**1430**	1830	2230
Q – Malin Head, Eire	0240	**0640**	**1040**	1440	**1840**	**2240**
S – Pinneberg, Hamburg	**0300**	**0700**	**1100**	**1500**	**1900**	**2300**
T – Oostende, Belgium (Note 3)	0310	**0710**	1110	1510	**1910**	2310
V – Oostende, Belgium (Note 2)	0330	0730	1130	1530	1930	2330
W – Valentia, Eire	0340	**0740**	**1140**	1540	**1940**	**2340**

Notes:
1 In English, no weather; only Nav warnings for waters from Cap Gris Nez to Île de Bréhat.
2 No weather information, only Nav warnings.
3 Forecasts and strong wind warnings for Thames and Dover, plus Nav info for Belgium.

METAREA II (Co-ordinator – France)

A – Corsen, Le Stiff, France	**0000**	**0400**	**0800**	**1200**	**1600**	**2000**
E – Corsen, *Le Stiff, France (In French)*	*0040*	*0440*	*0840*	*1240*	*1640*	*2040*
D – Coruña, Spain	**0030**	**0430**	**0830**	1230	1630	**2030**
W – Coruña, *Spain (in Spanish)*	*0340*	*0740*	*1140*	*1540*	*1940*	*2340*
F – Horta, Açores, Portugal	**0050**	**0450**	**0850**	1250	1650	**2050**
G – Tarifa, Spain (English & Spanish)	0100	0500	0900	1300	1700	2100
R – Monsanto, Portugal	**0250**	**0650**	1050	1450	1850	2250

INTERNET WEATHER SOURCES

The Internet provides a useful back-up for GMDSS services as well as information not available by conventional means.

www.metoffice.gov.uk/weather/marine/ has texts of all high seas, shipping and inshore waters forecasts, warnings, weather actuals from coastal stations, light vessels and data buoys. www. bbc.co.uk/weather/coast/ has texts of Navtex broadcasts.

National meteorological services provide the best forecasts for their own waters.

Other useful websites include:
www.franksweather.co.uk/
www.weatheronline.com/ www.saildocs.com/
www.mailasail.com/ www.grib.us/
www.passageweather.com/
www.windfinder.com/ www.xcweather.co.uk/
www.windguru.com/ www.theyr.com /
www.wetterzentrale.de/topkarten/tknf.html

Broadcasts of shipping and inshore waters forecasts by HM Coastguard

HM CG Centres routinely broadcast MSI every 3 hours at the local times below.

Each broadcast contains one of 3 different Groups of MSI:

Group A, the full broadcast, contains the Shipping forecast, a new Inshore waters forecast and 24 hrs outlook, Gale warnings, a 3 day forecast for Fishermen in the winter months*, Navigational (WZ) warnings and Subfacts & Gunfacts where relevant ‡. 'A' broadcast times are in bold type.

Group B contains a new Inshore waters forecast, plus the previous outlook, and Gale warnings. 'B' broadcast times are in plain type.

Group C is a repeat of the Inshore forecast and Gale warnings (as per the previous Group A or B) plus new Strong wind warnings. 'C' broadcast times are italicised.

Notes
*Fisherman's 3 day forecast (1 Oct-31 Mar).
‡ Subfacts & Gunfacts.

Coastguard	Shipping forecast areas	Inshore areas	B	C	A	C	B	C	A	C
South Coast			B	C	A	C	B	C	A	C
Falmouth‡	Portland, Plymouth, Sole, Shannon, Fastnet	8, 9	0110	0410	0710	1010	1310	1610	1910	2210
Brixham‡	Same as Falmouth CG	8, 9	0110	0410	0710	1010	1310	1610	1910	2210
Portland	Plymouth, Portland, Wight	6–8	0130	0430	0730	1030	1330	1630	1930	2230
Solent	Plymouth, Portland, Wight	6–8	0130	0430	0730	1030	1330	1630	1930	2230
Dover	Dover, Wight, Thames, Humber	5, 6	0110	0410	0710	1010	1310	1610	1910	2210
East Coast			B	C	A	C	B	C	A	C
Thames	Dover, Wight, Thames, Humber	5, 6	0110	0410	0710	1010	1310	1610	1910	2210
Humber	Thames, Humber, German Bight, Dogger, Tyne	3–5	0150	0450	0750	1050	1350	1650	1950	2250
Aberdeen‡	Tyne, Forth, Cromarty, Forties, Fair Isle	1, 2	0130	0430	0730	1030	1330	1630	1930	2230
Shetland	Cromarty, Viking, Fair Isle, Faeroes	1, 16	0110	0410	0710	1010	1310	1610	1910	2210
West Coast			B	C	A	C	B	C	A	C
Stornoway‡	Rockall, Malin, Hebrides, Bailey, Fair Is, Faeroes, SE Iceland	15, 16	0110	0410	0710	1010	1310	1610	1910	2210
Belfast‡	Irish Sea, Malin	12–14	0110	0410	0710	1010	1310	1610	1910	2210
Liverpool	Irish Sea	11, 12	0130	0430	0730	1030	1330	1630	1930	2230
Holyhead	Irish Sea	10, 11	0130	0450	0730	1050	1330	1650	1930	2250
Milford Hvn	Lundy, Fastnet, Irish Sea	9, 10	0150	0450	0750	1050	1350	1650	1950	2250
Swansea	Lundy, Fastnet, Irish Sea	9, 10	0150	0450	0750	1050	1350	1650	1950	2250

WEATHER

Remote CG transmitters and their VHF working channels

MSI broadcasts are transmitted via remote aerial sites geographically selected to give optimum coverage. The table below lists their positions and the VHF broadcast channel to be used. It will be one of channels 10, 23, 84 or 86 and is also specified in a prior announcement on Ch 16.

To minimise the risk of missing a broadcast, pre-select Ch 16 on Dual watch with the relevant (clearest) channel; and/or monitor the prior announcement to verify the working channel. **MF frequencies** (*kHz*), as quoted below, are also used for the broadcasts, primarily for fishermen.

Falmouth CG

Trevose Head	84	50°33'N 05°02'W
St Mary's (Scilly)	86	49°56'N 06°18'W
Lizard*	*1880kHz,* 23	49°58'N 05°12'W
Falmouth	84	50°09'N 05°03'W

Brixham CG

Fowey	10	50°20'N 04°38'W
Rame Head	86	50°19'N 04°13'W
East Prawle	84	50°13'N 03°42'W
Dartmouth	10	50°21'N 03°35'W
Berry Head	23	50°24'N 03°29'W

Portland CG

Beer Head	86	50°41'N 03°05'W
Grove Pt (Portland Bill)	84	50°33'N 02°25'W

Solent CG

Needles	86	50°39'N 01°35'W
Boniface (Ventnor, IoW)	23	50°36'N 01°12'W
Newhaven	86	50°47'N 00°03'E

Dover CG

Fairlight (Hastings)	84	50°52'N 00°39'E
Langdon (Dover)	86	51°08'N 01°21'E

Thames CG

Shoeburyness	23	51°31'N 00°47'E
Bradwell (R Blackwater)	86	51°44'N 00°53'E
Walton-on-the-Naze	23	51°51'N 01°17'E
Bawdsey (R Deben)	84	52°00'N 01°25'E

Humber CG

Lowestoft	23	52°29'N 01°46'E
Great Yarmouth	86	52°36'N 01°43'E
Trimingham (Cromer)	23	52°54'N 01°21'E
Langham (Blakeney)	86	52°57'N 00°58'E
Guy's Head (Wisbech)	23	52°48'N 00°13'E
Skegness	84	53°09'N 00°20'E
Easington (Spurn Hd)	86	53°39'N 00°06'E
Flamborough*	*1925kHz,* 23	54°07'N 00°05'W
Ravenscar	86	54°24'N 00°30'W
Boulby	23	54°34'N 00°51'W
Cullercoats (Blyth)	86	55°04'N 01°28'W
Newton	23	55°31'N 01°37'W

Aberdeen CG

St Abbs/Cross Law	86	55°54'N 02°12'W
Craigkelly (Burntisland)	23	56°04'N 03°14'W
Fife Ness	84	56°17'N 02°35'W
Inverbervie	23	56°51'N 02°16'W
Greg Ness*	*2226kHz,* 86	57°08'N 02°03'W
Windyheads Hill	23	57°39'N 02°14'W
Rosemarkie (Cromarty)	86	57°38'N 04°05'W

Noss Head (Wick)	84	58°29'N 03°03'W
Durness (Loch Eriboll)	23	58°34'N 04°44'W

Shetland CG

Wideford Hill (Kirkwall)	86	58°59'N 03°01'W
Fitful Head (Sumburgh)	23	59°54'N 01°23'W
Lerwick (Shetland)	84	60°10'N 01°08'W
Collafirth*	*2226kHz,* 86	60°32'N 01°23'W
Saxa Vord (Unst)	23	60°42'N 00°51'W

Stornoway CG

Butt of Lewis	*1743kHz,* 10	58°28'N 06°14'W
Portnaguran (Stornoway)	23	58°15'N 06°10'W
Forsnaval (W Lewis)	84	58°13'N 07°00'W
Melvaig (Loch Ewe)	86	57°50'N 05°47'W
Rodel (S Harris)	84	57°45'N 06°57'W
Clettreval (N Uist)	23	57°37'N 07°26'W
Skriag (Portree, Skye)	10	57°23'N 06°15'W
Drumfearn (SE Skye)	23	57°12'N 05°48'W
Barra	10	57°01'N 07°30'W
Arisaig (S of Mallaig)	86	56°55'N 06°50'W
Glengorm (N Mull)	23	56°38'N 06°08'W
Tiree	*1883kHz,* 86	56°31'N 06°57'W
Torosay (E Mull)	10	56°27'N 05°43'W

Belfast CG

Clyde (Greenock)	84	55°58'N 04°48'W
South Knapdale (Loch Fyne)	23	55°55'N 05°28'W
Kilchiaran (W Islay)	84	55°46'N 06°27'W
Lawhill (Ardrossan)	86	55°42'N 04°50'W
Rhu Staffnish (Kintyre)	10	55°22'N 05°32'W
Navar (Lower L Erne)	86	54°28'N 07°54'W
Limvady (Lough Foyle)	84	55°06'N 06°53'W
West Torr (Fair Head)	86	55°12'N 06°06'W
Black Mountain (Belfast)	23	54°35'N 06°01'W
Orlock Point (Bangor)	84	54°40'N 05°35'W
Slievemartin (Rostrevor)	86	54°06'N 06°10'W

Liverpool CG

Caldbeck (Carlisle)	23	54°46'N 03°07'W
Snaefell (Isle of Man)	86	54°16'N 04°28'W
Langthwaite (Lancaster)	84	54°02'N 02°46'W
Moel-y-Parc (Anglesey)	23	53°13'N 04°28'W

Holyhead CG

Great Ormes Head	86	53°20'N 03°51'W
South Stack (Holyhead)	23	53°19'N 04°41'W

Continued opposite top

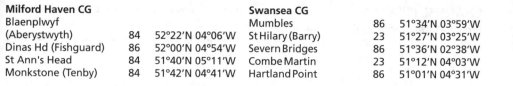

Milford Haven CG		
Blaenplwyf		
(Aberystwyth)	84	52°22'N 04°06'W
Dinas Hd (Fishguard)	86	52°00'N 04°54'W
St Ann's Head	84	51°40'N 05°11'W
Monkstone (Tenby)	84	51°42'N 04°41'W

Swansea CG		
Mumbles	86	51°34'N 03°59'W
St Hilary (Barry)	23	51°27'N 03°25'W
Severn Bridges	86	51°36'N 02°38'W
Combe Martin	23	51°12'N 04°03'W
Hartland Point	86	51°01'N 04°31'W

Inshore waters forecasts: Area boundaries used by the Coastguard

WEATHER

95

CHANNEL ISLANDS

Jersey Meteorological department

From the CI and UK call ☎ 0900 669 0022 (60p per min) for the Channel Islands recorded shipping forecast. For Guernsey only, call ☎ 06969 8800; it is chargeable. For more detailed info call ☎ +44 1534 448770, 🖷 448778.

Forecasts include: general situation, 24hr forecast for wind, weather, vis, sea state, swell, sea temperature, plus 2 & 4 day outlooks and St Helier tide times/heights. The area is bounded by 50°N, 03°W and the mainland from Cap de la Hague to Ile de Bréhat.

Weather broadcasts and bulletins

BBC Radio Guernsey 93·2 MHz, 1116 kHz
Bulletins for the waters around Guernsey, Herm and Sark are broadcast Mon-Fri at 0630, 0730 and 0830 LT; Sat/Sun at 0730 and 0830 LT. They contain forecast, synopsis, coastal forecast, storm warnings and wind strength.

In the summer coastal reports are included from: Portland, Chan lt V, Alderney, Guernsey, Jersey, Cherbourg, Cap de la Hague and Dinard. ☎ 01481 200600

BBC Radio Jersey 1026 kHz, 88·8 MHz.
Storm warnings on receipt. Wind info for Jersey waters: Mon-Fri 0725, 0825, 1325, 1725 LT; Sat/Sun 0725, 0825. ☎ 01534 870000

Shipping forecast for local waters: Mon-Fri @ H+00 (0600-1900, after the news) and 0625 & 1625 LT; Sat/Sun @ H+00 (0700-1300, after the news) and 0725 LT.

Jersey Coastguard Ch 25, 82. Gale warnings at 0307, 0907, 1507, 2107UT. Gale warnings, synopsis, 24h forecast, outlook for next 24 hrs, plus reports from observation stations, are broadcast on request and at 0645*, 0745*, 0845*, 1245, 1845, 2245 UT; *broadcast 1 hr earlier when DST in force. ☎ 01534 447705.

IRELAND

Met Éireann (Irish Met Office) is at Glasnevin Hill, Dublin 9, Ireland. ☎ 1 806 4200, 🖷 1 806 4247, www.met.ie. General forecasting division: ☎ 1 806 4255, 🖷 1 806 4275 (H24, charges may apply).

Coast radio stations

CRS and their VHF channels are listed below (anti-clockwise from Malin Head) and shown overleaf. Weather bulletins for 30M offshore and the Irish Sea are broadcast on VHF at 0103, 0403, 0703, 1003, 1303, 1603, 1903 and 2203UT after an announcement on Ch 16. Broadcasts are made 1 hour earlier when DST is in force. Bulletins include gale warnings, synopsis and a 24-hour forecast.

Malin Head	23	Bantry	23
Glen Head	24	Mizen Head	04
Donegal Bay	02	Cork	26
Belmullet	83	Mine Head	83
Clifden	26	Rosslare	23
Galway	04	Wicklow Head	02
Shannon	28	Dublin	83
Valentia	24	Carlingford	04

Gale warnings are broadcast on these VHF channels on receipt and at 0033, 0633, 1233 and 1833 UT, after an announcement Ch 16.

MF Valentia Radio broadcasts forecasts for sea areas Shannon and Fastnet on 1752 kHz at 0833 & 2033 UT, and on request.

Gale warnings are broadcast on 1752 kHz on receipt and at 0303, 0903, 1503 and 2103 (UT) after an announcement on 2182 kHz.

Malin Head does not broadcast weather information on 1677 kHz. At Dublin there is no MF transmitter.

Radio Telefís Éireann (RTE) Radio 1

RTE Radio 1 broadcasts weather bulletins daily at 0602, 1253 & 2355LT on 252kHz (LW) Summerhill (15M W ofDublin airport) and FM (88·2-95·2MHz).

Bulletins contain a situation, forecast and coastal reports. Forecasts include: wind, weather, vis, swell (if higher than 4m) and a 24 hrs outlook.

Gale warnings are included in hourly news bulletins on FM & MF.

Coastal reports include wind, weather, visibility, pressure and pressure tendency. The change over the last 3 hrs is described as:

Steady	=	0–0·4hPa
Rising/falling slowly	=	0·5–1·9
Rising/falling	=	2·0–3·4
Rising/falling rapidly	=	3·5–5·9
Rising/falling very rapidly	=	> 6·0

Weather by telephone

The latest sea area forecast and gale warnings are available as recorded messages H24 from Weatherdial.

Dial ☎ 1550 123 plus the suffixes below:

850	Munster
851	Leinster
852	Connaught
853	Ulster
854	Dublin (plus winds in Dublin Bay and HW times)
855	Coastal waters and Irish Sea.

Weather by fax

Similar information, plus isobaric, swell and wave charts and any small craft warnings (>F6 up to 10M offshore; Apr-Sep inc) is available H24 by Weatherdial Fax.

Dial 📠 1550 131 838 (from within ROI only). From the menu below select the required 4-digit product code (see 0400 for full listing):

0015:	Latest analysis chart
0016:	Forecast valid for next 24 hrs

0017:	Forecast valid for next 36 hrs
0018:	Forecast valid for next 48 hrs
0021:	Forecasts for coastal waters and Irish Sea
0031, 0032, 0033, 0034:	Forecast (days 1-4) for sea/swell wave hts/periods

5-day forecasts (plain language, farming/national)
0001: Munster. 0002: Leinster. 0003: Connaught.
0004: Ulster. 0005: Dublin.

Sea Planners provide graphic forecasts for up to 5 days (updated at 0430 daily) of expected winds and waves at the following seven offshore positions:

0041:	53°N 05°30'W
0042:	51°N 06°W
0043:	51°N 10°30'W
0044:	53°N 11°W
0045:	54°N 11°W
0046:	55°N 10°W
0047:	56°N 08°W

WEATHER

Provinces, headlands, sea areas and coastal stations referred to in weather broadcasts are shown here. Forecasts for coastal waters cover areas within 30M of the shore.

DENMARK

Gale warnings and forecasts are broadcast on receipt, on request and at 0133, 0533, 0933, 1333, 1733, 2133 UT in Danish/English by remote CRS, callsign *Lyngby Radio:*

Areas	VHF Channels
2 South Baltic	02, 04,
3 West Baltic	01, 02, 03, 04, 61, 85
4 The Belts & Sound	01, 02, 03, 04, 05, 07, 28, 65, 83, 85
5 Kattegat	03, 04, 05, 07, 64, 65, 66, 83
6 Skagerrack	01, 02, 04, 64, 66
8 Fisher	01, 02, 23, 26
9 German Bight	02, 23

Forecast areas: see above. Skagen and Blåvand CRS broadcast on MF gale warnings for all areas on receipt.

Areas 2–5 are north of the Kiel Canal and east of 10°E.

MF: Blåvand 1734 kHz, Skagen 1758 kHz, Skamlebæk 1704 kHz and Rønne 2586 kHz broadcast gale warnings for all areas in Danish/**English** on receipt.

KEY:
2 S Baltic
3 W Baltic
4 The Belts and the Sound
5 Kattegat
6 Skagerrak
8 Fisher

KEY:
9 German Bight
13 Forties
14 Dogger
15 Humber

Danmarks Radio, Programme 1
Kalundborg (55°44'N 11°E) broadcasts on LW 243 kHz:
• Gale warnings, weather reports and forecast for areas 2-6, 8, 9 and 13-15 at 0545, 0845, 1145, 1745LT.
• A 5 day forecast for areas 2-6, 8 and 9 at 1145 & 1745LT.

Danmarks Meteorologiske Institut (DM)
provides marine forecasts in Danish, **English** and German on www.dmi.dk/dmi/index/

GERMANY

Deutsche Wetterdienst (DWD)

DWD (German weather service) provides Met info through a databank which is updated twice daily; more often for weather reports and text forecasts.

DWD ☎ +49 (0) 69 8062 6201. 🖷 +49 (0) 69 8062 6193. www.dwd.de seeschifffahrt@dwd.de.

Traffic Centres

Traffic Centres, below, broadcast local storm warnings, weather bulletins, visibility (and when appropriate ice reports) in German or **English** on request.

Traffic Centre	VHF Ch	Every
German Bight Traffic	80	H+00
Cuxhaven-Elbe Traffic	71 (outer Elbe)	H+35
Brunsbüttel-Elbe Traffic	68 (lower Elbe)	H+05
Kiel Kanal II (E-bound)	02	H+15 & H+45
Kiel Kanal III (W-bound)	03	H+20 & H+50
Bremerhaven-Weser Traffic	02, 04, 05, 07, 21, 22, 82	H+20
Bremen-Weser Traffic	19, 78, 81	H+30
Hunte Traffic	63	H+30
Jade Traffic	20, 63	H+10
Ems Traffic	15, 18, 20, 21	H+50

Coast Radio Stations

DP07 (Seefunk) has commercial CRS, below, at:

Nordfriesland (Sylt) Ch 26. **Elbe-Weser** Ch 01, 24. **Hamburg** (Control centre) Ch 83. **Bremen** Ch 25. **Borkum** Ch 28.

DP07 broadcasts (only in German): gale and strong wind warnings on receipt. At 0745®, 0945, 1245, 1645 and 1945® UT for Fisher, German Bight and Humber, DP07 broadcasts: a synopsis, 12hr forecast, 24hrs outlook and coastal station reports. ®summer only. Also a 4–5 day outlook for the North Sea (and Baltic) at 0945 and 1645.

Radio broadcasting: Nord Deutscher Rundfunk (NDR)
NDR 1 Welle Nord (FM)

A summary, outlook and wind forecast for the German Bight are broadcast after the news at H (0600-2200LT) and at H +30 (0530-17300LT) by:

Sylt 90·9 MHz; **Helgoland** 88·9 MHz; **Hamburg**

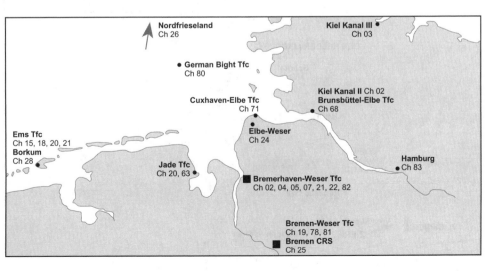

89·5 MHz; **Flensburg** 89·6 MHz; **Heide** 90·5 MHz; **Kiel** 91·3 MHz.

NDR Info (AM)

Synopsis, forecast and coastal station reports for the North Sea (and Baltic) are broadcast at 0005, 0830 and 2205 UT on 972 (Hamburg) & 702 (Flensburg) kHz.

Radio Bremen (MW and FM)

Warnings of extreme weather conditions in German Bight, with associated hazards, are broadcast after the news by: **Bremerhaven** 936 kHz; 89·3, 92·1, 95·4 & 100·8 MHz; and by **Bremen** 88·3, 93·8, 96·7 & 101·2 MHz.

Telephone forecasts (Marineweather)

For wind forecast and outlook (1 April – 30 Sept) call 0190 1160 (only within Germany) plus two digits for the following areas:

45	North Frisian Islands and Helgoland
46	R Elbe, Cuxhaven to Hamburg
47	Weser , Jade Bay and Helgoland
48	East Frisians and Ems Estuary
53	For pleasure craft

For year-round weather synopsis, forecast and outlook, call 0190 1169 plus two digits:

20	General information
21	North Sea and Baltic
22	German Bight, Fisher and SW North Sea
31	Reports for North Sea and Baltic

For the latest wind warnings (greater than F6) and storm warnings for individual areas of the North Sea coasts, call +49 (0) 69 8062 6101 (H24). If no warning is in force, a wind forecast for the German Bight, west and southern Baltic is given.

NETHERLANDS
VHF MSI broadcasts

Forecasts for 7 areas to 30M offshore and 3 inland waterways (IJsselmeer, Marken and Zierikzee) are broadcast in **English** and Dutch at 0805, 1305, 1905, 2305 LT on VHF as shown below, **without** prior announcement on Ch 16 or 70.

VHF Ch 23: Schiermonnikoog, Kornwerderzand, Wezep, Huisduinen (Den Helder), IJmuiden, Renesse, Woensdrecht.
VHF Ch 83: Appingedam, West Terschelling, Hoorn, Schoorl, Scheveningen, Westkapelle.
All stations monitor Ch 16.

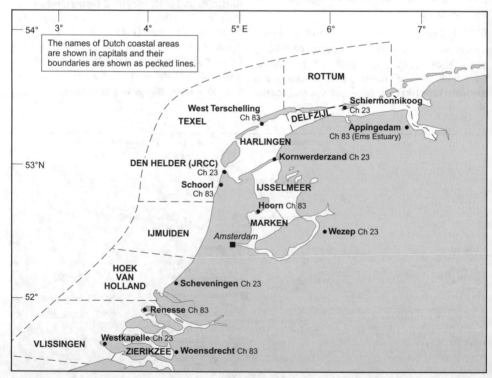

The names of Dutch coastal areas are shown in capitals and their boundaries are shown as pecked lines.

MF weather broadcasts

Forecasts for areas Dover, Thames, Humber, German Bight, Dogger, Fisher, Forties and Viking are broadcast by Scheveningen in **English** at 0940 & 2140 UT on 3673 kHz. Gale warnings for these areas are broadcast in **English** on receipt and at 0333, 0733, 1133, 1533, 1933 and 2333 UT.

Radio Noord-Holland (FM)

Coastal forecasts for northern areas, gale warnings and wind strength are broadcast in Dutch, Mon-Fri at 0730, 0838, 1005, 1230 and 1705LT; Sat/Sun 1005, by: **Haarlem** 97.6 MHz and **Wieringermeer** 93.9 MHz.

Omroep Zeeland (FM)

Coastal forecasts for southern areas, synopsis, gale warnings and wind strength are broadcast in Dutch, Mon-Fri at 0715, 0915, 1215 and 1715LT; Sat/Sun 1015, by:

Philippine 97.8 MHz and **Goes** 101.9 MHz.

BELGIUM, Coast radio stations

Oostende Radio, after prior notice on VHF 16, 24, DSC 70 and 2182kHz, broadcasts in **English** and Dutch on VHF 27, MF 2256, 2376 and 2761 kHz: Strong wind warnings on receipt and after the next 2 silent periods. Forecasts for Thames, Dover and the Belgian coast at 0720 LT and 0820, 1720 UT.

Antwerpen Radio broadcasts in **English** and Dutch on VHF Ch 24 for the Schelde estuary: Gale warnings on receipt and at every H+55. Also strong wind warnings (F6+) on receipt and at every H+55.

FRANCE

Le Guide Marine is a useful, free annual booklet which summarises the various means by which weather forecasts and warnings are broadcast or otherwise disseminated. It is available from marinas or Météo-France, 1 quai Branly, 75340 Paris. ☎ 01.45.56.74.36; 🖷 01.45.56.71.70. marine@meteo. fr www.meteo.fr

CROSS VHF and MF broadcasts

CROSS broadcasts Met bulletins in French, after an announcement on Ch 16. In the English Channel broadcasts can be given in English, on request Ch 16. Broadcasts include: Any gale warnings, general situation, 24 hrs forecast (actual weather, wind, sea state and vis) and further trends for coastal waters, which extend 20M offshore. VHF channels, remote stations and local times are shown below.

Gale warnings feature in Special Met Bulletins (*Bulletins Météorologique Spéciaux* or BMS). They are broadcast in French by all CROSS on VHF at H+03 and at other times on MF frequencies as shown below.

CROSS GRIS-NEZ Ch 79
Belgian border to Baie de la Somme

Dunkerque	0720, 1603, 1920
St Frieux	0710, 1545, 1910

Baie de la Somme to Cap de la Hague
L'Ailly
0703, 1533, 1903
Gale warnings for areas 12-13 are broadcast in French on MF 1650 & 2677 kHz at 0833 & 2033LT

CROSS JOBOURG Ch 80
Baie de la Somme to Cap de la Hague

Antifer	0803, 1633, 2003
Port-en-Bessin	0745, 1615, 1945
Jobourg	0733, 1603, 1933

Cap de la Hague to Pointe de Penmarc'h

Jobourg	0715, 1545, 1915
Granville	0703, 1533, 1903

Gale warnings for areas 13-14 in **English** on receipt and at H+20 and H+50. No gale warnings on MF.

French forecast areas

Map showing VHF channels and coastal stations. All times are local.

- Dunkerque 0720 1603 1920
- GRIZ-NEZ 0710 1545 1910
- **VHF Ch 79**
- **VHF Ch 80**
- **VHF Ch 79**
- JOBOURG 0733 1603 1933 / 0715 1545 1915
- Antifer 0803 1633 2003
- L'Ailly 0703 1533 1903
- Port-en-Bessin 0745 1615 1945
- Île de Batz 0515 0733 1133 1603 1933
- Le Stiff 0503 0715 1115 1545 1915
- Bodic 0533 0745 1145 1615 1945
- Granville 0703 1533 1903
- Cap Fréhel 0545 0803 1203 1633 2003
- CORSEN (MF)
- Pte du Raz 0445 0703 1103 1533 1903
- Penmarc'h 0703 1533 1903
- Île de Groix 0715 1545 1915
- ÉTEL
- Belle Île 0733 1603 1933
- St Nazaire 0745 1615 1945
- **VHF Ch 80**
- Île d'Yeu 0803 1633 2003
- Sables d'Olonne 0815 1645 2015
- **All times are local**
- Chassiron 0703 1533 1903
- **VHF Ch 79**

CROSS CORSEN Ch 79

Cap de la Hague to Pte de Penmarc'h (Times in bold = 1 May to 30 Sep only).

Cap Fréhel 0545, 0803, **1203**, 1633, 2003 Bodic 0533, 0745, **1145**, 1615, 1945

Ile de Batz   0515, 0733, **1133**, 1603, 1933
Le Stiff   0503, 0715, **1115**, 1545, 1915
Pte du Raz   0445, 0703, **1103**, 1533, 1903

Corsen broadcasts gale warnings for areas 13-22 in French at 0815 and 2015LT on MF 1650 & 2677 kHz.

CROSS ÉTEL Ch 80

Pte de Penmarc'h to l'Anse de l'Aiguillon (46° 15'N 01°10'W). Étel has no MF freqs

Penmarc'h   0703, 1533, 1903
Ile de Groix   0715, 1545, 1915
Belle Ile   0733, 1603, 1933
Saint-Nazaire   0745, 1615, 1945
Ile d'Yeu   0803, 1633, 2003
Les Sables d'Olonne   0815, 1645, 2015

CROSS ÉTEL Ch 79   L'Anse de l'Aiguillon to Spanish border

Chassiron   0703, 1533, 1903
Ch 63   Pointe de Penmarc'h to the Spanish border (A continuously transmitted weather bulletin).

Commercial radio broadcasting
Radio France (Inter-Service-Mer)

Broadcasts in French on LW 162 kHz at 2003LT daily: gale warnings, synopsis, 24 hrs forecast and outlook for all areas.

MF broadcasts are made at 0640LT by:

Brest	1404 kHz
Rennes	711 kHz

Local radio (FM)

France Blue Cotentin broadcasts daily at 0834 LT:

Coastal forecast, gale warnings, visibility, wind strength, tidal information, small craft warnings, in French, for the Cherbourg peninsula on the following frequencies:

St Vaast-la-Hougue	95·0 MHz
Cherbourg	95·0, 100·7 MHz
Cap de la Hague	99·8 MHz
Carteret	99·9 MHz

Forecasts by telephone

For recorded Inshore and Coastal forecasts. Dial 08·92·68·02·dd (dd is the number, as given, for the *département*); press the * key then 1 to access the main menu. Follow instructions:

For Inshore (*rivage*) or Coastal (*côte*) bulletins, say 'STOP' as your choice is spoken.

Inshore bulletins contain 7 day forecasts, tide times, actual reports, sea temperature, surf conditions, etc.

Coastal bulletins contain strong wind/gale warnings, general synopsis, 24 hrs forecast and outlook. Five bulletins cover the N & W coasts, out to 20M offshore.

For Offshore bulletins (*large*), out to 200M offshore, dial ☎ 08·92·68·08·77. Select one of three offshore areas (English Channel & southern North Sea, Bay of Biscay or the N part of the western Mediterranean) by saying 'STOP' as it is named. Offshore bulletins contain strong wind/gale warnings, the general synopsis and forecast, and the outlook for up to 7 days.

WEATHER

Forecast areas for the Eastern Atlantic and Coastal/Offshore Areas off France, Spain, Portugal and North West Africa

WEATHER VOCABULARY

ENGLISH	GERMAN	FRENCH	DUTCH
Air mass	Luftmasse	Masse d'air	Luchtmassa
Anticyclone	Antizyklonisch	Anticyclone	Hogedrukgebied
Area	Gebiet	Zone	Gebied
Backing wind	Rückdrehender Wind	Vent reculant	Krimpende wind
Barometer	Barometer	Baromètre	Barometer
Breeze	Brise	Brise	Bries
Calm	Flaute	Calme	Kalmte
Centre	Zentrum	Centre	Centum
Clouds	Wolken	Nuages	Wolken
Cold	Kalt	Froid	Koud
Cold front	Kaltfront	Front froid	Kou front
Cyclonic	Zyklonisch	Cyclonique	Cycloonachtig
Decrease	Abnahme	Affaiblissement	Afnemen
Deep	Tief	Profond	Diep
Deepening	Vertiefend	Approfondissant	Verdiepend
Depression	Sturmtief	Dépression	Depressie
Direction	Richtung	Direction	Richting
Dispersing	Auflösend	Se dispersant	Oplossend
Disturbance	Störung	Perturbation	Verstoving
Drizzle	Niesel	Bruine	Motregen
East	Ost	Est	Oosten
Extending	Ausdehnung	S'étendant	Uitstrekkend
Extensive	Ausgedehnt	Etendu	Uitgebreid
Falling	Fallend	Descendant	Dalen
Filling	Auffüllend	Secomblant	Vullend
Fog	Nebel	Brouillard	Nevel
Fog bank	Nebelbank	Ligne de brouillard	Mist bank
Forecast	Vorhersage	Prévision	Vooruitzicht
Frequent	Häufig	Fréquent	Veelvuldig
Fresh	Frisch	Frais	Fris
Front	Front	Front	Front
Gale	Sturm	Coup de vent	Storm
Gale warning	Sturmwarnung	Avis de coup de vent	Stormwaarschuwing
Good	Gut	Bon	Goed
Gradient	Druckunterschied	Gradient	Gradiatie
Gust, squall	Bö	Rafalle	Windvlaag
Hail	Hagel	Grêle	Hagel
Haze	Diesig	Brume	Nevel
Heavy	Schwer	Abondant	Zwaar
High	Hoch	Anticyclone	Hoog
Increasing	Zunehmend	Augmentant	Toenemend
Isobar	Isobar	Isobare	Isobar
Isolated	Vereinzelt	Isolé	Verspreid
Lightning	Blitze	Eclair de foudre	Bliksem
Local	Örtlich	Locale	Plaatselijk
Low	Tief	Dépression	Laag
Mist	Dunst	Brume légere	Mist
Moderate	Mäßig	Modéré	Matig
Moderating	Abnehmend	Se modérant	Matigend
Moving	Bewegend	Se déplacant	Bewegend
North	Nord	Nord	Noorden
Occluded	Okklusion	Couvert	Bewolkt
Poor	Schlecht	Mauvais	Slecht
Precipitation	Niederschlag	Précipitation	Neerslag
Pressure	Druck	Pression	Druk
Rain	Regen	Pluie	Regen
Ridge	Hochdruckbrücke	Crête	Rug
Rising	Ansteigend	Montant	Stijgen
Rough	Rauh	Agitée	Ruw
Sea	See	Mer	Zee
Seaway	Seegang	Haute mer	Zee

ENGLISH	GERMAN	FRENCH	DUTCH
Scattered	Vereinzelt	Sporadiques	Verspreid
Shower	Schauer	Averse	Bui
Slight	Leicht	Un peu	Licht
Slow	Langsam	Lent	Langzaam
Snow	Schnee	Neige	Sneeuw
South	Süd	Sud	Zuiden
Storm	Sturm	Tempête	Storm
Sun	Sonne	Soleil	Zon
Swell	Schwell	Houle	Deining
Thunder	Donner	Tonnerre	Donder
Thunderstorm	Gewitter	Orage	Onweer
Trough	Trog, Tiefausläufer	Creux	Trog
Variable	Umlaufend	Variable	Veranderlijk
Veering	Rechtdrehend	Virement de vent	Ruimende wind
Warm front	Warmfront	Front chaud	Warm front
Weather	Wetter	Temps	Weer
Wind	Wind	Vent	Wind
Weather report	Wetterbericht	Météo	Weer bericht meteorologica

WEATHER

Chapter 3 – Communications

COMMUNICATIONS

RADIO OPERATION

Avoiding interference

Before transmitting, first listen on the VHF channel. If occupied, wait for a break before transmitting, or choose another channel. If you cause interference you must comply immediately with any request from a Coastguard or Coast radio station to stop transmitting.

Control of communications

Ship-to-Shore: Communications between ship and shore stations are controlled by the latter, except in distress, urgency or safety cases.

Intership: The ship *called* controls communication. If you call another ship, then it has control. If you are called by a ship, you assume control. If a shore-based station breaks in, both ships must comply with instructions given.

Radio confidentiality

Private conversations heard on the radio must not be reproduced, passed on or otherwise used.

Making yourself understood

Clear R/T speech is vital. If a message cannot be understood by the receiver it is useless. Messages which have to be written down at the receiving station should be spoken slowly. This gives time for it to be written down by the receiving operator. If the transmitting operator himself writes it down all should be well. The average reading speed is 250 words a minute, whilst average writing speed is only 20.

When speaking, consider the following:

* **What** to say, ie *voice Procedure*

* **How** to say it, ie *voice Technique*

Voice Procedure is discussed below and overleaf. It includes procedural words, callsigns, making contact etc.

Voice Technique depends on a few simple rules:

Hold the microphone a few inches in front of the mouth and speak directly into it at a normal level. Speak clearly so that there can be no confusion. The voice should be pitched up at a higher level than normal. Do not drop the voice pitch at the end of a phrase or sentence. Emphasise words with weak syllables; 'Tower', if badly pronounced, could sound like 'tar'. Non Anglophones, or people with strong regional accents must try to pronounce words as clearly as possible.

Difficult words may be spelled phonetically, preceded with 'I spell'. If the word can be pronounced, include it before and after it has been spelt. For example, the message 'I will berth on the yacht *Coila*' would be sent as: 'I will berth on the yacht *Coila* – I spell – Charlie Oscar India Lima Alfa – *Coila*'.

The phonetic alphabet (ITU)

The syllables to emphasise are underlined

Letter	Morse	Phonetic	Spoken as
A	•–	Alfa	AL-fah
B	–•••	Bravo	BRAH-voh
C	–•–•	Charlie	CHAR-lee
D	–••	Delta	DELL-tah
E	•	Echo	ECK-oh
F	••–•	Foxtrot	FOKS-trot
G	––•	Golf	GOLF
H	••••	Hotel	hoh-TELL
I	••	India	IN-dee-ah
J	•–––	Juliett	JEW-lee-ett
K	–•–	Kilo	KEY-loh
L	•–••	Lima	LEE-mah
M	––	Mike	MIKE
N	–•	November	no-VEM-ber
O	–––	Oscar	OSS-car
P	•––•	Papa	pa-PAH
Q	––•–	Quebec	keh-BECK
R	•–•	Romeo	ROW-me-oh
S	•••	Sierra	see-AIR-rah
T	–	Tango	TANG-go
U	••–	Uniform	OO-nee-form
V	•••–	Victor	VIK-tah
W	•––	Whiskey	WISS-key
X	–••–	X-ray	ECKS-ray
Y	–•––	Yankee	YANG-key
Z	––••	Zulu	ZOO-loo

Phonetic numerals

When numerals are transmitted, the following pronunciations make them easier to understand.

No	Morse	Spoken	No	Morse	Spoken
1	•natural––––	WUN	6	–••••	SIX
2	••–––	TOO	7	––•••	SEV-EN
3	•••––	TREE	8	–––••	AIT
4	••••–	FOW-ER	9	––––•	NIN-ER
5	•••••	FIFE	0	–––––	ZERO

Numerals are transmitted digit by digit except that multiples of thousands may be spoken as follows:

Numeral	Spoken as
44	FOW-ER FOW-ER
90	NIN-ER ZERO
136	WUN TREE SIX
500	FIFE ZERO ZERO
1478	WUN FOW-ER SEV-EN AIT
7000	SEV-EN THOU-SAND

Punctuation

Punctuation marks should be used only where their omission would cause confusion.

Mark	Word	Spoken as
.	Decimal	DAY-SEE-MAL
,	Comma	COMMA
.	Stop	STOP

Procedural words or 'prowords'

These are used to shorten transmissions

All after and **All before.** Used after proword *'say again'* to request repetition of a part of a message

Correct Reply to repeat of message that was preceded by prowords *'read back for check'* when it has been correctly repeated. Often said twice

Correction Cancel the last word or group of words. The correct word or group follows. Spoken when an error has been made in a transmission.

I say again I repeat the transmission or the part indicated (see 'All after' and 'All before').

I spell I shall spell the next word or group of letters phonetically

Out This is the end of working to you

Over Invitation to reply

Read back If the receiver is doubtful about accuracy of all or part of message he may repeat it back to the sending station, preceding the repetition with prowords *'I read back'*

Station calling Used when a station is uncertain of the calling station's identification/callsign

This is This transmission is from the station whose callsign or name immediately follows

Wait If a called station cannot accept traffic immediately, it will reply **'WAIT.......MINUTES'**, with reason if delay may exceed 10 minutes

Word after or Word before Used after the proword *'say again'* to request repetition

Wrong Reply to repetition of message preceded by prowords *'read back'* when it has been incorrectly repeated

Calls, calling and callsigns

Shore stations normally use a callsign of their geographic name followed by Coastguard or Radio, eg Solent Coastguard, Dublin Radio etc. Vessels usually identify themselves by the ship's name but the International callsign may be used in certain cases. If two yachts have the same or confusingly similar names, give your International callsign when starting communications, and thereafter use your ship's name as callsign.

'All ships' broadcast

Address used by Coastguard Radio where broadcast information is to be received or used by all who intercept it, eg gale warnings etc. No reply is needed.

Communicating with a coast radio station

Call initially on a working channel or very briefly on channel 16 to establish a working channel.

- Pause to check the working channel is clear before transmitting
- Use low power *(1 watt)* if close enough , ie up to 10 miles away. High power *(25 watts)* drains more from the battery
- The callsign of calling station up to three times only, and prowords 'This is'
- Say how many R/T calls you have to make
- Proword 'Over'

Using high power decreases battery state and the range your VHF will achieve. Continued calling also clutters up the channel and denies access to other users.

Aerial faults commonly reduce your transmitting range. Possibly the station aerial for the channel chosen is directionally orientated and you are on the wrong side. Try another channel or station. Call again when closer.

RADIO DATA

SHORT, MEDIUM and LONG RANGE RADIO COMMUNICATIONS

A suitable radio receiver on board will provide weather forecasts and time signals at scheduled times on a number of frequencies in various wavebands. With a maritime receiver you are not limited to the familiar BBC and commercial broadcasts. HM Coastguard transmit navigation warnings, storm warnings and weather messages for shipping in their respective sea areas.

Short range radiotelephony (RT) transmits and receives on VHF channels in the marine VHF (Very High Frequency) band. The equipment and procedures are simple, but range is normally limited to about 20 miles from ship to shore, rather less from ship to ship. Interconnection with national telephone systems is possible on certain VHF/RT channels when a yacht is within range of a Coast Radio Station, although there are now no such stations on the mainland of the UK, France or the Netherlands. Mobile telephones are now by far the most common form of ship to shore communication.

Medium range two-way communication operate in the marine MF (medium frequency) RT band, the 2MHz 'trawler band'. Single sideband techniques are employed on these medium frequencies and SSB equipment is essential. The effective range depends on the power of the transmitter and the sensitivity of the associated receiver; in general this might be up to 200 miles from certain (but not all) Coast Radio Stations.

THE MARINE VHF BAND

VHF is used by most vessels, Coast Radio Stations, CG centres and other rescue services. Its range is slightly better than the line of sight between the transmitting and receiving aerials. A good aerial, as high as possible, is most important.

In the Marine VHF band (156·00–174·00 MHz) the individual frequencies are separated from their neighbours by exactly 25kHz 'elbow-room' to eliminate mutual interference. Each frequency is given a channel number, not necessarily consecutive. Thus 55 channels are available, plus some with special purposes (see below).

VHF Channel Grouping

Channels are grouped for three main purposes, but some can be used for more than one purpose. They are listed below in their preferred order of usage:

• **Public correspondence** (ie link calls via CRS into the shore telephone system): Ch 26, 27, 25, 24, 23, 28, 04, 01, 03, 02, 07, 05, 84, 87, 86, 83, 85, 88, 61, 64, 65, 62, 66, 63, 60, 82, 78, 81.

• **Inter-ship:** Ch 06, 08, 10, 13, 09, 72, 73, 67, 69, 77, 15, 17. Remember these, so that if another vessel calls you, you can swiftly nominate a working channel from within this group.

• **Port Operations:**
Ch 12, 14, 11, 13, 09, 68, 71, 74, 69, 73, 17, 15, 20, 22, 18, 19, 21, 05, 07, 02, 03, 01, 04, 78, 82, 79, 81, 80, 60, 63, 66, 62, 65, 64, 61, 84.

Special purposes. The following channels have one specific purpose only:

Ch 0 (156·00 MHz): SAR ops, not available to yachts.

Ch's 10 (156·500 MHz), **23** (161·750 MHz) **84** (161·825 MHz) and **86** (161·925 MHz): for MSI broadcasts by HMCG.

Ch 13 (156·650 MHz): Intership safety of navigation (sometimes referred to as bridge-to-bridge); a possible channel for calling a merchant ship if no contact on Ch 16.

Ch 16 (156·80 MHz): Distress, Safety and calling. *See Chapter 4 for Distress and Safety.* Ch 16 will be monitored by ships, CG centres (and, in some areas, any remaining Coast Radio Stations) for Distress and Safety until at least 2005, in parallel with DSC Ch 70. Yachts should monitor Ch 16. After an initial call, the stations concerned **must** switch to a working channel, except for Safety matters.

Ch 67 (156·375 MHz): the Small Craft Safety channel in the UK, accessed via Ch 16.

Ch 70 (156·525 MHz): exclusively for digital selective calling for Distress and Safety purposes.

Ch 80 (157·025 MHz): the primary working channel between yachts and UK marinas.

Ch M (157·85 MHz): the secondary working channel between yachts and UK marinas; previously known as Ch 37.

Ch M2 (161·425 MHz): for race control, with Ch M as stand-by. YCs may apply to use Ch M2.

SILENCE PERIODS

The periods are the 3 minutes immediately after the whole and half hours, ie H to H+03 and H+30 to H+33, when no transmissions should be made.

MEDIUM RANGE MF RADIO

Single sideband MF/RT provides communications in the offshore waters of the UK and Western Europe where small craft may be out of VHF contact. A receiver alone gives the ability to hear weather bulletins, storm and navigation warnings for local sea areas broadcast from CRS in the 1.6 to 4.0MHz maritime band, ie on frequencies from 1605 to 4200 kHz.

MF transmissions tend to follow the curvature of the earth, which makes them suitable for direction-finding. For this reason, and because of their good range, the marine Distress R/T frequency (2182 kHz) is in the MF band.

TRAFFIC LISTS

If a Coast Radio station has messages for a vessel, but is unable to contact her, that vessel's name will be added to the Traffic List broadcast at (usually) two hour intervals. This is not a system much used by yachts and small craft.

LONG RANGE HF RADIO

HF radios use short wave frequencies in the 4, 8, 12, 16 and 22 MHz bands, as chosen to suit propagation conditions. HF is more expensive than MF and requires more power, but can provide worldwide coverage. A good installation and skilled operating techniques are essential for satisfactory results.

GLOBAL COMMUNICATIONS

Once out of range of VHF/MF or wireless telephony/broadband service, the yachtsman's communications options are limited to MF/HF radio and satellite systems (Satcoms).

A yachtsman embarking on an extended offshore venture would usually choose a mix of equipment for sensible reasons of redundancy, this will allow a choice of listening and transmitting, via terrestrial and satellite radio systems, to meet his needs at various times and in different circumstances. A typical setup might include a fixed or handheld satcoms transceiver, a HF SSB transceiver and receiver. For data capability, these would be interfaced to an on-board PC.

HF/single sideband radio (HF-SSB)

HF SSB radios use frequencies in the 4, 8, 12, 16 and 22 MHz bands (short wave), provide worldwide coverage and usually include MF frequencies as well.

Despite rapid growth in marine satellite communications, HF SSB remains a popular choice amongst long-distance cruisers, providing a cost-free voice (and limited email) capability for cruisers, sometimes operating over vast distances. Operators have the Long Range Certificate (LRC) or General Operators Certificate (GOC). To use Amateur (ham) bands (giving more frequencies and higher power, therefore range) operators must take the ham examination.

Using HF SSB radio for email requires a radio modem, often proprietary to the supplier. Though slow and requiring some skill to operate effectively, the almost-nil operating costs appeal to many and SSB radio has a strong following amongst blue-water cruisers. Established suppliers include Sailmail and Globe Wireless.

HF SSB radio is also extensively used for receipt of weatherfax images, although a receive-only SSB radio (with an adequate, grounded antenna installation) may be used rather than a full transceiver. Though declining in popularity, several useful weatherfax transmitting stations remain, including Northwood, UK and Offenbach, Germany.

Satellite Communications (Satcoms)

Satellite communications systems operate over **Ultra High Frequency (UHF)** radio using digital technology that makes them simpler-to-operate and more reliable for voice (and data) communications than HF SSB radio; they operate with either a dedicated ship installation or a standalone handheld terminal. Apart from the equipment purchase (and installation if necessary), ongoing costs usually include a monthly service fee and usage charges that will be related to either the amount of satellite time used, or the volume of data transmitted and received.

For two-way voice communications, the 'Ship Station' (aka 'Mobile Earth Station') transmits to a visible satellite that is simultaneously in sight of a 'Land Earth Station', eg Goonhilly, Cornwall. From there, the call is routed to its destination through the normal terrestrial telephone network.

The satellite 'constellations' have different architectures. Inmarsat for example has four geostationary (GEO) satellites, one each positioned over the Pacific and Indian oceans and two over the Atlantic. Because they are comparatively high up 19,400M (36,000km), each satellite has a large signal 'footprint', overlapping the next one and thus world-wide coverage is provided (although not in the polar regions above about 70°N and 70°S).

Other systems employ many more Low Earth Orbit (LEO) satellites orbiting the Earth about 540M (1,000km) above the surface.

The smaller, low-data rate, handheld voice terminals incorporate an omni-directional antenna that works best with an unobstructed view of the satellite. Fixed installations use an external gyro-stabilised antenna (to keep it pointing at the satellite as the boat moves); more powerful systems that support higher data rates employ antenna radomes that are really too large for installation aboard a 10–15m yacht.

The GMDSS provides automatic distress, urgency and safety communications, with some satcom systems (eg Inmarsat C) providing a red button that alerts a Maritime Rescue Coordination Centre (MRCC) when pressed.

There are several service providers, each offering an array of capabilities. The table opposite provides a useful summary of systems that might be used aboard a 10–20m yacht.

This is a fast moving market place and you should check with manufacturers/retailers for up-to-date specifications and prices.

COMMUNICATIONS

COMMUNICATIONS

	Wired Broadband	Wi-Fi	Cellular GSM	Cellular GPRS	Cellular 3G	Wi-Max
[1] typical, **if** in coverage area [2] using VOIP [3] Likely to be expensive						
Range offshore[1] (NM)	0	0-1	0-15	0-15	0-15	0-30
Voice communication	Y[2]	Y[2]	Y	Y	Y	Y[2]
Text messages	Y	Y	Y	Y	Y	Y
Light email traffic	Y	Y	Y[3]	Y	Y	Y
Text weather forecasts	Y	Y	Y[3]	Y	Y	Y
Heavy email traffic	Y	Y	✗	Y[3]	Y	Y
Graphical weather forecasts	Y	Y	✗	Y[3]	Y	Y
Full web browsing	Y	Y	✗	Y[3]	Y	Y

SATELLITE COMMUNICATION SERVICES

System	Antenna	Satellites	Coverage	GMDSS	Phone (voice)	Fax	SMS text	Position tracking	Data rate
INMARSAT C	Omni-directional	4 GEO	Global excepting polar regions	Yes	No	Yes	Yes	Yes (GPS)	Very low, uneconomic for email
INMARSAT Mini-M	Gyro-stabilised 40cms diameter	4 GEO	Global excepting polar regions	No	Yes	Yes	No	No	2.4kbps
INMARSAT D+	Omni-directional	4 GEO	Global excepting polar regions	No	No	No	No	Yes (GPS)	Very low, uneconomic for email
Fleet 33	Gyro-stabilised 40cms diameter	4 GEO	Global excepting polar regions	No	Yes	Yes	Yes	No	9.6kbps uncom-pressed
Iridium	Omni-directional	66 LEO	Global	No	Yes	Out only	Yes	No	Data kit required 2.4kbps, higher with compression
Globalstar	Omni-directional	40 LEO	Global excepting polar regions	No	Yes	Yes	Yes	To 10km	9.6kbps uncom-pressed, 38.6kbps compressed, 56k with data kit
Thuraya	Omni-directional	1 GEO	Europe, N Africa & Middle East, India	No	Yes	Yes	Yes	Yes (GPS)	9.6kbps (144kbps possible with land *DSL receiver)

*DSL (Digital Subscriber Line) allows broadband Internet access via normal copper telephone lines. It is used in the wireless/Satcoms arena to denote broadband-like speeds over the wireless link. This usually means data transfer speeds of 5 to 24mbps which is fast for Satcoms.

PORT and/or MARINA VHF channels and telephone details

In larger ports it is sensible to monitor the VTS channel (if any) or the primary port channel (in bold) before changing to a marina channel. Times are local, unless marked UT. Abbreviations are at the front of the book. Telephone codes are shown only once unless more than one applies.

ENGLAND – SOUTH COAST

ISLES OF SCILLY, St Mary's HM Ch 14 (0800-1700); ☎ 01720 422768. *Falmouth CG* covers Scilly and the TSS off Land's End on Ch 23.
Tresco HM ☎ 07778 601237.

NEWLYN HM Ch 09, **12** (M-F: 0800-1700, Sat: 0800-1200). ☎ 01736 362523.

PENZANCE HM Ch 09, **12** (M-F: 0830-1730 and HW –2 to +1). ☎ 01736 366113.

FALMOUTH *Falmouth Hbr Radio* Ch 11, **12**, 14 (M-F 0800-1700). ☎ 01326 312285.
Ch 80: Falmouth ☎ 316620 and Port Pendennis marinas ☎ 311113. **Ch 12**: Visitors Yacht Haven ☎ 310991; St Mawes HM ☎ 270553. **Ch M** (HO): Mylor Yacht Hbr ☎ 372121.

TRURO HM *Carrick One* Ch 12. ☎ 01872 272130. **Ch M** (HO): Malpas Marine ☎ 271260.

MEVAGISSEY HM Ch 14 (Summer: 0900-2100, Winter: 0900-1700). ☎ 01726 843305.

CHARLESTOWN HM Ch 14, HW –2 to +1, only when a vessel is expected. ☎ 01726 70241.

FOWEY HM Ch 12 (0900-1700); also Hbr Patrol (0900-2000). ☎ 01726 832471. Water taxi: Ch 06.

LOOE. HM Ch 16, occas. ☎ 01503 262839.

PLYMOUTH *Long Room Port Control* Ch 14 H24, ☎ 01752 836528. **QAB** Ch 80, ☎ 671142. **Sutton Hbr lock**: Ch 12 H24, ☎ 204702. **Cattewater HM** Ch 14 (M-F 0900-1700), ☎ 836528. **Plymouth Yacht Haven**, Ch 80, M; ☎ 404231. **Mayflower marina**, Ch 80; ☎ 556633.

SALCOMBE HM & launch: Ch 14, May to mid-Sep: 7/7, 0600-2100; otherwise: M-F 0900-1600; ☎ 01548 843791. *Hbr Taxi* Ch 12. Fuel barge Ch 06, ☎ 07801 798862. *Egremont* (ICC) Ch M.

DARTMOUTH HM *Dartnav* Ch 11, 7/7 0730-dusk; ☎ 01803 832337. Darthaven marina Ch 80, ☎ 752242. Dart marina Ch 80, ☎ 837161. Noss marina ☎ 839087. Fuel barge Ch 06. Water taxi Ch 08.

TORBAY HBRS Brixham Marina Ch 80, ☎ 01803 882929; YC, ☎ 853332, & Water taxi *Shuttle* Ch M. Torquay Marina Ch 80, ☎ 200210. Fuel Ch M.

EXETER Exmouth Marina Ch 14, ☎ 01395 269314. **Retreat BY**: Ch M, ☎ 01392 874720. **Port of Exeter** HM Ch 12, M-F: 0730-1730 and when vessel due; ☎ 274306.

LYME REGIS HM Ch 14. Summer 0800-2000, winter 1000-1500. ☎ 01297 442137.

BRIDPORT HM Ch 11. ☎ 01308 423222.

PORTLAND PORT Port Control Ch 74 (H24). ☎ 01305 824044. **Sailing Academy** ☎ 866000.

WEYMOUTH HM & Town Bridge: Ch 12, M-F 0800-2000 summer & when vessel due; ☎ 01305 838423. **Marina** Ch 80, ☎ 767576. **Fuel** Ch 60.

POOLE
HM Ch 14 (H24); Code 01202 ☎ 440233.
Poole Bridge Ch12.
Marinas Ch 80 M: Salterns ☎ 709971. Parkstone YC ☎ 743610. Poole Quay ☎ 649488. Cobbs Quay ☎ 674299.

YARMOUTH (IoW)
HM & Yar bridge **Ch 68** H24. ☎ 01983 760321. Water taxi **Ch 15.**

LYMINGTON
Marinas Ch 80, M: Yacht Haven ☎ 01590 677071. Berthon Marina ☎ 01590 673312.

COWES
Harbour Radio, Chain Ferry & Folly Inn Ch 69 Mon-Fri: 0800-1700. Marinas **Ch 80, M**. Tel code 01983: Yacht Haven ☎ 299975. Shepards ☎ 297821. East Cowes ☎ 293983. Island Hbr **Ch 80**, ☎ 822999. Water Taxi **Ch 06.**

NEWPORT HM & Yacht Hbr Ch 69 0800-1600. ☎ 01983 525994.

RYDE HM Ch 80. Summer 0900-2000, Winter HX. ☎ 01983 613879. Access HW±2.

BEMBRIDGE Marina **Ch 80,** ☎ 01983 822828. Water Taxi **Ch 80.**

SOUTHAMPTON
Port Ops and VTS Ch 12 14. Marinas **Ch 80, M**. Tel code 02380: Hythe ☎ 207073. Ocean Village ☎ 229385. Shamrock Quay ☎ 229461. Kemp's ☎ 632323. Town Quay ☎ 234397.

HAMBLE
Hbr Radio Ch 68 Apr-Sep daily 0600-2200; Oct-Mar 0700-1830. Marinas **Ch 80, M**. Tel code 02380: Hamble Pt ☎ 452464. Port Hamble ☎ 452741. Mercury ☎ 455994. Water Taxi **Ch 77,** ☎ 454512. Tel code 01489: Universal ☎ 574272. Swanwick ☎ 884081.

PORTSMOUTH
VTS **Ch 11** (& *QHM* if essential). Marinas **80**. Tel code 02392: Haslar ☎ 601201. Gosport ☎ 524811. Royal Clarence ☎ 523810. Port Solent ☎ 210765. THE CAMBER (Commercial Hbr): *Portsmouth Hbr Radio* **Ch 11** 14 (H24).

LANGSTONE HBR
HM **Ch 12**. Summer, daily 0830-1700; Winter, M-F 0830-1700; Sat/Sun 0830-1300. Southsea Marina **Ch 80, M**, ☎ 02392 822719.

CHICHESTER
HM *Chichester Hbr Radio* **Ch 14**. 1 Apr-Sep: M-Fri: 0830-1700. Sat: 0900-1300. 1 Oct - 31 Mar: 0900-1300, 1400-1700. Marinas **Ch 80, M**. Sparkes ☎ 02392 463572. Tel code 01243: Northney ☎ 466321. Emsworth Yacht Hbr ☎ 377727. Thornham ☎ 375335. Birdham Pool ☎ 512310. Chichester ☎ 512731. Water taxi **Ch 08** 0900-1800, mobile 07970 378350

LITTLEHAMPTON HM/Bridge **Ch 71** 0900-1700. Marina **Ch 80, M**; ☎ 01903 241663.

SHOREHAM HM & lock *Shoreham Hbr Radio* **Ch 14** (H24). Marina ☎ 01273 593801.

BRIGHTON
Marina *Brighton Control* **Ch M 80**; ☎ 01273 819919.

NEWHAVEN HM & Bridge *Newhaven Radio* **Ch 12**. HM / Port Control 612926 (H24). Marina **Ch 80, M**; ☎ 01273 513881.

EASTBOURNE
Sovereign Hbr, inc lock/berthing: **Ch 17**. ☎ 01323 470099.

RYE *Hbr Radio,* **Ch 14** 0900-1700 or when ship due. ☎ 01797 225225.

FOLKESTONE
Port Control **Ch 15** for entry; ☎ 01303 254597.

DOVER
Port Control **Ch 74** for entry. Marina Ch 80; ☎ 01304 241663.

RAMSGATE
Port Control **Ch 14**. Marina **Ch 80**; ☎ 01843 572110.

ENGLAND – EAST COAST

WHITSTABLE
Hbr Radio Ch 09 12, Mon-Fri: 0830-1700 and −3HW+1. ☎ 01227 274086.

MEDWAY
Medway VTS **Ch 74**. Kingsferry Bridge (W Swale) **Ch 10** H24. Marinas **Ch 80, M**. Tel code 01634: Gillingham ☎ 280022. Hoo ☎ 250311. Chatham ☎ 899200.

PORT OF LONDON
LONDON VTS: Ch 69 from sea to Sea Reach No 4 buoy. **Ch 68** Sea Reach No 4 to Crayford Ness. **Ch 14**, 22, W of Crayford Ness.
Thames Barrier Ch 14. ☎ 020 8855 0315.

RIVER THAMES
Patrol Launches *Thames Patrol* **Ch 06, 13, 14, 68**
King George V Dock lock *KG Control* **Ch 13**.
West India Dock lock **Ch 13**
Greenwich Yacht Club **Ch M**

Thames lock (Brentford) **Ch 74** Summer 0800-1800; Winter 0800-1630.
Cadogan Pier **Ch 14** 0900-1700.
Marinas Ch 80, M; Tel code 0207: Gallions Point ☎ 4767054. Poplar Dock ☎ 5151046. South Dock ☎ 2522244. Limehouse Basin ☎ 3089930. St Katherine Haven ☎ 2645312. Chelsea Hbr ☎ 2259100. Brentford Dock ☎ 0208 2328941.

RIVER ROACH Havengore Bridge **Ch 72** *Shoe Bridge* HW±2. ☎ 01702 383436.

BURNHAM-ON-CROUCH
Ch 80: HM Launch 0900-1700. Yacht Hbr ☎ 01621 782150. Essex Marina ☎ 01702 258531.

RIVER BLACKWATER
Marinas **Ch 80, M**; Tel code 01621: Tollesbury ☎ 869202. Bradwell ☎ 776235. **Ch M**: Blackwater ☎ 740264. Heybridge Lock, **Ch 80** ☎ 853506.

RIVER COLNE
Brightlingsea Hbr Radio **Ch 68** 0800-2000. ☎ 01206 302200, mob 07952 734814.

WALTON BACKWATERS
Titchmarsh Marina **Ch 80**, ☎ 01255 672185.

RIVERS STOUR AND ORWELL
HARWICH VTS **Ch 71**, 11, 20, H24
SUNK VTS **Ch 14**, H24
Orwell Navigation Service **Ch 68**, H24
Marinas **Ch 80, M**. Tel code 01473: Shotley ☎ 788982. Suffolk Hbr ☎ 659240. Woolverstone ☎ 780206. Fox's ☎ 689111. Neptune ☎ 215204. Ipswich Haven ☎ 236644.

RIVER DEBEN HM ☎ (01473) 736257.
Tidemill Yacht Hbr ☎ 01394 385745.

SOUTHWOLD *Port Radio* **Ch 09** 12. HM ☎ 01502 724712.

LOWESTOFT
Hbr Control **Ch 11**, **14**. HM ☎ 01502 572286.
Royal Norfolk & Suffolk YC **Ch 80**. ☎ 566726. Haven Marina **Ch 80** ☎ 580300. **Mutford Bridge & Lock Ch 73** ☎ 531778.

GREAT YARMOUTH
Yarmouth Radio **Ch 12**. HM ☎ 01493 335511. *Haven & Breydon bridges* **Ch 12**.

WELLS-NEXT-THE-SEA
Wells Hbr **Ch 12**, HJ, HW±2 and when vessel expected. HM ☎ 01328 711646.

WISBECH Ch 09 HW−3 when vessel expected. HM 01945 588059. Sutton Bridge **Ch 09**

KING'S LYNN
Harbour Radio **Ch 14** 11 Mon-Fri: 0800-1700 and −3HW+1. HM ☎ 01553 773411.

BOSTON
Port Control **Ch 12** Mon-Fri 0800-1700 and HW HW -2½ to HW + 1½. HM ☎ 01205 362328.
Grand Sluice **Ch 74** only when lock operates. Marina ☎ 364420.

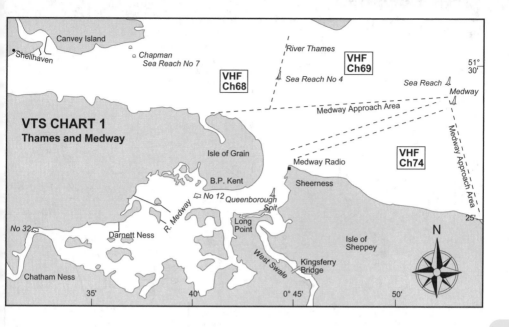

VHF Ch68

VHF Ch69

VHF Ch74

VTS CHART 1
Thames and Medway

Canvey Island

Shellhaven

Chapman
Sea Reach No 7

River Thames

Sea Reach No 4

Sea Reach

Medway

Medway Approach Area

Medway Approach Area

Isle of Grain

Medway Radio

Sheerness

B.P. Kent

No 12 Queenborough
Spit

Long
Point

Isle of
Sheppey

No 32

R. Medway

Darnett Ness

West Swale

Kingsferry
Bridge

Chatham Ness

51°
30'

25'

N

35'   40'   0° 45'   50'

Ford Motor Works
Dagenham

51°
30'

VHF Ch68

VHF Ch14

Crayfordness

Woolwich Radio

Port Control London

River Thames

West
Blyth

N

Tilbury Dock

Port Control London

Royal Terrace
Pier

Shornmead

10'   15'   0° 20'   25'   30'

N

River Thames

Waterloo Bridge

London Bridge

West India
Dock Lock

Thames Barrier
Control Zone

Tower
Bridge

Surrey
Entrance

Isle
of
Dogs

Blackwall Point

K.G.V.
Dock Lock

Thames
Barrier

Margaret Ness

51°
30'

Vauxhall Bridge

VHF Ch14

51°
30'

Putney Bridge

10'   05'   0°   05'

VTS CHART 2

Humber Estuary and Approaches VTS and TSS

= Recommended route for vessels <20m in and out

RIVER HUMBER
VTS 1, Ch 14 to seaward of Clee Ness Lt F
VTS 2, Ch 12 Clee Ness–Gainsborough (R Trent) &
Goole (R Ouse). MSI broadcasts Ch 12 & 14 every
2 hrs from 0103LT.
Grimsby Docks Radio **Ch 74**; 18 79 H24
Marinas: Grimsby, Meridian Quay **Ch 74,** ☎ 01472
268424. **Hull, Ch 80,** ☎ 01482 330508.
South Ferriby, Sluice **Ch 74. Brough,** Humber Yawl
club ☎ 01482 667224. **Goole** Boathouse ☎ 01405
763985.

BRIDLINGTON
HM, call Ch 16; work **Ch 12.** ☎ 01262 670148.

SCARBOROUGH
HM *Scarborough Port Control* **Ch 12** H24. ☎ 01723
373530.

WHITBY HM, Bridge & Marina **Ch 11,** 12 H24. ☎
01947 602354.

RIVER TEES and HARTLEPOOL
Monitor *Tees Port control* **Ch 14,** 08, 11, 12, 22.
Hartlepool Marina **Ch 80, M** H24. ☎ 01429 865744.

SEAHAM
HM **Ch 12,** M-F 0800-1700. ☎ 0191 5161700.

SUNDERLAND
Hbr Radio **Ch 14** (H24). Marina **Ch 80, M.**
☎ 0191 5144721.

RIVER TYNE
Tyne VTS **Ch 12,** 08, 11, inc Info service.
Royal Quays Marina **Ch 80** ☎ 0191 2728282.
St Peter's Marina **Ch 80** ☎ 0191 2654472.
Newcastle City Marina ☎ 0191 2211348.

BLYTH
Port control **Ch 12,** 11. ☎ 01670 352066. Marina
☎ 01670 353636 (R Northumberland YC).

WARKWORTH HARBOUR (Amble)
HM Ch 16, work **Ch 14.** ☎ 01665 710306. Marina
Ch 80, ☎ 01665 712168.

BERWICK-UPON-TWEED
HM **Ch 12,** M-F 0800-1700. ☎ 01289 307404.

SCOTLAND
EYEMOUTH HM **Ch 12,** 06 HO. ☎ 01890 750223.

FIRTH OF FORTH
Forth and Tay Navigation **Ch 71**; may work 12, 20.

PORT EDGAR Marina **Ch 80, M.** ☎ 0131 313330.

GRANTON, Royal Forth YC, Call *Boswell* **Ch M.** ☎
0131 5523006.

GRANGEMOUTH Docks **Ch 14.** ☎ 01324 498566.

FORTH & CLYDE CANAL *Carron Sea Lock* **Ch 74.**
☎ 01324 483034.

METHIL Docks **Ch 14.** ☎ 01324 498585.

ANSTRUTHER Ch 11. ☎ 01333 310836.

DUNDEE *Harbour Radio* **Ch 12.** ☎ 01382 224121.
Royal Tay YC Ch M. ☎ 01382 477516.

PERTH *Perth Harbour* **Ch 09.** ☎ 01738 624056.

ARBROATH *Port Control* **Ch 11.** ☎ 01241 872166.

MONTROSE *Port Control* **Ch 12.** ☎ 01674 672302.

STONEHAVEN HM **Ch 11.** ☎ 01569 762741.

ABERDEEN VTS **Ch 12,** ☎ 01224 597000.

PETERHEAD *Peterhead Hbrs* **Ch 14** for cl'nce to
enter/exit. Marina ☎ 01779 477868.

FRASERBURGH Ch 12 H24, ☎ 01346 515858.

MACDUFF Ch 12 H24, ☎ 01261 832236.

BANFF Ch 12, ☎ 01261 815544.

WHITEHILLS *Whitehills Hbr Radio* **Ch 14,** ☎ 01261
861291.

BUCKIE Ch 12, 16 (H24), ☎ 01542 831700.

LOSSIEMOUTH
HM **Ch 12** 0700-1700. Marina, ☎ 01343 813066.

HOPEMAN and BURGHEAD
Same HM: *Burghead Radio* **Ch 14** HX, ☎ 01343
835337.

NAIRN HM/Marina ☎ 01667 454330. No VHF.

INVERNESS
HM **Ch 12,** M-Fri 0900-1700; Tel code 01463:
☎ 715715.
Clachnaharry Sealock **Ch 74,** ☎ 713896. HW ±4.
Inverness Marina **Ch 12.**
Seaport Marina ☎ 239745.
Caley Marina ☎ 236539.

HELMSDALE Ch 13, ☎ 01431 821692.

WICK Ch 14 HM, ☎ 01955 602030.

SCRABSTER HM **Ch 12** H24, Call on arr/dep.
☎ 01847 892779.

ORKNEY HARBOURS NAVIGATION SERVICE
Orkney Harbour Radio **Ch 09 11** 12
Stromness HM **Ch 14** M-Fri 0900-1700; ☎ 07810
465825. Marina, ☎ 465825.
Kirkwall *Hbr Radio* **Ch 14,** ☎ 872292. M-Fri, 0800-
1700.
Westray Pier, *Pierowall Hbr* **Ch 14** when vessel
expected. ☎ 01857 677216.

SHETLAND
Lerwick Hbr Radio **Ch 12** ☎ 01595 692991.
Scalloway Hbr Radio **Ch 09, 12,** M-F 0700-1800, Sat
0900-1230. Piermaster ☎ 01595 744221.
Sullom Voe VTS **Ch 14** for tfc info, weather & radar
assistance on request. ☎ 01806 242551.
Balta Sound Harbour **Ch 16, 20** HO

OUTER HEBRIDES
STORNOWAY HM **Ch 12** H24, ☎ 01851 702688.

Loch Maddy, N Uist **Ch 12,** ☎ 01876 500337.

St Kilda, *Kilda Radio* **Ch 16,** ☎ 01870 604406.

MAINLAND
Kinlochbervie Ch 14 HX, ☎ 01971 521235.

Loch Inver Ch 09 HX, ☎ 01571 844247.

ULLAPOOL **Ch 14, ☎** 01854 612724.

Loch Gairloch **Hbr Ch 16, ☎** 01445 712140.

ISLE OF SKYE
Portree **Ch 12** (occas), **☎** 01478 612926.

Kyle Akin **Ch 11, ☎** 01599 534167.

KYLE OF LOCH ALSH Ch 11, ☎ 01599 534589.

Mallaig **Ch 09** HO, **☎** 01687 462154.

Tiree, Gott Bay Pier, **Ch 31, ☎** 01879 230337.

Coll, Arinagour Pier, **Ch 31, ☎** 01879 230347.

L Sunart, Salen Bay, **Ch 16, ☎** 01967 431510.

ISLAND OF MULL
Tobermory, **Ch 12, M** HJ, **☎** 01688 302017.

Loch Lathaich; Sound of Iona; Craignure Pier.

Corpach basin & lock/Caledonian Canal **Ch 74, ☎** 01397 772249.

DUNSTAFFNAGE Marina, **Ch M, ☎** 01631 566555.

Oban *North Bay* **Ch 12.** Marina, **☎** 01631 565333.

L Melfort, Kilmelford Haven, **Ch M, ☎** 01852 200248.

L Shuna, Craobh Marina, **Ch M, ☎** 01852 500222.

L Craignish, Ardfern **Ch 80, M, ☎** 01852 500247.

CRINAN CANAL, **Ch 74.** BWB, **☎** 01546 603210.

Islay, Port Ellen, **☎** 01496 300301; no VHF.

Tarbert, Loch Fyne **Ch 14, ☎** 01880 820344.

Portavadie Marina **Ch 80, ☎** 01700 811075.

CAMPBELTOWN **Ch 12,** 13, **☎** 01586 552552.

ROTHESAY, Bute **Ch 12, ☎** 01700 500630.

LARGS Yacht Haven **Ch 80, M, ☎** 01475 675333.

KIP Marina **Ch 80, M, ☎** 01475 521485.

HOLY LOCH Marina **Ch 80, M, ☎** 01369 701800.

RHU Marina **Ch 80, M, ☎** 01436 820238.

ARDROSSAN Marina **Ch 80, M, ☎** 01294 607077.

IRVINE HM/Bridge **Ch 12, ☎** 01292 487286.

TROON **Ch 14.** Marina **Ch 80, M, ☎** 01294 315553.

GIRVAN HM **Ch 12, ☎** 01465 713648.

KIRKCUDBRIGHT HM **Ch 12, ☎** 01557 331135.

ENGLAND W COAST AND WALES

MARYPORT Marina **Ch 80, ☎** 01900 814431.

WORKINGTON HM **Ch 14, ☎** 01900 602301.

WHITEHAVEN Marina **Ch 12, ☎** 01946 692435.

ISLE OF MAN (Tel code 01624) If unable to contact IoM hbrs below, call Douglas.

Douglas *Hbr Control* **Ch 12** H24.

Port St Mary HM **Ch 12** HJ, **☎** 833205.

Peel HM **Ch 12** HJ, **☎** 842338.

Ramsey HM **Ch 12** 0800-1600. HO, **☎** 812245.

MAINLAND
GLASSON DOCK Marina **Ch 69, ☎** 01524 751491.

FLEETWOOD *Fleetwood Dock Radio (*HW±2) **Ch 12** for Marina, **☎** 01253 879062.

PRESTON Lock *Riversway* **Ch 14.** Marina **Ch 80, ☎** 01772 733595.

LIVERPOOL *Mersey Radio* **Ch 12.** Info **Ch 09.** Radar **Ch 18.** Liverpool Marina (Brunswick Dock) **Ch M, ☎** 0151 7076777. Albert Dock **Ch M, ☎** 0151 7096558; access via Canning Dock lock.

CONWY HM **Ch 14.** Marinas, both **Ch 80:** Conwy, **☎** 01492 593000. Deganwy 576888.

MENAI STRAIT and ANGLESEY
Beaumaris/Menai HM **Ch 69, ☎** 01248 712312.

Caernarfon, HM & Victoria Dock **Ch 80, ☎** 01286 672118. Mon-Fri: 0900-1700 Sat: 0900-1200

HOLYHEAD *Port Control* **Ch 14, ☎** 01407 606700. Marina 764242.

MAINLAND
PWLLHELI, HM **Ch 12, ☎** 701219 . Marina **Ch 80, M, ☎** 01758 704081.

PORTHMADOG *Hbr* **Ch 12, ☎** 01766 512927.

BARMOUTH HM *Barmouth Hbr* **Ch 12, ☎** 01341 280671.

ABERDOVEY *Aberdovey Hbr* **Ch 12, ☎** 01654 767626.

ABERYSTWYTH HM **Ch 14.** Marina **Ch 80, ☎** 01970 611422.

FISHGUARD HM **Ch 14.**

MILFORD HAVEN Monitor *Port Control* (and *Patrol launch*) **Ch 12,** whilst under way. **Milford Docks** *Pierhead* **Ch 18.** Milford Dock Marina **Ch 14, ☎** 01646 696312. Neyland Yacht Haven **Ch 80, M, ☎** 01646 601601.

Tenby **Ch 80, ☎** 01834 842717.

Saundersfoot **Ch 11**

SWANSEA Tawe Lock **Ch 18.** Marina **Ch 80, ☎** 01792 470310.

BARRY *Barry Radio* **Ch 11.** HM **☎** 01446 732665.

CARDIFF *Cardiff Radio* **Ch 14.** Barrage control **Ch 18.** Penarth Marina **Ch 80, ☎** 02920 705021.

NEWPORT HM **Ch 71, ☎** 0870 6096699.

SHARPNESS *Sharpness Radio* **Ch 13** for lock. Marina, **☎** 01453 811476. Canal **Ch 74**

BRISTOL *Bristol VTS* **Ch 12 ☎** 0117 980 2638. *City Docks Radio* **Ch 14** (low power) to confirm. *Bristol Floating Hbr* **Ch 73.** Bristol Marina **Ch 80, ☎** 0117 9213198.

PORTISHEAD Marina **Ch 80, ☎** 0198 4631264.

BURNHAM-ON-SEA HM **Ch 08, ☎** 01938 822666.

WATCHET Marina **Ch 80, ☎** 01984 631264.

ILFRACOMBE HM **Ch 80, ☎** 01271 862108.

APPLEDORE-BIDEFORD HM *Two Rivers* **Ch 12,** Appledore ☎ 01237 428700.

BUDE HM **Ch 12,** ☎ 01288 353111.

PADSTOW HM **Ch 12,** ☎ 01841 532239.

ST IVES HM **Ch 12,** ☎ 07793 515460.

IRELAND

ROSSAVEEL Ch 12, ☎ 091 572108.

GALWAY, HM **Ch 12,** ☎ 091 561874.

SHANNON ESTUARY *Shannon Ports Radio* **Ch 11** (HO), ☎ 087 2560427.

KILRUSH Marina **Ch 80,** ☎ 06590 52072.

LIMERICK HBR Ch 12 13, ☎ 061 315377.

MFENIT HM **Ch 14, M,** ☎ 066 7136231.

DINGLE HM **Ch 14** (no calls req'd), ☎ 087 2325844.

CAHERSIVEEN (Valentia) Marina Ch 80, ☎ 066 9472777.

BANTRY BAY, Lawrence Cove Marina **Ch M,** ☎ 027 75044.

CASTLETOWN BEARHAVEN ⚓, ☎ 027 70220.

CROOKHAVEN ⚓, ☎ 028 35319.

SCHULL ⚓, mobile ☎ 086 1039105.

BALTIMORE Ch 09, mobile 087 2351485.

GLANDORE HM **Ch 06,** ☎ 028 34737.

COURTMACSHERRY HM ☎ 08610 40812.

KINSALE HM **Ch 14** ☎ 021 4772503. Marinas **Ch M:** KYC ☎ 4772196. Castlepark ☎ 4774959.

CORK *Cork Hbr Radio* **Ch 12,** 14 H24. HM ☎ 021 4273125. Marinas **Ch M:** Crosshaven ☎ 4831161. Salve ☎ 4831145. Royal Cork YC ☎ 4831023. East Ferry ☎ 4813390. Cork Hbr ☎ (087) 3669009.

YOUGHAL HM/Pilots **Ch 14** Mon-Fri 0900-1700 and when ships expected. ☎ 024 92577.

DUNMORE EAST HM/Pilots **Ch 14** ☎ 051 383166.

WATERFORD & NEW ROSS Ch 12, 14. ☎ 051 873501.

KILMORE QUAY Ch 09. Marina, ☎ 053 29955.

ROSSLARE HM **Ch 12** H24, ☎ 053 33114.

WEXFORD Hbr Boat club. **Ch 16,** ☎ 053 22039.

ARKLOW HM **Ch 12,** ☎ 0402 32466. Marina 39901.

WICKLOW HM **Ch 14** 12, ☎ 0404 67455.

DUN LAOGHAIRE HM **Ch 14,** ☎ 01 2801130. Marina **Ch M,** ☎ 2020040. YCs: National 2805725; R. St George 2801811; R. Irish 2809452; DL Motor 2801371.

Greystones Marina, ☎ 353 (086) 2718161

DUBLIN HM and VTS *Dublin VTS* **Ch 12,** 13. Poolbeg Marina **Ch M,** ☎ 01 6689983. Lifting bridge *Eastlink* **Ch 12, 13.** City moorings, ☎ 01 8183300.

HOWTH HM **Ch 11.** Marina Ch M, 80, ☎ 01 8392777.

MALAHIDE Marina **Ch 80, M,** ☎ 01 8454129.

CARLINGFORDFORD LOUGH
Carlingford Marina Ch M, ☎ 042 9373072.

Warrenpoint Ch 12, ☎ 028 41752878.

Kilkeel Ch 12, ☎ 028 41762287.

ARDGLASS (Phennick Cove) HM **Ch 12.** Marina **Ch M, 80,** ☎ 028 44842332.

STRANGFORD LOUGH
HM **Ch 12 14,** ☎ 028 44881637.

Portaferry Marina Ch 80, M, ☎ 07703 209780.

Donaghadee Copelands Marina, ☎ 028 91882184.

BELFAST VTS *Belfast Hbr Radio* **Ch 12. Marinas Ch 80, M:** Carrickfergus, ☎ 028 93366666. Bangor, ☎ 028 91453217.

LARNE *Port Control* **Ch 14,** 11.

Glenarm HM/Marina, mobile ☎ 07703 606763.

Ballycastle HM/Marina, mob ☎ 07803 505084.

PORTRUSH HM **Ch 12,** ☎ 028 70822307.

COLERAINE HM **Ch 12.** Marina, ☎ 028 70832086.

LONDONDERRY *Hbr radio* **Ch 14,** ☎ 028 71860313.

L SWILLY Fahan Marina, ☎ 074 9360008.

KILLYBEGS HM **Ch 14,** ☎ 07497 31032.

Burton Port HM **Ch 06, 12, 14,** ☎ 075 42155.

SLIGO HM **Ch 12,** 14, ☎ 071 9153819.

DENMARK

Skagen HM **Ch 12** 13 HX, ☎ 98 941346.

Hirtshals HM **Ch 12** 13 HX, ☎ 98 941422.

Torup Strand HM **Ch 12** 13 HX.

Hanstholm HM **Ch 12** 13 HX, ☎ 97 961833/96550710.

THYBORØN HM **Ch 12** 13 H24, ☎ 97 831188.

Thisted (Limfjord) Ch 12 13 HX, ☎ 97 911400.

Torsminde HM **Ch 12** 13, ☎ 24 233345.

Hvide Sande HM **Ch 12** (0700-1700), ☎ 97 311633 H24.

ESBJERG *Hbr Control* **Ch 12** 13 14 H24, ☎ 75 124000. **Fanø** HM, ☎ 75 163100.

Rømø HM **Ch 10, 12, 13** HX, ☎ 74 755245.

GERMANY

HELGOLAND HM **Ch 67,** ☎ 04725 81593583. **May-Aug** Mon-Thu 0700-1200, 1300-2000. Fri-Sun 0700-1200.
Sep-Apr Mon-Thu 0700-1200, 1300-1600. Fri 0700-1200.

List HM **Ch 11**, ☎ 046 51870374.
Hörnum HM **67**, ☎ 046 51881027.
Wyk HM **Ch 11**, ☎ 046 81500430.
Pellworm HM **Ch 11**, ☎ 048 44726.
Husum HM **Ch 11**, ☎ 048 16670.
R. Eider sealock **Ch 14**, ☎ 04833 4535211.
Büsum HM **Ch 11**, ☎ 048 413607.

INNER DEUTSCHE BUCHT (GERMAN BIGHT)
VTS, Eastern part **Ch 80**, ☎ 04421 489282.
VTS, Western part **Ch 79**

BRUNSBÜTTEL WSA (hbr info) ☎ 04852 8850.

NORD-OSTSEE KANAL (KIEL CANAL)
VTS Canal I   **Ch 13**, ☎ 04852 885371.
VTS Canal II   **Ch 02**, ☎ 04852 885369.
VTS Canal III   **Ch 03**, ☎ 0431 3603456.
VTS Canal IV   **Ch 12**, ☎ 0431 3603465.
Brieholz, **Ch 73**. Ostermoor, **Ch 73**.
Kiel-Holtenau, HM ☎ 0431 363830.

RIVER ELBE
CUXHAVEN HM **Ch 69** HX, ☎ 04721 500150. Lock
Ch 69, ☎ 500120. Cuxhaven Marina, ☎ 175 90
20015. YC Marina, ☎ 34111. R. Stör Lock **Ch 09**
Bridge opens on request. **Glückstadt** HM **Ch 08**,
☎ 04124 913200.

HAMBURG Port HM **Ch 12**, ☎ 040 7411540.
VTS *Hamburg Port Traffic* **Ch 13**, **14**, **74**. Wedel
Yacht Hbr, ☎ 040 1034438. City Sporthafen, ☎
040 364297.

BREMERHAVEN *Weser VTS* **Ch 22**. Port **Ch 12**, ☎
0471 59613401. **HM**, ☎ 59613416. **Locks Ch 69**,
70. Marinas Weser YC, ☎ 23531. NYC, ☎ 77555.
WVW, ☎ 73268.

BREMEN *Port Radio* **Ch 03**, ☎ 0421 3618504.

JADE VTS *Jade Traffic* **Ch 63, 20.**

WILHEMSHAVEN
Port **Ch 11**, ☎ 04421 154580. **Sealock Ch 13.**
Bridges **Ch 11**. Marinas Nassauhafen, ☎ 41439.
Wiking Sportsboothafen, ☎ 41301.

HOOKSIEL Ch 63. Alterhafen Marina.

WANGEROOGE HM **Ch 17**, ☎ 04469 1322.

SPIEKEROOG HM No VHF, ☎ 04976 9193133.

DORNUMER-ACCUMERSIEL HM No VHF, ☎
04933 2510. YC ☎ 2240.

LANGEOOG HM **Ch 17**, ☎ 04972 301.

NORDERNEY HM **Ch 17**, ☎ 04932 82826.

NORDDEICH HM **Ch 17**, ☎ 04931 81317.

BORKUM HM **Ch 14**, ☎ 04922 81317.

EMS VTS *Ems Traffic* **Ch 15, 18, 20, 21**

EMDEN HM & locks **Ch 13**, ☎ 04921 897260.
YC Marina, ☎ 997147. Mariners' Club, ☎
953795. City Marina, ☎ 8907211.

NETHERLANDS
DELFZIJL/EEMSHAVEN VTS is not compulsory
for leisure craft. **Delfzijl Radar Ch 03** gives radar
assistance when visibility falls below 2000m.
Eemshaven Radar Ch 01. Port Control Ch 66
broadcasts info every even H+10.

DELFZIJL HBR. HM **Ch 14**; ☎ 0596 640400. **Locks**
Ch 26, M-Sat H24, Sun & hols on request; ☎
693293. **Bridges:** Weiwerder **Ch 11**. Heemskes &
Handelshaven **Ch 14**. **Farmsumerhaven**, Ch 66,
☎ 640494.

EEMSHAVEN HM **Ch 14**; ☎ 516142. Radar **Ch 19**.

LAUWERSOOG. HM, *Havendienst*, **Ch 09**; ☎ 0519
39023. Mon 0000-1700; Tu-Wed 0800-1700; Th-Sat
0700-1500.

TERSCHELLING VTS Call/monitor *Brandaris* **Ch 02**;
☎ 0562 443100. **Marina**, **Ch 31**; ☎ 443337.

VLIELAND. HM **Ch 12. Marina**, **Ch 31**; ☎ 0562
451729.

HARLINGEN HM **Ch 11** (not on Sun); ☎ 0517
413423. **Locks Ch 22.**

OUDESCHILD HM **Ch 12**; ☎ 0222 312710. **Marina**,
Ch 31; ☎ 0222 321227. See Den Helder VTS.

DEN HELDER VTS. Monitor *Tfc Centre* **Ch 62**, H24;
broadcasts info and gives radar surveillance. **PORT**
CONTROL Ch 14; ☎ 0223 62770. **Marina** ☎ 652645.
Bridge: Moormanbrug **Ch 18. Lock:** Koopvaarders
Ch 22.

IJSSELMEER Den Oever lock Ch 20, ☎ 0227
511383. **Port Ch 11**, ☎ 511303. Marina ☎ 511789
Kornwerderzand lock Ch 18, ☎ 0517 57441.

ENKHUIZEN Naviduct (also Krabbersgat) **Ch 22**.

IJMUIDEN VTS. Traffic Centre Ch 07, Roads (W
of IJmuiden buoy). Thence **Port Control Ch 61** to
Noordzeesluizen (locks).

Seaport Marina Ch 75, ☎ 0255 560300.

NORDZEEKANAAL VTS
Noordzeesluizen. *Sluis IJmuiden* **Ch 22**
Noordzeekanaal. **Ch 03**, from locks to km 11·2.

AMSTERDAM Port Control Ch 68 (Km 11·2 to
Oranjesluisen). **Port Info Ch 14**. Access to Standing
Mast route: **Westerkeersluis Ch 22**. Haarlem hbr
Ch 18. Westerdoksbrug ☎ 6241457, **Ch 22, 69**
Marinas: Amsterdam Marina ☎ 6310767. **Marina**
Het Realeneiland, ☎ 6238855. Sixhaven, ☎ 020
6329429. WV Aeolus, ☎ 6360791. Aquadam, ☎
6320616. Access to Markermeer: **Oranjesluiser**
Ch 18.

SCHEVENINGEN. Traffic Centre & Port Ch 21; ☎ 070
3527711. **Marina Ch 31**; ☎ 070 3520017.

HOEK VAN HOLLAND ROADSTEAD
To cross the mouth of the Maas, call *Maas Entrance*
Ch 03, with vessel's name, position and course
Follow a track close W of a line joining buoys MV
MVN and Indusbank N. See VTS Chart No 4. Whilst

VTS CHART 3

Netherlands – Scheldemond (VTS-SM)

Westerschelde

ANTWERPEN Traffic Centre Ch 12

HANSWEERT Traffic Centre Ch 65

TERNEUZEN Traffic Centre Ch 03

VLISSINGEN Traffic Centre Ch 14

STEENBANK Traffic Centre Ch 64

ZEEBRUGGE Traffic Centre Ch 69

WANDELAAR Traffic Centre Ch 65

Wandelaar Approach Ch 60

BELGIUM

Antwerp

Rotterdam

Scheveningen

Hoek van Holland

Haringvliet

Grevelingemeer

Oosterschelde

Veerse Meer

Westerschelde

Vlissingen

Zeebrugge

Oostende

Nieuwpoort

Dunkerque

Maas Centre

Maas Centre

ITZ

Roompot Lock

SBO

Schouwenbank

OG13

W4

NE Akkaert

Westpit

A1 bis

Goote Bank

KB

AN

West Hinder Lt

Twin

Sandettie N

Foxtrot 3 DW

Wind farm under construction

NHR-SE

Noord Hinder

NOORD HINDER JUNCTION

NHR-S

NHR-N

Outer Gabbard

N. Galloper

DW

TSS NORTH HINDER NORTH

NORTH HINDER SOUTH TSS

WEST HINDER TSS

Euro

WEST OUTER

WEST INNER

Maas Junction

MW1

MW2

MW3

MW4

MW5

TSS MAAS NORTHWEST

TSS MAAS NORTH

MN2

MN3

COMMUNICATIONS

121

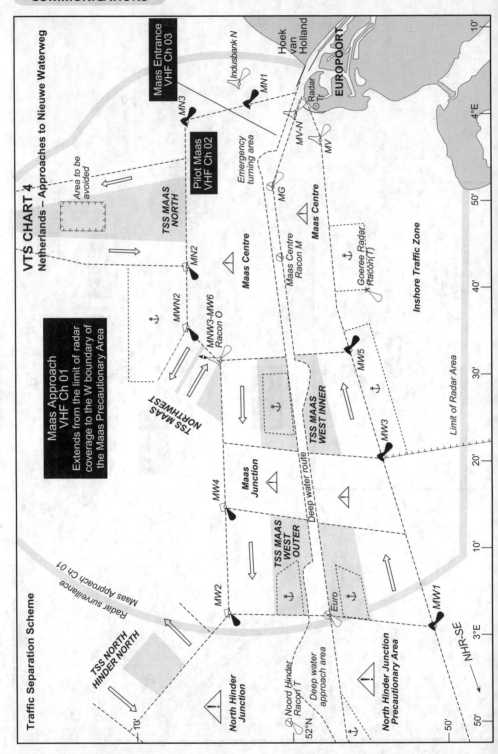

VTS CHART 4
Netherlands – Approaches to Nieuwe Waterweg

Traffic Separation Scheme

Maas Approach
VHF Ch 01
Extends from the limit of radar
coverage to the W boundary of
the Maas Precautionary Area

Pilot Maas
VHF Ch 02

Maas Entrance
VHF Ch 03

Radar surveillance
Maas Approach Ch 01

TSS NORTH
HINDER NORTH

North Hinder
Junction

North Hinder Junction
Precautionary Area

NHR-SE

Noord Hinder
Racon T

Deep water
approach area

Euro

52°N

50'

3°E

10'

20'

30'

40'

50'

4°E

10'

TSS MAAS
NORTHWEST

TSS MAAS
WEST OUTER

TSS MAAS
WEST INNER

Maas
Junction

Deep water route

MW1

MW2

MW3

MW4

MW5

MWN2

MWN3-MW6
Racon O

MN2

MN3

MN1

Indusbank N

Area to be
avoided

TSS MAAS
NORTH

Maas Centre

Maas Centre

Maas Centre
Racon M

Emergency
turning area

MG

MV-N

MV

Radar
Tr

EUROPOORT

Hoek
van
Holland

Goeree Radar
Racon (T)

Inshore Traffic Zone

Limit of Radar Area

122

crossing, maintain continuous listening watch and keep a very sharp lookout.

NIEUWE WATERWEG VTS. Outer areas as shown on VTS Charts 3 & 4: **Maas Approach** Ch 01. **Pilot Maas** Ch 02. **Maas Entrance** Ch 03. **HCC** *Central Traffic Control* Ch 14 19. Report to/monitor continuously the relevant Tfc Centre, as listed from seaward to City Marina: Rozenburg Ch 65; Maassluis Ch 80; Botlek Ch 61; Eemhaven Ch 63; Waalhaven Ch 60; Maasbruggen Ch 81.

ROTTERDAM Rotterdam **Tfc Centre** Ch 11. **Hbr Coordination Centre (HCC)** Ch 19. **Marinas/ Yacht hbrs: Vlaardingen** ☎ 010 2484333; **Lock** Ch 20. **Spuihaven** ☎ 4667765, mob 0644326722. **Coolhaven** ☎ 4764146. **Veerhaven** ☎ 4365446, mob 0653536107. **City Marina** ☎ 48540986, via Erasmus bridge Ch 18.

STELLENDAM Haringvliet lock & lifting bridge: *Goereese Sluis* Ch 20, ☎ 0187 497350. Opening hrs: M-F 0000-2200. 1 Nov - 1 Apr: Sat 0800-2200; Sun 0800-1000, 1600-1800. 1 Apr - 1 Nov: Sat & Sun 0800-2000. **Marina** Ch 31, ☎ 493769.

OOSTERSCHELDE Lock *Roompotsluis* Ch 18, ☎ 0111 659265. Opening hours: Mon & Thu, 0000-2200; Tue & Sun, 0600-0000; Wed H24; Fri & Sat: 0600-2200.
Roompot Marina Ch 31.

WESTERSCHELDE VTS See VTS Chart No 3. Reporting is not compulsory for leisure craft, but they should monitor the VHF channel for the appropriate Traffic Area. Each Traffic Area is controlled by a Traffic Centre and bounded by buoys. *In emergency call the relevant Traffic Centre:* Ch 67.
Tfc Centre Steenbank & Radar Ch 64.
Tfc Centre Vlissingen Ch 14. **Radar** Ch 21. **Info broadcast** Ch 14 H+55.
Tfc Centre Terneuzen & Radar Ch 03. **Info broadcast** Ch 11 H+00.
Tfc Centre Hansweert Ch 65.
Antwerpen, Zeebrugge and Wandelaar Traffic Areas are listed under Belgium.

VLISSINGEN De Ruyter Marina no VHF, ☎ 0118 414498, mobile 06 5353 7181. *Flushing Port Control* Ch 09. **Sealocks & canal bridge** Ch 22. **VVW Schelde Marina** Ch 14, ☎ 465912 / 0638 195369.

BRESKENS Marina, Ch 31, ☎ 0117 381902.

TERNEUZEN Port control Ch 11. **Marina**, ☎ 0115 697089. **Oostsluis** (E lock, small craft) Ch 18.

BELGIUM

ANTWERPEN, Tfc Centre Zandvliet Ch 12. **Info broadcast** Ch 12 H+35.

ANTWERPEN PORT Calling and safety Ch 74. **Royerssluis** Ch 22. **Siberia & Londen bridges** Ch 62. **Willemdok Marina** Ch 23, ☎ 03 2315066. **Linkeroever Marina** Ch 09, ☎ 03 2190895.

ZEEBRUGGE Tfc Centre Zeebrugge Ch 69. **Info broadcasts** Ch 69 H+15.

ZEEBRUGGE Port Control Ch 71 H24, ☎ 050 546867/550801. **Marina** ☎ 544903. **E lock** Ch 68.

BLANKENBERGE Marinas: VNZ, ☎ 050 429150, & **SYCB,** ☎ 411420, Ch 31. **VVW** ☎ 417536, Ch 23.

WANDELAAR Tfc Centre Wandelaar Ch 65. **Wandelaar Approach** Ch 60.

OOSTENDE Port Control Ch 09 H24, ☎ 059 566313. **Mercator lock,** ☎ 321669, & **marina,** ☎ 705762: Ch 14 H24. **Marinas: RNSYC,** ☎ 505912. **RYCO,** ☎ 321452.

NIEUWPOORT Port HM Ch 60 H24, ☎ 058 233000. **Marinas: KYCN,** Ch 23, ☎ 234413. **WSKLM,** Ch 23, ☎ 5233641. **VVW-N,** Ch 08, ☎ 235232.

NORTH FRANCE

DUNKERQUE Port & VTS Ch 73, H24. The VTS does not affect leisure craft, but monitor Ch 73. **Marinas** Ch 09: Grande Large ☎ 03.28.63.23.00. YCMN ☎ 03.28.66.79.90. **Trystram lock** Ch 14.

GRAVELINES HM/Marina, Ch 09, ☎ 03·59·73·42·42.

CALAIS VTS, Port Control & Marina Ch 17 H24, ☎ 03.21.34.55.23.

BOULOGNE Boulogne Port, ☎ 03.21.31.52.43, Ch 12, H24. **Marina** Ch 09, ☎ 06.76.98.74.98 / 03.21.99.66.50.

LE TOUQUET/ÉTAPLES-SUR-MER Ch 09, 77. **Étaples Marina,** ☎ 03.21.84.54.03.

LE TRÉPORT Marina/lock Ch 12, 72, ☎ 02.35.50.63.06

DIEPPE Port HM Ch 12, HO. **Marina** Ch 09, ☎ 02.35.40.19.79.

ST VALÉRY-EN-CAUX Entry gate & marina Ch 09, ☎ 02.35.97.01.30.

FÉCAMP Port HM, Ch 10, **12,** ☎ 02.35.28.25.53. **Marina & Bérigny lock,** Ch 09, ☎ 02.35.28.13.58.

LE HAVRE Control Tower Ch **12,** 20. **Port Ops** Ch 67, 69. **Marina,** Ch 09, ☎ 02.35.21.23.95.

LA SEINE VTS Rouen Port Control Ch 73 (Estuary), 68 (River). **Honfleur radar** Ch 15, 19, **73.**

HONFLEUR HM Ch **17,** 73 HX, ☎ 02.31.14.61.09. **Lock,** ☎ 02.31.98.72.82, & **Bridge** Ch 17 H24.

ROUEN Port HM Ch 73, 68 H24. **Halte Nautique,** ☎ 02.35.07.33.94. **Marina** ☎ 02.35.08.30.59.

ROUEN – PARIS, LOCKS Amfreville Ch 18. **Notre-Dame-de-la-Garenne** Ch 22. **Mericourt** Ch 18. **Andrésy** Ch 22. **Bougival** Ch 22. **Chatou** Ch 18. **Suresnes** Ch 22. **PARIS-ARSENAL Marina** Ch 09, ☎ 01.43.41.39.32.

DEAUVILLE Port Deauville lock, ☎ 02.31.88.95.66; **Marina** ☎ 02.31.98.30.01, Ch 09 0800-1730. **Port Morny** gate ☎ 02.31.88.57.89; Marina, Ch 09, ☎ 02.31.98.50.40.

DIVES-SUR-MER. Marina Ch 09, ☎ 02.31.24.48.00.

OUISTREHAM Port 74; lock Ch 12, ☎ 02.31.36.22.00. Marina Ch 09, ☎ 02.31.96.91.37. Canal Ch 68. CAEN HM/Marina Ch 74, ☎ 02.31.95.24.47.

COURSEULLES-SUR-MER Marina Ch 09, ☎ 02.31.37.51.69.

PORT-EN-BESSIN HM, ☎ 02.31.21.70.49. Gate/bridge Ch 18, ☎ 02.31.21.71.77.

GRANDCAMP Marina Ch 09, ☎ 02.31.22.63.16.

CARENTAN Lock Ch 09, ☎ 02.33.71.10.85. Marina Ch 09, ☎ 02.33.42.24.44.

ST VAAST-LA-HOUGUE Marina Ch 09, ☎ 02.33.21.61.00.

BARFLEUR HM, ☎ 02.33.54.08.29. No VHF.

CHERBOURG VTS (yachts to monitor) Vigie du Homet Ch 12 H24. Marina Chantereyne Ch 09, ☎ 02.33.87.65.70. Gate (B du Commerce) Ch 06.

OMONVILLE-LA-ROGUE No VHF/Tel. 6 W ☎s.

DIÉLETTE Marina Ch 09, ☎ 02.33.53.68.78.

CARTERET Marina Ch 09, ☎ 02.33.04.70.84.

PORTBAIL Yacht hbr Ch 09, ☎ 02.33.04.83.48.

GRANVILLE Port HM Ch 12. Marina Ch 09, ☎ 02.33.50.20.06.

ST MALO Port HM Ch 12 H24. Marinas Ch 09: Bas Sablons, ☎ 02.99.81.71.34. Bassin Vauban, ☎ 02.99.56.51.91. DINARD, ☎ 02.99.46.65.55.

R RANCE barrage lock Ch 13, ☎ 02.99.46.21.87. Chatelier lock Ch 14, ☎ 02.99.39.55.66.

ST CAST-LE-GUILDO Marina ☎ 02 96 81 04 43

DAHOUËT Marina Ch 09, ☎ 02.96.72.82.85.

LE LÉGUÉ HM/Marina Ch 12, ☎ 02.96.77.49.85.

BINIC Marina Ch 09, ☎ 02.96.73.61.86.

ST QUAY-PORTRIEUX Marina ☎ 02.96.70.81.30. Ch 09.

PAIMPOL Lock/Marina Ch 09, ☎ 02.96.20.47.65.

LÉZARDRIEUX Marina Ch 09, ☎ 02.96.20.14.22.

PONTRIEUX Lock/Marina Ch 12, ☎ 02.96.95.34.87.

TRÉGUIER Marina Ch 09, ☎ 02.96.92.42.37.

PERROS-GUIREC Marina Ch 09, ☎ 02.96.49.80.50.

PLOUMANAC'H Marina Ch 09, ☎ 02.96.91.44.31.

TRÉBEURDEN Marina Ch 09, ☎ 02.96.23.64.00.

MORLAIX Lock, ☎ 06.77.50.15.90 / 02.98.88.15.10. Marina Ch 09, ☎ 02.98.62.13.14.

ROSCOFF HM/S Basin Ch 09, ☎ 02.98.69.76.37.

BLOSCON Marina Ch 09, ☎ 02.98.62.39.39. Ferry Port Ch 12, ☎ 02.98.61.27.84.

L'ABERWRACH Marina Ch 09, ☎ 02.98.04.91.62.

ALDERNEY, Braye Hbr, Alderney Coastguard Ch 67, ☎ 01481 822620. Otherwise, try Guernsey Coastguard. Alderney Port Control Ch 74.

GUERNSEY Beaucette Marina, Ch 80, ☎ 01481 245000. St Sampson Ch 12 H24 via St Peter Port Control Ch 12 H24, ☎ 720229. Victoria Marina Ch 80 HO, ☎ 725987. Guernsey Coastguard Ch 20 H24 (Ch 62 for emergecy link calls).

JERSEY St Helier Port Control Ch 14 H24; 8M max range. St Helier Marina, ☎ 01534 447730/447708, has no VHF; call Ch 14 only if essential. Gorey Ch 74, ☎ 853616.

BREST VTS Brest Port Ch 08 H24. Marinas Ch 09. Marina du Chateau, ☎ 02·98·33·12·50. Port du Moulin Blanc, ☎ 02·98·33·12·50.

CAMARET Marina Ch 09, ☎ 02.98.27.95.99.

MORGAT Marina Ch 09, ☎ 02.98.27.01.97.

DOUARNENEZ HM Ch 12. Marinas Ch 09: Tréboul ☎ 02.98.74.02.56; Port Rhu ☎ 02.98.92.00.67.

AUDIERNE HM Ch 09. Marina ☎ 02.98.74.04.93. Ste Evette ☎ 02.98.70.00.28.

LOCTUDY Marina Ch 09, ☎ 02.98.87.51.36.

BENODÉT Marinas Ch 09: Penfoul ☎ 02.98.57.05.78. Ste Marine ☎ 02.98.56.38.72.

PORT-LA-FORÊT Marina Ch 09, ☎ 02.98.56.98.45.

CONCARNEAU Marina Ch 09, ☎ 02.98.97.57.96.

LORIENT Port Ch 12. Marinas Ch 09: Ban-Gâvres ☎ 02.97.65.48.25. Kernével ☎ 02.97.65.48.25. Port Louis ☎ 02.97.83.59.55. Locmiquélic ☎ 02.97.33.59.51. Lorient ☎ 02.97.21.10.14.

PORT TUDY Marina Ch 09, ☎ 02.97.86.54.62.

RIVER ÉTEL Marina Ch 13, ☎ 02.97.55.46.62.

BELLE ILE Sauzon HM Ch 09, ☎ 02.97.31.63.40. Le Palais HM Ch 09, ☎ 02.97.31.42.90.

PORT HALIGUEN Marina Ch 09, ☎ 02.97.50.20.56.

LA TRINITÉ Marina Ch 09, ☎ 02.97.55.71.49.

VANNES Marina Ch 09 (0800-1200, 1500-1900 July-Aug), ☎ 02.97.01.55.20.

CROUESTY Marina Ch 09, ☎ 02.97.53.73.33.

LA VILAINE Arzal Marina Ch 09, ☎ 02.97.45.02.97.

PIRIAC Marina Ch 09, ☎ 02.40.23.52.32.

LA TURBALLE Marina Ch 09, ☎ 02.40.23.41.65.

LE CROISIC Marina Ch 09, ☎ 09.81.12.75.92.

LE POULIGUEN Marina Ch 09, ☎ 02.40.11.97.97.

PORNICHET Marina Ch 09, ☎ 02.40.61.03.20.

ST-NAZAIRE VTS Loire Ports Control Ch 14. Port HM Ch 14, ☎ 02.40.00.45.89.

PORNIC Marina Ch 09, ☎ 02.40.82.05.40.

L'HERBAUDIÈRE Marina Ch 09, ☎ 02.51.39.05.05.

PORT JOINVILLE Marina Ch 09, ☎ 02.51.58.38.11.

ST GILLES-CROIX-DE-VIE Marina Ch 09, ☎ 02.51.55.30.83.

LES SABLES D'OLONNE Port HM Ch 12, ☎ 02.51.95.11.79. Marina Ch 09, ☎ 02.51.32.51.16.

BOURGENAY Marina Ch 09, ☎ 02.51.22.20.36.

ILE DE RÉ Ars-en-Ré Ch 09, ☎ 05.46.29.08.52.
St Martin Ch 09, ☎ 05.46.09.26.69.

LA ROCHELLE Marinas Ch 09: Port des Minimes ☎ 05.46.44.41.20. Vieux Port ☎ 05.46.41.32.05.

ROCHEFORT Marina Ch 09, ☎ 05.46.83.99.06.

ILE D'OLÉRON St Denis Ch 09, ☎ 05.46.47.97.97.
Boyardville Ch 09, ☎ 05.46.76.48.56.

LA GIRONDE VTS Ch 12 (yachts to monitor).
Radar *Bordeaux Port Control* Ch 12 on request.
Depths in Gironde broadcast Ch 17 every 5 mins.

ROYAN Marina Ch 09, ☎ 05.46.38.72.22.

COAST RADIO STATIONS

Coast Radio Stations (CRS) deal with public correspondence (and a few other things). They enable a yachtsman to be linked by radio into the public telephone system in order to converse with a subscriber ashore, ie he can make or receive a Link call.

However the mobile 'phone has to a great extent rendered Link calls obsolescent. Thus there are no longer any CRS in the UK, France and Netherlands. In Germany a limited service is provided by a commercial company (see below).

CRS still operate in the Channel Islands, Ireland*, Denmark, Belgium, Spain and Portugal; see below. But they too may gradually be withdrawn. *In Ireland CRS no longer handle commercial link calls, but Medico link calls are still available on both VHF and MF.

The CG does **not** handle Link calls, except in Denmark and Belgium where the functions of CG and CRS have always been co-located.

CHANNEL ISLANDS

GUERNSEY COASTGUARD 49°27'·00N 02°32'00W ☎ 01481 720672 ▦ 01534 714177
Emergency link calls on **Ch 62** only. Ch 20 is used for navigation, pilotage and ships' business

JERSEY COAST GUARD 49°10'·85N 02°14'30W
☎ 01534 447705 ▦ 01534 499089
Link calls on **Ch 25** only

REPUBLIC OF IRELAND

A Coast Radio service is provided by the Dept of the Marine, Leeson Lane, Dublin 2, Eire. ☎ +353 (0)1 662 0922; ext 670 for enquiries. Broadcasts are made on a working channel/frequency following a prior announcement on Ch 16 and 2182 kHz. Ch 67 is used for Safety messages only.
VHF calls to an Irish Coast Radio Station should be made on a working channel. Only use Ch 16 in case of difficulty or in emergency.

NW and SE Ireland

Weather broadcasts at 0103, 0403, 0703, 1003, 1303, 1603, 1903, 2203 UT and at 0033, 0633, 1233, 1833 UT on the VHF Channels below. Nav warnings are broadcast at 0033, 0433, 0833, 1233, 1633 and 2033 UT.

Clifden Radio	53°30'N 09°56'W	Ch 26
Belmullet Radio	54°16'N 10°03'W	Ch 83
Donegal Bay	54°22'N 08°31'W	Ch 02
Glen Head Radio	54°44'N 08°43'W	Ch 24
MALIN HD RADIO	55°22'N 07°21'W	Ch 23
MF 1677 kHz, ☎ +353 (0) 77 70103		
MMSI 002500100 DSC: 2187·5 kHz		
Carlingford Radio	54°05'N 06°19'W	Ch 04
DUBLIN RADIO	53°23'N 06°04'W	Ch 83
Wicklow Hd Radio	52°58'N 06°00'W	Ch 02
Rosslare Radio	52°15'N 06°20'W	Ch 23
Mine Hd Radio	52°00'N 07°35'W	Ch 83

SW Ireland

Weather is broadcast at 0103, 0403, 0703, 1003, 1303, 1603, 1903, 2203 and at 0033, 0633, 1233, 1833 UT on the VHF Channels listed. Navwarnings are broadcast every 4 hrs from 0233.

Cork Radio	51°51'N 08°29'W	Ch 26
Mizen Radio	51°34'N 09°33'W	Ch 04
Bantry Radio	51°38'N 10°00'W	Ch 23
VALENTIA RADIO	51°56'N 10°21'W	Ch 24
MF 1752 kHz, ☎ + 353 (0) 66947 6109		
MMSI 002500200, DSC: 2187·5 kHz		
Shannon Radio	52°31'N 09°36'W	Ch 28
Galway Bay Radio	53°18'N 09°07'W	Ch 04

DENMARK

All VHF/MF CRS are remotely controlled from Lyngby Radio (55°50N 11°25'E) (MMSI 002191000). The callsign for all stations is Lyngby Radio. Call on working frequencies to help keep Ch 16 clear. The stations listed below monitor Ch 16 H24 and Ch 70 DSC. Traffic lists are broadcast on all VHF channels every odd H+05. All MF stations, except Skagen, keep watch H24 on 2182 kHz. Blåvand, Skagen and Lyngby also monitor MF 2187·5 kHz DSC. MF DSC Public correspondence facilities are available from Blåvand and Skagen on 1624·5 and 2177 kHz.

VHF & MF CRS		
Skagen	57°44'N 10°35'E	Ch 04
	MF: Tx 1758, Rx 2102	
Hirtshals	57°31'N 09°57'E	Ch 66
Hanstholm	57°07'N 08°39'E	Ch 01
Bovbjerg	56°32'N 08°10'E	Ch 02
	MF: Tx 1767, Rx 2111	
Blåvand	55°33'N 08°07'E	Ch 23
	MF: Tx 1734, Rx 2078	

GERMANY

CRS: DPO7 – Seefunk (Hamburg) *(MMSI 002113100)*. All stns monitor DSC Ch 70 and 16. Traffic lists are broadcast (LT): 0745, 0945, 1245, 1645, 1945 and H & H+30 on request Ch 16.

Nordfriesland	54°31'N 08°41'E	Ch 26
Elbe-Weser	53°50'N 08°39'E	Ch 24
Hamburg	53°33'N 09°58'E	Ch 83
Bremen	53°05'N 08°48'E	Ch 25
Accumersiel	53°40'N 07°29'E	Ch 28
Borkum	53°35'N 06°40'E	Ch 61

SHAPES

◆	Towing vessel - length of tow > 200m	**Rule 24**
▼	Yacht under sail *and* power	**Rule 25**
✕	Vessel fishing or trawling	**Rule 26**
✕+▲	Vessel fishing with outlying gear >150m long	**Rule 26**
●◆●	Vessel restricted in her ability to manoeuvre	**Rule 27**
●●	Vessel not under command	**Rule 27**
▮	Vessel constrained by her draught	**Rule 28**
●	Vessel at anchor	**Rule 30**

SOUND SIGNALS

MANOEUVRING AND WARNING Rule 34

•	A short blast = about 1 second.
–	A prolonged blast = 4 – 6 seconds.
•	I am altering course to **Starboard**
••	I am altering course to **Port**
•••	My engines are going **Astern**
•••••	I do not understand your intentions/actions

Note: The above sound signals may be supplemented by light signals flashed on an all-round white light with least range of 5 miles.

In a narrow channel

– – •	I intend to overtake on your starboard side.
– – ••	I intend to overtake on your port side.
– • – •	I agree with your overtaking signal
–	Warning by vessel nearing a bend where other vessels may not be seen
–	Approaching vessel acknowledges.

VESSELS IN RESTRICTED VISIBILITY Rule 35

–	Power-driven vessel making way.
– –	Power-driven vessel underway, but stopped and not making way.
– ••	**A sailing vessel**; vessels not under command; restricted in ability to manoeuvre; constrained by draught; engaged in fishing, towing or pushing.
– •••	Vessel being towed or, if more than one vessel is towed, the last vessel in the tow.

VESSELS AT ANCHOR

🔔	Bell, ring for 5 seconds every minute
🔔	Vessel >100m: Bell forward, ring for 5 seconds every minute; plus
⊙	Gong aft, for 5 seconds every minute.
• – •	Optional extra to warn any approaching vessel

Sailing vessels < 12m at ⚓ do not have to sound the above fog signals. But if they do not, they *must* make an efficient noise every 2 minutes.

INTERNATIONAL PORT TRAFFIC SIGNALS (IPTS)

IPTS are widely used on the Continent, but less so around the UK. They may also be used to control traffic at locks and bridges.

- The main movement signal is always 3 lights in a vertical column, to which no extra light shall be added. Thus it is always recognisable as IPTS, as distinct from some kind of navigational lights.

- Red lights ⓡ indicate *Do not proceed.*

- Green lights ⓖ indicate *Proceed, subject to the conditions stipulated.* To avoid confusion ⓡ and ⓖ lights are never displayed together.

- Signals may be omni-directional ie seen by all vessels simultaneously; or directional, ie seen only from outside or from inside the harbour.

- Some ports may only use signals 2 and 4, or only Signal 1 when necessary

- Signal 1 *Serious Emergency* must show at least 60 flashes/minute.

- All other signals may be fixed or slow occulting, eg every 10s (helpful when background glare poses a problem), but never a mixture of both.

- Signal 5 assumes that VHF, signal lamp, loud-hailer, auxiliary signal or other means of communication will specifically inform a vessel that she may proceed.

- Exemption signals. A single ⓨ light, shown to the left of signals 2 or 5 and level with the upper light, means *Vessels which can safely navigate outside the main channel need not comply with the main message.* This signal is obviously important to small craft, which nevertheless have a clear duty to keep clear of manoeuvring vessels.

- Auxiliary signals (only ⓦ and/or ⓨ lights) may be locally authorised and displayed to the right of the main signal. Their meanings must be promulgated.

No	Lights		Main message
1	⨳ⓡ⨳ ⨳ⓡ⨳ ⨳ⓡ⨳	Flashing	Serious emergency – all vessels to stop or divert according to instructions
2	ⓡ ⓡ ⓡ	Fixed or Slow Occulting	Vessels shall not proceed (*Note:* Some ports may use an exemption signal, as in 2a below)
3	ⓖ ⓖ ⓖ	Fixed or Slow Occulting	Vessels may proceed. One-way traffic
4	ⓖ ⓖ ⓦ	Fixed or Slow Occulting	Vessels may proceed. Two-way traffic
5	ⓖ ⓦ ⓖ	Fixed or Slow Occulting	A vessel may proceed only when she has received specific orders to do so. (*Note:* Some ports may use an exemption signal, as in 5a below)
Exemption signals and messages			
2a	ⓨ ⓡ ⓡ ⓡ	Fixed or Slow Occulting	Vessels shall not proceed, except that vessels which navigate outside the main channel need not comply with the main message
5a	ⓨ ⓖ ⓦ ⓖ	Fixed or Slow Occulting	A vessel may proceed when she has received specific orders to do so, except that vessels which navigate outside the main channel need not comply with the main message
Auxiliary signals and messages			
White and/or yellow lights, displayed with the main lights			

COMMUNICATIONS

Chapter 4 – Safety

LOOKOUT

The International Regulations for the Prevention of Collisions at Sea clearly define the requirement:

Rule 5 – Every vessel shall at all times maintain a proper lookout by sight and hearing as well as by all available means in the prevailing circumstances and conditions so as to make a full appraisal of the situation and of the risk of collision.

In UK waters in the last 3 years, three serious incidents have been investigated, in which small craft have been in collision with larger vessels.

i) On 11 Feb 2011 the container ship *MV Boxford* collided with the fishing vessel *Admiral Blake* south of Start Pt. The fishing vessel was badly damaged and 2 crew members thrown overboard. They were safely recovered. The MAIB reported:

• Boxford's bridge team was unaware of the presence of *Admiral Blake* until shortly before the collision. Neither the visual nor the radar lookout was fully effective and the master, who was probably fatigued, inaccurately assessed the fishing vessel's proximity and movement.
• Had *Admiral Blake* been transmitting on her Automatic Identification System (AIS), *Boxford's* master would have been aware of the fishing vessel's presence much earlier. This would have allowed him more time to accurately assess the situation and to take appropriate action.

ii) On 6 Aug 2011, during Cowes week, the yacht *Atlanta of Chester* was in collision with the tanker *Hanne Knutsen* off Cowes. The yacht was dismasted and two crew members fell overboard. They were swiftly recovered. The yacht's skipper was prosecuted by the MCA in October 2013.

iii) On 5 Aug 2010 the ro-ro ferry *Scottish Viking* was in collision with the fishing vessel *Homeland* about 4 miles off St Abb's Head. The *Homeland* sank and a crew member was lost. The MAIB reported:

• *Scottish Viking's* watchkeeper did not: determine at an early stage if there was a risk of collision with *Homeland*; sufficiently monitor or plot *Homeland's* track; and, once a risk of collision was deemed to exist, take sufficient action to avoid collision.

• *Homeland's* watchkeeper did not: determine at an early stage if there was a risk of collision with *Scottish Viking*; maintain a proper lookout from the wheelhouse; or detect or recognise a risk of collision with *Scottish Viking* until it was too late to take effective action.

See full MAIB reports at: *http://www.maib.gov.uk/ publications/investigation_reports/*

These followed reported events in earlier years: In 2007 the LPG carrier *Gas Monarch* collided with the yacht *Whispa* off Lowestoft in restricted visibility. Later that year a bulk carrier *Alam Pintar* collided with a fishing vessel *Etoiles des Ondes* in the English Channel north of Cherbourg. The fishing vessel sank and a crew member was lost. In 2006 the yacht *Ouzo* sank and its crew of three were lost following a close quarters situation and possible collision with the ferry *Pride of Bilbao* south of St Catherine's Pt on the Isle of Wight.

These incidents emphasize the need for a proper lookout at all times in any condition of visibility. The purpose is 'to make a full appraisal of the situation and of the risk of collision'. A yacht or small craft must determine if it has been 'seen' by a vessel and monitor the avoiding action in accordance with Rule 8. If uncertain of another vessel's intentions, steps must be taken draw attention to the situation in time to allow action under Rule 17. Closing speed can be deceptive in small boats:

1Nm is covered in 3 minutes at a speed of 20kts.

On yachts, small workboats and fishing vessels it is a task which falls to everyone on board. Do the crew know what to look for, and do they have the confidence to draw attention to it? Other vessels and navigational marks are of obvious interest, so too are hazards such as fishing gear and debris, but will they recognise the unusual or untoward? A distress signal may be seen by a crew member, or a boat may appear 'odd', both drawing attention to a fellow seafarer in need of assistance.

It is not uncommon for a hazard to be recognised and then lost sight of as a new priority emerges. GPS, chartplotters, radar and now AIS add to the electronic comfort blanket that has multiplied the means of gathering information, and the amount of time spent in the process. Together with the radio they are a source of not only information, but also distraction to the short-handed skipper. A tactful reminder of 'that ship' may be welcome!

DISTRESS, URGENCY, SAFETY

MAYDAY (Distress) must only be used if a ship or person is in *grave and imminent danger and requires immediate assistance*. It may be appropriate for a man overboard if not quickly recovered.

PAN-PAN (Urgency) is appropriate for *a very urgent message concerning the safety of a vessel or person.*

SÉCURITÉ (Safety) is used typically by coast stations to announce navigational or weather warnings. May also be used by vessels to report a hazard.

DISTRESS CALL BY RADIO

A distress call may only be made with the skipper's authority, and only if the **boat or a person** is in **grave and imminent danger**. The initial call may be made by DSC or voice.

Distress alert by DSC

Depending on the particular layout of your radio, a distress alert is typically sent as follows:

Briefly press the red, guarded Distress button. The set will automatically switch to Ch 70. Press *again* for 5 seconds to transmit a basic distress alert* with position and time. The set then reverts to Ch 16.

*If time permits, select the nature of the distress from the menu (eg Collision, Fire, Flooding) then press the Distress button for 5 seconds to send a full distress alert.

A CG/CRS should automatically send a distress acknowledgement on Ch 70 before replying on Ch 16. Ships in range should reply directly on Ch 16. If a distress acknowledgement is not received from a CG/CRS, the distress alert will automatically be repeated by the radio every four minutes.

When a DSC distress acknowledgement has been received, or after about 15 seconds, the vessel in distress should transmit a MAYDAY message by voice on Ch 16 (see below), including its MMSI and callsign.

False alerts

If a distress alert is inadvertently transmitted, an All Stations voice message on VHF Ch 16 cancelling the false alert must be sent at once: 'Cancel my Distress Alert of (date/time (GMT/UT)'.

MAYDAY call by voice

The MAYDAY message format below should be displayed near the radio. A MAYDAY call by voice should usually be sent on VHF Ch 16. A distress call has priority over all other transmissions. If you hear a MAYDAY call, immediately cease all transmissions that may interfere with the call, listen on the frequency concerned and note down the details.

Before making the call check that the radio is ON, and that HIGH POWER (25 watts) and Ch 16 are selected.

Press and hold down the transmit button, and say slowly and distinctly:

MAYDAY MAYDAY MAYDAY

THIS IS ....
(name of boat, spoken three times)

MAYDAY ....
(name of boat spoken once)

MY POSITION IS ....
(latitude and longitude or true bearing and distance *from* a known point)

Nature of distress ....
(sinking, on fire etc)

Help required ....
(immediate assistance)

Number of persons on board ....

Any other important, helpful information ..
(you are taking to the liferaft; distress rockets are being fired etc)

OVER

Release the transmit button and listen.

MAYDAY acknowledgement
An acknowledgement should be expected:

MAYDAY ....
(name of vessel sending the distress message, spoken three times)

THIS IS ....
(name of station acknowledging, spoken three times)

RECEIVED MAYDAY

If an acknowledgement is not received, check the set and repeat the distress call.

If you hear a distress message, write down the details and, if you can help, acknowledge accordingly but only after giving an opportunity for the nearest Coastguard station or more suitable vessel to do so.

MAYDAY relay
If you hear a distress message from a vessel which is not acknowledged, you should pass on the message as follows:

MAYDAY RELAY ....
(spoken three times)

THIS IS ....
(name of vessel re-transmitting the distress message, spoken three times), followed by the intercepted message.

HELICOPTER RESCUE

- **COMMUNICATE ON CHANNEL 16**
- Use flares or smoke when helicopter is seen or heard
- Helicopter may ask you to drop sails and motor on a specific course
- You may be asked to stream the casualty astern in the dinghy
- Brief your crew early (too noisy when helicopter is close)
- **MAINTAIN YOUR COURSE** and do not get distracted
- Weighted line lowered
- Let it touch boat or water first (to earth any static charge)
- Take in slack line only
- **PULL LINE IN AS DIRECTED**
- **DO NOT SECURE IT TO THE BOAT**
- **DO EXACTLY AS YOU ARE TOLD**
  Note: The text and sketch relate to a Hi-line transfer, one of several techniques which may be used

SAFETY

URGENT MEDICAL HELP - PAN PAN

- **Send an URGENCY call by DSC**, if possible, and/or...
- **Make a PAN PAN voice call:**
- **CHANNEL 16, HIGH POWER (25W)** (if necessary, turn off dual watch)
- **PAN PAN** .... (repeat 3 times)
- **ALL STATIONS** .... (repeat 3 times)
- **THIS IS** .... (vessel's name; repeat 3 times)
- **OVER**
  Next message should include:
  Yacht's name, callsign, nationality
  Yacht's position and nearest harbour
  Patient's details, symptoms and advice wanted
  The medication you have on board

FIRST AID

The objectives of First Aid at sea are to:

• **Preserve life** • **Prevent further damage**
• **Relieve pain and distress**
• **Deliver a live casualty ashore**

With any casualty be calm, reassuring and methodical. First ensure your own safety and that of the vessel. If in doubt call for advice and assistance.

Completion of a First Aid Course is strongly recommended. In the UK, RYA approved, one-day, basic training is available through sailing clubs and schools. The St Johns Ambulance and British Red Cross provide a variety of recognised courses.

MEDICAL ADVICE can be obtained almost anywhere in European waters by making an All Stations 'PAN PAN' call or a DSC Urgency Alert to the Coastguard or to a Coast Radio Station. You will then be connected to a doctor or to the nearest hospital.

The Urgency signal 'PAN PAN' is always advised, especially abroad, because it is internationally understood and eliminates most language problems; it is also free.

If you are not qualified to judge how serious the casualty's condition is, get the best possible advice and/or help as quickly as possible. **Urgent help needed** is shown against the more serious medical problems.

Be ready to describe the patient's symptoms, eg consciousness, pulse rate, breathing rate, temperature, skin colour, site and type of injury, any pain, amount of blood lost etc. If a doctor needs to come aboard, or a casualty has to be landed, the Coastguard will arrange.

If non-urgent, wait until in harbour. Consider calling the port authority before arrival so that a doctor or paramedic can meet you on arrival.

MEDICAL CARE ABROAD It is advisable for each person on board to carry the European Health Insurance Card (EHIC) which entitles you to medical treatment on a reciprocal basis, although it may not cover the full charge. See *www.dh.gov.uk* for full details.

EMERGENCY RESUSCITATION (ABC)

The immediate procedure for any collapsed or apparently unconscious person is: Assess whether or not the casualty is conscious. Carefully shake his/her shoulders and ask loudly 'What's happened?' or 'Are you all right?' or give a command such as 'Open your eyes'. An unconscious casualty will not respond.

A = Airway

Remove any visible obstruction from the casualty's mouth (leave well-fitting dentures in place). Listen at the mouth for breathing. Tilt the head backwards, using head tilt and chin lift to maintain a clear airway.

Look, listen and feel for *no more than 10 seconds* to determine if the casualty is breathing normally. If in any doubt, act as if it is *not* normal.

If breathing, place casualty in recovery position. Check the area is clear of danger.

B = Breathing and C = Circulation

If not breathing and the airway is clear, start chest compressions. This situation is called **cardiac arrest**. The casualty will be unconscious and may appear very pale, grey or bluish in colour. An artificial circulation will have to be provided by chest compression. If the circulation stops, the breathing will also stop. Casualties with cardiac arrest will need both rescue breathing and chest compression, a combination known as Cardio Pulmonary Resuscitation (**CPR**).

External chest compression

To start external chest compression, lay the casualty face up on a hard, flat surface. Kneel beside casualty. Place the heel of your hand on top of the other hand and interlock your fingers. Apply pressure at the centre of the chest.

Depress breastbone 5–6cm (2-2½in) then release.

With either one or two operators give 30 chest compressions and continue cycles of 2 breaths to 30 compressions. Use a compression rate of 100 per minute. Chest compression should be combined with rescue breaths; after 30 compressions, give 2 effective rescue breaths (2 breaths should not take more than 5 seconds). *Do not stop.*

Action plan for the resuscitation of adults

Casualty unconscious but is breathing normally:

• *Urgent help needed*
• Turn casualty into the recovery position
• Check for continued breathing

Casualty is unconscious and not breathing:

• *Urgent help needed*
• Start chest compressions
• After 30 compressions, give 2 rescue breaths

Continue with chest compressions and rescue breaths in a ratio of 30:2. If you are untrained, or are unwilling to give rescue breaths, give chest compressions only. Stop to re-check casualty only if he/she starts to show signs of regaining consciousness; coughing, opening eyes, speaking or moving purposefully *and* starts to breath normally. If so place the casualty in the recovery position. Otherwise, *do not interrupt resuscitation*.

BITES AND STINGS Injected poison from bites and stings usually only causes local swelling and discomfort, but some people may react severely. For insect stings, resuscitate if collapse occurs; otherwise give rest, painkillers, antihistamines (eg chlorpheniramine).

BLEEDING – OPEN WOUND Bleeding is often very dramatic, but is virtually always controllable.
• Apply firm continuous direct pressure; bandage on a large pad. If bleeding continues, bandage more pads on top of initial pads; then press directly over wound for at least 10 minutes (blood takes this long to clot).
• Elevate if wound is on a limb.
• Do *not* apply a tourniquet. This practice is out of date due to the danger of losing a limb.

BLEEDING – INTERNAL (CLOSED INJURY)
Follows fractured bones, crush injuries, or rupture of organs such as the liver or spleen. Treat for shock which may appear rapidly. *Urgent help needed*.

BURNS AND SCALDS Move the victim into fresh air to avoid inhaling smoke.

ABC – Airway, Breathing, Circulation
• Stop further injury: dip the whole of the burnt part into cold water for 10–15 minutes. Seawater is excellent but may be very painful.
• Remove only loose clothing. Do not pull off clothing stuck to the skin.
• Cover with sterile dressing. If skin is broken or blistered, use sterile paraffin gauze beneath the dressing. Separate burnt fingers with paraffin gauze. Never use adhesive dressings.
• Do not prick blisters or apply ointments.
• Elevate burnt limb and immobilise.
• Give strong painkillers.
• Treat for shock: give frequent and copious drinks of water.
• Start giving antibiotics for major burns. If burns extensive or deep, *urgent help needed*.

CHOKING If blockage by some object (eg a peanut) is suspected, turn the casualty on his side and give up to 5 sharp back slaps with the flat of the hand between the shoulder blades. Check mouth and remove any obstruction.

If unsuccessful, wrap both arms around the victim's waist from behind, and give 5 sharp upward thrusts with both fists into the abdomen above the navel but below the ribs so as to cause coughing. Clear object from mouth.

CUTS AND WOUNDS Often dramatic but only potentially serious if nerves, tendons or blood vessels are severed.

Clean thoroughly with antiseptic. Remove dirt or other foreign bodies. Small clean cuts can be closed using as many Steristrips as necessary to keep the skin edges together. Skin must be dry. Leave for 5 days at least. Larger deep cuts may require stitches; apply a dressing and seek help. Do not try amateur surgery at sea.

Ragged lacerations or very dirty wounds – do not attempt to close these. Clean as well as possible, sprinkle antibiotic powder in wound and apply a dressing. Seek help. If in doubt a wound is best left open and lightly covered to keep it clean and dry.

Fingers and toes Blood may collect under the nail following an injury. Release the blood by piercing the nail with a red hot needle or paper clip. It will not hurt!

DENTAL PAIN seems worse at sea; prevention is better than cure. Dentanurse is an emergency treatment pack which enables an amateur to make temporary repairs, eg replacing crowns, lost fillings. It contains zinc oxide and Eugenol.

Throbbing toothache made worse by hot or cold or when bitten on. Clean out any cavity and apply temporary filling. Take painkiller.

Dull toothache tender to bite on; gum swollen or red with possible discharge. Treat as above but also take an antibiotic.

Broken tooth or filling Cover exposed surfaces with zinc oxide paste. Teeth knocked out should be put in a clean container with milk or moist gauze for a dentist to re-implant asap. This can be attempted onboard - ideally within 1 hour

Bleeding gums Clean teeth more thoroughly. Use regular hot salt water rinses and antibiotics.

Pain round wisdom tooth Clean area with toothbrush; use hot salt water rinses; take antibiotics and painkillers.

Mouth ulcers Hot salt water rinses.

DIARRHOEA Can become serious, especially in young children if much fluid is lost. Stop food, give plenty of fluid. Plain water is usually sufficient, or add salt (1 teaspoonful/litre) and sugar (4–5 teaspoons/litre). Lomotil or Imodium tablets are very effective in adults.

DROWNING ABC Clear seaweed, dentures. If not breathing start mouth to mouth ventilation as soon as possible and in the water if practicable. If no pulse, start chest compression as soon as on board. Keep the head low so that vomit is not inhaled and water can drain.

If stomach is bulging, turn casualty on to side to empty water and avoid inhaling it. Prevent cooling. Remove wet clothes; wrap casualty in blankets to warm him/her.

SAFETY

133

Continue resuscitation until the casualty revives or death is certain. Hypothermia may mimic death. Do not abandon resuscitation until the casualty has been warmed or signs of death persist despite attempts at warming.

Once revived, put in the recovery position.

Any person rescued from drowning may collapse in the next 24 hours as the lungs react to inhaled water. *Urgent help needed*.

EYE INJURIES are potentially serious. Never put old or previously opened ointment or drops into an eye; serious infection could result.

Foreign object Flush with clean water, pull the lower lid out to inspect, remove object with a clean tissue. For objects under upper eyelid, ask casualty to grasp lashes and pull the upper lid over the lower lid. An eye-bath is very effective. Blinking under water may help. After removal of object, insert sterile antibiotic ointment inside pulled out lower lid. Cover with pad.

Corrosive fluid Flush continuously with water for 15 minutes. Give painkillers and chloramphenicol ointment; cover with pad. *Seek help asap*.

Conjunctivitis Sticky, weeping eye with yellow discharge. Chloramphenicol 4 times a day.

FISH HOOKS Push the hook round until the point and barb can be cut off; withdraw the hook. Dress the holes and give an antibiotic.

FRACTURES AND DISLOCATIONS Fracture is a broken bone. Dislocation is a displaced joint. Both produce pain (aggravated by attempted movement), localised swelling, abnormal shape, and a grating feeling on movement (if it is a fracture). Blood vessels or nerves around the fracture or dislocation may also be damaged causing a cold, pale, or numb limb below the site of the injury.

Fractures of large bones such as the femur (upper leg) will result in major internal bleeding and may cause shock. When complications occur *urgent help is needed*.

Early application of a splint and raising the injured limb where possible will reduce pain and complications. Treat for shock and pain.

Specific fractures and dislocations

Cheek Caused by a direct blow. Rarely serious but requires specialist care.

Jaw Beware of associated brain or spinal injury. Remove blood and teeth fragments; leave loose teeth in place; protect broken teeth. Ensure airway is clear. Start regular antiseptic mouth washes and antibiotics. Support jaw with bandage over top of the head. Give only fluids by mouth.

Neck May result from a direct blow, a fall or a whiplash type injury. If conscious, casualty may complain of pain, tingling, numbness or weakness in limbs below the injury. *Mishandling may damage the spinal cord, causing paralysis or death*. Avoid movement and support the head. Immobilise by wrapping a folded towel around the neck. If movement is necessary then lift the victim as one rigid piece, never allowing the neck to bend. *Urgent help needed*.

Nose Control bleeding by pinching.

Ribs Very painful. Strapping is not advised.

Spine Fracture of the spine below the neck, may cause *paralysis or death*. Mishandling of the victim may greatly worsen the damage. Avoid movement if possible. Lift the casualty without allowing the spine to sag. *Urgent help needed*.

Collar bone Support arm in sling.

Dislocated shoulder If this has happened before, the casualty may remedy the dislocation himself; otherwise do not attempt to remedy it in case a fracture exists.

Upper arm Support the arm with a collar and cuff inside the shirt, ie tie a clove hitch around the wrist and loop the ends behind the neck.

Forearm and wrist Splint (eg with battens or wood). Do not bandage tightly. Elevate or support in a sling.

Fingers Elevate hand and, unless badly crushed, leave unbandaged; keep moving. If very wobbly, bandage to adjacent finger.

Lower limb

Thigh Shock may be considerable. Strap to other leg with padding between. Gently straighten the lower leg. If necessary apply traction at the ankle to help straighten the leg. Do not bandage too tightly.

Knee Twisting injuries or falls damage the ligaments and cartilages of the knee. Very painful and swollen. Treat as for fracture.

Lower leg Pad very well. Splint using oar, broom handle or similar pieces of wood.

Ankle Fracture or severe sprain may be indistinguishable. Immobilise in neutral position with foot at right angles. Raise the limb.

HEART ATTACK Severe 'crushing' chest pain; may spread to shoulders, neck or arms. Sweating, then bluish lips, then collapse. Breathing and heart may stop. Give one 300mg aspirin tablet (to chew) *Urgent help needed*.

Rest, reassure. If unconscious: recovery position; observe breathing and pulse. If breathing stops or no pulse, start mouth to mouth ventilation and chest compression immediately; do not stop.

STROKE Symptoms: if a person develops **sudden** onset weakness on one side of the body, problems with speech &/or visual problems: *think of stroke*.

Recognise a stroke using the FAST test:
- Face – Has side of face fallen; can they smile?
- Arms – Can both arms be raised and kept up?
- Speech – Is it slurred or muddled?
- Time – To call for help.

Place in recovery position and check airway. *Urgent help needed* – specialist treatment within 4½ hours can reverse the effects of a stroke. If you are more than 4½ hours from help, and the casualty is conscious and able to swallow, give 300mg of asprin even if he/she is improving.

HEAT STROKE Cool casualty by spraying with cold water or wrap the casualty in a cold wet sheet until their temperature under the tongue falls to 38°C. Encourage drinking (1 teaspoon of salt/ half litre of water). If casualty stops sweating, has a rapid pounding pulse and is becoming unconscious: *Urgent help needed.*

HYPOTHERMIA Symptoms: unreasonable behaviour, apathy and confusion; unsteady gait, stumbling; slurring of speech; pale, cold skin; slow, weak pulse; slow breathing; shivering. It leads to collapse, unconsciousness and ultimately death.

ABC Put in recovery position. If not breathing, start mouth to mouth ventilation. Be prepared to use chest compressions.

Remove wet clothing. Avoid wind chill. Dry and wrap in blankets or sleeping bag plus warm hat and cover, if available, in foil survival bag. *Urgent help needed.*

Give hot sweet drinks if conscious. Do not give alcohol, rub or place very hot objects against skin.

SEASICKNESS is aggravated by anxiety, fatigue and boredom. Symptoms: lethargy, dizziness, headache and nausea/vomiting. Help prevent with anti-seasickness pills, avoiding rich foods and alcohol. Take frequent small amounts of fluid and food. Keep warm; keep busy. Prolonged seasickness may cause serious loss of fluid – seek advice.

SHOCK can result from almost any accident or medical emergency; it can lead to collapse.

Signs and symptoms Thirst, apathy, nausea, restlessness. Pale, cold, clammy skin, sweating. Rapid, weak pulse. Rapid, shallow breathing. Dull, sunken eyes, bluish lips.

ABC Control any bleeding. Lay the casualty flat or in recovery position; raise legs 20°. Splint any fractures; avoid movement. Avoid chilling, keep warm. Give pain killers. Reassure the casualty. Do not let the casualty eat, drink, smoke or move unnecessarily. If complaining of thirst, moisten the lips with a little water. Note: Fluids may be life saving in cases of dehydration (eg diarrhoea, vomiting, severe burns).

FIRST AID KIT

Stow the following items in a waterproof container, readily accessible and clearly marked:

Triangular bandage x 2 (doubles as a sling)
Crepe bandage 75mm x 2
Gauze bandage 50mm x 2
Elastoplast 75mm x 1
Band Aids (or similar) various shapes and sizes
Wound dressings, 1 large, 1 medium
Sterile non-adhesive dressing (Melolin) x 5
Steristrips x 5 packs
Cotton wool. Safety pins. Thermometer.
Scissors and forceps, good quality stainless steel
Disposable gloves
Antiseptic solution (eg Savlon)
Sunscreen with high protection factor
Antifungal powder or cream (athlete's foot)
Insect repellent (DEET, diethyltoluamide)
Individual choice of anti-seasick tablets
Antibiotic eye ointment (prescription only)

Additional items for extended cruising
Vaccinations – a course may need to start as much as 6 months before departure.
Syringes 2ml x 2 (if carrying injections)
Dental kit – see Dental pain.

DRUGS AND MEDICATION

Paracetamol, painkiller. 1-2 500mg tablets 4 hrly.
Asprin, blood thiner. 300mg single dose for heart attack or stroke.
Ibuprofen, anti-inflammatory. 400mg every 8 hours (avoid if history of asthma or stomach ulcer).
*Dihydrocodeine, strong painkiller. 1-2 30mg tablets 4 hourly.
Certirizine, antihistamine. 10mg once a day.
Aludrox, indigestion. 1-2 before meals.
Loperamide, diarrhoea. 2 x 2mg capsules initially, then 1 after each loose stool; max 8 day.
Senokot, constipation. 2-4 tablets per day.
*Amoxycillin, antibiotic. 2 x 250mg capsules 8 hourly (beware penicillin allergy)
*Erythromycin, antibiotic for penicillin-allergic adults. 4 x 250mg tablets daily.
Cinnarizine, seasickness. 2 x 15mg tablets before sailing, then 1 every 8 hours.
*Scopolamine patches, seasickness. 1 patch behind ear 5-6 hours before voyage; replace after 72 hrs if necessary.
Chloramphenicol ointment 1%, eye infection, apply 3-4 times/day
*   Only available on prescription.

OBSERVATION FORM

The information recorded by you on this form will be invaluable in helping doctors and/or paramedics ashore to diagnose the problem and arrange the best possible treatment for your casualty.

This is particularly important if there may be a considerable time lapse between requesting medical help and the casualty reaching hospital.

- Keep photocopies of this form in your First Aid kit so as to preserve the original.
  Whilst awaiting help, record your careful

observations by ticking or annotating the various boxes at 10 minute intervals. This will help doctors detect any improvement or deterioration in the casualty's condition.

- If within radio range of shore attempt to pass the observations via the Coastguard to a medical authority; or ask a ship to relay.

- Before the casualty is taken off the yacht ensure that this form and personal documents (money, passport, EHIC and mobile 'phone) are securely tied to him/her.

DATE .... CASUALTY'S NAME .... AGE .... M/F ....

Times of observations @ 10 minute intervals:		10	20	30	40	50	60
EYES Observe for reactions whilst testing other responses	Open spontaneously						
	Open when spoken to						
	Open to painful stimulus						
	Nil response						
MOVEMENT Apply painful stimulus: Pinch ear lobe or skin on back of hand	Obeys commands						
	Responds						
	Nil response						
SPEECH Speak clearly and directly, close to the casualty's ear	Responds sensibly to queries						
	Seems confused						
	Uses inappropriate words						
	Incomprehensible sounds						
	Nil response						
PULSE (Beats per minute) Take adult's pulse at wrist or neck. Note rate and whether beats are: weak (w); strong (s); regular (reg) or irregular (irreg)	Over 110						
	101-110						
	91-100						
	81-90						
	71-80						
	61-70						
	Below 61						
BREATHING (Breaths per minute) Note rate and whether breathing is: quiet (q); noisy (n); easy (e); or difficult (d)	Over 40						
	31-40						
	21-30						
	11-20						
	Below 11						

GMDSS

The Global Maritime Distress and Safety System (GMDSS) is a sophisticated, but complex, semi-automatic, third-generation communications system. Although not compulsory for yachts, its potential for saving life, particularly when far offshore and out of VHF range, is so great that every yachtsman should seriously consider it. Equipment costs continue to fall. Training courses, leading to the award of the Short Range Certificate (SRC) of Competence, are widely available. The Long Range Certificate covers MF, HF, SatCom, EPIRBs and SART.

Recommended reading:

- *ALRS, Vol 5* (UK Hydrographic Office)
- *GMDSS: a User's Handbook* (Bréhaut/ACN)
- *GMDSS for small craft* (Clemmetsen/ Fernhurst)
- *Reeds VHF/DSC Handbook* (Fletcher/ACN)

Purpose

GMDSS enables a coordinated SAR operation to be mounted rapidly and reliably anywhere at sea. To this end, terrestrial and satellite communications and navigation equipment is used to alert SAR authorities ashore and ships in the vicinity to a Distress incident or Urgency situation. GMDSS also promulgates Maritime Safety Information.

Sea areas

For the purposes of GMDSS, the world's sea areas are divided into 4 categories (A1-4), defined mainly by the range of radio communications. These are:

A1 An area within R/T coverage of at least one VHF Coastguard or Coast radio station in which continuous VHF alerting is available via DSC. Range: 20–50M from the CG/CRS.

A2 An area, excluding sea area A1, within R/T coverage of at least one MF CG/ CRS in which continuous DSC alerting is available. Range: approx 50–250M from the CG/CRS.

A3 An area between 76°N and 76°S, excluding sea areas A1 and A2, within coverage of HF or an Inmarsat satellite in which continuous alerting is available.

A4 An area outside sea areas A1, A2 and A3, ie the polar regions, within coverage of HF.

In each category of sea area certain types of radio equipment must be carried by GMDSS vessels: in A1 areas VHF DSC; A2 areas VHF and MF DSC; A3 areas VHF, MF and HF or SatCom; A4 VHF, MF and HF.

Most UK yachtsmen will operate in A1 areas (the English Channel, for example, is an A1 area) where a simple VHF radio and a Navtex receiver will initially meet GMDSS requirements. As equipment becomes more affordable, yachtsmen may decide to fit GMDSS. This will become increasingly necessary as the present system for sending and receiving Distress calls is run down. The CG will continue a loudspeaker watch on VHF Ch 16 until further notice.

Functions

Regardless of the sea areas in which they operate, vessels complying with GMDSS must be able to perform certain functions:

- transmit ship-to-shore Distress alerts by two independent means
- receive shore-to-ship Distress alerts
- transmit & receive ship-to-ship Distress alerts
- transmit signals for locating incidents
- transmit and receive communications for SAR co-ordination
- transmit/receive maritime safety info, eg navigation and weather warnings

Distress alerts

A Distress alert is simply a Distress call using DSC. It is transmitted on Ch 70 and is automatically repeated five times. Whenever possible, a Distress alert should always include the last known position and time in UT. The position is normally entered automatically from an interfaced GPS, but can be entered manually if required. The nature of the distress can also be selected from the receiver's menu. The vessel's identity (MMSI number) is automatically included.

GMDSS requires participating ships to be able to send Distress alerts by two out of three independent means. These are:

- Digital Selective Calling (DSC) using terrestrial communications, ie VHF Ch 70, MF 2187·5 kHz, or HF distress and alerting frequencies in the 4, 6, 8,12 and 16 MHz bands.
- Emergency Position Indicating Radio Beacons (EPIRBs). See below.
- Inmarsat, via ship terminals.

Digital Selective Calling

DSC is an essential component of GMDSS. It is so called because information is sent by a burst of digital code; selective because it can be addressed to a specific DSC-equipped vessel or to a selected group of vessels.

In all DSC messages every vessel and relevant shore station has a 9-digit identification number, or MMSI (Maritime Mobile Service Identity), which is in effect an automatic, electronic callsign.

DSC is used to transmit Distress alerts from ships, to receive Distress acknowledgements from ships or shore stations; to send Urgency and Safety alerts; to relay Distress alerts; and for routine calling & answering. A thorough working knowledge is needed.

Maritime Safety Information (MSI)

MSI consists of the vital navigational, weather and safety messages which traditionally were sent to vessels at sea by CRS in Morse, but by R/T on VHF and MF in more recent years – and now by GMDSS. For navigation and weather warnings see this and chapter 2 respectively.

GMDSS transmits MSI in English by two independent but complementary means, Navtex and SafetyNet.

- Navtex on MF (518 kHz and 490 kHz) which can be received out to about 300 miles offshore, see Chapter 2.
- SafetyNet uses Inmarsat-C satellites to cover beyond MF range, except Area A4. Enhanced Group Calling (EGC) is a part of SafetyNet which enables MSI to be sent to selected groups of users in any of the four oceans.

Emergency Position Indicating Radio Beacons (EPIRB) may be hand-held or float-free, they transmit on 406 MHz. (Note that 121·5 MHz, 243·0 MHz and L-band EPIRBS are no longer used.) Most EPIRBs have a built in GPS and about 48 hours of battery life. They communicate via the Cospas-Sarsat (C/S) network of geostationary and polar orbit satellites. Although C/S will relay an EPIRB signal to earth with no delay, the position of a non-GPS EPIRB may take several hours to determine. The cost of an EPIRB ranges from less than £300 to more than £1000 for float-free, GPS models.

An EPIRB transmits data which is uniquely coded to identify the individual beacon and, because it may be transmitting from anywhere in the world, it must be registered. The UK registration centre is:

The EPIRB Registry, The Maritime and Coastguard Agency, MRCC Falmouth, Pendennis Point, Castle Drive, Falmouth, Cornwall TR11 4WZ; n 01326 211569; email: epirb@mcga.gov.uk.

It is just as important that any changes are immediately notified. False alerts caused by inadvertent or incorrect use of EPIRBs put a significant burden on SAR Centres and may coincide with an actual distress situation.

All crew members should be aware of the proper use of the particular EPIRB onboard. Make sure that testing is adequately supervised; that the EPIRB is correctly installed and maintained; and that it is not activated if assistance is already available. If an EPIRB is activated accidentally, make every effort to advise the nearest MRCC of the false alert as soon as possible.

Personal Locator Beacons (PLB) operate on the same principle. They must also be registered but they do not have a vessel-specific MMSI. A PLB with GPS costs about £200.

Search And Rescue Transponders (SART) are radar transceivers which operate on 9 GHz and respond to 3 cm (X-band) radars, like a small portable Racon (see Chapter 3). They are primarily intended for use in liferafts to help searching ships and aircraft find survivors. The transmitted signal shows on a radar screen as 12 dots radiating out from the SART's position. A SART costs about £500.

HM COASTGUARD – MRCC CONTACT DETAILS

EASTERN REGION

PORTLAND COASTGUARD

50°36'N 02°27'W. DSC MMSI 002320012
Custom House Quay, Weymouth DT4 8BE.
☎ 01305 760439. 📠 01305 760452.
Area: Topsham to Chewton Bunney (50°44'N 01°42'W)

SOLENT COASTGUARD

50°48'N 01°12'W. DSC MMSI 002320011
44A Marine Parade West, Lee-on-Solent, PO13 9NR.
☎ 02392 552100. 📠 02392 554131.
Area: Chewton Bunney to Beachy Hd.
Call on Ch 67 to keep Ch 16 clear.

DOVER COASTGUARD
50°08'N 01°20'E. DSC MMSI 002320010
Langdon Battery, Dover CT15 5NA.
☎ 01304 210008. 🖷 01304 225762.
Area: Beachy Head to Reculver Towers (51°23'N 01°12'E). Operates Channel Navigation Information Service.

THAMES COASTGUARD
51°51'N 01°17'E. MMSI 002320009
East Terrace, Walton-on-the-Naze CO14 8PY.
☎ 01255 675518. 🖷 01255 675249.
Area: Reculver Towers to Southwold.

LONDON COASTGUARD
51°30'N 00°03'E. MMSI 002320063
Thames Barrier Navigation Centre, Unit 28,
34 Bowater Rd, Woolwich, London SE18 5TF.
☎ 0208 312 7380. 🖷 0208 312 7679.
Area: River Thames from Shell Haven Pt (N bank) & Egypt Bay (S bank) up-river to Teddington Lock.

†HUMBER COASTGUARD
54°06'N 00°11'W. MMSI 002320007
Lime Kiln Lane, Bridlington,
N Humberside YO15 2LX.
☎ 01262 672317. 🖷 01262 606915.
Area: Southwold to Scottish border.

SCOTLAND & NORTHERN IRELAND

†ABERDEEN COASTGUARD
57°08'N 02°05'W. MMSI 002320004
Marine House, Blaikies Quay, Aberdeen AB11 5PB.
☎ 01224 592334. 🖷 01224 212862.
Area: S of Brora to English/Scottish border.

†SHETLAND COASTGUARD
60°09'N 01°08'W. MMSI 002320001
Knab Road, Lerwick ZE1 0AX.
☎ 01595 692976. 🖷 01595 694810.
Area: Orkney, Fair Isle and Shetland and mainland from C Wrath to S of Brora, incl Pentland Firth.

†*STORNOWAY COASTGUARD
58°12'N 06°22'W. MMSI 002320024
Battery Pt, Stornoway, Isle of Lewis H51 2RT.
☎ 01851 702013. 🖷 01851 704387.
Area: Cape Wrath to Ardnamurchan Pt, Western Isles and St Kilda; Ardnamurchan Pt to Mull of Galloway inc islands shared with Belfast CG.

†*BELFAST COASTGUARD
54°40'N 05°40'W. MMSI 002320021
Bregenz House, Quay St, Bangor, Co Down BT20 5ED.
☎ 02891 463933. 🖷 02891 465886.
Area: Carlingford Lough to Lough Foyle.

WESTERN REGION

LIVERPOOL COASTGUARD
53°30'N 03°03'W. MMSI 002320019
Hall Rd West, Crosby, Liverpool L23 8SY.
☎ 0151 9313341. 🖷 0151 9313347
Area: Mull of Galloway to Queensferry (near Chester).

†HOLYHEAD COASTGUARD
53°19'N 04°38'W. MMSI 002320018
Prince of Wales Rd, Holyhead,
Anglesey LL65 1ET.
☎ 01407 762051. 🖷 01407 764373.
Area: Queensferry to Friog (S of Barmouth).

†MILFORD HAVEN COASTGUARD
51°42'N 05°03'W. MMSI 002320017
Gorsewood Drive, Hakin,
Milford Haven, SA73 2HD.
☎ 01646 690909. 🖷 01646 692176.
Area: Friog to River Towy (11M N of Worms Head).

SWANSEA COASTGUARD
51°34'N 03°58'W. MMSI 002320016
Tutt Head, Mumbles, Swansea SA3 4EX.
☎ 01792 366534. 🖷 01792 369005.
Area: River Towy to Marsland Mouth (near Bude).

†*FALMOUTH COASTGUARD
50°09'N 05°03'W. MMSI 002320014
Pendennis Point, Castle Drive,
Falmouth TR11 4WZ.
☎ 01326 317575. 🖷 01326 318342.
Area: Marsland Mouth (near Bude) to Dodman Point.

*BRIXHAM COASTGUARD
50°24'N 03°31'W. DSC MMSI 002320013
King's Quay, Brixham TQ5 9TW.
☎ 01803 882704. 🖷 01803 882780.
Area: Dodman Point to Topsham (R. Exe).

NOTES: †Monitors DSC MF 2187.5 kHz.
*Broadcasts Gunfacts/Subfacts.

SAFETY

NATIONAL COASTWATCH INSTITUTION

The National Coastwatch Institution (NCI) - www. nci.org.uk is a voluntary organisation keeping a visual watch along the UK's coast assisting the preservation and protection of life at sea. There are 49 operational stations (2013) manned by over 2000 volunteers. They are marked on the Area maps by ©, for Coastwatch. All NCI stations monitor VHF Ch 16 and will provide actual weather and sea state on request. Many are equipped with AIS Ⓐ, DSC Ⓓ and radar Ⓡ. Contact details:

Area 1

St Mary's	01720 422641
Gwennap Head ⒶⒹⓇ	01736 871351
Penzance ⒶⒹ	01736 367063
Bass Point (Lizard) ⒶⒹⓇ	01326 290212
Nare Point (Helford)ⒶⒹⓇ	01326 231113
Portscatho (w/ends only)	01872 580180
Charlestown Ⓡ	01726 817068
Polruan (Fowey) ⒶⓇ	01726 870291
Rame Head (Plymouth) ⒶⒹⓇ	01752 823706
Prawle Point (Salcombe) ⒶⒹⓇ	01548 511259
Froward Pt (Dartmouth) ⒶⒹⓇ	07976 505649
Torbay ⒶⒹⓇ	01803 411145
Teignmouth ⒶⒹⓇ	01626 772377
Exmouth Ⓓ	01395 222492
West Bay Ⓓ	07745 756872
Portland Bill ⒶⒹⓇ	01305 860178
St Alban's Head ⒶⒹⓇ	01929 439220

Area 2

Peveril Pt (Swanage) ⒶⒹⓇ	01929 422596
Needles Ⓐ	01983 754321
Calshot ⒶⒹⓇ	02380 893562
Lee on Solent ⒶⒹ	02392 556758
Gosport	02392 765194

Area 3

Shoreham ⒶⒹⓇ	01273 463292
Newhaven ⒶⓇ	01273 516464
Folkestone (Copt Pt) ⒶⒹ	01303 227132

Area 4

Herne Bay (w/ends only) ⒶⒹⓇ	01227 744454
Whitstable (w/ends only) Ⓓ	07864 646209
Holehaven (Canvey IS)ⒶⒹ	01268 696971
Southend (w/ends only) ⒶⒹ	07815 945210
Felixstowe Ⓓ	01394 670808
Gorleston (Gt Yarmouth) ⒶⒹⓇ	01493 440384
Caister ⒶⒹ	07527 977613
Mundesley ⒶⒹⓇ	01263 722399
Wells-next-the-Sea ⒶⒹⓇ	01328 710587
Skegness ⒶⒹⓇ	01754 610900
Mablethorpe ⒶⒹ	07958 038564
Hartlepool Ⓡ	01429 274931
Sunderland Life Brigade ⒶⓇ	01915 672579
Berwick (w/e; limited hrs)	07738 269071

Area 8

Rossall Point (Fleetwood) ⒶⒹⓇ	01253 681378
Porth Dinllean Ⓓ	07773 362005
Rhoscolyn Ⓐ	07887 955496
Morfa Bychan (Porthmadog) Ⓓ	07521 446050
Wooltack Point (St Brides) Ⓓ	01646 636802
Worms Head (Gower) Ⓓ	01792 390167

Area 9

Nells Point (Barry) ⒶⒹ	01446 420746
Boscastle ⒶⒹⓇ	01840 250965
Stepper Point (Padstow) ⒶⒹⓇ	01841 530039
St Agnes Head ⒶⓇ	01872 552073
St Ives ⒶⓇ	01736 799398
Cape Cornwall ⒶⒹⓇ	01736 787890

Royal National Lifeboat Institution

The RNLI is a registered charity which saves life at sea. It provides, on call H24, a lifeboat service up to 50M off the UK and Irish coasts.

There are over 230 lifeboat stations, 130 all-weather and 191 inshore LBs from 4·9 to 17·0m LOA, plus 3 hovercraft. There are 131 LBs in the reserve fleet. All new LBs are capable of at least 25 knots.

When launched on service, lifeboats >10m keep watch on VHF and MF DSC as well as VHF Ch 16. They can also use alternative frequencies to contact other vessels, SAR aircraft, HM CG, Coast radio stations or other SAR agencies. All lifeboats show a quick-flashing blue light when on operational service.

The RNLI also actively promotes safety at sea by providing a free comprehensive safety service to members and the general public including advice, publications and demonstrations. The RNLI aims to save lives and prevent accidents by helping people be prepared through water safety awareness.

A useful A5 size, ring-bound RNLI Handbook covers emergencies, first aid, seamanship, weather, navigation and engines. It is recommended.

For more details of how the RNLI can help you to be safer at sea, to support the work of the RNLI by becoming a Shoreline Member, Offshore Member or a Governor call the RNLI on 0845 122 6999, or visit www.rnli.org.uk.

The headquarters are at: RNLI, West Quay Road, Poole, Dorset BH15 1HZ.

THE CHANNEL ISLANDS

Guernsey and Jersey Coastguard stations direct SAR operations in the North and South of the CI area respectively, they also provide communications on VHF and DSC.

Close liaison is maintained with adjacent French SAR authorities. A distress situation may be controlled by the Channel Islands or France, whichever is more appropriate. For example a British yacht in difficulty in French waters may be handled by St Peter Port or Jersey so as to avoid language problems; and vice versa for a French yacht.

GUERNSEY CG 49°27'·00N 02°32'00W. DSC MMSI 002320064. ☎ 01481 720672. ᠍ 714177. Area: Channel Islands North.

JERSEY CG   49°10'·85N 02°14'30W. DSC MMSI 002320060. ☎: 01534 447705/04. ᠍: 499089. Area: Channel Islands South.

SEARCH AND RESCUE ABROAD
THE IRISH REPUBLIC

The Irish CG co-ordinates SAR operations around the coast of Ireland via Dublin MRCC, Malin Head and Valentia MRSCs and remote sites. It may liaise with the UK and France during any rescue operation within 100M of the Irish coast.

It is part of the Dept of Marine, Leeson Lane, Dublin 2. ☎ (01) 6620922; ᠍ (01) 6620795. The Irish EPIRB Registry is co-located; ☎ (01) 6199280; ᠍ (01) 6621571.

The MRCC/MRSCs are co-located with the Coast radio stations of the same name and manned by the same staff. All stations keep watch H24 on VHF Ch 16 and DSC Ch 70. If ashore dial 999 or 112 in an emergency and ask for Marine Rescue.

Details of the MRCC/MRSCs are as follows:

DUBLIN (MRCC)
53°20'N 06°15W. DSC MMSI 002500300 (+2187·5 kHz).
☎ +353 1 662 0922/3; ᠍ +353 1 662 0795.
Area: Carlingford Lough to Youghal.

VALENTIA (MRSC)
51°56'N 10°21'W. DSC MMSI 002500200 (+2187·5 kHz).
☎ +353 669 476 109; ᠍ +353 669 476 289.
Area: Youghal to Slyne Head.

MALIN HEAD (MRSC)
55°22'N 07°20W. DSC MMSI 002500100 (+2187·5 kHz).
☎ +353 749 370103; ᠍ +353 749 370221.
Area: Slyne Head to Lough Foyle.

SAR resources

The Irish CG provides some 50 units around the coast and is on call H24. The RNLI maintains 4 stations around the coast and operates 42 lifeboats; six community-run inshore rescue boats are also available.

Sikorsky S-61 helicopters, based at Dublin, Waterford, Shannon and Sligo, can respond within 15 to 45 minutes and operate to a radius of 200M. They are equipped with infrared search equipment and can uplift 30 survivors.

Military and civilian aircraft and vessels, together with the Garda and lighthouse service, can also be called upon.

Some stations provide specialist cliff climbing services. They are manned by volunteers, who are trained in first aid and equipped with inflatables, breeches buoys, cliff ladders, etc. Their ☎ numbers (the Leader's residence) are given, where appropriate, under each port.

Irish Coastguard centres

DENMARK

The national SAR agency is: Ministry of Defence, 42 Holmens Kanal, DK-1060 København K.
☎ +45 339 23320; ᠍ +45 333 20655.

The SAR coordinator for Denmark is JRCC Denmark, ☎ +45 894 33099; ᠍ +45 894 33230; mas@sok.dk. JRCC has no direct communications with vessels in distress, but operates via two MRSCs and several Coast radio stations (CRS). MSC North, ☎ +45 992 21520; ᠍ +45 992 21538, MOCN@mil.dk deals with the W coast of Denmark.

Lyngby Radio

This is the main Danish CRS and is DSC VHF/MF/ HF equipped (☎ +45 452 89800; 🖻 +45 458 82485, lyngby-radio@tdc.dk MMSI 002191000).

It operates through remote sites at Skagen, Hirtshals, Hantsholm, Bovbjerg and Blavand, all of which guard Ch 16 H24 and use callsign *Lyngby Radio*. Their VHF and MF frequencies are shown in the chartlet below.

There are at least 12 lifeboats stationed at the major harbours along the west coast. They are designed to double up as Pilot boats.

Firing practice areas

There are 4 such areas on the W coast as in the chartlet and listed below. Firing times are broadcast daily by Danmarks Radio 1 after the weather at 1645UT. Times can also be obtained from the Range office Ch 16 or ☎.

Ⓐ   Tranum & Blokhus ☎ 982 35088 or call *Tranum.*

Ⓑ   Nymindegab ☎ 7652 3334 or call *Nymindegab.*

Ⓒ   Oksbøl ☎ 765 41213 or call *Oksbøl.*

Ⓓ   Rømø E ☎ 7375 5219 – or call *Fly Rømø*; Rømø W ☎ 745 41340 .

Danish Coastguard centres

GERMANY

The national SAR agency is: *Deutsche Gesellschaft zur Rettung Schiffbrüchiger* (DGzRS), the German Sea Rescue Service. Werderstrasse 2, Hermann-Helms-Haus, D-28199 Bremen. info@seenotretter. de. ☎ +49 421 536870 (emergency), 421 53707-0 (ops); 🖻 421 537 07690.

DGzRS is responsible for coordinating SAR operations, supported by ships and SAR helicopters of the German Navy.

Bremen MRCC(☎+49421536870;MMSI002111240), using callsign *Bremen Rescue,* maintains an H24 watch on Ch 16 and DSC Ch 70 via remote Coast radio stations at:

Blumenthal / Borkum / Cuxhaven / Helgoland / kampen / Norderney / Stade / Wangerooge / Westerhever.

There are 21 offshore lifeboats, LOA 23–44m, and 21 smaller <10m lifeboats, based at List, Amrum, Helgoland, Cuxhaven, Bremerhaven, Wilhelmshaven, Langeoog, Norderney and Borkum. There are also many inshore lifeboats.

German Coastguard stations

THE NETHERLANDS

The national SAR agency is: SAR Commission, Directorate Transport Safety (DGG), PO Box 20904, 2500 EX The Hague, Netherlands.

The Netherlands CG at Den Helder, co-located with the Navy HQ, coordinates SAR operations as the Dutch JRCC for A1 and A2 Sea Areas. (JRCC = Joint Rescue Coordination Centre – marine & aeronautical.) Callsign is *Netherlands Coastguard,* but *Den Helder Rescue* during SAR operations.

The JRCC keeps a listening watch H24 on DSC Ch 70, and MF DSC 2187·5 kHz (but not on 2182 kHz); MMSI 002442000.

West Terschelling
Ch 16 70 83
2187·5 2182 kHz

Schiermonnikoog
Ch 16 70 23

Appingedam
Ch 16 70 83
2187·5 2182 kHz

DEN HELDER (JRCC)
Ch 16 70 23

Kornwerderzand
Ch 16 70 23

Schoorl
Ch 16 70 83

Hoorn
Ch 16 70 83

Wezep
Ch 16 70 23

Amsterdam

Scheveningen
Ch 16 70 23
3673kHz

Noordwijk
2187·5 2182 kHz

Renesse
Ch 16 70 83

Westkapelle
Ch 16 70 23

Woensdrecht
Ch 16 70 83

Coastguard Operations can be contacted H24 via:

In emergency:
☎ + 31 9000 111 or dial 112.

Operational telephone number:
☎ + 31 223 542300. 🖷 + 31 223 658358; ccc@ kustwacht.nl If using a mobile phone, call 9000 111, especially if the International emergency number 112 is subject to delays.

Admin/info (HO)
☎+ 31 223 658300. 🖷+31 223 658303. info@ kustwacht.nl PO Box 10000, 1780 CA Den Helder.

Remote CG stations are shown above. Working channels are VHF 23 and 83.

Netherlands Coastguard stations

Medical advice
Call initially on Ch 16, DSC Ch 70 or 2187·5 kHz (MMSI 002442000). Working chans are VHF Ch 23 & 83 or MF 2824 kHz (transmit), 2520 kHz (receive).

Resources
The Dutch Lifeboat Ass'n (KNRM) manages 26 lifeboat stations and 13 inshore lifeboat stations along the coast. The 60 lifeboats include 13m LOA water-jet, rigid inflatables capable of 36 kn. Helicopters, fixed wing aircraft and ships of the RNLN can be called upon; also Air Force helos at Leeuwarden. The area of activity extends across the Dutch Continental Shelf and into the Waddenzee, IJsselmeer and estuaries of Zuid Holland and Zeeland.

BELGIUM
The Belgian CG coordinates SAR operations from Oostende MRCC, callsign *Coastguard Oostende*. The MRCC and *Oostende Radio* (Coast radio station) both keep listening watch H24 on Ch 16, 67, 2182 kHz and DSC Ch 70 and 2187·5 kHz.

Coast Radio stations

OOSTENDE Radio
☎ 50 558241; 🖷 50 558748.
Ch 16, DSC Ch 70 and MF DSC 2187·5 kHz.
MMSI 002050480.

Antwerpen Radio (remotely controlled by Oostende CRS) MMSI 002050485. Ch 16, DSC Ch 70.

Coastguard stations

MRCC OOSTENDE
☎ +32 59 701000; 🖷 +32 59 703605.
MMSI 002059981.

RCC Brussels (COSPAS/SARSAT agency)
☎ +32 2 751 4615; 🖷 +32 2 7524201.

Resources
Offshore and inshore lifeboats are based at Nieuwpoort, Oostende and Zeebrugge.

The Belgian Air Force provides helicopters from Koksijde near the French border. The Belgian Navy also participates in SAR operations as required.

FRANCE – CROSS

Four CROSS (Centres Régionaux Opérationnels de Surveillance et de Sauvetage, ie an MRCC) provide a permanent, H24, all weather operational presence along the N and W coasts and liaise with foreign CGs.

CROSS' main functions include:

- Co-ordinating SAR operations.
- Navigational surveillance.
- Broadcasting navigational warnings.
- Broadcasting weather information.
- Anti-pollution control.
- Marine and fishery surveillance.

All centres keep watch on VHF Ch 16 as well as Ch 70 (DSC) and co-ordinate SAR on Ch 15, 67, 68, 73. They also broadcast gale warnings, weather forecasts and local navigational warnings.

CROSSA Étel specialises in medical advice and responds to alerts from Cospas/Sarsat satellites.

CROSS can be contacted by R/T, by ☎, through Coast Radio Stations, via the National Gendarmerie or Affaires Maritimes, or via a Semaphore station. Call *Semaphore* stations on Ch 16 (working Ch 10) or by ☎ as listed later in this section.

CROSS also monitor TSS in the Dover Strait, off Casquets and off Ouessant using, for example, the callsign *Corsen Traffic*.

For medical advice call CROSS which will contact a doctor or SAMU (Service d'Aide Médicale Urgente). In harbour/marina SAMU responds faster to a medical emergency than calling a doctor. Simply dial 15.

CROSS stations (Emergency ☎ 112).

CROSS Gris-Nez
50°52'N 01°35'E   MMSI 002275100
☎ 03 21 87 21 87; ☒ 03 21 87 78 55
Belgian border to Cap d'Antifer.

NavWarnings Ch 79 at every H+10 via Dunkerque, Saint-Frieux and L'Ailly. CROSS Gris-Nez responds to COSPAS/SARSAT alerts.

CROSS Jobourg
49°41'N 01°54'W   MMSI 002275200
☎ 02 33 52 16 16; ☒ 02 33 52 71 72
Cap de la Hague to Mont St Michel

NavWarnings Ch 80 every H+20 and H+50 via Antifer, Ver-sur-Mer, Gatteville, Jobourg, Granville and Roche Douvres.

CROSS Corsen
48°24'N 04°47'W   MMSI 002275300
☎ 02 98 89 31 31; ☒ 02 98 89 65 75
Mont St Michel to Pointe de Penmarc'h.

NavWarnings Ch 79 every H+10 and H+40 via Cap Fréhel, Bodic, Ile de Batz, Le Stiff and Pte du Raz.

CROSS Étel
47°39'N 03°12'W   MMSI 002275000
☎ 02 97 55 35 35; ☒ 02 97 55 49 34
Pte de Penmarc'h to the Spanish border

NavWarnings Ch 79 for Landes range activity via Chassiron 1903.

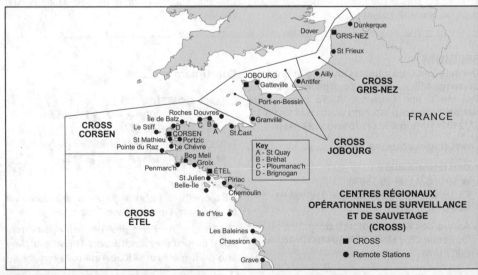

CROSS locations and areas of responsibility

Semaphore stations keep visual, radar and radio watch (Ch 16); are equipped with VHF DF; relay emergency calls to CROSS; show gale warning signals, repeat forecasts and offer local weather reports. Hours sunrise-sunset, but * H24.

* Dunkerque	03·28·66·86·18
* Boulogne	03·21·31·32·10
* Ault	03·22·60·47·33
* Dieppe	02·35·84·23·82
* Fécamp	02·35·28·00·91
* La Hève	02·35·46·07·81
* Villerville	02·31·88·11·13
* Port-en-Bessin	02·31·21·81·51
* St-Vaast	02·33·54·44·50
* Barfleur	02·33·54·04·37
* Le Homet	02·33·92·60·08
* La Hague	02·33·52·71·07
* Barneville-Carteret	02·33·53·85·08
* Granville Le Roc	02·33·50·05·85
St-Cast	02·96·41·85·30
* St Quay-Portrieux	02·96·70·42·18
Bréhat	02·96·20·00·12
* Ploumanac'h	02·96·91·46·51
Batz	02·98·61·76·06
* Brignogan	02·98·83·50·84
* Ouessant Stiff	02·98·48·81·50
* St-Mathieu	02·98·89·01·59
* Portzic (Ch 08)	02·98·22·21·47
Toulinguet	02·98·27·90·02
Cap-de-la-Chèvre	02·98·27·09·55
* Pointe-du-Raz	02·98·70·66·57
* Penmarc'h	02·98·58·61·00
Beg Meil	02·98·94·98·92
Étel Mât Fenoux	02·97·55·35·39
* Beg Melen (Groix)	02·97·86·80·13
Talut (Belle-Île)	02·97·31·85·07
* St-Julien	02·97·50·09·35
Piriac-sur-Mer	02·40·23·59·87
* Chemoulin	02·40·91·99·00
* St-Sauveur (Yeu)	02·51·58·31·01
Les Baleines (Ré)	05·46·29·42·06
* Chassiron (Oléron)	05·46·47·85·43

Lifeboats

The lifeboat service Société National de Sauvetage en Mer (SNSM) comes under CROSS, At sea all vessels must call CROSS to call upon the services of SNSM, they should not be contacted directly in an emergency. A hefty charge may be levied if a SNSM lifeboat attends a vessel not in distress.

Navigation warnings

Long-range warnings are broadcast by SafetyNet for Navarea II, which includes the W coast of France. The N coast is in Navarea I.

Avurnavs (AVis URgents aux NAVigateurs) are regional, coastal and local warnings issued by Cherbourg and Brest and broadcast by Niton and Brest Navtex and on MF. Warnings are prefixed by 'Sécurité Avurnav'.

EMERGENCY VHF DF SERVICE

A yacht in emergency can call CROSS on VHF Ch 16, 11 or 67 to obtain a true bearing of the yacht *from* the DF station. These monitor Ch 16 and other continuously scanned frequencies, which include Ch 1-29, 36, 39, 48, 50, 52, 55, 56 and 60-88. The Semaphore stations overleaf are also equipped with VHF DF.

HJ = Day service only.

VHF DF stations, are listed below geographically from NE to W then S:

Station	Lat/Long	Hrs
Dunkerque	51°03'.40N 02°20'.40E	H24
*Gris-Nez	50°52'.20N 01°35'.01E	H24
Boulogne	50°44'.00N 01°36'.00E	H24
Ault	50°06'.50N 01°27'.50E	H24
Dieppe	49°56'.00N 01°05'.20E	H24
Fécamp	49°46'.10N 00°22'.20E	H24
La Hève	49°30'.60N 00°04'.20E	H24
Villerville	49°23'.20N 00°06'.50E	H24
Port-en-Bessin	49°21'.10N 00°46'.30W	H24
Saint-Vaast	49°34'.50N 01°16'.50W	H24
Barfleur	49°41'.90N 01°15'.90W	H24
Levy	49°41'.70N 01°28'.20W	H24
†Homet	49°39'.50N 01°37'.90W	H24
*Jobourg	49°41'.50N 01°54'.50W	H24
La Hague	49°43'.60N 01°56'.30W	H24
Carteret	49°22'.40N 01°48'.30W	H24
Le Roc	48°50'.10N 01°36'.90W	H24
Grouin/Cancale	48°42'.60N 01°50'.60W	HJ
Saint-Cast	48°38'.60N 02°14'.70W	H24
St-Quay-Port'x	48°39'.30N 02°49'.50W	HJ
Bréhat	48°51'.30N 03°00'.10W	H24
Ploumanac'h	48°49'.50N 03°28'.20W	HJ
Batz	48°44'.80N 04°00'.60W	H24
Brignogan	48°40'.60N 04°19'.70W	HJ
Creac'h (Ushant)	48°27'.60N 05°07'.70W	H24
*Creac'h	48°27'.60N 05°07'.80W	H24
†Saint-Mathieu	48°19'.80N 04°46'.20W	H24
Toulinguet	48°16'.80N 04°37'.50W	HJ
Cap de la Chèvre	48°10'.20N 04°33'.00W	HJ
Pointe du Raz	48°02'.30N 04°43'.80W	H24
Penmarc'h	47°47'.90N 04°22'.40W	H24
Beg-Meil	47°51'.30N 03°58'.40W	HJ
Beg Melen	47°39'.20N 03°30'.10W	H24
*Etel	47°39'.80N 03°12'.00W	H24
Saint-Julien	47°29'.70N 03°07'.50W	HJ
Taillefer	47°21'.80N 03°09'.00W	H24
Le Talut	47°17'.70N 03°13'.00W	H24
Piriac	47°22'.50N 02°33'.40W	H24
Chemoulin	47°14'.10N 02°17'.80W	H24
Saint-Sauveur	46°41'.70N 02°18'.80W	H24
Les Baleines	46°14'.60N 01°33'.70W	HJ
Chassiron	46°02'.80N 01°24'.50W	H24

Chapter 5 – Tides

2014 TIDAL COEFFICIENTS

Date	Jan am	Jan pm	Feb am	Feb pm	Mar am	Mar pm	Apr am	Apr pm	May am	May pm	June am	June pm	July am	July pm	Aug am	Aug pm	Sept am	Sept pm	Oct am	Oct pm	Nov am	Nov pm	Dec am	Dec pm
1	96	100	113	114	108	112	108	106	94	91	76	72	73	71	70	67	60	55	53	49	51		59	
2	104	107	113	110	114	115	102	98	86	82	69	65	68	65	63	59	50	46	45		54	59	62	66
3	108	108	106	101	114	112	92	86	77	71	61	57	62	58	55	51	43		44	46	65	72	70	74
4	106	103	94	87	108	102	79	72	66	60	53	49	55	52	48	45	43	44	50	57	78	84	78	82
5	99	94	79	71	96	89	64	57	54	49	46	43	48	46	44		49	56	65	73	90	94	85	88
6	88	82	63	55	80	72	50	44	44	40	42		44		44	47	63	72	81	89	98	100	89	90
7	74	68	48	42	64	56	38	34	37		41	42	44	45	51	57	81	89	96	102	101	101	90	90
8	61	55	38		48	41	32		36	36	44	47	47	51	64	72	97	104	106	109	100	98	88	86
9	50	47	36	37	35	32	32	35	38	42	52	57	56	62	80	88	109	113	111	111	95	90	84	80
10	45		40	45	32		39	45	46	52	62	68	68	74	95	101	115	115	109	106	86	80	77	73
11	45	48	50	55	34	38	51	57	57	63	73	79	81	87	106	110	114	111	102	96	75	68	68	64
12	50	54	60	65	43	50	62	68	68	74	84	89	92	98	112	113	106	100	90	82	62	56	59	55
13	58	62	70	74	55	61	74	79	79	84	93	96	101	105	112	110	93	85	75	67	50	45	50	46
14	66	70	78	81	67	72	83	87	88	91	98	100	106	107	106	101	77	68	59	52	40	37	42	40
15	73	75	84	86	77	81	91	93	94	96	100	99	106	104	94	86	60	51	45	39	35	35	38	37
16	78	79	87	88	85	88	95	96	97	97	98	95	101	96	79	70	44	38	35		36		39	
17	81	82	89	88	91	93	96	95	96	94	92	87	91	84	62	54	35		33	33	39	43	41	45
18	82	82	87	86	94	94	93	90	91	87	83	78	78	71	48		34	36	36	40	48	53	50	55
19	81	80	83	80	93	92	87	82	83	78	73	68	64	58	43	40	40	44	45	50	59	64	61	66
20	78	76	76	72	90	87	77	71	73	68	64		53		40	41	50	55	56	61	69	74	72	78
21	73	70	67	62	83	78	66	60	64	61	60	58	50	48	45	49	61	66	66	71	79	83	83	87
22	66	62	57	52	73	67	56	53	59		57	58	48	50	55	59	71	75	76	80	86	89	91	95
23	59	54	48	46	61	55	53		59	60	59	61	53	56	64	68	79	82	83	86	91	92	97	99
24	51	48	46		51	48	54	58	62	65	64	67	60	64	73	76	84	86	88	90	93	93	99	99
25	46	46	49	54	47		63	69	69	72	70	72	68	71	79	81	88	89	91	91	91	89	97	95
26	47		61	70	50	55	75	81	76	79	75	77	74	76	83	84	89	88	90	89	86	83	91	87
27	51	57	79	87	62	70	86	91	82	84	78	79	78	80	85	85	87	85	86	83	78	74	82	77
28	64	72	95	102	78	85	94	97	86	86	80	80	80	81	85	84	82	79	79	75	69	65	72	67
29	80	88			93	99	98	99	87	86	79	79	81	80	82	80	74	70	69	64	61	59	62	59
30	95	101			104	107	98	96	85	84	77	76	79	78	77	74	64	59	59	55	57	58	57	
31	107	111			109	109			81	79			76	73	69	65			52	50			56	57

Tidal coefficients indicate the magnitude of the tide on any particular day without having to look up and calculate the range, and thus determine whether it is springs, neaps or somewhere in between. This table is valid for all areas covered by this Almanac. Typical values are:

120	Very big spring tide
95	**Mean spring tide**
70	Average tide
45	**Mean neap tide**
20	Very small neap tide

TIDES

TIDAL CALCULATIONS

Find the height at a given time (STANDARD PORT)

1. On Standard Curve diagram, plot heights of HW and LW occuring either side of required time and join by sloping line.
2. Enter HW Time and sufficient others to bracket required time.
3. From required time, proceed vertically to curves, using heights plotted in (1) to help interpolation between Spring and Neaps. Do NOT extrapolate.
4. Proceed horizontally to sloping line, thence vertically to Height scale.
5. Read off height.

EXAMPLE:

Find the height of tide at ULLAPOOL at 1900 on 6th January

From tables	JANUARY	
	0420	4.6
ULLAPOOL **6**	1033	1.6
	1641	4.6
	F 2308	1.2

Find the time for a given height (STANDARD PORT)

1. On Standard Curve diagram, plot heights of HW and LW occurring either side of required even and join by sloping line.
2. Enter HW time and those for half-tidal cycle covering required event.
3. From required height, proceed vertically to sloping line, thence horizontally to curves, using heights plotted in (1) to assist interpolation between Spring and Neaps. Do NOT extrapolate.
4. Proceed vertically to Time scale.
5. Read off time.

EXAMPLE:

Find the time at which the afternoon tide at ULLAPOOL falls to 3.7m on 6 January

From tables	JANUARY	
ULLAPOOL	**6** 0420 1033 1641 F 2308	4.6 1.6 4.6 1.2

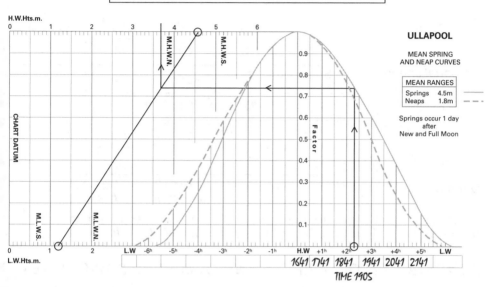

ULLAPOOL

MEAN SPRING AND NEAP CURVES

MEAN RANGES
Springs 4.5m
Neaps 1.8m

Springs occur 1 day after New and Full Moon

Find the time and height of HW and LW at a Secondary Port

EXAMPLE:

Find the time and height of the afternoon HW and LW at ST MARY's (Isles of Scilly) on 14th July (BST)

Note: *The data used in this example do not refer to the year of these tables.*

From tables	JULY	
PLYMOUTH (DEVONPORT)	**14** 0309 0927 1532 SA 2149	1.0 5.3 1.1 5.0

From tables										
Location	Lat	Long	High Water		Low Water		MHWS	MHWN	MLWN	MLWS
DEVONPORT *Standard port*	50°22'N	4°11'W	0000 and 1200	0600 and 1800	0000 and 1200	0600 and 1800	5.5	4.4	2.2	0.8
St Mary's, *Scilly*	49° 55'N	6°19'W	–0035	–0100	–0040	–0025	+0.2	–0.1	–0.2	–0.1

TIDES

TIDAL PREDICTION FORM (NP 204)

STANDARD PORT ...*Devonport*... TIME/HEIGHT REQUIRED ...*pm*...

SECONDARY PORT ...*St Mary's*... DATE *14 July* ...TIME ZONE ...*B.S.T*...

	TIME		HEIGHT		
STANDARD PORT	HW	LW	HW	LW	RANGE
	1 2149	2 1532	3 5·0	4 1·1	5 3·9
Seasonal change	Standard Ports -		6 0·0	6 0·0	
DIFFERENCES	7* -0044	8 -0032	9 0·1	10 -0·1	
Seasonal change *	Secondary Ports +		11 0·0	11 0·0	
SECONDARY PORT	12 2105	13 1500	14 5·1	15 1·0	
Duration	16 0605		LW 1500 UT = 1600 BST HW 2105 UT = 2205 BST		

* The seasonal changes are generally less than – 0.1m and for most purposes can be ignored. See Admiraly Tide Tables Vol 1. for details

CLEARANCE BELOW BRIDGES AND OVERHEAD POWER LINES

Vertical clearance heights are above the level of HAT (Highest Astronomical Tide) instead of MHWS as in the past. HAT is always a higher level than MHWS, as shown in the diagram on the back cover flap. It helps to draw such a diagram and insert the relevant dimensions when calculating overhead clearances. The Height of HAT above Chart Datum is stated at the foot of each page of Standard port tide tables. New editions of Admiralty charts are referenced to HAT; earlier editions to MHWS. Check the title block under **Heights**.

INTERMEDIATE TIMES/HEIGHTS (SECONDARY PORT)

These are the same as the appropriate calculations for a Standard Port except that the Standard Curve diagram for the Standard Port must be entered with HW and LW heights and times for the Secondary Port obtained on Form N.P. 204. When interpolating between the Spring and Neap curves the Range at the Standard Port must be used.

EXAMPLE:

Find the height of the tide at PADSTOW at 1100 on 28th February. Find the time at which the morning tide at PADSTOW falls to 4.9m on 28th February.

Note: The data in these examples do not refer to the year of these tables.

From tables	FEBRUARY	
MILFORD HAVEN		
	28 0315	1.1
	0922	6.6
	1538	1.3
	TU 2145	6.3

From tables

Location	Lat	Long	High Water		Low Water		MHWS	MHWN	MLWN	MLWS
			0100	0700	0100	0700				
MILFORD HAVEN	51°42'N	5°03'W	and	and	and	and	7.0	5.2	2.5	0.7
Standard port			1300	1900	1300	1900				
River Camel										
Padstow	50°33'N	4°56'W	−0055	−0050	−0040	−0050	+0.3	+0.4	+0.1	+0.1
Wadebridge	50°31'N	4°50'W	−0052	−0052	+0235	+0245	−3.8	−3.8	−2.5	−0.4

TIDAL PREDICTION FORM (NP 204)

STANDARD PORT ....*Milford Haven*.... TIME/HEIGHT REQUIRED ....*1100 : 4.9*

SECONDARY PORT ....*Padstow*.... DATE *28 Feb* .... TIME ZONE ....*UT*

	TIME		HEIGHT		
	HW	LW	HW	LW	RANGE
STANDARD PORT	¹ 0922	² 1538	³ 6.6	⁴ 1.3	⁵ 5.3
Seasonal change	Standard Ports +		⁶ 0.0	⁶ 0.0	
DIFFERENCES	⁷* −0052	⁸ —	⁹ +0.3	¹⁰ +0.1	
Seasonal change *	Secondary Ports −		¹¹ 0.0	¹¹ 0.0	
SECONDARY PORT	¹² 0830	¹³ —	¹⁴ 6.9	¹⁵ 1.4	
Duration	¹⁶ —				

H.W.Hts.m.

MILFORD HAVEN

MEAN SPRING
AND NEAP CURVES

MEAN RANGES
Springs 6.3m
Neaps 2.7m

Springs occur 2 days
after
New and Full Moon

M.H.W.N. M.H.W.S. CHART DATUM M.L.W.S. M.L.W.N. Factor

L.W. −5ʰ −4ʰ −3ʰ −2ʰ −1ʰ H.W. +1ʰ +2ʰ +3ʰ +4ʰ +5ʰ L.W.

0830 0930 1030 1130

L.W.Hts.m.

Height 4.9m

TIDES

SPECIAL INSTRUCTIONS FOR PLACES BETWEEN BOURNEMOUTH AND SELSEY BILL

• Owing to the rapid change of tidal characteristics and distortion of the tidal curve in this area, curves are shown for individual ports. It is a characteristic of the tide here that Low Water is more sharply defined than High Water and these curves have therefore been drawn with their times relative to that of Low Water.

• Apart from differences caused by referring the times to Low Water the procedure for obtaining intermediate heights at places whose curves are shown is identical to that used for normal Secondary Ports.

• The **height** differences for ports between Bournemouth and Yarmouth always refer to the higher High Water, i.e. that which is shown as reaching a factor of 1.0 on the curves. Note that the **time** differences, which are not required for this calculation, also refer to the higher High Water.

• The tide at ports between Bournemouth and Christchurch shows considerable change of shape and duration between Springs and Neaps and it is not practical to define the tide with only two curves. A third curve has therefore been drawn for the range at Portsmouth at which the two High Waters are equal at the port concerned – this range being marked on the body of the graph. Interpolation here should be between this 'critical' curve and either the Spring or Neap curve as appropriate. Note that while the critical curve extends throughout the tidal cycle the Spring and Neap curves stop at the higher High Water. Thus for a range at Portsmouth of 3.5m the factor for 7 hours after LW at Bournemouth should be referred to the following Low Water, whereas had the range at Portsmouth been 2.5, it should be referred to the preceding Low Water.

NOTES

1. NEWPORT. Owing to the constriction of the River Medina, Newport requires slightly different treatment since the harbour dries out at 1.4m. The calculation should be performed using the Low Water Time and Height Differences for Cowes and the High Water Height Differences for Newport. Any calculated heights which fall below 1.4m should be treated as 1.4m

2. CHRISTCHURCH (Tuckton). Low Waters do not fall below 0.7m except under very low river flow conditions.

To find the Height of tide at a given time at any Secondary Port between Bournemouth and Selsey Bill

1. Complete top section of N.P. 204 (as below). Omit HW time column (Boxes 1,7,12)
2. On Standard Curve diagram (previous page), plot Secondary Port HW and LW heights and join by sloping line.
3. From the time required, using Secondary Port LW time, proceed vertically to curve, interpolating as necessary using Range at Portsmouth. Do NOT extrapolate.
4. Proceed horizontally to sloping line, thence vertically to Height Scale.
5. Read off height.

EXAMPLE:
Find the height of tide at LYMINGTON at 0200 UT on 18th November

From tables	NOVEMBER	
	0110	4.6
PORTSMOUTH	**18** 0613	1.1
	1318	4.6
	SA 1833	1.0

From tables Location	Lat	Long	High Water		Low Water		MHWS	MHWN	MLWN	MLWS
			0000	0600	0500	1100				
PORTSMOUTH	50°48′N	1°07′W	and	and	and	and	4.7	3.8	1.9	0.8
Standard port			1200	1800	1700	2300				
Lymington	50°46′N	1°32′W	−0110	+0005	−0020	−0020	−1.7	−1.2	−0.5	−0.1

STANDARD PORT ...._Portsmouth_.... TIME/HEIGHT REQUIRED.... _0200_

SECONDARY PORT.._Lymington_.. DATE _18 Nov_.. TIME ZONE.... _UT_

	TIME		HEIGHT		
STANDARD PORT	HW	LW	HW	LW	RANGE
	1 –	2 _0613_	3 _4·6_	4 _1·1_	5 _3·5_
Seasonal change	Standard Ports -		6 _0·0_	6 _0·0_	
DIFFERENCES	7* –	8 _−0020_	9 _−1·7_	10 _−0·2_	
Seasonal change *	Secondary Ports +		11 _0·0_	11 _0·0_	
SECONDARY PORT	12 –	13 _0553_	14 _2·9_	15 _0·9_	
Duration	16 –				

* The Seasonal changes are generally less than ± 0.1m and for most purposes can be ignored. See Admiralty Tide Tables Vol 1 for full details.

TIDAL CURVES -
BOURNEMOUTH TO FRESHWATER

Bournemouth

Mean level
Range at Portsmouth
Sp — 3.9 m
— 2.8 m
Critical curve
Np — — — 1.9 m

Christchurch (Ent) (Quay) (Tuckton)

Mean level
Range at Portsmouth
Sp — 3.9 m
— 2.6 m
Critical curve
Np — — — 1.9 m

Hurst Point / Totland Bay / Freshwater

Mean level
Range at Portsmouth
Sp — 3.9 m
Np — — — 1.9 m

Note: The curves for Lymington and Yarmouth are on page 152, together with a worked example.

154

TIDAL CURVES -
BUCKLERS HARD TO SELSEY BILL

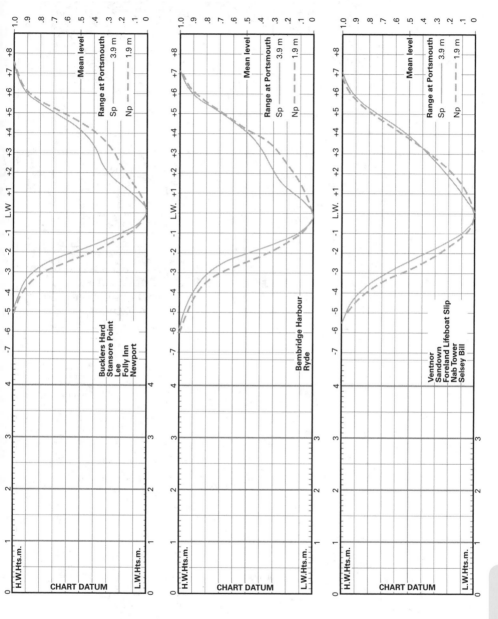

ENGLISH CHANNEL AND SOUTH BRITTANY

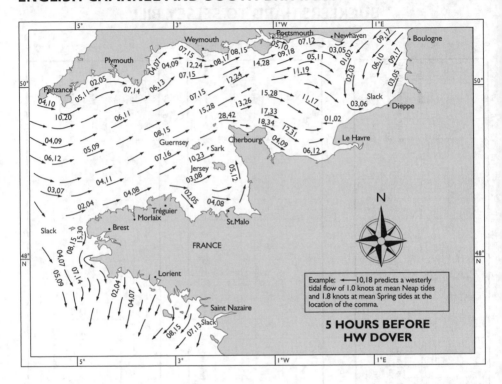

Example: ←—10,18 predicts a westerly tidal flow of 1.0 knots at mean Neap tides and 1.8 knots at mean Spring tides at the location of the comma.

5 HOURS BEFORE HW DOVER

4 HOURS BEFORE HW DOVER

ENGLISH CHANNEL AND SOUTH BRITTANY

3 HOURS BEFORE HW DOVER

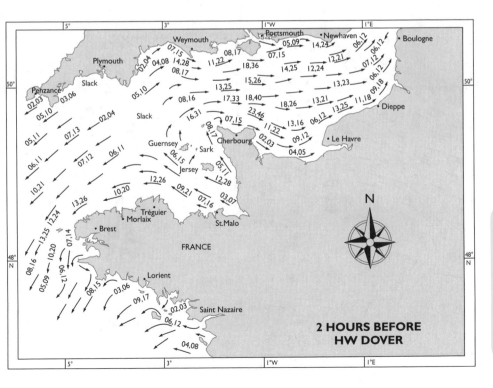

2 HOURS BEFORE HW DOVER

ENGLISH CHANNEL AND SOUTH BRITTANY

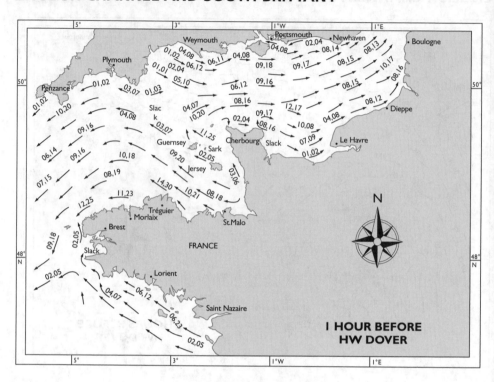

I HOUR BEFORE HW DOVER

HW DOVER

ENGLISH CHANNEL AND SOUTH BRITTANY

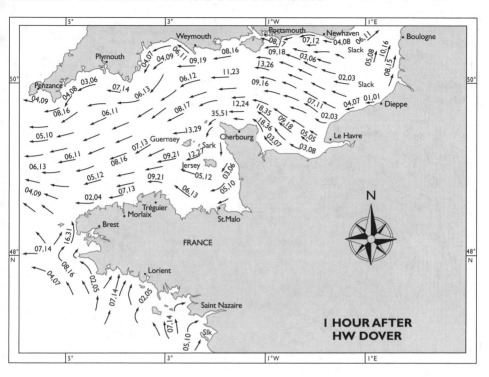

1 HOUR AFTER HW DOVER

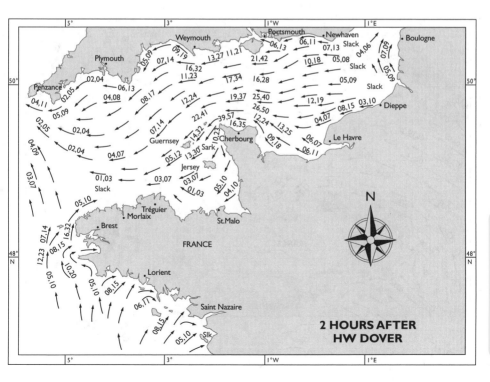

2 HOURS AFTER HW DOVER

ENGLISH CHANNEL AND SOUTH BRITTANY

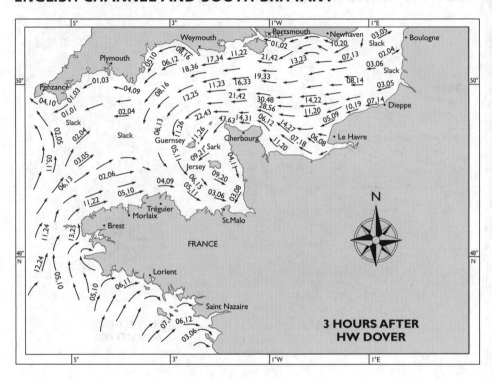

3 HOURS AFTER HW DOVER

4 HOURS AFTER HW DOVER

ENGLISH CHANNEL AND SOUTH BRITTANY

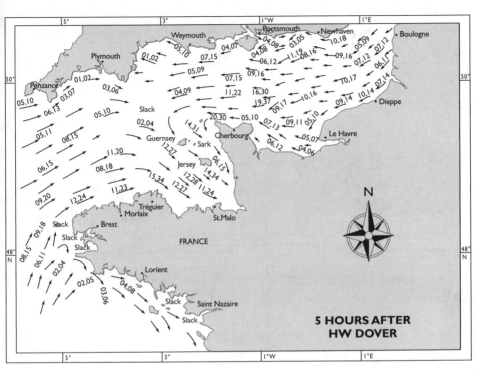

5 HOURS AFTER
HW DOVER

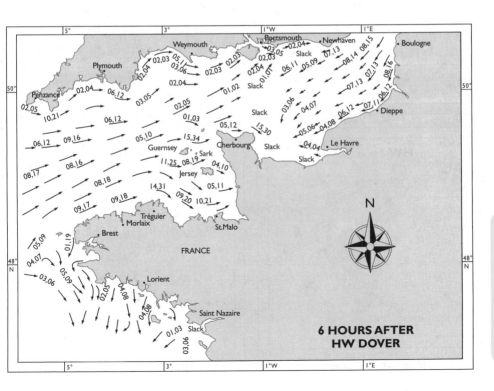

6 HOURS AFTER
HW DOVER

PORTLAND

HW-5 (0600 before HW Portland) (0145 after HW Dover)

5 hours before HW Plymouth (Devonport)

HW-4 (0500 before HW Portland) (0245 after HW Dover)

4 hours before HW Plymouth (Devonport)

HW-3 (0400 before HW Portland) (0345 after HW Dover)

3 hours before HW Plymouth (Devonport)

HW-2 (0300 before HW Portland) (0445 after HW Dover)

2 hours before HW Plymouth (Devonport)

HW-1 (0200 before HW Portland) (0545 after HW Dover)

1 hour before HW Plymouth (Devonport)

HW (0100 before HW Portland) (0540 before HW Dover)

HW Plymouth (Devonport)

1 hour after HW Plymouth (Devonport)

2 hours after HW Plymouth (Devonport)

3 hours after HW Plymouth (Devonport)

4 hours HW Plymouth (Devonport)

5 hours after HW Plymouth (Devonport)

6 hours after HW Plymouth (Devonport)

TIDES

ISLE OF WIGHT

5 HOURS BEFORE HW PORTSMOUTH

Example: ◄——10,18 predicts a westerly tidal flow of 1.0 knots at mean Neap tides and 1.8 knots at mean Spring tides at the location of the comma.

4 HOURS BEFORE HW PORTSMOUTH

ISLE OF WIGHT

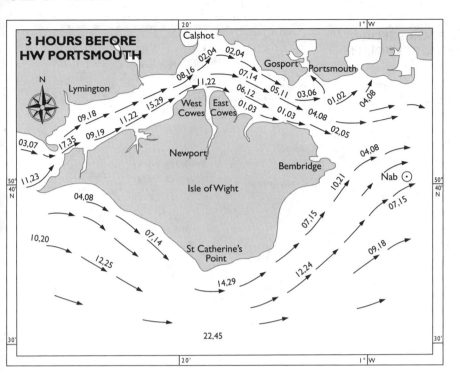

3 HOURS BEFORE HW PORTSMOUTH

N

Calshot
Lymington
Gosport
Portsmouth
West Cowes
East Cowes
Newport
Isle of Wight
Bembridge
Nab ⊙
St Catherine's Point

02,04 02,04
08,16 07,14 05,11 03,06 01,02 04,08
11,22 06,12 01,03 04,08
09,18 15,29 01,03 01,03 04,08 02,05
03,07 17,35 09,19 11,22
11,23
04,08
10,20 07,14
12,25
14,29 12,24
22,45
04,08
10,21 07,15
07,15
09,18

50°40'N
30'
20' 1°W

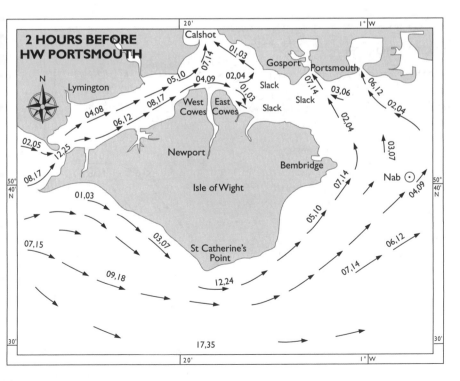

2 HOURS BEFORE HW PORTSMOUTH

N

Calshot
Lymington
Gosport
Portsmouth
West Cowes
East Cowes
Newport
Isle of Wight
Bembridge
Nab ⊙
St Catherine's Point
Slack
Slack
Slack

01,03
07,14
05,10 04,09 02,04
04,08 08,17 06,12 01,03 07,14 03,06 06,12 02,04
02,05 12,25 02,04
08,17 03,07
01,03
07,15 03,07
09,18 12,24
07,14 07,14
17,35
05,10 06,12
04,09

50°40'N
30'
20' 1°W

ISLE OF WIGHT

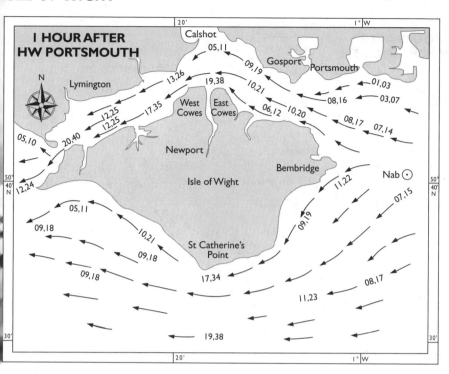

1 HOUR AFTER HW PORTSMOUTH

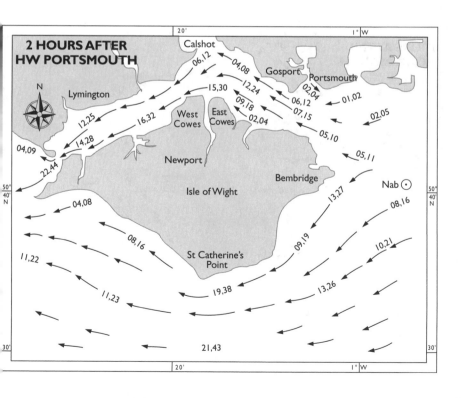

2 HOURS AFTER HW PORTSMOUTH

ISLE OF WIGHT

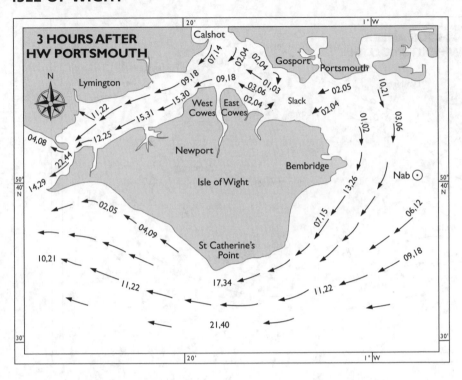

3 HOURS AFTER HW PORTSMOUTH

4 HOURS AFTER HW PORTSMOUTH

5 HOURS AFTER HW PORTSMOUTH

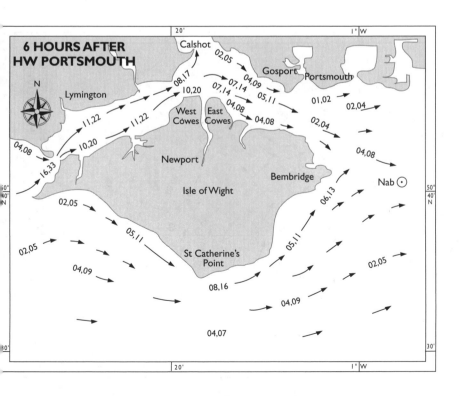

6 HOURS AFTER HW PORTSMOUTH

CHANNEL ISLANDS

Example: ←—10,18 predicts a westerly tidal flow of 1.0 knots at mean
Neap tides and 1.8 knots at mean Spring tides at the location of the comma.

4 HOURS BEFORE HW DOVER

5 HOURS BEFORE HW DOVER

CHANNEL ISLANDS

CHANNEL ISLANDS

HW DOVER

1 HOUR BEFORE HW DOVER

CHANNEL ISLANDS

2 HOURS AFTER HW DOVER

1 HOUR AFTER HW DOVER

CHANNEL ISLANDS

6 HOURS AFTER HW DOVER

5 HOURS AFTER HW DOVER

NORTH SEA

5 HOURS BEFORE HW DOVER

Example: ←—10,18 predicts a westerly tidal flow of 1.0 knots at mean Neap tides and 1.8 knots at mean Spring tides at the location of the comma.

4 HOURS BEFORE HW DOVER

NORTH SEA

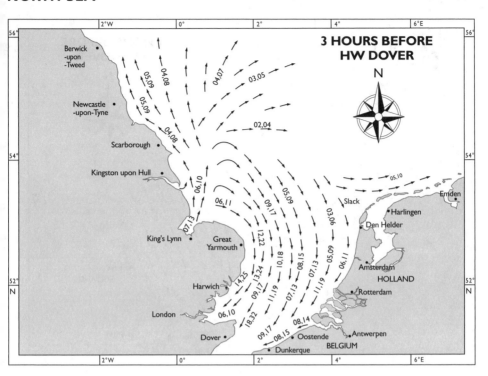

3 HOURS BEFORE HW DOVER

2 HOURS BEFORE HW DOVER

NORTH SEA

NORTH SEA

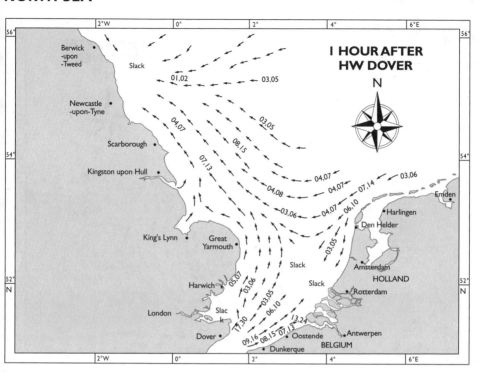

I HOUR AFTER HW DOVER

N

2 HOURS AFTER HW DOVER

N

NORTH SEA

3 HOURS AFTER HW DOVER

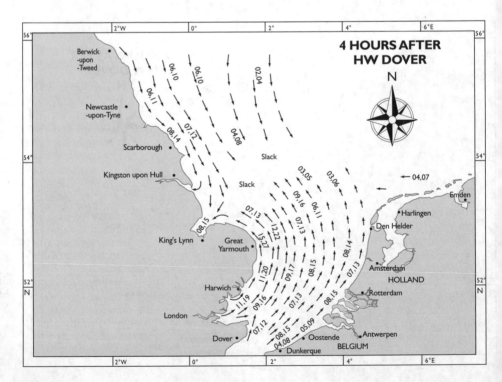

4 HOURS AFTER HW DOVER

NORTH SEA

SCOTLAND

Example: ◄——10,18 predicts a westerly tidal flow of 1.0 knots at mean Neap tides and 1.8 knots at mean Spring tides at the location of the comma.

4 HOURS BEFORE HW DOVER

5 HOURS BEFORE HW DOVER

SCOTLAND

HW DOVER

I HOUR BEFORE HW DOVER

SCOTLAND

SCOTLAND

4 HOURS AFTER HW DOVER

3 HOURS AFTER HW DOVER

SCOTLAND

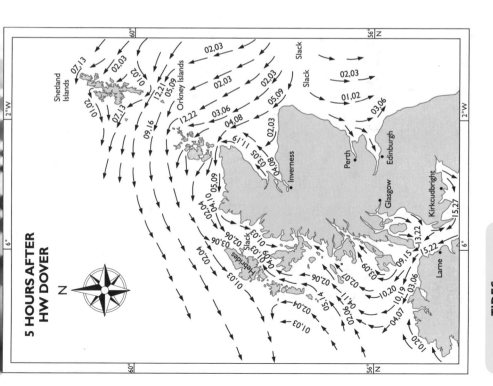

WEST UK AND IRELAND

4 HOURS BEFORE HW DOVER

5 HOURS BEFORE HW DOVER

Example:— 10,18 predicts a westerly tidal flow of 1.0 knots at mean Neap tides and 1.8 knots at mean Spring tides at the location of the comma.

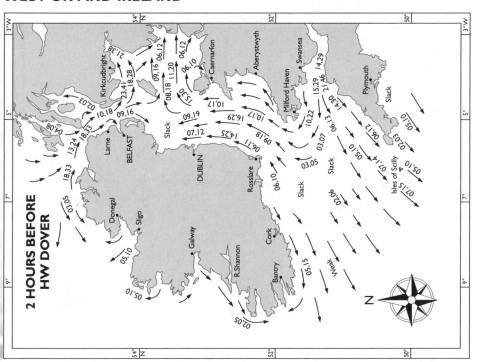

2 HOURS BEFORE HW DOVER

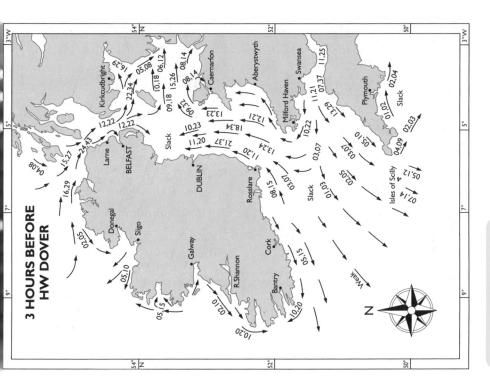

3 HOURS BEFORE HW DOVER

WEST UK AND IRELAND

WEST UK AND IRELAND

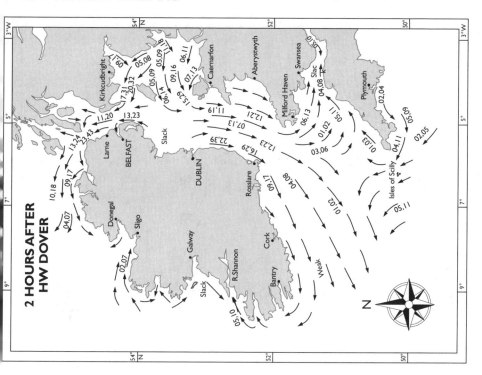

2 HOURS AFTER HW DOVER

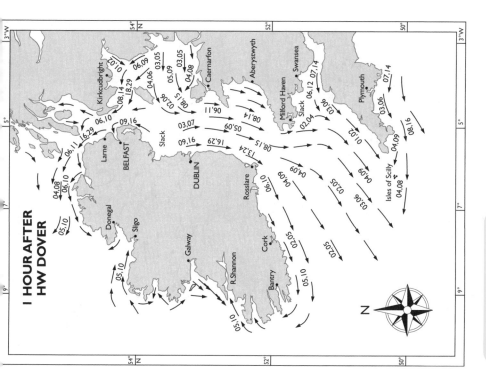

1 HOUR AFTER HW DOVER

WEST UK AND IRELAND

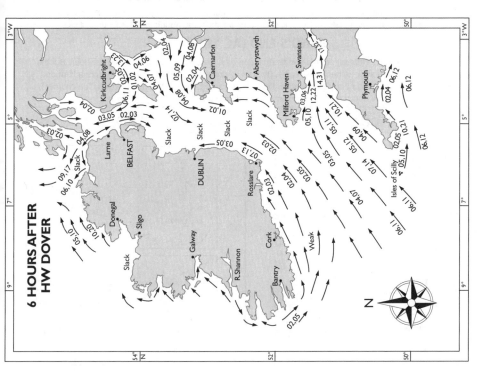

6 HOURS AFTER
HW DOVER

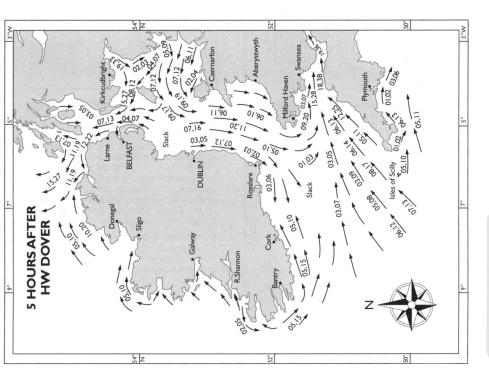

5 HOURS AFTER
HW DOVER

TIDES

TIDAL GATES – SOUTHERN ENGLAND

A guide to the time of tide turn at tidal gates, the approximate maximum strength of the tidal flow (spring rates shown - neaps are approximately 60% of these), and the position and timing of races, counter tides, etc.

LAND'S END (AC 1148)

Tidal streams set hard north/south round Land's End, and east/west around Gwennap and Pendeen. But the inshore currents run counter to the tidal streams. By staying close inshore, this tidal gate favours a N-bound passage. With careful timing nearly 9½hrs of fair tide can be carried, from HWD–3 to HWD+5. The chartlets, referenced to HW Dover, depict both tidal streams and inshore currents.

FLOOD	EBB

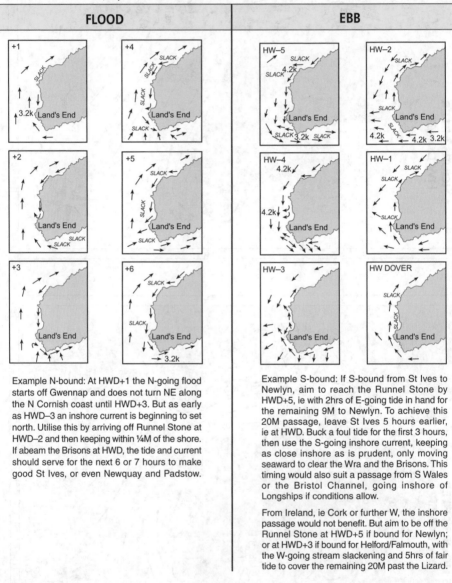

Example N-bound: At HWD+1 the N-going flood starts off Gwennap and does not turn NE along the N Cornish coast until HWD+3. But as early as HWD–3 an inshore current is beginning to set north. Utilise this by arriving off Runnel Stone at HWD–2 and then keeping within ¼M of the shore. If abeam the Brisons at HWD, the tide and current should serve for the next 6 or 7 hours to make good St Ives, or even Newquay and Padstow.

Example S-bound: If S-bound from St Ives to Newlyn, aim to reach the Runnel Stone by HWD+5, ie with 2hrs of E-going tide in hand for the remaining 9M to Newlyn. To achieve this 20M passage, leave St Ives 5 hours earlier, ie at HWD. Buck a foul tide for the first 3 hours, then use the S-going inshore current, keeping as close inshore as is prudent, only moving seaward to clear the Wra and the Brisons. This timing would also suit a passage from S Wales or the Bristol Channel, going inshore of Longships if conditions allow.

From Ireland, ie Cork or further W, the inshore passage would not benefit. But aim to be off the Runnel Stone at HWD+5 if bound for Newlyn; or at HWD+3 if bound for Helford/Falmouth, with the W-going stream slackening and 5hrs of fair tide to cover the remaining 20M past the Lizard.

With acknowledgements to the Royal Cruising Club Pilotage Foundation for their kind permission to use the tidal stream chartlets and text written by Hugh Davies, as first published in Yachting Monthly *magazine.*

TIDAL GATES – SOUTHERN ENGLAND

A guide to the time of tide turn at tidal gates, the approximate maximum strength of the tidal flow (spring rates shown - neaps are approximately 60% of these), and the position and timing of races, counter tides, etc.

FLOOD	EBB

THE LIZARD (AC 777, 2345)

Drying rocks lie approx 5 cables S of the Lizard lt ho and extend westwards. 49°57'N is about as far N as yachts may safely pass inshore of the Race, which extends 2-3M to seaward of these rocks. Race conditions may also exist SE of the Lizard with short, heavy seas in westerlies. If passing S of the Race, route via 49°55'N 05°13'W to clear the worst of the Race.

Inshore the E-going Channel flood, 2kn max @ springs, begins at HW Dover +0145; and outside the Race at approx HWD +0300.	Inshore the W-going Channel ebb, 3kn max @ springs, begins at HW Dover –0345; and outside the Race at HWD –0240.

START POINT (AC 1634)

Start Pt, and to a lesser extent Prawle Pt (3.3M WSW), can be slow to round when W-bound with a fair tide against a W'ly wind raising a bad sea. Drying rocks extend 3 cables SSE of the lt ho and a Race may extend up to 1.7M ESE and 1.0M S of the lt ho. It is safe to pass between the Race and the rocks, but in bad weather wiser to go outside the Race. The Skerries Bank (least depth 2.1m) lies 8 cables NE of Start Pt. On both the flood and the ebb back eddies form between Start Pt and Hallsands, 1M NW.

The NE-going Channel flood, 3.1kn max @ springs, begins at HW Dover +0430.	The SW-going Channel ebb, 2.2kn max @ springs, begins at HW Dover –0140, but an hour earlier it is possible to round Start Pt close inshore using the back eddy.

PORTLAND (AC 2255)

Tidal streams off Portland Bill run very strongly. The notorious Portland Race is caused by the almost constant strong southerly flow down both sides of the Bill meeting the main E and W-going streams in the English Channel. The violence of the race is increased by the sudden decrease in depth on Portland Ledge. The tidal stream chartlets on Pages 158–159 show that the race shifts to the E on the flood, and to the W on the ebb. Even in calm weather the race can be dangerous for small craft; in heavy weather or with wind against tide the whole area should be given a wide berth. In such conditions, pass at least 3 miles S of the Bill and do not pass between Portland and The Shambles bank.

In settled weather, with winds <F4/5, but not at springs nor with wind against tide, passage may be made very close S of the Bill in the narrow stretch of relatively smooth water N of the race. Night passage should not be attempted due to numerous fishing floats which may be semi-submerged.

Seaward of the race the Channel flood sets east from HW Plymouth -1 to HW +5; the ebb sets west from HW Plymouth +5 to HW -1.

Inshore passage

E-bound across Lyme Bay timing is critical to be close inshore about 2M north of the Bill by HW Plymouth –2 to achieve passage around the Bill between HW Plymouth –2 to HW+1.	W-bound timing is easier if starting from Portland Hbr, Weymouth or Lulworth Cove. Aim to be close inshore about 2M north of the Bill at HW Plymouth +4, and make the passage between HW Plymouth +5 and HW–5.

When using the inshore passage be particularly wary of being set S into the race itself.

ST ALBAN'S HEAD (AC 2610)

A sometimes vicious Race forms over St Alban's Ledge, a rocky dorsal ridge (least depth 8.5m) which extends approx 4M SW from St Alban's Head. Three yellow naval target buoys (DZ A, B and C) straddle the middle and outer sections, but are only occasionally used. In settled weather and at neaps the Race may be barely perceptible in which case it can be crossed with impunity. Avoid it either by keeping to seaward via 50°31'.40N 02°07'.80W; or by using the narrow inshore passage at the foot of St Alban's Head.

Based on a position 1M S of St Alban's Head, the tidal stream windows are:

ESE-going stream starts at HW Portsmouth +0530. Spring rates are the same, max 4kn. Along the W side of St Alban's Head the stream runs almost continuously SE due to a back eddy.	WNW-going stream starts at HW Portsmouth. Overfalls extend 2.5M further SW than on the E-going stream and are more dangerous to small craft. Slack water lasts barely half an hour.

The inshore passage lies as close to the foot of St Alban's Head as feels comfortable. It may be hard to see the width of clear water in the inshore passage until committed to it, but except in onshore gales when it is better to stay offshore, the passage will be swiftly made with only a few, if any, overfalls. The NCI station on the Head (☎ 01929 439220) may advise on conditions.

TIDAL GATES – SOUTHERN ENGLAND

A guide to the time of tide turn at tidal gates, the approximate maximum strength of the tidal flow (spring rates shown - neaps are approximately 60% of these), and the position and timing of races, counter tides, etc.

FLOOD	EBB

THE NEEDLES CHANNEL (AC 2035)

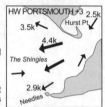

The Needles Channel lies between the SW Shingles PHM buoy and the Bridge WCM buoy. Once through this narrow section the channel widens with the Island shore to starboard and the long, drying 1.2m, Shingles bank to port. Abeam Hurst Castle the channel again narrows (assisted by The Trap, a shoal spit south of Hurst Castle) before opening out into the west Solent.

Study carefully the hourly tidal stream chartlets for the Isle of Wight on pp.186-191 and the values shown on AC 2035 at tidal diamonds B, C, D and E.

The ENE-going flood runs from HW Portsmouth +5 until HW P –1½, at springs reaching 3.1kn at The Bridge and 3.9kn at Hurst.	The WSW-going ebb runs from HW P –1 until HW P +4½, reaching 4.4kn at Hurst and 3.4kn at The Bridge, both spring rates. The ebb sets strongly WSW across the Shingles which with adequate rise is routinely crossed by racing yachts; but cruisers should stay clear even in calm conditions when any swell causes the sea to break heavily.

Prevailing W/SW winds, even if only F4, against the ebb raise dangerous breaking seas in the Needles Channel and at The Bridge, a shallow ridge extending 9 cables west from the Needles light. Worst conditions are often found just after LW slack. In such conditions it is safer to go via the North Channel to Hurst. In W/SW gales avoid the Needles altogether by sheltering at Poole or going east-about via Nab Tower.

ON PASSAGE UP CHANNEL

The following 3 tidal gates (Looe Channel, Beachy Head and Dungeness) are components in the tidal conveyor belt which, if stepped onto at the outset, can enable a fastish yacht to carry a fair tide for 88M from Selsey Bill to Dover. Go through the Looe at slackish water, HW Portsmouth +4½ (HW Dover +5). Based on a mean SOG of 7 knots, Beachy Head will be passed at HW D –1, Dungeness at HW D +3 and Dover at HW +5½, only bucking the first of the ebb in the last hour. A faster boat could make Ramsgate. The down-Channel passage is less rewarding and many yachts will pause at Brighton.

LOOE CHANNEL (AC 2045, 1652)

This channel is little shorter than the detour south of the Owers, but is much used by yachts on passage from/to points east of the Solent. Although adequately lit, it is best not attempted at night due to many lobster floats; nor in onshore gales as searoom is limited by extensive shoals on which the sea breaks.

	The E-going flood runs from HW Portsmouth +4½ (HW Dover +5) until HW P –1½ (HW D –1), at springs reaching 2.4kn near the Boulder and Street light buoys which mark its narrow western end; they may be hard to see in other than good visibility. Max neap rate is 1.2kn.	The W-going ebb runs from HW P –1½ (HW D –1) until HW P +4½ (HW D +5), at springs reaching 2.6kn near Boulder and Street. Max neap rate is 1.3kn.	

At the wider eastern end of the channel (near E Borough Head buoy) rates are greatly reduced.

BEACHY HEAD (AC 1652, 536)

Stay at least 5 cables to seaward of the towering chalk cliffs to avoid isolated boulders and rocky, part-drying ridges such as Head Ledge. The lt ho stands on a drying rock ledge. Close inshore many fishing floats are a trap for the unwary. In bad weather stay 2M offshore to avoid overfalls caused by a ridge of uneven ground which extends 1M SSE from Beachy Head.

2M south of Beachy Head the E-going flood starts at HW Dover +0530, max spring rate 2.6kn.	The W-going ebb starts at HW Dover +0030, max spring rate 2.0kn.

Between 5M and 7M east of Beachy Head avoid breakers and eddies caused by the Horse of Willingdon, Royal Sovereign and other shoals.

DUNGENESS (AC 536, 1892)

Tidal stream atlases: Dungeness is on the east and west edges respectively of NP 250 (English Channel) and NP 233 (Dover Strait). The nearest tidal stream diamond (2.2M SE of Dungeness) is 'H' on AC 536 and 'B' on AC 1892; their positions and values are the same.

The NE-going flood starts at HW Dover –0100, max spring rate 1.9kn.	The SW-going ebb starts at HW Dover +0430, max spring rate 2.1kn.

TIDAL GATES – NORTH EAST SCOTLAND

A guide to the time of tide turn at tidal gates, and in straits and estuaries, showing the approximate strength of the tidal flow (spring rates shown - neaps are approximately 60% of these), and the position and timing of races, counter tides etc.

FLOOD	EBB

FIRTHS of FORTH (AC 175) & TAY (AC 1481)

Tidal streams are quite weak in the outer part of the Firth, increasing as the narrows at islands and the bridges are approached.
Apart from the stream of the Tay, which attains 5 knots in most places, the coastwise tidal streams between Fife Ness and Arbroath are weak.

(a) Dover –0225 to Dover +0330
(b) Dover –0200 to Dover +0400
(c) Dover –0210 to Dover +0420
(d) Dover –0110 to Dover +0520

(a) Dover +0330 to Dover –0225
(b) Dover +0400 to Dover –0200
(c) Dover +0420 to Dover –0210
(d) Dover +0520 to Dover –0110

PASSAGES FROM FORTH & TAY

Northbound. Leave before HW (Dover +0400) to be at N Carr at Dover +0600. Bound from Forth to Tay aim to arrive at Abertay By at LW slack (Dover –0200).
Southbound. Leave before LW (Dover -0200) to be at Bass Rk at HW Dover. Similar timings if bound from Tay to Forth, leave late in ebb to pick up early flood off St Andrews to N Carr and into Forth.

INVERNESS & CROMARTY FIRTHS (AC 1077)

Tidal streams in the Inverness Firth and approaches are not strong, except in the Cromarty Firth Narrows, the Fort George Narrows and the Kessock Road, including off the entrance to the Caledonian Canal.

(a) Dover –0555 to Dover +0030
(b) Dover –0400 to Dover +0115
(c) Dover –0400 to Dover –0220
(d) Dover –0430 to Dover +0100

(a) Dover +0030 to Dover –0555
(b) Dover +0115 to Dover –0400
(c) Dover +0115 to Dover –0440
(d) Dover –0130 to Dover +0545

PENTLAND FIRTH & ORKNEYS (AC 1954)

The tide flows strongly around and through the Orkney Islands. The Pentland Firth is a dangerous area for all craft, tidal flows reach 12 knots between Duncansby Head and S Ronaldsay. W of Dunnet Hd & Hoy is less violent. There is little tide within Scapa Flow.

(a) Dover –0500 to Dover +0100
(b) Dover +0530 to Dover –0110
(c) Dover –0530 to Dover +0040

(a) Dover +0115 to Dover –0535
(b) Dover –0110 to Dover +0530
(c) Dover +0040 to Dover –0530

SHETLAND ISLANDS (AC 219)

The tidal flow around the Shetland Islands rotates as the cycle progresses. When the flood begins, at –0400 HW Dover, the tidal flow is to the E, at HW Dover it is S, at Dover +0300 it is W, and at –0600 Dover it is N.

(a) Dover –0410 to Dover +0020
(b) Dover –0400 to Dover +0030
(c) Dover –0530 to Dover +0100
(d) Dover –0400 to Dover –0200

(a) Dover +0050 to Dover –0410
(b) Dover +0130 to Dover –0500
(c) Dover +0100 to Dover –0530
(d) Dover +0200 to Dover +0500

Violent Race

TIDES

TIDAL GATES – NORTH WEST SCOTLAND

A guide to the time of tide turn at tidal gates, the approximate maximum strength of the tidal flow (spring rates shown – neaps are approximately 60% of these), and the position and timing of races, counter tides, etc.

FLOOD	EBB

SOUND OF HARRIS (AC 2802)

 HW Dover –0600

The behaviour of tidal streams in the Sd of Harris varies from day to night, springs to neaps, and winter to summer. The following data applies to daylight, in summer at spring tides in the Cope Channel. Further information can be sought in the Admiralty West of Scotland Pilot.
HW Dover - HW D +0200: SE stream.
HW D +0300 - HW D +0600: Incoming stream from both ends.
HW D –0600 - HW D –0500: NW stream.
HW D –0500 - HW Dover: Outgoing stream from both ends.
At neaps in summer the stream will run SE for most of the day.
Tide rates shown are the maxima likely to be encountered at any time.

 HW Dover

THE LITTLE MINCH (AC 1795)

The N going stream on both shores begins at HW Dover +0430 (HW Ullapool -0345), with the strongest flow from mid channel to the Skye coast. There is a W going counter tide E of Vaternish Point.

The S going stream on both shores begins at HW Dover –0130 (HW Ullapool +0240), with the strongest flow from mid channel to the Skye coast. The E going stream in Sound of Scalpay runs at up to 2k.The E going flood and W going ebb in Sound of Scalpay run at up to 2k.

KYLE OF LOCHALSH & KYLERHEA (AC 2540)

NOTE: THESE STREAMS ARE SUBJECT TO VARIATION

N going stream in Kyle Rhea begins HW Dover +0140 (HW Ullapool +0555) and runs for 6 hours. The E going stream in Kyle Akin begins (Sp) HW Dover +0350 (HW Ullapool –0415). (Nps) HW Dover –0415 (HW Ullapool).

S going stream in Kyle Rhea begins HW Dover -0415 (HW Ullapool) and runs for 6 hours. The W going stream in Kyle Akin begins (Sp) HW Dover –0015 (HW Ullapool +0400). (Nps) HW Dover +0140 (HW Ullapool +0555).

ARDNAMURCHAN POINT (AC 2171)

The N going stream off Ardnamurchan begins at HW Dover +0130 (HW Oban –0525). The E going stream in the Sound of Mull begins at HW Dover +0555 (HW Oban –0100).

The S going stream off Ardnamurchan begins at HW Dover –0430 (HW Oban +0100). The W going stream in the Sound of Mull begins at HW Dover –0130 (HW Oban +0400).

SOUND OF MULL – EAST (AC 2171)

The N going stream in the Firth of Lorne begins at HW Dover –0100 (HW Oban +0430). The W going stream in the Sound of Mull begins at HW Dover +0105 (HW Oban –0550). The ingoing tides at Lochs Feochan, Etive and Creran begin at HW Dover +0300, –0100 & +0030.

The S going stream in the Firth of Lorne begins at HW Dover +0500 (HW Oban –0155). The E going stream in the Sound of Mull begins at HW Dover +0555 (HW Oban –0025). The outgoing tides at Lochs Feochan, Etive and Creran begin at HW Dover –0500, –0520 & –0505.

SOUND OF LUING & DORUS MOR (AC 2343)

The N or W going stream begins as follows:
Dorus Mor: HW Dover –0200 (HW Oban +0330). Springs: 8 knots.
Corryvreckan: HW D –0120 (HW O +0410). Sp: 8.5 knots.
Cuan Sound: HW D –0110 (HW O +0420). Sp: 6 knots.
Sound of Jura: HW D –0130 (HW O +0400). Sp: 4 knots.
Sound of Luing: HW D –0100 (HW O +0430). Sp: 7 knots.
The S or E going stream begins as follows:
Dorus Mor: HW Dover +0440 (HW Oban –0215). Springs: 8 knots.
Corryvreckan: HW D +0445 (HW O –0210). Sp: 8.5 knots.
Cuan Sound: HW D +0455 (HW O –0200). Sp: 6 knots.
Sound of Jura: HW D +0450 (HW O –0205). Sp: 4 knots.
Sound of Luing: HW D +0500 (HW O –0155). Sp: 7 knots.

TIDAL GATES – SOUTH WEST SCOTLAND

A guide to the time of tide turn at tidal gates, the approximate maximum strength of the tidal flow (spring rates shown - neaps are approximately 60% of these), and the position and timing of races, counter tides, etc.

FLOOD	EBB

SOUNDS OF ISLAY AND GIGHA (AC 2168)

Main flood begins +0015 HW Dover (HW Oban +0545). Streams turn approx 1 hr earlier in Gigha Sd & at Kintyre & Jura shores. S going stream for 9hrs close inshore between Gigha and Machrihanish starting HW Dover (HW Oban –0530).

Main ebb begins HW Dover –0545 (HW Oban –0015). Streams turn 1 hr earlier in Gigha Sd, Kintyre & Jura shores. Overfalls off McArthur's Hd.

NORTH CHANNEL – NORTH (AC 2798)

Main flood begins HW Dover –0600 (HW Greenock +0505). Races off Mull of Kintyre, Altacarry Hd & Fair Hd. Counter tides in bays of Antrim coast. W-going streams in Rathlin Sd, counter tide from Sanda Sd to Machrihanish last 1h30 - 2 hrs.

Main ebb begins HW Dover (HW Greenock –0120). Races off Mull of Kintyre & Altacarry Hd. Counter tides in bays of Antrim coast, counter tide from Macrihanish to Sanda Sd last 1h30 - 2 hrs.

NORTH CHANNEL – SOUTH (AC 2198)

Irish coast - flood begins HW Dover +0610 (HW Belfast –0600). Scottish coast - HW Dover +0430 (HW Greenock +0310). Races off Copeland Is. & Mull of Galloway. Counter tide off Donaghadee and Island Magee last 3 hrs of flood.

Irish coast - ebb begins HW Dover –0015 (HW Belfast). Scottish coast - HW Dover –0130 (HW Greenock –0250). Races off Copeland Is. & Mull of Galloway. Flood begins 2 hrs early close inshore N of Mull of Galloway.

APPROACHES TO STRANGFORD LOUGH (AC 2156)

The tide cycle is approx 3 hours later than in the N Channel

Flood runs for 6 hours from HW Dover –0345 (HW Belfast –0330), with a maximum rate of 7.5 knots at Rue Point. The strong flow flattens the sea in onshore winds and entrance can be made in strong winds.

Ebb runs for 6 hours from HW Dover +0215 (HW Belfast +0230), max rate 7.5k, E of Angus Rk. If entering against ebb use West Channel with care. Smoothest water near Bar Pladdy Buoy when leaving.

ISLE OF MAN – NORTH (AC 2094)

E going stream at Point of Ayre begins HW Dover –0545 (HW Liverpool –0600). Counter tide inside banks E of Point. In Ramsey Bay the S Going tide runs for 3h from +0530 Dover (+0515 Liverpool).

W going stream at Point of Ayre begins HW Dover +0015 (HW Liverpool). Counter tide inside banks W of Point. In Ramsey Bay the N going tide runs for 9h from –0330 Dover (–0345 Liverpool).

ISLE OF MAN – SOUTH (AC 2094)

E going stream begins –0600 Dover (Liverpool +0610). Overfalls and race E of Chicken Rock. Calf Sound: The E going stream begins earlier, at approximately Dover +0400 (Liverpool +0345).

W going stream begins +0015 Dover (HW Liverpool). Overfalls and race N of Chicken Rock. Calf Sound:The W going stream begins earlier, at approximately –0130 Dover (–0145 Liverpool). Note: all times may vary due to weather conditions.

TIDES

199

MENAI STRAIT (AC 1464) – TIDAL GATES

FLOOD

(T): turning → : < 2k ➡ : 2-4k ⫸ : 4k +

LOCAL LW: Caernarfon: HW Dover –0555. Port Dinorwic: –0620. Menai: –0540. Beaumaris: –0605.

SLACK WATER IN THE SWELLIES: HW Dover –0200 to –0230.

LOCAL HW: Belan: HW Dover –0115. Caernarfon: –0105. Port Dinorwic: –0050.

THE SWELLIES

WESTBOUND: Leave or pass Beaumaris in time to arrive at the Swellies by HW Dover –0230 to –0200. If in doubt about passage speed, leave early; the adverse tide will check your progress. For a first time passage this is useful, as the yacht's speed over the ground is reduced. Late arrival will mean a faster passage, but with perhaps less control.

EASTBOUND: Leave or pass Port Dinorwic in time to arrive at Menai Bridge by HW Dover –0230 to –0200. Progress towards the Swellies should be closely monitored, as you are travelling with the last of the flood. Early arrival will mean a fast, perhaps dangerous passage, being late may make it impossible.

EBB

(T): turning → : < 2k ➡ : 2-4k ⦀➡ : 4k +

LOCAL HW TIMES: Menai: Dover – 0005.   Beaumaris: Dover – 0010

HW DOVER
+ 0100

HW DOVER
+ 0200

HW DOVER
+ 0300

HW DOVER
+ 0400

HW DOVER
+ 0500

LOCAL LW TIMES: Belan: Dover + 0520.

CAERNARFON BAR

CAERNARFON BAR is without question highly dangerous in certain conditions. Buoys are located to suit changing channel; positions obtainable from Caernarfon Port Radio - VHF Ch 16; 06, 12: 2h–HW, or when vessel expected. Beware cross track tides near high water. Bar impassable during or after fresh or strong onshore weather. Keep strictly in channel.

OUTWARD BOUND: Do not leave Belan Narrows after half tide, better as soon as possible after the ebb commences, which gives maximum depth and duration of fair tide if bound S & W.

INWARD BOUND: Locating the bar buoys may be difficult; head for Llanddwyn I. until they are located. Only cross after half tide (HW Dover –0400), which inevitably limits onward passage to max of 3 hours.

TIDES

TIDAL GATES – IRISH SEA

A guide to the time of tide turn at tidal gates, the approximate strength of the tidal flow (spring rates shown – neaps are approximately 60% of these), and the position and timing of races, counter tides, etc.

FLOOD	EBB

DUBLIN BAY (AC 1415)

Tide between Rosbeg bank and Howth Hd (a) runs NE from HW Dublin +0300 for 9h30. In Howth Sd (b) the stream is NW going from +0430 to –0130.
New flood and ebb tides begin close to the S shore and N of Baily up to 1h before HW Dublin .

The tide between Rosbeg bank and Howth Hd (a) runs SW from HW Dublin for 3h. In Howth Sd (b) the stream is SE going from –0130 to +0430.
Strengths of streams increase S of Dublin Bay, and decrease N of it.

N W ANGLESEY (AC 1977)

Flood tide close to the coast runs at over 5k springs, and at about 2.5k 7 miles offshore. The brief period of slack water offshore is 1h before HW Dover (1h15 before HW L'pool). Slack water lasts longer in Holyhead Bay.

Ebb tide close to the coast runs at over 5k springs, and at about 2.5k 7 miles offshore. Slack water is 5h after HW Dover (4h45 after HW L'pool). There is no significant counter tide in Holyhead Bay, but the ebb starts first there, giving about 9h W-going tide N of the harbour (a).

BARDSEY SOUND (AC 1971)

The tide turns to the NW or NE (flood) as follows:
at (a): HW Dover +0300;
at (b): HW D +0500;
at (c): –0545 HW D.
These times are approximate. There is a strong eddy down tide of Bardsey Island and overfalls throughout the area.

The tide turns to the SW or SE (ebb) as follows:
at (a): HW Dover –0300;
at (b): HW D –0100 ;
at (c): at HW D –0030.
These times are approximate. There is a strong eddy down tide of Bardsey Island and overfalls throughout the area.

S W WALES (AC 1478)

The tide turns to the S or SE (Bristol Channel flood) as follows:
at (a): HW Dover –0200;
at (b) & (c): HW D –0100 ;
at (d): –0300 HW D

The tide turns to the N or NW (Bristol Channel ebb) as follows:
at (a): HW Dover +0400;
at (b) & (c): HW D +0500 ;
at (d): +0300 HW D

CARNSORE POINT (AC 2049)

The tide turns to the NE or N (Irish Sea flood) as follows:
at (a): HW Dover +0500; at (b): HW D +0520; at (c): HW D +0600; at (d): –0600 HW D. NE going streams are shorter in duration and weaker than SE going - careful passage planning is essential.

The tide turns to the SW or S as follows:
at (a): –0200 HW D ; at (b): HW D –0020; at (c): –0015 HW D; at (d): –0300 HW Dover. Leaving Rosslare at –0300 HW D a yacht can carry a fair tide for about 8h until HW D +0515 off Hook Head.

NOTE: The tide turns on St Patrick's Bridge (e) up to 2 hours earlier than in Saltee Sound

CORK COAST (AC 2049)

The tide, which flows coastwise, turns to the NE at HW Dover +0045. There is an eddy 5 miles ESE of Old Head of Kinsale at HW Dover +0400. The ingoing Cork Harbour tide begins at HW Dover +0055.

The tide turns SW at HW Dover +0500. The outgoing Cork Harbour tide begins at HW Dover –0540.

SECONDARY PORTS: TIME & HEIGHT DIFFERENCES
SOUTH COAST OF ENGLAND *Time zone UT*

Location	Lat	Long	High Water		Low Water		MHWS	MHWN	MLWN	MLWS
			0000	0600	0000	0600				
PLYMOUTH (DEVONPORT)	50 22N	4 11W	and	and	and	and	5.5	4.4	2.2	0.8
Standard port			1200	1800	1200	1800				
Isles of Scilly, St Mary's	49 55N	6 19W	−0052	−0103	−0048	−0045	+0.2	−0.1	−0.2	−0.1
Penzance & Newlyn	50 06N	5 33W	−0053	−0108	−0035	−0036	0.0	−0.1	−0.2	0.0
Porthleven	50 05N	5 19W	−0045	−0105	−0030	−0025	0.0	−0.1	−0.2	0.0
Lizard Point	49 57N	5 12W	−0045	−0100	−0030	−0030	−0.2	−0.2	−0.3	−0.2
Coverack	50 01N	5 05W	−0030	−0050	−0020	−0015	−0.2	−0.2	−0.3	−0.2
Helford River Entrance	50 05N	5 05W	−0030	−0035	−0015	−0010	−0.2	−0.2	−0.3	−0.2
FALMOUTH	50 09N	5 03W	*Standard port (no Secondaries)*							
River Fal, Truro	50 16N	5 03W	−0020	−0025	Dries	Dries	−2.0	−2.0	Dries	
Mevagissey	50 16N	4 47W	−0015	−0020	−0010	−0005	−0.1	−0.1	−0.2	−0.1
Par	50 21N	4 42W	−0010	−0015	−0010	−0005	−0.4	−0.4	−0.4	−0.2
River Fowey, Fowey	50 20N	4 38W	−0010	−0015	−0010	−0005	−0.1	−0.1	−0.2	−0.2
Lostwithiel	50 24N	4 40W	+0005	−0010	Dries	Dries	−4.1	−4.1	Dries	
Looe	50 21N	4 27W	−0010	−0010	−0005	−0005	−0.1	−0.2	−0.2	−0.2
Whitsand Bay	50 20N	4 15W	0000	0000	0000	0000	0.0	+0.1	−0.1	+0.2
River Tamar										
Saltash	50 24N	4 12W	0000	+0010	0000	−0005	+0.1	+0.1	+0.1	+0.1
Cargreen	50 26N	4 12W	0000	+0010	+0020	+0020	0.0	0.0	−0.1	0.0
Cotehele Quay	50 29N	4 13W	0000	+0020	+0045	+0045	−0.9	−0.9	−0.8	−0.4
River Tavy, Lopwell	50 28N	4 09W	No data	No data	Dries	Dries	−2.6	−2.7	Dries	
River Lynher, Jupiter Point	50 23N	4 14W	+0010	+0005	0000	−0005	0.0	0.0	+0.1	0.0
St Germans	50 23N	4 18W	0000	0000	+0020	+0020	−0.3	−0.1	0.0	+0.2
Turnchapel	50 22N	4 07W	0000	0000	+0010	−0015	0.0	+0.1	+0.2	+0.1
Bovisand Pier	50 20N	4 08W	−0010	−0010	−0008	−0009	−0.1	0.0	+0.2	+0.2
River Yealm, Entrance	50 18N	4 04W	+0006	+0006	+0002	+0002	−0.1	−0.1	−0.1	−0.1
			0100	0600	0100	0600				
PLYMOUTH (DEVONPORT)	50 22N	4 11W	and	and	and	and	5.5	4.4	2.2	0.8
Standard port			1300	1800	1300	1800				
Salcombe	50 13N	3 47W	0000	+0010	+0005	−0005	−0.2	−0.3	−0.1	−0.1
Start Point	50 13N	3 39W	+0015	+0015	+0005	+0010	−0.1	−0.2	+0.1	+0.2
River Dart										
DARTMOUTH	50 21N	3 34W	*Standard port (no Secondaries)*							
Greenway Quay	50 23N	3 35W	+0030	+0045	+0025	+0005	−0.6	−0.6	−0.2	−0.2
Totnes	50 26N	3 41W	+0030	+0040	+0115	+0030	−2.0	−2.1	Dries	
Torquay	50 28N	3 31W	+0025	+0045	+0010	0000	−0.6	−0.7	−0.2	−0.1
Teignmouth, Approaches	50 33N	3 29W	+0020	+0050	+0025	0000	−0.9	−0.8	−0.2	−0.1
Teignmouth, New Quay	50 33N	3 30W	+0025	+0055	+0040	+0005	−0.8	−0.8	−0.2	+0.1
Exmouth Approaches	50 36N	3 23W	+0030	+0050	+0015	+0005	−0.9	−1.0	−0.5	−0.3
River Exe										
Exmouth Dock	50 37N	3 25W	+0035	+0055	+0050	+0020	−1.5	−1.6	−0.9	−0.5
Starcross	50 38N	3 27W	+0040	+0100	+0055	+0025	−1.4	−1.5	−0.8	−0.1
Turf Lock	50 40N	3 28W	+0045	+0100	+0034	No data	−1.6	−1.6	−1.2	No data
Topsham	50 41N	3 28W	+0045	+0105	No data	No data	−1.5	−1.6	No data	
Lyme Regis	50 43N	2 56W	+0040	+0100	+0005	−0005	−1.2	−1.3	−0.5	−0.2
Bridport (West Bay)	50 42N	2 45W	+0025	+0040	0000	0000	−1.4	−1.4	−0.6	−0.1
Chesil Beach	50 37N	2 33W	+0040	+0055	−0005	+0010	−1.6	−1.5	−0.5	0.0
Chesil Cove	50 34N	2 28W	+0035	+0050	−0010	+0005	−1.5	−1.6	−0.5	−0.2
			0100	0700	0100	0700				
PORTLAND	50 34N	2 26W	and	and	and	and	2.1	1.4	0.8	0.1
Standard port			1300	1900	1300	1900				
Lulworth Cove, Mupe Bay	50 37N	2 14W	+0005	+0015	−0005	0000	+0.1	+0.1	+0.2	+0.1
			—	—	0500	1100				
POOLE HARBOUR	50 42N	1 59W			and	and	2.2	1.7	1.2	0.6
Standard port			—	—	1700	2300				
Swanage	50 37N	1 57W	—	—	−0045	+0050	−0.1	+0.1	+0.2	+0.2
Poole Harbour Entrance	50 41N	1 57W	—	—	−0025	−0010	0.0	0.0	0.0	0.0
Ro-Ro terminal	50 42N	1 59W	*Standard port*							
Pottery Pier	50 42N	1 59W	—	—	+0010	+0010	−0.2	0.0	+0.1	+0.2
Wareham, River Frome	50 41N	2 06W	—	—	+0130	+0045	0.0	0.0	0.0	+0.3
Cleavel Point	50 40N	2 00W	—	—	−0005	−0005	−0.1	−0.2	0.0	−0.1
			0000	0600	0500	1100				
PORTSMOUTH	50 48N	1 07W	and	and	and	and	4.7	3.8	1.9	0.8
Standard port			1200	1800	1700	2300				
Bournemouth	50 43N	1 52W	−0240	+0055	−0050	−0030	−2.6	−2.0	−0.6	−0.2
Christchurch Entrance	50 43N	1 45W	−0230	+0030	−0035	−0035	−2.9	−2.4	−1.2	−0.2

TIDES

Location	Lat	Long	High Water		Low Water		MHWS	MHWN	MLWN	MLWS
Christchurch Quay	50 44N	1 47W	−0210	+0100	+0105	+0055	−2.9	−2.4	−1.0	0.0
Christchurch, Tuckton	50 44N	1 47W	−0205	+0110	+0110	+0105	−3.0	−2.5	−1.0	+0.1
Hurst Point	50 42N	1 33W	−0115	−0005	−0030	−0025	−2.0	−1.5	−0.5	−0.1
Lymington	50 46N	1 32W	−0110	+0005	−0020	−0020	−1.6	−1.2	−0.4	−0.1
Bucklers Hard	50 48N	1 25W	−0040	−0010	+0010	−0010	−1.0	−0.8	−0.2	−0.3
Stansore Point	50 47N	1 20W	−0030	−0010	−0005	−0015	−0.8	−0.5	−0.3	−0.3
Isle of Wight										
Yarmouth	50 42N	1 30W	−0105	+0005	−0025	−0030	−1.7	−1.2	−0.3	0.0
Totland Bay	50 41N	1 33W	−0130	−0045	−0035	−0045	−2.2	−1.7	−0.4	−0.1
Freshwater	50 40N	1 31W	−0210	+0025	−0040	−0020	−2.1	−1.5	−0.4	0.0
Ventnor	50 36N	1 12W	−0025	−0030	−0025	−0030	−0.8	−0.6	−0.2	+0.2
Sandown	50 39N	1 09W	0000	+0005	+0010	+0025	−0.6	−0.5	−0.2	0.0
Foreland Lifeboat Slip	50 41N	1 04W	−0005	0000	+0005	+0010	+0.1	+0.1	0.0	+0.1
Bembridge Harbour	50 42N	1 07W	+0020	0000	+0100	+0020	−1.5	−1.4	−1.3	−1.0
Ryde	50 44N	1 10W	−0010	−0010	−0005	−0005	−0.1	0.0	0.0	0.0
Medina River										
Cowes	50 46N	1 18W	−0015	+0015	0000	−0020	−0.5	−0.3	−0.1	0.0
Folly Inn	50 44N	1 17W	−0015	+0015	0000	−0020	−0.6	−0.4	−0.1	+0.2
Newport	50 42N	1 17W	No data	No data	No data	No data	−0.6	−0.4	+0.1	+0.8
			0400	1100	0000	0600				
SOUTHAMPTON	50 53N	1 24W	and	and	and	and	4.5	3.7	1.8	0.5
Standard port			1600	2300	1200	1800				
Calshot Castle	50 49N	1 18W	0000	+0025	0000	0000	0.0	0.0	+0.2	+0.3
Redbridge	50 55N	1 28W	−0020	+0005	0000	−0005	−0.1	−0.1	−0.1	−0.1
River Hamble										
Warsash	50 51N	1 18W	+0020	+0010	+0010	0000	0.0	+0.1	+0.1	+0.3
Bursledon	50 53N	1 18W	+0020	+0020	+0010	+0010	+0.1	+0.1	+0.2	+0.2
			0500	1000	0000	0600				
PORTSMOUTH	50 48N	1 07W	and	and	and	and	4.7	3.8	1.9	0.8
Standard port			1700	2200	1200	1800				
Lee-on-the-Solent	50 48N	1 12W	−0005	+0005	−0015	−0010	−0.2	−0.1	+0.1	+0.2
Chichester Harbour Entrance	50 47N	0 56W	−0010	+0005	+0015	+0020	+0.2	+0.2	0.0	+0.1
Northney	50 50N	0 58W	+0020	+0010	0000	+0005	0.0	−0.2	−0.2	−0.4
Bosham	50 50N	0 52W	+0010	+0005	No data	No data	0.0	−0.1	No data	
Itchenor	50 48N	0 52W	+0005	0000	−0010	+0005	−0.1	−0.2	−0.2	−0.3
Dell Quay	50 49N	0 49W	+0015	+0010	no data	No data	0.0	−0.1	No data	
Selsey Bill	50 43N	0 47W	+0010	−0010	+0035	+0020	+0.5	+0.3	−0.1	−0.2
Nab Tower	50 40N	0 57W	+0015	0000	+0015	+0015	−0.2	0.0	+0.2	0.0
			0500	1000	0000	0600				
SHOREHAM	50 50N	0 15W	and	and	and	and	6.3	4.8	1.9	0.6
Standard port			1700	2200	1200	1800				
Pagham	50 46N	0 43W	+0015	0000	−0015	−0025	−0.7	−0.5	−0.1	−0.1
Bognor Regis	50 47N	0 40W	+0010	−0005	−0005	−0020	−0.6	−0.5	−0.2	−0.1
River Arun										
Littlehampton Entrance	50 48N	0 33W	+0010	0000	−0005	−0010	−0.4	−0.4	−0.2	−0.2
Littlehampton UMA wharf	50 49N	0 33W	+0015	+0005	0000	+0045	−0.7	−0.7	−0.3	+0.2
Arundel	50 51N	0 33W	No data	+0120	No data	No data	−3.1	−2.8	No data	
Worthing	50 48N	0 22W	+0010	0000	−0005	−0010	−0.1	−0.2	0.0	0.0
Brighton	50 49N	0 08W	−0002	−0002	0000	0000	+0.2	+0.2	+0.1	+0.1
Newhaven	50 47N	0 04E	−0003	−0005	0000	+0005	+0.5	+0.4	+0.2	+0.2
Eastbourne	50 46N	0 17E	−0010	−0005	+0015	+0020	+1.1	+0.6	+0.2	+0.1
			0000	0600	0100	0700				
DOVER	51 07N	1 19E	and	and	and	and	6.8	5.3	2.1	0.8
Standard port			1200	1800	1300	1900				
Hastings	50 51N	0 36E	0000	−0010	−0030	−0030	+0.8	+0.5	+0.1	−0.1
Rye Approaches	50 55N	0 47E	+0005	−0010	No data	No data	+1.0	+0.7	No data	
Rye Harbour	50 56N	0 48E	+0005	−0010	Dries	Dries	−1.4	−1.7	Dries	
Dungeness	50 55N	0 58E	−0010	−0015	−0020	−0010	+1.0	+0.6	+0.4	+0.1
Folkestone	51 05N	1 12E	−0020	−0005	−0010	−0010	+0.4	+0.4	0.0	−0.1
Deal	51 13N	1 25E	+0012	+0010	+0004	+0002	−0.5	−0.3	0.0	+0.1
Richborough	51 18N	1 21E	+0015	+0015	+0030	+0030	−3.4	−2.6	−1.7	−0.7
Ramsgate	51 20N	1 25E	+0030	+0030	+0017	+0007	−1.6	−1.3	−0.7	−0.2

EAST COAST ENGLAND *Time Zone UT*

Location	Lat	Long	High Water		Low Water		MHWS	MHWN	MLWN	MLWS
			0100	0700	0100	0700				
MARGATE	51 23N	1 23E	and	and	and	and	4.8	3.9	1.4	0.5
Standard port			1300	1900	1300	1900				
Herne Bay	51 23N	1 07E	+0022	+0020	+0019	+0017	+0.6	+0.3	+0.2	+0.1
Whitstable approaches	51 22N	1 02E	+0042	+0029	+0025	+0050	+0.6	+0.6	+0.1	0.0

204

Location	Lat	Long	High Water		Low Water		MHWS	MHWN	MLWN	MLWS
			0200	0800	0200	0700				
SHEERNESS	51 27N	0 45E	and	and	and	and	5.8	4.7	1.5	0.6
Standard port			1400	2000	1400	1900				
River Swale										
Grovehurst Jetty	51 22N	0 46E	–0007	0000	0000	+0016	0.0	0.0	0.0	–0.1
Faversham	51 19N	0 54E	No data	No data	No data	No data	–0.2	–0.2	No data	
River Medway										
Bee Ness	51 25N	0 39E	+0002	+0002	0000	+0005	+0.2	+0.1	0.0	0.0
Bartlett Creek	51 23N	0 38E	+0016	+0008	No data	No data	+0.1	0.0	No data	
Darnett Ness	51 24N	0 36E	+0004	+0004	0000	+0010	+0.2	+0.1	0.0	–0.1
Chatham, Lock approaches	51 24N	0 33E	+0010	+0012	+0012	+0018	+0.3	+0.1	–0.1	–0.2
Upnor	51 25N	0 32E	+0015	+0015	+0015	+0025	+0.2	+0.2	–0.1	–0.1
Rochester, Strood Pier	51 24N	0 30E	+0018	+0018	+0018	+0028	+0.2	+0.2	–0.2	–0.3
Wouldham	51 21N	0 27E	+0030	+0025	+0035	+0120	–0.2	–0.3	–1.0	–0.3
New Hythe	51 19N	0 28E	+0035	+0035	+0220	+0240	–1.6	–1.7	–1.2	–0.3
Allington Lock	51 17N	0 30E	+0050	+0035	No data	No data	–2.1	–2.2	–1.3	–0.4
River Thames										
Southend–on–Sea	51 31N	0 43E	–0005	–0005	–0005	–0005	+0.1	0.0	–0.1	–0.1
Coryton	51 30N	0 31E	+0005	+0010	+0010	+0010	+0.4	+0.3	0.0	0.0
			0300	0900	0400	1100				
LONDON BRIDGE	51 30N	0 05W	and	and	and	and	7.1	5.9	1.3	0.5
Standard port			1500	2100	1600	2300				
Tilbury	51 27N	0 22E	–0055	–0040	–0050	–0115	–0.7	–0.5	+0.1	0.0
North Woolwich	51 30N	0 05E	–0020	–0020	–0035	–0045	–0.1	0.0	+0.2	0.0
Albert bridge	51 29N	0 10W	+0025	+0020	+0105	+0110	–0.9	–0.8	–0.7	–0.4
Hammersmith bridge	51 29N	0 14W	+0040	+0035	+0205	+0155	–1.4	–1.3	–1.0	–0.5
Kew bridge	51 29N	0 17W	+0055	+0050	+0255	+0235	–1.8	–1.8	–1.2	–0.5
Richmond lock	51 28N	0 19W	+0105	+0055	+0325	+0305	–2.2	–2.7	–0.9	–0.5
			0200	0700	0100	0700				
SHEERNESS	51 27N	0 45E	and	and	and	and	5.8	4.7	1.5	0.6
Standard port			1400	1900	1300	1900				
Thames Estuary Shivering Sand	51 30N	1 05E	–0025	–0019	–0008	–0026	–0.6	–0.6	–0.1	–0.1
			0000	0600	0500	1100				
WALTON–ON–THE–NAZE	51 51N	1 17E	and	and	and	and	4.2	3.4	1.1	0.4
Standard port			1200	1800	1700	2300				
Whitaker Beacon	51 40N	1 06E	+0022	+0024	+0033	+0027	+0.6	+0.5	+0.2	+0.1
Holliwell Point	51 38N	0 56E	+0034	+0037	+0100	+0037	+1.1	+0.9	+0.3	+0.1
River Roach Rochford	51 35N	0 43E	+0050	+0040	Dries	Dries	–0.8	–1.1	Dries	
River Crouch										
Burnham-on-Crouch	51 37N	0 48E	+0050	+0035	+0115	+0050	+1.0	+0.8	–0.1	–0.2
North Fambridge	51 38N	0 41E	+0115	+0050	+0130	+0100	+1.1	+0.8	0.0	–0.1
Hullbridge	51 38N	0 38E	+0115	+0050	+0135	+0105	+1.1	+0.8	0.0	–0.1
Battlesbridge	51 37N	0 34E	+0120	+0110	Dries	Dries	–1.8	–2.0	Dries	
River Blackwater										
Bradwell Waterside	51 45N	0 54E	+0035	+0023	+0047	+0004	+1.0	+0.8	+0.2	0.0
Osea Island	51 43N	0 46E	+0057	+0045	+0050	+0007	+1.1	+0.9	+0.1	0.0
Maldon	51 44N	0 42E	+0107	+0055	No data	No data	–1.3	–1.1	No data	
West Mersea	51 47N	0 54E	+0035	+0015	+0055	+0010	+0.9	+0.4	+0.1	+0.1
River Colne										
Brightlingsea	51 48N	1 00E	+0025	+0021	+0046	+0004	+0.8	+0.4	+0.1	0.0
Colchester	51 53N	0 56E	+0035	+0025	Dries	Dries	0.0	–0.3	Dries	
Clacton–on–Sea	51 47N	1 10E	+0012	+0010	+0025	+0008	+0.3	+0.1	+0.1	+0.1
Bramble Creek	51 53N	1 14E	+0010	–0007	–0005	+0010	+0.3	+0.3	+0.3	+0.3
Sunk Head	51 47N	1 30E	0000	+0002	–0002	+0002	–0.3	–0.3	–0.1	–0.1
Harwich	51 57N	1 17E	+0007	+0002	–0010	–0012	–0.2	0.0	0.0	0.0
Mistley	51 57N	1 05E	+0032	+0027	–0010	–0012	0.0	0.0	–0.1	–0.1
Ipswich	52 03N	1 10E	+0022	+0027	0000	+0012	0.0	0.0	–0.1	–0.1
			0100	0700	0100	0700				
WALTON–ON–THE–NAZE	51 51N	1 17E	and	and	and	and	4.2	3.4	1.1	0.4
Standard port			1300	1900	1300	1900				
Felixstowe Pier	51 57N	1 21E	–0005	–0007	–0018	–0020	–0.5	–0.4	0.0	0.0
River Deben										
Woodbridge Haven	51 59N	1 24E	0000	–0005	–0020	–0025	–0.5	–0.5	–0.1	+0.1
Woodbridge	52 05N	1 19E	+0045	+0025	+0025	–0020	–0.2	–0.3	–0.2	0.0
Bawdsey	52 01N	1 26E	–0016	–0020	–0030	–0032	–0.8	–0.6	–0.1	–0.1
Orford Haven										
Bar	52 02N	1 28E	–0026	–0030	–0036	–0038	–1.0	–0.8	–0.1	0.0
Orford Quay	52 05N	1 32E	+0040	+0040	+0055	+0055	–1.4	–1.1	0.0	+0.2
Slaughden Quay	52 08N	1 36E	+0105	+0105	+0125	+0125	–1.3	–0.8	–0.1	+0.2
Iken Cliffs	52 09N	1 31E	+0130	+0130	+0155	+0155	–1.3	–1.0	0.0	+0.2

TIDES

Location	Lat	Long	High Water		Low Water		MHWS	MHWN	MLWN	MLWS
			0300	0900	0200	0800				
LOWESTOFT	52 28N	1 45E	and	and	and	and	2.4	2.1	1.0	0.5
Standard port			1500	2100	1400	2000				
Orford Ness	52 05N	1 35E	+0135	+0135	+0135	+0125	+0.4	+0.6	−0.1	0.0
Aldeburgh	52 09N	1 36E	+0130	+0130	+0115	+0120	+0.3	+0.2	−0.1	−0.2
Minsmere Sluice	52 14N	1 38E	+0110	+0110	+0110	+0110	0.0	−0.1	−0.2	−0.2
Southwold	52 19N	1 40E	+0105	+0105	+0055	+0055	0.0	0.0	−0.1	0.0
Great Yarmouth										
Gorleston-on-Sea	52 34N	1 44E	−0035	−0035	−0030	−0030	0.0	0.0	0.0	0.0
Britannia Pier	52 36N	1 45E	−0105	−0100	−0040	−0055	+0.1	+0.1	0.0	0.0
Caister-on-Sea	52 39N	1 44E	−0120	−0120	−0100	−0100	0.0	−0.1	0.0	0.0
Winterton-on-Sea	52 43N	1 42E	−0225	−0215	−0135	−0135	+0.8	+0.5	+0.2	+0.1
			0100	0700	0100	0700				
IMMINGHAM	53 38N	0 11W	and	and	and	and	7.3	5.8	2.6	0.9
Standard port			1300	1900	1300	1900				
Cromer	52 56N	1 18E	+0044	+0032	+0108	+0059	−2.3	−1.8	−0.7	0.0
Blakeney Bar	52 59N	0 59E	+0035	+0025	+0030	+0040	−1.6	−1.3	*No data*	
Blakeney	52 57N	1 01E	+0115	+0055	*No data*	*No data*	−3.9	−3.8	*No data*	
Wells Bar	52 59N	0 49E	+0020	+0020	+0020	+0020	−1.3	−1.0	*No data*	
Wells	52 57N	0 51E	+0035	+0045	+0340	+0310	−3.8	−3.8	*Not below CD*	
Burnham Overy Staithe	52 58N	0 48E	+0045	+0055	*No data*	*No data*	−5.0	−4.9	*No data*	
The Wash										
Hunstanton	52 56N	0 29E	+0010	+0020	+0105	+0025	+0.1	−0.2	−0.1	0.0
West Stones	52 50N	0 21E	+0025	+0025	+0115	+0040	−0.3	−0.4	−0.3	+0.2
King's Lynn	52 45N	0 24E	+0030	+0030	+0305	+0140	−0.5	−0.8	−0.8	+0.1
Outer Westmark Knock	52 53N	0 13E	+0010	+0015	+0040	+0020	−0.2	−0.5	−0.6	−0.4
Wisbech Cut	52 48N	0 13E	+0020	+0010	+0120	+0055	−0.3	−0.7	−0.4	*No data*
Port Sutton bridge	52 46N	0 12E	+0030	+0020	+0130	+0105	−0.3	−0.6	−0.6	+0.3
Wisbech	52 40N	0 09E	+0055	+0040	*Dries*	*Dries*	−0.2	−0.6	*Dries*	*Dries*
Lawyer's Creek	52 53N	0 05E	+0010	+0020	*No data*	*No data*	−0.3	−0.6	*No data*	
Tabs Head	52 56N	0 05E	0000	+0005	+0125	+0020	+0.2	−0.2	−0.2	−0.2
Boston	52 58N	0 01E	0000	+0010	+0140	+0050	−0.5	−1.0	−0.9	−0.5
Skegness	53 09N	0 21E	+0010	+0015	+0030	+0020	−0.4	−0.5	−0.1	0.0
Inner Dowsing Light Tower	53 19N	0 35E	0000	0000	+0010	+0010	−0.9	−0.7	−0.1	+0.3
River Humber										
Bull Sand Fort	53 34N	0 04E	−0020	−0030	−0035	−0015	−0.4	−0.3	+0.1	+0.2
Grimsby	53 35N	0 04W	−0012	−0012	−0015	−0013	−0.3	−0.2	+0.1	+0.4
Hull, King George Dock	53 44N	0 16W	+0010	+0010	+0021	+0017	+0.3	+0.2	−0.1	−0.2
Hull, Albert Dock	53 44N	0 21W	+0019	+0019	+0033	+0027	+0.3	+0.1	−0.1	−0.2
Humber Bridge	53 43N	0 27W	+0027	+0022	+0049	+0039	−0.1	−0.4	−0.7	−0.6
River Trent										
Burton Stather	53 39N	0 42W	+0105	+0050	+0240	+0205	−2.0	−2.7	−2.2	−1.1
Flixborough Wharf	53 37N	0 42W	+0100	+0115	+0305	+0220	−2.3	−2.6	−2.2	−0.9
Keadby	53 36N	0 44W	+0130	+0115	+0320	+0235	−2.8	−3.3	−2.3	−0.9
Owston Ferry	53 29N	0 46W	+0155	+0145	*Dries*	*Dries*	−3.5	−3.9	*Dries*	
River Ouse										
Blacktoft	53 42N	0 43W	+0100	+0055	+0325	+0255	−1.6	−1.8	−2.2	−1.1
Goole	53 42N	0 52W	+0130	+0115	+0355	+0350	−1.6	−2.1	−1.9	−0.6
			0000	0600	0000	0600				
R TEES ENTRANCE	54 38N	1 09W	and	and	and	and	5.5	4.3	2.0	0.9
Standard port			1200	1800	1200	1800				
Bridlington	54 05N	0 11W	+0100	+0050	+0055	+0050	+0.6	+0.4	+0.3	+0.2
Filey Bay	54 13N	0 16W	+0042	+0042	+0047	+0034	+0.3	+0.6	+0.4	+0.1
Scarborough	54 17N	0 23W	+0040	+0040	+0030	+0030	+0.2	+0.3	+0.3	0.0
Whitby	54 29N	0 37W	+0020	+0020	+0018	+0017	+0.1	+0.1	+0.2	+0.1
Middlesborough Dock ent	54 35N	1 13W	0000	+0002	0000	−0003	+0.1	+0.2	+0.1	−0.1
Tees (Newport) Bridge	54 34N	1 16W	−0002	+0004	+0005	−0003	+0.1	+0.2	0.0	−0.1
Hartlepool	54 42N	1 12W	−0004	−0004	−0006	−0006	−0.1	−0.1	−0.2	−0.1
Seaham	54 50N	1 19W	−0015	−0015	−0015	−0015	−0.3	−0.2	0.0	−0.2
Sunderland	54 55N	1 22W	−0017	−0017	−0016	−0016	−0.2	−0.1	0.0	0.0
			0200	0800	0100	0800				
R TYNE, NORTH SHIELDS	55 00N	1 26W	and	and	and	and	5.0	3.9	1.8	0.7
Standard port			1400	2000	1300	2000				
Newcastle-upon-Tyne	54 58N	1 36W	+0003	+0003	+0008	+0008	+0.3	+0.2	+0.1	+0.1
Blyth	55 07N	1 29W	+0005	−0007	−0001	+0009	0.0	0.0	−0.1	+0.1
Coquet Island	55 20N	1 32W	−0010	−0010	−0020	−0020	+0.1	+0.1	0.0	+0.1
Amble	55 20N	1 34W	−0013	−0013	−0016	−0020	0.0	0.0	+0.1	+0.1

Location	Lat	Long	High Water		Low Water		MHWS	MHWN	MLWN	MLWS
North Sunderland	55 35N	1 39W	−0048	−0044	−0058	−0102	−0.2	−0.2	−0.2	0.0
Holy Island	55 40N	1 48W	−0043	−0039	−0105	−0110	−0.2	−0.2	−0.3	−0.1
Berwick	55 46N	1 59W	−0053	−0053	−0109	−0109	−0.3	−0.1	−0.5	−0.1

SCOTLAND *Time Zone UT*

Location	Lat	Long	High Water		Low Water		MHWS	MHWN	MLWN	MLWS
			0300	0900	0300	0900				
LEITH	55 59N	3 11W	and	and	and	and	5.6	4.4	2.0	0.8
Standard port			1500	2100	1500	2100				
Eyemouth	55 52N	2 05W	−0005	+0007	+0012	+0008	−0.4	−0.3	0.0	+0.1
Dunbar	56 00N	2 31W	−0005	+0003	+0003	−0003	−0.3	−0.3	0.0	+0.1
Fidra	56 04N	2 47W	−0001	0000	−0002	+0001	−0.2	−0.2	0.0	0.0
Cockenzie	55 58N	2 57W	−0007	−0015	−0013	−0005	−0.2	0.0	*No data*	
Granton	55 59N	3 13W	0000	0000	0000	0000	0.0	0.0	0.0	0.0
River Forth Grangemouth	56 02N	3 41W	+0015	+0010	−0050	−0045	0.0	−0.1	−0.2	−0.2
Kincardine	56 04N	3 43W	+0015	+0030	−0030	−0030	0.0	−0.2	−0.5	−0.3
Alloa	56 06N	3 48W	+0040	+0040	+0025	+0025	−0.2	−0.5	*No data*	−0.7
Stirling	56 07N	3 56W	+0100	+0100	*No data*		−2.9	−3.1	−2.3	−0.7
Firth of Forth										
Burntisland	56 03N	3 14W	+0013	+0004	−0002	+0007	+0.1	0.0	+0.1	+0.2
Kirkcaldy	56 09N	3 09W	+0005	0000	−0004	−0001	−0.3	−0.3	−0.2	−0.2
Methil	56 11N	3 00W	−0005	−0001	−0001	−0001	−0.1	−0.1	−0.1	−0.1
Anstruther Easter	56 13N	2 42W	−0018	−0012	−0006	−0008	−0.3	−0.2	0.0	0.0
			0000	0600	0100	0700				
ABERDEEN	57 09N	2 04W	and	and	and	and	4.3	3.4	1.6	0.6
Standard port			1200	1800	1300	1900				
River Tay										
Bar	56 28N	2 38W	+0100	+0100	+0050	+0110	+0.9	+0.8	+0.3	+0.1
Dundee	56 27N	2 58W	+0140	+0120	+0055	+0145	+1.2	+1.0	+0.5	+0.4
Newburgh	56 21N	3 14W	+0215	+0200	+0250	+0335	−0.2	−0.4	−1.1	−0.5
Perth	56 24N	3 25W	+0220	+0225	+0510	+0530	−0.9	−1.4	−1.2	−0.3
Arbroath	56 33N	2 35W	+0056	+0037	+0034	+0055	+1.0	+0.8	+0.4	+0.2
Montrose	56 42N	2 28W	+0050	+0045	+0035	+0030	+0.6	+0.4	+0.3	+0.2
Stonehaven	56 58N	2 12W	+0013	+0008	+0013	+0009	+0.2	+0.2	+0.1	0.0
Peterhead	57 30N	1 46W	−0035	−0045	−0035	−0040	−0.3	−0.2	0.0	+0.1
Fraserburgh	57 41N	2 00W	−0122	−0118	−0115	−0115	−0.5	−0.4	−0.1	+0.2
			0200	0900	0400	0900				
ABERDEEN	57 09N	2 04W	and	and	and	and	4.3	3.4	1.6	0.6
Standard port			1400	2100	1600	2100				
Banff	57 40N	2 31W	−0100	−0150	−0150	−0050	−0.4	−0.2	−0.1	+0.2
Whitehills	57 41N	2 35W	−0122	−0137	−0117	−0127	−0.4	−0.3	+0.1	+0.1
Buckie	57 41N	2 57W	−0130	−0145	−0125	−0140	−0.2	−0.2	0.0	+0.1
Lossiemouth	57 43N	3 18W	−0125	−0200	−0130	−0130	−0.2	−0.2	0.0	0.0
Burghead	57 42N	3 29W	−0120	−0150	−0135	−0120	−0.2	−0.2	0.0	0.0
Nairn	57 36N	3 52W	−0120	−0150	−0135	−0130	0.0	−0.1	0.0	+0.1
McDermott Base	57 36N	3 59W	−0110	−0140	−0120	−0115	−0.1	−0.1	+0.1	+0.3
			0300	1000	0000	0700				
ABERDEEN	57 09N	2 04W	and	and	and	and	4.3	3.4	1.6	0.6
Standard port			1500	2200	1200	1900				
Inverness Firth										
Fortrose	57 35N	4 08W	−0125	−0125	−0125	−0125	0.0	0.0	*No data*	
Inverness	57 30N	4 15W	−0050	−0150	−0200	−0150	+0.5	+0.3	+0.2	+0.1
Cromarty Firth										
Cromarty	57 42N	4 03W	−0120	−0155	−0155	−0120	0.0	0.0	+0.1	+0.2
Invergordon	57 41N	4 10W	−0105	−0200	−0200	−0110	+0.1	+0.1	+0.1	+0.1
Dingwall	57 36N	4 25W	−0045	−0145	*No data*	*No data*	+0.1	+0.2	*No data*	
			0300	0800	0200	0800				
ABERDEEN	57 09N	2 04W	and	and	and	and	4.3	3.4	1.6	0.6
Standard port			1500	2000	1400	2000				
Dornoch Firth										
Portmahomack	57 50N	3 50W	−0120	−0210	−0140	−0110	−0.2	−0.1	+0.1	+0.1
Meikle Ferry	57 51N	4 08W	−0100	−0140	−0120	−0055	+0.1	0.0	−0.1	0.0
Golspie	57 58N	3 59W	−0130	−0215	−0155	−0130	−0.3	−0.3	−0.1	0.0
			0000	0700	0200	0700				
WICK	58 26N	3 05W	and	and	and	and	3.5	2.8	1.4	0.7
Standard port			1200	1900	1400	1900				
Helmsdale	58 07N	3 39W	+0025	+0015	+0035	+0030	+0.5	+0.3	+0.1	−0.1
Duncansby Head	58 39N	3 02W	−0115	−0115	−0110	−0110	−0.4	−0.4	*No data*	
Orkney Islands										
Muckle Skerry	58 41N	2 55W	−0025	−0025	−0020	−0020	−0.9	−0.8	−0.4	−0.3

Location	Lat	Long	High Water		Low Water		MHWS	MHWN	MLWN	MLWS
Burray Ness	58 51N	2 52W	+0005	+0005	+0015	+0015	−0.2	−0.3	−0.1	−0.1
Deer Sound	58 58N	2 50W	−0040	−0040	−0035	−0035	−0.3	−0.3	−0.1	−0.1
Kirkwall	58 59N	2 58W	−0042	−0042	−0041	−0041	−0.5	−0.4	−0.1	−0.1
Egilsay	59 09N	2 57W	−0125	−0125	−0125	−0125	−0.1	0.0	+0.2	+0.1
Whitehall	58 09N	2 36W	−0030	−0030	−0025	−0030	−0.1	0.0	+0.2	+0.2
Loth	59 11N	2 42W	−0045	−0045	−0055	−0105	−0.4	−0.3	+0.1	+0.2
Kettletoft Pier	59 14N	2 36W	−0030	−0025	−0025	−0025	0.0	0.0	+0.2	+0.2
Rapness	59 15N	2 52W	−0205	−0205	−0205	−0200	+0.1	+0.1	+0.2	0.0
Pierowall	59 19N	2 59W	−0150	−0150	−0145	−0145	+0.2	0.0	0.0	−0.1
Tingwall	59 05N	3 03W	−0200	−0125	−0145	−0125	−0.4	−0.4	−0.1	−0.1
Stromness	58 58N	3 18W	−0225	−0135	−0205	−0205	+0.1	−0.1	0.0	0.0
St Mary's	58 54N	2 55W	−0140	−0140	−0140	−0140	−0.2	−0.2	0.0	−0.1
Widewall Bay	58 49N	3 01W	−0155	−0155	−0150	−0150	+0.1	−0.1	−0.1	−0.3
Bur Wick	58 44N	2 58W	−0100	−0100	−0150	−0150	−0.1	−0.1	+0.2	+0.1
			0000	0600	0100	0800				
LERWICK	60 09N	1 08W	and	and	and	and	2.1	1.7	0.9	0.5
Standard port			1200	1800	1300	2000				
Fair Isle	59 32N	1 36W	−0006	−0015	−0031	−0037	+0.1	0.0	+0.1	+0.1
Shetland Islands										
Sumburgh (Grutness Voe)	59 53N	1 17W	+0006	+0008	+0004	−0002	−0.3	−0.3	−0.2	−0.1
Dury Voe	60 21N	1 10W	−0015	−0015	−0010	−0010	0.0	−0.1	0.0	−0.2
Out Skerries	60 25N	0 45W	−0025	−0025	−0010	−0010	+0.1	0.0	0.0	−0.1
Toft Pier	60 28N	1 12W	−0105	−0100	−0125	−0115	+0.2	+0.1	−0.1	−0.1
Burra Voe (Yell Sound)	60 30N	1 03W	−0025	−0025	−0025	−0025	+0.2	+0.1	0.0	−0.1
Mid Yell	60 36N	1 03W	−0030	−0020	−0035	−0025	+0.3	+0.2	+0.2	+0.1
Balta Sound	60 46N	0 50W	−0040	−0045	−0040	−0045	+0.3	+0.2	+0.1	0.0
Burra Firth	60 48N	0 52W	−0110	−0110	−0115	−0115	+0.4	+0.2	0.0	0.0
Bluemull Sound	60 42N	1 00W	−0135	−0135	−0155	−0155	+0.5	+0.2	+0.1	0.0
Sullom Voe	60 27N	1 18W	−0135	−0125	−0135	−0120	0.0	0.0	−0.2	−0.2
Hillswick	60 29N	1 29W	−0220	−0220	−0200	−0200	−0.1	−0.1	−0.1	−0.1
Scalloway	60 08N	1 16W	−0150	−0150	−0150	−0150	−0.5	−0.4	−0.3	0.0
Bay of Quendale	59 54N	1 21W	−0025	−0025	−0030	−0030	−0.4	−0.3	0.0	+0.1
Foula	60 07N	2 03W	−0140	−0140	−0130	−0130	−0.1	−0.1	0.0	0.0
			0200	0700	0100	0700				
WICK	58 26N	3 05W	and	and	and	and	3.5	2.8	1.4	0.7
Standard port			1400	1900	1300	1900				
Stroma	58 40N	3 08W	−0115	−0115	−0110	−0110	−0.4	−0.5	−0.1	−0.2
Gills Bay	58 38N	3 10W	−0150	−0150	−0202	−0202	+0.7	+0.7	+0.6	+0.3
Scrabster	58 37N	3 33W	−0255	−0225	−0240	−0230	+1.5	+1.2	+0.8	+0.3
Sule Skerry	59 05N	4 24W	−0320	−0255	−0315	−0250	+0.4	+0.3	+0.2	+0.1
Loch Eriboll Portnancon	58 30N	4 42W	−0340	−0255	−0315	−0255	+1.6	+1.3	+0.8	+0.4
Kyle of Durness	58 36N	4 47W	−0350	−0350	−0315	−0315	+1.1	+0.7	+0.4	−0.1
Rona	59 08N	5 49W	−0350	−0350	−0350	−0340	−0.3	−0.4	−0.2	−0.4
			0100	0700	0300	0900				
STORNOWAY	58 12N	6 23W	and	and	and	and	4.8	3.7	2.0	0.7
Standard port			1300	1900	1500	2100				
Outer Hebrides										
Loch Shell	58 00N	6 25W	−0013	0000	0000	−0017	0.0	−0.1	−0.1	0.0
E Loch Tarbert	57 54N	6 48W	−0025	−0010	−0010	−0020	+0.2	0.0	+0.1	+0.1
Leverburgh	57 46N	7 02W	−0041	−0020	−0015	−0025	−0.2	−0.2	−0.2	−0.1
Bays Loch	57 43N	7 10W	−0038	−0013	−0014	−0027	−0.1	−0.2	−0.2	−0.1
Loch Maddy	57 36N	7 09W	−0044	−0014	−0016	−0030	0.0	−0.1	−0.1	0.0
Loch Carnan	57 22N	7 16W	−0050	−0010	−0020	−0040	−0.3	−0.5	−0.1	−0.1
Loch Skiport	57 20N	7 16W	−0100	−0025	−0024	−0024	−0.2	−0.4	−0.3	−0.2
Loch Boisdale	57 09N	7 16W	−0055	−0030	−0020	−0040	−0.7	−0.7	−0.3	−0.2
Barra (North Bay)	57 00N	7 24W	−0103	−0031	−0034	−0048	−0.6	−0.5	−0.2	−0.1
Castle Bay	56 57N	7 29W	−0115	−0040	−0045	−0100	−0.5	−0.6	−0.3	−0.1
Barra Head	56 47N	7 38W	−0115	−0040	−0045	−0055	−0.8	−0.7	−0.2	+0.1
Shillay	57 32N	7 42W	−0103	−0043	−0047	−0107	−0.6	−0.7	−0.7	−0.3
Balivanich	57 29N	7 23W	−0103	−0017	−0031	−0045	−0.7	−0.6	−0.5	−0.2
Scolpaig	57 39N	7 29W	−0033	−0033	−0040	−0040	−1.0	−0.9	−0.5	0.0
W Loch Tarbert	57 55N	6 55W	−0015	−0015	−0046	−0046	−1.1	−0.9	−0.5	0.0
Little Bernera	58 16N	6 52W	−0021	−0011	−0017	−0027	−0.5	−0.6	−0.4	−0.2
Carloway	58 17N	6 47W	−0040	+0020	−0035	−0015	−0.7	−0.5	−0.3	0.0
St Kilda Village Bay	57 48N	8 34W	−0040	−0040	−0045	−0045	−1.4	−1.1	−0.8	−0.3
Flannan Isles	58 17N	7 35W	−0026	−0016	−0016	−0026	−0.9	−0.7	−0.6	−0.2
Rockall	57 36N	13 41W	−0055	−0055	−0105	−0105	−1.8	−1.5	−0.9	−0.2

Location	Lat	Long	High Water		Low Water		MHWS	MHWN	MLWN	MLWS
			0000	0600	0300	0900				
ULLAPOOL	57 54N	5 09W	and	and	and	and	**5.2**	**3.9**	**2.1**	**0.7**
Standard port			1200	1800	1500	2100				
Loch Bervie	58 27N	5 03W	+0017	+0020	+0015	+0015	−0.4	−0.2	−0.1	+0.1
Loch Laxford	58 24N	5 05W	+0015	+0015	+0005	+0005	−0.3	−0.4	−0.2	0.0
Eddrachillis Bay										
Badcall Bay	58 19N	5 08W	+0005	+0005	+0005	+0005	−0.7	−0.5	−0.5	+0.2
Loch Nedd	58 14N	5 10W	0000	0000	0000	0000	−0.3	−0.2	−0.2	0.0
Loch Inver	58 09N	5 18W	−0005	−0005	−0005	−0005	−0.2	0.0	0.0	+0.1
Summer Isles Tanera Mor	58 01N	5 24W	−0005	−0005	−0010	−0010	−0.1	+0.1	0.0	+0.1
Loch Ewe Mellon Charles	57 51N	5 38W	−0005	−0010	−0005	−0005	−0.1	−0.1	−0.1	+0.1
Loch Gairloch Gairloch	57 43N	5 41W	−0020	−0020	−0010	−0010	0.0	+0.1	−0.3	−0.1
Loch Torridon Shieldaig	57 31N	5 39W	−0020	−0020	−0015	−0015	+0.4	+0.3	+0.1	0.0
Inner Sound Applecross	57 26N	5 49W	−0010	−0015	−0010	−0010	0.0	0.0	0.0	+0.1
Loch Carron Plockton	57 21N	5 39W	+0005	−0025	−0005	−0010	+0.5	+0.5	+0.5	+0.2
Rona Loch a' Bhraige	57 35N	5 58W	−0020	0000	−0010	0000	−0.1	−0.1	−0.1	−0.2
Skye										
Broadford Bay	57 15N	5 54W	−0015	−0015	−0010	−0015	+0.2	+0.1	+0.1	0.0
Portree	57 24N	6 11W	−0025	−0025	−0025	−0025	+0.1	−0.2	−0.2	0.0
Loch Snizort (Uig Bay)	57 35N	6 22W	−0045	−0020	−0005	−0025	+0.1	−0.4	−0.2	0.0
Loch Dunvegan	57 27N	6 38W	−0105	−0030	−0020	−0040	0.0	−0.1	0.0	0.0
Loch Harport	57 20N	6 25W	−0115	−0035	−0020	−0100	−0.1	−0.1	0.0	+0.1
Soay Camus nan Gall	57 09N	6 13W	−0055	−0025	−0025	−0045	−0.4	−0.2	No data	
Loch Alsh										
Kyle of Lochalsh	57 17N	5 43W	−0040	−0020	−0005	−0025	+0.1	0.0	0.0	−0.1
Dornie Bridge	57 17N	5 31W	−0040	−0010	−0005	−0020	+0.1	−0.1	0.0	0.0
Kyle Rhea Glenelg Bay	57 13N	5 38W	−0105	−0035	−0035	−0055	−0.4	−0.4	−0.9	−0.1
Loch Hourn	57 06N	5 34W	−0125	−0050	−0040	−0110	−0.2	−0.1	−0.1	+0.1
			0000	0600	0100	0700				
OBAN	56 25N	5 29W	and	and	and	and	**4.0**	**2.9**	**1.8**	**0.7**
Standard port			1200	1800	1300	1900				
Loch Nevis										
Inverie Bay	57 02N	5 41W	+0030	+0020	+0035	+0020	+1.0	+0.9	+0.2	0.0
Mallaig	57 00N	5 50W	+0017	+0017	+0030	+0024	+1.0	+0.7	+0.3	+0.1
Eigg Bay of Laig	56 55N	6 10W	+0015	+0030	+0040	+0005	+0.7	+0.6	−0.2	− 0.2
Loch Moidart	56 47N	5 53W	+0015	+0015	+0040	+0020	+0.8	+0.6	− 0.2	−0.2
Coll Loch Eatharna	56 37N	6 31W	+0025	+0010	+0015	+0025	+0.4	+0.3	No data	
Tiree Gott Bay	56 31N	6 48W	0000	+0010	+0005	+0010	0.0	+0.1	0.0	0.0
			0100	0700	0100	0800				
OBAN	56 25N	5 29W	and	and	and	and	**4.0**	**2.9**	**1.8**	**0.7**
Standard port			1300	1900	1300	2000				
Mull										
Carsaig Bay	56 19N	5 58W	−0015	−0005	−0030	+0020	+0.1	+0.2	0.0	−0.1
Iona	56 20N	6 23W	−0010	−0005	−0020	+0015	0.0	+0.1	−0.3	−0.2
Bunessan	56 19N	6 14W	−0015	−0015	−0010	−0015	+0.3	+0.1	0.0	−0.1
Ulva Sound	56 29N	6 08W	−0010	−0015	0000	−0005	+0.4	+0.3	0.0	−0.1
Loch Sunart Salen	56 43N	5 47W	−0015	+0015	+0010	+0005	+0.6	+0.5	−0.1	−0.1
Sound of Mull										
Tobermory	56 37N	6 04W	+0025	+0010	+0015	+0025	+0.5	+0.6	+0.1	+0.2
Salen	56 31N	5 57W	+0045	+0015	+0020	+0030	+0.2	+0.2	−0.1	0.0
Loch Aline	56 32N	5 46W	+0012	+0012	No data	No data	+0.5	+0.3	No data	
Craignure	56 28N	5 42W	+0030	+0005	+0010	+0015	0.0	+0.1	−0.1	−0.1
Loch Linnhe										
Corran	56 43N	5 14W	+0007	+0007	+0004	+0004	+0.4	+0.4	−0.1	0.0
Corpach	56 51N	5 07W	0000	+0020	+0040	0000	0.0	0.0	−0.2	−0.2
Loch Eil Head	56 51N	5 20W	+0025	+0045	+0105	+0025	No data		No data	
Loch Leven Head	56 43N	5 00W	+0045	+0045	+0045	+0045	No data		No data	
Loch Linnhe Port Appin	56 33N	5 25W	−0005	−0005	−0030	0000	+0.2	+0.2	+0.1	+0.1
Loch Creran										
Barcaldine Pier	56 32N	5 19W	+0010	+0020	+0040	+0015	+0.1	+0.1	0.0	+0.1
Loch Creran Head	56 33N	5 16W	+0015	+0025	+0120	+0020	−0.3	−0.3	−0.4	−0.3
Loch Etive										
Dunstaffnage Bay	56 27N	5 26W	+0005	0000	0000	+0005	+0.1	+0.1	+0.1	+0.1
Connel	56 27N	5 24W	+0020	+0005	+0010	+0015	−0.3	−0.2	−0.1	+0.1
Bonawe	56 27N	5 13W	+0150	+0205	+0240	+0210	−2.0	−1.7	−1.3	−0.5
Seil Sound	56 18N	5 35W	−0035	−0015	−0040	−0015	−1.3	−0.9	−0.7	−0.3
Colonsay Scalasaig	56 04N	6 11W	−0020	−0005	−0015	+0005	−0.3	−0.2	−0.3	0.0
Jura Glengarrisdale Bay	56 07N	5 47W	−0020	0000	−0010	0000	−0.4	−0.2	0.0	−0.2

TIDES

Location	Lat	Long	High Water		Low Water		MHWS	MHWN	MLWN	MLWS
Islay										
Rubha A'Mhail	55 56N	6 07W	−0020	0000	+0005	−0015	−0.3	−0.1	−0.3	−0.1
Ardnave Point	55 52N	6 20W	−0035	+0010	0000	−0025	−0.4	−0.2	−0.3	−0.1
Orsay	55 41N	6 31W	−0110	−0110	−0040	−0040	−1.4	−0.6	−0.5	−0.2
Bruichladdich	55 46N	6 22W	−0105	−0035	−0110	−0110	−1.8	−1.3	−0.4	+0.3
Port Ellen	55 38N	6 11W	−0530	−0050	−0045	−0530	−3.1	−2.1	−1.3	−0.4
Port Askaig	55 51N	6 06W	−0030	−0035	−0015	−0025	−1.8	−1.3	−0.7	−0.2
Sound of Jura										
Craighouse	55 50N	5 57W	−0230	−0250	−0150	−0230	−3.0	−2.4	−1.3	−0.6
Loch Melfort	56 15N	5 29W	−0055	−0025	−0040	−0035	−1.2	−0.8	−0.5	−0.1
Loch Beag	56 09N	5 36W	−0110	−0045	−0035	−0045	−1.6	−1.2	−0.8	−0.4
Carsaig Bay	56 02N	5 38W	−0105	−0040	−0050	−0050	−2.1	−1.6	−1.0	−0.4
Sound of Gigha	55 41N	5 44W	−0450	−0210	−0130	−0410	−2.5	−1.6	−1.0	−0.1
Machrihanish	55 25N	5 45W	−0520	−0350	−0340	−0540	Mean range 0.5 metres			
			0000	**0600**	**0000**	**0600**				
GREENOCK	55 57N	4 46W	and	and	and	and	**3.4**	**2.8**	**1.0**	**0.3**
Standard port			**1200**	**1800**	**1200**	**1800**				
Firth of Clyde										
Southend, Kintyre	55 19N	5 38W	−0030	−0010	+0005	+0035	−1.3	−1.2	−0.5	−0.2
Campbeltown	55 25N	5 36W	−0025	−0005	−0015	+0005	−0.5	−0.3	+0.1	+0.2
Carradale	55 36N	5 28W	−0015	−0005	−0005	+0005	−0.3	−0.2	+0.1	+0.1
Loch Ranza	55 43N	5 18W	−0015	−0005	−0010	−0005	−0.4	−0.3	−0.1	0.0
Loch Fyne										
East Loch Tarbert	55 52N	5 24W	−0005	−0005	0000	−0005	+0.2	+0.1	0.0	0.0
Inveraray	56 14N	5 04W	+0011	+0011	+0034	+0034	−0.1	+0.1	−0.5	−0.2
Kyles of Bute										
Rubha a'Bhodaich	55 55N	5 09W	−0020	−0010	−0007	−0007	−0.2	−0.1	+0.2	+0.2
Tighnabruich	55 55N	5 13W	+0007	−0010	−0002	−0015	0.0	+0.2	+0.4	+0.5
Firth of Clyde – continued										
Millport	55 45N	4 56W	−0005	−0025	−0025	−0005	0.0	−0.1	0.0	+0.1
Rothesay Bay	55 50N	5 03W	−0020	−0015	−0010	−0002	+0.2	+0.2	+0.2	+0.2
Wemyss Bay	55 53N	4 53W	−0005	−0005	−0005	−0005	0.0	0.0	+0.1	+0.1
Loch Long										
Coulport	56 03N	4 53W	−0011	−0011	−0008	−0008	0.0	0.0	0.0	0.0
Lochgoilhead	56 10N	4 54W	+0015	0000	−0005	−0005	−0.2	−0.3	−0.3	−0.3
Arrochar	56 12N	4 45W	−0005	−0005	−0005	−0005	0.0	0.0	−0.1	−0.1
Gare Loch										
Rhu Marina	56 01N	4 46W	−0007	−0007	−0007	−0007	−0.1	−0.1	−0.1	−0.2
Faslane	56 04N	4 49W	−0010	−0010	−0010	−0010	0.0	0.0	−0.1	−0.2
Garelochhead	56 05N	4 50W	0000	0000	0000	0000	0.0	0.0	0.0	−0.1
River Clyde										
Helensburgh	56 00N	4 44W	0000	0000	0000	0000	0.0	0.0	0.0	0.0
Port Glasgow	55 56N	4 41W	+0010	+0005	+0010	+0020	+0.2	+0.1	0.0	0.0
Bowling	55 56N	4 29W	+0020	+0010	+0030	+0055	+0.6	+0.5	+0.3	+0.1
Clydebank (Rothesay Dock)	55 54N	4 24W	+0025	+0015	+0035	+0100	+1.1	+0.9	+0.6	+0.3
Glasgow	55 51N	4 16W	+0025	+0015	+0035	+0105	+1.4	+1.1	+0.8	+0.4
Firth of Clyde – continued										
Brodick Bay	55 35N	5 08W	−0013	−0013	−0008	−0008	−0.2	−0.1	0.0	+0.1
Lamlash	55 32N	5 07W	−0016	−0036	−0024	−0004	−0.2	−0.2	No data	
Ardrossan	55 38N	4 49W	−0020	−0010	−0010	−0010	−0.2	−0.2	+0.1	+0.1
Irvine	55 36N	4 42W	−0020	−0020	−0030	−0010	−0.3	−0.3	−0.1	0.0
Troon	55 33N	4 41W	−0025	−0025	−0020	−0020	−0.2	−0.2	0.0	0.0
Ayr	55 28N	4 39W	−0025	−0025	−0030	−0015	−0.4	−0.3	+0.1	+0.1
Girvan	55 15N	4 52W	−0025	−0040	−0035	−0010	−0.3	−0.3	−0.1	0.0
Loch Ryan Stranraer	54 55N	5 02W	−0030	−0025	−0010	−0010	−0.2	−0.1	0.0	+0.1
			0000	**0600**	**0200**	**0800**				
LIVERPOOL	53 27N	3 01W	and	and	and	and	**9.4**	**7.5**	**3.2**	**1.1**
Standard port			**1200**	**1800**	**1400**	**2000**				
Portpatrick	54 51N	5 07W	+0038	+0032	+0009	−0008	−5.5	−4.4	−2.0	−0.6
Luce Bay										
Drummore	54 42N	4 53W	+0035	+0045	+0010	+0015	−3.5	−2.6	−1.2	−0.5
Port William	54 46N	4 35W	+0035	+0035	+0020	−0005	−3.0	−2.3	−1.1	Nodata
Wigtown Bay										
Isle of Whithorn	54 42N	4 22W	+0025	+0030	+0020	0000	−2.5	−2.1	−1.1	−0.4
Garlieston	54 47N	4 22W	+0030	+0040	+0025	0000	−2.4	−1.8	−0.8	Nodata
Solway Firth										
Kirkcudbright Bay	54 48N	4 04W	+0020	+0020	+0005	−0005	−1.9	−1.6	−0.8	−0.3
Hestan Islet	54 50N	3 48W	+0030	+0030	+0015	+0020	−1.1	−1.2	−0.8	−0.2
Southerness Point	54 52N	3 36W	+0035	+0035	+0025	+0005	−0.8	−0.8	No data	

Location	Lat	Long	High Water		Low Water		MHWS	MHWN	MLWN	MLWS
Annan Waterfoot	54 58N	3 16W	+0055	+0110	+0215	+0305	−2.3	−2.7	−3.0	
Torduff Point	54 58N	3 09W	+0110	+0145	+0515	+0405	−4.2	−5.0		
Redkirk	54 59N	3 06W	+0115	+0220	+0710	+0440	−5.6	−6.3		
WEST COAST OF ENGLAND										
Silloth	54 52N	3 24W	+0035	+0045	+0040	+0050	−0.2	−0.4	−0.9	−0.3
Maryport	54 43N	3 30W	+0021	+0036	+0017	+0002	−0.8	−0.9	−0.7	−0.2
Workington	54 39N	3 34W	+0029	+0027	+0014	+0004	−1.1	−1.1	−0.5	−0.1
Whitehaven	54 33N	3 36W	+0010	+0020	+0005	0000	−1.4	−1.2	−0.8	−0.1
Tarn Point	54 17N	3 25W	+0010	+0010	+0005	−0005	−1.1	−1.1	−0.7	−0.2
Duddon Bar	54 09N	3 20W	+0007	+0007	+0005	−0001	−0.9	−0.9	−0.6	−0.2
			0000	0600	0200	0700				
LIVERPOOL	53 27N	3 01W	and	and	and	and	9.4	7.5	3.2	2.1
Standard port			1200	1800	1400	1900				
Barrow-in-Furness	54 06N	3 12W	+0020	+0020	+0010	+0010	+0.1	−0.2	−0.2	0.0
Ulverston	54 11N	3 04W	+0025	+0045	*No data*	no data	−0.1	−0.2	*No data*	
Arnside	54 12N	2 51W	+0105	+0140	*No data*	no data	+0.4	+0.1	*No data*	
Morecambe	54 04N	2 53W	+0010	+0015	+0025	+0010	+0.1	−0.1	−0.3	0.0
Heysham	54 02N	2 55W	+0014	+0012	+0002	−0003	+0.2	−0.1	−0.2	0.0
River Lune Glasson Dock	54 00N	2 51W	+0025	+0035	+0215	+0235	−2.8	−3.1	*No data*	
Lancaster	54 03N	2 49W	+0115	+0035	*Dries*	Dries	−5.1	−5.0	*Dries*	
River Wyre										
Wyre Lighthouse	53 57N	3 02W	−0005	−0005	0000	−0005	−0.2	−0.2	*No data*	
Fleetwood	53 56N	3 00W	−0004	−0004	−0006	−0006	−0.2	−0.2	−0.1	+0.1
Blackpool	53 49N	3 04W	−0010	0000	−0010	−0020	−0.5	−0.5	−0.4	−0.1
River Ribble Preston	53 45N	2 45W	+0015	+0015	+0330	+0305	−4.1	−4.2	−3.1	−1.0
Liverpool Bay										
Southport	53 39N	3 01W	−0015	−0005	*No data*	No data	−0.4	−0.4	*No data*	
Formby	53 32N	3 07W	−0010	−0005	−0025	−0025	−0.4	−0.2	−0.3	−0.1
River Mersey										
Alfred Dock	53 24N	3 01W	+0007	+0007	0000	0000	−0.1	−0.1	−0.3	−0.2
Eastham	53 19N	2 57W	+0014	+0014	+0006	+0006	+0.2	0.0	−0.4	−0.5
Hale Head	53 19N	2 48W	+0035	+0030	*No data*	No data	−2.5	−2.6	*No data*	
Widnes	53 21N	2 44W	+0045	+0050	+0355	+0340	−4.3	−4.5	−2.8	−0.6
Fiddler's Ferry	53 22N	2 40W	+0105	+0120	+0535	+0445	−6.0	−6.4	−2.7	−0.6
River Dee										
Hilbre Island	53 23N	3 14W	−0011	−0008	−0013	−0018	−0.4	−0.3	−0.1	+0.2
Chester	53 12N	2 54W	+0110	+0110	+0455	+0455	−5.4	−5.5	*Dries*	
Connah's Quay (Wales)	53 13N	3 03W	+0005	+0020	+0350	+0335	−4.7	−4.5	*Dries*	
Mostyn Docks (Wales)	53 19N	3 16W	−0015	−0010	−0025	−0025	−0.9	−0.8	*No data*	
Isle of Man Peel	54 14N	4 42W	+0010	+0010	−0020	−0030	−4.2	−3.2	−1.7	−0.7
Ramsey	54 19N	4 22W	+0010	+0020	−0010	−0020	−2.0	−1.6	−0.9	−0.2
Douglas	54 09N	4 28W	+0010	+0020	−0020	−0030	−2.5	−2.1	−0.8	−0.3
Port St Mary	54 04N	4 44W	+0010	+0020	−0015	−0035	−3.5	−2.7	−1.6	−0.6
Calf Sound	54 04N	4 48W	+0010	+0010	−0020	−0030	−3.3	−2.7	−1.2	−0.5
Port Erin	54 05N	4 46W	+0018	+0010	−0013	−0028	−4.1	−3.3	−1.6	−0.6
WALES										
Colwyn Bay	53 18N	3 43W	−0015	−0015	*No data*	No data	−1.6	−1.4	*No data*	
Llandudno	53 20N	3 50W	−0019	−0021	−0031	−0038	−1.7	−1.6	−0.9	−0.6
			0000	0600	0500	1100				
HOLYHEAD	53 19N	4 37W	and	and	and	and	5.6	4.4	2.0	0.7
Standard port			1200	1800	1700	2300				
Conwy	53 17N	3 50W	+0025	+0035	+0120	+0105	+2.3	+1.8	+0.6	+0.4
Menai Strait										
Beaumaris	53 16N	4 05W	+0025	+0010	+0055	+0035	+2.0	+1.6	+0.5	+0.1
Menai Bridge	53 13N	4 10W	+0030	+0010	+0100	+0035	+1.7	+1.4	+0.3	0.0
Port Dinorwic	53 11N	4 13W	−0015	−0025	+0030	0000	0.0	0.0	0.0	+0.1
Caernarfon	53 09N	4 16W	−0030	−0030	+0015	−0005	−0.4	−0.4	−0.1	−0.1
Fort Belan	53 07N	4 20W	−0040	−0015	−0025	−0005	−1.0	−0.9	−0.2	−0.1
Trwyn Dinmor	53 19N	4 03W	+0025	+0015	+0050	+0035	+1.9	+1.5	+0.5	+0.2
Moelfre	53 20N	4 14W	+0025	+0020	+0050	+0035	+1.9	+1.4	+0.5	+0.2
Amlwch	53 25N	4 20W	+0020	+0010	+0035	+0025	+1.6	+ 1.3	+0.5	+0.2
Cemaes Bay	53 25N	4 27W	+0020	+0025	+0040	+0035	+1.0	+0.7	+0.3	+0.1
Trearddur Bay	53 16N	4 37W	−0045	−0025	−0015	−0015	−0.4	−0.4	0.0	+0.1
Porth Trecastell	53 12N	4 30W	−0045	−0025	−0005	−0015	−0.6	−0.6	0.0	0.0
Llanddwyn Island	53 08N	4 25W	−0115	−0055	−0030	−0020	−0.7	−0.5	−0.1	0.0
Trefor	53 00N	4 25W	−0115	−0100	−0030	−0020	−0.8	−0.9	−0.2	−0.1
Porth Dinllaen	52 57N	4 34W	−0120	−0105	−0035	−0025	−1.0	−1.0	−0.2	−0.2
Porth Ysgaden	52 54N	4 39W	−0125	−0110	−0040	−0035	−1.1	−1.0	−0.1	−0.1
Bardsey Island	52 46N	4 47W	−0220	−0240	−0145	−0140	−1.2	−1.2	−0.5	−0.1

TIDES

Location	Lat	Long	High Water		Low Water		MHWS	MHWN	MLWN	MLWS
MILFORD HAVEN	51 42N	5 03W	0100 and 1300	0800 and 2000	0100 and 1300	0700 and 1900	7.0	5.2	2.5	0.7
Standard port										
Cardigan Bay										
Aberdaron	52 48N	4 43W	+0210	+0200	+0240	+0310	−2.4	−1.9	−0.6	−0.2
St Tudwal's Roads	52 49N	4 29W	+0155	+0145	+0240	+0310	−2.2	−1.9	−0.7	−0.2
Pwllheli	52 53N	4 24W	+0210	+0150	+0245	+0320	−2.0	−1.8	−0.6	−0.1
Criccieth	52 55N	4 14W	+0210	+0155	+0255	+0320	−2.0	−1.8	−0.7	−0.3
Porthmadog	52 55N	4 08W	+0235	+0210	No data	No data	−1.9	−1.8	No data	
Barmouth	52 43N	4 03W	+0207	+0200	+0300	+0233	−2.0	−1.5	−0.6	0.0
Aberdovey	52 33N	4 03W	+0215	+0200	+0230	+0305	−2.0	−1.7	−0.5	0.0
Aberystwyth	52 24N	4 05W	+0145	+0130	+0210	+0245	−2.0	−1.7	−0.7	0.0
New Quay	52 13N	4 21W	+0150	+0125	+0155	+0230	−2.1	−1.8	−0.6	−0.1
Aberporth	52 08N	4 33W	+0135	+0120	+0150	+0220	−2.1	−1.8	−0.6	−0.1
Port Cardigan	52 07N	4 41W	+0140	+0120	+0220	+0130	−2.3	−1.8	−0.5	0.0
Cardigan (Town)	52 05N	4 40W	+0220	+0150	No data	No data	−2.2	−1.6	No data	
Fishguard	52 01N	4 59W	+0115	+0100	+0110	+0135	−2.2	−1.8	−0.5	+0.1
Porthgain	51 57N	5 11W	+0055	+0045	+0045	+0100	−2.5	−1.8	−0.6	0.0
Ramsey Sound	51 53N	5 19W	+0030	+0030	+0030	+0030	−1.9	−1.3	−0.3	0.0
Solva	51 52N	5 12W	+0015	+0010	+0035	+0015	−1.5	−1.0	−0.2	0.0
Little Haven	51 46N	5 07W	+0010	+0010	+0025	+0015	−1.1	−0.8	−0.2	0.0
Martin's Haven	51 44N	5 15W	+0010	+0010	+0015	+0015	−0.8	−0.5	+0.1	+0.1
Skomer Island	51 44N	5 17W	−0005	−0005	+0005	+0005	−0.4	−0.1	0.0	0.0
Dale Roads	51 42N	5 09W	−0005	−0005	−0008	−0008	0.0	0.0	0.0	−0.1
Cleddau River										
Neyland	51 42N	4 57W	+0002	+0010	0000	0000	0.0	0.0	0.0	0.0
Black Tar	51 45N	4 54W	+0010	+0020	+0005	0000	+0.1	+0.1	0.0	−0.1
Haverfordwest	51 48N	4 58W	+0010	+0025	*Dries*	*Dries*	−4.8	−4.9	*Dries*	
Stackpole Quay	51 37N	4 54W	−0005	+0025	−0010	−0010	+0.9	+0.7	+0.2	+0.3
Tenby	51 40N	4 42W	−0015	−0010	−0015	−0020	+1.4	+1.1	+0.5	+0.2
Towy River										
Ferryside	51 46N	4 22W	0000	−0010	+0220	0000	−0.3	−0.7	−1.7	−0.6
Carmarthen	51 51N	4 18W	+0010	0000	*Dries*	*Dries*	−4.4	−4.8	*Dries*	
Burry Inlet										
Burry Port	51 41N	4 15W	+0003	+0003	+0007	+0007	+1.6	+1.4	+0.5	+0.4
Llanelli	51 40N	4 10W	−0003	−0003	+0150	+0020	+0.8	+0.6	No data	
Mumbles	51 34N	3 58W	+0001	+0003	−0012	−0005	+2.5	+2.0	+0.8	+0.4
River Neath Entrance	51 37N	3 51W	+0002	+0011	*Dries*	*Dries*	+2.7	+2.2	*Dries*	
Port Talbot	51 35N	3 49W	0000	+0005	−0010	−0005	+2.7	+2.1	+1.0	+0.4
Porthcawl	51 28N	3 42W	+0005	+0010	−0010	−0005	+2.9	+2.3	+0.8	+0.3
BRISTOL, AVONMOUTH	51 30N	2 44W	0600 and 1800	1100 and 2300	0300 and 1500	0800 and 2000	13.2	9.8	3.8	1.0
Standard port										
Barry	51 23N	3 16W	−0025	−0025	−0130	−0045	−1.5	−1.1	0.0	+0.2
Flat Holm	51 23N	3 07W	−0015	−0015	−0035	−0035	−1.4	−1.0	−0.5	0.0
Steep Holm	51 20N	3 06W	−0020	−0020	−0040	−0040	−1.7	−1.1	−0.5	−0.4
Cardiff	51 27N	3 10W	−0015	−0015	−0035	−0030	−0.9	−0.7	+0.2	+0.2
Newport	51 33N	2 59W	−0005	−0010	−0015	−0015	−0.9	−0.9	−0.2	−0.2
River Wye Chepstow	51 39N	2 40W	+0020	+0020	No data	No data		No data	No data	
BRISTOL, AVONMOUTH	51 30N	2 44W	0000 and 1200	0600 and 1800	0000 and 1200	0700 and 1900	13.2	9.8	3.8	1.0
Standard port										

WEST COAST OF ENGLAND

Location	Lat	Long	High Water		Low Water		MHWS	MHWN	MLWN	MLWS
River Severn										
Sudbrook	51 35N	2 43W	+0010	+0010	+0025	+0015	+0.2	+0.1	−0.1	+0.1
Beachley (Aust)	51 36N	2 38W	+0010	+0015	+0040	+0025	−0.2	−0.2	−0.5	−0.3
Inward Rocks	51 39N	2 37W	+0020	+0020	+0105	+0045	−1.0	−1.1	−1.4	−0.6
Narlwood Rocks	51 39N	2 36W	+0025	+0025	+0120	+0100	−1.9	−2.0	−2.3	−0.8
White House	51 40N	2 33W	+0025	+0025	+0145	+0120	−3.0	−3.1	−3.6	−1.0
Berkeley	51 42N	2 30W	+0030	+0045	+0245	+0220	−3.8	−3.9	−3.4	−0.5
Sharpness Dock	51 43N	2 29W	+0035	+0050	+0305	+0245	−3.9	−4.2	−3.3	−0.4
Wellhouse Rock	51 44N	2 29W	+0040	+0055	+0320	+0305	−4.1	−4.4	−3.1	−0.2
Epney	51 42N	2 24W	+0130	No data	No data	No data	−9.4	No data	No data	
Minsterworth	51 50N	2 23W	+0140	No data	No data	No data	−10.1	No data	No data	
Llanthony	51 51N	2 21W	+0215	No data	No data	No data	−10.7	No data	No data	
BRISTOL, AVONMOUTH	51 30N	2 44W	0200 and 1400	0800 and 2000	0300 and 1500	0800 and 2000	13.2	9.8	3.8	1.0
Standard port										
River Avon										
Shirehampton	51 29N	2 41W	0000	0000	+0035	+0010	−0.7	−0.7	−0.8	0.0
Sea Mills	51 29N	2 39W	+0005	+0005	+0105	+0030	−1.4	−1.5	−1.7	−0.1
Cumberland Basin Entrance	51 27N	2 37W	+0010	+0010	*Dries*	*Dries*	−2.9	−3.0	*Dries*	
Portishead	51 30N	2 45W	−0002	0000	No data	No data	−0.1	−0.1	No data	

Location	Lat	Long	High Water		Low Water		MHWS	MHWN	MLWN	MLWS
Clevedon	51 27N	2 52W	−0010	−0020	−0025	−0015	−0.4	−0.2	+0.2	0.0
St Thomas Head	51 24N	2 56W	0000	0000	−0030	−0030	−0.4	−0.2	+0.1	+0.1
English & Welsh Grounds	51 28N	2 59W	−0008	−0008	−0030	−0030	−0.5	−0.8	−0.3	0.0
Weston-super-Mare	51 21N	2 59W	−0020	−0030	−0130	−0030	−1.2	−1.0	−0.8	−0.2
River Parrett										
Burnham-on-Sea	51 14N	3 00W	−0020	−0025	−0030	0000	−2.3	−1.9	−1.4	−1.1
Bridgwater	51 08N	3 00W	−0015	−0030	+0305	+0455	−8.6	−8.1	*Dries*	
Hinkley Point	51 13N	3 08W	−0032	−0028	−0055	−0049	−1.4	−1.1	−0.1	0.0
Minehead	51 13N	3 28W	−0037	−0052	−0155	−0045	−2.6	−1.9	−0.2	0.0
Porlock Bay	51 13N	3 38W	−0045	−0055	−0205	−0050	−3.0	−2.2	−0.1	−0.1
Lynmouth	51 14N	3 50W	−0055	−0115	*No data*	*No data*	−3.6	−2.7	*No data*	
			0100	**0700**	**0100**	**0700**				
MILFORD HAVEN	51 42N	5 03W	and	and	and	and	**7.0**	**5.2**	**2.5**	**0.7**
Standard port			**1300**	**1900**	**1300**	**1900**				
Ilfracombe	51 13N	4 07W	−0016	−0016	−0041	−0031	+2.3	+1.8	+0.6	+0.3
Rivers Taw & Torridge										
Appledore	51 03N	4 12W	−0020	−0025	+0015	−0045	+0.5	0.0	−0.9	−0.5
Yelland Marsh	51 04N	4 10W	−0010	−0015	+0100	−0015	+0.1	−0.4	−1.2	−0.6
Fremington	51 05N	4 07W	−0010	−0015	+0030	−0030	−1.1	−1.8	−2.2	−0.5
Barnstaple	51 05N	4 04W	0000	−0015	−0155	−0245	−2.9	−3.8	−2.2	−0.4
Bideford	51 01N	4 12W	−0020	−0025	0000	0000	−1.1	−1.6	−2.5	−0.7
Clovelly	51 00N	4 24W	−0030	−0030	−0020	−0040	+1.3	+1.1	+0.2	+0.2
Lundy	51 10N	4 39W	−0025	−0025	−0035	−0030	+1.0	+0.8	+0.2	+0.1
Bude	50 50N	4 33W	−0040	−0040	−0035	−0045	+0.7	+0.6	*No data*	
Boscastle	50 41N	4 42W	−0045	−0010	−0110	−0100	+0.3	+0.4	+0.2	+0.2
Port Isaac	50 35N	4 50W	−0100	−0100	−0100	−0100	+0.5	+0.6	0.0	+0.2
River Camel										
Padstow	50 33N	4 56W	−0055	−0050	−0040	−0050	+0.3	+0.4	+0.1	+0.1
Wadebridge	50 31N	4 50W	−0052	−0052	+0235	+0245	−3.8	−3.8	−2.5	−0.4
Newquay	50 25N	5 05W	−0100	−0110	−0105	−0050	0.0	+0.1	0.0	−0.1
Perranporth	50 21N	5 09W	−0100	−0110	−0110	−0050	−0.1	0.0	0.0	+0.1
St Ives	50 13N	5 29W	−0050	−0115	−0105	−0040	−0.4	−0.3	−0.1	−0.1
Cape Cornwall	50 08N	5 42 W	−0130	−0145	−0120	−0120	−1.0	−0.9	−0.5	−0.1
Sennen Cove	50 05N	5 42W	−0130	−0145	−0125	−0125	−0.9	−0.4	*No data*	

IRELAND

Location	Lat	Long	High Water		Low Water		MHWS	MHWN	MLWN	MLWS
			0000	**0700**	**0000**	**0500**				
DUBLIN, NORTH WALL	53 21N	6 13W	and	and	and	and	**4.1**	**3.4**	**1.5**	**0.7**
Standard port			**1200**	**1900**	**1200**	**1700**				
Courtown	52 39N	6 13W	−0328	−0242	−0158	−0138	−2.8	−2.4	−0.5	0.0
Arklow	52 48N	6 08W	−0315	−0201	−0140	−0134	−2.7	−2.2	−0.6	−0.1
Wicklow	52 59N	6 02W	−0019	−0019	−0024	−0026	−1.4	−1.1	−0.4	0.0
Greystones	53 09N	6 04W	−0008	−0008	−0008	−0008	−0.5	−0.4	*No data*	
Dun Laoghaire	53 18N	6 08W	−0006	−0001	−0002	−0003	0.0	0.0	0.0	+0.1
Dublin Bar	53 21N	6 09W	−0006	−0001	−0002	−0003	0.0	0.0	0.0	+0.1
Howth	53 23N	6 04W	−0007	−0005	+0001	+0005	0.0	−0.1	−0.2	−0.2
Malahide	53 27N	6 09W	+0002	+0003	+0009	+0009	+0.1	−0.2	−0.4	−0.2
Balbriggan	53 37N	6 11W	−0021	−0015	+0010	+0002	+0.3	+0.2	*No data*	
River Boyne Bar	53 43N	6 14W	−0005	0000	+0020	+0030	+0.4	+0.3	−0.1	−0.2
Dunany Point	53 52N	6 14W	−0028	−0018	−0008	−0006	+0.7	+0.9	*No data*	
Dundalk Soldiers Point	54 00N	6 21W	−0010	−0010	0000	+0045	+1.0	+0.8	+0.1	−0.1

NORTHERN IRELAND

Location	Lat	Long	High Water		Low Water		MHWS	MHWN	MLWN	MLWS
Carlingford Lough										
Cranfield Point	54 01N	6 04W	−0027	−0011	+0005	−0010	+0.7	+0.9	+0.3	+0.2
Warrenpoint	54 06N	6 15W	−0020	−0010	+0025	+0035	+1.0	+0.7	+0.2	+0.0
Newry (Victoria Lock)	54 09N	6 19W	+0005	+0015	+0045	*Dries*	+1.2	+0.9	+0.1	*Dries*
			0100	**0700**	**0000**	**0600**				
BELFAST	54 36N	5 55W	and	and	and	and	**3.5**	**3.0**	**1.1**	**0.4**
Standard port			**1300**	**1900**	**1200**	**1800**				
Kilkeel	54 03N	5 59W	+0040	+0030	+0010	+0010	+1.2	+1.1	+0.4	+0.4
Newcastle	54 12N	5 53W	+0025	+0035	+0020	+0040	+1.6	+1.1	+0.4	+0.1
Killough Harbour	54 15N	5 38W	0000	+0020	*No data*	*No data*	+1.8	+1.6	*No data*	
Ardglass	54 16N	5 36W	+0010	+0015	+0005	+0010	+1.7	+1.2	+0.6	+0.3
Strangford Lough										
Killard Point	54 19N	5 31W	+0011	+0021	+0005	+0025	+1.0	+0.8	+0.1	+0.1
Strangford	54 22N	5 33W	+0147	+0157	+0148	+0208	+0.1	+0.1	−0.2	0.0
Quoile Barrier	54 22N	5 41W	+0150	+0200	+0150	+0300	+0.2	+0.2	−0.3	−0.1
Killyleagh	54 24N	5 39W	+0157	+0207	+0211	+0231	+0.3	+0.3	*No data*	
South Rock	54 24N	5 25W	+0023	+0023	+0025	+0025	+1.0	+0.8	+0.1	+0.1
Portavogie	54 27N	5 26W	+0010	+0020	+0010	+0020	+1.2	+0.9	+0.3	+0.2
Donaghadee	54 39N	5 32W	+0020	+0020	+0023	+0023	+0.5	+0.4	+0.1	+0.1
Carrickfergus	54 43N	5 48W	+0005	+0005	+0005	+0005	−0.3	−0.3	−0.2	−0.1
Larne	54 51N	5 48W	+0005	0000	+0010	−0005	−0.7	−0.5	−0.3	0.0
Red Bay	55 04N	6 03W	+0022	−0010	+0007	−0017	−1.9	−1.5	−0.8	−0.2

TIDES

Location	Lat	Long	High Water		Low Water		MHWS	MHWN	MLWN	MLWS
Cushendun	55 08N	6 02W	+0010	−0030	0000	−0025	−1.7	−1.5	−0.6	−0.2
Portrush	55 12N	6 40W	−0433	−0433	−0433	−0433	−1.6	−1.6	−0.3	0.0
Coleraine	55 08N	6 40W	−0403	−0403	−0403	−0403	−1.3	−1.2	−0.2	0.0
			0200	0900	0200	0800				
GALWAY	53 16N	9 03W	and	and	and	and	5.1	3.9	2.0	0.8
Standard port			1400	2100	1400	2000				
Londonderry	55 00N	7 19W	+0254	+0319	+0322	+0321	−2.4	−1.8	−0.8	−0.1

IRELAND

Inishtrahull	55 26N	7 14W	+0100	+0100	+0115	+0200	−1.8	−1.4	−0.4	−0.4
Bulbinbeg	55 22N	7 20W	+0120	+0120	+0135	+0135	−1.3	−1.1	−0.4	−0.3
Trawbreaga Bay	55 19N	7 23W	+0115	+0059	+0109	+0125	−1.1	−0.8	No data	
Lough Swilly										
Rathmullan	55 06N	7 32W	+0125	+0050	+0126	+0118	−0.8	−0.7	−0.1	−0.3
Fanad Head	55 17N	7 38W	+0115	+0040	+0125	+0120	−1.1	−0.9	−0.5	−0.3
Mulroy Bay Bar	55 15N	7 46W	+0108	+0052	+0102	+0118	−1.2	−1.0	No data	
Fanny's Bay	55 12N	7 49W	+0145	+0129	+0151	+0207	−2.2	−1.7	No data	
Seamount Bay	55 11N	7 44W	+0210	+0154	+0226	+0242	−3.1	−2.3	No data	
Cranford Bay	55 09N	7 42W	+0329	+0313	+0351	+0407	−3.7	−2.8		
No data										
Sheephaven Downies Bay	55 11N	7 50W	+0057	+0043	+0053	+0107	−1.1	−0.9	No data	
Inishbofin Bay	55 10N	8 10W	+0040	+0026	+0032	+0046	−1.2	−0.9	No data	
			0600	1100	0000	0700				
GALWAY	53 16N	9 03W	and	and	and	and	5.1	3.9	2.0	0.8
Standard port			1800	2300	1200	1900				
Gweedore Harbour	55 04N	8 19W	+0048	+0100	+0055	+0107	−1.3	−1.0	−0.5	−0.3
Burtonport	54 59N	8 26W	+0042	+0055	+0115	+0055	−1.2	−1.0	−0.6	−0.3
Loughros More Bay	54 47N	8 30W	+0042	+0054	+0046	+0058	−1.1	−0.9	No data	
Donegal Bay										
Killybegs	54 38N	8 26W	+0040	+0050	+0055	+0035	−1.0	−0.9	−0.5	−0.2
Donegal Hbr, Salt Hill Quay	54 38N	8 12W	+0038	+0050	+0052	+0104	−1.2	−0.9	No data	
Mullaghmore	54 28N	8 27W	+0036	+0048	+0047	+0059	−1.4	−1.0	−0.4	−0.4
Sligo Hbr (Oyster Island)	54 18N	8 34W	+0043	+0055	+0042	+0054	−1.0	−0.9	−0.5	−0.3
Ballysadare Bay, Culleenamore	54 16N	8 36W	+0059	+0111	+0111	+0123	−1.2	−0.9	No data	
Killala Bay (Inishcrone)	54 13N	9 06W	+0035	+0055	+0030	+0050	−1.3	−1.2	−0.7	−0.4
Broadhaven	54 16N	9 53W	+0035	+0035	+0040	+0040	−1.4	−1.0	−0.6	−0.2
Blacksod Bay										
Blacksod Quay	54 06N	10 04W	+0025	+0035	+0040	+0040	−1.2	−1.0	−0.6	−0.4
Inishbiggle	54 00N	9 53W	+0055	+0100	+0125	+0110	−1.3	− 0.9	−0.5	−0.2
Clare Island	53 48N	9 57W	+0015	+0021	+0039	+0027	−0.6	−0.4	−0.1	0.0
Clew Bay Inishgort	53 50N	9 40W	+0035	+0045	+0115	+0100	−0.7	−0.5	−0.2	0.0
Killary Harbour	53 38N	9 53W	+0021	+0015	+0035	+0029	−1.0	−0.8	−0.4	−0.3
Inishbofin Bofin Harbour	53 37N	10 12W	+0013	+0009	+0021	+0017	−1.0	−0.8	−0.4	−0.3
Clifden Bay	53 29N	10 04W	+0005	+0005	+0016	+0016	−0.7	−0.5	No data	
Slyne Head	53 24N	10 14W	+0002	+0002	+0010	+0010	−0.7	−0.5	No data	
Roundstone Bay	53 23N	9 55W	+0003	+0003	+0008	+0008	−0.7	−0.5	−0.3	−0.3
Kilkieran Cove	53 19N	9 44W	+0005	+0005	+0016	+0016	−0.3	−0.2	−0.1	−0.2
Aran Islands Killeany Bay	53 07N	9 40W	0000	0000	+0001	−0001	−0.1	+0.1	+0.1	+0.2
Liscannor	52 56N	9 23W	−0003	−0007	+0006	+0002	−0.4	−0.3	No data	
Seafield Point	52 48N	9 30W	−0006	−0014	+0004	−0004	−0.5	−0.4	No data	
Kilrush	52 38N	9 30W	−0006	+0027	+0057	−0016	−0.1	−0.2	−0.3	−0.1
Limerick Dock	52 40N	8 38W	+0135	+0141	+0141	+0219	+1.0	+0.7	−0.8	−0.2
			0500	1100	0500	1100				
COBH	51 51N	8 18 W	and	and	and	and	4.1	3.2	1.3	0.4
Standard port			1700	2300	1700	2300				
Tralee Bay Fenit Pier	52 16N	9 52W	−0057	−0017	−0029	−0109	+0.5	+0.2	+0.3	+0.1
Smerwick Harbour	52 12N	10 24W	−0107	−0027	−0041	−0121	−0.3	−0.4	No data	
Dingle Harbour	52 07N	10 15W	−0111	−0041	−0049	−0119	−0.1	0.0	+0.3	+0.4
Castlemaine Hbr Cromane Pt	52 08N	9 54W	−0026	−0006	−0017	−0037	+0.4	+0.2	+0.4	+0.2
Valentia Harbour										
Knights Town	51 56N	10 18W	−0118	−0038	−0056	−0136	−0.6	−0.4	−0.1	0.0
Ballinskelligs Bay Castle	51 49N	10 16W	−0119	−0039	−0054	−0134	−0.5	−0.5	−0.1	0.0
Kenmare River										
West Cove	51 46N	10 03W	−0113	−0033	−0049	−0129	−0.6	−0.5	−0.1	0.0
Dunkerron Harbour	51 52N	9 39W	−0117	−0027	−0050	−0140	−0.2	−0.3	+0.1	0.0
Coulagh Bay										
Ballycrovane Hbr	51 43N	9 57W	−0116	−0036	−0053	−0133	−0.6	−0.5	−0.1	0.0
Black Ball Harbour	51 36N	10 02W	−0115	−0035	−0047	−0127	−0.7	−0.6	−0.1	+0.1
Bantry Bay										
Castletown Bearhaven	51 39N	9 54W	−0048	−0012	−0025	−0101	−0.8	−0.6	−0.2	0.0
Bantry	51 41N	9 28W	−0045	−0025	−0040	−0105	−0.7	−0.6	−0.2	+0.1

Location	Lat	Long	High Water		Low Water		MHWS	MHWN	MLWN	MLWS
Dunmanus Bay										
Dunbeacon Harbour	51 37N	9 33W	−0057	−0025	−0032	−0104	−0.8	−0.7	−0.3	−0.1
Dunmanus Harbour	51 32N	9 40W	−0107	−0031	−0044	−0120	−0.7	−0.6	−0.2	0.0
Crookhaven	51 28N	9 44W	−0057	−0033	−0048	−0112	−0.8	−0.6	−0.4	−0.1
Skull	51 31N	9 32W	−0040	−0015	−0015	−0110	−0.9	−0.6	−0.2	0.0
Baltimore	51 29N	9 23W	−0025	−0005	−0010	−0050	−0.6	−0.3	+0.1	+0.2
Castletownshend	51 32N	9 10W	−0020	−0030	−0020	−0050	−0.4	−0.2	+0.1	+0.3
Clonakilty Bay	51 35N	8 50W	−0033	−0011	−0019	−0041	−0.3	−0.2	*No data*	
Courtmacsherry	51 38N	8 43W	−0025	−0008	−0008	−0015	−0.1	−0.1	−0.0	+0.1
Kinsale	51 42N	8 31W	−0019	−0005	−0009	−0023	−0.2	0.0	−0.1	+0.2
Roberts Cove	51 45N	8 19W	−0005	−0005	−0005	−0005	−0.1	0.0	0.0	+0.1
Cork Harbour										
Ringaskiddy	51 50N	8 19W	+0005	+0020	+0007	+0013	+0.1	+0.1	+0.1	+0.1
Marino Point	51 53N	8 20W	0000	+0010	0000	+0010	+0.1	+0.1	0.0	0.0
Cork City	51 54N	8 27W	+0005	+0010	+0020	+0010	+0.4	+0.4	+0.3	+0.2
Ballycotton	51 50N	8 01W	−0011	+0001	+0003	−0009	0.0	0.0	−0.1	0.0
Youghal	51 57N	7 51W	0000	+0010	+0010	0000	−0.2	−0.1	−0.1	−0.1
Dungarvan Harbour	52 05N	7 34W	+0004	+0012	+0007	−0001	0.0	+0.1	−0.2	0.0
Waterford Harbour										
Dunmore East	52 09N	6 59W	+0008	+0003	0000	0000	+0.1	0.0	+0.1	+0.2
Cheekpoint	52 16N	7 00W	+0026	+0021	+0019	+0022	+0.5	+0.4	+0.3	+0.2
Kilmokea Point	52 17N	7 00W	+0026	+0022	+0020	+0020	+0.2	+0.1	+0.1	+0.1
Waterford	52 16N	7 07W	+0053	+0032	+0015	+0100	+0.6	+0.6	+0.4	+0.2
New Ross	52 24N	6 57W	+0100	+0030	+0055	+0130	+0.3	+0.4	+0.3	+0.4
Baginbun Head	52 10N	6 50W	+0003	+0003	−0008	−0008	−0.2	−0.1	+0.2	+0.2
Great Saltee	52 07N	6 37W	+0019	+0009	−0004	+0006	−0.3	−0.4	*No data*	
Carnsore Point	52 10N	6 22W	+0029	+0019	−0002	+0008	−1.1	−1.0	*No data*	
Rosslare Europort	52 15N	6 21W	+0045	+0035	+0015	−0005	−2.2	−1.8	−0.5	−0.1
Wexford Harbour	52 20N	6 27W	+0126	+0126	+0118	+0108	−2.1	−1.7	−0.3	+0.1

DENMARK *Time zone −0100*

			0300	0700	0100	0800				
ESBJERG	55 28N	8 27E	and	and	and	and	1.9	1.5	0.5	0.1
Standard port			1500	1900	1300	2000				
Hirtshals	57 36N	9 58E	+0055	+0320	+0340	+0100	−1.6	−1.3	−0.4	−0.1
Hanstholm	57 07N	8 36E	+0100	+0340	+0340	+0130	−1.6	−1.2	−0.4	−0.1
Thyborøn	56 42N	8 13E	+0120	+0230	+0410	+0210	−1.5	−1.2	−0.4	−0.1
Torsminde	56 22N	8 07E	+0045	+0050	+0040	+0010	−1.3	−1.0	−0.4	−0.1
Hvide Sande	56 00N	8 08E	0000	+0010	−0015	−0025	−1.1	−0.8	−0.3	−0.1
Blavands Huk	55 33N	8 05E	−0120	−0110	−0050	−0100	−0.1	−0.1	−0.2	−0.1
Esbjerg, Gradyb Bar	55 26N	8 15E	−0130	−0115	*No data*	*No data*	−0.4	−0.3	−0.2	−0.1
Havneby (Rømø)	55 05N	8 34E	−0040	−0005	0000	−0020	0.0	+0.1	−0.2	−0.2
Hojer	54 58N	8 40E	−0020	+0015	*No data*	*No data*	+0.5	+0.6	−0.1	−0.1

GERMANY *Time zone −0100*

			0100	0600	0100	0800				
HELGOLAND	54 11N	7 53E	and	and	and	and	3.2	2.8	0.9	0.5
Standard port			1300	1800	1300	2000				
Lister Tief, List	55 01N	8 26E	+0252	+0240	+0201	+0210	−0.7	−0.6	−0.3	0.0
Hörnum	54 45N	8 18E	+0223	+0218	+0131	+0137	−0.4	−0.3	−0.2	0.0
Amrum - Hafen	54 38N	8 23E	+0138	+0137	+0128	+0134	+0.2	+0.2	−0.1	0.0
Dagebüll	54 44N	8 41E	+0226	+0217	+0211	+0225	+0.7	+0.7	+0.1	+0.1
Suderoogsand	54 25N	8 30E	+0116	+0102	+0038	+0122	+0.5	+0.1	+0.1	0.1
River Hever, Husum	54 28N	9 01E	+0205	+0152	+0118	+0200	+1.1	+1.0	+0.1	−0.0
Suederhoeft	54 16N	8 42E	+0103	+0056	+0051	+0112	+0.7	+0.6	−0.2	0.0
Eidersperrwerk	54 16N	8 51E	+0120	+0115	+0130	+0155	+0.7	+0.6	−0.1	0.0
Linnenplate	54 13N	8 40E	+0047	+0046	+0034	+0046	+0.7	+0.6	−0.1	−0.1
Büsum	54 07N	8 52E	+0054	+0049	−0001	+0027	+0.9	+0.8	+0.1	0.0

			0200	0800	0200	0900				
CUXHAVEN	53 52N	8 43E	and	and	and	and	3.8	3.3	0.9	0.5
Standard port			1400	2000	1400	2100				
River Elbe Großer Vogelsand	54 00N	8 29E	−0044	−0046	−0101	−0103	0.0	+0.1	+0.1	0.0
Scharhörn	53 58N	8 28E	−0045	−0047	−0101	−0103	+0.1	+0.1	+0.1	0.0
Otterndorf	53 50N	8 52E	+0029	+0029	+0027	+0027	−0.1	−0.1	−0.1	0.0
Brunsbüttel	53 53N	9 08E	+0057	+0105	+0121	+0112	−0.2	−0.1	−0.1	0.0
Glückstadt	53 47N	9 25E	+0205	+0214	+0220	+0213	−0.1	0.0	−0.1	+0.1
Stadersand	53 38N	9 32E	+0241	+0245	+0300	+0254	0.0	+0.1	−0.2	0.0
Schulau	53 34N	9 42E	+0304	+0315	+0337	+0321	+0.2	+0.3	−0.3	−0.1
Seemannshoeft	53 32N	9 53E	+0324	+0332	+0403	+0347	+0.4	+0.4	−0.4	−0.2
Hamburg	53 33N	9 58E	+0338	+0346	+0422	+0406	+0.4	+0.5	−0.4	−0.2

TIDES

215

TIDES

Location	Lat	Long	High Water		Low Water		MHWS	MHWN	MLWN	MLWS
WILHELMSHAVEN	53 31N	8 09E	0200 and 1400	0800 and 2000	0200 and 1400	0900 and 2100	4.8	4.2	1.1	0.5
Standard port										
River Weser										
Alter Weser lt ho	53 32N	8 08E	−0055	−0048	−0015	−0029	−1.1	−0.9	−0.1	0.0
Dwarsgat	53 43N	8 18E	−0015	+0002	−0006	−0001	−0.5	−0.4	−0.1	0.0
Bremerhaven	53 33N	8 34E	+0029	+0046	+0033	+0038	−0.1	0.0	−0.1	0.0
Nordenham	53 28N	8 29E	+0051	+0109	+0055	+0058	0.0	+0.1	−0.2	−0.1
Brake	53 19N	8 29E	+0120	+0119	+0143	+0155	−0.2	−0.1	−0.4	−0.2
Elsfleth	53 16N	8 29E	+0137	+0137	+0206	+0216	−0.2	−0.1	−0.4	−0.2
Vegesack	53 10N	8 37E	+0208	+0204	+0250	+0254	−0.1	−0.1	−0.5	−0.2
Bremen	53 07N	8 43E	+0216	+0211	+0311	+0314	0.0	0.0	−0.6	−0.3
River Jade										
Wangerooge East	53 46N	7 59E	−0058	−0053	−0024	−0034	−1.0	−0.8	−0.1	0.0
Wangerooge West	53 47N	7 52E	−0101	−0058	−0035	−0045	−1.1	−0.9	−0.1	0.0
Schillig	53 42N	8 03E	−0031	−0025	−0006	−0014	−0.7	−0.6	−0.1	0.0
Hooksiel	53 39N	8 05E	−0023	−0022	−0008	−0012	−0.5	−0.4	0.0	0.0
HELGOLAND	54 11N	7 53E	0200 and 1400	0700 and 1900	0200 and 1400	0800 and 2000	3.2	2.8	0.9	0.5
Standard port										
East Frisian Islands and coast										
Spiekeroog	53 45N	7 41E	+0003	−0003	−0031	−0012	+0.3	+0.3	0.0	−0.1
Neuharlingersiel	53 42N	7 42E	+0014	+0008	−0024	−0013	+0.5	+0.4	−0.1	−0.1
Langeoog	53 43N	7 30E	+0003	−0001	−0034	−0018	+0.3	+0.3	0.0	0.0
Norderney (Riffgat)	53 42N	7 09E	−0024	−0030	−0056	−0045	0.0	0.0	−0.1	−0.1
Norddeich Hafen	53 39N	7 09E	−0018	−0017	−0029	−0012	+0.1	+0.1	−0.1	−0.1
Juist	53 40N	7 00E	−0026	−0032	−0019	−0008	+0.1	+0.1	0.0	−0.1
River Ems										
Memmert	53 38N	6 54E	−0032	−0038	−0114	−0103	+0.1	+0.1	0.0	−0.1
Borkum (Fischerbalje)	53 33N	6 45E	−0048	−0052	−0124	−0105	0.0	0.0	0.0	0.0
Emshorn	53 30N	6 50E	−0037	−0041	−0108	−0047	+0.1	+0.1	−0.1	0.0
Knock	53 20N	7 02E	+0018	+0005	−0028	+0004	+0.6	+0.6	0.0	0.0
Emden	53 20N	7 11E	+0041	+0028	−0011	+0022	+0.8	+0.8	0.0	−0.1

NETHERLANDS *Time zone −0100*

Location	Lat	Long	High Water		Low Water		MHWS	MHWN	MLWN	MLWS
HELGOLAND	54 11N	7 53E	0200 and 1400	0700 and 1900	0200 and 1400	0800 and 2000	3.2	2.8	0.9	0.5
Standard port										
Delfzijl	53 20N	6 56E	+0020	−0005	−0040	0000	+0.5	+0.6	−0.1	−0.1
Eemshaven	53 27N	6 50E	−0025	−0045	−0115	−0045	0.0	+0.1	−0.1	−0.1
Huibertgat	53 35N	6 24E	−0150	−0150	−0210	−0210	−0.5	−0.4	−0.2	−0.2
Schiermonnikoog	53 28N	6 12E	−0120	−0130	−0240	−0220	−0.3	−0.2	−0.2	−0.2
Waddenzee										
Lauwersoog	53 25N	6 12E	−0130	−0145	−0235	−0220	−0.3	−0.2	−0.2	0.0
Nes	53 26N	5 47E	−0135	−0150	−0245	−0225	−0.3	−0.2	−0.2	0.0
West Terschelling	53 22N	5 13E	−0220	−0250	−0335	−0310	−0.8	−0.6	−0.3	−0.2
Vlieland-Haven	53 18N	5 06E	−0250	−0320	−0355	−0330	−0.8	−0.6	−0.3	−0.1
Harlingen	53 10N	5 25E	−0155	−0245	−0210	−0130	−0.8	−0.7	−0.4	−0.1
Kornwerderzand	53 04N	5 20E	−0210	−0315	−0300	−0215	−1.0	−0.8	−0.4	−0.2
Den Oever	52 56N	5 02E	−0245	−0410	−0400	−0305	−1.2	−1.0	−0.5	−0.2
Oudeschild	53 02N	4 51E	−0310	−0420	−0445	−0400	−1.4	−1.1	−0.4	−0.2
Den Helder	52 58N	4 45E	−0410	−0520	−0520	−0430	−1.3	−1.1	−0.4	−0.2
Noordwinning (Platform K13–A)	53 13N	3 13E	−0420	−0430	−0520	−0530	−1.4	−1.4	−0.3	−0.3
VLISSINGEN	51 27N	3 36E	0300 and 1500	0900 and 2100	0400 and 1600	1000 and 2200	4.9	4.1	1.0	0.5
Standard port										
IJmuiden	52 28N	4 33E	+0145	+0140	+0305	+0325	−2.9	−2.4	−0.8	−0.3
Scheveningen	52 06N	4 16E	+0105	+0100	+0220	+0245	−2.8	−2.3	−0.8	−0.2
Europlatform	52 00N	3 17E	+0005	−0005	−0030	−0055	−2.8	−2.3	−0.6	−0.1
Nieuwe Waterweg										
HOEK VAN HOLLAND			*Standard port, no Secondaries*							
Maassluis	51 55N	4 15E	+0155	+0115	+0100	+0310	−2.9	−2.3	−0.8	−0.2
Nieuwe Maas, Vlaardingen	51 54N	4 21E	+0150	+0120	+0130	+0330	−2.9	−2.3	−0.8	−0.2
Haringvlietsluizen	51 50N	4 03E	+0015	+0015	+0015	−0020	−2.0	−1.9	−0.7	−0.2
Ooster Schelde										
Roompot Buiten	51 37N	3 40E	−0015	+0005	+0005	−0020	−1.3	−1.1	−0.4	−0.1
Walcheren, Westkapelle	51 32N	3 26E	−0025	−0015	−0010	−0025	−0.6	−0.6	−0.2	−0.1
Westerschelde										
Terneuzen	51 20N	3 50E	+0020	+0020	+0020	+0030	+0.3	+0.4	0.0	+0.1
Hansweert	51 27N	4 00E	+0100	+0050	+0040	+0100	+0.6	+0.7	0.0	0.0
Bath	51 24N	4 13E	+0125	+0115	+0115	+0140	+1.1	+1.0	+0.1	+0.1

Location	Lat	Long	High Water		Low Water		MHWS	MHWN	MLWN	MLWS
BELGIUM *Time zone –0100*										
Antwerpen	51 21N	4 14E	+0128	+0116	+0121	+0144	+1.2	+1.0	+0.1	+0.1
Blankenberge	51 19N	3 07E	–0040	–0040	–0040	–0040	–0.3	0.0	+0.3	+0.2
			0300	0900	0300	0900				
ZEEBRUGGE	51 21N	3 12E	and	and	and	and	4.8	4.0	1.1	0.5
Standard port			1500	2100	1500	2100				
Oostende	51 14N	2 56E	–0019	–0019	–0008	–0008	+0.4	+0.3	+0.2	+0.1
Nieuwpoort	51 09N	2 43E	–0031	–0031	–0010	–0010	+0.7	+0.5	+0.3	+0.1
FRANCE *Time zone –0100*										
			0200	0800	0200	0900				
DUNKERQUE	51 03N	2 22E	and	and	and	and	6.0	5.0	1.5	0.6
Standard port			1400	2000	1400	2100				
Gravelines	51 01N	2 06E	–0010	–0015	–0010	–0005	+0.5	+0.3	+0.1	0.0
Sandettie Bank	51 15N	2 03E	–0010	–0015	–0015	–0010	+0.6	–0.6	–0.2	–0.1
Calais	50 58N	1 51E	–0020	–0030	–0015	–0005	+1.2	+0.9	+0.6	+0.3
Wissant	50 53N	1 40E	–0035	–0050	–0030	–0010	+1.9	+1.5	+0.8	+0.4
Boulogne	50 44N	1 35E	–0045	–0100	–0045	–0025	+2.8	+2.2	+1.1	+0.5
			0100	0600	0100	0700				
DIEPPE	49 56N	1 05E	and	and	and	and	9.3	7.4	2.5	0.8
Standard port			1300	1800	1300	1900				
Le Touquet, Étaples	50 31N	1 35E	+0005	+0015	+0030	+0030	+0.2	+0.3	+0.4	+0.4
Berck	50 24N	1 34E	+0005	+0015	+0030	+0030	+0.5	+0.5	+0.4	+0.4
La Somme										
Le Hourdel	50 13N	1 34E	+0020	+0020	No data	No data	+0.8	+0.6	No data	
St Valéry	50 11N	1 37E	+0035	+0035	No data	No data	+0.9	+0.7	No data	
Cayeux	50 11N	1 29E	0000	+0005	+0015	+0010	+0.5	+0.6	+0.4	+0.4
Le Tréport	50 04N	1 22E	+0005	0000	+0007	+0007	+0.1	+0.1	0.0	+0.1
St Valéry–en–Caux	49 52N	0 42E	–0005	–0005	–0015	–0020	–0.5	–0.4	–0.1	–0.1
Fécamp	49 46N	0 22E	–0015	–0010	–0030	–0040	–1.0	–0.6	+0.3	+0.4
Etretat	49 42N	0 12E	–0020	–0020	–0045	–0050	–1.2	–0.8	+0.3	+0.4
			0000	0500	0000	0700				
LE HAVRE	49 29N	0 07E	and	and	and	and	7.9	6.6	2.8	1.2
Standard port			1200	1700	1200	1900				
Antifer (Le Havre)	49 39N	0 09E	+0025	+0015	+0005	–0005	+0.1	0.0	0.0	0.0
La Seine										
Chenal du Rouen	49 26N	0 07E	0000	0000	0000	+0015	0.0	–0.1	0.0	–0.1
Honfleur	49 25N	0 14E	–0150	–0135	+0025	+0040	0.0	0.0	+0.1	+0.4
Tancarville	49 28N	0 28E	–0135	–0120	+0030	+0145	+0.1	+0.1	+0.3	+1.0
Quilleboeuf	49 28N	0 32E	–0055	–0110	+0105	+0210	+0.1	+0.1	+0.5	+1.4
Vatteville	49 29N	0 40E	+0015	–0040	+0205	+0240	–0.1	–0.1	+0.9	+2.2
Caudebec	49 32N	0 44E	–0005	–0030	+0220	+0300	–0.1	–0.1	+1.0	+2.3
Heurteauville	49 27N	0 49E	+0055	+0005	+0250	+0330	–0.2	–0.1	+1.2	+2.6
Duclair	49 29N	0 53E	+0210	+0145	+0350	+0410	–0.2	0.0	+1.5	+3.2
Rouen	49 27N	1 06E	+0305	+0240	+0505	+0515	–0.1	+0.2	+1.6	+3.3
Trouville	49 22N	0 05E	–0100	–0010	0000	+0005	+0.4	+0.3	+0.3	+0.1
Dives	49 18N	0 05W	–0100	–0010	0000	0000	+0.3	+0.2	+0.2	+0.1
Ouistreham	49 17N	0 15W	–0045	–0010	–0005	0000	–0.3	–0.3	–0.2	–0.3
Courseulles-sur-Mer	49 20N	0 27W	–0045	–0015	–0020	–0025	–0.5	–0.5	–0.1	–0.1
Arromanches	49 21N	0 37W	–0055	–0025	–0025	–0035	–0.6	–0.6	–0.2	–0.2
Port-en-Bessin	49 21N	0 45W	–0055	–0030	–0030	–0035	–0.7	–0.7	–0.2	–0.1
Alpha-Baie de Seine	49 49N	0 20W	+0030	+0020	–0005	–0020	–1.0	–0.9	–0.4	–0.2
			0300	1000	0400	1000				
CHERBOURG	49 39N	1 38W	and	and	and	and	6.4	5.0	2.5	1.1
Standard port			1500	2200	1600	2200				
Rade de la Capelle	49 25N	1 05W	+0115	+0050	+0130	+0115	+0.8	+0.9	+0.1	+0.1
Iles Saint Marcouf	49 30N	1 08W	+0120	+0050	+0125	+0110	+0.6	+0.7	+0.1	+0.1
St Vaast-la-Hougue	49 34N	1 16W	+0120	+0050	+0120	+0115	+0.3	+0.5	0.0	–0.1
Barfleur	49 40N	1 15W	+0110	+0055	+0050	+0050	+0.1	+0.3	0.0	0.0
Omonville	49 42N	1 50W	–0010	–0010	–0015	–0015	–0.1	–0.1	0.0	0.0
Goury	49 43N	1 57W	–0100	–0040	–0105	–0120	+1.7	+1.6	+1.0	+0.3
CHANNEL ISLANDS *Time zone UT*										
			0300	0900	0200	0900				
ST HELIER	49 11N	2 07W	and	and	and	and	11.0	8.1	4.0	1.4
Standard port			1500	2100	1400	2100				
Alderney, Braye	49 43N	2 12W	+0050	+0040	+0025	+0105	–4.8	–3.4	–1.5	–0.5
Sark, Maseline Pier	49 26N	2 21W	+0005	+0015	+0005	+0010	–2.1	–1.5	–0.6	–0.3
Guernsey, ST PETER PORT	49 27N	2 31W	Standard port (no Secondaries)							

TIDES

TIDES

Location	Lat	Long	High Water		Low Water		MHWS	MHWN	MLWN	MLWS
Jersey										
St Catherine Bay	49 13N	2 01W	0000	+0010	+0010	+0010	0.0	–0.1	0.0	+0.1
Bouley Bay	49 15N	2 05W	+0002	+0002	+0004	+0004	–0.3	–0.3	–0.1	–0.1
Les Ecrehou	49 17N	1 56W	+0005	+0009	+0011	+0009	–0.2	+0.1	–0.2	0.0
Les Minquiers	48 57N	2 08W	–0014	–0018	–0001	–0008	+0.5	+0.6	+0.1	+0.1

FRANCE *Time zone –0100*

Location	Lat	Long	High Water		Low Water		MHWS	MHWN	MLWN	MLWS
			0100	0800	0300	0800				
ST MALO	48 38N	2 02W	and	and	and	and	12.2	9.3	4.2	1.5
Standard port			1300	2000	1500	2000				
Les Ardentes	48 58N	1 52W	+0010	+0010	+0020	+0010	0.0	–0.1	0.0	–0.1
Iles Chausey	48 52N	1 49W	+0005	+0005	+0015	+0015	+0.8	+0.7	+0.6	+0.4
Diélette	49 33N	1 52W	+0045	+0035	+0020	+0035	–2.5	–1.9	–0.7	–0.3
Carteret	49 22N	1 47W	+0030	+0020	+0015	+0030	–1.6	–1.2	–0.5	–0.2
Portbail	49 18N	1 45W	+0030	+0025	+0025	+0030	–0.8	–0.6	–0.2	–0.1
St Germain sur Ay	49 14N	1 36W	+0025	+0025	+0035	+0035	–0.7	–0.5	0.0	+0.1
Le Sénéquet	49 05N	1 40W	+0015	+0015	+0025	+0025	–0.3	–0.3	+0.1	+0.1
Regnéville sur Mer	49 01N	1 33W	+0010	+0010	+0030	+0020	+0.5	+0.4	+0.2	0.0
Granville	48 50N	1 36W	+0005	+0005	+0020	+0010	+0.7	+0.5	+0.3	+0.1
Cancale	48 40N	1 51W	0000	0000	+0010	+0010	+0.8	+0.6	+0.3	+0.1
Ile des Hebihens	48 37N	2 11W	0000	0000	–0005	–0005	–0.2	–0.2	–0.1	–0.1
St Cast	48 38N	2 15W	0000	0000	–0005	–0005	–0.2	–0.2	–0.1	–0.1
Erquy	48 38N	2 28W	–0010	–0005	–0025	–0015	–0.6	–0.5	0.0	0.0
Dahouët	48 35N	2 34W	–0010	–0010	–0025	–0020	–0.9	–0.7	–0.2	–0.2
Le Légué (Buoy)	48 34N	2 41W	–0010	–0005	–0020	–0015	–0.8	–0.5	–0.2	–0.1
Binic	48 36N	2 49W	–0010	–0010	–0030	–0015	–0.8	–0.7	–0.2	–0.2
St Quay-Portrieux	48 38N	2 49W	–0010	–0005	–0025	–0020	–0.9	–0.7	–0.2	–0.1
Paimpol	48 47N	3 02W	–0010	–0005	–0035	–0025	–1.4	–1.0	–0.4	–0.2
Ile de Bréhat	48 50N	3 00W	–0015	–0005	–0040	–0030	–1.6	–1.2	–0.5	–0.0
Les Héaux de Bréhat	48 55N	3 05W	–0020	–0020	–0055	–0045	–2.4	–1.7	–0.7	–0.3
Lézardrieux	48 47N	3 06W	–0020	–0015	–0055	–0045	–1.7	–1.3	–0.5	–0.2
Port-Béni	48 51N	3 10W	–0025	–0025	–0105	–0050	–2.4	–1.7	–0.6	–0.2
Tréguier	48 47N	3 13W	–0020	–0020	–0100	–0045	–2.3	–1.6	–0.6	–0.2
Perros-Guirec	48 49N	3 28W	–0040	–0045	–0120	–0105	–2.9	–2.0	–0.8	–0.3
Ploumanac'h	48 50N	3 29W	–0035	–0040	–0120	–0100	–2.9	–2.0	–0.7	–0.2
			0000	0600	0000	0600				
BREST	48 23N	4 30W	and	and	and	and	7.0	5.5	2.7	1.1
Standard port			1200	1800	1200	1800				
Trébeurden	48 46N	3 35W	+0100	+0110	+0120	+0100	+2.2	+1.8	+0.8	+0.3
Locquirec	48 42N	3 38W	+0100	+0110	+0120	+0100	+2.1	+1.7	+0.7	+0.2
Anse de Primel	48 43N	3 50W	+0100	+0110	+0120	+0100	+2.0	+1.6	+0.7	+0.2
Chateau du Taureau (Morlaix)	48 41N	3 53W	+0055	+0105	+0115	+0055	+1.9	+1.6	+0.7	+0.2
Roscoff	48 43N	3 58W	+0055	+0105	+0115	+0055	+1.8	+1.5	+0.7	+0.2
Ile de Batz	48 44N	4 00W	+0045	+0100	+0105	+0055	+1.9	+1.5	+0.8	+0.3
Brignogan	48 40N	4 19W	+0040	+0045	+0100	+0040	+1.4	+1.1	+0.5	+0.1
L'Aber Wrac'h	48 36N	4 34W	+0030	+0030	+0040	+0035	+0.7	+0.6	+0.1	–0.1
Aber Benoit	48 35N	4 37W	+0022	+0025	+0035	+0020	+0.9	+0.8	+0.3	+0.1
Portsall	48 34N	4 43W	+0015	+0020	+0025	+0015	+0.5	+0.4	0.0	–0.1
L'Aber-Ildut	48 28N	4 45W	+0010	+0010	+0023	+0010	+0.3	+0.2	–0.1	–0.1
Ouessant, Baie de Lampaul	48 27N	5 06W	+0010	+0010	0000	+0005	–0.1	–0.1	–0.1	–0.1
Molene	48 24N	4 58W	+0015	+0010	+0020	+0020	+0.3	+0.3	+0.1	+0.1
Le Conquet	48 22N	4 47W	0000	0000	+0005	+0005	–0.2	–0.2	–0.1	0.0
Le Trez Hir	48 21N	4 42W	–0005	–0005	–0010	–0010	–0.4	–0.4	–0.2	–0.1
Camaret	48 17N	4 35W	–0010	–0010	–0015	–0010	–0.4	–0.4	–0.3	–0.1
Morgat	48 13N	4 30W	–0005	–0010	–0020	–0005	–0.5	–0.4	–0.2	0.0
Douarnenez	48 06N	4 19W	–0010	–0010	–0020	–0010	–0.4	–0.4	–0.2	–0.1
Ile de Sein	48 02N	4 51W	–0005	–0005	–0015	–0010	–0.9	–0.7	–0.4	–0.2
Anse de Feunteun Aod	48 02N	4 42W	–0030	–0040	–0035	–0025	–1.4	–1.2	–0.6	–0.2
Audierne	48 01N	4 33W	–0035	–0030	–0035	–0030	–1.8	–1.4	–0.7	–0.3
Le Guilvinec	47 48N	4 17W	–0010	–0025	–0025	–0015	–1.9	–1.5	–0.7	–0.2
Lesconil	47 48N	4 13W	–0010	–0030	–0030	–0020	–2.0	–1.5	–0.7	–0.2
Pont l'Abbe River, Loctudy	47 50N	4 10W	–0010	–0030	–0030	–0020	–2.1	–1.7	–0.8	–0.4
Odet River										
Bénodet	47 53N	4 07W	0000	0000	–0025	–0015	–1.8	–1.4	–0.6	–0.2
Corniguel	47 58N	4 06W	+0015	+0010	–0015	–0010	–2.1	–1.7	–1.1	–0.8

Location	Lat	Long	High Water		Low Water		MHWS	MHWN	MLWN	MLWS
Concarneau	47 52N	3 55W	−0010	−0030	−0030	−0020	−2.0	−1.6	−0.8	−0.3
Iles de Glenan, Ile de Penfret	47 44N	3 57W	−0005	−0030	−0030	−0020	−2.0	−1.6	−0.8	−0.3
Port Louis	47 42N	3 21W	+0005	−0020	−0020	−0010	−1.9	−1.5	−0.7	−0.2
Lorient	47 45N	3 21W	+0005	−0020	−0020	−0010	−1.9	−1.5	−0.7	−0.3
Hennebont	47 48N	3 17W	+0015	−0015	+0005	+0005	−2.0	−1.6	−0.9	−0.3
Ile de Groix, Port Tudy	47 39N	3 27W	0000	−0025	−0025	−0015	−1.9	−1.5	−0.7	−0.2
Port d'Etel	47 39N	3 12W	+0020	−0010	+0030	+0010	−2.1	−1.4	−0.5	+0.4
Port Haliguen	47 29N	3 06W	+0010	−0020	−0015	−0010	−1.7	−1.3	−0.7	−0.3
Port Maria	47 29N	3 08W	+0010	−0025	−0025	−0015	−1.7	−1.4	−0.7	−0.2
Belle Ile, Le Palais	47 21N	3 09W	−0005	−0025	−0025	−0010	−1.9	−1.4	−0.8	−0.3
Crac'h River, La Trinité	47 35N	3 01W	+0025	−0020	−0015	−0010	−1.7	−1.2	−0.6	−0.3
Golfe du Morbihan										
Port Navalo	47 33N	2 55W	+0030	−0005	−0010	−0005	−2.1	−1.6	−0.9	−0.4
Auray	47 40N	2 59W	+0035	0000	+0015	−0005	−2.3	−1.9	−1.2	−0.5
Arradon	47 37N	2 50W	+0135	+0145	+0140	+0115	−3.9	−3.1	−1.9	−0.8
Vannes	47 39N	2 46W	+0200	+0150	+0140	+0120	−3.8	−3.0	−2.1	−0.9
St Armel (Le Passage)	47 36N	2 43W	+0200	+0200	+0210	+0135	−3.8	−3.0	−2.0	−0.9
Le Logeo	47 33N	2 51W	+0140	+0140	+0145	+0115	−4.1	−3.2	−2.1	−0.9
Port du Crouesty	47 32N	2 54W	+0010	−0025	−0025	−0030	−1.7	−1.3	−0.7	−0.4
Ile de Houat	47 24N	2 57W	+0005	−0025	−0025	−0010	−1.8	−1.4	−0.7	−0.4
Ile de Hoëdic	47 20N	2 52W	+0010	−0035	−0025	−0020	−1.9	−1.5	−0.8	−0.4
Pénerf	47 31N	2 37W	+0015	−0025	−0015	−0015	−1.6	−1.2	−0.7	−0.4
Tréhiguier	47 30N	2 27W	+0035	−0020	−0005	−0010	−1.5	−1.1	−0.6	−0.4
Le Croisic	47 18N	2 31W	+0015	−0040	−0020	−0015	−1.6	−1.2	−0.7	−0.4
Le Pouliguen	47 17N	2 25W	+0020	−0025	−0020	−0025	−1.6	−1.2	−0.7	−0.4
Le Grand-Charpentier	47 13N	2 19W	+0015	−0045	−0025	−0020	−1.6	−1.2	−0.7	−0.4
Pornichet	47 16N	2 21W	+0020	−0045	−0022	−0022	−1.5	−1.1	−0.6	−0.3
La Loire										
St Nazaire	47 16N	2 12W	+0030	−0040	−0010	−0010	−1.2	−0.9	−0.5	−0.3
Donges	47 18N	2 05W	+0035	−0035	+0005	+0005	−1.1	−0.8	−0.6	−0.5
Cordemais	47 17N	1 54W	+0055	−0005	+0105	+0030	−0.8	−0.6	−0.8	−0.5
Le Pellerin	47 12N	1 46W	+0110	+0010	+0145	+0100	−0.8	−0.6	−1.0	−0.5
Nantes (Chantenay)	47 12N	1 35W	+0135	+0055	+0215	+0125	−0.7	−0.4	−0.9	−0.2
			0500	**1100**	**0500**	**1100**				
BREST	48 23N	4 30W	and	and	and	and	7.0	5.5	2.7	1.1
Standard port			**1700**	**2300**	**1700**	**2300**				
Pointe de Saint–Gildas	47 08N	2 15W	−0045	+0025	−0020	−0020	−1.4	−1.1	−0.6	−0.3
Pornic	47 06N	2 07W	−0050	+0030	−0010	−0010	−1.2	−0.9	−0.5	−0.3
Ile de Noirmoutier, L'Herbaudière	47 02N	2 18W	−0045	+0025	−0020	−0020	−1.5	−1.1	−0.6	−0.3
Fromentine	46 54N	2 10W	−0045	+0020	−0015	+0005	−1.8	−1.4	−0.9	−0.2
Ile de Yeu, Port Joinville	46 44N	2 21W	−0040	+0015	−0030	−0035	−2.0	−1.5	−0.8	−0.4
St Gilles-Croix-de-Vie	46 41N	1 56W	−0030	+0015	−0030	−0030	−1.9	−1.4	−0.7	−0.4
Les Sables d'Olonne	46 30N	1 48W	−0030	+0015	−0035	−0035	−1.8	−1.4	−0.7	−0.4
			0000	**0600**	**0000**	**0500**				
POINTE DE GRAVE	45 34N	1 04W	and	and	and	and	5.3	4.4	2.1	1.0
Standard port			**1200**	**1800**	**1200**	**1700**				
Ile de Ré, St Martin	46 12N	1 22W	+0005	−0030	−0025	−0030	+0.6	+0.3	+0.2	−0.1
La Pallice	46 10N	1 13W	+0015	−0030	−0020	−0025	+0.7	+0.5	+0.3	−0.1
La Rochelle	46 09N	1 09W	+0015	−0030	−0020	−0025	+0.7	+0.5	+0.3	−0.1
Ile d'Aix	46 01N	1 10W	+0015	−0040	−0025	−0030	+0.8	+0.5	+0.3	−0.1
La Charente, Rochefort	45 57N	0 58W	+0035	−0010	+0125	+0030	+1.2	+0.9	+0.1	−0.2
Le Chapus	45 51N	1 11W	+0015	−0040	−0015	−0025	+0.7	+0.6	+0.4	+0.2
La Cayenne	45 47N	1 08W	+0030	−0015	−0005	−0010	+0.3	+0.2	+0.3	0.0
Pointe de Gatseau	45 48N	1 14W	+0015	0000	−0020	−0015	0.0	−0.1	+0.2	+0.1
Cordouan	45 35N	1 10W	−0010	−0010	−0025	−0015	−0.4	−0.4	−0.1	−0.2
La Gironde										
Royan	45 37N	1 01W	0000	−0005	0000	0000	−0.1	−0.1	0.0	0.0
Richard	45 27N	0 56W	+0020	+0020	+0035	+0030	0.0	−0.1	−0.4	−0.5
Lamena	45 20N	0 48W	+0035	+0045	+0125	+0100	+0.3	+0.1	−0.5	−0.3
Pauillac	45 12N	0 45W	+0100	+0100	+0205	+0135	+0.2	0.0	−1.0	−0.5
La Reuille	45 03N	0 36W	+0135	+0145	+0305	+0230	−0.1	−0.3	−1.3	−0.7
La Garonne										
Le Marquis	45 00N	0 33W	+0145	+0150	+0320	+0245	−0.2	−0.4	− 1.5	−0.9
Bordeaux	44 52N	0 33W	+0200	+0225	+0405	+0330	0.0	−0.2	−1.7	−1.0

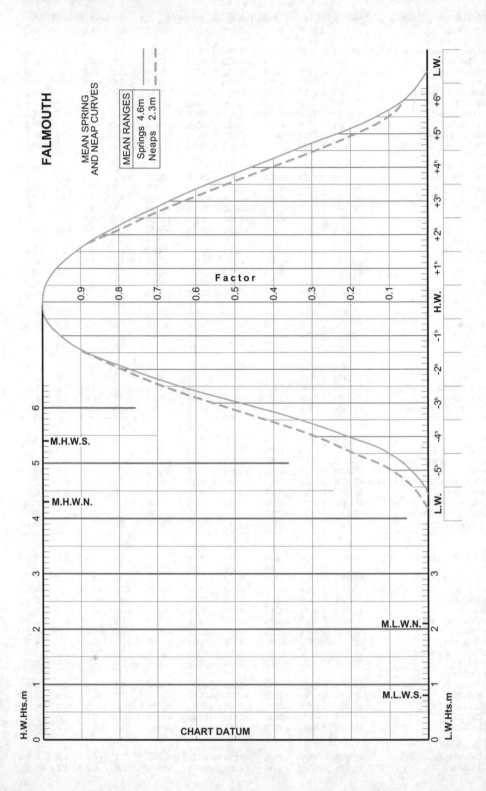

FALMOUTH

MEAN SPRING
AND NEAP CURVES

MEAN RANGES	
Springs	4.6m
Neaps	2.3m

Factor

FALMOUTH

LAT 50°09'N   LONG 5°03'W

TIMES AND HEIGHTS OF HIGH AND LOW WATERS

Dates in amber are **SPRINGS**
Dates in yellow are **NEAPS**

2014

JANUARY

Day	Time	m	Time	m	Time	m	Time	m
1 W	0438	5.2	1125	0.4	1706	5.1	●2349	0.4
16 TH	0515	5.0	1157	0.8	1736	4.8	○	
2 TH	0529	5.4	1217	0.2	1758	5.2		
17 F	0009	0.8	0553	5.0	1232	0.8	1813	4.8
3 F	0038	0.2	0619	5.5	1306	0.1	1847	5.2
18 SA	0041	0.8	0628	5.1	1301	0.8	1847	4.8
4 SA	0125	0.2	0707	5.5	1352	0.1	1934	5.1
19 SU	0108	0.8	0701	5.0	1327	0.8	1919	4.8
5 SU	0209	0.3	0752	5.4	1435	0.3	2018	5.0
20 M	0135	0.9	0730	4.9	1354	0.9	1947	4.7
6 M	0251	0.5	0836	5.2	1518	0.5	2101	4.8
21 TU	0204	1.0	0757	4.8	1425	1.0	2012	4.6
7 TU	0334	0.7	0921	4.9	1602	0.8	2148	4.5
22 W	0237	1.1	0823	4.7	1459	1.1	2036	4.4
8 W	0420	1.1	1009	4.6	1651	1.2	◐2242	4.2
23 TH	0315	1.2	0855	4.6	1541	1.3	2120	4.3
9 TH	0514	1.4	1107	4.3	1748	1.5	2352	4.1
24 F	0402	1.4	0953	4.4	1634	1.5	◐2237	4.2
10 F	0617	1.6	1223	4.1	1856	1.6		
25 SA	0505	1.6	1112	4.3	1748	1.6	2356	4.2
11 SA	0115	4.0	0730	1.7	1344	4.1	2012	1.6
26 SU	0628	1.7	1230	4.2	1914	1.6		
12 SU	0222	4.2	0847	1.5	1446	4.2	2120	1.4
27 M	0113	4.3	0754	1.5	1348	4.4	2034	1.3
13 M	0314	4.4	0949	1.3	1535	4.4	2211	1.2
28 TU	0226	4.6	0910	1.2	1458	4.6	2142	1.0
14 TU	0357	4.7	1037	1.1	1618	4.6	2255	1.0
29 W	0328	4.9	1015	0.8	1558	4.8	2243	0.6
15 W	0437	4.9	1119	0.9	1658	4.7	2334	0.9
30 TH	0423	5.2	1113	0.4	1652	5.1	●2337	0.3
31 F	0514	5.4	1206	0.1	1743	5.2		

FEBRUARY

Day	Time	m	Time	m	Time	m	Time	m
1 SA	0027	0.1	0603	5.6	1254	-0.1	1830	5.3
16 SU	0018	0.7	0608	5.1	1238	0.6	1827	4.9
2 SU	0113	0.0	0649	5.6	1338	-0.1	1914	5.2
17 M	0047	0.7	0640	5.0	1305	0.6	1858	4.9
3 M	0154	0.0	0732	5.5	1418	0.0	1954	5.1
18 TU	0115	0.7	0708	5.0	1333	0.7	1923	4.8
4 TU	0232	0.2	0812	5.3	1455	0.3	2031	4.9
19 W	0144	0.7	0732	4.9	1403	0.7	1941	4.7
5 W	0309	0.5	0849	5.0	1532	0.7	2108	4.7
20 TH	0216	0.8	0750	4.8	1435	0.9	1957	4.6
6 TH	0348	0.9	0927	4.6	1612	1.1	○2150	4.4
21 F	0251	1.1	0815	4.7	1512	1.1	2035	4.5
7 F	0434	1.4	0904	4.4	1701	1.5	2245	4.1
22 SA	0333	1.2	0904	4.4	1600	1.4	○2144	4.3
8 SA	0531	1.7	1113	3.9	1803	1.8		
23 SU	0430	1.5	1002	4.1	1707	1.6	2323	4.1
9 SU	0005	3.9	0641	1.9	1259	3.8	1919	1.9
24 M	0553	1.7	1205	4.1	1840	1.7		
10 M	0148	1.8	0803	1.8	1421	3.9	2042	1.7
25 TU	0049	4.2	0730	1.5	1331	4.2	2014	1.4
11 TU	0249	4.2	0920	1.5	1514	4.2	2144	1.4
26 W	0208	4.5	0855	1.0	1444	4.5	2129	1.0
12 W	0336	4.5	1012	1.2	1558	4.5	2231	1.1
27 TH	0312	4.8	1002	0.7	1544	4.8	2230	0.6
13 TH	0417	4.8	1055	1.0	1638	4.7	2311	0.9
28 F	0407	5.2	1059	0.3	1636	5.0	2323	0.3
14 F	0456	4.9	1134	0.8	1717	4.8	○2347	0.8
15 SA	0533	5.0	1208	0.7	1754	4.9		

MARCH

Day	Time	m	Time	m	Time	m	Time	m
1 SA	0456	5.4	1150	0.0	1724	5.2	●	
16 SU	0507	5.0	1138	0.6	1728	4.9	○2351	0.6
2 SU	0011	0.0	0543	5.5	1236	-0.1	1809	5.3
17 M	0542	5.0	1210	0.6	1801	4.9		
3 M	0055	-0.1	0628	5.5	1317	-0.1	1850	5.3
18 TU	0023	0.6	0614	5.0	1241	0.5	1832	4.9
4 TU	0134	0.0	0709	5.5	1355	0.0	1926	5.2
19 W	0054	0.5	0645	5.0	1311	0.5	1858	4.9
5 W	0209	0.2	0745	5.3	1428	0.3	2001	5.0
20 TH	0125	0.6	0711	5.0	1343	0.6	1920	4.9
6 TH	0243	0.5	0819	5.0	1500	0.7	2034	4.8
21 F	0158	0.7	0733	4.8	1416	0.8	1943	4.8
7 F	0317	0.9	0852	4.6	1535	1.1	2111	4.5
22 SA	0234	0.8	0802	4.7	1453	1.0	2024	4.6
8 SA	0357	1.3	0931	4.3	1617	1.6	◐2158	4.2
23 SU	0316	1.1	0855	4.4	1540	1.3	2133	4.4
9 SU	0450	1.7	1024	3.9	1716	1.9	2302	3.9
24 M	0413	1.4	1022	4.1	1647	1.6	◐2304	4.2
10 M	0600	2.0	1145	3.7	1832	2.0		
25 TU	0535	1.6	1152	4.0	1819	1.7		
11 TU	0055	3.9	0719	1.9	1349	3.8	1954	1.9
26 W	0031	4.2	0714	1.5	1318	4.2	1957	1.5
12 W	0218	4.1	0839	1.7	1448	4.1	2106	1.6
27 TH	0151	4.5	0840	1.1	1431	4.4	2112	1.0
13 TH	0309	4.4	0938	1.3	1533	4.4	2158	1.2
28 F	0255	4.8	0945	0.7	1528	4.8	2212	0.6
14 F	0351	4.7	1023	1.0	1614	4.6	2240	1.0
29 SA	0348	5.1	1040	0.3	1617	5.0	2304	0.3
15 SA	0430	4.9	1103	0.8	1651	4.8	2318	0.8
30 SU	0437	5.3	1129	0.1	1703	5.2	●2350	0.1
31 M	0522	5.4	1213	0.0	1745	5.3		

APRIL

Day	Time	m	Time	m	Time	m	Time	m
1 TU	0033	0.0	0605	5.4	1254	0.0	1823	5.3
16 W	0546	5.0	1216	0.5	1803	5.0		
2 W	0111	0.1	0644	5.3	1330	0.2	1859	5.2
17 TH	0033	0.5	0622	5.0	1252	0.5	1837	5.0
3 TH	0146	0.3	0720	5.1	1402	0.5	1933	5.1
18 F	0109	0.5	0657	5.0	1327	0.5	1910	5.0
4 F	0218	0.6	0752	4.9	1432	0.8	2006	4.9
19 SA	0146	0.6	0732	4.8	1403	0.7	1946	4.9
5 SA	0251	0.9	0824	4.6	1503	1.2	2041	4.6
20 SU	0225	0.7	0813	4.7	1444	0.9	2033	4.7
6 SU	0326	1.3	0901	4.3	1539	1.6	2124	4.3
21 M	0311	1.0	0908	4.4	1534	1.2	2136	4.5
7 M	0412	1.7	0950	4.0	1632	1.9	◐2220	4.0
22 TU	0410	1.3	1020	4.2	1642	1.5	◐2252	4.3
8 TU	0518	1.9	1058	3.8	1747	2.0	2336	3.9
23 W	0528	1.4	1141	4.1	1805	1.5		
9 W	0634	1.9	1252	3.8	1905	2.0		
24 TH	0014	4.3	0655	1.3	1303	4.2	1933	1.4
10 TH	0127	4.0	0748	1.7	1411	4.0	2016	1.7
25 F	0131	4.5	0817	1.1	1413	4.4	2048	1.0
11 F	0231	4.3	0851	1.4	1500	4.3	2113	1.4
26 SA	0234	4.7	0921	0.7	1508	4.7	2148	0.7
12 SA	0317	4.5	0941	1.1	1541	4.6	2200	1.1
27 SU	0328	4.9	1016	0.5	1556	4.9	2240	0.4
13 SU	0357	4.7	1023	0.9	1619	4.8	2242	0.8
28 M	0415	5.1	1105	0.3	1639	5.1	2327	0.3
14 M	0434	4.9	1103	0.7	1654	4.9	2320	0.7
29 TU	0500	5.1	1149	0.2	1720	5.1	●	
15 TU	0510	5.0	1140	0.5	1729	5.0	○2357	0.5
30 W	0010	0.2	0542	5.1	1230	0.3	1758	5.2

Chart Datum: 2·91 metres below Ordnance Datum (Newlyn)
HAT is 5·7 metres above Chart Datum

TIDES

TIME ZONE (UT)
For Summer Time add ONE hour in **non-shaded areas**

FALMOUTH
LAT 50°09′N   LONG 5°03′W
TIMES AND HEIGHTS OF HIGH AND LOW WATERS

Dates in amber are **SPRINGS**
Dates in yellow are **NEAPS**

2014

MAY

Day	Time	m	Day	Time	m
1 TH	0048 / 0621 / 1306 / 1835	0.3 / 5.1 / 5.1 / 5.1	16	0015 / 0602 / 1236 / 1820	0.4 / 5.0 / 0.5 / 5.2
2 F	0123 / 0657 / 1338 / 1909	0.4 / 4.9 / 0.6 / 5.0	17 SA	0058 / 0647 / 1317 / 1903	0.4 / 5.0 / 0.5 / 5.1
3 SA	0156 / 0730 / 1409 / 1943	0.7 / 4.8 / 0.9 / 4.9	18 SU	0140 / 0731 / 1359 / 1948	0.5 / 4.9 / 0.6 / 5.1
4 SU	0228 / 0803 / 1438 / 2017	1.0 / 4.6 / 1.2 / 4.7	19 M	0224 / 0818 / 1444 / 2036	0.6 / 4.7 / 0.8 / 4.9
5 M	0301 / 0839 / 1511 / 2057	1.3 / 4.3 / 1.5 / 4.4	20 TU	0313 / 0910 / 1535 / 2133	0.8 / 4.5 / 1.0 / 4.7
6 TU	0339 / 0924 / 1554 / 2146	1.5 / 4.1 / 1.8 / 4.2	21 W	0410 / 1013 / 1637 / 2239	1.0 / 4.3 / 1.2 / 4.5
7 W	0434 / 1022 / 1658 / 2248	1.8 / 3.9 / 1.9 / 4.1	22 TH	0517 / 1125 / 1746 / 2352	1.2 / 4.2 / 1.3 / 4.4
8 TH	0543 / 1133 / 1811	1.9 / 3.9 / 1.9	23 F	0629 / 1240 / 1901	1.2 / 4.2 / 1.3
9 F	0000 / 0652 / 1258 / 1920	4.0 / 1.8 / 4.0 / 1.8	24 SA	0106 / 0744 / 1348 / 2015	4.5 / 1.1 / 4.4 / 1.1
10 SA	0120 / 0756 / 1406 / 2021	4.2 / 1.5 / 4.2 / 1.5	25 SU	0211 / 0851 / 1445 / 2120	4.6 / 0.9 / 4.6 / 0.9
11 SU	0223 / 0852 / 1455 / 2114	4.4 / 1.3 / 4.5 / 1.2	26 M	0306 / 0949 / 1534 / 2215	4.7 / 0.7 / 4.8 / 0.7
12 M	0310 / 0941 / 1536 / 2203	4.6 / 1.0 / 4.7 / 1.0	27 TU	0354 / 1040 / 1617 / 2303	4.8 / 0.6 / 4.9 / 0.6
13 TU	0353 / 1027 / 1615 / 2248	4.8 / 0.8 / 4.9 / 0.7	28 W	0439 / 1125 / 1658 / 2347	4.9 / 0.6 / 5.0 / 0.5
14	0435 / 1111 / 1655 / 2332	4.9 / 0.6 / 5.0 / 0.6	29 TH	0521 / 1207 / 1736	4.9 / 0.5 / 5.0
15 TH	0518 / 1154 / 1737	5.0 / 0.5 / 5.1	30 F	0027 / 0600 / 1245 / 1814	0.6 / 4.9 / 0.4 / 5.0
			31 SA	0104 / 0637 / 1318 / 1850	0.6 / 4.8 / 0.8 / 5.0

JUNE

Day	Time	m	Day	Time	m
1 SU	0137 / 0712 / 1349 / 1924	0.8 / 4.7 / 1.0 / 4.9	16 M	0137 / 0725 / 1357 / 1942	0.3 / 5.0 / 0.4 / 5.3
2 M	0208 / 0746 / 1417 / 1958	1.0 / 4.6 / 1.2 / 4.7	17 TU	0223 / 0813 / 1443 / 2031	0.4 / 4.9 / 0.6 / 5.1
3 TU	0238 / 0820 / 1447 / 2034	1.2 / 4.4 / 1.4 / 4.6	18 W	0311 / 0903 / 1531 / 2121	0.5 / 4.8 / 0.7 / 4.9
4 W	0310 / 0900 / 1522 / 2116	1.4 / 4.3 / 1.6 / 4.4	19 TH	0401 / 0957 / 1623 / 2218	0.8 / 4.6 / 1.0 / 4.7
5 TH	0352 / 0948 / 1610 / 2208	1.6 / 4.1 / 1.7 / 4.3	20 F	0457 / 1059 / 1721 / 2323	1.0 / 4.4 / 1.2 / 4.5
6 F	0448 / 1045 / 1713 / 2307	1.7 / 4.1 / 1.8 / 4.2	21	0557 / 1209 / 1825	1.2 / 4.3 / 1.3
7	0553 / 1148 / 1822	1.7 / 4.1 / 1.8	22 SU	0035 / 0704 / 1319 / 1935	4.4 / 1.2 / 4.3 / 1.3
8 SU	0010 / 0700 / 1253 / 1928	4.2 / 1.6 / 4.2 / 1.6	23 M	0145 / 0816 / 1421 / 2048	4.4 / 1.2 / 4.4 / 1.2
9 M	0116 / 0802 / 1355 / 2029	4.3 / 1.4 / 4.4 / 1.4	24 TU	0245 / 0921 / 1513 / 2150	4.4 / 1.1 / 4.6 / 1.1
10 TU	0218 / 0900 / 1450 / 2126	4.5 / 1.1 / 4.6 / 1.1	25 W	0335 / 1016 / 1558 / 2242	4.6 / 1.0 / 4.7 / 0.9
11 W	0313 / 0954 / 1540 / 2219	4.7 / 0.8 / 4.8 / 0.8	26 TH	0420 / 1104 / 1639 / 2328	4.6 / 0.9 / 4.9 / 0.8
12 TH	0405 / 1045 / 1628 / 2311	4.9 / 0.7 / 5.0 / 0.6	27 F	0502 / 1147 / 1718	4.7 / 0.8 / 4.9
13 F	0456 / 1136 / 1717	5.0 / 0.5 / 5.2	28	0009 / 0542 / 1225 / 1756	0.8 / 4.8 / 0.8 / 5.0
14	0001 / 0546 / 1225 / 1806	0.4 / 5.1 / 0.4 / 5.3	29 SU	0046 / 0620 / 1259 / 1833	0.8 / 4.8 / 0.9 / 5.0
15	0050 / 0637 / 1311 / 1855	0.3 / 5.1 / 0.4 / 5.3	30 M	0119 / 0656 / 1329 / 1907	0.9 / 4.7 / 1.0 / 4.9

JULY

Day	Time	m	Day	Time	m
1 TU	0148 / 0730 / 1356 / 1940	1.0 / 4.7 / 1.1 / 4.9	16	0215 / 0800 / 1433 / 2016	0.1 / 5.1 / 0.3 / 5.4
2 W	0214 / 0802 / 1422 / 2011	1.1 / 4.6 / 1.2 / 4.7	17 TH	0259 / 0845 / 1516 / 2102	0.3 / 5.0 / 0.5 / 5.1
3 TH	0243 / 0835 / 1453 / 2046	1.2 / 4.5 / 1.3 / 4.6	18 F	0343 / 0930 / 1601 / 2149	0.6 / 4.7 / 0.8 / 4.8
4 F	0317 / 0912 / 1532 / 2128	1.3 / 4.4 / 1.5 / 4.5	19 SA	0430 / 1020 / 1651 / 2244	0.9 / 4.5 / 1.1 / 4.5
5 SA	0401 / 1000 / 1621 / 2221	1.5 / 4.2 / 1.6 / 4.4	20 SU	0522 / 1124 / 1749 / 2355	1.2 / 4.3 / 1.4 / 4.2
6	0457 / 1059 / 1725 / 2323	1.6 / 4.2 / 1.7 / 4.3	21 M	0623 / 1244 / 1856	1.5 / 4.2 / 1.6
7 M	0606 / 1202 / 1838	1.6 / 4.2 / 1.7	22 TU	0117 / 0735 / 1357 / 2016	4.1 / 1.6 / 4.2 / 1.6
8 TU	0029 / 0717 / 1310 / 1949	4.3 / 1.5 / 4.4 / 1.5	23 W	0225 / 0853 / 1454 / 2130	4.2 / 1.5 / 4.4 / 1.4
9 W	0138 / 0825 / 1415 / 2055	4.4 / 1.3 / 4.6 / 1.2	24 TH	0318 / 0955 / 1540 / 2224	4.3 / 1.3 / 4.6 / 1.2
10 TH	0244 / 0927 / 1514 / 2157	4.6 / 1.1 / 4.8 / 0.9	25 F	0403 / 1041 / 1621 / 2310	4.5 / 1.1 / 4.8 / 1.0
11 F	0343 / 1026 / 1608 / 2255	4.8 / 0.8 / 5.1 / 0.6	26 SA	0444 / 1127 / 1700 / 2350	4.7 / 0.9 / 5.0 / 0.9
12	0439 / 1122 / 1701 / 2351	5.0 / 0.5 / 5.3 / 0.4	27 SU	0523 / 1205 / 1738	4.8 / 0.9 / 5.0
13 SU	0532 / 1215 / 1753	5.1 / 0.3 / 5.4	28	0026 / 0601 / 1238 / 1815	0.8 / 4.8 / 0.9 / 5.1
14	0042 / 0624 / 1304 / 1842	0.2 / 5.2 / 0.2 / 5.5	29 TU	0057 / 0637 / 1307 / 1849	0.8 / 4.8 / 0.9 / 5.0
15	0130 / 0714 / 1350 / 1930	0.1 / 5.2 / 0.2 / 5.5	30 W	0124 / 0711 / 1332 / 1919	0.9 / 4.8 / 1.0 / 5.0
			31 TH	0149 / 0741 / 1357 / 1947	1.0 / 4.7 / 1.1 / 4.9

AUGUST

Day	Time	m	Day	Time	m
1 F	0215 / 0807 / 1426 / 2014	1.0 / 4.6 / 1.1 / 4.8	16 SA	0318 / 0857 / 1535 / 2115	0.6 / 4.9 / 0.8 / 4.8
2 SA	0247 / 0834 / 1500 / 2045	1.2 / 4.5 / 1.3 / 4.6	17 SU	0358 / 0938 / 1620 / 2159	1.0 / 4.6 / 1.2 / 4.4
3 SU	0324 / 0910 / 1542 / 2131	1.3 / 4.4 / 1.5 / 4.5	18 M	0445 / 1030 / 1714 / 2259	1.4 / 4.3 / 1.6 / 4.1
4 M	0411 / 1010 / 1638 / 2241	1.5 / 4.3 / 1.6 / 4.3	19 TU	0544 / 1151 / 1820	1.7 / 4.1 / 1.9
5	0516 / 1123 / 1754 / 2356	1.7 / 4.3 / 1.7 / 4.3	20 W	0047 / 0655 / 1331 / 1942	3.9 / 1.9 / 4.1 / 1.9
6 W	0637 / 1238 / 1918	1.7 / 4.3 / 1.6	21 TH	0205 / 0823 / 1433 / 2110	4.0 / 1.8 / 4.3 / 1.6
7 TH	0112 / 0757 / 1351 / 2034	4.4 / 1.5 / 4.6 / 1.4	22 F	0300 / 0933 / 1520 / 2204	4.2 / 1.5 / 4.6 / 1.3
8 F	0226 / 0908 / 1457 / 2142	4.6 / 1.2 / 4.9 / 1.0	23 SA	0344 / 1022 / 1601 / 2247	4.5 / 1.2 / 4.8 / 1.1
9 SA	0329 / 1012 / 1553 / 2243	4.8 / 0.8 / 5.2 / 0.6	24 SU	0423 / 1103 / 1639 / 2325	4.7 / 1.0 / 5.0 / 0.9
10 SU	0425 / 1110 / 1646 / 2339	5.1 / 0.5 / 5.4 / 0.3	25 M	0501 / 1139 / 1717	4.9 / 0.9 / 5.1
11 M	0518 / 1203 / 1737	5.2 / 0.2 / 5.6	26 TU	0000 / 0538 / 1213 / 1752	0.9 / 4.9 / 0.8 / 5.1
12	0030 / 0608 / 1251 / 1826	0.1 / 5.3 / 0.1 / 5.7	27 W	0030 / 0615 / 1241 / 1826	0.8 / 5.0 / 0.8 / 5.1
13 W	0116 / 0655 / 1335 / 1912	0.0 / 5.4 / 0.0 / 5.6	28 TH	0057 / 0647 / 1306 / 1855	0.8 / 5.0 / 0.9 / 5.1
14	0159 / 0739 / 1416 / 1955	0.0 / 5.3 / 0.2 / 5.5	29 F	0122 / 0716 / 1333 / 1922	0.9 / 4.9 / 0.9 / 5.0
15	0239 / 0819 / 1455 / 2035	0.2 / 5.1 / 0.4 / 5.2	30 SA	0150 / 0740 / 1402 / 1945	0.9 / 4.8 / 1.0 / 4.9
			31 SU	0220 / 0759 / 1435 / 2006	1.0 / 4.7 / 1.0 / 4.7

Chart Datum: 2·91 metres below Ordnance Datum (Newlyn)
HAT is 5·7 metres above Chart Datum

FALMOUTH
LAT 50°09'N   LONG 5°03'W
TIMES AND HEIGHTS OF HIGH AND LOW WATERS

Dates in amber are **SPRINGS**
Dates in yellow are **NEAPS**

2014

SEPTEMBER

#	Day	Time m	Time m	Time m	Time m	#	Day	Time m	Time m	Time m	Time m
1	M	0255 1.2	0826 4.6	1513 1.4	2046 4.5	16	TU	0409 1.6	0946 4.4	1639 1.7	◗ 2211 4.0
2	TU	0338 1.5	0929 4.4	1604 1.6	◗ 2209 4.3	17	W	0505 1.9	1049 4.1	1745 2.0	2349 3.8
3	W	0438 1.7	1055 4.3	1721 1.8	2335 4.2	18	TH	0616 2.1	1250 4.0	1904 2.0	
4	TH	0606 1.8	1216 4.3	1856 1.7		19	F	0138 3.9	0739 2.0	1404 4.2	2034 1.8
5	F	0057 4.3	0738 1.6	1334 4.5	2020 1.4	20	SA	0235 4.2	0859 1.7	1454 4.5	2132 1.4
6	SA	0214 4.5	0855 1.3	1442 4.9	2130 1.0	21	SU	0319 4.5	0949 1.4	1536 4.8	2214 1.1
7	SU	0317 4.8	0959 0.9	1539 5.2	2229 0.6	22	M	0359 4.7	1030 1.1	1614 5.0	2252 0.9
8	M	0411 5.1	1055 0.5	1630 5.5	2323 0.2	23	TU	0436 4.9	1108 0.9	1651 5.1	2327 0.8
9	TU	0500 5.3	1146 0.2	1719 5.6 ○		24	W	0513 5.0	1141 0.8	1727 5.2	● 2358 0.7
10	W	0012 0.0	0548 5.4	1233 0.0	1806 5.7	25	TH	0548 5.1	1212 0.8	1800 5.1	
11	TH	0057 -0.1	0632 5.5	1316 0.0	1850 5.6	26	F	0027 0.7	0620 5.1	1242 0.8	1830 5.1
12	F	0137 0.0	0713 5.4	1354 0.2	1930 5.4	27	SA	0057 0.7	0649 5.0	1311 0.8	1859 5.0
13	SA	0214 0.3	0749 5.2	1431 0.5	2007 5.1	28	SU	0127 0.8	0716 5.0	1342 0.9	1925 4.9
14	SU	0250 0.7	0824 5.0	1507 0.9	2041 4.8	29	M	0159 1.0	0740 4.9	1415 1.0	1951 4.7
15	M	0326 1.1	0901 4.7	1548 1.3	2120 4.4	30	TU	0234 1.2	0813 4.7	1454 1.3	2036 4.5

OCTOBER

#	Day	Time m	Time m	Time m	Time m	#	Day	Time m	Time m	Time m	Time m
1	W	0316 1.4	0916 4.5	1545 1.5	◗ 2158 4.3	16	TH	0425 2.0	1007 4.2	1707 2.0	2245 3.8
2	TH	0416 1.7	1038 4.4	1702 1.8	2322 4.2	17	F	0534 2.2	1124 4.0	1821 2.1	
3	F	0546 1.9	1158 4.3	1840 1.7		18	SA	0051 3.9	0650 2.1	1316 4.1	1937 1.9
4	SA	0045 4.2	0721 1.7	1318 4.5	2006 1.4	19	SU	0159 4.1	0805 1.9	1417 4.4	2042 1.6
5	SU	0202 4.5	0840 1.3	1426 4.9	2114 0.9	20	M	0248 4.4	0904 1.5	1503 4.6	2131 1.3
6	M	0303 4.8	0942 0.9	1522 5.2	2211 0.5	21	TU	0329 4.7	0950 1.2	1544 4.9	2212 1.0
7	TU	0354 5.1	1037 0.5	1612 5.4	2303 0.3	22	W	0407 4.9	1031 1.0	1621 5.0	2250 0.8
8	W	0441 5.3	1126 0.2	1659 5.5	● 2350 0.1	23	TH	0443 5.0	1108 0.8	1656 5.1	2326 0.7
9	TH	0525 5.4	1211 0.1	1744 5.5		24	F	0517 5.1	1144 0.7	1731 5.1	
10	F	0033 0.1	0607 5.4	1253 0.1	1826 5.5	25	SA	0000 0.7	0551 5.1	1219 0.7	1806 5.1
11	SA	0113 0.2	0645 5.4	1331 0.3	1905 5.3	26	SU	0035 0.7	0625 5.1	1253 0.7	1841 5.0
12	SU	0149 0.5	0721 5.2	1406 0.6	1939 5.0	27	M	0109 0.7	0658 5.1	1328 0.8	1916 4.9
13	M	0222 0.8	0755 5.0	1441 0.9	2013 4.7	28	TU	0144 0.9	0734 5.0	1404 0.9	1954 4.7
14	TU	0256 1.2	0831 4.8	1519 1.3	2050 4.4	29	W	0222 1.1	0817 4.8	1446 1.1	2045 4.5
15	W	0335 1.6	0912 4.5	1605 1.7	◗ 2137 4.1	30	TH	0307 1.3	0913 4.6	1539 1.4	2152 4.3
						31	F	0408 1.6	1023 4.5	1653 1.6	◗ 2309 4.2

NOVEMBER

#	Day	Time m	Time m	Time m	Time m	#	Day	Time m	Time m	Time m	Time m
1	SA	0530 1.7	1140 4.4	1821 1.6		16	SU	0556 2.1	1147 4.1	1840 1.9	
2	SU	0030 4.2	0657 1.6	1257 4.5	1943 1.3	17	M	0052 4.0	0707 2.0	1312 4.2	1946 1.7
3	M	0144 4.5	0806 1.3	1406 4.8	2052 1.0	18	TU	0201 4.2	0811 1.7	1416 4.4	2042 1.4
4	TU	0245 4.7	0920 0.9	1503 5.0	2149 0.7	19	W	0250 4.5	0905 1.4	1503 4.7	2130 1.2
5	W	0335 5.0	1014 0.6	1553 5.2	2240 0.4	20	TH	0331 4.7	0952 1.1	1545 4.8	2214 0.9
6	TH	0420 5.2	1104 0.4	1639 5.3	○ 2327 0.3	21	F	0409 4.9	1035 0.9	1624 5.0	2255 0.7
7	F	0503 5.3	1149 0.3	1723 5.3		22	SA	0446 5.1	1117 0.7	1703 5.1	● 2336 0.6
8	SA	0010 0.3	0542 5.3	1231 0.3	1803 5.2	23	SU	0525 5.2	1158 0.6	1745 5.1	
9	SU	0050 0.4	0620 5.3	1309 0.4	1841 5.1	24	M	0016 0.6	0604 5.2	1239 0.6	1826 5.1
10	M	0125 0.6	0656 5.2	1345 0.7	1916 4.9	25	TU	0056 0.6	0646 5.2	1319 0.6	1909 5.0
11	TU	0158 0.9	0731 5.0	1419 0.9	1950 4.7	26	W	0136 0.7	0728 5.1	1401 0.7	1953 4.8
12	W	0231 1.2	0807 4.8	1454 1.3	2027 4.5	27	TH	0218 0.9	0814 5.0	1445 0.9	2043 4.6
13	TH	0305 1.5	0846 4.6	1533 1.6	2110 4.2	28	F	0305 1.1	0906 4.8	1537 1.1	2141 4.4
14	F	0346 1.8	0933 4.4	1623 1.8	◗ 2207 4.0	29	SA	0401 1.3	1006 4.6	1641 1.3	2249 4.3
15	SA	0444 2.0	1033 4.2	1729 2.0	2320 3.9	30	SU	0509 1.5	1115 4.5	1754 1.4	

DECEMBER

#	Day	Time m	Time m	Time m	Time m	#	Day	Time m	Time m	Time m	Time m
1	M	0004 4.2	0624 1.5	1229 4.5	1910 1.3	16	TU	0558 2.0	1154 4.2	1842 1.8	
2	TU	0117 4.4	0742 1.4	1339 4.6	2022 1.1	17	W	0041 4.1	0711 1.9	1302 4.3	1948 1.6
3	W	0221 4.6	0852 1.1	1441 4.7	2123 0.9	18	TH	0149 4.3	0816 1.6	1407 4.4	2047 1.3
4	TH	0314 4.8	0951 0.9	1533 4.9	2217 0.7	19	F	0245 4.5	0913 1.3	1503 4.6	2139 1.1
5	F	0400 4.9	1042 0.7	1620 5.0	2305 0.6	20	SA	0332 4.8	1005 1.0	1552 4.8	2228 0.8
6	SA	0443 5.1	1129 0.5	1703 5.0	2349 0.5	21	SU	0417 5.0	1054 0.8	1639 5.0	2316 0.6
7	SU	0522 5.1	1212 0.5	1744 5.0		22	M	0502 5.2	1141 0.6	1726 5.1 ●	
8	M	0029 0.6	0600 5.2	1251 0.6	1821 4.9	23	TU	0002 0.5	0547 5.3	1228 0.4	1813 5.1
9	TU	0105 0.7	0637 5.1	1326 0.7	1858 4.9	24	W	0048 0.4	0633 5.3	1313 0.4	1900 5.1
10	W	0138 0.9	0713 5.1	1359 0.9	1932 4.7	25	TH	0131 0.4	0719 5.3	1357 0.4	1946 5.0
11	TH	0209 1.1	0748 4.9	1430 1.1	2008 4.6	26	F	0214 0.5	0805 5.2	1442 0.5	2032 4.8
12	F	0238 1.3	0824 4.8	1501 1.3	2046 4.4	27	SA	0259 0.7	0853 5.1	1529 0.7	2122 4.6
13	SA	0309 1.5	0904 4.6	1536 1.6	2132 4.2	28	SU	0348 0.9	0944 4.8	1621 1.0	◗ 2219 4.4
14	SU	0349 1.7	0952 4.4	1624 1.8	2228 4.1	29	M	0434 1.2	1043 4.6	1720 1.2	2326 4.2
15	M	0446 1.9	1050 4.2	1729 1.9	2332 4.0	30	TU	0547 1.4	1152 4.4	1828 1.4	
						31	W	0041 4.2	0659 1.5	1308 4.3	1944 1.3

Chart Datum: 2·91 metres below Ordnance Datum (Newlyn)
HAT is 5·7 metres above Chart Datum

TIDES

PLYMOUTH
DEVONPORT
MEAN SPRING
AND NEAP CURVES

MEAN RANGES
Springs 4.7m
Neaps 2.2m

Factor

0.9 0.8 0.7 0.6 0.5 0.4 0.3 0.2 0.1

L.W. +5ʰ +4ʰ +3ʰ +2ʰ +1ʰ H.W. -1ʰ -2ʰ -3ʰ -4ʰ -5ʰ L.W.

H.W.Hts.m.

M.H.W.S.
M.H.W.N.

M.L.W.N.
M.L.W.S.

L.W.Hts.m.

CHART DATUM

PLYMOUTH (DEVONPORT)

LAT 50°22'N   LONG 4°11'W

TIMES AND HEIGHTS OF HIGH AND LOW WATERS

Dates in amber are **SPRINGS**
Dates in yellow are **NEAPS**

2014

JANUARY

Day	Time m	Time m	Time m	Time m		Day	Time m	Time m	Time m	Time m
1 W	0513 5.6	1135 0.8	1741 5.5	●2358 0.8		16 TH	0543 5.3	1210 1.2	1805 5.1	○
2 TH	0604 5.8	1227 0.6	1833 5.6			17 F	0022 1.2	0619 5.4	1244 1.1	1841 5.2
3 F	0048 0.6	0654 5.8	1316 0.5	1923 5.6		18 SA	0054 1.2	0655 5.4	1314 1.2	1917 5.2
4 SA	0135 0.6	0742 5.9	1402 0.5	2011 5.5		19 SU	0122 1.2	0730 5.3	1342 1.2	1951 5.1
5 SU	0220 0.7	0830 5.8	1447 0.6	2057 5.4		20 M	0149 1.3	0802 5.3	1409 1.3	2022 5.0
6 M	0303 0.9	0915 5.6	1530 0.9	2142 5.2		21 TU	0217 1.4	0832 5.2	1436 1.4	2051 4.9
7 TU	0346 1.2	1001 5.3	1614 1.2	2227 4.9		22 W	0246 1.5	0904 5.0	1507 1.5	2123 4.8
8 W	0430 1.5	1048 5.0	1700 1.6	☾2319 4.7		23 TH	0321 1.6	0941 4.9	1546 1.7	2205 4.7
9 TH	0521 1.9	1145 4.7	1755 1.9			24 F	0406 1.8	1029 4.7	1634 1.9	☾2301 4.6
10 F	0023 4.5	0623 2.1	1255 4.5	1903 2.1		25 SA	0507 2.0	1132 4.6	1748 2.0	
11 SA	0134 4.5	0744 2.2	1405 4.5	2023 2.1		26 SU	0013 4.5	0635 2.1	1249 4.5	1923 2.0
12 SU	0239 4.6	0903 2.0	1507 4.6	2130 1.9		27 M	0136 4.6	0807 1.9	1413 4.7	2045 1.8
13 M	0335 4.8	1002 1.8	1600 4.8	2222 1.6		28 TU	0255 4.9	0922 1.6	1532 4.9	2154 1.4
14 TU	0423 5.0	1050 1.5	1646 4.9	2307 1.4		29 W	0401 5.2	1027 1.1	1633 5.2	2254 1.0
15 W	0505 5.2	1132 1.3	1727 5.1	2346 1.3		30 TH	0458 5.5	1124 0.7	●1729 5.4	2347 0.6
						31 F	0550 5.8	1215 0.4	1821 5.6	

FEBRUARY

Day	Time m	Time m	Time m	Time m		Day	Time m	Time m	Time m	Time m
1 SA	0036 0.4	0640 5.9	1303 0.2	1909 5.6		16 SU	0034 1.0	0637 5.4	1254 1.0	1858 5.2
2 SU	0122 0.3	0728 5.9	1348 0.2	1955 5.6		17 M	0104 1.0	0712 5.4	1322 1.0	1931 5.2
3 M	0205 0.3	0812 5.8	1429 0.3	2036 5.5		18 TU	0131 1.0	0744 5.3	1349 1.0	2001 5.1
4 TU	0244 0.6	0854 5.6	1508 0.6	2114 5.3		19 W	0158 1.1	0813 5.2	1416 1.1	2029 5.0
5 W	0322 0.9	0932 5.3	1545 1.0	2148 5.0		20 TH	0227 1.2	0843 5.1	1446 1.2	2058 4.9
6 TH	0359 1.3	1007 5.0	1623 1.5	☾2222 4.7		21 F	0300 1.3	0918 4.9	1522 1.4	2136 4.8
7 F	0441 1.7	1045 4.6	1708 1.9	2307 4.5		22 SA	0341 1.6	1003 4.7	1607 1.7	2229 4.6
8 SA	0533 2.1	1147 4.3	1806 2.2			23 SU	0437 1.8	1105 4.5	1712 2.0	2341 4.5
9 SU	0032 4.3	0643 2.3	1326 4.2	1922 2.3		24 M	0600 2.0	1224 4.4	1850 2.1	
10 M	0203 4.3	0820 2.3	1439 4.3	2056 2.2		25 TU	0109 4.5	0744 1.9	1357 4.6	2026 1.8
11 TU	0307 4.6	0939 2.0	1536 4.5	2159 1.8		26 W	0236 4.8	0908 1.6	1517 4.8	2141 1.4
12 W	0358 4.8	1030 1.6	1624 4.8	2246 1.5		27 TH	0345 5.1	1014 1.1	1621 5.1	2241 0.9
13 TH	0442 5.1	1112 1.3	1706 5.0	2326 1.2		28 F	0442 5.5	1109 0.6	1715 5.4	2333 0.5
14 F	0522 5.2	1150 1.1	1745 5.1	○						
15 SA	0002 1.1	0600 5.3	1224 1.0	1822 5.2						

MARCH

Day	Time m	Time m	Time m	Time m		Day	Time m	Time m	Time m	Time m
1 SA	0534 5.7	1159 0.3	1804 5.6	●		16 SU	0535 5.3	1154 0.9	1757 5.2	○
2 SU	0020 0.3	0622 5.8	1245 0.1	1849 5.7		17 M	0007 0.9	0613 5.3	1227 0.8	1834 5.2
3 M	0104 0.2	0707 5.9	1327 0.1	1931 5.6		18 TU	0040 0.8	0649 5.3	1258 0.8	1908 5.3
4 TU	0144 0.2	0749 5.8	1406 0.3	2009 5.5		19 W	0111 0.8	0722 5.3	1328 0.8	1939 5.2
5 W	0221 0.4	0827 5.5	1441 0.6	2040 5.3		20 TH	0141 0.9	0754 5.3	1358 0.9	2008 5.2
6 TH	0255 0.8	0858 5.2	1515 1.0	2107 5.1		21 F	0212 1.0	0826 5.1	1429 1.1	2040 5.1
7 F	0329 1.2	0926 4.9	1549 1.5	2135 4.8		22 SA	0246 1.1	0903 5.0	1506 1.3	2119 4.9
8 SA	0406 1.6	0957 4.6	1628 1.9	☾2213 4.5		23 SU	0328 1.4	0950 4.7	1552 1.6	2211 4.7
9 SU	0454 2.1	1044 4.2	1722 2.2	2311 4.3		24 M	0424 1.7	1051 4.5	1656 1.9	☾2321 4.5
10 M	0559 2.3	1222 4.0	1833 2.4			25 TU	0546 1.9	1211 4.4	1831 2.1	
11 TU	0113 4.0	0720 2.3	1406 4.1	1959 2.3		26 W	0052 4.5	0729 1.9	1347 4.5	2011 1.8
12 W	0243 4.1	0901 2.1	1507 4.4	2123 2.0		27 TH	0220 4.8	0853 1.5	1505 4.8	2125 1.4
13 TH	0328 4.7	0958 1.7	1556 4.7	2215 1.6		28 F	0328 5.1	0957 1.0	1605 5.1	2223 0.9
14 F	0414 4.9	1041 1.4	1639 4.9	2256 1.3		29 SA	0424 5.4	1050 0.6	1656 5.4	2313 0.6
15 SA	0455 5.1	1119 1.1	1719 5.1	2333 1.1		30 SU	0514 5.6	1138 0.3	●1742 5.6	2359 0.3
						31 M	0600 5.7	1222 0.2	1825 5.6	

APRIL

Day	Time m	Time m	Time m	Time m		Day	Time m	Time m	Time m	Time m
1 TU	0041 0.2	0643 5.7	1303 0.2	1904 5.6		16 W	0013 0.8	0623 5.3	1233 0.8	1842 5.3
2 W	0120 0.3	0723 5.6	1340 0.4	1938 5.5		17 TH	0050 0.7	0701 5.3	1308 0.8	1917 5.4
3 TH	0156 0.5	0757 5.4	1414 0.7	2006 5.3		18 F	0125 0.7	0737 5.3	1343 0.9	1951 5.3
4 F	0229 0.8	0826 5.1	1446 1.1	2032 5.1		19 SA	0201 0.8	0810 5.3	1419 1.0	2028 5.2
5 SA	0302 1.2	0853 4.8	1518 1.5	2101 4.9		20 SU	0240 1.0	0856 5.1	1459 1.3	2111 5.1
6 SU	0337 1.6	0926 4.6	1555 1.9	2139 4.6		21 M	0325 1.3	0944 4.8	1548 1.6	2202 4.9
7 M	0421 2.0	1011 4.3	1645 2.2	☾2230 4.4		22 TU	0423 1.6	1045 4.6	1653 1.8	☾2310 4.7
8 TU	0522 2.2	1119 4.1	1752 2.4	2346 4.2		23 W	0539 1.8	1205 4.4	1818 2.0	
9 W	0635 2.3	1318 4.1	1907 2.3			24 TH	0037 4.6	0710 1.7	1332 4.5	1949 1.8
10 TH	0143 4.3	0752 2.1	1428 4.3	2022 2.1		25 F	0200 4.8	0830 1.4	1443 4.8	2101 1.4
11 F	0248 4.6	0903 1.8	1520 4.6	2125 1.7		26 SA	0306 5.0	0933 1.1	1541 5.0	2159 1.1
12 SA	0337 4.8	0955 1.5	1605 4.8	2214 1.4		27 SU	0401 5.4	1026 0.8	1631 5.3	2249 0.8
13 SU	0422 5.0	1038 1.2	1647 5.0	2256 1.1		28 M	0451 5.4	1114 0.6	1717 5.4	2335 0.6
14 M	0504 5.2	1118 1.0	1728 5.2	2336 0.9		29 TU	0536 5.5	1157 0.5	1759 5.5	●
15 TU	0545 5.3	1156 0.8	1806 5.3	○		30 W	0017 0.5	0618 5.5	1238 0.5	1836 5.5

Chart Datum: 3·22 metres below Ordnance Datum (Newlyn)
HAT is 5·9 metres above Chart Datum

TIDES

TIDES

PLYMOUTH (DEVONPORT)
LAT 50°22'N   LONG 4°11'W
TIMES AND HEIGHTS OF HIGH AND LOW WATERS

Dates in amber are **SPRINGS**
Dates in yellow are **NEAPS**

2014

MAY

Time	m	Time	m
1 TH 0057 0.6 / 0656 5.4 / 1315 0.7 / 1908 5.4		**16** F 0030 0.7 / 0640 5.3 / 1251 0.7 / 1858 5.5	
2 F 0132 0.7 / 0729 5.2 / 1349 0.9 / 1937 5.3		**17** SA 0113 0.7 / 0723 5.3 / 1332 0.8 / 1939 5.5	
3 SA 0205 1.0 / 0759 5.0 / 1420 1.2 / 2005 5.2		**18** SU 0155 0.7 / 0807 5.3 / 1415 0.9 / 2021 5.4	
4 SU 0237 1.3 / 0830 4.8 / 1452 1.5 / 2037 5.0		**19** M 0239 0.9 / 0853 5.1 / 1459 1.1 / 2107 5.3	
5 M 0311 1.6 / 0905 4.6 / 1526 1.8 / 2115 4.8		**20** TU 0327 1.1 / 0943 4.9 / 1549 1.4 / 2159 5.1	
6 TU 0351 1.9 / 0948 4.4 / 1610 2.1 / 2201 4.5		**21** W 0422 1.3 / 1042 4.7 / 1648 1.6 / 2301 4.9	
7 W 0444 2.1 / 1045 4.2 / 1710 2.3 / 2300 4.4		**22** TH 0528 1.5 / 1153 4.6 / 1758 1.8	
8 TH 0550 2.2 / 1204 4.2 / 1820 2.3		**23** F 0017 4.8 / 0643 1.6 / 1308 4.6 / 1917 1.8	
9 F 0020 4.3 / 0658 2.1 / 1330 4.3 / 1928 2.1		**24** SA 0133 4.8 / 0758 1.5 / 1414 4.7 / 2030 1.6	
10 SA 0148 4.5 / 0803 1.9 / 1432 4.5 / 2031 1.9		**25** SU 0238 4.9 / 0903 1.3 / 1512 4.9 / 2131 1.3	
11 SU 0250 4.7 / 0901 1.6 / 1523 4.8 / 2127 1.6		**26** M 0335 5.0 / 0959 1.1 / 1604 5.1 / 2224 1.1	
12 M 0342 4.9 / 0953 1.3 / 1610 5.0 / 2217 1.3		**27** TU 0426 5.1 / 1048 0.9 / 1650 5.2 / 2311 0.9	
13 TU 0429 5.1 / 1041 1.1 / 1654 5.2 / 2303 1.1		**28** W 0512 5.2 / 1133 0.8 / 1732 5.3 / ● 2355 0.8	
14 W 0514 5.2 / 1126 0.9 / 1736 5.3 / ○ 2347 0.8		**29** TH 0554 5.2 / 1214 0.8 / 1810 5.4	
15 TH 0558 5.3 / 1209 0.8 / 1818 5.4		**30** F 0034 0.8 / 0632 5.2 / 1252 0.9 / 1843 5.3	
		31 SA 0111 0.9 / 0706 5.1 / 1326 1.1 / 1914 5.3	

JUNE

Time	m	Time	m
1 SU 0145 1.1 / 0739 5.0 / 1358 1.2 / 1946 5.2		**16** M 0150 0.6 / 0800 5.4 / 1411 0.7 / 2015 5.6	
2 M 0217 1.3 / 0813 4.9 / 1429 1.4 / 2020 5.1		**17** TU 0237 0.6 / 0849 5.3 / 1457 0.9 / 2103 5.5	
3 TU 0248 1.5 / 0849 4.7 / 1500 1.7 / 2056 4.9		**18** W 0324 0.8 / 0938 5.1 / 1544 1.1 / 2152 5.3	
4 W 0322 1.7 / 0929 4.6 / 1536 1.9 / 2137 4.7		**19** TH 0413 1.1 / 1031 4.9 / 1634 1.4 / ● 2246 5.0	
5 TH 0402 1.9 / 1015 4.4 / 1622 2.1 / ● 2224 4.6		**20** F 0506 1.3 / 1129 4.8 / 1731 1.6 / 2350 4.8	
6 F 0457 2.0 / 1111 4.3 / 1725 2.2 / 2322 4.5		**21** SA 0608 1.6 / 1235 4.6 / 1838 1.8	
7 SA 0604 2.0 / 1218 4.3 / 1835 2.1		**22** SU 0100 4.7 / 0718 1.7 / 1341 4.6 / 1952 1.8	
8 SU 0030 4.5 / 0710 1.9 / 1329 4.5 / 1941 2.0		**23** M 0207 4.7 / 0829 1.6 / 1441 4.7 / 2101 1.7	
9 M 0146 4.6 / 0813 1.9 / 1433 4.7 / 2043 1.7		**24** TU 0307 4.7 / 0931 1.5 / 1536 4.9 / 2200 1.5	
10 TU 0253 4.8 / 0912 1.5 / 1528 4.9 / 2140 1.4		**25** W 0401 4.9 / 1024 1.3 / 1625 5.0 / 2250 1.3	
11 W 0351 5.0 / 1007 1.2 / 1619 5.1 / 2234 1.1		**26** TH 0449 5.0 / 1111 1.2 / 1708 5.2 / 2335 1.1	
12 TH 0444 5.1 / 1059 1.0 / 1708 5.3 / 2325 0.9		**27** F 0532 5.0 / 1154 1.1 / 1747 5.3 ○	
13 F 0534 5.3 / 1149 0.8 / 1755 5.5 ○		**28** 0016 1.0 / 0610 5.1 / 1233 1.1 / 1822 5.3	
14 SA 0015 0.7 / 0623 5.4 / 1238 0.7 / 1842 5.6		**29** SU 0053 1.0 / 0647 5.1 / 1307 1.1 / 1856 5.3	
15 SU 0103 0.6 / 0712 5.4 / 1324 0.7 / 1928 5.6		**30** M 0127 1.1 / 0722 5.0 / 1338 1.2 / 1930 5.2	

JULY

Time	m	Time	m
1 TU 0157 1.2 / 0757 5.0 / 1407 1.3 / 2004 5.2		**16** W 0226 0.4 / 0837 5.4 / 1445 0.6 / 2051 5.6	
2 W 0225 1.3 / 0832 4.8 / 1435 1.5 / 2038 5.0		**17** TH 0310 0.6 / 0922 5.3 / 1528 0.8 / 2136 5.4	
3 TH 0253 1.5 / 0907 4.7 / 1504 1.6 / 2113 4.9		**18** F 0353 0.9 / 1008 5.1 / 1611 1.2 / 2222 5.1	
4 F 0324 1.6 / 0945 4.6 / 1538 1.8 / 2151 4.8		**19** SA 0438 1.2 / 1057 4.8 / 1659 1.5 / ● 2314 4.8	
5 SA 0403 1.8 / 1028 4.5 / 1624 2.0 / ● 2238 4.6		**20** SU 0529 1.6 / 1155 4.6 / 1756 1.8	
6 SU 0457 1.9 / 1122 4.4 / 1730 2.1 / 2337 4.5		**21** M 0022 4.5 / 0631 1.9 / 1304 4.5 / 1908 2.0	
7 M 0612 2.0 / 1227 4.5 / 1851 2.0		**22** TU 0136 4.4 / 0749 2.0 / 1411 4.5 / 2030 2.0	
8 TU 0047 4.5 / 0728 1.9 / 1340 4.6 / 2004 1.8		**23** W 0242 4.5 / 0904 1.8 / 1511 4.7 / 2138 1.8	
9 W 0206 4.6 / 0837 1.6 / 1449 4.8 / 2110 1.5		**24** TH 0339 4.6 / 1003 1.6 / 1602 4.9 / 2232 1.5	
10 TH 0318 4.8 / 0940 1.4 / 1550 5.1 / 2211 1.2		**25** F 0428 4.8 / 1052 1.4 / 1646 5.1 / 2317 1.3	
11 F 0420 5.1 / 1038 1.1 / 1645 5.4 / 2308 0.9		**26** SA 0511 4.9 / 1135 1.2 / 1726 5.2 / ● 2358 1.1	
12 SA 0515 5.3 / 1133 0.8 / 1737 5.6 ○		**27** SU 0550 5.0 / 1213 1.1 / 1803 5.3	
13 SU 0001 0.6 / 0608 5.4 / 1226 0.6 / 1827 5.7		**28** M 0035 1.0 / 0627 5.1 / 1248 1.1 / 1838 5.3	
14 M 0052 0.4 / 0659 5.5 / 1315 0.5 / 1916 5.8		**29** TU 0107 1.0 / 0703 5.1 / 1318 1.1 / 1913 5.3	
15 TU 0140 0.3 / 0749 5.5 / 1401 0.5 / 2004 5.8		**30** W 0135 1.1 / 0738 5.1 / 1344 1.2 / 1946 5.2	
		31 TH 0200 1.2 / 0811 5.0 / 1410 1.3 / 2018 5.1	

AUGUST

Time	m	Time	m
1 F 0225 1.3 / 0843 4.9 / 1436 1.4 / 2048 5.0		**16** SA 0327 0.8 / 0937 5.2 / 1544 1.1 / 2150 5.1	
2 SA 0252 1.4 / 0914 4.8 / 1506 1.6 / 2121 4.9		**17** SU 0406 1.3 / 1015 4.9 / 1626 1.5 / ● 2229 4.7	
3 SU 0326 1.6 / 0951 4.6 / 1545 1.7 / 2203 4.7		**18** M 0451 1.7 / 1101 4.6 / 1716 2.0 / 2325 4.4	
4 M 0409 1.8 / 1039 4.5 / 1637 2.0 / ● 2258 4.6		**19** TU 0547 2.1 / 1218 4.4 / 1823 2.2	
5 TU 0512 2.0 / 1143 4.5 / 1758 2.1		**20** W 0103 4.2 / 0701 2.3 / 1341 4.4 / 1956 2.2	
6 W 0009 4.5 / 0644 2.0 / 1300 4.5 / 1932 2.0		**21** TH 0219 4.3 / 0836 2.1 / 1446 4.5 / 2118 2.0	
7 TH 0133 4.6 / 0809 1.8 / 1419 4.8 / 2048 1.7		**22** F 0318 4.5 / 0942 1.8 / 1539 4.8 / 2212 1.6	
8 F 0256 4.8 / 0921 1.5 / 1528 5.1 / 2154 1.2		**23** SA 0407 4.8 / 1031 1.5 / 1624 5.0 / 2256 1.3	
9 SA 0402 5.0 / 1023 1.1 / 1627 5.4 / 2254 0.8		**24** SU 0449 4.9 / 1112 1.2 / 1703 5.2 / 2335 1.1	
10 SU 0500 5.3 / 1120 0.7 / 1720 5.6 / ○ 2348 0.5		**25** M 0527 5.1 / 1150 1.1 / 1741 5.3 ●	
11 M 0553 5.5 / 1211 0.5 / 1811 5.8		**26** 0010 1.0 / 0604 5.2 / 1223 1.0 / 1817 5.4	
12 0037 0.2 / 0643 5.6 / 1300 0.3 / 1900 5.9		**27** W 0041 1.0 / 0640 5.2 / 1253 1.0 / 1852 5.4	
13 W 0124 0.1 / 0731 5.6 / 1344 0.3 / 1947 5.9		**28** TH 0108 1.0 / 0715 5.2 / 1319 1.1 / 1925 5.3	
14 TH 0208 0.3 / 0816 5.6 / 1426 0.4 / 2031 5.7		**29** F 0134 1.1 / 0747 5.1 / 1345 1.2 / 1956 5.2	
15 F 0248 0.5 / 0858 5.4 / 1505 0.7 / 2111 5.4		**30** SA 0159 1.2 / 0817 5.0 / 1411 1.3 / 2024 5.1	
		31 SU 0226 1.3 / 0846 4.9 / 1441 1.4 / 2056 5.0	

Chart Datum: 3·22 metres below Ordnance Datum (Newlyn)
HAT is 5·9 metres above Chart Datum

SEPTEMBER

Time m — Time m

Day	Time 1 m	Time 2 m	Time 3 m	Time 4 m	Day	Time 1 m	Time 2 m	Time 3 m	Time 4 m
1 M	0258 1.5	0920 4.8	1517 1.6	2136 4.8	16 TU	0414 1.9	1005 4.6	1641 2.1	☽ 2225 4.3
2 TU	0338 1.7	1008 4.6	1606 1.9	☾ 2232 4.6	17 W	0506 2.3	1101 4.4	1744 2.4	
3 W	0435 2.0	1112 4.5	1721 2.1	2344 4.4	18 TH	0007 4.1	0617 2.5	1302 4.3	1908 2.4
4 TH	0609 2.2	1231 4.5	1909 2.1		19 F	0151 4.2	0752 2.4	1416 4.5	2047 2.1
5 F	0113 4.5	0750 2.0	1359 4.7	2032 1.7	20 SA	0252 4.4	0911 2.0	1511 4.7	2143 1.8
6 SA	0242 4.7	0907 1.6	1512 5.1	2140 1.2	21 SU	0340 4.7	1001 1.7	1556 5.0	2226 1.4
7 SU	0350 5.1	1009 1.1	1611 5.4	2239 0.8	22 M	0422 5.0	1042 1.4	1637 5.2	2304 1.2
8 M	0445 5.4	1104 0.7	1703 5.7	2330 0.4	23 TU	0501 5.2	1119 1.2	1715 5.4	2338 1.0
9 TU	0535 5.6	1154 0.4	1753 5.9	○	24 W	0538 5.3	1153 1.0	1753 5.4	●
10 W	0018 0.2	0623 5.7	1240 0.2	1840 5.9	25 TH	0010 1.0	0615 5.3	1224 1.0	1828 5.4
11 TH	0103 0.1	0708 5.8	1323 0.2	1924 5.9	26 F	0040 1.0	0650 5.3	1254 1.0	1902 5.4
12 F	0144 0.3	0750 5.6	1402 0.4	2005 5.7	27 SA	0108 1.0	0722 5.3	1322 1.1	1934 5.3
13 SA	0222 0.5	0827 5.5	1439 0.7	2042 5.4	28 SU	0136 1.1	0752 5.2	1351 1.2	2004 5.2
14 SU	0258 0.9	0900 5.2	1516 1.2	2113 5.0	29 M	0205 1.2	0823 5.1	1423 1.3	2038 5.0
15 M	0334 1.4	0930 4.9	1554 1.6	2144 4.7	30 TU	0238 1.5	0859 5.0	1500 1.6	2121 4.8

OCTOBER

Time m — Time m

Day	Time 1 m	Time 2 m	Time 3 m	Time 4 m	Day	Time 1 m	Time 2 m	Time 3 m	Time 4 m
1 W	0320 1.7	0948 4.8	1550 1.9	☾ 2216 4.6	16 TH	0430 2.3	1018 4.5	1707 2.4	2255 4.2
2 TH	0417 2.0	1051 4.6	1705 2.1	2328 4.4	17 F	0536 2.5	1134 4.3	1820 2.5	
3 F	0548 2.2	1211 4.6	1851 2.1		18 SA	0104 4.2	0654 2.5	1331 4.4	1945 2.3
4 SA	0101 4.5	0734 2.1	1342 4.8	2017 1.7	19 SU	0214 4.4	0816 2.3	1433 4.7	2055 2.0
5 SU	0230 4.8	0851 1.6	1455 5.1	2124 1.3	20 M	0305 4.7	0916 1.9	1521 4.9	2143 1.6
6 M	0334 5.1	0952 1.2	1554 5.5	2220 0.8	21 TU	0349 5.0	1001 1.6	1605 5.1	2223 1.4
7 TU	0427 5.4	1045 0.8	1645 5.7	2310 0.5	22 W	0430 5.2	1042 1.3	1646 5.3	2301 1.2
8 W	0515 5.6	1133 0.5	1733 5.8	○ 2356 0.3	23 TH	0510 5.3	1119 1.1	1725 5.4	● 2337 1.0
9 TH	0600 5.7	1217 0.4	1818 5.9		24 F	0548 5.4	1155 1.0	1804 5.4	
10 F	0038 0.3	0642 5.8	1259 0.4	1900 5.8	25 SA	0011 1.0	0624 5.4	1230 1.0	1840 5.4
11 SA	0119 0.5	0721 5.7	1338 0.6	1938 5.6	26 SU	0045 1.0	0659 5.4	1303 1.0	1915 5.4
12 SU	0156 0.7	0755 5.5	1414 0.9	2012 5.3	27 M	0118 1.1	0733 5.4	1337 1.1	1950 5.3
13 M	0230 1.1	0825 5.3	1449 1.3	2041 5.0	28 TU	0152 1.2	0808 5.3	1414 1.3	2028 5.1
14 TU	0304 1.5	0853 5.0	1525 1.7	2111 4.7	29 W	0229 1.4	0848 5.2	1455 1.5	2113 4.9
15 W	0341 1.9	0929 4.8	1609 2.1	☾ 2152 4.4	30 TH	0313 1.7	0937 5.0	1547 1.8	2208 4.7
					31 F	0412 2.0	1038 4.8	1659 2.0	☾ 2318 4.6

NOVEMBER

Time m — Time m

Day	Time 1 m	Time 2 m	Time 3 m	Time 4 m	Day	Time 1 m	Time 2 m	Time 3 m	Time 4 m
1 SA	0534 2.2	1154 4.7	1831 2.0		16 SU	0601 2.5	1205 4.5	1842 2.4	
2 SU	0047 4.6	0711 2.1	1321 4.9	1954 1.8	17 M	0110 4.4	0712 2.4	1333 4.6	1949 2.2
3 M	0210 4.8	0828 1.7	1433 5.1	2101 1.4	18 TU	0217 4.6	0817 2.1	1435 4.8	2048 1.9
4 TU	0313 5.1	0930 1.3	1532 5.4	2157 1.0	19 W	0309 4.8	0913 1.8	1526 5.0	2138 1.6
5 W	0406 5.4	1022 1.0	1624 5.6	2247 0.8	20 TH	0355 5.1	1001 1.5	1613 5.2	2223 1.3
6 TH	0453 5.6	1110 0.7	1711 5.7	2332 0.6	21 F	0439 5.3	1045 1.3	1657 5.3	2305 1.2
7 F	0537 5.7	1155 0.6	1756 5.7		22 SA	0520 5.4	1128 1.1	1739 5.4	● 2346 1.0
8 SA	0015 0.6	0617 5.7	1237 0.7	1837 5.6	23 SU	0600 5.5	1209 1.0	1820 5.4	
9 SU	0055 0.7	0655 5.6	1315 0.8	1914 5.4	24 M	0026 1.0	0639 5.6	1250 1.0	1900 5.4
10 M	0131 0.9	0728 5.5	1351 1.0	1946 5.2	25 TU	0106 1.0	0719 5.6	1330 1.0	1941 5.4
11 TU	0205 1.2	0757 5.3	1426 1.3	2016 5.0	26 W	0146 1.1	0759 5.5	1412 1.1	2024 5.2
12 W	0238 1.6	0828 5.1	1501 1.7	2049 4.8	27 TH	0228 1.3	0843 5.4	1457 1.3	2110 5.1
13 TH	0313 1.9	0905 4.9	1540 2.0	2130 4.6	28 F	0314 1.5	0932 5.2	1548 1.5	2203 4.9
14 F	0354 2.2	0950 4.7	1629 2.3	☾ 2223 4.4	29 SA	0409 1.8	1028 5.0	1649 1.7	☾ 2307 4.7
15 SA	0451 2.4	1047 4.5	1732 2.4	2336 4.3	30 SU	0516 2.0	1136 4.9	1803 1.9	

DECEMBER

Time m — Time m

Day	Time 1 m	Time 2 m	Time 3 m	Time 4 m	Day	Time 1 m	Time 2 m	Time 3 m	Time 4 m
1 M	0023 4.7	0637 2.0	1253 4.9	1922 1.8	16 TU	0609 2.4	1212 4.5	1848 2.2	
2 TU	0139 4.8	0757 1.9	1405 5.0	2032 1.6	17 W	0106 4.5	0720 2.3	1328 4.6	1953 2.1
3 W	0245 5.0	0903 1.6	1507 5.1	2132 1.3	18 TH	0216 4.6	0824 2.0	1437 4.7	2053 1.8
4 TH	0341 5.2	1000 1.3	1602 5.3	2224 1.1	19 F	0314 4.9	0922 1.7	1536 4.9	2147 1.5
5 F	0430 5.4	1050 1.1	1651 5.4	2311 1.0	20 SA	0406 5.1	1015 1.4	1628 5.1	2238 1.3
6 SA	0515 5.5	1135 1.0	1736 5.4	2354 0.9	21 SU	0453 5.3	1105 1.2	1716 5.3	2326 1.1
7 SU	0556 5.6	1218 0.9	1817 5.4		22 M	0538 5.5	1153 0.9	1803 5.4	
8 M	0034 1.0	0633 5.6	1257 1.0	1854 5.3	23 TU	0013 0.9	0623 5.6	1240 0.8	1848 5.5
9 TU	0111 1.1	0707 5.5	1333 1.1	1927 5.2	24 W	0058 0.8	0708 5.7	1325 0.7	1934 5.5
10 W	0145 1.3	0738 5.4	1407 1.3	1959 5.1	25 TH	0143 0.9	0753 5.7	1410 0.8	2019 5.4
11 TH	0217 1.5	0811 5.3	1439 1.5	2033 4.9	26 F	0227 1.0	0838 5.6	1455 0.9	2106 5.3
12 F	0248 1.7	0847 5.1	1512 1.8	2111 4.7	27 SA	0312 1.1	0925 5.5	1542 1.1	2154 5.1
13 SA	0321 1.9	0926 4.9	1549 2.0	2155 4.6	28 SU	0359 1.4	1015 5.2	1632 1.4	☾ 2248 4.9
14 SU	0401 2.2	1012 4.7	1632 2.2	2247 4.4	29 M	0452 1.7	1113 5.0	1729 1.7	2351 4.9
15 M	0457 2.3	1106 4.6	1738 2.3	2351 4.4	30 TU	0556 1.9	1221 4.8	1839 1.9	
					31 W	0103 4.7	0715 2.0	1334 4.7	1957 1.9

Chart Datum: 3·22 metres below Ordnance Datum (Newlyn)
HAT is 5·9 metres above Chart Datum

TIDES

DARTMOUTH

MEAN SPRING
AND NEAP CURVES

MEAN RANGES
Springs 4.3m
Neaps 1.8m

DARTMOUTH

LAT 50°21'N   LONG 3°35'W

TIMES AND HEIGHTS OF HIGH AND LOW WATERS

Dates in amber are **SPRINGS**
Dates in yellow are **NEAPS**

2014

JANUARY

Day	Time m	Time m	Time m	Time m		Day	Time m	Time m	Time m	Time m
1 W ●	0536 5.0	1134 0.6	1805 4.9	2357 0.6		16 TH O	0607 4.7	1209 1.0	1830 4.5	
2 TH	0629 5.2	1226 0.4	1857 5.0			17 F	0021 1.0	0644 4.8	1244 0.9	1905 4.6
3 F	0048 0.4	0718 5.3	1316 0.3	1946 5.0		18 SA	0054 1.0	0719 4.8	1314 1.0	1940 4.6
4 SA	0134 0.4	0805 5.3	1401 0.3	2033 4.9		19 SU	0122 1.0	0753 4.7	1341 1.0	2013 4.5
5 SU	0219 0.5	0851 5.2	1445 0.4	2118 4.8		20 M	0148 1.1	0824 4.6	1408 1.1	2044 4.4
6 M	0301 0.7	0935 5.0	1527 0.7	2202 4.6		21 TU	0216 1.2	0853 4.6	1434 1.2	2112 4.3
7 TU	0343 1.0	1020 4.7	1611 1.0	2246 4.3		22 W	0244 1.3	0925 4.4	1505 1.3	2143 4.2
8 W ◐	0426 1.3	1106 4.4	1656 1.4	2336 4.1		23 TH	0319 1.4	1001 4.3	1543 1.5	2224 4.1
9 TH	0517 1.7	1201 4.1	1750 1.7			24 F ◐	0403 1.6	1048 4.1	1632 1.7	2319 4.0
10 F	0039 3.9	0618 1.9	1310 3.9	1859 1.9		25 SA	0503 1.8	1149 4.0	1743 1.8	
11 SA	0150 3.9	0740 1.9	1422 3.9	2019 1.9		26 SU	0029 3.9	0631 1.9	1304 3.9	1919 1.8
12 SU	0257 4.0	0900 1.8	1526 4.0	2128 1.7		27 M	0152 4.0	0803 1.7	1430 4.1	2042 1.6
13 M	0355 4.2	1000 1.6	1621 4.2	2220 1.4		28 TU	0314 4.3	0919 1.4	1550 4.3	2152 1.2
14 TU	0445 4.4	1049 1.3	1709 4.4	2306 1.2		29 W	0422 4.6	1025 0.9	1655 4.6	2253 0.8
15 W	0528 4.6	1131 1.1	1751 4.5	2345 1.1		30 TH ●	0521 4.9	1123 0.5	1753 4.8	2346 0.4
						31 F	0615 5.2	1214 0.2	1846 5.0	

FEBRUARY

Day	Time m	Time m	Time m	Time m		Day	Time m	Time m	Time m	Time m
1 SA	0036 0.2	0704 5.3	1303 0.0	1933 5.0		16 SU	0034 0.8	0701 4.8	1254 0.8	1922 4.6
2 SU	0122 0.1	0751 5.3	1347 0.0	2017 5.0		17 M	0104 0.8	0736 4.8	1322 0.8	1954 4.6
3 M	0204 0.1	0834 5.2	1428 0.1	2057 4.9		18 TU	0130 0.8	0807 4.7	1348 0.8	2023 4.5
4 TU	0242 0.4	0915 5.0	1506 0.4	2135 4.7		19 W	0157 0.9	0835 4.6	1415 0.9	2051 4.4
5 W	0320 0.7	0952 4.7	1542 0.8	2207 4.4		20 TH	0226 1.0	0904 4.5	1444 1.0	2119 4.3
6 TH	0356 1.1	1026 4.4	1620 1.3	2241 4.1		21 F	0258 1.1	0938 4.3	1520 1.2	2156 4.2
7 F	0437 1.5	1103 4.0	1704 1.7	2325 3.9		22 SA	0338 1.4	1022 4.1	1604 1.5	2248 4.0
8 SA	0528 1.9	1203 3.7	1801 2.0			23 SU	0433 1.6	1123 3.9	1708 1.8	2358 3.9
9 SU	0047 3.7	0639 2.1	1342 3.6	1918 2.1		24 M	0555 1.8	1240 3.8	1846 1.9	
10 M	0220 3.7	0816 2.1	1457 3.7	2053 2.0		25 TU	0124 3.9	0740 1.7	1414 3.9	2022 1.6
11 TU	0326 4.0	0937 1.8	1556 3.9	2157 1.6		26 W	0254 4.2	0905 1.4	1537 4.2	2139 1.2
12 W	0419 4.2	1029 1.4	1646 4.2	2245 1.3		27 TH	0406 4.5	1012 0.9	1643 4.5	2240 0.7
13 TH	0504 4.5	1111 1.1	1729 4.4	2325 1.0		28 F	0504 4.9	1108 0.4	1739 4.8	2332 0.3
14 F	0546 4.6	1149 0.9	1810 4.5	O						
15 SA	0001 0.9	0625 4.6	1223 0.8	1847 4.6						

MARCH

Day	Time m	Time m	Time m	Time m		Day	Time m	Time m	Time m	Time m
1 SA ●	0558 5.1	1158 0.1	1829 5.0			16 SU O	0559 4.7	1153 0.7	1822 4.6	
2 SU	0019 0.1	0647 5.2	1245 -0.1	1913 5.1		17 M	0006 0.7	0638 4.7	1226 0.6	1858 4.6
3 M	0104 0.0	0731 5.3	1327 -0.1	1954 5.0		18 TU	0040 0.6	0713 4.7	1258 0.6	1932 4.7
4 TU	0143 0.0	0811 5.2	1405 0.1	2031 4.9		19 W	0111 0.6	0745 4.7	1328 0.6	2002 4.7
5 W	0220 0.2	0849 4.9	1439 0.4	2101 4.7		20 TH	0140 0.7	0816 4.7	1357 0.7	2030 4.6
6 TH	0253 0.6	0919 4.6	1513 0.8	2128 4.5		21 F	0211 0.8	0848 4.5	1428 0.9	2101 4.5
7 F	0327 1.0	0946 4.3	1546 1.3	2155 4.2		22 SA	0244 0.9	0924 4.4	1504 1.1	2139 4.3
8 SA	0403 1.4	1016 4.0	1625 1.7	2232 3.9		23 SU	0326 1.2	1009 4.1	1549 1.4	2230 4.1
9 SU	0450 1.9	1102 3.6	1718 2.0	2329 3.7		24 M ◐	0421 1.5	1109 3.9	1652 1.7	2338 3.9
10 M	0554 2.1	1238 3.4	1829 2.2			25 TU	0541 1.7	1227 3.8	1827 1.9	
11 TU	0128 3.6	0716 2.1	1423 3.5	1955 2.1		26 W	0107 3.9	0725 1.7	1404 3.9	2007 1.6
12 W	0251 3.8	0858 1.9	1526 3.8	2120 1.8		27 TH	0238 4.2	0850 1.3	1524 4.2	2122 1.2
13 TH	0348 4.1	0956 1.5	1617 4.1	2213 1.4		28 F	0348 4.5	0955 0.8	1626 4.5	2221 0.7
14 F	0435 4.3	1040 1.2	1701 4.3	2255 1.1		29 SA	0446 4.8	1049 0.4	1719 4.8	2312 0.4
15 SA	0518 4.5	1118 0.9	1743 4.5	2332 0.9		30 SU ●	0537 5.0	1137 0.1	1806 4.9	2358 0.1
						31 M	0625 5.1	1221 0.0	1850 5.0	

APRIL

Day	Time m	Time m	Time m	Time m		Day	Time m	Time m	Time m	Time m
1 TU	0041 0.0	0707 5.1	1303 0.0	1928 5.0		16 W	0012 0.6	0648 4.7	1233 0.6	1906 4.7
2 W	0120 0.1	0746 5.0	1339 0.2	2001 4.9		17 TH	0050 0.5	0725 4.7	1308 0.6	1940 4.8
3 TH	0155 0.3	0819 4.8	1413 0.5	2028 4.7		18 F	0125 0.5	0800 4.7	1342 0.7	2013 4.7
4 F	0228 0.6	0848 4.5	1444 0.9	2053 4.5		19 SA	0200 0.6	0836 4.6	1418 0.8	2050 4.6
5 SA	0300 1.0	0914 4.2	1516 1.3	2122 4.3		20 SU	0238 0.8	0917 4.4	1457 1.1	2132 4.5
6 SU	0334 1.4	0946 4.0	1552 1.7	2159 4.0		21 M	0323 1.1	1004 4.2	1545 1.4	2221 4.3
7 M	0418 1.8	1030 3.7	1641 2.0	2248 3.8		22 TU ◐	0420 1.4	1103 4.0	1649 1.6	2328 4.1
8 TU	0518 2.0	1136 3.5	1747 2.2			23 W	0534 1.6	1221 3.8	1813 1.8	
9 W	0002 3.6	0631 2.1	1334 3.5	1903 2.1		24 TH	0052 4.0	0706 1.5	1348 3.9	1945 1.6
10 TH	0159 3.7	0748 1.9	1446 3.7	2018 1.9		25 F	0217 4.2	0827 1.2	1501 4.2	2058 1.2
11 F	0307 4.0	0900 1.6	1540 4.0	2122 1.5		26 SA	0325 4.4	0931 0.9	1601 4.4	2157 0.9
12 SA	0357 4.2	0953 1.3	1626 4.2	2212 1.2		27 SU	0422 4.7	1024 0.6	1653 4.7	2248 0.6
13 SU	0444 4.4	1037 1.0	1710 4.4	2255 0.9		28 M	0514 4.8	1113 0.4	1741 4.8	2334 0.4
14 M	0527 4.6	1117 0.8	1752 4.6	2335 0.7		29 TU ●	0600 4.9	1156 0.3	1824 4.9	
15 TU O	0610 4.7	1155 0.6	1831 4.7			30 W	0016 0.3	0643 4.9	1238 0.3	1900 4.9

Chart Datum: 2·62 metres below Ordnance Datum (Newlyn)
HAT is 5·3 metres above Chart Datum

TIDES

TIME ZONE (UT)	DARTMOUTH	Dates in amber are SPRINGS
For Summer Time add ONE hour in **non-shaded** areas	LAT 50°21'N LONG 3°35'W	Dates in yellow are NEAPS
	TIMES AND HEIGHTS OF HIGH AND LOW WATERS	**2014**

MAY

Time	m	Time	m
1 TH 0057 / 0720 / 1315 / 1932	0.4 / 4.8 / 0.5 / 4.8	**16** F 0030 / 0704 / 1251 / 1922	0.5 / 4.7 / 0.5 / 4.9
2 F 0131 / 0752 / 1348 / 2000	0.5 / 4.6 / 0.7 / 4.7	**17** SA 0113 / 0746 / 1331 / 2002	0.5 / 4.7 / 0.6 / 4.9
3 SA 0204 / 0821 / 1419 / 2027	0.8 / 4.4 / 1.0 / 4.6	**18** SU 0154 / 0829 / 1414 / 2043	0.5 / 4.7 / 0.7 / 4.8
4 SU 0235 / 0851 / 1450 / 2058	1.1 / 4.2 / 1.3 / 4.4	**19** M 0237 / 0914 / 1457 / 2128	0.7 / 4.5 / 0.9 / 4.7
5 M 0309 / 0926 / 1524 / 2135	1.4 / 4.0 / 1.6 / 4.2	**20** TU 0325 / 1003 / 1546 / 2218	0.9 / 4.3 / 1.2 / 4.5
6 TU 0348 / 1007 / 1607 / 2220	1.7 / 3.8 / 1.9 / 3.9	**21** W 0419 / 1100 / 1644 / 2319	1.1 / 4.1 / 1.4 / 4.3
7 W 0440 / 1103 / 1706 / 2318	1.9 / 3.6 / 2.1 / 3.8	**22** TH 0524 / 1209 / 1753	1.3 / 4.0 / 1.6
8 TH 0545 / 1220 / 1815	2.0 / 3.6 / 2.1	**23** F 0033 / 0639 / 1323 / 1913	4.2 / 1.4 / 4.0 / 1.6
9 F 0036 / 0654 / 1346 / 1924	3.7 / 1.9 / 3.7 / 1.9	**24** SA 0149 / 0754 / 1431 / 2027	4.2 / 1.3 / 4.1 / 1.4
10 SA 0205 / 0759 / 1450 / 2028	3.9 / 1.7 / 3.9 / 1.7	**25** SU 0256 / 0900 / 1531 / 2129	4.3 / 1.1 / 4.3 / 1.1
11 SU 0309 / 0858 / 1543 / 2124	4.1 / 1.4 / 4.2 / 1.4	**26** M 0355 / 0957 / 1625 / 2222	4.4 / 0.9 / 4.5 / 0.9
12 M 0402 / 0951 / 1631 / 2215	4.3 / 1.1 / 4.4 / 1.1	**27** TU 0448 / 1047 / 1713 / 2310	4.6 / 0.7 / 4.6 / 0.7
13 TU 0451 / 1040 / 1717 / 2302	4.5 / 0.9 / 4.6 / 0.8	**28** W 0535 / 1132 / 1756 / 2354	4.6 / 0.6 / 4.7 / 0.6
14 W 0537 / 1125 / 1800 / 2346	4.6 / 0.7 / 4.7 / 0.6	**29** TH 0619 / 1213 / 1835	4.6 / 0.6 / 4.8
15 TH 0623 / 1208 / 1843	4.7 / 0.6 / 4.8	**30** F 0034 / 0656 / 1252 / 1907	0.6 / 4.6 / 0.7 / 4.7
		31 SA 0111 / 0730 / 1326 / 1938	0.7 / 4.5 / 0.9 / 4.7

JUNE

Time	m	Time	m
1 SU 0144 / 0802 / 1357 / 2008	0.9 / 4.4 / 1.0 / 4.6	**16** M 0149 / 0822 / 1410 / 2037	0.4 / 4.8 / 0.5 / 5.0
2 M 0216 / 0835 / 1428 / 2042	1.1 / 4.3 / 1.2 / 4.5	**17** TU 0235 / 0853 / 1455 / 2124	0.4 / 4.7 / 0.7 / 4.9
3 TU 0246 / 0910 / 1458 / 2117	1.3 / 4.1 / 1.5 / 4.3	**18** W 0322 / 0958 / 1541 / 2211	0.6 / 4.5 / 0.9 / 4.7
4 W 0320 / 0949 / 1533 / 2157	1.5 / 4.0 / 1.7 / 4.1	**19** TH 0410 / 1049 / 1630 / 2304	0.9 / 4.3 / 1.2 / 4.4
5 TH 0359 / 1034 / 1619 / 2243	1.7 / 3.8 / 1.9 / 4.0	**20** F 0502 / 1146 / 1726	1.1 / 4.2 / 1.4
6 F 0453 / 1129 / 1721 / 2339	1.8 / 3.7 / 2.0 / 3.9	**21** SA 0006 / 0603 / 1250 / 1834	4.2 / 1.4 / 4.0 / 1.6
7 SA 0559 / 1234 / 1831	1.8 / 3.7 / 1.9	**22** SU 0115 / 0714 / 1357 / 1948	4.1 / 1.5 / 4.0 / 1.6
8 SU 0045 / 0706 / 1345 / 1937	3.9 / 1.7 / 3.9 / 1.8	**23** M 0224 / 0825 / 1459 / 2058	4.1 / 1.4 / 4.1 / 1.5
9 M 0203 / 0809 / 1451 / 2040	4.0 / 1.5 / 4.1 / 1.5	**24** TU 0326 / 0929 / 1556 / 2158	4.1 / 1.3 / 4.3 / 1.3
10 TU 0312 / 0909 / 1548 / 2138	4.2 / 1.2 / 4.3 / 1.2	**25** W 0422 / 1022 / 1647 / 2249	4.3 / 1.1 / 4.4 / 1.1
11 W 0412 / 1005 / 1641 / 2233	4.4 / 1.0 / 4.5 / 0.9	**26** TH 0512 / 1110 / 1731 / 2334	4.4 / 1.0 / 4.6 / 0.9
12 TH 0506 / 1058 / 1731 / 2324	4.5 / 0.8 / 4.7 / 0.7	**27** F 0556 / 1153 / 1812	4.4 / 0.9 / 4.7
13 F 0558 / 1148 / 1820	4.7 / 0.6 / 4.7	**28** SA 0015 / 0635 / 1233 / 1847	0.8 / 4.5 / 0.9 / 4.7
14 SA 0014 / 0648 / 1238 / 1906	0.5 / 4.8 / 0.5 / 5.0	**29** SU 0053 / 0711 / 1307 / 1920	0.6 / 4.5 / 0.9 / 4.7
15 SU 0103 / 0736 / 1324 / 1951	0.4 / 4.8 / 0.5 / 5.0	**30** M 0127 / 0745 / 1337 / 1953	0.9 / 4.4 / 1.0 / 4.6

JULY

Time	m	Time	m
1 TU 0156 / 0819 / 1406 / 2026	1.0 / 4.4 / 1.1 / 4.6	**16** W 0225 / 0858 / 1443 / 2112	0.2 / 4.8 / 0.4 / 5.0
2 W 0224 / 0853 / 1433 / 2059	1.1 / 4.2 / 1.3 / 4.4	**17** TH 0308 / 0942 / 1526 / 2156	0.4 / 4.7 / 0.6 / 4.8
3 TH 0251 / 0928 / 1502 / 2134	1.3 / 4.1 / 1.4 / 4.3	**18** F 0350 / 1027 / 1608 / 2241	0.7 / 4.5 / 1.0 / 4.5
4 F 0322 / 1004 / 1535 / 2210	1.4 / 4.0 / 1.6 / 4.2	**19** SA 0434 / 1115 / 1655 / 2332	1.0 / 4.2 / 1.3 / 4.2
5 SA 0400 / 1047 / 1621 / 2256	1.6 / 3.9 / 1.8 / 4.0	**20** SU 0525 / 1211 / 1751	1.4 / 4.0 / 1.6
6 SU 0453 / 1139 / 1725 / 2354	1.7 / 3.8 / 1.9 / 3.9	**21** M 0038 / 0627 / 1319 / 1904	3.9 / 1.7 / 3.9 / 1.8
7 M 0607 / 1243 / 1847	1.8 / 3.9 / 1.8	**22** TU 0152 / 0745 / 1428 / 2027	3.8 / 1.8 / 3.9 / 1.8
8 TU 0102 / 0724 / 1356 / 2000	3.9 / 1.7 / 4.0 / 1.6	**23** W 0300 / 0901 / 1530 / 2136	3.9 / 1.6 / 4.1 / 1.6
9 W 0223 / 0834 / 1508 / 2107	4.0 / 1.4 / 4.2 / 1.3	**24** TH 0359 / 1001 / 1623 / 2231	4.0 / 1.4 / 4.3 / 1.3
10 TH 0338 / 0938 / 1611 / 2209	4.2 / 1.2 / 4.5 / 1.0	**25** F 0450 / 1051 / 1709 / 2316	4.2 / 1.2 / 4.5 / 1.1
11 F 0442 / 1037 / 1708 / 2307	4.5 / 0.9 / 4.8 / 0.7	**26** SA 0534 / 1134 / 1750 / 2357	4.3 / 1.0 / 4.6 / 0.9
12 SA 0539 / 1132 / 1801	4.7 / 0.6 / 5.0	**27** SU 0615 / 1212 / 1828	4.4 / 0.9 / 4.7
13 SU 0000 / 0633 / 1225 / 1852	0.4 / 4.8 / 0.4 / 5.1	**28** M 0035 / 0652 / 1248 / 1902	0.8 / 4.5 / 0.9 / 4.7
14 M 0052 / 0723 / 1315 / 1939	0.2 / 4.9 / 0.3 / 5.2	**29** TU 0107 / 0727 / 1318 / 1937	0.8 / 4.5 / 0.9 / 4.7
15 TU 0139 / 0811 / 1400 / 2026	0.1 / 4.9 / 0.3 / 5.2	**30** W 0134 / 0801 / 1343 / 2008	0.9 / 4.5 / 1.0 / 4.6
		31 TH 0159 / 0833 / 1409 / 2040	1.0 / 4.4 / 1.1 / 4.5

AUGUST

Time	m	Time	m
1 F 0224 / 0904 / 1434 / 2109	1.1 / 4.3 / 1.2 / 4.4	**16** SA 0325 / 0957 / 1541 / 2209	0.6 / 4.6 / 0.9 / 4.5
2 SA 0250 / 0935 / 1504 / 2141	1.2 / 4.2 / 1.4 / 4.3	**17** SU 0403 / 1034 / 1623 / 2248	1.1 / 4.3 / 1.3 / 4.1
3 SU 0324 / 1010 / 1542 / 2222	1.4 / 4.0 / 1.5 / 4.1	**18** M 0447 / 1119 / 1712 / 2342	1.5 / 4.0 / 1.8 / 3.8
4 M 0406 / 1057 / 1633 / 2316	1.6 / 3.9 / 1.8 / 4.0	**19** TU 0542 / 1234 / 1818	1.9 / 3.8 / 2.0
5 TU 0508 / 1200 / 1753	1.8 / 3.9 / 1.9	**20** W 0118 / 0657 / 1357 / 1952	3.6 / 2.1 / 3.8 / 2.0
6 W 0025 / 0640 / 1315 / 1928	3.9 / 1.8 / 3.9 / 1.8	**21** TH 0237 / 0833 / 1505 / 2115	3.7 / 1.9 / 3.9 / 1.8
7 TH 0149 / 0805 / 1437 / 2045	3.9 / 1.6 / 4.2 / 1.5	**22** F 0338 / 0940 / 1559 / 2210	3.9 / 1.7 / 4.2 / 1.4
8 F 0315 / 0918 / 1548 / 2152	4.2 / 1.3 / 4.5 / 1.0	**23** SA 0428 / 1030 / 1646 / 2255	4.1 / 1.3 / 4.4 / 1.1
9 SA 0423 / 1021 / 1649 / 2253	4.4 / 0.9 / 4.8 / 0.6	**24** SU 0512 / 1111 / 1726 / 2334	4.3 / 1.0 / 4.6 / 0.9
10 SU 0523 / 1119 / 1744 / 2347	4.7 / 0.5 / 5.0 / 0.3	**25** M 0551 / 1149 / 1805	4.5 / 0.9 / 4.7
11 M 0618 / 1210 / 1836	4.9 / 0.3 / 5.2	**26** TU 0009 / 0629 / 1222 / 1842	0.8 / 4.6 / 0.8 / 4.8
12 TU 0037 / 0707 / 1300 / 1924	0.0 / 5.0 / 0.1 / 5.3	**27** W 0041 / 0704 / 1253 / 1916	0.8 / 4.6 / 0.8 / 4.8
13 W 0124 / 0754 / 1343 / 2009	-0.1 / 5.0 / 0.1 / 5.3	**28** TH 0108 / 0738 / 1319 / 1948	0.9 / 4.6 / 0.9 / 4.7
14 TH 0207 / 0838 / 1425 / 2052	0.0 / 5.0 / 0.2 / 5.1	**29** F 0133 / 0809 / 1344 / 2018	0.9 / 4.5 / 1.0 / 4.6
15 F 0246 / 0919 / 1503 / 2132	0.3 / 4.8 / 0.5 / 4.8	**30** SA 0158 / 0839 / 1410 / 2046	1.0 / 4.4 / 1.1 / 4.5
		31 SU 0225 / 0907 / 1439 / 2117	1.1 / 4.3 / 1.2 / 4.4

Chart Datum: 2·62 metres below Ordnance Datum (Newlyn)
HAT is 5·3 metres above Chart Datum

TIME ZONE (UT)	DARTMOUTH	Dates in amber are SPRINGS
For Summer Time add ONE hour in **non-shaded areas**	LAT 50°21'N LONG 3°35'W	Dates in yellow are NEAPS
	TIMES AND HEIGHTS OF HIGH AND LOW WATERS	**2014**

SEPTEMBER

Time m	Time m
1 0256 1.3 / 0940 4.2 / M 1515 1.4 / 2156 4.2	**16** 0411 1.7 / 1024 4.0 / TU 1637 1.9 / ☽ 2244 3.7
2 0335 1.5 / 1027 4.0 / TU 1603 1.7 / ☾ 2250 4.0	**17** 0502 2.1 / 1119 3.8 / W 1739 2.2
3 0431 1.8 / 1130 3.9 / W 1717 1.9	**18** 0023 3.5 / 0612 2.3 / TH 1317 3.7 / 1904 2.2
4 0001 3.8 / 0604 2.0 / TH 1246 3.9 / 1905 1.9	**19** 0208 3.6 / 0811 2.2 / F 1434 3.9 / 2044 1.9
5 0128 3.9 / 0746 1.8 / F 1416 4.1 / 2029 1.5	**20** 0311 3.8 / 0908 1.8 / SA 1530 4.1 / 2141 1.6
6 0300 4.1 / 0904 1.4 / SA 1531 4.5 / 2138 1.0	**21** 0400 4.1 / 0959 1.5 / SU 1617 4.4 / 2224 1.2
7 0411 4.5 / 1007 0.9 / SU 1632 4.8 / 2238 0.6	**22** 0444 4.4 / 1041 1.2 / M 1659 4.6 / 2303 1.0
8 0508 4.8 / 1103 0.5 / M 1726 5.1 / 2329 0.2	**23** 0524 4.6 / 1118 1.0 / TU 1739 4.8 / 2337 0.8
9 0559 5.0 / 1153 0.2 / TU 1818 5.3 / ○	**24** 0602 4.7 / 1152 0.8 / W 1818 4.8 / ●
10 0017 0.0 / 0648 5.1 / W 1240 0.0 / 1904 5.3	**25** 0009 0.8 / 0640 4.7 / TH 1223 0.8 / 1853 4.8
11 0103 -0.1 / 0732 5.1 / TH 1323 0.0 / 1947 5.3	**26** 0040 0.8 / 0714 4.7 / F 1254 0.8 / 1926 4.8
12 0143 0.1 / 0812 5.0 / F 1401 0.2 / 2027 5.1	**27** 0108 0.8 / 0745 4.7 / SA 1322 0.9 / 1957 4.7
13 0221 0.3 / 0849 4.9 / SA 1437 0.5 / 2103 4.8	**28** 0135 0.9 / 0814 4.6 / SU 1350 1.0 / 2026 4.6
14 0256 0.7 / 0921 4.6 / SU 1514 1.0 / 2134 4.4	**29** 0204 1.0 / 0845 4.5 / M 1422 1.1 / 2059 4.4
15 0331 1.2 / 0950 4.3 / M 1551 1.4 / 2204 4.1	**30** 0236 1.3 / 0920 4.4 / TU 1458 1.4 / 2141 4.2

OCTOBER

Time m	Time m
1 0318 1.5 / 1007 4.2 / W 1547 1.7 / ☽ 2235 4.0	**16** 0426 2.1 / 1037 3.9 / TH 1703 2.2 / 2313 3.6
2 0414 1.8 / 1109 4.0 / TH 1701 1.9 / 2345 3.8	**17** 0531 2.3 / 1151 3.7 / F 1815 2.3
3 0543 2.0 / 1227 4.0 / F 1847 1.9	**18** 0119 3.6 / 0650 2.3 / SA 1347 3.8 / 1941 2.1
4 0116 3.9 / 0730 1.9 / SA 1358 4.2 / 2013 1.5	**19** 0231 3.8 / 0812 2.1 / SU 1451 4.1 / 2052 1.8
5 0248 4.2 / 0848 1.4 / SU 1514 4.5 / 2121 1.1	**20** 0324 4.1 / 0913 1.7 / M 1541 4.3 / 2141 1.4
6 0354 4.5 / 0950 1.0 / M 1615 4.9 / 2218 0.6	**21** 0410 4.4 / 0959 1.4 / TU 1626 4.5 / 2221 1.2
7 0449 4.8 / 1044 0.6 / TU 1708 5.1 / 2309 0.3	**22** 0452 4.6 / 1041 1.1 / W 1709 4.7 / 2300 1.0
8 0539 5.0 / 1132 0.3 / W 1757 5.2 / ○ 2355 0.1	**23** 0533 4.7 / 1118 0.9 / TH 1749 4.8 / 2336 0.8
9 0625 5.1 / 1216 0.2 / TH 1843 5.3	**24** 0613 4.8 / 1154 0.8 / F 1829 4.8
10 0038 0.1 / 0706 5.2 / F 1259 0.2 / 1924 5.2	**25** 0010 0.8 / 0649 4.8 / SA 1230 0.8 / 1904 4.8
11 0119 0.3 / 0744 5.1 / SA 1337 0.4 / 2001 5.0	**26** 0045 0.8 / 0723 4.8 / SU 1303 0.8 / 1938 4.8
12 0155 0.5 / 0817 4.9 / SU 1413 0.7 / 2034 4.7	**27** 0118 0.9 / 0756 4.8 / M 1336 0.9 / 2012 4.7
13 0228 0.9 / 0847 4.7 / M 1447 1.1 / 2102 4.4	**28** 0151 1.0 / 0830 4.7 / TU 1413 1.1 / 2050 4.5
14 0302 1.3 / 0914 4.4 / TU 1523 1.5 / 2132 4.1	**29** 0228 1.2 / 0909 4.6 / W 1453 1.3 / 2134 4.3
15 0338 1.7 / 0949 4.2 / W 1606 1.9 / ☽ 2211 3.8	**30** 0311 1.5 / 0957 4.4 / TH 1544 1.6 / 2227 4.1
	31 0409 1.8 / 1056 4.2 / F 1655 1.8 / ☽ 2335 4.0

NOVEMBER

Time m	Time m
1 0529 2.0 / 1210 4.1 / SA 1827 1.8	**16** 0556 2.3 / 1221 3.9 / SU 1838 2.2
2 0102 4.0 / 0707 1.9 / SU 1337 4.3 / 1950 1.6	**17** 0125 3.8 / 0708 2.2 / M 1349 4.0 / 1945 2.0
3 0227 4.2 / 0824 1.5 / M 1451 4.5 / 2058 1.2	**18** 0235 4.0 / 0813 1.9 / TU 1453 4.2 / 2045 1.7
4 0332 4.5 / 0928 1.1 / TU 1552 4.8 / 2155 0.8	**19** 0328 4.2 / 0910 1.6 / W 1546 4.4 / 2136 1.4
5 0427 4.8 / 1020 0.8 / W 1646 5.0 / 2246 0.6	**20** 0416 4.5 / 0959 1.3 / TH 1634 4.6 / 2221 1.1
6 0516 5.0 / 1109 0.5 / TH 1734 5.1 / ○ 2331 0.4	**21** 0501 4.7 / 1044 1.1 / F 1720 4.7 / 2304 1.0
7 0601 5.1 / 1154 0.4 / F 1821 5.1	**22** 0544 4.8 / 1127 0.9 / SA 1803 4.8 / ● 2345 0.8
8 0014 0.4 / 0642 5.1 / SA 1237 0.5 / 1901 5.0	**23** 0625 4.9 / 1208 0.8 / SU 1845 4.8
9 0055 0.5 / 0719 5.0 / SU 1315 0.6 / 1938 4.8	**24** 0025 0.8 / 0703 5.0 / M 1250 0.8 / 1924 4.8
10 0130 0.7 / 0751 4.9 / M 1350 0.8 / 2008 4.6	**25** 0106 0.8 / 0742 5.0 / TU 1329 0.8 / 2004 4.8
11 0204 1.0 / 0819 4.7 / TU 1425 1.1 / 2038 4.4	**26** 0145 0.9 / 0821 4.9 / W 1411 0.9 / 2046 4.6
12 0236 1.4 / 0850 4.5 / W 1459 1.5 / 2110 4.2	**27** 0227 1.1 / 0904 4.8 / TH 1455 1.1 / 2131 4.5
13 0311 1.7 / 0926 4.3 / TH 1537 1.8 / 2150 4.0	**28** 0312 1.3 / 0952 4.6 / F 1545 1.3 / 2222 4.3
14 0351 2.0 / 1009 4.1 / F 1626 2.1 / ☽ 2242 3.8	**29** 0406 1.6 / 1047 4.4 / SA 1645 1.5 / ☽ 2325 4.1
15 0447 2.2 / 1105 3.9 / SA 1727 2.2 / 2353 3.7	**30** 0512 1.8 / 1153 4.3 / SU 1758 1.7

DECEMBER

Time m	Time m
1 0039 4.1 / 0633 1.8 / M 1308 4.3 / 1918 1.6	**16** 0007 3.8 / 0604 2.2 / TU 1228 3.9 / 1844 2.0
2 0155 4.2 / 0753 1.7 / TU 1422 4.4 / 2029 1.4	**17** 0121 3.9 / 0716 2.1 / W 1344 4.0 / 1949 1.9
3 0304 4.4 / 0900 1.4 / W 1526 4.5 / 2130 1.1	**18** 0234 4.0 / 0820 1.8 / TH 1455 4.1 / 2050 1.6
4 0401 4.6 / 0958 1.1 / TH 1623 4.7 / 2222 0.9	**19** 0333 4.3 / 0919 1.5 / F 1556 4.3 / 2145 1.3
5 0452 4.8 / 1049 0.9 / F 1714 4.8 / 2310 0.8	**20** 0427 4.5 / 1013 1.2 / SA 1650 4.5 / 2237 1.1
6 0539 4.9 / 1134 0.8 / SA 1800 4.8 / ○ 2353 0.7	**21** 0516 4.7 / 1104 1.0 / SU 1740 4.7 / 2325 0.9
7 0621 5.0 / 1217 0.7 / SU 1842 4.8	**22** 0602 4.9 / 1152 0.7 / M 1828 4.8 / ●
8 0034 0.8 / 0657 5.0 / M 1257 0.8 / 1918 4.7	**23** 0012 0.7 / 0648 5.0 / TU 1240 0.6 / 1912 4.9
9 0111 0.9 / 0731 4.9 / TU 1332 0.9 / 1950 4.6	**24** 0058 0.6 / 0732 5.1 / W 1325 0.5 / 1957 4.9
10 0144 1.1 / 0801 4.8 / W 1406 1.1 / 2021 4.5	**25** 0142 0.7 / 0815 5.1 / TH 1409 0.6 / 2041 4.8
11 0216 1.3 / 0833 4.7 / TH 1437 1.3 / 2054 4.3	**26** 0226 0.8 / 0859 5.0 / F 1453 0.7 / 2127 4.7
12 0246 1.5 / 0908 4.6 / F 1510 1.6 / 2132 4.1	**27** 0310 0.9 / 0945 4.9 / SA 1539 0.9 / 2213 4.5
13 0319 1.7 / 0946 4.3 / SA 1546 1.8 / 2214 4.0	**28** 0356 1.2 / 1034 4.6 / SU 1628 1.2 / ☽ 2306 4.3
14 0358 2.0 / 1031 4.1 / SU 1632 2.0 / 2305 3.8	**29** 0448 1.5 / 1131 4.4 / M 1725 1.5
15 0453 2.1 / 1124 4.0 / M 1733 2.1	**30** 0007 4.1 / 0551 1.7 / TU 1237 4.2 / 1835 1.7
	31 0118 4.1 / 0711 1.8 / W 1350 4.1 / 1953 1.7

Chart Datum: 2·62 metres below Ordnance Datum (Newlyn)
HAT is 5·3 metres above Chart Datum

231

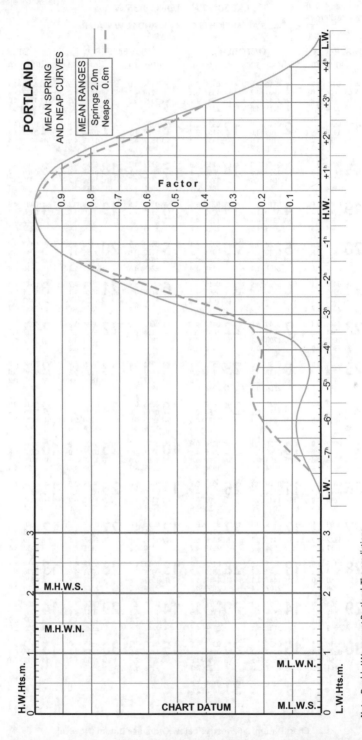

PORTLAND

MEAN SPRING
AND NEAP CURVES

MEAN RANGES
Springs 2.0m
Neaps 0.6m

Factor

0.9 0.8 0.7 0.6 0.5 0.4 0.3 0.2 0.1

L.W. +4ʰ +3ʰ +2ʰ +1ʰ H.W. -1ʰ -2ʰ -3ʰ -4ʰ -5ʰ -6ʰ -7ʰ L.W.

H.W.Hts.m.

M.H.W.S.

M.H.W.N.

CHART DATUM

L.W.Hts.m.

M.L.W.N.

M.L.W.S.

Note - Double LWs occur at Portland. The predictions
are for the first LW. The second LW occurs from 3
to 4 Hrs later and may, at Springs, on occasions be
lower than the first.

PORTLAND

LAT 50°34′N   LONG 2°26′W

TIMES AND HEIGHTS OF HIGH AND LOW WATERS

Dates in amber are **SPRINGS**
Dates in yellow are **NEAPS**

2014

JANUARY

Day	Time	m	Time	m	Time	m	Time	m
1 W ●	0606	2.2	1114	0.4	1835	2.1	2334	0.3
16 TH ○	0641	2.1	1143	0.4	1914	1.9	2356	0.3
2 TH	0656	2.3	1204	0.3	1929	2.1		
17 F	0718	2.1	1222	0.4	1949	1.9		
3 F	0020	0.2	0747	2.4	1250	0.3	2023	2.2
18 SA	0032	0.3	0754	2.1	1255	0.3	2022	1.9
4 SA	0105	0.2	0839	2.4	1335	0.1	2112	2.2
19 SU	0103	0.3	0827	2.0	1324	0.3	2052	1.8
5 SU	0148	0.2	0928	2.3	1420	0.2	2154	2.1
20 M	0133	0.4	0856	1.9	1353	0.3	2116	1.7
6 M	0231	0.3	1010	2.2	1505	0.3	2233	1.9
21 TU	0203	0.4	0919	1.8	1424	0.3	2138	1.7
7 TU	0313	0.5	1051	2.0	1552	0.4	2314	1.7
22 W	0234	0.4	0944	1.8	1458	0.3	2208	1.6
8 W ☽	0358	0.6	1134	1.8	1641	0.5		
23 TH	0308	0.5	1022	1.7	1538	0.4	2250	1.5
9 TH	0003	1.6	0449	0.8	1232	1.5	1739	0.7
24 F ☾	0352	0.6	1111	1.6	1631	0.5	2347	1.5
10 F	0116	1.5	0557	0.9	1355	1.4	1845	0.8
25 SA	0458	0.7	1214	1.5	1736	0.5		
11 SA	0234	1.5	0716	0.9	1508	1.4	1950	0.7
26 SU	0108	1.4	0614	0.7	1344	1.4	1850	0.6
12 SU	0337	1.6	0823	0.8	1611	1.5	2047	0.7
27 M	0243	1.5	0740	0.7	1514	1.5	2019	0.6
13 M	0432	1.7	0919	0.8	1706	1.6	2139	0.6
28 TU	0353	1.7	0912	0.6	1623	1.6	2134	0.5
14 TU	0520	1.9	1011	0.6	1753	1.8	2229	0.5
29 W	0454	1.9	1012	0.5	1727	1.8	2231	0.4
15 W	0602	2.0	1100	0.5	1835	1.8	2315	0.4
30 TH ●	0550	2.1	1105	0.3	1825	2.0	2322	0.2
31 F	0644	2.3	1152	0.1	1922	2.1		

FEBRUARY

Day	Time	m	Time	m	Time	m	Time	m
1 SA	0007	0.1	0739	2.4	1236	0.0	2018	2.2
16 SU	0013	0.2	0740	2.1	1235	0.2	2010	2.0
2 SU	0050	0.1	0832	2.4	1318	0.0	2101	2.2
17 M	0045	0.2	0814	2.0	1304	0.2	2039	1.9
3 M	0131	0.1	0917	2.4	1359	0.0	2136	2.2
18 TU	0115	0.2	0840	2.0	1333	0.2	2057	1.8
4 TU	0210	0.2	0953	2.2	1439	0.1	2207	2.0
19 W	0146	0.2	0858	1.9	1404	0.2	2113	1.8
5 W	0246	0.3	1025	2.0	1518	0.3	2236	1.8
20 TH	0217	0.3	0923	1.8	1436	0.2	2141	1.7
6 TH ☽	0322	0.5	1055	1.7	1558	0.5	2307	1.6
21 F	0249	0.3	0959	1.7	1511	0.3	2221	1.6
7 F	0358	0.7	1132	1.5	1643	0.7	2348	1.4
22 SA ☾	0325	0.4	1046	1.6	1556	0.4	2313	1.5
8 SA	0443	0.8	1227	1.3	1757	0.8		
23 SU	0422	0.5	1146	1.4	1701	0.5		
9 SU	0059	1.3	0643	0.9	1434	1.2	1918	0.8
24 M	0025	1.4	0544	0.7	1323	1.3	1822	0.6
10 M	0304	1.4	0757	0.9	1548	1.3	2019	0.7
25 TU	0220	1.4	1019	0.6	1502	1.4	2016	0.6
11 TU	0407	1.5	0854	0.7	1645	1.5	2114	0.6
26 W	0336	1.6	0918	0.5	1612	1.6	2126	0.5
12 W	0457	1.7	0947	0.6	1732	1.6	2205	0.5
27 TH	0439	1.8	1004	0.4	1715	1.8	2219	0.3
13 TH	0540	1.9	1036	0.4	1815	1.8	2253	0.4
28 F	0537	2.1	1051	0.2	1813	2.0	2307	0.2
14 F ○	0621	2.0	1122	0.3	1856	1.9	2336	0.3
15 SA	0701	2.1	1202	0.3	1934	1.9		

MARCH

Day	Time	m	Time	m	Time	m	Time	m
1 SA ●	0631	2.3	1136	0.1	1908	2.2	2352	0.1
16 SU ○	0637	2.0	1135	0.2	1910	2.0	2349	0.2
2 SU	0725	2.4	1218	0.0	1958	2.3		
17 M	0718	2.1	1209	0.2	1949	2.0		
3 M	0032	0.0	0816	2.4	1257	-0.1	2039	2.3
18 TU	0022	0.2	0755	2.1	1239	0.1	2022	2.0
4 TU	0110	0.0	0857	2.3	1334	0.0	2112	2.2
19 W	0053	0.1	0819	2.0	1310	0.1	2037	2.0
5 W	0145	0.1	0930	2.2	1409	0.1	2137	2.0
20 TH	0126	0.1	0836	2.0	1343	0.1	2052	1.9
6 TH	0218	0.2	0954	1.9	1443	0.3	2200	1.8
21 F	0159	0.2	0905	1.9	1417	0.2	2123	1.8
7 F	0250	0.4	1020	1.7	1515	0.5	2229	1.6
22 SA	0234	0.2	0944	1.7	1452	0.3	2204	1.7
8 SA	0320	0.6	1054	1.5	1545	0.6	2305	1.5
23 SU	0313	0.4	1033	1.6	1536	0.4	2256	1.5
9 SU	0349	0.7	1138	1.3	1616	0.8	2353	1.3
24 M ☾	0409	0.5	1136	1.4	1640	0.6		
10 M	0614	0.9	1250	1.1	1846	0.8		
25 TU	0007	1.4	0531	0.6	1321	1.3	1807	0.7
11 TU	0118	1.3	0731	0.8	1524	1.2	1951	0.8
26 W	0204	1.4	0951	0.6	1452	1.4	2007	0.6
12 W	0332	1.4	0827	0.7	1620	1.4	2046	0.6
27 TH	0320	1.6	0909	0.5	1558	1.6	2110	0.5
13 TH	0426	1.6	0918	0.6	1705	1.6	2137	0.5
28 F	0423	1.8	0948	0.3	1658	1.8	2201	0.3
14 F	0511	1.7	1008	0.4	1748	1.7	2226	0.4
29 SA	0520	2.0	1033	0.2	1753	2.0	2248	0.2
15 SA	0555	1.9	1054	0.3	1830	1.9	2311	0.3
30 SU ●	0614	2.2	1116	0.0	1844	2.2	2332	0.1
31 M	0706	2.3	1156	0.0	1931	2.2		

APRIL

Day	Time	m	Time	m	Time	m	Time	m
1 TU	0010	0.0	0753	2.3	1232	0.0	2012	2.2
16 W	0728	2.1	1212	0.2	1958	2.1		
2 W	0045	0.1	0832	2.2	1306	0.1	2043	2.2
17 TH	0030	0.1	0754	2.1	1247	0.1	2017	2.1
3 TH	0119	0.1	0900	2.1	1340	0.2	2106	2.0
18 F	0106	0.1	0818	2.0	1323	0.2	2038	2.0
4 F	0151	0.2	0924	1.9	1412	0.3	2131	1.8
19 SA	0144	0.2	0853	1.9	1401	0.2	2114	1.9
5 SA	0223	0.4	0953	1.7	1441	0.5	2201	1.7
20 SU	0224	0.2	0938	1.8	1442	0.3	2158	1.8
6 SU	0251	0.5	1028	1.5	1506	0.6	2238	1.5
21 M	0310	0.4	1030	1.6	1531	0.5	2252	1.6
7 M	0320	0.7	1111	1.3	1537	0.7	2322	1.4
22 TU ☾	0410	0.5	1135	1.4	1635	0.6		
8 TU	0407	0.8	1208	1.2	1636	0.8		
23 W	0002	1.5	0526	0.6	1314	1.4	1754	0.7
9 W	0023	1.3	0702	0.8	1356	1.2	1920	0.8
24 TH	0146	1.5	0951	0.5	1435	1.5	1930	0.7
10 TH	0209	1.3	0758	0.7	1537	1.3	2016	0.7
25 F	0300	1.6	0840	0.5	1538	1.6	2044	0.6
11 F	0334	1.5	0849	0.5	1625	1.5	2107	0.5
26 SA	0401	1.8	0924	0.3	1634	1.8	2138	0.4
12 SA	0430	1.7	0936	0.4	1711	1.7	2155	0.4
27 SU	0458	1.9	1008	0.2	1728	2.0	2226	0.3
13 SU	0519	1.8	1021	0.3	1756	1.9	2239	0.3
28 M	0552	2.1	1051	0.2	1817	2.1	2309	0.2
14 M	0606	1.9	1102	0.2	1840	2.0	2319	0.3
29 TU ●	0642	2.2	1130	0.1	1903	2.2	2346	0.1
15 TU ○	0650	2.0	1138	0.2	1922	2.1	2355	0.2
30 W	0727	2.2	1206	0.1	1942	2.2		

Chart Datum: 0·93 metres below Ordnance Datum (Newlyn)
HAT is 2·5 metres above Chart Datum

TIDES

PORTLAND
LAT 50°34'N   LONG 2°26'W
TIMES AND HEIGHTS OF HIGH AND LOW WATERS

Dates in amber are **SPRINGS**
Dates in yellow are **NEAPS**

2014

MAY

Time	m	Time	m
1 0021	0.2	**16** 0010	0.2
0804	2.1	0730	2.1
TH 1239	0.2	F 1227	0.2
2013	2.1	1959	2.2
2 0055	0.2	**17** 0051	0.2
0831	2.0	0806	2.0
F 1313	0.2	SA 1309	0.2
2040	2.0	2032	2.1
3 0130	0.3	**18** 0134	0.2
0858	1.8	0848	2.0
SA 1346	0.4	SU 1352	0.2
2109	1.9	2113	2.1
4 0203	0.4	**19** 0219	0.2
0931	1.7	0937	1.8
SU 1416	0.5	M 1437	0.3
2141	1.7	2200	1.9
5 0232	0.5	**20** 0309	0.3
1007	1.5	1030	1.7
M 1441	0.6	TU 1528	0.5
2218	1.5	2252	1.8
6 0301	0.6	**21** 0406	0.4
1048	1.4	1132	1.6
TU 1515	0.7	W 1626	0.6
2259	1.5	2355	1.7
7 0345	0.7	**22** 0510	0.5
1138	1.3	1253	1.5
W 1609	0.8	TH 1731	0.7
2349	1.4		
8 0624	0.8	**23** 0118	1.6
1248	1.2	0623	0.6
TH 1722	0.8	F 1409	1.5
		1844	0.7
9 0059	1.4	**24** 0232	1.6
0725	0.7	0747	0.5
F 1422	1.3	SA 1511	1.6
1940	0.8	2001	0.7
10 0230	1.4	**25** 0334	1.7
0815	0.6	0849	0.5
SA 1532	1.5	SU 1607	1.8
2031	0.6	2106	0.6
11 0338	1.6	**26** 0432	1.8
0901	0.5	0937	0.4
SU 1627	1.7	M 1701	1.9
2118	0.5	2158	0.5
12 0436	1.7	**27** 0527	1.9
0943	0.4	1021	0.3
M 1718	1.8	TU 1750	2.0
2202	0.4	2244	0.4
13 0528	1.9	**28** 0617	2.0
1024	0.3	1102	0.3
TU 1806	2.0	W 1835	2.1
2246	0.4	2324	0.4
14 0615	2.0	**29** 0701	2.0
1106	0.2	1140	0.2
W 1849	2.1	TH 1915	2.1
2328	0.3		
15 0656	2.0	**30** 0001	0.3
1147	0.2	0739	2.0
TH 1929	2.2	F 1217	0.2
		1949	2.1
		31 0037	0.3
		0809	1.9
		SA 1253	0.3
		2020	2.0

JUNE

Time	m	Time	m
1 0114	0.3	**16** 0127	0.1
0840	1.8	0851	2.0
SU 1328	0.4	M 1343	0.2
2052	1.9	2117	2.2
2 0148	0.4	**17** 0213	0.2
0913	1.7	0940	2.0
M 1359	0.5	TU 1429	0.3
2126	1.8	2202	2.1
3 0219	0.5	**18** 0301	0.2
0948	1.6	1028	1.8
TU 1426	0.5	W 1516	0.4
2200	1.7	2248	2.0
4 0248	0.5	**19** 0352	0.3
1026	1.5	1119	1.7
W 1459	0.6	TH 1607	0.5
2235	1.6	2339	1.8
5 0326	0.6	**20** 0446	0.4
1107	1.4	1221	1.6
TH 1545	0.7	F 1702	0.7
2316	1.5		
6 0417	0.6	**21** 0043	1.6
1158	1.3	0546	0.5
F 1644	0.7	SA 1333	1.5
		1805	0.8
7 0007	1.3	**22** 0158	1.6
0519	0.6	0652	0.6
SA 1311	1.3	SU 1439	1.6
1752	0.7	1917	0.8
8 0116	1.5	**23** 0305	1.6
0629	0.6	0801	0.6
SU 1433	1.5	M 1539	1.7
1908	0.7	2027	0.7
9 0235	1.5	**24** 0406	1.6
0752	0.5	0859	0.5
M 1537	1.6	TU 1634	1.8
2025	0.6	2128	0.7
10 0343	1.6	**25** 0503	1.7
0854	0.4	0950	0.5
TU 1633	1.8	W 1725	1.9
2123	0.5	2220	0.6
11 0443	1.8	**26** 0554	1.8
0946	0.4	1036	0.4
W 1726	1.9	TH 1810	2.0
2215	0.4	2306	0.5
12 0538	1.9	**27** 0639	1.9
1037	0.3	1119	0.3
TH 1815	2.1	F 1851	2.1
2306	0.3	2347	0.4
13 0627	2.0	**28** 0719	1.9
1127	0.2	1159	0.3
F 1900	2.2	SA 1928	2.1
2355	0.2		
14 0714	2.1	**29** 0025	0.3
1213	0.2	0753	0.3
SA 1945	2.3	SU 1237	0.3
		2003	2.1
15 0041	0.1	**30** 0102	0.3
0802	2.1	0825	1.8
SU 1258	0.2	M 1312	0.3
2031	2.3	2037	2.0

JULY

Time	m	Time	m
1 0135	0.3	**16** 0200	0.1
0857	1.7	0939	2.1
TU 1344	0.4	W 1414	0.2
2110	1.9	2157	2.3
2 0204	0.4	**17** 0245	0.1
0929	1.7	1018	2.0
W 1412	0.4	TH 1457	0.3
2140	1.8	2236	2.1
3 0232	0.4	**18** 0330	0.2
1000	1.6	1058	1.8
TH 1443	0.5	F 1542	0.5
2209	1.7	2317	1.9
4 0305	0.4	**19** 0417	0.4
1033	1.5	1144	1.6
F 1521	0.5	SA 1630	0.6
2241	1.6		
5 0347	0.4	**20** 0006	1.6
1114	1.4	0510	0.6
SA 1611	0.6	SU 1247	1.5
2326	1.5	1728	0.8
6 0441	0.5	**21** 0118	1.5
1209	1.4	0613	0.7
SU 1711	0.7	M 1405	1.5
		1842	0.9
7 0023	1.5	**22** 0237	1.4
0543	0.5	0723	0.7
M 1326	1.4	TU 1513	1.5
1819	0.7	1957	0.8
8 0137	1.5	**23** 0344	1.4
0651	0.5	0826	0.7
TU 1447	1.5	W 1611	1.7
1932	0.7	2101	0.7
9 0259	1.5	**24** 0443	1.5
0806	0.5	0921	0.6
W 1552	1.7	TH 1702	1.8
2051	0.6	2156	0.6
10 0409	1.7	**25** 0534	1.7
0918	0.4	1011	0.5
TH 1652	1.9	F 1749	1.9
2156	0.5	2245	0.5
11 0512	1.8	**26** 0619	1.8
1018	0.3	1059	0.4
F 1747	2.1	SA 1830	2.1
2253	0.3	2330	0.4
12 0609	1.9	**27** 0700	1.9
1112	0.2	1142	0.3
SA 1839	2.2	SU 1909	2.1
2344	0.2		
13 0703	2.0	**28** 0010	0.3
1201	0.2	0738	1.9
SU 1931	2.3	M 1220	0.2
		1946	2.1
14 0031	0.1	**29** 0046	0.2
0759	2.1	0811	1.9
M 1246	0.1	TU 1255	0.2
2025	2.4	2021	2.0
15 0116	0.0	**30** 0117	0.1
0854	2.1	0841	1.8
TU 1331	0.1	W 1326	0.3
2115	2.4	2052	1.9
		31 0144	0.3
		0909	1.8
		TH 1354	0.3
		2118	1.8

AUGUST

Time	m	Time	m
1 0211	0.3	**16** 0301	0.2
0932	1.7	1027	1.9
F 1424	0.4	SA 1511	0.4
2139	1.7	2248	1.9
2 0241	0.3	**17** 0342	0.4
0957	1.6	1059	1.7
SA 1456	0.4	SU 1552	0.6
2208	1.7	2324	1.6
3 0316	0.4	**18** 0427	0.6
1033	1.5	1141	1.5
SU 1536	0.5	M 1644	0.8
2250	1.6		
4 0403	0.4	**19** 0017	1.4
1123	1.5	0532	0.8
M 1634	0.6	TU 1306	1.4
2345	1.5	1815	0.9
5 0505	0.5	**20** 0212	1.3
1231	1.4	0653	0.8
TU 1744	0.7	W 1448	1.4
		1934	0.9
6 0058	1.4	**21** 0327	1.3
0615	0.6	0758	0.8
W 1409	1.5	TH 1551	1.5
1902	0.7	2035	0.8
7 0235	1.4	**22** 0425	1.5
0737	0.6	0854	0.7
TH 1526	1.6	F 1642	1.7
2042	0.6	2128	0.6
8 0351	1.6	**23** 0514	1.6
0904	0.5	0945	0.5
F 1629	1.9	SA 1726	1.9
2148	0.5	2218	0.4
9 0457	1.9	**24** 0557	1.8
1005	0.4	1034	0.4
SA 1727	2.1	SU 1807	2.0
2242	0.3	2305	0.3
10 0556	1.9	**25** 0638	1.9
1058	0.2	1119	0.3
SU 1822	2.2	M 1847	2.1
2331	0.1	2348	0.2
11 0652	2.1	**26** 0716	2.0
1146	0.1	1200	0.2
M 1915	2.4	TU 1925	2.1
12 0016	0.0	**27** 0024	0.3
0749	2.2	0752	2.0
TU 1231	0.0	W 1234	0.2
2010	2.5	2001	2.1
13 0059	0.0	**28** 0053	0.2
0842	2.2	0825	1.9
W 1313	0.0	TH 1304	0.2
2100	2.4	2031	2.0
14 0141	0.0	**29** 0119	0.2
0922	2.2	0846	1.9
TH 1354	0.1	F 1332	0.3
2140	2.3	2053	1.9
15 0222	0.1	**30** 0146	0.3
0957	2.1	0901	1.8
F 1433	0.2	SA 1402	0.3
2215	2.1	2110	1.8
		31 0215	0.3
		0923	1.7
		SU 1432	0.4
		2139	1.7

Chart Datum: 0·93 metres below Ordnance Datum (Newlyn)
HAT is 2·5 metres above Chart Datum

TIME ZONE (UT)
For Summer Time add ONE hour in **non-shaded areas**

PORTLAND
LAT 50°34′N   LONG 2°26′W
TIMES AND HEIGHTS OF HIGH AND LOW WATERS

Dates in amber are **SPRINGS**
Dates in yellow are **NEAPS**

2014

SEPTEMBER

Time	m	Time	m	Time	m	Time	m
1 M	0246 0.4 / 0959 1.6 / 1506 0.5 / 2222 1.6	**16** TU	0337 0.7 / 1056 1.5 / 1559 0.8 / ☽ 2330 1.3				
2 TU	0324 0.4 / 1049 1.5 / 1559 0.6 / ☽ 2318 1.5	**17** W	0418 0.9 / 1146 1.4 / 1755 0.9				
3 W	0426 0.6 / 1155 1.4 / 1716 0.7	**18** TH	0055 1.2 / 0625 0.9 / 1409 1.3 / 1908 0.9				
4 TH	0035 1.3 / 0843 0.8 / 1343 1.4 / 1847 0.7	**19** F	0314 1.3 / 0730 0.9 / 1528 1.5 / 2005 0.7				
5 F	0227 1.4 / 0725 0.7 / 1509 1.6 / 2052 0.6	**20** SA	0407 1.5 / 0825 0.7 / 1617 1.6 / 2057 0.6				
6 SA	0342 1.6 / 0856 0.6 / 1612 1.8 / 2139 0.4	**21** SU	0450 1.6 / 0916 0.6 / 1659 1.8 / 2147 0.4				
7 SU	0444 1.8 / 0951 0.4 / 1710 2.1 / 2227 0.3	**22** M	0531 1.8 / 1006 0.4 / 1740 2.0 / 2235 0.3				
8 M	0542 2.0 / 1042 0.3 / 1805 2.3 / 2313 0.1	**23** TU	0610 2.0 / 1052 0.3 / 1820 2.1 / 2319 0.3				
9 TU	0635 2.2 / 1129 0.1 / 1857 2.4 / ○ 2358 0.0	**24** W	0649 2.1 / 1133 0.3 / 1900 2.1 / ● 2355 0.2				
10 W	0727 2.3 / 1212 0.0 / 1949 2.5	**25** TH	0726 2.1 / 1208 0.3 / 1937 2.1				
11 TH	0038 0.0 / 0815 2.3 / 1252 0.0 / 2037 2.4	**26** F	0024 0.2 / 0759 2.1 / 1238 0.3 / 2007 2.1				
12 F	0117 0.0 / 0855 2.3 / 1329 0.1 / 2116 2.3	**27** SA	0052 0.3 / 0819 2.0 / 1309 0.3 / 2025 2.0				
13 SA	0153 0.1 / 0925 2.1 / 1405 0.3 / 2147 2.1	**28** SU	0122 0.3 / 0832 1.9 / 1340 0.3 / 2046 1.9				
14 SU	0228 0.3 / 0949 1.9 / 1440 0.4 / 2214 1.8	**29** M	0152 0.3 / 0858 1.9 / 1413 0.4 / 2120 1.8				
15 M	0302 0.5 / 1018 1.7 / 1516 0.6 / 2246 1.6	**30** TU	0224 0.4 / 0936 1.8 / 1450 0.5 / 2205 1.6				

OCTOBER

Time	m	Time	m
1 W	0259 0.5 / 1027 1.6 / 1542 0.6 / ☽ 2304 1.5	**16** TH	0318 0.9 / 1112 1.5 / 1728 0.9 / 2359 1.3
2 TH	0357 0.7 / 1134 1.5 / 1701 0.7	**17** F	0550 1.0 / 1215 1.4 / 1838 0.9
3 F	0029 1.3 / 0817 0.9 / 1326 1.5 / 2101 0.7	**18** SA	0247 1.3 / 0659 1.0 / 1416 1.4 / 1935 0.8
4 SA	0220 1.4 / 0720 0.8 / 1453 1.6 / 2046 0.6	**19** SU	0340 1.4 / 0755 0.8 / 1534 1.5 / 2027 0.6
5 SU	0330 1.6 / 0842 0.7 / 1556 1.8 / 2123 0.4	**20** M	0418 1.6 / 0846 0.7 / 1620 1.7 / 2115 0.5
6 M	0429 1.8 / 0934 0.5 / 1653 2.0 / 2207 0.3	**21** TU	0457 1.8 / 0935 0.6 / 1705 1.9 / 2201 0.4
7 TU	0523 2.1 / 1022 0.3 / 1746 2.2 / 2252 0.2	**22** W	0537 2.0 / 1021 0.5 / 1749 2.0 / 2245 0.3
8 W	0614 2.2 / 1108 0.2 / 1837 2.3 / ○ 2335 0.1	**23** TH	0617 2.1 / 1102 0.4 / 1831 2.1 / ● 2321 0.3
9 TH	0701 2.3 / 1150 0.2 / 1926 2.4	**24** F	0656 2.2 / 1139 0.4 / 1909 2.1 / 2354 0.3
10 F	0013 0.1 / 0745 2.4 / 1228 0.2 / 2011 2.3	**25** SA	0730 2.2 / 1212 0.3 / 1939 2.1
11 SA	0049 0.1 / 0821 2.3 / 1303 0.2 / 2046 2.2	**26** SU	0026 0.3 / 0750 2.1 / 1246 0.3 / 2000 2.0
12 SU	0123 0.3 / 0849 2.2 / 1338 0.3 / 2114 2.0	**27** M	0100 0.3 / 0811 2.1 / 1323 0.3 / 2031 2.0
13 M	0156 0.4 / 0915 2.0 / 1413 0.5 / 2143 1.8	**28** TU	0136 0.4 / 0844 2.0 / 1402 0.4 / 2110 1.8
14 TU	0228 0.6 / 0947 1.8 / 1448 0.6 / 2218 1.6	**29** W	0213 0.5 / 0927 1.9 / 1445 0.5 / 2200 1.7
15 W	0256 0.8 / 1026 1.6 / 1524 0.8 / ☽ 2301 1.4	**30** TH	0255 0.6 / 1019 1.7 / 1541 0.6 / 2300 1.5
		31 F	0355 0.8 / 1124 1.6 / 1653 0.7 / ☽

NOVEMBER

Time	m	Time	m
1 SA	0024 1.4 / 0800 1.0 / 1304 1.5 / 2034 0.7	**16** SU	0030 1.3 / 0621 1.0 / 1245 1.4 / 1903 0.8
2 SU	0205 1.5 / 0645 0.9 / 1432 1.6 / 2016 0.6	**17** M	0209 1.4 / 0723 0.9 / 1415 1.5 / 1955 0.7
3 M	0311 1.7 / 0816 0.8 / 1534 1.8 / 2058 0.5	**18** TU	0321 1.6 / 0815 0.8 / 1525 1.6 / 2042 0.6
4 TU	0407 1.9 / 0912 0.6 / 1631 2.0 / 2143 0.4	**19** W	0411 1.7 / 0902 0.7 / 1620 1.7 / 2126 0.5
5 W	0500 2.1 / 1001 0.5 / 1725 2.1 / 2227 0.3	**20** TH	0458 1.9 / 0946 0.6 / 1711 1.9 / 2207 0.4
6 TH	0549 2.2 / 1046 0.4 / 1816 2.2 / ○ 2310 0.2	**21** F	0543 2.1 / 1027 0.5 / 1758 2.0 / 2245 0.4
7 F	0635 2.3 / 1127 0.3 / 1903 2.3 / 2347 0.2	**22** SA	0624 2.2 / 1109 0.5 / 1839 2.1 / ● 2325 0.4
8 SA	0716 2.3 / 1204 0.3 / 1944 2.2	**23** SU	0700 2.2 / 1149 0.4 / 1914 2.1
9 SU	0022 0.3 / 0750 2.3 / 1240 0.3 / 2018 2.1	**24** M	0004 0.3 / 0729 2.2 / 1230 0.3 / 1946 2.1
10 M	0057 0.3 / 0820 2.2 / 1316 0.4 / 2047 2.0	**25** TU	0045 0.3 / 0800 2.2 / 1312 0.3 / 2023 2.0
11 TU	0132 0.5 / 0851 2.0 / 1352 0.5 / 2119 1.8	**26** W	0126 0.4 / 0839 2.1 / 1355 0.3 / 2107 1.9
12 W	0204 0.6 / 0926 1.9 / 1428 0.6 / 2156 1.6	**27** TH	0209 0.5 / 0925 2.0 / 1443 0.4 / 2157 1.8
13 TH	0231 0.8 / 1003 1.7 / 1502 0.7 / 2236 1.5	**28** F	0256 0.6 / 1016 1.9 / 1537 0.5 / 2254 1.7
14 F	0254 0.9 / 1045 1.6 / 1540 0.8 / ☽ 2324 1.4	**29** SA	0350 0.7 / 1116 1.7 / 1638 0.6 / ●
15 SA	0336 1.0 / 1135 1.5 / 1804 0.9	**30** SU	0005 1.6 / 0454 0.8 / 1234 1.6 / 2001 0.7

DECEMBER

Time	m	Time	m
1 M	0133 1.6 / 0606 0.9 / 1400 1.6 / 1905 0.6	**16** TU	0041 1.4 / 0517 0.9 / 1252 1.4 / 1800 0.7
2 TU	0242 1.7 / 0728 0.9 / 1506 1.7 / 2021 0.6	**17** W	0207 1.5 / 0637 0.9 / 1418 1.5 / 1950 0.7
3 W	0340 1.8 / 0844 0.8 / 1606 1.8 / 2114 0.5	**18** TH	0315 1.6 / 0818 0.8 / 1527 1.6 / 2037 0.6
4 TH	0434 2.0 / 0938 0.7 / 1702 1.9 / 2200 0.4	**19** F	0412 1.8 / 0906 0.7 / 1627 1.7 / 2125 0.5
5 F	0524 2.1 / 1025 0.6 / 1755 2.0 / 2244 0.4	**20** SA	0503 2.0 / 0954 0.6 / 1723 1.8 / 2214 0.4
6 SA	0610 2.2 / 1107 0.5 / 1842 2.1 / ○ 2324 0.4	**21** SU	0550 2.1 / 1044 0.5 / 1812 2.0 / 2303 0.4
7 SU	0652 2.3 / 1146 0.4 / 1924 2.1	**22** M	0633 2.2 / 1132 0.4 / 1857 2.0 / ● 2350 0.3
8 M	0001 0.3 / 0729 2.2 / 1223 0.4 / 1959 2.0	**23** TU	0714 2.3 / 1219 0.3 / 1939 2.1
9 TU	0038 0.4 / 0802 2.2 / 1300 0.4 / 2030 1.9	**24** W	0035 0.3 / 0756 2.3 / 1304 0.2 / 2023 2.1
10 W	0114 0.4 / 0835 2.1 / 1338 0.5 / 2102 1.8	**25** TH	0119 0.3 / 0839 2.3 / 1349 0.2 / 2108 2.0
11 TH	0147 0.5 / 0909 1.9 / 1413 0.5 / 2136 1.7	**26** F	0203 0.3 / 0925 2.2 / 1435 0.3 / 2154 1.9
12 F	0215 0.6 / 0944 1.8 / 1444 0.6 / 2212 1.6	**27** SA	0248 0.4 / 1013 2.1 / 1524 0.3 / 2243 1.8
13 SA	0240 0.7 / 1020 1.7 / 1513 0.7 / 2250 1.5	**28** SU	0335 0.5 / 1103 1.9 / 1616 0.4 / ☽ 2338 1.7
14 SU	0315 0.8 / 1058 1.6 / 1555 0.7 / ☽ 2336 1.4	**29** M	0427 0.7 / 1204 1.7 / 1712 0.6
15 M	0408 0.9 / 1145 1.5 / 1652 0.7	**30** TU	0049 1.6 / 0529 0.8 / 1322 1.6 / 1817 0.7
		31 W	0204 1.6 / 0642 0.9 / 1435 1.5 / 1932 0.7

Chart Datum: 0·93 metres below Ordnance Datum (Newlyn)
HAT is 2·5 metres above Chart Datum

TIDES

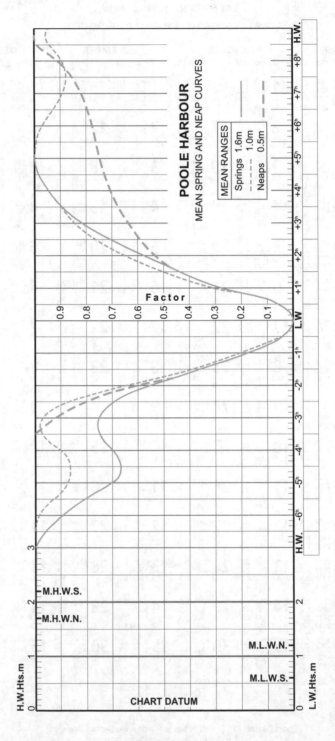

POOLE HARBOUR
MEAN SPRING AND NEAP CURVES

MEAN RANGES	
Springs	1.6m
	1.0m
Neaps	0.5m

Note - Sea level is above mean tide level from 2 hrs after LW to 2 hrs before the next LW. HW occurs between 5 hrs after LW and 3 hrs before the next LW, the time shown is approximate and should be checked for suitability.

POOLE HARBOUR

LAT 50°43′N   LONG 1°59′W

TIMES AND HEIGHTS OF HIGH AND LOW WATERS

Dates in amber are **SPRINGS**
Dates in yellow are **NEAPS**

2014

JANUARY

Day	Time m	Day	Time m
1	0329 0.5 W 1556 0.3 ● 2119 2.2	16	0413 0.8 TH 1634 0.6 ○ 2114 2.0
2	0419 0.4 TH 1644 0.2 2204 2.3	17	0449 0.8 F 1707 0.6 2157 2.0
3	0506 0.4 1018 2.5 F 1730 0.2 2247 2.3	18	0521 0.8 1003 2.1 SA 1737 0.6 2238 2.0
4	0554 0.5 1100 2.4 SA 1816 0.2 2330 2.2	19	0553 0.8 1043 2.1 SU 1808 0.6 2319 1.9
5	0642 0.6 1141 2.3 SU 1903 0.4	20	0626 0.8 1109 2.0 M 1842 0.6
6	0433 2.1 0732 0.7 M 1217 2.2 1953 0.5	21	0405 1.9 0702 0.8 TU 1021 1.9 1920 0.7
7	0518 2.1 0824 0.9 TU 1247 2.0 2046 0.7	22	0447 2.0 0742 0.9 W 1039 1.9 2002 0.7
8	0604 2.1 0923 1.0 W 1825 1.8 ◐ 2147 0.9	23	0531 1.9 0921 1.0 TH 1117 1.8 2050 0.8
9	0654 2.0 1030 1.1 TH 1922 1.8 2257 1.1	24	0619 1.9 F 1207 1.8 ◐ 2149 1.0
10	0750 2.0 1138 1.2 F 2030 1.8	25	0708 1.9 1027 1.1 SA 1935 1.7 2300 1.0
11	0004 1.1 0856 2.0 SA 1241 1.1 2143 1.8	26	0802 1.8 1140 1.0 SU 2034 1.7
12	0105 1.1 1003 1.9 SU 1339 1.0 2248 1.8	27	0011 1.0 0623 1.8 M 1250 0.9 1852 1.7
13	0200 1.0 1104 1.9 M 1429 1.0 2343 1.9	28	0119 0.9 0704 1.9 TU 1354 0.7 1938 1.9
14	0248 1.0 0621 TU 1515 0.8 1900 1.8	29	0220 0.7 0751 2.1 W 1451 0.5 2025 2.0
15	0333 0.9 0717 2.0 W 1557 0.7 2042 1.9	30	0315 0.5 0838 2.3 TH 1542 0.3 ● 2108 2.2
		31	0405 0.4 0922 2.4 F 1629 0.1 2150 2.3

FEBRUARY

Day	Time m	Day	Time m
1	0451 0.3 1004 2.5 SA 1713 0.0 2230 2.3	16	0459 0.7 0944 2.2 SU 1715 0.5 2213 2.1
2	0537 0.3 1044 2.5 SU 1757 0.1 2309 2.3	17	0530 0.6 1023 2.2 M 1746 0.5 2250 2.1
3	0621 0.4 1121 2.4 M 1841 0.2 2346 2.1	18	0602 0.6 1058 2.1 TU 1818 0.5 2326 2.0
4	0706 0.5 1156 2.2 TU 1926 0.5	19	0636 0.6 1126 2.0 W 1853 0.6
5	0452 2.0 0753 0.7 W 1220 2.0 2013 0.7	20	0422 1.9 0713 0.7 TH 1018 1.9 1932 0.7
6	0534 2.0 0844 0.9 TH 1755 1.8 ◐ 2106 1.0	21	0505 1.9 0754 0.8 F 1054 1.9 2016 0.8
7	0619 1.9 0944 1.1 F 1847 1.8 2213 1.2	22	0550 1.9 0843 0.9 SA 1814 1.8 ◐ 2110 1.0
8	0710 1.9 1101 1.2 SA 1954 1.8 2335 1.3	23	0637 1.8 0947 1.0 SU 1904 1.8 2224 1.1
9	0816 1.8 1215 1.2 SU 2112 1.8	24	0725 1.8 1109 1.0 M 1957 1.7 2349 1.1
10	0045 1.2 0931 1.8 M 1317 1.1 2220 1.8	25	0610 1.8 1230 0.9 TU 1853 1.7
11	0142 1.1 1037 1.8 TU 1409 0.9 2318 1.8	26	0105 1.0 0652 1.9 W 1338 0.7 1931 1.9
12	0231 1.0 1134 1.8 W 1455 0.8 2035 1.7	27	0208 0.8 0738 2.0 TH 1435 0.5 2013 2.0
13	0315 0.9 0653 1.9 TH 1536 1.0	28	0301 0.6 0824 2.2 F 1525 0.2 2053 2.2
14	0354 0.8 0803 2.0 F 1613 0.6 ○ 2052 2.0		

MARCH

Day	Time m	Day	Time m
1	0349 0.4 0905 2.4 SA 1611 0.1 ● 2131 2.3	16	0401 0.7 0838 2.1 SU 1617 0.5 ○ 2106 2.1
2	0433 0.3 0945 2.5 SU 1653 0.0 2209 2.3	17	0433 0.6 0921 2.2 M 1649 0.5 2145 2.2
3	0516 0.2 1023 2.5 M 1736 0.1 2245 2.3	18	0505 0.5 1001 2.2 TU 1721 0.4 2223 2.2
4	0558 0.3 1059 2.4 TU 1817 0.3 2319 2.2	19	0539 0.5 1039 2.2 W 1755 0.5 2259 2.1
5	0640 0.5 1133 2.2 W 1859 0.5 2348 2.0	20	0613 0.5 1115 2.1 TH 1830 0.6 2335 2.0
6	0723 0.7 1159 1.9 TH 1942 0.8	21	0649 0.6 1151 1.9 F 1908 0.7 2219 1.9
7	0503 1.9 0808 0.9 F 1725 1.8 2028 1.0	22	0730 0.7 1704 1.9 SA 1952 0.9 2300 1.8
8	0542 1.9 0857 1.0 SA 1810 1.8 ◐ 2122 1.2	23	0818 0.8 1750 1.9 SU 2046 1.0
9	0621 1.8 1004 1.2 SU 1910 1.8 2258 1.4	24	0609 1.8 0920 1.0 M 1841 1.9 ◐ 2205 1.2
10	0633 1.7 1141 1.2 M 2039 1.8	25	0655 1.7 1051 1.0 TU 1933 1.8 2338 1.1
11	0021 1.3 0900 1.7 TU 1249 1.1 2149 1.8	26	0550 1.8 1213 0.9 W 2025 1.8
12	0119 1.2 1010 1.7 W 1342 1.0 2247 1.8	27	0052 1.0 0634 1.9 TH 1319 0.7 1918 1.9
13	0207 1.1 1107 1.7 TH 1428 0.9 2339 1.9	28	0151 0.8 0720 2.0 F 1415 0.5 1955 2.0
14	0249 1.0 0637 1.8 F 1508 0.7 1950 1.8	29	0243 0.6 0804 2.1 SA 1504 0.3 2033 2.2
15	0327 0.8 0745 1.9 SA 1544 0.6 2026 2.0	30	0330 0.4 0845 2.3 SU 1549 0.2 ● 2109 2.3
		31	0413 0.3 0923 2.4 M 1632 0.2 2143 2.3

APRIL

Day	Time m	Day	Time m
1	0454 0.3 1000 2.4 TU 1713 0.3 2217 2.3	16	0440 0.5 0940 2.2 W 1656 0.5 2156 2.3
2	0535 0.3 1036 2.3 W 1753 0.4 2249 2.2	17	0516 0.4 1020 2.2 TH 1733 0.5 2236 2.2
3	0616 0.5 1110 2.1 TH 1834 0.7 2318 2.0	18	0553 0.5 1101 2.1 F 1812 0.6 2315 2.1
4	0656 0.6 1142 1.9 F 1915 0.9 2251 1.9	19	0632 0.5 1143 2.0 SA 1853 0.8 2356 2.0
5	0737 0.8 1656 1.9 SA 1958 1.1	20	0716 0.7 1648 2.0 SU 1941 0.9
6	0504 1.8 0821 1.0 SU 1733 1.9 2045 1.3	21	0042 1.9 0807 0.8 M 1735 2.0 2042 1.1
7	0530 1.8 0910 1.1 M 1807 1.9 ◐ 2144 1.4	22	0138 1.8 0914 0.9 TU 1828 2.0 ◐ 2205 1.2
8	0557 1.7 1015 1.2 TU 1839 1.8 2342 1.4	23	0239 1.8 1036 0.9 W 1925 1.9 2324 1.1
9	0633 1.6 1206 1.2 W 2109 1.8	24	0522 1.8 1150 0.9 TH 2027 1.9
10	0045 1.3 0933 1.6 TH 1304 1.1 2209 1.8	25	0030 1.0 0612 1.9 F 1254 0.8 1858 1.9
11	0134 1.2 1031 1.7 F 1351 1.0 2300 1.9	26	0128 0.9 0659 1.9 SA 1349 0.6 1934 2.0
12	0216 1.0 0636 1.7 SA 1431 0.8 1922 1.9	27	0220 0.7 0744 2.0 SU 1439 0.5 2011 2.1
13	0253 0.9 0726 1.9 SU 1508 0.7 1958 2.0	28	0307 0.5 0824 2.1 M 1526 0.4 2044 2.2
14	0329 0.7 0815 2.0 M 1544 0.6 2037 2.2	29	0351 0.4 0901 2.2 TU 1609 0.4 ● 2116 2.3
15	0404 0.6 0858 2.1 TU 1620 0.5 2117 2.2	30	0433 0.4 0937 2.2 W 1651 0.5 ○ 2147 2.3

Chart Datum: 1·40 metres below Ordnance Datum (Newlyn)
HAT is 2·6 metres above Chart Datum

TIDES

TIME ZONE (UT)
For Summer Time add ONE hour in **non-shaded areas**

POOLE HARBOUR
LAT 50°43'N LONG 1°59'W
TIMES AND HEIGHTS OF HIGH AND LOW WATERS

Dates in amber are **SPRINGS**
Dates in yellow are **NEAPS**

2014

MAY

Day	Time m	Time m	Time m	Day	Time m	Time m	Time m
1 TH	0514 0.4	1012 2.2	1732 0.6 / 2220 2.2	16 F	0456 0.4	1005 2.2	1715 0.6 / 2218 2.3
2 F	0554 0.5	1048 2.1	1812 0.8 / 2251 2.1	17 SA	0538 0.4	1049 2.2	1759 0.7 / 2302 2.3
3 SA	0633 0.7	1126 1.9	1852 1.0 / 2229 1.9	18 SU	0621 0.5	1134 2.1	1846 0.8 / 2346 2.2
4 SU	0711 0.8	1629 1.9	1933 1.1 / 2244 1.8	19 M	0709 0.6	1638 2.0	1939 0.9
5 M	0751 0.9	1702 1.9	2017 1.3 / 2318 1.8	20 TU	0032 2.1 / 0803 0.7	1727 2.1	2041 1.1
6 TU	0836 1.0	1738 1.9	2107 1.3	21 W	0119 1.9 / 0906 0.8	1820 2.1	2151 1.1
7 W	0541 1.7 / 0927 1.1	1822 1.9	2205 1.4	22 TH	0208 1.8 / 1015 0.9	1915 2.1	2259 1.1
8 TH	0631 1.7 / 1027 1.2	1922 1.9	2318 1.4	23 F	0258 1.8 / 1123 0.9	2014 2.0	
9 F	0744 1.6 / 1138 1.2	2059 1.9		24 SA	0003 1.0 / 0552 1.8	1225 0.8	2119 2.0
10 SA	0034 1.3 / 0934 1.6	1248 1.1	2205 1.9	25 SU	0101 0.9 / 0642 1.8	1322 0.8	1916 2.0
11 SU	0125 1.1 / 0627 1.7	1340 0.9	1857 1.9	26 M	0155 0.8 / 0726 1.9	1415 0.7	1951 2.0
12 M	0209 0.9 / 0707 1.8	1426 0.8	1929 2.0	27 TU	0244 0.7 / 0807 2.0	1503 0.7	2023 2.1
13 TU	0252 0.8 / 0752 2.0	1509 0.7	2008 2.2	28 W	0331 0.6 / 0843 2.1	1549 0.7	2050 2.2
14 W	0334 0.6 / 0837 2.1	1552 0.6	2051 2.3	29 TH	0414 0.6 / 0916 2.1	1632 0.6	2117 2.2
15 TH	0415 0.5 / 0921 2.2	1634 0.5	2135 2.3	30 F	0455 0.6 / 0950 2.1	1713 0.6	2152 2.2
				31 SA	0534 0.6 / 1027 2.1	1753 0.9	2229 2.1

JUNE

Day	Time m	Time m	Time m	Day	Time m	Time m	Time m
1 SU	0612 0.7 / 1108 2.0	1831 1.0	2301 2.0	16 M	0610 0.4 / 1123 2.2	1836 0.7	2336 2.3
2 M	0648 0.8 / 1605 1.9	1908 1.1	2228 1.9	17 TU	0659 0.5 / 1208 2.1	1928 0.8	
3 TU	0724 0.9 / 1637 2.0	1949 1.2	2257 1.8	18 W	0018 2.2 / 0751 0.6	1716 2.1	2025 0.9
4 W	0806 0.9 / 1716 2.0	2034 1.2	2335 1.8	19 TH	0059 2.1 / 0847 0.7	1805 2.1	2126 1.0
5 TH	0852 1.0 / 1802 2.0	2125 1.3		20 F	0137 1.9 / 0948 0.8	1856 2.1	2230 1.1
6 F	0620 1.7 / 0946 1.1	1854 2.0	2222 1.3	21 SA	0720 1.8 / 1053 0.9	1952 2.1	2334 1.1
7 SA	0720 1.7 / 1044 1.1	1953 1.9	2324 1.2	22 SU	0822 1.8 / 1157 1.0	2051 2.1	
8 SU	0828 1.7 / 1147 1.1	2100 1.9		23 M	0034 1.0 / 0932 1.8	1257 1.0	2156 2.0
9 M	0026 1.1 / 0939 1.7	1248 1.1	2206 1.9	24 TU	0131 0.9 / 1042 1.8	1353 1.0	2300 2.0
10 TU	0124 1.0 / 0509 1.8	1345 0.9	1905 2.0	25 W	0224 0.8 / 1143 1.9	1444 0.9	2010 2.0
11 W	0216 0.8 / 0733 1.8	1438 0.8	1945 2.1	26 TH	0312 0.7 / 0834 1.8	1532 0.9	2025 2.1
12 TH	0305 0.6 / 0822 2.0	1526 0.6	2034 2.3	27 F	0357 0.7 / 0901 2.0	1616 0.9	2042 2.2
13 F	0353 0.5 / 0908 2.2	1614 0.6	2121 2.4	28 SA	0439 0.6 / 0929 2.0	1657 0.9	2125 2.2
14 SA	0438 0.4 / 0955 2.3	1700 0.6	2208 2.4	29 SU	0517 0.6 / 1006 2.1	1735 0.9	2209 2.2
15 SU	0524 0.3 / 1039 2.3	1747 0.6	2252 2.4	30 M	0552 0.7 / 1046 2.0	1809 1.0	2250 2.1

JULY

Day	Time m	Time m	Time m	Day	Time m	Time m	Time m
1 TU	0624 0.7 / 1129 2.0	1843 1.0	2315 2.0	16 W	0642 0.3 / 1150 2.3	1909 0.7	
2 W	0658 0.8 / 1613 2.0	1919 1.0	2241 1.9	17 TH	0001 2.3 / 0730 0.5	1656 2.1	2001 0.8
3 TH	0736 0.8 / 1653 2.0	2001 1.1	2308 1.8	18 F	0038 2.1 / 0821 0.7	1742 2.1	2056 1.0
4 F	0819 0.9 / 1737 2.0	2048 1.1	2343 1.8	19 SA	0106 1.9 / 0918 0.9	1830 2.1	2159 1.1
5 SA	0908 1.0 / 1826 2.0	2142 1.2		20 SU	0656 1.9 / 1022 1.0	1923 2.1	2305 1.1
6 SU	0650 1.8 / 1005 1.0	1919 2.0	2242 1.2	21 M	0758 1.9 / 1130 1.1	2022 2.0	
7 M	0750 1.8 / 1106 1.1	2018 1.9	2344 1.1	22 TU	0010 1.1 / 0908 1.9	1235 1.2	2126 2.0
8 TU	0855 1.9 / 1210 1.0	2121 1.9		23 W	0110 1.0 / 1017 1.9	1335 1.1	2231 2.0
9 W	0047 1.0 / 1002 1.8	1312 1.0	1849 2.0	24 TH	0206 0.9 / 1124 2.0	1428 1.1	2002 1.9
10 TH	0147 0.8 / 0720 1.9	1411 0.8	1933 2.1	25 F	0255 0.8 / 1214 1.9	1516 1.0	1855 2.0
11 F	0242 0.6 / 0811 2.0	1506 0.7	2023 2.3	26 SA	0340 0.7 / 1301 1.9	1600 0.9	2003 2.1
12 SA	0334 0.4 / 0858 2.2	1557 0.6	2111 2.4	27 SU	0421 0.6 / 0906 2.0	1639 0.9	2101 2.2
13 SU	0422 0.3 / 0944 2.3	1646 0.5	2157 2.5	28 M	0457 0.6 / 0942 2.1	1714 0.9	2148 2.2
14 M	0509 0.2 / 1027 2.4	1733 0.5	2240 2.5	29 TU	0530 0.6 / 1021 2.1	1745 0.9	2229 2.2
15 TU	0555 0.2 / 1109 2.3	1821 0.5	2322 2.5	30 W	0559 0.7 / 1101 2.1	1816 0.9	2306 2.1
				31 TH	0630 0.7 / 1139 2.0	1849 0.9	2242 2.0

AUGUST

Day	Time m	Time m	Time m	Day	Time m	Time m	Time m
1 F	0705 0.7 / 1627 2.0	1928 0.9	2239 1.9	16 SA	0016 2.2 / 0753 0.7	1714 2.1	2024 0.9
2 SA	0745 0.8 / 1710 2.0	2011 1.0	2304 1.9	17 SU	0039 1.9 / 0845 0.9	1800 2.1	2124 1.1
3 SU	0830 0.9 / 1756 2.0	2102 1.1		18 M	0627 1.6 / 0949 1.2	1850 2.0	2236 1.2
4 M	0620 1.8 / 0924 1.0	1846 2.0	2202 1.1	19 TU	0730 1.4 / 1105 1.3	1950 2.0	2347 1.2
5 TU	0714 1.8 / 1029 1.1	1939 1.9	2310 1.1	20 W	0844 1.9 / 1217 1.3	2101 1.9	
6 W	0815 1.8 / 1138 1.1	2036 1.9		21 TH	0050 1.1 / 0954 1.9	1318 1.2	2208 1.9
7 TH	0018 1.0 / 0922 1.8	1246 1.0	1837 2.0	22 F	0146 1.0 / 1055 2.0	1410 1.1	2309 1.9
8 F	0124 0.9 / 0713 1.9	1352 0.9	1923 2.1	23 SA	0235 0.9 / 1149 2.0	1457 1.0	1834 2.0
9 SA	0224 0.6 / 0801 2.0	1450 0.7	2012 2.3	24 SU	0319 0.7 / 1236 2.0	1539 0.9	1936 2.1
10 SU	0318 0.4 / 0847 2.2	1542 0.6	2058 2.5	25 M	0359 0.6 / 0834 2.0	1617 0.8	2036 2.1
11 M	0406 0.2 / 0930 2.3	1630 0.4	2142 2.6	26 TU	0433 0.6 / 0914 2.1	1649 0.6	2124 2.3
12 TU	0452 0.1 / 1011 2.4	1715 0.4	2224 2.6	27 W	0504 0.6 / 0954 2.2	1718 0.8	2206 2.3
13 W	0536 0.1 / 1051 2.4	1800 0.4	2304 2.6	28 TH	0533 0.6 / 1032 2.2	1748 0.8	2243 2.2
14 TH	0620 0.2 / 1129 2.3	1845 0.5	2342 2.4	29 F	0603 0.6 / 1108 2.1	1820 0.8	2314 2.1
15 F	0705 0.4 / 1205 2.2	1932 0.7		30 SA	0636 0.7 / 1600 2.0	1855 0.8	2210 2.0
				31 SU	0712 0.6 / 1642 2.0	1935 0.9	2232 1.9

Chart Datum: 1·40 metres below Ordnance Datum (Newlyn)
HAT is 2·6 metres above Chart Datum

TIME ZONE (UT)
For Summer Time add ONE hour in **non-shaded areas**

POOLE HARBOUR
LAT 50°43′N   LONG 1°59′W
TIMES AND HEIGHTS OF HIGH AND LOW WATERS

Dates in amber are **SPRINGS**
Dates in yellow are **NEAPS**
2014

SEPTEMBER

Day	Time m	Time m	Time m	Time m
1 M	0754 0.9	1726 2.0	2021 1.0	
16 TU	0556 1.9	0914 1.3	1813 2.0	☽ 2201 1.2
2 TU	0550 1.9	1813 1.9	☾ 2122 1.1	
17 W	0658 1.9	1039 1.4	1914 1.9	2320 1.2
3 W	0640 1.9	0952 1.2	1901 1.9	2240 1.1
18 TH	0819 1.9	1155 1.4	2037 1.9	
4 TH	0736 1.8	1114 1.2	1748 1.9	2358 1.0
19 F	0025 1.2	0928 2.0	1255 1.3	2146 1.9
5 F	0838 1.8	1231 1.1	1823 2.0	
20 SA	0120 1.0	1027 2.0	1346 1.2	2244 1.9
6 SA	0107 0.9	0705 1.9	1338 1.0	1909 2.1
21 SU	0208 0.9	1119 2.0	1432 1.1	1825 1.9
7 SU	0207 0.6	0748 2.1	1434 0.7	1957 2.3
22 M	0251 0.8	1206 2.0	1512 0.9	1919 2.0
8 M	0259 0.4	0831 2.2	1524 0.5	2042 2.5
23 TU	0330 0.7	0800 2.1	1548 0.8	2013 2.2
9 TU	0346 0.2	0911 2.4	1610 0.4	O 2123 2.6
24 W	0404 0.6	0843 2.2	1620 0.7	● 2059 2.3
10 W	0431 0.1	0950 2.5	1654 0.3	2204 2.6
25 TH	0434 0.6	0924 2.3	1650 0.7	2141 2.3
11 TH	0514 0.1	1028 2.5	1737 0.4	2243 2.4
26 F	0505 0.6	1002 2.3	1721 0.7	2220 2.3
12 F	0556 0.3	1104 2.4	1820 0.5	2320 2.4
27 SA	0537 0.6	1039 2.2	1754 0.7	2256 2.2
13 SA	0639 0.5	1138 2.2	1904 0.7	2355 2.1
28 SU	0610 0.7	1112 2.1	1828 0.7	2331 2.0
14 SU	0724 0.8	1645 2.0	1952 0.9	
29 M	0646 0.8	1142 2.0	1907 0.8	
15 M	0508 1.9	0814 1.8	1727 2.0	2048 1.1
30 TU	0440 2.0	0727 0.9	1659 2.0	1952 0.9

OCTOBER

Day	Time m	Time m	Time m	Time m
1 W	0525 2.0	0816 1.1	1744 1.9	☾ 2049 1.1
16 TH	0618 2.0	0956 1.5	1729 1.8	2240 1.3
2 TH	0614 1.9	0925 1.2	1829 1.9	2217 1.1
17 F	0740 1.9	1123 1.4	1757 1.8	2351 1.2
3 F	0707 1.9	1101 1.3	1730 1.9	2341 1.0
18 SA	0852 2.0	1225 1.4	2115 1.8	
4 SA	0807 1.9	1219 1.2	1807 2.0	
19 SU	0047 1.1	0952 2.0	1316 1.3	2213 1.8
5 SU	0049 0.8	0651 2.0	1322 1.0	1853 2.1
20 M	0135 1.0	1043 2.0	1400 1.1	1832 1.8
6 M	0146 0.6	0730 2.1	1415 0.7	1938 2.2
21 TU	0217 0.9	1129 2.0	1439 1.0	1907 2.0
7 TU	0237 0.4	0811 2.2	1504 0.5	2022 2.4
22 W	0254 0.8	0734 2.1	1515 0.8	1952 2.1
8 W	0324 0.3	0849 2.4	1549 0.4	O 2103 2.5
23 TH	0329 0.7	0812 2.2	1549 0.7	● 2036 2.2
9 TH	0408 0.2	0926 2.4	1632 0.4	2142 2.5
24 F	0404 0.6	0853 2.3	1623 0.6	2117 2.3
10 F	0450 0.3	1003 2.5	1714 0.4	2221 2.5
25 SA	0438 0.6	0933 2.3	1657 0.6	2158 2.3
11 SA	0532 0.4	1037 2.4	1756 0.5	2258 2.3
26 SU	0514 0.6	1011 2.3	1733 0.6	2239 2.2
12 SU	0615 0.6	1109 2.2	1838 0.7	2334 2.1
27 M	0550 0.7	1050 2.2	1810 0.7	2321 2.1
13 M	0658 0.9	1131 2.0	1923 0.9	
28 TU	0629 0.8	1130 2.1	1850 0.7	
14 TU	0443 2.0	0745 1.1	1654 1.9	2012 1.1
29 W	0423 2.0	0713 1.0	1215 2.0	1937 0.9
15 W	0527 2.0	0838 1.3	1730 1.9	☽ 2111 1.2
30 TH	0509 2.0	0805 1.1	1312 1.9	2036 1.0
31 F	0600 2.0	0919 1.3	1811 1.9	☾ 2200 1.0

NOVEMBER

Day	Time m	Time m	Time m	Time m
1 SA	0654 2.0	1048 1.3	1704 1.9	2320 1.0
16 SU	0630 1.9	1134 1.4	1833 1.7	2353 1.2
2 SU	0756 2.0	1200 1.1	1748 1.9	
17 M	0857 1.9	1233 1.3	2124 1.7	
3 M	0025 0.8	0634 2.0	1300 1.0	1835 2.0
18 TU	0047 1.1	0956 1.9	1318 1.2	2221 1.8
4 TU	0121 0.7	0711 2.1	1353 0.8	1920 2.1
19 W	0131 1.0	1046 1.9	1358 1.0	1856 1.8
5 W	0213 0.5	0750 2.2	1442 0.6	2003 2.2
20 TH	0212 0.9	0714 2.0	1437 0.9	1933 2.0
6 TH	0300 0.5	0828 2.3	1527 0.5	O 2043 2.3
21 F	0253 0.8	0744 2.1	1516 0.7	2015 2.1
7 F	0346 0.4	0903 2.4	1611 0.4	2121 2.4
22 SA	0334 0.7	0822 2.2	1557 0.6	● 2058 2.2
8 SA	0429 0.5	0937 2.4	1653 0.4	2159 2.3
23 SU	0414 0.6	0907 2.3	1636 0.5	2142 2.2
9 SU	0511 0.6	1010 2.3	1734 0.5	2236 2.2
24 M	0454 0.6	0952 2.3	1716 0.5	2227 2.2
10 M	0554 0.8	1042 2.2	1816 0.7	2315 2.1
25 TU	0536 0.7	1037 2.3	1758 0.5	2312 2.1
11 TU	0636 1.0	1108 2.1	1857 0.8	
26 W	0619 0.8	1122 2.2	1842 0.6	
12 W	0420 2.0	0719 1.1	1041 1.9	1940 1.0
27 TH	0414 2.0	0707 0.9	1208 2.1	1930 0.7
13 TH	0458 2.0	0805 1.3	1107 1.8	2025 1.1
28 F	0500 2.1	0802 1.0	1257 2.0	2028 0.8
14 F	0532 2.0	0854 1.4	1717 1.8	☽ 2116 1.2
29 SA	0550 2.1	0909 1.2	1349 1.9	☾ 2138 0.9
15 SA	0558 2.0	0957 1.5	1753 1.8	2222 1.2
30 SU	0643 2.1	1024 1.2	1443 1.8	2251 0.9

DECEMBER

Day	Time m	Time m	Time m	Time m
1 M	0740 2.0	1133 1.1	1732 1.8	2357 0.9
16 TU	0715 1.9	1059 1.3	1947 1.7	2325 1.1
2 TU	0843 2.0	1235 1.0	1820 1.9	
17 W	0825 1.9	1206 1.2	2111 1.7	
3 W	0056 0.8	0656 2.0	1330 0.9	1906 2.0
18 TH	0029 1.1	0945 1.9	1307 1.1	2222 1.8
4 TH	0150 0.7	0734 2.1	1421 0.7	1948 2.0
19 F	0127 1.0	0657 1.9	1359 0.9	1918 1.8
5 F	0239 0.7	0811 2.1	1508 0.6	2028 2.1
20 SA	0218 0.8	0723 2.0	1448 0.7	2000 2.0
6 SA	0327 0.6	0844 2.2	1553 0.5	2104 2.1
21 SU	0307 0.7	0805 2.2	1534 0.5	2046 2.1
7 SU	0411 0.6	0914 2.3	1636 0.5	2139 2.2
22 M	0354 0.6	0855 2.3	1619 0.4	2132 2.2
8 M	0454 0.7	0944 2.3	1717 0.5	2215 2.1
23 TU	0438 0.6	0944 2.4	1702 0.3	2217 2.2
9 TU	0536 0.8	1018 2.2	1757 0.6	2254 2.0
24 W	0524 0.6	1029 2.4	1747 0.3	2301 2.2
10 W	0616 0.9	1053 2.1	1835 0.7	2346 2.1
25 TH	0610 0.6	1113 2.3	1832 0.4	2346 2.1
11 TH	0358 1.9	0654 1.0	1027 2.0	1911 0.8
26 F	0657 0.7	1157 2.3	1920 0.5	
12 F	0430 2.0	0733 1.1	1044 1.9	1950 0.9
27 SA	0449 2.0	0749 0.8	1239 2.1	2012 0.6
13 SA	0501 2.0	0814 1.2	1118 1.8	2032 1.0
28 SU	0536 2.0	0846 1.0	1321 2.0	☾ 2111 0.8
14 SU	0538 2.0	0901 1.3	1751 1.8	☽ 2122 1.1
29 M	0625 2.1	0952 1.1	1404 1.8	☽ 2219 0.9
15 M	0622 2.0	0956 1.3	1843 1.7	2221 1.1
30 TU	0717 2.0	1102 1.1	1940 1.8	2328 0.9
31 W	0815 2.0	1208 1.0	2049 1.9	

Chart Datum: 1·40 metres below Ordnance Datum (Newlyn)
HAT is 2·6 metres above Chart Datum

TIDES

SOUTHAMPTON
MEAN SPRING AND NEAP CURVES

MEAN RANGES
Springs 4.0m
Neaps 1.9m

Factor

0.9 0.8 0.7 0.6 0.5 0.4 0.3 0.2 0.1

H.W. +6h +5h +4h +3h +2h +1h L.W. -1h -2h -3h -4h -5h H.W.

M.H.W.S.
M.H.W.N.

M.L.W.N.

M.L.W.S.

CHART DATUM

H.W.Hts.m.
L.W.Hts.m.

Note - Double HWs occur at Southampton. The predictions are for the first HW.

SOUTHAMPTON

LAT 50°53′N   LONG 1°24′W

TIMES AND HEIGHTS OF HIGH AND LOW WATERS

Dates in amber are **SPRINGS**
Dates in yellow are **NEAPS**

2014

JANUARY

Day	Time m	Time m	Time m	Time m
1 W	0348 0.8	1025 4.8	1614 0.5	● 2250 4.8
2 TH	0437 0.6	1108 4.8	1702 0.3	2336 4.8
3 F	0524 0.5	1154 4.9	1748 0.2	
4 SA	0022 4.8	0611 0.5	1240 4.8	1834 0.3
5 SU	0111 4.7	0656 0.6	1329 4.7	1919 0.5
6 M	0204 4.6	0743 0.8	1422 4.5	2006 0.8
7 TU	0310 4.5	0831 1.1	1526 4.3	2056 1.1
8 W	0531 4.4	0926 1.4	1648 4.1	◑ 2154 1.5
9 TH	0549 4.2	1030 1.7	1748 3.9	2300 1.7
10 F	0624 4.1	1141 1.8	1846 3.8	
11 SA	0011 1.9	0719 4.0	1251 1.8	1956 3.8
12 SU	0116 1.8	0825 4.0	1351 1.6	2239 4.0
13 M	0213 1.7	1045 4.1	1442 1.4	2328 4.1
14 TU	0302 1.5	1000 4.2	1528 1.2	2213 4.2
15 W	0349 1.3	1035 4.3	1612 1.0	2317 4.3
16 TH	0431 1.1	1112 4.4	1652 0.9	○ 2349 4.4
17 F	0510 1.1	1148 4.4	1730 0.9	
18 SA	0021 4.4	0545 1.1	1219 4.4	1801 0.9
19 SU	0046 4.4	0612 1.1	1247 4.4	1825 1.0
20 M	0109 4.4	0638 1.1	1316 4.4	1851 1.0
21 TU	0138 4.4	0709 1.1	1350 4.4	1925 1.0
22 W	0216 4.4	0746 1.1	1432 4.3	2005 1.1
23 TH	0300 4.3	0830 1.2	1519 4.2	2052 1.3
24 F	0351 4.2	0922 1.5	1614 4.0	◑ 2148 1.5
25 SA	0448 4.1	1028 1.7	1718 3.9	2301 1.7
26 SU	0559 4.0	1148 1.8	2002 3.9	
27 M	0026 1.8	0817 4.1	1310 1.6	2053 4.1
28 TU	0145 1.5	0856 4.3	1419 1.2	2127 4.3
29 W	0247 1.2	0932 4.5	1515 0.8	2159 4.5
30 TH	0339 0.8	1012 4.7	1604 0.4	● 2239 4.7
31 F	0426 0.5	1053 4.8	1650 0.2	2321 4.8

FEBRUARY

Day	Time m	Time m	Time m	Time m
1 SA	0511 0.3	1137 4.9	1734 0.0	
2 SU	0005 4.8	0555 0.2	1221 4.8	1817 0.1
3 M	0051 4.7	0638 0.3	1308 4.7	1859 0.3
4 TU	0140 4.6	0720 0.5	1357 4.5	1941 0.6
5 W	0238 4.4	0803 0.9	1456 4.3	2025 1.0
6 TH	0455 4.3	0851 1.2	1642 4.1	◑ 2117 1.4
7 F	0505 4.1	0947 1.6	1720 3.9	2218 1.8
8 SA	0543 3.9	1056 1.9	1811 3.7	2334 2.0
9 SU	0635 3.8	1218 2.0	1913 3.6	
10 M	0052 2.0	0737 3.7	1327 1.8	2157 3.8
11 TU	0154 1.9	1012 3.9	1421 1.6	2255 4.0
12 W	0244 1.6	0935 4.0	1508 1.3	2334 4.1
13 TH	0329 1.3	1009 4.2	1550 1.0	2243 4.2
14 F	0410 1.1	1047 4.3	1629 0.8	○ 2315 4.4
15 SA	0448 0.9	1123 4.4	1706 0.7	2349 4.4
16 SU	0521 0.9	1155 4.4	1737 0.7	
17 M	0016 4.4	0549 0.9	1222 4.4	1804 0.8
18 TU	0041 4.4	0615 0.8	1251 4.5	1830 0.7
19 W	0111 4.5	0646 0.8	1326 4.5	1902 0.7
20 TH	0148 4.5	0722 0.8	1406 4.5	1940 0.8
21 F	0231 4.4	0803 0.9	1452 4.3	2024 1.0
22 SA	0320 4.3	0851 1.2	1546 4.1	◑ 2115 1.4
23 SU	0418 4.1	0950 1.6	1651 3.9	2224 1.8
24 M	0533 3.9	1118 1.8	1940 3.8	
25 TU	0010 1.9	0757 4.0	1302 1.6	2036 4.0
26 W	0143 1.6	0843 4.2	1412 1.2	2118 4.3
27 TH	0239 1.2	0919 4.4	1503 0.8	2149 4.5
28 F	0327 0.8	0957 4.6	1549 0.4	2225 4.7

MARCH

Day	Time m	Time m	Time m	Time m
1 SA	0412 0.4	1037 4.7	1633 0.1	● 2304 4.7
2 SU	0454 0.2	1115 4.8	1715 0.0	2347 4.7
3 M	0536 0.1	1202 4.7	1756 0.0	
4 TU	0030 4.7	0617 0.2	1246 4.6	1836 0.2
5 W	0115 4.5	0656 0.4	1333 4.4	1916 0.6
6 TH	0205 4.4	0736 0.8	1428 4.3	1957 1.0
7 F	0418 4.3	0818 1.1	1625 4.1	2042 1.4
8 SA	0430 4.0	0907 1.5	1654 3.9	◑ 2139 1.8
9 SU	0507 3.8	1011 1.9	1739 3.7	2254 2.1
10 M	0557 3.6	1134 2.0	1835 3.6	
11 TU	0021 2.1	0656 3.6	1254 1.9	1947 3.6
12 W	0129 2.0	0802 3.6	1357 1.7	2216 3.9
13 TH	0220 1.7	0900 3.8	1440 1.4	2300 4.1
14 F	0303 1.4	0941 4.1	1522 1.1	2209 4.2
15 SA	0343 1.1	1019 4.3	1601 0.8	2243 4.4
16 SU	0419 0.9	1055 4.4	1637 0.7	○ 2317 4.4
17 M	0452 0.8	1127 4.4	1709 0.6	2346 4.5
18 TU	0522 0.7	1156 4.5	1738 0.6	
19 W	0014 4.5	0552 0.6	1227 4.6	1808 0.6
20 TH	0046 4.6	0625 0.6	1303 4.6	1842 0.6
21 F	0124 4.6	0701 0.6	1345 4.5	1920 0.7
22 SA	0207 4.5	0742 0.8	1432 4.4	2003 1.0
23 SU	0257 4.3	0828 1.1	1528 4.1	2054 1.4
24 M	0358 4.0	0928 1.5	1642 3.9	◑ 2207 1.8
25 TU	0525 3.8	1105 1.7	1917 3.9	
26 W	0010 1.9	0732 3.9	1250 1.6	2017 4.1
27 TH	0130 1.6	0824 4.1	1354 1.2	2103 4.3
28 F	0222 1.2	0902 4.3	1443 0.8	2134 4.5
29 SA	0308 0.8	0939 4.5	1528 0.5	2208 4.6
30 SU	0352 0.5	1019 4.6	1612 0.2	● 2246 4.7
31 M	0433 0.2	1100 4.6	1653 0.1	2327 4.7

APRIL

Day	Time m	Time m	Time m	Time m
1 TU	0514 0.2	1142 4.6	1733 0.2	
2 W	0008 4.6	0554 0.3	1225 4.5	1813 0.4
3 TH	0049 4.5	0633 0.5	1310 4.4	1852 0.7
4 F	0133 4.3	0711 0.8	1404 4.2	1930 1.0
5 SA	0223 4.2	0748 1.1	1604 4.2	2011 1.4
6 SU	0348 4.0	0832 1.4	1628 4.0	2102 1.8
7 M	0428 3.8	0929 1.8	1707 3.8	◑ 2211 2.1
8 TU	0519 3.6	1043 2.0	1758 3.7	2334 2.2
9 W	0617 3.5	1203 2.0	1859 3.7	
10 TH	0051 2.1	0721 3.6	1310 1.8	2132 3.8
11 F	0146 1.8	0822 3.8	1402 1.6	2058 4.0
12 SA	0230 1.5	0910 4.0	1446 1.2	2135 4.2
13 SU	0309 1.2	0950 4.2	1525 1.0	2211 4.4
14 M	0345 0.9	1026 4.4	1602 0.8	2245 4.5
15 TU	0420 0.7	1058 4.5	1638 0.6	○ 2316 4.6
16 W	0454 0.6	1130 4.5	1712 0.6	2347 4.6
17 TH	0529 0.5	1205 4.6	1747 0.6	
18 F	0023 4.7	0606 0.5	1245 4.6	1824 0.6
19 SA	0104 4.6	0645 0.6	1329 4.6	1905 0.8
20 SU	0150 4.5	0728 0.8	1419 4.4	1951 1.1
21 M	0243 4.3	0817 1.1	1522 4.2	2047 1.5
22 TU	0350 4.1	0922 1.4	1801 4.1	◑ 2208 1.8
23 W	0516 3.9	1052 1.6	1858 4.1	2343 1.8
24 TH	0703 3.9	1217 1.5	1957 4.2	
25 F	0059 1.6	0801 4.1	1323 1.3	2045 4.3
26 SA	0155 1.3	0842 4.2	1416 1.0	2117 4.5
27 SU	0243 0.9	0921 4.3	1503 0.7	2151 4.5
28 M	0328 0.6	1002 4.4	1547 0.5	2229 4.6
29 TU	0411 0.5	1043 4.4	1629 0.5	● 2308 4.5
30 W	0452 0.4	1127 4.4	1711 0.6	2348 4.5

Chart Datum: 2·74 metres below Ordnance Datum (Newlyn)
HAT is 5·0 metres above Chart Datum

TIDES

TIME ZONE (UT)	SOUTHAMPTON	Dates in amber are SPRINGS
For Summer Time add ONE hour in **non-shaded areas**	LAT 50°53'N LONG 1°24'W	Dates in yellow are NEAPS
	TIMES AND HEIGHTS OF HIGH AND LOW WATERS	**2014**

MAY

Time	m	Time	m
1 0532 TH 1211 1751	0.5 4.4 0.7	**16** 0509 1146 F 1730	0.4 4.7 0.6
2 0027 0612 F 1258 1830	4.4 0.6 4.3 0.9	**17** 0004 0551 SA 1230 1812	4.7 0.4 4.7 0.6
3 0106 0649 SA 1515 1909	4.3 0.9 4.3 1.2	**18** 0048 0634 SU 1317 1858	4.7 0.5 4.6 0.8
4 0149 0724 SU 1543 1946	4.2 1.1 4.3 1.4	**19** 0137 0721 M 1411 1947	4.6 0.7 4.5 1.0
5 0237 0802 M 1605 2029	4.0 1.4 4.1 1.7	**20** 0232 0813 TU 1515 2045	4.4 1.0 4.3 1.3
6 0335 0849 TU 1636 2125	3.9 1.6 4.0 2.0	**21** 0337 0915 W 1751 2154	4.2 1.2 4.3 1.5
7 0437 0952 W 1723 2231	3.7 1.8 3.9 2.1	**22** 0453 1026 TH 1841 2307	4.0 1.4 4.2 1.6
8 0538 1059 TH 1820 2339	3.6 1.9 3.8 2.1	**23** 0623 1138 F 1934	4.0 1.5 4.3
9 0642 1205 F 1921	3.6 1.9 3.9	**24** 0018 0733 SA 1245 2022	1.6 4.0 1.4 4.3
10 0044 0746 SA 1306 2018	1.9 3.7 1.7 4.0	**25** 0122 0821 SU 1344 2057	1.4 4.1 1.2 4.4
11 0139 0839 SU 1358 2102	1.7 3.9 1.4 4.2	**26** 0215 0904 M 1435 2132	1.2 4.2 1.1 4.4
12 0224 0921 M 1444 2140	1.3 4.1 1.2 4.4	**27** 0303 0948 TU 1522 2212	0.9 4.2 0.9 4.4
13 0306 0957 TU 1526 2214	1.0 4.3 0.9 4.5	**28** 0348 1033 W 1607 2252	0.8 4.3 0.8 4.4
14 0347 1031 W 1607 2247	0.7 4.5 0.7 4.6	**29** 0431 1122 TH 1650 2332	0.7 4.3 0.8 4.4
15 0428 1107 TH 1648 2324	0.5 4.6 0.6 4.7	**30** 0513 1351 F 1733	0.7 4.4 0.9
		31 0010 0554 SA 1416 1813	4.3 0.8 4.4 1.0

JUNE

Time	m	Time	m
1 0047 0631 SU 1449 1850	4.3 0.9 4.3 1.2	**16** 0034 0626 M 1304 1850	4.7 0.4 4.7 0.7
2 0125 0713 M 1523 1924	4.2 1.1 4.3 1.4	**17** 0123 0705 TU 1357 1939	4.6 0.5 4.6 0.8
3 0204 0737 TU 1550 1958	4.1 1.3 4.2 1.6	**18** 0216 0802 W 1458 2031	4.5 0.7 4.5 1.1
4 0247 0814 W 1547 2040	4.0 1.4 4.1 1.7	**19** 0317 0857 TH 1739 2129	4.3 1.0 4.5 1.3
5 0335 0901 TH 1637 2134	3.9 1.6 4.0 1.9	**20** 0428 0956 F 1819 2232	4.1 1.3 4.3 1.5
6 0431 1001 F 1738 2236	3.7 1.8 3.9 1.9	**21** 0548 1101 SA 1857 2340	4.0 1.4 4.3 1.6
7 0550 1105 SA 1842 2339	3.7 1.8 3.9 1.9	**22** 0656 1208 SU 1942	4.0 1.4 4.2
8 0712 1207 SU 1942	3.7 1.7 4.0	**23** 0047 0758 M 1312 2030	1.6 4.0 1.5 4.2
9 0039 0812 M 1307 2032	1.7 3.9 1.6 4.2	**24** 0147 0853 TU 1409 2114	1.4 4.0 1.4 4.2
10 0137 0857 TU 1403 2111	1.4 4.1 1.3 4.3	**25** 0240 0942 W 1501 2156	1.2 4.1 1.3 4.3
11 0230 0932 W 1454 2146	1.1 4.3 1.1 4.5	**26** 0328 1029 TH 1548 2237	1.0 4.2 1.1 4.3
12 0320 1008 TH 1543 2224	0.8 4.5 0.8 4.6	**27** 0413 1117 F 1634 2315	0.9 4.2 1.0 4.3
13 0407 1047 F 1630 2304	0.6 4.6 0.6 4.7	**28** 0456 1215 SA 1716 2353	0.8 4.3 1.0 4.3
14 0453 1130 SA 1717 2348	0.4 4.7 0.6 4.8	**29** 0537 1336 SU 1756	0.8 4.3 1.1
15 0539 1216 SU 1803	0.3 4.7 0.6	**30** 0028 0615 M 1419 1832	4.3 0.9 4.3 1.2

JULY

Time	m	Time	m
1 0102 0646 TU 1339 1901	4.2 1.1 4.3 1.3	**16** 0104 0658 W 1338 1922	4.7 0.3 4.7 0.6
2 0135 0712 W 1406 1928	4.2 1.2 4.3 1.4	**17** 0155 0744 TH 1434 2009	4.6 0.4 4.6 0.8
3 0209 0742 TH 1440 2003	4.1 1.2 4.2 1.4	**18** 0252 0832 F 1717 2101	4.4 0.8 4.5 1.1
4 0249 0821 F 1521 2048	4.1 1.3 4.2 1.5	**19** 0404 0926 SA 1745 2159	4.2 1.2 4.4 1.4
5 0335 0910 SA 1609 2143	4.0 1.5 4.1 1.7	**20** 0525 1027 SU 1805 2305	4.0 1.5 4.2 1.7
6 0427 1009 SU 1703 2247	3.9 1.6 4.0 1.8	**21** 0622 1134 M 1853	3.9 1.7 4.1
7 0528 1117 M 1813 2354	3.8 1.7 4.0 1.7	**22** 0015 0728 TU 1243 1954	1.7 3.8 1.8 4.0
8 0756 1224 TU 2009	3.8 1.7 4.1	**23** 0122 0748 W 1347 2055	1.7 3.9 1.7 4.0
9 0059 0848 W 1329 2051	1.5 4.0 1.5 4.3	**24** 0220 1112 TH 1442 2139	1.5 4.1 1.5 4.1
10 0202 0922 TH 1430 2127	1.3 4.2 1.2 4.5	**25** 0309 1200 F 1530 2216	1.2 4.2 1.3 4.2
11 0300 0954 F 1525 2206	0.9 4.4 0.9 4.6	**26** 0355 1058 SA 1616 2253	1.0 4.2 1.1 4.3
12 0352 1033 SA 1616 2248	0.6 4.6 0.7 4.8	**27** 0437 1132 SU 1658 2331	0.9 4.3 1.1 4.3
13 0441 1116 SU 1704 2332	0.3 4.7 0.5 4.8	**28** 0517 1208 M 1736	0.8 4.4 1.0
14 0528 1200 M 1751	0.2 4.8 0.4	**29** 0005 0554 TU 1239 1810	4.3 0.8 4.4 1.1
15 0017 0613 TU 1247 1836	4.8 0.1 4.8 0.4	**30** 0037 0624 W 1304 1835	4.3 1.0 4.4 1.2
		31 0105 0645 TH 1330 1859	4.3 1.0 4.4 1.2

AUGUST

Time	m	Time	m
1 0137 0712 F 1402 1931	4.3 1.1 4.4 1.2	**16** 0227 0806 SA 1648 2032	4.4 0.8 4.5 1.1
2 0214 0748 SA 1441 2012	4.3 1.1 4.3 1.3	**17** 0456 0856 SU 1703 2126	4.2 1.3 4.3 1.5
3 0258 0831 SU 1528 2100	4.2 1.2 4.2 1.4	**18** 0504 1104 M 1727 2231	4.0 0.8 4.1 1.8
4 0350 0923 M 1621 2200	4.1 1.5 4.1 1.6	**19** 0552 1104 TU 1814 2346	3.8 1.7 3.9 1.9
5 0447 1030 TU 1723 2314	3.9 1.7 4.0 1.8	**20** 0651 1218 W 1912	3.7 2.0 3.9
6 0558 1150 TU 1954	3.8 1.8 4.0	**21** 0057 0945 TH 1325 2200	1.7 3.9 1.9 3.9
7 0032 0836 TH 1307 2041	1.7 4.0 1.7 4.2	**22** 0157 1046 F 1421 2258	1.7 4.0 1.7 4.0
8 0146 0920 F 1417 2114	1.4 4.2 1.4 4.4	**23** 0247 1133 SA 1510 2152	1.4 4.2 1.4 4.2
9 0248 0946 SA 1514 2151	1.0 4.5 1.0 4.6	**24** 0332 1037 SU 1553 2228	1.1 4.3 1.2 4.3
10 0340 1020 SU 1604 2232	0.6 4.7 0.7 4.8	**25** 0413 1101 M 1634 2305	0.9 4.4 1.0 4.4
11 0428 1100 M 1650 2314	0.3 4.8 0.4 4.9	**26** 0452 1135 TU 1711 2340	0.8 4.4 1.0 4.4
12 0512 1143 TU 1735 2358	0.1 4.9 0.3 4.9	**27** 0528 1207 W 1742	0.8 4.5 1.0
13 0556 1228 W 1818	0.1 4.8 0.3	**28** 0010 0556 TH 1232 1807	4.4 0.9 4.5 1.0
14 0044 0639 TH 1316 1900	4.8 0.2 4.7 0.5	**29** 0037 0618 F 1258 1831	4.4 1.0 4.5 1.0
15 0132 0721 F 1409 1945	4.6 0.5 4.6 0.7	**30** 0108 0645 SA 1330 1903	4.5 1.0 4.5 1.0
		31 0145 0720 SU 1409 1942	4.4 1.0 4.5 1.1

Chart Datum: 2·74 metres below Ordnance Datum (Newlyn)
HAT is 5·0 metres above Chart Datum

TIME ZONE (UT)
For Summer Time add ONE hour in **non-shaded areas**

SOUTHAMPTON
LAT 50°53'N   LONG 1°24'W
TIMES AND HEIGHTS OF HIGH AND LOW WATERS

Dates in amber are **SPRINGS**
Dates in yellow are **NEAPS**

2014

SEPTEMBER

Time	m	Time	m
1 M 0229 1455 2026	4.4 4.4 1.3	**16** TU 0440 1653 ☽2158	4.0 4.0 1.9
2 TU 0319 0849 1549 ☽2121	4.2 4.2 4.2 1.6	**17** W 0521 1738 2315	3.9 3.8 2.0
3 W 0419 0952 1654 2241	4.0 1.8 4.0 1.9	**18** TH 0613 1151 1833	3.7 2.2 3.7
4 TH 0536 1127 1933	3.8 2.0 4.0	**19** F 0026 0910 1258 1936	2.0 3.8 2.1 3.7
5 F 0018 0817 1301 2026	1.8 4.0 1.8 4.2	**20** SA 0127 1011 1355 2230	1.8 4.0 1.8 4.0
6 SA 0138 0906 1409 2101	1.5 4.3 1.5 4.4	**21** SU 0218 1056 1443 2124	1.5 4.2 1.5 4.1
7 SU 0236 0935 1501 2135	1.0 4.5 1.0 4.6	**22** M 0303 1129 1526 2201	1.2 4.3 1.2 4.3
8 M 0325 1005 1548 2214	0.6 4.7 0.6 4.8	**23** TU 0344 1029 1605 2238	1.0 4.4 1.0 4.4
9 TU 0410 1042 1633 ○2255	0.3 4.9 0.4 4.9	**24** W 0422 1103 1640 ●2313	0.9 4.5 0.9 4.5
10 W 0453 1124 1715 2338	0.1 4.9 0.2 4.9	**25** TH 0457 1135 1711 2343	0.8 4.6 0.9 4.5
11 TH 0535 1207 1756	0.1 4.8 0.3	**26** F 0525 1202 1738	0.9 4.6 0.9
12 F 0022 0616 1252 1837	4.8 0.3 4.7 0.5	**27** SA 0011 0552 1229 1806	4.6 0.9 4.6 0.9
13 SA 0108 0657 1341 1919	4.6 0.6 4.6 0.8	**28** SU 0043 0622 1303 1840	4.6 0.9 4.6 0.9
14 SU 0201 0740 1614 2003	4.4 0.9 4.5 1.1	**29** M 0122 0657 1343 1918	4.6 1.0 4.6 1.0
15 M 0423 0826 1625 2053	4.2 1.1 4.2 1.5	**30** TU 0206 0738 1430 2002	4.5 1.2 4.4 1.3

OCTOBER

Time	m	Time	m
1 W 0257 0825 1526 ☽2055	4.3 1.5 4.2 1.6	**16** TH 0451 1002 1703 2236	4.0 2.1 3.8 2.1
2 TH 0401 0929 1638 2222	4.0 1.9 4.0 1.9	**17** F 0537 1118 1755 2348	3.8 2.2 3.7 2.1
3 F 0654 1122 1910	4.0 2.1 4.0	**18** SA 0634 1225 1855	3.8 2.2 3.7
4 SA 0010 0756 1252 2007	1.8 4.1 1.8 4.2	**19** SU 0050 0742 1323 1957	2.0 3.9 2.0 3.8
5 SU 0122 0849 1352 2044	1.5 4.4 1.5 4.4	**20** M 0143 1014 1411 2051	1.7 4.2 1.7 4.1
6 M 0216 0921 1442 2117	1.1 4.6 1.1 4.6	**21** TU 0229 0922 1453 2132	1.5 4.3 1.4 4.3
7 TU 0303 0948 1527 2155	0.7 4.8 0.7 4.7	**22** W 0310 0957 1531 2211	1.2 4.6 1.2 4.4
8 W 0348 1024 1611 ○2235	0.5 4.9 0.4 4.8	**23** TH 0348 1032 1606 ●2245	1.0 4.6 1.0 4.5
9 TH 0430 1104 1652 2318	0.3 4.9 0.3 4.8	**24** F 0422 1104 1639 2316	0.9 4.6 0.9 4.6
10 F 0512 1145 1733	0.3 4.8 0.4	**25** SA 0455 1134 1711 2348	0.9 4.7 0.8 4.7
11 SA 0001 0553 1228 1814	4.7 0.5 4.7 0.6	**26** SU 0527 1206 1745	0.8 4.7 0.8
12 SU 0046 0633 1313 1854	4.6 0.7 4.6 0.9	**27** M 0023 0603 1242 1822	4.7 0.9 4.7 0.8
13 M 0137 0715 1407 1935	4.4 1.1 4.4 1.2	**28** TU 0104 0641 1324 1902	4.7 1.0 4.6 1.0
14 TU 0356 0852 1549 2022	4.3 1.4 4.2 1.6	**29** W 0150 0724 1413 1948	4.5 1.2 4.5 1.2
15 W 0415 0852 1617 ☽2121	4.1 1.9 4.0 1.9	**30** TH 0245 0814 1511 2043	4.4 1.5 4.2 1.6
		31 F 0354 0923 1627 ☽2211	4.2 1.9 4.0 1.8

NOVEMBER

Time	m	Time	m
1 SA 0634 1105 1845 2344	4.2 2.0 4.0 1.8	**16** SU 0555 1135 1818 2359	3.9 2.2 3.7 2.1
2 SU 0733 1226 1943	4.3 2.1 4.1	**17** M 0654 1238 1920	3.9 2.1 3.8
3 M 0053 0828 1326 2024	1.5 4.4 1.5 4.3	**18** TU 0057 0755 1328 2019	1.9 4.1 1.9 4.0
4 TU 0149 0904 1417 2059	1.3 4.6 1.2 4.5	**19** W 0146 0846 1412 2106	1.7 4.3 1.6 4.2
5 W 0238 0931 1504 2139	1.0 4.7 0.9 4.6	**20** TH 0229 0927 1452 2146	1.4 4.4 1.3 4.4
6 TH 0323 1007 1548 ○2220	0.7 4.8 0.6 4.6	**21** F 0310 1004 1531 2220	1.2 4.6 1.0 4.5
7 F 0407 1045 1631 2302	0.6 4.8 0.5 4.6	**22** SA 0350 1036 1610 ●2253	1.0 4.7 0.8 4.6
8 SA 0449 1124 1712 2346	0.6 4.7 0.5 4.6	**23** SU 0429 1109 1650 2328	0.9 4.7 0.7 4.7
9 SU 0531 1207 1754	0.7 4.6 0.7	**24** M 0508 1146 1729	0.8 4.7 0.6
10 M 0031 0613 1249 1833	4.5 0.9 4.5 0.9	**25** TU 0007 0549 1227 1810	4.7 0.8 4.8 0.6
11 TU 0122 0653 1333 1912	4.4 1.2 4.4 1.2	**26** W 0051 0632 1311 1854	4.7 0.9 4.8 0.8
12 W 0334 0735 1424 1954	4.4 1.5 4.2 1.5	**27** TH 0140 0718 1400 1942	4.6 1.1 4.7 1.1
13 TH 0355 0820 1526 2041	4.2 1.8 4.0 1.8	**28** F 0235 0810 1458 2037	4.5 1.4 4.3 1.3
14 F 0419 0916 1623 ☽2143	4.1 2.1 3.9 2.0	**29** SA 0342 0914 1608 ☽2148	4.3 1.7 4.2 1.6
15 SA 0503 1031 1718 2253	4.0 2.3 3.8 2.1	**30** SU 0615 1031 1817 2307	4.3 1.8 4.1 1.6

DECEMBER

Time	m	Time	m
1 M 0706 1149 1910	4.3 1.7 4.1	**16** TU 0617 1121 1847 2351	4.0 2.1 3.7 2.0
2 TU 0018 0758 1255 2000	1.6 4.4 1.6 4.2	**17** W 0719 1224 1953	4.0 2.0 3.9
3 W 0119 0839 1351 2043	1.4 4.5 1.3 4.3	**18** TH 0051 0817 1321 2048	1.9 4.1 1.7 4.0
4 TH 0212 0914 1441 2126	1.2 4.5 1.1 4.4	**19** F 0146 0903 1413 2129	1.6 4.3 1.4 4.2
5 F 0300 0952 1527 2211	1.1 4.6 0.9 4.4	**20** SA 0236 0940 1501 2201	1.3 4.5 1.1 4.4
6 SA 0347 1032 1612 ○2256	0.9 4.6 0.7 4.5	**21** SU 0323 1014 1548 2235	1.1 4.6 0.8 4.6
7 SU 0431 1113 1654 2344	0.9 4.6 0.7 4.5	**22** M 0409 1050 1633 ●2312	0.9 4.8 0.6 4.7
8 M 0514 1153 1736	0.9 4.5 0.8	**23** TU 0454 1129 1718 2354	0.7 4.9 0.5 4.8
9 TU 0210 0556 1231 1817	4.5 1.0 4.5 0.9	**24** W 0539 1212 1802	0.7 4.9 0.4
10 W 0239 0636 1309 1854	4.5 1.2 4.4 1.1	**25** TH 0038 0624 1257 1847	4.8 0.7 4.8 0.5
11 TH 0313 0713 1350 1928	4.4 1.4 4.3 1.3	**26** F 0127 0710 1346 1933	4.7 0.8 4.7 0.7
12 F 0239 0747 1434 2002	4.3 1.6 4.1 1.5	**27** SA 0219 0759 1440 2023	4.6 1.0 4.5 1.0
13 SA 0330 0825 1523 2044	4.2 1.8 4.0 1.7	**28** SU 0321 0853 1544 2121	4.4 1.3 4.3 1.3
14 SU 0422 0913 1622 ☽2139	4.1 2.0 3.8 1.9	**29** M 0553 0956 1705 2228	4.4 1.5 4.1 1.5
15 M 0517 1015 1736 2245	4.0 2.1 3.8 2.0	**30** TU 0632 1109 1828 2341	4.3 1.7 4.0 1.6
		31 W 0715 1224 1929	4.3 1.7 4.0

Chart Datum: 2·74 metres below Ordnance Datum (Newlyn)
HAT is 5·0 metres above Chart Datum

TIDES

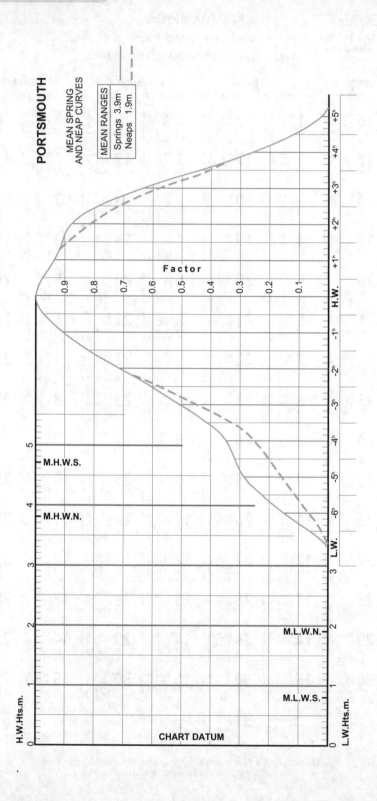

PORTSMOUTH

MEAN SPRING
AND NEAP CURVES

MEAN RANGES
Springs 3.9m
Neaps 1.9m

Factor

0.9 0.8 0.7 0.6 0.5 0.4 0.3 0.2 0.1

H.W.Hts.m.

M.H.W.S.

M.H.W.N.

CHART DATUM

L.W.Hts.m.

M.L.W.N.

M.L.W.S.

TIME ZONE (UT)	PORTSMOUTH	Dates in amber are SPRINGS
For Summer Time add ONE hour in **non-shaded areas**	LAT 50°48′N LONG 1°07′W	Dates in yellow are NEAPS
	TIMES AND HEIGHTS OF HIGH AND LOW WATERS	**2014**

JANUARY

#	Time	m	#	Time	m
1 W ●	0352 1047 1620 2317	0.9 4.9 0.6 4.8	**16** TH ○	0438 1131 1658	1.2 4.5 1.0
2 TH	0442 1132 1707	0.7 5.0 0.4	**17** F	0000 0515 1209 1732	4.5 1.1 4.5 0.9
3 F	0005 0529 1219 1753	4.9 0.6 5.0 0.4	**18** SA	0038 0548 1243 1804	4.5 1.1 4.5 0.9
4 SA	0056 0616 1307 1839	4.9 0.6 4.9 0.4	**19** SU	0111 0617 1313 1833	4.5 1.1 4.5 1.0
5 SU	0152 0702 1359 1925	4.9 0.7 4.8 0.6	**20** M	0141 0647 1343 1902	4.5 1.1 4.4 1.0
6 M	0255 0751 1458 2014	4.8 0.9 4.6 0.9	**21** TU	0212 0718 1416 1935	4.5 1.1 4.4 1.0
7 TU	0353 0843 1559 2108	4.7 1.2 4.4 1.2	**22** W	0247 0754 1455 2013	4.4 1.2 4.3 1.1
8 W ◑	0443 0945 1656 2213	4.5 1.5 4.2 1.5	**23** TH	0330 0837 1542 2058	4.3 1.3 4.1 1.3
9 TH	0534 1055 1755 2323	4.3 1.6 4.0 1.7	**24** F ◐	0421 0929 1641 2154	4.2 1.5 4.0 1.5
10 F	0631 1204 1858	4.2 1.8 3.9	**25** SA	0522 1035 1752 2308	4.1 1.7 3.9 1.7
11 SA	0029 0732 1307 2004	1.8 4.1 1.7 3.9	**26** SU	0633 1202 1911	4.0 1.7 3.9
12 SU	0129 0833 1404 2108	1.8 4.1 1.6 4.0	**27** M	0040 0747 1323 2027	1.7 4.1 1.5 4.1
13 M	0224 0926 1454 2200	1.7 4.2 1.4 4.2	**28** TU	0151 0852 1425 2127	1.5 4.4 1.2 4.4
14 TU	0313 1010 1539 2242	1.5 4.3 1.2 4.3	**29** W	0250 0945 1519 2218	1.2 4.6 0.8 4.6
15 W	0358 1051 1620 2322	1.3 4.4 1.1 4.4	**30** TH ●	0342 1032 1608 2305	0.9 4.8 0.5 4.8
			31 F	0431 1117 1655 2352	0.6 4.8 0.3 4.9

FEBRUARY

#	Time	m	#	Time	m
1 SA	0517 1203 1739	0.5 4.9 0.2	**16** SU	0012 0524 1220 1740	4.5 0.9 4.5 0.8
2 SU	0039 0601 1249 1822	4.9 0.4 4.9 0.3	**17** M	0044 0555 1251 1811	4.5 0.9 4.5 0.8
3 M	0131 0644 1339 1905	4.9 0.5 4.8 0.4	**18** TU	0114 0624 1320 1840	4.5 0.9 4.5 0.8
4 TU	0228 0728 1433 1949	4.8 0.7 4.6 0.7	**19** W	0144 0655 1351 1911	4.5 0.9 4.5 0.8
5 W	0321 0814 1529 2035	4.7 1.0 4.4 1.1	**20** TH	0216 0729 1427 1947	4.5 0.9 4.4 0.9
6 TH	0407 0904 1623 2129	4.5 1.3 4.2 1.4	**21** F	0255 0809 1512 2030	4.4 1.0 4.2 1.1
7 F	0453 1009 1719 2242	4.2 1.6 4.0 1.8	**22** SA ◐	0344 0857 1610 2122	4.2 1.3 4.1 1.4
8 SA	0548 1127 1823 2357	4.0 1.8 3.8 1.9	**23** SU	0448 0959 1726 2232	4.0 1.6 3.9 1.7
9 SU	0655 1237 1935	3.8 1.9 3.7	**24** M	0606 1133 1854	3.9 1.7 3.9
10 M	0105 0803 1341 2043	1.9 3.8 1.7 3.8	**25** TU	0028 0729 1312 2014	1.8 4.0 1.5 4.1
11 TU	0206 0902 1434 2138	1.8 4.0 1.5 4.0	**26** W	0144 0837 1414 2114	1.5 4.2 1.2 4.3
12 W	0256 0949 1513 2221	1.6 4.1 1.3 4.2	**27** TH	0241 0929 1506 2203	1.2 4.5 0.8 4.6
13 TH	0339 1031 1558 2259	1.4 4.3 1.1 4.4	**28** F	0331 1016 1553 2248	0.8 4.7 0.5 4.8
14 F ○	0417 1109 1635 2337	1.2 4.4 0.9 4.5			
15 SA	0453 1146 1709	1.0 4.5 0.8			

MARCH

#	Time	m	#	Time	m
1 SA ●	0416 1100 1638 2333	0.6 4.8 0.3 4.9	**16** SU ○	0424 1121 1640 2342	1.0 4.4 0.8 4.5
2 SU	0500 1144 1721	0.4 4.9 0.4	**17** M	0457 1154 1714	0.8 4.5 0.7
3 M	0018 0542 1230 1802	4.9 0.3 4.8 0.3	**18** TU	0014 0529 1225 1746	4.6 0.7 4.5 0.7
4 TU	0105 0623 1317 1843	4.9 0.4 4.8 0.4	**19** W	0045 0601 1256 1817	4.6 0.7 4.6 0.7
5 W	0154 0704 1407 1923	4.8 0.6 4.6 0.7	**20** TH	0116 0633 1329 1850	4.6 0.7 4.6 0.7
6 TH	0240 0744 1457 2003	4.6 0.9 4.5 1.1	**21** F	0150 0709 1408 1927	4.5 0.7 4.5 0.9
7 F	0323 0826 1547 2048	4.4 1.2 4.2 1.4	**22** SA	0230 0749 1456 2011	4.4 0.9 4.3 1.1
8 SA	0406 0916 1639 2149	4.2 1.6 4.0 1.8	**23** SU	0321 0837 1558 2103	4.3 1.2 4.1 1.4
9 SU	0457 1040 1743 2323	3.9 1.8 3.7 2.0	**24** M ◐	0428 0938 1715 2219	4.0 1.5 4.0 1.7
10 M	0610 1202 1902	3.6 1.9 3.6	**25** TU	0549 1127 1842	3.9 1.7 3.9
11 TU	0036 0729 1309 2013	2.0 3.6 1.9 3.7	**26** W	0024 0712 1258 1958	1.8 4.0 1.5 4.1
12 W	0141 0834 1405 2111	1.9 3.8 1.7 4.0	**27** TH	0133 0818 1357 2057	1.5 4.2 1.2 4.4
13 TH	0232 0924 1449 2154	1.7 4.0 1.4 4.2	**28** F	0226 0910 1448 2145	1.2 4.4 0.9 4.6
14 F	0312 1006 1528 2233	1.4 4.2 1.1 4.4	**29** SA	0313 0956 1534 2229	0.9 4.6 0.6 4.8
15 SA	0349 1045 1605 2309	1.2 4.4 0.9 4.5	**30** SU ●	0357 1040 1617 2312	0.6 4.7 0.4 4.8
			31 M	0440 1124 1700 2355	0.4 4.8 0.4 4.8

APRIL

#	Time	m	#	Time	m
1 TU	0521 1209 1740	0.4 4.7 0.4	**16** W	0502 1158 1720	0.7 4.6 0.7
2 W	0038 0601 1255 1819	4.8 0.5 4.7 0.6	**17** TH	0015 0537 1234 1756	4.7 0.6 4.6 0.7
3 TH	0121 0639 1343 1857	4.7 0.7 4.6 0.8	**18** F	0051 0614 1313 1833	4.7 0.6 4.6 0.7
4 F	0202 0717 1429 1935	4.6 0.9 4.5 1.1	**19** SA	0130 0653 1357 1914	4.6 0.7 4.6 0.9
5 SA	0243 0754 1515 2016	4.4 1.2 4.3 1.4	**20** SU	0215 0736 1451 2000	4.5 0.9 4.4 1.1
6 SU	0324 0836 1600 2105	4.1 1.5 4.1 1.8	**21** M	0311 0827 1557 2058	4.3 1.1 4.3 1.4
7 M	0409 0933 1655 2236	3.9 1.8 3.8 2.0	**22** TU ◐	0418 0932 1710 2223	4.1 1.4 4.1 1.7
8 TU	0508 1115 1815 2357	3.6 2.0 3.7 2.1	**23** W	0534 1114 1826	4.0 1.6 4.1
9 W	0645 1225 1935	1.9 1.9 3.7	**24** TH	0001 0650 1232 1937	1.7 4.0 1.4 4.3
10 TH	0102 0759 1322 2035	2.0 3.7 1.8 3.9	**25** F	0108 0755 1332 2036	1.5 4.2 1.2 4.4
11 F	0154 0853 1409 2122	1.8 3.9 1.5 4.2	**26** SA	0202 0849 1423 2124	1.2 4.3 1.0 4.6
12 SA	0236 0937 1450 2201	1.5 4.1 1.3 4.3	**27** SU	0250 0935 1510 2207	1.0 4.5 0.8 4.7
13 SU	0314 1016 1529 2237	1.2 4.3 1.0 4.5	**28** M	0335 1020 1554 2249	0.8 4.6 0.7 4.7
14 M	0350 1051 1607 2310	1.0 4.4 0.9 4.6	**29** TU ●	0418 1105 1637 2331	0.6 4.6 0.7 4.7
15 TU	0426 1124 1644 2342	0.8 4.6 0.7 4.6	**30** W	0459 1151 1718	0.6 4.6 0.7

Chart Datum: 2·73 metres below Ordnance Datum (Newlyn)
HAT is 5·1 metres above Chart Datum

TIDES

TIME ZONE (UT)	PORTSMOUTH	Dates in amber are **SPRINGS**
For Summer Time add ONE hour in **non-shaded areas**	**LAT 50°48′N LONG 1°07′W**	Dates in yellow are **NEAPS**

TIMES AND HEIGHTS OF HIGH AND LOW WATERS   2014

MAY

Day	Time	m	Day	Time	m
1 TH	0013	4.7	**16** F	0517	0.6
	0539	0.7		1214	4.7
	1237	4.6		1738	0.7
	1757	0.8			
2 F	0054	4.6	**17** SA	0030	4.8
	0617	0.8		0558	0.5
	1323	4.6		1300	4.7
	1835	1.0		1820	0.7
3 SA	0134	4.5	**18** SU	0115	4.7
	0654	1.0		0642	0.6
	1407	4.5		1350	4.7
	1913	1.2		1905	0.9
4 SU	0213	4.4	**19** M	0204	4.8
	0729	1.2		0728	0.8
	1449	4.3		1450	4.6
	1951	1.5		1955	1.1
5 M	0252	4.2	**20** TU	0302	4.4
	0808	1.4		0821	1.0
	1530	4.2		1555	4.5
	2033	1.7		2054	1.3
6 TU	0334	4.0	**21** W	0408	4.3
	0854	1.6		0926	1.3
	1615	4.0		1659	4.4
	2130	1.9		2209	1.5
7 W	0424	3.8	**22** TH	0516	4.1
	0959	1.8		1045	1.4
	1711	3.9		1804	4.3
	2256	2.0		2327	1.6
8 TH	0528	3.6	**23** F	0624	4.1
	1126	1.9		1158	1.4
	1832	3.8		1909	4.3
9 F	0006	2.0	**24** SA	0034	1.5
	0705	3.6		0727	4.1
	1229	1.8		1300	1.3
	1948	3.9		2008	4.4
10 SA	0103	1.8	**25** SU	0133	1.3
	0813	3.8		0824	4.2
	1321	1.6		1355	1.2
	2041	4.1		2100	4.5
11 SU	0150	1.6	**26** M	0224	1.2
	0901	4.0		0915	4.3
	1408	1.4		1444	1.1
	2123	4.3		2145	4.6
12 M	0233	1.3	**27** TU	0312	1.0
	0942	4.2		1003	4.4
	1451	1.2		1531	1.0
	2200	4.5		2228	4.6
13 TU	0314	1.1	**28** W	0356	0.9
	1018	4.4		1050	4.5
	1533	1.0		1615	1.0
	2235	4.6		2310	4.6
14 W	0355	0.8	**29** TH	0439	0.8
	1055	4.5		1136	4.5
	1615	0.8		1658	1.0
	2312	4.7		2352	4.6
15 TH	0436	0.7	**30** F	0521	0.8
	1133	4.7		1222	4.5
	1656	0.7		1739	1.0
	2350	4.8			
			31 SA	0032	4.5
				0559	0.9
				1306	4.5
				1817	1.1

JUNE

Day	Time	m	Day	Time	m
1 SU	0112	4.5	**16** M	0101	4.8
	0635	1.0		0632	0.5
	1348	4.5		1342	4.8
	1853	1.3		1856	0.7
2 M	0149	4.4	**17** TU	0152	4.7
	0709	1.2		0719	0.6
	1427	4.4		1442	4.8
	1928	1.4		1946	0.9
3 TU	0225	4.3	**18** W	0250	4.6
	0743	1.3		0810	0.8
	1504	4.3		1544	4.7
	2005	1.6		2040	1.1
4 W	0305	4.1	**19** TH	0352	4.4
	0822	1.5		0907	1.1
	1543	4.2		1641	4.6
	2048	1.7		2143	1.3
5 TH	0350	4.0	**20** F	0454	4.3
	0910	1.6		1014	1.3
	1628	4.1		1737	4.5
	2141	1.8		2252	1.5
6 F	0442	3.8	**21** SA	0556	4.2
	1008	1.8		1123	1.4
	1721	4.0		1836	4.4
	2246	1.9		2359	1.5
7 SA	0542	3.8	**22** SU	0658	4.1
	1119	1.8		1227	1.5
	1823	4.0		1936	4.3
	2357	1.9			
8 SU	0654	3.8	**23** M	0102	1.5
	1226	1.7		0759	4.1
	1932	4.1		1326	1.5
				2032	4.3
9 M	0057	1.7	**24** TU	0159	1.4
	0805	3.9		0858	4.2
	1323	1.5		1421	1.4
	2032	4.2		2123	4.4
10 TU	0150	1.4	**25** W	0250	1.2
	0859	4.1		0951	4.3
	1413	1.3		1511	1.3
	2119	4.4		2209	4.4
11 W	0240	1.2	**26** TH	0338	1.1
	0945	4.4		1039	4.3
	1502	1.1		1557	1.2
	2203	4.6		2252	4.5
12 TH	0327	0.9	**27** F	0422	1.0
	1029	4.5		1123	4.4
	1550	0.9		1641	1.1
	2247	4.7		2333	4.5
13 F	0414	0.7	**28** SA	0504	0.9
	1114	4.7		1205	4.5
	1636	0.8		1723	1.1
	2330	4.8			
14 SA	0500	0.5	**29** SU	0013	4.5
	1200	4.8		0542	0.9
	1723	0.7		1247	4.5
				1800	1.1
15 SU	0014	4.8	**30** M	0052	4.4
	0545	0.5		0617	1.0
	1248	4.8		1326	4.5
	1809	0.7		1834	1.2

JULY

Day	Time	m	Day	Time	m
1 TU	0128	4.4	**16** W	0135	4.8
	0649	1.1		0704	0.4
	1403	4.5		1425	4.9
	1905	1.3		1929	0.7
2 W	0201	4.3	**17** TH	0231	4.7
	0719	1.2		0751	0.7
	1436	4.4		1526	4.8
	1937	1.4		2019	0.9
3 TH	0236	4.2	**18** F	0331	4.5
	0752	1.3		0843	1.0
	1511	4.3		1618	4.7
	2013	1.5		2114	1.2
4 F	0316	4.1	**19** SA	0430	4.4
	0832	1.4		0942	1.3
	1552	4.2		1708	4.5
	2057	1.6		2218	1.5
5 SA	0403	4.0	**20** SU	0528	4.2
	0918	1.5		1050	1.5
	1640	4.2		1803	4.3
	2150	1.7		2326	1.6
6 SU	0457	3.9	**21** M	0629	4.0
	1016	1.6		1157	1.7
	1734	4.1		1903	4.1
	2254	1.7			
7 M	0600	3.9	**22** TU	0032	1.7
	1126	1.7		0735	3.9
	1836	4.1		1301	1.7
				2005	4.1
8 TU	0006	1.7	**23** W	0135	1.6
	0710	3.9		0843	4.0
	1239	1.6		1400	1.7
	1943	4.2		2103	4.2
9 W	0113	1.5	**24** TH	0231	1.5
	0821	4.1		0942	4.1
	1342	1.5		1454	1.5
	2047	4.3		2151	4.3
10 TH	0212	1.3	**25** F	0320	1.3
	0921	4.3		1025	4.1
	1438	1.2		1541	1.4
	2140	4.5		2233	4.4
11 F	0306	1.0	**26** SA	0404	1.1
	1012	4.5		1105	4.2
	1531	1.0		1624	1.2
	2227	4.7		2313	4.4
12 SA	0358	0.7	**27** SU	0445	1.0
	1059	4.7		1144	4.2
	1622	0.8		1704	1.1
	2312	4.8		2353	4.5
13 SU	0446	0.5	**28** M	0522	0.9
	1146	4.8		1223	4.5
	1710	0.6		1740	1.1
	2358	4.9			
14 M	0533	0.4	**29** TU	0030	4.5
	1234	4.9		0555	0.9
	1756	0.5		1301	4.5
				1812	1.1
15 TU	0044	4.9	**30** W	0105	4.4
	0618	0.3		0637	1.0
	1327	4.9		1335	4.5
	1842	0.6		1840	1.1
			31 TH	0135	4.4
				0653	1.0
				1405	4.5
				1909	1.2

AUGUST

Day	Time	m	Day	Time	m
1 F	0206	4.3	**16** SA	0305	4.6
	0723	1.1		0815	1.0
	1438	4.4		1548	4.6
	1942	1.2		2044	1.2
2 SA	0242	4.3	**17** SU	0402	4.4
	0758	1.2		0909	1.3
	1516	4.4		1635	4.4
	2020	1.3		2144	1.5
3 SU	0325	4.2	**18** M	0458	4.1
	0839	1.3		1018	1.7
	1601	4.2		1727	4.2
	2108	1.5		2256	1.7
4 M	0418	4.0	**19** TU	0600	3.9
	0930	1.5		1131	1.9
	1654	4.1		1830	4.0
	2207	1.6			
5 TU	0521	3.9	**20** W	0006	1.8
	1036	1.7		0710	3.8
	1758	4.0		1238	2.0
	2323	1.7		1938	3.9
6 W	0636	3.9	**21** TH	0111	1.8
	1204	1.8		0824	3.8
	1912	4.1		1341	1.9
				2041	4.0
7 TH	0046	1.6	**22** F	0209	1.6
	0758	4.0		0930	4.1
	1322	1.6		1435	1.7
	2025	4.3		2131	4.2
8 F	0155	1.3	**23** SA	0258	1.4
	0906	4.3		1007	4.3
	1424	1.3		1521	1.4
	2122	4.5		2212	4.3
9 SA	0252	1.0	**24** SU	0341	1.2
	0957	4.6		1043	4.4
	1519	1.0		1602	1.2
	2210	4.7		2252	4.4
10 SU	0344	0.7	**25** M	0420	1.0
	1043	4.8		1120	4.5
	1608	0.7		1640	1.1
	2255	4.9		2330	4.3
11 M	0432	0.4	**26** TU	0456	0.9
	1129	4.9		1157	4.6
	1655	0.5		1714	1.0
	2339	4.9			
12 TU	0517	0.3	**27** W	0006	4.5
	1215	5.0		0528	0.9
	1740	0.4		1232	4.6
				1745	1.0
13 W	0025	4.9	**28** TH	0039	4.5
	0601	0.3		0558	0.9
	1305	5.0		1304	4.6
	1824	0.5		1813	1.0
14 TH	0113	4.9	**29** F	0108	4.5
	0644	0.4		0627	1.0
	1359	4.9		1333	4.5
	1908	0.6		1842	1.0
15 F	0206	4.7	**30** SA	0136	4.5
	0728	0.6		0655	1.0
	1458	4.8		1403	4.5
	1954	0.9		1913	1.1
			31 SU	0209	4.4
				0728	1.1
				1438	4.5
				1949	1.1

Chart Datum: 2·73 metres below Ordnance Datum (Newlyn)
HAT is 5·1 metres above Chart Datum

TIME ZONE (UT)
For Summer Time add ONE hour in **non-shaded areas**

PORTSMOUTH
LAT 50°48'N   LONG 1°07'W
TIMES AND HEIGHTS OF HIGH AND LOW WATERS

Dates in amber are **SPRINGS**
Dates in yellow are **NEAPS**
2014

SEPTEMBER

Day	Time m	Day	Time m
1 M	0250 4.3 / 0807 1.2 / 2033 1.3	16 TU	0426 4.1 / 0942 1.8 / 2224 1.9 ◗
2 TU	0343 4.1 / 0855 1.5 / 1619 4.1 / 2130 1.6 ◗	17 W	0526 3.9 / 1104 2.0 / 1750 3.8 / 2337 2.0
3 W	0452 4.0 / 0959 1.8 / 1728 4.0 / 2249 1.8	18 TH	0639 3.8 / 1212 2.1 / 1906 3.7
4 TH	0615 3.9 / 1147 1.9 / 1851 4.0	19 F	0042 1.9 / 0756 3.8 / 1315 2.0 / 2014 3.9
5 F	0035 1.7 / 0744 4.0 / 1314 1.7 / 2009 4.2	20 SA	0140 1.8 / 0905 4.1 / 1410 1.8 / 2107 4.1
6 SA	0144 1.4 / 0850 4.3 / 1414 1.4 / 2105 4.5	21 SU	0229 1.5 / 0943 4.3 / 1455 1.5 / 2149 4.3
7 SU	0239 1.0 / 0940 4.6 / 1505 1.0 / 2152 4.7	22 M	0311 1.3 / 1018 4.5 / 1534 1.3 / 2228 4.4
8 M	0328 0.7 / 1025 4.9 / 1552 0.7 / 2236 4.9	23 TU	0349 1.1 / 1053 4.6 / 1610 1.1 / 2305 4.5
9 TU	0414 0.4 / 1109 5.0 / 1637 0.5 / 2319 5.0 ○	24 W	0425 1.0 / 1128 4.7 / 1644 1.0 / 2340 4.6 ●
10 W	0458 0.3 / 1153 5.0 / 1720 0.4	25 TH	0458 0.9 / 1201 4.7 / 1716 1.0
11 TH	0004 5.0 / 0540 0.3 / 1239 5.0 / 1802 0.5	26 F	0011 4.6 / 0530 0.6 / 1232 4.7 / 1746 0.9
12 F	0050 4.9 / 0622 0.6 / 1328 4.9 / 1844 0.6	27 SA	0040 4.6 / 0600 0.9 / 1301 4.6 / 1816 0.9
13 SA	0140 4.8 / 0703 0.7 / 1419 4.8 / 1927 0.8	28 SU	0110 4.6 / 0631 1.0 / 1331 4.6 / 1848 1.0
14 SU	0235 4.6 / 0746 1.1 / 1509 4.6 / 2011 1.2	29 M	0144 4.5 / 0705 1.1 / 1406 4.4 / 1925 1.1
15 M	0331 4.4 / 0834 1.5 / 1555 4.3 / 2105 1.6	30 TU	0226 4.4 / 0744 1.2 / 1452 4.4 / 2009 1.3

OCTOBER

Day	Time m	Day	Time m
1 W	0322 4.2 / 0833 1.5 / 1553 4.2 / 2105 1.6 ◗	16 TH	0446 4.0 / 1031 2.1 / 1700 3.8 / 2302 2.0
2 TH	0437 4.1 / 0939 1.9 / 1709 4.0 / 2231 1.8	17 F	0557 3.8 / 1141 2.2 / 1822 3.7
3 F	0603 4.0 / 1151 2.0 / 1834 4.0	18 SA	0006 2.0 / 0714 3.9 / 1242 2.1 / 1937 3.8
4 SA	0025 1.7 / 0727 4.1 / 1303 1.7 / 1948 4.2	19 SU	0103 1.9 / 0821 4.0 / 1336 1.9 / 2036 4.0
5 SU	0127 1.4 / 0831 4.4 / 1358 1.4 / 2044 4.5	20 M	0152 1.7 / 0909 4.3 / 1420 1.7 / 2122 4.2
6 M	0220 1.1 / 0921 4.7 / 1447 1.1 / 2131 4.7	21 TU	0234 1.5 / 0948 4.5 / 1459 1.4 / 2202 4.4
7 TU	0307 0.8 / 1004 4.9 / 1532 0.8 / 2215 4.9	22 W	0313 1.2 / 1024 4.6 / 1535 1.2 / 2238 4.5
8 M	0352 0.6 / 1047 5.0 / 1616 0.6 / 2258 4.9 ○	23 TH	0350 1.1 / 1058 4.7 / 1611 1.0 / 2312 4.6 ●
9 TH	0435 0.5 / 1130 5.0 / 1659 0.5 / 2343 4.9	24 F	0427 1.0 / 1130 4.7 / 1646 0.9 / 2343 4.7
10 F	0517 0.5 / 1213 5.0 / 1740 0.6	25 SA	0502 0.9 / 1200 4.8 / 1720 0.9
11 SA	0028 4.9 / 0558 0.6 / 1258 4.9 / 1820 0.7	26 SU	0015 4.7 / 0536 0.9 / 1233 4.8 / 1754 0.8
12 SU	0116 4.8 / 0638 0.9 / 1342 4.7 / 1901 1.0	27 M	0050 4.7 / 0611 1.0 / 1307 4.7 / 1830 0.9
13 M	0207 4.6 / 0719 1.2 / 1427 4.6 / 1942 1.3	28 TU	0129 4.7 / 0649 1.1 / 1347 4.6 / 1910 1.0
14 TU	0259 4.4 / 0803 1.5 / 1513 4.3 / 2027 1.6	29 W	0216 4.5 / 0732 1.3 / 1436 4.4 / 1956 1.3
15 W	0350 4.2 / 0859 1.9 / 1602 4.1 / 2136 1.9 ◗	30 TH	0317 4.4 / 0823 1.6 / 1540 4.2 / 2053 1.5
		31 F	0432 4.2 / 0933 1.9 / 1655 4.1 / 2222 1.7 ◗

NOVEMBER

Day	Time m	Day	Time m
1 SA	0548 4.2 / 1131 1.9 / 1813 4.1	16 SU	0614 3.9 / 1200 2.1 / 1844 3.7
2 SU	0001 1.7 / 0703 4.3 / 1240 1.7 / 1923 4.2	17 M	0017 2.0 / 0730 4.0 / 1254 2.0 / 1954 3.9
3 M	0103 1.5 / 0807 4.5 / 1335 1.4 / 2021 4.4	18 TU	0108 1.8 / 0827 4.2 / 1339 1.8 / 2048 4.1
4 TU	0155 1.2 / 0859 4.7 / 1424 1.2 / 2109 4.6	19 W	0153 1.6 / 0913 4.4 / 1420 1.5 / 2132 4.3
5 W	0243 1.0 / 0943 4.8 / 1510 0.9 / 2155 4.7	20 TH	0235 1.4 / 0951 4.5 / 1459 1.3 / 2210 4.4
6 TH	0329 0.8 / 1025 4.9 / 1554 0.8 / 2240 4.7 ○	21 F	0316 1.2 / 1025 4.7 / 1539 1.1 / 2244 4.6
7 F	0413 0.7 / 1107 4.9 / 1637 0.7 / 2325 4.8	22 SA	0356 1.0 / 1059 4.7 / 1618 0.9 / 2318 4.7 ●
8 SA	0455 0.7 / 1150 4.9 / 1719 0.7	23 SU	0436 0.9 / 1134 4.8 / 1658 0.8 / 2355 4.8
9 SU	0011 4.8 / 0537 0.7 / 1233 4.8 / 1759 0.8	24 M	0516 0.9 / 1210 4.8 / 1738 0.7
10 M	0058 4.7 / 0617 1.0 / 1315 4.7 / 1839 1.0	25 TU	0035 4.8 / 0556 0.9 / 1250 4.8 / 1818 0.8
11 TU	0146 4.6 / 0657 1.2 / 1357 4.5 / 1917 1.2	26 W	0120 4.8 / 0639 1.0 / 1334 4.7 / 1902 0.9
12 W	0232 4.5 / 0737 1.5 / 1439 4.3 / 1957 1.5	27 TH	0211 4.7 / 0725 1.2 / 1426 4.6 / 1949 1.1
13 TH	0318 4.3 / 0822 1.8 / 1523 4.1 / 2043 1.8	28 F	0314 4.5 / 0817 1.4 / 1529 4.4 / 2046 1.3
14 F	0405 4.1 / 0924 2.1 / 1613 3.9 / 2156 2.0 ◗	29 SA	0422 4.4 / 0924 1.6 / 1639 4.2 / 2200 1.5
15 SA	0501 4.0 / 1055 2.2 / 1715 3.8 / 2318 2.0	30 SU	0528 4.4 / 1053 1.7 / 1748 4.2 / 2326 1.6

DECEMBER

Day	Time m	Day	Time m
1 M	0634 4.4 / 1208 1.7 / 1854 4.2	16 TU	0601 4.0 / 1147 2.1 / 1833 3.8
2 TU	0032 1.5 / 0737 4.5 / 1308 1.5 / 1954 4.3	17 W	0011 1.9 / 0717 4.0 / 1248 1.9 / 1958 3.9
3 W	0129 1.4 / 0833 4.6 / 1400 1.3 / 2049 4.4	18 TH	0107 1.8 / 0825 4.1 / 1338 1.7 / 2056 4.1
4 TH	0220 1.2 / 0922 4.7 / 1448 1.1 / 2139 4.5	19 F	0157 1.6 / 0913 4.4 / 1424 1.4 / 2140 4.3
5 F	0307 1.1 / 1006 4.7 / 1534 1.0 / 2227 4.6	20 SA	0244 1.3 / 0953 4.5 / 1510 1.1 / 2220 4.5
6 SA	0353 1.0 / 1049 4.8 / 1619 0.9 / 2314 4.6	21 SU	0330 1.1 / 1033 4.7 / 1555 0.9 / 2259 4.7
7 SU	0437 1.0 / 1131 4.7 / 1702 0.8 / 2359 4.7	22 M	0416 0.9 / 1113 4.8 / 1640 0.7 / 2340 4.8 ●
8 M	0520 1.0 / 1213 4.7 / 1743 0.9	23 TU	0501 0.8 / 1153 4.9 / 1724 0.6
9 TU	0044 4.6 / 0600 1.1 / 1254 4.6 / 1821 1.0	24 W	0023 4.8 / 0545 0.7 / 1236 4.9 / 1808 0.5
10 W	0128 4.6 / 0639 1.3 / 1334 4.5 / 1857 1.1	25 TH	0110 4.8 / 0629 0.8 / 1322 4.8 / 1853 0.6
11 TH	0209 4.5 / 0715 1.4 / 1412 4.4 / 1932 1.3	26 F	0203 4.8 / 0716 0.9 / 1414 4.7 / 1939 0.8
12 F	0249 4.4 / 0751 1.6 / 1450 4.2 / 2008 1.5	27 SA	0303 4.7 / 0806 1.1 / 1513 4.5 / 2031 1.0
13 SA	0327 4.3 / 0830 1.8 / 1532 4.1 / 2050 1.7	28 SU	0405 4.6 / 0903 1.3 / 1618 4.4 / 2132 1.3 ◗
14 SU	0410 4.1 / 0919 2.0 / 1621 3.9 / 2144 1.9	29 M	0504 4.5 / 1014 1.5 / 1722 4.2 / 2247 1.5
15 M	0501 4.0 / 1026 2.1 / 1719 3.8 / 2258 2.0	30 TU	0603 4.4 / 1131 1.6 / 1825 4.1 / 2359 1.6
		31 W	0705 4.3 / 1238 1.6 / 1929 4.1

TIDES

Chart Datum: 2·73 metres below Ordnance Datum (Newlyn)
HAT is 5·1 metres above Chart Datum

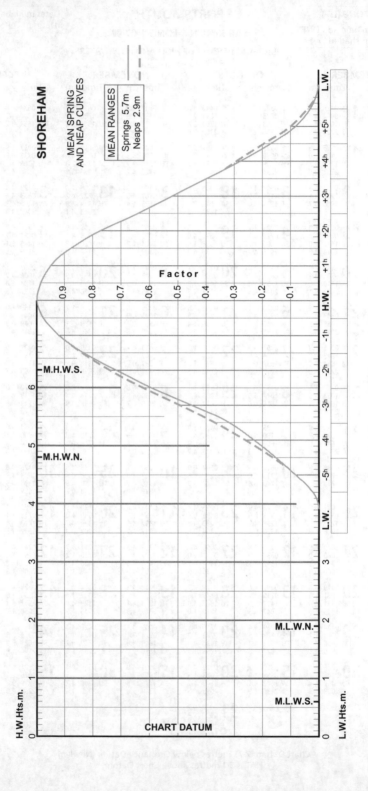

SHOREHAM

MEAN SPRING
AND NEAP CURVES

MEAN RANGES
Springs 5.7m
Neaps 2.9m

Factor

SHOREHAM

LAT 50°50'N   LONG 0°15'W

TIMES AND HEIGHTS OF HIGH AND LOW WATERS

Dates in amber are **SPRINGS**
Dates in yellow are **NEAPS**

2014

JANUARY

#	Time m	#	Time m
1	0431 0.8 / 1040 6.5 / W 1658 0.5 / ● 2311 6.5	16	0515 1.1 / 1124 5.9 / TH 1735 0.9 / ○ 2348 6.0
2	0521 0.6 / 1129 6.6 / TH 1748 0.4	17	0550 1.0 / 1154 6.0 / F 1810 0.9
3	0001 6.6 / 0610 0.5 / F 1219 6.7 / 1836 0.3	18	0018 6.0 / 0624 1.0 / SA 1223 6.0 / 1844 0.9
4	0051 6.7 / 0659 0.5 / SA 1308 6.6 / 1925 0.3	19	0046 6.0 / 0657 1.0 / SU 1251 5.9 / 1916 0.9
5	0140 6.6 / 0748 0.6 / SU 1357 6.4 / 2015 0.5	20	0112 6.0 / 0728 1.1 / M 1321 5.9 / 1946 1.0
6	0227 6.5 / 0838 0.8 / M 1445 6.2 / 2104 0.7	21	0141 5.9 / 0758 1.2 / TU 1353 5.8 / 2014 1.1
7	0315 6.2 / 0930 1.0 / TU 1535 5.8 / 2155 1.0	22	0215 5.8 / 0830 1.3 / W 1430 5.7 / 2048 1.2
8	0405 5.9 / 1025 1.3 / W 1628 5.5 / ◑ 2251 1.4	23	0254 5.7 / 0911 1.4 / TH 1513 5.5 / 2132 1.4
9	0459 5.5 / 1128 1.6 / TH 1728 5.1 / 2357 1.7	24	0341 5.5 / 1003 1.6 / F 1605 5.2 / ◑ 2228 1.7
10	0602 5.2 / F 1840 4.9	25	0441 5.2 / 1111 1.8 / SA 1716 5.0 / 2344 1.8
11	0109 1.8 / 0716 5.1 / SA 1347 1.7 / 2001 5.0	26	0605 5.1 / 1235 1.7 / SU 1854 5.0
12	0214 1.8 / 0829 5.2 / SU 1446 1.6 / 2105 5.2	27	0112 1.7 / 0732 5.3 / M 1354 1.5 / 2010 5.3
13	0309 1.6 / 0925 5.5 / M 1536 1.4 / 2156 5.5	28	0227 1.5 / 0839 5.7 / TU 1500 1.1 / 2113 5.8
14	0357 1.4 / 1011 5.7 / TU 1620 1.1 / 2238 5.7	29	0327 1.1 / 0937 6.1 / W 1555 0.7 / 2209 6.2
15	0438 1.2 / 1050 5.8 / W 1659 1.0 / 2315 5.9	30	0420 0.7 / 1030 6.4 / TH 1646 0.4 / ● 2302 6.5
		31	0509 0.5 / 1121 6.6 / F 1734 0.2 / 2351 6.7

FEBRUARY

#	Time m	#	Time m
1	0557 0.3 / 1209 6.7 / SA 1822 0.2	16	0603 0.9 / 1200 6.0 / SU 1822 0.8
2	0039 6.8 / 0646 0.3 / SU 1257 6.7 / 1908 0.2	17	0021 6.1 / 0635 0.9 / M 1230 6.1 / 1853 0.8
3	0124 6.8 / 0730 0.4 / M 1342 6.6 / 1953 0.3	18	0048 6.1 / 0705 0.9 / TU 1300 6.1 / 1921 0.8
4	0207 6.5 / 0815 0.5 / TU 1424 6.3 / 2037 0.6	19	0118 6.1 / 0732 0.9 / W 1332 6.0 / 1948 0.9
5	0248 6.3 / 0858 0.8 / W 1507 6.0 / 2120 0.9	20	0151 6.0 / 0804 1.0 / TH 1407 5.9 / 2022 1.0
6	0330 5.9 / 0943 1.2 / TH 1552 5.5 / ◐ 2206 1.3	21	0228 5.9 / 0843 1.1 / F 1447 5.7 / 2105 1.2
7	0417 5.5 / 1034 1.6 / F 1645 5.1 / 2300 1.7	22	0312 5.6 / 0932 1.4 / SA 1537 5.4 / 2159 1.5
8	0513 5.0 / 1143 1.9 / SA 1749 4.8	23	0408 5.3 / 1037 1.6 / SU 1643 5.0 / 2314 1.8
9	0023 2.0 / 0621 4.8 / SU 1315 2.0 / 1910 4.7	24	0528 5.0 / 1204 1.8 / M 1827 4.9
10	0147 2.0 / 0750 4.8 / M 1421 1.8 / 2041 4.9	25	0050 1.8 / 0711 5.1 / TU 1335 1.6 / 1955 5.2
11	0248 1.8 / 0903 5.1 / TU 1514 1.5 / 2136 5.3	26	0213 1.5 / 0826 5.5 / W 1446 1.2 / 2102 5.7
12	0337 1.5 / 0952 5.4 / W 1559 1.2 / 2218 5.6	27	0315 1.1 / 0927 5.9 / TH 1542 0.7 / 2159 6.1
13	0418 1.3 / 1030 5.7 / TH 1638 1.0 / 2254 5.8	28	0407 0.7 / 1020 6.3 / F 1631 0.4 / 2250 6.5
14	0455 1.1 / 1103 5.9 / F 1713 0.9 / ○ 2326 6.0		
15	0529 0.9 / 1133 6.0 / SA 1748 0.8 / 2355 6.0		

MARCH

#	Time m	#	Time m
1	0454 0.4 / 1109 6.6 / SA 1718 0.2 / ● 2337 6.7	16	0503 0.9 / 1104 5.9 / SU 1721 0.8 / ○ 2324 6.1
2	0540 0.2 / 1156 6.7 / SU 1803 0.1	17	0537 0.8 / 1135 6.1 / M 1755 0.7 / 2353 6.1
3	0021 6.8 / 0624 0.2 / M 1240 6.7 / 1846 0.2	18	0610 0.7 / 1206 6.1 / TU 1828 0.7
4	0103 6.7 / 0707 0.3 / TU 1322 6.6 / 1928 0.3	19	0023 6.2 / 0640 0.7 / W 1239 6.2 / 1856 0.7
5	0142 6.6 / 0748 0.5 / W 1401 6.3 / 2007 0.5	20	0055 6.2 / 0709 0.7 / TH 1312 6.2 / 1927 0.7
6	0219 6.3 / 0826 0.7 / TH 1438 6.0 / 2045 0.9	21	0130 6.2 / 0745 0.8 / F 1349 6.1 / 2004 0.9
7	0256 5.9 / 0904 1.1 / F 1519 5.6 / 2125 1.3	22	0208 6.0 / 0826 0.9 / SA 1431 5.8 / 2049 1.1
8	0337 5.4 / 0947 1.5 / SA 1607 5.1 / ◐ 2212 1.7	23	0252 5.7 / 0915 1.2 / SU 1521 5.5 / 2145 1.5
9	0430 4.9 / 1042 1.9 / SU 1709 4.7 / 2317 2.1	24	0349 5.3 / 1020 1.5 / M 1630 5.1 / ◑ 2301 1.7
10	0537 4.6 / 1210 2.1 / M 1821 4.6	25	0511 5.0 / 1147 1.7 / TU 1812 5.0
11	0111 2.2 / 0654 4.5 / TU 1350 2.0 / 1959 4.7	26	0037 1.8 / 0654 5.0 / W 1319 1.5 / 1940 5.2
12	0221 2.0 / 0829 4.8 / W 1446 1.7 / 2106 5.1	27	0158 1.4 / 0812 5.4 / TH 1429 1.1 / 2049 5.7
13	0311 1.6 / 0923 5.2 / TH 1531 1.4 / 2149 5.5	28	0259 1.0 / 0913 5.8 / F 1524 0.7 / 2144 6.1
14	0352 1.3 / 1002 5.5 / F 1610 1.1 / 2224 5.8	29	0349 0.6 / 1005 6.2 / SA 1612 0.4 / 2232 6.5
15	0428 1.1 / 1034 5.8 / SA 1646 0.9 / 2255 5.9	30	0435 0.4 / 1053 6.4 / SU 1657 0.3 / ● 2317 6.6
		31	0520 0.3 / 1138 6.6 / M 1740 0.2 / 2359 6.7

APRIL

#	Time m	#	Time m
1	0602 0.3 / 1220 6.6 / TU 1822 0.3	16	0543 0.7 / 1143 6.2 / W 1800 0.7 / 2359 6.3
2	0039 6.6 / 0642 0.4 / W 1300 6.4 / 1901 0.4	17	0617 0.6 / 1219 6.3 / TH 1835 0.7
3	0116 6.4 / 0721 0.5 / TH 1337 6.2 / 1939 0.7	18	0035 6.3 / 0653 0.6 / F 1257 6.2 / 1912 0.7
4	0150 6.1 / 0757 0.8 / F 1412 6.0 / 2015 0.9	19	0113 6.2 / 0733 0.6 / SA 1337 6.1 / 1954 0.8
5	0224 5.8 / 0833 1.1 / SA 1450 5.6 / 2053 1.3	20	0155 6.0 / 0817 0.8 / SU 1423 5.9 / 2043 1.1
6	0301 5.4 / 0913 1.4 / SU 1535 5.2 / 2138 1.7	21	0243 5.7 / 0910 1.1 / M 1517 5.6 / 2141 1.3
7	0349 5.0 / 1003 1.8 / M 1633 4.8 / 2236 2.0	22	0342 5.4 / 1014 1.3 / TU 1628 5.3 / ◑ 2255 1.6
8	0457 4.6 / 1109 2.0 / TU 1740 4.6 / 2355 2.2	23	0503 5.1 / 1135 1.5 / W 1757 5.2
9	0609 4.5 / 1250 2.1 / W 1852 4.7	24	0021 1.6 / 0635 5.1 / TH 1259 1.4 / 1920 5.3
10	0139 2.1 / 0722 4.6 / TH 1406 1.8 / 2007 5.0	25	0137 1.4 / 0752 5.3 / F 1407 1.1 / 2027 5.7
11	0235 1.7 / 0829 5.0 / F 1455 1.5 / 2101 5.3	26	0237 1.0 / 0853 5.7 / SA 1501 0.8 / 2122 6.0
12	0318 1.4 / 0916 5.3 / SA 1535 1.2 / 2140 5.7	27	0328 0.7 / 0946 6.0 / SU 1550 0.6 / 2210 6.3
13	0356 1.1 / 0954 5.7 / SU 1613 1.0 / 2215 5.9	28	0414 0.5 / 1033 6.2 / M 1635 0.5 / 2254 6.4
14	0432 0.9 / 1030 5.9 / M 1649 0.8 / 2250 6.1	29	0458 0.5 / 1117 6.3 / TU 1718 0.5 / ● 2336 6.4
15	0507 0.8 / 1106 6.1 / TU 1725 0.7 / ○ 2324 6.2	30	0540 0.6 / 1159 6.3 / W 1759 0.5

Chart Datum: 3·27 metres below Ordnance Datum (Newlyn)
HAT is 6·9 metres above Chart Datum

TIDES

TIME ZONE (UT)
For Summer Time add ONE hour in **non-shaded areas**

SHOREHAM
LAT 50°50′N   LONG 0°15′W
TIMES AND HEIGHTS OF HIGH AND LOW WATERS

Dates in amber are **SPRINGS**
Dates in yellow are **NEAPS**

2014

MAY

Day	Time	m	Time	m		Day	Time	m	Time	m
1 TH	0015	6.4	0619	0.5		16 F	0557	0.5	1203	6.3
	1238	6.3	1837	0.7			1817	0.6		
2 F	0051	6.2	0657	0.6		17 SA	0019	6.4	0639	0.5
	1314	6.1	1914	0.8			1246	6.3	1901	0.6
3 SA	0124	6.0	0732	0.8		18 SU	0102	6.3	0724	0.5
	1349	5.9	1949	1.0			1332	6.2	1948	0.7
4 SU	0157	5.7	0808	1.0		19 M	0148	6.1	0813	0.7
	1425	5.7	2027	1.3			1421	6.1	2039	0.9
5 M	0231	5.4	0847	1.3		20 TU	0239	5.9	0907	0.9
	1506	5.4	2111	1.6			1517	5.8	2137	1.1
6 TU	0314	5.1	0933	1.6		21 W	0339	5.6	1008	1.1
	1557	5.1	2203	1.9			1621	5.6	2245	1.3
7 W	0414	4.8	1030	1.8		22 TH	0450	5.3	1119	1.3
	1659	4.8	2306	2.0			1734	5.4	2359	1.4
8 TH	0525	4.6	1138	2.0		23 F	0609	5.2	1232	1.3
	1804	4.8					1851	5.5		
9 F	0021	2.0	0631	4.7		24 SA	0110	1.3	0724	5.3
	1255	1.9	1907	5.0			1339	1.2	1958	5.6
10 SA	0137	1.8	0733	4.9		25 SU	0211	1.1	0828	5.5
	1402	1.7	2004	5.2			1436	1.1	2056	5.8
11 SU	0232	1.5	0826	5.2		26 M	0304	0.9	0923	5.7
	1451	1.4	2052	5.6			1527	0.9	2146	6.0
12 M	0316	1.2	0913	5.5		27 TU	0352	0.8	1012	5.9
	1534	1.2	2136	5.8			1613	0.8	2232	6.1
13 TU	0356	1.0	0957	5.8		28 W	0437	0.7	1058	6.0
	1615	1.0	2217	6.1			1657	0.8	2314	6.2
14 W	0436	0.8	1039	6.0		29 TH	0519	0.7	1139	6.1
	1655	0.8	2257	6.2			1738	0.8	2353	6.1
15 TH	0515	0.6	1121	6.2		30 F	0559	0.7	1218	6.1
	1735	0.7	2337	6.3			1817	0.9		
						31 SA	0029	6.0	0636	0.8
							1254	6.0	1853	0.9

JUNE

Day	Time	m	Time	m		Day	Time	m	Time	m
1 SU	0102	5.9	0712	0.9		16 M	0055	6.4	0715	0.4
	1329	5.9	1928	1.1			1327	6.4	1940	0.6
2 M	0134	5.7	0747	1.0		17 TU	0144	6.3	0806	0.5
	1402	5.7	2005	1.2			1417	6.3	2031	0.7
3 TU	0206	5.5	0825	1.2		18 W	0235	6.1	0858	0.7
	1437	5.5	2045	1.4			1510	6.1	2126	0.9
4 W	0242	5.3	0906	1.4		19 TH	0330	5.8	0954	0.9
	1517	5.3	2131	1.6			1605	5.9	2226	1.1
5 TH	0326	5.0	0953	1.6		20 F	0429	5.6	1056	1.1
	1606	5.1	2224	1.8			1705	5.7	2332	1.3
6 F	0424	4.8	1049	1.8		21 SA	0535	5.3	1202	1.3
	1709	5.0	2325	1.9			1812	5.5		
7 SA	0538	4.8	1152	1.8		22 SU	0040	1.4	0648	5.2
	1815	5.0					1309	1.4	1923	5.4
8 SU	0030	1.8	0644	4.9		23 M	0144	1.4	0800	5.2
	1258	1.8	1915	5.2			1411	1.4	2028	5.5
9 M	0134	1.6	0743	5.1		24 TU	0241	1.2	0901	5.4
	1400	1.6	2010	5.4			1505	1.3	2124	5.7
10 TU	0231	1.4	0836	5.4		25 W	0333	1.1	0954	5.6
	1454	1.3	2101	5.7			1554	1.1	2212	5.8
11 W	0320	1.1	0926	5.7		26 TH	0419	1.0	1040	5.8
	1543	1.1	2148	6.0			1639	1.0	2256	5.9
12 TH	0407	0.8	1014	6.0		27 F	0501	0.9	1122	5.9
	1629	0.9	2234	6.2			1720	1.0	2334	5.9
13 F	0453	0.6	1102	6.2		28 SA	0541	0.9	1200	6.0
	1715	0.7	2320	6.4			1758	1.0		
14 SA	0539	0.5	1150	6.4		29 SU	0009	5.9	0617	0.9
	1803	0.6					1236	6.0	1834	1.0
15 SU	0007	6.4	0626	0.4		30 M	0042	5.9	0652	0.9
	1239	6.4	1850	0.6			1308	5.9	1908	1.0

JULY

Day	Time	m	Time	m		Day	Time	m	Time	m
1 TU	0111	5.8	0727	1.0		16 W	0135	6.5	0752	0.3
	1338	5.8	1944	1.1			1406	6.6	2017	0.5
2 W	0141	5.6	0802	1.1		17 TH	0224	6.3	0841	0.5
	1406	5.7	2020	1.2			1453	6.4	2107	0.7
3 TH	0212	5.5	0837	1.2		18 F	0312	6.0	0932	0.7
	1438	5.6	2057	1.4			1541	6.1	2200	1.0
4 F	0248	5.4	0914	1.4		19 SA	0403	5.7	1026	1.1
	1516	5.4	2139	1.6			1633	5.7	2259	1.3
5 SA	0331	5.2	0958	1.6		20 SU	0500	5.3	1127	1.4
	1603	5.2	2231	1.7			1731	5.4		
6 SU	0425	5.0	1053	1.7		21 M	0006	1.6	0606	5.0
	1704	5.1	2334	1.8			1238	1.7	1840	5.2
7 M	0540	4.9	1201	1.8		22 TU	0117	1.6	0728	5.0
	1823	5.1					1347	1.7	1959	5.1
8 TU	0043	1.7	0700	5.0		23 W	0220	1.6	0842	5.1
	1314	1.7	1932	5.3			1446	1.6	2105	5.3
9 W	0151	1.5	0805	5.3		24 TH	0315	1.4	0938	5.4
	1420	1.5	2032	5.6			1537	1.4	2156	5.6
10 TH	0252	1.2	0902	5.7		25 F	0401	1.2	1024	5.7
	1518	1.2	2126	6.0			1622	1.2	2239	5.7
11 F	0345	0.9	0956	6.0		26 SA	0443	1.0	1105	5.9
	1610	0.9	2217	6.2			1702	1.1	2317	5.9
12 SA	0435	0.6	1048	6.3		27 SU	0521	0.9	1141	6.0
	1700	0.6	2307	6.4			1739	1.0	2350	5.9
13 SU	0524	0.4	1139	6.5		28 M	0557	0.9	1214	6.0
	1749	0.5	2357	6.5			1813	1.0		
14 M	0613	0.3	1229	6.6		29 TU	0019	5.9	0631	0.9
	1838	0.4					1244	6.0	1847	1.0
15 TU	0046	6.6	0702	0.3		30 W	0047	6.0	0704	0.9
	1318	6.6	1927	0.4			1309	6.0	1920	1.0
						31 TH	0114	5.8	0736	1.0
							1335	5.9	1952	1.1

AUGUST

Day	Time	m	Time	m		Day	Time	m	Time	m
1 F	0143	5.8	0806	1.1		16 SA	0249	6.1	0903	0.8
	1405	5.8	2022	1.2			1513	6.1	2127	1.0
2 SA	0216	5.6	0836	1.2		17 SU	0335	5.7	0950	1.2
	1440	5.7	2057	1.4			1600	5.7	2218	1.4
3 SU	0255	5.5	0914	1.4		18 M	0426	5.3	1044	1.6
	1522	5.5	2142	1.5			1653	5.3	2323	1.8
4 M	0343	5.2	1005	1.6		19 TU	0528	4.9	1200	1.8
	1615	5.3	2242	1.7			1758	4.9		
5 TU	0445	5.0	1112	1.8		20 W	0048	1.9	0648	4.8
	1728	5.1	2359	1.8			1323	2.0	1925	4.8
6 W	0619	4.9	1237	1.8		21 TH	0159	1.8	0821	4.9
	1901	5.2					1427	1.8	2045	5.1
7 TH	0121	1.6	0741	5.2		22 F	0255	1.6	0920	5.3
	1357	1.6	2011	5.5			1518	1.6	2138	5.4
8 F	0232	1.3	0846	5.6		23 SA	0341	1.4	1005	5.6
	1502	1.2	2110	5.9			1602	1.3	2219	5.7
9 SA	0330	0.9	0943	6.0		24 SU	0421	1.1	1043	5.9
	1556	0.9	2204	6.3			1640	1.1	2255	5.9
10 SU	0421	0.6	1036	6.4		25 M	0458	0.9	1117	6.0
	1645	0.6	2255	6.5			1715	0.9	2326	6.0
11 M	0509	0.3	1126	6.6		26 TU	0532	0.9	1148	6.1
	1734	0.4	2345	6.7			1749	0.9	2353	6.0
12 TU	0557	0.2	1215	6.8		27 W	0606	0.8	1214	6.1
	1821	0.3					1823	0.9		
13 W	0033	6.7	0644	0.2		28 TH	0019	6.1	0639	0.9
	1302	6.8	1908	0.3			1239	6.1	1854	0.9
14 TH	0120	6.6	0731	0.3		29 F	0047	6.0	0709	0.9
	1347	6.7	1955	0.4			1306	6.1	1923	1.0
15 F	0205	6.4	0817	0.5		30 SA	0117	6.0	0735	1.0
	1430	6.5	2041	0.7			1336	6.0	1951	1.1
						31 SU	0149	5.9	0804	1.1
							1410	5.9	2025	1.2

Chart Datum: 3·27 metres below Ordnance Datum (Newlyn)
HAT is 6·9 metres above Chart Datum

TIME ZONE (UT)	SHOREHAM	Dates in amber are SPRINGS
For Summer Time add ONE hour in **non-shaded areas**	LAT 50°50'N LONG 0°15'W	Dates in yellow are NEAPS
	TIMES AND HEIGHTS OF HIGH AND LOW WATERS	**2014**

SEPTEMBER

Time	m		Time	m
1 0227	5.7	**16** 0354	5.3
0844	1.3	1001	1.7
M 1451	5.6	TU 1617	5.1
2110	1.4	◖ 2231	1.9
2 0312	5.4	**17** 0453	4.9
0935	1.6	1106	2.1
TU 1541	5.3	W 1721	4.8
◖ 2208	1.7		
3 0412	5.1	**18** 0002	2.2
1042	1.9	0604	4.7
W 1652	5.0	TH 1252	2.2
2327	1.9	1838	4.7
4 0551	4.9	**19** 0131	2.1
1213	1.9	0747	4.8
TH 1838	5.0	F 1402	2.0
		2017	4.9
5 0059	1.7	**20** 0229	1.8
0724	5.1	0852	5.2
F 1341	1.7	SA 1454	1.7
1955	5.4	2112	5.3
6 0217	1.4	**21** 0315	1.5
0833	5.6	0937	5.6
SA 1448	1.3	SU 1536	1.4
2058	5.9	2152	5.6
7 0315	0.9	**22** 0355	1.2
0930	6.1	1013	5.9
SU 1541	0.8	M 1614	1.1
2152	6.3	2226	5.9
8 0405	0.5	**23** 0430	1.0
1022	6.5	1045	6.1
M 1629	0.5	TU 1648	1.0
2242	6.6	2255	6.0
9 0451	0.3	**24** 0505	0.9
1110	6.8	1114	6.1
TU 1715	0.4	W 1722	0.9
○ 2329	6.7	● 2323	6.1
10 0537	0.2	**25** 0539	0.9
1156	6.9	1140	6.2
W 1801	0.3	TH 1756	0.9
		2352	6.1
11 0015	6.8	**26** 0612	0.9
0622	0.2	1208	6.2
TH 1241	6.9	F 1828	0.9
1845	0.3		
12 0100	6.7	**27** 0022	6.2
0706	0.3	0641	0.9
F 1323	6.7	SA 1239	6.2
1929	0.5	1856	0.9
13 0142	6.5	**28** 0054	6.1
0748	0.6	0709	1.0
SA 1403	6.4	SU 1311	6.1
2011	0.7	1927	1.0
14 0222	6.2	**29** 0128	6.0
0830	0.9	0742	1.1
SU 1443	6.1	M 1346	6.0
2052	1.1	2004	1.1
15 0305	5.7	**30** 0206	5.9
0912	1.3	0824	1.3
M 1526	5.6	TU 1428	5.7
2137	1.5	2050	1.4

OCTOBER

Time	m		Time	m
1 0252	5.5	**16** 0419	5.0
0917	1.6	1022	2.1
W 1519	5.4	TH 1644	4.8
◖ 2149	1.7	2256	2.2
2 0355	5.2	**17** 0525	4.8
1026	1.9	1144	2.3
TH 1633	5.0	F 1754	4.6
2308	1.9		
3 0535	5.0	**18** 0041	2.2
1158	1.9	0639	4.8
F 1821	5.0	SA 1324	2.2
		1913	4.8
4 0042	1.8	**19** 0152	2.0
0707	5.2	0803	5.1
SA 1325	1.7	SU 1420	1.8
1940	5.4	2028	5.1
5 0159	1.4	**20** 0242	1.7
0817	5.7	0854	5.5
SU 1431	1.2	M 1504	1.5
2043	5.8	2111	5.5
6 0257	0.9	**21** 0323	1.4
0914	6.1	0932	5.8
M 1523	0.8	TU 1543	1.2
2136	6.2	2145	5.8
7 0346	0.6	**22** 0400	1.2
1004	6.5	1004	6.0
TU 1610	0.6	W 1618	1.0
2225	6.5	2218	6.0
8 0431	0.4	**23** 0435	1.0
1050	6.7	1036	6.2
W 1654	0.4	TH 1653	0.9
○ 2311	6.7	● 2251	6.1
9 0515	0.3	**24** 0510	0.9
1134	6.8	1108	6.2
TH 1738	0.3	F 1728	0.9
2355	6.7	2325	6.2
10 0559	0.4	**25** 0544	0.9
1216	6.8	1141	6.3
F 1821	0.4	SA 1801	0.8
		2359	6.3
11 0037	6.6	**26** 0616	0.9
0640	0.5	1215	6.5
SA 1257	6.6	SU 1835	0.8
1902	0.6		
12 0118	6.4	**27** 0034	6.3
0721	0.7	0650	1.0
SU 1335	6.3	M 1251	6.2
1942	0.8	1910	0.9
13 0156	6.1	**28** 0112	6.2
0800	1.0	0729	1.1
M 1412	6.0	TU 1330	6.1
2021	1.1	1951	1.0
14 0236	5.8	**29** 0154	6.0
0840	1.4	0814	1.2
TU 1452	5.6	W 1414	5.8
2102	1.5	2040	1.3
15 0322	5.4	**30** 0244	5.7
0925	1.8	0908	1.5
W 1541	5.1	TH 1509	5.5
◖ 2151	1.9	2139	1.5
		31 0348	5.4
		1017	1.9
		F 1622	5.2
		◖ 2254	1.7

NOVEMBER

Time	m		Time	m
1 0517	5.2	**16** 0548	4.9
1141	1.8	1203	2.2
SA 1759	5.1	SU 1815	4.7
2 0020	1.7	**17** 0040	2.1
0644	5.4	0651	5.0
SU 1302	1.6	M 1326	2.0
1918	5.4	1918	4.9
3 0135	1.4	**18** 0151	1.9
0755	5.7	0751	5.3
M 1407	1.3	TU 1421	1.7
2023	5.7	2014	5.2
4 0234	1.1	**19** 0241	1.6
0852	6.1	0840	5.6
TU 1501	0.9	W 1505	1.4
2117	6.1	2100	5.6
5 0324	0.8	**20** 0324	1.4
0942	6.4	0922	5.9
W 1549	0.7	TH 1545	1.2
2206	6.4	2142	5.9
6 0410	0.6	**21** 0403	1.2
1028	6.6	1001	6.1
TH 1634	0.5	F 1623	1.0
○ 2252	6.5	2222	6.1
7 0454	0.6	**22** 0440	1.0
1111	6.6	1039	6.3
F 1717	0.5	SA 1700	0.9
2335	6.5	● 2301	6.2
8 0537	0.6	**23** 0518	0.9
1153	6.6	1117	6.4
SA 1800	0.6	SU 1739	0.8
		2341	6.3
9 0017	6.5	**24** 0556	0.9
0618	0.7	1156	6.4
SU 1232	6.4	M 1818	0.7
1839	0.7		
10 0056	6.3	**25** 0021	6.4
0657	0.9	0636	0.9
M 1309	6.2	TU 1237	6.3
1918	0.9	1859	0.8
11 0133	6.1	**26** 0103	6.3
0734	1.1	0720	1.0
TU 1344	5.9	W 1320	6.2
1955	1.1	1945	0.9
12 0211	5.9	**27** 0149	6.2
0813	1.4	0808	1.1
W 1422	5.6	TH 1408	6.0
2034	1.4	2034	1.0
13 0253	5.5	**28** 0240	5.9
0856	1.7	0902	1.3
TH 1506	5.2	F 1502	5.7
2119	1.7	2132	1.3
14 0343	5.2	**29** 0340	5.7
0947	1.9	1006	1.5
F 1603	4.9	SA 1608	5.4
◖ 2214	2.0	◖ 2239	1.4
15 0443	5.0	**30** 0453	5.5
1048	2.2	1119	1.6
SA 1709	4.7	SU 1728	5.3
2320	2.1	2353	1.5

DECEMBER

Time	m		Time	m
1 0612	5.5	**16** 0556	5.0
1233	1.5	1209	2.1
M 1848	5.3	TU 1826	4.8
2 0105	1.5	**17** 0038	2.0
0724	5.6	0658	5.1
TU 1340	1.4	W 1317	1.9
1956	5.5	1926	5.0
3 0208	1.3	**18** 0145	1.9
0826	5.9	0754	5.4
W 1438	1.1	TH 1418	1.6
2055	5.8	2021	5.3
4 0302	1.1	**19** 0242	1.6
0920	6.1	0845	5.7
TH 1529	0.9	F 1508	1.3
2147	6.0	2110	5.7
5 0351	0.9	**20** 0330	1.3
1008	6.3	0931	6.0
F 1615	0.8	SA 1554	1.1
2234	6.2	2156	6.0
6 0436	0.8	**21** 0413	1.1
1052	6.3	1015	6.2
SA 1700	0.7	SU 1637	0.8
○ 2318	6.3	2241	6.2
7 0519	0.8	**22** 0456	0.9
1133	6.3	1059	6.4
SU 1742	0.7	M 1720	0.7
2359	6.3	● 2326	6.4
8 0600	0.8	**23** 0540	0.8
1212	6.3	1142	6.5
M 1821	0.8	TU 1804	0.6
9 0038	6.2	**24** 0011	6.5
0637	1.0	0624	0.7
TU 1248	6.1	W 1227	6.5
1858	0.9	1849	0.5
10 0114	6.1	**25** 0057	6.5
0713	1.1	0711	0.7
W 1322	5.9	TH 1313	6.4
1934	1.0	1937	0.6
11 0149	5.9	**26** 0143	6.4
0750	1.3	0759	0.8
TH 1355	5.7	F 1401	6.3
2011	1.2	2026	0.7
12 0224	5.7	**27** 0233	6.2
0829	1.5	0851	0.9
F 1431	5.4	SA 1452	6.0
2051	1.4	2119	0.9
13 0302	5.5	**28** 0326	6.0
0913	1.7	0948	1.1
SA 1512	5.2	SU 1549	5.7
2137	1.7	◖ 2217	1.1
14 0348	5.2	**29** 0425	5.8
1004	1.9	1052	1.4
SU 1606	4.9	M 1654	5.4
◖ 2229	1.7	2322	1.4
15 0449	5.0	**30** 0532	5.5
1103	2.0	1201	1.5
M 1718	4.8	TU 1807	5.3
2331	2.0		
		31 0033	1.5
		0646	5.4
		W 1311	1.5
		1925	5.2

Chart Datum: 3·27 metres below Ordnance Datum (Newlyn)
HAT is 6·9 metres above Chart Datum

TIDES

251

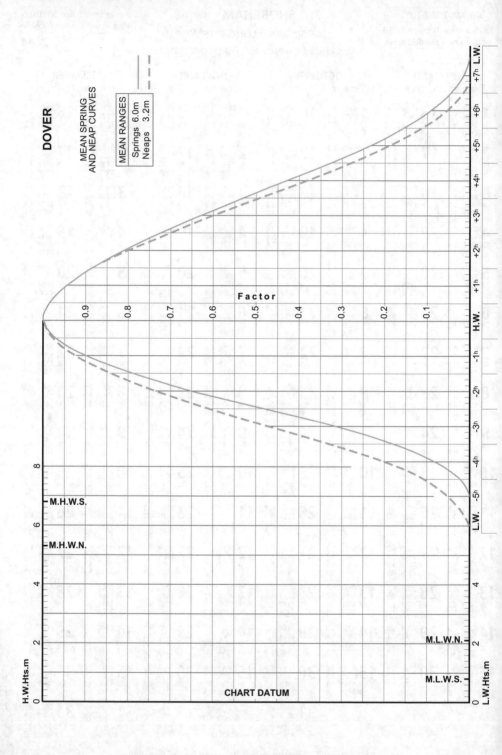

DOVER

MEAN SPRING
AND NEAP CURVES

MEAN RANGES
Springs 6.0m
Neaps   3.2m

Factor

0.9 0.8 0.7 0.6 0.5 0.4 0.3 0.2 0.1

H.W.Hts.m

M.H.W.S.

M.H.W.N.

CHART DATUM

L.W.Hts.m

M.L.W.N.

M.L.W.S.

+7ʰ L.W. +6ʰ +5ʰ +4ʰ +3ʰ +2ʰ +1ʰ H.W. -1ʰ -2ʰ -3ʰ -4ʰ -5ʰ L.W.

DOVER
LAT 51°07′N   LONG 1°19′E
TIMES AND HEIGHTS OF HIGH AND LOW WATERS

Dates in amber are SPRINGS
Dates in yellow are NEAPS

2014

JANUARY

Time m | Time m

Day	T1	m	T2	m	T3	m	T4	m
1 W ●	0534	1.0	1026	6.8	1804	0.8	2252	6.9
2 TH	0631	0.8	1114	6.9	1859	0.7	2340	7.0
3 F	0724	0.6	1202	7.0	1950	0.7		
4 SA	0027	7.1	0814	0.5	1251	6.9	2036	0.7
5 SU	0114	7.1	0901	0.6	1339	6.7	2118	0.8
6 M	0203	6.9	0945	0.7	1430	6.5	2200	1.0
7 TU	0253	6.7	1029	1.0	1523	6.2	2243	1.3
8 W ☽	0346	6.4	1116	1.3	1620	5.9	2333	1.7
9 TH	0444	6.0	1209	1.7	1725	5.6		
10 F	0032	2.0	0550	5.7	1311	1.9	1839	5.4
11 SA	0139	2.1	0706	5.6	1417	2.0	1954	5.5
12 SU	0248	2.0	0820	5.6	1525	1.9	2056	5.7
13 M	0355	1.8	0919	5.8	1627	1.7	2145	6.0
14 TU	0451	1.6	1006	6.0	1715	1.5	2226	6.2
15 W	0535	1.4	1754	1.4	2302	6.4		
16 TH	0612	1.2	1149	6.3	1827	1.3	2335	6.5 ○
17 F	0645	1.2	1149	6.3	1858	1.2		
18 SA	0007	6.5	0716	1.1	1219	6.3	1929	1.2
19 SU	0035	6.5	0749	1.1	1246	6.3	2002	1.2
20 M	0101	6.5	0823	1.2	1310	6.3	2034	1.3
21 TU	0127	6.4	0856	1.2	1339	6.2	2107	1.3
22 W	0159	6.4	0930	1.3	1414	6.2	2142	1.5
23 TH	0239	6.3	1007	1.6	1458	6.0	2222	1.7
24 F	0327	6.1	1052	1.7	1552	5.7	2313	1.9 ◐
25 SA	0428	5.8	1153	1.9	1706	5.5		
26 SU	0026	2.1	0556	5.6	1317	1.9	1853	5.5
27 M	0156	2.0	0725	5.8	1437	1.7	2006	5.8
28 TU	0310	1.7	0832	6.1	1546	1.4	2105	6.1
29 W	0418	1.3	0930	6.4	1653	1.1	2158	6.5
30 TH	0524	0.9	1022	6.7	1757	0.8	2246	6.8 ●
31 F	0625	0.6	1110	6.9	1853	0.6	2332	7.1

FEBRUARY

Time m | Time m

Day	T1	m	T2	m	T3	m	T4	m
1 SA	0719	0.4	1155	7.0	1942	0.5		
2 SU	0016	7.2	0807	0.3	1239	7.0	2024	0.5
3 M	0100	7.2	0849	0.3	1322	6.8	2102	0.6
4 TU	0143	7.1	0927	0.5	1407	6.6	2138	0.8
5 W	0228	6.8	1004	0.8	1453	6.3	2214	1.1
6 TH	0314	6.4	1042	1.2	1543	6.0	2254	1.6
7 F	0406	6.0	1128	1.7	1640	5.6	2345	2.0
8 SA	0506	5.6	1226	2.1	1748	5.3		
9 SU	0054	2.2	0619	5.3	1335	2.2	1908	5.2
10 M	0209	2.2	0746	5.3	1446	2.1	2027	5.4
11 TU	0320	2.0	0901	5.5	1552	1.9	2125	5.7
12 W	0421	1.7	0950	5.8	1648	1.6	2207	6.1
13 TH	0510	1.4	1026	6.1	1731	1.4	2241	6.3
14 F	0549	1.2	1056	6.2	1807	1.2	2312	6.4
15 SA	0624	1.1	1125	6.3	1839	1.1	2341	6.5
16 SU	0657	1.0	1153	6.4	1911	1.1		
17 M	0009	6.5	0730	1.0	1221	6.4	1943	1.0
18 TU	0035	6.6	0804	1.0	1246	6.4	2015	1.0
19 W	0102	6.6	0836	1.0	1314	6.5	2047	1.1
20 TH	0134	6.6	0907	1.1	1349	6.5	2119	1.2
21 F	0212	6.5	0941	1.3	1431	6.3	2157	1.5
22 SA	0257	6.3	1023	1.6	1522	5.9	2245	1.8 ◐
23 SU	0355	5.9	1119	1.8	1631	5.5	2353	2.0
24	0524	5.5	1241	2.0	1831	5.4		
25 TU	0126	2.0	0714	5.6	1413	1.9	1952	5.6
26 W	0249	1.7	0826	5.9	1529	1.5	2055	6.1
27 TH	0404	1.3	0925	6.3	1642	1.1	2149	6.5
28 F	0515	0.9	1017	6.6	1747	0.8	2236	6.8

MARCH

Time m | Time m

Day	T1	m	T2	m	T3	m	T4	m
1 SA ●	0615	0.5	1102	6.5	1840	0.5	2320	7.1
2 SU	0706	0.3	1144	7.0	1926	0.4		
3 M	0001	7.2	0750	0.2	1223	7.0	2005	0.4
4 TU	0042	7.2	0828	0.3	1302	6.9	2040	0.5
5 W	0122	7.0	0903	0.5	1342	6.7	2112	0.7
6 TH	0202	6.8	0935	0.8	1424	6.4	2144	1.1
7 F	0244	6.4	1007	1.3	1510	6.1	2216	1.5
8 SA	0331	6.0	1043	1.7	1603	5.7	2258	1.9 ◐
9 SU	0429	5.5	1135	2.2	1707	5.3		
10 M	0006	2.3	0538	5.2	1253	2.4	1821	5.1
11 TU	0130	2.4	0701	5.1	1409	2.3	1945	5.3
12 W	0243	2.1	0830	5.3	1553	2.0	2053	5.6
13 TH	0346	1.8	0923	5.7	1614	1.7	2137	5.9
14 F	0437	1.5	0957	6.0	1700	1.4	2211	6.2
15 SA	0519	1.2	1026	6.2	1739	1.2	2241	6.4
16 SU ○	0557	1.1	1055	6.3	1814	1.1	2311	6.5
17 M	0633	0.9	1125	6.4	1848	1.0	2340	6.6
18 TU	0708	0.9	1153	6.5	1922	0.9		
19 W	0008	6.7	0742	0.8	1222	6.6	1955	0.9
20 TH	0039	6.7	0815	0.9	1253	6.7	2027	1.0
21 F	0113	6.7	0847	1.0	1330	6.6	2101	1.1
22 SA	0152	6.6	0922	1.2	1413	6.4	2141	1.3
23 SU	0238	6.3	1005	1.5	1506	6.0	2230	1.6
24 M	0338	5.8	1100	1.8	1620	5.6	2337	1.9 ◐
25 TU	0517	5.5	1222	2.0	1814	5.4		
26 W	0109	2.0	0702	5.5	1355	1.9	1935	5.7
27 TH	0232	1.7	0815	5.9	1513	1.6	2040	6.1
28 F	0350	1.3	0914	6.2	1626	1.2	2133	6.5
29 SA	0501	0.9	1004	6.6	1729	0.8	2220	6.8
30 SU	0558	0.6	1048	6.8	1819	0.6	2303	7.0 ●
31 M	0646	0.4	1127	6.9	1903	0.5	2343	7.1

APRIL

Time m | Time m

Day	T1	m	T2	m	T3	m	T4	m
1 TU	0728	0.3	1204	6.9	1941	0.5		
2 W	0022	7.0	0804	0.4	1241	6.8	2014	0.6
3 TH	0101	6.9	0836	0.7	1320	6.7	2046	0.8
4 F	0139	6.7	0906	1.0	1359	6.5	2114	1.1
5 SA	0218	6.3	0932	1.3	1442	6.2	2142	1.5
6 SU	0302	5.9	1000	1.7	1531	5.8	2217	1.9
7 M	0356	5.5	1040	2.1	1631	5.4	2313	2.2 ◐
8 TU	0502	5.2	1157	2.4	1739	5.2		
9 W	0044	2.4	0616	5.1	1327	2.4	1852	5.2
10 TH	0201	2.2	0733	5.2	1435	2.1	2002	5.5
11 F	0302	1.9	0833	5.6	1532	1.8	2052	5.8
12 SA	0354	1.5	0914	5.9	1620	1.5	2130	6.1
13 SU	0440	1.3	0948	6.1	1703	1.3	2203	6.3
14 M	0523	1.1	1021	6.3	1743	1.1	2236	6.5
15 TU	0604	0.9	1054	6.5	1822	1.0	2309	6.6 ○
16 W	0643	0.8	1126	6.6	1859	0.9	2343	6.7
17 TH	0721	0.8	1200	6.7	1936	0.9		
18 F	0018	6.8	0756	0.8	1237	6.7	2012	0.9
19 SA	0056	6.7	0831	0.9	1318	6.7	2050	1.0
20 SU	0140	6.6	0910	1.1	1406	6.4	2132	1.2
21 M	0231	6.2	0955	1.4	1504	6.1	2224	1.5
22 TU	0338	5.9	1053	1.7	1619	5.8	2333	1.8 ◐
23 W	0511	5.6	1213	1.9	1750	5.6		
24 TH	0056	1.8	0644	5.6	1337	1.8	1911	5.8
25 F	0214	1.6	0757	5.9	1451	1.6	2017	6.1
26 SA	0329	1.3	0856	6.1	1601	1.2	2112	6.4
27 SU	0438	1.0	0945	6.4	1702	1.0	2200	6.6
28 M	0535	0.7	1028	6.6	1753	0.8	2243	6.8
29 TU	0623	0.6	1106	6.7	1837	0.7	2324	6.8 ●
30 W	0703	0.6	1143	6.7	1915	0.7		

TIDES

Chart Datum: 3·67 metres below Ordnance Datum (Newlyn)
HAT is 7·4 metres above Chart Datum

TIDES

TIME ZONE (UT)
For Summer Time add ONE hour in **non-shaded areas**

DOVER
LAT 51°07′N   LONG 1°19′E
TIMES AND HEIGHTS OF HIGH AND LOW WATERS

Dates in amber are SPRINGS
Dates in yellow are NEAPS

2014

MAY

Day	Time	m	Time	m	Time	m	Time	m
1 TH	0002	6.8	0738	0.7	1221	6.7	1949	0.8
2 F	0041	6.7	0810	0.9	1259	6.6	2020	1.0
3 SA	0118	6.5	0837	1.1	1338	6.5	2048	1.2
4 SU	0155	6.2	0901	1.4	1418	6.2	2116	1.4
5 M	0236	5.9	0929	1.7	1502	5.9	2150	1.7
6 TU	0325	5.6	1007	2.0	1554	5.6	2237	2.0
7 W	0425	5.3	1100	2.2	1655	5.4	◐ 2347	2.2
8 TH	0532	5.2	1225	2.3	1801	5.3		
9 F	0108	2.1	0639	5.2	1343	2.2	1904	5.5
10 SA	0213	1.9	0739	5.5	1444	1.9	1959	5.7
11 SU	0309	1.6	0827	5.8	1536	1.7	2043	6.0
12 M	0359	1.4	0908	6.0	1625	1.4	2123	6.3
13 TU	0448	1.1	0946	6.3	1711	1.2	2202	6.5
14 W	0535	1.0	1024	6.5	1755	1.0	○ 2241	6.6
15 TH	0619	0.9	1102	6.6	1838	0.9	2321	6.8
16 F	0702	0.8	1142	6.8	1920	0.8		
17 SA	0002	6.8	0742	0.8	1225	6.8	2002	0.8
18 SU	0046	6.7	0823	0.9	1312	6.7	2045	0.9
19 M	0135	6.6	0906	1.0	1403	6.6	2132	1.0
20 TU	0231	6.3	0955	1.2	1502	6.3	2226	1.3
21 W	0336	6.0	1052	1.5	1608	6.1	◑ 2329	1.5
22 TH	0453	5.8	1201	1.7	1720	5.9		
23 F	0040	1.5	0616	5.7	1312	1.7	1837	5.9
24 SA	0149	1.5	0729	5.8	1420	1.6	1948	6.0
25 SU	0259	1.3	0830	6.0	1527	1.4	2047	6.2
26 M	0408	1.2	0922	6.2	1631	1.2	2138	6.4
27 TU	0508	1.0	1006	6.3	1725	1.1	2223	6.5
28 W	0557	1.0	1046	6.5	1810	1.0	● 2305	6.6
29 TH	0638	1.0	1124	6.5	1850	1.0	2344	6.5
30 F	0714	1.0	1202	6.6	1926	1.0		
31 SA	0022	6.5	0745	1.1	1241	6.6	1957	1.1

JUNE

Day	Time	m	Time	m	Time	m	Time	m
1 SU	0059	6.4	0812	1.3	1318	6.5	2026	1.2
2 M	0135	6.2	0837	1.4	1355	6.3	2055	1.4
3 TU	0211	6.0	0906	1.6	1431	6.1	2129	1.5
4 W	0249	5.8	0943	1.7	1510	5.9	2210	1.7
5 TH	0336	5.5	1027	1.9	1600	5.6	◑ 2301	1.9
6 F	0437	5.4	1123	2.1	1701	5.5		
7 SA	0008	2.0	0544	5.3	1238	2.2	1806	5.5
8 SU	0120	1.9	0647	5.4	1351	2.0	1906	5.6
9 M	0223	1.7	0742	5.6	1452	1.8	1959	5.9
10 TU	0320	1.5	0830	5.9	1548	1.5	2047	6.2
11 W	0414	1.3	0915	6.1	1640	1.3	2133	6.4
12 TH	0507	1.1	0959	6.4	1731	1.0	2219	6.6
13 F	0557	0.9	1044	6.7	1820	0.9	○ 2304	6.8
14 SA	0647	0.8	1130	6.8	1909	0.7	2351	6.8
15 SU	0735	0.8	1216	6.9	1958	0.7		
16 M	0039	6.8	0822	0.8	1305	6.9	2046	0.7
17 TU	0130	6.7	0909	0.9	1356	6.8	2134	0.8
18 W	0224	6.5	0954	1.0	1450	6.6	2223	0.9
19 TH	0322	6.3	1044	1.2	1547	6.4	◐ 2317	1.2
20 F	0425	6.0	1139	1.4	1648	6.1		
21 SA	0015	1.4	0535	5.8	1241	1.6	1756	5.9
22 SU	0118	1.5	0651	5.7	1345	1.7	1911	5.9
23 M	0223	1.6	0759	5.7	1452	1.7	2020	5.9
24 TU	0333	1.5	0857	5.9	1558	1.5	2118	6.1
25 W	0438	1.4	0946	6.1	1657	1.3	2207	6.2
26 TH	0531	1.3	1028	6.3	1746	1.2	2250	6.3
27 F	0614	1.2	1107	6.4	1828	1.1	● 2328	6.4
28 SA	0650	1.2	1145	6.5	1904	1.1		
29 SU	0004	6.3	0721	1.2	1222	6.5	1935	1.1
30 M	0040	6.3	0749	1.3	1257	6.5	2005	1.2

JULY

Day	Time	m	Time	m	Time	m	Time	m
1 TU	0112	6.2	0816	1.3	1329	6.4	2035	1.2
2 W	0141	6.1	0846	1.4	1357	6.2	2109	1.3
3 TH	0208	5.9	0920	1.5	1427	6.1	2145	1.5
4 F	0240	5.8	0958	1.7	1504	6.0	2226	1.6
5 SA	0323	5.7	1041	1.9	1553	5.8	◐ 2314	1.8
6 SU	0421	5.5	1135	2.0	1657	5.6		
7 M	0019	1.9	0543	5.4	1251	2.1	1813	5.6
8 TU	0136	1.9	0659	5.5	1408	2.0	1921	5.8
9 W	0243	1.7	0759	5.8	1514	1.7	2020	6.0
10 TH	0344	1.4	0853	6.1	1613	1.4	2114	6.3
11 F	0443	1.2	0943	6.4	1710	1.1	● 2312	6.3
12 SA	0540	0.9	1032	6.7	1806	0.8	○ 2254	6.8
13 SU	0636	0.8	1120	6.9	1902	0.6	2342	6.9
14 M	0730	0.7	1207	7.0	1954	0.5		
15 TU	0030	6.9	0818	0.6	1254	7.1	2042	0.4
16 W	0119	6.8	0902	0.6	1342	7.0	2126	0.5
17 TH	0208	6.7	0943	0.8	1431	6.9	2209	0.7
18 F	0300	6.4	1024	1.0	1522	6.6	2254	1.0
19 SA	0354	6.1	1111	1.3	1617	6.3	◐ 2344	1.4
20 SU	0455	5.8	1205	1.7	1718	5.9		
21 M	0043	1.7	0604	5.6	1309	1.9	1830	5.7
22 TU	0148	1.9	0722	5.5	1418	1.9	1951	5.6
23 W	0258	1.8	0833	5.6	1528	1.8	2101	5.8
24 TH	0409	1.7	0928	5.9	1633	1.6	2154	6.0
25 F	0506	1.5	1013	6.2	1725	1.4	2236	6.2
26 SA	0551	1.4	1051	6.4	1807	1.2	2312	6.3
27 SU	0628	1.3	1126	6.5	1842	1.2	2344	6.3
28 M	0658	1.3	1200	6.5	1913	1.1		
29 TU	0015	6.3	0725	1.3	1230	6.5	1942	1.1
30 W	0045	6.3	0753	1.2	1300	6.5	2013	1.1
31 TH	0109	6.2	0824	1.3	1324	6.4	2045	1.2

AUGUST

Day	Time	m	Time	m	Time	m	Time	m
1 F	0132	6.2	0856	1.3	1350	6.3	2118	1.3
2 SA	0202	6.1	0930	1.5	1424	6.3	2153	1.5
3 SU	0240	6.0	1007	1.7	1507	6.1	2233	1.7
4 M	0329	5.8	1051	1.9	1602	5.8	◐ 2325	1.9
5 TU	0434	5.5	1153	2.1	1721	5.6		
6 W	0043	2.0	0621	5.4	1325	2.1	1855	5.6
7 TH	0210	1.9	0739	5.7	1445	1.8	2005	5.9
8 F	0320	1.6	0839	6.0	1551	1.5	2104	6.3
9 SA	0424	1.3	0932	6.4	1654	1.1	2157	6.6
10 SU	0526	1.0	1022	6.8	1755	0.8	○ 2246	6.8
11 M	0625	0.7	1108	7.0	1852	0.5	2332	7.0
12 TU	0718	0.6	1153	7.2	1943	0.4		
13 W	0016	7.0	0804	0.5	1238	7.2	2028	0.3
14 TH	0101	6.9	0844	0.5	1323	7.2	2108	0.4
15 F	0146	6.8	0921	0.7	1408	7.0	2146	0.7
16 SA	0233	6.5	0958	1.0	1455	6.7	2225	1.1
17 SU	0323	6.2	1039	1.4	1546	6.4	◑ 2309	1.5
18 M	0419	5.8	1128	1.8	1643	5.8		
19 TU	0005	1.9	0523	5.5	1233	2.1	1752	5.5
20 W	0114	2.2	0641	5.3	1347	2.2	1919	5.4
21 TH	0228	2.2	0805	5.5	1502	2.0	2046	5.6
22 F	0340	1.9	0908	5.8	1609	1.7	2140	5.9
23 SA	0440	1.7	0953	6.1	1702	1.5	2219	6.1
24 SU	0526	1.4	1030	6.4	1743	1.3	2250	6.3
25 M	0602	1.3	1102	6.5	1816	1.2	● 2318	6.4
26 TU	0632	1.3	1133	6.6	1847	1.1	2347	6.4
27 W	0659	1.2	1202	6.6	1917	1.1		
28 TH	0013	6.4	0729	1.2	1228	6.6	1948	1.1
29 F	0037	6.3	0800	1.2	1252	6.5	2020	1.1
30 SA	0101	6.4	0832	1.2	1319	6.5	2051	1.2
31 SU	0131	6.4	0903	1.4	1353	6.5	2123	1.4

Chart Datum: 3·67 metres below Ordnance Datum (Newlyn)
HAT is 7·4 metres above Chart Datum

DOVER

LAT 51°07'N   LONG 1°19'E

TIMES AND HEIGHTS OF HIGH AND LOW WATERS

Dates in amber are **SPRINGS**
Dates in yellow are **NEAPS**

2014

SEPTEMBER

Day	Time m	Time m	Time m	Time m
1 M	0209 6.3	0938 1.6	1434 6.3	2201 1.6
2 TU ◐	0256 6.0	1021 1.8	1527 5.9	2250 1.9
3 W	0358 5.6	1119 2.1	1645 5.6	
4 TH	0001 2.1	0556 5.4	1249 2.2	1841 5.6
5 F	0143 2.1	0723 5.6	1421 1.9	1955 5.9
6 SA	0301 1.7	0826 6.1	1533 1.5	2055 6.3
7 SU	0409 1.3	0920 6.5	1640 1.1	2147 6.6
8 M	0512 1.0	1008 6.9	1742 0.7	2234 6.9
9 TU ○	0609 0.7	1053 7.1	1837 0.6	2318 7.0
10 W	0659 0.6	1136 7.3	1925 0.4	2359 7.1
11 TH	0742 0.5	1218 7.3	2007 0.4	
12 F	0039 7.0	0820 0.6	1301 7.2	2044 0.5
13 SA	0121 6.9	0855 0.8	1343 7.0	2119 0.8
14 SU	0205 6.6	0929 1.1	1427 6.6	2153 1.2
15 M	0253 6.3	1006 1.5	1516 6.2	2232 1.7
16 TU ◗	0346 5.9	1049 1.9	1612 5.7	2323 2.2
17 W	0448 5.5	1152 2.3	1719 5.4	
18 TH	0037 2.5	0600 5.3	1314 2.4	1839 5.2
19 F	0156 2.4	0725 5.4	1431 2.2	2018 5.4
20 SA	0308 2.2	0838 5.7	1537 1.9	2114 5.8
21 SU	0407 1.8	0924 6.1	1629 1.5	2151 6.1
22 M	0453 1.5	1000 6.3	1710 1.3	2219 6.3
23 TU	0530 1.4	1031 6.5	1744 1.2	2246 6.4
24 W ●	0601 1.2	1100 6.6	1816 1.1	2314 6.5
25 TH	0631 1.2	1128 6.6	1849 1.1	2341 6.5
26 F	0703 1.1	1155 6.7	1923 1.0	
27 SA	0007 6.6	0736 1.1	1223 6.7	1955 1.1
28 SU	0035 6.6	0808 1.2	1253 6.7	2027 1.2
29 M	0108 6.6	0841 1.3	1328 6.6	2100 1.4
30 TU	0147 6.4	0917 1.5	1411 6.3	2138 1.6

OCTOBER

Day	Time m	Time m	Time m	Time m
1 W	0235 6.1	1001 1.8	1505 5.9	2228 1.9
2 TH	0340 5.7	1100 2.1	1631 5.6	2337 2.2
3 F	0538 5.5	1227 2.2	1829 5.6	
4 SA	0120 2.2	0703 5.7	1401 1.9	1941 5.9
5 SU	0242 1.8	0808 6.1	1515 1.5	2042 6.3
6 M	0351 1.4	0902 6.5	1623 1.1	2133 6.6
7 TU	0453 1.0	0950 6.9	1724 0.8	2218 6.9
8 W ○	0548 0.8	1035 7.1	1816 0.6	2259 7.0
9 TH	0635 0.7	1116 7.2	1902 0.5	2338 7.1
10 F	0717 0.6	1157 7.2	1942 0.5	
11 SA	0017 7.0	0754 0.7	1238 7.1	2017 0.7
12 SU	0058 6.9	0828 0.9	1319 6.9	2050 1.0
13 M	0140 6.7	0901 1.2	1401 6.5	2121 1.4
14 TU	0225 6.3	0934 1.6	1448 6.1	2152 1.8
15 W ◐	0316 6.0	1010 1.9	1543 5.7	2231 2.2
16 TH	0414 5.6	1103 2.3	1646 5.4	2342 2.6
17 F	0520 5.4	1229 2.5	1758 5.2	
18 SA	0112 2.6	0634 5.4	1349 2.3	1920 5.3
19 SU	0225 2.4	0748 5.6	1453 2.0	2026 5.7
20 M	0324 2.0	0841 5.9	1544 1.7	2107 6.0
21 TU	0411 1.6	0919 6.2	1628 1.4	2139 6.2
22 W	0451 1.5	0952 6.4	1707 1.2	2209 6.4
23 TH ●	0527 1.3	1023 6.6	1745 1.1	2240 6.6
24 F	0603 1.2	1054 6.7	1822 1.0	2310 6.7
25 SA	0639 1.1	1125 6.7	1858 1.0	2341 6.7
26 SU	0714 1.1	1158 6.8	1933 1.1	
27 M	0014 6.8	0749 1.1	1233 6.7	2007 1.1
28 TU	0052 6.7	0825 1.2	1313 6.6	2043 1.3
29 W	0135 6.5	0905 1.4	1359 6.3	2125 1.6
30 TH	0227 6.2	0952 1.6	1458 6.0	2215 1.8
31 F ◗	0337 5.9	1051 1.9	1627 5.7	2324 2.1

NOVEMBER

Day	Time m	Time m	Time m	Time m
1 SA	0512 5.7	1214 2.0	1808 5.7	
2 SU	0057 2.1	0636 5.8	1339 1.8	1921 5.9
3 M	0216 1.8	0743 6.1	1452 1.5	2022 6.2
4 TU	0325 1.5	0840 6.5	1600 1.2	2114 6.5
5 W	0428 1.2	0929 6.7	1701 0.9	2159 6.7
6 TH	0523 1.0	1015 6.9	1753 0.8	2240 6.8
7 F	0610 0.8	1057 7.0	1838 0.7	2319 6.9
8 SA	0652 0.7	1138 7.0	1917 0.8	2358 6.9
9 SU	0730 0.9	1217 6.9	1952 1.0	
10 M	0037 6.8	0805 1.0	1257 6.7	2023 1.2
11 TU	0118 6.7	0837 1.3	1338 6.4	2051 1.5
12 W	0200 6.4	0907 1.6	1421 6.1	2118 1.8
13 TH	0246 6.1	0939 1.8	1511 5.8	2151 2.1
14 F ◐	0338 5.8	1022 2.1	1609 5.5	2239 2.4
15 SA	0437 5.5	1125 2.3	1715 5.3	2357 2.6
16 SU	0543 5.4	1248 2.3	1823 5.3	
17 M	0124 2.5	0649 5.5	1357 2.1	1926 5.5
18 TU	0229 2.2	0746 5.7	1454 1.9	2016 5.8
19 W	0323 1.9	0831 6.0	1544 1.6	2056 6.1
20 TH	0411 1.6	0910 6.3	1630 1.3	2133 6.3
21 F	0454 1.4	0947 6.5	1714 1.2	2208 6.5
22 SA ○	0536 1.2	1023 6.6	1756 1.0	2244 6.7
23 SU	0617 1.1	1101 6.8	1837 1.0	2321 6.8
24 M	0657 1.0	1139 6.8	1916 1.0	
25 TU	0000 6.9	0736 1.0	1220 6.8	1955 1.1
26 W	0043 6.8	0817 1.1	1305 6.7	2035 1.2
27 TH	0130 6.7	0901 1.2	1355 6.4	2120 1.4
28 F	0224 6.5	0950 1.4	1454 6.2	2211 1.6
29 SA ◐	0327 6.2	1048 1.6	1608 5.8	2314 1.8
30 SU	0440 6.0	1157 1.7	1734 5.8	

DECEMBER

Day	Time m	Time m	Time m	Time m
1 M	0029 1.9	0559 5.9	1310 1.7	1851 5.8
2 TU	0142 1.8	0712 6.0	1420 1.6	1956 6.0
3 W	0251 1.7	0814 6.2	1531 1.4	2052 6.2
4 TH	0359 1.4	0909 6.4	1637 1.2	2141 6.4
5 F	0458 1.2	0957 6.6	1731 1.0	2223 6.6
6 SA	0547 1.1	1041 6.7	1816 1.0	2303 6.7
7 SU	0631 1.0	1122 6.7	1855 1.0	2342 6.7
8 M	0710 1.0	1201 6.7	1929 1.1	
9 TU	0020 6.7	0745 1.1	1240 6.5	2000 1.3
10 W	0059 6.6	0816 1.2	1317 6.4	2027 1.4
11 TH	0137 6.5	0845 1.4	1355 6.1	2053 1.6
12 F	0215 6.3	0916 1.6	1435 5.9	2125 1.8
13 SA	0255 6.0	0952 1.8	1520 5.6	2205 2.0
14 SU	0341 5.8	1038 2.0	1618 5.4	2255 2.2
15 M	0440 5.5	1137 2.1	1725 5.3	
16 TU	0003 2.4	0547 5.4	1310 2.2	1830 5.3
17 W	0124 2.3	0650 5.5	1401 2.0	1928 5.5
18 TH	0232 2.1	0745 5.8	1500 1.7	2017 5.8
19 F	0330 1.8	0832 6.0	1555 1.5	2101 6.1
20 SA	0422 1.5	0917 6.3	1646 1.2	2143 6.4
21 SU	0511 1.2	1000 6.6	1734 1.1	2224 6.6
22 M ●	0557 1.0	1043 6.7	1820 0.9	2307 6.7
23 TU	0644 0.9	1126 6.8	1906 0.9	2350 6.8
24 W	0730 0.8	1211 6.8	1951 0.9	
25 TH	0036 7.0	0815 0.8	1258 6.7	2034 0.9
26 F	0124 6.9	0902 0.9	1348 6.6	2119 1.0
27 SA	0214 6.8	0949 1.0	1442 6.4	2205 1.2
28 SU ◗	0309 6.5	1039 1.2	1542 6.1	2257 1.5
29 M	0410 6.2	1135 1.4	1651 5.9	2358 1.7
30 TU	0518 6.0	1238 1.6	1809 5.7	
31 W	0104 1.9	0634 5.9	1345 1.7	1924 5.7

Chart Datum: 3·67 metres below Ordnance Datum (Newlyn)
HAT is 7·4 metres above Chart Datum

TIDES

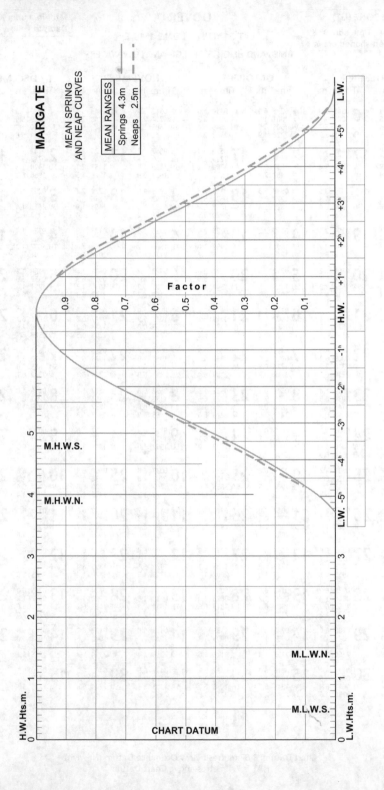

MARGATE

MEAN SPRING
AND NEAP CURVES

MEAN RANGES	
Springs	4.3m
Neaps	2.5m

MARGATE

LAT 51°23'N LONG 1°23'E

TIMES AND HEIGHTS OF HIGH AND LOW WATERS

Dates in amber are **SPRINGS**
Dates in yellow are **NEAPS**

2014

JANUARY

Day	Time m	Time m	Time m	Time m
1 W ●	0536 0.6	1137 4.8	1749 0.7	2356 4.8
2 TH	0629 0.5	1229 4.9	1837 0.6	
3 F	0043 4.9	0719 0.4	1322 5.0	1924 0.6
4 SA	0132 4.9	0808 0.3	1413 5.0	2010 0.7
5 SU	0220 4.9	0855 0.3	1502 4.9	2055 0.8
6 M	0307 4.9	0942 0.4	1550 4.7	2141 0.9
7 TU	0354 4.7	1029 0.5	1640 4.5	2229 1.1
8 W ◗	0445 4.6	1120 0.7	1735 4.3	2326 1.2
9 TH	0546 4.4	1218 0.9	1838 4.2	
10 F	0038 1.3	0653 4.2	1324 1.1	1944 4.1
11 SA	0154 1.4	0808 4.1	1428 1.2	2049 4.1
12 SU	0303 1.3	0911 4.2	1528 1.2	2150 4.2
13 M	0407 1.1	1013 4.2	1622 1.1	2242 4.4
14 TU	0500 0.9	1103 4.3	1706 1.1	2322 4.5
15 W	0543 0.8	1143 4.4	1745 1.0	2355 4.5
16 TH ○	0620 0.7	1216 4.5	1820 0.9	
17 F	0025 4.6	0653 0.6	1248 4.5	1851 0.9
18 SA	0058 4.7	0724 0.6	1321 4.6	1921 0.9
19 SU	0133 4.7	0754 0.6	1357 4.6	1952 0.9
20 M	0209 4.7	0825 0.6	1434 4.5	2026 0.9
21 TU	0244 4.6	0858 0.6	1508 4.4	2102 1.0
22 W	0315 4.5	0933 0.7	1541 4.3	2139 1.1
23 TH	0349 4.4	1011 0.8	1618 4.2	2222 1.2
24 F ◗	0431 4.3	1056 0.9	1705 4.1	2316 1.3
25 SA	0526 4.2	1157 1.1	1805 4.1	
26 SU	0029 1.3	0634 4.1	1317 1.1	1928 4.0
27 M	0201 1.3	0805 4.1	1438 1.0	2051 4.1
28 TU	0320 1.1	0924 4.3	1546 0.9	2158 4.4
29 W	0426 0.8	1031 4.6	1644 0.8	2255 4.6
30 TH ●	0526 0.6	1129 4.8	1737 0.6	2346 4.8
31 F	0620 0.4	1222 4.9	1826 0.6	

FEBRUARY

Day	Time m	Time m	Time m	Time m
1 SA	0034 4.9	0708 0.3	1312 5.0	1911 0.6
2 SU	0122 5.0	0755 0.2	1400 5.0	1956 0.6
3 M	0207 5.0	0838 0.2	1445 4.9	2037 0.7
4 TU	0250 5.0	0917 0.3	1527 4.7	2117 0.8
5 W	0331 4.9	0954 0.5	1607 4.5	2158 0.9
6 TH ◗	0414 4.6	1032 0.6	1649 4.3	2244 1.1
7 F	0503 4.4	1121 1.0	1745 4.1	2346 1.3
8 SA	0607 4.1	1229 1.3	1856 3.9	
9 SU	0109 1.4	0723 3.9	1346 1.4	2008 3.9
10 M	0228 1.4	0841 4.0	1457 1.4	2117 4.0
11 TU	0342 1.2	0951 4.1	1559 1.3	2216 4.2
12 W	0441 1.0	1045 4.3	1649 1.1	2302 4.4
13 TH	0524 0.8	1126 4.4	1728 1.0	2338 4.5
14 F ○	0559 0.7	1159 4.4	1802 1.0	
15 SA	0008 4.6	0630 0.6	1228 4.5	1832 0.9
16 SU	0040 4.7	0700 0.6	1300 4.6	1902 0.8
17 M	0113 4.7	0730 0.5	1334 4.6	1933 0.8
18 TU	0148 4.7	0800 0.5	1410 4.6	2007 0.8
19 W	0221 4.7	0832 0.5	1443 4.5	2041 0.8
20 TH	0251 4.6	0904 0.6	1512 4.4	2116 0.9
21 F ◗	0322 4.5	0939 0.8	1546 4.3	2155 1.0
22 SA	0402 4.4	1022 0.9	1632 4.2	2246 1.1
23 SU	0457 4.3	1121 1.1	1733 4.1	2357 1.2
24 M	0609 4.1	1244 1.2	1857 4.0	
25 TU	0135 1.2	0745 4.1	1416 1.1	2028 4.1
26 W	0302 1.0	0911 4.3	1530 1.0	2141 4.3
27 TH	0413 0.7	1023 4.5	1630 0.8	2242 4.6
28 F	0514 0.5	1120 4.8	1722 0.7	2334 4.8

MARCH

Day	Time m	Time m	Time m	Time m
1 SA	0606 0.3	1209 4.9	1810 0.6	
2 SU	0020 4.9	0651 0.2	1256 4.9	1853 0.6
3 M	0104 5.0	0733 0.2	1339 4.9	1936 0.6
4 TU	0147 5.1	0811 0.3	1420 4.8	2016 0.6
5 W	0228 5.0	0844 0.4	1457 4.7	2054 0.7
6 TH	0306 4.8	0915 0.6	1531 4.5	2130 0.8
7 F	0344 4.6	0949 0.8	1606 4.3	2210 1.0
8 SA ◗	0426 4.4	1031 1.1	1650 4.1	2301 1.2
9 SU	0520 4.1	1129 1.4	1756 3.9	
10 M	0017 1.4	0639 3.8	1256 1.6	1923 3.8
11 TU	0147 1.4	0805 3.8	1422 1.5	2036 3.9
12 W	0305 1.3	0918 4.0	1530 1.4	2139 4.1
13 TH	0406 1.0	1015 4.2	1622 1.2	2230 4.3
14 F	0451 0.8	1058 4.3	1703 1.0	2310 4.4
15 SA	0528 0.7	1132 4.4	1737 0.9	2343 4.5
16 SU ○	0601 0.6	1202 4.5	1809 0.9	
17 M	0015 4.6	0630 0.5	1234 4.5	1840 0.8
18 TU	0049 4.7	0702 0.5	1308 4.6	1913 0.7
19 W	0124 4.8	0733 0.5	1344 4.6	1947 0.7
20 TH	0159 4.7	0805 0.5	1418 4.6	2023 0.7
21 F	0231 4.6	0839 0.6	1449 4.5	2059 0.8
22 SA	0304 4.6	0916 0.7	1525 4.4	2140 0.9
23 SU	0348 4.4	1001 0.9	1614 4.2	2232 1.0
24 M ◗	0445 4.3	1102 1.1	1716 4.1	2346 1.1
25 TU	0601 4.1	1228 1.2	1840 4.0	
26 W	0122 1.1	0735 4.1	1359 1.2	2009 4.1
27 TH	0248 0.9	0901 4.3	1513 1.0	2123 4.3
28 F	0359 0.6	1010 4.6	1613 0.9	2224 4.6
29 SA	0457 0.5	1105 4.7	1704 0.7	2315 4.7
30 SU	0545 0.3	1151 4.8	1749 0.6	2359 4.9
31 M	0627 0.3	1234 4.8	1832 0.6	

APRIL

Day	Time m	Time m	Time m	Time m
1 TU	0041 5.0	0704 0.3	1313 4.8	1914 0.5
2 W	0123 5.0	0739 0.4	1351 4.8	1955 0.5
3 TH	0203 4.9	0811 0.5	1425 4.7	2032 0.6
4 F	0241 4.8	0842 0.7	1458 4.5	2107 0.8
5 SA	0318 4.6	0915 0.9	1532 4.3	2143 0.9
6 SU	0357 4.3	0953 1.1	1612 4.1	2227 1.1
7 M ◗	0443 4.0	1043 1.4	1704 3.9	2329 1.3
8 TU	0547 3.8	1153 1.6	1824 3.7	
9 W	0055 1.4	0718 3.7	1332 1.6	1950 3.8
10 TH	0217 1.3	0833 3.9	1449 1.5	2054 4.0
11 F	0320 1.1	0931 4.1	1544 1.2	2147 4.2
12 SA	0409 0.9	1018 4.2	1628 1.1	2232 4.4
13 SU	0450 0.7	1057 4.4	1706 0.9	2310 4.5
14 M	0526 0.6	1131 4.5	1742 0.8	2345 4.6
15 TU ○	0600 0.5	1205 4.6	1817 0.7	
16 W	0021 4.7	0633 0.5	1241 4.6	1853 0.6
17 TH	0059 4.8	0706 0.5	1318 4.7	1930 0.6
18 F	0138 4.8	0742 0.5	1356 4.6	2008 0.6
19 SA	0217 4.7	0820 0.6	1433 4.5	2049 0.6
20 SU	0259 4.6	0902 0.7	1516 4.4	2134 0.7
21 M	0347 4.5	0951 0.9	1606 4.3	2230 0.8
22 TU ◗	0445 4.3	1054 1.1	1708 4.2	2346 0.9
23 W	0559 4.2	1216 1.2	1828 4.1	
24 TH	0111 0.9	0726 4.2	1340 1.2	1950 4.2
25 F	0230 0.7	0844 4.3	1452 1.0	2100 4.3
26 SA	0338 0.6	0950 4.5	1551 0.9	2201 4.5
27 SU	0433 0.5	1044 4.6	1642 0.8	2252 4.7
28 M	0519 0.5	1129 4.6	1727 0.7	2336 4.8
29 TU ●	0558 0.5	1209 4.7	1811 0.6	
30 W	0017 4.8	0633 0.5	1245 4.7	1854 0.5

Chart Datum: 2·50 metres below Ordnance Datum (Newlyn)
HAT is 5·2 metres above Chart Datum

TIDES

TIME ZONE (UT)	MARGATE	Dates in amber are SPRINGS
For Summer Time add ONE hour in **non-shaded areas**	**LAT 51°23′N LONG 1°23′E** TIMES AND HEIGHTS OF HIGH AND LOW WATERS	Dates in yellow are NEAPS **2014**

MAY

Time	m	Time	m	Time	m	Time	m
1 0059	4.8	**16** 0036	4.8				
0708	0.5	0645	0.5				
TH 1320	4.7	F 1256	4.7				
1935	0.5	1916	0.5				
2 0139	4.8	**17** 0122	4.8				
0742	0.6	0725	0.5				
F 1355	4.7	SA 1339	4.7				
2013	0.6	2000	0.5				
3 0217	4.7	**18** 0208	4.8				
0815	0.8	0808	0.6				
SA 1430	4.5	SU 1423	4.7				
2048	0.7	2045	0.5				
4 0254	4.5	**19** 0256	4.7				
0848	0.9	0854	0.7				
SU 1506	4.4	M 1510	4.6				
2122	0.8	2135	0.5				
5 0332	4.3	**20** 0347	4.6				
0924	1.1	0946	0.8				
M 1544	4.2	TU 1600	4.5				
2201	0.9	2233	0.6				
6 0414	4.1	**21** 0444	4.4				
1008	1.3	1047	1.0				
TU 1629	4.1	W 1659	4.3				
2252	1.1	◑ 2341	0.7				
7 0504	3.9	**22** 0553	4.3				
1105	1.4	1159	1.1				
W 1724	3.9	TH 1811	4.3				
◑ 2358	1.2						
8 0612	3.8	**23** 0054	0.7				
1217	1.6	0709	4.3				
TH 1844	3.8	F 1316	1.1				
		1925	4.3				
9 0116	1.2	**24** 0206	0.7				
0737	3.8	0820	4.3				
F 1347	1.5	SA 1425	1.1				
2002	3.9	2032	4.4				
10 0227	1.1	**25** 0310	0.6				
0840	4.0	0923	4.4				
SA 1456	1.3	SU 1526	1.0				
2059	4.1	2134	4.5				
11 0322	0.9	**26** 0405	0.6				
0931	4.2	1019	4.5				
SU 1547	1.1	M 1620	0.9				
2148	4.3	2229	4.5				
12 0409	0.8	**27** 0451	0.7				
1016	4.3	1106	4.5				
M 1631	0.9	TU 1708	0.7				
2232	4.4	2315	4.6				
13 0450	0.7	**28** 0530	0.7				
1057	4.5	1146	4.5				
TU 1713	0.8	W 1753	0.6				
2314	4.6	● 2357	4.7				
14 0529	0.6	**29** 0606	0.7				
1136	4.6	1220	4.6				
W 1754	0.7	TH 1837	0.6				
○ 2354	4.7						
15 0607	0.5	**30** 0037	4.7				
1215	4.6	0643	0.7				
TH 1835	0.6	F 1255	4.6				
		1917	0.5				
		31 0117	4.7				
		0719	0.7				
		SA 1330	4.6				
		1955	0.6				

JUNE

Time	m	Time	m
1 0155	4.6	**16** 0201	4.9
0753	0.8	0800	0.6
SU 1407	4.6	M 1414	4.8
2030	0.6	2043	0.3
2 0232	4.5	**17** 0252	4.8
0826	0.9	0847	0.7
M 1443	4.5	TU 1502	4.8
2103	0.7	2133	0.4
3 0310	4.3	**18** 0342	4.7
0900	1.0	0937	0.8
TU 1521	4.4	W 1551	4.7
2139	0.8	2226	0.4
4 0349	4.2	**19** 0436	4.6
0941	1.1	1032	0.9
W 1601	4.2	TH 1645	4.6
2221	0.9	◑ 2324	0.5
5 0432	4.1	**20** 0537	4.4
1028	1.3	1133	1.0
TH 1646	4.1	F 1748	4.5
◑ 2313	1.0		
6 0521	3.9	**21** 0028	0.7
1124	1.4	0643	4.3
F 1738	4.0	SA 1244	1.1
		1856	4.4
7 0014	1.1	**22** 0134	0.7
0621	3.9	0749	4.3
SA 1232	1.4	SU 1355	1.1
1844	3.9	2002	4.3
8 0124	1.1	**23** 0237	0.8
0737	3.9	0853	4.3
SU 1351	1.4	M 1500	1.1
2000	4.0	2107	4.4
9 0231	1.1	**24** 0334	0.9
0841	4.1	0953	4.3
M 1501	1.2	TU 1600	1.0
2101	4.2	2208	4.4
10 0327	0.8	**25** 0425	0.9
0936	4.3	1045	4.4
TU 1556	1.0	W 1653	0.8
2154	4.4	2300	4.5
11 0416	0.7	**26** 0508	0.9
1025	4.4	1127	4.5
W 1646	0.8	TH 1741	0.7
2244	4.5	2343	4.5
12 0502	0.7	**27** 0547	0.8
1110	4.6	1202	4.5
TH 1733	0.7	F 1823	0.6
2332	4.7	●	
13 0546	0.6	**28** 0021	4.6
1154	4.7	0624	0.8
F 1821	0.6	SA 1235	4.6
○		1901	0.6
14 0020	4.8	**29** 0058	4.6
0629	0.6	0700	0.8
SA 1240	4.8	SU 1309	4.6
1907	0.5	1937	0.6
15 0110	4.9	**30** 0134	4.6
0714	0.6	0733	0.8
SU 1326	4.8	M 1345	4.6
1955	0.4	2010	0.6

JULY

Time	m	Time	m
1 0210	4.5	**16** 0242	4.9
0806	0.9	0836	0.6
TU 1422	4.6	W 1450	4.9
2042	0.6	2121	0.3
2 0247	4.4	**17** 0330	4.8
0839	0.9	0922	0.7
W 1459	4.5	TH 1537	4.9
2115	0.7	2207	0.4
3 0324	4.3	**18** 0418	4.6
0916	1.0	1009	0.9
TH 1535	4.4	F 1624	4.7
2152	0.8	2256	0.6
4 0402	4.2	**19** 0509	4.4
0957	1.1	1102	1.0
F 1613	4.3	SA 1718	4.6
2234	0.9	◑ 2351	0.8
5 0443	4.1	**20** 0609	4.2
1043	1.3	1206	1.2
SA 1656	4.2	SU 1822	4.4
◑ 2324	1.0		
6 0530	4.0	**21** 0054	1.0
1139	1.4	0713	4.2
SU 1748	4.1	M 1320	1.2
		1930	4.3
7 0024	1.1	**22** 0201	1.1
0628	4.0	0820	4.2
M 1250	1.4	TU 1432	1.2
1854	4.1	2041	4.2
8 0136	1.1	**23** 0305	1.1
0745	4.0	0926	4.2
TU 1412	1.3	W 1541	1.1
2012	4.1	2150	4.3
9 0246	1.0	**24** 0403	1.1
0856	4.2	1024	4.3
W 1522	1.1	TH 1642	0.9
2120	4.3	2247	4.4
10 0347	0.8	**25** 0452	1.1
0956	4.4	1111	4.4
TH 1622	0.9	F 1729	0.8
2220	4.5	2331	4.5
11 0440	0.7	**26** 0532	1.0
1049	4.6	1147	4.5
F 1716	0.7	SA 1808	0.7
2316	4.7	●	
12 0530	0.7	**27** 0007	4.5
1138	4.7	0607	0.9
SA 1808	0.5	SU 1218	4.6
○		1842	0.6
13 0008	4.8	**28** 0039	4.6
0617	0.6	0641	0.9
SU 1226	4.8	M 1249	4.7
1858	0.4	1915	0.6
14 0101	4.9	**29** 0111	4.6
0704	0.6	0713	0.9
M 1315	4.9	TU 1324	4.7
1947	0.3	1946	0.6
15 0152	5.0	**30** 0146	4.6
0750	0.6	0745	0.9
TU 1403	5.0	W 1400	4.7
2034	0.3	2017	0.6
		31 0222	4.6
		0819	0.9
		TH 1435	4.6
		2048	0.7

AUGUST

Time	m	Time	m
1 0258	4.5	**16** 0350	4.7
0852	0.9	0942	0.8
F 1509	4.5	SA 1557	4.8
2121	0.7	2217	0.7
2 0332	4.3	**17** 0433	4.4
0928	1.0	1028	1.0
SA 1542	4.4	SU 1645	4.6
2157	0.9	◑ 2303	0.9
3 0406	4.2	**18** 0524	4.2
1008	1.2	1126	1.2
SU 1620	4.3	M 1744	4.3
2239	1.0		
4 0448	4.1	**19** 0006	1.2
1056	1.3	0631	4.0
M 1708	4.2	TU 1242	1.3
◑ 2333	1.1	1857	4.1
5 0542	4.1	**20** 0123	1.4
1202	1.4	0744	4.0
TU 1810	4.1	W 1402	1.3
		2015	4.1
6 0047	1.2	**21** 0237	1.4
0655	4.0	0855	4.1
W 1330	1.3	TH 1519	1.2
1932	4.1	2130	4.2
7 0212	1.1	**22** 0343	1.3
0821	4.1	0958	4.3
TH 1454	1.1	F 1623	1.0
2054	4.3	2229	4.4
8 0322	1.0	**23** 0434	1.2
0931	4.3	1048	4.4
F 1601	0.9	SA 1710	0.8
2203	4.5	2314	4.5
9 0422	0.8	**24** 0515	1.1
1031	4.6	1127	4.5
SA 1700	0.7	SU 1746	0.7
2303	4.7	2348	4.5
10 0514	0.7	**25** 0549	1.0
1123	4.7	1158	4.6
SU 1755	0.5	M 1818	0.7
○ 2357	4.9	●	
11 0603	0.7	**26** 0017	4.6
1211	4.9	0621	0.9
M 1845	0.3	TU 1227	4.7
		1848	0.6
12 0047	5.0	**27** 0046	4.6
0649	0.6	0652	0.9
TU 1259	5.0	W 1259	4.8
1931	0.3	1918	0.6
13 0137	5.0	**28** 0119	4.7
0734	0.6	0723	0.8
W 1347	5.1	TH 1334	4.8
2016	0.2	1948	0.6
14 0224	5.0	**29** 0154	4.6
0818	0.6	0756	0.8
TH 1432	5.1	F 1409	4.7
2058	0.3	2019	0.6
15 0308	4.8	**30** 0229	4.6
0900	0.7	0829	0.9
F 1515	5.0	SA 1442	4.6
2137	0.5	2050	0.7
		31 0300	4.4
		0840	1.0
		SU 1512	4.5
		2123	0.9

Chart Datum: 2·50 metres below Ordnance Datum (Newlyn)
HAT is 5·2 metres above Chart Datum

MARGATE

LAT 51°23'N   LONG 1°23'E

TIMES AND HEIGHTS OF HIGH AND LOW WATERS

Dates in amber are **SPRINGS**
Dates in yellow are **NEAPS**

2014

SEPTEMBER

Day	Time m	Time m	Day	Time m	Time m
1 M	0330 4.3 / 0940 1.1	1547 4.4 / 2202 1.0	16 TU	0436 4.2 / 1049 1.2	1706 4.2 / ◑ 2313 1.4
2 TU	0411 4.2 / 1025 1.2	1636 4.3 / ◑ 2254 1.2	17 W	0539 4.0 / 1200 1.4	1819 4.0
3 W	0506 4.1 / 1128 1.3	1740 4.2	18 TH	0035 1.6 / 0732 3.9	1325 1.4 / 1944 4.0
4 TH	0010 1.3 / 0620 4.0	1301 1.3 / 1907 4.1	19 F	0203 1.6 / 0817 4.0	1445 1.3 / 2059 4.1
5 F	0145 1.3 / 0753 4.1	1431 1.1 / 2036 4.3	20 SA	0314 1.5 / 0921 4.2	1549 1.1 / 2159 4.3
6 SA	0302 1.1 / 0910 4.3	1543 0.9 / 2150 4.6	21 SU	0408 1.3 / 1014 4.4	1636 0.9 / 2244 4.5
7 SU	0404 0.9 / 1013 4.6	1644 0.6 / 2250 4.8	22 M	0449 1.1 / 1056 4.5	1714 0.8 / 2319 4.5
8 M	0457 0.8 / 1106 4.8	1737 0.4 / 2342 4.9	23 TU	0525 1.0 / 1129 4.6	1747 0.7 / 2348 4.6
9 TU	0544 0.7 / 1153 4.9	1825 0.3 / ○	24 W	0557 0.9 / 1200 4.7	1818 0.6 / ●
10 W	0029 5.0 / 0629 0.6	1239 5.1 / 1908 0.3	25 TH	0017 4.7 / 0628 0.8	1232 4.8 / 1848 0.6
11 TH	0115 5.0 / 0714 0.6	1324 5.1 / 1949 0.3	26 F	0049 4.7 / 0700 0.8	1307 4.8 / 1918 0.6
12 F	0158 5.0 / 0757 0.6	1408 5.1 / 2027 0.4	27 SA	0124 4.7 / 0733 0.8	1342 4.8 / 1949 0.7
13 SA	0239 4.8 / 0838 0.7	1449 5.0 / 2101 0.6	28 SU	0158 4.6 / 0807 0.8	1416 4.7 / 2021 0.8
14 SU	0316 4.6 / 0917 0.8	1529 4.8 / 2136 0.9	29 M	0229 4.5 / 0842 0.9	1448 4.6 / 2056 0.9
15 M	0352 4.4 / 0958 1.0	1613 4.5 / 2217 1.1	30 TU	0301 4.4 / 0920 1.0	1526 4.5 / 2137 1.0

OCTOBER

Day	Time m	Time m	Day	Time m	Time m
1 W	0345 4.3 / 1007 1.1	1618 4.3 / ◑ 2231 1.2	16 TH	0448 4.0 / 1117 1.3	1733 4.0 / 2336 1.7
2 TH	0443 4.1 / 1111 1.2	1725 4.2 / 2348 1.4	17 F	0606 3.8 / 1237 1.4	1901 3.9
3 F	0558 4.0 / 1243 1.2	1853 4.2	18 SA	0113 1.8 / 0823 3.9	1358 1.3 / 2015 4.0
4 SA	0122 1.4 / 0730 4.1	1411 1.0 / 2021 4.3	19 SU	0234 1.6 / 0837 4.0	1503 1.2 / 2115 4.2
5 SU	0242 1.2 / 0848 4.3	1524 0.8 / 2135 4.6	20 M	0331 1.4 / 0931 4.2	1553 1.0 / 2203 4.4
6 M	0344 1.0 / 0951 4.6	1624 0.6 / 2233 4.8	21 TU	0416 1.2 / 1017 4.4	1635 0.8 / 2242 4.5
7 TU	0436 0.8 / 1044 4.8	1715 0.4 / 2322 4.9	22 W	0454 1.0 / 1055 4.5	1712 0.7 / 2315 4.6
8 W	0523 0.7 / 1131 4.9	1800 0.4 / ○	23 TH	0530 0.9 / 1129 4.6	1746 0.7 / ● 2346 4.7
9 TH	0006 5.0 / 0608 0.6	1215 5.0 / 1840 0.4	24 F	0604 0.8 / 1203 4.7	1818 0.7
10 F	0048 4.9 / 0652 0.6	1258 5.1 / 1918 0.5	25 SA	0020 4.7 / 0638 0.8	1239 4.8 / 1849 0.7
11 SA	0127 4.9 / 0735 0.6	1342 5.0 / 1954 0.6	26 SU	0055 4.8 / 0713 0.7	1317 4.8 / 1922 0.7
12 SU	0205 4.8 / 0816 0.8	1423 4.9 / 2028 0.8	27 M	0131 4.7 / 0749 0.7	1355 4.7 / 1958 0.7
13 M	0240 4.6 / 0855 0.8	1503 4.7 / 2101 1.0	28 TU	0206 4.6 / 0828 0.7	1434 4.6 / 2037 0.9
14 TU	0316 4.5 / 0933 0.9	1541 4.5 / 2140 1.2	29 W	0245 4.5 / 0910 0.8	1519 4.5 / 2122 1.0
15 W	0357 4.2 / 1017 1.1	1631 4.2 / ◑ 2228 1.5	30 TH	0333 4.4 / 1000 0.9	1612 4.4 / 2219 1.2
			31 F	0430 4.2 / 1106 1.0	1718 4.3 / ◑ 2332 1.3

NOVEMBER

Day	Time m	Time m	Day	Time m	Time m
1 SA	0541 4.1 / 1229 1.0	1840 4.2	16 SU	0624 3.8 / 1256 1.3	1919 3.9
2 SU	0059 1.3 / 0707 4.2	1350 0.9 / 2003 4.4	17 M	0130 1.7 / 0744 3.9	1410 1.2 / 2023 4.0
3 M	0217 1.2 / 0823 4.3	1500 0.7 / 2113 4.5	18 TU	0243 1.5 / 0843 4.1	1506 1.1 / 2115 4.2
4 TU	0320 1.0 / 0926 4.5	1600 0.6 / 2211 4.7	19 W	0335 1.3 / 0933 4.2	1554 0.9 / 2200 4.4
5 W	0414 0.9 / 1021 4.7	1650 0.5 / 2300 4.8	20 TH	0420 1.1 / 1017 4.4	1636 0.8 / 2240 4.5
6 TH	0502 0.8 / 1109 4.8	1733 0.5 / ○ 2343 4.8	21 F	0500 0.9 / 1057 4.5	1714 0.8 / 2317 4.6
7 F	0548 0.6 / 1153 4.9	1812 0.6	22 SA	0539 0.8 / 1136 4.6	1750 0.7 / 2354 4.7
8 SA	0021 4.8 / 0632 0.6	1236 4.9 / 1849 0.6	23 SU	0618 0.7 / 1215 4.7	1826 0.7
9 SU	0058 4.8 / 0716 0.5	1318 4.9 / 1926 0.7	24 M	0031 4.8 / 0656 0.7	1257 4.8 / 1902 0.7
10 M	0135 4.8 / 0758 0.6	1400 4.8 / 2001 0.9	25 TU	0111 4.8 / 0737 0.6	1341 4.8 / 1942 0.7
11 TU	0211 4.6 / 0836 0.7	1439 4.6 / 2035 1.0	26 W	0152 4.7 / 0819 0.6	1427 4.7 / 2026 0.8
12 W	0248 4.5 / 0912 0.9	1518 4.4 / 2110 1.2	27 TH	0237 4.6 / 0905 0.6	1516 4.6 / 2114 0.9
13 TH	0327 4.3 / 0951 1.0	1600 4.2 / 2152 1.4	28 F	0325 4.5 / 0958 0.7	1608 4.5 / 2209 1.1
14 F	0410 4.1 / 1038 1.1	1649 4.0 / ◑ 2246 1.6	29 SA	0419 4.4 / 1100 0.8	1709 4.4 / 2314 1.2
15 SA	0504 4.0 / 1140 1.3	1754 3.9 / 2354 1.7	30 SU	0524 4.3 / 1211 0.8	1823 4.3

DECEMBER

Day	Time m	Time m	Day	Time m	Time m
1 M	0031 1.3 / 0641 4.3	1324 0.8 / 1939 4.3	16 TU	0002 1.6 / 0615 3.9	1255 1.2 / 1912 3.9
2 TU	0147 1.2 / 0754 4.3	1432 0.8 / 2047 4.4	17 W	0122 1.6 / 0738 3.9	1408 1.2 / 2021 4.0
3 W	0254 1.1 / 0900 4.4	1532 0.7 / 2148 4.5	18 TH	0243 1.4 / 0843 4.1	1508 1.1 / 2117 4.2
4 TH	0352 1.0 / 0959 4.5	1624 0.7 / 2240 4.6	19 F	0340 1.2 / 0937 4.2	1559 0.9 / 2206 4.4
5 F	0445 0.8 / 1051 4.6	1709 0.7 / 2324 4.7	20 SA	0430 1.0 / 1026 4.4	1644 0.8 / 2251 4.6
6 SA	0533 0.7 / 1137 4.7	1749 0.7 / ○	21 SU	0516 0.8 / 1112 4.6	1727 0.8 / 2333 4.7
7 SU	0001 4.7 / 0618 0.6	1219 4.8 / 1827 0.8	22 M	0601 0.7 / 1157 4.7	1808 0.7
8 M	0037 4.7 / 0701 0.6	1300 4.8 / 1905 0.8	23 TU	0014 4.8 / 0644 0.6	1244 4.8 / 1849 0.7
9 TU	0112 4.7 / 0742 0.6	1339 4.7 / 1940 0.9	24 W	0057 4.8 / 0729 0.5	1332 4.9 / 1933 0.7
10 W	0149 4.7 / 0818 0.7	1417 4.6 / 2013 1.0	25 TH	0142 4.9 / 0814 0.4	1421 4.9 / 2018 0.7
11 TH	0225 4.6 / 0852 0.7	1455 4.4 / 2047 1.1	26 F	0228 4.8 / 0901 0.4	1510 4.8 / 2105 0.8
12 F	0303 4.4 / 0926 0.8	1533 4.3 / 2124 1.2	27 SA	0316 4.7 / 0951 0.5	1600 4.6 / 2155 0.9
13 SA	0341 4.4 / 1004 1.0	1613 4.1 / 2207 1.4	28 SU	0406 4.6 / 1044 0.6	1654 4.5 / ◑ 2251 1.1
14 SU	0424 4.2 / 1051 1.1	1700 4.0 / ◑ 2259 1.5	29 M	0503 4.5 / 1145 0.7	1758 4.3 / 2358 1.2
15 M	0513 4.0 / 1147 1.2	1756 3.9	30 TU	0612 4.4 / 1252 0.8	1909 4.3
			31 W	0113 1.2 / 0723 4.3	1400 0.9 / 2017 4.3

Chart Datum: 2·50 metres below Ordnance Datum (Newlyn)
HAT is 5·2 metres above Chart Datum

TIDES

SHEERNESS

MEAN SPRING
AND NEAP CURVES

MEAN RANGES
Springs 5.2m
Neaps 3.2m

Factor

0.9 0.8 0.7 0.6 0.5 0.4 0.3 0.2 0.1

H.W.Hts.m.

M.H.W.S.

M.H.W.N.

M.L.W.N.

M.L.W.S.

CHART DATUM

L.W.Hts.m.

L.W.

H.W.

L.W.

TIME ZONE (UT)
For Summer Time add ONE hour in **non-shaded areas**

SHEERNESS
LAT 51°27′N LONG 0°45′E
TIMES AND HEIGHTS OF HIGH AND LOW WATERS

Dates in amber are SPRINGS
Dates in yellow are NEAPS

2014

JANUARY	FEBRUARY	MARCH	APRIL
Time m Time m	Time m Time m	Time m Time m	Time m Time m

JANUARY

1 W — 0603 0.7, 1208 5.9, 1827 0.7 ●
16 TH — 0030 5.5, 0643 0.8, 1252 5.5, ○ 1844 1.0
2 TH — 0032 5.9, 0700 0.5, 1259 6.1, 1918 0.6
17 F — 0105 5.6, 0718 0.8, 1325 5.6, 1916 0.9
3 F — 0119 6.0, 0752 0.4, 1348 6.2, 2005 0.6
18 SA — 0136 5.6, 0751 0.7, 1357 5.6, 1949 0.9
4 SA — 0205 6.0, 0842 0.3, 1436 6.2, 2050 0.6
19 SU — 0207 5.6, 0824 0.7, 1429 5.6, 2022 0.9
5 SU — 0251 6.0, 0928 0.3, 1524 6.1, 2132 0.7
20 M — 0238 5.7, 0857 0.7, 1502 5.6, 2056 0.9
6 M — 0337 5.9, 1012 0.4, 1612 5.9, 2213 0.8
21 TU — 0310 5.5, 0929 0.8, 1536 5.5, 2127 1.0
7 TU — 0424 5.7, 1054 0.6, 1702 5.6, 2255 1.1
22 W — 0344 5.4, 0959 0.9, 1612 5.4, 2157 1.1
8 W — 0515 5.5, 1756 5.4, ◐ 2344 1.2
23 TH — 0420 5.3, 1029 1.0, 1653 5.2, 2232 1.2
9 TH — 0612 5.3, 1856 5.1
24 F — 0504 5.2, 1201 1.2, 1743 5.1, ◑ 2321 1.3
10 F — 0045 1.4, 0717 5.1, 1338 1.3, 2002 5.0
25 SA — 0600 5.1, 1846 5.0
11 SA — 0159 1.5, 0828 4.9, 1447 1.3, 2111 5.0
26 SU — 0028 1.4, 0713 5.0, 1324 1.3, 2002 5.0
12 SU — 0312 1.4, 0940 5.0, 1552 1.3, 2215 5.1
27 M — 0205 1.4, 0836 5.0, 1500 1.2, 2118 5.1
13 M — 0420 1.3, 1042 5.1, 1648 1.3, 2308 5.3
28 TU — 0333 1.2, 0952 5.3, 1612 1.0, 2226 5.4
14 TU — 0518 1.1, 1132 5.3, 1733 1.2, 2352 5.4
29 W — 0446 0.9, 1059 5.6, 1716 0.8, 2326 5.6
15 W — 0604 0.9, 1215 5.4, 1811 1.1
30 TH — 0553 0.7, 1156 5.9, 1814 0.7 ●
31 F — 0018 5.8, 0652 0.4, 1248 6.1, 1905 0.6

FEBRUARY

1 SA — 0105 6.0, 0743 0.2, 1335 6.2, 1952 0.5
16 SU — 0115 5.6, 0731 0.6, 1335 5.7, 1931 0.8
2 SU — 0150 6.1, 0829 0.1, 1421 6.2, 2035 0.5
17 M — 0146 5.7, 0804 0.6, 1406 5.7, 2005 0.8
3 M — 0234 6.1, 0912 0.1, 1505 6.1, 2114 0.6
18 TU — 0217 5.7, 0838 0.6, 1438 5.7, 2039 0.8
4 TU — 0317 6.0, 0950 0.3, 1548 5.9, 2151 0.7
19 W — 0248 5.7, 0911 0.6, 1511 5.6, 2109 0.9
5 W — 0359 5.9, 1025 0.5, 1632 5.7, 2226 0.9
20 TH — 0321 5.6, 0938 0.8, 1546 5.5, 2135 1.0
6 TH — 0444 5.6, 1059 0.8, 1718 5.3, ◐ 2305 1.1
21 F — 0357 5.5, 1003 0.9, 1625 5.4, 2206 1.1
7 F — 0533 5.3, 1138 1.1, 1810 5.0, 2355 1.4
22 SA — 0439 5.4, 1036 1.1, 1711 5.2, 2251 1.2
8 SA — 0632 5.0, 1235 1.4, 1913 4.8
23 SU — 0532 5.2, 1129 1.2, 1811 5.0, 2356 1.3
9 SU — 0107 1.5, 0746 4.7, 1355 1.6, 2027 4.7
24 M — 0644 5.0, 1250 1.4, 1929 4.9
10 M — 0236 1.5, 0908 4.7, 1513 1.6, 2143 4.8
25 TU — 0135 1.4, 0811 5.0, 1436 1.3, 2053 5.0
11 TU — 0354 1.4, 1019 4.9, 1619 1.4, 2243 5.1
26 W — 0315 1.2, 0936 5.2, 1553 1.1, 2208 5.3
12 W — 0457 1.1, 1112 5.2, 1711 1.2, 2330 5.3
27 TH — 0434 0.9, 1046 5.6, 1701 0.9, 2309 5.6
13 TH — 0545 0.9, 1155 5.4, 1752 1.1
28 F — 0544 0.6, 1143 5.9, 1800 0.7
14 F — 0009 5.4, 0624 0.8, 1231 5.5, ○ 1826 1.0
15 SA — 0044 5.6, 0658 0.7, 1304 5.6, 1858 0.9

MARCH

1 SA — 0001 5.8, 0639 0.3, 1233 6.1, ● 1849 0.6
16 SU — 0016 5.5, 0631 0.7, 1236 5.6, ○ 1836 0.9
2 SU — 0048 6.0, 0726 0.2, 1318 6.2, 1934 0.5
17 M — 0049 5.6, 0705 0.6, 1308 5.7, 1910 0.8
3 M — 0131 6.1, 0809 0.1, 1401 6.2, 2015 0.4
18 TU — 0121 5.7, 0740 0.5, 1340 5.8, 1946 0.7
4 TU — 0212 6.2, 0848 0.2, 1442 6.1, 2053 0.5
19 W — 0153 5.8, 0816 0.5, 1413 5.8, 2021 0.7
5 W — 0253 6.1, 0923 0.3, 1521 5.9, 2127 0.6
20 TH — 0226 5.8, 0849 0.6, 1447 5.8, 2053 0.8
6 TH — 0333 5.9, 0953 0.6, 1600 5.6, 2158 0.8
21 F — 0301 5.7, 0919 0.7, 1523 5.7, 2121 0.9
7 F — 0413 5.6, 1021 0.9, 1639 5.3, 2231 1.0
22 SA — 0339 5.6, 0946 0.9, 1602 5.5, 2154 0.9
8 SA — 0457 5.3, 1054 1.2, 1723 5.0, ◐ 2312 1.3
23 SU — 0423 5.5, 1022 1.0, 1649 5.3, 2240 1.1
9 SU — 0550 4.9, 1141 1.5, 1820 4.7
24 M — 0518 5.2, 0734 1.1, 1748 5.0, ◑ 2347 1.2
10 M — 0013 1.5, 0700 4.6, 1257 1.7, 1936 4.5
25 TU — 0630 5.0, 1239 1.4, 1906 4.9
11 TU — 0154 1.6, 0827 4.6, 1433 1.7, 2100 4.6
26 W — 0127 1.3, 0757 5.0, 1417 1.4, 2032 4.9
12 W — 0320 1.4, 0945 4.8, 1545 1.5, 2209 4.9
27 TH — 0303 1.1, 0922 5.3, 1534 1.2, 2149 5.2
13 TH — 0425 1.2, 1042 5.1, 1641 1.3, 2259 5.2
28 F — 0422 0.8, 1030 5.6, 1642 0.9, 2250 5.5
14 F — 0515 1.0, 1126 5.3, 1726 1.1, 2340 5.4
29 SA — 0528 0.5, 1126 5.8, 1741 0.6, 2341 5.8
15 SA — 0556 0.8, 1203 5.5, 1802 1.0
30 SU — 0620 0.4, 1214 6.0, 1829 0.6 ●
31 M — 0027 5.9, 0704 0.3, 1257 6.1, 1912 0.5

APRIL

1 TU — 0109 6.1, 0744 0.3, 1337 6.1, 1952 0.4
16 W — 0054 5.7, 0713 0.6, 1314 5.8, 1925 0.7
2 W — 0150 6.1, 0820 0.3, 1416 6.0, 2029 0.5
17 TH — 0129 5.8, 0752 0.6, 1350 5.9, 2004 0.6
3 TH — 0229 6.0, 0853 0.5, 1453 5.8, 2104 0.6
18 F — 0206 5.9, 0829 0.6, 1426 5.8, 2042 0.7
4 F — 0308 5.8, 0922 0.7, 1529 5.6, 2134 0.8
19 SA — 0245 5.8, 0904 0.7, 1505 5.7, 2117 0.7
5 SA — 0346 5.6, 0948 1.0, 1604 5.3, 2203 1.0
20 SU — 0327 5.7, 0939 0.8, 1547 5.6, 2156 0.8
6 SU — 0427 5.3, 1019 1.2, 1643 5.0, 2239 1.2
21 M — 0415 5.6, 1020 1.0, 1636 5.3, 2245 0.9
7 M — 0514 4.9, 1101 1.5, 1732 4.7, ◐ 2331 1.4
22 TU — 0513 5.3, 1116 1.2, 1736 5.1, ◑ 2353 1.1
8 TU — 0616 4.6, 1203 1.7, 1841 4.5
23 W — 0624 5.2, 1232 1.4, 1852 5.0
9 W — 0053 1.6, 0734 4.5, 1338 1.8, 2005 4.5
24 TH — 0124 1.1, 0745 5.2, 1358 1.3, 2013 5.0
10 TH — 0235 1.5, 0855 4.7, 1501 1.7, 2120 4.7
25 F — 0249 0.9, 0903 5.3, 1511 1.2, 2126 5.3
11 F — 0342 1.2, 0958 5.0, 1601 1.4, 2217 5.0
26 SA — 0402 0.7, 1010 5.6, 1618 1.0, 2228 5.5
12 SA — 0434 1.0, 1046 5.3, 1649 1.2, 2302 5.3
27 SU — 0505 0.6, 1105 5.8, 1716 0.8, 2319 5.7
13 SU — 0518 0.8, 1126 5.5, 1730 1.0, 2341 5.5
28 M — 0556 0.5, 1152 5.9, 1805 0.7
14 M — 0558 0.7, 1203 5.6, 1808 0.9
29 TU — 0005 5.8, 0638 0.5, 1235 5.9, ● 1848 0.6
15 TU — 0018 5.6, 0635 0.7, 1239 5.8, ○ 1846 0.8
30 W — 0048 5.9, 0715 0.6, 1314 5.9, 1929 0.5

Chart Datum: 2·90 metres below Ordnance Datum (Newlyn)
HAT is 6·3 metres above Chart Datum

TIDES

TIME ZONE (UT)
For Summer Time add ONE hour in **non-shaded areas**

SHEERNESS
LAT 51°27'N LONG 0°45'E
TIMES AND HEIGHTS OF HIGH AND LOW WATERS

Dates in amber are **SPRINGS**
Dates in yellow are **NEAPS**

2014

MAY

Day	Time	m	Time	m	Time	m	Time	m
1 TH	0128	5.9	0751	0.6	1352	5.9	2007	0.5
2 F	0208	5.9	0823	0.7	1427	5.7	2043	0.6
3 SA	0246	5.7	0853	0.9	1502	5.6	2114	0.8
4 SU	0324	5.5	0920	1.1	1535	5.4	2142	1.0
5 M	0402	5.3	0950	1.2	1612	5.1	2215	1.1
6 TU	0445	5.0	1029	1.4	1655	4.9	2259	1.4
7 W ☽	0537	4.8	1121	1.6	1752	4.7		
8 TH	0000	1.4	0640	4.6	1231	1.8	1905	4.6
9 F	0128	1.4	0752	4.7	1358	1.7	2020	4.7
10 SA	0246	1.3	0900	4.9	1508	1.5	2124	4.9
11 SU	0344	1.1	0957	5.2	1603	1.3	2217	5.2
12 M	0434	0.9	1045	5.4	1651	1.1	2304	5.4
13 TU	0520	0.8	1129	5.6	1737	0.9	2346	5.6
14 W ○	0604	0.7	1210	5.8	1822	0.8		
15 TH	0027	5.7	0647	0.6	1250	5.9	1906	0.7
16 F	0109	5.9	0730	0.6	1330	5.9	1951	0.6
17 SA	0151	5.9	0812	0.6	1410	5.9	2035	0.5
18 SU	0234	5.9	0853	0.7	1452	5.8	2119	0.6
19 M	0321	5.9	0935	0.8	1538	5.6	2204	0.6
20 TU	0412	5.7	1020	1.0	1629	5.5	2255	0.7
21 W ☽	0509	5.5	1113	1.1	1728	5.3	2358	0.8
22 TH	0616	5.4	1219	1.3	1837	5.2		
23 F	0112	0.9	0727	5.3	1332	1.3	1950	5.2
24 SA	0225	0.9	0839	5.4	1442	1.2	2100	5.3
25 SU	0334	0.8	0944	5.5	1548	1.1	2203	5.4
26 M	0436	0.8	1041	5.6	1649	1.0	2257	5.5
27 TU	0528	0.8	1130	5.7	1741	0.8	2346	5.6
28 W	0610	0.8	1213	5.7	1827	0.7		
29 TH	0030	5.7	0648	0.8	1254	5.7	1909	0.6
30 F	0111	5.7	0723	0.8	1331	5.7	1948	0.6
31 SA	0151	5.7	0756	0.8	1406	5.6	2024	0.7

JUNE

Day	Time	m	Time	m	Time	m	Time	m
1 SU	0228	5.6	0828	0.9	1440	5.5	2056	0.8
2 M	0304	5.5	0857	1.1	1513	5.4	2126	0.9
3 TU	0340	5.4	0928	1.2	1548	5.3	2158	1.0
4 W	0419	5.2	1004	1.3	1627	5.1	2236	1.1
5 TH	0502	5.0	1048	1.5	1712	4.9	2323	1.2
6 F	0553	4.9	1140	1.6	1809	4.8		
7 SA	0022	1.3	0653	4.8	1246	1.7	1917	4.7
8 SU	0136	1.3	0800	4.9	1403	1.6	2027	4.9
9 M	0249	1.2	0905	5.1	1513	1.4	2130	5.1
10 TU	0350	1.0	1003	5.3	1612	1.2	2226	5.3
11 W	0444	0.9	1055	5.6	1707	1.0	2317	5.6
12 TH	0535	0.8	1144	5.7	1759	0.8		
13 F	0006	5.7	0624	0.7	1230	5.9	1851	0.7
14 SA	0053	5.9	0712	0.6	1314	5.9	1941	0.5
15 SU	0139	6.0	0759	0.6	1358	5.9	2030	0.4
16 M	0226	6.1	0844	0.6	1443	5.9	2119	0.4
17 TU	0315	6.0	0929	0.7	1530	5.8	2206	0.4
18 W	0405	5.9	1014	0.8	1619	5.7	2254	0.5
19 TH ☽	0459	5.7	1102	1.0	1713	5.5	2346	0.6
20 F	0558	5.5	1156	1.1	1814	5.4		
21 SA	0046	0.8	0701	5.4	1300	1.2	1921	5.3
22 SU	0152	0.9	0808	5.3	1408	1.3	2030	5.2
23 M	0259	1.0	0914	5.3	1517	1.2	2137	5.3
24 TU	0402	1.0	1015	5.4	1622	1.1	2238	5.4
25 W	0459	1.0	1109	5.5	1721	1.0	2330	5.5
26 TH	0545	1.0	1156	5.6	1810	0.9		
27 F	0016	5.5	0624	1.0	1237	5.6	1853	0.8
28 SA	0058	5.6	0659	1.0	1314	5.6	1931	0.7
29 SU	0136	5.6	0733	1.0	1349	5.6	2007	0.7
30 M	0211	5.6	0805	1.0	1421	5.6	2040	0.7

JULY

Day	Time	m	Time	m	Time	m	Time	m
1 TU	0245	5.6	0837	1.0	1453	5.5	2111	0.8
2 W	0318	5.5	0909	1.1	1526	5.4	2142	0.9
3 TH	0353	5.4	0942	1.2	1600	5.3	2215	1.0
4 F	0431	5.2	1018	1.3	1639	5.2	2253	1.1
5 SA	0513	5.1	1100	1.4	1724	5.0	2337	1.2
6 SU	0603	5.0	1151	1.5	1820	4.9		
7 M	0033	1.3	0705	4.9	1258	1.6	1930	4.9
8 TU	0150	1.3	0815	5.0	1422	1.5	2044	5.0
9 W	0308	1.2	0924	5.2	1536	1.3	2152	5.3
10 TH	0412	1.0	1026	5.5	1640	1.0	2253	5.5
11 F	0511	0.9	1121	5.7	1741	0.8	2348	5.8
12 SA	0606	0.7	1212	5.9	1839	0.7		
13 SU	0039	6.0	0657	0.7	1300	6.0	1933	0.4
14 M	0128	6.1	0747	0.6	1346	6.1	2023	0.2
15 TU	0216	6.2	0833	0.6	1431	6.1	2110	0.2
16 W	0303	6.2	0917	0.6	1516	6.0	2155	0.2
17 TH	0350	6.0	0959	0.7	1603	5.9	2238	0.4
18 F	0439	5.8	1041	0.9	1651	5.7	2322	0.6
19 SA ☽	0531	5.6	1127	1.1	1745	5.5		
20 SU	0010	0.9	0628	5.4	1222	1.3	1847	5.3
21 M	0110	1.1	0732	5.2	1331	1.4	1957	5.1
22 TU	0219	1.3	0841	5.1	1446	1.4	2111	5.1
23 W	0328	1.3	0949	5.2	1600	1.3	2219	5.2
24 TH	0431	1.3	1049	5.3	1705	1.1	2316	5.4
25 F	0523	1.2	1138	5.5	1756	0.9		
26 SA ●	0002	5.5	0604	1.1	1220	5.6	1837	0.8
27 SU	0043	5.6	0639	1.1	1257	5.6	1913	0.8
28 M	0118	5.6	0712	1.0	1330	5.7	1947	0.7
29 TU	0150	5.6	0744	1.0	1401	5.7	2019	0.7
30 W	0222	5.6	0817	0.9	1431	5.7	2051	0.7
31 TH	0253	5.6	0849	1.0	1502	5.6	2123	0.8

AUGUST

Day	Time	m	Time	m	Time	m	Time	m
1 F	0326	5.5	0921	1.1	1534	5.5	2153	0.9
2 SA	0400	5.4	0952	1.2	1609	5.4	2223	1.0
3 SU	0438	5.3	1024	1.3	1648	5.2	2257	1.2
4 M	0523	5.1	1106	1.4	1738	5.1	2344	1.3
5 TU	0619	5.0	1205	1.5	1844	5.0		
6 W	0055	1.4	0730	5.0	1333	1.5	2005	5.0
7 TH	0231	1.3	0848	5.1	1507	1.3	2124	5.2
8 F	0346	1.1	1000	5.4	1620	1.1	2233	5.5
9 SA	0450	0.9	1102	5.6	1727	0.8	2333	5.8
10 SU ○	0549	0.8	1155	5.9	1828	0.5		
11 M	0025	6.1	0643	0.7	1244	6.1	1921	0.3
12 TU	0114	6.2	0732	0.6	1332	6.2	2009	0.2
13 W	0200	6.3	0817	0.5	1413	6.2	2053	0.1
14 TH	0244	6.2	0859	0.6	1456	6.2	2135	0.2
15 F	0328	6.1	0939	0.7	1540	6.1	2213	0.4
16 SA	0413	5.9	1016	0.9	1625	5.8	2249	0.7
17 SU ☽	0459	5.6	1055	1.1	1714	5.5	2328	1.0
18 M	0550	5.3	1142	1.3	1811	5.2		
19 TU	0019	1.3	0651	5.0	1248	1.5	1922	4.9
20 W	0133	1.6	0803	4.9	1415	1.5	2043	4.9
21 TH	0253	1.6	0919	5.0	1536	1.4	2158	5.1
22 F	0403	1.5	1025	5.2	1645	1.2	2256	5.3
23 SA	0459	1.3	1116	5.4	1735	1.0	2342	5.5
24 SU	0542	1.2	1157	5.6	1815	0.9		
25 M ●	0021	5.6	0617	1.1	1234	5.7	1849	0.7
26 TU	0055	5.7	0650	1.0	1306	5.7	1921	0.7
27 W	0125	5.7	0721	0.9	1336	5.8	1953	0.7
28 TH	0155	5.8	0754	0.9	1406	5.8	2026	0.7
29 F	0226	5.8	0828	0.9	1437	5.7	2059	0.7
30 SA	0258	5.7	0903	0.9	1508	5.7	2129	0.9
31 SU	0331	5.6	0927	1.1	1542	5.6	2155	1.0

Chart Datum: 2·90 metres below Ordnance Datum (Newlyn)
HAT is 6·3 metres above Chart Datum

TIME ZONE (UT)
For Summer Time add ONE hour in **non-shaded areas**

SHEERNESS
LAT 51°27'N LONG 0°45'E
TIMES AND HEIGHTS OF HIGH AND LOW WATERS

Dates in amber are **SPRINGS**
Dates in yellow are **NEAPS**

2014

SEPTEMBER

#	Time	m	Time	m	#	Time	m	Time	m
1 M	0407	5.5	0955	1.2	16 TU	0510	5.2	1104	1.3
	1621	5.4	2224	1.2		1735	5.1	☽ 2330	1.5
2 TU	0450	5.3	1033	1.3	17 W	0606	4.9	1202	1.6
	1709	5.2	☽ 2308	1.3		1844	4.8		
3 W	0543	5.1	1813	5.0	18 TH	0039	1.8	0718	4.7
						1338	1.7	2006	4.7
4 TH	0019	1.5	0654	5.0	19 F	0213	1.8	0840	4.7
	1259	1.5	1936	5.0		1505	1.5	2126	4.9
5 F	0202	1.5	0818	5.0	20 SA	0328	1.6	0951	5.0
	1445	1.4	2102	5.2		1612	1.2	2227	5.2
6 SA	0323	1.3	0936	5.3	21 SU	0427	1.4	1045	5.3
	1603	1.0	2216	5.6		1703	1.0	2313	5.5
7 SU	0430	1.0	1041	5.6	22 M	0513	1.2	1127	5.5
	1713	0.7	2316	5.9		1744	0.9	2351	5.6
8 M	0532	0.8	1136	5.9	23 TU	0550	1.1	1203	5.7
	1813	0.5				1819	0.8		
9 TU	0008	6.1	0625	0.7	24 W	0024	5.7	0623	1.0
	1224	6.1	○ 1903	0.3		1236	5.7	● 1851	0.7
10 W	0055	6.3	0712	0.6	25 TH	0055	5.8	0656	0.9
	1308	6.2	1948	0.2		1307	5.8	1924	0.7
11 TH	0139	6.3	0756	0.5	26 F	0126	5.8	0730	0.9
	1351	6.3	2030	0.2		1339	5.8	1958	0.7
12 F	0221	6.2	0837	0.6	27 SA	0158	5.9	0805	0.8
	1433	6.2	2108	0.4		1411	5.8	2032	0.7
13 SA	0302	6.1	0914	0.7	28 SU	0231	5.8	0838	0.9
	1515	6.1	2142	0.6		1445	5.8	2103	0.9
14 SU	0343	5.8	0949	0.9	29 M	0305	5.7	0908	1.1
	1557	5.8	2213	0.9		1521	5.7	2131	1.0
15 M	0425	5.5	1024	1.1	30 TU	0342	5.6	0937	1.2
	1642	5.5	2246	1.2		1602	5.5	2202	1.2

OCTOBER

#	Time	m	Time	m	#	Time	m	Time	m
1 W	0425	5.4	1017	1.3	16 TH	0521	4.9	1120	1.5
	1651	5.3	☽ 2249	1.4		1803	4.8	2345	1.8
2 TH	0518	5.1	1116	1.4	17 F	0627	4.7	1239	1.7
	1755	5.1				1918	4.7		
3 F	0001	1.6	0628	5.0	18 SA	0115	2.0	0747	4.6
	1245	1.5	1917	5.0		1421	1.6	2037	4.8
4 SA	0139	1.6	0753	5.0	19 SU	0243	1.8	0903	4.8
	1427	1.3	2044	5.2		1528	1.4	2143	5.0
5 SU	0301	1.3	0913	5.3	20 M	0345	1.6	1002	5.1
	1546	1.0	2157	5.6		1620	1.1	2233	5.3
6 M	0408	1.1	1019	5.6	21 TU	0434	1.3	1048	5.4
	1655	0.7	2257	5.9		1704	1.0	2314	5.5
7 TU	0509	0.9	1113	5.9	22 W	0515	1.1	1128	5.6
	1752	0.5	2347	6.1		1742	0.9	2349	5.7
8 W	0603	0.8	1201	6.0	23 TH	0552	1.0	1203	5.7
	○ 1840	0.4				● 1818	0.8		
9 TH	0032	6.2	0649	0.6	24 F	0023	5.8	0628	0.9
	1245	6.2	1922	0.4		1238	5.8	1853	0.7
10 F	0115	6.2	0732	0.6	25 SA	0058	5.9	0705	0.9
	1328	6.2	2002	0.4		1313	5.8	1930	0.7
11 SA	0156	6.1	0812	0.6	26 SU	0132	5.9	0743	0.8
	1409	6.2	2037	0.6		1348	5.9	2007	0.8
12 SU	0235	6.0	0850	0.7	27 M	0207	5.9	0821	0.8
	1451	6.0	2110	0.8		1425	5.8	2042	0.9
13 M	0314	5.8	0924	0.9	28 TU	0244	5.8	0856	0.9
	1532	5.7	2139	1.1		1505	5.8	2115	1.0
14 TU	0352	5.5	0956	1.1	29 W	0323	5.6	0932	1.0
	1614	5.4	2208	1.3		1550	5.6	2153	1.2
15 W	0432	5.2	1031	1.3	30 TH	0408	5.4	1015	1.1
	1703	5.1	☽ 2248	1.6		1642	5.4	2242	1.3
					31 F	0502	5.2	1115	1.2
						1746	5.2	☽ 2350	1.5

NOVEMBER

#	Time	m	Time	m	#	Time	m	Time	m
1 SA	0611	5.0	1238	1.3	16 SU	0004	1.9	0645	4.6
	1904	5.2				1304	1.6	1932	4.7
2 SU	0115	1.5	0731	5.1	17 M	0132	1.9	0759	4.7
	1409	1.2	2024	5.3		1429	1.5	2041	4.8
3 M	0234	1.4	0848	5.3	18 TU	0249	1.7	0905	4.9
	1524	0.9	2134	5.5		1529	1.3	2139	5.1
4 TU	0341	1.2	0954	5.5	19 W	0346	1.5	1000	5.1
	1631	0.8	2234	5.8		1618	1.1	2229	5.4
5 W	0443	1.0	1050	5.7	20 TH	0434	1.2	1048	5.4
	1727	0.6	2325	5.9		1703	0.9	2312	5.6
6 TH	0537	0.8	1139	5.9	21 F	0518	1.1	1130	5.6
	○ 1814	0.6				1744	0.9	2352	5.7
7 F	0010	6.0	0625	0.7	22 SA	0601	0.9	1210	5.7
	1224	6.0	1855	0.6		● 1825	0.8		
8 SA	0053	6.0	0708	0.6	23 SU	0031	5.8	0643	0.8
	1307	6.0	1932	0.6		1251	5.8	1905	0.7
9 SU	0132	6.0	0750	0.6	24 M	0110	5.9	0726	0.7
	1349	6.0	2007	0.7		1331	5.9	1946	0.7
10 M	0211	5.9	0828	0.7	25 TU	0149	5.9	0809	0.7
	1430	5.9	2039	0.9		1412	5.9	2026	0.8
11 TU	0248	5.7	0903	0.9	26 W	0229	5.8	0852	0.7
	1510	5.7	2108	1.1		1456	5.9	2106	0.9
12 W	0324	5.5	0933	1.0	27 TH	0311	5.7	0935	0.8
	1550	5.4	2137	1.3		1543	5.7	2149	1.0
13 TH	0401	5.2	1004	1.2	28 F	0358	5.5	1022	0.9
	1633	5.1	2213	1.5		1636	5.6	2237	1.2
14 F	0443	5.0	1044	1.4	29 SA	0451	5.4	1117	1.0
	1723	4.9	☽ 2300	1.7		1736	5.4	☽ 2336	1.3
15 SA	0536	4.8	1140	1.5	30 SU	0554	5.2	1226	1.0
	1823	4.7				1845	5.3		

DECEMBER

#	Time	m	Time	m	#	Time	m	Time	m
1 M	0047	1.4	0706	5.2	16 TU	0013	1.8	0649	4.7
	1342	1.0	1958	5.3		1303	1.5	1934	4.7
2 TU	0201	1.4	0819	5.2	17 W	0129	1.8	0801	4.7
	1454	1.0	2107	5.4		1424	1.4	2040	4.9
3 W	0310	1.3	0927	5.4	18 TH	0248	1.6	0907	4.9
	1601	0.9	2209	5.5		1528	1.2	2141	5.2
4 TH	0415	1.1	1027	5.5	19 F	0350	1.4	1006	5.2
	1659	0.9	2303	5.7		1623	1.1	2235	5.4
5 F	0514	1.0	1120	5.6	20 SA	0445	1.1	1058	5.4
	1748	0.8	2350	5.7		1713	0.9	2324	5.6
6 SA	0605	0.8	1207	5.7	21 SU	0535	1.0	1146	5.6
	○ 1829	0.8				1800	0.8		
7 SU	0033	5.8	0650	0.7	22 M	0009	5.8	0624	0.8
	1252	5.8	1906	0.8		1232	5.8	● 1845	0.7
8 M	0114	5.8	0731	0.7	23 TU	0053	5.9	0714	0.6
	1334	5.8	1941	0.9		1317	5.9	1931	0.7
9 TU	0152	5.7	0810	0.7	24 W	0135	5.9	0802	0.5
	1413	5.7	2013	1.0		1402	6.0	2016	0.7
10 W	0227	5.6	0844	0.8	25 TH	0218	5.9	0850	0.5
	1451	5.6	2043	1.1		1447	6.0	2059	0.7
11 TH	0301	5.5	0914	0.9	26 F	0302	5.9	0936	0.5
	1528	5.4	2112	1.2		1535	5.9	2143	0.8
12 F	0335	5.3	0943	1.0	27 SA	0348	5.8	1021	0.6
	1605	5.3	2145	1.3		1625	5.8	2227	1.0
13 SA	0412	5.2	1017	1.1	28 SU	0438	5.6	1109	0.7
	1646	5.1	2224	1.5		1720	5.5	☽ 2316	1.2
14 SU	0454	5.0	1100	1.3	29 M	0534	5.4	1202	0.9
	1733	4.9	2313	1.6		1821	5.3		
15 M	0546	4.8	1153	1.4	30 TU	0014	1.3	0638	5.3
	1829	4.8				1307	1.0	1927	5.2
					31 W	0124	1.3	0749	5.2
						1418	1.1	2036	5.2

Chart Datum: 2·90 metres below Ordnance Datum (Newlyn)
HAT is 6·3 metres above Chart Datum

TIDES

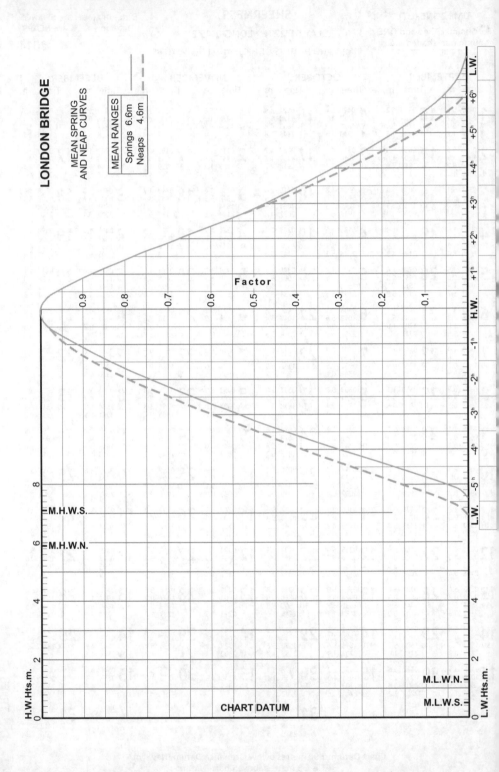

LONDON BRIDGE

MEAN SPRING
AND NEAP CURVES

MEAN RANGES	
Springs	6.6m
Neaps	4.6m

LONDON BRIDGE
LAT 51°30'N   LONG 0°05'W
TIMES AND HEIGHTS OF HIGH AND LOW WATERS

Dates in amber are **SPRINGS**
Dates in yellow are **NEAPS**

2014

JANUARY

Day	Time m	Time m	Time m	Time m
1 W ●	0104 6.9	0755 0.6	1329 7.3	2014 0.7
16 TH ○	0154 6.7	0823 0.7	1411 6.8	2032 1.1
2 TH	0157 7.1	0854 0.6	1420 7.4	2109 0.7
17 F	0229 6.7	0901 0.7	1445 6.8	2106 1.1
3 F	0247 7.2	0946 0.2	1510 7.5	2158 0.6
18 SA	0300 6.8	0936 0.6	1516 6.9	2137 1.0
4 SA	0334 7.2	1033 0.1	1559 7.5	2242 0.6
19 SU	0330 6.8	1008 0.6	1546 6.9	2208 1.0
5 SU	0420 7.2	1115 0.1	1646 7.4	2321 0.7
20 M	0400 6.8	1038 0.6	1618 6.9	2239 1.0
6 M	0505 7.1	1153 0.2	1734 7.2	
21 TU	0431 6.8	1106 0.6	1651 6.8	2309 1.1
7 TU	0000 0.8	0550 6.9	1230 0.4	1823 6.9
22 W	0505 6.6	1131 0.7	1727 6.6	2338 1.2
8 W ◑	0040 1.0	0640 6.7	1310 0.6	1916 6.6
23 TH	0541 6.5	1158 0.8	1807 6.4	
9 TH	0125 1.2	0735 6.4	1357 0.9	2013 6.3
24 F ◑	0011 1.2	0623 6.4	1234 0.9	1853 6.2
10 F	0221 1.4	0837 6.2	1454 1.2	2114 6.1
25 SA	0055 1.3	0714 6.2	1321 1.0	1952 6.0
11 SA	0327 1.5	0943 6.1	1557 1.3	2222 6.0
26 SU	0154 1.5	0823 6.1	1430 1.3	2116 6.0
12 SU	0438 1.5	1052 6.1	1704 1.3	2333 6.1
27 M	0321 1.5	0955 6.2	1616 1.3	2235 6.2
13 M	0550 1.2	1157 6.3	1811 1.3	
28 TU	0504 1.3	1110 6.5	1736 1.0	2346 6.5
14 TU	0029 6.4	0651 1.0	1249 6.5	1907 1.1
29 W	0627 0.9	1216 6.9	1854 0.9	
15 W	0115 6.5	0740 0.8	1333 6.7	1952 1.1
30 TH ●	0048 6.8	0743 0.6	1315 7.2	2003 0.7
31 F	0144 7.1	0844 0.2	1408 7.4	2059 0.6

FEBRUARY

Day	Time m	Time m	Time m	Time m
1 SA	0233 7.3	0935 0.0	1457 7.5	2147 0.5
16 SU	0240 6.9	0915 0.6	1454 6.9	2125 0.9
2 SU	0319 7.4	1020 -0.1	1543 7.6	2230 0.5
17 M	0310 6.9	0949 0.5	1523 7.0	2157 0.9
3 M	0402 7.4	1100 -0.1	1628 7.5	2308 0.5
18 TU	0339 7.0	1021 0.4	1555 7.0	2229 0.8
4 TU	0444 7.4	1134 0.1	1711 7.2	2341 0.7
19 W	0410 7.0	1049 0.5	1628 6.9	2257 0.9
5 W	0525 7.1	1203 0.4	1753 6.9	
20 TH	0444 6.9	1112 0.6	1703 6.7	2323 1.0
6 TH	0013 0.9	0607 6.8	1231 0.7	1836 6.5
21 F	0520 6.7	1136 0.7	1741 6.5	2353 1.1
7 F	0047 1.1	0653 6.5	1304 1.0	1924 6.2
22 SA ◐	0600 6.6	1209 0.8	1825 6.3	
8 SA	0128 1.4	0749 6.2	1353 1.3	2021 5.9
23 SU	0032 1.1	0650 6.4	1253 1.0	1921 6.1
9 SU	0229 1.6	0856 5.9	1506 1.6	2130 5.7
24 M	0126 1.3	0755 6.2	1358 1.3	2040 5.9
10 M	0350 1.6	1011 5.8	1622 1.6	2253 5.8
25 TU	0249 1.5	0928 6.2	1553 1.4	2209 6.1
11 TU	0506 1.4	1127 6.1	1736 1.4	2328 6.4
26 W	0441 1.3	1050 6.4	1718 1.1	2328 6.4
12 W	0000 6.1	0616 1.1	1226 6.4	1839 1.2
27 TH	0613 0.9	1202 6.8	1842 0.9	
13 TH	0050 6.5	0712 0.8	1311 6.8	1929 1.1
28 F	0034 6.8	0731 0.4	1303 7.2	1949 0.6
14 F ○	0132 6.7	0758 0.7	1350 6.7	2012 1.0
15 SA	0208 6.8	0838 0.6	1424 6.8	2050 1.0

MARCH

Day	Time m	Time m	Time m	Time m
1 SA ●	0128 7.1	0828 0.1	1354 7.4	2043 0.5
16 SU	0140 6.8	0808 0.6	1356 6.8	2027 0.9
2 SU	0215 7.3	0917 0.0	1440 7.5	2130 0.4
17 M	0213 6.9	0848 0.5	1427 6.9	2105 0.9
3 M	0258 7.5	1000 -0.1	1523 7.5	2211 0.4
18 TU	0244 7.0	0924 0.5	1458 7.0	2141 0.8
4 TU	0339 7.5	1037 0.0	1603 7.4	2248 0.4
19 W	0315 7.1	0958 0.4	1531 7.0	2215 0.7
5 W	0418 7.5	1107 0.3	1642 7.2	2318 0.6
20 TH	0349 7.1	1027 0.5	1606 6.9	2244 0.8
6 TH	0457 7.3	1128 0.5	1720 6.8	2343 0.8
21 F	0424 7.1	1052 0.6	1642 6.8	2310 0.8
7 F	0536 6.9	1149 0.8	1757 6.4	
22 SA	0502 6.9	1118 0.7	1720 6.5	2340 0.9
8 SA	0010 1.0	0616 6.5	1218 1.0	1837 6.1
23 SU	0544 6.7	1152 0.9	1805 6.3	
9 SU	0044 1.2	0704 6.1	1259 1.4	1927 5.8
24 M ◐	0018 1.0	0635 6.5	1238 1.1	1902 6.1
10 M	0134 1.5	0808 5.8	1404 1.7	2037 5.6
25 TU	0112 1.2	0743 6.2	1347 1.4	2021 5.9
11 TU	0258 1.7	0928 5.7	1541 1.8	2204 5.6
26 W	0239 1.4	0913 6.2	1539 1.4	2151 6.1
12 W	0425 1.5	1048 5.9	1700 1.6	2322 6.0
27 TH	0425 1.1	1035 6.5	1702 1.1	2311 6.4
13 TH	0535 1.2	1152 6.2	1806 1.3	
28 F	0600 0.8	1147 6.8	1825 0.8	
14 F	0017 6.4	0635 0.9	1242 6.5	1859 1.1
29 SA	0017 6.8	0712 0.4	1247 7.1	1929 0.6
15 SA ●	0102 6.6	0725 0.7	1322 6.7	1945 1.0
30 SU ●	0109 7.1	0806 0.1	1336 7.2	2021 0.5
31 M	0154 7.2	0852 0.1	1419 7.3	2107 0.4

APRIL

Day	Time m	Time m	Time m	Time m
1 TU	0235 7.4	0933 0.2	1459 7.3	2148 0.4
16 W	0216 7.1	0856 0.5	1434 7.0	2121 0.7
2 W	0313 7.5	1007 0.3	1537 7.2	2223 0.4
17 TH	0252 7.2	0934 0.5	1511 7.0	2159 0.6
3 TH	0352 7.5	1033 0.5	1613 7.1	2252 0.5
18 F	0330 7.2	1007 0.5	1548 6.9	2233 0.6
4 F	0430 7.2	1051 0.7	1648 6.8	2314 0.7
19 SA	0408 7.2	1037 0.6	1626 6.8	2303 0.7
5 SA	0507 6.9	1114 0.8	1723 6.4	2340 0.9
20 SU	0449 7.0	1108 0.7	1708 6.5	2334 0.7
6 SU	0546 6.5	1144 1.1	1800 6.1	
21 M	0535 6.8	1146 0.9	1755 6.3	
7 M ◑	0012 1.1	0628 6.1	1221 1.4	1844 5.8
22 TU ◑	0014 0.8	0629 6.6	1237 1.2	1854 6.1
8 TU	0056 1.4	0723 5.8	1314 1.7	1946 5.6
23 W	0111 1.0	0740 6.4	1353 1.4	2012 6.1
9 W	0203 1.6	0841 5.6	1442 1.9	2114 5.5
24 TH	0241 1.1	0902 6.4	1523 1.3	2135 6.2
10 TH	0339 1.5	1000 5.7	1616 1.7	2233 5.8
25 F	0408 0.9	1017 6.6	1641 1.1	2250 6.5
11 F	0451 1.2	1107 6.1	1724 1.4	2335 6.2
26 SA	0534 0.7	1127 6.8	1759 0.9	2354 6.8
12 SA	0550 0.9	1201 6.4	1821 1.1	
27 SU	0645 0.4	1226 7.0	1903 0.7	
13 SU	0023 6.5	0644 0.7	1245 6.6	1911 0.9
28 M	0047 7.0	0738 0.3	1315 7.0	1955 0.5
14 M	0105 6.8	0732 0.6	1322 6.8	1957 0.9
29 TU ●	0131 7.1	0823 0.4	1357 7.1	2041 0.5
15 TU ○	0141 6.9	0816 0.6	1358 6.9	2040 0.8
30 W	0211 7.2	0902 0.5	1436 7.0	2122 0.4

TIDES

Chart Datum: 3·20 metres below Ordnance Datum (Newlyn)
HAT is 7·7 metres above Chart Datum

LONDON BRIDGE
LAT 51°30′N   LONG 0°05′W
TIMES AND HEIGHTS OF HIGH AND LOW WATERS

TIME ZONE (UT)
For Summer Time add ONE hour in **non-shaded areas**

Dates in amber are SPRINGS
Dates in yellow are NEAPS

2014

MAY

Day	Time m	Time m	Time m	Time m	Day	Time m	Time m	Time m	Time m
1 TH	0250 7.3	0935 0.6	1512 7.1	2158 0.4	16 F	0232 7.3	0912 0.6	1454 7.0	2145 0.5
2 F	0328 7.3	0959 0.7	1547 6.9	2227 0.5	17 SA	0314 7.3	0953 0.6	1536 7.0	2225 0.4
3 SA	0405 7.2	1019 0.8	1621 6.7	2250 0.7	18 SU	0358 7.3	1030 0.6	1619 6.8	2303 0.4
4 SU	0443 6.9	1046 0.9	1655 6.4	2316 0.8	19 M	0443 7.1	1108 0.7	1703 6.7	2339 0.5
5 M	0520 6.5	1118 1.1	1730 6.2	2348 1.0	20 TU	0532 7.0	1151 0.9	1753 6.5	
6 TU	0559 6.2	1153 1.3	1810 6.0		21 W	0022 0.6	0628 6.7	1244 1.1	1851 6.4
7 W	0026 1.2	0645 5.9	1238 1.6	1900 5.7	22 TH	0120 0.7	0735 6.6	1350 1.2	2002 6.3
8 TH	0119 1.4	0747 5.7	1340 1.8	2014 5.6	23 F	0232 0.8	0845 6.6	1502 1.2	2114 6.4
9 F	0237 1.4	0906 5.7	1506 1.8	2140 5.7	24 SA	0343 0.8	0953 6.6	1613 1.1	2223 6.3
10 SA	0358 1.3	1013 6.0	1628 1.6	2245 6.0	25 SU	0455 0.7	1101 6.7	1726 0.9	2327 6.7
11 SU	0501 1.0	1111 6.3	1733 1.3	2339 6.4	26 M	0609 0.7	1202 6.7	1833 0.8	
12 M	0557 0.8	1201 6.6	1830 1.1		27 TU	0023 6.8	0705 0.7	1254 6.8	1928 0.6
13 TU	0025 6.7	0650 0.7	1247 6.8	1924 0.9	28 W	0110 6.9	0752 0.7	1337 6.8	2015 0.5
14 W	0108 6.9	0741 0.6	1330 6.9	2014 0.8	29 TH	0152 7.0	0831 0.8	1416 6.9	2057 0.5
15 TH	0150 7.1	0828 0.6	1412 7.0	2101 0.6	30 F	0230 7.1	0905 0.8	1452 6.9	2135 0.5
					31 SA	0308 7.1	0933 0.9	1526 6.8	2206 0.6

JUNE

Day	Time m	Time m	Time m	Time m	Day	Time m	Time m	Time m	Time m
1 SU	0345 7.0	0957 0.9	1600 6.7	2232 0.7	16 M	0350 7.4	1029 0.6	1613 7.0	2304 0.1
2 M	0421 6.8	1026 1.0	1633 6.5	2300 0.7	17 TU	0438 7.3	1111 0.6	1659 6.9	2345 0.2
3 TU	0457 6.6	1059 1.1	1707 6.4	2331 0.8	18 W	0527 7.2	1153 0.7	1747 6.8	
4 W	0533 6.4	1134 1.2	1744 6.2		19 TH	0027 0.3	0620 7.0	1240 0.8	1841 6.7
5 TH	0005 1.0	0613 6.2	1212 1.4	1826 6.0	20 F	0115 0.5	0719 6.8	1333 1.0	1942 6.6
6 F	0045 1.1	0700 6.0	1257 1.5	1918 5.8	21 SA	0210 0.6	0821 6.5	1434 1.1	2046 6.5
7 SA	0136 1.2	0802 5.8	1356 1.7	2031 5.7	22 SU	0309 0.8	0924 6.5	1539 1.1	2151 6.5
8 SU	0244 1.3	0917 5.9	1511 1.6	2150 5.9	23 M	0412 0.9	1030 6.4	1648 1.1	2257 6.5
9 M	0403 1.1	1022 6.1	1636 1.4	2252 6.3	24 TU	0521 1.0	1136 6.5	1800 1.0	2358 6.6
10 TU	0508 0.9	1120 6.4	1746 1.1	2347 6.6	25 W	0629 1.0	1232 6.6	1901 0.8	
11 W	0608 0.8	1214 6.7	1850 0.9		26 TH	0050 6.7	0721 0.9	1319 6.7	1951 0.6
12 TH	0038 6.9	0706 0.7	1305 6.9	1949 0.7	27 F	0136 6.9	0804 0.9	1400 6.7	2035 0.5
13 F	0128 7.1	0804 0.7	1354 7.0	2043 0.5	28 SA	0216 6.9	0842 0.9	1437 6.8	2114 0.5
14 SA	0215 7.3	0857 0.6	1441 7.1	2134 0.3	29 SU	0254 7.0	0916 1.0	1511 6.9	2148 0.6
15 SU	0303 7.4	0945 0.6	1527 7.1	2221 0.2	30 M	0329 6.9	0945 1.0	1543 6.7	2218 0.6

JULY

Day	Time m	Time m	Time m	Time m	Day	Time m	Time m	Time m	Time m
1 TU	0402 6.8	1014 1.0	1614 6.7	2247 0.6	16 W	0426 7.5	1106 0.4	1645 7.3	2338 -0.1
2 W	0435 6.7	1046 1.0	1646 6.6	2317 0.7	17 TH	0513 7.3	1146 0.5	1731 7.1	
3 TH	0508 6.6	1119 1.1	1720 6.4	2346 0.8	18 F	0015 0.1	0601 7.1	1226 0.7	1818 6.9
4 F	0544 6.4	1151 1.2	1757 6.3		19 SA	0054 0.4	0653 6.8	1309 0.9	1912 6.7
5 SA	0016 0.9	0623 6.2	1226 1.3	1839 6.1	20 SU	0137 0.7	0748 6.5	1359 1.1	2011 6.5
6 SU	0052 1.0	0704 6.0	1311 1.4	1931 5.9	21 M	0229 0.9	0848 6.3	1500 1.3	2115 6.3
7 M	0141 1.1	0814 5.9	1410 1.5	2045 5.9	22 TU	0330 1.1	0953 6.1	1608 1.3	2223 6.3
8 TU	0250 1.2	0934 6.0	1533 1.5	2207 6.1	23 W	0436 1.2	1106 6.2	1722 1.1	2333 6.4
9 W	0421 1.1	1042 6.3	1705 1.2	2313 6.5	24 TH	0549 1.2	1209 6.4	1833 0.9	
10 TH	0532 0.9	1145 6.6	1818 0.9		25 F	0031 6.6	0652 1.1	1300 6.6	1927 0.7
11 F	0013 6.9	0638 0.8	1244 6.8	1927 0.6	26 SA	0119 6.8	0740 1.0	1343 6.7	2012 0.6
12 SA	0108 7.2	0746 0.7	1337 7.0	2030 0.4	27 SU	0201 6.9	0822 1.0	1420 6.8	2052 0.5
13 SU	0201 7.4	0846 0.6	1427 7.2	2125 0.2	28 M	0238 6.9	0900 1.0	1454 6.8	2128 0.5
14 M	0250 7.5	0938 0.5	1515 7.3	2214 0.0	29 TU	0311 6.9	0932 1.0	1524 6.9	2200 0.5
15 TU	0339 7.6	1024 0.5	1601 7.3	2258 -0.1	30 W	0340 6.9	1003 0.9	1553 6.9	2230 0.5
					31 TH	0410 6.9	1033 0.9	1623 6.8	2259 0.5

AUGUST

Day	Time m	Time m	Time m	Time m	Day	Time m	Time m	Time m	Time m
1 F	0441 6.8	1103 1.0	1655 6.7	2325 0.7	16 SA	0535 7.0	1203 0.7	1750 7.1	
2 SA	0515 6.6	1131 1.1	1729 6.5	2349 0.8	17 SU	0022 0.5	0619 6.7	1239 0.9	1836 6.7
3 SU	0551 6.4	1159 1.2	1807 6.3		18 M	0055 0.9	0708 6.3	1319 1.2	1930 6.4
4 M	0018 0.9	0632 6.2	1236 1.3	1853 6.2	19 TU	0140 1.2	0804 6.0	1415 1.4	2034 6.1
5 TU	0059 1.0	0725 6.0	1327 1.4	1954 6.0	20 W	0245 1.5	0910 5.8	1528 1.5	2147 6.0
6 W	0157 1.2	0843 5.9	1441 1.5	2124 6.1	21 TH	0359 1.5	1030 5.9	1644 1.3	2304 6.2
7 TH	0337 1.5	1007 6.1	1631 1.3	2243 6.4	22 F	0515 1.4	1141 6.2	1759 1.0	
8 F	0504 1.1	1119 6.4	1751 0.9	2350 6.8	23 SA	0008 6.5	0622 1.1	1235 6.5	1858 0.7
9 SA	0617 0.9	1223 6.8	1911 0.6		24 SU	0057 6.8	0715 1.0	1319 6.7	1945 0.6
10 SU	0051 7.2	0733 0.7	1320 7.1	2017 0.3	25 M	0139 6.9	0759 0.9	1357 6.9	2025 0.5
11 M	0145 7.4	0834 0.6	1410 7.3	2112 0.0	26 TU	0215 6.9	0838 0.9	1430 6.9	2102 0.5
12 TU	0235 7.6	0926 0.4	1457 7.4	2200 -0.2	27 W	0246 6.9	0914 0.9	1500 7.0	2136 0.5
13 W	0322 7.6	1012 0.4	1541 7.5	2242 -0.2	28 TH	0314 7.0	0946 0.9	1528 7.0	2207 0.5
14 TH	0407 7.4	1052 0.4	1624 7.5	2320 -0.1	29 F	0343 7.0	1017 0.9	1557 7.0	2236 0.5
15 F	0451 7.4	1129 0.5	1706 7.3	2352 0.2	30 SA	0414 6.9	1047 0.9	1627 6.9	2300 0.7
					31 SU	0447 6.7	1112 1.0	1703 6.7	2322 0.8

Chart Datum: 3·20 metres below Ordnance Datum (Newlyn)
HAT is 7·7 metres above Chart Datum

TIME ZONE (UT)
For Summer Time add ONE hour in **non-shaded areas**

LONDON BRIDGE
LAT 51°30'N   LONG 0°05'W
TIMES AND HEIGHTS OF HIGH AND LOW WATERS

Dates in amber are **SPRINGS**
Dates in yellow are NEAPS
2014

SEPTEMBER

Day	Time m	Time m	Time m	Time m
1 M	0522 6.5	1137 1.1	1741 6.6	2349 0.9
2 TU	0602 6.3	1210 1.2	1826 6.4 ◗	
3 W	0027 1.1	0652 6.0	1257 1.3	1924 6.2
4 TH	0122 1.3	0802 5.9	1406 1.5	2050 6.1
5 F	0306 1.5	0936 6.0	1605 1.3	2218 6.4
6 SA	0443 1.2	1055 6.3	1731 0.9	2331 6.8
7 SU	0601 0.9	1204 6.8	1857 0.5	
8 M	0034 7.2	0718 0.7	1301 7.1	2001 0.2
9 TU	0128 7.4	0817 0.5	1350 7.3	2053 0.0 ○
10 W	0215 7.6	0907 0.4	1435 7.5	2139 -0.1
11 TH	0300 7.6	0952 0.5	1517 7.6	2219 0.0
12 F	0343 7.5	1032 0.4	1558 7.6	2254 0.2
13 SA	0424 7.3	1107 0.5	1638 7.4	2322 0.5
14 SU	0503 7.0	1137 0.7	1719 7.1	2344 0.8
15 M	0542 6.6	1205 0.9	1802 6.7	
16 TU	0010 1.1	0623 6.2	1239 1.2	1849 6.3 ◖
17 W	0048 1.4	0713 5.9	1326 1.4	1951 5.9
18 TH	0150 1.7	0821 5.6	1444 1.6	2108 5.8
19 F	0321 1.8	0945 5.6	1606 1.4	2226 6.0
20 SA	0441 1.6	1103 6.0	1717 1.1	2335 6.3
21 SU	0548 1.3	1201 6.4	1819 0.8	
22 M	0027 6.7	0643 1.0	1248 6.7	1909 0.6
23 TU	0109 6.8	0730 0.9	1327 6.8	1952 0.6
24 W	0145 6.9	0811 0.9	1401 6.9	2031 0.6 ●
25 TH	0216 7.0	0849 0.9	1431 7.0	2107 0.5
26 F	0245 7.0	0925 0.8	1500 7.1	2140 0.5
27 SA	0315 7.0	0959 0.8	1532 7.1	2210 0.6
28 SU	0348 7.0	1029 0.8	1606 7.1	2235 0.7
29 M	0422 6.8	1055 0.9	1642 6.9	2259 0.9
30 TU	0458 6.6	1120 1.0	1721 6.7	2329 1.0

OCTOBER

Day	Time m	Time m	Time m	Time m
1 W	0538 6.3	1153 1.1	1808 6.5 ○	
2 TH	0008 1.2	0629 6.1	1240 1.2	1906 6.3
3 F	0104 1.5	0737 5.9	1347 1.4	2031 6.2
4 SA	0252 1.6	0911 6.0	1547 1.3	2157 6.4
5 SU	0424 1.3	1033 6.3	1712 0.9	2311 6.8
6 M	0543 1.0	1142 6.7	1836 0.5	
7 TU	0014 7.1	0656 0.7	1258 7.0	1937 0.2
8 W	0108 7.3	0754 0.5	1327 7.3	2028 0.1 ○
9 TH	0154 7.4	0840 0.4	1411 7.4	2112 0.7
10 F	0236 7.4	0929 0.4	1452 7.6	2151 0.3
11 SA	0317 7.4	1009 0.4	1532 7.6	2224 0.5
12 SU	0355 7.2	1043 0.5	1612 7.4	2247 0.7
13 M	0433 6.9	1110 0.7	1651 7.1	2306 1.0
14 TU	0509 6.5	1134 0.9	1731 6.7	2333 1.2
15 W	0546 6.2	1204 1.2	1815 6.3 ◖	
16 TH	0008 1.5	0628 5.9	1245 1.4	1908 5.9
17 F	0059 1.8	0727 5.6	1349 1.6	2022 5.7
18 SA	0221 2.0	0854 5.5	1522 1.6	2139 5.8
19 SU	0357 1.9	1014 5.7	1634 1.3	2248 6.1
20 M	0507 1.5	1118 6.1	1733 1.0	2345 6.4
21 TU	0604 1.2	1208 6.5	1826 0.8	
22 W	0030 6.7	0654 1.0	1251 6.7	1913 0.7
23 TH	0109 6.8	0739 0.9	1327 6.9	1956 0.7 ●
24 F	0143 6.9	0821 0.7	1400 7.0	2035 0.7
25 SA	0216 7.0	0901 0.8	1434 7.1	2112 0.7
26 SU	0251 7.0	0939 0.8	1509 7.2	2144 0.7
27 M	0327 7.0	1013 0.7	1546 7.2	2214 0.8
28 TU	0403 6.8	1043 0.8	1625 7.1	2243 0.9
29 W	0441 6.6	1111 0.9	1708 6.9	2318 1.0
30 TH	0524 6.4	1146 0.9	1757 6.6 ◖	
31 F	0002 1.2	0616 6.2	1234 1.1	1858 6.4 ◐

NOVEMBER

Day	Time m	Time m	Time m	Time m
1 SA	0102 1.5	0723 6.0	1347 1.2	2018 6.3
2 SU	0239 1.6	0851 6.1	1529 1.1	2137 6.5
3 M	0402 1.4	1009 6.3	1648 0.8	2248 6.7
4 TU	0518 1.1	1118 6.7	1807 0.6	2352 7.0
5 W	0630 0.8	1216 6.9	1909 0.4	
6 TH	0046 7.1	0729 0.6	1305 7.1	1959 0.4 ○
7 F	0133 7.2	0819 0.5	1348 7.3	2043 0.5
8 SA	0214 7.2	0904 0.5	1429 7.4	2121 0.6
9 SU	0253 7.2	0944 0.5	1509 7.4	2153 0.8
10 M	0331 7.0	1019 0.6	1548 7.3	2214 0.9
11 TU	0407 6.8	1045 0.7	1627 7.0	2235 1.1
12 W	0441 6.5	1108 0.9	1706 6.6	2305 1.3
13 TH	0516 6.3	1137 1.1	1745 6.3	2340 1.5
14 F	0553 6.0	1214 1.2	1829 6.0 ◖	
15 SA	0021 1.7	0638 5.8	1302 1.4	1925 5.8
16 SU	0118 1.9	0743 5.5	1414 1.6	2043 5.7
17 M	0239 2.0	0917 5.6	1540 1.5	2152 5.9
18 TU	0410 1.8	1025 5.9	1644 1.2	2252 6.2
19 W	0516 1.5	1122 6.2	1739 1.0	2345 6.5
20 TH	0612 1.2	1209 6.6	1831 0.7	
21 F	0030 6.7	0703 1.0	1252 6.8	1919 0.8
22 SA	0112 6.9	0752 0.9	1331 7.0	2004 0.7 ●
23 SU	0152 7.0	0838 0.8	1411 7.1	2047 0.8
24 M	0232 7.0	0922 0.7	1452 7.2	2127 0.8
25 TU	0313 7.0	1003 0.6	1533 7.3	2204 0.8
26 W	0353 6.9	1040 0.7	1616 7.2	2240 0.8
27 TH	0434 6.7	1115 0.6	1701 7.0	2320 1.0
28 F	0519 6.6	1152 0.7	1752 6.7	
29 SA	0007 1.2	0610 6.4	1241 0.9	1852 6.6 ◗
30 SU	0107 1.4	0713 6.3	1349 1.0	2003 6.5

DECEMBER

Day	Time m	Time m	Time m	Time m
1 M	0220 1.4	0830 6.2	1505 1.0	2114 6.5
2 TU	0335 1.4	0943 6.4	1615 0.9	2222 6.6
3 W	0448 1.2	1051 6.5	1730 0.8	2328 6.7
4 TH	0601 1.0	1152 6.7	1837 0.7	
5 F	0026 6.8	0702 0.8	1245 6.9	1930 0.7
6 SA	0114 6.9	0754 0.6	1330 7.0	2015 0.8 ○
7 SU	0157 6.9	0841 0.5	1412 7.1	2054 0.9
8 M	0236 6.9	0922 0.5	1452 7.2	2127 1.0
9 TU	0312 6.9	0958 0.6	1530 7.1	2151 1.1
10 W	0346 6.8	1027 0.7	1607 6.9	2215 1.1
11 TH	0420 6.6	1050 0.8	1643 6.7	2246 1.2
12 F	0452 6.4	1119 0.9	1718 6.5	2319 1.3
13 SA	0526 6.2	1151 1.0	1755 6.3	2355 1.5
14 SU	0604 6.1	1227 1.2	1838 6.0 ◖	
15 M	0036 1.6	0649 5.8	1311 1.3	1930 5.9
16 TU	0126 1.8	0748 5.7	1409 1.5	2044 5.8
17 W	0232 1.9	0921 5.7	1533 1.4	2155 5.9
18 TH	0406 1.8	1029 6.0	1647 1.2	2256 6.2
19 F	0524 1.5	1126 6.3	1746 1.0	2352 6.5
20 SA	0625 1.1	1218 6.7	1842 0.9	
21 SU	0043 6.8	0723 1.0	1306 7.0	1937 0.8
22 M	0131 6.9	0817 0.7	1353 7.2	2029 0.8 ●
23 TU	0218 7.0	0909 0.6	1438 7.3	2118 0.8
24 W	0302 7.1	0956 0.4	1524 7.4	2204 0.7
25 TH	0346 7.1	1041 0.3	1610 7.4	2246 0.7
26 F	0430 7.0	1121 0.3	1656 7.2	2327 0.8
27 SA	0514 6.9	1200 0.4	1745 7.0	
28 SU	0010 0.9	0601 6.7	1243 0.5	1839 6.8 ◗
29 M	0058 1.1	0650 6.6	1333 0.7	1941 6.6
30 TU	0155 1.3	0803 6.4	1432 0.9	2046 6.4
31 W	0301 1.4	0912 6.0	1537 1.0	2152 6.4

Chart Datum: 3·20 metres below Ordnance Datum (Newlyn)
HAT is 7·7 metres above Chart Datum

TIDES

WALTON-ON-THE-NAZE

MEAN SPRING
AND NEAP CURVES

MEAN RANGES	
Springs	3.8m
Neaps	2.3m

WALTON-ON-THE-NAZE

LAT 51°51′N   LONG 1°17′E

TIMES AND HEIGHTS OF HIGH AND LOW WATERS

Dates in amber are **SPRINGS**
Dates in yellow are **NEAPS**

2014

JANUARY

Day				
1 W	0505 0.5	1200 4.4	1719 0.5	● 2340 4.3
2 TH	0558 0.3	1200 4.5	1809 0.5	
3 F	0029 4.4	0649 0.2	1250 4.6	1856 0.5
4 SA	0117 4.5	0738 0.1	1339 4.6	1943 0.6
5 SU	0204 4.5	0826 0.1	1428 4.5	2029 0.7
6 M	0251 4.4	0913 0.2	1518 4.3	2116 0.8
7 TU	0338 4.2	1001 0.3	1610 4.1	2206 0.9
8 W	0429 4.1	1052 0.5	1706 3.9	◐ 2302 1.0
9 TH	0525 3.9	1148 0.7	1807 3.7	
10 F	0006 1.1	0631 3.7	1251 0.8	1914 3.6
11 SA	0119 1.1	0743 3.6	1400 1.0	2025 3.6
12 SU	0235 1.1	0850 3.7	1510 1.0	2126 3.7
13 M	0344 0.9	0946 3.8	1605 1.0	2216 3.9
14 TU	0435 0.7	1033 3.9	1647 0.9	2259 4.0
15 W	0516 0.6	1113 4.0	1723 0.8	2336 4.0
16 TH	0552 0.5	1149 4.0	1756 0.8	○
17 F	0011 4.1	0624 0.4	1225 4.1	1826 0.8
18 SA	0044 4.2	0655 0.4	1259 4.1	1855 0.8
19 SU	0117 4.2	0726 0.4	1333 4.1	1924 0.7
20 M	0149 4.1	0757 0.4	1406 4.0	1955 0.8
21 TU	0222 4.1	0828 0.4	1439 4.0	2029 0.8
22 W	0255 4.0	0900 0.5	1516 3.9	2106 0.9
23 TH	0332 3.9	0937 0.6	1557 3.8	2149 1.0
24 F	0415 3.8	1023 0.7	1647 3.7	◑ 2245 1.1
25 SA	0510 3.7	1127 0.8	1751 3.6	
26 SU	0004 1.1	0620 3.7	1253 0.9	1906 3.6
27 M	0137 1.0	0742 3.7	1410 0.8	2025 3.7
28 TU	0251 0.8	0859 3.8	1515 0.7	2137 3.9
29 W	0355 0.6	1003 4.1	1614 0.6	2236 4.1
30 TH	0454 0.4	1058 4.3	1708 0.6	● 2327 4.3
31 F	0548 0.2	1149 4.5	1758 0.5	

FEBRUARY

Day				
1 SA	0015 4.4	0638 0.1	1237 4.6	1844 0.5
2 SU	0101 4.6	0725 0.0	1324 4.6	1929 0.5
3 M	0146 4.6	0809 0.0	1410 4.5	2012 0.6
4 TU	0229 4.5	0850 0.1	1455 4.3	2053 0.7
5 W	0312 4.3	0929 0.3	1541 4.1	2135 0.8
6 TH	0356 4.1	1009 0.5	1629 3.9	◑ 2222 0.9
7 F	0444 3.9	1056 0.8	1718 3.8	2318 1.0
8 SA	0543 3.6	1156 1.0	1825 3.4	
9 SU	0029 1.1	0658 3.4	1308 1.1	1942 3.4
10 M	0156 1.1	0818 3.5	1434 1.2	2057 3.5
11 TU	0323 1.0	0923 3.6	1542 1.1	2153 3.7
12 W	0417 0.8	1013 3.7	1627 1.0	2237 3.9
13 TH	0457 0.6	1054 3.9	1704 0.9	2315 4.0
14 F	0530 0.5	1131 4.0	1736 0.8	○ 2349 4.1
15 SA	0601 0.4	1205 4.0	1806 0.7	
16 SU	0022 4.2	0630 0.4	1238 4.1	1834 0.7
17 M	0056 4.2	0700 0.3	1311 4.1	1904 0.6
18 TU	0128 4.2	0731 0.3	1343 4.1	1935 0.6
19 W	0200 4.2	0801 0.4	1416 4.0	2008 0.7
20 TH	0232 4.1	0831 0.4	1451 4.0	2044 0.7
21 F	0307 4.1	0906 0.5	1531 3.9	2124 0.8
22 SA	0349 4.0	0949 0.7	1618 3.8	◑ 2216 0.9
23 SU	0441 3.8	1053 0.8	1718 3.6	2332 1.0
24 M	0550 3.7	1223 1.0	1834 3.5	
25 TU	0110 1.0	0717 3.6	1348 0.9	2004 3.5
26 W	0232 0.8	0845 3.8	1458 0.8	2123 3.8
27 TH	0341 0.5	0952 4.0	1559 0.7	2223 4.0
28 F	0441 0.3	1047 4.3	1653 0.6	2313 4.3

MARCH

Day				
1 SA	0533 0.1	1135 4.4	1741 0.5	● 2358 4.4
2 SU	0620 0.0	1220 4.5	1827 0.5	
3 M	0041 4.6	0703 0.0	1304 4.5	1909 0.4
4 TU	0123 4.6	0743 0.1	1347 4.4	1951 0.5
5 W	0203 4.5	0820 0.2	1428 4.3	2029 0.5
6 TH	0243 4.4	0853 0.4	1509 4.0	2106 0.6
7 F	0322 4.1	0927 0.6	1551 3.8	2146 0.8
8 SA	0406 3.9	1008 0.8	1638 3.6	◑ 2235 0.9
9 SU	0500 3.6	1104 1.1	1736 3.4	2340 1.1
10 M	0612 3.3	1220 1.3	1849 3.3	
11 TU	0107 1.1	0736 3.3	1349 1.3	2013 3.3
12 W	0240 1.0	0851 3.5	1507 1.2	2118 3.5
13 TH	0344 0.8	0945 3.7	1558 1.0	2207 3.7
14 F	0426 0.6	1028 3.8	1637 0.9	2246 3.9
15 SA	0500 0.5	1104 3.9	1710 0.8	2321 4.0
16 SU	0531 0.4	1138 4.0	1740 0.7	○ 2355 4.1
17 M	0601 0.4	1212 4.1	1810 0.6	
18 TU	0028 4.2	0631 0.3	1246 4.2	1842 0.6
19 W	0103 4.3	0702 0.3	1320 4.2	1915 0.5
20 TH	0136 4.3	0733 0.3	1355 4.1	1950 0.5
21 F	0211 4.2	0805 0.4	1431 4.0	2026 0.6
22 SA	0248 4.1	0842 0.5	1511 3.9	2108 0.7
23 SU	0331 4.0	0929 0.7	1558 3.8	2202 0.8
24 M	0425 3.9	1036 0.9	1657 3.6	◑ 2318 0.9
25 TU	0534 3.7	1206 1.0	1815 3.5	
26 W	0054 0.8	0705 3.6	1330 1.0	1948 3.5
27 TH	0216 0.7	0833 3.8	1440 0.9	2106 3.8
28 F	0326 0.5	0939 4.0	1541 0.7	2205 4.0
29 SA	0424 0.3	1031 4.2	1634 0.6	2253 4.2
30 SU	0513 0.2	1117 4.3	1721 0.5	● 2337 4.4
31 M	0557 0.1	1200 4.4	1806 0.5	

APRIL

Day				
1 TU	0017 4.5	0637 0.1	1241 4.4	1848 0.4
2 W	0058 4.5	0714 0.2	1322 4.3	1929 0.4
3 TH	0136 4.4	0748 0.4	1401 4.2	2006 0.5
4 F	0214 4.3	0819 0.5	1439 4.0	2041 0.6
5 SA	0253 4.1	0850 0.7	1517 3.8	2117 0.7
6 SU	0334 3.8	0927 0.9	1559 3.6	2159 0.8
7 M	0424 3.6	1017 1.1	1652 3.4	◑ 2257 1.0
8 TU	0530 3.4	1129 1.3	1800 3.3	
9 W	0017 1.1	0648 3.3	1301 1.4	1915 3.3
10 TH	0144 1.0	0802 3.4	1420 1.2	2026 3.4
11 F	0252 0.8	0903 3.6	1518 1.1	2122 3.6
12 SA	0342 0.7	0951 3.7	1602 0.9	2207 3.8
13 SU	0422 0.5	1030 3.9	1638 0.8	2246 4.0
14 M	0456 0.5	1107 4.0	1712 0.7	2323 4.1
15 TU	0529 0.4	1143 4.1	1746 0.6	○ 2359 4.2
16 W	0602 0.3	1219 4.2	1821 0.5	
17 TH	0037 4.3	0635 0.3	1258 4.2	1857 0.5
18 F	0115 4.3	0709 0.4	1336 4.2	1935 0.5
19 SA	0154 4.3	0746 0.4	1416 4.1	2016 0.5
20 SU	0235 4.2	0829 0.6	1459 3.9	2102 0.5
21 M	0322 4.1	0922 0.8	1548 3.8	2200 0.6
22 TU	0418 3.9	1031 0.9	1649 3.6	◑ 2316 0.7
23 W	0529 3.7	1152 1.0	1806 3.6	
24 TH	0042 0.7	0655 3.7	1309 1.0	1930 3.6
25 F	0158 0.5	0814 3.8	1418 0.9	2043 3.8
26 SA	0306 0.4	0919 3.8	1519 0.8	2142 4.0
27 SU	0403 0.4	1012 4.1	1613 0.7	2231 4.2
28 M	0450 0.3	1057 4.2	1700 0.6	2314 4.3
29 TU	0532 0.3	1138 4.3	1745 0.5	● 2354 4.4
30 W	0610 0.4	1218 4.3	1828 0.4	○ 2359 4.2

Chart Datum: 2·16 metres below Ordnance Datum (Newlyn)
HAT is 4·7 metres above Chart Datum

TIDES

TIDES

WALTON-ON-THE-NAZE
LAT 51°51'N LONG 1°17'E
TIMES AND HEIGHTS OF HIGH AND LOW WATERS

Dates in amber are **SPRINGS**
Dates in yellow are **NEAPS**

2014

MAY

Day	Time	m	Time	m	Day	Time	m	Time	m
1 TH	0033	4.4	1258	4.2	16 F	0014	4.4	1239	4.3
	0646	0.4	1908	0.4		0613	0.4	1844	0.4
2 F	0112	4.3	1336	4.1	17 SA	0058	4.4	1323	4.2
	0720	0.5	1946	0.4		0653	0.4	1927	0.4
3 SA	0149	4.2	1412	4.0	18 SU	0142	4.4	1407	4.2
	0751	0.7	2021	0.5		0736	0.5	2013	0.4
4 SU	0228	4.1	1448	3.9	19 M	0228	4.3	1454	4.1
	0821	0.8	2054	0.6		0824	0.6	2104	0.4
5 M	0308	3.9	1527	3.7	20 TU	0318	4.2	1545	3.9
	0855	0.9	2132	0.7		0919	0.8	2203	0.5
6 TU	0353	3.6	1615	3.5	21 W	0415	4.0	1645	3.8
	0938	1.1	2221	0.8		1022	0.9	2312	0.5
7 W	0450	3.5	1716	3.4	22 TH	0523	3.9	1753	3.8
	1036	1.2	2327	0.9		1132	1.0		
8 TH	0559	3.4	1824	3.4	23 F	0025	0.5	1244	1.0
	1158	1.4				0636	3.8	1905	3.8
9 F	0049	1.0	1327	1.3	24 SA	0134	0.5	1352	0.9
	0707	3.4	1929	3.4		0748	3.9	2015	3.9
10 SA	0159	0.9	1431	1.1	25 SU	0240	0.5	1455	0.8
	0809	3.5	2029	3.6		0854	3.9	2116	4.0
11 SU	0253	0.7	1520	1.0	26 M	0338	0.5	1552	0.7
	0903	3.7	2122	3.8		0949	4.0	2207	4.1
12 M	0339	0.6	1603	0.8	27 TU	0427	0.5	1642	0.6
	0950	3.9	2208	4.0		1036	4.1	2252	4.2
13 TU	0420	0.5	1642	0.7	28 W	0508	0.5	1727	0.5
	1032	4.0	2250	4.1		1119	4.1	2333	4.2
14 W	0458	0.5	1722	0.6	29 TH	0546	0.6	1810	0.4
	1114	4.1	2332	4.3		1159	4.2		
15 TH	0536	0.4	1803	0.5	30 F	0012	4.3	1238	4.2
	1156	4.2				0622	0.6	1851	0.4
					31 SA	0051	4.2	1315	4.1
						0657	0.6	1928	0.4

JUNE

Day	Time	m	Time	m	Day	Time	m	Time	m
1 SU	0129	4.2	1350	4.1	16 M	0131	4.5	1359	4.3
	0730	0.7	2003	0.5		0731	0.5	2013	0.2
2 M	0207	4.0	1426	4.0	17 TU	0220	4.5	1447	4.3
	0800	0.8	2035	0.5		0820	0.6	2104	0.2
3 TU	0245	3.9	1503	3.9	18 W	0311	4.3	1537	4.2
	0831	0.9	2110	0.6		0911	0.7	2158	0.3
4 W	0326	3.8	1544	3.7	19 TH	0406	4.2	1631	4.1
	0910	1.0	2151	0.7		1006	0.8	2257	0.4
5 TH	0412	3.6	1634	3.6	20 F	0506	4.0	1730	4.0
	0956	1.1	2242	0.8		1107	0.9	2359	0.5
6 F	0506	3.5	1732	3.5	21 SA	0611	3.9	1836	3.9
	1053	1.2	2347	0.9		1213	1.0		
7 SA	0609	3.5	1835	3.5	22 SU	0103	0.6	1322	1.0
	1210	1.3				0718	3.8	1944	3.9
8 SU	0101	0.9	1334	1.2	23 M	0208	0.7	1429	0.9
	0712	3.5	1937	3.6		0825	3.8	2049	3.9
9 M	0204	0.8	1435	1.0	24 TU	0312	0.7	1534	0.8
	0812	3.6	2036	3.7		0926	3.9	2145	4.0
10 TU	0257	0.7	1527	0.9	25 W	0406	0.8	1629	0.7
	0908	3.8	2131	3.9		1017	4.0	2233	4.0
11 W	0345	0.6	1615	0.7	26 TH	0450	0.8	1716	0.6
	1000	4.0	2221	4.1		1102	4.1	2316	4.1
12 TH	0431	0.6	1702	0.6	27 F	0529	0.7	1757	0.5
	1049	4.1	2309	4.3		1143	4.1	2355	4.1
13 F	0515	0.5	1749	0.4	28 SA	0604	0.7	1835	0.4
	1137	4.2	2356	4.4		1220	4.1		
14 SA	0600	0.5	1836	0.3	29 SU	0033	4.2	1257	4.2
	1224	4.3				0639	0.7	1910	0.4
15 SU	0043	4.5	1312	4.4	30 M	0111	4.1	1331	4.1
	0644	0.5	1924	0.3		0711	0.8	1943	0.5

JULY

Day	Time	m	Time	m	Day	Time	m	Time	m
1 TU	0147	4.1	1405	4.1	16 W	0207	4.6	1431	4.5
	0741	0.8	2015	0.5		0809	0.6	2053	0.2
2 W	0223	4.0	1440	4.0	17 TH	0256	4.4	1518	4.4
	0811	0.8	2047	0.5		0856	0.7	2140	0.2
3 TH	0259	3.9	1516	3.9	18 F	0346	4.2	1607	4.3
	0845	0.9	2122	0.6		0944	0.8	2229	0.4
4 F	0336	3.8	1555	3.8	19 SA	0440	4.0	1700	4.1
	0924	1.0	2201	0.7		1037	0.9	2323	0.6
5 SA	0419	3.7	1641	3.7	20 SU	0539	3.9	1802	3.9
	1010	1.1	2249	0.8		1138	1.0		
6 SU	0510	3.6	1737	3.6	21 M	0024	0.8	1246	1.0
	1107	1.2	2354	0.9		0643	3.7	1911	3.8
7 M	0614	3.6	1844	3.6	22 TU	0131	0.9	1401	1.0
	1225	1.2				0754	3.7	2022	3.8
8 TU	0112	0.9	1350	1.1	23 W	0245	1.0	1519	0.9
	0722	3.6	1953	3.7		0902	3.8	2124	3.8
9 W	0218	0.8	1454	0.9	24 TH	0348	1.0	1619	0.8
	0830	3.7	2058	3.9		0958	3.9	2216	3.9
10 TH	0316	0.7	1551	0.7	25 F	0436	0.9	1705	0.6
	0933	3.9	2157	4.1		1045	4.0	2301	4.0
11 F	0409	0.6	1645	0.5	26 SA	0514	0.9	1743	0.5
	1029	4.1	2250	4.3		1126	4.1	2339	4.1
12 SA	0500	0.6	1737	0.4	27 SU	0547	0.8	1817	0.5
	1121	4.2	2341	4.5		1202	4.1		
13 SU	0549	0.6	1828	0.2	28 M	0016	4.1	1237	4.2
	1210	4.4				0619	0.8	1849	0.4
14 M	0030	4.6	1258	4.5	29 TU	0051	4.2	1310	4.2
	0636	0.5	1917	0.2		0650	0.8	1920	0.4
15 TU	0119	4.6	1345	4.5	30 W	0126	4.1	1343	4.2
	0723	0.5	2006	0.1		0720	0.8	1950	0.5
					31 TH	0159	4.1	1415	4.1
						0749	0.8	2020	0.5

AUGUST

Day	Time	m	Time	m	Day	Time	m	Time	m
1 F	0231	4.0	1447	4.1	16 SA	0320	4.3	1537	4.3
	0821	0.8	2050	0.6		0919	0.7	2154	0.5
2 SA	0304	3.9	1521	4.0	17 SU	0409	4.0	1626	4.1
	0856	0.9	2123	0.7		1006	0.8	2241	0.8
3 SU	0342	3.8	1601	3.9	18 M	0502	3.8	1723	3.9
	0935	1.0	2203	0.8		1100	1.0	2337	1.0
4 M	0427	3.7	1650	3.8	19 TU	0604	3.6	1835	3.7
	1024	1.1	2259	0.9		1207	1.1		
5 TU	0525	3.6	1754	3.7	20 W	0047	1.2	1328	1.1
	1133	1.2				0718	3.5	1953	3.6
6 W	0021	1.0	1308	1.1	21 TH	0213	1.2	1459	1.0
	0637	3.6	1912	3.7		0835	3.6	2103	3.7
7 TH	0146	1.0	1426	1.0	22 F	0327	1.1	1602	0.8
	0756	3.7	2031	3.8		0936	3.8	2157	3.9
8 F	0252	0.8	1530	0.7	23 SA	0416	1.0	1646	0.7
	0910	3.8	2138	4.1		1024	3.9	2241	4.0
9 SA	0351	0.7	1630	0.5	24 SU	0454	0.9	1721	0.6
	1012	4.1	2235	4.3		1104	4.1	2319	4.1
10 SU	0445	0.7	1724	0.3	25 M	0526	0.9	1752	0.5
	1105	4.3	2326	4.5		1139	4.2	2353	4.1
11 M	0535	0.6	1815	0.2	26 TU	0557	0.8	1822	0.5
	1153	4.4				1211	4.2		
12 TU	0014	4.6	1240	4.6	27 W	0027	4.2	1244	4.3
	0622	0.6	1902	0.1		0627	0.8	1851	0.4
13 W	0102	4.7	1325	4.7	28 TH	0100	4.2	1316	4.3
	0708	0.5	1948	0.1		0656	0.7	1920	0.5
14 TH	0148	4.6	1409	4.6	29 F	0131	4.2	1347	4.2
	0752	0.6	2031	0.2		0726	0.7	1949	0.5
15 F	0234	4.5	1453	4.5	30 SA	0203	4.1	1418	4.2
	0835	0.6	2112	0.3		0758	0.8	2017	0.6
					31 SU	0235	4.0	1452	4.1
						0831	0.8	2048	0.7

Chart Datum: 2·16 metres below Ordnance Datum (Newlyn)
HAT is 4·7 metres above Chart Datum

TIME ZONE (UT)	WALTON-ON-THE-NAZE	Dates in amber are SPRINGS
For Summer Time add ONE hour in **non-shaded areas**	LAT 51°51′N LONG 1°17′E	Dates in yellow are NEAPS
	TIMES AND HEIGHTS OF HIGH AND LOW WATERS	**2014**

SEPTEMBER

Day	Time	m	Time	m	Time	m	Time	m
1 M	0312	3.9	0907	0.9	1530	4.0	2126	0.8
16 TU	0422	3.7	1024	0.9	1644	3.8	◐2250	1.2
2 TU	0354	3.8	0953	1.0	1618	3.9	◑2220	1.0
17 W	0520	3.5	1126	1.1	1755	3.6		
3 W	0449	3.7	1059	1.1	1720	3.7	2344	1.1
18 TH	0001	1.4	0633	3.4	1247	1.1	1917	3.5
4 TH	0601	3.6	1236	1.1	1841	3.7		
19 F	0130	1.4	0755	3.5	1419	1.1	2033	3.6
5 F	0119	1.1	0727	3.6	1402	0.9	2011	3.8
20 SA	0252	1.3	0903	3.6	1529	0.9	2130	3.8
6 SA	0231	1.0	0851	3.8	1511	0.7	2123	4.1
21 SU	0346	1.1	0953	3.8	1614	0.7	2214	4.0
7 SU	0333	0.8	0955	4.0	1612	0.4	2220	4.3
22 M	0425	1.0	1033	4.0	1649	0.6	2252	4.1
8 M	0427	0.7	1047	4.3	1705	0.4	2309	4.5
23 TU	0500	0.9	1108	4.1	1720	0.5	2325	4.1
9 TU	0517	0.6	1133	4.5	1755	0.2	○2355	4.6
24 W	0531	0.8	1141	4.2	1750	0.5	●2358	4.2
10 W	0603	0.5	1217	4.6	1840	0.1		
25 TH	0601	0.7	1213	4.3	1819	0.5		
11 TH	0040	4.6	0648	0.5	1301	4.7	1923	0.2
26 F	0030	4.2	0631	0.7	1247	4.3	1848	0.5
12 F	0125	4.6	0731	0.5	1343	4.7	2002	0.3
27 SA	0103	4.2	0703	0.7	1319	4.3	1917	0.5
13 SA	0208	4.4	0813	0.6	1424	4.5	2039	0.5
28 SU	0136	4.2	0736	0.7	1353	4.3	1947	0.6
14 SU	0251	4.2	0854	0.7	1506	4.3	2116	0.7
29 M	0210	4.1	0810	0.7	1428	4.2	2020	0.7
15 M	0334	4.0	0936	0.8	1551	4.1	2157	0.9
30 TU	0247	4.0	0848	0.8	1508	4.1	2101	0.9

OCTOBER

Day	Time	m	Time	m	Time	m	Time	m
1 W	0330	3.9	0935	0.9	1557	4.0	◐2158	1.0
16 TH	0435	3.5	1046	1.0	1713	3.5	2310	1.4
2 TH	0424	3.7	1042	1.0	1659	3.8	2324	1.2
17 F	0543	3.4	1159	1.1	1831	3.4		
3 F	0535	3.6	1216	1.0	1821	3.7		
18 SA	0039	1.5	0659	3.4	1324	1.1	1946	3.5
4 SA	0056	1.2	0705	3.6	1341	0.8	1953	3.8
19 SU	0202	1.4	0812	3.5	1435	1.0	2049	3.7
5 SU	0209	1.0	0829	3.8	1450	0.6	2105	4.1
20 M	0304	1.2	0909	3.7	1528	0.8	2137	3.9
6 M	0311	0.9	0933	4.0	1551	0.4	2202	4.3
21 TU	0350	1.0	0954	3.9	1609	0.7	2217	4.0
7 TU	0406	0.7	1025	4.3	1644	0.3	2250	4.5
22 W	0428	0.9	1031	4.0	1644	0.6	2252	4.1
8 W	0455	0.6	1111	4.5	1731	0.2	○2334	4.5
23 TH	0502	0.8	1107	4.2	1716	0.6	●2326	4.2
9 TH	0542	0.5	1153	4.6	1814	0.2		
24 F	0534	0.7	1142	4.3	1747	0.5		
10 F	0017	4.6	0626	0.5	1235	4.6	1854	0.3
25 SA	0001	4.3	0607	0.6	1218	4.3	1818	0.5
11 SA	0100	4.5	0710	0.5	1316	4.6	1932	0.5
26 SU	0037	4.3	0642	0.6	1255	4.4	1850	0.6
12 SU	0141	4.4	0752	0.5	1356	4.5	2007	0.6
27 M	0114	4.3	0718	0.6	1332	4.3	1924	0.6
13 M	0221	4.2	0831	0.6	1437	4.2	2040	0.8
28 TU	0152	4.2	0755	0.6	1411	4.3	2002	0.7
14 TU	0301	4.0	0909	0.7	1519	4.0	2117	1.0
29 W	0231	4.1	0838	0.6	1455	4.2	2049	0.9
15 W	0343	3.7	0952	0.8	1608	3.7	◑2204	1.2
30 TH	0316	3.9	0929	0.7	1545	4.0	2150	1.1
31 F	0410	3.7	1038	0.8	1648	3.8	◐2309	1.2

NOVEMBER

Day	Time	m	Time	m	Time	m	Time	m
1 SA	0520	3.6	1202	0.8	1809	3.8		
16 SU	0602	3.4	1226	1.0	1848	3.4		
2 SU	0031	1.2	0644	3.6	1319	0.7	1933	3.9
17 M	0104	1.5	0709	3.0	1338	1.0	1951	3.5
3 M	0144	1.1	0804	3.8	1427	0.5	2043	4.1
18 TU	0214	1.3	0812	0.9	1436	0.9	2047	3.7
4 TU	0247	0.9	0909	4.0	1528	0.4	2141	4.2
19 W	0307	1.1	0905	0.8	1524	0.8	2134	3.9
5 W	0343	0.8	1002	4.2	1620	0.4	2230	4.3
20 TH	0351	1.0	0951	0.9	1605	0.7	2216	4.0
6 TH	0434	0.7	1048	4.4	1706	0.4	○2314	4.4
21 F	0430	0.8	1033	4.1	1643	0.6	2256	4.2
7 F	0522	0.5	1131	4.5	1749	0.4	2356	4.4
22 SA	0508	0.7	1113	4.2	1718	0.6	●2335	4.3
8 SA	0607	0.5	1211	4.5	1828	0.5		
23 SU	0546	0.6	1153	4.3	1754	0.6		
9 SU	0036	4.4	0651	0.4	1252	4.5	1905	0.6
24 M	0016	4.3	0625	0.5	1235	4.4	1830	0.6
10 M	0117	4.3	0732	0.5	1332	4.3	1940	0.8
25 TU	0058	4.3	0706	0.4	1317	4.4	1910	0.6
11 TU	0155	4.2	0811	0.5	1412	4.2	2012	0.9
26 W	0140	4.3	0749	0.4	1401	4.4	1954	0.7
12 W	0232	4.0	0846	0.6	1452	4.0	2044	1.0
27 TH	0224	4.2	0835	0.5	1448	4.3	2045	0.8
13 TH	0310	3.8	0924	0.7	1537	3.8	2123	1.2
28 F	0310	4.0	0929	0.5	1539	4.1	2143	1.0
14 F	0355	3.6	1009	0.9	1631	3.6	◑2216	1.4
29 SA	0404	3.9	1032	0.6	1640	3.9	◐2251	1.1
15 SA	0454	3.5	1109	1.0	1739	3.4	2330	1.5
30 SU	0507	3.8	1144	0.6	1752	3.9		

DECEMBER

Day	Time	m	Time	m	Time	m	Time	m
1 M	0003	1.1	0621	3.8	1254	0.6	1907	3.9
16 TU	0608	3.4	1233	1.0	1848	3.5		
2 TU	0115	1.1	0736	3.8	1400	0.6	2017	3.9
17 W	0107	1.4	0713	3.5	1342	0.9	1949	3.6
3 W	0220	1.0	0843	3.9	1502	0.6	2118	4.1
18 TH	0217	1.2	0815	3.6	1438	0.9	2047	3.7
4 TH	0321	0.8	0939	4.1	1557	0.6	2211	4.2
19 F	0311	1.0	0911	3.8	1528	0.8	2140	3.9
5 F	0416	0.7	1028	4.2	1645	0.6	2256	4.2
20 SA	0359	0.8	1001	4.0	1613	0.7	2228	4.1
6 SA	0506	0.6	1112	4.3	1728	0.6	○2338	4.3
21 SU	0444	0.7	1048	4.1	1655	0.6	2315	4.2
7 SU	0552	0.5	1153	4.3	1807	0.6		
22 M	0529	0.5	1134	4.2	1737	0.6	●	
8 M	0019	4.3	0635	0.4	1234	4.3	1844	0.7
23 TU	0000	4.4	0613	0.4	1220	4.4	1819	0.6
9 TU	0057	4.2	0715	0.4	1312	4.2	1918	0.8
24 W	0046	4.4	0658	0.3	1306	4.5	1903	0.6
10 W	0134	4.2	0752	0.5	1351	4.1	1950	0.9
25 TH	0131	4.4	0744	0.2	1352	4.5	1949	0.6
11 TH	0209	4.1	0825	0.5	1429	4.0	2019	1.0
26 F	0217	4.3	0832	0.2	1440	4.4	2038	0.7
12 F	0245	3.9	0859	0.6	1509	3.8	2053	1.1
27 SA	0303	4.2	0923	0.3	1531	4.2	2130	0.8
13 SA	0323	3.8	0936	0.7	1552	3.7	2135	1.2
28 SU	0353	4.1	1018	0.4	1626	4.0	◐2228	0.9
14 SU	0408	3.6	1021	0.8	1643	3.5	2226	1.3
29 M	0448	4.0	1118	0.5	1729	3.9	2332	1.0
15 M	0504	3.5	1119	0.9	1744	3.5	2333	1.4
30 TU	0553	3.9	1223	0.6	1837	3.8		
31 W	0041	1.0	0704	3.8	1329	0.7	1948	3.8

Chart Datum: 2·16 metres below Ordnance Datum (Newlyn)
HAT is 4·7 metres above Chart Datum

TIDES

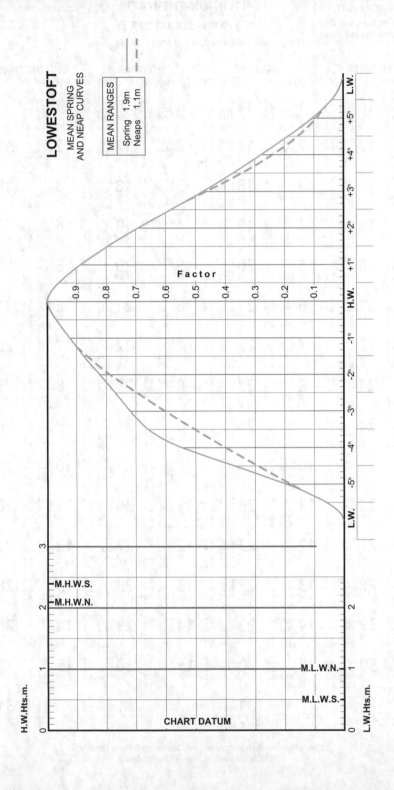

LOWESTOFT
MEAN SPRING
AND NEAP CURVES

MEAN RANGES
Spring 1.9m
Neaps 1.1m

Factor

0.9 0.8 0.7 0.6 0.5 0.4 0.3 0.2 0.1

H.W. -1ʰ -2ʰ -3ʰ -4ʰ -5ʰ L.W.

L.W. +5ʰ +4ʰ +3ʰ +2ʰ +1ʰ H.W.

H.W.Hts.m.

M.H.W.S.
M.H.W.N.

M.L.W.N.
M.L.W.S.

CHART DATUM

L.W.Hts.m.

LOWESTOFT

LAT 52°28′N   LONG 1°45′E

TIMES AND HEIGHTS OF HIGH AND LOW WATERS

Dates in amber are **SPRINGS**
Dates in yellow are **NEAPS**

2014

JANUARY

Time m   Time m

1 W ●	0248 0.7 / 0854 2.5 / 1507 0.7 / 2113 2.6	16 TH ○	0339 0.7 / 0953 2.3 / 1539 0.9 / 2148 2.5
2 TH	0342 0.5 / 0946 2.6 / 1557 0.6 / 2158 2.7	17 F	0414 0.7 / 1025 2.3 / 1607 0.9 / 2220 2.6
3 F	0434 0.4 / 1037 2.6 / 1644 0.7 / 2245 2.7	18 SA	0447 0.6 / 1055 2.3 / 1636 0.9 / 2253 2.6
4 SA	0523 0.3 / 1126 2.6 / 1730 0.7 / 2331 2.8	19 SU	0520 0.6 / 1126 2.3 / 1708 0.9 / 2328 2.6
5 SU	0611 0.3 / 1215 2.5 / 1814 0.8	20 M	0553 0.6 / 1158 2.3 / 1742 0.9
6 M	0017 2.7 / 0658 0.4 / 1306 2.4 / 1857 0.9	21 TU	0004 2.5 / 0626 0.7 / 1234 2.3 / 1819 0.9
7 TU	0105 2.7 / 0747 0.5 / 1403 2.3 / 1943 1.0	22 W	0042 2.5 / 0702 0.7 / 1312 2.2 / 1859 1.0
8 W ◐	0156 2.6 / 0841 0.6 / 1519 2.2 / 2036 1.1	23 TH	0122 2.4 / 0742 0.8 / 1355 2.2 / 1945 1.1
9 TH	0257 2.4 / 0945 0.8 / 1630 2.2 / 2148 1.2	24 F ◐	0207 2.4 / 0830 0.9 / 1449 2.2 / 2039 1.1
10 F	0416 2.3 / 1054 0.9 / 1731 2.2 / 2314 1.2	25 SA	0303 2.3 / 0932 0.9 / 1608 2.1 / 2151 1.2
11 SA	0530 1.0 / 1157 1.0 / 1829 2.2	26 SU	0422 1.0 / 1055 1.0 / 1727 2.2 / 2326 1.1
12 SU	0025 1.1 / 0640 2.2 / 1255 1.0 / 1923 2.3	27 M	0544 2.3 / 1205 0.9 / 1825 2.3
13 M	0127 1.0 / 0747 2.3 / 1347 1.0 / 2007 2.4	28 TU	0035 0.9 / 0649 2.3 / 1304 0.9 / 1916 2.4
14 TU	0218 0.9 / 0837 2.3 / 1430 1.0 / 2044 2.4	29 W	0137 0.8 / 0750 2.4 / 1359 0.8 / 2006 2.5
15 W	0300 0.8 / 0917 2.4 / 1507 1.0 / 2117 2.5	30 TH ●	0236 0.6 / 0846 2.5 / 1453 0.7 / 2055 2.6
		31 F	0331 0.4 / 0937 2.6 / 1544 0.7 / 2141 2.7

FEBRUARY

Time m   Time m

1 SA	0422 0.2 / 1023 2.6 / 1630 0.6 / 2227 2.8	16 SU	0423 0.6 / 1029 2.3 / 1618 0.8 / 2230 2.6
2 SU	0508 0.2 / 1108 2.6 / 1713 0.6 / 2312 2.8	17 M	0455 0.5 / 1059 2.4 / 1650 0.6 / 2305 2.6
3 M	0552 0.2 / 1153 2.5 / 1754 0.7 / 2357 2.8	18 TU	0528 0.6 / 1131 2.3 / 1724 0.6 / 2340 2.5
4 TU	0635 0.3 / 1238 2.4 / 1834 0.8	19 W	0600 0.6 / 1205 2.3 / 1759 0.8
5 W	0042 2.7 / 0718 0.5 / 1326 2.3 / 1916 0.9	20 TH	0016 2.6 / 0634 0.7 / 1242 2.3 / 1836 0.9
6 TH ◑	0131 2.6 / 0803 0.7 / 1421 2.2 / 2003 1.0	21 F	0055 2.4 / 0711 0.7 / 1323 2.2 / 1919 0.9
7 F	0228 2.4 / 0857 0.9 / 1535 2.1 / 2103 1.1	22 SA	0140 2.4 / 0755 0.8 / 1413 2.2 / 2012 1.0
8 SA	0349 2.2 / 1013 1.1 / 1645 2.1 / 2239 1.2	23 SU	0236 2.3 / 0852 1.0 / 1516 2.1 / 2120 1.0
9 SU	0510 2.2 / 1130 1.1 / 1748 2.1	24 M	0357 2.2 / 1018 1.0 / 1643 2.2 / 2303 1.0
10 M	0000 1.1 / 0629 2.2 / 1235 1.2 / 1851 2.2	25 TU	0531 2.2 / 1144 1.0 / 1753 2.2
11 TU	0105 1.0 / 0739 2.2 / 1330 1.1 / 1943 2.3	26 W	0018 0.8 / 0642 2.3 / 1248 1.0 / 1851 2.3
12 W	0157 0.9 / 0826 2.2 / 1414 1.1 / 2022 2.3	27 TH	0122 0.7 / 0744 2.4 / 1346 0.9 / 1945 2.4
13 TH	0240 0.8 / 0903 2.3 / 1450 1.0 / 2054 2.4	28 F	0223 0.5 / 0837 2.5 / 1440 0.8 / 2035 2.6
14 F	0316 0.7 / 0933 2.3 / 1519 0.9 / 2124 2.5 ○		
15 SA	0350 0.6 / 1001 2.3 / 1548 0.8 / 2156 2.5		

MARCH

Time m   Time m

1 SA ●	0316 0.3 / 0922 2.5 / 1529 0.6 / 2122 2.7	16 SU ○	0319 0.6 / 0932 2.3 / 1523 0.8 / 2129 2.5
2 SU	0404 0.2 / 1005 2.5 / 1613 0.6 / 2208 2.8	17 M	0352 0.5 / 1000 2.4 / 1556 0.7 / 2204 2.5
3 M	0447 0.2 / 1047 2.5 / 1654 0.5 / 2252 2.8	18 TU	0426 0.5 / 1030 2.4 / 1630 0.7 / 2240 2.5
4 TU	0528 0.2 / 1128 2.5 / 1733 0.6 / 2337 2.7	19 W	0500 0.5 / 1104 2.4 / 1706 0.7 / 2316 2.5
5 W	0608 0.4 / 1209 2.4 / 1812 0.6	20 TH	0535 0.5 / 1139 2.4 / 1742 0.7 / 2354 2.5
6 TH	0021 2.6 / 0646 0.6 / 1251 2.3 / 1851 0.7	21 F	0609 0.6 / 1216 2.3 / 1820 0.7
7 F	0108 2.4 / 0725 0.8 / 1335 2.2 / 1935 0.9	22 SA	0035 2.4 / 0647 0.7 / 1259 2.3 / 1903 0.8
8 SA	0203 2.3 / 0809 1.0 / 1427 2.1 / 2029 1.0	23 SU	0123 2.4 / 0731 0.9 / 1347 2.2 / 1956 0.8
9 SU	0322 2.2 / 0908 1.2 / 1540 2.1 / 2158 1.1	24 M ◐	0223 2.3 / 0827 1.0 / 1447 2.2 / 2108 0.9
10 M	0447 2.1 / 1058 1.3 / 1654 2.1 / 2331 1.0	25 TU	0352 2.2 / 0950 1.1 / 1605 2.2 / 2250 0.8
11 TU	0606 2.1 / 1209 1.3 / 1800 2.1	26 W	0526 2.2 / 1125 1.1 / 1723 2.2
12 W	0033 0.9 / 0717 2.2 / 1306 1.2 / 1901 2.2	27 TH	0002 0.7 / 0635 2.3 / 1231 1.0 / 1825 2.3
13 TH	0126 0.9 / 0803 2.2 / 1350 1.1 / 1947 2.3	28 F	0106 0.6 / 0734 2.4 / 1330 0.9 / 1922 2.4
14 F	0209 0.8 / 0838 2.3 / 1424 1.0 / 2022 2.3	29 SA	0204 0.4 / 0822 2.4 / 1423 0.8 / 2013 2.5
15 SA	0245 0.7 / 0906 2.3 / 1453 0.9 / 2055 2.4	30 SU ●	0256 0.3 / 0903 2.5 / 1510 0.7 / 2101 2.6
		31 M	0341 0.3 / 0943 2.5 / 1553 0.6 / 2147 2.7

APRIL

Time m   Time m

1 TU	0423 0.3 / 1023 2.5 / 1634 0.5 / 2233 2.7	16 W	0356 0.5 / 1003 2.4 / 1610 0.6 / 2216 2.5
2 W	0502 0.4 / 1103 2.5 / 1713 0.5 / 2318 2.6	17 TH	0434 0.5 / 1039 2.5 / 1650 0.6 / 2255 2.5
3 TH	0539 0.5 / 1142 2.4 / 1751 0.6	18 F	0511 0.5 / 1116 2.5 / 1729 0.6 / 2337 2.5
4 F	0002 2.5 / 0614 0.7 / 1221 2.3 / 1830 0.7	19 SA	0550 0.6 / 1156 2.4 / 1811 0.6
5 SA	0049 2.3 / 0649 0.9 / 1300 2.3 / 1911 0.8	20 SU	0023 2.4 / 0630 0.8 / 1240 2.4 / 1858 0.7
6 SU	0141 2.2 / 0727 1.1 / 1343 2.2 / 2000 0.9	21 M	0115 2.3 / 0716 0.9 / 1330 2.3 / 1954 0.7
7 M	0254 2.1 / 0811 1.2 / 1437 2.1 / 2110 1.0	22 TU ◐	0220 2.2 / 0812 1.1 / 1428 2.3 / 2108 0.7
8 TU	0417 2.1 / 0921 1.4 / 1549 2.1 / 2252 1.0	23 W	0354 2.2 / 0930 1.2 / 1537 2.2 / 2235 0.7
9 W	0528 2.1 / 1132 1.3 / 1703 2.1 / 2354 0.9	24 TH	0517 2.2 / 1101 1.2 / 1654 2.2 / 2343 0.6
10 TH	0636 2.1 / 1228 1.3 / 1804 2.1	25 F	0622 2.3 / 1208 1.1 / 1800 2.3
11 F	0044 0.8 / 0727 2.2 / 1312 1.2 / 1857 2.2	26 SA	0044 0.5 / 0717 2.4 / 1308 1.0 / 1858 2.4
12 SA	0128 0.8 / 0803 2.2 / 1347 1.0 / 1941 2.3	27 SU	0141 0.5 / 0803 2.4 / 1402 0.8 / 1951 2.5
13 SU	0206 0.7 / 0832 2.3 / 1420 0.9 / 2020 2.4	28 M	0232 0.4 / 0843 2.4 / 1450 0.7 / 2042 2.5
14 M	0242 0.6 / 0859 2.3 / 1454 0.8 / 2058 2.4	29 TU ●	0317 0.4 / 0922 2.5 / 1534 0.6 / 2130 2.6
15 TU ○	0319 0.5 / 0931 2.3 / 1531 0.7 / 2137 2.5	30 W	0358 0.5 / 1001 2.5 / 1615 0.6 / 2216 2.5

Chart Datum: 1·50 metres below Ordnance Datum (Newlyn)
HAT is 2·9 metres above Chart Datum

TIDES

TIDES

TIME ZONE (UT)
For Summer Time add ONE hour in **non-shaded** areas

LOWESTOFT
LAT 52°28'N   LONG 1°45'E
TIMES AND HEIGHTS OF HIGH AND LOW WATERS

Dates in amber are **SPRINGS**
Dates in yellow are **NEAPS**

2014

MAY

Day	Time m	Time m	Time m	Time m
1 TH	0436 0.5	1039 2.5	1655 0.5	2302 2.5
2 F	0512 0.7	1117 2.4	1733 0.6	2346 2.4
3 SA	0545 0.8	1153 2.4	1811 0.6	
4 SU	0031 2.3	0617 0.9	1231 2.4	1851 0.7
5 M	0119 2.2	0651 1.1	1311 2.3	1935 0.8
6 TU	0217 2.1	0731 1.2	1358 2.2	2029 0.9
7 W	0335 2.1	0819 1.3	1453 2.2	☽ 2150 0.9
8 TH	0444 2.1	0927 1.4	1603 2.1	2305 0.9
9 F	0543 2.1	1129 1.3	1713 2.1	2357 0.9
10 SA	0635 2.2	1219 1.2	1810 2.2	
11 SU	0042 0.8	0717 2.2	1302 1.1	1859 2.2
12 M	0123 0.7	0752 2.2	1342 1.0	1945 2.3
13 TU	0204 0.6	0826 2.4	1424 0.8	2028 2.4
14 W	0246 0.6	0901 2.4	1507 0.7	○ 2111 2.4
15 TH	0328 0.5	0938 2.5	1551 0.6	2154 2.5
16 F	0410 0.5	1016 2.5	1636 0.5	2239 2.5
17 SA	0452 0.6	1057 2.5	1721 0.5	2326 2.5
18 SU	0535 0.7	1140 2.5	1808 0.5	
19 M	0016 2.4	0619 0.8	1226 2.5	1857 0.5
20 TU	0111 2.4	0706 0.9	1316 2.4	1954 0.5
21 W	0215 2.3	0800 1.0	1411 2.4	☽ 2101 0.6
22 TH	0344 2.2	0907 1.1	1514 2.3	2214 0.6
23 F	0459 2.3	1029 1.2	1628 2.3	2319 0.6
24 SA	0601 2.3	1140 1.1	1737 2.3	
25 SU	0019 0.6	0655 2.3	1243 1.0	1837 2.4
26 M	0116 0.6	0742 2.4	1341 0.9	1934 2.4
27 TU	0208 0.6	0823 2.4	1431 0.8	2028 2.4
28 W	0253 0.6	0903 2.5	● 1517 0.6	2118 2.4
29 TH	0334 0.7	0941 2.5	1559 0.6	2205 2.4
30 F	0412 0.7	1019 2.5	1639 0.6	2249 2.4
31 SA	0447 0.8	1055 2.5	1717 0.6	2332 2.3

JUNE

Day	Time m	Time m	Time m	Time m
1 SU	0519 0.9	1130 2.5	1754 0.6	
2 M	0012 2.2	0548 1.0	1206 2.4	1831 0.7
3 TU	0053 2.2	0621 1.0	1244 2.4	1910 0.7
4 W	0136 2.1	0658 1.1	1327 2.3	1953 0.8
5 TH	0228 2.1	0742 1.2	1414 2.3	☽ 2045 0.9
6 F	0343 2.1	0834 1.3	1508 2.2	2151 0.9
7 SA	0449 2.1	0940 1.3	1616 2.2	2300 0.9
8 SU	0542 2.1	1110 1.3	1725 2.2	2355 0.8
9 M	0630 2.2	1215 1.2	1821 2.2	
10 TU	0043 0.8	0713 2.2	1307 1.0	1912 2.3
11 W	0130 0.7	0754 2.4	1356 0.9	2001 2.3
12 TH	0217 0.6	0834 2.4	1445 0.7	2050 2.4
13 F	0304 0.6	0915 2.5	1535 0.6	○ 2139 0.6
14 SA	0351 0.6	0957 2.6	1624 0.5	2228 2.5
15 SU	0437 0.6	1041 2.6	1713 0.4	2317 2.5
16 M	0523 0.7	1126 2.6	1802 0.3	
17 TU	0007 2.5	0608 0.8	1213 2.6	1851 0.4
18 W	0100 2.4	0654 0.9	1301 2.6	1944 0.4
19 TH	0159 2.3	0743 1.0	1353 2.5	☽ 2041 0.5
20 F	0317 2.3	0840 1.1	1451 2.4	2146 0.6
21 SA	0432 2.2	0951 1.1	1603 2.4	2252 0.7
22 SU	0533 2.3	1109 1.1	1717 2.3	2354 0.7
23 M	0629 2.3	1218 1.1	1822 2.3	
24 TU	0052 0.8	0721 2.3	1321 1.0	1925 2.3
25 W	0146 0.8	0806 2.4	1416 0.8	2023 2.3
26 TH	0234 0.8	0846 2.4	1503 0.7	2112 2.3
27 F	0315 0.8	0924 2.5	1545 0.6	● 2156 2.3
28 SA	0352 0.9	1000 2.5	1625 0.6	2236 2.3
29 SU	0425 0.9	1035 2.5	1701 0.6	2314 2.3
30 M	0455 0.6	1108 2.5	1736 0.6	2348 2.3

JULY

Day	Time m	Time m	Time m	Time m
1 TU	0524 0.9	1142 2.5	1810 0.6	
2 W	0022 2.2	0555 1.0	1219 2.5	1843 0.7
3 TH	0058 2.2	0631 1.0	1258 2.4	1920 0.8
4 F	0137 2.2	0712 1.1	1340 2.4	2001 0.8
5 SA	0223 2.1	0758 1.2	1426 2.3	☽ 2051 0.9
6 SU	0325 2.1	0853 1.2	1521 2.3	2154 0.9
7 M	0448 2.1	1005 1.3	1636 2.2	2307 0.9
8 TU	0546 2.1	1132 1.2	1747 2.2	
9 W	0008 1.0	0636 2.3	1236 1.0	1845 2.3
10 TH	0102 0.8	0724 2.4	1332 0.9	1941 2.4
11 F	0153 0.8	0809 2.5	1427 0.7	2035 2.4
12 SA	0244 0.7	0854 2.6	1521 0.5	○ 2127 2.5
13 SU	0335 0.7	0939 2.7	1613 0.4	2217 2.6
14 M	0423 0.6	1025 2.7	1702 0.3	2305 2.6
15 TU	0510 0.7	1110 2.8	1750 0.2	2352 2.5
16 W	0554 0.7	1155 2.8	1837 0.3	
17 TH	0040 2.5	0637 0.8	1242 2.7	1923 0.4
18 F	0133 2.4	0722 0.9	1331 2.6	2013 0.5
19 SA	0235 2.3	0811 1.0	1427 2.5	☽ 2111 0.7
20 SU	0355 2.2	0913 1.1	1540 2.4	2220 0.8
21 M	0459 2.2	1038 1.2	1700 2.3	2328 0.9
22 TU	0559 2.3	1156 1.1	1812 2.3	
23 W	0030 1.0	0657 2.3	1304 1.0	1924 2.3
24 TH	0129 1.0	0748 2.4	1402 0.9	2021 2.3
25 F	0218 1.0	0829 2.4	1449 0.8	2105 2.3
26 SA	0259 1.0	0906 2.5	1529 0.7	● 2143 2.3
27 SU	0334 0.9	0939 2.5	1606 0.6	2218 2.4
28 M	0404 0.9	1012 2.6	1640 0.6	2249 2.3
29 TU	0433 0.9	1044 2.6	1713 0.6	2319 2.3
30 W	0501 0.9	1118 2.6	1744 0.6	2350 2.3
31 TH	0533 0.9	1153 2.6	1816 0.7	

AUGUST

Day	Time m	Time m	Time m	Time m
1 F	0023 2.3	0607 1.0	1230 2.5	1848 0.7
2 SA	0059 2.3	0645 1.0	1308 2.5	1925 0.8
3 SU	0140 2.2	0728 1.1	1351 2.4	2008 0.9
4 M	0229 2.2	0818 1.2	1442 2.3	☽ 2102 1.0
5 TU	0334 2.2	0922 1.2	1551 2.3	2217 1.0
6 W	0459 2.2	1054 1.2	1718 2.3	2337 1.0
7 TH	0601 2.3	1211 1.0	1826 2.3	
8 F	0038 0.9	0654 2.4	1312 0.9	1927 2.4
9 SA	0133 0.9	0744 2.5	1410 0.7	2024 2.5
10 SU	0227 0.8	0833 2.6	1506 0.5	○ 2115 2.6
11 M	0319 0.7	0919 2.7	1558 0.3	2201 2.6
12 TU	0408 0.7	1005 2.8	1646 0.2	2246 2.6
13 W	0452 0.7	1050 2.9	1731 0.2	2330 2.6
14 TH	0535 0.7	1135 2.9	1814 0.3	
15 F	0015 2.5	0616 0.7	1221 2.8	1857 0.4
16 SA	0102 2.4	0658 0.8	1309 2.7	1941 0.6
17 SU	0154 2.3	0745 1.0	1404 2.5	☽ 2032 0.8
18 M	0301 2.3	0841 1.1	1519 2.4	2139 1.0
19 TU	0416 2.2	1006 1.1	1644 2.3	☽ 2300 1.1
20 W	0521 2.3	1134 1.1	1801 2.2	
21 TH	0010 1.2	0624 2.3	1243 1.0	1916 2.3
22 F	0111 1.2	0722 2.4	1341 0.9	2009 2.3
23 SA	0200 1.1	0806 2.4	1427 0.8	2049 2.3
24 SU	0239 1.1	0842 2.5	1505 0.7	2123 2.4
25 M	0312 1.0	0913 2.6	1540 0.7	● 2153 2.4
26 TU	0340 0.9	0944 2.6	1612 0.6	2220 2.4
27 W	0408 0.9	1017 2.6	1643 0.6	2248 2.4
28 TH	0438 0.8	1051 2.6	1714 0.6	2319 2.4
29 F	0511 0.9	1126 2.6	1746 0.7	2352 2.4
30 SA	0545 0.9	1202 2.6	1818 0.7	
31 SU	0027 2.4	0621 0.9	1240 2.6	1853 0.8

Chart Datum: 1·50 metres below Ordnance Datum (Newlyn)
HAT is 2·9 metres above Chart Datum

LOWESTOFT

LAT 52°28'N   LONG 1°45'E

TIMES AND HEIGHTS OF HIGH AND LOW WATERS

Dates in amber are **SPRINGS**
Dates in yellow are **NEAPS**

2014

SEPTEMBER

Day	Time m	Time m	Time m	Time m
1 M	0107 2.3	0702 1.0	1322 2.4	1934 0.9
16 TU	0210 2.3	0814 1.0	1458 2.3	◐ 2047 1.2
2 TU	0153 2.3	0751 1.1	1413 2.4	◑ 2025 1.0
17 W	0319 2.3	0933 1.1	1625 2.2	2224 1.3
3 W	0250 2.3	0853 1.1	1522 2.3	2134 1.1
18 TH	0432 2.3	1107 1.1	1741 2.2	2344 1.3
4 TH	0407 2.3	1027 1.1	1700 2.3	2309 1.1
19 F	0537 2.3	1213 1.0	1854 2.3	
5 F	0525 2.3	1150 1.0	1814 2.4	
20 SA	0044 1.3	0639 2.3	1308 0.9	1946 2.3
6 SA	0017 1.1	0624 2.4	1253 0.8	1917 2.4
21 SU	0133 1.2	0729 2.4	1354 0.8	2025 2.4
7 SU	0115 1.0	0718 2.5	1352 0.6	2011 2.5
22 M	0211 1.1	0807 2.5	1432 0.8	2056 2.4
8 M	0210 0.9	0808 2.7	1448 0.4	2058 2.6
23 TU	0242 1.0	0840 2.5	1506 0.7	2122 2.4
9 TU	0302 0.8	0856 2.8	1538 0.3	○ 2141 2.6
24 W	0311 0.9	0913 0.6	1538 0.6	● 2148 2.5
10 W	0349 0.7	0943 2.9	1624 0.4	2224 2.6
25 TH	0341 0.9	0948 0.6	1610 0.6	2217 2.5
11 TH	0432 0.6	1029 2.9	1707 0.3	2306 2.6
26 F	0414 0.8	1024 0.8	1643 0.6	2249 2.5
12 F	0514 0.6	1114 2.9	1748 0.4	2348 2.5
27 SA	0449 0.8	1100 0.8	1716 0.7	2323 2.5
13 SA	0555 0.7	1200 2.8	1828 0.5	
28 SU	0525 0.8	1137 2.6	1750 0.7	2359 2.4
14 SU	0031 2.5	0636 0.8	1248 2.6	1908 0.8
29 M	0602 0.9	1216 2.5	1826 0.8	
15 M	0117 2.4	0721 1.0	1343 2.5	1952 1.0
30 TU	0039 2.4	0643 0.9	1301 2.4	1907 0.9

OCTOBER

Day	Time m	Time m	Time m	Time m
1 W	0126 2.4	0733 1.0	1355 2.4	◑ 1958 1.1
16	0224 2.3	0856 1.1	1557 2.2	2101 1.4
2 TH	0221 2.3	0836 1.0	1507 2.3	2104 1.2
17 F	0331 2.3	1030 1.1	1708 2.2	2304 1.5
3 F	0329 2.3	1010 1.0	1651 2.3	2242 1.2
18 SA	0443 2.3	1135 1.0	1816 2.3	
4 SA	0448 2.3	1130 0.9	1803 2.4	2355 1.2
19 SU	0006 1.4	0544 2.3	1228 0.9	1911 2.3
5 SU	0555 2.4	1233 0.7	1903 2.5	
20 M	0055 1.3	0637 2.3	1313 0.9	1951 2.4
6 M	0054 1.1	0651 2.5	1331 0.6	1953 2.5
21 TU	0133 1.2	0722 2.4	1352 0.8	2021 2.4
7 TU	0150 0.9	0743 2.7	1426 0.5	2037 2.6
22 W	0206 1.1	0802 2.5	1427 0.7	2047 2.5
8 W	0241 0.8	0832 2.8	1515 0.4	○ 2119 2.6
23 TH	0238 1.0	0840 2.5	1501 0.7	● 2115 2.5
9 TH	0328 0.7	0921 2.8	1600 0.3	2200 2.7
24 F	0313 0.9	0918 0.6	1537 0.6	2147 2.6
10 F	0411 0.6	1008 2.8	1641 0.4	2241 2.6
25 SA	0351 0.8	0957 2.6	1613 0.6	2221 2.6
11 SA	0453 0.6	1055 2.8	1720 0.5	2322 2.6
26 SU	0430 0.8	1036 2.6	1650 0.7	2257 2.6
12 SU	0535 0.7	1141 2.6	1758 0.7	
27 M	0509 0.8	1116 2.6	1727 0.8	2336 2.6
13 M	0003 2.5	0615 0.7	1230 2.5	1835 0.9
28 TU	0550 0.8	1159 2.5	1806 0.9	
14 TU	0045 2.5	0659 0.8	1324 2.4	1914 1.1
29 W	0018 2.5	0634 0.8	1248 2.4	1849 1.0
15 W	0130 2.4	0749 1.0	1433 2.3	◑ 1959 1.3
30 TH	0105 2.5	0726 0.9	1345 2.4	1940 1.1
31 F	0159 2.4	0830 0.9	1459 2.3	◐ 2044 1.2

NOVEMBER

Day	Time m	Time m	Time m	Time m
1 SA	0301 2.4	0954 0.9	1639 2.3	2212 1.3
16	0340 2.3	1047 1.0	1725 2.2	2306 1.5
2 SU	0415 2.4	1109 0.8	1747 2.4	2329 1.2
17 M	0451 2.3	1142 1.0	1819 2.4	
3 M	0526 2.5	1210 0.7	1844 2.5	
18 TU	0003 1.4	0549 2.3	1228 0.9	1903 2.3
4 TU	0030 1.1	0625 2.5	1308 0.6	1933 2.5
19 W	0047 1.3	0640 2.3	1309 0.9	1939 2.4
5 W	0127 1.0	0719 2.6	1402 0.5	2016 2.6
20 TH	0126 1.1	0726 2.4	1347 0.8	2011 2.4
6 TH	0220 0.9	0811 2.7	1451 0.5	○ 2057 2.6
21 F	0206 1.0	0809 2.5	1426 0.7	2044 2.5
7 F	0308 0.7	0902 2.7	1535 0.5	2137 2.6
22 SA	0247 0.9	0852 2.5	1506 0.7	● 2119 2.6
8 SA	0353 0.6	0951 2.7	1616 0.6	2218 2.6
23 SU	0330 0.8	0934 2.5	1547 0.7	2157 2.6
9 SU	0436 0.6	1039 2.6	1654 0.7	2258 2.6
24 M	0413 0.7	1017 2.6	1628 0.7	2236 2.6
10 M	0517 0.6	1126 2.5	1731 0.8	2338 2.6
25 TU	0458 0.7	1102 2.6	1710 0.7	2317 2.6
11 TU	0558 0.7	1213 2.4	1805 1.0	
26 W	0543 0.6	1149 2.5	1753 0.8	
12 W	0017 2.6	0639 0.8	1303 2.3	1840 1.1
27 TH	0001 2.6	0631 0.7	1240 2.4	1837 1.0
13 TH	0058 2.5	0724 0.9	1359 2.2	1918 1.3
28 F	0049 2.6	0723 0.7	1336 2.4	1927 1.1
14 F	0143 2.4	0817 1.0	1513 2.1	◑ 2003 1.4
29 SA	0140 2.5	0823 0.7	1445 2.3	◑ 2024 1.2
15 SA	0236 2.3	0930 1.0	1624 2.2	2102 1.5
30 SU	0237 2.5	0933 0.7	1618 2.3	2137 1.2

DECEMBER

Day	Time m	Time m	Time m	Time m
1 M	0345 2.4	1044 0.7	1725 2.3	2257 1.2
16	0349 2.3	1040 1.0	1723 2.2	2236 1.4
2 TU	0500 2.4	1146 0.7	1821 2.4	
17 W	0502 2.2	1138 1.0	1812 2.2	2355 1.3
3 W	0004 1.1	0603 2.5	1244 0.7	1911 2.4
18 TH	0602 2.3	1226 0.9	1856 2.3	
4 TH	0105 1.0	0701 2.5	1339 0.7	1956 2.5
19 F	0047 1.1	0653 2.3	1312 0.8	1937 2.4
5 F	0202 0.9	0757 2.5	1429 0.7	2038 2.5
20 SA	0136 1.0	0742 2.4	1356 0.8	2016 2.5
6 SA	0252 0.8	0851 2.5	1517 0.7	○ 2119 2.6
21 SU	0223 0.9	0830 2.4	1441 0.7	2056 2.5
7 SU	0338 0.7	0941 2.5	1554 0.8	2159 2.6
22 M	0311 0.7	0917 2.5	1526 0.7	● 2136 2.6
8 M	0421 0.6	1028 2.5	1632 0.8	2238 2.6
23 TU	0400 0.6	1004 2.5	1612 0.7	2218 2.7
9 TU	0502 0.6	1113 2.4	1706 0.9	2315 2.6
24 W	0448 0.5	1051 2.6	1657 0.7	2302 2.7
10 W	0541 0.7	1155 2.4	1738 1.0	2352 2.5
25 TH	0536 0.5	1139 2.5	1742 0.8	2346 2.7
11 TH	0620 0.7	1236 2.3	1809 1.1	
26 F	0624 0.5	1228 2.5	1826 0.9	
12 F	0029 2.5	0658 0.8	1319 2.2	1843 1.2
27 SA	0033 2.7	0713 0.5	1320 2.4	1912 1.0
13 SA	0110 2.4	0739 0.9	1406 2.2	1923 1.2
28 SU	0122 2.6	0806 0.6	1420 2.3	◐ 2002 1.1
14 SU	0155 2.4	0826 1.0	1510 2.1	2011 1.3
29 M	0215 2.5	0906 0.7	1544 2.2	2103 1.2
15 M	0246 2.3	0927 1.0	1626 2.1	2109 1.4
30 TU	0318 2.5	1014 0.7	1656 2.2	2222 1.2
31 W	0438 2.4	1121 0.8	1755 2.2	2340 1.1

Chart Datum: 1·50 metres below Ordnance Datum (Newlyn)
HAT is 2·9 metres above Chart Datum

TIDES

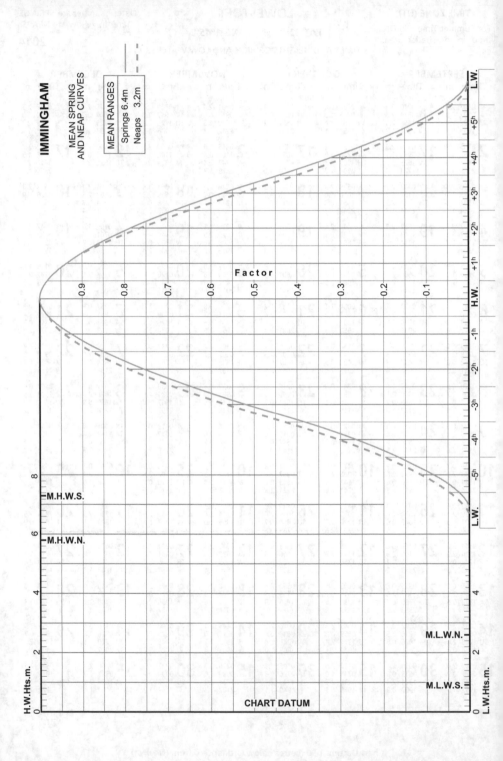

IMMINGHAM

MEAN SPRING
AND NEAP CURVES

MEAN RANGES	
Springs	6.4m
Neaps	3.2m

IMMINGHAM
LAT 53°38'N   LONG 0°11'W
TIMES AND HEIGHTS OF HIGH AND LOW WATERS
2014

JANUARY

Day	Time m	Time m	Time m	Time m
1 W ●	0521 7.2	1141 1.1	1741 7.4	
2 TH	0012 0.9	0613 7.4	1232 1.0	1827 7.6
3 F	0104 0.6	0703 7.5	1320 0.9	1912 7.7
4 SA	0153 0.5	0751 7.4	1405 0.9	1956 7.7
5 SU	0240 0.5	0838 7.3	1441 1.1	2041 7.6
6 M	0325 0.8	0925 7.0	1533 1.4	2128 7.3
7 TU	0411 1.1	1016 6.7	1618 1.6	2220 6.9
8 W ◑	0500 1.6	1113 6.3	1708 2.2	2321 6.5
9 TH	0554 2.0	1215 6.0	1808 2.5	
10 F	0029 6.2	0658 2.3	1319 5.9	1925 2.6
11 SA	0141 6.0	0809 2.4	1423 5.9	2044 2.5
12 SU	0249 6.0	0912 2.3	1522 6.1	2147 2.2
13 M	0350 6.2	1005 2.1	1613 6.4	2238 1.9
14 TU	0441 6.4	1051 1.9	1657 6.7	2323 1.6
15 W	0524 6.5	1133 1.8	1736 6.9	
16 TH ○	0005 1.4	0602 6.6	1212 1.6	1811 7.0
17 F	0044 1.3	0636 6.7	1248 1.6	1845 7.0
18 SA	0120 1.3	0709 6.7	1320 1.6	1917 7.0
19 SU	0152 1.3	0741 6.7	1349 1.6	1948 7.0
20 M	0222 1.4	0814 6.7	1417 1.6	2018 6.9
21 TU	0249 1.5	0845 6.6	1447 1.7	2047 6.8
22 W	0319 1.6	0919 6.4	1521 1.9	2122 6.6
23 TH	0355 1.8	0959 6.2	1602 2.1	2206 6.4
24 F ◑	0442 2.0	1048 6.0	1657 2.3	2302 6.2
25 SA	0546 2.2	1154 5.9	1809 2.5	
26 SU	0015 6.0	0701 2.3	1321 5.9	1931 2.5
27 M	0150 6.0	0819 2.2	1439 6.1	2051 2.2
28 TU	0313 6.3	0929 1.9	1543 6.5	2203 1.7
29 W	0419 6.7	1031 1.6	1638 7.0	2306 1.2
30 TH ●	0516 7.1	1127 1.2	1728 7.4	
31 F	0002 0.8	0607 7.3	1219 0.9	1814 7.7

FEBRUARY

Day	Time m	Time m	Time m	Time m
1 SA	0053 0.4	0654 7.5	1306 0.7	1859 7.8
2 SU	0140 0.3	0738 7.5	1350 0.7	1942 7.9
3 M	0223 0.4	0820 7.4	1432 0.8	2024 7.7
4 TU	0304 0.6	0900 7.1	1510 1.1	2107 7.4
5 W	0343 1.0	0942 6.8	1548 1.5	2151 7.0
6 TH ◑	0420 1.6	1027 6.3	1628 2.0	2242 6.5
7 F	0502 2.1	1121 5.9	1716 2.4	2347 6.0
8 SA	0556 2.5	1229 5.7	1821 2.7	
9 SU	0105 5.7	0711 2.8	1341 5.6	2004 2.8
10 M	0222 5.7	0839 2.7	1449 5.8	2124 2.5
11 TU	0330 5.9	0941 2.6	1547 6.1	2217 2.1
12 W	0424 6.1	1030 2.2	1634 6.5	2302 1.7
13 TH	0506 6.4	1113 1.8	1714 6.7	2344 1.4
14 F	0542 6.6	1152 1.6	1749 6.9	
15 SA	0023 1.3	0614 6.7	1229 1.5	1822 7.0
16 SU ○	0100 1.2	0646 6.8	1302 1.4	1855 7.1
17 M	0133 1.2	0718 6.9	1331 1.4	1927 7.1
18 TU	0202 1.2	0749 6.9	1359 1.4	1956 7.1
19 W	0228 1.3	0819 6.8	1428 1.4	2026 7.0
20 TH	0255 1.4	0850 6.7	1459 1.6	2059 6.8
21 F	0326 1.6	0927 6.5	1537 1.8	2141 6.6
22 SA	0407 1.9	1013 6.2	1626 2.1	2235 6.2
23 SU	0508 2.2	1114 5.9	1738 2.3	2347 5.9
24 M	0630 2.4	1239 5.8	1906 2.4	
25 TU	0135 5.9	0756 2.4	1414 6.0	2034 2.1
26 W	0307 6.2	0913 2.0	1524 6.4	2151 1.6
27 TH	0413 6.6	1017 1.6	1621 6.9	2253 1.1
28 F	0507 7.0	1112 1.2	1711 7.3	2347 0.6

MARCH

Day	Time m	Time m	Time m	Time m
1 SA ●	0555 7.3	1202 0.8	1758 7.6	
2 SU	0035 0.4	0638 7.5	1249 0.7	1841 7.8
3 M	0120 0.3	0718 7.5	1331 0.6	1924 7.8
4 TU	0201 0.4	0756 7.4	1411 0.7	2004 7.7
5 W	0238 0.7	0831 7.2	1447 1.0	2044 7.4
6 TH	0311 1.1	0906 6.8	1520 1.4	2123 6.9
7 F	0342 1.6	0942 6.4	1554 1.8	2207 6.4
8 SA	0418 2.1	1025 6.0	1637 2.2	2304 5.9
9 SU	0505 2.6	1130 5.6	1735 2.6	
10 M	0027 5.5	0611 2.9	1258 5.5	1856 2.8
11 TU	0152 5.4	0747 3.0	1413 5.6	2052 2.6
12 W	0302 5.7	0912 2.6	1515 5.9	2149 2.2
13 TH	0358 6.0	1004 2.2	1605 6.3	2234 1.8
14 F	0441 6.3	1045 1.8	1647 6.6	2315 1.4
15 SA ●	0516 6.6	1127 1.6	1721 6.8	2355 1.2
16 SU ○	0547 6.7	1204 1.4	1755 7.0	
17 M	0032 1.1	0619 6.9	1239 1.3	1829 7.1
18 TU	0107 1.1	0651 7.0	1310 1.2	1903 7.1
19 W	0137 1.1	0723 7.0	1341 1.2	1935 7.2
20 TH	0206 1.1	0754 7.0	1412 1.2	2008 7.1
21 F	0235 1.3	0827 6.9	1445 1.3	2044 6.9
22 SA	0308 1.5	0904 6.7	1524 1.5	2127 6.6
23 SU	0349 1.8	0951 6.4	1614 1.9	2222 6.2
24 M	0448 2.2	1051 6.0	1726 2.2	2339 5.8
25 TU	0611 2.5	1216 5.9	1853 2.2	
26 W	0134 5.8	0739 2.4	1352 6.0	2021 2.0
27 TH	0258 6.2	0856 2.1	1504 6.4	2136 1.5
28 F	0400 6.6	0959 1.6	1601 6.9	2235 1.0
29 SA	0452 7.0	1053 1.2	1651 7.3	2326 0.7
30 SU	0536 7.2	1142 0.9	1737 7.5	
31 M	0013 0.5	0616 7.4	1228 0.7	1821 7.6

APRIL

Day	Time m	Time m	Time m	Time m
1 TU	0056 0.5	0654 7.4	1310 0.7	1903 7.6
2 W	0135 0.6	0729 7.3	1349 0.8	1943 7.5
3 TH	0210 0.9	0803 7.1	1423 1.0	2021 7.2
4 F	0241 1.2	0834 6.9	1455 1.3	2059 6.8
5 SA	0310 1.7	0906 6.5	1528 1.7	2138 6.3
6 SU	0343 2.1	0943 6.1	1609 2.1	2226 5.8
7 M ◐	0426 2.5	1035 5.8	1702 2.4	2341 5.4
8 TU	0527 2.9	1201 5.5	1813 2.7	
9 W	0112 5.4	0646 3.0	1329 5.5	1943 2.6
10 TH	0224 5.6	0820 2.8	1435 5.8	2103 2.2
11 F	0321 5.9	0925 2.4	1526 6.1	2154 1.9
12 SA	0405 6.2	1012 2.0	1608 6.4	2238 1.5
13 SU	0441 6.5	1054 1.7	1646 6.7	2320 1.3
14 M	0515 6.7	1133 1.5	1724 6.9	2359 1.1
15 TU	0550 6.9	1210 1.3	1802 7.0	
16 W	0036 1.0	0624 7.1	1247 1.1	1839 7.2
17 TH	0112 1.0	0659 7.1	1323 1.1	1916 7.2
18 F	0146 1.0	0734 7.1	1359 1.0	1954 7.1
19 SA	0220 1.2	0810 7.1	1438 1.1	2036 7.0
20 SU	0258 1.4	0850 6.9	1521 1.4	2123 6.6
21 M	0343 1.8	0939 6.5	1615 1.6	2222 6.2
22 TU	0442 2.1	1040 6.2	1725 1.9	2344 5.9
23 W	0559 2.4	1202 6.1	1845 1.9	
24 TH	0124 6.0	0720 2.4	1329 6.2	2004 1.7
25 F	0239 6.2	0834 2.1	1439 6.5	2112 1.4
26 SA	0339 6.6	0936 1.7	1537 6.8	2210 1.1
27 SU	0430 6.9	1030 1.3	1629 7.1	2300 0.9
28 M	0513 7.1	1119 1.1	1716 7.2	2347 0.8
29 TU	0552 7.2	1205 0.9	1801 7.3	
30 W ○	0029 0.8	0628 7.2	1249 0.9	1843 7.3

Chart Datum: 3·90 metres below Ordnance Datum (Newlyn)
HAT is 8·0 metres above Chart Datum

TIDES

TIDES

TIME ZONE (UT)
For Summer Time add ONE hour in **non-shaded areas**

IMMINGHAM
LAT 53°38'N LONG 0°11'W
TIMES AND HEIGHTS OF HIGH AND LOW WATERS

Dates in amber are **SPRINGS**
Dates in yellow are **NEAPS**

2014

MAY

Day	Time m	Day	Time m
1 TH	0108 0.9 / 0704 7.2 / 1328 0.9 / 1924 7.2	16 F	0048 1.0 / 0638 7.2 / 1308 0.9 / 1902 7.2
2 F	0143 1.1 / 0737 7.0 / 1403 1.1 / 2002 6.9	17 SA	0129 1.0 / 0718 7.3 / 1351 0.9 / 1946 7.2
3 SA	0214 1.4 / 0808 6.9 / 1436 1.3 / 2038 6.6	18 SU	0210 1.1 / 0758 7.2 / 1436 0.9 / 2032 7.0
4 SU	0244 1.7 / 0839 6.6 / 1509 1.6 / 2115 6.3	19 M	0252 1.3 / 0842 7.1 / 1523 1.1 / 2123 6.7
5 M	0317 2.0 / 0914 6.3 / 1548 1.9 / 2157 5.9	20 TU	0340 1.6 / 0932 6.8 / 1618 1.3 / 2223 6.4
6 TU	0356 2.4 / 0959 6.0 / 1636 2.2 / 2255 5.6	21 W	0436 1.9 / 1032 6.5 / 1721 1.5 / 2340 6.2
7 W	0448 2.7 / 1104 5.7 / 1737 2.4	22 TH	0543 2.2 / 1146 6.3 / 1829 1.6
8 TH	0013 5.5 / 0555 2.9 / 1228 5.6 / 1846 2.4	23 F	0059 6.1 / 0655 2.2 / 1303 6.3 / 1939 1.6
9 F	0128 5.5 / 0711 2.8 / 1339 5.7 / 1957 2.3	24 SA	0209 6.2 / 0806 2.1 / 1411 6.4 / 2044 1.5
10 SA	0229 5.8 / 0823 2.6 / 1437 6.0 / 2101 2.0	25 SU	0310 6.4 / 0910 1.8 / 1512 6.6 / 2142 1.4
11 SU	0319 6.1 / 0923 2.2 / 1525 6.3 / 2153 1.7	26 M	0402 6.6 / 1006 1.6 / 1607 6.8 / 2234 1.3
12 M	0402 6.4 / 1012 1.9 / 1610 6.5 / 2240 1.4	27 TU	0447 6.8 / 1057 1.3 / 1657 6.9 / 2321 1.2
13 TU	0442 6.7 / 1058 1.6 / 1653 6.8 / 2324 1.2	28 W	0527 6.9 / 1145 1.2 / 1743 6.9
14 W	0521 6.9 / 1142 1.3 / 1736 7.0	29 TH	0004 1.2 / 0605 7.0 / 1229 1.1 / 1826 6.9
15 TH	0007 1.1 / 0600 7.1 / 1225 1.1 / 1818 7.1	30 F	0044 1.3 / 0641 7.0 / 1310 1.1 / 1907 6.9
		31 SA	0120 1.4 / 0716 7.0 / 1347 1.2 / 1944 6.7

JUNE

Day	Time m	Day	Time m
1 SU	0153 1.5 / 0748 6.9 / 1421 1.3 / 2019 6.6	16 M	0200 1.0 / 0749 7.5 / 1432 0.6 / 2029 7.2
2 M	0224 1.7 / 0820 6.7 / 1454 1.5 / 2054 6.4	17 TU	0245 1.1 / 0835 7.4 / 1521 0.7 / 2120 7.0
3 TU	0255 1.9 / 0854 6.5 / 1530 1.8 / 2132 6.1	18 W	0332 1.3 / 0924 7.1 / 1611 1.0 / 2216 6.7
4 W	0331 2.2 / 0933 6.2 / 1612 2.0 / 2218 5.9	19 TH	0423 1.6 / 1020 6.9 / 1706 1.2 / 2319 6.4
5 TH	0414 2.4 / 1022 6.0 / 1702 2.1 / 2315 5.7	20 F	0520 1.9 / 1124 6.6 / 1806 1.5
6 F	0509 2.6 / 1125 5.8 / 1800 2.2	21 SA	0026 6.2 / 0624 2.2 / 1233 6.4 / 1909 1.7
7 SA	0022 5.7 / 0613 2.7 / 1236 5.8 / 1901 2.2	22 SU	0132 6.1 / 0735 2.2 / 1342 6.3 / 2014 1.8
8 SU	0129 5.8 / 0721 2.6 / 1342 5.9 / 2005 2.1	23 M	0234 6.2 / 0843 2.1 / 1447 6.3 / 2115 1.8
9 M	0229 6.0 / 0827 2.4 / 1441 6.1 / 2105 1.8	24 TU	0332 6.3 / 0944 1.9 / 1547 6.4 / 2209 1.7
10 TU	0322 6.3 / 0928 2.0 / 1535 6.4 / 2200 1.6	25 W	0421 6.5 / 1038 1.6 / 1641 6.5 / 2257 1.6
11 W	0410 6.6 / 1024 1.7 / 1626 6.7 / 2252 1.4	26 TH	0504 6.7 / 1127 1.4 / 1729 6.6 / 2342 1.6
12 TH	0455 6.9 / 1116 1.4 / 1715 6.9 / 2341 1.2	27 F	0544 6.8 / 1212 1.3 / 1812 6.7
13 F	0539 7.1 / 1207 1.0 / 1804 7.1	28 SA	0023 1.5 / 0621 6.9 / 1254 1.2 / 1850 6.7
14 SA	0029 1.0 / 0622 7.3 / 1256 0.8 / 1852 7.3	29 SU	0101 1.5 / 0656 7.0 / 1332 1.2 / 1926 6.7
15 SU	0115 0.9 / 0705 7.4 / 1345 0.7 / 1941 7.3	30 M	0135 1.6 / 0731 7.0 / 1407 1.3 / 1959 6.6

JULY

Day	Time m	Day	Time m
1 TU	0206 1.7 / 0802 6.8 / 1439 1.4 / 2032 6.5	16 W	0233 0.9 / 0823 7.7 / 1509 0.5 / 2107 7.2
2 W	0236 1.8 / 0834 6.7 / 1511 1.6 / 2106 6.4	17 TH	0318 1.1 / 0910 7.5 / 1555 0.8 / 2155 6.9
3 TH	0307 1.9 / 0909 6.5 / 1545 1.8 / 2144 6.2	18 F	0403 1.4 / 1000 7.1 / 1642 1.2 / 2248 6.6
4 F	0343 2.1 / 0947 6.3 / 1625 1.9 / 2228 6.0	19 SA	0451 1.8 / 1057 6.7 / 1734 1.6 / 2347 6.2
5 SA	0427 2.3 / 1033 6.1 / 1713 2.1 / 2322 5.9	20 SU	0548 2.2 / 1201 6.3 / 1833 2.0
6 SU	0522 2.5 / 1132 5.9 / 1811 2.2	21 M	0050 6.0 / 0657 2.4 / 1312 6.1 / 1941 2.0
7 M	0029 5.8 / 0628 2.6 / 1244 5.9 / 1916 2.2	22 TU	0156 5.9 / 0817 2.4 / 1423 6.0 / 2049 2.3
8 TU	0141 5.9 / 0739 2.5 / 1359 6.0 / 2023 2.0	23 W	0259 6.1 / 0925 2.2 / 1531 6.1 / 2147 2.2
9 W	0245 6.1 / 0850 2.2 / 1506 6.3 / 2127 1.8	24 TH	0355 6.3 / 1021 1.9 / 1628 6.3 / 2237 2.0
10 TH	0342 6.5 / 0956 1.8 / 1606 6.6 / 2226 1.5	25 F	0442 6.6 / 1110 1.6 / 1715 6.5 / 2322 1.8
11 F	0433 6.8 / 1056 1.4 / 1702 6.9 / 2321 1.3	26 SA	0523 6.8 / 1154 1.4 / 1756 6.6
12 SA	0522 7.2 / 1153 1.0 / 1755 7.2	27 SU	0003 1.6 / 0600 6.9 / 1236 1.2 / 1831 6.7
13 SU	0013 1.0 / 0608 7.4 / 1246 0.6 / 1845 7.3	28 M	0042 1.6 / 0635 7.0 / 1313 1.2 / 1904 6.7
14 M	0102 0.7 / 0653 7.6 / 1336 0.4 / 1934 7.4	29 TU	0117 1.5 / 0709 7.0 / 1348 1.2 / 1936 6.7
15 TU	0149 0.8 / 0741 7.7 / 1423 0.4 / 2020 7.4	30 W	0147 1.6 / 0741 7.0 / 1420 1.3 / 2007 6.7
		31 TH	0215 1.6 / 0813 6.9 / 1449 1.4 / 2039 6.6

AUGUST

Day	Time m	Day	Time m
1 F	0243 1.7 / 0843 6.8 / 1516 1.6 / 2112 6.5	16 SA	0337 1.3 / 0935 7.2 / 1610 1.3 / 2211 6.6
2 SA	0314 1.9 / 0915 6.6 / 1547 1.8 / 2148 6.3	17 SU	0419 1.8 / 1027 6.7 / 1653 1.6 / 2303 6.2
3 SU	0351 2.1 / 0954 6.4 / 1628 2.0 / 2232 6.1	18 M	0506 2.2 / 1128 6.2 / 1745 2.4
4 M	0440 2.3 / 1044 6.1 / 1723 2.2 / 2331 5.9	19 TU	0007 5.9 / 0610 2.6 / 1243 5.8 / 1857 2.7
5 TU	0545 2.5 / 1152 5.9 / 1834 2.3	20 W	0118 5.8 / 0748 2.7 / 1400 5.7 / 2022 2.7
6 W	0052 5.8 / 0702 2.5 / 1324 5.9 / 1949 2.3	21 TH	0227 5.9 / 0906 2.4 / 1511 5.9 / 2126 2.5
7 TH	0213 6.0 / 0821 2.3 / 1449 6.2 / 2102 2.0	22 F	0328 6.2 / 1002 2.0 / 1610 6.2 / 2216 2.2
8 F	0319 6.4 / 0937 1.9 / 1556 6.5 / 2207 1.7	23 SA	0418 6.5 / 1049 1.7 / 1656 6.4 / 2301 1.9
9 SA	0415 6.8 / 1042 1.4 / 1654 6.9 / 2305 1.3	24 SU	0459 6.8 / 1131 1.4 / 1734 6.5 / 2341 1.7
10 SU	0505 7.3 / 1140 0.9 / 1746 7.2 / 2358 1.0	25 M	0536 7.0 / 1201 1.2 / 1807 6.6
11 M	0553 7.6 / 1232 0.5 / 1835 7.5	26 TU	0019 1.5 / 0610 7.1 / 1249 1.1 / 1838 6.9
12 TU	0046 0.8 / 0638 7.8 / 1321 0.3 / 1920 7.6	27 W	0055 1.5 / 0643 7.1 / 1324 1.2 / 1909 6.9
13 W	0133 0.7 / 0722 7.9 / 1406 0.2 / 2003 7.5	28 TH	0125 1.5 / 0716 7.1 / 1355 1.2 / 1940 6.9
14 TH	0216 0.7 / 0806 7.9 / 1449 0.4 / 2044 7.3	29 F	0153 1.5 / 0748 7.1 / 1422 1.3 / 2010 6.8
15 F	0257 0.9 / 0850 7.6 / 1529 0.8 / 2126 7.0	30 SA	0219 1.6 / 0817 6.9 / 1447 1.5 / 2040 6.7
		31 SU	0248 1.7 / 0848 6.8 / 1514 1.7 / 2113 6.5

Chart Datum: 3·90 metres below Ordnance Datum (Newlyn)
HAT is 8·0 metres above Chart Datum

TIME ZONE (UT)	IMMINGHAM	Dates in amber are SPRINGS
For Summer Time add ONE hour in **non-shaded areas**	LAT 53°38′N LONG 0°11′W	Dates in yellow are NEAPS
	TIMES AND HEIGHTS OF HIGH AND LOW WATERS	**2014**

SEPTEMBER

Time m | Time m

Day	Times (m)	Day	Times (m)
1 M	0323 1.9 / 0925 6.6 / 1551 1.9 / 2154 6.3	**16** TU ☽	0428 2.2 / 1054 6.1 / 1653 2.6 / 2320 5.9
2 TU ☽	0408 2.2 / 1013 6.2 / 1643 2.3 / 2249 6.0	**17** W	0525 2.6 / 1211 5.7 / 1758 3.0
3 W	0512 2.4 / 1121 5.9 / 1759 2.5	**18** TH	0039 5.7 / 0656 2.8 / 1332 5.6 / 1940 3.0
4 TH	0008 5.8 / 0635 2.5 / 1304 5.8 / 1924 2.5	**19** F	0153 5.8 / 0839 2.6 / 1444 5.8 / 2059 2.8
5 F	0145 6.0 / 0802 2.3 / 1439 6.1 / 2044 2.2	**20** SA	0257 6.1 / 0935 2.2 / 1542 6.1 / 2151 2.3
6 SA	0258 6.4 / 0922 1.8 / 1546 6.6 / 2151 1.8	**21** SU	0349 6.4 / 1020 1.8 / 1628 6.4 / 2234 2.0
7 SU	0356 6.9 / 1020 1.3 / 1642 7.0 / 2248 1.4	**22** M	0431 6.7 / 1102 1.5 / 1705 6.7 / 2314 1.7
8 M	0446 7.3 / 1123 0.8 / 1732 7.3 / 2339 1.0	**23** TU	0507 6.9 / 1141 1.3 / 1737 6.9 / 2352 1.5
9 TU ○	0533 7.7 / 1213 0.4 / 1817 7.5	**24** W ●	0541 7.1 / 1218 1.2 / 1808 7.0
10 W	0027 0.8 / 0618 7.9 / 1300 0.3 / 1859 7.6	**25** TH	0027 1.4 / 0615 7.2 / 1254 1.1 / 1839 7.0
11 TH	0110 0.7 / 0702 8.0 / 1343 0.3 / 1938 7.6	**26** F	0059 1.4 / 0649 7.2 / 1326 1.2 / 1911 7.1
12 F	0154 0.7 / 0744 7.9 / 1422 0.6 / 2016 7.4	**27** SA	0128 1.4 / 0722 7.2 / 1354 1.3 / 1942 7.0
13 SA	0233 0.9 / 0827 7.6 / 1454 1.0 / 2053 7.1	**28** SU	0157 1.5 / 0754 7.1 / 1420 1.4 / 2012 6.9
14 SU	0310 1.3 / 0909 7.2 / 1534 1.5 / 2132 6.7	**29** M	0228 1.6 / 0827 6.9 / 1450 1.6 / 2046 6.7
15 M	0346 1.7 / 0956 6.6 / 1609 2.0 / 2218 6.2	**30** TU	0304 1.7 / 0906 6.6 / 1527 1.9 / 2127 6.5

OCTOBER

Time m | Time m

Day	Times (m)	Day	Times (m)
1 W ☽	0349 2.0 / 0956 6.3 / 1618 2.3 / 2222 6.2	**16** TH	0449 2.5 / 1133 5.7 / 1709 3.0 / 2349 5.7
2 TH	0454 2.3 / 1107 5.9 / 1734 2.6 / 2340 5.9	**17** F	0600 2.8 / 1254 5.5 / 1829 3.2
3 F	0619 2.4 / 1257 5.8 / 1903 2.6	**18** SA	0111 5.7 / 0743 2.7 / 1405 5.7 / 2010 3.0
4 SA	0119 6.1 / 0746 2.2 / 1425 6.1 / 2024 2.3	**19** SU	0218 5.9 / 0854 2.3 / 1504 6.0 / 2114 2.6
5 SU	0234 6.5 / 0905 1.7 / 1530 6.6 / 2131 1.9	**20** M	0312 6.3 / 0942 2.0 / 1552 6.3 / 2200 2.2
6 M	0333 6.9 / 1007 1.2 / 1624 7.0 / 2227 1.4	**21** TU	0355 6.6 / 1024 1.6 / 1630 6.6 / 2241 1.9
7 TU	0424 7.3 / 1100 0.8 / 1711 7.3 / 2317 1.1	**22** W	0433 6.8 / 1105 1.4 / 1704 6.9 / 2320 1.6
8 W ○	0511 7.6 / 1148 0.6 / 1754 7.5	**23** TH ●	0509 7.0 / 1143 1.3 / 1737 7.0
9 TH	0005 0.8 / 0556 7.8 / 1234 0.5 / 1833 7.6	**24** F	0546 7.1 / 1220 1.2 / 1811 7.1
10 F	0049 0.7 / 0640 7.8 / 1316 0.6 / 1911 7.5	**25** SA	0031 1.3 / 0622 7.2 / 1255 1.2 / 1844 7.2
11 SA	0131 0.8 / 0723 7.7 / 1354 0.8 / 1947 7.4	**26** SU	0105 1.3 / 0659 7.2 / 1327 1.3 / 1917 7.2
12 SU	0209 1.0 / 0804 7.4 / 1428 1.2 / 2022 7.1	**27** M	0139 1.3 / 0735 7.1 / 1359 1.4 / 1951 7.1
13 M	0244 1.3 / 0845 7.0 / 1459 1.7 / 2057 6.8	**28** TU	0215 1.4 / 0814 7.0 / 1434 1.6 / 2028 6.9
14 TU	0318 1.7 / 0928 6.6 / 1532 2.1 / 2135 6.4	**29** W	0255 1.6 / 0857 6.7 / 1514 1.9 / 2111 6.7
15 W ☽	0357 2.1 / 1020 6.0 / 1612 2.6 / 2227 6.0	**30** TH	0343 1.8 / 0950 6.4 / 1606 2.2 / 2206 6.4
		31 F ☽	0447 2.1 / 1103 6.0 / 1717 2.5 / 2320 6.2

NOVEMBER

Time m | Time m

Day	Times (m)	Day	Times (m)
1 SA	0605 2.2 / 1242 6.0 / 1840 2.6	**16** SU	0009 5.7 / 0627 2.6 / 1311 5.6 / 1848 3.0
2 SU	0050 6.2 / 0726 2.0 / 1402 6.2 / 1958 2.4	**17** M	0123 5.8 / 0742 2.5 / 1413 5.9 / 2006 2.8
3 M	0206 6.5 / 0840 1.7 / 1506 6.6 / 2106 2.0	**18** TU	0222 6.0 / 0847 2.2 / 1505 6.2 / 2109 2.5
4 TU	0307 6.9 / 0941 1.3 / 1600 6.9 / 2203 1.6	**19** W	0312 6.3 / 0938 1.9 / 1548 6.5 / 2159 2.1
5 W	0400 7.2 / 1034 1.0 / 1647 7.2 / 2254 1.2	**20** TH	0355 6.6 / 1024 1.6 / 1628 6.7 / 2242 1.8
6 TH ○	0449 7.4 / 1122 0.9 / 1729 7.3 / 2342 1.0	**21** F	0437 6.8 / 1106 1.4 / 1706 7.0 / 2324 1.6
7 F	0536 7.5 / 1207 0.9 / 1808 7.4	**22** SA ●	0518 7.0 / 1147 1.3 / 1743 7.1
8 SA	0027 0.9 / 0620 7.5 / 1249 1.0 / 1845 7.4	**23** SU	0005 1.4 / 0559 7.1 / 1227 1.2 / 1821 7.3
9 SU	0110 1.0 / 0703 7.4 / 1326 1.1 / 1922 7.3	**24** M	0046 1.2 / 0641 7.2 / 1305 1.2 / 1858 7.3
10 M	0148 1.1 / 0745 7.2 / 1400 1.4 / 1956 7.1	**25** TU	0126 1.1 / 0723 7.2 / 1344 1.3 / 1936 7.3
11 TU	0223 1.4 / 0824 6.9 / 1431 1.7 / 2029 6.9	**26** W	0208 1.2 / 0806 7.1 / 1424 1.4 / 2016 7.2
12 W	0256 1.7 / 0903 6.5 / 1502 2.1 / 2103 6.6	**27** TH	0252 1.3 / 0853 6.9 / 1507 1.7 / 2101 7.0
13 TH	0333 2.0 / 0947 6.1 / 1539 2.4 / 2146 6.2	**28** F	0342 1.5 / 0946 6.6 / 1558 2.0 / 2155 6.7
14 F ☽	0418 2.3 / 1043 5.8 / 1627 2.8 / 2246 5.9	**29** SA ☽	0440 1.7 / 1054 6.3 / 1700 2.3 / 2301 6.5
15 SA	0518 2.5 / 1158 5.6 / 1731 3.0	**30** SU	0548 1.8 / 1215 6.2 / 1812 2.4

DECEMBER

Time m | Time m

Day	Times (m)	Day	Times (m)
1 M	0020 6.4 / 0700 1.9 / 1329 6.2 / 1927 2.4	**16** TU	0010 5.8 / 0637 2.5 / 1307 5.7 / 1853 2.9
2 TU	0134 6.5 / 0810 1.8 / 1434 6.4 / 2037 2.1	**17** W	0121 5.8 / 0742 2.4 / 1409 5.9 / 2003 2.7
3 W	0240 6.6 / 0912 1.6 / 1532 6.6 / 2138 1.8	**18** TH	0223 6.0 / 0844 2.1 / 1504 6.2 / 2107 2.4
4 TH	0338 6.8 / 1007 1.4 / 1621 6.9 / 2232 1.5	**19** F	0318 6.3 / 0940 1.9 / 1552 6.5 / 2203 2.0
5 F	0430 7.0 / 1057 1.3 / 1705 7.1 / 2322 1.3	**20** SA	0408 6.6 / 1030 1.6 / 1637 6.8 / 2254 1.7
6 SA ○	0519 7.1 / 1142 1.3 / 1745 7.2	**21** SU	0455 6.9 / 1118 1.4 / 1720 7.1 / 2342 1.3
7 SU	0008 1.2 / 0605 7.1 / 1225 1.3 / 1824 7.2	**22** M ●	0542 7.1 / 1203 1.2 / 1802 7.3
8 M	0052 1.1 / 0648 7.1 / 1303 1.4 / 1901 7.2	**23** TU	0030 1.1 / 0628 7.2 / 1249 1.1 / 1843 7.4
9 TU	0131 1.2 / 0728 7.0 / 1337 1.5 / 1936 7.1	**24** W	0117 0.9 / 0713 7.3 / 1332 1.1 / 1924 7.5
10 W	0206 1.3 / 0805 6.8 / 1409 1.7 / 2008 7.0	**25** TH	0203 0.8 / 0759 7.2 / 1416 1.2 / 2007 7.5
11 TH	0239 1.5 / 0840 6.6 / 1439 1.9 / 2040 6.8	**26** F	0248 0.9 / 0846 7.1 / 1500 1.3 / 2052 7.3
12 F	0313 1.8 / 0916 6.3 / 1513 2.2 / 2116 6.5	**27** SA	0336 1.0 / 0936 6.8 / 1546 1.6 / 2142 7.1
13 SA	0351 2.0 / 0958 6.0 / 1552 2.4 / 2200 6.2	**28** SU ☽	0427 1.5 / 1033 6.5 / 1639 1.9 / 2240 6.8
14 SU	0437 2.3 / 1051 5.8 / 1641 2.7 / 2257 5.9	**29** M	0524 1.6 / 1140 6.3 / 1740 2.2 / 2348 6.5
15 M	0534 2.4 / 1157 5.7 / 1743 2.9	**30** TU	0628 1.9 / 1249 6.1 / 1851 2.4
		31 W	0101 6.3 / 0737 2.0 / 1357 6.1 / 2006 2.3

Chart Datum: 3·90 metres below Ordnance Datum (Newlyn)
HAT is 8·0 metres above Chart Datum

TIDES

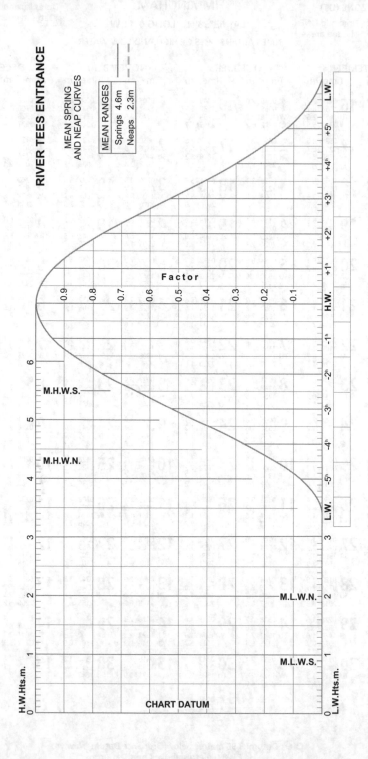

RIVER TEES ENTRANCE

MEAN SPRING
AND NEAP CURVES

MEAN RANGES
Springs 4.6m
Neaps 2.3m

Factor

0.9 0.8 0.7 0.6 0.5 0.4 0.3 0.2 0.1

M.H.W.S.

M.H.W.N.

M.L.W.N.

M.L.W.S.

H.W.Hts.m.

L.W.Hts.m.

CHART DATUM

RIVER TEES

LAT 54°38′N   LONG 1°09′W

TIMES AND HEIGHTS OF HIGH AND LOW WATERS

2014

JANUARY

Day	Time	m	Time	m
1 W	0258 / 0921 / 1517 / ● 2150	5.4 / 0.9 / 5.6 / 0.6	**16** TH	0345 / 0952 / 1557 / ○ 2217	5.0 / 1.4 / 5.2 / 1.1
2 TH	0350 / 1009 / 1605 / 2239	5.6 / 0.8 / 5.7 / 0.4	**17** F	0420 / 1023 / 1628 / 2250	5.0 / 1.3 / 5.3 / 1.0
3 F	0441 / 1057 / 1652 / 2327	5.6 / 0.7 / 5.8 / 0.3	**18** SA	0452 / 1054 / 1658 / 2323	5.1 / 1.3 / 5.3 / 1.0
4 SA	0530 / 1143 / 1739	5.6 / 0.8 / 5.8	**19** SU	0524 / 1125 / 1730 / 2355	5.0 / 1.3 / 5.2 / 1.0
5 SU	0015 / 0619 / 1229 / 1826	0.4 / 5.5 / 1.0 / 5.7	**20** M	0558 / 1158 / 1804	5.0 / 1.4 / 5.2
6 M	0102 / 0709 / 1316 / 1915	0.5 / 5.3 / 1.2 / 5.5	**21** TU	0028 / 0634 / 1235 / 1841	1.1 / 4.9 / 1.5 / 5.1
7 TU	0150 / 0802 / 1406 / 2008	0.8 / 5.0 / 1.5 / 5.2	**22** W	0105 / 0715 / 1311 / 1922	1.2 / 4.8 / 1.6 / 4.9
8 W	0243 / 0857 / 1502 / ◐ 2107	1.2 / 4.7 / 1.8 / 4.9	**23** TH	0146 / 0800 / 1354 / 2010	1.4 / 4.6 / 1.8 / 4.7
9 TH	0342 / 0958 / 1608 / 2212	1.5 / 4.5 / 2.0 / 4.6	**24** F	0235 / 0854 / 1448 / ◑ 2109	1.6 / 4.5 / 2.0 / 4.6
10 F	0452 / 1106 / 1724 / 2325	1.8 / 4.4 / 2.1 / 4.4	**25** SA	0336 / 0956 / 1601 / 2219	1.8 / 4.4 / 2.0 / 4.5
11 SA	0607 / 1216 / 1838	1.9 / 4.4 / 2.0	**26** SU	0450 / 1103 / 1724 / 2334	1.8 / 4.4 / 2.0 / 4.5
12 SU	0038 / 0710 / 1317 / 1937	4.5 / 1.9 / 4.6 / 1.7	**27** M	0606 / 1211 / 1841	1.7 / 4.6 / 1.7
13 M	0139 / 0800 / 1407 / 2025	4.6 / 1.7 / 4.8 / 1.5	**28** TU	0046 / 0715 / 1315 / 1949	4.7 / 1.5 / 4.9 / 1.3
14 TU	0228 / 0841 / 1448 / 2105	4.7 / 1.6 / 5.0 / 1.3	**29** W	0151 / 0816 / 1412 / 2048	5.0 / 1.2 / 5.2 / 0.9
15 W	0308 / 0918 / 1525 / 2142	4.9 / 1.5 / 5.1 / 1.2	**30** TH	0248 / 0909 / 1503 / ● 2140	5.3 / 0.9 / 5.4 / 0.5
			31 F	0339 / 0958 / 1551 / 2229	5.5 / 0.7 / 5.8 / 0.3

FEBRUARY

Day	Time	m	Time	m
1 SA	0428 / 1044 / 1637 / 2314	5.7 / 0.6 / 5.9 / 0.1	**16** SU	0429 / 1034 / 1637 / 2259	5.1 / 1.1 / 5.3 / 0.8
2 SU	0514 / 1127 / 1721 / 2357	5.7 / 0.6 / 5.9 / 0.2	**17** M	0459 / 1105 / 1706 / 2330	5.1 / 1.1 / 5.3 / 0.8
3 M	0559 / 1209 / 1806	5.6 / 0.7 / 5.8	**18** TU	0530 / 1136 / 1737	5.1 / 1.1 / 5.3
4 TU	0039 / 0644 / 1251 / 1850	0.4 / 5.4 / 1.0 / 5.6	**19** W	0002 / 0604 / 1210 / 1811	0.9 / 5.1 / 1.2 / 5.2
5 W	0122 / 0729 / 1334 / 1938	0.8 / 5.1 / 1.3 / 5.2	**20** TH	0038 / 0641 / 1245 / 1850	1.0 / 4.9 / 1.3 / 5.1
6 TH	0206 / 0818 / 1422 / ◐ 2031	1.2 / 4.7 / 1.6 / 4.8	**21** F	0116 / 0724 / 1325 / 1938	1.2 / 4.8 / 1.5 / 4.8
7 F	0256 / 0913 / 1521 / 2133	1.6 / 4.4 / 1.9 / 4.5	**22** SA	0202 / 0815 / 1416 / ◑ 2037	1.5 / 4.6 / 1.7 / 4.6
8 SA	0401 / 1017 / 1638 / 2246	2.0 / 4.2 / 2.1 / 4.2	**23** SU	0300 / 0918 / 1525 / 2152	1.7 / 4.4 / 1.9 / 4.4
9 SU	0524 / 1132 / 1805	2.2 / 4.2 / 2.1	**24** M	0418 / 1031 / 1657 / 2313	1.9 / 4.3 / 1.9 / 4.4
10 M	0007 / 0641 / 1246 / 1913	4.2 / 2.1 / 4.3 / 1.9	**25** TU	0544 / 1147 / 1825	1.9 / 4.5 / 1.6
11 TU	0118 / 0736 / 1343 / 2004	4.3 / 2.0 / 4.6 / 1.6	**26** W	0032 / 0700 / 1257 / 1937	4.6 / 1.6 / 4.8 / 1.2
12 W	0209 / 0820 / 1427 / 2046	4.6 / 1.7 / 4.8 / 1.4	**27** TH	0140 / 0802 / 1357 / 2035	4.9 / 1.3 / 5.2 / 0.8
13 TH	0250 / 0858 / 1505 / 2122	4.8 / 1.5 / 5.0 / 1.2	**28** F	0236 / 0854 / 1448 / 2126	5.3 / 0.9 / 5.5 / 0.4
14 F	0326 / 0932 / 1538 / 2157	4.9 / 1.4 / 5.2 / 1.0			
15 SA	0359 / 1004 / 1608 / 2229	5.0 / 1.2 / 5.3 / 0.9			

MARCH

Day	Time	m	Time	m
1 SA	0325 / 0941 / 1534 / ● 2212	5.5 / 0.7 / 5.7 / 0.2	**16** SU	0331 / 0939 / 1541 / ○ 2201	5.0 / 1.1 / 5.2 / 0.8
2 SU	0410 / 1025 / 1618 / 2254	5.6 / 0.5 / 5.9 / 0.1	**17** M	0401 / 1010 / 1610 / 2232	5.2 / 1.0 / 5.3 / 0.7
3 M	0452 / 1106 / 1700 / 2334	5.6 / 0.5 / 5.9 / 0.2	**18** TU	0431 / 1042 / 1640 / 2304	5.2 / 0.9 / 5.3 / 0.7
4 TU	0533 / 1146 / 1742	5.5 / 0.6 / 5.7	**19** W	0502 / 1114 / 1712 / 2337	5.2 / 0.9 / 5.3 / 0.8
5 W	0012 / 0614 / 1224 / 1824	0.5 / 5.3 / 0.8 / 5.5	**20** TH	0537 / 1148 / 1749	5.2 / 1.0 / 5.3
6 TH	0050 / 0655 / 1303 / 1909	0.8 / 5.1 / 1.1 / 5.2	**21** F	0013 / 0614 / 1225 / 1830	0.9 / 5.1 / 1.1 / 5.1
7 F	0128 / 0738 / 1346 / 1958	1.3 / 4.8 / 1.4 / 4.8	**22** SA	0053 / 0656 / 1307 / 1920	1.1 / 4.9 / 1.3 / 4.9
8 SA	0210 / 0827 / 1438 / ◐ 2056	1.7 / 4.4 / 1.8 / 4.4	**23** SU	0138 / 0748 / 1359 / 2022	1.4 / 4.7 / 1.5 / 4.6
9 SU	0306 / 0928 / 1552 / 2207	2.1 / 4.2 / 2.1 / 4.1	**24** M	0237 / 0852 / 1510 / ◑ 2138	1.7 / 4.4 / 1.7 / 4.4
10 M	0432 / 1044 / 1723 / 2330	2.4 / 4.1 / 2.1 / 4.0	**25** TU	0358 / 1008 / 1643 / 2301	1.9 / 4.4 / 1.7 / 4.4
11 TU	0602 / 1217 / 1840	2.3 / 4.3 / 1.9	**26** W	0527 / 1127 / 1811	1.9 / 4.5 / 1.5
12 W	0045 / 0705 / 1310 / 1934	4.2 / 2.0 / 4.4 / 1.6	**27** TH	0021 / 0643 / 1239 / 1921	4.6 / 1.6 / 4.8 / 1.1
13 TH	0141 / 0752 / 1358 / 2017	4.4 / 1.8 / 4.7 / 1.4	**28** F	0127 / 0743 / 1339 / 2018	4.9 / 1.3 / 5.1 / 0.7
14 F	0223 / 0832 / 1437 / 2055	4.7 / 1.6 / 4.9 / 1.1	**29** SA	0220 / 0835 / 1430 / 2106	5.2 / 1.0 / 5.4 / 0.5
15 SA	0259 / 0907 / 1511 / 2129	4.9 / 1.3 / 5.1 / 0.9	**30** SU	0306 / 0920 / 1515 / ● 2150	5.4 / 0.7 / 5.6 / 0.3
			31 M	0348 / 1003 / 1557 / 2230	5.5 / 0.6 / 5.7 / 0.3

APRIL

Day	Time	m	Time	m
1 TU	0428 / 1043 / 1638 / 2308	5.5 / 0.5 / 5.7 / 0.4	**16** W	0402 / 1018 / 1616 / 2239	5.3 / 0.8 / 5.4 / 0.6
2 W	0507 / 1121 / 1719 / 2344	5.4 / 0.6 / 5.6 / 0.7	**17** TH	0437 / 1054 / 1653 / 2315	5.3 / 0.8 / 5.4 / 0.7
3 TH	0544 / 1158 / 1800	5.3 / 0.8 / 5.3	**18** F	0514 / 1131 / 1734 / 2354	5.3 / 0.8 / 5.3 / 0.9
4 F	0019 / 0622 / 1237 / 1843	1.0 / 5.1 / 1.0 / 5.0	**19** SA	0554 / 1212 / 1820	5.2 / 0.9 / 5.1
5 SA	0054 / 0702 / 1317 / 1929	1.3 / 4.8 / 1.3 / 4.7	**20** SU	0036 / 0639 / 1259 / 1914	1.1 / 5.0 / 1.1 / 4.9
6 SU	0131 / 0747 / 1405 / 2022	1.7 / 4.5 / 1.7 / 4.4	**21** M	0125 / 0732 / 1355 / 2017	1.4 / 4.8 / 1.3 / 4.6
7 M	0217 / 0841 / 1510 / ◐ 2128	2.1 / 4.3 / 1.9 / 4.1	**22** TU	0226 / 0835 / 1507 / ◑ 2130	1.7 / 4.6 / 1.5 / 4.5
8 TU	0334 / 0952 / 1634 / 2245	2.3 / 4.1 / 2.0 / 4.0	**23** W	0345 / 0949 / 1630 / 2248	1.9 / 4.5 / 1.5 / 4.4
9 W	0509 / 1113 / 1753	2.4 / 4.1 / 1.9	**24** TH	0507 / 1107 / 1751	1.9 / 4.6 / 1.3
10 TH	0001 / 0622 / 1223 / 1852	4.1 / 2.2 / 4.3 / 1.7	**25** F	0004 / 0620 / 1218 / 1859	4.6 / 1.6 / 4.8 / 1.0
11 F	0101 / 0714 / 1316 / 1939	4.3 / 1.9 / 4.5 / 1.4	**26** SA	0108 / 0720 / 1319 / 1955	4.9 / 1.4 / 5.1 / 0.8
12 SA	0146 / 0757 / 1359 / 2020	4.6 / 1.6 / 4.8 / 1.2	**27** SU	0200 / 0812 / 1409 / 2043	5.1 / 1.1 / 5.3 / 0.6
13 SU	0224 / 0834 / 1435 / 2056	4.8 / 1.4 / 5.0 / 1.0	**28** M	0245 / 0858 / 1455 / 2126	5.3 / 0.9 / 5.4 / 0.6
14 M	0257 / 0909 / 1509 / 2130	5.0 / 1.1 / 5.1 / 0.8	**29** TU	0326 / 0940 / 1537 / ● 2206	5.3 / 0.7 / 5.5 / 0.6
15 TU	0329 / 0943 / 1542 / ○ 2204	5.2 / 0.7 / 5.3 / 0.7	**30** W	0405 / 1020 / 1618 / 2242	5.4 / 0.7 / 5.4 / 0.7

Chart Datum: 2·85 metres below Ordnance Datum (Newlyn)
HAT is 6·1 metres above Chart Datum

TIDES

TIME ZONE (UT)	RIVER TEES	Dates in amber are SPRINGS
For Summer Time add ONE hour in **non-shaded areas**	LAT 54°38′N LONG 1°09′W	Dates in yellow are NEAPS
	TIMES AND HEIGHTS OF HIGH AND LOW WATERS	**2014**

MAY

Time	m		Time	m
1 TH 0441 1059 1658 2317	5.3 0.7 5.4 0.9	**16** F 0415 1037 1639 2258	5.4 0.7 5.4 0.7
2 F 0517 1136 1738 2351	5.2 0.8 5.2 1.1	**17** SA 0456 1120 1726 2341	5.4 0.6 5.3 0.8
3 SA 0553 1214 1820	5.1 1.0 4.9	**18** SU 0540 1206 1816	5.3 0.7 5.2
4 SU 0024 0631 1254 1904	1.4 4.9 1.3 4.7	**19** M 0027 0627 1257 1910	1.0 5.2 0.8 5.0
5 M 0100 0714 1338 1952	1.7 4.6 1.5 4.4	**20** TU 0119 0721 1354 2011	1.3 5.0 1.0 4.8
6 TU 0143 0803 1432 2048	2.0 4.4 1.7 4.2	**21** W 0218 0822 1459 2117	1.6 4.8 1.2 4.6
7 W 0241 0903 1541 2153	2.2 4.3 1.9 4.1	**22** TH 0328 0931 1611 2228	1.7 4.7 1.3 4.5
8 TH 0405 1013 1653 2303	2.3 4.2 1.9 4.1	**23** F 0441 1043 1724 2339	1.8 4.7 1.3 4.6
9 F 0522 1123 1758	2.2 4.2 1.7	**24** SA 0552 1153 1832	1.7 4.8 1.2
10 SA 0006 0623 1223 1851	4.3 2.0 4.4 1.5	**25** SU 0043 0654 1256 1930	4.8 1.5 4.9 1.1
11 SU 0058 0713 1312 1937	4.5 1.7 4.6 1.3	**26** M 0137 0749 1350 2020	4.9 1.3 5.1 1.0
12 M 0141 0756 1355 2018	4.7 1.5 4.9 1.1	**27** TU 0224 0837 1438 2103	5.1 1.1 5.1 1.0
13 TU 0220 0836 1435 2057	5.0 1.2 5.1 0.9	**28** W 0306 0921 1521 2143	5.2 1.0 5.2 1.0
14 W 0258 0916 1515 2137	5.2 1.0 5.2 0.7	**29** TH 0344 1001 1602 2220	5.2 0.9 5.2 1.0
15 TH 0336 0956 1556 2217	5.3 0.8 5.4 0.7	**30** F 0420 1040 1641 2255	5.2 0.9 5.1 1.1
		31 SA 0454 1118 1720 2328	5.2 0.9 5.0 1.3

JUNE

Time	m		Time	m
1 SU 0529 1155 1759	5.1 1.0 4.9	**16** M 0529 1202 1809	5.6 0.5 5.4
2 M 0001 0606 1233 1839	1.4 5.0 1.2 4.8	**17** TU 0020 0617 1253 1902	0.9 5.5 0.6 5.2
3 TU 0036 0646 1313 1923	1.6 4.8 1.4 4.6	**18** W 0111 0709 1346 1957	1.1 5.3 0.7 5.0
4 W 0116 0731 1358 2011	1.8 4.7 1.6 4.4	**19** TH 0205 0806 1443 2057	1.4 5.1 1.0 4.8
5 TH 0203 0822 1450 2104	2.0 4.5 1.7 4.3	**20** F 0305 0908 1545 2200	1.6 4.9 1.2 4.6
6 F 0303 0920 1551 2204	2.1 4.4 1.8 4.2	**21** SA 0411 1015 1652 2307	1.7 4.7 1.4 4.6
7 SA 0415 1023 1655 2305	2.2 4.3 1.8 4.3	**22** SU 0521 1125 1802	1.8 4.7 1.4
8 SU 0523 1126 1756	2.1 4.4 1.6	**23** M 0014 0629 1234 1905	4.6 1.7 4.7 1.4
9 M 0003 0623 1224 1850	4.4 1.9 4.6 1.4	**24** TU 0114 0729 1334 1959	4.7 1.5 4.8 1.4
10 TU 0056 0715 1316 1941	4.7 1.6 4.8 1.2	**25** W 0205 0820 1424 2044	4.9 1.3 4.9 1.3
11 W 0144 0804 1406 2028	4.9 1.3 5.0 1.0	**26** TH 0249 0905 1508 2124	5.0 1.2 5.0 1.3
12 TH 0229 0852 1453 2115	5.1 1.0 5.2 0.9	**27** F 0327 0945 1548 2201	5.1 1.1 5.0 1.3
13 F 0314 0939 1541 2201	5.3 0.8 5.4 0.8	**28** SA 0403 1023 1626 2235	5.2 1.0 5.0 1.3
14 SA 0358 1026 1629 2247	5.5 0.6 5.5 0.7	**29** SU 0436 1100 1702 2308	5.2 1.0 5.0 1.3
15 SU 0443 1113 1718 2333	5.6 0.5 5.5 0.8	**30** M 0509 1135 1738 2340	5.2 1.0 5.0 1.4

JULY

Time	m		Time	m
1 TU 0543 1210 1814	5.1 1.1 4.9	**16** W 0008 0602 1240 1845	0.7 5.7 0.4 5.4
2 W 0013 0620 1246 1853	1.5 5.0 1.2 4.8	**17** TH 0055 0651 1327 1935	0.9 5.6 0.6 5.2
3 TH 0050 0700 1325 1935	1.6 4.9 1.4 4.6	**18** F 0143 0743 1418 2029	1.2 5.3 0.9 4.9
4 F 0130 0744 1408 2022	1.8 4.7 1.5 4.5	**19** SA 0236 0841 1514 2127	1.5 5.0 1.3 4.7
5 SA 0217 0834 1459 2115	1.9 4.6 1.7 4.4	**20** SU 0337 0945 1618 2231	1.7 4.7 1.6 4.5
6 SU 0315 0932 1559 2214	2.1 4.5 1.8 4.3	**21** M 0448 1056 1731 2342	1.9 4.5 1.8 4.4
7 M 0425 1036 1705 2316	2.1 4.4 1.7 4.4	**22** TU 0605 1211 1843	1.9 4.5 1.8
8 TU 0535 1141 1809	2.0 4.5 1.6	**23** W 0050 0712 1319 1940	4.5 1.7 4.6 1.7
9 W 0016 0639 1244 1909	4.6 1.7 4.7 1.4	**24** TH 0146 0806 1411 2026	4.7 1.5 4.8 1.6
10 TH 0114 0738 1342 2005	4.8 1.4 5.0 1.2	**25** F 0232 0850 1455 2106	4.9 1.3 4.9 1.5
11 F 0206 0833 1436 2058	5.1 1.0 5.2 1.0	**26** SA 0311 0929 1533 2142	5.1 1.1 5.0 1.4
12 SA 0255 0925 1528 2148	5.4 0.7 5.4 0.8	**27** SU 0346 1005 1608 2215	5.2 1.0 5.1 1.3
13 SU 0342 1016 1618 2236	5.6 0.5 5.6 0.7	**28** M 0418 1039 1642 2247	5.2 1.0 5.1 1.3
14 M 0429 1104 1707 2322	5.7 0.3 5.6 0.7	**29** TU 0449 1112 1714 2318	5.3 1.0 5.1 1.3
15 TU 0516 1152 1756	5.8 0.3 5.6	**30** W 0520 1144 1747 2349	5.2 1.0 5.1 1.3
		31 TH 0553 1217 1822	5.2 1.1 5.0

AUGUST

Time	m		Time	m
1 F 0022 0628 1252 1900	1.4 5.1 1.2 4.9	**16** SA 0116 0717 1348 1956	1.1 5.4 1.0 5.0
2 SA 0059 0708 1332 1943	1.6 4.9 1.4 4.7	**17** SU 0204 0811 1439 2050	1.5 5.0 1.5 4.7
3 SU 0140 0753 1417 2033	1.7 4.7 1.6 4.5	**18** M 0302 0913 1540 2153	1.7 4.7 1.9 4.4
4 M 0229 0848 1514 2131	1.9 4.6 1.8 4.4	**19** TU 0415 1026 1658 2306	2.0 4.4 2.1 4.3
5 TU 0334 0955 1623 2236	2.0 4.5 1.9 4.4	**20** W 0539 1148 1817	2.0 4.3 2.1
6 W 0455 1108 1737 2344	2.0 4.5 1.8 4.5	**21** TH 0022 0652 1301 1918	4.4 1.8 4.5 2.0
7 TH 0612 1220 1847	1.8 4.7 1.6	**22** F 0123 0747 1354 2005	4.6 1.6 4.7 1.8
8 F 0048 0720 1326 1948	4.8 1.4 5.0 1.3	**23** SA 0210 0830 1435 2045	4.9 1.4 4.9 1.6
9 SA 0146 0819 1423 2043	5.1 1.0 5.3 1.0	**24** SU 0250 0907 1512 2120	5.1 1.2 5.0 1.4
10 SU 0238 0913 1514 2134	5.4 0.6 5.5 0.8	**25** M 0325 0942 1546 2153	5.2 1.0 5.1 1.3
11 M 0326 1003 1603 2221	5.7 0.3 5.7 0.6	**26** TU 0356 1015 1617 2223	5.3 0.9 5.2 1.2
12 TU 0413 1050 1650 2306	5.9 0.2 5.8 0.6	**27** W 0425 1045 1646 2253	5.3 0.9 5.2 1.2
13 W 0458 1135 1736 2349	6.0 0.1 5.7 0.6	**28** TH 0454 1116 1717 2324	5.3 0.9 5.2 1.2
14 TH 0543 1218 1822	5.9 0.3 5.6	**29** F 0524 1147 1750 2356	5.3 1.0 5.1 1.2
15 F 0032 0629 1302 1908	0.8 5.7 0.6 5.3	**30** SA 0557 1221 1827	5.2 1.1 5.0
		31 SU 0030 0634 1259 1907	1.4 5.1 1.3 4.9

Chart Datum: 2·85 metres below Ordnance Datum (Newlyn)
HAT is 6·1 metres above Chart Datum

RIVER TEES

LAT 54°38′N   LONG 1°09′W

TIMES AND HEIGHTS OF HIGH AND LOW WATERS

2014

SEPTEMBER

Day	Time m	Day	Time m
1 M	0109 1.6 / 0719 4.9 / 1343 1.6 / 1955 4.7	16 TU	0227 1.7 / 0841 4.6 / 1458 2.1 / ◑ 2111 4.4
2 TU	0156 1.8 / 0814 4.6 / 1437 1.8 / ◑ 2054 4.5	17 W	0339 2.0 / 0953 4.3 / 1618 2.3 / 2225 4.2
3 W	0259 1.9 / 0925 4.5 / 1550 2.0 / 2203 4.4	18 TH	0506 2.1 / 1116 4.2 / 1744 2.3 / 2345 4.3
4 TH	0427 2.0 / 1045 4.4 / 1714 2.4 / 2316 4.5	19 F	0623 1.9 / 1232 4.3 / 1849 2.2
5 F	0553 1.7 / 1203 4.6 / 1830 1.7	20 SA	0051 4.5 / 0718 1.7 / 1327 4.6 / 1937 1.9
6 SA	0027 4.8 / 0705 1.4 / 1312 5.0 / 1932 1.4	21 SU	0141 4.8 / 0801 1.4 / 1409 4.8 / 2017 1.7
7 SU	0128 5.1 / 0805 0.9 / 1408 5.3 / 2026 1.1	22 M	0221 5.0 / 0839 1.2 / 1445 5.0 / 2053 1.4
8 M	0220 5.5 / 0857 0.5 / 1458 5.6 / 2115 0.8	23 TU	0257 5.2 / 0914 1.0 / 1518 5.2 / 2126 1.3
9 TU	0308 5.8 / 0945 0.3 / 1544 5.8 / ○ 2201 0.6	24 W	0328 5.3 / 0946 0.9 / 1548 5.3 / ● 2157 1.1
10 W	0353 6.0 / 1029 0.2 / 1628 5.8 / 2244 0.5	25 TH	0358 5.4 / 1016 0.9 / 1617 5.3 / 2228 1.1
11 TH	0436 6.0 / 1112 0.2 / 1711 5.8 / 2326 0.6	26 F	0426 5.4 / 1047 0.9 / 1647 5.3 / 2259 1.1
12 F	0520 5.9 / 1153 0.4 / 1754 5.6	27 SA	0457 5.4 / 1119 0.9 / 1720 5.3 / 2332 1.1
13 SA	0007 0.7 / 0604 5.7 / 1233 0.7 / 1837 5.3	28 SU	0531 5.3 / 1154 1.1 / 1757 5.2
14 SU	0049 1.0 / 0650 5.4 / 1315 1.2 / 1922 5.0	29 M	0007 1.2 / 0610 5.1 / 1232 1.3 / 1837 5.0
15 M	0134 1.4 / 0741 5.0 / 1400 1.6 / 2012 4.7	30 TU	0047 1.4 / 0656 4.9 / 1316 1.6 / 1925 4.8

OCTOBER

Day	Time m	Day	Time m
1 W	0136 1.6 / 0755 4.7 / 1410 1.9 / ◑ 2024 4.6	16 TH	0300 1.9 / 0916 4.3 / 1527 2.4 / 2137 4.3
2 TH	0240 1.8 / 0907 4.5 / 1526 2.1 / 2136 4.5	17 F	0421 2.1 / 1033 4.2 / 1655 2.5 / 2255 4.3
3 F	0409 1.9 / 1029 4.5 / 1654 2.1 / 2253 4.6	18 SA	0539 2.0 / 1149 4.3 / 1808 2.3
4 SA	0537 1.6 / 1149 4.6 / 1811 1.8	19 SU	0006 4.4 / 0638 1.8 / 1248 4.5 / 1900 2.1
5 SU	0006 4.8 / 0649 1.3 / 1257 5.0 / 1913 1.5	20 M	0102 4.7 / 0725 1.5 / 1334 4.7 / 1943 1.8
6 M	0108 5.2 / 0747 0.9 / 1351 5.3 / 2006 1.0	21 TU	0145 4.9 / 0805 1.3 / 1412 5.0 / 2021 1.5
7 TU	0201 5.5 / 0837 0.6 / 1439 5.6 / 2054 0.9	22 W	0223 5.1 / 0841 1.1 / 1445 5.1 / 2056 1.3
8 W	0248 5.7 / 0923 0.4 / 1523 5.7 / ○ 2139 0.7	23 TH	0257 5.2 / 0915 1.0 / 1516 5.3 / 2129 1.2
9 TH	0332 5.9 / 1006 0.3 / 1605 5.7 / 2222 0.6	24 F	0329 5.3 / 0947 0.9 / 1547 5.4 / 2203 1.0
10 F	0415 5.9 / 1050 0.4 / 1646 5.7 / 2303 0.6	25 SA	0401 5.4 / 1020 0.9 / 1620 5.4 / 2237 1.0
11 SA	0457 5.8 / 1126 0.6 / 1726 5.5 / 2343 0.8	26 SU	0435 5.4 / 1055 0.9 / 1655 5.4 / 2313 1.0
12 SU	0541 5.5 / 1204 1.0 / 1806 5.3	27 M	0513 5.3 / 1132 1.0 / 1734 5.3 / 2352 1.1
13 M	0023 1.0 / 0625 5.2 / 1242 1.4 / 1848 5.1	28 TU	0556 5.2 / 1212 1.3 / 1816 5.2
14 TU	0106 1.3 / 0714 4.9 / 1332 1.8 / 1934 4.8	29 W	0035 1.2 / 0646 5.0 / 1258 1.5 / 1905 5.0
15 W	0156 1.7 / 0809 4.5 / 1412 2.1 / ◑ 2028 4.5	30 TH	0126 1.4 / 0745 4.8 / 1354 1.8 / 2004 4.8
		31 F	0232 1.6 / 0856 4.6 / 1508 2.0 / ◑ 2113 4.7

NOVEMBER

Day	Time m	Day	Time m
1 SA	0353 1.6 / 1013 4.5 / 1631 2.0 / 2229 4.7	16 SU	0438 2.0 / 1050 4.2 / 1708 2.4 / 2306 4.3
2 SU	0515 1.5 / 1129 4.7 / 1746 1.9 / 2341 4.9	17 M	0545 1.9 / 1154 4.4 / 1812 2.2
3 M	0626 1.2 / 1236 4.9 / 1850 1.6	18 TU	0009 4.5 / 0639 1.7 / 1248 4.6 / 1902 2.0
4 TU	0045 5.1 / 0724 1.0 / 1332 5.2 / 1944 1.3	19 W	0101 4.7 / 0725 1.5 / 1331 4.8 / 1945 1.7
5 W	0140 5.4 / 0815 0.8 / 1419 5.4 / 2033 1.0	20 TH	0144 4.9 / 0805 1.3 / 1409 5.0 / 2024 1.4
6 TH	0229 5.5 / 0901 0.7 / 1503 5.5 / ○ 2118 0.8	21 F	0224 5.1 / 0843 1.1 / 1444 5.2 / 2102 1.2
7 F	0314 5.6 / 0943 0.7 / 1543 5.6 / 2201 0.8	22 SA	0302 5.2 / 0920 1.0 / 1520 5.4 / ● 2140 1.0
8 SA	0357 5.6 / 1023 0.8 / 1623 5.6 / 2242 0.8	23 SU	0340 5.3 / 0957 0.9 / 1558 5.5 / 2259 0.8
9 SU	0439 5.5 / 1101 0.9 / 1701 5.5 / 2322 0.9	24 M	0420 5.4 / 1036 0.9 / 1636 5.5 / 2300 0.8
10 M	0521 5.4 / 1137 1.2 / 1739 5.3	25 TU	0503 5.4 / 1117 1.0 / 1717 5.5 / 2343 1.0
11 TU	0002 1.0 / 0604 5.1 / 1213 1.5 / 1818 5.1	26 W	0549 5.3 / 1200 1.2 / 1802 5.4
12 W	0043 1.3 / 0649 4.9 / 1250 1.8 / 1900 4.9	27 TH	0029 1.0 / 0640 5.1 / 1248 1.4 / 1851 5.2
13 TH	0128 1.5 / 0738 4.6 / 1331 2.1 / 1948 4.7	28 F	0122 1.1 / 0738 4.9 / 1343 1.6 / 1947 5.0
14 F	0220 1.8 / 0834 4.4 / 1427 2.3 / ◑ 2046 4.5	29 SA	0223 1.3 / 0842 4.7 / 1449 1.9 / ◑ 2052 4.9
15 SA	0326 2.0 / 0940 4.2 / 1548 2.5 / 2155 4.3	30 SU	0332 1.4 / 0951 4.6 / 1602 2.0 / 2202 4.8

DECEMBER

Day	Time m	Day	Time m
1 M	0445 1.4 / 1102 4.7 / 1715 1.9 / 2313 4.8	16 TU	0435 2.0 / 1047 4.3 / 1703 2.3 / 2306 4.4
2 TU	0557 1.3 / 1210 4.8 / 1823 1.7	17 W	0540 1.9 / 1148 4.4 / 1808 2.1
3 W	0021 5.0 / 0700 1.2 / 1310 5.0 / 1923 1.5	18 TH	0007 4.5 / 0637 1.7 / 1243 4.6 / 1903 1.9
4 TH	0121 5.1 / 0754 1.1 / 1400 5.2 / 2015 1.2	19 F	0103 4.7 / 0727 1.5 / 1330 4.9 / 1952 1.6
5 F	0214 5.2 / 0841 1.0 / 1445 5.3 / 2102 1.1	20 SA	0152 4.9 / 0813 1.3 / 1414 5.1 / 2037 1.3
6 SA	0301 5.3 / 0924 1.0 / 1526 5.4 / ○ 2145 0.9	21 SU	0238 5.1 / 0857 1.1 / 1457 5.3 / 2122 1.0
7 SU	0344 5.3 / 1004 1.1 / 1605 5.4 / 2226 0.9	22 M	0323 5.3 / 0940 1.0 / 1539 5.5 / ● 2206 0.8
8 M	0425 5.3 / 1040 1.2 / 1641 5.4 / 2305 0.9	23 TU	0408 5.4 / 1023 0.9 / 1621 5.6 / 2251 0.6
9 TU	0505 5.2 / 1115 1.3 / 1717 5.3 / 2343 1.0	24 W	0454 5.5 / 1107 0.9 / 1705 5.6 / 2337 0.5
10 W	0545 5.1 / 1149 1.5 / 1753 5.2	25 TH	0542 5.4 / 1152 1.0 / 1750 5.6
11 TH	0021 1.2 / 0625 4.9 / 1223 1.7 / 1832 5.0	26 F	0023 0.6 / 0631 5.3 / 1239 1.1 / 1838 5.5
12 F	0100 1.4 / 0707 4.7 / 1259 1.9 / 1914 4.9	27 SA	0113 0.8 / 0724 5.1 / 1329 1.4 / 1930 5.3
13 SA	0142 1.6 / 0753 4.5 / 1342 2.1 / 2003 4.7	28 SU	0206 1.0 / 0821 4.9 / 1426 1.6 / ◑ 2029 5.1
14 SU	0230 1.8 / 0846 4.4 / 1437 2.3 / 2058 4.5	29 M	0305 1.2 / 0923 4.7 / 1530 1.8 / 2133 4.9
15 M	0328 1.9 / 0944 4.3 / 1548 2.4 / 2200 4.4	30 TU	0412 1.4 / 1029 4.6 / 1641 1.9 / 2243 4.7
		31 W	0525 1.6 / 1139 4.6 / 1756 1.8 / 2356 4.7

Chart Datum: 2·85 metres below Ordnance Datum (Newlyn)
HAT is 6·1 metres above Chart Datum

TIDES

RIVER TYNE (NORTH SHIELDS)

MEAN SPRING
AND NEAP CURVES

MEAN RANGES	
Springs	4.3m
Neaps	2.1m

JANUARY

#	Time	m	Time	m	#	Time	m	Time	m
1 ●	0245 0908 W 1503 2136	5.1 0.9 5.3 0.6			16 ○	0333 0940 TH 1544 2207	4.7 1.3 4.6 1.0		
2	0335 0956 TH 1548 2226	5.3 0.8 5.4 0.4			17	0406 1012 F 1615 2240	4.8 1.2 5.0 0.9		
3	0424 1043 F 1633 2314	5.4 0.7 5.5 0.3			18	0438 1042 SA 1645 2312	4.8 1.2 5.0 0.9		
4	0513 1128 SA 1720	5.3 0.8 5.5			19	0511 1113 SU 1717 2344	4.8 1.2 5.0 1.0		
5	0002 0602 SU 1214 1808	0.4 5.2 1.0 5.4			20	0544 1144 M 1750	4.7 1.3 4.9		
6	0050 0654 M 1300 1900	0.6 5.0 1.2 5.2			21	0018 0618 TU 1217 1824	1.0 4.6 1.4 4.8		
7	0140 0748 TU 1350 1956	0.8 4.7 1.4 4.9			22	0054 0656 W 1253 1903	1.2 4.5 1.5 4.7		
8	0234 0846 W 1448 ◐ 2057	1.2 4.5 1.7 4.6			23	0133 0739 TH 1335 1950	1.3 4.4 1.7 4.5		
9	0335 0948 TH 1557 2205	1.5 4.3 1.9 4.4			24	0221 0831 F 1430 ◑ 2048	1.5 4.3 1.8 4.4		
10	0443 1056 F 1714 2319	1.7 4.2 1.9 4.3			25	0322 0935 SA 1544 2200	1.7 4.2 1.9 4.0		
11	0554 1205 SA 1828	1.8 4.2 1.9			26	0439 1048 SU 1712 2321	1.7 4.2 1.9 4.3		
12	0031 0658 SU 1305 1929	4.3 1.8 4.4 1.7			27	0556 1202 M 1830	1.6 4.3 1.6		
13	0130 0749 M 1354 2017	4.4 1.7 4.4 1.5			28	0038 0704 TU 1307 1937	4.5 1.4 4.6 1.2		
14	0218 0831 TU 1435 2058	4.5 1.5 4.7 1.3			29	0142 0804 W 1401 2035	4.8 1.2 4.9 0.8		
15	0257 0907 W 1511 2134	4.6 1.4 4.8 1.1			30	0235 0856 TH 1449 ● 2126	5.1 0.9 5.2 0.5		
					31	0324 0944 F 1534 2214	5.3 0.7 5.4 0.3		

FEBRUARY

#	Time	m	Time	m	#	Time	m	Time	m
1	0411 1029 SA 1618 2300	5.4 0.6 5.6 0.2			16	0415 1023 SU 1623 2249	4.8 1.0 5.0 0.8		
2	0456 1112 SU 1703 2345	5.3 0.6 5.6 0.2			17	0446 1052 M 1653 2320	4.8 1.0 5.0 0.8		
3	0542 1153 M 1749	5.2 0.7 5.4			18	0517 1123 TU 1725 2352	4.8 1.0 5.0 0.8		
4	0027 0627 TU 1235 1835	0.4 5.0 0.9 5.2			19	0549 1154 W 1758	4.8 1.1 4.9		
5	0110 0714 W 1318 1925	0.8 4.7 1.2 4.9			20	0026 0624 TH 1229 1836	1.0 4.7 1.2 4.8		
6	0155 0805 TH 1407 ● 2021	1.2 4.5 1.5 4.6			21	0102 0705 F 1308 1921	1.2 4.5 1.4 4.6		
7	0246 0902 F 1508 2125	1.6 4.2 1.8 4.2			22	0146 0754 SA 1400 ◐ 2019	1.4 4.4 1.6 4.4		
8	0351 1009 SA 1628 2241	1.9 4.0 2.0 4.0			23	0245 0857 SU 1512 2134	1.6 4.2 1.8 4.2		
9	0510 1125 SU 1757	2.0 4.0 2.0			24	0406 1015 M 1646 2302	1.8 4.1 1.8 4.2		
10	0003 0630 M 1237 1908	4.0 2.0 4.1 1.8			25	0534 1137 TU 1814	1.7 4.2 1.5		
11	0111 0729 TU 1333 1959	4.1 1.8 4.3 1.5			26	0026 0649 W 1249 1925	4.4 1.5 4.5 1.1		
12	0200 0813 W 1416 2039	4.3 1.6 4.6 1.3			27	0131 0750 TH 1345 2022	4.7 1.2 4.9 0.7		
13	0240 0849 TH 1452 2114	4.6 1.4 4.7 1.1			28	0223 0842 F 1433 2112	5.0 0.9 5.2 0.4		
14	0314 0922 F 1524 ○ 2147	4.6 1.3 4.9 0.9							
15	0345 0953 SA 1554 2218	4.8 1.1 5.0 0.8							

MARCH

#	Time	m	Time	m	#	Time	m	Time	m
1 ●	0310 0927 SA 1517 2158	5.2 0.7 5.4 0.2			16	0318 0929 SU 1528 ○ 2151	4.7 1.1 4.9 0.7		
2	0353 1010 SU 1600 2241	5.3 0.5 5.5 0.1			17	0348 0959 M 1558 2222	4.8 0.9 5.0 0.7		
3	0435 1051 M 1643 2322	5.3 0.5 5.5 0.2			18	0418 1030 TU 1628 2254	4.9 0.9 5.0 0.6		
4	0516 1131 TU 1726	5.2 0.6 5.4			19	0450 1102 W 1701 2327	4.9 0.8 5.0 0.7		
5	0000 0557 W 1210 1810	0.5 5.0 0.8 5.1			20	0523 1135 TH 1737	4.9 0.9 5.0		
6	0038 0640 TH 1249 1856	0.8 4.7 1.1 4.8			21	0001 0559 F 1211 1817	0.9 4.8 1.0 4.8		
7	0117 0725 F 1332 1947	1.2 4.5 1.4 4.5			22	0039 0640 SA 1253 1906	1.1 4.6 1.2 4.6		
8	0200 0816 SA 1426 ● 2048	1.6 4.2 1.7 4.1			23	0125 0730 SU 1347 2006	1.3 4.4 1.4 4.4		
9	0256 0919 SU 1540 2201	2.0 4.0 1.9 3.9			24	0225 0834 M 1459 ◐ 2124	1.6 4.2 1.6 4.2		
10	0419 1036 M 1713 2325	2.2 3.9 2.0 3.8			25	0348 0953 TU 1632 2252	1.8 4.1 1.6 4.2		
11	0552 1157 TU 1835	2.2 3.9 1.8			26	0518 1116 W 1759	1.8 4.2 1.4		
12	0040 0700 W 1301 1929	4.0 2.0 4.2 1.6			27	0013 0633 TH 1230 1909	4.4 1.5 4.5 1.0		
13	0133 0747 TH 1348 2011	4.2 1.7 4.4 1.3			28	0116 0733 F 1327 2005	4.7 1.2 4.8 0.7		
14	0213 0824 F 1425 2046	4.4 1.5 4.6 1.1			29	0207 0823 SA 1415 2053	4.9 0.9 5.1 0.4		
15	0247 0858 SA 1458 2119	4.6 1.2 4.8 0.9			30	0251 0908 SU 1458 ● 2136	5.1 0.7 5.3 0.3		
					31	0332 0950 M 1541 2217	5.2 0.5 5.4 0.3		

APRIL

#	Time	m	Time	m	#	Time	m	Time	m
1	0411 1030 TU 1622 2255	5.2 0.5 5.4 0.4			16	0350 1007 W 1604 2229	5.0 0.8 5.0 0.6		
2	0450 1108 W 1704 2332	5.1 0.6 5.2 0.6			17	0424 1043 TH 1641 2305	5.0 0.7 5.0 0.7		
3	0529 1146 TH 1747	5.0 0.7 5.0			18	0500 1120 F 1722 2343	5.0 0.7 5.0 0.8		
4	0006 0607 F 1224 1831	1.0 4.8 1.0 4.7			19	0540 1201 SA 1807	4.9 0.8 4.9		
5	0042 0649 SA 1305 1919	1.3 4.5 1.3 4.4			20	0025 0624 SU 1248 1859	1.1 4.8 1.0 4.6		
6	0121 0735 SU 1353 2014	1.6 4.3 1.6 4.1			21	0114 0716 M 1345 2003	1.3 4.6 1.2 4.4		
7	0210 0833 M 1455 ◐ 2120	2.0 4.0 1.8 3.9			22	0215 0820 TU 1456 ◑ 2119	1.6 4.4 1.3 4.3		
8	0322 0943 TU 1618 2236	2.2 3.9 1.9 3.8			23	0334 0936 W 1621 2239	1.8 4.3 1.3 4.2		
9	0456 1102 W 1741 2353	2.2 3.9 1.8 3.9			24	0459 1055 TH 1740 2354	1.7 4.3 1.2 4.4		
10	0614 1214 TH 1844	2.1 4.0 1.6			25	0611 1206 F 1847	1.5 4.5 1.0		
11	0052 0708 F 1307 1931	4.1 1.8 4.2 1.4			26	0055 0711 SA 1306 1942	4.6 1.3 4.7 0.8		
12	0136 0750 SA 1348 2010	4.3 1.5 4.5 1.1			27	0146 0802 SU 1355 2030	4.8 1.0 4.9 0.6		
13	0213 0826 SU 1424 2045	4.5 1.3 4.7 0.9			28	0230 0847 M 1440 2113	5.0 0.8 5.1 0.6		
14	0246 0859 M 1457 2119	4.7 1.1 4.8 0.8			29	0309 0929 TU 1522 ● 2152	5.0 0.7 5.1 0.6		
15	0318 0933 TU 1530 ○ 2154	4.9 0.9 5.0 0.6			30	0348 1009 W 1604 2229	5.1 0.6 5.1 0.7		

Chart Datum: 2·60 metres below Ordnance Datum (Newlyn)
HAT is 5·7 metres above Chart Datum

TIDES

285

TIDES

NORTH SHIELDS
LAT 55°00'N LONG 1°26'W
TIMES AND HEIGHTS OF HIGH AND LOW WATERS

Dates in amber are **SPRINGS**
Dates in yellow are **NEAPS**

2014

MAY

Day	Time m	Day	Time m
1 TH	0425 5.0 / 1048 0.7 / 1645 5.1 / 2304 0.9	**16** F	0402 5.1 / 1027 0.6 / 1626 5.1 / 2247 0.7
2 F	0503 4.9 / 1125 0.8 / 1727 4.8 / 2338 1.1	**17** SA	0442 5.1 / 1110 0.6 / 1712 5.0 / 2330 0.8
3 SA	0540 4.8 / 1203 1.0 / 1809 4.6	**18** SU	0525 5.0 / 1156 0.6 / 1801 4.9
4 SU	0013 1.3 / 0619 4.6 / 1242 1.2 / 1853 4.4	**19** M	0016 1.0 / 0612 4.9 / 1247 0.8 / 1856 4.7
5 M	0050 1.6 / 0702 4.4 / 1325 1.4 / 1943 4.2	**20** TU	0107 1.2 / 0706 4.8 / 1343 0.9 / 1958 4.6
6 TU	0134 1.9 / 0753 4.2 / 1418 1.6 / 2040 4.0	**21** W	0206 1.3 / 0808 4.6 / 1449 1.1 / 2107 4.4
7 W	0232 2.1 / 0853 4.0 / 1524 1.7 / 2144 3.9	**22** TH	0317 1.6 / 0918 4.5 / 1602 1.1 / 2218 4.3
8 TH	0350 2.2 / 1001 3.9 / 1638 1.8 / 2252 3.9	**23** F	0432 1.7 / 1031 4.5 / 1715 1.1 / 2328 4.4
9 F	0510 2.1 / 1111 4.0 / 1745 1.6 / 2356 4.0	**24** SA	0543 1.6 / 1141 4.5 / 1821 1.0
10 SA	0615 1.9 / 1213 4.1 / 1840 1.4	**25** SU	0030 4.5 / 0645 1.4 / 1243 4.6 / 1918 1.0
11 SU	0049 4.2 / 0705 1.7 / 1303 4.3 / 1926 1.2	**26** M	0123 4.7 / 0740 1.2 / 1336 4.7 / 2007 0.9
12 M	0132 4.5 / 0748 1.4 / 1345 4.5 / 2007 1.0	**27** TU	0209 4.8 / 0828 0.9 / 1423 4.8 / 2050 0.9
13 TU	0210 4.7 / 0827 1.2 / 1425 4.7 / 2047 0.8	**28** W	0250 4.9 / 0911 0.9 / 1507 4.9 / 2130 0.9
14 W	0247 4.9 / 0906 0.9 / 1503 4.9 / 2126 0.7	**29** TH	0328 4.9 / 0952 0.8 / 1549 4.9 / 2206 1.0
15 TH	0324 5.0 / 0946 0.8 / 1543 5.0 / 2206 0.7	**30** F	0405 4.9 / 1031 0.8 / 1629 4.8 / 2241 1.1
		31 SA	0441 4.9 / 1107 0.8 / 1708 4.7 / 2315 1.2

JUNE

Day	Time m	Day	Time m
1 SU	0518 4.8 / 1143 0.9 / 1748 4.6 / 2348 1.3	**16** M	0513 5.2 / 1150 0.4 / 1753 5.1
2 M	0555 4.7 / 1220 1.1 / 1829 4.4	**17** TU	0007 0.9 / 0601 5.2 / 1241 0.5 / 1847 4.9
3 TU	0024 1.5 / 0634 4.6 / 1300 1.2 / 1912 4.3	**18** W	0056 1.1 / 0653 5.0 / 1334 0.7 / 1944 4.7
4 W	0104 1.7 / 0718 4.4 / 1345 1.4 / 2000 4.1	**19** TH	0150 1.3 / 0751 4.9 / 1432 0.9 / 2045 4.5
5 TH	0150 1.9 / 0809 4.2 / 1437 1.6 / 2054 4.0	**20** F	0251 1.5 / 0855 4.7 / 1536 1.1 / 2150 4.4
6 F	0248 2.0 / 0906 4.1 / 1538 1.6 / 2153 4.0	**21** SA	0400 1.6 / 1003 4.5 / 1644 1.2 / 2256 4.3
7 SA	0359 2.1 / 1008 4.1 / 1643 1.6 / 2255 4.0	**22** SU	0511 1.6 / 1113 4.4 / 1751 1.3
8 SU	0511 2.0 / 1112 4.1 / 1745 1.5 / 2355 4.2	**23** M	0002 4.4 / 0619 1.5 / 1221 4.5 / 1853 1.3
9 M	0613 1.8 / 1212 4.3 / 1840 1.4	**24** TU	0100 4.5 / 0720 1.4 / 1320 4.5 / 1946 1.3
10 TU	0048 4.4 / 0706 1.5 / 1307 4.5 / 1930 1.2	**25** W	0150 4.6 / 0812 1.2 / 1411 4.6 / 2031 1.2
11 W	0136 4.6 / 0755 1.3 / 1355 4.7 / 2017 1.0	**26** TH	0233 4.7 / 0857 1.1 / 1455 4.7 / 2111 1.2
12 TH	0219 4.8 / 0842 1.0 / 1441 4.9 / 2103 0.8	**27** F	0312 4.8 / 0937 0.9 / 1535 4.7 / 2147 1.2
13 F	0301 5.0 / 0928 0.7 / 1527 5.1 / 2148 0.7	**28** SA	0348 4.9 / 1015 0.9 / 1613 4.7 / 2221 1.2
14 SA	0343 5.2 / 1015 0.5 / 1614 5.2 / 2234 0.7	**29** SU	0423 4.9 / 1050 0.9 / 1650 4.7 / 2254 1.2
15 SU	0427 5.2 / 1102 0.4 / 1702 5.2 / 2320 0.8	**30** M	0457 4.9 / 1124 0.9 / 1725 4.7 / 2326 1.3

JULY

Day	Time m	Day	Time m
1 TU	0531 4.8 / 1158 1.0 / 1802 4.6 / 2359 1.3	**16** W	0545 5.4 / 1226 0.3 / 1829 5.1
2 W	0607 4.7 / 1233 1.1 / 1840 4.5	**17** TH	0038 0.9 / 0635 5.3 / 1315 0.5 / 1921 4.8
3 TH	0034 1.5 / 0645 4.6 / 1313 1.2 / 1921 4.3	**18** F	0127 1.1 / 0729 5.0 / 1406 0.8 / 2017 4.6
4 F	0114 1.6 / 0728 4.5 / 1355 1.4 / 2007 4.2	**19** SA	0221 1.4 / 0828 4.8 / 1503 1.2 / 2116 4.4
5 SA	0200 1.8 / 0816 4.3 / 1446 1.5 / 2059 4.1	**20** SU	0324 1.6 / 0933 4.5 / 1608 1.4 / 2222 4.3
6 SU	0257 1.9 / 0912 4.2 / 1545 1.6 / 2159 4.1	**21** M	0438 1.7 / 1045 4.3 / 1719 1.6 / 2331 4.2
7 M	0408 2.0 / 1016 4.1 / 1652 1.6 / 2303 4.1	**22** TU	0555 1.7 / 1200 4.3 / 1829 1.7
8 TU	0522 1.9 / 1125 4.2 / 1758 1.5	**23** W	0037 4.3 / 0704 1.6 / 1306 4.3 / 1928 1.6
9 W	0007 4.3 / 0629 1.6 / 1233 4.4 / 1858 1.3	**24** TH	0132 4.5 / 0759 1.4 / 1359 4.4 / 2015 1.5
10 TH	0105 4.5 / 0728 1.3 / 1332 4.6 / 1954 1.1	**25** F	0217 4.7 / 0843 1.2 / 1443 4.6 / 2054 1.4
11 F	0156 4.8 / 0823 1.0 / 1425 4.9 / 2045 0.9	**26** SA	0256 4.8 / 0921 1.0 / 1520 4.7 / 2129 1.3
12 SA	0242 5.1 / 0914 0.7 / 1514 5.1 / 2134 0.7	**27** SU	0331 4.9 / 0956 0.9 / 1555 4.7 / 2202 1.2
13 SU	0327 5.3 / 1003 0.4 / 1602 5.3 / 2221 0.6	**28** M	0403 5.0 / 1029 0.8 / 1628 4.8 / 2233 1.1
14 M	0412 5.4 / 1051 0.2 / 1650 5.3 / 2307 0.6	**29** TU	0435 5.0 / 1101 0.8 / 1700 4.8 / 2303 1.1
15 TU	0458 5.5 / 1139 0.2 / 1739 5.2 / 2352 0.7	**30** W	0506 5.0 / 1133 0.9 / 1733 4.7 / 2334 1.2
		31 TH	0539 4.9 / 1206 0.9 / 1807 4.6

AUGUST

Day	Time m	Day	Time m
1 F	0007 1.3 / 0613 4.8 / 1241 1.1 / 1843 4.5	**16** SA	0100 1.0 / 0703 5.1 / 1335 0.9 / 1943 4.7
2 SA	0042 1.4 / 0651 4.7 / 1318 1.2 / 1923 4.4	**17** SU	0149 1.3 / 0759 4.7 / 1426 1.3 / 2039 4.4
3 SU	0122 1.6 / 0734 4.5 / 1402 1.4 / 2011 4.3	**18** M	0248 1.6 / 0903 4.4 / 1528 1.7 / 2144 4.2
4 M	0211 1.8 / 0827 4.3 / 1456 1.6 / 2109 4.2	**19** TU	0404 1.8 / 1016 4.2 / 1644 1.9 / 2257 4.1
5 TU	0317 1.9 / 0933 4.2 / 1607 1.7 / 2218 4.2	**20** W	0530 1.9 / 1137 4.1 / 1805 2.0
6 W	0440 1.9 / 1050 4.2 / 1724 1.7 / 2331 4.3	**21** TH	0011 4.2 / 0646 1.9 / 1249 4.2 / 1909 1.8
7 TH	0600 1.7 / 1209 4.4 / 1835 1.5	**22** F	0111 4.4 / 0741 1.5 / 1343 4.4 / 1956 1.7
8 F	0039 4.5 / 0708 1.3 / 1316 4.6 / 1936 1.2	**23** SA	0158 4.6 / 0824 1.3 / 1424 4.5 / 2035 1.5
9 SA	0136 4.8 / 0807 0.9 / 1411 4.9 / 2030 1.0	**24** SU	0236 4.8 / 0900 1.1 / 1500 4.7 / 2108 1.3
10 SU	0225 5.1 / 0900 0.6 / 1500 5.2 / 2118 0.7	**25** M	0309 4.9 / 0933 0.9 / 1532 4.8 / 2139 1.2
11 M	0310 5.4 / 0949 0.3 / 1546 5.4 / 2205 0.6	**26** TU	0340 5.0 / 1004 0.8 / 1602 4.9 / 2209 1.1
12 TU	0354 5.6 / 1036 0.1 / 1632 5.4 / 2249 0.5	**27** W	0410 5.1 / 1035 0.8 / 1632 4.9 / 2239 1.0
13 W	0439 5.6 / 1121 0.1 / 1718 5.3 / 2332 0.6	**28** TH	0440 5.1 / 1105 0.8 / 1703 4.9 / 2309 1.1
14 TH	0525 5.6 / 1205 0.3 / 1804 5.2	**29** F	0511 5.0 / 1137 0.9 / 1735 4.8 / 2340 1.1
15 F	0015 0.8 / 0612 5.4 / 1250 0.5 / 1852 4.9	**30** SA	0544 4.9 / 1209 1.0 / 1809 4.7
		31 SU	0014 1.3 / 0620 4.8 / 1245 1.1 / 1847 4.6

Chart Datum: 2·60 metres below Ordnance Datum (Newlyn)
HAT is 5·7 metres above Chart Datum

NORTH SHIELDS

LAT 55°00′N LONG 1°26′W

TIMES AND HEIGHTS OF HIGH AND LOW WATERS

Dates in amber are **SPRINGS**
Dates in yellow are **NEAPS**

2014

SEPTEMBER

Day	Time m	Time m	Time m	Time m	Day	Time m	Time m	Time m	Time m
1 M	0052 1.4	0702 4.6	1326 1.4	1933 4.4	16	0213 1.6	0832 4.3	1442 1.9	2103 4.2 ◐
2 TU	0140 1.6	0756 4.6	1419 1.6	2031 4.3 ◐	17 W	0326 1.9	0944 4.0	1601 2.2	2216 4.1
3 W	0245 1.8	0905 4.2	1532 1.8	2143 4.2	18 TH	0456 1.9	1106 4.0	1731 2.2	2336 4.1
4 TH	0412 1.8	1029 4.2	1659 1.8	2304 4.3	19 F	0617 1.8	1221 4.1	1842 2.0	
5 F	0540 1.6	1153 4.4	1817 1.6		20 SA	0041 4.3	0713 1.6	1317 4.3	1930 1.8
6 SA	0017 4.5	0653 1.3	1302 4.7	1920 1.3	21 SU	0130 4.5	0755 1.3	1358 4.5	2009 1.6
7 SU	0117 4.9	0752 0.8	1356 5.0	2013 1.0	22 M	0209 4.7	0831 1.1	1433 4.7	2042 1.4
8 M	0206 5.2	0844 0.5	1443 5.3	2101 0.7	23 TU	0242 4.9	0904 1.0	1504 4.8	2114 1.2
9 TU	0251 5.5	0931 0.4	1527 5.4	2145 0.6 ○	24 W	0313 5.0	0935 0.8	1534 4.9	2144 1.1 ●
10 W	0335 5.6	1015 0.1	1610 5.5	2228 0.5	25 TH	0342 5.1	1006 0.8	1603 5.0	2214 1.0
11 TH	0418 5.7	1058 0.2	1653 5.4	2310 0.8	26 F	0413 5.1	1037 0.8	1634 5.0	2245 1.0
12 F	0502 5.6	1139 0.4	1736 5.2	2351 0.7	27 SA	0445 5.1	1109 0.8	1706 5.0	2318 1.0
13 SA	0548 5.3	1220 0.7	1820 5.0		28 SU	0519 5.0	1142 1.0	1740 4.9	2353 1.2
14 SU	0033 1.0	0636 5.0	1217 1.1	1907 4.7	29 M	0557 4.9	1217 1.2	1819 4.8	
15 M	0119 1.3	0730 4.7	1346 1.5	2000 4.4	30 TU	0032 1.3	0642 4.7	1300 1.4	1906 4.6

OCTOBER

Day	Time m	Time m	Time m	Time m	Day	Time m	Time m	Time m	Time m
1 W	0122 1.5	0738 4.5	1354 1.7	2004 4.4 ◐	16	0245 1.9	0906 4.0	1507 2.3	2128 4.1
2 TH	0229 1.7	0850 4.3	1510 1.9	2118 4.3	17 F	0406 2.0	1020 3.9	1639 2.3	2245 4.1
3 F	0355 1.7	1016 4.2	1640 1.9	2240 4.3	18 SA	0528 1.9	1137 4.0	1758 2.2	2357 4.2
4 SA	0523 1.5	1138 4.4	1759 1.7	2355 4.6	19 SU	0630 1.7	1237 4.2	1853 2.0	
5 SU	0636 1.2	1245 4.7	1902 1.4		20 M	0051 4.4	0717 1.5	1323 4.5	1935 1.7
6 M	0056 4.9	0734 0.8	1339 5.0	1954 1.1	21 TU	0134 4.6	0755 1.3	1400 4.7	2011 1.5
7 TU	0147 5.2	0824 0.5	1424 5.2	2041 0.8	22 W	0210 4.8	0830 1.1	1432 4.8	2045 1.3
8 W	0232 5.4	0909 0.4	1506 5.4	2125 0.6 ○	23 TH	0243 5.0	0903 0.9	1504 5.0	2117 1.1 ●
9 TH	0315 5.6	0952 0.3	1547 5.4	2207 0.6	24 F	0315 5.1	0936 0.8	1535 5.1	2150 1.0
10 F	0358 5.6	1033 0.4	1627 5.4	2248 0.6	25 SA	0348 5.1	1010 0.8	1607 5.1	2224 0.9
11 SA	0441 5.5	1112 0.6	1708 5.2	2328 0.8	26 SU	0423 5.1	1044 0.9	1641 5.1	2300 1.0
12 SU	0526 5.2	1150 0.9	1749 5.0		27 M	0501 5.1	1120 1.0	1718 5.0	2339 1.2
13 M	0009 1.0	0612 4.9	1228 1.3	1832 4.8	28 TU	0543 4.9	1159 1.2	1759 4.9	
14 TU	0052 1.3	0703 4.6	1308 1.7	1921 4.5	29 W	0023 1.2	0631 4.8	1245 1.4	1847 4.7
15 W	0142 1.6	0800 4.3	1357 2.0	2019 4.2 ◐	30 TH	0115 1.3	0729 4.5	1340 1.7	1946 4.6
					31 F	0220 1.5	0841 4.4	1453 1.9	2058 4.4 ◐

NOVEMBER

Day	Time m	Time m	Time m	Time m	Day	Time m	Time m	Time m	Time m
1 SA	0341 1.5	1001 4.3	1619 1.9	2217 4.5	16	0422 1.9	1036 4.0	1652 2.3	2254 4.1
2 SU	0503 1.4	1118 4.5	1735 1.8	2331 4.6	17 M	0530 1.8	1142 4.1	1759 2.1	2358 4.3
3 M	0613 1.2	1224 4.7	1839 1.5		18 TU	0627 1.7	1236 4.3	1852 1.9	
4 TU	0034 4.9	0712 0.9	1318 4.9	1933 1.2	19 W	0050 4.4	0713 1.4	1321 4.5	1935 1.6
5 W	0127 5.1	0802 0.8	1404 5.1	2021 1.0	20 TH	0134 4.6	0754 1.3	1359 4.8	2014 1.4
6 TH	0214 5.3	0848 0.6	1446 5.2	2105 0.8 ○	21 F	0212 4.8	0832 1.1	1434 4.9	2051 1.2
7 F	0258 5.4	0930 0.6	1526 5.3	2148 0.7	22 SA	0249 5.0	0909 1.0	1509 5.1	2128 1.0 ●
8 SA	0341 5.4	1009 0.7	1605 5.2	2229 0.7	23 SU	0327 5.1	0946 0.9	1544 5.2	2207 0.9
9 SU	0424 5.2	1047 0.9	1644 5.2	2309 0.8	24 M	0406 5.1	1025 0.9	1621 5.2	2248 0.9
10 M	0507 5.1	1123 1.2	1723 5.0	2349 1.0	25 TU	0448 5.1	1106 1.0	1701 5.2	2331 0.9
11 TU	0551 4.8	1158 1.4	1803 4.8		26 W	0534 5.0	1148 1.1	1746 5.1	
12 W	0029 1.3	0637 4.6	1239 1.7	1846 4.6	27 TH	0018 0.9	0624 4.9	1236 1.4	1834 5.0
13 TH	0113 1.5	0727 4.3	1319 2.0	1937 4.4	28 F	0111 1.1	0721 4.7	1329 1.6	1931 4.8
14 F	0204 1.7	0824 4.1	1413 2.2	2036 4.2 ◐	29 SA	0211 1.2	0827 4.5	1434 1.8	2037 4.7 ◐
15 SA	0308 1.9	0927 4.0	1528 2.3	2144 4.1	30 SU	0322 1.3	0939 4.4	1550 1.9	2150 4.6

DECEMBER

Day	Time m	Time m	Time m	Time m	Day	Time m	Time m	Time m	Time m
1 M	0436 1.3	1051 4.5	1705 1.8	2303 4.6	16	0422 1.9	1036 4.0	1649 2.2	2253 4.1
2 TU	0546 1.3	1158 4.6	1813 1.6		17 W	0527 1.8	1139 4.2	1757 2.1	2358 4.2
3 W	0010 4.7	0648 1.2	1256 4.7	1912 1.4	18 TH	0626 1.6	1235 4.4	1854 1.8	
4 TH	0109 4.9	0742 1.1	1345 4.9	2004 1.2	19 F	0054 4.4	0716 1.5	1324 4.6	1942 1.6
5 F	0200 5.0	0829 1.0	1429 5.0	2051 1.0	20 SA	0143 4.6	0802 1.3	1406 4.8	2027 1.3
6 SA	0246 5.1	0911 1.0	1509 5.1	2134 0.9 ○	21 SU	0227 4.9	0846 1.1	1450 5.0	2110 1.0
7 SU	0329 5.1	0950 1.0	1548 5.2	2215 0.9	22 M	0310 5.0	0928 0.9	1525 5.2	2154 0.8 ●
8 M	0411 5.0	1026 1.1	1625 5.1	2253 0.9	23 TU	0353 5.2	1011 0.9	1606 5.3	2239 0.6
9 TU	0451 4.9	1101 1.3	1702 5.0	2330 1.0	24 W	0438 5.2	1055 0.9	1648 5.3	2324 0.6
10 W	0531 4.8	1135 1.4	1739 4.9		25 TH	0525 5.2	1139 1.0	1733 5.3	
11 TH	0007 1.2	0611 4.6	1209 1.6	1817 4.8	26 F	0011 0.6	0614 5.1	1225 1.1	1821 5.2
12 F	0046 1.3	0654 4.5	1246 1.8	1900 4.6	27 SA	0101 0.8	0707 4.9	1315 1.3	1914 5.0
13 SA	0128 1.5	0741 4.3	1329 2.0	1948 4.4	28 SU	0155 1.0	0806 4.7	1410 1.5	2014 4.8 ◑
14 SU	0217 1.7	0834 4.1	1423 2.1	2045 4.2	29 M	0256 1.2	0910 4.5	1516 1.7	2122 4.7
15 M	0316 1.8	0932 4.0	1532 2.3	2147 4.1	30	0404 1.4	1018 4.4	1631 1.8	2234 4.5
					31 W	0515 1.5	1128 4.4	1745 1.7	2347 4.5

Chart Datum: 2·60 metres below Ordnance Datum (Newlyn)
HAT is 5·7 metres above Chart Datum

TIDES

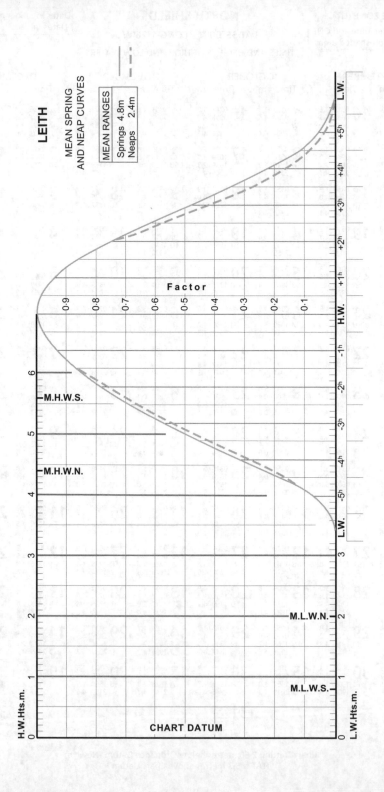

LEITH

MEAN SPRING
AND NEAP CURVES

MEAN RANGES
Springs 4.8m
Neaps 2.4m

Factor

TIME ZONE (UT)	SCOTLAND – LEITH	Dates in amber are SPRINGS
For Summer Time add ONE hour in **non-shaded areas**	LAT 55°59'N LONG 3°11'W	Dates in yellow are NEAPS
	TIMES AND HEIGHTS OF HIGH AND LOW WATERS	**2014**

JANUARY
Time m — Time m

Day		Day	
1 W	0156 5.7 / 0759 0.9 / 1413 5.8 / ● 2030 0.7	**16** TH	0245 5.2 / 0816 1.4 / 1501 5.3 / ○ 2050 1.1
2 TH	0244 5.9 / 0851 0.8 / 1459 5.9 / 2123 0.4	**17** F	0317 5.2 / 0848 1.3 / 1532 5.4 / 2121 1.0
3 F	0331 6.0 / 0940 0.7 / 1545 6.0 / 2213 0.3	**18** SA	0349 5.3 / 0921 1.2 / 1604 5.4 / 2153 0.9
4 SA	0419 5.9 / 1027 0.7 / 1632 6.0 / 2301 0.4	**19** SU	0422 5.2 / 0953 1.2 / 1636 5.3 / 2225 1.0
5 SU	0508 5.8 / 1112 0.9 / 1722 5.8 / 2347 0.6	**20** M	0456 5.2 / 1022 1.3 / 1709 5.3 / 2256 1.1
6 M	0559 5.5 / 1155 1.2 / 1814 5.6	**21** TU	0532 5.1 / 1046 1.5 / 1743 5.1 / 2323 1.3
7 TU	0032 0.9 / 0654 5.2 / 1238 1.5 / 1912 5.3	**22** W	0611 5.0 / 1111 1.6 / 1821 5.0 / 2353 1.4
8 W	0119 1.3 / 0753 5.0 / 1327 1.8 / ◐ 2016 5.0	**23** TH	0654 4.9 / 1146 1.8 / 1905 4.9
9 TH	0215 1.7 / 0855 4.8 / 1435 2.0 / 2121 4.8	**24** F	0034 1.6 / 0743 4.7 / 1240 2.0 / ◑ 1959 4.7
10 F	0330 1.9 / 0958 4.7 / 1555 2.1 / 2227 4.7	**25** SA	0137 1.8 / 0843 4.6 / 1403 2.1 / 2111 4.6
11 SA	0447 2.0 / 1104 4.7 / 1710 2.0 / 2335 4.7	**26** SU	0311 2.0 / 0955 4.6 / 1559 2.1 / 2232 4.7
12 SU	0552 2.0 / 1209 4.8 / 1814 1.8	**27** M	0448 1.8 / 1108 4.8 / 1722 1.8 / 2346 4.9
13 M	0037 4.8 / 0638 1.8 / 1304 5.0 / 1904 1.6	**28** TU	0557 1.6 / 1213 5.1 / 1829 1.4
14 TU	0128 4.9 / 0713 1.7 / 1349 5.1 / 1944 1.4	**29** W	0049 5.3 / 0654 1.3 / 1309 5.4 / 1928 0.9
15 W	0210 5.1 / 0744 1.5 / 1427 5.3 / 2018 1.2	**30** TH	0143 5.6 / 0748 1.0 / 1358 5.7 / ● 2023 0.5
		31 F	0230 5.8 / 0838 0.7 / 1444 6.0 / 2114 0.2

FEBRUARY
Time m — Time m

Day		Day	
1 SA	0316 6.0 / 0926 0.5 / 1542 6.1 / 2200 0.1	**16** SU	0326 5.3 / 0906 1.0 / 1542 5.4 / 2136 0.8
2 SU	0402 6.0 / 1010 0.5 / 1615 6.1 / 2244 0.2	**17** M	0358 5.3 / 0938 1.0 / 1613 5.4 / 2208 0.8
3 M	0448 5.8 / 1052 0.7 / 1702 5.9 / 2325 0.4	**18** TU	0430 5.3 / 1006 1.1 / 1645 5.4 / 2236 0.9
4 TU	0535 5.6 / 1129 0.9 / 1751 5.7	**19** W	0505 5.3 / 1024 1.2 / 1718 5.3 / 2256 1.1
5 W	0002 0.8 / 0624 5.3 / 1202 1.3 / 1843 5.3	**20** TH	0542 5.1 / 1044 1.3 / 1756 5.2 / 2317 1.3
6 TH	0032 1.3 / 0717 4.9 / 1237 1.6 / ◐ 1940 5.0	**21** F	0622 5.0 / 1117 1.5 / 1839 5.0 / 2354 1.5
7 F	0106 1.7 / 0814 4.7 / 1333 2.0 / 2042 4.7	**22** SA	0709 4.8 / 1205 1.7 / 1932 4.8 / ○
8 SA	0208 2.1 / 0915 4.5 / 1505 2.2 / 2148 4.4	**23** SU	0053 1.8 / 0805 4.6 / 1320 2.0 / 2040 4.6
9 SU	0355 2.3 / 1022 4.4 / 1644 2.2 / 2301 4.4	**24** M	0237 2.0 / 0920 4.5 / 1532 2.0 / 2208 4.6
10 M	0519 2.0 / 1137 4.5 / 1759 1.9	**25** TU	0430 2.0 / 1042 4.6 / 1711 1.7 / 2328 4.8
11 TU	0016 4.5 / 0615 2.0 / 1243 4.7 / 1851 1.7	**26** W	0543 1.7 / 1154 4.9 / 1821 1.3
12 W	0112 4.7 / 0654 1.8 / 1330 5.0 / 1930 1.4	**27** TH	0034 5.2 / 0641 1.3 / 1252 5.3 / 1920 0.8
13 TH	0153 4.9 / 0727 1.6 / 1408 5.2 / 2002 1.2	**28** F	0127 5.5 / 0733 0.9 / 1341 5.7 / 2011 0.4
14 F	0226 5.1 / 0759 1.3 / 1441 5.3 / ○ 2032 1.0		
15 SA	0256 5.2 / 0832 1.2 / 1512 5.4 / 2104 0.9		

MARCH
Time m — Time m

Day		Day	
1 SA	0213 5.8 / 0821 0.6 / 1426 5.9 / ● 2057 0.2	**16** SU	0229 5.2 / 0811 1.1 / 1542 5.4 / ○ 2039 0.8
2 SU	0257 5.9 / 0906 0.4 / 1511 6.1 / 2141 0.1	**17** M	0259 5.3 / 0845 0.9 / 1517 5.4 / 2113 0.7
3 M	0341 5.9 / 0949 0.4 / 1556 6.1 / 2222 0.2	**18** TU	0331 5.4 / 0919 0.9 / 1548 5.5 / 2145 0.7
4 TU	0425 5.8 / 1029 0.5 / 1641 5.9 / 2259 0.5	**19** W	0404 5.4 / 0948 0.9 / 1621 5.5 / 2215 0.8
5 W	0509 5.5 / 1104 0.8 / 1727 5.6 / 2329 0.9	**20** TH	0439 5.4 / 1009 1.0 / 1657 5.4 / 2236 1.0
6 TH	0554 5.2 / 1130 1.1 / 1815 5.3 / 2347 1.3	**21** F	0516 5.3 / 1028 1.1 / 1736 5.3 / 2256 1.2
7 F	0641 4.9 / 1157 1.5 / 1906 4.9	**22** SA	0558 5.1 / 1102 1.3 / 1822 5.1 / 2334 1.5
8 SA	0016 1.8 / 0733 4.6 / 1245 1.9 / ◐ 2003 4.6	**23** SU	0644 4.9 / 1153 1.5 / 1916 4.9
9 SU	0109 2.2 / 0832 4.4 / 1403 2.2 / 2106 4.3	**24** M	0040 1.8 / 0741 4.7 / 1317 1.8 / ◑ 2026 4.6
10 M	0244 2.4 / 0937 4.3 / 1612 2.2 / 2216 4.2	**25** TU	0234 2.0 / 0857 4.5 / 1527 1.8 / 2152 4.6
11 TU	0440 2.4 / 1052 4.3 / 1731 2.0 / 2340 4.3	**26** W	0415 2.0 / 1022 4.6 / 1700 1.5 / 2312 4.8
12 W	0543 2.2 / 1208 4.5 / 1824 1.7	**27** TH	0525 1.7 / 1134 4.9 / 1808 1.2
13 TH	0043 4.6 / 0627 1.9 / 1301 4.8 / 1903 1.5	**28** F	0017 5.1 / 0621 1.3 / 1233 5.3 / 1903 0.8
14 F	0125 4.8 / 0703 1.6 / 1340 5.0 / 1936 1.2	**29** SA	0109 5.4 / 0711 1.0 / 1322 5.6 / 1952 0.5
15 SA	0158 5.0 / 0737 1.3 / 1414 5.2 / 2007 1.0	**30** SU	0154 5.6 / 0759 0.7 / 1407 5.8 / ● 2036 0.3
		31 M	0236 5.8 / 0844 0.5 / 1451 5.9 / 2118 0.2

APRIL
Time m — Time m

Day		Day	
1 TU	0318 5.8 / 0927 0.4 / 1535 5.9 / 2156 0.4	**16** W	0304 5.5 / 0856 0.8 / 1523 5.5 / 2121 0.7
2 W	0401 5.6 / 1006 0.5 / 1620 5.7 / 2230 0.7	**17** TH	0339 5.5 / 0932 0.8 / 1600 5.5 / 2156 0.8
3 TH	0443 5.5 / 1040 0.8 / 1704 5.5 / 2255 1.0	**18** F	0416 5.5 / 1005 0.8 / 1639 5.5 / 2231 0.9
4 F	0525 5.2 / 1105 1.1 / 1749 5.2 / 2309 1.4	**19** SA	0455 5.4 / 1037 0.9 / 1722 5.4 / 2305 1.2
5 SA	0609 4.9 / 1129 1.4 / 1836 4.9 / 2339 1.8	**20** SU	0539 5.2 / 1116 1.1 / 1811 5.2 / 2351 1.5
6 SU	0656 4.7 / 1211 1.7 / 1927 4.5	**21** M	0628 5.0 / 1217 1.4 / 1908 4.9
7 M	0028 2.1 / 0750 4.4 / 1314 2.0 / ◑ 2024 4.3	**22** TU	0101 1.8 / 0726 4.8 / 1341 1.6 / ◑ 2017 4.6
8 TU	0143 2.4 / 0852 4.3 / 1510 2.2 / 2126 4.2	**23** W	0228 1.9 / 0842 4.7 / 1519 1.6 / 2137 4.7
9 W	0346 2.4 / 0959 4.2 / 1645 2.0 / 2237 4.2	**24** TH	0352 1.9 / 1003 4.7 / 1640 1.4 / 2251 4.9
10 TH	0459 2.2 / 1113 4.4 / 1740 1.8 / 2350 4.4	**25** F	0459 1.6 / 1112 5.0 / 1745 1.1 / 2355 5.1
11 F	0549 1.9 / 1215 4.6 / 1823 1.5	**26** SA	0555 1.3 / 1211 5.2 / 1841 0.9
12 SA	0041 4.7 / 0629 1.6 / 1301 4.9 / 1859 1.3	**27** SU	0047 5.3 / 0646 1.1 / 1302 5.4 / 1928 0.7
13 SU	0120 5.0 / 0706 1.4 / 1339 5.1 / 1934 1.0	**28** M	0133 5.5 / 0735 0.8 / 1348 5.6 / 2011 0.6
14 M	0155 5.2 / 0743 1.1 / 1414 5.3 / 2009 0.8	**29** TU	0216 5.6 / 0821 0.6 / 1433 5.6 / ● 2052 0.6
15 TU	0229 5.3 / 0819 0.9 / 1449 5.4 / ○ 2044 0.7	**30** W	0257 5.6 / 0905 0.6 / 1517 5.6 / 2129 0.7

Chart Datum: 2·90 metres below Ordnance Datum (Newlyn)
HAT is 6·3 metres above Chart Datum

TIDES

TIME ZONE (UT)
For Summer Time add ONE hour in **non-shaded** areas

SCOTLAND – LEITH
LAT 55°59'N   LONG 3°11'W
TIMES AND HEIGHTS OF HIGH AND LOW WATERS

Dates in amber are **SPRINGS**
Dates in yellow are **NEAPS**

2014

MAY

Day	Time	m	Time	m	Time	m	Time	m
1 TH	0339	5.5	0944	0.6	1600	5.5	2200	0.9
16 F	0316	5.6	0918	0.7	1541	5.6	2142	0.7
2 F	0420	5.4	1018	0.8	1643	5.3	2223	1.2
17 SA	0356	5.6	1004	0.6	1625	5.6	2227	0.9
3 SA	0500	5.2	1044	1.1	1725	5.1	2242	1.4
18 SU	0439	5.5	1051	0.7	1711	5.5	2314	1.1
4 SU	0540	5.0	1110	1.3	1808	4.9	2313	1.7
19 M	0525	5.4	1141	0.9	1802	5.3		
5 M	0623	4.8	1147	1.5	1853	4.6	2357	2.0
20 TU	0003	1.4	0616	5.2	1236	1.1	1859	5.1
6 TU	0712	4.6	1239	1.8	1944	4.4		
21 W	0101	1.6	0716	5.0	1341	1.3	2006 ☽	4.9
7 W	0058	2.2	0807	4.4	1348	2.0	2039 ☽	4.3
22 TH	0209	1.8	0828	4.9	1457	1.3	2118	4.8
8 TH	0225	2.4	0908	4.3	1531	2.0	2139	4.3
23 F	0322	1.8	0941	4.9	1612	1.3	2226	4.9
9 F	0401	2.3	1012	4.4	1643	1.8	2243	4.4
24 SA	0428	1.7	1048	5.0	1717	1.2	2329	5.0
10 SA	0501	2.0	1116	4.5	1732	1.6	2343	4.6
25 SU	0527	1.5	1149	5.1	1814	1.1		
11 SU	0548	1.8	1211	4.7	1815	1.4		
26 M	0025	5.1	0621	1.3	1243	5.2	1903	1.0
12 M	0034	4.9	0630	1.5	1259	5.0	1854	1.1
27 TU	0114	5.3	0713	1.0	1332	5.3	1946	1.0
13 TU	0119	5.1	0710	1.2	1341	5.2	1934	0.9
28 W	0158	5.4	0800	0.9	1418	5.4	2025 ●	1.0
14 W	0159	5.3	0751	1.0	1421	5.4	2015 ○	0.8
29 TH	0240	5.4	0844	0.8	1501	5.4	2100	1.0
15 TH	0237	5.5	0834	0.8	1501	5.5	2058	0.7
30 F	0320	5.4	0923	0.8	1543	5.3	2130	1.1
31 SA	0400	5.3	0956	0.8	1623	5.2	2155	1.2

JUNE

Day	Time	m	Time	m	Time	m	Time	m
1 SU	0437	5.2	1024	1.0	1701	5.1	2221	1.4
16 M	0425	5.7	1049	0.4	1700	5.7	2307	0.9
2 M	0515	5.1	1053	1.2	1740	4.9	2253	1.6
17 TU	0513	5.6	1139	0.5	1751	5.5	2355	1.1
3 TU	0554	4.9	1127	1.4	1821	4.8	2332	1.8
18 W	0605	5.5	1229	0.8	1846	5.3		
4 W	0637	4.7	1210	1.5	1906	4.6		
19 TH	0045	1.3	0702	5.3	1324	1.0	1948 ☽	5.1
5 TH	0020	2.0	0724	4.6	1303	1.7	1955 ☽	4.5
20 F	0141	1.6	0808	5.1	1426	1.3	2053	4.9
6 F	0124	2.2	0818	4.5	1407	1.9	2051	4.4
21 SA	0247	1.7	0917	5.0	1536	1.4	2158	4.8
7 SA	0243	2.2	0918	4.4	1524	1.9	2150	4.5
22 SU	0356	1.7	1023	4.9	1645	1.5	2301	4.9
8 SU	0401	2.1	1021	4.5	1634	1.7	2251	4.6
23 M	0501	1.7	1126	4.9	1747	1.5		
9 M	0501	1.9	1122	4.7	1729	1.5	2350	4.8
24 TU	0002	5.0	0601	1.5	1227	5.0	1838	1.4
10 TU	0552	1.6	1219	4.9	1817	1.3		
25 W	0056	5.1	0652	1.3	1320	5.1	1921	1.4
11 W	0043	5.1	0639	1.3	1310	5.1	1903	1.1
26 TH	0143	5.2	0744	1.1	1406	5.1	1958	1.3
12 TH	0130	5.3	0727	1.0	1357	5.4	1951	0.9
27 F	0226	5.3	0826	1.0	1448	5.2	2032 ●	1.2
13 F	0214	5.5	0817	0.8	1441	5.6	2041 ○	0.8
28 SA	0305	5.3	0903	0.9	1526	5.2	2102	1.2
14 SA	0256	5.7	0908	0.6	1526	5.7	2130	0.7
29 SU	0341	5.3	0935	0.8	1602	5.2	2132	1.2
15 SU	0340	5.7	0959	0.4	1612	5.8	2219	0.8
30 M	0416	5.3	1005	1.0	1637	5.1	2203	1.3

JULY

Day	Time	m	Time	m	Time	m	Time	m
1 TU	0451	5.2	1035	1.0	1713	5.1	2234	1.4
16 W	0458	5.9	1125	0.3	1734	5.7	2337	0.9
2 W	0527	5.1	1108	1.2	1751	5.0	2307	1.5
17 TH	0548	5.7	1211	0.6	1826	5.4		
3 TH	0604	5.0	1143	1.3	1831	4.8	2343	1.7
18 F	0021	1.1	0642	5.5	1257	0.9	1922	5.2
4 F	0645	4.8	1224	1.5	1916	4.7		
19 SA	0108	1.5	0743	5.2	1347	1.3	2024 ☽	4.9
5 SA	0028	1.9	0731	4.7	1314	1.7	2005 ☽	4.6
20 SU	0206	1.7	0849	4.9	1452	1.7	2127	4.8
6 SU	0131	2.1	0825	4.6	1416	1.8	2103	4.6
21 M	0322	1.9	0955	4.8	1610	1.9	2231	4.7
7 M	0251	2.1	0930	4.5	1532	1.8	2207	4.6
22 TU	0439	1.9	1103	4.7	1721	1.9	2338	4.8
8 TU	0412	2.0	1039	4.6	1647	1.7	2311	4.8
23 W	0549	1.7	1210	4.8	1818	1.8		
9 W	0519	1.8	1144	4.8	1748	1.5		
24 TH	0039	4.9	0647	1.5	1308	4.9	1900	1.6
10 TH	0011	5.0	0615	1.4	1244	5.1	1842	1.2
25 F	0130	5.1	0733	1.3	1354	5.0	1934	1.5
11 F	0106	5.3	0710	1.1	1337	5.4	1934 ●	1.0
26 SA	0211	5.2	0810	1.1	1433	5.1	2006	1.3
12 SA	0154	5.5	0805	0.7	1424	5.7	2027 ○	0.8
27 SU	0248	5.3	0843	1.0	1507	5.2	2039	1.2
13 SU	0239	5.8	0903	0.4	1510	5.9	2117	0.6
28 M	0322	5.4	0914	0.9	1539	5.2	2111	1.1
14 M	0324	5.9	0950	0.2	1557	5.9	2206	0.6
29 TU	0354	5.4	0944	0.9	1611	5.2	2144	1.1
15 TU	0410	6.0	1039	0.2	1644	5.9	2252	0.7
30 W	0426	5.3	1015	0.9	1645	5.2	2214	1.2
31 TH	0459	5.3	1046	1.0	1720	5.1	2242	1.3

AUGUST

Day	Time	m	Time	m	Time	m	Time	m
1 F	0534	5.2	1115	1.2	1758	5.0	2306	1.5
16 SA	0618	5.5	1223	1.0	1853	5.2		
2 SA	0611	5.0	1144	1.3	1839	4.9	2336	1.7
17 SU	0032	1.4	0715	5.2	1301	1.5	1951 ☽	4.9
3 SU	0652	4.9	1221	1.6	1925	4.8		
18 M	0123	1.8	0819	4.8	1355	1.9	2053	4.7
4 M	0022	1.9	0741	4.7	1316	1.8	2019 ☽	4.6
19 TU	0245	2.0	0925	4.6	1530	2.2	2158	4.6
5 TU	0139	2.1	0845	4.6	1438	1.9	2125	4.6
20 W	0422	2.0	1036	4.5	1657	2.2	2310	4.6
6 W	0326	2.1	1002	4.6	1615	1.9	2237	4.7
21 TH	0540	1.9	1151	4.6	1758	2.0		
7 TH	0455	1.8	1117	4.8	1728	1.7	2345	5.0
22 F	0018	4.8	0637	1.6	1252	4.8	1840	1.8
8 F	0601	1.5	1223	5.1	1827	1.4		
23 SA	0110	5.0	0717	1.4	1337	5.0	1912	1.6
9 SA	0044	5.3	0700	1.0	1319	5.4	1920	1.0
24 SU	0151	5.2	0750	1.2	1413	5.1	1944	1.3
10 SU	0135	5.6	0755	0.6	1407	5.8	2011 ○	0.7
25 M	0226	5.3	0819	1.0	1444	5.2	2016 ●	1.2
11 M	0221	5.9	0847	0.3	1453	6.0	2101	0.5
26 TU	0258	5.4	0849	0.9	1513	5.3	2050	1.1
12 TU	0305	6.1	0936	0.0	1538	6.0	2148	0.4
27 W	0329	5.5	0920	0.8	1544	5.4	2123	1.0
13 W	0351	6.1	1021	0.0	1624	6.0	2232	0.5
28 TH	0400	5.4	0951	0.8	1617	5.3	2153	1.1
14 TH	0438	6.1	1105	0.2	1711	5.8	2314	0.7
29 F	0432	5.4	1021	0.9	1651	5.3	2215	1.2
15 F	0527	5.9	1146	0.6	1800	5.5	2353	1.0
30 SA	0505	5.3	1045	1.1	1727	5.2	2234	1.3
31 SU	0541	5.2	1104	1.3	1806	5.1	2301	1.5

Chart Datum: 2·90 metres below Ordnance Datum (Newlyn)
HAT is 6·3 metres above Chart Datum

| TIME ZONE (UT)
For Summer Time add ONE
hour in **non-shaded areas** | **SCOTLAND – LEITH**
LAT 55°59'N   LONG 3°11'W
TIMES AND HEIGHTS OF HIGH AND LOW WATERS | Dates in amber are **SPRINGS**
Dates in yellow are **NEAPS**
2014 |

SEPTEMBER

Time	m		Time	m
1 M	0623 5.0 1134 1.5 1850 4.9 2343 1.7	**16** TU	0040 1.8 0747 4.7 1257 2.1 2017 4.6
2 TU	0712 4.8 1226 1.8 1943 4.7	**17** W	0158 2.1 0851 4.5 1429 2.4 2122 4.5
3 W	0051 2.0 0814 4.7 1402 2.1 2050 4.6	**18** TH	0359 2.2 1000 4.4 1623 2.4 2233 4.5
4 TH	0256 2.1 0934 4.6 1556 2.0 2209 4.7	**19** F	0518 2.0 1119 4.5 1727 2.2 2346 4.7
5 F	0441 1.8 1056 4.8 1713 1.8 2322 4.9	**20** SA	0611 1.7 1225 4.7 1811 2.0
6 SA	0551 1.4 1205 5.1 1812 1.4	**21** SU	0041 4.9 0649 1.5 1310 4.9 1846 1.7
7 SU	0024 5.3 0649 1.0 1301 5.5 1903 1.1	**22** M	0123 5.1 0721 1.2 1345 5.1 1919 1.4
8 M	0115 5.7 0741 0.5 1348 5.8 1952 0.7	**23** TU	0158 5.3 0750 1.0 1415 5.3 1952 1.2
9 TU	0200 6.0 0830 0.2 1432 6.0 ○ 2040 0.5	**24** W	0230 5.4 0821 0.9 1444 5.4 ● 2026 1.0
10 W	0245 6.2 0916 0.0 1516 6.0 2126 0.4	**25** TH	0301 5.5 0852 0.8 1516 5.5 2100 1.0
11 TH	0330 6.2 0959 0.1 1600 6.0 2209 0.4	**26** F	0332 5.5 0924 0.8 1548 5.5 2130 1.0
12 F	0416 6.1 1040 0.3 1646 5.8 2250 0.7	**27** SA	0405 5.5 0954 0.9 1622 5.4 2154 1.1
13 SA	0504 5.8 1117 0.7 1733 5.5 2326 1.0	**28** SU	0440 5.4 1017 1.0 1659 5.3 2212 1.2
14 SU	0554 5.5 1146 1.2 1822 5.2 2357 1.4	**29** M	0518 5.3 1036 1.3 1738 5.2 2241 1.4
15 M	0648 5.1 1210 1.7 1917 4.9	**30** TU	0601 5.1 1108 1.5 1823 5.0 2326 1.6

OCTOBER

Time	m		Time	m
1 W	0652 4.9 1202 1.9 1916 4.8	**16** TH	0104 2.1 0812 4.5 1322 2.5 2041 4.5
2 TH	0041 1.9 0755 4.7 1353 2.1 2023 4.7	**17** F	0308 2.2 0915 4.3 1528 2.6 2146 4.4
3 F	0247 2.0 0916 4.7 1539 2.1 2146 4.8	**18** SA	0434 2.1 1025 4.4 1643 2.4 2256 4.6
4 SA	0427 1.7 1037 4.9 1654 1.8 2301 5.0	**19** SU	0528 1.9 1136 4.6 1733 2.1 2358 4.8
5 SU	0536 1.3 1145 5.2 1752 1.5	**20** M	0609 1.6 1228 4.8 1813 1.8
6 M	0002 5.3 0632 0.9 1241 5.5 1842 1.1	**21** TU	0045 5.0 0643 1.4 1307 5.1 1849 1.5
7 TU	0054 5.7 0722 0.6 1328 5.8 1930 0.8	**22** W	0123 5.2 0716 1.2 1341 5.3 1925 1.3
8 W	0139 5.9 0808 0.4 1411 5.9 ○ 2018 0.6	**23** TH	0158 5.4 0749 1.0 1414 5.4 ● 2000 1.1
9 TH	0224 6.1 0852 0.3 1453 6.0 2103 0.5	**24** F	0232 5.5 0822 0.9 1447 5.5 2035 1.0
10 F	0309 6.1 0934 0.3 1537 5.9 2147 0.5	**25** SA	0307 5.5 0856 0.8 1522 5.6 2110 1.0
11 SA	0355 5.9 1013 0.6 1621 5.7 2226 0.8	**26** SU	0342 5.6 0930 0.9 1557 5.6 2142 1.0
12 SU	0442 5.7 1045 1.0 1706 5.4 2300 1.1	**27** M	0419 5.5 1001 1.1 1635 5.5 2211 1.1
13 M	0530 5.4 1105 1.4 1752 5.2 2326 1.4	**28** TU	0500 5.4 1030 1.3 1716 5.4 2246 1.3
14 TU	0620 5.0 1126 1.8 1842 4.9	**29** W	0546 5.3 1108 1.6 1802 5.2 2339 1.5
15 W	0003 1.8 0714 4.7 1211 2.2 ● 1938 4.6	**30** TH	0639 5.1 1217 1.9 1856 5.0
		31 F	0101 1.7 0742 4.9 1346 2.1 ● 2004 4.8

NOVEMBER

Time	m		Time	m
1 SA	0236 1.7 0900 4.8 1515 2.1 2125 4.9	**16** SU	0316 2.2 0926 4.4 1540 2.5 2157 4.5
2 SU	0405 1.6 1016 4.9 1628 1.9 2238 5.0	**17** M	0430 2.0 1028 4.5 1645 2.3 2300 4.6
3 M	0513 1.3 1123 5.2 1727 1.6 2340 5.3	**18** TU	0520 1.8 1128 4.7 1734 2.0 2356 4.8
4 TU	0610 1.0 1218 5.4 1819 1.3	**19** W	0602 1.6 1220 4.9 1816 1.7
5 W	0033 5.6 0659 0.8 1307 5.6 1908 1.0	**20** TH	0043 5.0 0639 1.4 1304 5.2 1855 1.5
6 TH	0121 5.7 0745 0.7 1351 5.8 ○ 1956 0.8	**21** F	0126 5.2 0716 1.2 1343 5.4 1934 1.2
7 F	0207 5.8 0828 0.6 1433 5.8 2043 0.7	**22** SA	0205 5.4 0754 1.0 1421 5.5 ● 2013 1.0
8 SA	0252 5.8 0909 0.7 1516 5.8 2126 0.7	**23** SU	0244 5.5 0833 0.9 1458 5.6 2054 0.9
9 SU	0338 5.7 0945 0.9 1559 5.6 2205 0.9	**24** M	0322 5.6 0914 0.9 1536 5.7 2137 0.9
10 M	0423 5.5 1013 1.2 1642 5.4 2237 1.1	**25** TU	0403 5.6 0956 1.0 1616 5.6 2222 0.9
11 TU	0507 5.3 1030 1.5 1725 5.2 2301 1.4	**26** W	0447 5.6 1041 1.2 1700 5.5 2310 1.1
12 W	0553 5.0 1056 1.8 1810 5.0 2333 1.6	**27** TH	0535 5.4 1135 1.4 1747 5.4
13 TH	0640 4.8 1136 2.1 1859 4.7	**28** F	0002 1.2 0627 5.2 1224 1.7 1841 5.2
14 F	0021 1.9 0731 4.6 1233 2.3 ● 1954 4.6	**29** SA	0102 1.4 0728 5.0 1329 1.9 ● 1945 5.0
15 SA	0128 2.1 0826 4.4 1354 2.5 2055 4.5	**30** SU	0214 1.5 0839 4.9 1443 2.0 2101 5.0

DECEMBER

Time	m		Time	m
1 M	0333 1.5 0951 4.9 1555 1.9 2213 5.0	**16** TU	0256 2.1 0930 4.5 1537 2.4 2201 4.5
2 TU	0443 1.4 1057 5.1 1659 1.7 2317 5.2	**17** W	0416 2.0 1031 4.6 1646 2.2 2303 4.6
3 W	0544 1.3 1156 5.2 1756 1.5	**18** TH	0515 1.8 1131 4.8 1739 1.9
4 TH	0014 5.3 0637 1.2 1248 5.4 1849 1.2	**19** F	0002 4.8 0603 1.6 1227 5.0 1826 1.6
5 F	0106 5.4 0724 1.1 1335 5.5 1940 1.0	**20** SA	0055 5.1 0647 1.4 1315 5.3 1910 1.3
6 SA	0154 5.5 0806 1.0 1418 5.6 2026 0.9	**21** SU	0141 5.3 0731 1.2 1358 5.5 1956 1.1
7 SU	0240 5.6 0844 1.0 1501 5.6 2109 0.9	**22** M	0224 5.5 0816 1.0 1439 5.7 ● 2043 0.8
8 M	0323 5.5 0918 1.1 1542 5.5 2146 0.9	**23** TU	0306 5.7 0903 0.9 1519 5.8 2132 0.7
9 TU	0405 5.4 0945 1.3 1622 5.4 2217 1.1	**24** W	0349 5.8 0950 0.9 1601 5.8 2221 0.6
10 W	0445 5.3 1007 1.4 1700 5.3 2241 1.2	**25** TH	0434 5.8 1037 1.0 1646 5.8 2309 0.7
11 TH	0525 5.1 1035 1.6 1739 5.1 2311 1.4	**26** F	0521 5.6 1124 1.1 1734 5.7 2357 0.8
12 F	0606 4.9 1110 1.8 1821 4.9 2349 1.6	**27** SA	0612 5.4 1211 1.4 1826 5.5
13 SA	0650 4.7 1153 2.1 1908 4.7	**28** SU	0047 1.1 0709 5.2 1303 1.6 ● 1925 5.2
14 SU	0038 1.8 0738 4.6 1250 2.3 ● 2000 4.6	**29** M	0144 1.3 0813 5.0 1405 1.8 2035 5.1
15 M	0139 2.0 0832 4.5 1407 2.4 2059 4.5	**30** TU	0253 1.6 0922 4.9 1518 1.9 2147 5.0
		31 W	0409 1.7 1029 4.9 1630 1.9 2254 4.9

Chart Datum: 2·90 metres below Ordnance Datum (Newlyn)
HAT is 6·3 metres above Chart Datum

TIDES

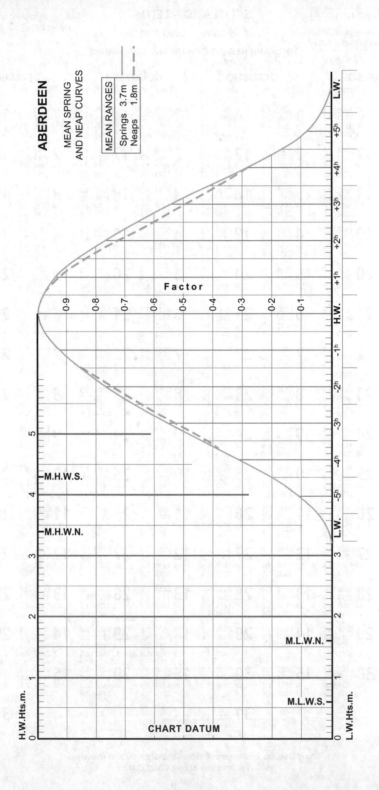

ABERDEEN

MEAN SPRING
AND NEAP CURVES

MEAN RANGES
Springs   3.7m
Neaps   1.8m

TIME ZONE (UT)	SCOTLAND – ABERDEEN	Dates in amber are SPRINGS
For Summer Time add ONE hour in **non-shaded areas**	LAT 57°09'N LONG 2°04'W	Dates in yellow are NEAPS
	TIMES AND HEIGHTS OF HIGH AND LOW WATERS	**2014**

JANUARY

Time	m	Time	m
1 0040 0643 W 1256 ● 1910	4.4 0.9 4.5 0.6	**16** 0127 0717 TH 1337 ○ 1943	4.0 1.2 4.2 1.0
2 0129 0730 TH 1341 1959	4.5 0.8 4.6 0.4	**17** 0200 0748 F 1408 2015	4.0 1.2 4.2 0.9
3 0218 0816 F 1427 2047	4.6 0.7 4.7 0.4	**18** 0232 0819 SA 1439 2047	4.0 1.1 4.2 0.9
4 0307 0902 SA 1514 2136	4.5 0.8 4.7 0.4	**19** 0305 0850 SU 1510 2119	4.0 1.1 4.2 0.9
5 0357 0948 SU 1602 2225	4.4 0.9 4.6 0.6	**20** 0338 0921 M 1543 2153	4.0 1.2 4.2 1.0
6 0449 1036 M 1655 2316	4.2 1.1 4.4 0.8	**21** 0413 0954 TU 1618 2228	3.9 1.3 4.1 1.1
7 0543 1129 TU 1751	4.0 1.3 4.2	**22** 0451 1031 W 1658 2308	3.8 1.4 3.9 1.2
8 0011 0640 W 1228 ◑ 1852	1.1 3.8 1.5 3.9	**23** 0536 1114 TH 1746 2357	3.7 1.5 3.8 1.4
9 0111 0743 TH 1334 2000	1.3 3.6 1.7 3.7	**24** 0630 1211 F 1847 ○	3.6 1.7 3.7
10 0218 0852 F 1452 2115	1.6 3.6 1.8 3.6	**25** 0100 0734 SA 1326 1958	1.5 3.5 1.7 3.6
11 0336 1002 SA 1611 2227	1.6 3.6 1.7 3.6	**26** 0214 0843 SU 1449 2115	1.6 3.6 1.7 3.6
12 0440 1100 SU 1709 2325	1.6 3.7 1.5 3.7	**27** 0331 0955 M 1609 2231	1.5 3.7 1.5 3.8
13 0528 1147 M 1755	1.5 3.9 1.3	**28** 0443 1100 TU 1716 2335	1.3 3.9 1.2 4.1
14 0011 0608 TU 1228 1833	3.8 1.4 4.0 1.2	**29** 0541 1154 W 1810	1.1 4.2 0.8
15 0051 0643 W 1304 1909	3.9 1.3 4.1 1.1	**30** 0029 0631 TH 1242 ● 1900	4.3 0.9 4.4 0.5
		31 0118 0717 F 1328 1947	4.5 0.7 4.6 0.3

FEBRUARY

Time	m	Time	m
1 0205 0802 SA 1412 2033	4.5 0.6 4.7 0.2	**16** 0209 0758 SU 1417 2024	4.1 1.0 4.3 0.7
2 0250 0845 SU 1457 2117	4.5 0.6 4.7 0.3	**17** 0239 0828 M 1447 2055	4.1 0.9 4.3 0.7
3 0336 0927 M 1542 2202	4.4 0.7 4.6 0.5	**18** 0310 0858 TU 1519 2126	4.1 1.0 4.2 0.8
4 0422 1010 TU 1630 2246	4.2 0.9 4.4 0.7	**19** 0343 0930 W 1553 2159	4.0 1.0 4.1 0.9
5 0510 1056 W 1721 2333	4.0 1.1 4.1 1.1	**20** 0419 1006 TH 1632 2236	3.9 1.1 4.0 1.1
6 0601 1147 TH 1818 ◐	3.8 1.4 3.8	**21** 0500 1045 F 1718 2322	3.8 1.3 3.9 1.2
7 0025 0658 F 1249 1921	1.4 3.6 1.6 3.6	**22** 0551 1138 SA 1817 ◯	3.7 1.4 3.7
8 0128 0805 SA 1406 2037	1.7 3.4 1.8 3.4	**23** 0023 0655 SU 1253 1933	1.5 3.5 1.6 3.6
9 0250 0921 SU 1543 2200	1.8 3.4 1.8 3.4	**24** 0143 0811 M 1423 2055	1.6 3.5 1.6 3.6
10 0415 1032 M 1649 2306	1.8 3.5 1.6 3.5	**25** 0311 0929 TU 1554 2218	1.6 3.6 1.4 3.7
11 0509 1126 TU 1737 2355	1.7 3.7 1.4 3.7	**26** 0429 1041 W 1703 2324	1.4 3.8 1.0 4.0
12 0550 1208 W 1815	1.5 3.9 1.2	**27** 0528 1138 TH 1758	1.1 4.1 0.7
13 0034 0625 TH 1245 1850	3.8 1.3 4.0 1.0	**28** 0017 0617 F 1227 1845	4.2 0.9 4.4 0.4
14 0108 0658 F 1317 1922	3.9 1.2 4.1 0.9		
15 0139 0728 SA 1347 1953	4.0 1.1 4.2 0.8		

MARCH

Time	m	Time	m
1 0103 0701 SA 1311 ● 1930	4.4 0.6 4.6 0.2	**16** 0112 0704 SU 1322 ○ 1925	4.0 1.0 4.1 0.7
2 0147 0744 SU 1354 2013	4.5 0.5 4.7 0.2	**17** 0142 0734 M 1352 1956	4.1 0.9 4.2 0.6
3 0228 0824 M 1437 2054	4.5 0.5 4.7 0.3	**18** 0212 0805 TU 1423 2028	4.1 0.8 4.3 0.6
4 0310 0904 TU 1520 2134	4.4 0.6 4.6 0.5	**19** 0243 0836 W 1456 2100	4.1 0.8 4.2 0.7
5 0351 0944 W 1605 2213	4.2 0.7 4.3 0.8	**20** 0317 0909 TH 1532 2134	4.1 0.8 4.2 0.8
6 0435 1026 TH 1652 2254	4.0 1.0 4.1 1.1	**21** 0353 0945 F 1613 2212	4.0 0.9 4.0 1.0
7 0521 1112 F 1745 2340	3.8 1.2 3.7 1.5	**22** 0435 1028 SA 1702 2300	3.9 1.1 3.9 1.2
8 0614 1208 SA 1846 ◑	3.5 1.5 3.5	**23** 0525 1123 SU 1804	3.7 1.2 3.7
9 0038 0716 SU 1321 1957	1.8 3.4 1.7 3.3	**24** 0003 0630 M 1240 ○ 1921	1.5 3.6 1.4 3.5
10 0157 0831 M 1459 2122	1.9 3.3 1.8 3.4	**25** 0126 0747 TU 1410 2044	1.6 3.5 1.4 3.5
11 0340 0952 TU 1620 2237	1.9 3.4 1.6 3.4	**26** 0256 0907 W 1540 2207	1.6 3.6 1.2 3.7
12 0443 1054 W 1710 2328	1.7 3.5 1.4 3.5	**27** 0414 1022 TH 1648 2310	1.4 3.8 0.9 3.9
13 0526 1140 TH 1749	1.5 3.7 1.3	**28** 0512 1120 F 1741	1.1 4.0 0.6
14 0007 0601 F 1218 1823	3.7 1.3 3.9 1.0	**29** 0001 0559 SA 1209 1827	4.1 0.9 4.3 0.4
15 0041 0633 SA 1251 ● 1854	3.9 1.1 4.0 0.8	**30** 0045 0643 SU 1252 ● 1910	4.3 0.7 4.5 0.3
		31 0125 0724 M 1334 1950	4.4 0.5 4.5 0.3

APRIL

Time	m	Time	m
1 0204 0803 TU 1416 2028	4.4 0.5 4.5 0.4	**16** 0144 0742 W 1400 2002	4.2 0.7 4.2 0.6
2 0243 0842 W 1458 2105	4.3 0.5 4.4 0.6	**17** 0218 0817 TH 1437 2038	4.2 0.7 4.2 0.7
3 0322 0921 TH 1541 2142	4.2 0.7 4.2 0.9	**18** 0254 0854 F 1517 2116	4.2 0.7 4.2 0.8
4 0402 1001 F 1627 2219	4.0 0.9 4.0 1.2	**19** 0333 0935 SA 1602 2159	4.1 0.8 4.1 1.0
5 0444 1043 SA 1716 2301	3.8 1.1 3.7 1.5	**20** 0417 1023 SU 1655 2250	4.0 0.9 3.9 1.2
6 0532 1134 SU 1813 2353	3.6 1.4 3.4 1.7	**21** 0510 1122 M 1800 2355	3.8 1.1 3.7 1.4
7 0631 1239 M 1917 ◑	3.4 1.6 3.2	**22** 0616 1235 TU 1914 ○	3.7 1.2 3.6
8 0105 0738 TU 1400 2031	1.9 3.3 1.7 3.2	**23** 0114 0730 W 1359 2031	1.6 3.6 1.2 3.6
9 0237 0855 W 1530 2150	2.0 3.3 1.6 3.3	**24** 0237 0846 TH 1520 2149	1.5 3.6 1.1 3.7
10 0401 1008 TH 1630 2248	1.8 3.4 1.4 3.4	**25** 0352 0959 F 1627 2251	1.4 3.8 0.9 3.9
11 0451 1106 F 1712 2331	1.6 3.6 1.2 3.6	**26** 0450 1059 SA 1720 2340	1.2 4.0 0.7 4.0
12 0529 1142 SA 1748	1.4 3.7 1.0	**27** 0539 1149 SU 1806	0.9 4.1 0.6
13 0007 0602 SU 1218 1821	3.8 1.2 3.9 0.8	**28** 0023 0623 M 1234 1848	4.1 0.7 4.3 0.5
14 0040 0635 M 1252 1854	3.9 1.0 4.0 0.7	**29** 0103 0704 TU 1316 ● 1926	4.2 0.6 4.3 0.6
15 0112 0708 TU 1325 ○ 1928	4.1 0.8 4.2 0.6	**30** 0141 0744 W 1358 2004	4.2 0.6 4.3 0.7

Chart Datum: 2·25 metres below Ordnance Datum (Newlyn)
HAT is 4·8 metres above Chart Datum

TIDES

TIME ZONE (UT)	SCOTLAND – ABERDEEN	Dates in amber are SPRINGS
For Summer Time add ONE hour in **non-shaded areas**	LAT 57°09′N LONG 2°04′W TIMES AND HEIGHTS OF HIGH AND LOW WATERS	Dates in yellow are NEAPS **2014**

MAY

Day	Time	m	Day	Time	m
1 TH	0219 / 0823 / 1439 / 2039	4.2 / 0.6 / 4.2 / 0.8	**16** F	0156 / 0801 / 1422 / 2021	4.3 / 0.6 / 4.3 / 0.7
2 F	0256 / 0901 / 1521 / 2114	4.1 / 0.7 / 4.0 / 1.0	**17** SA	0236 / 0844 / 1507 / 2104	4.3 / 0.6 / 4.2 / 0.8
3 SA	0334 / 0939 / 1604 / 2150	4.0 / 0.9 / 3.8 / 1.2	**18** SU	0318 / 0930 / 1556 / 2151	4.2 / 0.6 / 4.1 / 0.9
4 SU	0413 / 1020 / 1650 / 2229	3.8 / 1.0 / 3.6 / 1.4	**19** M	0405 / 1022 / 1652 / 2244	4.1 / 0.7 / 4.0 / 1.1
5 M	0457 / 1105 / 1741 / 2316	3.7 / 1.2 / 3.5 / 1.6	**20** TU	0500 / 1121 / 1755 / 2346	4.0 / 0.8 / 3.8 / 1.3
6 TU	0549 / 1200 / 1838	3.5 / 1.4 / 3.3	**21** W	0603 / 1228 / 1901	3.8 / 0.9 / 3.7 ☽
7 W	0016 / 0649 / 1306 / 1939	1.8 / 3.4 / 1.5 / 3.2	**22** TH	0057 / 0711 / 1340 / 2011	1.5 / 3.7 / 1.0 / 3.6
8 TH	0133 / 0755 / 1419 / 2047	1.9 / 3.3 / 1.5 / 3.3	**23** F	0210 / 0822 / 1453 / 2123	1.5 / 3.7 / 1.0 / 3.7
9 F	0252 / 0904 / 1528 / 2153	1.9 / 3.3 / 1.4 / 3.4	**24** SA	0323 / 0934 / 1601 / 2226	1.4 / 3.8 / 1.0 / 3.8
10 SA	0358 / 1009 / 1623 / 2245	1.7 / 3.4 / 1.3 / 3.5	**25** SU	0426 / 1037 / 1657 / 2318	1.2 / 3.9 / 0.9 / 3.9
11 SU	0447 / 1059 / 1706 / 2328	1.5 / 3.6 / 1.1 / 3.7	**26** M	0519 / 1131 / 1745	1.1 / 4.0 / 0.9
12 M	0527 / 1141 / 1745	1.3 / 3.7 / 0.9	**27** TU	0002 / 0605 / 1218 / 1827	4.0 / 0.9 / 4.1 / 0.8
13 TU	0005 / 0604 / 1221 / 1822	3.9 / 1.0 / 4.0 / 0.8	**28** W	0043 / 0648 / 1302 / 1905	4.1 / 0.8 / 4.1 / 0.8 ●
14 W	0042 / 0642 / 1259 / 1901	4.1 / 0.8 / 4.1 / 0.7 ○	**29** TH	0122 / 0728 / 1343 / 1942	4.1 / 0.7 / 4.1 / 0.9
15 TH	0118 / 0721 / 1339 / 1940	4.2 / 0.7 / 4.2 / 0.6	**30** F	0159 / 0806 / 1424 / 2017	4.1 / 0.7 / 4.0 / 1.0
			31 SA	0235 / 0843 / 1504 / 2052	4.1 / 0.8 / 3.9 / 1.1

JUNE

Day	Time	m	Day	Time	m
1 SU	0311 / 0920 / 1543 / 2127	4.0 / 0.8 / 3.8 / 1.2	**16** M	0306 / 0925 / 1548 / 2142	4.4 / 0.4 / 4.3 / 0.8
2 M	0348 / 0958 / 1625 / 2203	3.9 / 1.0 / 3.7 / 1.4	**17** TU	0355 / 1016 / 1642 / 2233	4.3 / 0.5 / 4.1 / 1.0
3 TU	0428 / 1038 / 1709 / 2244	3.8 / 1.1 / 3.6 / 1.5	**18** W	0448 / 1111 / 1740 / 2329	4.2 / 0.6 / 4.0 / 1.2
4 W	0513 / 1124 / 1758 / 2332	3.7 / 1.2 / 3.5 / 1.6	**19** TH	0546 / 1210 / 1840	4.1 / 0.8 / 3.8 ☽
5 TH	0605 / 1217 / 1851	3.5 / 1.4 / 3.4 ☽	**20** F	0031 / 0649 / 1314 / 1943	1.3 / 3.9 / 1.0 / 3.7
6 F	0032 / 0702 / 1318 / 1948	1.8 / 3.4 / 1.4 / 3.3	**21** SA	0138 / 0756 / 1421 / 2051	1.4 / 3.8 / 1.1 / 3.6
7 SA	0142 / 0802 / 1422 / 2050	1.8 / 3.4 / 1.4 / 3.4	**22** SU	0250 / 0907 / 1531 / 2158	1.5 / 3.7 / 1.2 / 3.7
8 SU	0251 / 0906 / 1523 / 2151	1.7 / 3.4 / 1.4 / 3.5	**23** M	0401 / 1016 / 1634 / 2255	1.4 / 3.7 / 1.2 / 3.8
9 M	0353 / 1009 / 1619 / 2244	1.6 / 3.5 / 1.2 / 3.7	**24** TU	0501 / 1115 / 1726 / 2344	1.2 / 3.8 / 1.2 / 3.9
10 TU	0447 / 1103 / 1708 / 2331	1.4 / 3.7 / 1.1 / 3.9	**25** W	0550 / 1206 / 1809	1.1 / 3.9 / 1.1
11 W	0534 / 1151 / 1754	1.1 / 3.9 / 0.9	**26** TH	0027 / 0634 / 1250 / 1848	4.0 / 1.0 / 3.9 / 1.1
12 TH	0014 / 0619 / 1237 / 1839	4.1 / 0.9 / 4.1 / 0.8	**27** F	0106 / 0718 / 1331 / 1924	4.1 / 0.9 / 3.9 / 1.1 ●
13 F	0056 / 0704 / 1323 / 1923	4.2 / 0.7 / 4.2 / 0.7 ○	**28** SA	0142 / 0750 / 1409 / 1958	4.1 / 0.8 / 3.9 / 1.1
14 SA	0138 / 0749 / 1409 / 2008	4.3 / 0.5 / 4.3 / 0.7	**29** SU	0217 / 0826 / 1445 / 2031	4.1 / 0.8 / 3.9 / 1.1
15 SU	0221 / 0836 / 1457 / 2055	4.4 / 0.4 / 4.3 / 0.7	**30** M	0251 / 0900 / 1521 / 2104	4.1 / 0.8 / 3.9 / 1.1

JULY

Day	Time	m	Day	Time	m
1 TU	0325 / 0935 / 1557 / 2138	4.0 / 0.9 / 3.8 / 1.2	**16** W	0339 / 1002 / 1624 / 2215	4.5 / 0.3 / 4.3 / 0.8
2 W	0401 / 1011 / 1636 / 2214	4.0 / 1.0 / 3.7 / 1.3	**17** TH	0430 / 1052 / 1717 / 2305	4.4 / 0.5 / 4.1 / 1.0
3 TH	0439 / 1049 / 1718 / 2253	3.8 / 1.1 / 3.6 / 1.5	**18** F	0524 / 1144 / 1812	4.2 / 0.8 / 3.9
4 F	0523 / 1133 / 1805 / 2341	3.7 / 1.2 / 3.5 / 1.6	**19** SA	0001 / 0623 / 1241 / 1911	1.2 / 4.0 / 1.0 / 3.7 ☽
5 SA	0613 / 1224 / 1858	3.6 / 1.3 / 3.5 ☽	**20** SU	0104 / 0728 / 1344 / 2017	1.4 / 3.8 / 1.3 / 3.6
6 SU	0040 / 0711 / 1324 / 1956	1.7 / 3.5 / 1.4 / 3.4	**21** M	0216 / 0840 / 1458 / 2127	1.5 / 3.6 / 1.5 / 3.6
7 M	0150 / 0814 / 1429 / 2058	1.7 / 3.5 / 1.4 / 3.5	**22** TU	0338 / 0956 / 1612 / 2233	1.5 / 3.6 / 1.5 / 3.7
8 TU	0301 / 0921 / 1535 / 2202	1.6 / 3.5 / 1.4 / 3.6	**23** W	0445 / 1102 / 1708 / 2326	1.4 / 3.6 / 1.4 / 3.8
9 W	0409 / 1029 / 1637 / 2259	1.5 / 3.7 / 1.2 / 3.8	**24** TH	0537 / 1154 / 1753	1.2 / 3.7 / 1.3
10 TH	0509 / 1127 / 1732 / 2350	1.2 / 3.9 / 0.9 / 4.0	**25** F	0011 / 0619 / 1238 / 1831	3.9 / 1.1 / 3.8 / 1.2
11 F	0601 / 1220 / 1822	0.9 / 4.1 / 0.9	**26** SA	0050 / 0657 / 1316 / 1905	4.0 / 0.9 / 3.9 / 1.2 ●
12 SA	0036 / 0649 / 1309 / 1909	4.3 / 0.6 / 4.3 / 0.7 ○	**27** SU	0125 / 0732 / 1350 / 1938	4.1 / 0.8 / 4.0 / 1.1
13 SU	0121 / 0737 / 1357 / 1955	4.4 / 0.4 / 4.4 / 0.6	**28** M	0157 / 0805 / 1423 / 2010	4.2 / 0.8 / 4.0 / 1.0
14 M	0206 / 0825 / 1445 / 2041	4.6 / 0.2 / 4.5 / 0.6	**29** TU	0229 / 0837 / 1455 / 2041	4.2 / 0.8 / 4.0 / 1.0
15 TU	0252 / 0913 / 1534 / 2127	4.6 / 0.2 / 4.4 / 0.7	**30** W	0300 / 0909 / 1528 / 2112	4.2 / 0.8 / 3.9 / 1.1
			31 TH	0333 / 0942 / 1602 / 2144	4.1 / 0.9 / 3.9 / 1.2

AUGUST

Day	Time	m	Day	Time	m
1 F	0408 / 1016 / 1639 / 2219	4.0 / 1.0 / 3.8 / 1.3	**16** SA	0459 / 1112 / 1739 / 2329	4.3 / 0.9 / 3.9 / 1.2
2 SA	0446 / 1054 / 1721 / 2300	3.9 / 1.1 / 3.7 / 1.4	**17** SU	0556 / 1204 / 1836	4.0 / 1.2 / 3.7 ☽
3 SU	0531 / 1138 / 1811 / 2351	3.8 / 1.3 / 3.6 / 1.6	**18** M	0029 / 0659 / 1306 / 1940	1.5 / 3.7 / 1.5 / 3.5
4 M	0627 / 1235 / 1910	3.6 / 1.4 / 3.5 ☽	**19** TU	0142 / 0812 / 1421 / 2053	1.6 / 3.5 / 1.7 / 3.5
5 TU	0100 / 0733 / 1345 / 2016	1.7 / 3.5 / 1.5 / 3.5	**20** W	0314 / 0934 / 1550 / 2207	1.7 / 3.4 / 1.8 / 3.6
6 W	0220 / 0847 / 1500 / 2126	1.7 / 3.5 / 1.5 / 3.6	**21** TH	0429 / 1045 / 1650 / 2305	1.5 / 3.5 / 1.6 / 3.7
7 TH	0340 / 1003 / 1614 / 2233	1.5 / 3.7 / 1.4 / 3.8	**22** F	0520 / 1138 / 1734 / 2351	1.3 / 3.7 / 1.5 / 3.9
8 F	0450 / 1110 / 1715 / 2329	1.2 / 3.9 / 1.1 / 4.1	**23** SA	0601 / 1219 / 1811	1.1 / 3.8 / 1.3
9 SA	0546 / 1205 / 1807	0.9 / 4.1 / 0.9	**24** SU	0029 / 0636 / 1255 / 1844	4.0 / 1.0 / 3.9 / 1.2
10 SU	0018 / 0635 / 1255 / 1854	4.3 / 0.5 / 4.4 / 0.7	**25** M	0103 / 0709 / 1327 / 1916	4.1 / 0.8 / 4.0 / 1.1 ●
11 M	0104 / 0723 / 1342 / 1939	4.5 / 0.3 / 4.5 / 0.6	**26** TU	0134 / 0740 / 1357 / 1946	4.2 / 0.8 / 4.1 / 1.0
12 TU	0149 / 0809 / 1427 / 2023	4.7 / 0.1 / 4.6 / 0.5	**27** W	0204 / 0810 / 1427 / 2015	4.3 / 0.7 / 4.1 / 1.0
13 W	0234 / 0855 / 1513 / 2107	4.8 / 0.1 / 4.5 / 0.6	**28** TH	0234 / 0841 / 1458 / 2046	4.3 / 0.8 / 4.1 / 1.0
14 TH	0319 / 0940 / 1559 / 2151	4.7 / 0.3 / 4.3 / 0.7	**29** F	0306 / 0912 / 1530 / 2117	4.2 / 0.8 / 4.0 / 1.1
15 F	0407 / 1025 / 1647 / 2237	4.5 / 0.5 / 4.1 / 0.9	**30** SA	0339 / 0944 / 1604 / 2150	4.1 / 0.9 / 4.0 / 1.2
			31 SU	0416 / 1019 / 1644 / 2229	4.0 / 1.1 / 3.9 / 1.3

Chart Datum: 2·25 metres below Ordnance Datum (Newlyn)
HAT is 4·8 metres above Chart Datum

SCOTLAND – ABERDEEN
LAT 57°09′N   LONG 2°04′W
TIMES AND HEIGHTS OF HIGH AND LOW WATERS

Dates in amber are **SPRINGS**
Dates in yellow are **NEAPS**

2014

SEPTEMBER

Day	Time m	Time m	Time m	Time m
1 M	0500 3.9	1101 1.3	1731 3.7	2318 1.5
16 TU	0631 3.6	1223 1.7	1901 3.5	◑
2 TU	0555 3.7	1157 1.5	1831 3.6	◐
17 W	0106 1.7	0741 3.4	1338 1.9	2012 3.5
3 W	0026 1.6	0706 3.6	1311 1.6	1942 3.6
18 TH	0239 1.7	0903 3.4	1516 2.0	2131 3.5
4 TH	0152 1.6	0825 3.6	1437 1.6	2057 3.6
19 F	0403 1.6	1019 3.5	1624 1.8	2235 3.7
5 F	0321 1.5	0946 3.7	1557 1.5	2210 3.8
20 SA	0454 1.4	1113 3.6	1709 1.6	2323 3.8
6 SA	0434 1.2	1056 3.9	1700 1.2	2310 4.1
21 SU	0534 1.2	1153 3.8	1746 1.4	
7 SU	0531 0.8	1151 4.2	1751 1.0	
22 M	0001 4.0	0608 1.0	1227 3.9	1819 1.3
8 M	0000 4.4	0629 0.5	1238 4.4	1836 0.7
23 TU	0035 4.1	0640 0.9	1258 4.1	1850 1.1
9 TU	0046 4.6	0705 0.3	1322 4.6	○ 1920 0.6
24 W	0107 4.2	0711 0.8	1328 4.2	● 1920 1.0
10 W	0129 4.8	0749 0.2	1405 4.6	2002 0.5
25 TH	0137 4.3	0741 0.7	1358 4.2	1950 0.9
11 TH	0213 4.8	0831 0.2	1447 4.5	2044 0.6
26 F	0208 4.3	0812 0.7	1428 4.2	2021 0.9
12 F	0257 4.7	0913 0.4	1530 4.4	2126 0.7
27 SA	0240 4.3	0841 0.8	1500 4.2	2053 1.0
13 SA	0343 4.5	0955 0.7	1615 4.2	2210 0.9
28 SU	0315 4.2	0916 0.9	1535 4.1	2128 1.1
14 SU	0433 4.2	1038 1.0	1704 3.9	2258 1.2
29 M	0354 4.1	0952 1.1	1615 4.0	2208 1.2
15 M	0528 3.9	1125 1.4	1758 3.7	2356 1.5
30 TU	0439 3.9	1035 1.3	1701 3.9	2259 1.4

OCTOBER

Day	Time m	Time m	Time m	Time m
1 W	0537 3.8	1132 1.5	1802 3.7	
16 TH	0027 1.7	0704 3.4	1250 2.0	1925 3.5
2 TH	0008 1.5	0650 3.6	1250 1.7	1916 3.6
17 F	0146 1.8	0817 3.4	1417 2.1	2039 3.5
3 F	0135 1.5	0810 3.6	1418 1.7	2033 3.7
18 SA	0315 1.7	0934 3.4	1543 2.0	2151 3.6
4 SA	0303 1.4	0931 3.7	1539 1.6	2147 3.9
19 SU	0416 1.5	1034 3.6	1635 1.8	2245 3.7
5 SU	0416 1.1	1040 4.0	1642 1.3	2249 4.1
20 M	0459 1.3	1117 3.8	1715 1.6	2327 3.9
6 M	0512 0.8	1133 4.2	1732 1.0	2340 4.4
21 TU	0535 1.2	1154 3.9	1750 1.4	
7 TU	0601 0.5	1218 4.4	1818 0.8	
22 W	0003 4.1	0608 1.0	1227 4.1	1821 1.2
8 W	0025 4.6	0644 0.4	1301 4.5	○ 1900 0.6
23 TH	0037 4.2	0639 0.9	1258 4.2	● 1853 1.0
9 TH	0109 4.7	0726 0.3	1341 4.6	1941 0.6
24 F	0110 4.3	0711 0.8	1329 4.3	1926 0.9
10 F	0152 4.7	0807 0.4	1421 4.5	2022 0.6
25 SA	0143 4.3	0744 0.8	1401 4.3	1959 0.9
11 SA	0236 4.6	0846 0.6	1502 4.4	2103 0.7
26 SU	0219 4.3	0818 0.8	1435 4.3	2035 0.9
12 SU	0321 4.4	0925 0.9	1544 4.2	2145 0.9
27 M	0257 4.3	0854 1.0	1512 4.3	2113 1.0
13 M	0409 4.1	1004 1.2	1629 4.0	2231 1.2
28 TU	0339 4.2	0934 1.1	1553 4.2	2157 1.1
14 TU	0501 3.9	1048 1.5	1719 3.8	2323 1.4
29 W	0427 4.0	1020 1.3	1642 4.0	2251 1.2
15 W	0600 3.6	1140 1.8	1819 3.6	◐
30 TH	0527 3.9	1119 1.6	1742 3.9	2359 1.4
31 F	0639 3.7	1234 1.7	1855 3.8	

NOVEMBER

Day	Time m	Time m	Time m	Time m
1 SA	0120 1.4	0754 3.7	1357 1.7	2009 3.8
16 SU	0202 1.7	0831 3.4	1430 2.1	2047 3.5
2 SU	0242 1.3	0911 3.8	1515 1.6	2122 3.9
17 M	0313 1.7	0938 3.5	1542 1.9	2153 3.6
3 M	0353 1.1	1019 4.0	1619 1.4	2227 4.1
18 TU	0411 1.5	1032 3.7	1634 1.7	2245 3.8
4 TU	0451 0.9	1112 4.2	1712 1.2	2320 4.3
19 W	0454 1.3	1115 3.9	1715 1.5	2328 3.9
5 W	0540 0.7	1158 4.3	1759 0.9	
20 TH	0532 1.2	1152 4.0	1751 1.3	
6 TH	0007 4.5	0624 0.6	1240 4.4	○ 1842 0.8
21 F	0006 4.1	0608 1.0	1228 4.2	1827 1.1
7 F	0052 4.5	0705 0.6	1320 4.4	1923 0.7
22 SA	0044 4.2	0644 0.9	1303 4.3	● 1904 1.0
8 SA	0135 4.5	0744 0.7	1359 4.4	2004 0.7
23 SU	0122 4.3	0721 0.9	1338 4.4	1942 0.9
9 SU	0219 4.4	0822 0.9	1438 4.4	2044 0.8
24 M	0201 4.4	0800 0.9	1415 4.4	2023 0.8
10 M	0302 4.3	0859 1.1	1517 4.3	2125 1.0
25 TU	0243 4.3	0840 1.0	1455 4.4	2106 0.8
11 TU	0347 4.1	0936 1.3	1558 4.1	2206 1.2
26 W	0329 4.3	0923 1.1	1539 4.3	2153 0.9
12 W	0435 3.9	1015 1.5	1643 3.9	2252 1.4
27 TH	0420 4.1	1011 1.3	1628 4.2	2246 1.0
13 TH	0526 3.7	1100 1.8	1735 3.7	2346 1.6
28 F	0518 4.0	1108 1.5	1726 4.1	2349 1.1
14 F	0623 3.5	1157 2.0	1834 3.6	◐
29 SA	0624 3.9	1215 1.6	1833 4.0	
15 SA	0050 1.7	0723 3.4	1311 2.1	1938 3.5
30 SU	0100 1.2	0732 3.8	1329 1.7	1943 3.9

DECEMBER

Day	Time m	Time m	Time m	Time m
1 M	0213 1.2	0844 3.8	1443 1.6	2055 3.9
16 TU	0201 1.7	0830 3.5	1428 2.0	2047 3.5
2 TU	0325 1.2	0953 3.9	1553 1.5	2204 4.0
17 W	0306 1.6	0934 3.6	1537 1.9	2152 3.6
3 W	0428 1.1	1050 4.0	1652 1.3	2303 4.1
18 TH	0405 1.5	1030 3.7	1633 1.7	2249 3.8
4 TH	0520 1.0	1139 4.2	1742 1.1	2353 4.2
19 F	0455 1.4	1117 3.9	1720 1.5	2337 3.9
5 F	0606 1.0	1222 4.3	1828 1.0	
20 SA	0539 1.2	1159 4.1	1803 1.2	
6 SA	0039 4.3	0647 1.0	1303 4.4	○ 1910 0.9
21 SU	0021 4.1	0621 1.0	1239 4.3	1845 1.0
7 SU	0123 4.3	0725 1.0	1341 4.4	1950 0.8
22 M	0104 4.3	0703 0.9	1319 4.4	● 1928 0.8
8 M	0205 4.3	0802 1.1	1419 4.4	2029 0.9
23 TU	0148 4.4	0746 0.9	1359 4.5	2013 0.6
9 TU	0246 4.2	0837 1.1	1456 4.3	2106 1.0
24 W	0232 4.4	0829 0.9	1442 4.5	2058 0.6
10 W	0327 4.1	0912 1.3	1533 4.2	2144 1.1
25 TH	0319 4.4	0914 0.9	1526 4.5	2146 0.6
11 TH	0408 3.9	0948 1.5	1612 4.0	2223 1.2
26 F	0409 4.3	1001 1.1	1615 4.4	2237 0.7
12 F	0452 3.8	1026 1.6	1655 3.9	2306 1.4
27 SA	0503 4.1	1052 1.2	1709 4.3	2332 0.9
13 SA	0539 3.6	1110 1.8	1745 3.7	2357 1.5
28 SU	0602 4.0	1150 1.4	1810 4.1	
14 SU	0631 3.5	1205 1.9	1841 3.6	◐
29 M	0034 1.1	0704 3.8	1256 1.6	1915 4.0
15 M	0056 1.6	0728 3.4	1315 2.0	1941 3.5
30 TU	0141 1.3	0811 3.7	1408 1.6	2027 3.9

Chart Datum: 2·25 metres below Ordnance Datum (Newlyn)
HAT is 4·8 metres above Chart Datum

TIDES

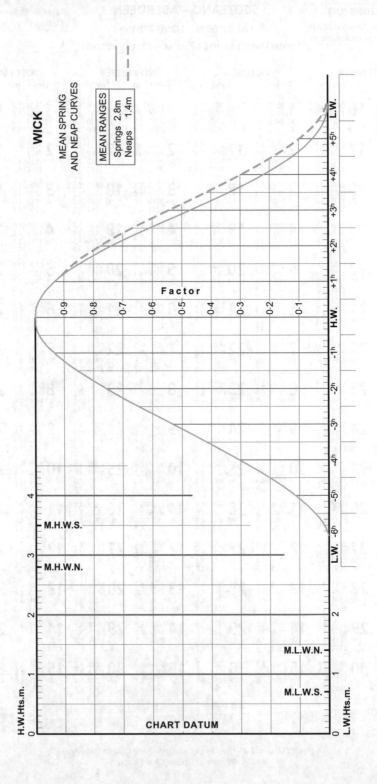

WICK

MEAN SPRING
AND NEAP CURVES

MEAN RANGES	
Springs	2.8m
Neaps	1.4m

TIMES AND HEIGHTS OF HIGH AND LOW WATERS

2014

JANUARY

Time	m	Time	m
1 0428 0.8 / 1050 3.7 / W 1657 0.6 / ● 2324 3.7		**16** 0459 1.1 / 1129 3.5 / TH 1730 0.9 / ○ 2351 3.3	
2 0514 0.7 / 1138 3.8 / TH 1745 0.5		**17** 0531 1.1 / 1202 3.5 / F 1802 0.8	
3 0014 3.7 / 0559 0.7 / F 1225 3.9 / 1832 0.4		**18** 0024 3.3 / 0601 1.0 / SA 1235 3.5 / 1834 0.8	
4 0103 3.7 / 0645 0.8 / SA 1312 3.9 / 1921 0.4		**19** 0057 3.3 / 0632 1.0 / SU 1306 3.5 / 1906 0.8	
5 0151 3.6 / 0730 0.8 / SU 1359 3.8 / 2011 0.6		**20** 0130 3.2 / 0703 1.1 / M 1339 3.4 / 1939 0.9	
6 0240 3.4 / 0816 1.0 / M 1448 3.6 / 2103 0.8		**21** 0204 3.1 / 0736 1.1 / TU 1413 3.3 / 2013 1.0	
7 0332 3.2 / 0907 1.2 / TU 1540 3.4 / 2159 1.0		**22** 0241 3.1 / 0811 1.2 / W 1450 3.2 / 2052 1.1	
8 0427 3.1 / 1006 1.4 / W 1639 3.2 / ◐ 2302 1.2		**23** 0323 3.0 / 0852 1.3 / TH 1535 3.1 / 2140 1.2	
9 0527 2.9 / 1119 1.5 / TH 1743 3.1		**24** 0413 2.9 / 0945 1.4 / F 1630 3.0 / ◑ 2249 1.3	
10 0015 1.3 / 0632 2.9 / F 1245 1.5 / 1853 3.0		**25** 0516 2.9 / 1110 1.5 / SA 1741 2.9	
11 0131 1.4 / 0742 2.9 / SA 1403 1.4 / 2008 3.0		**26** 0009 1.3 / 0627 2.9 / SU 1242 1.5 / 1900 3.0	
12 0230 1.4 / 0845 3.1 / SU 1459 1.3 / 2110 3.0		**27** 0125 1.3 / 0738 3.0 / M 1403 1.3 / 2016 3.1	
13 0315 1.3 / 0935 3.2 / M 1543 1.2 / 2159 3.1		**28** 0233 1.1 / 0845 3.2 / TU 1507 1.0 / 2125 3.3	
14 0353 1.3 / 1017 3.3 / TU 1621 1.1 / 2240 3.2		**29** 0329 1.0 / 0944 3.4 / W 1559 0.7 / 2222 3.5	
15 0427 1.2 / 1055 3.3 / W 1656 0.9 / 2317 3.2		**30** 0417 0.8 / 1036 3.7 / TH 1647 0.5 / ● 2313 3.6	
		31 0502 0.7 / 1124 3.8 / F 1733 0.3	

FEBRUARY

Time	m	Time	m
1 0000 3.7 / 0545 0.6 / SA 1211 3.9 / 1818 0.2		**16** 0002 3.3 / 0541 0.9 / SU 1213 3.5 / 1810 0.7	
2 0047 3.7 / 0627 0.6 / SU 1256 3.9 / 1902 0.3		**17** 0033 3.3 / 0611 0.8 / M 1244 3.5 / 1840 0.7	
3 0131 3.6 / 0709 0.7 / M 1340 3.8 / 1945 0.5		**18** 0105 3.3 / 0641 0.8 / TU 1316 3.4 / 1911 0.7	
4 0215 3.4 / 0750 0.8 / TU 1425 3.7 / 2029 0.7		**19** 0137 3.2 / 0713 0.9 / W 1349 3.4 / 1944 0.8	
5 0259 3.2 / 0833 1.0 / W 1511 3.4 / 2114 1.0		**20** 0212 3.2 / 0747 1.0 / TH 1425 3.3 / 2020 0.9	
6 0347 3.0 / 0922 1.2 / TH 1603 3.2 / ◑ 2208 1.2		**21** 0251 3.1 / 0826 1.1 / F 1509 3.1 / 2103 1.1	
7 0442 2.9 / 1029 1.4 / F 1705 2.9 / 2316 1.5		**22** 0338 3.0 / 0914 1.2 / SA 1603 3.0 / ◐ 2204 1.3	
8 0546 2.8 / 1159 1.5 / SA 1818 2.8		**23** 0438 2.9 / 1031 1.4 / SU 1714 2.9 / 2336 1.4	
9 0046 1.6 / 0659 2.8 / SU 1338 1.5 / 1940 2.7		**24** 0553 2.8 / 1218 1.3 / M 1841 2.8	
10 0206 1.5 / 0814 2.9 / M 1441 1.3 / 2051 2.8		**25** 0105 1.3 / 0712 2.9 / TU 1350 1.2 / 2004 3.0	
11 0257 1.4 / 0912 3.0 / TU 1527 1.2 / 2141 2.9		**26** 0220 1.2 / 0825 3.1 / W 1456 0.9 / 2115 3.2	
12 0336 1.3 / 0956 3.2 / W 1604 1.0 / 2222 3.1		**27** 0316 1.0 / 0927 3.3 / TH 1547 0.6 / 2210 3.4	
13 0410 1.2 / 1034 3.3 / TH 1637 0.9 / 2257 3.2		**28** 0403 0.8 / 1020 3.6 / F 1633 0.4 / 2258 3.5	
14 0441 1.0 / 1109 3.4 / F 1709 0.8 / ○ 2330 3.2			
15 0511 0.9 / 1141 3.5 / SA 1740 0.7			

MARCH

Time	m	Time	m
1 0445 0.6 / 1107 3.8 / SA 1716 0.2 / ● 2343 3.6		**16** 0447 0.9 / 1115 3.4 / SU 1712 0.6 / ○ 2335 3.3	
2 0526 0.5 / 1152 3.9 / SU 1757 0.2		**17** 0517 0.8 / 1147 3.4 / M 1742 0.6	
3 0025 3.6 / 0606 0.5 / M 1236 3.9 / 1837 0.3		**18** 0006 3.3 / 0547 0.7 / TU 1220 3.5 / 1813 0.5	
4 0106 3.5 / 0646 0.5 / TU 1318 3.7 / 1916 0.5		**19** 0039 3.3 / 0619 0.7 / W 1254 3.4 / 1845 0.6	
5 0146 3.4 / 0725 0.7 / W 1400 3.5 / 1954 0.7		**20** 0112 3.3 / 0653 0.7 / TH 1329 3.4 / 1919 0.7	
6 0225 3.2 / 0804 0.9 / TH 1443 3.3 / 2032 1.0		**21** 0148 3.2 / 0729 0.8 / F 1408 3.3 / 1957 0.8	
7 0307 3.0 / 0848 1.1 / F 1530 3.0 / 2115 1.3		**22** 0228 3.1 / 0810 0.9 / SA 1453 3.1 / 2041 1.0	
8 0356 2.9 / 0946 1.3 / SA 1628 2.8 / ◐ 2215 1.5		**23** 0315 3.0 / 0901 1.1 / SU 1549 2.9 / 2143 1.2	
9 0458 2.7 / 1112 1.4 / SU 1740 2.6 / 2344 1.6		**24** 0413 2.9 / 1023 1.2 / M 1704 2.8 / ◑ 2318 1.4	
10 0612 2.7 / 1258 1.4 / M 1904 2.6		**25** 0529 2.8 / 1208 1.2 / TU 1831 2.8	
11 0129 1.6 / 0731 2.7 / TU 1411 1.3 / 2022 2.7		**26** 0050 1.4 / 0650 2.9 / W 1336 1.0 / 1953 2.9	
12 0231 1.5 / 0838 2.8 / W 1459 1.1 / 2115 2.8		**27** 0205 1.2 / 0805 3.0 / TH 1440 0.8 / 2101 3.1	
13 0312 1.3 / 0927 3.0 / TH 1537 1.0 / 2155 3.0		**28** 0259 1.0 / 0908 3.3 / F 1530 0.5 / 2153 3.3	
14 0346 1.1 / 1006 3.1 / F 1610 0.8 / 2231 3.1		**29** 0345 0.8 / 1001 3.5 / SA 1613 0.4 / 2239 3.4	
15 0417 1.0 / 1043 3.3 / SA 1641 0.7 / 2303 3.2		**30** 0426 0.6 / 1048 3.6 / SU 1654 0.3 / ● 2321 3.5	
		31 0506 0.5 / 1132 3.7 / M 1733 0.3	

APRIL

Time	m	Time	m
1 0001 3.5 / 0545 0.4 / TU 1215 3.7 / 1810 0.4		**16** 0525 0.6 / 1156 3.4 / W 1747 0.5	
2 0040 3.5 / 0624 0.5 / W 1256 3.6 / 1847 0.6		**17** 0014 3.4 / 0600 0.6 / TH 1234 3.4 / 1822 0.6	
3 0117 3.4 / 0702 0.6 / TH 1336 3.4 / 1922 0.8		**18** 0050 3.4 / 0638 0.6 / F 1314 3.3 / 1900 0.7	
4 0154 3.2 / 0741 0.8 / F 1417 3.2 / 1957 1.0		**19** 0129 3.3 / 0718 0.6 / SA 1357 3.2 / 1942 0.8	
5 0233 3.1 / 0822 1.0 / SA 1501 2.9 / 2034 1.2		**20** 0211 3.2 / 0805 0.8 / SU 1446 3.1 / 2031 1.0	
6 0316 2.9 / 0914 1.2 / SU 1553 2.7 / 2124 1.5		**21** 0300 3.1 / 0903 0.9 / M 1545 2.9 / 2136 1.2	
7 0411 2.7 / 1029 1.3 / M 1701 2.6 / ◑ 2246 1.6		**22** 0400 3.0 / 1027 1.0 / TU 1659 2.8 / ◑ 2305 1.3	
8 0522 2.6 / 1157 1.3 / TU 1817 2.5		**23** 0513 2.9 / 1156 1.0 / W 1819 2.8	
9 0023 1.6 / 0637 2.6 / W 1323 1.3 / 1934 2.6		**24** 0029 1.3 / 0630 2.9 / TH 1316 0.9 / 1935 2.9	
10 0147 1.5 / 0748 2.7 / TH 1419 1.1 / 2035 2.7		**25** 0142 1.2 / 0742 3.0 / F 1419 0.7 / 2040 3.0	
11 0236 1.3 / 0844 2.8 / F 1500 1.0 / 2119 2.9		**26** 0238 1.0 / 0846 3.2 / SA 1509 0.6 / 2132 3.2	
12 0314 1.2 / 0928 3.0 / SA 1536 0.8 / 2156 3.0		**27** 0324 0.8 / 0941 3.3 / SU 1552 0.5 / 2217 3.3	
13 0347 1.0 / 1007 3.1 / SU 1608 0.7 / 2231 3.1		**28** 0406 0.7 / 1028 3.4 / M 1631 0.5 / 2259 3.4	
14 0419 0.8 / 1043 3.3 / M 1640 0.6 / 2305 3.3		**29** 0447 0.6 / 1113 3.5 / TU 1708 0.5 / ● 2338 3.4	
15 0451 0.7 / 1119 3.4 / TU 1713 0.5 / ● 2339 3.3		**30** 0526 0.5 / 1155 3.4 / W 1745 0.6	

Chart Datum: 1·71 metres below Ordnance Datum (Newlyn)
HAT is 4·0 metres above Chart Datum

TIDES

297

TIME ZONE (UT)
For Summer Time add ONE hour in **non-shaded areas**

SCOTLAND – WICK
LAT 58°26'N   LONG 3°05'W
TIMES AND HEIGHTS OF HIGH AND LOW WATERS

Dates in amber are **SPRINGS**
Dates in yellow are **NEAPS**

2014

MAY

Time	m	Time	m
1 TH 0015 / 0605 / 1235 / 1820	3.4 / 0.5 / 3.4 / 0.7	**16** F 0545 / 1217 / 1805	0.5 / 3.4 / 0.6
2 F 0052 / 0644 / 1314 / 1855	3.3 / 0.6 / 3.2 / 0.9	**17** SA 0032 / 0627 / 1303 / 1847	3.5 / 0.5 / 3.4 / 0.7
3 SA 0127 / 0722 / 1354 / 1929	3.2 / 0.7 / 3.1 / 1.0	**18** SU 0115 / 0714 / 1350 / 1933	3.4 / 0.5 / 3.3 / 0.8
4 SU 0204 / 0802 / 1435 / 2005	3.1 / 0.9 / 2.9 / 1.2	**19** M 0201 / 0805 / 1442 / 2025	3.3 / 0.6 / 3.1 / 1.0
5 M 0245 / 0849 / 1522 / 2049	3.0 / 1.0 / 2.7 / 1.4	**20** TU 0251 / 0907 / 1541 / 2129	3.2 / 0.7 / 3.0 / 1.1
6 TU 0332 / 0949 / 1619 / 2152	2.8 / 1.2 / 2.6 / 1.5	**21** W 0349 / 1020 / 1649 / 2244	3.1 / 0.8 / 2.9 / 1.2
7 W 0431 / 1101 / 1726 / 2316	2.7 / 1.2 / 2.5 / 1.6	**22** TH 0457 / 1135 / 1759	3.0 / 0.8 / 2.8
8 TH 0540 / 1214 / 1834	2.6 / 1.2 / 2.5	**23** F 0000 / 0607 / 1249 / 1907	1.3 / 0.8 / 0.8 / 2.9
9 F 0036 / 0647 / 1321 / 1936	1.5 / 2.7 / 1.1 / 2.6	**24** SA 0113 / 0716 / 1354 / 2012	1.2 / 3.0 / 0.8 / 3.0
10 SA 0143 / 0748 / 1413 / 2029	1.4 / 2.7 / 1.0 / 2.8	**25** SU 0214 / 0822 / 1446 / 2108	1.1 / 3.1 / 0.7 / 3.1
11 SU 0232 / 0841 / 1455 / 2114	1.2 / 2.9 / 0.9 / 2.9	**26** M 0305 / 0920 / 1530 / 2155	0.9 / 3.2 / 0.7 / 3.2
12 M 0312 / 0927 / 1533 / 2154	1.1 / 3.0 / 0.8 / 3.1	**27** TU 0350 / 1011 / 1610 / 2237	0.8 / 3.2 / 0.7 / 3.3
13 TU 0349 / 1010 / 1609 / 2233	0.9 / 3.2 / 0.7 / 3.3	**28** W 0431 / 1056 / 1647 / 2317	0.7 / 3.3 / 0.7 / 3.3
14 W 0426 / 1052 / 1646 / 2312	0.7 / 3.3 / 0.6 / 3.4	**29** TH 0511 / 1137 / 1723 / 2354	0.6 / 3.3 / 0.8 / 3.4
15 TH 0504 / 1134 / 1724 / 2351	0.6 / 3.3 / 0.5 / 3.5	**30** F 0550 / 1217 / 1759	0.6 / 3.2 / 0.8
		31 SA 0030 / 0628 / 1255 / 1832	3.3 / 0.7 / 3.1 / 0.9

JUNE

Time	m	Time	m
1 SU 0105 / 0705 / 1333 / 1906	3.3 / 0.7 / 3.0 / 1.0	**16** M 0104 / 0709 / 1342 / 1924	3.6 / 0.4 / 3.4 / 0.7
2 M 0141 / 0743 / 1411 / 1941	3.2 / 0.8 / 2.9 / 1.1	**17** TU 0151 / 0801 / 1434 / 2015	3.5 / 0.4 / 3.3 / 0.9
3 TU 0218 / 0824 / 1453 / 2020	3.1 / 0.9 / 2.8 / 1.3	**18** W 0241 / 0858 / 1528 / 2110	3.4 / 0.5 / 3.1 / 1.0
4 W 0300 / 0911 / 1539 / 2107	2.9 / 1.0 / 2.7 / 1.4	**19** TH 0335 / 1001 / 1628 / 2215	3.3 / 0.7 / 3.0 / 1.2
5 TH 0347 / 1009 / 1633 / 2212	2.8 / 1.1 / 2.6 / 1.5	**20** F 0436 / 1107 / 1730 / 2325	3.2 / 0.8 / 2.9 / 1.2
6 F 0443 / 1113 / 1734 / 2328	2.7 / 1.2 / 2.6 / 1.5	**21** SA 0541 / 1216 / 1835	3.0 / 0.9 / 2.9
7 SA 0547 / 1216 / 1835	2.7 / 1.2 / 2.7	**22** SU 0040 / 0649 / 1326 / 1941	1.2 / 3.0 / 1.0 / 2.9
8 SU 0038 / 0649 / 1317 / 1933	1.4 / 2.7 / 1.1 / 2.8	**23** M 0152 / 0759 / 1424 / 2042	1.2 / 3.0 / 1.0 / 3.0
9 M 0141 / 0749 / 1410 / 2027	1.3 / 2.8 / 1.0 / 3.0	**24** TU 0250 / 0903 / 1512 / 2134	1.1 / 3.0 / 1.0 / 3.1
10 TU 0234 / 0846 / 1457 / 2117	1.1 / 3.0 / 0.9 / 3.1	**25** W 0338 / 0956 / 1553 / 2218	0.9 / 3.1 / 1.0 / 3.2
11 W 0320 / 0939 / 1540 / 2203	1.0 / 3.1 / 0.8 / 3.3	**26** TH 0420 / 1041 / 1630 / 2259	0.8 / 3.1 / 0.9 / 3.3
12 TH 0404 / 1028 / 1623 / 2248	0.8 / 3.3 / 0.7 / 3.4	**27** F 0459 / 1122 / 1705 / 2336	0.7 / 3.1 / 0.9 / 3.3
13 F 0448 / 1117 / 1707 / 2333	0.5 / 3.4 / 0.6 / 3.5	**28** SA 0536 / 1200 / 1740	0.7 / 3.1 / 0.9
14 SA 0534 / 1205 / 1752	0.4 / 3.5 / 0.6	**29** SU 0011 / 0611 / 1237 / 1813	3.3 / 0.7 / 3.1 / 0.9
15 SU 0018 / 0620 / 1253 / 1837	3.6 / 0.4 / 3.5 / 0.6	**30** M 0046 / 0646 / 1312 / 1845	3.3 / 0.7 / 3.1 / 1.0

JULY

Time	m	Time	m
1 TU 0120 / 0721 / 1347 / 1918	3.3 / 0.7 / 3.0 / 1.0	**16** W 0137 / 0747 / 1417 / 1956	3.7 / 0.3 / 3.4 / 0.8
2 W 0154 / 0757 / 1423 / 1953	3.2 / 0.8 / 2.9 / 1.1	**17** TH 0225 / 0837 / 1506 / 2044	3.6 / 0.5 / 3.2 / 0.9
3 TH 0230 / 0835 / 1502 / 2031	3.1 / 0.9 / 2.9 / 1.2	**18** F 0315 / 0931 / 1559 / 2141	3.4 / 0.7 / 3.1 / 1.1
4 F 0310 / 0919 / 1546 / 2116	3.0 / 1.0 / 2.8 / 1.3	**19** SA 0411 / 1031 / 1657 / 2248	3.2 / 0.9 / 2.9 / 1.2
5 SA 0356 / 1013 / 1638 / 2219	2.9 / 1.1 / 2.7 / 1.4	**20** SU 0513 / 1138 / 1759	3.0 / 1.1 / 2.8
6 SU 0451 / 1118 / 1738 / 2338	2.8 / 1.2 / 2.7 / 1.4	**21** M 0008 / 0621 / 1255 / 1907	1.3 / 2.9 / 1.2 / 2.8
7 M 0556 / 1223 / 1842	2.8 / 1.2 / 2.8	**22** TU 0133 / 0737 / 1404 / 2016	1.3 / 2.8 / 1.2 / 2.9
8 TU 0051 / 0704 / 1327 / 1944	1.4 / 2.8 / 1.1 / 2.9	**23** W 0238 / 0847 / 1456 / 2114	1.2 / 2.9 / 1.2 / 3.1
9 W 0159 / 0811 / 1427 / 2043	1.2 / 2.9 / 1.0 / 3.1	**24** TH 0327 / 0942 / 1538 / 2200	1.0 / 3.0 / 1.2 / 3.2
10 TH 0258 / 0914 / 1519 / 2138	1.0 / 3.1 / 0.9 / 3.3	**25** F 0408 / 1027 / 1614 / 2241	0.9 / 3.0 / 1.1 / 3.3
11 F 0348 / 1010 / 1607 / 2228	0.8 / 3.3 / 0.8 / 3.4	**26** SA 0444 / 1106 / 1648 / 2317	0.8 / 3.1 / 1.0 / 3.4
12 SA 0436 / 1103 / 1653 / 2316	0.6 / 3.4 / 0.7 / 3.6	**27** SU 0518 / 1141 / 1720 / 2351	0.7 / 3.2 / 1.0 / 3.4
13 SU 0524 / 1152 / 1739	0.4 / 3.5 / 0.6	**28** M 0551 / 1215 / 1752	0.7 / 3.2 / 0.9
14 M 0003 / 0610 / 1241 / 1824	3.7 / 0.2 / 3.6 / 0.6	**29** TU 0024 / 0623 / 1248 / 1823	3.4 / 0.7 / 3.2 / 0.9
15 TU 0050 / 0658 / 1329 / 1909	3.8 / 0.2 / 3.5 / 0.6	**30** W 0057 / 0655 / 1320 / 1854	3.4 / 0.7 / 3.1 / 0.9
		31 TH 0129 / 0727 / 1353 / 1926	3.3 / 0.7 / 3.1 / 1.0

AUGUST

Time	m	Time	m
1 F 0202 / 0800 / 1428 / 2000	3.2 / 0.8 / 3.0 / 1.1	**16** SA 0251 / 0855 / 1526 / 2106	3.5 / 0.8 / 3.1 / 1.1
2 SA 0238 / 0807 / 1507 / 2038	3.1 / 0.9 / 2.9 / 1.2	**17** SU 0342 / 0948 / 1619 / 2211	3.2 / 1.1 / 3.0 / 1.3
3 SU 0319 / 0920 / 1553 / 2126	3.0 / 1.1 / 2.9 / 1.3	**18** M 0443 / 1053 / 1721 / 2335	3.0 / 1.3 / 2.8 / 1.4
4 M 0409 / 1019 / 1649 / 2240	2.9 / 1.2 / 2.8 / 1.4	**19** TU 0554 / 1216 / 1832	2.8 / 1.5 / 2.8
5 TU 0513 / 1137 / 1757	2.8 / 1.3 / 2.8	**20** W 0112 / 0714 / 1342 / 1947	1.4 / 2.7 / 1.5 / 2.9
6 W 0012 / 0630 / 1254 / 1908	1.4 / 2.8 / 1.2 / 2.9	**21** TH 0222 / 0830 / 1439 / 2050	1.2 / 2.8 / 1.4 / 3.0
7 TH 0134 / 0746 / 1405 / 2015	1.3 / 2.9 / 1.1 / 3.1	**22** F 0311 / 0925 / 1521 / 2138	1.1 / 2.9 / 1.3 / 3.1
8 F 0242 / 0857 / 1504 / 2116	1.0 / 3.1 / 1.0 / 3.3	**23** SA 0349 / 1007 / 1555 / 2218	1.0 / 3.0 / 1.2 / 3.3
9 SA 0336 / 0957 / 1553 / 2210	0.7 / 3.3 / 0.8 / 3.5	**24** SU 0423 / 1044 / 1627 / 2254	0.8 / 3.1 / 1.0 / 3.4
10 SU 0424 / 1049 / 1639 / 2259	0.5 / 3.5 / 0.7 / 3.7	**25** M 0455 / 1118 / 1658 / 2328	0.7 / 3.2 / 1.0 / 3.4
11 M 0510 / 1137 / 1723 / 2347	0.3 / 3.6 / 0.6 / 3.8	**26** TU 0526 / 1150 / 1728 / 2359	0.7 / 3.3 / 1.0 / 3.5
12 TU 0555 / 1223 / 1806	0.2 / 3.7 / 0.5	**27** W 0556 / 1221 / 1758	0.6 / 3.3 / 0.8
13 W 0033 / 0639 / 1309 / 1849	3.9 / 0.2 / 3.6 / 0.5	**28** TH 0031 / 0626 / 1252 / 1828	3.5 / 0.6 / 3.3 / 0.9
14 TH 0118 / 0723 / 1354 / 1932	3.8 / 0.3 / 3.5 / 0.7	**29** F 0102 / 0657 / 1323 / 1900	3.3 / 0.7 / 3.2 / 0.9
15 F 0204 / 0808 / 1438 / 2016	3.7 / 0.5 / 3.3 / 0.8	**30** SA 0135 / 0729 / 1357 / 1933	3.3 / 0.8 / 3.2 / 1.0
		31 SU 0210 / 0803 / 1434 / 2010	3.2 / 0.9 / 3.1 / 1.1

Chart Datum: 1·71 metres below Ordnance Datum (Newlyn)
HAT is 4·0 metres above Chart Datum

SCOTLAND – WICK
LAT 58°26′N   LONG 3°05′W
TIMES AND HEIGHTS OF HIGH AND LOW WATERS
2014

SEPTEMBER
Time	m	Time	m
1 0251	3.1	**16** 0412	2.9
0842	1.1	1001	1.5
M 1518	3.0	TU 1641	2.9
2055	1.2	☽ 2259	1.4
2 0340	3.0	**17** 0523	2.7
0935	1.3	1126	1.6
TU 1613	2.9	W 1752	2.8
☽ 2201	1.4		
3 0445	2.9	**18** 0040	1.4
1101	1.4	0643	2.7
W 1722	2.9	TH 1309	1.6
2347	1.4	1909	2.8
4 0608	2.8	**19** 0155	1.3
1231	1.4	0803	2.8
TH 1840	2.9	F 1414	1.5
		2018	3.0
5 0118	1.2	**20** 0244	1.2
0730	2.9	0859	2.9
F 1349	1.3	SA 1456	1.4
1952	3.1	2109	3.1
6 0228	1.0	**21** 0322	1.0
0844	3.1	0941	3.0
SA 1449	1.1	SU 1531	1.2
2056	3.3	2150	3.2
7 0321	0.7	**22** 0355	0.9
0942	3.3	1017	3.2
SU 1537	0.9	M 1602	1.1
2151	3.6	2226	3.4
8 0408	0.4	**23** 0426	0.8
1032	3.5	1049	3.3
M 1621	0.7	TU 1633	1.0
2241	3.8	2259	3.4
9 0451	0.3	**24** 0457	0.7
1118	3.7	1121	3.3
TU 1703	0.5	W 1703	0.9
○ 2327	3.9	● 2332	3.5
10 0534	0.2	**25** 0527	0.7
1202	3.7	1152	3.4
W 1745	0.5	TH 1733	0.8
11 0012	3.9	**26** 0004	3.5
0615	0.2	0557	0.7
TH 1245	3.7	F 1223	3.4
1826	0.5	1804	0.8
12 0057	3.9	**27** 0037	3.5
0656	0.4	0628	0.7
F 1326	3.5	SA 1256	3.4
1907	0.6	1837	0.9
13 0140	3.7	**28** 0111	3.4
0736	0.6	0701	0.8
SA 1408	3.4	SU 1330	3.3
1949	0.8	1911	0.9
14 0225	3.4	**29** 0149	3.3
0817	0.9	0736	1.0
SU 1451	3.2	M 1408	3.3
2035	1.1	1950	1.0
15 0314	3.2	**30** 0231	3.2
0901	1.2	0817	1.1
M 1540	3.0	TU 1452	3.1
2135	1.3	2038	1.2

OCTOBER
Time	m	Time	m
1 0323	3.0	**16** 0447	2.7
0910	1.3	1028	1.7
W 1547	3.0	TH 1707	2.8
☽ 2147	1.3	2345	1.5
2 0431	2.9	**17** 0601	2.7
1039	1.5	1204	1.8
TH 1656	3.0	F 1821	2.8
2334	1.3		
3 0555	2.9	**18** 0109	1.4
1213	1.5	0717	2.7
F 1816	3.0	SA 1331	1.7
		1930	2.9
4 0102	1.2	**19** 0205	1.3
0717	3.0	0819	2.9
SA 1331	1.3	SU 1422	1.5
1930	3.1	2028	3.0
5 0211	0.9	**20** 0247	1.1
0828	3.2	0905	3.0
SU 1431	1.1	M 1500	1.3
2035	3.4	2113	3.2
6 0303	0.7	**21** 0322	1.0
0924	3.4	0943	3.2
M 1519	0.9	TU 1533	1.2
2131	3.6	2152	3.3
7 0348	0.5	**22** 0355	0.9
1013	3.6	1017	3.3
TU 1602	0.8	W 1605	1.1
2221	3.8	2228	3.4
8 0430	0.4	**23** 0426	0.8
1057	3.7	1050	3.4
W 1643	0.6	TH 1637	0.9
○ 2307	3.9	● 2303	3.5
9 0510	0.4	**24** 0457	0.7
1139	3.7	1123	3.5
TH 1724	0.6	F 1709	0.9
2351	3.9	2338	3.5
10 0550	0.4	**25** 0529	0.7
1219	3.7	1156	3.5
F 1805	0.6	SA 1743	0.8
11 0034	3.8	**26** 0014	3.5
0628	0.6	0603	0.8
SA 1259	3.6	SU 1231	3.5
1845	0.7	1818	0.8
12 0117	3.6	**27** 0053	3.5
0705	0.8	0639	0.9
SU 1338	3.4	M 1308	3.5
1926	0.9	1857	0.9
13 0200	3.4	**28** 0134	3.4
0743	1.1	0718	1.0
M 1419	3.3	TU 1349	3.4
2010	1.1	1940	1.0
14 0247	3.1	**29** 0220	3.3
0822	1.3	0802	1.2
TU 1503	3.1	W 1435	3.3
2103	1.3	2032	1.1
15 0340	2.9	**30** 0315	3.1
0911	1.6	0858	1.4
W 1558	2.9	TH 1529	3.1
☽ 2218	1.4	2146	1.4
		31 0422	3.0
		1022	1.5
		F 1637	3.1
		☽ 2318	1.2

NOVEMBER
Time	m	Time	m
1 0542	3.0	**16** 0618	2.7
1149	1.5	1215	1.8
SA 1754	3.1	SU 1832	2.9
2 0040	1.1	**17** 0107	1.4
0657	3.0	0721	2.8
SU 1307	1.4	M 1329	1.6
1906	3.2	1933	3.0
3 0148	0.9	**18** 0201	1.2
0806	3.2	0816	3.0
M 1408	1.2	TU 1420	1.5
2012	3.4	2027	3.1
4 0242	0.8	**19** 0243	1.1
0903	3.4	0901	3.1
TU 1458	1.0	W 1501	1.3
2110	3.5	2113	3.2
5 0327	0.7	**20** 0320	1.0
0951	3.5	0941	3.3
W 1543	0.9	TH 1537	1.2
2201	3.6	2155	3.3
6 0408	0.6	**21** 0355	0.9
1035	3.6	1018	3.4
TH 1625	0.8	F 1612	1.0
○ 2248	3.7	2235	3.4
7 0448	0.6	**22** 0430	0.9
1116	3.7	1055	3.5
F 1706	0.7	SA 1648	0.9
2333	3.7	● 2315	3.5
8 0526	0.7	**23** 0506	0.8
1156	3.7	1133	3.6
SA 1747	0.7	SU 1726	0.8
		2356	3.6
9 0015	3.6	**24** 0543	0.8
0603	0.8	1211	3.7
SU 1235	3.6	M 1806	0.8
1827	0.9		
10 0057	3.5	**25** 0039	3.5
0639	1.0	0623	0.9
M 1312	3.5	TU 1253	3.6
1907	0.9	1849	0.8
11 0138	3.3	**26** 0125	3.5
0715	1.2	0707	1.0
TU 1351	3.4	W 1336	3.6
1949	1.0	1937	0.8
12 0221	3.1	**27** 0213	3.4
0751	1.4	0754	1.1
W 1432	3.2	TH 1423	3.5
2035	1.2	2031	0.9
13 0308	3.0	**28** 0307	3.2
0833	1.5	0849	1.3
TH 1519	3.1	F 1516	3.4
2134	1.3	2139	1.0
14 0404	2.8	**29** 0410	3.1
0930	1.7	0959	1.4
F 1617	2.9	SA 1619	3.3
☽ 2244	1.4	● 2255	1.1
15 0510	2.7	**30** 0520	3.0
1052	1.8	1118	1.5
SA 1725	2.9	SU 1730	3.2
2358	1.4		

DECEMBER
Time	m	Time	m
1 0010	1.1	**16** 0617	2.8
0630	3.1	1215	1.7
M 1234	1.4	TU 1832	2.9
1839	3.2		
2 0121	1.0	**17** 0101	1.4
0738	3.1	0717	2.9
TU 1343	1.3	W 1326	1.6
1947	3.3	1933	3.0
3 0220	1.0	**18** 0158	1.3
0839	3.3	0813	3.0
W 1440	1.2	TH 1423	1.5
2050	3.4	2030	3.1
4 0308	0.9	**19** 0245	1.2
0930	3.4	0902	3.2
TH 1528	1.0	F 1509	1.3
2145	3.5	2123	3.2
5 0350	0.9	**20** 0327	1.1
1016	3.5	0947	3.4
F 1612	0.9	SA 1550	1.1
2234	3.5	2211	3.4
6 0429	0.9	**21** 0407	0.9
1058	3.6	1030	3.5
SA 1653	0.8	SU 1631	0.9
○ 2318	3.5	2257	3.5
7 0507	0.9	**22** 0447	0.9
1137	3.6	1113	3.7
SU 1734	0.8	M 1714	0.7
		● 2342	3.6
8 0000	3.5	**23** 0529	0.8
0543	1.0	1156	3.7
M 1215	3.6	TU 1757	0.6
1813	0.8		
9 0040	3.4	**24** 0028	3.6
0618	1.1	0612	0.8
TU 1252	3.5	W 1240	3.8
1851	0.9	1843	0.6
10 0118	3.3	**25** 0115	3.6
0653	1.2	0657	0.9
W 1328	3.5	TH 1325	3.8
1929	1.0	1931	0.6
11 0157	3.2	**26** 0203	3.5
0727	1.3	0743	1.0
TH 1405	3.3	F 1412	3.7
2009	1.1	2022	0.7
12 0237	3.0	**27** 0255	3.3
0803	1.4	0833	1.1
F 1445	3.2	SA 1502	3.5
2053	1.2	2120	0.8
13 0322	2.9	**28** 0350	3.2
0845	1.5	0931	1.3
SA 1531	3.1	SU 1559	3.4
2146	1.3	☽ 2225	1.0
14 0414	2.8	**29** 0452	3.1
0941	1.7	1041	1.4
SU 1624	3.0	M 1703	3.3
☽ 2250	1.4	2336	1.1
15 0514	2.8	**30** 0558	3.0
1048	1.7	1157	1.4
M 1727	2.9	TU 1812	3.2
2356	1.4		
		31 0050	1.2
		0705	3.0
		W 1317	1.4
		1923	3.2

Chart Datum: 1·71 metres below Ordnance Datum (Newlyn)
HAT is 4·0 metres above Chart Datum

TIDES

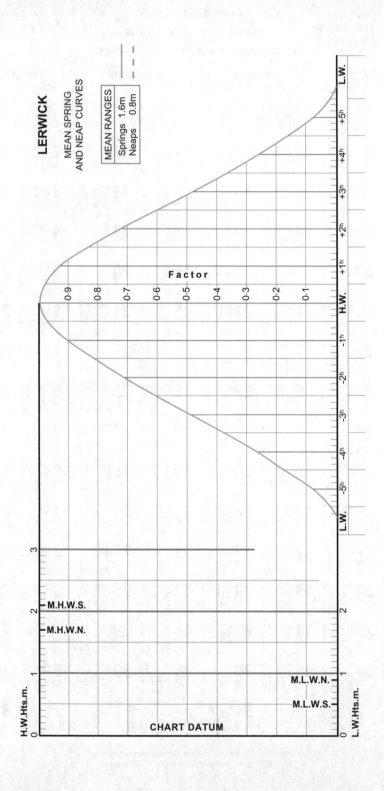

LERWICK

MEAN SPRING
AND NEAP CURVES

MEAN RANGES	
Springs	1.6m
Neaps	0.8m

SCOTLAND – LERWICK

TIME ZONE (UT) — For Summer Time add ONE hour in **non-shaded areas**

LAT 60°09'N   LONG 1°08'W

TIMES AND HEIGHTS OF HIGH AND LOW WATERS

Dates in amber are **SPRINGS**
Dates in yellow are **NEAPS**

2014

JANUARY

Date				
1 W	0412 0.6	1641 0.4	● 2302 2.3	
2 TH	0459 0.6	1113 2.5	1729 0.3	2355 2.3
3 F	0545 0.6	1816 0.3		
4 SA	0045 2.3	0630 0.6	1251 2.5	1903 0.3
5 SU	0135 2.2	0716 0.6	1340 2.4	1951 0.4
6 M	0223 2.1	0803 0.7	1429 2.3	2042 0.5
7 TU	0312 2.0	0853 0.8	1520 2.1	2138 0.7
8 W	0404 1.9	0952 0.9	1615 2.0	● 2245 0.8
9 TH	0503 1.8	1109 1.0	1722 1.9	
10 F	0004 0.9	0613 1.8	1238 1.0	1839 1.8
11 SA	0116 1.0	0721 1.8	1349 1.0	1950 1.8
12 SU	0213 1.0	0820 1.9	1445 0.9	2049 1.9
13 M	0301 0.9	0910 2.0	1530 0.8	2138 1.9
14 TU	0341 0.9	0952 2.1	1609 0.7	2219 2.0
15 W	0416 0.9	1030 2.2	1644 0.7	2256 2.0
16 TH	0449 0.8	1106 2.2	1716 0.6	○ 2331 2.0
17 F	0521 0.8	1140 2.2	1748 0.6	
18 SA	0004 2.0	0551 0.8	1212 2.2	1820 0.6
19 SU	0037 2.0	0621 0.8	1242 2.2	1852 0.6
20 M	0108 2.0	0653 0.8	1314 2.1	1926 0.6
21 TU	0141 2.0	0727 0.8	1348 2.1	2003 0.7
22 W	0218 1.9	0805 0.9	1427 2.0	2045 0.8
23 TH	0302 1.9	0850 0.9	1515 1.9	2133 0.8
24 F	0354 1.8	0945 1.0	1613 1.9	○ 2233 0.9
25 SA	0455 1.8	1100 1.0	1722 1.8	2353 0.9
26 SU	0606 1.8	1236 1.0	1844 1.8	
27 M	0110 0.9	0721 1.9	1350 0.9	2000 1.9
28 TU	0215 0.8	0825 2.0	1450 0.7	2103 2.0
29 W	0310 0.7	0920 2.2	1542 0.5	2159 2.2
30 TH	0359 0.6	1012 2.3	1630 0.3	● 2252 2.3
31 F	0445 0.5	1101 2.4	1716 0.2	2342 2.3

FEBRUARY

Date				
1 SA	0529 0.5	1149 2.5	1800 0.2	
2 SU	0028 2.3	0612 0.4	1235 2.5	1844 0.2
3 M	0113 2.2	0655 0.5	1320 2.4	1927 0.3
4 TU	0156 2.1	0738 0.6	1405 2.3	2012 0.5
5 W	0239 2.0	0824 0.7	1451 2.1	2059 0.7
6 TH	0324 1.9	0915 0.8	1540 1.9	○ 2153 0.9
7 F	0415 1.8	1023 1.0	1639 1.8	2308 1.0
8 SA	0521 1.7	1201 1.0	1800 1.7	
9 SU	0039 1.1	0643 1.7	1325 1.0	1925 1.7
10 M	0150 1.0	0753 1.8	1427 0.9	2030 1.7
11 TU	0243 1.0	0847 1.9	1513 0.8	2118 1.8
12 W	0324 0.9	0931 2.0	1551 0.7	2159 1.9
13 TH	0359 0.8	1010 2.1	1623 0.6	2235 2.0
14 F	0430 0.7	1045 2.1	1654 0.5	○ 2308 2.0
15 SA	0500 0.7	1118 2.2	1724 0.5	2340 2.0
16 SU	0529 0.6	1149 2.2	1755 0.5	
17 M	0011 2.0	0559 0.6	1220 2.2	1826 0.5
18 TU	0041 2.0	0630 0.6	1250 2.1	1859 0.5
19 W	0112 2.0	0704 0.6	1323 2.1	1934 0.6
20 TH	0147 2.0	0742 0.7	1401 2.0	2014 0.6
21 F	0227 1.9	0825 0.8	1446 1.9	2059 0.8
22 SA	0316 1.8	0918 0.9	1544 1.8	○ 2156 0.9
23 SU	0416 1.8	1028 0.9	1656 1.7	2315 0.9
24 M	0530 1.7	1210 0.9	1824 1.7	
25 TU	0050 0.9	0655 1.8	1334 0.8	1949 1.8
26 W	0201 0.8	0808 1.9	1437 0.6	2053 1.9
27 TH	0257 0.7	0906 2.1	1529 0.4	2148 2.1
28 F	0345 0.6	0957 2.2	1615 0.2	2237 2.2

MARCH

Date				
1 SA	0429 0.4	1046 2.3	1658 0.1	● 2323 2.2
2 SU	0511 0.3	1131 2.4	1739 0.1	
3 M	0006 2.2	0551 0.3	1215 2.4	1820 0.2
4 TU	0047 2.2	0632 0.4	1258 2.3	1900 0.3
5 W	0126 2.1	0714 0.5	1339 2.2	1941 0.5
6 TH	0204 2.0	0757 0.6	1422 2.0	2023 0.7
7 F	0245 1.9	0844 0.7	1508 1.8	2108 0.9
8 SA	0330 1.8	0944 0.9	1600 1.7	○ 2210 1.0
9 SU	0425 1.7	1114 0.9	1713 1.5	2349 1.1
10 M	0551 1.6	1247 0.9	1853 1.5	
11 TU	0116 1.1	0718 1.6	1356 0.9	2001 1.6
12 W	0216 1.0	0816 1.7	1444 0.8	2050 1.7
13 TH	0259 0.9	0902 1.8	1522 0.7	2130 1.8
14 F	0333 0.8	0941 1.9	1554 0.6	2205 1.9
15 SA	0404 0.7	1017 2.0	1624 0.5	2239 1.9
16 SU	0433 0.6	1051 2.1	1655 0.4	○ 2311 2.0
17 M	0504 0.5	1123 2.1	1726 0.4	2341 2.0
18 TU	0536 0.5	1154 2.1	1758 0.4	
19 W	0012 2.0	0609 0.5	1227 2.1	1832 0.4
20 TH	0045 2.0	0644 0.5	1302 2.1	1909 0.5
21 F	0120 2.0	0724 0.5	1342 2.0	1949 0.6
22 SA	0200 1.9	0809 0.6	1430 1.9	2036 0.7
23 SU	0248 1.8	0903 0.7	1530 1.8	2134 0.8
24 M	0349 1.7	1013 0.8	1645 1.7	○ 2254 0.9
25 TU	0504 1.7	1155 0.7	1814 1.6	
26 W	0034 0.9	0634 1.7	1319 0.6	1937 1.7
27 TH	0145 0.8	0750 1.8	1420 0.5	2039 1.9
28 F	0240 0.6	0848 2.0	1511 0.3	2130 2.0
29 SA	0327 0.5	0939 2.1	1555 0.2	2217 2.1
30 SU	0409 0.4	1027 2.2	1636 0.2	● 2300 2.1
31 M	0450 0.3	1111 2.3	1716 0.2	2340 2.1

APRIL

Date				
1 TU	0531 0.3	1153 2.2	1755 0.2	
2 W	0018 2.1	0611 0.3	1235 2.2	1833 0.4
3 TH	0054 2.1	0651 0.4	1315 2.0	1911 0.5
4 F	0131 2.0	0733 0.5	1356 1.9	1949 0.7
5 SA	0209 1.9	0818 0.6	1439 1.7	2030 0.9
6 SU	0251 1.8	0911 0.8	1528 1.6	2122 1.0
7 M	0340 1.6	1025 0.8	1628 1.5	○ 2248 1.0
8 TU	0442 1.6	1149 0.8	1801 1.5	
9 W	0021 1.0	0624 1.5	1303 0.8	1920 1.5
10 TH	0132 1.0	0735 1.6	1358 0.7	2012 1.6
11 F	0221 0.9	0824 1.7	1440 0.6	2053 1.7
12 SA	0258 0.7	0905 1.8	1515 0.5	2129 1.8
13 SU	0331 0.6	0943 1.9	1549 0.4	2204 1.9
14 M	0404 0.5	1018 2.0	1622 0.4	2238 2.0
15 TU	0437 0.5	1054 2.0	1657 0.3	○ 2311 2.0
16 W	0512 0.4	1130 2.1	1732 0.3	2346 2.1
17 TH	0549 0.4	1207 2.1	1809 0.4	
18 F	0021 2.1	0628 0.4	1248 2.0	1848 0.4
19 SA	0100 2.0	0711 0.6	1333 1.9	1932 0.6
20 SU	0142 1.9	0800 0.6	1426 1.8	2022 0.7
21 M	0232 1.9	0856 0.5	1528 1.7	2121 0.8
22 TU	0335 1.8	1007 0.6	1639 1.6	○ 2240 0.9
23 W	0448 1.7	1139 0.6	1802 1.6	
24 TH	0013 0.8	0612 1.7	1257 0.5	1917 1.7
25 F	0123 0.7	0727 1.8	1358 0.4	2017 1.8
26 SA	0219 0.6	0827 1.9	1449 0.4	2107 1.9
27 SU	0306 0.5	0919 2.0	1533 0.3	2153 2.0
28 M	0350 0.4	1007 2.1	1614 0.3	2235 2.0
29 TU	0431 0.3	1051 2.1	1653 0.3	● 2314 2.1
30 W	0512 0.3	1133 2.1	1731 0.4	2351 2.1

Chart Datum: 1·22 metres below Ordnance Datum (Local)
HAT is 2·5 metres above Chart Datum

TIDES

TIME ZONE (UT) For Summer Time add ONE hour in non-shaded areas	SCOTLAND – LERWICK LAT 60°09'N LONG 1°08'W TIMES AND HEIGHTS OF HIGH AND LOW WATERS	Dates in amber are SPRINGS Dates in yellow are NEAPS 2014

MAY

Day	Time m	Time m	Time m	Time m	Day	Time m	Time m	Time m	Time m
1 TH	0552 0.3	1213 2.0	1808 0.5		16 F	0532 0.3	1152 2.1	1751 0.4	
2 F	0026 2.0	0631 0.4	1253 1.9	1845 0.6	17 SA	0003 2.1	0615 0.3	1239 2.0	1834 0.4
3 SA	0103 2.0	0712 0.5	1333 1.8	1921 0.7	18 SU	0047 2.1	0702 0.3	1330 2.0	1920 0.5
4 SU	0140 1.9	0755 0.6	1415 1.7	2000 0.8	19 M	0134 2.0	0753 0.3	1425 1.9	2012 0.6
5 M	0220 1.8	0842 0.7	1500 1.6	2045 0.9	20 TU	0227 1.9	0849 0.4	1524 1.8	2110 0.7
6 TU	0305 1.7	0940 0.7	1550 1.5	2149 1.0	21 W	0327 1.8	0956 0.5	1627 1.7	2219 0.8
7 W	0357 1.6	1050 0.8	1651 1.5	☽ 2316 1.0	22 TH	0433 1.8	1115 0.5	1738 1.7	2342 0.8
8 TH	0501 1.5	1157 0.8	1816 1.5		23 F	0548 1.7	1230 0.5	1849 1.7	
9 F	0028 1.0	0631 1.5	1257 0.7	1921 1.6	24 SA	0055 0.7	0701 1.7	1333 0.5	1949 1.8
10 SA	0127 0.9	0735 1.6	1348 0.6	2008 1.6	25 SU	0156 0.7	0803 1.8	1426 0.5	2041 1.8
11 SU	0214 0.8	0822 1.7	1431 0.6	2048 1.8	26 M	0247 0.6	0858 1.9	1512 0.5	2128 1.9
12 M	0254 0.7	0904 1.8	1511 0.5	2127 1.9	27 TU	0333 0.5	0948 1.9	1553 0.5	2211 2.0
13 TU	0333 0.6	0945 1.9	2205 2.0		28 W	0416 0.4	1034 1.9	1632 0.5	2251 2.0
14 W	0412 0.4	1026 2.0	1629 0.4	○ 2243 2.1	29 TH	0456 0.4	1116 1.9	1710 0.5	2328 2.0
15 TH	0451 0.4	1108 2.0	1709 0.4	2323 2.1	30 F	0536 0.4	1156 1.9	1747 0.6	
					31 SA	0005 2.0	0614 0.4	1235 1.9	1822 0.6

JUNE

Day	Time m	Time m	Time m	Time m	Day	Time m	Time m	Time m	Time m
1 SU	0041 2.0	0653 0.5	1313 1.8	1858 0.7	16 M	0037 2.2	0653 0.2	1324 2.0	1909 0.5
2 M	0117 1.9	0732 0.5	1351 1.7	1934 0.8	17 TU	0128 2.1	0743 0.2	1417 1.9	1959 0.6
3 TU	0154 1.8	0814 0.6	1432 1.7	2014 0.8	18 W	0220 2.1	0836 0.3	1510 1.9	2052 0.7
4 W	0235 1.8	0859 0.7	1515 1.6	☽ 2101 0.9	19 TH	0315 2.0	0935 0.4	1605 1.8	2152 0.7
5 TH	0321 1.7	0953 0.7	1604 1.6	☽ 2202 0.9	20 F	0413 1.9	1043 0.5	1707 1.7	2306 0.8
6 F	0413 1.6	1056 0.7	1700 1.5	2322 0.9	21 SA	0520 1.8	1158 0.6	1814 1.7	
7 SA	0514 1.6	1200 0.7	1807 1.6		22 SU	0026 0.8	0632 1.8	1307 0.7	1918 1.7
8 SU	0031 0.9	0626 1.6	1257 0.7	1913 1.6	23 M	0134 0.7	0740 1.8	1404 0.7	2015 1.8
9 M	0128 0.8	0733 1.7	1349 0.6	2005 1.7	24 TU	0231 0.7	0840 1.8	1454 0.7	2106 1.9
10 TU	0218 0.7	0826 1.8	1436 0.6	2051 1.9	25 W	0320 0.6	0934 1.8	1537 0.7	2152 2.0
11 W	0304 0.6	0915 1.9	1522 0.5	2135 2.0	26 TH	0404 0.5	1020 1.9	1617 0.6	2233 2.0
12 TH	0349 0.5	1003 2.0	1606 0.5	2220 2.1	27 F	0444 0.5	1101 1.9	1654 0.6	○ 2311 2.0
13 F	0433 0.4	1051 2.1	1651 0.4	2304 2.2	28 SA	0521 0.5	1140 1.9	○ 2347 2.0	
14 SA	0519 0.3	1141 2.1	1736 0.4	○ 2350 2.2	29 SU	0557 0.4	1216 1.9	1803 0.7	
15 SU	0605 0.2	1232 2.1	1822 0.4		30 M	0022 2.0	0632 0.5	1251 1.9	1836 0.7

JULY

Day	Time m	Time m	Time m	Time m	Day	Time m	Time m	Time m	Time m
1 TU	0056 2.0	0707 0.5	1326 1.8	1909 0.7	16 W	0116 2.3	0726 0.2	1359 2.0	1940 0.5
2 W	0130 1.9	0743 0.5	1401 1.8	1944 0.8	17 TH	0205 2.2	0815 0.3	1447 1.9	2028 0.6
3 TH	0206 1.9	0822 0.6	1440 1.7	2023 0.8	18 F	0255 2.1	0907 0.5	1537 1.8	2122 0.7
4 F	0247 1.8	0905 0.7	1523 1.7	2110 0.9	19 SA	0348 1.9	1007 0.6	1632 1.8	☽ 2230 0.8
5 SA	0334 1.7	0956 0.7	1613 1.6	☽ 2208 0.9	20 SU	0450 1.8	1121 0.8	1736 1.7	2357 0.8
6 SU	0428 1.7	1059 0.8	1710 1.6	2327 0.9	21 M	0603 1.7	1239 0.8	1847 1.7	
7 M	0531 1.7	1208 0.8	1815 1.7		22 TU	0115 0.8	0719 1.7	1345 0.9	1951 1.8
8 TU	0044 0.9	0644 1.7	1311 0.7	1922 1.7	23 W	0219 0.8	0825 1.7	1438 0.8	2047 1.9
9 W	0146 0.8	0753 1.8	1407 0.7	2020 1.9	24 TH	0309 0.7	0920 1.8	1523 0.8	2134 2.0
10 TH	0240 0.7	0851 1.9	1459 0.6	2111 2.0	25 F	0352 0.6	1004 1.8	1602 0.7	2215 2.0
11 F	0330 0.5	0945 2.0	1549 0.5	2200 2.0	26 SA	0429 0.5	1044 1.9	1637 0.7	● 2253 2.1
12 SA	0419 0.3	1038 2.1	1636 0.5	○ 2249 2.2	27 SU	0503 0.5	1120 1.9	1710 0.7	2328 2.1
13 SU	0506 0.2	1130 2.2	1723 0.4	2338 2.3	28 M	0536 0.5	1154 1.9	1741 0.7	
14 M	0553 0.1	1221 2.2	1808 0.4		29 TU	0001 2.1	0608 0.5	1226 1.9	1811 0.6
15 TU	0026 2.3	0639 0.1	1310 2.1	1853 0.4	30 W	0033 2.1	0640 0.5	1258 1.9	1843 0.7
					31 TH	0104 2.0	0713 0.5	1329 1.9	1915 0.7

AUGUST

Day	Time m	Time m	Time m	Time m	Day	Time m	Time m	Time m	Time m
1 F	0136 2.0	0748 0.6	1404 1.8	1952 0.8	16 SA	0230 2.1	0836 0.6	1504 1.9	2054 0.7
2 SA	0213 1.9	0827 0.7	1444 1.8	2033 0.8	17 SU	0321 2.0	0929 0.8	1554 1.8	☽ 2157 0.7
3 SU	0257 1.8	0911 0.7	1531 1.7	2124 0.9	18 M	0418 1.8	1038 0.9	1654 1.7	2330 0.9
4 M	0350 1.8	1005 0.8	1627 1.7	☽ 2231 0.9	19 TU	0532 1.7	1209 1.0	1812 1.7	
5 TU	0453 1.7	1118 0.9	1731 1.7		20 W	0057 0.9	0659 1.6	1324 1.0	1926 1.8
6 W	0003 0.9	0608 1.7	1239 0.9	1845 1.8	21 TH	0203 0.8	0809 1.7	1421 1.0	2025 1.9
7 TH	0121 0.8	0729 1.8	1345 0.8	1954 1.9	22 F	0253 0.7	0901 1.8	1506 0.9	2112 1.9
8 F	0222 0.8	0835 1.9	1443 0.7	2052 2.0	23 SA	0333 0.7	0943 1.8	1543 0.8	2153 2.0
9 SA	0316 0.6	0932 2.0	1534 0.6	2144 2.2	24 SU	0408 0.6	1020 1.9	1616 0.7	2230 2.1
10 SU	0405 0.3	1024 2.1	1621 0.5	○ 2234 2.3	25 M	0439 0.5	1054 2.0	1646 0.7	● 2304 2.1
11 M	0451 0.2	1115 2.2	1706 0.4	2322 2.4	26 TU	0510 0.5	1126 2.0	1716 0.6	2336 2.2
12 TU	0536 0.1	1203 2.2	1750 0.4		27 W	0540 0.5	1157 2.0	1746 0.6	
13 W	0010 2.2	0620 0.1	1249 2.2	1833 0.4	28 TH	0006 2.1	0610 0.6	1227 2.0	1816 0.6
14 TH	0057 2.1	0704 0.2	1334 2.1	1917 0.5	29 F	0036 2.1	0642 0.6	1257 2.0	1849 0.7
15 F	0143 2.3	0749 0.4	1418 2.1	2003 0.6	30 SA	0108 2.1	0716 0.6	1330 2.0	1925 0.7
					31 SU	0144 2.0	0754 0.7	1408 1.9	2006 0.8

Chart Datum: 1·22 metres below Ordnance Datum (Local)
HAT is 2·5 metres above Chart Datum

TIME ZONE (UT)
For Summer Time add ONE hour in **non-shaded areas**

SCOTLAND – LERWICK
LAT 60°09'N   LONG 1°08'W
TIMES AND HEIGHTS OF HIGH AND LOW WATERS

Dates in amber are **SPRINGS**
Dates in yellow are **NEAPS**
2014

SEPTEMBER

Time m		Time m	
1 M	0227 1.9 / 0837 0.8 / 1454 1.9 / 2056 0.9	**16** TU	0347 1.8 / 0954 1.0 / 1611 1.8 / ☽ 2256 1.0
2 TU	0320 1.8 / 0929 0.9 / 1550 1.8 / ☽ 2200 0.9	**17** W	0457 1.7 / 1129 1.1 / 1729 1.7
3 W	0427 1.7 / 1040 0.9 / 1657 1.8 / 2334 0.9	**18** TH	0028 0.9 / 0630 1.6 / 1255 1.1 / 1855 1.8
4 TH	0547 1.7 / 1215 1.0 / 1817 1.8	**19** F	0136 0.9 / 0743 1.7 / 1356 1.0 / 1956 1.8
5 F	0103 0.8 / 0714 1.8 / 1330 0.9 / 1934 1.9	**20** SA	0227 0.8 / 0833 1.8 / 1441 0.9 / 2044 1.9
6 SA	0207 0.7 / 0822 1.9 / 1428 0.8 / 2035 2.1	**21** SU	0306 0.7 / 0914 1.9 / 1518 0.9 / 2125 2.0
7 SU	0301 0.5 / 0918 2.1 / 1518 0.6 / 2128 2.2	**22** M	0339 0.6 / 0950 2.0 / 1549 0.8 / 2201 2.1
8 M	0348 0.3 / 1008 2.2 / 1603 0.5 / 2217 2.3	**23** TU	0409 0.6 / 1024 2.0 / 1619 0.7 / 2235 2.1
9 TU	0432 0.2 / 1055 2.3 / 1647 0.4 / ○ 2304 2.4	**24** W	0439 0.5 / 1055 2.1 / 1649 0.6 / ● 2307 2.2
10 W	0515 0.1 / 1140 2.3 / 1729 0.4 / 2349 2.5	**25** TH	0510 0.5 / 1126 2.1 / 1720 0.6 / 2338 2.2
11 TH	0557 0.2 / 1223 2.3 / 1811 0.4	**26** F	0541 0.5 / 1156 2.1 / 1752 0.6
12 F	0034 2.4 / 0639 0.3 / 1305 2.2 / 1854 0.4	**27** SA	0010 2.2 / 0614 0.5 / 1227 2.1 / 1826 0.6
13 SA	0119 2.3 / 0721 0.5 / 1346 2.1 / 1938 0.6	**28** SU	0044 2.1 / 0649 0.6 / 1301 2.1 / 1904 0.7
14 SU	0204 2.1 / 0804 0.7 / 1429 2.0 / 2027 0.7	**29** M	0122 2.1 / 0727 0.7 / 1339 2.0 / 1947 0.7
15 M	0253 1.9 / 0852 0.9 / 1516 1.9 / 2127 0.9	**30** TU	0206 2.0 / 0811 0.8 / 1424 2.0 / 2038 0.8

OCTOBER

Time m		Time m	
1 W	0303 1.9 / 0905 0.9 / 1522 1.9 / ☽ 2143 0.9	**16** TH	0417 1.7 / 1034 1.2 / 1635 1.8 / 2338 1.0
2 TH	0413 1.8 / 1017 1.0 / 1632 1.8 / 2316 0.9	**17** F	0543 1.6 / 1206 1.2 / 1807 1.7
3 F	0535 1.7 / 1157 1.0 / 1755 1.8	**18** SA	0051 0.9 / 0702 1.7 / 1317 1.1 / 1918 1.8
4 SA	0046 0.8 / 0702 1.8 / 1313 0.9 / 1915 1.9	**19** SU	0147 0.9 / 0756 1.8 / 1407 1.0 / 2009 1.9
5 SU	0150 0.6 / 0807 2.0 / 1411 0.8 / 2017 2.1	**20** M	0228 0.8 / 0838 1.9 / 1445 0.9 / 2051 2.0
6 M	0243 0.5 / 0900 2.1 / 1500 0.7 / 2109 2.2	**21** TU	0303 0.7 / 0915 2.0 / 1518 0.8 / 2128 2.1
7 TU	0329 0.4 / 0948 2.2 / 1549 0.5 / 2157 2.3	**22** W	0335 0.6 / 0950 2.1 / 1550 0.7 / 2204 2.1
8 W	0412 0.3 / 1033 2.3 / 1626 0.4 / ○ 2244 2.4	**23** TH	0407 0.6 / 1023 2.1 / 1622 0.7 / ● 2238 2.2
9 TH	0453 0.3 / 1115 2.3 / 1708 0.4 / 2329 2.4	**24** F	0440 0.5 / 1055 2.2 / 1656 0.6 / 2312 2.2
10 F	0534 0.3 / 1156 2.3 / 1750 0.4	**25** SA	0514 0.5 / 1128 2.2 / 1731 0.6 / 2348 2.2
11 SA	0012 2.4 / 0613 0.5 / 1236 2.2 / 1832 0.5	**26** SU	0550 0.6 / 1202 2.2 / 1809 0.6
12 SU	0056 2.2 / 0654 0.6 / 1315 2.2 / 1916 0.6	**27** M	0026 2.2 / 0627 0.6 / 1239 2.2 / 1849 0.6
13 M	0140 2.1 / 0735 0.8 / 1356 2.1 / 2003 0.7	**28** TU	0108 2.1 / 0708 0.7 / 1319 2.1 / 1935 0.7
14 TU	0227 2.0 / 0818 1.0 / 1440 1.9 / 2059 0.9	**29** W	0157 2.0 / 0755 0.8 / 1406 2.1 / 2028 0.7
15 W	0317 1.8 / 0912 1.0 / 1531 1.8 / ☽ 2213 1.0	**30** TH	0257 1.9 / 0850 0.8 / 1505 2.0 / 2132 0.8
		31 F	0405 1.8 / 0959 1.0 / 1615 1.9 / ☽ 2258 0.8

NOVEMBER

Time m		Time m	
1 SA	0521 1.8 / 1132 1.0 / 1734 1.9	**16** SU	0600 1.7 / 1214 1.2 / 1819 1.8
2 SU	0024 0.8 / 0642 1.9 / 1250 1.0 / 1852 2.0	**17** M	0047 0.9 / 0708 1.7 / 1316 1.1 / 1923 1.8
3 M	0128 0.7 / 0746 2.0 / 1350 0.9 / 1956 2.1	**18** TU	0138 0.9 / 0756 1.8 / 1403 1.0 / 2011 1.9
4 TU	0222 0.6 / 0839 2.1 / 1440 0.7 / 2050 2.2	**19** W	0220 0.8 / 0837 1.9 / 1443 0.9 / 2052 2.0
5 W	0308 0.5 / 0926 2.2 / 1526 0.6 / 2139 2.3	**20** TH	0259 0.7 / 0914 2.1 / 1520 0.8 / 2132 2.1
6 TH	0351 0.5 / 1010 2.3 / 1609 0.5 / ○ 2226 2.3	**21** F	0336 0.7 / 0951 2.2 / 1557 0.7 / 2210 2.2
7 F	0432 0.5 / 1052 2.3 / 1651 0.5 / 2311 2.3	**22** SA	0413 0.6 / 1027 2.2 / 1635 0.6 / ● 2250 2.2
8 SA	0512 0.6 / 1132 2.3 / 1733 0.5 / 2354 2.3	**23** SU	0451 0.6 / 1105 2.3 / 1714 0.6 / 2331 2.2
9 SU	0551 0.6 / 1210 2.3 / 1815 0.5	**24** M	0530 0.6 / 1143 2.3 / 1755 0.5
10 M	0036 2.2 / 0630 0.7 / 1249 2.2 / 1857 0.6	**25** TU	0015 2.2 / 0611 0.7 / 1224 2.3 / 1839 0.5
11 TU	0119 2.1 / 0709 0.9 / 1328 2.1 / 1941 0.7	**26** W	0103 2.2 / 0655 0.7 / 1308 2.2 / 1927 0.6
12 W	0202 1.9 / 0749 1.0 / 1410 2.0 / 2030 0.8	**27** TH	0155 2.1 / 0743 0.8 / 1357 2.2 / 2019 0.6
13 TH	0248 1.8 / 0834 1.1 / 1455 1.9 / 2127 0.9	**28** F	0251 2.0 / 0837 0.8 / 1454 2.1 / 2119 0.7
14 F	0338 1.7 / 0934 1.2 / 1547 1.8 / ☽ 2235 1.0	**29** SA	0353 1.9 / 0939 1.0 / 1558 2.0 / ☽ 2232 0.7
15 SA	0438 1.7 / 1057 1.2 / 1651 1.8 / 2345 1.0	**30** SU	0500 1.9 / 1057 1.0 / 1709 2.0 / 2354 0.8

DECEMBER

Time m		Time m	
1 M	0613 1.9 / 1220 1.0 / 1825 2.0	**16** TU	0549 1.7 / 1214 1.2 / 1808 1.8
2 TU	0103 0.7 / 0719 1.9 / 1326 0.9 / 1932 2.0	**17** W	0043 1.0 / 0700 1.8 / 1315 1.1 / 1920 1.8
3 W	0200 0.7 / 0815 2.0 / 1422 0.8 / 2031 2.1	**18** TH	0136 0.9 / 0754 1.9 / 1406 1.0 / 2014 1.9
4 TH	0250 0.7 / 0905 2.1 / 1511 0.7 / 2124 2.2	**19** F	0223 0.8 / 0839 2.0 / 1452 0.9 / 2101 2.0
5 F	0334 0.7 / 0951 2.2 / 1556 0.6 / 2213 2.2	**20** SA	0307 0.8 / 0921 2.1 / 1534 0.8 / 2147 2.1
6 SA	0415 0.7 / 1034 2.3 / 1638 0.6 / ○ 2258 2.2	**21** SU	0350 0.7 / 1003 2.2 / 1617 0.6 / 2232 2.2
7 SU	0454 0.7 / 1113 2.3 / 1720 0.6 / 2341 2.2	**22** M	0433 0.6 / 1046 2.3 / 1700 0.5 / ● 2319 2.3
8 M	0533 0.7 / 1151 2.3 / 1800 0.6	**23** TU	0515 0.6 / 1129 2.4 / 1744 0.4
9 TU	0020 2.1 / 0610 0.8 / 1229 2.2 / 1840 0.6	**24** W	0007 2.3 / 0559 0.6 / 1214 2.4 / 1829 0.4
10 W	0100 2.1 / 0646 0.9 / 1306 2.2 / 1920 0.7	**25** TH	0056 2.2 / 0644 0.7 / 1301 2.4 / 1916 0.4
11 TH	0138 2.0 / 0723 0.9 / 1343 2.1 / 2000 0.8	**26** F	0147 2.2 / 0730 0.7 / 1350 2.3 / 2006 0.5
12 F	0218 1.9 / 0800 1.0 / 1423 2.0 / 2044 0.9	**27** SA	0238 2.1 / 0820 0.8 / 1442 2.2 / 2100 0.6
13 SA	0300 1.8 / 0843 1.1 / 1507 1.9 / 2135 0.9	**28** SU	0332 2.0 / 0915 0.9 / 1539 2.1 / ☽ 2202 0.7
14 SU	0347 1.8 / 0938 1.2 / 1556 1.8 / ☽ 2237 1.0	**29** M	0431 1.9 / 1020 1.0 / 1642 2.0 / 2317 0.8
15 M	0441 1.7 / 1057 1.2 / 1655 1.8 / 2343 1.0	**30** TU	0538 1.9 / 1145 1.0 / 1755 1.9
		31 W	0035 0.8 / 0648 1.9 / 1304 1.0 / 1909 1.9

Chart Datum: 1·22 metres below Ordnance Datum (Local)
HAT is 2·5 metres above Chart Datum

TIDES

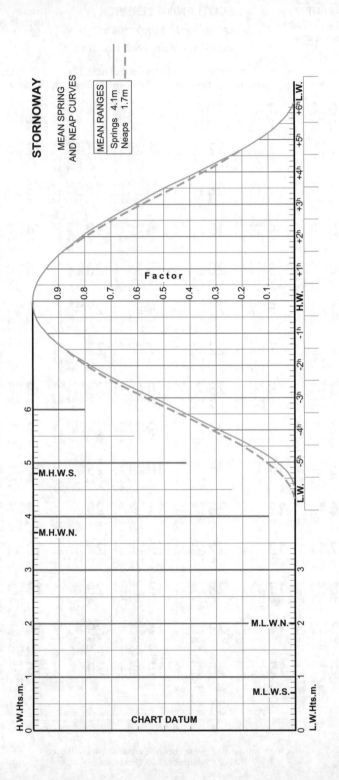

STORNOWAY

MEAN SPRING
AND NEAP CURVES

MEAN RANGES
Springs 4.1m
Neaps   1.7m

SCOTLAND – STORNOWAY

LAT 58°12′N   LONG 6°23′W

TIMES AND HEIGHTS OF HIGH AND LOW WATERS

Dates in amber are **SPRINGS**
Dates in yellow are **NEAPS**

2014

JANUARY

Day	Time	m	Time	m	Time	m	Time	m
1	0023	0.9	0621	5.1	W 1248	0.8	● 1847	5.0
16	0100	1.3	0659	4.7	TH 1331	1.2	○ 1917	4.5
2	0109	0.7	0706	5.3	TH 1335	0.6	1934	5.0
17	0132	1.2	0727	4.8	F 1403	1.1	1947	4.5
3	0154	0.6	0751	5.4	F 1422	0.5	2022	5.0
18	0204	1.2	0754	4.8	SA 1435	1.1	2017	4.5
4	0239	0.7	0837	5.4	SA 1509	0.5	2110	4.8
19	0235	1.2	0823	4.7	SU 1506	1.1	2049	4.4
5	0324	0.8	0926	5.2	SU 1556	0.7	2201	4.6
20	0306	1.2	0854	4.7	M 1539	1.2	2124	4.3
6	0411	1.1	1019	4.9	M 1644	1.0	2258	4.3
21	0339	1.3	0928	4.5	TU 1613	1.3	2203	4.2
7	0500	1.4	1118	4.6	TU 1735	1.3		
22	0416	1.5	1008	4.4	W 1651	1.5	2251	4.0
8	0004	4.0	0555	1.7	W 1227	4.3	◑ 1832	1.7
23	0457	1.7	1055	4.2	TH 1736	1.7	2352	3.9
9	0119	3.8	0701	2.0	TH 1340	4.1	1939	1.9
24	0547	1.9	1159	4.0	F 1832 ◐	1.8		
10	0236	3.8	0821	2.1	F 1453	4.0	2058	2.0
25	0108	3.8	0653	2.1	SA 1323	3.9	1948	1.9
11	0346	3.9	0944	2.1	SA 1559	4.0	2210	1.9
26	0225	3.9	0818	2.1	SU 1447	3.9	2113	1.9
12	0441	4.1	1048	1.9	SU 1652	4.1	2304	1.8
27	0333	4.1	0943	1.9	M 1601	4.1	2224	1.6
13	0524	4.3	1138	1.7	M 1736	4.2	2347	1.6
28	0433	4.4	1051	1.5	TU 1702	4.4	2321	1.3
14	0559	4.5	1219	1.5	TU 1813	4.3		
29	0523	4.7	1147	1.1	W 1752	4.7		
15	0025	1.4	0630	4.6	W 1257	1.3	1846	4.4
30	0011	0.9	0609	5.1	TH 1238	0.7	● 1838	4.9
31	0057	0.7	0652	5.4	F 1324	0.4	1921	5.1

FEBRUARY

Day	Time	m	Time	m	Time	m	Time	m
1	0141	0.5	0735	5.5	SA 1409	0.3	2004	5.1
16	0143	1.0	0732	4.8	SU 1411	0.9	1952	4.6
2	0224	0.5	0818	5.5	SU 1451	0.3	2046	4.9
17	0213	0.9	0759	4.8	M 1441	0.9	2022	4.6
3	0306	0.6	0902	5.3	M 1534	0.5	2130	4.7
18	0244	0.9	0829	4.8	TU 1511	0.9	2054	4.5
4	0348	0.8	0949	5.0	TU 1616	0.8	2216	4.4
19	0316	1.0	0901	4.6	W 1544	1.0	2130	4.4
5	0432	1.1	1040	4.6	W 1659	1.2	2312	4.0
20	0351	1.2	0939	4.5	TH 1619	1.2	2213	4.2
6	0520	1.5	1143	4.2	TH 1747 ◐	1.6		
21	0430	1.4	1024	4.2	F 1700	1.5	2309	4.0
7	0026	3.8	0617	1.9	F 1300	3.9	1844	2.0
22	0516	1.6	1125	4.0	SA 1752 ◐	1.7		
8	0152	3.7	0734	2.2	SA 1420	3.7	2005	2.2
23	0026	3.8	0618	1.9	SU 1256	3.8	1906	1.9
9	0312	3.7	0915	2.2	SU 1534	3.7	2140	2.2
24	0153	3.8	0747	2.0	M 1431	3.8	2046	1.9
10	0417	3.9	1031	2.0	M 1634	3.8	2243	2.0
25	0310	4.0	0926	1.8	TU 1551	3.9	2209	1.6
11	0504	4.1	1122	1.8	TU 1719	4.0	2329	1.7
26	0415	4.3	1040	1.4	W 1653	4.3	2308	1.3
12	0541	4.3	1202	1.5	W 1756	4.2		
27	0508	4.7	1136	1.0	TH 1741	4.6	2357	0.7
13	0006	1.5	0612	4.5	TH 1238	1.3	1827	4.4
28	0553	5.0	1223	0.6	F 1824	4.8		
14	0041	1.3	0640	4.6	F 1311	1.1	○ 1856	4.5
15	0113	1.1	0706	4.7	SA 1341	0.9	1924	4.6

MARCH

Day	Time	m	Time	m	Time	m	Time	m
1	0041	0.6	0634	5.3	SA 1308	0.3	● 1903	5.0
16	0047	1.0	0639	4.6	SU 1313	0.8	○ 1857	4.6
2	0124	0.4	0715	5.4	SU 1349	0.2	1941	5.0
17	0118	0.9	0705	4.7	M 1343	0.7	1925	4.7
3	0205	0.3	0756	5.4	M 1429	0.2	2020	4.9
18	0149	0.8	0733	4.8	TU 1413	0.7	1955	4.7
4	0245	0.4	0837	5.2	TU 1507	0.4	2058	4.7
19	0220	0.7	0804	4.8	W 1444	0.7	2028	4.6
5	0325	0.6	0919	4.8	W 1546	0.8	2138	4.4
20	0254	0.8	0839	4.6	TH 1517	0.8	2105	4.5
6	0406	1.0	1006	4.4	TH 1625	1.2	2223	4.1
21	0330	0.9	0919	4.4	F 1554	1.0	2149	4.3
7	0449	1.4	1102	4.0	F 1706	1.6	2325	3.8
22	0410	1.2	1008	4.2	SA 1635	1.3	2246	4.1
8	0540	1.8	1217	3.7	SA 1756 ◐	2.0		
23	0458	1.4	1116	3.9	SU 1727 ◐	1.7		
9	0058	3.6	0649	2.1	SU 1341	3.5	1906	2.2
24	0003	3.9	0601	1.7	M 1250	3.7	◑ 1843	1.9
10	0226	3.5	0834	2.2	M 1500	3.5	2055	2.3
25	0131	3.8	0733	1.8	TU 1421	3.7	2027	1.9
11	0339	3.7	1003	2.0	TU 1605	3.6	2214	2.1
26	0249	4.0	0913	1.6	W 1539	3.9	2151	1.6
12	0433	3.9	1056	1.8	W 1654	3.8	2302	1.8
27	0355	4.2	1025	1.3	TH 1639	4.2	2250	1.3
13	0513	4.1	1136	1.5	TH 1731	4.0	2341	1.5
28	0448	4.6	1118	0.9	F 1725	4.5	2338	0.9
14	0545	4.3	1211	1.2	F 1802	4.3		
29	0533	4.9	1204	0.6	SA 1805	4.7		
15	0015	1.3	0612	4.5	SA 1243	1.0	1830	4.4
30	0022	0.6	0614	5.1	SU 1247	0.3	● 1842	4.9
31	0104	0.4	0654	5.2	M 1326	0.3	1918	4.9

APRIL

Day	Time	m	Time	m	Time	m	Time	m
1	0144	0.4	0733	5.1	TU 1404	0.3	1954	4.8
16	0124	0.7	0709	4.7	W 1346	0.6	1932	4.8
2	0223	0.5	0813	4.9	W 1440	0.5	2030	4.7
17	0158	0.6	0744	4.7	TH 1420	0.6	2008	4.7
3	0302	0.7	0854	4.6	TH 1517	0.8	2107	4.4
18	0235	0.7	0824	4.6	F 1456	0.7	2048	4.6
4	0342	1.0	0938	4.3	F 1553	1.2	2147	4.1
19	0315	0.8	0911	4.4	SA 1535	1.0	2136	4.4
5	0423	1.3	1029	3.9	SA 1632	1.5	2236	3.9
20	0359	1.0	1007	4.1	SU 1620	1.3	2236	4.2
6	0510	1.7	1137	3.6	SU 1716	1.9	2353	3.6
21	0451	1.3	1121	3.9	M 1716	1.6	2351	4.0
7	0610	2.0	1256	3.4	M 1816	2.2		
22	0557	1.5	1246	3.7	TU 1832 ◐	1.8		
8	0126	3.5	0738	2.1	TU 1413	3.4	1949	2.3
23	0111	4.0	0723	1.6	W 1407	3.7	2006	1.9
9	0244	3.6	0915	2.0	W 1522	3.5	2125	2.2
24	0225	4.0	0852	1.5	TH 1520	3.9	2126	1.6
10	0346	3.7	1016	1.8	TH 1616	3.7	2223	1.9
25	0331	4.2	1001	1.2	F 1619	4.1	2226	1.3
11	0432	3.9	1059	1.5	F 1657	3.9	2305	1.6
26	0426	4.4	1055	0.9	SA 1706	4.4	2317	1.1
12	0508	4.1	1135	1.2	SA 1730	4.2	2342	1.3
27	0513	4.7	1141	0.7	SU 1746	4.6		
13	0539	4.3	1209	1.0	SU 1800	4.4		
28	0002	0.8	0555	4.8	M 1224	0.6	1822	4.7
14	0016	1.1	0607	4.5	M 1241	0.8	1829	4.6
29	0045	0.7	0635	4.8	TU 1303	0.5	● 1858	4.8
15	0050	0.9	0637	4.6	TU 1313	0.7	○ 1859	4.7
30	0125	0.6	0714	4.8	W 1340	0.6	1933	4.7

TIDES

Chart Datum: 2·71 metres below Ordnance Datum (Local)
HAT is 5·5 metres above Chart Datum

SCOTLAND – STORNOWAY
LAT 58°12′N   LONG 6°23′W
TIMES AND HEIGHTS OF HIGH AND LOW WATERS

TIME ZONE (UT)
For Summer Time add ONE hour in **non-shaded areas**

Dates in amber are **SPRINGS**
Dates in yellow are **NEAPS**

2014

MAY

Day	Time m	Day	Time m
1 TH	0204 0.6 / 0753 4.6 / 1416 0.7 / 2007 4.6	16 F	0140 0.6 / 0731 4.7 / 1400 0.6 / 1953 4.9
2 F	0243 0.8 / 0833 4.4 / 1451 0.9 / 2043 4.4	17 SA	0221 0.6 / 0817 4.6 / 1441 0.7 / 2038 4.8
3 SA	0321 1.0 / 0916 4.1 / 1527 1.2 / 2120 4.2	18 SU	0306 0.7 / 0909 4.4 / 1524 0.9 / 2129 4.6
4 SU	0402 1.3 / 1003 3.9 / 1605 1.5 / 2204 4.0	19 M	0354 0.8 / 1008 4.2 / 1613 1.2 / 2229 4.4
5 M	0445 1.5 / 1059 3.7 / 1647 1.8 / 2300 3.8	20 TU	0448 1.0 / 1117 4.0 / 1709 1.4 / 2338 4.2
6 TU	0537 1.8 / 1207 3.5 / 1737 2.0	21 W	0551 1.3 / 1231 3.8 / 1818 1.7
7 W ☽	0018 3.6 / 0643 1.9 / 1318 3.4 / 1846 2.2	22 TH	0050 4.1 / 0704 1.4 / 1345 3.8 / 1937 1.7
8 TH	0137 3.6 / 0804 1.9 / 1426 3.5 / 2014 2.2	23 F	0200 4.1 / 0821 1.4 / 1455 3.9 / 2054 1.7
9 F	0244 3.6 / 0916 1.8 / 1526 3.6 / 2127 2.0	24 SA	0306 4.2 / 0931 1.3 / 1556 4.0 / 2200 1.5
10 SA	0339 3.8 / 1010 1.6 / 1614 3.8 / 2220 1.8	25 SU	0405 4.3 / 1029 1.2 / 1647 4.2 / 2255 1.3
11 SU	0423 3.9 / 1052 1.3 / 1653 4.1 / 2303 1.5	26 M	0455 4.4 / 1118 1.0 / 1729 4.4 / 2344 1.1
12 M	0501 4.2 / 1131 1.1 / 1727 4.3 / 2343 1.2	27 TU	0540 4.5 / 1202 0.9 / 1807 4.5
13 TU	0536 4.4 / 1207 0.9 / 1801 4.5	28 W ●	0028 0.9 / 0621 4.5 / 1242 0.9 / 1842 4.6
14 W ○	0021 1.0 / 0611 4.5 / 1244 0.7 / 1835 4.7	29 TH	0110 0.9 / 0700 4.5 / 1320 0.9 / 1916 4.6
15 TH	0100 0.8 / 0649 4.6 / 1322 0.6 / 1912 4.8	30 F	0149 0.9 / 0738 4.4 / 1355 1.0 / 1950 4.6
		31 SA	0227 0.9 / 0816 4.3 / 1430 1.1 / 2024 4.5

JUNE

Day	Time m	Day	Time m
1 SU	0304 1.0 / 0855 4.1 / 1506 1.2 / 2059 4.3	16 M	0258 0.5 / 0902 4.6 / 1516 0.8 / 2119 4.9
2 M	0342 1.2 / 0937 4.0 / 1542 1.4 / 2137 4.2	17 TU	0347 0.6 / 0958 4.4 / 1604 1.0 / 2215 4.7
3 TU	0422 1.4 / 1023 3.8 / 1621 1.6 / 2222 4.0	18 W	0439 0.8 / 1059 4.2 / 1657 1.2 / 2317 4.5
4 W ☽	0505 1.5 / 1117 3.6 / 1705 1.8 / 2317 3.8	19 TH	0534 1.0 / 1206 4.0 / 1757 1.5
5 TH ●	0556 1.7 / 1219 3.5 / 1757 2.0	20 F	0024 4.3 / 0636 1.3 / 1316 3.8 / 1904 1.7
6 F	0025 3.7 / 0655 1.8 / 1326 3.5 / 1904 2.1	21 SA	0134 4.1 / 0744 1.4 / 1427 3.8 / 2019 1.7
7 SA	0136 3.7 / 0804 1.8 / 1429 3.6 / 2018 2.0	22 SU	0242 4.1 / 0856 1.5 / 1533 3.9 / 2133 1.7
8 SU	0239 3.7 / 0909 1.7 / 1525 3.8 / 2125 1.9	23 M	0346 4.1 / 1002 1.5 / 1629 4.1 / 2237 1.5
9 M	0334 3.8 / 1005 1.5 / 1613 4.0 / 2221 1.7	24 TU	0442 4.1 / 1057 1.4 / 1715 4.2 / 2330 1.4
10 TU	0423 4.0 / 1053 1.3 / 1655 4.2 / 2310 1.4	25 W	0529 4.2 / 1144 1.3 / 1755 4.4
11 W	0508 4.2 / 1137 1.1 / 1735 4.5 / 2356 1.1	26 TH	0016 1.2 / 0610 4.3 / 1226 1.2 / 1830 4.5
12 TH	0552 4.4 / 1219 0.9 / 1816 4.7	27 F ○	0058 1.1 / 0648 4.3 / 1303 1.1 / 1903 4.6
13 F ○	0040 0.8 / 0636 4.6 / 1303 0.7 / 1857 4.9	28 SA	0136 1.0 / 0724 4.3 / 1338 1.1 / 1934 4.6
14 SA	0126 0.6 / 0722 4.7 / 1346 0.6 / 1941 5.0	29 SU	0211 1.0 / 0758 4.3 / 1412 1.1 / 2005 4.5
15 SU	0211 0.5 / 0811 4.7 / 1430 0.7 / 2028 5.0	30 M	0246 1.0 / 0832 4.2 / 1446 1.2 / 2037 4.5

JULY

Day	Time m	Day	Time m
1 TU	0321 1.1 / 0908 4.1 / 1520 1.3 / 2110 4.4	16 W	0333 0.4 / 0936 4.6 / 1549 0.8 / 2152 4.9
2 W	0356 1.2 / 0946 4.0 / 1556 1.4 / 2147 4.2	17 TH	0420 0.6 / 1031 4.3 / 1637 1.0 / 2249 4.6
3 TH	0433 1.3 / 1030 3.9 / 1634 1.6 / 2230 4.0	18 F	0509 0.9 / 1133 4.1 / 1730 1.3 / 2355 4.3
4 F	0514 1.5 / 1123 3.7 / 1717 1.8 / 2323 3.9	19 SA	0602 1.3 / 1243 3.9 / 1831 1.6
5 SA ●	0601 1.7 / 1226 3.6 / 1810 1.9	20 SU	0106 4.1 / 0704 1.6 / 1358 3.8 / 1944 1.9
6 SU	0029 3.8 / 0658 1.8 / 1333 3.6 / 1915 2.0	21 M	0219 3.9 / 0818 1.8 / 1511 3.8 / 2109 1.9
7 M	0142 3.7 / 0807 1.8 / 1437 3.7 / 2031 2.0	22 TU	0330 3.8 / 0936 1.8 / 1613 3.9 / 2223 1.8
8 TU	0250 3.8 / 0917 1.7 / 1536 3.9 / 2142 1.8	23 W	0430 3.9 / 1040 1.7 / 1702 4.1 / 2319 1.6
9 W	0352 3.9 / 1019 1.5 / 1628 4.2 / 2243 1.5	24 TH	0519 4.0 / 1128 1.5 / 1742 4.3
10 TH	0448 4.1 / 1112 1.2 / 1715 4.5 / 2336 1.2	25 F	0004 1.4 / 0558 4.1 / 1210 1.4 / 1816 4.5
11 F	0539 4.4 / 1201 1.0 / 1800 4.8	26 SA ●	0044 1.2 / 0633 4.2 / 1247 1.2 / 1846 4.6
12 SA ○	0026 0.8 / 0626 4.6 / 1248 0.7 / 1843 5.0	27 SU	0119 1.1 / 0705 4.4 / 1321 1.1 / 1915 4.6
13 SU	0114 0.5 / 0712 4.8 / 1333 0.6 / 1928 5.2	28 M	0153 1.0 / 0736 4.4 / 1353 1.1 / 1943 4.7
14 M	0201 0.3 / 0759 4.8 / 1418 0.5 / 2014 5.2	29 TU	0224 0.9 / 0806 4.4 / 1425 1.1 / 2011 4.6
15 TU	0247 0.3 / 0847 4.8 / 1503 0.6 / 2101 5.1	30 W	0256 1.0 / 0838 4.3 / 1456 1.1 / 2041 4.5
		31 TH	0327 1.0 / 0911 4.2 / 1529 1.2 / 2114 4.4

AUGUST

Day	Time m	Day	Time m
1 F	0400 1.2 / 0949 4.1 / 1604 1.4 / 2151 4.2	16 SA	0439 0.9 / 1052 4.2 / 1701 1.3 / 2322 4.3
2 SA	0436 1.3 / 1033 3.9 / 1642 1.6 / 2236 4.0	17 SU ◐	0526 1.4 / 1205 3.9 / 1757 1.7
3 SU	0517 1.5 / 1130 3.8 / 1728 1.8 / 2334 3.9	18 M	0038 3.9 / 0622 1.8 / 1327 3.8 / 1910 2.0
4 M ●	0606 1.7 / 1242 3.7 / 1827 2.0	19 TU	0157 3.7 / 0735 2.0 / 1445 3.7 / 2046 2.1
5 TU	0053 3.7 / 0712 1.9 / 1357 3.8 / 1945 2.0	20 W	0312 3.7 / 0909 2.1 / 1553 3.9 / 2209 1.9
6 W	0218 3.7 / 0836 1.9 / 1505 3.9 / 2111 1.9	21 TH	0415 3.8 / 1021 1.9 / 1644 4.0 / 2304 1.7
7 TH	0333 3.9 / 0954 1.7 / 1606 4.2 / 2224 1.6	22 F	0503 3.9 / 1110 1.7 / 1723 4.2 / 2346 1.4
8 F	0436 4.1 / 1055 1.4 / 1658 4.5 / 2322 1.2	23 SA	0541 4.1 / 1150 1.5 / 1756 4.4
9 SA	0528 4.4 / 1146 1.0 / 1744 4.9	24 SU	0023 1.2 / 0613 4.3 / 1226 1.3 / 1824 4.6
10 SU ○	0013 0.8 / 0614 4.7 / 1233 0.7 / 1828 5.2	25 M ●	0057 1.0 / 0643 4.4 / 1259 1.1 / 1851 4.7
11 M	0100 0.4 / 0658 4.9 / 1318 0.5 / 1910 5.4	26 TU	0128 0.9 / 0711 4.5 / 1330 1.0 / 1917 4.7
12 TU	0145 0.2 / 0741 5.0 / 1401 0.4 / 1954 5.4	27 W	0158 0.9 / 0739 4.6 / 1400 1.0 / 1944 4.7
13 W	0229 0.2 / 0824 4.9 / 1444 0.4 / 2038 5.3	28 TH	0228 0.9 / 0807 4.5 / 1431 1.0 / 2012 4.7
14 TH	0312 0.3 / 0908 4.7 / 1528 0.6 / 2126 5.0	29 F	0257 0.9 / 0838 4.5 / 1502 1.1 / 2044 4.6
15 F	0354 0.6 / 0956 4.5 / 1613 0.9 / 2218 4.7	30 SA	0328 1.0 / 0913 4.3 / 1536 1.2 / 2119 4.4
		31 SU	0402 1.2 / 0954 4.2 / 1613 1.6 / 2202 4.2

Chart Datum: 2·71 metres below Ordnance Datum (Local)
HAT is 5·5 metres above Chart Datum

SCOTLAND – STORNOWAY

LAT 58°12′N   LONG 6°23′W

TIMES AND HEIGHTS OF HIGH AND LOW WATERS

Dates in amber are **SPRINGS**
Dates in yellow are **NEAPS**

2014

SEPTEMBER

Day	WD	Time m	Time m	Time m	Time m
1	M	0441 1.4	1047 4.0	1657 1.6	2259 3.9
2	TU	0527 1.7	1200 3.8	1753 1.9	◐
3	W	0026 3.7	0632 1.9	1326 3.8	1913 2.0
4	TH	0202 3.7	0807 2.0	1442 3.9	2052 1.9
5	F	0321 3.9	0936 1.8	1547 4.2	2210 1.5
6	SA	0425 4.1	1039 1.5	1640 4.6	2308 1.1
7	SU	0516 4.5	1130 1.1	1727 5.0	2357 0.7
8	M	0559 4.8	1216 0.7	1809 5.3	
9	TU	0042 0.4	0639 5.0	1300 0.5	○ 1850 5.5
10	W	0125 0.2	0719 5.1	1342 0.4	1932 5.5
11	TH	0206 0.2	0758 5.1	1423 0.4	2014 5.3
12	F	0246 0.3	0839 4.9	1505 0.6	2058 5.0
13	SA	0326 0.6	0921 4.6	1548 0.9	2147 4.6
14	SU	0407 1.1	1010 4.2	1633 1.3	2247 4.2
15	M	0451 1.5	1117 3.9	1726 1.7	
16	TU	0006 3.8	0540 1.9	1248 3.8	◑ 1835 2.1
17	W	0128 3.6	0649 2.2	1411 3.7	2014 2.2
18	TH	0245 3.6	0830 2.3	1522 3.8	2144 2.0
19	F	0350 3.7	0953 2.1	1616 4.0	2239 1.8
20	SA	0439 3.9	1045 1.9	1657 4.2	2320 1.5
21	SU	0517 4.1	1124 1.6	1729 4.4	2355 1.3
22	M	0548 4.3	1159 1.4	1758 4.6	
23	TU	0028 1.1	0616 4.5	1232 1.2	1824 4.7
24	W	0059 0.9	0643 4.6	1303 1.0	● 1850 4.8
25	TH	0128 0.8	0711 4.7	1334 1.0	1917 4.8
26	F	0158 0.8	0739 4.7	1405 0.9	1946 4.8
27	SA	0228 0.9	0810 4.7	1437 1.0	2019 4.7
28	SU	0300 1.0	0845 4.6	1512 1.1	2056 4.5
29	M	0334 1.2	0926 4.4	1551 1.3	2142 4.2
30	TU	0413 1.4	1019 4.2	1636 1.6	2245 4.0

OCTOBER

Day	WD	Time m	Time m	Time m	Time m
1	W	0501 1.7	1133 4.0	1734 1.8	◑
2	TH	0017 3.8	0607 2.0	1302 3.9	1856 2.0
3	F	0150 3.7	0746 2.1	1419 4.0	2036 1.8
4	SA	0308 3.9	0917 1.9	1525 4.3	2153 1.5
5	SU	0410 4.2	1021 1.5	1621 4.6	2250 1.1
6	M	0500 4.5	1111 1.2	1707 5.0	2337 0.7
7	TU	0541 4.8	1157 0.8	1750 5.2	
8	W	0021 0.6	0619 5.0	1240 0.6	○ 1830 5.4
9	TH	0103 0.3	0657 5.1	1322 0.5	1911 5.3
10	F	0142 0.4	0734 5.1	1403 0.5	1952 5.2
11	SA	0221 0.6	0812 4.9	1443 0.7	2034 4.9
12	SU	0259 0.8	0851 4.7	1525 1.0	2121 4.5
13	M	0338 1.2	0934 4.4	1609 1.4	2215 4.1
14	TU	0419 1.6	1027 4.1	1658 1.7	2326 3.8
15	W	0505 2.0	1151 3.8	1759 2.0	◐
16	TH	0046 3.6	0603 2.3	1320 3.7	1924 2.2
17	F	0202 3.6	0732 2.4	1434 3.8	2058 2.1
18	SA	0310 3.7	0906 2.2	1535 3.9	2200 1.9
19	SU	0404 3.9	1007 2.1	1620 4.1	2244 1.7
20	M	0445 4.1	1050 1.8	1656 4.3	2321 1.4
21	TU	0518 4.3	1128 1.5	1727 4.5	2355 1.2
22	W	0548 4.5	1202 1.3	1756 4.6	
23	TH	0026 1.0	0616 4.7	1235 1.1	● 1823 4.8
24	F	0058 0.9	0657 4.9	1308 1.0	1853 4.8
25	SA	0129 0.8	0715 4.9	1342 0.9	1926 4.7
26	SU	0202 0.9	0748 4.9	1417 0.9	2002 4.7
27	M	0236 1.0	0826 4.8	1455 1.0	2045 4.5
28	TU	0314 1.2	0910 4.6	1536 1.2	2136 4.3
29	W	0356 1.4	1005 4.4	1625 1.4	2243 4.0
30	TH	0446 1.7	1116 4.2	1725 1.7	
31	F	0008 3.9	0553 2.6	1238 4.1	◑ 1844 1.8

NOVEMBER

Day	WD	Time m	Time m	Time m	Time m
1	SA	0133 3.9	0724 2.1	1354 4.2	2014 1.7
2	SU	0247 4.0	0850 1.9	1501 4.4	2129 1.5
3	M	0351 4.2	0956 1.6	1559 4.6	2227 1.2
4	TU	0441 4.5	1050 1.3	1648 4.8	2316 0.9
5	W	0523 4.8	1137 1.0	1732 5.0	
6	TH	0000 0.7	0602 4.9	1222 0.8	○ 1814 5.1
7	F	0041 0.7	0638 5.0	1304 0.7	1854 5.1
8	SA	0120 0.7	0715 5.0	1345 0.8	1935 5.0
9	SU	0158 0.9	0751 4.9	1426 0.9	2016 4.7
10	M	0235 1.0	0829 4.7	1506 1.1	2059 4.4
11	TU	0313 1.3	0907 4.5	1548 1.4	2146 4.2
12	W	0352 1.6	0951 4.3	1633 1.7	2241 3.9
13	TH	0434 1.9	1045 4.0	1724 1.9	2349 3.7
14	F	0524 2.2	1204 3.9	1828 2.1	◐
15	SA	0103 3.6	0629 2.4	1327 3.8	1946 2.1
16	SU	0213 3.6	0754 2.4	1435 3.8	2101 2.0
17	M	0315 3.8	0910 2.3	1531 4.0	2157 1.8
18	TU	0404 4.0	1006 2.0	1616 4.1	2241 1.6
19	W	0444 4.2	1050 1.8	1653 4.3	2319 1.4
20	TH	0518 4.5	1130 1.5	1726 4.5	2354 1.2
21	F	0550 4.7	1207 1.3	1759 4.7	
22	SA	0029 1.0	0621 4.9	1244 1.1	● 1834 4.8
23	SU	0105 0.9	0656 5.0	1322 1.0	1912 4.8
24	M	0142 0.9	0733 5.0	1402 0.9	1953 4.8
25	TU	0220 0.9	0814 5.0	1443 0.9	2040 4.6
26	W	0301 1.1	0901 4.9	1528 1.0	2133 4.5
27	TH	0346 1.3	0955 4.7	1618 1.2	2236 4.2
28	F	0437 1.6	1059 4.5	1716 1.4	2349 3.7
29	SA	0540 1.8	1211 4.4	1825 1.6	◑
30	SU	0106 4.0	0655 2.0	1325 4.3	1942 1.6

DECEMBER

Day	WD	Time m	Time m	Time m	Time m
1	M	0220 4.0	0816 1.9	1434 4.4	2056 1.6
2	TU	0327 4.2	0928 1.8	1537 4.5	2201 1.4
3	W	0423 4.4	1028 1.5	1632 4.6	2254 1.2
4	TH	0509 4.6	1120 1.3	1720 4.7	2341 1.1
5	F	0549 4.8	1208 1.1	1803 4.8	
6	SA	0023 1.0	0626 4.9	1252 1.0	○ 1843 4.8
7	SU	0103 1.0	0702 4.9	1333 1.0	1923 4.8
8	M	0140 1.1	0737 4.9	1412 1.0	2001 4.6
9	TU	0217 1.2	0812 4.8	1450 1.1	2039 4.5
10	W	0253 1.3	0846 4.7	1528 1.3	2119 4.3
11	TH	0329 1.5	0922 4.5	1608 1.5	2201 4.1
12	F	0407 1.7	1003 4.3	1650 1.7	2251 3.9
13	SA	0449 1.9	1052 4.1	1738 1.9	2352 3.7
14	SU	0537 2.1	1159 3.9	1835 2.0	◐
15	M	0103 3.7	0639 2.3	1318 3.8	1943 2.1
16	TU	0213 3.7	0755 2.3	1428 3.9	2053 2.0
17	W	0313 3.9	0908 2.2	1526 4.0	2153 1.9
18	TH	0404 4.1	1008 2.0	1616 4.1	2241 1.6
19	F	0447 4.3	1057 1.7	1659 4.3	2324 1.4
20	SA	0525 4.6	1141 1.5	1740 4.5	
21	SU	0005 1.2	0602 4.8	1225 1.2	1820 4.7
22	M	0046 1.0	0641 5.0	1307 0.9	● 1902 4.8
23	TU	0127 0.8	0721 5.2	1350 0.8	1946 4.9
24	W	0208 0.8	0804 5.2	1435 0.7	2033 4.8
25	TH	0251 0.9	0851 5.2	1520 0.8	2123 4.7
26	F	0336 1.0	0941 5.0	1609 0.9	2218 4.5
27	SA	0425 1.3	1037 4.8	1701 1.1	2320 4.2
28	SU	0520 1.5	1142 4.6	1759 1.4	◑
29	M	0032 4.0	0623 1.8	1254 4.4	1904 1.6
30	TU	0147 4.0	0737 1.9	1407 4.3	2019 1.7
31	W	0301 4.0	0857 1.9	1517 4.2	2133 1.7

Chart Datum: 2·71 metres below Ordnance Datum (Local)
HAT is 5·5 metres above Chart Datum

TIDES

ULLAPOOL
MEAN SPRING
AND NEAP CURVES

MEAN RANGES	
Springs	4.5m
Neaps	1.8m

TIME ZONE (UT)	SCOTLAND – ULLAPOOL	Dates in amber are SPRINGS
For Summer Time add ONE hour in **non-shaded areas**	LAT 57°54′N LONG 5°09′W	Dates in yellow are NEAPS
	TIMES AND HEIGHTS OF HIGH AND LOW WATERS	**2014**

JANUARY

Day	Time m	Time m	Time m	Time m
1	0030 1.0	0627 5.5	W 1254 0.8	● 1854 5.4
16	0107 1.4	0705 5.0	TH 1337 1.3	○ 1925 4.9
2	0117 0.8	0712 5.7	TH 1342 0.6	1941 5.4
17	0140 1.3	0733 5.1	F 1409 1.2	1955 4.9
3	0202 0.7	0757 5.8	F 1429 0.5	2028 5.4
18	0212 1.2	0801 5.1	SA 1440 1.1	2025 4.9
4	0247 0.7	0844 5.7	SA 1515 0.6	2117 5.2
19	0243 1.2	0829 5.1	SU 1512 1.2	2056 4.8
5	0333 0.9	0933 5.5	SU 1602 0.7	2208 5.0
20	0314 1.3	0900 5.0	M 1543 1.3	2130 4.7
6	0420 1.1	1025 5.2	M 1650 1.1	2303 4.7
21	0347 1.4	0934 4.8	TU 1617 1.4	2208 4.5
7	0509 1.5	1125 4.9	TU 1741 1.4	
22	0423 1.6	1013 4.7	W 1655 1.6	2255 4.4
8	0007 4.4	0605 1.8	W 1232 4.6	1838 1.8
23	0505 1.8	1100 4.5	TH 1740 1.8	2356 4.2
9	0121 4.2	0711 2.1	TH 1345 4.3	1945 2.0
24	0556 2.0	1205 4.3	F 1838 2.0	◐
10	0240 4.1	0830 2.2	F 1501 4.2	2104 2.1
25	0112 4.1	0702 2.2	SA 1330 4.2	1953 2.1
11	0350 4.2	0950 2.2	SA 1607 4.3	2215 2.1
26	0227 4.2	0826 2.2	SU 1452 4.2	2118 2.0
12	0445 4.4	1054 2.0	SU 1700 4.4	2310 1.9
27	0336 4.4	0949 2.0	M 1606 4.4	2230 1.7
13	0528 4.6	1143 1.8	M 1743 4.5	2354 1.7
28	0437 4.7	1057 1.6	TU 1707 4.7	2328 1.4
14	0604 4.8	1225 1.6	TU 1820 4.7	
29	0529 5.1	1153 1.2	W 1758 5.0	
15	0032 1.5	0636 4.9	W 1302 1.4	1853 4.8
30	0018 1.0	0615 5.5	TH 1244 0.7	● 1844 5.3
31	0105 0.7	0659 5.7	F 1330 0.4	1928 5.5

FEBRUARY

Day	Time m	Time m	Time m	Time m
1	0149 0.5	0742 5.9	SA 1415 0.3	2010 5.5
16	0151 1.1	0738 5.1	SU 1417 0.9	1959 5.0
2	0232 0.5	0825 5.8	SU 1458 0.3	2053 5.3
17	0221 1.0	0805 5.1	M 1446 0.9	2029 5.0
3	0314 0.6	0909 5.6	M 1540 0.5	2137 5.1
18	0251 1.0	0835 5.1	TU 1516 1.0	2100 4.9
4	0357 0.9	0955 5.3	TU 1622 0.9	2223 4.8
19	0323 1.1	0907 5.0	W 1549 1.1	2136 4.7
5	0441 1.2	1047 4.9	W 1706 1.3	2318 4.4
20	0358 1.2	0945 4.8	TH 1625 1.3	2219 4.5
6	0529 1.6	1149 4.5	TH 1754 1.7	
21	0437 1.5	1030 4.5	F 1707 1.6	2314 4.3
7	0028 4.1	0626 2.0	F 1303 4.1	1852 2.1
22	0525 1.7	1131 4.3	SA 1759 1.9	◑
8	0152 4.0	0743 2.3	SA 1425 4.0	2013 2.3
23	0031 4.1	0627 2.0	SU 1302 4.1	1914 2.1
9	0317 4.0	0913 2.3	SU 1543 4.0	2145 2.3
24	0156 4.1	0755 2.1	M 1434 4.1	2053 2.1
10	0421 4.1	1035 2.1	M 1641 4.1	2250 2.1
25	0314 4.3	0932 1.9	TU 1555 4.3	2215 1.8
11	0509 4.3	1126 1.9	TU 1726 4.3	2336 1.8
26	0421 4.6	1045 1.5	W 1658 4.6	2315 1.4
12	0546 4.6	1207 1.6	W 1803 4.5	
27	0514 5.0	1141 1.1	TH 1747 5.0	
13	0014 1.6	0617 4.8	TH 1244 1.4	1834 4.7
28	0004 1.0	0559 5.4	F 1230 0.6	1829 5.3
14	0049 1.4	0646 4.9	F 1316 1.2	○ 1904 4.9
15	0120 1.2	0712 5.1	SA 1347 1.0	1932 5.0

MARCH

Day	Time m	Time m	Time m	Time m
1	0050 0.6	0641 5.7	SA 1314 0.3	● 1909 5.4
16	0055 1.1	0645 5.0	SU 1319 0.9	○ 1905 5.0
2	0132 0.4	0722 5.8	SU 1355 0.2	1948 5.5
17	0126 0.9	0712 5.1	M 1349 0.8	1932 5.1
3	0212 0.4	0803 5.7	M 1435 0.2	2026 5.3
18	0156 0.8	0740 5.1	TU 1419 0.7	2002 5.1
4	0252 0.5	0844 5.5	TU 1514 0.5	2105 5.1
19	0227 0.8	0811 5.1	W 1450 0.8	2035 5.0
5	0332 0.7	0926 5.2	W 1552 0.8	2146 4.8
20	0301 0.9	0846 5.0	TH 1523 0.9	2111 4.9
6	0413 1.1	1012 4.8	TH 1632 1.2	2231 4.4
21	0337 1.0	0926 4.8	F 1600 1.1	2155 4.6
7	0457 1.5	1108 4.3	F 1714 1.7	2331 4.1
22	0418 1.2	1015 4.5	SA 1643 1.4	2251 4.4
8	0548 1.9	1220 4.0	SA 1805 2.1	◑
23	0506 1.5	1122 4.2	SU 1736 1.7	
9	0056 3.9	0656 2.2	SU 1344 3.8	1917 2.4
24	0009 4.2	0610 1.8	M 1255 4.0	◐ 1852 2.0
10	0229 3.8	0837 2.3	M 1507 3.8	2103 2.4
25	0135 4.1	0739 1.9	TU 1424 4.0	2035 2.1
11	0346 3.9	1005 2.2	TU 1613 3.9	2220 2.2
26	0254 4.2	0918 1.8	W 1544 4.2	2159 1.8
12	0439 4.1	1059 1.9	W 1700 4.2	2309 1.9
27	0402 4.5	1029 1.4	TH 1644 4.5	2258 1.4
13	0519 4.4	1140 1.6	TH 1737 4.4	2348 1.6
28	0456 4.9	1124 1.0	F 1731 4.8	2346 1.0
14	0551 4.6	1216 1.3	F 1809 4.6	
29	0541 5.2	1210 0.6	SA 1811 5.1	
15	0022 1.3	0619 4.8	SA 1248 1.1	1837 4.8
30	0030 0.7	0622 5.4	SU 1253 0.4	● 1848 5.3
31	0112 0.5	0701 5.5	M 1333 0.3	1925 5.3

APRIL

Day	Time m	Time m	Time m	Time m
1	0152 0.4	0740 5.5	TU 1410 0.4	2001 5.2
16	0131 0.7	0716 5.1	W 1352 0.6	1938 5.1
2	0231 0.5	0820 5.3	W 1447 0.6	2037 5.0
17	0205 0.7	0751 5.1	TH 1426 0.7	2014 5.1
3	0309 0.7	0901 5.0	TH 1524 0.9	2114 4.8
18	0242 0.7	0831 4.9	F 1503 0.8	2055 5.0
4	0349 1.0	0945 4.6	F 1601 1.2	2154 4.5
19	0322 0.8	0917 4.7	SA 1543 1.0	2143 4.7
5	0430 1.4	1036 4.2	SA 1641 1.6	2243 4.1
20	0406 1.1	1014 4.5	SU 1629 1.3	2243 4.5
6	0517 1.8	1141 3.9	SU 1727 2.0	2356 3.9
21	0458 1.3	1127 4.2	M 1726 1.7	2358 4.3
7	0616 2.1	1257 3.7	M 1828 2.3	◐
22	0604 1.6	1250 4.0	TU 1842 1.9	○
8	0126 3.7	0742 2.2	TU 1418 3.7	2003 2.4
23	0117 4.2	0729 1.7	W 1410 4.0	2015 1.9
9	0251 3.8	0916 2.1	W 1529 3.8	2134 2.3
24	0232 4.3	0857 1.6	TH 1525 4.2	2134 1.7
10	0354 3.9	1018 1.9	TH 1623 4.0	2231 2.0
25	0339 4.5	1006 1.3	F 1625 4.4	2235 1.4
11	0440 4.2	1103 1.6	F 1703 4.3	2313 1.7
26	0435 4.7	1101 1.0	SA 1712 4.7	2325 1.1
12	0516 4.4	1140 1.3	SA 1737 4.5	2350 1.4
27	0521 5.0	1148 0.8	SU 1752 4.9	
13	0546 4.6	1214 1.1	SU 1807 4.7	
28	0010 0.8	0603 5.1	M 1230 0.6	1828 5.1
14	0024 1.1	0614 4.8	M 1247 0.9	1835 4.9
29	0053 0.6	0643 5.2	TU 1310 0.6	● 1904 5.1
15	0057 0.9	0644 5.0	TU 1319 0.7	○ 1905 5.1
30	0133 0.6	0722 5.1	W 1347 0.6	1939 5.1

Chart Datum: 2·75 metres below Ordnance Datum (Newlyn)
HAT is 5·9 metres above Chart Datum

TIDES

TIDES

SCOTLAND – ULLAPOOL
LAT 57°54'N   LONG 5°09'W
TIMES AND HEIGHTS OF HIGH AND LOW WATERS

Dates in amber are **SPRINGS**
Dates in yellow are **NEAPS**

2014

MAY

Day	Time	m	Time	m	Time	m	Time	m
1 TH	0211	0.7	0801	5.0	1423	0.8	2014	4.9
2 F	0249	0.8	0841	4.7	1459	1.0	2050	4.7
3 SA	0328	1.1	0923	4.5	1536	1.3	2128	4.5
4 SU	0408	1.3	1010	4.2	1615	1.6	2211	4.2
5 M	0451	1.6	1105	4.0	1657	1.9	2306	4.0
6 TU	0542	1.9	1210	3.8	1749	2.1		
7 W ☽	0021	3.8	0646	2.0	1320	3.7	1859	2.3
8 TH	0140	3.8	0808	2.1	1430	3.7	2026	2.3
9 F	0251	3.8	0920	1.9	1532	3.9	2137	2.1
10 SA	0347	4.0	1014	1.7	1619	4.1	2228	1.8
11 SU	0431	4.2	1058	1.5	1658	4.4	2311	1.5
12 M	0508	4.4	1136	1.2	1733	4.6	2350	1.2
13 TU	0543	4.7	1213	1.0	1807	4.9		
14 W ○	0028	1.0	0618	4.9	1251	0.8	1841	5.1
15 TH	0107	0.8	0656	5.0	1329	0.7	1919	5.2
16 F	0147	0.6	0738	5.0	1408	0.7	1959	5.2
17 SA	0229	0.6	0824	4.9	1449	0.8	2045	5.1
18 SU	0313	0.7	0916	4.8	1533	1.0	2136	4.9
19 M	0401	0.9	1016	4.5	1622	1.2	2237	4.7
20 TU	0455	1.1	1124	4.3	1719	1.5	2345	4.5
21 W ☾	0558	1.3	1235	4.2	1829	1.7		
22 TH	0056	4.4	0710	1.5	1348	4.1	1948	1.8
23 F	0207	4.4	0826	1.5	1500	4.2	2103	1.7
24 SA	0315	4.4	0936	1.4	1602	4.3	2208	1.5
25 SU	0414	4.5	1035	1.2	1652	4.5	2303	1.3
26 M	0504	4.7	1125	1.1	1735	4.7	2352	1.1
27 TU	0548	4.8	1209	1.0	1813	4.9		
28 W ●	0036	1.0	0629	4.8	1250	0.9	1848	4.9
29 TH	0117	0.9	0708	4.8	1327	0.9	1923	4.9
30 F	0156	0.9	0746	4.8	1404	1.0	1957	4.9
31 SA	0233	1.0	0824	4.6	1439	1.1	2031	4.7

JUNE

Day	Time	m	Time	m	Time	m	Time	m
1 SU	0310	1.1	0903	4.5	1515	1.3	2106	4.6
2 M	0348	1.2	0944	4.3	1552	1.5	2144	4.4
3 TU	0427	1.4	1029	4.1	1631	1.7	2228	4.2
4 W ☽	0510	1.6	1122	4.0	1715	1.9	2322	4.0
5 TH ☽	0559	1.8	1223	3.8	1808	2.1		
6 F	0031	3.9	0659	1.9	1329	3.8	1914	2.2
7 SA	0142	3.9	0808	1.9	1432	3.9	2029	2.1
8 SU	0246	3.9	0914	1.8	1529	4.1	2134	2.0
9 M	0341	4.1	1010	1.6	1617	4.3	2229	1.7
10 TU	0430	4.3	1058	1.4	1700	4.6	2317	1.4
11 W	0515	4.5	1143	1.1	1741	4.8		
12 TH	0002	1.1	0558	4.8	1227	0.9	1821	5.1
13 F ○	0048	0.8	0643	4.9	1310	0.7	1903	5.2
14 SA	0133	0.6	0729	5.0	1354	0.7	1948	5.3
15 SU	0218	0.5	0818	5.0	1439	0.7	2036	5.3
16 M	0305	0.5	0910	4.9	1525	0.8	2127	5.2
17 TU	0354	0.6	1006	4.7	1614	1.0	2223	5.0
18 W	0445	0.9	1106	4.5	1707	1.3	2325	4.7
19 TH ☾	0541	1.1	1211	4.3	1807	1.5		
20 F	0031	4.5	0642	1.4	1320	4.2	1915	1.7
21 SA	0140	4.4	0750	1.5	1431	4.1	2029	1.8
22 SU	0250	4.3	0902	1.6	1538	4.2	2141	1.7
23 M	0355	4.3	1008	1.6	1634	4.4	2244	1.6
24 TU	0450	4.4	1104	1.5	1720	4.5	2336	1.4
25 W	0537	4.5	1151	1.4	1800	4.7		
26 TH	0022	1.2	0618	4.6	1233	1.3	1836	4.8
27 F ●	0104	1.1	0656	4.7	1311	1.2	1909	4.8
28 SA	0142	1.0	0732	4.7	1347	1.2	1941	4.9
29 SU	0217	1.0	0806	4.6	1421	1.2	2012	4.8
30 M	0252	1.1	0840	4.6	1455	1.2	2043	4.7

JULY

Day	Time	m	Time	m	Time	m	Time	m
1 TU	0326	1.1	0915	4.5	1529	1.3	2116	4.6
2 W	0401	1.3	0953	4.3	1604	1.5	2153	4.5
3 TH	0438	1.4	1036	4.2	1643	1.6	2236	4.3
4 F	0518	1.6	1127	4.1	1726	1.8	2328	4.1
5 SA ☽	0605	1.8	1229	4.0	1819	2.0		
6 SU ☽	0035	4.0	0702	1.9	1336	3.9	1924	2.1
7 M	0149	4.0	0812	1.9	1440	4.0	2039	2.1
8 TU	0256	4.0	0923	1.8	1539	4.2	2149	1.9
9 W	0358	4.1	1025	1.6	1632	4.5	2249	1.6
10 TH	0454	4.5	1119	1.3	1720	4.8	2342	1.2
11 F	0545	4.7	1208	1.0	1806	5.1		
12 SA ○	0032	0.8	0632	4.9	1256	0.8	1850	5.4
13 SU	0120	0.5	0719	5.2	1341	0.6	1935	5.5
14 M	0207	0.3	0806	5.2	1426	0.5	2021	5.5
15 TU	0253	0.3	0854	5.2	1512	0.6	2109	5.4
16 W	0339	0.4	0944	5.0	1558	0.8	2200	5.2
17 TH	0426	0.7	1038	4.7	1646	1.1	2257	4.9
18 F	0515	1.0	1138	4.4	1739	1.4		
19 SA ☾	0002	4.6	0608	1.4	1246	4.2	1840	1.7
20 SU	0112	4.3	0710	1.7	1400	4.1	1954	1.9
21 M	0226	4.1	0824	1.9	1515	4.1	2116	2.0
22 TU	0338	4.1	0942	1.9	1618	4.2	2228	1.8
23 W	0438	4.2	1046	1.8	1707	4.4	2324	1.6
24 TH	0526	4.3	1136	1.6	1747	4.6		
25 F	0009	1.4	0606	4.5	1218	1.5	1821	4.7
26 SA ●	0049	1.2	0641	4.6	1255	1.3	1852	4.8
27 SU	0125	1.1	0713	4.7	1329	1.2	1921	4.9
28 M	0158	1.0	0744	4.8	1402	1.1	1949	4.9
29 TU	0230	1.0	0814	4.7	1433	1.1	2018	4.9
30 W	0301	1.0	0845	4.7	1504	1.2	2047	4.8
31 TH	0332	1.1	0918	4.6	1537	1.3	2120	4.7

AUGUST

Day	Time	m	Time	m	Time	m	Time	m
1 F	0405	1.2	0954	4.4	1611	1.6	2157	4.5
2 SA	0441	1.4	1038	4.3	1651	1.6	2242	4.3
3 SU	0522	1.6	1134	4.1	1737	1.8	2340	4.1
4 M	0612	1.8	1245	4.0	1836	2.0		
5 TU	0101	4.0	0719	2.0	1400	4.0	1953	2.1
6 W	0224	4.0	0842	2.0	1508	4.2	2118	2.0
7 TH	0338	4.1	1000	1.8	1610	4.5	2229	1.6
8 F	0441	4.4	1102	1.5	1703	4.8	2328	1.2
9 SA	0534	4.8	1153	1.1	1750	5.2		
10 SU ○	0018	0.8	0620	5.1	1241	0.8	1834	5.5
11 M	0106	0.4	0704	5.3	1326	0.5	1917	5.7
12 TU	0151	0.2	0747	5.4	1410	0.4	2001	5.8
13 W	0235	0.2	0830	5.3	1453	0.4	2045	5.6
14 TH	0318	0.3	0915	5.1	1536	0.6	2133	5.3
15 F	0401	0.6	1003	4.8	1621	1.0	2225	4.9
16 SA	0445	1.0	1059	4.5	1710	1.4	2328	4.5
17 SU ☾	0533	1.4	1207	4.2	1806	1.8		
18 M	0042	4.2	0629	1.9	1327	4.0	1918	2.1
19 TU ●	0202	4.0	0744	2.2	1450	4.0	2050	2.2
20 W	0320	4.0	0915	2.2	1558	4.1	2212	2.0
21 TH	0422	4.1	1028	2.0	1649	4.3	2308	1.8
22 F	0510	4.2	1118	1.8	1729	4.5	2351	1.5
23 SA	0548	4.6	1158	1.5	1802	4.7		
24 SU	0028	1.3	0620	4.6	1234	1.4	1831	4.9
25 M	0102	1.1	0650	4.8	1307	1.2	1858	5.0
26 TU	0133	1.0	0718	4.9	1338	1.1	1924	5.0
27 W	0204	0.9	0746	4.9	1408	1.0	1950	5.0
28 TH	0233	0.9	0814	4.9	1438	1.0	2019	5.0
29 F	0303	1.0	0845	4.8	1509	1.1	2050	4.9
30 SA	0334	1.1	0919	4.7	1543	1.3	2126	4.7
31 SU	0408	1.3	0959	4.6	1621	1.4	2208	4.5

Chart Datum: 2·75 metres below Ordnance Datum (Newlyn)
HAT is 5·9 metres above Chart Datum

SCOTLAND – ULLAPOOL
LAT 57°54'N   LONG 5°09'W
TIMES AND HEIGHTS OF HIGH AND LOW WATERS

Dates in amber are **SPRINGS**
Dates in yellow are **NEAPS**

2014

SEPTEMBER

Day	Time m	Time m	Time m	Time m	Day	Time m	Time m	Time m	Time m
1 M	0447 1.5	1050 4.3	1705 1.7	2305 4.2	16 TU	0009 4.1	0550 2.0	1246 4.0	◑ 1841 2.2
2 TU	0535 1.8	1203 4.1	1802 2.0 ◑		17 W	0131 3.9	0700 2.3	1414 3.9	2017 2.3
3 W	0032 4.0	0640 2.1	1329 4.1	1921 2.1	18 TH	0252 3.9	0839 2.4	1528 4.0	2146 2.1
4 TH	0205 4.0	0814 2.1	1445 4.2	2057 2.0	19 F	0357 4.0	1000 2.2	1622 4.2	2242 1.9
5 F	0325 4.2	0943 1.9	1551 4.5	2215 1.6	20 SA	0445 4.2	1052 2.0	1703 4.4	2324 1.6
6 SA	0430 4.5	1046 1.5	1646 4.9	2313 1.2	21 SU	0523 4.4	1132 1.7	1736 4.6	
7 SU	0521 4.8	1138 1.1	1733 5.3		22 M	0000 1.4	0554 4.7	1207 1.4	1804 4.8
8 M	0002 0.7	0604 5.2	1224 0.8	1816 5.6	23 TU	0033 1.1	0623 4.9	1240 1.2	1831 5.0
9 TU	0048 0.4	0645 5.4	1307 0.5	○ 1857 5.8	24 W	0104 1.0	0650 5.0	1311 1.1	● 1857 5.1
10 W	0131 0.2	0725 5.5	1349 0.4	1939 5.8	25 TH	0134 0.9	0717 5.1	1341 1.0	1924 5.1
11 TH	0212 0.2	0804 5.5	1431 0.4	2021 5.6	26 F	0203 0.9	0746 5.1	1412 1.0	1953 5.1
12 F	0253 0.4	0845 5.2	1512 0.6	2105 5.3	27 SA	0234 0.9	0816 5.0	1444 1.0	2026 5.0
13 SA	0333 0.7	0928 4.9	1555 1.0	2154 4.9	28 SU	0306 1.0	0851 4.9	1519 1.2	2103 4.8
14 SU	0414 1.1	1017 4.6	1641 1.4	2254 4.5	29 M	0341 1.2	0931 4.7	1558 1.4	2148 4.5
15 M	0458 1.6	1121 4.2	1733 1.8		30 TU	0421 1.5	1023 4.5	1643 1.6	2249 4.3

OCTOBER

Day	Time m	Time m	Time m	Time m	Day	Time m	Time m	Time m	Time m
1 W	0510 1.8	1137 4.3	1742 1.9 ◑		16 TH	0047 3.9	0615 2.4	1320 3.9	1928 2.3
2 TH	0021 4.1	0617 2.1	1306 4.2	1903 2.1	17 F	0207 3.8	0745 2.5	1441 4.0	2059 2.3
3 F	0152 4.0	0755 2.2	1424 4.3	2041 1.9	18 SA	0317 4.0	0915 2.4	1543 4.1	2203 2.0
4 SA	0311 4.2	0925 2.0	1532 4.6	2158 1.6	19 SU	0410 4.2	1015 2.2	1628 4.3	2248 1.8
5 SU	0415 4.5	1028 1.6	1628 4.9	2255 1.2	20 M	0451 4.4	1058 1.9	1704 4.6	2326 1.5
6 M	0505 4.9	1119 1.2	1714 5.3	2343 0.8	21 TU	0524 4.6	1135 1.6	1734 4.8	
7 TU	0547 5.2	1204 0.8	1757 5.6		22 W	0000 1.3	0554 4.9	1209 1.4	1802 4.9
8 W	0027 0.5	0625 5.4	1247 0.6	○ 1837 5.7	23 TH	0032 1.1	0622 5.0	1242 1.2	● 1830 5.1
9 TH	0109 0.4	0702 5.5	1329 0.5	1918 5.7	24 F	0104 1.0	0651 5.2	1315 1.0	1900 5.2
10 F	0149 0.4	0740 5.5	1410 0.6	1959 5.5	25 SA	0136 0.9	0721 5.2	1348 1.0	1932 5.2
11 SA	0227 0.6	0818 5.3	1450 0.7	2041 5.2	26 SU	0208 0.9	0754 5.2	1423 1.0	2009 5.1
12 SU	0306 0.9	0858 5.0	1532 1.1	2127 4.8	27 M	0243 1.0	0832 5.1	1501 1.1	2051 4.9
13 M	0346 1.3	0940 4.7	1615 1.4	2221 4.4	28 TU	0321 1.2	0915 4.9	1543 1.3	2141 4.6
14 TU	0427 1.7	1033 4.4	1704 1.8	2329 4.1	29 W	0404 1.5	1009 4.7	1631 1.5	2248 4.4
15 W	0515 2.1	1150 4.1	1805 2.2 ◑		30 TH	0455 1.8	1121 4.5	1731 1.8 ◑	
					31 F	0012 4.2	0603 2.1	1244 4.4	◑ 1849 1.9

NOVEMBER

Day	Time m	Time m	Time m	Time m	Day	Time m	Time m	Time m	Time m
1 SA	0135 4.2	0733 2.2	1359 4.4	2018 1.8	16 SU	0217 3.9	0806 2.5	1442 4.1	2105 2.2
2 SU	0251 4.3	0859 2.0	1508 4.6	2133 1.6	17 M	0321 4.1	0921 2.4	1540 4.2	2201 2.0
3 M	0355 4.6	1004 1.7	1606 4.9	2232 1.3	18 TU	0410 4.3	1015 2.1	1624 4.4	2246 1.7
4 TU	0446 4.9	1057 1.4	1656 5.2	2321 1.0	19 W	0449 4.5	1058 1.8	1700 4.6	2324 1.5
5 W	0529 5.1	1145 1.1	1740 5.4		20 TH	0523 4.8	1137 1.6	1733 4.8	
6 TH	0006 0.8	0607 5.3	1229 0.9	○ 1821 5.5	21 F	0000 1.3	0555 5.0	1214 1.3	1806 5.0
7 F	0048 0.7	0644 5.4	1311 0.8	1901 5.5	22 SA	0036 1.1	0627 5.2	1251 1.1	1841 5.1
8 SA	0127 0.7	0720 5.4	1352 0.8	1942 5.3	23 SU	0112 1.0	0702 5.3	1329 1.0	● 1918 5.2
9 SU	0205 0.9	0758 5.3	1432 0.9	2023 5.1	24 M	0149 0.9	0739 5.4	1408 0.9	2000 5.1
10 M	0243 1.1	0835 5.1	1512 1.2	2106 4.8	25 TU	0227 1.0	0820 5.3	1450 1.0	2046 5.0
11 TU	0321 1.4	0914 4.8	1554 1.4	2153 4.5	26 W	0309 1.1	0907 5.2	1535 1.1	2139 4.8
12 W	0401 1.7	0957 4.5	1638 1.7	2247 4.2	27 TH	0354 1.4	1001 5.0	1625 1.3	2242 4.6
13 TH	0444 2.0	1050 4.3	1729 2.0	2352 4.0	28 F	0446 1.6	1105 4.8	1722 1.5	2354 4.4
14 F	0535 2.3	1206 4.1	1832 2.2 ◑		29 SA	0549 1.9	1218 4.6	1830 1.7 ◑	
15 SA	0104 3.9	0641 2.5	1329 4.0	1950 2.3	30 SU	0108 4.3	0705 2.0	1331 4.6	1947 1.8

DECEMBER

Day	Time m	Time m	Time m	Time m	Day	Time m	Time m	Time m	Time m
1 M	0223 4.4	0825 2.0	1441 4.6	2101 1.7	16 TU	0215 4.0	0805 2.5	1433 4.1	2058 2.2
2 TU	0331 4.5	0936 1.8	1545 4.8	2206 1.5	17 W	0317 4.2	0917 2.3	1533 4.2	2158 2.0
3 W	0427 4.7	1036 1.6	1640 4.9	2300 1.3	18 TH	0409 4.4	1015 2.1	1622 4.4	2247 1.8
4 TH	0514 4.9	1128 1.4	1727 5.1	2347 1.2	19 F	0451 4.6	1104 1.8	1705 4.6	2330 1.5
5 F	0555 5.1	1214 1.2	1810 5.2		20 SA	0530 4.9	1148 1.5	1746 4.9	
6 SA	0030 1.1	0632 5.2	1258 1.1	1851 5.2	21 SU	0011 1.3	0608 5.2	1231 1.2	1826 5.1
7 SU	0110 1.1	0708 5.3	1339 1.0	1930 5.1	22 M	0053 1.1	0647 5.4	1314 1.0	● 1909 5.2
8 M	0148 1.1	0743 5.2	1418 1.1	2008 5.0	23 TU	0134 0.9	0727 5.5	1357 0.8	1953 5.3
9 TU	0225 1.2	0818 5.1	1456 1.2	2047 4.8	24 W	0216 0.9	0811 5.6	1441 0.7	2039 5.2
10 W	0301 1.4	0852 5.0	1534 1.4	2126 4.6	25 TH	0259 0.9	0857 5.5	1527 0.8	2129 5.1
11 TH	0338 1.6	0928 4.8	1613 1.6	2208 4.4	26 F	0345 1.1	0947 5.3	1615 1.0	2224 4.8
12 F	0416 1.8	1008 4.5	1654 1.8	2256 4.2	27 SA	0434 1.3	1044 5.1	1706 1.2	2326 4.6
13 SA	0458 2.0	1057 4.3	1741 2.0	2356 4.1	28 SU	0529 1.6	1158 4.8	1804 1.5 ◑	
14 SU	0547 2.3	1203 4.2	1838 2.2 ◑		29 M	0035 4.4	0632 1.9	1300 4.6	1910 1.7
15 M	0106 4.0	0649 2.4	1322 4.1	1947 2.2	30 TU	0150 4.3	0747 2.0	1412 4.5	2024 1.8
					31 W	0305 4.4	0905 2.0	1524 4.5	2138 1.8

Chart Datum: 2·75 metres below Ordnance Datum (Newlyn)
HAT is 5·9 metres above Chart Datum

TIDES

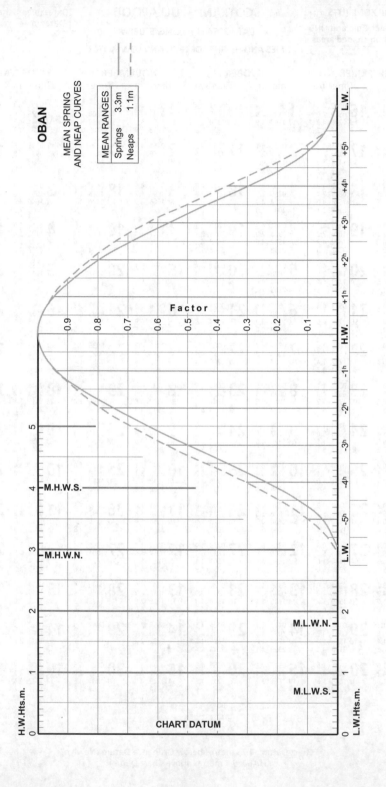

OBAN

MEAN SPRING
AND NEAP CURVES

MEAN RANGES	
Springs	3.3m
Neaps	1.1m

Factor

0.9 0.8 0.7 0.6 0.5 0.4 0.3 0.2 0.1

H.W.Hts.m.

M.H.W.S.

M.H.W.N.

CHART DATUM

M.L.W.N.

M.L.W.S.

L.W.Hts.m.

L.W.   +5ʰ +4ʰ +3ʰ +2ʰ +1ʰ H.W. -1ʰ -2ʰ -3ʰ -4ʰ -5ʰ L.W.

SCOTLAND – OBAN

LAT 56°25'N   LONG 5°29'W

TIMES AND HEIGHTS OF HIGH AND LOW WATERS

Dates in amber are **SPRINGS**
Dates in yellow are **NEAPS**

2014

JANUARY

Time	m	Time	m
1 0519 / 1133 / W 1735 / ● 2355	4.1 / 0.7 / 4.0 / 0.6	**16** 0542 / 1226 / TH 1808 / ○	3.9 / 1.3 / 3.9
2 0603 / 1223 / TH 1818	4.2 / 0.6 / 4.1	**17** 0019 / 0617 / F 1259 / 1842	1.0 / 4.0 / 1.3 / 3.9
3 0040 / 0646 / F 1311 / 1900	0.5 / 4.3 / 0.6 / 4.0	**18** 0055 / 0651 / SA 1331 / 1914	1.0 / 4.0 / 1.3 / 3.9
4 0127 / 0729 / SA 1358 / 1943	0.4 / 4.2 / 0.6 / 3.9	**19** 0128 / 0722 / SU 1402 / 1944	1.0 / 4.0 / 1.4 / 3.8
5 0214 / 0814 / SU 1445 / 2026	0.5 / 4.1 / 0.8 / 3.9	**20** 0158 / 0752 / M 1429 / 2012	1.1 / 3.9 / 1.5 / 3.7
6 0301 / 0900 / M 1533 / 2110	0.7 / 3.9 / 1.0 / 3.5	**21** 0226 / 0820 / TU 1449 / 2043	1.2 / 3.8 / 1.6 / 3.5
7 0351 / 0949 / TU 1624 / 2159	0.9 / 3.6 / 1.3 / 3.2	**22** 0258 / 0852 / W 1519 / 2119	1.3 / 3.6 / 1.7 / 3.4
8 0445 / 1048 / W 1719 / ◐ 2259	1.2 / 3.3 / 1.5 / 3.0	**23** 0338 / 0931 / TH 1604 / 2203	1.5 / 3.5 / 1.8 / 3.2
9 0545 / 1213 / TH 1820	1.5 / 3.1 / 1.7	**24** 0429 / 1021 / F 1710 / ◐ 2302	1.6 / 3.3 / 1.9 / 3.1
10 0025 / 0657 / F 1347 / 1928	2.9 / 1.7 / 3.1 / 1.8	**25** 0536 / 1131 / SA 1834	1.7 / 3.2 / 1.9
11 0152 / 0825 / SA 1500 / 2039	2.9 / 1.7 / 3.1 / 1.7	**26** 0033 / 0654 / SU 1324 / 1954	3.0 / 1.7 / 3.1 / 1.7
12 0256 / 0941 / SU 1549 / 2138	3.1 / 1.7 / 3.3 / 1.6	**27** 0231 / 0815 / M 1501 / 2106	3.2 / 1.5 / 3.3 / 1.5
13 0344 / 1034 / M 1624 / 2224	3.3 / 1.6 / 3.4 / 1.4	**28** 0337 / 0930 / TU 1600 / 2206	3.5 / 1.3 / 3.5 / 1.1
14 0426 / 1117 / TU 1658 / 2304	3.5 / 1.5 / 3.6 / 1.3	**29** 0427 / 1033 / W 1647 / 2258	3.8 / 1.0 / 3.8 / 0.8
15 0505 / 1153 / W 1733 / 2342	3.7 / 1.4 / 3.8 / 1.1	**30** 0512 / 1126 / TH 1729 / ● 2345	4.1 / 0.7 / 4.0 / 0.5
		31 0554 / 1214 / F 1809	4.3 / 0.5 / 4.1

FEBRUARY

Time	m	Time	m
1 0030 / 0635 / SA 1259 / 1848	0.3 / 4.4 / 0.4 / 4.1	**16** 0032 / 0632 / SU 1307 / 1854	0.8 / 4.0 / 1.1 / 3.9
2 0115 / 0715 / SU 1342 / 1927	0.3 / 4.3 / 0.5 / 4.0	**17** 0104 / 0701 / M 1335 / 1920	0.8 / 4.0 / 1.1 / 3.9
3 0158 / 0755 / M 1424 / 2005	0.3 / 4.2 / 0.6 / 3.8	**18** 0131 / 0727 / TU 1358 / 1945	0.9 / 3.9 / 1.2 / 3.8
4 0241 / 0835 / TU 1506 / 2042	0.5 / 3.9 / 0.9 / 3.6	**19** 0158 / 0754 / W 1417 / 2015	0.9 / 3.8 / 1.2 / 3.7
5 0325 / 0915 / W 1549 / 2120	0.8 / 3.6 / 1.1 / 3.4	**20** 0229 / 0825 / TH 1447 / 2050	1.1 / 3.7 / 1.4 / 3.5
6 0411 / 1000 / TH 1637 / ◑ 2203	1.1 / 3.3 / 1.4 / 3.1	**21** 0309 / 0902 / F 1530 / 2132	1.2 / 3.5 / 1.5 / 3.3
7 0503 / 1056 / F 1732 / 2303	1.5 / 3.0 / 1.7 / 2.9	**22** 0358 / 0948 / SA 1629 / ◑ 2228	1.4 / 3.3 / 1.7 / 3.1
8 0607 / 1250 / SA 1836	1.7 / 2.8 / 1.8	**23** 0506 / 1055 / SU 1757 / 2357	1.6 / 3.0 / 1.7 / 3.0
9 0054 / 0742 / SU 1445 / 1952	2.8 / 1.9 / 2.9 / 1.8	**24** 0634 / 1257 / M 1928	1.6 / 2.9 / 1.7
10 0228 / 0932 / M 1545 / 2112	2.9 / 1.8 / 3.0 / 1.7	**25** 0216 / 0803 / TU 1500 / 2048	3.1 / 1.5 / 3.1 / 1.4
11 0328 / 1026 / TU 1616 / 2207	3.1 / 1.6 / 3.2 / 1.5	**26** 0327 / 0923 / W 1558 / 2153	3.4 / 1.2 / 3.4 / 1.1
12 0410 / 1106 / W 1645 / 2249	3.3 / 1.5 / 3.5 / 1.3	**27** 0417 / 1024 / TH 1641 / 2245	3.8 / 0.9 / 3.6 / 0.7
13 0449 / 1140 / TH 1718 / 2325	3.6 / 1.3 / 3.7 / 1.1	**28** 0500 / 1114 / F 1718 / 2332	4.1 / 0.6 / 3.9 / 0.4
14 0525 / 1210 / F 1752 / ○ 2359	3.8 / 1.2 / 3.8 / 0.9		
15 0600 / 1238 / SA 1825	3.9 / 1.1 / 3.9		

MARCH

Time	m	Time	m
1 0540 / 1159 / SA 1754 / ●	4.3 / 0.4 / 4.0	**16** 0536 / 1210 / SU 1800 / ○	3.8 / 0.9 / 3.9
2 0016 / 0618 / SU 1241 / 1830	0.2 / 4.3 / 0.3 / 4.1	**17** 0004 / 0607 / M 1238 / 1828	0.7 / 3.9 / 0.9 / 3.9
3 0059 / 0656 / M 1320 / 1906	0.2 / 4.3 / 0.4 / 4.0	**18** 0035 / 0635 / TU 1304 / 1853	0.7 / 4.0 / 0.9 / 3.9
4 0140 / 0732 / TU 1358 / 1940	0.3 / 4.1 / 0.5 / 3.9	**19** 0105 / 0701 / W 1329 / 1919	0.7 / 3.9 / 0.9 / 3.8
5 0220 / 0808 / W 1437 / 2014	0.5 / 3.9 / 0.8 / 3.7	**20** 0135 / 0730 / TH 1355 / 1951	0.7 / 3.8 / 1.0 / 3.7
6 0300 / 0843 / TH 1516 / 2048	0.8 / 3.6 / 1.0 / 3.5	**21** 0210 / 0804 / F 1429 / 2029	0.9 / 3.7 / 1.1 / 3.6
7 0341 / 0921 / F 1601 / 2125	1.2 / 3.3 / 1.3 / 3.2	**22** 0252 / 0843 / SA 1512 / 2114	1.0 / 3.4 / 1.3 / 3.4
8 0429 / 1006 / SA 1653 / ◑ 2213	1.5 / 3.0 / 1.6 / 3.0	**23** 0345 / 0931 / SU 1612 / 2213	1.2 / 3.2 / 1.4 / 3.1
9 0527 / 1121 / SU 1755 / 2338	1.8 / 2.7 / 1.8 / 2.8	**24** 0457 / 1041 / M 1738 / ◑ 2343	1.4 / 2.9 / 1.6 / 3.0
10 0650 / 1413 / M 1908	2.0 / 2.7 / 1.8	**25** 0625 / 1251 / TU 1907	1.5 / 2.8 / 1.5
11 0155 / 0914 / TU 1518 / 2033	2.8 / 1.9 / 2.9 / 1.7	**26** 0158 / 0753 / W 1448 / 2028	3.1 / 1.4 / 3.0 / 1.3
12 0307 / 1007 / W 1553 / 2139	3.0 / 1.7 / 3.1 / 1.5	**27** 0308 / 0910 / TH 1544 / 2134	3.4 / 1.2 / 3.3 / 1.0
13 0349 / 1044 / TH 1622 / 2223	3.2 / 1.5 / 3.3 / 1.3	**28** 0358 / 1008 / F 1625 / 2227	3.7 / 0.9 / 3.5 / 0.7
14 0426 / 1115 / F 1654 / 2259	3.5 / 1.3 / 3.6 / 1.0	**29** 0441 / 1055 / SA 1700 / 2314	4.0 / 0.6 / 3.8 / 0.5
15 0502 / 1143 / SA 1728 / 2332	3.7 / 1.1 / 3.7 / 0.9	**30** 0520 / 1138 / SU 1734 / ● 2357	4.1 / 0.5 / 3.9 / 0.3
		31 0557 / 1217 / M 1808	4.2 / 0.4 / 4.0

APRIL

Time	m	Time	m
1 0039 / 0633 / TU 1255 / 1842	0.3 / 4.2 / 0.4 / 4.0	**16** 0005 / 0609 / W 1234 / 1827	0.6 / 3.9 / 0.7 / 3.9
2 0119 / 0707 / W 1332 / 1916	0.4 / 4.0 / 0.6 / 3.9	**17** 0041 / 0639 / TH 1305 / 1858	0.6 / 3.9 / 0.7 / 3.9
3 0158 / 0741 / TH 1409 / 1948	0.6 / 3.8 / 0.8 / 3.8	**18** 0119 / 0712 / F 1339 / 1935	0.6 / 3.8 / 0.8 / 3.8
4 0236 / 0815 / F 1447 / 2022	0.9 / 3.5 / 1.0 / 3.6	**19** 0200 / 0751 / SA 1420 / 2017	0.7 / 3.6 / 0.9 / 3.6
5 0315 / 0852 / SA 1531 / 2059	1.3 / 3.3 / 1.3 / 3.3	**20** 0248 / 0835 / SU 1508 / 2106	0.9 / 3.4 / 1.1 / 3.4
6 0401 / 0934 / SU 1620 / 2144	1.6 / 3.0 / 1.5 / 3.1	**21** 0345 / 0928 / M 1609 / 2208	1.1 / 3.1 / 1.2 / 3.2
7 0457 / 1034 / M 1718 / ◑ 2248	1.8 / 2.7 / 1.7 / 2.9	**22** 0455 / 1039 / TU 1724 / ◑ 2335	1.3 / 2.9 / 1.4 / 3.1
8 0610 / 1320 / TU 1825	2.0 / 2.7 / 1.8	**23** 0614 / 1238 / W 1845	1.4 / 2.8 / 1.4
9 0051 / 0830 / W 1434 / 1938	2.8 / 1.9 / 2.8 / 1.7	**24** 0132 / 0736 / TH 1421 / 2003	3.2 / 1.3 / 2.9 / 1.3
10 0228 / 0932 / TH 1517 / 2050	2.9 / 1.7 / 3.0 / 1.6	**25** 0241 / 0849 / F 1519 / 2111	3.4 / 1.2 / 3.2 / 1.0
11 0315 / 1009 / F 1551 / 2142	3.1 / 1.5 / 3.2 / 1.3	**26** 0334 / 0945 / SA 1601 / 2206	3.6 / 1.0 / 3.4 / 0.8
12 0354 / 1039 / SA 1624 / 2222	3.4 / 1.3 / 3.4 / 1.1	**27** 0418 / 1032 / SU 1636 / 2253	3.8 / 0.8 / 3.6 / 0.7
13 0431 / 1107 / SU 1658 / 2257	3.6 / 1.1 / 3.6 / 0.9	**28** 0458 / 1113 / M 1710 / 2337	3.9 / 0.7 / 3.8 / 0.6
14 0506 / 1135 / M 1730 / 2331	3.8 / 0.9 / 3.8 / 0.7	**29** 0535 / 1152 / TU 1745 / ●	4.0 / 0.6 / 3.9
15 0539 / 1204 / TU 1800 / ○	3.9 / 0.8 / 3.9	**30** 0019 / 0610 / W 1230 / 1819	0.6 / 4.0 / 0.6 / 3.9

TIDES

Chart Datum: 2·10 metres below Ordnance Datum (Newlyn)
HAT is 4·5 metres above Chart Datum

TIME ZONE (UT)	SCOTLAND – OBAN	Dates in amber are SPRINGS
For Summer Time add ONE hour in non-shaded areas	LAT 56°25'N LONG 5°29'W	Dates in yellow are NEAPS
	TIMES AND HEIGHTS OF HIGH AND LOW WATERS	2014

MAY

Day	Time m	Time m	Time m	Time m
1 TH	0059 0.7	0645 3.9	1306 0.7	1853 3.9
16 F	0022 0.6	0622 3.9	1246 0.6	1844 3.9
2 F	0138 0.9	0719 3.7	1343 0.9	1927 3.8
17 SA	0107 0.6	0701 3.8	1328 0.6	1925 3.9
3 SA	0215 1.1	0754 3.5	1422 1.0	2002 3.6
18 SU	0154 0.6	0744 3.6	1413 0.7	2011 3.7
4 SU	0254 1.4	0831 3.3	1504 1.3	2040 3.4
19 M	0245 0.8	0831 3.4	1504 0.9	2102 3.6
5 M	0338 1.6	0913 3.1	1550 1.5	2123 3.2
20 TU	0342 1.0	0925 3.2	1601 1.0	2202 3.4
6 TU	0429 1.8	1005 2.9	1642 1.6	2216 3.0
21 W	0445 1.1	1031 3.0	1706 1.2	2319 3.2
7 W	0533 2.0	1126 2.8	1740 1.7	2330 2.9
22 TH	0556 1.3	1205 2.9	1819 1.3	
8 TH	0653 2.0	1330 2.8	1842 1.8	
23 F	0058 3.2	0709 1.3	1342 2.9	1933 1.3
9 F	0111 2.9	0821 1.8	1429 2.9	1945 1.7
24 SA	0211 3.3	0820 1.2	1446 3.1	2044 1.2
10 SA	0224 3.1	0914 1.6	1511 3.1	2044 1.5
25 SU	0309 3.4	0918 1.0	1533 3.3	2143 1.1
11 SU	0313 3.3	0952 1.2	1549 3.3	2133 1.3
26 M	0356 3.6	1007 1.0	1611 3.5	2234 1.0
12 M	0355 3.5	1026 1.2	1625 3.5	2216 1.0
27 TU	0438 3.7	1049 0.9	1648 3.6	2319 0.9
13 TU	0434 3.7	1058 1.0	1700 3.7	2258 0.8
28 W	0516 3.7	1128 0.9	1724 3.8	
14 W	0510 3.8	1131 0.8	1733 3.8	2339 0.7
29 TH	0001 0.9	0551 3.8	1206 0.9	1800 3.8
15 TH	0546 3.9	1207 0.7	1807 3.9	
30 F	0042 1.0	0627 3.8	1244 0.9	1835 3.9
31 SA	0120 1.1	0702 3.7	1322 1.0	1910 3.8

JUNE

Day	Time m	Time m	Time m	Time m
1 SU	0158 1.2	0738 3.6	1400 1.1	1946 3.7
16 M	0147 0.5	0738 3.7	1404 0.5	2005 3.9
2 M	0236 1.4	0815 3.4	1440 1.2	2023 3.6
17 TU	0237 0.6	0824 3.5	1454 0.6	2055 3.7
3 TU	0316 1.6	0855 3.3	1521 1.4	2102 3.4
18 W	0330 0.8	0915 3.3	1547 0.8	2149 3.5
4 W	0401 1.8	0938 3.1	1605 1.6	2145 3.3
19 TH	0427 1.0	1012 3.1	1645 1.0	2253 3.3
5 TH	0452 1.9	1030 3.0	1653 1.7	2236 3.1
20 F	0528 1.2	1124 2.9	1749 1.2	
6 F	0551 1.9	1142 2.9	1747 1.7	2341 3.1
21 SA	0017 3.2	0634 1.3	1252 2.9	1859 1.3
7 SA	0658 1.9	1314 2.9	1845 1.7	
22 SU	0138 3.2	0743 1.4	1407 3.0	2013 1.4
8 SU	0107 3.1	0802 1.8	1421 3.0	1944 1.6
23 M	0245 3.2	0848 1.4	1504 3.1	2123 1.3
9 M	0221 3.2	0857 1.6	1510 3.2	2043 1.4
24 TU	0339 3.3	0942 1.2	1549 3.3	2219 1.3
10 TU	0317 3.4	0943 1.3	1553 3.4	2138 1.2
25 W	0423 3.4	1028 1.2	1629 3.5	2307 1.2
11 W	0404 3.6	1025 1.1	1634 3.6	2230 0.9
26 TH	0502 3.5	1108 1.1	1707 3.6	2349 1.2
12 TH	0448 3.7	1106 0.9	1714 3.8	2320 0.7
27 F	0538 3.6	1147 1.0	1744 3.8	
13 F	0530 3.8	1148 0.7	1755 3.9	
28 SA	0027 1.2	0613 3.7	1225 1.0	1820 3.8
14 SA	0009 0.6	0611 3.9	1232 0.5	1836 4.0
29 SU	0104 1.2	0649 3.7	1303 1.0	1856 3.9
15 SU	0058 0.5	0654 3.8	1317 0.5	1919 4.0
30 M	0140 1.3	0724 3.7	1340 1.0	1931 3.8

JULY

Day	Time m	Time m	Time m	Time m
1 TU	0216 1.4	0759 3.6	1415 1.1	2005 3.7
16 W	0223 0.5	0811 3.7	1439 0.4	2040 3.9
2 W	0252 1.5	0833 3.5	1450 1.3	2039 3.6
17 TH	0311 0.7	0855 3.5	1528 0.7	2127 3.6
3 TH	0328 1.6	0908 3.3	1526 1.4	2113 3.5
18 F	0401 0.9	0943 3.2	1619 0.9	2220 3.4
4 F	0406 1.7	0947 3.2	1606 1.6	2152 3.3
19 SA	0455 1.2	1040 3.0	1717 1.2	2329 3.1
5 SA	0452 1.8	1033 3.0	1655 1.7	2240 3.2
20 SU	0554 1.4	1159 2.9	1822 1.4	
6 SU	0551 1.9	1135 3.0	1753 1.7	2344 3.1
21 M	0102 3.0	0701 1.5	1328 2.9	1941 1.6
7 M	0658 1.8	1311 3.0	1858 1.7	
22 TU	0226 3.0	0814 1.6	1440 3.0	2109 1.6
8 TU	0119 3.1	0805 1.7	1433 3.1	2005 1.5
23 W	0332 3.1	0920 1.5	1533 3.1	2213 1.5
9 W	0244 3.3	0907 1.4	1530 3.3	2111 1.3
24 TH	0415 3.2	1011 1.3	1614 3.3	2300 1.4
10 TH	0344 3.4	1000 1.2	1618 3.6	2213 1.0
25 F	0450 3.4	1053 1.2	1652 3.6	2339 1.3
11 F	0434 3.6	1049 0.9	1703 3.8	2308 0.8
26 SA	0524 3.6	1131 1.0	1730 3.7	
12 SA	0520 3.8	1135 0.6	1746 4.0	2359 0.5
27 SU	0014 1.2	0559 3.7	1208 0.9	1805 3.9
13 SU	0603 3.9	1220 0.4	1829 4.2	
28 M	0047 1.2	0633 3.8	1244 0.9	1839 3.9
14 M	0048 0.4	0645 3.9	1306 0.3	1912 4.2
29 TU	0120 1.2	0706 3.8	1318 0.9	1912 3.9
15 TU	0136 0.4	0728 3.8	1352 0.3	1955 4.1
30 W	0153 1.2	0737 3.8	1350 1.0	1942 3.9
31 TH	0224 1.3	0806 3.6	1419 1.1	2011 3.7

AUGUST

Day	Time m	Time m	Time m	Time m
1 F	0251 1.4	0835 3.5	1449 1.3	2040 3.6
16 SA	0331 0.9	0910 3.4	1553 1.0	2143 3.4
2 SA	0315 1.6	0908 3.4	1524 1.4	2114 3.5
17 SU	0420 1.2	0956 3.1	1645 1.3	2238 3.0
3 SU	0351 1.7	0949 3.2	1610 1.6	2157 3.3
18 M	0515 1.4	1100 2.9	1746 1.6	
4 M	0448 1.8	1042 3.0	1709 1.7	2254 3.1
19 TU	0016 2.8	0619 1.6	1249 2.8	1907 1.8
5 TU	0607 1.8	1202 3.0	1823 1.7	
20 W	0213 2.8	0735 1.7	1424 2.9	2104 1.8
6 W	0025 3.0	0728 1.7	1410 3.1	1941 1.6
21 TH	0331 2.9	0856 1.6	1523 3.1	2206 1.6
7 TH	0228 3.1	0842 1.5	1519 3.3	2057 1.4
22 F	0406 3.1	0953 1.4	1559 3.3	2248 1.5
8 F	0337 3.3	0944 1.2	1609 3.6	2204 1.1
23 SA	0433 3.3	1036 1.2	1635 3.5	2323 1.3
9 SA	0427 3.6	1037 0.8	1653 3.9	2300 0.7
24 SU	0504 3.6	1113 1.0	1710 3.8	2354 1.1
10 SU	0511 3.8	1124 0.5	1735 4.2	2349 0.5
25 M	0538 3.8	1147 0.9	1745 3.9 ●	
11 M	0551 3.9	1209 0.3	1816 4.3	
26 TU	0023 1.1	0611 3.9	1220 0.8	1818 4.0
12 TU	0035 0.3	0631 4.0	1253 0.2	1856 4.3
27 W	0053 1.0	0642 3.9	1252 0.8	1848 4.0
13 W	0120 0.3	0710 4.0	1337 0.2	1937 4.2
28 TH	0124 1.1	0711 3.9	1322 0.9	1916 3.9
14 TH	0203 0.4	0749 3.8	1421 0.4	2017 4.0
29 F	0152 1.1	0736 3.8	1348 1.0	1942 3.8
15 F	0246 0.6	0829 3.6	1505 0.6	2058 3.7
30 SA	0214 1.2	0803 3.6	1417 1.1	2009 3.7
31 SU	0236 1.6	0835 3.5	1452 1.3	2042 3.5

Chart Datum: 2·10 metres below Ordnance Datum (Newlyn)
HAT is 4·5 metres above Chart Datum

SCOTLAND – OBAN
LAT 56°25'N   LONG 5°29'W
TIMES AND HEIGHTS OF HIGH AND LOW WATERS

Dates in amber are **SPRINGS**
Dates in yellow are **NEAPS**

2014

SEPTEMBER

Day	Time m	Time m	Time m	Time m		Day	Time m	Time m	Time m	Time m
1 M	0312 1.5	0915 3.3	1537 1.5	2123 3.3		**16** TU	0438 1.5	1009 3.0	1714 1.8	◐ 2304 2.8
2 TU	0405 1.7	1007 3.1	1639 1.7	◑ 2220 3.1		**17** W	0540 1.7	1152 2.8	1836 2.0	
3 W	0530 1.8	1128 3.0	1802 1.7	2357 2.9		**18** TH	0150 2.7	0820 1.7	1406 2.9	2051 1.9
4 TH	0701 1.7	1402 3.1	1929 1.7			**19** F	0303 2.9	0820 1.7	1507 3.1	2148 1.7
5 F	0229 3.0	0822 1.5	1508 3.4	2050 1.4		**20** SA	0340 3.1	0925 1.5	1539 3.3	2226 1.5
6 SA	0334 3.3	0929 1.2	1557 3.7	2155 1.1		**21** SU	0408 3.3	1010 1.3	1611 3.6	2258 1.3
7 SU	0419 3.6	1022 0.8	1639 4.0	2248 0.7		**22** M	0439 3.6	1047 1.1	1645 3.8	2326 1.2
8 M	0457 3.8	1109 0.5	1719 4.3	2333 0.5		**23** TU	0512 3.8	1120 0.9	1719 3.9	2354 1.0
9 TU	0534 4.0	1153 0.3	1757 4.4	○		**24** W	0545 3.9	1152 0.9	1752 4.0	●
10 W	0016 0.3	0610 4.1	1236 0.2	1835 4.4		**25** TH	0022 1.0	0615 4.0	1223 0.8	1821 4.1
11 TH	0058 0.3	0647 4.1	1318 0.3	1913 4.3		**26** F	0052 1.0	0642 3.9	1253 0.9	1847 4.0
12 F	0138 0.4	0724 4.0	1400 0.4	1950 4.0		**27** SA	0119 1.0	0707 3.9	1322 0.9	1914 3.9
13 SA	0218 0.6	0800 3.8	1442 0.7	2027 3.7		**28** SU	0143 1.1	0736 3.8	1353 1.1	1944 3.8
14 SU	0300 0.9	0837 3.5	1526 1.1	2106 3.4		**29** M	0212 1.2	0811 3.6	1431 1.2	2020 3.6
15 M	0346 1.2	0917 3.3	1615 1.5	2152 3.0		**30** TU	0250 1.4	0852 3.4	1519 1.4	2102 3.3

OCTOBER

Day	Time m	Time m	Time m	Time m		Day	Time m	Time m	Time m	Time m
1 W	0344 1.6	0947 3.2	1625 1.6	◑ 2202 3.0		**16** TH	0503 1.7	1045 3.0	1800 2.1	
2 TH	0506 1.7	1111 3.1	1752 1.7	2345 2.9		**17** F	0105 2.8	0609 1.8	1319 3.0	2009 2.1
3 F	0637 1.7	1343 3.2	1920 1.6			**18** SA	0219 2.9	0727 1.8	1431 3.1	2116 1.9
4 SA	0219 3.0	0800 1.5	1448 3.5	2038 1.4		**19** SU	0304 3.1	0840 1.7	1509 3.3	2154 1.7
5 SU	0319 3.3	0908 1.2	1537 3.8	2139 1.1		**20** M	0337 3.3	0932 1.5	1542 3.5	2225 1.5
6 M	0402 3.6	1002 0.9	1619 4.1	2228 0.8		**21** TU	0409 3.5	1012 1.3	1616 3.7	2253 1.3
7 TU	0438 3.8	1050 0.6	1644 4.3	2312 0.6		**22** W	0443 3.7	1047 1.1	1650 3.9	2321 1.1
8 W	0512 4.0	1134 0.4	1735 4.4	○ 2353 0.5		**23** TH	0516 3.9	1120 1.0	1723 4.0	● 2350 1.0
9 TH	0548 4.1	1216 0.4	1811 4.4			**24** F	0547 4.0	1153 0.9	1753 4.1	
10 F	0032 0.5	0623 4.1	1258 0.5	1847 4.2		**25** SA	0020 0.9	0614 4.0	1226 0.9	1822 4.0
11 SA	0111 0.6	0659 4.0	1339 0.7	1922 4.0		**26** SU	0050 0.9	0643 4.0	1301 0.9	1853 4.0
12 SU	0150 0.7	0734 3.9	1420 1.0	1958 3.7		**27** M	0122 1.0	0716 3.9	1338 1.0	1927 3.8
13 M	0230 1.0	0809 3.7	1502 1.3	2035 3.4		**28** TU	0158 1.1	0755 3.8	1422 1.2	2007 3.6
14 TU	0315 1.3	0848 3.4	1548 1.6	2117 3.1		**29** W	0241 1.2	0841 3.6	1514 1.4	2055 3.3
15 W	0405 1.5	0935 3.2	1645 1.9	◑ 2215 2.9		**30** TH	0336 1.4	0938 3.4	1621 1.6	2157 3.1
						31 F	0448 1.5	1057 3.2	1740 1.6	◑ 2328 2.9

NOVEMBER

Day	Time m	Time m	Time m	Time m		Day	Time m	Time m	Time m	Time m
1 SA	0611 1.6	1311 3.3	1901 1.6			**16** SU	0114 2.9	0627 1.9	1317 3.1	2011 2.1
2 SU	0149 3.0	0731 1.5	1421 3.5	2016 1.4		**17** M	0217 3.1	0735 1.8	1423 3.3	2106 1.9
3 M	0254 3.2	0842 1.3	1513 3.8	2116 1.2		**18** TU	0259 3.2	0836 1.7	1505 3.5	2143 1.7
4 TU	0339 3.5	0940 1.0	1557 4.0	2205 1.0		**19** W	0336 3.4	0926 1.5	1543 3.6	2215 1.5
5 W	0415 3.7	1029 0.8	1636 4.1	2248 0.8		**20** TH	0412 3.6	1008 1.3	1620 3.8	2246 1.2
6 TH	0450 3.9	1115 0.7	1713 4.2	○ 2329 0.7		**21** F	0447 3.8	1047 1.1	1656 4.0	2318 1.1
7 F	0525 4.1	1158 0.7	1749 4.2			**22** SA	0521 3.9	1125 1.0	1730 4.0	● 2352 0.9
8 SA	0008 0.7	0601 4.1	1240 0.8	1824 4.1		**23** SU	0553 4.0	1204 0.9	1803 4.0	
9 SU	0047 0.8	0637 4.0	1320 1.0	1900 4.0		**24** M	0027 0.9	0627 4.0	1246 0.9	1838 4.0
10 M	0125 0.9	0712 4.0	1400 1.2	1935 3.8		**25** TU	0106 0.9	0704 4.0	1329 0.9	1917 3.9
11 TU	0205 1.1	0748 3.8	1441 1.5	2012 3.5		**26** W	0148 0.9	0746 3.9	1417 1.0	2001 3.7
12 W	0248 1.3	0827 3.6	1525 1.7	2053 3.3		**27** TH	0234 1.0	0833 3.8	1510 1.2	2049 3.4
13 TH	0334 1.5	0910 3.4	1616 2.0	2142 3.1		**28** F	0328 1.2	0928 3.6	1610 1.4	2147 3.2
14 F	0426 1.7	1004 3.2	1718 2.1	◑ 2253 2.9		**29** SA	0430 1.3	1037 3.4	1718 1.5	◑ 2300 3.0
15 SA	0524 1.8	1121 3.1	1838 2.2			**30** SU	0541 1.4	1222 3.4	1831 1.6	

DECEMBER

Day	Time m	Time m	Time m	Time m		Day	Time m	Time m	Time m	Time m
1 M	0048 3.0	0657 1.5	1347 3.5	1943 1.5		**16** TU	0041 3.0	0629 1.9	1257 3.2	1946 2.0
2 TU	0215 3.2	0812 1.4	1447 3.6	2047 1.4		**17** W	0205 3.1	0730 1.9	1415 3.3	2045 1.9
3 W	0310 3.4	0916 1.2	1537 3.8	2140 1.2		**18** TH	0258 3.3	0831 1.7	1509 3.5	2132 1.6
4 TH	0352 3.6	1011 1.1	1619 3.9	2226 1.1		**19** F	0342 3.5	0926 1.5	1553 3.6	2212 1.4
5 F	0429 3.8	1059 1.0	1657 4.0	2307 1.0		**20** SA	0422 3.7	1017 1.3	1634 3.8	2251 1.2
6 SA	0506 3.9	1143 1.0	1733 4.0	○ 2347 0.9		**21** SU	0501 3.9	1103 1.1	1713 3.9	2330 0.9
7 SU	0544 4.0	1225 1.1	1809 4.0			**22** M	0539 4.0	1149 0.9	1751 4.0	●
8 M	0026 0.9	0620 4.1	1305 1.2	1843 3.9		**23** TU	0010 0.7	0617 4.1	1235 0.8	1829 4.0
9 TU	0105 1.0	0656 4.0	1344 1.3	1919 3.8		**24** W	0053 0.7	0657 4.1	1321 0.7	1910 3.9
10 W	0144 1.1	0732 3.9	1422 1.5	1956 3.7		**25** TH	0137 0.7	0739 4.1	1408 0.8	1953 3.8
11 TH	0224 1.2	0809 3.8	1502 1.7	2034 3.5		**26** F	0224 0.7	0825 4.0	1458 0.9	2038 3.6
12 F	0305 1.4	0848 3.6	1545 1.9	2115 3.3		**27** SA	0314 0.9	0915 3.8	1551 1.1	2129 3.4
13 SA	0349 1.6	0930 3.5	1634 2.0	2203 3.2		**28** SU	0409 1.1	1012 3.5	1649 1.3	◑ 2228 3.2
14 SU	0437 1.8	1019 3.3	1731 2.1	◑ 2305 3.0		**29** M	0512 1.3	1128 3.4	1754 1.5	2345 3.0
15 M	0531 1.9	1124 3.2	1837 2.1			**30** TU	0622 1.4	1306 3.3	1903 1.6	
						31 W	0122 3.0	0738 1.5	1422 3.3	2012 1.6

TIDES

Chart Datum: 2·10 metres below Ordnance Datum (Newlyn)
HAT is 4·5 metres above Chart Datum

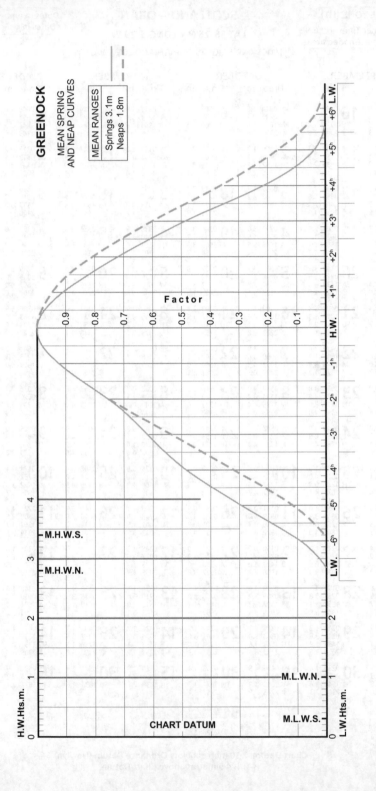

GREENOCK
MEAN SPRING
AND NEAP CURVES

MEAN RANGES
Springs 3.1m
Neaps 1.8m

TIME ZONE (UT)
For Summer Time add ONE hour in **non-shaded areas**

SCOTLAND – GREENOCK
LAT 55°57'N   LONG 4°46'W
TIMES AND HEIGHTS OF HIGH AND LOW WATERS

Dates in amber are **SPRINGS**
Dates in yellow are **NEAPS**

2014

JANUARY

Day	Time m	Time m
1 W ●	0500 0.4 / 1207 3.7 / 1734 0.2	16 TH ○ — 0037 3.3 / 0553 0.6 / 1234 3.6 / 1807 0.6
2 TH	0026 3.6 / 0548 0.3 / 1253 3.8 / 1820 0.0	17 F — 0112 3.3 / 0626 0.6 / 1306 3.6 / 1838 0.6
3 F	0118 3.6 / 0637 0.3 / 1338 3.9 / 1908 0.0	18 SA — 0145 3.3 / 0658 0.6 / 1338 3.7 / 1908 0.5
4 SA	0208 3.6 / 0725 0.3 / 1424 3.9 / 1957 0.0	19 SU — 0217 3.3 / 0729 0.6 / 1410 3.7 / 1939 0.5
5 SU	0256 3.6 / 0814 0.4 / 1509 3.9 / 2047 0.1	20 M — 0250 3.3 / 0803 0.6 / 1445 3.7 / 2013 0.5
6 M	0342 3.5 / 0904 0.5 / 1555 3.8 / 2140 0.2	21 TU — 0324 3.3 / 0840 0.6 / 1522 3.7 / 2052 0.5
7 TU	0427 3.4 / 0956 0.6 / 1643 3.6 / 2238 0.4	22 W — 0359 3.2 / 0922 0.7 / 1601 3.6 / 2136 0.6
8 W ◐	0513 3.3 / 1052 0.8 / 1734 3.4 / 2342 0.6	23 TH — 0437 3.2 / 1009 0.8 / 1642 3.4 / 2226 0.7
9 TH	0603 3.1 / 1157 0.9 / 1831 3.2	24 F ◐ — 0519 3.1 / 1102 0.9 / 1728 3.3 / 2323 0.8
10 F	0051 0.7 / 0700 3.0 / 1314 1.0 / 1943 3.0	25 SA — 0609 2.9 / 1204 1.0 / 1825 3.1
11 SA	0157 0.8 / 0815 3.0 / 1425 1.0 / 2109 3.0	26 SU — 0027 0.9 / 0719 2.9 / 1316 1.0 / 1939 3.0
12 SU	0256 0.8 / 0934 3.1 / 1525 0.9 / 2219 3.1	27 M — 0139 0.9 / 0853 2.9 / 1431 0.8 / 2107 3.1
13 M	0348 0.7 / 1033 3.2 / 1615 0.7 / 2312 3.2	28 TU — 0252 0.8 / 1008 3.1 / 1537 0.6 / 2223 3.2
14 TU	0434 0.6 / 1120 3.4 / 1658 0.6 / 2358 3.2	29 W — 0354 0.6 / 1104 3.4 / 1632 0.3 / 2324 3.3
15 W	0516 0.6 / 1159 3.5 / 1735 0.6	30 TH ● — 0448 0.4 / 1153 3.6 / 1720 0.0
		31 F — 0018 3.4 / 0536 0.2 / 1241 3.7 / 1806 -0.1

FEBRUARY

Day	Time m	Time m
1 SA	0109 3.5 / 0622 0.2 / 1326 3.8 / 1851 -0.2	16 SU — 0126 3.2 / 0635 0.5 / 1318 3.5 / 1843 0.4
2 SU	0156 3.5 / 0708 0.1 / 1411 3.9 / 1937 -0.1	17 M — 0156 3.3 / 0703 0.5 / 1349 3.6 / 1911 0.4
3 M	0240 3.5 / 0753 0.2 / 1455 3.9 / 2022 0.0	18 TU — 0225 3.3 / 0735 0.4 / 1423 3.6 / 1945 0.3
4 TU	0321 3.5 / 0839 0.2 / 1537 3.8 / 2110 0.1	19 W — 0256 3.3 / 0812 0.4 / 1459 3.6 / 2023 0.3
5 W	0400 3.4 / 0925 0.4 / 1619 3.6 / 2200 0.3	20 TH — 0329 3.3 / 0853 0.4 / 1537 3.6 / 2107 0.4
6 TH ◐	0439 3.3 / 1013 0.6 / 1702 3.4 / 2257 0.6	21 F — 0404 3.3 / 0939 0.5 / 1616 3.5 / 2156 0.5
7 F	0520 3.2 / 1109 0.8 / 1749 3.1	22 SA ◐ — 0441 3.2 / 1032 0.6 / 1700 3.3 / 2252 0.7
8 SA	0006 0.8 / 0607 3.0 / 1226 1.0 / 1845 2.9	23 SU — 0525 3.0 / 1134 0.8 / 1751 3.1 / 2356 0.8
9 SU	0124 0.9 / 0705 2.9 / 1354 1.0 / 2021 2.7	24 M — 0626 2.8 / 1247 0.8 / 1902 2.9
10 M	0230 0.9 / 0841 2.9 / 1501 0.9 / 2203 2.8	25 TU — 0112 0.9 / 0816 2.8 / 1410 0.7 / 2049 2.9
11 TU	0326 0.8 / 1008 3.0 / 1554 0.7 / 2257 3.1	26 W — 0235 0.8 / 0949 3.0 / 1522 0.4 / 2216 3.1
12 W	0414 0.7 / 1059 3.2 / 1637 0.6 / 2340 3.1	27 TH — 0342 0.6 / 1048 3.3 / 1617 0.1 / 2316 3.2
13 TH	0456 0.5 / 1141 3.4 / 1715 0.5	28 F — 0436 0.4 / 1138 3.5 / 1705 -0.1
14 F ○	0019 3.2 / 0533 0.5 / 1217 3.5 / 1747 0.5	
15 SA	0054 3.2 / 0605 0.5 / 1248 3.5 / 1816 0.5	

MARCH

Day	Time m	Time m
1 SA ●	0006 3.4 / 0522 0.2 / 1225 3.7 / 1749 -0.2	16 SU — 0027 3.2 / 0539 0.4 / 1222 3.4 / 1748 0.4
2 SU	0053 3.4 / 0606 0.1 / 1311 3.8 / 1831 -0.2	17 M — 0100 3.2 / 0607 0.4 / 1252 3.4 / 1814 0.3
3 M	0136 3.5 / 0648 0.0 / 1354 3.8 / 1913 -0.2	18 TU — 0130 3.3 / 0636 0.3 / 1324 3.5 / 1843 0.3
4 TU	0216 3.5 / 0729 0.1 / 1436 3.8 / 1955 0.0	19 W — 0158 3.3 / 0708 0.3 / 1400 3.5 / 1919 0.2
5 W	0253 3.5 / 0810 0.1 / 1516 3.7 / 2038 0.1	20 TH — 0229 3.4 / 0747 0.2 / 1438 3.6 / 2000 0.2
6 TH	0329 3.4 / 0852 0.2 / 1554 3.5 / 2123 0.3	21 F — 0302 3.4 / 0829 0.2 / 1517 3.5 / 2045 0.3
7 F	0406 3.4 / 0936 0.4 / 1634 3.3 / 2213 0.6	22 SA — 0337 3.4 / 0917 0.3 / 1557 3.4 / 2135 0.4
8 SA ◐	0445 3.2 / 1027 0.6 / 1727 3.0 / 2314 0.9	23 SU — 0415 3.3 / 1012 0.5 / 1641 3.3 / 2231 0.6
9 SU	0528 3.0 / 1131 0.9 / 1807 2.7	24 M ◐ — 0459 3.1 / 1115 0.6 / 1733 3.0 / 2337 0.8
10 M	0038 1.0 / 0620 2.9 / 1312 1.0 / 1918 2.6	25 TU — 0559 2.9 / 1231 0.7 / 1843 2.8
11 TU	0157 1.0 / 0733 2.8 / 1429 0.9 / 2135 2.6	26 W — 0056 0.9 / 0750 2.8 / 1355 0.5 / 2042 2.8
12 W	0258 0.9 / 0928 2.9 / 1524 0.7 / 2231 2.8	27 TH — 0221 0.8 / 0928 3.0 / 1505 0.3 / 2205 3.0
13 TH	0348 0.7 / 1029 3.1 / 1608 0.6 / 2313 3.0	28 F — 0328 0.6 / 1028 3.3 / 1600 0.0 / 2300 3.2
14 F	0430 0.6 / 1112 3.2 / 1646 0.4 / 2351 3.1	29 SA — 0421 0.3 / 1119 3.5 / 1646 -0.1 / 2348 3.3
15 SA	0507 0.5 / 1149 3.3 / 1719 0.4	30 SU ● — 0506 0.2 / 1205 3.6 / 1729 -0.2
		31 M — 0031 3.4 / 0547 0.1 / 1251 3.6 / 1810 -0.2

APRIL

Day	Time m	Time m
1 TU	0112 3.4 / 0627 0.0 / 1334 3.6 / 1849 -0.1	16 W — 0101 3.3 / 0610 0.2 / 1258 3.4 / 1818 0.2
2 W	0149 3.5 / 0705 0.0 / 1414 3.6 / 1929 0.1	17 TH — 0131 3.4 / 0646 0.2 / 1338 3.5 / 1858 0.2
3 TH	0224 3.5 / 0743 0.1 / 1453 3.5 / 2009 0.2	18 F — 0204 3.5 / 0727 0.1 / 1419 3.5 / 1942 0.2
4 F	0259 3.5 / 0822 0.2 / 1530 3.4 / 2052 0.4	19 SA — 0240 3.5 / 0812 0.1 / 1501 3.5 / 2030 0.3
5 SA	0335 3.4 / 0904 0.3 / 1609 3.2 / 2138 0.6	20 SU — 0318 3.5 / 0903 0.2 / 1544 3.4 / 2122 0.4
6 SU	0414 3.3 / 0952 0.5 / 1651 3.0 / 2232 0.8	21 M — 0359 3.4 / 1000 0.3 / 1631 3.2 / 2220 0.6
7 M ◐	0456 3.1 / 1051 0.8 / 1740 2.7 / 2341 1.0	22 TU ◐ — 0446 3.2 / 1106 0.4 / 1726 3.0 / 2326 0.8
8 TU	0545 2.9 / 1212 0.9 / 1843 2.6	23 W — 0549 3.0 / 1221 0.5 / 1841 2.9
9 W	0106 1.1 / 0648 2.8 / 1341 0.9 / 2027 2.6	24 TH — 0043 0.9 / 0731 2.9 / 1337 0.4 / 2027 2.8
10 TH	0218 1.0 / 0820 2.8 / 1442 0.7 / 2147 2.7	25 F — 0202 0.8 / 0902 3.0 / 1443 0.2 / 2143 3.0
11 F	0312 0.8 / 0942 2.9 / 1530 0.6 / 2235 2.9	26 SA — 0308 0.6 / 1004 3.2 / 1537 0.1 / 2237 3.2
12 SA	0357 0.6 / 1031 3.1 / 1609 0.4 / 2316 3.1	27 SU — 0402 0.4 / 1056 3.4 / 1625 0.0 / 2324 3.3
13 SU	0435 0.5 / 1111 3.2 / 1644 0.4 / 2354 3.2	28 M — 0448 0.2 / 1144 3.5 / 1708 0.0
14 M	0508 0.4 / 1146 3.3 / 1715 0.3	29 TU ● — 0007 3.4 / 0529 0.1 / 1230 3.5 / 1748 0.0
15 TU ○	0029 3.2 / 0538 0.3 / 1221 3.3 / 1744 0.3	30 W — 0046 3.4 / 0607 0.1 / 1313 3.5 / 1827 0.1

Chart Datum: 1·62 metres below Ordnance Datum (Newlyn)
HAT is 3·9 metres above Chart Datum

TIME ZONE (UT)	SCOTLAND – GREENOCK	Dates in amber are SPRINGS
For Summer Time add ONE hour in **non-shaded areas**	LAT 55°57′N LONG 4°46′W	Dates in yellow are NEAPS
	TIMES AND HEIGHTS OF HIGH AND LOW WATERS	**2014**

MAY

Day	Time m	Time m		Day	Time m	Time m
1 TH	0122 3.5 / 0643 0.1	1353 3.4 / 1905 0.2		16 F	0107 3.4 / 0628 0.1	1318 3.4 / 1841 0.2
2 F	0156 3.5 / 0719 0.2	1430 3.3 / 1944 0.3		17 SA	0144 3.5 / 0712 0.0	1404 3.4 / 1929 0.2
3 SA	0232 3.5 / 0757 0.2	1508 3.2 / 2026 0.5		18 SU	0224 3.6 / 0800 0.0	1450 3.4 / 2019 0.3
4 SU	0308 3.5 / 0838 0.3	1547 3.1 / 2111 0.6		19 M	0305 3.6 / 0852 0.1	1537 3.3 / 2113 0.4
5 M	0345 3.4 / 0924 0.5	1629 3.0 / 2200 0.8		20 TU	0349 3.5 / 0951 0.2	1627 3.2 / 2211 0.5
6 TU	0426 3.2 / 1018 0.6	1717 2.8 / 2257 0.9		21 W	0440 3.3 / 1055 0.3	1725 3.1 / 2313 0.7
7 W	0512 3.0 / 1124 0.8	1814 2.7		22 TH	0543 3.1 / 1205 0.3	1835 3.0
8 TH	0004 1.1 / 0607 2.9	1238 0.8 / 1924 2.6		23 F	0022 0.8 / 0707 3.0	1314 0.3 / 1957 2.9
9 F	0116 1.1 / 0716 2.8	1345 0.8 / 2044 2.7		24 SA	0135 0.8 / 0831 3.1	1417 0.2 / 2110 3.0
10 SA	0220 0.9 / 0833 2.9	1440 0.7 / 2146 2.9		25 SU	0242 0.7 / 0937 3.2	1513 0.2 / 2208 3.1
11 SU	0313 0.8 / 0936 3.0	1525 0.5 / 2234 3.0		26 M	0340 0.5 / 1033 3.3	1602 0.2 / 2258 3.2
12 M	0356 0.6 / 1025 3.1	1604 0.4 / 2317 3.2		27 TU	0429 0.4 / 1123 3.3	1648 0.2 / 2342 3.3
13 TU	0434 0.4 / 1107 3.2	1640 0.3 / 2355 3.2		28 W	0512 0.3 / 1209 3.3	1730 0.2
14 W	0510 0.3 / 1150 3.3	1717 0.2		29 TH	0021 3.4 / 0550 0.2	1253 3.3 / 1808 0.3
15 TH	0030 3.3 / 0547 0.2	1234 3.4 / 1757 0.2		30 F	0058 3.4 / 0625 0.2	1333 3.2 / 1846 0.4
				31 SA	0132 3.5 / 0700 0.3	1410 3.2 / 1924 0.4

JUNE

Day	Time m	Time m		Day	Time m	Time m
1 SU	0207 3.5 / 0736 0.3	1447 3.1 / 2004 0.5		16 M	0212 3.7 / 0748 -0.1	1442 3.4 / 2008 0.2
2 M	0243 3.5 / 0815 0.3	1525 3.1 / 2046 0.6		17 TU	0256 3.7 / 0840 -0.1	1532 3.3 / 2101 0.3
3 TU	0319 3.5 / 0858 0.4	1607 3.0 / 2131 0.7		18 W	0342 3.6 / 0936 0.0	1622 3.3 / 2155 0.4
4 W	0357 3.4 / 0945 0.5	1651 2.9 / 2220 0.8		19 TH	0432 3.5 / 1036 0.1	1715 3.2 / 2253 0.5
5 TH	0440 3.2 / 1039 0.7	1740 2.8 / 2313 0.9		20 F	0529 3.3 / 1141 0.2	1812 3.1 / 2356 0.7
6 F	0529 3.1 / 1139 0.7	1835 2.8		21 SA	0637 3.1 / 1246 0.3	1917 3.0
7 SA	0012 1.0 / 0626 3.0	1243 0.7 / 1937 2.8		22 SU	0104 0.7 / 0754 3.0	1350 0.4 / 2027 3.0
8 SU	0116 1.0 / 0731 2.9	1342 0.7 / 2045 2.8		23 M	0214 0.7 / 0909 3.1	1448 0.4 / 2135 3.0
9 M	0218 0.9 / 0838 3.0	1436 0.6 / 2146 3.0		24 TU	0317 0.6 / 1012 3.1	1541 0.4 / 2232 3.1
10 TU	0313 0.7 / 0939 3.1	1524 0.5 / 2237 3.1		25 W	0411 0.5 / 1106 3.2	1629 0.4 / 2320 3.2
11 W	0401 0.5 / 1033 3.2	1609 0.3 / 2322 3.2		26 TH	0456 0.4 / 1154 3.2	1713 0.4
12 TH	0446 0.3 / 1123 3.3	1653 0.3		27 F	0002 3.3 / 0536 0.4	1239 3.2 / 1753 0.4
13 F	0004 3.4 / 0529 0.1	1213 3.3 / 1739 0.2		28 SA	0039 3.4 / 0612 0.3	1318 3.1 / 1830 0.4
14 SA	0046 3.5 / 0613 0.0	1303 3.4 / 1827 0.2		29 SU	0113 3.5 / 0644 0.2	1353 3.1 / 1906 0.5
15 SU	0129 3.6 / 0700 -0.1	1352 3.4 / 1917 0.2		30 M	0146 3.5 / 0718 0.4	1427 3.1 / 1942 0.5

JULY

Day	Time m	Time m		Day	Time m	Time m
1 TU	0220 3.5 / 0753 0.4	1503 3.1 / 2020 0.5		16 W	0246 3.8 / 0822 -0.2	1520 3.4 / 2041 0.2
2 W	0254 3.5 / 0830 0.4	1541 3.1 / 2100 0.6		17 TH	0331 3.7 / 0914 -0.1	1606 3.3 / 2132 0.3
3 TH	0330 3.5 / 0911 0.5	1620 3.0 / 2143 0.6		18 F	0417 3.6 / 1009 0.1	1652 3.3 / 2226 0.4
4 F	0409 3.4 / 0956 0.5	1702 3.0 / 2229 0.7		19 SA	0506 3.4 / 1110 0.3	1739 3.1 / 2324 0.6
5 SA	0453 3.2 / 1046 0.6	1748 2.9 / 2321 0.9		20 SU	0601 3.2 / 1217 0.4	1830 3.0
6 SU	0543 3.1 / 1144 0.7	1840 2.9		21 M	0032 0.8 / 0708 3.0	1324 0.5 / 1932 2.9
7 M	0020 0.9 / 0642 3.0	1246 0.7 / 1942 2.8		22 TU	0147 0.8 / 0838 2.9	1426 0.6 / 2055 2.9
8 TU	0126 0.9 / 0751 2.9	1349 0.7 / 2053 2.9		23 W	0256 0.8 / 0956 3.0	1522 0.6 / 2207 3.0
9 W	0232 0.8 / 0901 3.0	1448 0.6 / 2200 3.0		24 TH	0353 0.6 / 1054 3.0	1612 0.5 / 2301 3.2
10 TH	0332 0.6 / 1006 3.1	1543 0.4 / 2255 3.2		25 F	0441 0.5 / 1142 3.1	1657 0.5 / 2345 3.3
11 F	0425 0.3 / 1104 3.2	1634 0.3 / 2343 3.4		26 SA	0521 0.4 / 1224 3.1	1737 0.4
12 SA	0513 0.1 / 1158 3.3	1724 0.2		27 SU	0022 3.4 / 0556 0.4	1302 3.1 / 1812 0.5
13 SU	0029 3.5 / 0559 -0.1	1251 3.4 / 1812 0.2		28 M	0055 3.5 / 0627 0.4	1334 3.1 / 1845 0.5
14 M	0115 3.7 / 0645 -0.2	1342 3.4 / 1902 0.1		29 TU	0125 3.5 / 0657 0.4	1405 3.1 / 1918 0.5
15 TU	0200 3.7 / 0733 -0.2	1432 3.4 / 1951 0.2		30 W	0156 3.5 / 0728 0.4	1437 3.1 / 1951 0.5
				31 TH	0229 3.6 / 0800 0.4	1511 3.2 / 2027 0.5

AUGUST

Day	Time m	Time m		Day	Time m	Time m
1 F	0304 3.6 / 0836 0.4	1545 3.2 / 2107 0.5		16 SA	0356 3.6 / 0937 0.2	1620 3.3 / 2153 0.4
2 SA	0342 3.5 / 0917 0.4	1623 3.1 / 2151 0.6		17 SU	0439 3.4 / 1034 0.4	1701 3.2 / 2248 0.6
3 SU	0421 3.4 / 1004 0.5	1704 3.0 / 2241 0.7		18 M	0526 3.3 / 1142 0.6	1747 3.1 / 2356 0.7
4 M	0506 3.2 / 1059 0.7	1751 2.9 / 2338 0.9		19 TU	0621 2.9 / 1256 0.8	1840 2.9
5 TU	0600 3.0 / 1201 0.8	1850 2.9		20 W	0121 0.9 / 0753 2.7	1403 0.9 / 1958 2.9
6 W	0044 0.9 / 0708 2.9	1310 0.8 / 2007 2.9		21 TH	0234 0.9 / 0943 2.8	1502 0.7 / 2140 3.0
7 TH	0159 0.8 / 0830 2.9	1420 0.7 / 2129 3.0		22 F	0333 0.7 / 1039 2.9	1553 0.6 / 2239 3.2
8 F	0309 0.6 / 0948 3.0	1524 0.5 / 2233 3.2		23 SA	0420 0.6 / 1124 3.1	1637 0.5 / 2324 3.3
9 SA	0408 0.3 / 1052 3.2	1619 0.4 / 2326 3.4		24 SU	0500 0.4 / 1203 3.1	1716 0.5
10 SU	0457 0.0 / 1147 3.3	1709 0.2		25 M	0001 3.4 / 0534 0.4	1239 3.2 / 1750 0.6
11 M	0014 3.6 / 0543 -0.2	1239 3.4 / 1756 0.1		26 TU	0033 3.5 / 0605 0.4	1310 3.2 / 1821 0.5
12 TU	0101 3.7 / 0628 -0.3	1328 3.4 / 1843 0.1		27 W	0102 3.5 / 0632 0.4	1339 3.2 / 1850 0.5
13 W	0146 3.8 / 0713 -0.3	1415 3.4 / 1930 0.1		28 TH	0132 3.6 / 0659 0.4	1408 3.2 / 1920 0.5
14 TH	0231 3.8 / 0759 -0.2	1458 3.4 / 2016 0.2		29 F	0204 3.6 / 0729 0.4	1438 3.3 / 1955 0.5
15 F	0314 3.8 / 0846 0.0	1540 3.4 / 2104 0.2		30 SA	0240 3.6 / 0804 0.4	1511 3.3 / 2034 0.5
				31 SU	0317 3.6 / 0844 0.4	1547 3.3 / 2118 0.6

Chart Datum: 1·62 metres below Ordnance Datum (Newlyn)
HAT is 3·9 metres above Chart Datum

TIME ZONE (UT)
For Summer Time add ONE hour in **non-shaded areas**

SCOTLAND – GREENOCK
LAT 55°57'N   LONG 4°46'W
TIMES AND HEIGHTS OF HIGH AND LOW WATERS

Dates in amber are **SPRINGS**
Dates in yellow are **NEAPS**

2014

SEPTEMBER
Time	m		Time	m
1 0355 0931 M 1625 2208	3.5 0.5 3.2 0.7	**16**	0456 1058 TU 1711 ◑ 2315	3.1 0.9 3.2 0.9
2 0437 1025 TU 1709 ◑ 2306	3.3 0.7 3.1 0.8	**17**	0547 1222 W 1802	2.8 1.0 3.0
3 0526 1128 W 1806	3.1 0.9 2.9	**18**	0049 1222 TH 1336 1908	1.0 1.1 1.0 2.9
4 0014 0632 TH 1242 1928	0.9 2.9 0.9 2.9	**19**	0207 0919 F 1436 2057	1.0 2.7 0.9 3.0
5 0135 0807 F 1401 2105	0.8 2.9 0.9 2.9	**20**	0305 1015 SA 1528 2207	0.8 2.9 0.8 3.2
6 0252 0939 SA 1510 2215	0.6 3.0 0.7 3.3	**21**	0352 1057 SU 1612 2253	0.6 3.1 0.6 3.3
7 0351 1043 SU 1606 2308	0.3 3.2 0.4 3.5	**22**	0432 1134 M 1650 2331	0.5 3.2 0.5 3.4
8 0440 1135 M 1654 2356	0.0 3.4 0.4 3.7	**23**	0507 1209 TU 1724	0.4 3.3 0.5
9 0525 1138 TU 1739 ○	-0.2 3.4 0.1	**24**	0004 0547 W 1241 ● 1753	3.5 -0.1 3.3 0.5
10 0043 0608 W 1308 1823	3.8 -0.2 3.5 0.1	**25**	0034 0604 TH 1311 1821	3.5 0.4 3.3 0.5
11 0128 0650 TH 1350 1906	3.8 -0.2 3.5 0.1	**26**	0105 0630 F 1338 1851	3.6 0.4 3.4 0.5
12 0212 0733 F 1430 1949	3.8 -0.1 3.5 0.2	**27**	0140 0701 SA 1408 1927	3.6 0.4 3.4 0.5
13 0253 0817 SA 1508 2033	3.7 0.1 3.5 0.3	**28**	0217 0738 SU 1441 2008	3.6 0.4 3.5 0.5
14 0333 0903 SU 1546 2119	3.6 0.3 3.4 0.4	**29**	0255 0820 M 1517 2053	3.6 0.5 3.4 0.5
15 0413 0954 M 1626 2210	3.4 0.5 3.3 0.7	**30**	0335 0907 TU 1556 2145	3.5 0.6 3.4 0.7

OCTOBER
Time	m		Time	m
1 0416 1002 W 1640 ◑ 2244	3.4 0.8 3.2 0.8	**16**	0522 1130 TH 1729 2358	2.9 1.2 3.1 1.1
2 0505 1106 TH 1735 2356	3.2 1.0 3.1 0.9	**17**	0626 1255 F 1830	2.7 1.2 3.0
3 0610 1222 F 1900	3.0 1.1 3.0	**18**	0125 0814 SA 1402 1953	1.1 2.7 1.1 3.0
4 0118 0753 SA 1346 2043	0.8 2.9 1.0 3.1	**19**	0228 0933 SU 1456 2118	0.9 2.9 1.0 3.1
5 0234 0929 SU 1456 2154	0.6 3.1 0.8 3.3	**20**	0317 1019 M 1541 2212	0.8 3.1 0.8 3.3
6 0333 1029 M 1551 2247	0.3 3.3 0.5 3.6	**21**	0358 1059 TU 1620 2253	0.6 3.3 0.7 3.4
7 0421 1117 TU 1638 2336	0.1 3.4 0.3 3.7	**22**	0434 1136 W 1655 2329	0.5 3.4 0.6 3.5
8 0505 1202 W 1721 ○	-0.1 3.5 0.2	**23**	0506 1210 TH 1726 ●	0.5 3.4 0.5
9 0023 0547 TH 1244 1802	3.8 -0.1 3.6 0.2	**24**	0003 0547 F 1242 1755	3.5 0.5 3.5 0.5
10 0108 0628 F 1324 1843	3.8 0.0 3.6 0.2	**25**	0039 0604 SA 1311 1828	3.6 0.5 3.5 0.5
11 0151 0708 SA 1401 1923	3.8 0.1 3.6 0.3	**26**	0117 0638 SU 1343 1906	3.6 0.4 3.6 0.5
12 0231 0749 SU 1438 2004	3.7 0.3 3.6 0.4	**27**	0157 0718 M 1419 1948	3.6 0.4 3.6 0.5
13 0310 0833 M 1516 2048	3.5 0.5 3.6 0.5	**28**	0238 0803 TU 1456 2036	3.6 0.4 3.6 0.5
14 0350 0920 TU 1556 2136	3.4 0.7 3.5 0.7	**29**	0320 0852 W 1537 2129	3.6 0.5 3.6 0.6
15 0432 1015 W 1640 ◑ 2235	3.1 1.0 3.3 0.9	**30**	0404 0947 TH 1623 2230	3.4 0.7 3.4 0.7
		31	0455 1051 F 1719 ◑ 2342	3.2 1.0 3.3 0.8

NOVEMBER
Time	m		Time	m
1 0600 1205 SA 1840	3.0 1.1 3.1	**16**	0021 0706 SU 1306 1856	1.1 2.8 1.3 3.1
2 0101 0737 SU 1326 2016	0.7 3.0 1.1 3.2	**17**	0134 0826 M 1410 2010	1.0 2.9 1.2 3.1
3 0212 0907 M 1436 2128	0.6 3.1 0.9 3.4	**18**	0231 0930 TU 1502 2117	0.9 3.1 1.0 3.2
4 0311 1007 TU 1533 2225	0.4 3.3 0.7 3.6	**19**	0318 1019 W 1545 2208	0.8 3.3 0.9 3.3
5 0401 1055 W 1621 2315	0.2 3.5 0.5 3.7	**20**	0358 1101 TH 1623 2252	0.7 3.4 0.7 3.4
6 0446 1139 TH 1705 ○	0.1 3.6 0.4	**21**	0434 1139 F 1658 2333	0.6 3.5 0.6 3.5
7 0002 0527 F 1221 1745	3.7 0.1 3.6 0.3	**22**	0507 1214 SA 1733 ●	0.5 3.6 0.5
8 0048 0608 SA 1259 1824	3.7 0.2 3.7 0.3	**23**	0015 0542 SU 1248 1809	3.6 0.5 3.6 0.4
9 0131 0647 SU 1336 1902	3.7 0.2 3.7 0.4	**24**	0058 0621 M 1324 1850	3.6 0.5 3.7 0.4
10 0211 0727 M 1413 1941	3.6 0.4 3.7 0.4	**25**	0142 0704 TU 1402 1935	3.6 0.5 3.8 0.4
11 0250 0808 TU 1451 2023	3.5 0.6 3.7 0.6	**26**	0226 0751 W 1443 2024	3.5 0.5 3.8 0.4
12 0329 0853 W 1530 2108	3.3 0.8 3.6 0.7	**27**	0310 0841 TH 1526 2118	3.6 0.6 3.7 0.5
13 0412 0942 TH 1612 2201	3.2 1.0 3.5 0.9	**28**	0357 0936 F 1613 2217	3.5 0.7 3.6 0.6
14 0459 1039 F 1658 ◑ 2305	3.0 1.2 3.3 1.0	**29**	0449 1036 SA 1708 ◑ 2325	3.3 0.9 3.4 0.6
15 0555 1150 SA 1752	2.9 1.3 3.2	**30**	0550 1144 SU 1819	3.2 1.0 3.3

DECEMBER
Time	m		Time	m
1 0037 1259 M 1944	0.6 1.1 3.3	**16**	0023 0719 TU 1302 1908	1.1 2.9 1.3 3.1
2 0146 0833 TU 1411 2100	0.6 3.1 1.0 3.4	**17**	0129 0829 W 1408 2014	1.0 3.0 1.2 3.1
3 0247 0939 W 1512 2202	0.5 3.3 0.8 3.5	**18**	0228 0933 TH 1503 2120	0.9 3.1 1.0 3.2
4 0340 1032 TH 1604 2256	0.4 3.4 0.6 3.5	**19**	0317 1026 F 1550 2217	0.8 3.3 0.8 3.3
5 0428 1119 F 1650 2346	0.3 3.5 0.5 3.6	**20**	0401 1110 SA 1633 2307	0.7 3.4 0.6 3.4
6 0512 1201 SA 1732 ○	0.3 3.6 0.4	**21**	0442 1150 SU 1713 2355	0.6 3.5 0.5 3.5
7 0033 0552 SU 1240 1809	3.6 0.4 3.7 0.4	**22**	0523 1229 M 1754 ●	0.5 3.7 0.4
8 0116 0632 M 1317 1846	3.5 0.5 3.7 0.5	**23**	0043 0606 TU 1309 1837	3.5 0.4 3.8 0.2
9 0155 0710 TU 1353 1922	3.4 0.6 3.8 0.5	**24**	0130 0652 W 1350 1923	3.6 0.4 3.8 0.2
10 0232 0748 W 1430 2001	3.4 0.6 3.7 0.6	**25**	0216 0739 TH 1433 2012	3.6 0.4 3.9 0.2
11 0310 0829 TH 1507 2043	3.3 0.7 3.7 0.6	**26**	0303 0829 F 1518 2103	3.6 0.5 3.8 0.3
12 0351 0912 F 1546 2129	3.2 0.9 3.6 0.8	**27**	0350 0921 SA 1605 2159	3.5 0.6 3.7 0.3
13 0434 0959 SA 1628 2219	3.1 1.0 3.5 0.9	**28**	0438 1016 SU 1656 ◑ 2300	3.4 0.7 3.6 0.3
14 0522 1052 SU 1714 ◑ 2318	3.0 1.1 3.3 1.0	**29**	0531 1118 M 1755	3.3 0.8 3.4
15 0616 1153 M 1807	2.9 1.3 3.2	**30**	0008 0632 TU 1228 1906	0.6 3.1 1.0 3.3
		31	0118 0748 W 1343 2028	0.6 1.0 1.0 3.2

Chart Datum: 1·62 metres below Ordnance Datum (Newlyn)
HAT is 3·9 metres above Chart Datum

TIDES

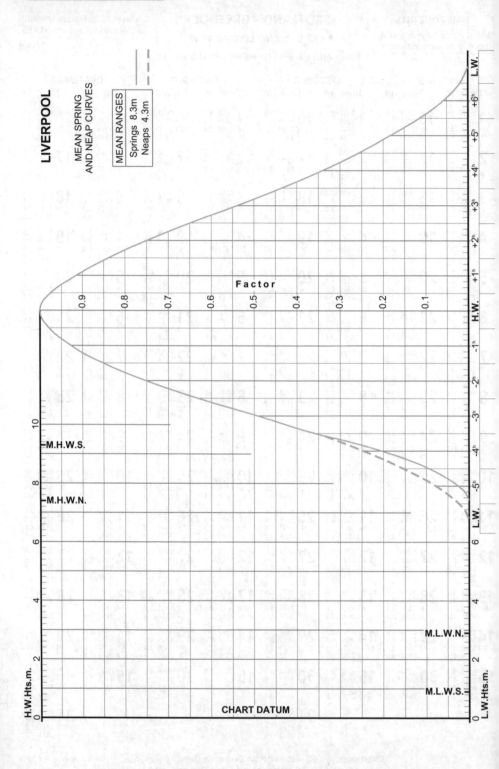

LIVERPOOL

MEAN SPRING
AND NEAP CURVES

MEAN RANGES
Springs 8.3m
Neaps 4.3m

Factor

L.W.

+6ʰ
+5ʰ
+4ʰ
+3ʰ
+2ʰ
+1ʰ

H.W.

-1ʰ
-2ʰ
-3ʰ
-4ʰ
-5ʰ

L.W.

=M.H.W.S.

=M.H.W.N.

M.L.W.N.=

M.L.W.S.=

H.W.Hts.m.

L.W.Hts.m.

CHART DATUM

LIVERPOOL (GLADSTONE DOCK)
LAT 53°27'N   LONG 3°01'W
TIMES AND HEIGHTS OF HIGH AND LOW WATERS

Dates in amber are **SPRINGS**
Dates in yellow are **NEAPS**

2014

JANUARY

Day	Time m	Time m	Time m	Time m		Day	Time m	Time m	Time m	Time m
1 W	0511 1.2	1037 9.6	1739 1.0	●2304 9.6		16 TH	0538 2.0	1117 9.0	1809 1.8	○2335 8.8
2 TH	0601 0.9	1125 9.9	1830 0.7	2354 9.7		17 F	0609 1.8	1149 9.1	1841 1.7	
3 F	0650 0.8	1214 10.1	1920 0.5			18 SA	0007 8.9	0640 1.7	1221 9.1	1911 1.6
4 SA	0043 9.7	0736 0.9	1302 10.0	2006 0.6		19 SU	0040 8.9	0713 1.7	1253 9.1	1943 1.6
5 SU	0131 9.5	0821 1.1	1350 9.8	2053 0.9		20 M	0112 8.8	0747 1.8	1324 8.9	2016 1.8
6 M	0219 9.2	0907 1.4	1439 9.5	2139 1.3		21 TU	0144 8.6	0822 2.0	1355 8.8	2050 2.0
7 TU	0308 8.8	0954 1.9	1530 9.0	2227 1.8		22 W	0219 8.4	0858 2.3	1430 8.5	2126 2.3
8 W	0401 8.3	1046 2.4	1626 8.5	◑2322 2.4		23 TH	0258 8.2	0937 2.6	1512 8.3	2208 2.6
9 TH	0501 7.9	1147 2.8	1729 8.1			24 F	0346 8.0	1026 2.9	1605 8.0	◑2303 2.9
10 F	0025 2.8	0610 7.6	1259 3.0	1841 7.8		25 SA	0448 7.7	1130 3.1	1716 7.8	
11 SA	0135 2.9	0725 7.7	1412 3.0	1952 7.8		26 SU	0020 3.0	0605 7.7	1255 3.0	1841 7.8
12 SU	0242 2.8	0830 7.9	1517 2.7	2054 8.0		27 M	0146 2.8	0724 8.0	1418 2.6	1959 8.1
13 M	0338 2.6	0923 8.2	1611 2.4	2144 8.3		28 TU	0258 2.3	0833 8.5	1529 2.0	2106 8.6
14 TU	0424 2.4	1006 8.6	1656 2.1	2226 8.5		29 W	0400 1.8	0932 9.1	1631 1.4	2203 9.1
15 W	0503 2.2	1043 8.8	1734 1.9	2302 8.7		30 TH	0457 1.2	1024 9.6	1728 0.9	●2255 9.5
						31 F	0549 0.8	1113 10.0	1819 0.4	2342 9.8

FEBRUARY

Day	Time m	Time m	Time m	Time m		Day	Time m	Time m	Time m	Time m
1 SA	0637 0.6	1200 10.2	1906 0.2			16 SU	0623 1.5	1200 9.2	1851 1.3	
2 SU	0028 9.8	0721 0.5	1246 10.2	1950 0.3		17 M	0017 9.0	0655 1.4	1230 9.2	1923 1.3
3 M	0112 9.7	0804 0.7	1333 10.0	2031 0.6		18 TU	0048 9.0	0729 1.4	1300 9.1	1955 1.4
4 TU	0155 9.4	0845 1.1	1413 9.6	2111 1.1		19 W	0119 8.9	0802 1.6	1331 9.0	2027 1.6
5 W	0237 8.9	0926 1.6	1457 9.1	2152 1.8		20 TH	0152 8.8	0836 1.8	1405 8.8	2059 2.0
6 TH	0321 8.4	1010 2.2	1546 8.5	◑2236 2.4		21 F	0229 8.5	0912 2.1	1445 8.5	2137 2.3
7 F	0413 7.9	1103 2.8	1644 7.8	2332 3.0		22 SA	0314 8.2	0956 2.5	1535 8.1	◑2227 2.7
8 SA	0519 7.4	1213 3.2	1756 7.4			23 SU	0414 7.9	1057 2.8	1646 7.7	2341 3.0
9 SU	0047 3.3	0640 7.3	1336 3.3	1919 7.3		24 M	0535 7.6	1223 2.9	1817 7.6	
10 M	0207 3.3	0759 7.5	1451 3.0	2032 7.6		25 TU	0116 2.9	0701 7.8	1356 2.6	1944 7.9
11 TU	0312 3.0	0900 7.9	1549 2.6	2126 8.0		26 W	0237 2.4	0816 8.3	1513 2.0	2055 8.5
12 W	0403 2.6	0945 8.3	1636 2.2	2208 8.3		27 TH	0344 1.8	0917 9.0	1617 1.3	2152 9.0
13 TH	0444 2.2	1023 8.7	1714 1.9	2243 8.6		28 F	0442 1.2	1010 9.5	1713 0.7	2241 9.5
14 F	0519 1.9	1057 8.9	1748 1.6	○2315 8.8						
15 SA	0551 1.7	1129 9.1	1820 1.4	2346 9.0						

MARCH

Day	Time m	Time m	Time m	Time m		Day	Time m	Time m	Time m	Time m
1 SA	0533 0.8	1057 9.9	1802 0.3	●2326 9.8		16 SU	0527 1.6	1102 9.0	1753 1.3	○2319 9.0
2 SU	0620 0.5	1142 10.1	1846 0.2			17 M	0601 1.3	1133 9.2	1826 1.1	2350 9.2
3 M	0008 9.8	0702 0.4	1225 10.1	1927 0.2		18 TU	0635 1.2	1204 9.2	1900 1.1	
4 TU	0049 9.7	0742 0.5	1306 9.9	2005 0.6		19 W	0022 9.2	0709 1.1	1236 9.2	1932 1.2
5 W	0128 9.4	0820 0.9	1346 9.5	2041 1.1		20 TH	0055 9.2	0743 1.3	1310 9.1	2005 1.4
6 TH	0205 9.0	0857 1.5	1426 9.0	2115 1.8		21 F	0130 9.0	0818 1.5	1346 8.9	2038 1.7
7 F	0244 8.5	0936 2.1	1509 8.4	2152 2.5		22 SA	0209 8.8	0855 1.8	1429 8.6	2117 2.1
8 SA	0330 7.9	1021 2.7	1601 7.7	◑2238 3.1		23 SU	0256 8.4	0940 2.2	1522 8.2	2207 2.6
9 SU	0430 7.4	1124 3.3	1711 7.2	2348 3.6		24 M	0357 8.0	1041 2.6	1634 7.7	◑2320 3.0
10 M	0550 7.1	1252 3.4	1838 7.0			25 TU	0518 7.7	1207 2.7	1805 7.6	
11 TU	0121 3.6	0717 7.2	1415 3.2	1959 7.3		26 W	0054 2.9	0643 7.9	1339 2.4	1930 7.9
12 W	0237 3.3	0826 7.6	1517 2.7	2058 7.7		27 TH	0218 2.4	0758 8.3	1455 1.9	2040 8.4
13 TH	0333 2.8	0915 8.1	1605 2.2	2141 8.2		28 F	0326 1.9	0859 8.9	1559 1.3	2135 9.0
14 F	0416 2.3	0955 8.5	1644 1.8	2216 8.5		29 SA	0424 1.3	0951 9.4	1653 0.8	2222 9.4
15 SA	0452 1.9	1030 8.8	1720 1.5	●2248 8.8		30 SU	0514 0.9	1037 9.7	1740 0.5	●2305 9.6
						31 M	0558 0.6	1121 9.9	1822 0.4	2345 9.7

APRIL

Day	Time m	Time m	Time m	Time m		Day	Time m	Time m	Time m	Time m
1 TU	0639 0.5	1202 9.9	1901 0.5			16 W	0612 1.1	1137 9.2	1836 1.0	2356 9.3
2 W	0023 9.6	0718 0.6	1241 9.6	1936 0.8		17 TH	0650 1.0	1214 9.3	1912 1.1	
3 TH	0100 9.3	0755 1.0	1319 9.3	2009 1.3		18 F	0033 9.3	0727 1.1	1253 9.2	1947 1.3
4 F	0136 9.0	0830 1.5	1357 8.8	2041 1.9		19 SA	0113 9.2	0805 1.3	1333 9.0	2024 1.6
5 SA	0212 8.5	0906 2.0	1438 8.3	2113 2.5		20 SU	0157 8.9	0846 1.6	1422 8.7	2106 2.0
6 SU	0255 8.0	0945 2.6	1526 7.7	2153 3.0		21 M	0248 8.6	0934 1.9	1519 8.2	2159 2.4
7 M	0348 7.5	1038 3.1	1628 7.2	◑2250 3.5		22 TU	0351 8.2	1037 2.3	1631 7.9	◑2310 2.7
8 TU	0501 7.1	1158 3.4	1748 6.9			23 W	0507 8.0	1201 2.4	1752 7.8	
9 W	0018 3.7	0624 7.1	1324 3.2	1910 7.1		24 TH	0035 2.7	0624 8.1	1320 2.2	1911 8.0
10 TH	0145 3.5	0737 7.4	1430 2.8	2015 7.5		25 F	0155 2.4	0735 8.4	1433 1.8	2018 8.4
11 F	0247 3.0	0833 7.8	1522 2.4	2102 8.0		26 SA	0302 1.9	0837 8.8	1535 1.4	2113 8.8
12 SA	0336 2.5	0917 8.2	1605 1.9	2141 8.4		27 SU	0400 1.5	0929 9.1	1629 1.1	2200 9.1
13 SU	0417 2.0	0955 8.6	1645 1.6	2215 8.7		28 M	0450 1.1	1016 9.4	1715 0.9	2242 9.3
14 M	0456 1.6	1029 8.9	1722 1.3	2248 9.0		29 TU	0535 0.9	1059 9.5	1756 0.9	●2321 9.4
15 TU	0534 1.3	1103 9.1	1759 1.1	○2321 9.2		30 W	0616 0.9	1139 9.4	1833 1.0	2359 9.3

Chart Datum: 4·93 metres below Ordnance Datum (Newlyn)
HAT is 10·3m above Chart Datum

TIDES

TIME ZONE (UT)
For Summer Time add ONE hour in **non-shaded areas**

LIVERPOOL (GLADSTONE DOCK)
LAT 53°27′N   LONG 3°01′W
TIMES AND HEIGHTS OF HIGH AND LOW WATERS

Dates in amber are **SPRINGS**
Dates in yellow are **NEAPS**

2014

MAY

Day	Time	m	Day	Time	m
1 TH	0655 / 1218 / 1908	1.0 / 9.3 / 1.2	16 F	0633 / 1156 / 1854	1.0 / 9.3 / 1.0
2 F	0035 / 0731 / 1256 / 1940	9.2 / 1.2 / 9.0 / 1.5	17 SA	0016 / 0715 / 1240 / 1934	9.5 / 0.9 / 9.3 / 1.1
3 SA	0110 / 0806 / 1333 / 2011	8.9 / 1.6 / 8.6 / 2.0	18 SU	0101 / 0758 / 1327 / 2016	9.4 / 1.0 / 9.1 / 1.4
4 SU	0146 / 0840 / 1411 / 2042	8.6 / 2.0 / 8.3 / 2.4	19 M	0149 / 0843 / 1418 / 2102	9.2 / 1.3 / 8.8 / 1.8
5 M	0226 / 0916 / 1455 / 2119	8.2 / 2.4 / 7.8 / 2.8	20 TU	0242 / 0935 / 1516 / 2156	8.9 / 1.6 / 8.5 / 2.1
6 TU	0314 / 1000 / 1549 / 2208	7.8 / 2.8 / 7.4 / 3.2	21 W	0343 / 1034 / 1621 / (2300	8.6 / 1.9 / 8.1 / 2.4
7 W	0414 / 1101 / 1655 / (2314	7.4 / 3.1 / 7.1 / 3.5	22 TH	0451 / 1143 / 1732	8.4 / 2.0 / 8.0
8 TH	0526 / 1217 / 1809	7.2 / 3.2 / 7.1	23 F	0013 / 0600 / 1256 / 1844	2.5 / 8.3 / 2.0 / 8.0
9 F	0034 / 0638 / 1330 / 1917	3.5 / 7.3 / 2.9 / 7.3	24 SA	0126 / 0709 / 1404 / 1951	2.4 / 8.4 / 1.9 / 8.2
10 SA	0148 / 0740 / 1430 / 2012	3.1 / 7.6 / 2.6 / 7.7	25 SU	0234 / 0812 / 1507 / 2049	2.1 / 8.6 / 1.7 / 8.5
11 SU	0247 / 0830 / 1520 / 2057	2.7 / 8.0 / 2.1 / 8.2	26 M	0334 / 0907 / 1602 / 2137	1.8 / 8.8 / 1.6 / 8.8
12 M	0336 / 0914 / 1606 / 2137	2.2 / 8.4 / 1.7 / 8.6	27 TU	0427 / 0955 / 1649 / 2221	1.6 / 8.9 / 1.5 / 9.0
13 TU	0423 / 0954 / 1650 / 2215	1.8 / 8.7 / 1.4 / 9.0	28 W	0513 / 1039 / 1730 / ● 2300	1.4 / 9.0 / 1.4 / 9.1
14 W	0507 / 1033 / 1732 / ○ 2254	1.4 / 9.0 / 1.2 / 9.2	29 TH	0555 / 1120 / 1807 / 2338	1.3 / 9.0 / 1.4 / 9.1
15 TH	0550 / 1114 / 1813 / 2334	1.1 / 9.2 / 1.0 / 9.4	30 F	0634 / 1158 / 1842	1.3 / 8.9 / 1.5
			31 SA	0013 / 0710 / 1235 / 1914	9.0 / 1.5 / 8.8 / 1.7

JUNE

Day	Time	m	Day	Time	m
1 SU	0049 / 0744 / 1311 / 1945	8.9 / 1.7 / 8.6 / 2.0	16 M	0051 / 0753 / 1320 / 2010	9.7 / 0.7 / 9.3 / 1.1
2 M	0124 / 0817 / 1348 / 2018	8.7 / 1.9 / 8.4 / 2.2	17 TU	0141 / 0840 / 1411 / 2057	9.5 / 0.9 / 9.1 / 1.4
3 TU	0201 / 0851 / 1428 / 2054	8.4 / 2.2 / 8.1 / 2.5	18 W	0233 / 0930 / 1504 / 2147	9.3 / 1.2 / 8.8 / 1.7
4 W	0243 / 0930 / 1512 / 2137	8.1 / 2.5 / 7.7 / 2.8	19 TH	0328 / 1023 / 1602 / (2243	9.0 / 1.5 / 8.4 / 2.1
5 TH	0330 / 1017 / 1604 / (2229	7.8 / 2.7 / 7.5 / 3.1	20 F	0427 / 1121 / 1705 / 2346	8.7 / 1.8 / 8.1 / 2.3
6 F	0428 / 1115 / 1705 / 2332	7.5 / 2.9 / 7.3 / 3.3	21 SA	0532 / 1225 / 1813	8.4 / 2.1 / 8.0
7 SA	0533 / 1223 / 1811	7.4 / 2.9 / 7.3	22 SU	0055 / 0639 / 1333 / 1921	2.5 / 8.2 / 2.2 / 8.0
8 SU	0043 / 0638 / 1332 / 1914	3.2 / 7.5 / 2.7 / 7.6	23 M	0205 / 0746 / 1438 / 2024	2.4 / 8.2 / 2.2 / 8.2
9 M	0153 / 0738 / 1433 / 2010	2.9 / 7.8 / 2.4 / 8.0	24 TU	0310 / 0846 / 1536 / 2117	2.2 / 8.3 / 2.1 / 8.4
10 TU	0254 / 0832 / 1528 / 2100	2.4 / 8.2 / 2.0 / 8.5	25 W	0406 / 0938 / 1625 / 2203	2.0 / 8.5 / 2.0 / 8.6
11 W	0349 / 0921 / 1619 / 2146	2.0 / 8.6 / 1.6 / 8.9	26 TH	0455 / 1023 / 1708 / 2243	1.8 / 8.6 / 1.9 / 8.8
12 TH	0441 / 1008 / 1707 / 2231	1.5 / 8.9 / 1.3 / 9.3	27 F	0538 / 1104 / 1746 / ● 2320	1.7 / 8.7 / 1.8 / 8.9
13 F	0530 / 1055 / 1753 / ○ 2316	1.2 / 9.2 / 1.1 / 9.5	28 SA	0617 / 1141 / 1820 / 2355	1.6 / 8.8 / 1.8 / 8.9
14 SA	0618 / 1142 / 1839	0.9 / 9.4 / 1.0	29 SU	0652 / 1216 / 1852	1.6 / 8.7 / 1.8
15 SU	0002 / 0705 / 1230 / 1924	9.7 / 0.7 / 9.4 / 1.0	30 M	0029 / 0724 / 1251 / 1923	8.9 / 1.6 / 8.7 / 1.9

JULY

Day	Time	m	Day	Time	m
1 TU	0103 / 0755 / 1325 / 1956	8.8 / 1.8 / 8.5 / 2.0	16 W	0126 / 0829 / 1355 / 2044	9.9 / 0.5 / 9.4 / 1.0
2 W	0138 / 0828 / 1401 / 2031	8.7 / 1.9 / 8.3 / 2.2	17 TH	0215 / 0914 / 1443 / 2130	9.6 / 0.9 / 9.0 / 1.4
3 TH	0213 / 0903 / 1438 / 2110	8.4 / 2.1 / 8.1 / 2.5	18 F	0305 / 1001 / 1534 / 2219	9.2 / 1.3 / 8.6 / 1.9
4 F	0251 / 0942 / 1520 / 2153	8.2 / 2.4 / 7.9 / 2.7	19 SA	0358 / 1051 / 1630 / (2315	8.8 / 1.9 / 8.2 / 2.3
5 SA	0335 / 1028 / 1609 / (2244	7.9 / 2.7 / 7.6 / 3.0	20 SU	0458 / 1150 / 1736	8.3 / 2.4 / 7.8
6 SU	0430 / 1124 / 1710 / 2348	7.7 / 2.8 / 7.5 / 3.1	21 M	0022 / 0606 / 1258 / 1848	2.7 / 7.9 / 2.7 / 7.7
7 M	0536 / 1235 / 1819	7.6 / 2.9 / 7.6	22 TU	0137 / 0719 / 1409 / 1959	2.8 / 7.8 / 2.7 / 7.8
8 TU	0102 / 0647 / 1348 / 1927	3.0 / 7.7 / 2.6 / 7.9	23 W	0248 / 0827 / 1513 / 2059	2.6 / 7.9 / 2.6 / 8.1
9 W	0216 / 0755 / 1454 / 2028	2.6 / 8.0 / 2.2 / 8.4	24 TH	0350 / 0923 / 1606 / 2147	2.3 / 8.1 / 2.4 / 8.4
10 TH	0320 / 0855 / 1552 / 2122	2.1 / 8.4 / 1.8 / 8.8	25 F	0440 / 1009 / 1650 / 2227	2.1 / 8.4 / 2.2 / 8.7
11 F	0419 / 0949 / 1646 / ● 2212	1.6 / 8.9 / 1.4 / 9.3	26 SA	0522 / 1048 / 1727 / 2303	1.8 / 8.6 / 2.0 / 8.9
12 SA	0514 / 1040 / 1737 / ○ 2301	1.1 / 9.2 / 1.1 / 9.7	27 SU	0559 / 1123 / 1800 / 2336	1.7 / 8.7 / 1.8 / 9.0
13 SU	0606 / 1130 / 1827 / 2349	0.7 / 9.5 / 0.8 / 9.9	28 M	0632 / 1156 / 1831	1.6 / 8.8 / 1.7
14 M	0656 / 1219 / 1914	0.5 / 9.6 / 0.7	29 TU	0009 / 0702 / 1228 / 1902	9.0 / 1.5 / 8.8 / 1.7
15 TU	0038 / 0743 / 1307 / 1959	10.0 / 0.4 / 9.6 / 0.8	30 W	0041 / 0732 / 1300 / 1935	9.0 / 1.6 / 8.8 / 1.7
			31 TH	0112 / 0804 / 1332 / 2009	8.9 / 1.6 / 8.6 / 1.9

AUGUST

Day	Time	m	Day	Time	m
1 F	0144 / 0836 / 1406 / 2044	8.7 / 1.9 / 8.4 / 2.1	16 SA	0236 / 0932 / 1502 / 2152	9.3 / 1.4 / 8.7 / 1.9
2 SA	0216 / 0911 / 1442 / 2122	8.5 / 2.1 / 8.2 / 2.4	17 SU	0325 / 1017 / 1552 / (2243	8.7 / 2.1 / 8.1 / 2.5
3 SU	0254 / 0950 / 1525 / 2206	8.2 / 2.5 / 8.0 / 2.7	18 M	0421 / 1110 / 1655 / 2348	8.1 / 2.7 / 7.7 / 2.9
4 M	0342 / 1038 / 1621 / 2303	7.9 / 2.8 / 7.7 / 3.0	19 TU	0531 / 1219 / 1813	7.6 / 3.1 / 7.4
5 TU	0445 / 1145 / 1733	7.7 / 2.9 / 7.6	20 W	0109 / 0652 / 1340 / 1932	3.1 / 7.4 / 3.2 / 7.6
6 W	0020 / 0606 / 1309 / 1852	3.0 / 7.6 / 2.9 / 7.8	21 TH	0227 / 0808 / 1450 / 2038	2.9 / 7.6 / 3.0 / 7.9
7 TH	0144 / 0727 / 1425 / 2003	2.8 / 7.8 / 2.5 / 8.3	22 F	0330 / 0907 / 1546 / 2127	2.5 / 7.9 / 2.6 / 8.3
8 F	0257 / 0836 / 1530 / 2103	2.2 / 8.3 / 2.0 / 8.8	23 SA	0420 / 0952 / 1630 / 2207	2.2 / 8.3 / 2.3 / 8.7
9 SA	0401 / 0935 / 1628 / 2157	1.6 / 8.9 / 1.5 / 9.4	24 SU	0501 / 1028 / 1706 / 2242	1.9 / 8.6 / 2.0 / 8.9
10 SU	0459 / 1028 / 1722 / ○ 2246	1.0 / 9.3 / 1.0 / 9.8	25 M	0535 / 1101 / 1738 / ● 2314	1.7 / 8.8 / 1.8 / 9.1
11 M	0553 / 1116 / 1812 / 2334	0.6 / 9.7 / 0.7 / 10.1	26 TU	0607 / 1132 / 1809 / 2345	1.5 / 8.9 / 1.6 / 9.2
12 TU	0642 / 1203 / 1859	0.2 / 9.8 / 0.5	27 W	0637 / 1202 / 1840	1.4 / 9.0 / 1.5
13 W	0020 / 0727 / 1248 / 1942	10.2 / 0.2 / 9.8 / 0.6	28 TH	0015 / 0707 / 1233 / 1913	9.0 / 1.4 / 9.0 / 1.5
14 TH	0106 / 0810 / 1333 / 2025	10.1 / 0.4 / 9.5 / 0.8	29 F	0045 / 0738 / 1304 / 1946	9.1 / 1.5 / 8.9 / 1.7
15 F	0151 / 0851 / 1416 / 2107	9.8 / 0.8 / 9.2 / 1.3	30 SA	0115 / 0810 / 1336 / 2020	8.9 / 1.7 / 8.7 / 1.9
			31 SU	0147 / 0843 / 1411 / 2056	8.7 / 2.0 / 8.9 / 2.2

Chart Datum: 4·93 metres below Ordnance Datum (Newlyn)
HAT is 10·3m above Chart Datum

LIVERPOOL (GLADSTONE DOCK)
LAT 53°27'N   LONG 3°01'W
TIMES AND HEIGHTS OF HIGH AND LOW WATERS

Dates in amber are **SPRINGS**
Dates in yellow are **NEAPS**

2014

SEPTEMBER

#	Time	m	#	Time	m
1	0224	8.5	**16**	0344	7.9
	0919	2.3		1028	3.0
M	1452	8.2	TU	1614	7.6
	2137	2.6	◑	2313	3.1
2	0310	8.1	**17**	0452	7.3
	1004	2.7		1135	3.5
TU	1546	7.9	W	1731	7.3
◐	2232	2.9			
3	0413	7.7	**18**	0036	3.3
	1108	3.0		0617	7.1
W	1701	7.7	TH	1303	3.6
	2349	3.0		1856	7.4
4	0540	7.5	**19**	0157	3.1
	1237	3.0		0740	7.3
TH	1827	7.8	F	1420	3.3
				2007	7.7
5	0120	2.8	**20**	0306	2.7
	0709	7.8		0841	7.8
F	1402	2.7	SA	1517	2.9
	1943	8.2		2059	8.2
6	0238	2.2	**21**	0350	2.3
	0823	8.3		0925	8.2
SA	1511	2.1	SU	1601	2.5
	2047	8.9		2139	8.6
7	0345	1.5	**22**	0430	1.9
	0922	8.9		1002	8.6
SU	1611	1.5	M	1637	2.1
	2141	9.5		2214	8.9
8	0443	0.9	**23**	0505	1.7
	1013	9.4		1034	8.9
M	1705	1.0	TU	1711	1.8
	2229	9.9		2246	9.1
9	0535	0.5	**24**	0537	1.5
	1059	9.8		1104	9.0
TU	1754	0.6	W	1743	1.6
○	2315	10.2	●	2317	9.2
10	0622	0.2	**25**	0609	1.3
	1143	9.9		1134	9.2
W	1839	0.5	TH	1817	1.4
	2359	10.3		2347	9.2
11	0705	0.2	**26**	0641	1.3
	1225	9.8		1205	9.2
TH	1921	0.5	F	1851	1.4
12	0042	10.1	**27**	0018	9.2
	0745	0.5		0714	1.4
F	1307	9.6	SA	1237	9.1
	2002	0.8		1925	1.5
13	0125	9.7	**28**	0050	9.1
	0823	1.0		0746	1.6
SA	1347	9.2	SU	1310	9.0
	2042	1.3		2000	1.8
14	0207	9.2	**29**	0125	8.9
	0901	1.6		0820	1.9
SU	1428	8.7	M	1347	8.8
	2124	2.0		2036	2.1
15	0252	8.6	**30**	0204	8.6
	0940	2.3		0856	2.3
M	1515	8.2	TU	1431	8.4
	2211	2.6		2118	2.4

OCTOBER

#	Time	m	#	Time	m
1	0253	8.2	**16**	0412	7.3
	0942	2.7		1044	3.6
W	1526	8.1	TH	1645	7.4
◑	2214	2.8		2352	3.4
2	0358	7.8	**17**	0531	7.1
	1047	3.0		1208	3.8
TH	1642	7.8	F	1807	7.3
	2332	2.9			
3	0526	7.6	**18**	0112	3.3
	1215	3.1		0654	7.2
F	1808	7.9	SA	1333	3.6
				1921	7.5
4	0102	2.7	**19**	0217	3.0
	0654	7.8		0801	7.6
SA	1341	2.7	SU	1434	3.2
	1924	8.3		2019	8.0
5	0220	2.1	**20**	0308	2.5
	0807	8.4		0849	8.0
SU	1451	2.1	M	1522	2.7
	2028	8.9		2103	8.4
6	0326	1.5	**21**	0351	2.1
	0905	8.9		0928	8.5
M	1551	1.6	TU	1602	2.3
	2122	9.5		2141	8.7
7	0423	1.0	**22**	0429	1.8
	0954	9.4		1002	8.8
TU	1644	1.1	W	1639	1.9
	2210	9.9		2215	9.0
8	0513	0.6	**23**	0505	1.5
	1039	9.7		1034	9.1
W	1732	0.8	TH	1716	1.6
○	2254	10.1	●	2248	9.2
9	0558	0.5	**24**	0540	1.4
	1121	9.8		1106	9.2
TH	1817	0.6	F	1753	1.4
	2337	10.1		2321	9.3
10	0639	0.5	**25**	0616	1.3
	1201	9.8		1139	9.3
F	1858	0.7	SA	1830	1.4
				2355	9.3
11	0019	9.9	**26**	0651	1.3
	0718	0.8		1214	9.3
SA	1241	9.6	SU	1907	1.4
	1938	1.0			
12	0100	9.5	**27**	0031	9.2
	0755	1.3		0726	1.5
SU	1319	9.2	M	1251	9.2
	2017	1.5		1945	1.6
13	0140	9.0	**28**	0110	9.0
	0830	1.9		0803	1.8
M	1357	8.8	TU	1332	9.0
	2057	2.1		2024	1.9
14	0222	8.5	**29**	0154	8.7
	0906	2.5		0842	2.2
TU	1440	8.3	W	1419	8.7
	2140	2.7		2110	2.2
15	0310	7.9	**30**	0247	8.3
	0946	3.1		0931	2.6
W	1534	7.8	TH	1517	8.4
◑	2235	3.2		2207	2.5
			31	0352	8.0
				1035	2.9
			F	1629	8.1
			◑	2321	2.6

NOVEMBER

#	Time	m	#	Time	m
1	0513	7.8	**16**	0008	3.4
	1156	3.0		0551	7.2
SA	1748	8.1	SU	1221	3.7
				1822	7.4
2	0043	2.5	**17**	0119	3.2
	0634	7.9		0703	7.4
SU	1318	2.7	M	1335	3.5
	1902	8.4		1926	7.7
3	0158	2.1	**18**	0217	2.8
	0745	8.4		0801	7.8
M	1428	2.3	TU	1432	3.0
	2006	8.9		2019	8.0
4	0303	1.6	**19**	0306	2.4
	0844	8.8		0847	8.2
TU	1529	1.8	W	1521	2.6
	2101	9.3		2103	8.4
5	0359	1.3	**20**	0350	2.0
	0934	9.2		0926	8.6
W	1622	1.4	TH	1606	2.1
	2150	9.6		2142	8.7
6	0449	1.0	**21**	0432	1.7
	1019	9.5		1003	9.0
TH	1711	1.1	F	1648	1.8
○	2235	9.7		2219	9.0
7	0533	0.9	**22**	0512	1.5
	1100	9.6		1039	9.2
F	1755	1.0	SA	1730	1.5
	2318	9.7	●	2257	9.2
8	0614	1.0	**23**	0553	1.3
	1140	9.6		1117	9.4
SA	1837	1.0	SU	1812	1.3
	2359	9.4		2336	9.3
9	0652	1.2	**24**	0632	1.3
	1218	9.4		1156	9.5
SU	1917	1.3	M	1854	1.3
10	0038	9.3	**25**	0017	9.3
	0728	1.6		0712	1.4
M	1255	9.2	TU	1238	9.5
	1955	1.6		1935	1.4
11	0117	8.9	**26**	0101	9.2
	0801	2.0		0752	1.6
TU	1332	8.8	W	1323	9.3
	2033	2.1		2019	1.5
12	0157	8.5	**27**	0149	9.0
	0835	2.5		0836	1.9
W	1412	8.4	TH	1412	9.1
	2111	2.6		2107	1.8
13	0240	8.0	**28**	0242	8.6
	0910	3.0		0925	2.3
TH	1459	8.0	F	1508	8.8
	2156	3.0		2202	2.1
14	0332	7.6	**29**	0343	8.3
	0956	3.4		1024	2.6
F	1557	7.6	SA	1613	8.5
◑	2254	3.3	◑	2307	2.3
15	0437	7.2	**30**	0453	8.1
	1100	3.7		1134	2.7
SA	1709	7.4	SU	1724	8.4

DECEMBER

#	Time	m	#	Time	m
1	0018	2.3	**16**	0004	3.3
	0607	8.0		0552	7.3
M	1249	2.7	TU	1222	3.6
	1834	8.4		1821	7.5
2	0130	2.2	**17**	0115	3.1
	0718	8.2		0659	7.5
TU	1400	2.4	W	1335	3.3
	1941	8.6		1925	7.7
3	0236	2.0	**18**	0218	2.8
	0821	8.5		0758	7.9
W	1505	2.1	TH	1438	2.9
	2040	8.9		2020	8.0
4	0335	1.7	**19**	0312	2.4
	0914	8.9		0848	8.3
TH	1602	1.8	F	1532	2.4
	2132	9.1		2109	8.4
5	0426	1.6	**20**	0401	2.0
	1001	9.1		0933	8.8
F	1652	1.5	SA	1622	2.0
	2219	9.2		2154	8.8
6	0511	1.5	**21**	0448	1.6
	1043	9.3		1016	9.2
SA	1738	1.4	SU	1711	1.6
○	2302	9.3		2238	9.1
7	0552	1.5	**22**	0533	1.4
	1123	9.3		1058	9.5
SU	1820	1.4	M	1757	1.2
	2343	9.2	●	2322	9.4
8	0630	1.6	**23**	0618	1.2
	1200	9.3		1142	9.7
M	1859	1.5	TU	1844	1.0
9	0021	9.1	**24**	0007	9.5
	0704	1.8		0701	1.1
TU	1236	9.2	W	1227	9.8
	1936	1.7		1929	1.0
10	0058	8.9	**25**	0053	9.5
	0737	2.0		0746	1.2
W	1311	9.0	TH	1314	9.7
	2010	2.0		2015	1.0
11	0134	8.6	**26**	0141	9.3
	0809	2.3		0830	1.4
TH	1348	8.7	F	1403	9.5
	2044	2.3		2101	1.3
12	0213	8.3	**27**	0232	9.0
	0842	2.7		0917	1.8
F	1428	8.4	SA	1455	9.3
	2120	2.6		2151	1.6
13	0256	7.9	**28**	0326	8.6
	0921	3.0		1008	2.1
SA	1513	8.0	SU	1551	8.9
	2202	2.9	◑	2245	1.9
14	0345	7.6	**29**	0426	8.3
	1009	3.3		1108	2.5
SU	1608	7.7	M	1654	8.6
◑	2257	3.2		2348	2.3
15	0444	7.3	**30**	0534	8.0
	1109	3.5		1216	2.7
M	1712	7.5	TU	1803	8.3
			31	0057	2.4
				0646	8.0
			W	1331	2.7
				1914	8.3

Chart Datum: 4·93 metres below Ordnance Datum (Newlyn)
HAT is 10·3m above Chart Datum

TIDES

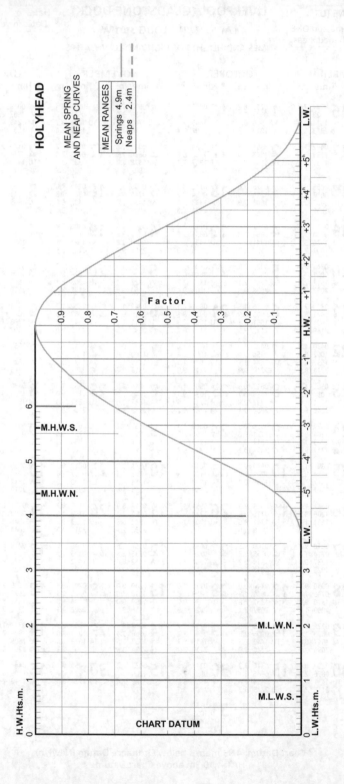

HOLYHEAD

MEAN SPRING
AND NEAP CURVES

MEAN RANGES	
Springs	4.9m
Neaps	2.4m

TIMES AND HEIGHTS OF HIGH AND LOW WATERS

2014

JANUARY

Day	Time m	Time m	Time m	Time m		Day	Time m	Time m	Time m	Time m
1 W	0335 0.8	0950 5.9	1600 0.6	●2217 5.8		**16** TH	0416 1.3	1031 5.5	1643 1.1	○2249 5.3
2 TH	0422 0.6	1036 6.1	1649 0.4	2305 5.9		**17** F	0447 1.2	1102 5.6	1715 1.1	2320 5.3
3 F	0509 0.5	1123 6.2	1738 0.3	2353 5.9		**18** SA	0519 1.1	1133 5.6	1747 1.0	2352 5.3
4 SA	0557 0.6	1211 6.2	1827 0.4			**19** SU	0551 1.2	1205 5.6	1819 1.1	
5 SU	0042 5.7	0644 0.7	1300 6.0	1917 0.6		**20** M	0025 5.3	0624 1.2	1239 5.5	1853 1.2
6 M	0133 5.5	0735 1.0	1350 5.6	2009 0.9		**21** TU	0101 5.2	0659 1.3	1314 5.4	1928 1.3
7 TU	0226 5.2	0828 1.3	1444 5.5	2105 1.2		**22** W	0138 5.0	0737 1.5	1352 5.2	2008 1.5
8 W	0323 4.9	0928 1.6	1544 5.2	☾2207 1.6		**23** TH	0219 4.9	0821 1.7	1435 5.0	2056 1.6
9 TH	0430 4.7	1036 1.9	1652 4.9	2315 1.8		**24** F	0309 4.7	0915 1.9	1530 4.8	☾2156 1.8
10 F	0544 4.6	1149 2.0	1807 4.7			**25** SA	0414 4.6	1024 2.0	1642 4.7	2310 1.9
11 SA	0025 1.9	0656 4.7	1301 2.0	1919 4.7		**26** SU	0535 4.6	1143 1.9	1808 4.7	
12 SU	0130 1.9	0756 4.9	1403 1.9	2017 4.8		**27** M	0027 1.7	0651 4.8	1259 1.7	1923 4.9
13 M	0224 1.7	0844 5.1	1454 1.6	2103 5.0		**28** TU	0134 1.5	0754 5.1	1403 1.3	2025 5.2
14 TU	0307 1.6	0924 5.2	1535 1.4	2142 5.1		**29** W	0232 1.1	0848 5.5	1459 0.9	2118 5.5
15 W	0344 1.4	0959 5.4	1611 1.2	2217 5.2		**30** TH	0323 0.8	0936 5.8	1549 0.5	●2206 5.7
						31 F	0409 0.5	1022 6.1	1636 0.3	2252 5.9

FEBRUARY

Day	Time m	Time m	Time m	Time m		Day	Time m	Time m	Time m	Time m
1 SA	0455 0.4	1108 6.3	1722 0.2	2337 5.9		**16** SU	0457 1.0	1110 5.6	1722 0.9	2328 5.4
2 SU	0540 0.4	1153 6.3	1808 0.2			**17** M	0528 0.9	1142 5.6	1753 0.9	
3 M	0022 5.8	0624 0.5	1239 6.1	1853 0.4		**18** TU	0000 5.4	0559 0.9	1215 5.6	1824 0.9
4 TU	0107 5.6	0710 0.7	1325 5.9	1939 0.8		**19** W	0034 5.3	0633 1.0	1249 5.5	1858 1.0
5 W	0153 5.3	0757 1.1	1413 5.5	2028 1.2		**20** TH	0109 5.2	0709 1.2	1325 5.3	1936 1.2
6 TH	0242 5.0	0850 1.4	1505 5.1	☾2122 1.6		**21** F	0148 5.1	0751 1.4	1406 5.1	2021 1.4
7 F	0339 4.7	0953 1.8	1607 4.7	2228 1.9		**22** SA	0235 4.9	0843 1.6	1458 4.9	☾2119 1.7
8 SA	0450 4.5	1109 2.1	1726 4.5	2344 2.1		**23** SU	0336 4.7	0951 1.8	1610 4.6	2236 1.9
9 SU	0615 4.4	1229 2.1	1852 4.4			**24** M	0459 4.6	1116 1.8	1745 4.6	
10 M	0059 2.1	0730 4.6	1341 1.9	1959 4.6		**25** TU	0003 1.8	0625 4.7	1240 1.6	1910 4.8
11 TU	0202 1.9	0824 4.8	1435 1.7	2048 4.8		**26** W	0118 1.6	0736 5.0	1349 1.2	2014 5.1
12 W	0249 1.7	0905 5.1	1510 1.4	2126 5.0		**27** TH	0218 1.2	0832 5.4	1446 0.8	2106 5.4
13 TH	0326 1.5	0940 5.3	1551 1.2	2158 5.1		**28** F	0308 0.8	0920 5.8	1534 0.4	2151 5.7
14 F	0357 1.2	1011 5.4	1622 1.0	○2228 5.3						
15 SA	0427 1.1	1040 5.5	1652 0.9	2258 5.4						

MARCH

Day	Time m	Time m	Time m	Time m		Day	Time m	Time m	Time m	Time m
1 SA	0354 0.5	1005 6.0	1619 0.2	●2234 5.8		**16** SU	0401 1.0	1013 5.5	1623 0.8	○2231 5.4
2 SU	0437 0.3	1049 6.2	1702 0.1	2316 5.9		**17** M	0431 0.9	1044 5.6	1653 0.7	2301 5.5
3 M	0519 0.2	1133 6.2	1745 0.2	2358 5.8		**18** TU	0502 0.8	1116 5.6	1725 0.7	2334 5.5
4 TU	0602 0.3	1216 6.0	1827 0.4			**19** W	0535 0.7	1147 5.6	1757 0.8	
5 W	0039 5.6	0644 0.6	1259 5.7	1908 0.8		**20** TH	0008 5.5	0610 0.8	1226 5.6	1832 0.9
6 TH	0121 5.3	0728 0.9	1343 5.4	1952 1.2		**21** F	0045 5.4	0648 0.9	1304 5.3	1912 1.1
7 F	0204 5.0	0816 1.3	1429 5.0	2039 1.6		**22** SA	0126 5.2	0732 1.1	1348 5.1	1959 1.3
8 SA	0252 4.7	0912 1.7	1525 4.6	☾2137 2.0		**23** SU	0214 5.0	0826 1.4	1443 4.8	2058 1.6
9 SU	0355 4.4	1024 2.1	1640 4.3	2255 2.3		**24** M	0315 4.8	0935 1.6	1558 4.6	☾2217 1.9
10 M	0519 4.3	1149 2.2	1814 4.2			**25** TU	0437 4.6	1101 1.7	1734 4.5	2345 1.8
11 TU	0020 2.3	0648 4.4	1306 2.0	1930 4.4		**26** W	0604 4.7	1224 1.5	1858 4.7	
12 W	0130 2.1	0751 4.6	1405 1.7	2022 4.6		**27** TH	0100 1.6	0716 5.0	1333 1.1	2000 5.1
13 TH	0221 1.8	0836 4.9	1448 1.4	2100 4.9		**28** F	0201 1.2	0813 5.4	1428 0.8	2050 5.3
14 F	0259 1.5	0912 5.1	1523 1.2	2132 5.1		**29** SA	0251 0.8	0901 5.7	1516 0.5	2133 5.6
15 SA	0331 1.2	0943 5.3	1554 1.0	2202 5.3		**30** SU	0335 0.5	0946 5.9	1559 0.3	●2214 5.7
						31 M	0417 0.4	1029 6.0	1640 0.3	2254 5.8

APRIL

Day	Time m	Time m	Time m	Time m		Day	Time m	Time m	Time m	Time m
1 TU	0459 0.3	1111 6.0	1720 0.4	2333 5.7		**16** W	0437 0.7	1050 5.6	1657 0.7	2309 5.6
2 W	0540 0.4	1153 5.8	1800 0.6			**17** TH	0513 0.6	1128 5.6	1734 0.7	2346 5.6
3 TH	0013 5.6	0621 0.6	1235 5.5	1839 0.9		**18** F	0552 0.7	1207 5.5	1813 0.8	
4 F	0052 5.4	0703 0.9	1316 5.2	1919 1.2		**19** SA	0027 5.5	0634 0.8	1251 5.3	1856 1.0
5 SA	0132 5.1	0747 1.3	1359 4.9	2002 1.6		**20** SU	0112 5.4	0722 1.0	1340 5.1	1947 1.3
6 SU	0215 4.8	0838 1.6	1449 4.5	2053 2.0		**21** M	0203 5.2	0819 1.2	1438 4.9	2048 1.5
7 M	0308 4.5	0940 1.9	1555 4.3	☾2200 2.3		**22** TU	0305 4.9	0928 1.4	1554 4.6	☾2205 1.8
8 TU	0421 4.3	1059 2.1	1720 4.1	2325 2.4		**23** W	0422 4.8	1048 1.4	1722 4.6	2326 1.7
9 W	0547 4.3	1217 2.0	1843 4.3			**24** TH	0543 4.9	1205 1.3	1839 4.8	
10 TH	0042 2.2	0701 4.5	1320 1.8	1942 4.5		**25** F	0038 1.5	0653 5.1	1312 1.1	1940 5.0
11 F	0139 1.9	0754 4.7	1407 1.5	2024 4.8		**26** SA	0139 1.3	0751 5.3	1407 0.9	2029 5.2
12 SA	0221 1.6	0834 5.0	1445 1.2	2058 5.0		**27** SU	0231 1.0	0841 5.5	1455 0.7	2113 5.4
13 SU	0257 1.3	0909 5.2	1519 1.0	2130 5.2		**28** M	0316 0.7	0926 5.6	1538 0.6	2153 5.6
14 M	0330 1.1	0942 5.4	1551 0.8	2201 5.4		**29** TU	0358 0.6	1009 5.7	1618 0.6	●2232 5.6
15 TU	0402 0.9	1015 5.5	1623 0.7	○2234 5.5		**30** W	0440 0.5	1051 5.7	1657 0.6	2311 5.6

Chart Datum: 3·05 metres below Ordnance Datum (Newlyn)
HAT is 6·3m above Chart Datum

TIDES

TIME ZONE (UT)
For Summer Time add ONE hour in **non-shaded areas**

WALES – HOLYHEAD
LAT 53°19′N   LONG 4°37′W
TIMES AND HEIGHTS OF HIGH AND LOW WATERS

Dates in amber are **SPRINGS**
Dates in yellow are **NEAPS**

2014

MAY

#	Time	m	#	Time	m
1 TH	0520 / 1132 / 1735 / 2350	0.6 / 5.5 / 0.8 / 5.5	16 F	0454 / 1110 / 1715 / 2329	0.6 / 5.6 / 0.7 / 5.7
2 F	0601 / 1212 / 1813	0.8 / 5.3 / 1.0	17 SA	0538 / 1154 / 1759	0.6 / 5.5 / 0.7
3 SA	0027 / 0640 / 1252 / 1851	5.4 / 1.0 / 5.1 / 1.3	18 SU	0014 / 0625 / 1243 / 1846	5.7 / 0.6 / 5.4 / 0.9
4 SU	0105 / 0722 / 1333 / 1932	5.2 / 1.3 / 4.9 / 1.6	19 M	0102 / 0716 / 1335 / 1939	5.6 / 0.8 / 5.2 / 1.1
5 M	0145 / 0808 / 1418 / 2018	4.9 / 1.5 / 4.6 / 1.9	20 TU	0155 / 0814 / 1434 / 2040	5.4 / 1.0 / 5.0 / 1.4
6 TU	0231 / 0901 / 1513 / 2113	4.7 / 1.8 / 4.4 / 2.1	21 W	0255 / 0919 / 1544 / 2149 ◐	5.2 / 1.1 / 4.8 / 1.6
7 W	0330 / 1005 / 1623 / 2222 ◐	4.5 / 1.9 / 4.2 / 2.3	22 TH	0404 / 1030 / 1701 / 2303	5.0 / 1.3 / 4.7 / 1.6
8 TH	0442 / 1117 / 1739 / 2338	4.4 / 2.0 / 4.3 / 2.3	23 F	0518 / 1142 / 1813	5.0 / 1.3 / 4.8
9 F	0556 / 1222 / 1845	4.4 / 1.8 / 4.4	24 SA	0012 / 0627 / 1247 / 1915	1.6 / 5.0 / 1.2 / 4.9
10 SA	0042 / 0658 / 1317 / 1936	2.1 / 4.6 / 1.6 / 4.7	25 SU	0115 / 0728 / 1345 / 2008	1.4 / 5.1 / 1.1 / 5.1
11 SU	0134 / 0748 / 1401 / 2018	1.8 / 4.8 / 1.4 / 4.9	26 M	0210 / 0821 / 1434 / 2053	1.2 / 5.3 / 1.0 / 5.3
12 M	0217 / 0830 / 1440 / 2055	1.5 / 5.0 / 1.1 / 5.2	27 TU	0259 / 0909 / 1518 / 2134	1.0 / 5.3 / 0.9 / 5.4
13 TU	0256 / 0909 / 1518 / 2131	1.2 / 5.2 / 0.9 / 5.4	28 W	0343 / 0952 / 1559 / 2214 ●	0.9 / 5.4 / 0.9 / 5.5
14 W	0334 / 0948 / 1555 / 2208 ○	0.9 / 5.4 / 0.8 / 5.5	29 TH	0424 / 1034 / 1637 / 2252	0.8 / 5.4 / 0.9 / 5.5
15 TH	0413 / 1028 / 1634 / 2247	0.7 / 5.5 / 0.7 / 5.7	30 F	0504 / 1114 / 1714 / 2329	0.8 / 5.3 / 1.0 / 5.4
			31 SA	0543 / 1152 / 1751	0.9 / 5.2 / 1.1

JUNE

#	Time	m	#	Time	m
1 SU	0005 / 0620 / 1230 / 1827	5.4 / 1.0 / 5.1 / 1.3	16 M	0002 / 0616 / 1234 / 1836	5.9 / 0.4 / 5.5 / 0.7
2 M	0042 / 0659 / 1308 / 1905	5.2 / 1.2 / 4.9 / 1.5	17 TU	0052 / 0708 / 1325 / 1928	5.8 / 0.5 / 5.4 / 0.9
3 TU	0119 / 0740 / 1348 / 1947	5.1 / 1.4 / 4.7 / 1.7	18 W	0143 / 0802 / 1421 / 2024	5.6 / 0.7 / 5.2 / 1.2
4 W	0200 / 0825 / 1434 / 2033	4.9 / 1.6 / 4.6 / 1.9	19 TH	0239 / 0901 / 1523 / 2126 ◐	5.4 / 0.9 / 4.9 / 1.4
5 TH	0248 / 0916 / 1529 / 2128 ◐	4.7 / 1.7 / 4.4 / 2.1	20 F	0342 / 1005 / 1631 / 2234	5.2 / 1.2 / 4.8 / 1.6
6 F	0345 / 1014 / 1633 / 2232	4.6 / 1.8 / 4.4 / 2.2	21 SA	0450 / 1113 / 1742 / 2344	5.0 / 1.3 / 4.7 / 1.6
7 SA	0451 / 1118 / 1741 / 2339	4.5 / 1.8 / 4.4 / 2.1	22 SU	0600 / 1219 / 1849	4.9 / 1.4 / 4.8
8 SU	0559 / 1219 / 1842	4.6 / 1.7 / 4.6	23 M	0051 / 0707 / 1322 / 1947	1.6 / 4.9 / 1.4 / 4.9
9 M	0041 / 0659 / 1314 / 1935	1.9 / 4.7 / 1.5 / 4.8	24 TU	0152 / 0805 / 1416 / 2037	1.4 / 5.0 / 1.3 / 5.1
10 TU	0136 / 0752 / 1403 / 2021	1.6 / 4.9 / 1.3 / 5.1	25 W	0245 / 0856 / 1503 / 2120	1.3 / 5.1 / 1.3 / 5.2
11 W	0224 / 0839 / 1448 / 2104	1.3 / 5.1 / 1.1 / 5.3	26 TH	0331 / 0940 / 1544 / 2159	1.2 / 5.1 / 1.2 / 5.3
12 TH	0309 / 0924 / 1532 / 2146	1.0 / 5.3 / 0.8 / 5.6	27 F	0412 / 1019 / 1621 / 2236 ●	1.1 / 5.2 / 1.1 / 5.4
13 F	0354 / 1009 / 1615 / 2230 ○	0.7 / 5.5 / 0.7 / 5.7	28 SA	0449 / 1057 / 1656 / 2311	1.0 / 5.2 / 1.1 / 5.4
14 SA	0440 / 1056 / 1701 / 2315	0.5 / 5.6 / 0.6 / 5.8	29 SU	0525 / 1132 / 1730 / 2345	1.0 / 5.2 / 1.2 / 5.4
15 SU	0527 / 1143 / 1748	0.4 / 5.6 / 0.6	30 M	0600 / 1207 / 1804	1.0 / 5.1 / 1.2

JULY

#	Time	m	#	Time	m
1 TU	0018 / 0634 / 1242 / 1839	5.3 / 1.1 / 5.0 / 1.3	16 W	0035 / 0651 / 1308 / 1910	6.0 / 0.3 / 5.6 / 0.7
2 W	0054 / 0711 / 1319 / 1917	5.2 / 1.2 / 4.9 / 1.5	17 TH	0125 / 0742 / 1359 / 2002	5.9 / 0.6 / 5.3 / 1.0
3 TH	0131 / 0750 / 1358 / 1957	5.1 / 1.4 / 4.8 / 1.7	18 F	0217 / 0836 / 1454 / 2058	5.6 / 0.9 / 5.1 / 1.3
4 F	0211 / 0832 / 1443 / 2043	5.0 / 1.5 / 4.7 / 1.8	19 SA	0314 / 0934 / 1555 / 2203 ◐	5.3 / 1.2 / 4.8 / 1.5
5 SA	0257 / 0921 / 1535 / 2138 ◐	4.8 / 1.7 / 4.5 / 2.0	20 SU	0418 / 1040 / 1706 / 2314	5.0 / 1.5 / 4.7 / 1.7
6 SU	0353 / 1019 / 1639 / 2242	4.7 / 1.8 / 4.5 / 2.0	21 M	0531 / 1150 / 1820	4.8 / 1.7 / 4.6
7 M	0501 / 1125 / 1749 / 2352	4.6 / 1.8 / 4.6 / 1.9	22 TU	0027 / 0647 / 1259 / 1927	1.8 / 4.7 / 1.7 / 4.8
8 TU	0613 / 1230 / 1855	4.6 / 1.7 / 4.7	23 W	0136 / 0753 / 1359 / 2022	1.7 / 4.7 / 1.7 / 4.9
9 W	0058 / 0718 / 1331 / 1951	1.7 / 4.8 / 1.5 / 5.0	24 TH	0233 / 0845 / 1449 / 2106	1.5 / 4.9 / 1.5 / 5.1
10 TH	0157 / 0815 / 1424 / 2041	1.4 / 5.0 / 1.2 / 5.3	25 F	0319 / 0928 / 1529 / 2144	1.3 / 5.0 / 1.4 / 5.3
11 F	0249 / 0907 / 1513 / 2128 ●	1.0 / 5.3 / 0.9 / 5.6	26 SA	0358 / 1005 / 1604 / 2218 ●	1.2 / 5.1 / 1.2 / 5.4
12 SA	0338 / 0955 / 1600 / 2214 ○	0.7 / 5.5 / 0.7 / 5.8	27 SU	0432 / 1038 / 1637 / 2250	1.0 / 5.2 / 1.1 / 5.4
13 SU	0426 / 1043 / 1647 / 2300	0.4 / 5.7 / 0.5 / 6.0	28 M	0504 / 1110 / 1708 / 2322	1.0 / 5.2 / 1.1 / 5.5
14 M	0514 / 1130 / 1733 / 2347	0.3 / 5.7 / 0.5 / 6.1	29 TU	0536 / 1141 / 1740 / 2354	1.0 / 5.2 / 1.1 / 5.5
15 TU	0603 / 1218 / 1821	0.2 / 5.7 / 0.5	30 W	0608 / 1214 / 1813	1.0 / 5.2 / 1.2
			31 TH	0027 / 0641 / 1249 / 1847	5.4 / 1.1 / 5.1 / 1.3

AUGUST

#	Time	m	#	Time	m
1 F	0102 / 0715 / 1325 / 1923	5.3 / 1.2 / 5.0 / 1.4	16 SA	0151 / 0805 / 1421 / 2028	5.6 / 0.9 / 5.1 / 1.2
2 SA	0138 / 0753 / 1404 / 2005	5.1 / 1.4 / 4.9 / 1.6	17 SU	0244 / 0859 / 1517 / 2130 ◐	5.2 / 1.4 / 4.9 / 1.6
3 SU	0218 / 0836 / 1450 / 2054	5.0 / 1.6 / 4.7 / 1.8	18 M	0345 / 1003 / 1626 / 2243	4.8 / 1.7 / 4.6 / 1.9
4 M	0307 / 0930 / 1548 / 2156 ◐	4.8 / 1.7 / 4.6 / 1.9	19 TU	0501 / 1117 / 1747 / 2156 ◐	4.6 / 2.0 / 4.5 / 1.9
5 TU	0412 / 1038 / 1702 / 2312	4.6 / 1.8 / 4.6 / 2.0	20 W	0002 / 0625 / 1233 / 1904	2.0 / 4.5 / 2.0 / 4.6
6 W	0535 / 1154 / 1820	4.6 / 1.8 / 4.7	21 TH	0117 / 0738 / 1340 / 2003	1.9 / 4.6 / 1.9 / 4.8
7 TH	0029 / 0653 / 1305 / 1926	1.8 / 4.7 / 1.6 / 5.0	22 F	0216 / 0831 / 1431 / 2048	1.7 / 4.8 / 1.7 / 5.1
8 F	0136 / 0759 / 1405 / 2022	1.4 / 5.0 / 1.3 / 5.3	23 SA	0301 / 0911 / 1510 / 2124	1.4 / 4.9 / 1.3 / 5.2
9 SA	0233 / 0853 / 1457 / 2111	1.0 / 5.3 / 0.9 / 5.6	24 SU	0337 / 0945 / 1544 / 2156	1.2 / 5.1 / 1.3 / 5.4
10 SU	0324 / 0941 / 1544 / 2157 ○	0.6 / 5.6 / 0.6 / 5.9	25 M	0409 / 1015 / 1614 / 2226 ●	1.1 / 5.2 / 1.2 / 5.4
11 M	0411 / 1027 / 1630 / 2243	0.3 / 5.8 / 0.4 / 6.2	26 TU	0439 / 1044 / 1643 / 2256	1.0 / 5.3 / 1.0 / 5.4
12 TU	0457 / 1113 / 1715 / 2328	0.1 / 5.9 / 0.3 / 6.2	27 W	0508 / 1114 / 1713 / 2327	0.9 / 5.4 / 1.0 / 5.4
13 W	0543 / 1158 / 1801	0.1 / 5.8 / 0.4	28 TH	0538 / 1145 / 1745 / 2359	0.9 / 5.4 / 1.0 / 5.5
14 TH	0015 / 0629 / 1244 / 1847	6.2 / 0.3 / 5.7 / 0.6	29 F	0610 / 1218 / 1818	1.0 / 5.3 / 1.1
15 F	0102 / 0716 / 1331 / 1935	5.9 / 0.6 / 5.4 / 0.9	30 SA	0032 / 0642 / 1254 / 1853	5.4 / 1.1 / 5.2 / 1.3
			31 SU	0108 / 0718 / 1331 / 1933	5.3 / 1.3 / 5.2 / 1.5

Chart Datum: 3·05 metres below Ordnance Datum (Newlyn)
HAT is 6·3m above Chart Datum

WALES – HOLYHEAD
LAT 53°19′N   LONG 4°37′W
TIMES AND HEIGHTS OF HIGH AND LOW WATERS

Dates in amber are **SPRINGS**
Dates in yellow are **NEAPS**

2014

SEPTEMBER

Day	Time m	Time m	Time m	Time m		Day	Time m	Time m	Time m	Time m
1 M	0147 5.1	1415 4.9	2021 1.7			16 TU	0311 4.7	0922 2.0	1543 4.6	2209 2.0
2 TU	0235 4.8	0853 1.7	1511 4.7	2124 1.9		17 W	0426 4.4	1037 2.2	1704 4.5	2331 2.1
3 W	0340 4.6	1003 1.9	1626 4.6	2244 1.9		18 TH	0556 4.3	1159 2.3	1830 4.5	
4 TH	0510 4.5	1128 1.9	1753 4.7			19 F	0047 2.0	0713 4.5	1311 2.2	1934 4.8
5 F	0008 1.8	0637 4.7	1246 1.7	1905 5.0		20 SA	0148 1.8	0806 4.7	1404 1.9	2020 5.0
6 SA	0119 1.4	0745 5.0	1348 1.4	2003 5.4		21 SU	0233 1.5	0846 4.9	1444 1.6	2056 5.2
7 SU	0217 1.0	0839 5.4	1440 1.0	2053 5.7		22 M	0309 1.3	0919 5.1	1517 1.4	2128 5.4
8 M	0307 0.6	0925 5.6	1527 0.6	2138 6.0		23 TU	0340 1.1	0948 5.3	1546 1.2	2158 5.5
9 TU	0353 0.3	1008 5.9	1611 0.4	2222 6.2		24 W	0409 1.0	1016 5.4	1616 1.1	2228 5.6
10 W	0437 0.1	1051 5.9	1654 0.3	2307 6.3		25 TH	0438 0.9	1046 5.5	1646 1.0	2259 5.6
11 TH	0520 0.2	1134 5.9	1738 0.4	2352 6.2		26 F	0508 0.9	1117 5.5	1718 1.0	2332 5.6
12 F	0604 0.4	1218 5.7	1823 0.6			27 SA	0540 0.9	1151 5.5	1752 1.0	
13 SA	0037 5.9	0647 0.7	1302 5.5	1909 0.9		28 SU	0006 5.5	0613 1.1	1227 5.4	1829 1.2
14 SU	0124 5.5	0733 1.1	1348 5.2	1959 1.3		29 M	0044 5.4	0651 1.2	1306 5.3	1910 1.3
15 M	0213 5.1	0823 1.5	1439 4.9	2057 1.7		30 TU	0125 5.1	0734 1.5	1351 5.1	2000 1.6

OCTOBER

Day	Time m	Time m	Time m	Time m		Day	Time m	Time m	Time m	Time m
1 W	0216 4.9	0829 1.7	1448 4.9	2105 1.8		16 TH	0344 4.4	0948 2.4	1611 4.5	2247 2.2
2 TH	0324 4.7	0941 2.0	1603 4.8	2226 1.9		17 F	0508 4.3	1110 2.5	1734 4.5	
3 F	0456 4.6	1108 2.0	1730 4.8	2350 1.7		18 SA	0003 2.1	0629 4.4	1226 2.4	1847 4.7
4 SA	0623 4.8	1226 1.8	1844 5.1			19 SU	0106 1.9	0728 4.6	1324 2.1	1940 4.9
5 SU	0101 1.3	0729 5.1	1329 1.4	1943 5.4		20 M	0154 1.7	0811 4.9	1408 1.8	2020 5.1
6 M	0159 1.0	0821 5.4	1421 1.0	2033 5.8		21 TU	0233 1.4	0846 5.1	1443 1.6	2055 5.3
7 TU	0248 0.6	0906 5.7	1507 0.7	2118 6.0		22 W	0306 1.2	0917 5.3	1516 1.3	2127 5.5
8 W	0332 0.4	0948 5.8	1551 0.5	2202 6.2		23 TH	0337 1.1	0947 5.5	1547 1.1	2159 5.6
9 TH	0415 0.3	1029 5.9	1634 0.4	2246 6.2		24 F	0408 1.0	1018 5.6	1620 1.0	2233 5.6
10 F	0457 0.4	1111 5.9	1717 0.5	2330 6.0		25 SA	0440 0.9	1051 5.7	1655 0.9	2308 5.6
11 SA	0538 0.6	1153 5.8	1801 0.7			26 SU	0515 0.9	1127 5.7	1732 1.0	2346 5.6
12 SU	0014 5.8	0620 0.9	1235 5.6	1845 1.0		27 M	0552 1.0	1206 5.6	1812 1.1	
13 M	0059 5.4	0703 1.3	1318 5.3	1932 1.4		28 TU	0026 5.4	0632 1.2	1248 5.5	1857 1.2
14 TU	0145 5.1	0748 1.7	1404 5.0	2025 1.7		29 W	0113 5.2	0719 1.4	1336 5.3	1950 1.4
15 W	0238 4.7	0841 2.1	1500 4.7	2130 2.0		30 TH	0207 5.0	0816 1.7	1434 5.1	2054 1.6
						31 F	0316 4.8	0926 1.9	1546 5.0	2211 1.7

NOVEMBER

Day	Time m	Time m	Time m	Time m		Day	Time m	Time m	Time m	Time m
1 SA	0442 4.7	1048 2.0	1707 5.0	2330 1.6		16 SU	0523 4.4	1122 2.5	1741 4.6	
2 SU	0603 4.9	1203 1.8	1820 5.2			17 M	0009 2.1	0632 4.8	1229 2.3	1845 4.8
3 M	0039 1.3	0709 5.1	1307 1.5	1920 5.4		18 TU	0105 1.9	0725 4.8	1322 2.1	1936 5.0
4 TU	0138 1.1	0802 5.4	1401 1.2	2013 5.7		19 W	0150 1.6	0807 5.0	1405 1.8	2018 5.2
5 W	0228 0.8	0847 5.6	1449 0.9	2100 5.9		20 TH	0229 1.4	0844 5.3	1443 1.5	2056 5.3
6 TH	0313 0.7	0929 5.8	1534 0.7	2144 6.0		21 F	0305 1.2	0918 5.5	1520 1.2	2133 5.5
7 F	0355 0.6	1010 5.9	1617 0.7	2228 5.9		22 SA	0340 1.1	0953 5.6	1557 1.1	2210 5.6
8 SA	0436 0.7	1051 5.9	1700 0.7	2311 5.8		23 SU	0417 0.9	1030 5.8	1636 0.9	2249 5.7
9 SU	0516 0.8	1131 5.8	1742 0.9	2354 5.6		24 M	0455 0.9	1109 5.8	1717 0.9	2331 5.6
10 M	0556 1.1	1212 5.6	1825 1.1			25 TU	0536 0.9	1151 5.8	1801 0.9	
11 TU	0036 5.3	0636 1.4	1252 5.4	1908 1.4		26 W	0016 5.5	0620 1.1	1236 5.7	1848 1.0
12 W	0119 5.1	0718 1.7	1333 5.2	1955 1.7		27 TH	0105 5.4	0709 1.3	1326 5.6	1942 1.2
13 TH	0205 4.8	0804 2.0	1421 4.9	2048 1.9		28 F	0200 5.2	0805 1.5	1422 5.4	2043 1.3
14 F	0259 4.5	0858 2.3	1517 4.7	2152 2.1		29 SA	0304 5.0	0910 1.7	1526 5.2	2152 1.5
15 SA	0407 4.4	1006 2.5	1628 4.6	2303 2.2		30 SU	0419 4.8	1022 1.8	1639 5.2	2305 1.5

DECEMBER

Day	Time m	Time m	Time m	Time m		Day	Time m	Time m	Time m	Time m
1 M	0535 4.9	1136 1.8	1752 5.2			16 TU	0521 4.5	1119 2.4	1740 4.6	
2 TU	0013 1.4	0643 5.0	1243 1.6	1857 5.3		17 W	0004 2.0	0627 4.6	1226 2.2	1844 4.8
3 W	0115 1.3	0741 5.2	1342 1.4	1955 5.4		18 TH	0102 1.8	0723 4.8	1322 2.0	1939 4.9
4 TH	0209 1.1	0830 5.4	1434 1.2	2045 5.6		19 F	0151 1.6	0810 5.1	1411 1.7	2027 5.1
5 F	0256 1.0	0914 5.6	1521 1.0	2131 5.6		20 SA	0235 1.4	0851 5.3	1455 1.4	2110 5.4
6 SA	0340 1.0	0955 5.7	1605 0.9	2215 5.6		21 SU	0317 1.1	0932 5.6	1538 1.1	2152 5.5
7 SU	0420 1.0	1035 5.7	1647 0.9	2256 5.6		22 M	0358 0.9	1012 5.8	1621 0.8	2235 5.7
8 M	0459 1.0	1114 5.7	1727 1.0	2336 5.5		23 TU	0440 0.8	1054 5.9	1705 0.7	2319 5.7
9 TU	0536 1.2	1152 5.6	1806 1.1			24 W	0524 0.8	1138 6.0	1751 0.6	
10 W	0015 5.3	0613 1.3	1229 5.5	1845 1.3		25 TH	0006 5.7	0609 0.8	1225 6.0	1839 0.7
11 TH	0053 5.1	0651 1.5	1306 5.3	1925 1.5		26 F	0055 5.6	0657 1.0	1313 5.9	1930 0.8
12 F	0133 4.9	0731 1.8	1345 5.1	2009 1.7		27 SA	0146 5.4	0750 1.2	1406 5.7	2025 1.0
13 SA	0216 4.8	0815 2.0	1430 4.9	2058 1.9		28 SU	0243 5.2	0847 1.4	1503 5.4	2126 1.3
14 SU	0308 4.6	0907 2.2	1524 4.8	2155 2.0		29 M	0348 4.9	0953 1.6	1609 5.2	2234 1.5
15 M	0411 4.5	1009 2.4	1629 4.6	2300 2.1		30 TU	0501 4.8	1105 1.8	1722 5.1	2345 1.6
						31 W	0614 4.9	1217 1.8	1835 5.1	

Chart Datum: 3·05 metres below Ordnance Datum (Newlyn)
HAT is 6·3m above Chart Datum

TIDES

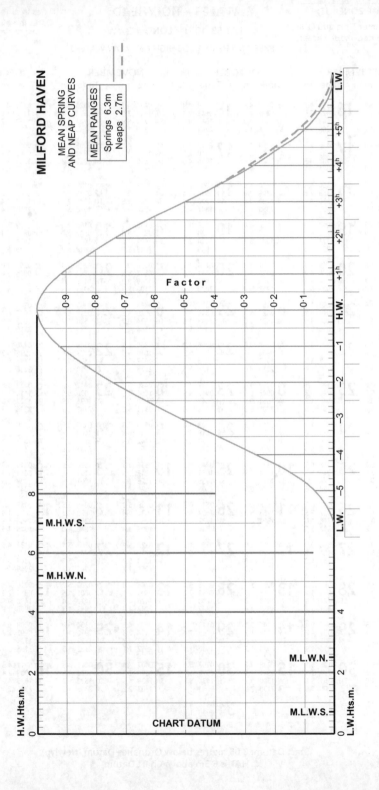

MILFORD HAVEN

MEAN SPRING
AND NEAP CURVES

MEAN RANGES	
Springs	6.3m
Neaps	2.7m

Factor

0·9 0·8 0·7 0·6 0·5 0·4 0·3 0·2 0·1

H.W. −1 −2 −3 −4 −5 L.W.

+5h +4h +3h +2h +1h H.W. L.W.

H.W.Hts.m.

M.H.W.S.

M.H.W.N.

CHART DATUM

L.W.Hts.m.

M.L.W.N.

M.L.W.S.

WALES – MILFORD HAVEN
LAT 51°42′N   LONG 5°03′W
TIMES AND HEIGHTS OF HIGH AND LOW WATERS

Dates in amber are SPRINGS
Dates in yellow are NEAPS

2014

JANUARY

Day	Time m	Time m	Time m	Time m
1 W ●	0540 7.2	1204 0.7	1807 7.2	
16 TH ○	0015 1.4	0621 6.6	1240 1.3	1839 6.6
2 TH	0028 0.7	0630 7.5	1255 0.5	1856 7.4
17 F	0049 1.2	0654 6.7	1312 1.2	1912 6.6
3 F	0116 0.5	0719 7.6	1343 0.4	1944 7.4
18 SA	0121 1.2	0725 6.8	1343 1.2	1943 6.6
4 SA	0203 0.5	0807 7.6	1430 0.4	2031 7.2
19 SU	0152 1.2	0756 6.8	1414 1.2	2014 6.5
5 SU	0249 0.7	0854 7.4	1517 0.7	2117 6.9
20 M	0224 1.2	0828 6.7	1445 1.3	2046 6.4
6 M	0334 1.0	0941 7.1	1603 1.0	2204 6.6
21 TU	0257 1.4	0900 6.5	1518 1.5	2119 6.2
7 TU	0421 1.3	1029 6.7	1651 1.5	2253 6.2
22 W	0331 1.6	0935 6.3	1553 1.7	2156 6.0
8 W ◑	0512 1.8	1121 6.2	1744 1.9	2349 5.8
23 TH	0409 1.8	1015 6.1	1634 2.0	2241 5.8
9 TH	0613 2.1	1848 2.2		
24 F ◑	0454 2.1	1105 5.8	1725 2.2	2339 5.5
10 F	0056 5.5	0726 2.4	1332 5.6	2002 2.3
25 SA	0556 2.3	1211 5.6	1837 2.4	
11 SA	0211 5.5	0844 2.4	1445 5.6	2113 2.2
26 SU	0055 5.4	0720 2.4	1332 5.5	2008 2.3
12 SU	0322 5.6	0950 2.2	1551 5.8	2211 2.0
27 M	0218 5.6	0847 2.1	1453 5.8	2126 1.9
13 M	0420 5.9	1043 1.9	1644 6.0	2258 1.8
28 TU	0331 6.1	0959 1.6	1603 6.2	2230 1.4
14 TU	0507 6.2	1127 1.6	1727 6.3	2339 1.5
29 W	0434 6.6	1059 1.1	1703 6.7	2325 0.9
15 W	0546 6.5	1204 1.5	1805 6.4	
30 TH ●	0529 7.1	1153 0.6	1756 7.1	
31 F	0016 0.5	0619 7.5	1243 0.3	1844 7.4

FEBRUARY

Day	Time m	Time m	Time m	Time m
1 SA	0103 0.3	0706 7.7	1330 0.1	1930 7.5
16 SU	0101 1.0	0704 6.8	1322 1.0	1920 6.8
2 SU	0148 0.2	0751 7.7	1414 0.2	2013 7.4
17 M	0132 0.9	0734 6.9	1352 0.9	1951 6.8
3 M	0231 0.3	0834 7.6	1456 0.4	2055 7.1
18 TU	0203 0.9	0804 6.9	1422 1.0	2022 6.7
4 TU	0313 0.6	0917 7.2	1536 0.8	2136 6.7
19 W	0235 1.0	0836 6.7	1454 1.2	2054 6.5
5 W	0353 1.1	0959 6.7	1616 1.3	2218 6.3
20 TH	0308 1.2	0909 6.5	1527 1.4	2129 6.3
6 TH ◑	0435 1.6	1043 6.2	1659 1.8	2304 5.8
21 F	0344 1.5	0947 6.3	1604 1.7	2210 6.0
7 F	0524 2.1	1135 5.7	1753 2.3	
22 SA ◑	0426 1.8	1034 5.9	1651 2.0	2304 5.7
8 SA	0003 5.4	0630 2.5	1243 5.3	1907 2.6
23 SU	0523 2.1	1137 5.6	1758 2.3	
9 SU	0124 5.1	0802 2.6	1407 5.1	2036 2.6
24 M	0020 5.4	0647 2.3	1304 5.4	1938 2.3
10 M	0250 5.3	0923 2.4	1525 5.4	2146 2.3
25 TU	0152 5.5	0826 2.1	1435 5.6	2108 2.0
11 TU	0357 5.6	1022 2.1	1623 5.7	2237 1.9
26 W	0314 5.9	0944 1.6	1550 6.1	2215 1.5
12 W	0446 6.0	1107 1.7	1707 6.1	2319 1.6
27 TH	0420 6.5	1045 1.0	1650 6.6	2311 0.9
13 TH	0526 6.3	1145 1.4	1745 6.3	2355 1.3
28 F	0515 7.0	1138 0.6	1741 7.1	
14 F ○	0601 6.6	1219 1.2	1819 6.5	
15 SA	0029 1.1	0633 6.7	1251 1.1	1850 6.7

MARCH

Day	Time m	Time m	Time m	Time m
1 SA ●	0000 0.5	0603 7.5	1226 0.2	1827 7.4
16 SU ○	0002 1.1	0605 6.7	1224 1.0	1822 6.7
2 SU	0046 0.2	0648 7.7	1310 0.1	1910 7.5
17 M	0035 0.9	0637 6.9	1255 0.8	1854 6.9
3 M	0129 0.1	0730 7.7	1351 0.1	1950 7.4
18 TU	0108 0.8	0708 7.0	1327 0.8	1925 6.9
4 TU	0209 0.2	0811 7.5	1430 0.4	2029 7.2
19 W	0140 0.7	0740 7.0	1359 0.8	1958 6.9
5 W	0247 0.6	0850 7.1	1507 0.8	2106 6.8
20 TH	0214 0.8	0813 6.9	1432 1.0	2031 6.8
6 TH	0324 1.0	0928 6.7	1542 1.3	2144 6.3
21 F	0248 1.0	0849 6.7	1506 1.2	2108 6.5
7 F	0401 1.5	1007 6.1	1619 1.8	2224 5.8
22 SA	0326 1.3	0928 6.4	1545 1.5	2151 6.2
8 SA ◑	0442 2.0	1052 5.6	1703 2.3	2314 5.4
23 SU	0411 1.6	1017 6.0	1633 1.9	2247 5.8
9 SU	0538 2.5	1151 5.1	1809 2.7	
24 M ○	0509 2.0	1121 5.6	1741 2.2	
10 M	0028 5.0	0707 2.7	1321 4.9	1946 2.8
25 TU	0003 5.5	0633 2.2	1248 5.4	1920 2.3
11 TU	0207 5.0	0846 2.6	1450 5.1	2111 2.5
26 W	0135 5.6	0810 2.0	1420 5.6	2050 2.0
12 W	0324 5.4	0951 2.2	1555 5.5	2207 2.1
27 TH	0257 5.9	0927 1.6	1534 6.0	2158 1.5
13 TH	0416 5.8	1038 1.8	1639 5.9	2251 1.7
28 F	0402 6.5	1028 1.0	1633 6.5	2253 1.0
14 F	0457 6.2	1117 1.5	1717 6.2	2328 1.3
29 SA	0456 7.0	1119 0.6	1722 7.0	2341 0.6
15 SA ●	0533 6.5	1152 1.2	1751 6.5	
30 SU	0543 7.3	1204 0.4	1806 7.2	
31 M	0025 0.3	0626 7.5	1247 0.2	1847 7.3

APRIL

Day	Time m	Time m	Time m	Time m
1 TU	0106 0.3	0707 7.4	1326 0.3	1925 7.3
16 W	0042 0.8	0641 7.0	1301 0.7	1900 7.0
2 W	0145 0.4	0746 7.3	1403 0.5	2002 7.1
17 TH	0118 0.7	0717 7.0	1337 0.8	1936 7.0
3 TH	0221 0.7	0823 7.0	1438 0.9	2038 6.8
18 F	0155 0.7	0755 6.9	1414 0.9	2014 6.9
4 F	0257 1.1	0859 6.5	1512 1.3	2113 6.4
19 SA	0234 0.9	0835 6.7	1453 1.1	2056 6.7
5 SA	0332 1.5	0936 6.1	1546 1.8	2151 5.9
20 SU	0316 1.2	0919 6.4	1536 1.4	2143 6.4
6 SU	0409 2.0	1017 5.6	1625 2.2	2236 5.5
21 M	0405 1.5	1011 6.0	1627 1.8	2242 6.0
7 M ◑	0457 2.4	1109 5.2	1720 2.6	2337 5.1
22 TU ◑	0505 1.8	1116 5.7	1736 2.1	2354 5.8
8 TU	0612 2.7	1225 4.9	1847 2.8	
23 W	0625 2.0	1236 5.5	1906 2.1	
9 W ○	0109 5.0	0748 2.7	1400 4.9	2018 2.6
24 TH	0116 5.8	0751 1.9	1359 5.6	2028 1.9
10 TH	0234 5.2	0904 2.4	1510 5.3	2124 2.3
25 F	0234 6.0	0904 1.5	1511 6.0	2135 1.5
11 F	0333 5.6	0957 2.0	1600 5.7	2212 1.9
26 SA	0338 6.4	1004 1.0	1609 6.4	2230 1.1
12 SA	0418 6.0	1039 1.6	1640 6.1	2253 1.5
27 SU	0432 6.8	1055 0.7	1659 6.8	2318 0.8
13 SU	0456 6.3	1116 1.3	1717 6.5	2330 1.2
28 M	0520 7.0	1140 0.7	1743 7.0	
14 M	0532 6.6	1151 1.0	1751 6.7	
29 TU ●	0002 0.7	0603 7.1	1221 0.7	1823 7.1
15 TU ○	0006 0.9	0606 6.8	1226 0.9	1825 6.9
30 W	0043 0.6	0643 7.1	1300 0.7	1901 7.0

Chart Datum: 3·71 metres below Ordnance Datum (Newlyn)
HAT is 7·9m above Chart Datum

TIDES

TIME ZONE (UT)	WALES – MILFORD HAVEN	Dates in amber are SPRINGS
For Summer Time add ONE hour in **non-shaded areas**	LAT 51°42′N LONG 5°03′W	Dates in yellow are NEAPS

WALES – MILFORD HAVEN
LAT 51°42′N   LONG 5°03′W
TIMES AND HEIGHTS OF HIGH AND LOW WATERS

2014

MAY

Day	Time	m	Time	m
1 TH	0121 / 0722 / 1337 / 1937	0.7 / 7.0 / 0.8 / 6.9		
16 F	0058 / 0658 / 1319 / 1919	0.7 / 7.0 / 0.7 / 7.1		
2 F	0158 / 0758 / 1412 / 2013	0.9 / 6.7 / 1.1 / 6.7		
17 SA	0141 / 0741 / 1401 / 2003	0.7 / 7.0 / 0.8 / 7.1		
3 SA	0233 / 0834 / 1445 / 2048	1.2 / 6.4 / 1.4 / 6.4		
18 SU	0225 / 0826 / 1444 / 2049	0.8 / 6.8 / 1.0 / 6.9		
4 SU	0307 / 0910 / 1519 / 2125	1.5 / 6.1 / 1.7 / 6.1		
19 M	0312 / 0915 / 1531 / 2140	1.0 / 6.6 / 1.3 / 6.6		
5 M	0344 / 0949 / 1556 / 2206	1.9 / 5.7 / 2.1 / 5.7		
20 TU	0402 / 1008 / 1624 / 2237	1.2 / 6.2 / 1.6 / 6.3		
6 TU	0427 / 1035 / 1643 / 2257	2.2 / 5.4 / 2.4 / 5.4		
21 W	0501 / 1109 / 1728 / 2342	1.5 / 5.9 / 1.8 / 6.1		
7 W	0525 / 1135 / 1750	2.5 / 5.1 / 2.6		
22 TH	0611 / 1218 / 1844	1.7 / 5.7 / 1.9		
8 TH	0004 / 0642 / 1253 / 1912	5.2 / 2.6 / 5.0 / 2.6		
23 F	0053 / 0725 / 1332 / 1959	6.0 / 1.7 / 5.7 / 1.9		
9 F	0127 / 0759 / 1410 / 2024	5.2 / 2.4 / 5.2 / 2.4		
24 SA	0205 / 0835 / 1441 / 2107	6.0 / 1.6 / 5.9 / 1.7		
10 SA	0236 / 0902 / 1509 / 2122	5.4 / 2.1 / 5.5 / 2.1		
25 SU	0310 / 0936 / 1542 / 2205	6.2 / 1.4 / 6.2 / 1.4		
11 SU	0329 / 0952 / 1556 / 2210	5.8 / 1.8 / 5.9 / 1.7		
26 M	0407 / 1029 / 1634 / 2255	6.4 / 1.2 / 6.4 / 1.2		
12 M	0414 / 1036 / 1638 / 2254	6.2 / 1.5 / 6.3 / 1.4		
27 TU	0457 / 1115 / 1720 / 2340	6.6 / 1.1 / 6.6 / 1.1		
13 TU	0455 / 1117 / 1718 / 2335	6.5 / 1.2 / 6.7 / 1.1		
28 W	0542 / 1157 / 1802	6.7 / 1.0 / 6.7		
14 W	0536 / 1157 / 1757	6.8 / 0.9 / 6.9		
29 TH	0021 / 0623 / 1237 / 1840	1.0 / 6.7 / 1.0 / 6.8		
15 TH	0016 / 0638 / 1238 / 1837	0.8 / 6.9 / 0.8 / 7.1		
30 F	0100 / 0701 / 1314 / 1917	1.0 / 6.7 / 1.1 / 6.7		
31 SA	0137 / 0737 / 1349 / 1952	1.1 / 6.5 / 1.2 / 6.6		

JUNE

Day	Time	m
1 SU	0212 / 0813 / 1423 / 2027	1.3 / 6.4 / 1.4 / 6.4
16 M	0217 / 0819 / 1437 / 2042	0.6 / 7.0 / 0.8 / 7.2
2 M	0246 / 0848 / 1456 / 2102	1.5 / 6.1 / 1.6 / 6.2
17 TU	0305 / 0908 / 1524 / 2132	0.7 / 6.8 / 1.0 / 6.9
3 TU	0321 / 0925 / 1532 / 2140	1.7 / 5.9 / 1.9 / 6.0
18 W	0355 / 0958 / 1615 / 2225	0.9 / 6.5 / 1.3 / 6.6
4 W	0359 / 1005 / 1613 / 2224	1.9 / 5.6 / 2.1 / 5.7
19 TH	0448 / 1052 / 1711 / 2321	1.2 / 6.2 / 1.6 / 6.3
5 TH	0445 / 1053 / 1703 / 2315	2.2 / 5.4 / 2.3 / 5.5
20 F	0547 / 1152 / 1815	1.5 / 5.9 / 1.8
6 F	0542 / 1150 / 1807	2.3 / 5.2 / 2.5
21 SA	0024 / 0652 / 1259 / 1926	6.1 / 1.8 / 5.7 / 1.9
7 SA	0017 / 0651 / 1259 / 1919	5.4 / 2.4 / 5.2 / 2.4
22 SU	0132 / 0801 / 1408 / 2037	5.9 / 1.8 / 5.7 / 1.8
8 SU	0127 / 0759 / 1408 / 2026	5.4 / 2.3 / 5.4 / 2.2
23 M	0239 / 0907 / 1514 / 2140	5.9 / 1.8 / 5.9 / 1.8
9 M	0233 / 0900 / 1507 / 2125	5.6 / 2.0 / 5.8 / 1.9
24 TU	0342 / 1004 / 1612 / 2235	6.0 / 1.7 / 6.1 / 1.6
10 TU	0329 / 0954 / 1558 / 2218	6.0 / 1.7 / 6.2 / 1.5
25 W	0437 / 1054 / 1702 / 2322	6.2 / 1.5 / 6.3 / 1.4
11 W	0420 / 1044 / 1646 / 2307	6.3 / 1.3 / 6.6 / 1.2
26 TH	0524 / 1137 / 1745	6.3 / 1.4 / 6.5
12 TH	0508 / 1131 / 1733 / 2355	6.6 / 1.0 / 6.9 / 0.9
27 F	0004 / 0605 / 1217 / 1823	1.2 / 6.4 / 1.3 / 6.6
13 F	0556 / 1217 / 1820	6.9 / 0.8 / 7.1
28 SA	0043 / 0643 / 1254 / 1859	1.2 / 6.5 / 1.2 / 6.6
14 SA	0042 / 0643 / 1304 / 1906	0.7 / 7.1 / 0.7 / 7.3
29 SU	0118 / 0719 / 1329 / 1933	1.2 / 6.5 / 1.2 / 6.6
15 SU	0130 / 0731 / 1350 / 1954	0.6 / 7.1 / 0.7 / 7.3
30 M	0152 / 0753 / 1402 / 2007	1.3 / 6.4 / 1.3 / 6.5

JULY

Day	Time	m
1 TU	0225 / 0826 / 1434 / 2040	1.4 / 6.3 / 1.4 / 6.4
16 W	0252 / 0853 / 1511 / 2116	0.4 / 7.1 / 0.7 / 7.2
2 W	0258 / 0900 / 1508 / 2114	1.5 / 6.1 / 1.6 / 6.2
17 TH	0338 / 0940 / 1557 / 2204	0.7 / 6.8 / 1.0 / 6.9
3 TH	0332 / 0935 / 1544 / 2151	1.7 / 5.9 / 1.8 / 6.0
18 F	0425 / 1028 / 1646 / 2254	1.1 / 6.4 / 1.4 / 6.4
4 F	0410 / 1015 / 1625 / 2233	1.9 / 5.7 / 2.0 / 5.8
19 SA	0515 / 1120 / 1741 / 2350	1.5 / 6.0 / 1.8 / 6.0
5 SA	0453 / 1101 / 1713 / 2324	2.1 / 5.5 / 2.2 / 5.6
20 SU	0614 / 1221 / 1848	1.9 / 5.7 / 2.1
6 SU	0547 / 1158 / 1816	2.3 / 5.4 / 2.4
21 M	0056 / 0723 / 1333 / 2006	5.7 / 2.1 / 5.5 / 2.2
7 M	0026 / 0656 / 1308 / 1931	5.5 / 2.3 / 5.4 / 2.3
22 TU	0209 / 0838 / 1447 / 2119	5.6 / 2.2 / 5.6 / 2.1
8 TU	0138 / 0810 / 1420 / 2043	5.5 / 2.2 / 5.6 / 2.1
23 W	0320 / 0943 / 1553 / 2218	5.6 / 2.0 / 5.8 / 1.9
9 W	0248 / 0918 / 1524 / 2147	5.8 / 1.9 / 6.0 / 1.7
24 TH	0420 / 1036 / 1646 / 2307	5.9 / 1.8 / 6.1 / 1.7
10 TH	0351 / 1017 / 1621 / 2244	6.1 / 1.5 / 6.4 / 1.3
25 F	0508 / 1120 / 1729 / 2348	6.1 / 1.6 / 6.4 / 1.5
11 F	0447 / 1111 / 1714 / 2337	6.5 / 1.1 / 6.9 / 0.9
26 SA	0549 / 1159 / 1807	6.3 / 1.4 / 6.5
12 SA	0540 / 1201 / 1805	6.9 / 0.8 / 7.2
27 SU	0024 / 0625 / 1235 / 1840	1.3 / 6.5 / 1.2 / 6.7
13 SU	0028 / 0630 / 1251 / 1854	0.6 / 7.1 / 0.6 / 7.4
28 M	0059 / 0659 / 1308 / 1913	1.2 / 6.5 / 1.2 / 6.7
14 M	0118 / 0719 / 1338 / 1942	0.4 / 7.3 / 0.4 / 7.5
29 TU	0131 / 0731 / 1340 / 1944	1.2 / 6.5 / 1.2 / 6.7
15 TU	0206 / 0807 / 1425 / 2029	0.3 / 7.2 / 0.5 / 7.5
30 W	0201 / 0802 / 1411 / 2015	1.2 / 6.5 / 1.2 / 6.6
31 TH	0232 / 0833 / 1443 / 2046	1.3 / 6.4 / 1.3 / 6.5

AUGUST

Day	Time	m
1 F	0304 / 0905 / 1516 / 2119	1.4 / 6.2 / 1.5 / 6.3
16 SA	0357 / 0958 / 1616 / 2223	1.1 / 6.5 / 1.4 / 6.4
2 SA	0337 / 0940 / 1552 / 2156	1.6 / 6.0 / 1.8 / 6.1
17 SU	0440 / 1045 / 1705 / 2314	1.6 / 6.0 / 1.9 / 5.9
3 SU	0414 / 1020 / 1634 / 2241	1.9 / 5.8 / 2.0 / 5.8
18 M	0532 / 1141 / 1807	2.1 / 5.6 / 2.3
4 M	0500 / 1111 / 1727 / 2338	2.1 / 5.5 / 2.3 / 5.5
19 TU	0017 / 0640 / 1256 / 1933	5.4 / 2.5 / 5.3 / 2.5
5 TU	0601 / 1219 / 1842	2.3 / 5.4 / 2.4
20 W	0137 / 0807 / 1421 / 2058	5.2 / 2.5 / 5.3 / 2.4
6 W	0054 / 0727 / 1341 / 2010	5.4 / 2.3 / 5.5 / 2.2
21 TH	0258 / 0921 / 1533 / 2201	5.3 / 2.3 / 5.6 / 2.1
7 TH	0217 / 0850 / 1458 / 2125	5.6 / 2.1 / 5.9 / 1.8
22 F	0402 / 1016 / 1627 / 2248	5.7 / 2.0 / 6.0 / 1.8
8 F	0330 / 0957 / 1602 / 2228	6.0 / 1.6 / 6.4 / 1.3
23 SA	0449 / 1100 / 1709 / 2328	6.0 / 1.7 / 6.3 / 1.5
9 SA	0432 / 1055 / 1659 / 2323	6.5 / 1.1 / 6.9 / 0.8
24 SU	0528 / 1138 / 1745	6.3 / 1.4 / 6.5
10 SU	0527 / 1146 / 1751	6.9 / 0.7 / 7.3
25 M	0003 / 0602 / 1212 / 1817	1.2 / 6.5 / 1.2 / 6.7
11 M	0014 / 0616 / 1236 / 1839	0.4 / 7.3 / 0.4 / 7.6
26 TU	0035 / 0635 / 1244 / 1848	1.1 / 6.7 / 1.1 / 6.8
12 TU	0103 / 0703 / 1322 / 1925	0.2 / 7.4 / 0.3 / 7.7
27 W	0106 / 0705 / 1315 / 1918	1.1 / 6.7 / 1.0 / 6.9
13 W	0149 / 0749 / 1407 / 2010	0.1 / 7.4 / 0.3 / 7.6
28 TH	0135 / 0735 / 1346 / 1948	1.0 / 6.7 / 1.1 / 6.8
14 TH	0233 / 0832 / 1450 / 2054	0.3 / 7.3 / 0.5 / 7.4
29 F	0205 / 0805 / 1417 / 2019	1.0 / 6.7 / 1.2 / 6.7
15 F	0315 / 0915 / 1533 / 2138	0.6 / 6.9 / 0.9 / 6.9
30 SA	0236 / 0836 / 1450 / 2050	1.3 / 6.5 / 1.3 / 6.5
31 SU	0308 / 0909 / 1524 / 2126	1.5 / 6.3 / 1.6 / 6.3

Chart Datum: 3·71 metres below Ordnance Datum (Newlyn)
HAT is 7·9m above Chart Datum

TIME ZONE (UT)
For Summer Time add ONE hour in **non-shaded** areas

WALES – MILFORD HAVEN
LAT 51°42'N   LONG 5°03'W
TIMES AND HEIGHTS OF HIGH AND LOW WATERS

Dates in amber are SPRINGS
Dates in yellow are NEAPS

2014

SEPTEMBER

Day	Time	m	Time	m	Day	Time	m	Time	m
1 M	0343	1.8	0948	6.0	16 TU	0451	2.3	1101	5.6
	1604	1.9	2208	5.9		1726	2.5	2336 ◑	5.3
2 TU	0426	2.1	1037	5.7	17 W	0555	2.7	1212	5.2
	1655	2.2	2305 ●	5.6		1853	2.8		
3 W	0525	2.4	1145	5.5	18 TH	0100	5.0	0728	2.8
	1810	2.4				1347	5.2	2029	2.7
4 TH	0024	5.4	0656	2.5	19 F	0229	5.2	0853	2.6
	1314	5.5	1949	2.3		1505	5.5	2134	2.3
5 F	0157	5.5	0831	2.2	20 SA	0335	5.5	0950	2.2
	1439	5.8	2110	1.9		1559	5.9	2222	1.9
6 SA	0316	5.9	0942	1.7	21 SU	0423	6.0	1034	1.8
	1547	6.4	2213	1.3		1641	6.3	2301	1.6
7 SU	0418	6.5	1040	1.1	22 M	0501	6.3	1111	1.5
	1644	7.0	2308	0.8		1717	6.6	2335	1.3
8 M	0511	7.0	1131	0.7	23 TU	0535	6.6	1145	1.2
	1734	7.0	2357	0.4		1750	6.8		
9 TU	0559	7.4	1218	0.4	24 W	0007	1.1	0607	6.8
	1821 ○	7.7				1218	1.1	1820 ●	6.9
10 W	0043	0.2	0644	7.5	25 TH	0038	1.0	0637	6.9
	1303	0.2	1905	7.8		1249	1.0	1851	7.0
11 TH	0127	0.1	0726	7.5	26 F	0109	1.0	0708	6.9
	1345	0.3	1948	7.7		1321	1.0	1922	7.0
12 F	0208	0.3	0807	7.0	27 SA	0140	1.0	0739	6.9
	1426	0.5	2029	7.3		1354	1.1	1953	6.9
13 SA	0248	0.7	0847	7.0	28 SU	0212	1.2	0811	6.8
	1506	0.9	2110	6.9		1428	1.2	2027	6.7
14 SU	0326	1.2	0927	6.5	29 M	0245	1.4	0846	6.5
	1546	1.5	2151	6.3		1504	1.5	2104	6.4
15 M	0405	1.7	1010	6.0	30 TU	0322	1.7	0926	6.2
	1630	2.0	2237	5.8		1546	1.8	2149	6.0

OCTOBER

Day	Time	m	Time	m	Day	Time	m	Time	m
1 W	0407	2.0	1017	5.9	16 TH	0510	2.7	1127	5.3
	1639	2.2	2247 ●	5.7		1804	2.8		
2 TH	0507	2.4	1127	5.6	17 F	0012	5.0	0634	2.9
	1756	2.4				1255	5.2	1938	2.8
3 F	0008	5.4	0639	2.5	18 SA	0144	5.1	0805	2.8
	1257	5.6	1934	2.3		1419	5.4	2053	2.5
4 SA	0141	5.5	0815	2.2	19 SU	0255	5.4	0911	2.4
	1422	5.9	2054	1.8		1519	5.7	2145	2.1
5 SU	0300	6.0	0926	1.7	20 M	0346	5.8	0959	2.0
	1530	6.5	2157	1.3		1605	6.1	2226	1.8
6 M	0401	6.5	1022	1.2	21 TU	0427	6.2	1039	1.7
	1626	7.0	2250	0.8		1643	6.5	2303	1.5
7 TU	0453	7.0	1112	0.8	22 W	0503	6.5	1115	1.4
	1715	7.4	2337	0.5		1718	6.7	2336	1.2
8 W	0539	7.3	1158	0.5	23 TH	0536	6.8	1149	1.2
	1801 ○	7.6				1751 ●	6.9		
9 TH	0021	0.3	0622	7.5	24 F	0009	1.1	0609	7.0
	1242	0.4	1843	7.6		1224	1.0	1824	7.0
10 F	0103	0.4	0703	7.5	25 SA	0043	1.0	0642	7.1
	1323	0.5	1924	7.5		1258	1.0	1858	7.0
11 SA	0143	0.6	0743	7.1	26 SU	0117	1.0	0717	7.1
	1402	0.7	2004	7.2		1334	1.0	1933	7.0
12 SU	0221	0.9	0821	6.9	27 M	0152	1.1	0753	7.0
	1441	1.1	2043	6.8		1412	1.2	2011	6.8
13 M	0257	1.3	0859	6.6	28 TU	0230	1.3	0832	6.8
	1519	1.6	2122	6.3		1452	1.4	2052	6.5
14 TU	0334	1.8	0939	6.1	29 W	0310	1.6	0916	6.5
	1559	2.1	2205	5.8		1538	1.7	2141	6.2
15 W	0415	2.3	1025	5.7	30 TH	0358	1.9	1010	6.1
	1649	2.5	2257 ◑	5.3		1634	2.0	2241	5.8
					31 F	0500	2.2	1119	5.9
						1748	2.2	2358 ◑	5.6

NOVEMBER

Day	Time	m	Time	m	Day	Time	m	Time	m
1 SA	0626	2.4	1239	5.8	16 SU	0037	5.1	0657	2.8
	1916	2.1				1313	5.3	1948	2.7
2 SU	0122	5.7	0754	2.2	17 M	0157	5.2	0812	2.7
	1400	6.0	2032	1.8		1424	5.5	2052	2.4
3 M	0238	6.0	0904	1.8	18 TU	0258	5.6	0912	2.3
	1507	6.4	2135	1.4		1519	5.8	2143	2.0
4 TU	0340	6.4	1002	1.4	19 W	0346	6.0	0959	2.0
	1604	6.8	2229	1.1		1603	6.2	2225	1.7
5 W	0432	6.8	1053	1.0	20 TH	0427	6.3	1041	1.6
	1654	7.1	2316	0.8		1643	6.5	2304	1.4
6 TH	0519	7.1	1138	0.8	21 F	0505	6.7	1121	1.3
	1740	7.3	○ 2359	0.7		1722	6.8	2342	1.2
7 F	0602	7.3	1221	0.7	22 SA	0542	6.9	1200	1.1
	1823	7.3				1800	7.0		
8 SA	0040	0.7	0642	7.3	23 SU	0020	1.0	0620	7.1
	1302	0.8	1903	7.2		1240	1.0	1839	7.1
9 SU	0119	0.9	0721	7.2	24 M	0059	1.0	0700	7.2
	1341	1.0	1942	7.0		1320	0.9	1919	7.1
10 M	0157	1.1	0759	6.9	25 TU	0139	1.0	0741	7.2
	1419	1.3	2020	6.7		1402	1.0	2002	6.9
11 TU	0233	1.4	0836	6.6	26 W	0221	1.1	0825	7.0
	1456	1.6	2058	6.3		1446	1.1	2048	6.7
12 W	0309	1.8	0914	6.3	27 TH	0305	1.4	0912	6.8
	1534	2.0	2138	5.9		1534	1.4	2138	6.4
13 TH	0346	2.2	0955	5.9	28 F	0354	1.7	1006	6.5
	1617	2.3	2223	5.5		1629	1.7	2235	6.1
14 F	0431	2.5	1046	5.6	29 SA	0453	1.9	1107	6.2
	1713	2.6	2321 ◑	5.2		1734	1.9	2341 ◑	5.9
15 SA	0535	2.8	1151	5.3	30 SU	0605	2.1	1217	6.1
	1829	2.8				1850	2.0		

DECEMBER

Day	Time	m	Time	m	Day	Time	m	Time	m
1 M	0055	5.8	0724	2.1	16 TU	0038	5.2	0700	2.7
	1330	6.1	2003	1.9		1309	5.4	1944	2.6
2 TU	0208	5.9	0837	1.9	17 W	0153	5.3	0812	2.6
	1439	6.3	2109	1.7		1419	5.5	2049	2.3
3 W	0314	6.2	0939	1.6	18 TH	0256	5.6	0913	2.3
	1541	6.5	2206	1.4		1518	5.8	2144	2.0
4 TH	0411	6.5	1034	1.4	19 F	0347	6.0	1006	1.9
	1635	6.7	2256	1.2		1608	6.2	2232	1.6
5 F	0500	6.8	1122	1.2	20 SA	0434	6.4	1054	1.5
	1723	6.9	2340	1.1		1655	6.5	2317	1.3
6 SA	0545	6.9	1205	1.1	21 SU	0519	6.8	1139	1.2
	1807 ○	6.9				1740	6.8		
7 SU	0021	1.0	0626	7.0	22 M	0001	1.0	0602	7.1
	1246	1.1	1847	6.9		1224	0.9	1824 ●	7.1
8 M	0101	1.1	0704	7.0	23 TU	0045	0.9	0647	7.3
	1325	1.1	1925	6.8		1309	0.7	1909	7.2
9 TU	0137	1.2	0741	6.9	24 W	0129	0.8	0732	7.4
	1401	1.3	2002	6.6		1354	0.7	1955	7.1
10 W	0213	1.4	0817	6.7	25 TH	0213	0.8	0818	7.3
	1436	1.5	2037	6.4		1440	0.7	2042	7.0
11 TH	0247	1.6	0852	6.5	26 F	0258	1.0	0905	7.1
	1511	1.8	2113	6.1		1527	0.9	2130	6.7
12 F	0321	1.9	0929	6.2	27 SA	0346	1.2	0955	6.9
	1548	2.0	2152	5.8		1617	1.2	2221	6.4
13 SA	0359	2.2	1010	5.9	28 SU	0437	1.5	1049	6.5
	1630	2.3	2236	5.5		1712	1.5	2317 ◑	6.1
14 SU	0445	2.4	1058	5.6	29 M	0537	1.9	1149	6.2
	1723	2.5	2330	5.3		1816	1.8		
15 M	0545	2.7	1157	5.4	30 TU	0021	5.8	0648	2.1
	1831	2.6				1257	6.0	1927	2.0
					31 W	0134	5.7	0805	2.1
						1409	5.9	2040	2.0

Chart Datum: 3·71 metres below Ordnance Datum (Newlyn)
HAT is 7·9m above Chart Datum

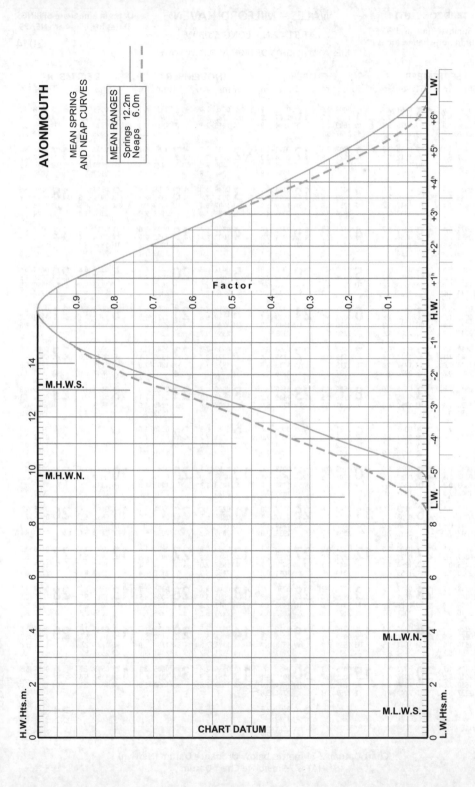

AVONMOUTH

MEAN SPRING
AND NEAP CURVES

MEAN RANGES	
Springs	12.2m
Neaps	6.0m

AVONMOUTH

LAT 51°30′N   LONG 2°44′W

TIMES AND HEIGHTS OF HIGH AND LOW WATERS

Dates in amber are **SPRINGS**
Dates in yellow are **NEAPS**

2014

JANUARY

Day					Day				
1 W ●	0104 1.4	0642 13.5	1908 13.6		**16** ○	0132 1.5	0712 12.6	1936 12.5	
2 TH	0159 1.0	0731 14.0	1425 0.8	1958 13.9	**17** F	0216 1.4	0750 12.7	1440 1.7	2013 12.4
3 F	0250 0.8	0820 14.2	1515 0.6	2046 14.0	**18** SA	0255 1.6	0825 12.6	1516 1.9	2047 12.3
4 SA	0336 0.7	0907 14.2	1600 0.6	2132 13.9	**19** SU	0326 1.8	0858 12.5	1543 2.1	2117 12.2
5 SU	0417 0.9	0952 13.9	1640 0.8	2216 13.4	**20** M	0348 2.0	0927 12.3	1601 2.2	2146 12.0
6 M	0454 1.1	1036 13.4	1716 1.3	2258 12.8	**21** TU	0408 2.0	0956 12.1	1623 2.2	2215 11.9
7 TU	0527 1.8	1120 12.6	1750 1.8	2342 11.9	**22** W	0437 2.1	1029 11.9	1654 2.2	2250 11.6
8 W ◑	0601 2.4	1209 11.7	1828 2.5		**23** TH	0512 2.2	1109 11.6	1732 2.4	2333 11.2
9 TH	0031 11.1	0642 3.0	1311 10.9	1915 3.1	**24** F ◐	0554 2.6	1157 11.1	1817 2.8	
10 F	0139 10.4	0739 3.6	1425 10.4	2019 3.5	**25** SA	0026 10.7	0646 3.2	1259 10.7	1915 3.4
11 SA	0255 10.2	0902 3.8	1533 10.4	2145 3.5	**26** SU	0135 10.3	0800 3.6	1416 10.5	2045 3.6
12 SU	0400 10.5	1032 3.5	1633 10.8	2258 3.0	**27** M	0305 10.5	0947 3.4	1548 10.8	2234 3.2
13 M	0458 11.1	1133 2.8	1727 11.4	2355 2.3	**28** TU	0429 11.3	1111 2.6	1730 11.7	2348 2.3
14 TU	0548 11.8	1224 2.2	1814 11.9		**29** W	0534 12.4	1218 1.8	1803 12.7	
15 W	0045 1.8	0631 12.3	1313 1.8	1857 12.3	**30** TH ●	0050 1.5	0629 13.3	1318 1.0	1856 13.5
					31 F	0147 0.9	0719 14.1	1414 0.5	1946 14.1

FEBRUARY

Day					Day				
1 SA	0239 0.4	0807 14.5	1504 0.2	2032 14.3	**16** SU	0237 1.3	0804 12.8	1500 1.6	2025 12.6
2 SU	0325 0.2	0852 14.6	1548 0.1	2116 14.2	**17** M	0313 1.5	0838 12.7	1531 1.8	2057 12.5
3 M	0406 0.4	0935 14.3	1625 0.4	2156 13.8	**18** TU	0338 1.7	0907 12.6	1550 2.0	2125 12.4
4 TU	0438 0.8	1015 13.7	1655 1.0	2233 13.1	**19** W	0355 1.8	0936 12.5	1605 1.9	2154 12.3
5 W	0504 1.4	1052 12.9	1720 1.6	2308 12.2	**20** TH	0418 1.7	1009 12.4	1632 1.9	2228 12.1
6 TH	0528 2.0	1129 11.8	1749 2.3	2344 11.3	**21** F	0450 1.8	1046 12.0	1706 2.0	2308 11.6
7 F	0600 2.7	1212 10.8	1827 3.0		**22** SA ◐	0528 2.2	1131 11.4	1747 2.5	2357 11.0
8 SA	0031 10.3	0645 3.5	1319 9.9	1920 3.7	**23** SU	0615 2.8	1228 10.7	1839 3.2	
9 SU	0153 9.6	0751 4.1	1453 9.6	2037 4.0	**24** M	0102 10.4	0721 3.5	1346 10.2	1958 3.8
10 M	0323 9.7	0927 4.1	1603 10.0	2214 3.6	**25** TU	0235 10.2	0920 3.6	1528 10.5	2217 3.4
11 TU	0429 10.4	1102 3.3	1702 10.7	2325 2.7	**26** W	0412 11.0	1057 2.7	1650 11.4	2334 2.4
12 W	0523 11.3	1158 2.5	1751 11.5		**27** TH	0520 12.1	1205 1.7	1750 12.6	
13 TH	0019 2.0	0609 12.0	1248 1.8	1834 12.1	**28** F	0035 1.4	0615 13.3	1303 0.8	1842 13.5
14 F ○	0108 1.5	0650 12.5	1336 1.5	1914 12.5					
15 SA	0155 1.3	0728 12.7	1420 1.5	1951 12.6					

MARCH

Day					Day				
1 SA ●	0131 0.6	0704 14.1	1357 0.2	1929 14.1	**16** SU ○	0127 1.3	0701 12.7	1353 1.4	1923 12.7
2 SU	0222 0.1	0750 14.5	1445 -0.1	2013 14.4	**17** M	0211 1.2	0738 12.8	1434 1.4	1959 12.8
3 M	0307 0.0	0833 14.6	1528 -0.1	2054 14.3	**18** TU	0250 1.3	0813 12.9	1509 1.6	2032 12.8
4 TU	0346 0.2	0913 14.3	1603 0.3	2132 13.9	**19** W	0320 1.5	0845 12.9	1532 1.7	2102 12.7
5 W	0417 0.7	0950 13.7	1629 1.0	2205 13.2	**20** TH	0341 1.5	0917 12.8	1549 1.7	2134 12.6
6 TH	0438 1.3	1022 12.8	1649 1.6	2235 12.3	**21** F	0403 1.6	0951 12.6	1613 1.7	2209 12.4
7 F	0456 1.9	1054 11.8	1721 2.0	2305 11.4	**22** SA	0433 1.6	1029 12.2	1646 1.9	2249 11.9
8 SA ◑	0524 2.5	1128 10.7	1745 2.9	2343 10.4	**23** SU	0510 2.0	1114 11.6	1726 2.4	2338 11.2
9 SU	0603 3.3	1217 9.7	1834 3.6		**24** M ◐	0556 2.6	1210 10.7	1818 3.2	
10 M	0043 9.5	0704 4.0	1355 9.1	1948 4.2	**25** TU	0043 10.4	0702 3.4	1329 10.1	1938 3.8
11 TU	0239 9.3	0832 4.2	1529 9.4	2121 4.0	**26** W	0221 10.2	0907 3.5	1515 10.4	2203 3.4
12 W	0355 9.9	1017 3.6	1610 11.0	2250 3.1	**27** TH	0355 10.9	1039 2.6	1633 11.4	2315 2.3
13 TH	0452 10.8	1127 2.7	1712 11.7	2349 2.2	**28** F	0502 12.1	1144 1.6	1732 12.5	
14 F	0540 11.7	1219 1.9	1806 12.0		**29** SA	0013 1.3	0555 13.1	1240 0.8	1822 13.4
15 SA	0040 1.6	0622 12.3	1308 1.5	1845 12.5	**30** SU ●	0107 0.6	0644 13.8	1332 0.2	1907 14.0
					31 M	0157 0.2	0728 14.2	1420 0.0	1950 14.1

APRIL

Day					Day				
1 TU	0242 0.1	0810 14.2	1502 0.1	2029 14.0	**16** W	0220 1.2	0746 13.0	1440 1.4	2006 13.0
2 W	0321 0.4	0849 13.9	1537 0.6	2105 13.6	**17** TH	0256 1.3	0823 13.0	1511 1.5	2041 13.0
3 TH	0352 0.9	0924 13.3	1602 1.2	2137 13.0	**18** F	0326 1.3	0900 13.0	1537 1.5	2118 12.9
4 F	0412 1.5	0955 12.5	1620 1.7	2205 12.2	**19** SA	0354 1.3	0938 12.8	1604 1.6	2156 12.6
5 SA	0429 1.9	1024 11.7	1641 2.2	2234 11.4	**20** SU	0425 1.5	1019 12.4	1637 1.9	2239 12.1
6 SU	0455 2.4	1056 10.8	1712 2.7	2308 10.6	**21** M	0504 1.9	1106 11.7	1718 2.4	2330 11.4
7 M	0531 3.0	1137 9.9	1755 3.4	2357 9.7	**22** TU ◐	0552 2.5	1202 10.9	1812 3.1	
8 TU	0625 3.7	1246 9.2	1904 4.0		**23** W	0036 10.7	0701 3.1	1321 10.4	1940 3.6
9 W	0133 9.2	0747 4.1	1438 9.2	2033 4.1	**24** TH	0209 10.5	0849 3.1	1455 10.6	2137 3.1
10 TH	0310 9.6	0914 3.8	1549 9.9	2157 3.4	**25** F	0332 11.1	1011 2.4	1608 11.4	2247 2.3
11 F	0412 10.5	1037 3.0	1643 10.8	2307 2.6	**26** SA	0436 12.0	1115 1.6	1706 12.3	2345 1.5
12 SA	0502 11.3	1139 2.2	1730 11.7		**27** SU	0531 12.8	1211 1.0	1757 13.0	
13 SU	0003 1.9	0547 12.0	1231 1.7	1812 12.3	**28** M	0038 0.9	0619 13.3	1303 0.6	1842 13.5
14 M	0052 1.5	0628 12.5	1350 1.2	1852 12.7	**29** TU ●	0128 0.6	0704 13.6	1350 0.6	1924 13.6
15 TU ○	0138 1.3	0708 12.8	1402 1.4	1929 12.9	**30** W	0214 0.6	0746 13.5	1433 0.6	2003 13.5

Chart Datum: 6·50 metres below Ordnance Datum (Newlyn)
HAT is 14·7m above Chart Datum

TIDES

TIDES

AVONMOUTH
LAT 51°30'N   LONG 2°44'W
TIMES AND HEIGHTS OF HIGH AND LOW WATERS

Dates in amber are **SPRINGS**
Dates in yellow are **NEAPS**

2014

MAY

Day	Time m	Day	Time m
1 TH	0254 0.8 / 0825 13.3 / 1510 0.9 / 2040 13.1	**16** F	0232 1.1 / 0803 13.2 / 1452 1.3 / 2024 13.3
2 F	0328 1.2 / 0900 12.8 / 1537 1.4 / 2112 12.7	**17** SA	0313 1.1 / 0846 13.2 / 1529 1.3 / 2106 13.2
3 SA	0351 1.7 / 0932 12.2 / 1557 1.9 / 2141 12.1	**18** SU	0350 1.1 / 0930 13.0 / 1603 1.5 / 2149 12.9
4 SU	0409 2.1 / 1002 11.6 / 1619 2.2 / 2210 11.5	**19** M	0428 1.3 / 1015 12.6 / 1640 1.8 / 2235 12.5
5 M	0434 2.4 / 1033 10.9 / 1648 2.5 / 2244 10.8	**20** TU	0509 1.7 / 1102 12.1 / 1722 2.2 / 2326 11.8
6 TU	0509 2.8 / 1111 10.3 / 1727 3.0 / 2326 10.2	**21** W	0557 2.1 / 1157 11.4 / 1815 2.7
7 W	0555 3.3 / 1203 9.7 / 1823 3.6	**22** TH	0029 11.2 / 0659 2.5 / 1306 10.9 / 1930 3.1
8 TH	0031 9.7 / 0702 3.7 / 1323 9.4 / 1942 3.9	**23** F	0149 11.0 / 0818 2.7 / 1426 10.9 / 2101 3.0
9 F	0203 9.7 / 0821 3.6 / 1449 9.8 / 2101 3.6	**24** SA	0303 11.2 / 0935 2.5 / 1536 11.2 / 2212 2.5
10 SA	0318 10.2 / 0935 3.2 / 1554 10.5 / 2212 2.9	**25** SU	0406 11.7 / 1040 2.0 / 1636 11.8 / 2313 1.9
11 SU	0416 10.9 / 1045 2.6 / 1647 11.3 / 2316 2.3	**26** M	0503 12.2 / 1138 1.6 / 1729 12.3
12 M	0507 11.7 / 1146 2.1 / 1735 12.0	**27** TU	0007 1.5 / 0553 12.6 / 1231 1.2 / 1815 12.8
13 TU	0011 1.8 / 0553 12.3 / 1239 1.7 / 1819 12.6	**28** W	0058 1.2 / 0639 12.8 / 1320 1.1 / 1859 13.0
14 W	0102 1.4 / 0637 12.7 / 1328 1.4 / 1901 13.0	**29** TH	0145 1.1 / 0722 12.8 / 1405 1.1 / 1939 12.9
15 TH	0149 1.2 / 0720 13.0 / 1412 1.3 / 1942 13.2	**30** F	0229 1.3 / 0803 12.7 / 1445 1.3 / 2017 12.8
		31 SA	0306 1.6 / 0840 12.4 / 1518 1.6 / 2051 12.4

JUNE

Day	Time m	Day	Time m
1 SU	0335 1.9 / 0914 12.0 / 1542 1.9 / 2123 12.0	**16** M	0347 0.8 / 0922 13.4 / 1605 1.1 / 2142 13.4
2 M	0356 2.2 / 0945 11.6 / 1604 2.2 / 2154 11.6	**17** TU	0430 0.9 / 1008 13.1 / 1645 1.4 / 2229 13.1
3 TU	0420 2.3 / 1016 11.2 / 1632 2.3 / 2226 11.2	**18** W	0511 1.2 / 1055 12.7 / 1725 1.7 / 2318 12.5
4 W	0451 2.5 / 1050 10.8 / 1707 2.6 / 2303 10.8	**19** TH	0554 1.6 / 1144 12.0 / 1809 2.2
5 TH	0531 2.8 / 1132 10.4 / 1751 3.0 / 2351 10.4	**20** F	0013 11.8 / 0641 2.1 / 1242 11.4 / 1902 2.7
6 F	0622 3.1 / 1225 10.1 / 1850 3.4	**21** SA	0119 11.3 / 0739 2.5 / 1351 11.0 / 2013 3.0
7 SA	0053 10.1 / 0726 3.3 / 1335 10.0 / 2003 3.5	**22** SU	0230 11.0 / 0849 2.7 / 1500 10.9 / 2132 3.0
8 SU	0208 10.2 / 0839 3.3 / 1450 10.3 / 2119 3.2	**23** M	0334 11.1 / 1001 2.7 / 1603 11.1 / 2240 2.7
9 M	0320 10.7 / 0952 2.9 / 1558 10.9 / 2229 2.7	**24** TU	0434 11.4 / 1105 2.3 / 1700 11.6 / 2338 2.2
10 TU	0423 11.3 / 1101 2.4 / 1656 11.7 / 2332 2.1	**25** W	0528 11.8 / 1201 1.9 / 1750 12.0
11 W	0519 12.0 / 1202 1.9 / 1748 12.4	**26** TH	0030 1.8 / 0616 12.1 / 1252 1.6 / 1836 12.4
12 TH	0028 1.6 / 0610 12.6 / 1257 1.5 / 1836 13.0	**27** F	0120 1.6 / 0701 12.3 / 1340 1.4 / 1918 12.4
13 F	0122 1.2 / 0659 13.1 / 1349 1.3 / 1923 13.4	**28** SA	0206 1.5 / 0742 12.4 / 1423 1.5 / 1957 12.6
14 SA	0213 1.0 / 0747 13.3 / 1438 1.1 / 2010 13.6	**29** SU	0247 1.7 / 0821 12.3 / 1502 1.6 / 2033 12.4
15 SU	0302 0.9 / 0835 13.4 / 1523 1.1 / 2056 13.6	**30** M	0323 1.9 / 0856 12.1 / 1532 1.9 / 2107 12.2

JULY

Day	Time m	Day	Time m
1 TU	0350 2.2 / 0928 11.8 / 1555 2.1 / 2138 11.9	**16** W	0424 0.5 / 0956 13.6 / 1640 0.9 / 2216 13.6
2 W	0410 2.3 / 0958 11.6 / 1618 2.2 / 2207 11.6	**17** TH	0502 0.8 / 1039 13.2 / 1715 1.3 / 2300 13.0
3 TH	0435 2.3 / 1029 11.3 / 1647 2.3 / 2239 11.3	**18** F	0537 1.3 / 1123 12.5 / 1749 1.9 / 2347 12.2
4 F	0507 2.4 / 1103 11.0 / 1724 2.5 / 2318 11.0	**19** SA	0614 1.9 / 1210 11.6 / 1827 2.5
5 SA	0547 2.6 / 1146 10.7 / 1809 2.9	**20** SU	0042 11.3 / 0656 2.6 / 1309 10.8 / 1917 3.2
6 SU	0008 10.7 / 0636 2.9 / 1241 10.4 / 1907 3.3	**21** M	0152 10.6 / 0753 3.2 / 1422 10.4 / 2032 3.6
7 M	0111 10.4 / 0740 3.2 / 1349 10.3 / 2024 3.4	**22** TU	0303 10.4 / 0911 3.4 / 1531 10.4 / 2205 3.5
8 TU	0225 10.5 / 0900 3.3 / 1508 10.6 / 2147 3.1	**23** W	0407 10.6 / 1031 3.1 / 1633 10.9 / 2311 2.9
9 W	0342 10.9 / 1022 2.9 / 1622 11.3 / 2300 2.5	**24** TH	0504 11.1 / 1133 2.5 / 1727 11.5
10 TH	0450 11.7 / 1133 2.3 / 1723 12.1	**25** F	0006 2.3 / 0555 11.7 / 1227 1.9 / 1814 12.1
11 F	0004 1.8 / 0548 12.4 / 1235 1.7 / 1817 13.0	**26** SA	0056 1.8 / 0640 12.1 / 1316 1.5 / 1857 12.5
12 SA	0104 1.3 / 0642 13.1 / 1333 1.3 / 1907 13.6	**27** SU	0144 1.5 / 0722 12.3 / 1403 1.4 / 1937 12.6
13 SU	0200 0.9 / 0734 13.5 / 1427 0.9 / 1957 13.9	**28** M	0228 1.5 / 0800 12.4 / 1445 1.5 / 2014 12.6
14 M	0253 0.6 / 0823 13.8 / 1517 0.7 / 2045 14.1	**29** TU	0308 1.7 / 0836 12.3 / 1521 1.7 / 2048 12.4
15 TU	0341 0.4 / 0911 13.8 / 1601 0.7 / 2131 14.0	**30** W	0340 2.0 / 0908 12.1 / 1547 2.0 / 2118 12.2
		31 TH	0401 2.2 / 0937 11.9 / 1604 2.1 / 2146 12.0

AUGUST

Day	Time m	Day	Time m
1 F	0416 2.2 / 1005 11.7 / 1626 2.1 / 2214 11.8	**16** SA	0513 1.3 / 1055 12.6 / 1721 1.9 / 2315 12.2
2 SA	0442 2.2 / 1035 11.5 / 1657 2.2 / 2249 11.5	**17** SU	0540 2.0 / 1133 11.6 / 1750 2.6 / 2359 11.1
3 SU	0516 2.3 / 1113 11.2 / 1735 2.6 / 2333 11.1	**18** M	0614 2.8 / 1220 10.6 / 1831 3.4
4 M	0557 2.7 / 1202 10.7 / 1823 3.1	**19** TU	0203 10.1 / 0703 3.5 / 1337 9.9 / 1932 4.1
5 TU	0029 10.6 / 0649 3.2 / 1304 10.3 / 1929 3.5	**20** W	0232 9.7 / 0815 4.0 / 1502 9.8 / 2118 4.2
6 W	0141 10.3 / 0806 3.6 / 1426 10.3 / 2109 3.5	**21** TH	0342 10.0 / 0956 3.9 / 1608 10.4 / 2248 3.4
7 TH	0309 10.5 / 0951 3.3 / 1555 10.9 / 2238 2.9	**22** F	0441 10.7 / 1108 2.9 / 1704 11.2 / 2343 2.5
8 F	0429 11.3 / 1114 2.6 / 1704 11.9 / 2348 2.0	**23** SA	0532 11.4 / 1202 2.1 / 1752 12.0
9 SA	0534 12.3 / 1220 1.8 / 1802 13.0	**24** SU	0032 1.8 / 0617 12.1 / 1252 1.5 / 1834 12.5
10 SU	0050 1.2 / 0629 13.1 / 1320 1.2 / 1853 13.8	**25** M	0120 1.4 / 0657 12.5 / 1339 1.3 / 1913 12.8
11 M	0148 0.7 / 0720 13.6 / 1415 0.7 / 1943 14.3	**26** TU	0205 1.3 / 0735 12.6 / 1423 1.3 / 1950 12.8
12 TU	0241 0.3 / 0808 14.1 / 1505 0.3 / 2029 14.5	**27** W	0247 1.5 / 0811 12.5 / 1502 1.5 / 2024 12.7
13 W	0329 0.1 / 0854 14.2 / 1549 0.3 / 2114 14.4	**28** TH	0322 1.8 / 0843 12.4 / 1532 1.8 / 2054 12.5
14 TH	0410 0.2 / 0937 13.9 / 1626 0.6 / 2156 13.9	**29** F	0345 2.1 / 0912 12.2 / 1549 2.1 / 2122 12.3
15 F	0444 0.7 / 1017 13.4 / 1656 1.2 / 2236 13.2	**30** SA	0356 2.2 / 0939 12.0 / 1605 2.1 / 2150 12.1
		31 SU	0417 2.2 / 1009 11.8 / 1633 2.3 / 2224 11.9

Chart Datum: 6·50 metres below Ordnance Datum (Newlyn)
HAT is 14·7m above Chart Datum

TIME ZONE (UT)	AVONMOUTH	Dates in amber are SPRINGS
For Summer Time add ONE hour in **non-shaded areas**	LAT 51°30'N LONG 2°44'W	Dates in yellow are NEAPS
	TIMES AND HEIGHTS OF HIGH AND LOW WATERS	**2014**

SEPTEMBER

Time m — Time m

1 0447 2.3 / 1046 11.5 / M 1707 2.4 / 2306 11.4
16 0535 3.0 / 1135 10.5 / TU 1751 3.5 ◐

2 0525 2.6 / 1132 10.9 / TU 1750 3.0 / ◑ 2359 10.7
17 0007 9.8 / 0619 3.7 / W 1238 9.6 / 1847 4.2

3 0613 3.2 / 1232 10.4 / W 1850 3.6
18 0153 9.2 / 0729 4.3 / TH 1430 9.4 / 2017 4.5

4 0110 10.1 / 0722 3.8 / TH 1357 10.1 / 2036 3.9
19 0313 9.5 / 0907 4.2 / F 1539 10.0 / 2218 3.8

5 0248 10.2 / 0933 3.7 / F 1537 10.7 / 2225 3.1
20 0413 10.3 / 1038 3.3 / SA 1635 10.9 / 2316 2.8

6 0416 11.1 / 1102 2.8 / SA 1649 11.9 / 2336 2.0
21 0504 11.2 / 1134 2.3 / SU 1724 11.8

7 0520 12.3 / 1206 1.8 / SU 1747 13.0
22 0005 1.9 / 0548 12.0 / M 1224 1.6 / 1806 12.5

8 0036 1.1 / 0614 13.3 / M 1304 1.0 / 1837 13.9
23 0051 1.4 / 0628 12.5 / TU 1310 1.3 / 1845 12.8

9 0131 0.4 / 0703 14.0 / TU 1357 0.4 / ○ 1925 14.5
24 0136 1.3 / 0706 12.7 / W 1355 1.3 / ● 1922 12.9

10 0222 0.0 / 0749 14.3 / W 1445 0.2 / 2010 14.7
25 0218 1.4 / 0742 12.8 / TH 1435 1.4 / 1957 12.9

11 0308 0.0 / 0832 14.3 / TH 1528 0.2 / 2052 14.5
26 0255 1.6 / 0815 12.6 / F 1508 1.7 / 2029 12.7

12 0347 0.3 / 0913 14.0 / F 1604 0.7 / 2132 13.9
27 0322 2.0 / 0846 12.5 / SA 1540 2.0 / 2058 12.6

13 0420 0.8 / 0950 13.4 / SA 1632 1.3 / 2209 13.1
28 0337 2.1 / 0915 12.4 / SU 1547 2.0 / 2130 12.4

14 0443 1.6 / 1024 12.5 / SU 1651 2.1 / 2243 12.0
29 0356 2.1 / 0948 12.1 / M 1614 2.1 / 2206 12.1

15 0505 2.3 / 1057 11.6 / M 1715 2.7 / 2319 10.9
30 0426 2.2 / 1021 11.7 / TU 1648 2.4 / 2248 11.5

OCTOBER

Time m — Time m

1 0503 2.6 / 1112 11.1 / W 1730 2.9 / ◑ 2340 10.8
16 0543 3.7 / 1150 9.8 / TH 1810 4.1

2 0550 3.3 / 1212 10.5 / TH 1828 3.6
17 0038 9.2 / 0645 4.3 / F 1337 9.3 / 1929 4.5

3 0005 10.1 / 0657 3.9 / F 1339 10.2 / 2018 3.9
18 0232 9.3 / 0813 4.4 / SA 1501 9.8 / 2103 4.2

4 0235 10.2 / 0922 3.8 / SA 1522 10.8 / 2210 3.1
19 0336 10.0 / 0944 3.7 / SU 1559 10.6 / 2233 3.3

5 0400 11.1 / 1045 2.8 / SU 1632 11.9 / 2317 2.0
20 0428 10.9 / 1054 2.8 / M 1648 11.5 / 2328 2.4

6 0502 12.3 / 1146 1.7 / M 1728 13.0
21 0514 11.7 / 1147 2.0 / TU 1733 12.2

7 0014 1.0 / 0554 13.3 / TU 1241 0.9 / 1817 13.9
22 0016 1.8 / 0556 12.4 / W 1235 1.6 / 1813 12.7

8 0107 0.4 / 0641 13.9 / W 1332 0.5 / ○ 1904 14.4
23 0102 1.5 / 0635 12.7 / TH 1320 1.4 / ● 1852 12.9

9 0156 0.1 / 0726 14.2 / TH 1420 0.3 / 1947 14.5
24 0145 1.4 / 0712 12.9 / F 1403 1.5 / 1929 13.0

10 0242 0.2 / 0808 14.2 / F 1503 0.5 / 2029 14.2
25 0224 1.6 / 0748 12.9 / SA 1440 1.6 / 2004 13.0

11 0321 0.5 / 0847 13.8 / SA 1539 0.9 / 2108 13.7
26 0256 1.8 / 0822 12.9 / SU 1510 1.8 / 2039 12.9

12 0353 1.1 / 0923 13.2 / SU 1606 1.6 / 2143 12.9
27 0321 1.9 / 0857 12.7 / M 1536 1.9 / 2115 12.7

13 0415 1.8 / 0956 12.4 / M 1625 2.2 / 2215 11.9
28 0345 2.0 / 0934 12.5 / TU 1605 2.0 / 2155 12.3

14 0435 2.4 / 1026 11.6 / TU 1647 2.8 / 2247 10.9
29 0416 2.2 / 1015 12.1 / W 1641 2.3 / 2238 11.8

15 0503 3.0 / 1101 10.7 / W 1720 3.4 / ◑ 2327 10.0
30 0454 2.6 / 1102 11.5 / TH 1724 2.8 / 2330 11.1

31 0542 3.2 / 1202 10.8 / F 1824 3.4

NOVEMBER

Time m — Time m

1 0038 10.5 / 0649 3.8 / SA 1326 10.5 / 2002 3.6
16 0106 9.4 / 0717 4.2 / SU 1355 9.6 / 2000 4.1

2 0215 10.4 / 0858 3.7 / SU 1459 11.0 / 2141 3.0
17 0238 9.6 / 0838 4.0 / M 1508 10.1 / 2117 3.7

3 0336 11.1 / 1017 2.8 / M 1607 11.8 / 2249 2.1
18 0341 10.3 / 0952 3.4 / TU 1604 10.9 / 2231 3.0

4 0438 12.1 / 1118 1.9 / TU 1704 12.7 / 2346 1.3
19 0433 11.2 / 1058 2.7 / W 1654 11.6 / 2331 2.3

5 0531 12.9 / 1213 1.2 / W 1755 13.4
20 0520 11.9 / 1153 2.1 / TH 1739 12.2

6 0039 0.8 / 0618 13.5 / TH 1305 0.8 / ○ 1841 13.9
21 0022 1.9 / 0602 12.5 / F 1243 1.7 / 1821 12.7

7 0128 0.5 / 0702 13.8 / F 1353 0.7 / 1925 13.9
22 0109 1.6 / 0643 12.9 / SA 1329 1.5 / ● 1903 13.0

8 0214 0.6 / 0744 13.8 / SA 1437 0.8 / 2007 13.7
23 0153 1.5 / 0724 13.2 / SU 1413 1.4 / 1944 13.1

9 0254 0.9 / 0823 13.5 / SU 1515 1.2 / 2046 13.3
24 0233 1.5 / 0803 13.2 / M 1453 1.5 / 2025 13.2

10 0328 1.4 / 0900 13.0 / M 1545 1.8 / 2121 12.6
25 0310 1.6 / 0844 13.2 / TU 1530 1.6 / 2106 13.0

11 0352 1.9 / 0932 12.4 / TU 1605 2.3 / 2153 11.9
26 0343 1.8 / 0926 13.0 / W 1606 1.7 / 2149 12.7

12 0413 2.4 / 1003 11.7 / W 1627 2.7 / 2224 11.2
27 0417 2.0 / 1010 12.6 / TH 1644 2.0 / 2234 12.3

13 0440 2.8 / 1036 11.0 / TH 1658 3.1 / 2300 10.4
28 0456 2.3 / 1058 12.1 / F 1727 2.3 / 2324 11.7

14 0515 3.3 / 1118 10.3 / F 1741 3.6 / ◑ 2348 9.8
29 0542 2.8 / 1153 11.5 / SA 1822 2.8

15 0605 3.8 / 1219 9.7 / SA 1842 4.0
30 0024 11.1 / 0643 3.2 / SU 1305 11.1 / 1934 3.1

DECEMBER

Time m — Time m

1 0144 10.8 / 0815 3.4 / M 1428 11.1 / 2102 3.0
16 0108 9.8 / 0733 3.8 / TU 1346 10.0 / 2012 3.8

2 0303 11.0 / 0941 3.0 / TU 1537 11.5 / 2214 2.5
17 0229 9.9 / 0850 3.7 / W 1503 10.3 / 2128 3.5

3 0408 11.6 / 1047 2.4 / W 1637 12.1 / 2315 2.0
18 0341 10.5 / 1004 3.2 / TH 1607 10.9 / 2240 2.9

4 0504 12.3 / 1144 1.9 / TH 1731 12.7
19 0440 11.3 / 1110 2.6 / F 1703 11.7 / 2342 2.3

5 0010 1.4 / 0554 12.8 / F 1237 1.4 / 1819 13.1
20 0531 12.1 / 1207 2.0 / SA 1753 12.4

6 0100 1.1 / 0639 13.2 / SA 1326 1.2 / ○ 1904 13.2
21 0036 1.8 / 0618 12.8 / SU 1300 1.6 / 1840 12.9

7 0147 1.0 / 0722 13.3 / SU 1412 1.2 / 1947 13.2
22 0127 1.5 / 0703 13.3 / M 1351 1.3 / ● 1927 13.3

8 0230 1.2 / 0803 13.2 / M 1454 1.5 / 2027 12.9
23 0216 1.3 / 0748 13.6 / TU 1440 1.2 / 2013 13.5

9 0308 1.5 / 0840 12.9 / TU 1528 1.9 / 2103 12.5
24 0301 1.3 / 0833 13.7 / W 1525 1.1 / 2058 13.5

10 0337 1.9 / 0915 12.5 / W 1553 2.3 / 2136 12.0
25 0343 1.3 / 0918 13.6 / TH 1607 1.2 / 2143 13.3

11 0359 2.2 / 0946 12.0 / TH 1614 2.5 / 2206 11.5
26 0422 1.5 / 1003 13.4 / F 1646 1.3 / 2227 13.0

12 0423 2.5 / 1017 11.5 / F 1641 2.7 / 2238 11.0
27 0459 1.7 / 1049 12.9 / SA 1726 1.7 / 2313 12.4

13 0454 2.7 / 1052 11.0 / SA 1716 3.0 / 2315 10.5
28 0538 2.0 / 1138 12.3 / SU 1809 2.1 / ◑

14 0533 3.1 / 1134 10.5 / SU 1800 3.3 / ◑
29 0003 11.7 / 0624 2.6 / M 1237 11.6 / 1900 2.6

15 0003 10.1 / 0624 3.5 / M 1231 10.1 / 1858 3.6
30 0107 11.1 / 0704 3.1 / TU 1350 11.1 / 2008 3.0

31 0224 10.8 / 0852 3.4 / W 1504 11.0 / 2132 3.1

Chart Datum: 6·50 metres below Ordnance Datum (Newlyn)
HAT is 14·7m above Chart Datum

TIDES

335

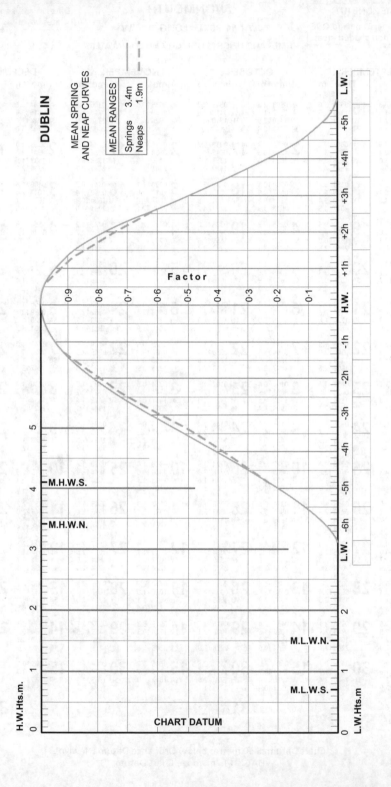

DUBLIN

MEAN SPRING
AND NEAP CURVES

MEAN RANGES	
Springs	3.4m
Neaps	1.9m

Factor

0·9 0·8 0·7 0·6 0·5 0·4 0·3 0·2 0·1

L.W. +5h +4h +3h +2h +1h H.W. -1h -2h -3h -4h -5h -6h L.W.

H.W.Hts.m.

M.H.W.S.

M.H.W.N.

M.L.W.N.

M.L.W.S.

CHART DATUM

L.W.Hts.m.

TIME ZONE (UT)	IRELAND – DUBLIN (NORTH WALL)	Dates in amber are SPRINGS
For Summer Time add ONE hour in **non-shaded areas**	LAT 53°21′N LONG 6°13′W	Dates in yellow are NEAPS
	TIMES AND HEIGHTS OF HIGH AND LOW WATERS	**2014**

JANUARY

Time m	Time m
1 0422 0.6 / 1101 4.3 / W 1649 0.4 / ● 2332 4.2	**16** 0515 1.0 / 1149 4.0 / TH 1740 0.9 / O
2 0508 0.5 / 1146 4.4 / TH 1736 0.3	**17** 0003 3.7 / 0544 1.0 / F 1219 4.0 / 1811 0.8
3 0020 4.2 / 0552 0.5 / F 1233 4.5 / 1823 0.3	**18** 0033 3.8 / 0611 0.9 / SA 1249 4.0 / 1841 0.8
4 0109 4.2 / 0639 0.5 / SA 1322 4.5 / 1913 0.3	**19** 0105 3.8 / 0639 0.9 / SU 1322 4.0 / 1910 0.8
5 0200 4.1 / 0729 0.7 / SU 1413 4.4 / 2006 0.4	**20** 0141 3.8 / 0711 1.0 / M 1400 3.9 / 1944 0.8
6 0255 4.0 / 0823 0.8 / M 1508 4.2 / 2101 0.6	**21** 0220 3.7 / 0748 1.0 / TU 1444 3.9 / 2023 0.9
7 0353 3.8 / 0920 1.0 / TU 1606 4.1 / 2158 0.9	**22** 0303 3.7 / 0831 1.1 / W 1524 3.8 / 2107 1.0
8 0455 3.7 / 1021 1.2 / W 1709 3.9 / ◐ 2259 1.1	**23** 0350 3.6 / 0919 1.2 / TH 1612 3.7 / 2156 1.1
9 0600 3.6 / 1127 1.4 / TH 1817 3.7	**24** 0443 3.5 / 1014 1.3 / F 1706 3.6 / ◐ 2255 1.2
10 0006 1.3 / 0705 3.6 / F 1239 1.5 / 1924 3.6	**25** 0544 3.4 / 1121 1.4 / SA 1811 3.5
11 0121 1.4 / 0809 3.6 / SA 1353 1.4 / 2031 3.6	**26** 0006 1.3 / 0654 3.5 / SU 1240 1.4 / 1926 3.5
12 0229 1.4 / 0909 3.7 / SU 1457 1.3 / 2132 3.6	**27** 0121 1.2 / 0804 3.6 / M 1354 1.2 / 2038 3.6
13 0323 1.3 / 1001 3.8 / M 1548 1.2 / 2222 3.6	**28** 0227 1.1 / 0905 3.8 / TU 1456 0.9 / 2139 3.8
14 0407 1.2 / 1043 3.9 / TU 1630 1.0 / 2301 3.7	**29** 0323 0.8 / 1047 4.1 / W 1551 0.6 / 2232 4.0
15 0443 1.1 / 1118 4.0 / W 1706 0.9 / 2333 3.7	**30** 0412 0.6 / 1047 4.3 / TH 1639 0.4 / ● 2320 4.1
	31 0456 0.4 / 1133 4.4 / F 1725 0.2

FEBRUARY

Time m	Time m
1 0006 4.2 / 0539 0.4 / SA 1218 4.5 / 1809 0.1	**16** 0007 3.8 / 0546 0.8 / SU 1224 4.0 / 1809 0.7
2 0051 4.2 / 0622 0.4 / SU 1304 4.4 / 1854 0.2	**17** 0036 3.8 / 0611 0.7 / M 1255 4.0 / 1837 0.6
3 0137 4.1 / 0708 0.5 / M 1351 4.3 / 1942 0.3	**18** 0110 3.8 / 0642 0.7 / TU 1331 4.0 / 1911 0.6
4 0224 4.0 / 0757 0.6 / TU 1441 4.2 / 2031 0.6	**19** 0148 3.8 / 0719 0.7 / W 1412 3.9 / 1950 0.7
5 0315 3.8 / 0850 0.8 / W 1533 4.0 / 2123 0.8	**20** 0230 3.7 / 0801 0.8 / TH 1455 3.8 / 2034 0.8
6 0410 3.6 / 0946 1.1 / TH 1632 3.7 / ◐ 2217 1.1	**21** 0316 3.7 / 0848 0.9 / F 1543 3.7 / 2123 0.9
7 0514 3.5 / 1048 1.3 / F 1739 3.5 / 2318 1.4	**22** 0407 3.6 / 0943 1.1 / SA 1637 3.6 / ◐ 2221 1.1
8 0622 3.4 / 1157 1.4 / SA 1850 3.4	**23** 0507 3.5 / 1050 1.2 / SU 1743 3.4 / 2333 1.3
9 0032 1.5 / SU 1321 1.5 / 1959 3.3	**24** 0620 3.4 / 1214 1.3 / M 1905 3.4
10 0201 1.5 / 0834 3.5 / M 1436 1.3 / 2106 3.4	**25** 0056 1.3 / 0738 3.5 / TU 1336 1.1 / 2023 3.5
11 0304 1.4 / 0932 3.7 / TU 1529 1.2 / 2200 3.5	**26** 0211 1.1 / 0847 3.7 / W 1445 0.8 / 2127 3.7
12 0348 1.3 / 1018 3.8 / W 1610 1.0 / 2240 3.6	**27** 0311 0.9 / 0944 4.0 / TH 1541 0.5 / 2221 3.9
13 0424 1.1 / 1055 3.9 / TH 1645 0.9 / 2312 3.6	**28** 0400 0.6 / 1034 4.2 / F 1628 0.3 / 2308 4.1
14 0454 1.0 / 1127 3.9 / F 1716 0.8 / O 2341 3.7	
15 0522 0.9 / 1156 4.0 / SA 1744 0.7	

MARCH

Time m	Time m
1 0444 0.4 / 1119 4.3 / SA 1711 0.1 / ● 2350 4.1	**16** 0454 0.8 / 1129 3.9 / SU 1711 0.6 / O 2339 3.8
2 0525 0.3 / 1202 4.4 / SU 1753 0.1	**17** 0518 0.7 / 1156 3.9 / M 1737 0.5
3 0031 4.1 / 0605 0.3 / M 1245 4.3 / 1834 0.2	**18** 0006 3.9 / 0544 0.6 / TU 1228 4.0 / 1807 0.5
4 0111 4.0 / 0648 0.3 / TU 1328 4.2 / 1916 0.3	**19** 0040 3.9 / 0616 0.5 / W 1305 4.0 / 1842 0.5
5 0153 3.9 / 0733 0.5 / W 1414 4.1 / 2001 0.6	**20** 0119 3.9 / 0655 0.5 / TH 1347 3.9 / 1923 0.6
6 0237 3.8 / 0822 0.7 / TH 1502 3.9 / 2048 0.8	**21** 0202 3.9 / 0739 0.6 / F 1433 3.8 / 2009 0.7
7 0326 3.6 / 0916 0.9 / F 1556 3.6 / 2140 1.1	**22** 0249 3.8 / 0828 0.7 / SA 1522 3.7 / 2101 0.9
8 0424 3.5 / 1014 1.1 / SA 1700 3.4 / ◐ 2237 1.4	**23** 0341 3.7 / 0927 0.9 / SU 1619 3.6 / 2202 1.1
9 0535 3.3 / 1119 1.3 / SU 1813 3.2 / 2344 1.6	**24** 0442 3.5 / 1037 1.1 / M 1729 3.4 / ◐ 2315 1.3
10 0648 3.3 / 1236 1.4 / M 1925 3.2	**25** 0556 3.5 / 1200 1.1 / TU 1852 3.4
11 0112 1.6 / 0756 3.3 / TU 1402 1.3 / 2032 3.2	**26** 0037 1.3 / 0717 3.5 / W 1322 1.0 / 2009 3.5
12 0233 1.5 / 0857 3.5 / W 1500 1.2 / 2129 3.4	**27** 0153 1.1 / 0828 3.7 / TH 1430 0.7 / 2115 3.7
13 0321 1.3 / 0946 3.6 / TH 1541 1.0 / 2211 3.5	**28** 0255 0.9 / 0929 3.9 / F 1525 0.5 / 2209 3.9
14 0357 1.1 / 1026 3.7 / F 1615 0.9 / 2245 3.6	**29** 0345 0.6 / 1018 4.0 / SA 1612 0.3 / 2255 4.0
15 0427 0.9 / 1100 3.8 / SA 1645 0.7 / 2314 3.7	**30** 0429 0.4 / 1106 4.2 / SU 1655 0.2 / ● 2335 4.0
	31 0509 0.3 / 1147 4.2 / M 1734 0.2

APRIL

Time m	Time m
1 0011 4.0 / 0549 0.3 / TU 1227 4.2 / 1813 0.3	**16** 0518 0.5 / 1203 4.0 / W 1740 0.4
2 0047 4.0 / 0629 0.3 / W 1308 4.1 / 1852 0.4	**17** 0013 4.0 / 0554 0.4 / TH 1244 4.0 / 1818 0.5
3 0125 3.9 / 0712 0.4 / TH 1350 3.9 / 1933 0.6	**18** 0055 4.0 / 0636 0.5 / F 1328 3.9 / 1902 0.6
4 0206 3.8 / 0759 0.6 / F 1436 3.8 / 2018 0.9	**19** 0140 4.0 / 0723 0.6 / SA 1417 3.9 / 1951 0.7
5 0252 3.7 / 0850 0.8 / SA 1527 3.5 / 2107 1.1	**20** 0230 3.9 / 0818 0.6 / SU 1510 3.7 / 2047 0.9
6 0343 3.5 / 0946 1.0 / SU 1625 3.3 / 2202 1.4	**21** 0325 3.8 / 0921 0.8 / M 1611 3.6 / 2150 1.1
7 0448 3.3 / 1046 1.2 / M 1735 3.2 / ◐ 2305 1.6	**22** 0427 3.7 / 1031 0.9 / TU 1721 3.5 / ◐ 2301 1.2
8 0604 3.2 / 1153 1.3 / TU 1847 3.1	**23** 0540 3.6 / 1148 0.9 / W 1840 3.5
9 0017 1.6 / 0714 3.3 / W 1309 1.3 / 1952 3.2	**24** 0017 1.2 / 0658 3.6 / TH 1303 0.9 / 1953 3.6
10 0138 1.5 / 0816 3.4 / TH 1414 1.2 / 2049 3.3	**25** 0130 1.1 / 0809 3.7 / F 1409 0.7 / 2057 3.7
11 0239 1.4 / 0909 3.5 / F 1501 1.0 / 2135 3.5	**26** 0232 1.0 / 0911 3.9 / SA 1505 0.6 / 2152 3.8
12 0319 1.1 / 0952 3.6 / SA 1537 0.8 / 2212 3.6	**27** 0325 0.8 / 1006 4.0 / SU 1553 0.5 / 2239 3.9
13 0352 0.9 / 1028 3.7 / SU 1608 0.7 / 2242 3.7	**28** 0411 0.6 / 1053 4.0 / M 1637 0.4 / 2319 3.9
14 0420 0.8 / 1059 3.8 / M 1637 0.6 / 2308 3.8	**29** 0454 0.5 / 1134 4.0 / TU 1716 0.4 / ● 2353 3.9
15 0447 0.6 / 1129 3.9 / TU 1707 0.5 / O 2337 3.9	**30** 0534 0.5 / 1211 4.0 / W 1754 0.5

Chart Datum: 0·20 metres above Ordnance Datum (Dublin)
HAT is 4·5m above Chart Datum

TIDES

TIME ZONE (UT)
For Summer Time add ONE hour in **non-shaded areas**

IRELAND – DUBLIN (NORTH WALL)
LAT 53°21'N   LONG 6°13'W
TIMES AND HEIGHTS OF HIGH AND LOW WATERS

Dates in amber are **SPRINGS**
Dates in yellow are NEAPS

2014

MAY

Day	Time	m	Day	Time	m
1 TH	0026 / 0614 / 1250 / 1831	3.9 / 0.5 / 3.9 / 0.6	16 F	0537 / 1226 / 1800	0.4 / 4.0 / 0.5
2 F	0102 / 0656 / 1330 / 1909	3.9 / 0.5 / 3.8 / 0.8	17 SA	0036 / 0622 / 1314 / 1846	4.1 / 0.4 / 4.0 / 0.6
3 SA	0142 / 0740 / 1413 / 1951	3.8 / 0.6 / 3.7 / 0.9	18 SU	0124 / 0713 / 1405 / 1937	4.1 / 0.5 / 3.9 / 0.7
4 SU	0224 / 0828 / 1500 / 2037	3.7 / 0.8 / 3.5 / 1.1	19 M	0216 / 0811 / 1501 / 2034	4.1 / 0.6 / 3.8 / 0.9
5 M	0311 / 0920 / 1552 / 2129	3.6 / 1.0 / 3.4 / 1.3	20 TU	0313 / 0914 / 1602 / 2137	4.0 / 0.7 / 3.7 / 1.0
6 TU	0406 / 1015 / 1653 / 2228	3.5 / 1.1 / 3.2 / 1.5	21 W	0415 / 1021 / 1710 / 2243	3.9 / 0.8 / 3.6 / 1.1
7 W	0513 / 1114 / 1801 / 2332	3.3 / 1.2 / 3.2 / 1.6	22 TH	0525 / 1130 / 1821 / 2353	3.8 / 0.8 / 3.6 / 1.2
8 TH	0626 / 1216 / 1907	3.3 / 1.2 / 3.2	23 F	0638 / 1239 / 1931	3.8 / 0.9 / 3.6
9 F	0038 / 0729 / 1317 / 2004	1.5 / 3.3 / 1.2 / 3.3	24 SA	0102 / 0747 / 1344 / 2034	1.2 / 3.8 / 0.8 / 3.7
10 SA	0139 / 0824 / 1409 / 2052	1.4 / 3.4 / 1.1 / 3.4	25 SU	0206 / 0851 / 1442 / 2131	1.1 / 3.8 / 0.8 / 3.8
11 SU	0229 / 0911 / 1452 / 2132	1.3 / 3.6 / 0.9 / 3.6	26 M	0303 / 0948 / 1533 / 2220	1.0 / 3.9 / 0.7 / 3.8
12 M	0309 / 0951 / 1529 / 2206	1.1 / 3.7 / 0.7 / 3.7	27 TU	0353 / 1038 / 1619 / 2303	0.8 / 3.9 / 0.7 / 3.9
13 TU	0344 / 1027 / 1604 / 2238	0.8 / 3.8 / 0.6 / 3.9	28 W	0439 / 1121 / 1659 / 2338	0.7 / 3.9 / 0.7 / 3.9
14 W	0418 / 1103 / 1640 / 2313	0.7 / 3.9 / 0.5 / 4.0	29 TH	0520 / 1157 / 1737	0.7 / 3.9 / 0.8
15 TH	0456 / 1143 / 1718 / 2352	0.5 / 4.0 / 0.5 / 4.1	30 F	0008 / 0600 / 1232 / 1812	3.9 / 0.7 / 3.8 / 0.8
			31 SA	0042 / 0640 / 1309 / 1848	3.9 / 0.7 / 3.7 / 0.9

JUNE

Day	Time	m	Day	Time	m
1 SU	0119 / 0721 / 1349 / 1926	3.9 / 0.7 / 3.7 / 1.0	16 M	0110 / 0703 / 1353 / 1922	4.3 / 0.4 / 4.0 / 0.6
2 M	0159 / 0805 / 1432 / 2007	3.8 / 0.8 / 3.6 / 1.1	17 TU	0202 / 0759 / 1448 / 2017	4.2 / 0.4 / 3.9 / 0.8
3 TU	0242 / 0851 / 1517 / 2053	3.7 / 0.9 / 3.5 / 1.2	18 W	0258 / 0859 / 1547 / 2117	4.2 / 0.6 / 3.8 / 0.9
4 W	0329 / 0940 / 1607 / 2144	3.6 / 1.0 / 3.4 / 1.4	19 TH	0358 / 1002 / 1650 / 2219	4.0 / 0.7 / 3.7 / 1.1
5 TH	0421 / 1033 / 1703 / 2242	3.5 / 1.1 / 3.3 / 1.5	20 F	0504 / 1105 / 1756 / 2324	3.9 / 0.8 / 3.7 / 1.2
6 F	0521 / 1128 / 1806 / 2343	3.4 / 1.2 / 3.2 / 1.5	21 SA	0614 / 1210 / 1903	3.8 / 0.9 / 3.6
7 SA	0627 / 1224 / 1908	3.4 / 1.2 / 3.3	22 SU	0032 / 0723 / 1316 / 2007	1.2 / 3.8 / 1.0 / 3.7
8 SU	0042 / 0729 / 1318 / 2002	1.5 / 3.4 / 1.1 / 3.4	23 M	0140 / 0828 / 1419 / 2106	1.2 / 3.8 / 1.0 / 3.7
9 M	0137 / 0824 / 1408 / 2049	1.4 / 3.5 / 1.0 / 3.6	24 TU	0243 / 0929 / 1514 / 2159	1.2 / 3.8 / 1.0 / 3.8
10 TU	0226 / 0912 / 1453 / 2131	1.2 / 3.7 / 0.9 / 3.8	25 W	0337 / 1022 / 1601 / 2244	1.0 / 3.8 / 1.0 / 3.9
11 W	0310 / 0958 / 1536 / 2212	0.9 / 3.8 / 0.7 / 3.9	26 TH	0425 / 1106 / 1643 / 2321	0.9 / 3.8 / 1.0 / 3.9
12 TH	0354 / 1042 / 1618 / 2253	0.7 / 3.9 / 0.6 / 4.1	27 F	0507 / 1142 / 1719 / 2351	0.9 / 3.7 / 0.9 / 3.9
13	0437 / 1126 / 1700 / 2336	0.5 / 4.0 / 0.5 / 4.2	28 SA	0545 / 1214 / 1753	0.8 / 3.7 / 0.9
14	0523 / 1212 / 1745	0.4 / 4.1 / 0.5	29 SU	0022 / 0622 / 1247 / 1825	3.9 / 0.8 / 3.7 / 0.9
15	0021 / 0611 / 1301 / 1831	4.3 / 0.4 / 4.1 / 0.5	30 M	0056 / 0659 / 1323 / 1858	3.9 / 0.8 / 3.7 / 1.0

JULY

Day	Time	m	Day	Time	m
1 TU	0133 / 0736 / 1401 / 1933	3.9 / 0.9 / 3.6 / 1.0	16 W	0143 / 0740 / 1427 / 1955	4.4 / 0.3 / 4.0 / 0.7
2 W	0212 / 0815 / 1441 / 2012	3.8 / 0.9 / 3.6 / 1.1	17 TH	0236 / 0836 / 1522 / 2051	4.3 / 0.5 / 3.9 / 0.8
3 TH	0254 / 0856 / 1524 / 2054	3.8 / 1.0 / 3.5 / 1.2	18 F	0334 / 0934 / 1620 / 2150	4.1 / 0.7 / 3.8 / 1.0
4 F	0339 / 0941 / 1611 / 2142	3.7 / 1.1 / 3.4 / 1.3	19 SA	0436 / 1034 / 1724 / 2252	3.9 / 0.9 / 3.6 / 1.2
5 SA	0429 / 1032 / 1704 / 2238	3.5 / 1.1 / 3.4 / 1.4	20 SU	0546 / 1137 / 1831	3.8 / 1.1 / 3.6
6	0526 / 1129 / 1804 / 2342	3.5 / 1.2 / 3.4 / 1.5	21	0000 / 0656 / 1245 / 1936	1.3 / 3.7 / 1.2 / 3.6
7 M	0631 / 1228 / 1909	3.4 / 1.2 / 3.4	22	0113 / 0805 / 1355 / 2040	1.4 / 3.6 / 1.3 / 3.6
8 TU	0048 / 0738 / 1328 / 2008	1.5 / 3.5 / 1.2 / 3.5	23 W	0225 / 0909 / 1455 / 2137	1.3 / 3.6 / 1.3 / 3.7
9 W	0149 / 0840 / 1422 / 2102	1.2 / 3.6 / 1.0 / 3.7	24 TH	0324 / 1005 / 1544 / 2224	1.2 / 3.6 / 1.2 / 3.8
10 TH	0244 / 0934 / 1513 / 2150	1.0 / 3.8 / 0.8 / 4.0	25 F	0411 / 1050 / 1625 / 2301	1.0 / 3.7 / 1.1 / 3.9
11 F	0335 / 1024 / 1600 / 2236	0.8 / 4.0 / 0.6 / 4.2	26 SA	0451 / 1124 / 1700 / 2332	0.9 / 3.7 / 1.0 / 3.9
12 SA	0423 / 1111 / 1645 / 2321	0.5 / 4.1 / 0.5 / 4.3	27 SU	0526 / 1153 / 1732	0.9 / 3.7 / 0.9
13 SU	0510 / 1158 / 1730	0.3 / 4.2 / 0.4	28	0001 / 0559 / 1223 / 1801	4.0 / 0.8 / 3.7 / 0.9
14	0006 / 0558 / 1246 / 1815	4.4 / 0.2 / 4.2 / 0.4	29 TU	0032 / 0631 / 1255 / 1829	4.0 / 0.8 / 3.7 / 0.9
15 TU	0053 / 0647 / 1335 / 1903	4.4 / 0.2 / 4.1 / 0.5	30 W	0104 / 0701 / 1329 / 1859	4.0 / 0.8 / 3.7 / 0.9
			31 TH	0141 / 0733 / 1406 / 1935	3.9 / 0.8 / 3.7 / 1.0

AUGUST

Day	Time	m	Day	Time	m
1 F	0221 / 0810 / 1447 / 2015	3.9 / 0.9 / 3.7 / 1.0	16 SA	0304 / 0902 / 1545 / 2120	4.1 / 0.7 / 3.8 / 1.0
2 SA	0304 / 0853 / 1532 / 2100	3.8 / 1.0 / 3.6 / 1.1	17 SU	0404 / 0958 / 1646 / 2221	3.8 / 1.0 / 3.6 / 1.2
3 SU	0351 / 0941 / 1621 / 2151	3.7 / 1.1 / 3.5 / 1.3	18 M	0513 / 1059 / 1754 / 2327	3.6 / 1.3 / 3.5 / 1.4
4 M	0444 / 1037 / 1717 / 2252	3.5 / 1.2 / 3.4 / 1.4	19 TU	0627 / 1207 / 1903	3.5 / 1.4 / 3.5
5 TU	0547 / 1143 / 1824	3.4 / 1.3 / 3.4	20 W	0045 / 0739 / 1327 / 2010	1.4 / 3.5 / 1.5 / 3.4
6 W	0007 / 0703 / 1254 / 1935	1.4 / 3.4 / 1.3 / 3.5	21 TH	0206 / 0849 / 1435 / 2110	1.4 / 3.5 / 1.4 / 3.4
7 TH	0121 / 0815 / 1359 / 2038	1.3 / 3.5 / 1.1 / 3.7	22 F	0307 / 0946 / 1525 / 2159	1.2 / 3.6 / 1.3 / 3.8
8 F	0226 / 0916 / 1456 / 2132	1.0 / 3.7 / 0.9 / 4.0	23 SA	0352 / 1029 / 1605 / 2238	1.0 / 3.6 / 1.1 / 3.9
9 SA	0322 / 1009 / 1545 / 2220	0.7 / 3.9 / 0.7 / 4.2	24 SU	0430 / 1102 / 1638 / 2309	0.9 / 3.7 / 1.0 / 4.0
10 SU	0411 / 1057 / 1631 / 2305	0.5 / 4.1 / 0.5 / 4.4	25 M	0502 / 1131 / 1709 / 2338	0.9 / 3.7 / 0.9 / 4.0
11 M	0458 / 1142 / 1714 / 2349	0.2 / 4.2 / 0.4 / 4.5	26 TU	0532 / 1158 / 1735	0.8 / 3.7 / 0.9
12 TU	0543 / 1227 / 1757	0.1 / 4.2 / 0.3	27 W	0006 / 0559 / 1226 / 1800	4.0 / 0.7 / 3.8 / 0.8
13 W	0033 / 0628 / 1313 / 1842	4.5 / 0.1 / 4.1 / 0.4	28 TH	0036 / 0625 / 1258 / 1829	4.0 / 0.7 / 3.8 / 0.8
14 TH	0120 / 0716 / 1400 / 1930	4.4 / 0.3 / 4.0 / 0.5	29 F	0111 / 0655 / 1334 / 1903	4.0 / 0.7 / 3.8 / 0.9
15 F	0210 / 0808 / 1450 / 2023	4.3 / 0.5 / 3.9 / 0.7	30 SA	0150 / 0733 / 1415 / 1943	3.9 / 0.8 / 3.7 / 0.9
			31 SU	0233 / 0815 / 1459 / 2028	3.8 / 0.9 / 3.7 / 1.0

Chart Datum: 0·20 metres above Ordnance Datum (Dublin)
HAT is 4·5m above Chart Datum

TIME ZONE (UT)	IRELAND – DUBLIN (NORTH WALL)	Dates in amber are SPRINGS
For Summer Time add ONE hour in **non-shaded areas**	LAT 53°21'N LONG 6°13'W	Dates in yellow are NEAPS
	TIMES AND HEIGHTS OF HIGH AND LOW WATERS	**2014**

SEPTEMBER

Time m   Time m

1 0320 3.7 / 1547 3.6 / 2119 1.2   **16** 0439 3.5 / 1022 1.4 / 1714 3.5 / ☽ 2256 1.3
M   TU

2 0413 3.6 / 1001 1.3 / 1643 3.5 / ☽ 2222 1.3   **17** 0555 3.3 / 1127 1.6 / 1825 3.4
TU   W

3 0517 3.4 / 1110 1.3 / 1750 3.4 / 2340 1.4   **18** 0011 1.4 / 0709 3.3 / 1249 1.6 / 1934 3.5
W   TH

4 0639 3.4 / 1228 1.4 / 1907 3.5   **19** 0138 1.4 / 0820 3.4 / 1406 1.5 / 2037 3.6
TH   F

5 0102 1.2 / 0757 3.5 / 1340 1.2 / 2016 3.7   **20** 0241 1.2 / 0918 3.5 / 1459 1.4 / 2128 3.8
F   SA

6 0213 1.0 / 0902 3.7 / 1441 1.0 / 2113 4.0   **21** 0326 1.0 / 1001 3.6 / 1539 1.2 / 2209 3.9
SA   SU

7 0311 0.7 / 0956 3.9 / 1531 0.7 / 2203 4.2   **22** 0402 0.9 / 1035 3.7 / 1612 1.0 / 2243 4.0
SU   M

8 0400 0.4 / 1043 4.1 / 1616 0.5 / 2249 4.4   **23** 0433 0.8 / 1115 3.8 / 1642 0.9 / 2313 4.0
M   TU

9 0444 0.2 / 1126 4.2 / 1658 0.3 / ○ 2331 4.5   **24** 0501 0.7 / 1132 3.8 / 1708 0.8 / ● 2340 4.0
TU   W

10 0526 0.1 / 1207 4.2 / 1740 0.3   **25** 0526 0.7 / 1158 3.9 / 1733 0.8
W   TH

11 0014 4.5 / 0608 0.1 / 1250 4.2 / 1822 0.3   **26** 0009 4.0 / 0552 0.7 / 1229 3.9 / 1801 0.7
TH   F

12 0058 4.4 / 0652 0.3 / 1333 4.1 / 1907 0.5   **27** 0044 4.0 / 0624 0.7 / 1305 3.9 / 1837 0.7
F   SA

13 0145 4.2 / 0738 0.5 / 1419 3.9 / 1957 0.7   **28** 0124 4.0 / 0702 0.7 / 1347 3.9 / 1918 0.8
SA   SU

14 0235 4.0 / 0828 0.8 / 1509 3.8 / 2052 0.9   **29** 0208 3.9 / 0746 0.9 / 1432 3.8 / 2004 0.9
SU   M

15 0332 3.8 / 0923 1.1 / 1606 3.6 / 2151 1.1   **30** 0257 3.8 / 0837 1.0 / 1521 3.7 / 2059 1.1
M   TU

OCTOBER

Time m   Time m

1 0352 3.6 / 0936 1.2 / 1618 3.6 / ☽ 2205 1.2   **16** 0519 3.3 / 1050 1.6 / 1744 3.5 / 2333 1.4
W   TH

2 0459 3.5 / 1048 1.4 / 1725 3.6 / 2324 1.3   **17** 0632 3.3 / 1202 1.7 / 1854 3.5
TH   F

3 0622 3.4 / 1207 1.4 / 1842 3.6   **18** 0051 1.4 / 0739 3.3 / 1322 1.6 / 1957 3.6
F   SA

4 0047 1.2 / 0741 3.5 / 1321 1.3 / 1954 3.8   **19** 0201 1.3 / 0838 3.5 / 1423 1.5 / 2051 3.7
SA   SU

5 0158 0.9 / 0846 3.7 / 1423 1.0 / 2054 4.0   **20** 0251 1.1 / 0924 3.6 / 1507 1.3 / 2136 3.8
SU   M

6 0256 0.6 / 0941 3.9 / 1515 0.8 / 2147 4.2   **21** 0328 0.9 / 1003 3.8 / 1542 1.1 / 2213 3.9
M   TU

7 0345 0.4 / 1028 4.1 / 1601 0.5 / 2233 4.3   **22** 0400 0.8 / 1036 3.9 / 1612 1.0 / 2246 4.0
TU   W

8 0428 0.3 / 1111 4.2 / 1643 0.4 / ○ 2316 4.4   **23** 0428 0.7 / 1104 3.9 / 1639 0.9 / ● 2314 4.0
W   TH

9 0509 0.2 / 1150 4.2 / 1724 0.4 / 2357 4.4   **24** 0455 0.7 / 1130 4.0 / 1707 0.8 / 2345 4.0
TH   F

10 0549 0.3 / 1228 4.2 / 1805 0.4   **25** 0525 0.6 / 1202 4.1 / 1739 0.7
F   SA

11 0039 4.3 / 0629 0.4 / 1309 4.1 / 1849 0.5   **26** 0021 4.0 / 0559 0.6 / 1240 4.1 / 1816 0.7
SA   SU

12 0124 4.1 / 0712 0.7 / 1352 4.0 / 1936 0.7   **27** 0103 4.0 / 0639 0.7 / 1323 4.1 / 1900 0.7
SU   M

13 0212 3.9 / 0758 0.9 / 1439 3.9 / 2028 0.9   **28** 0149 3.9 / 0724 0.9 / 1410 4.0 / 1950 0.8
M   TU

14 0305 3.7 / 0850 1.2 / 1531 3.7 / 2124 1.1   **29** 0241 3.8 / 0817 1.1 / 1502 3.9 / 2047 1.0
TU   W

15 0407 3.5 / 0947 1.4 / 1634 3.6 / ☽ 2225 1.3   **30** 0339 3.7 / 0919 1.2 / 1600 3.8 / 2154 1.1
W   TH

31 0447 3.6 / 1030 1.4 / 1705 3.7 / ☽ 2309 1.1
F

NOVEMBER

Time m   Time m

1 0605 3.6 / 1146 1.4 / 1819 3.8   **16** 0653 3.3 / 1225 1.7 / 1911 3.5
SA   SU

2 0027 1.1 / 0720 3.6 / 1258 1.3 / 1930 3.8   **17** 0103 1.4 / 0752 3.4 / 1331 1.6 / 2007 3.6
SU   M

3 0137 0.9 / 0827 3.8 / 1402 1.1 / 2034 4.0   **18** 0201 1.2 / 0842 3.6 / 1423 1.4 / 2056 3.7
M   TU

4 0236 0.7 / 0923 4.0 / 1456 0.9 / 2130 4.1   **19** 0246 1.1 / 0926 3.7 / 1504 1.3 / 2139 3.8
TU   W

5 0327 0.6 / 1013 4.1 / 1545 0.7 / 2220 4.2   **20** 0323 1.0 / 1002 3.9 / 1539 1.1 / 2216 3.9
W   TH

6 0412 0.5 / 1056 4.1 / 1629 0.6 / ○ 2304 4.2   **21** 0355 0.8 / 1034 4.0 / 1611 0.9 / 2249 4.0
TH   F

7 0454 0.5 / 1135 4.2 / 1711 0.6 / 2345 4.2   **22** 0427 0.7 / 1105 4.1 / 1645 0.8 / ● 2325 4.0
F   SA

8 0533 0.5 / 1212 4.2 / 1753 0.6   **23** 0502 0.7 / 1140 4.2 / 1721 0.7
SA   SU

9 0025 4.1 / 0610 0.6 / 1249 4.1 / 1834 0.6   **24** 0004 4.1 / 0539 0.7 / 1220 4.2 / 1802 0.6
SU   M

10 0107 4.0 / 0650 0.8 / 1329 4.0 / 1919 0.7   **25** 0048 4.1 / 0621 0.7 / 1305 4.2 / 1848 0.6
M   TU

11 0151 3.9 / 0733 1.0 / 1413 4.0 / 2007 0.9   **26** 0136 4.0 / 0708 0.8 / 1353 4.2 / 1939 0.7
TU   W

12 0240 3.7 / 0820 1.2 / 1501 3.8 / 2058 1.0   **27** 0229 3.9 / 0802 1.0 / 1446 4.1 / 2037 0.8
W   TH

13 0334 3.5 / 0914 1.4 / 1555 3.7 / 2154 1.2   **28** 0327 3.8 / 0902 1.1 / 1543 4.0 / 2140 0.9
TH   F

14 0438 3.4 / 1013 1.6 / 1658 3.5 / ☽ 2253 1.3   **29** 0433 3.7 / 1009 1.3 / 1646 3.9 / ☽ 2249 1.0
F   SA

15 0546 3.3 / 1118 1.7 / 1806 3.5 / 2357 1.4   **30** 0544 3.7 / 1119 1.3 / 1755 3.9
SA   SU

DECEMBER

Time m   Time m

1 0001 1.0 / 0655 3.7 / 1230 1.3 / 1905 3.9   **16** 0004 1.4 / 0657 3.4 / 1233 1.7 / 1913 3.4
M   TU

2 0111 1.0 / 0802 3.8 / 1337 1.2 / 2012 3.9   **17** 0103 1.4 / 0754 3.5 / 1331 1.6 / 2010 3.5
TU   W

3 0214 0.9 / 0902 3.9 / 1437 1.1 / 2114 4.0   **18** 0157 1.3 / 0844 3.6 / 1421 1.4 / 2100 3.6
W   TH

4 0309 0.8 / 0955 4.0 / 1530 1.0 / 2209 4.0   **19** 0243 1.1 / 0927 3.8 / 1505 1.2 / 2145 3.8
TH   F

5 0357 0.8 / 1042 4.1 / 1618 0.8 / 2256 4.1   **20** 0325 1.0 / 1005 4.0 / 1545 1.0 / 2227 3.9
F   SA

6 0440 0.8 / 1124 4.1 / 1701 0.7 / ○ 2337 4.0   **21** 0404 0.8 / 1043 4.1 / 1625 0.8 / 2308 4.0
SA   SU

7 0519 0.8 / 1159 4.1 / 1742 0.7   **22** 0443 0.7 / 1122 4.2 / 1706 0.6 / ● 2350 4.1
SU   M

8 0013 4.0 / 0555 0.8 / 1233 4.1 / 1822 0.7   **23** 0524 0.6 / 1203 4.3 / 1750 0.5
M   TU

9 0051 3.9 / 0632 0.9 / 1310 4.1 / 1903 0.8   **24** 0034 4.1 / 0607 0.6 / 1249 4.4 / 1836 0.4
TU   W

10 0131 3.8 / 0710 1.0 / 1349 4.0 / 1945 0.8   **25** 0123 4.1 / 0653 0.7 / 1337 4.3 / 1927 0.5
W   TH

11 0214 3.7 / 0751 1.1 / 1432 3.9 / 2030 1.0   **26** 0214 4.0 / 0745 0.8 / 1429 4.3 / 2021 0.6
TH   F

12 0300 3.6 / 0837 1.3 / 1517 3.8 / 2118 1.1   **27** 0310 3.9 / 0842 1.0 / 1524 4.2 / 2120 0.7
F   SA

13 0350 3.5 / 0929 1.5 / 1607 3.6 / 2210 1.2   **28** 0410 3.8 / 0943 1.1 / 1624 4.1 / ☽ 2222 0.9
SA   SU

14 0448 3.4 / 1028 1.6 / 1704 3.5 / ☽ 2305 1.3   **29** 0517 3.7 / 1049 1.2 / 1729 3.9 / 2329 1.0
SU   M

15 0554 3.3 / 1130 1.7 / 1809 3.4   **30** 0626 3.7 / 1159 1.3 / 1840 3.8
M   TU

31 0040 1.1 / 0734 3.7 / 1310 1.3 / 1951 3.8
W

Chart Datum: 0·20 metres above Ordnance Datum (Dublin)
HAT is 4·5m above Chart Datum

TIDES

339

COBH

MEAN SPRING
AND NEAP CURVES

MEAN RANGES	
Springs	3.7m
Neaps	1.9m

Factor

0·9 0·8 0·7 0·6 0·5 0·4 0·3 0·2 0·1

L.W. +6h +5h +4h +3h +2h +1h H.W. -1h -2h -3h -4h -5h L.W.

M.H.W.S.

M.H.W.N.

M.L.W.N.

M.L.W.S.

CHART DATUM

H.W.Hts.m.

L.W.Hts.m.

TIMES AND HEIGHTS OF HIGH AND LOW WATERS

2014

JANUARY

Day	DoW	Time m	Time m	Time m	Time m
1	W	0454 4.2	1127 0.4	1717 4.2	● 2350 0.3
16	TH	0535 4.1	1200 0.8	1748 4.0	○
2	TH	0545 4.4	1215 0.3	1806 4.3	
17	F	0009 0.7	0608 4.1	1230 0.8	1820 4.0
3	F	0037 0.2	0633 4.4	1303 0.3	1852 4.3
18	SA	0037 0.7	0640 4.1	1259 0.8	1851 4.0
4	SA	0124 0.2	0720 4.4	1349 0.3	1939 4.2
19	SU	0107 0.7	0710 4.1	1331 0.8	1921 4.0
5	SU	0211 0.3	0807 4.2	1436 0.4	2026 4.1
20	M	0140 0.8	0742 4.0	1406 0.9	1955 3.9
6	M	0259 0.4	0855 4.1	1524 0.6	2113 3.9
21	TU	0217 0.9	0817 4.0	1443 1.0	2031 3.9
7	TU	0349 0.6	0944 3.9	1613 0.8	2202 3.7
22	W	0257 1.0	0855 3.9	1523 1.1	2112 3.8
8	W	0442 0.8	1035 3.7	1707 1.0	◐ 2255 3.6
23	TH	0341 1.1	0939 3.8	1608 1.2	2159 3.7
9	TH	0540 1.0	1133 3.4	1808 1.1	2358 3.4
24	F	0433 1.2	1030 3.7	1702 1.3	◑ 2256 3.6
10	F	0646 1.1	1238 3.4	1917 1.2	
25	SA	0535 1.3	1131 3.6	1813 1.4	
11	SA	0110 3.4	0756 1.2	1348 3.4	2026 1.2
26	SU	0004 3.5	0648 1.3	1242 3.5	1930 1.3
12	SU	0221 3.4	0903 1.1	1450 3.5	2129 1.1
27	M	0119 3.6	0804 1.2	1356 3.6	2043 1.1
13	M	0321 3.6	1001 1.0	1545 3.7	2222 1.0
28	TU	0234 3.7	0916 0.9	1508 3.7	2149 0.8
14	TU	0412 3.8	1049 0.9	1632 3.8	2304 0.8
29	W	0342 3.9	1020 0.6	1611 4.0	2246 0.5
15	W	0456 3.9	1128 0.8	1713 3.9	2339 0.7
30	TH	0440 4.2	1114 0.4	1705 4.2	● 2337 0.2
31	F	0531 4.4	1203 0.2	1753 4.3	

FEBRUARY

Day	DoW	Time m	Time m	Time m	Time m
1	SA	0023 0.1	0618 4.4	1249 0.1	1837 4.3
16	SU	0016 0.6	0619 4.1	1237 0.6	1831 4.0
2	SU	0108 0.0	0702 4.4	1332 0.1	1921 4.3
17	M	0044 0.6	0647 4.1	1308 0.7	1900 4.0
3	M	0152 0.1	0746 4.3	1416 0.2	2003 4.2
18	TU	0116 0.6	0717 4.0	1341 0.7	1931 4.0
4	TU	0237 0.2	0829 4.2	1459 0.4	2045 4.0
19	W	0152 0.7	0749 4.0	1416 0.8	2005 4.0
5	W	0321 0.5	0913 4.0	1542 0.6	2128 3.8
20	TH	0231 0.8	0826 3.9	1454 0.9	2043 3.9
6	TH	0407 0.7	0957 3.7	1629 0.9	◐ 2214 3.6
21	F	0313 0.9	0908 3.8	1535 1.0	2127 3.8
7	F	0458 1.0	1047 3.5	1722 1.1	2308 3.4
22	SA	0402 1.0	0957 3.7	1627 1.2	◑ 2222 3.6
8	SA	0557 1.2	1148 3.3	1826 1.3	
23	SU	0501 1.2	1057 3.5	1735 1.3	2331 3.5
9	SU	0021 3.2	0708 1.3	1306 3.2	1941 1.3
24	M	0616 1.3	1211 3.3	1858 1.3	
10	M	0146 3.2	0825 1.3	1420 3.3	2057 1.2
25	TU	0051 3.4	0737 1.2	1334 3.4	2019 1.1
11	TU	0255 3.6	0935 1.1	1521 3.5	2159 1.0
26	W	0215 3.6	0856 0.9	1452 3.6	2130 0.8
12	W	0350 3.6	1027 0.9	1611 3.7	2245 0.8
27	TH	0327 3.8	1004 0.6	1557 3.9	2230 0.4
13	TH	0435 3.8	1108 0.8	1653 3.9	2321 0.7
28	F	0425 4.1	1059 0.3	1650 4.1	2321 0.2
14	F	0514 4.0	1141 0.7	1730 4.0	○ 2350 0.6
15	SA	0549 4.1	1209 0.6	1802 4.0	

MARCH

Day	DoW	Time m	Time m	Time m	Time m
1	SA	0514 4.3	1146 0.1	1736 4.3	●
16	SU	0521 4.0	1142 0.5	1737 4.0	○ 2350 0.5
2	SU	0006 0.0	0559 4.4	1230 0.0	1819 4.3
17	M	0552 4.0	1212 0.5	1807 4.0	
3	M	0049 0.0	0641 4.4	1311 0.0	1859 4.3
18	TU	0019 0.5	0620 4.0	1243 0.5	1836 4.0
4	TU	0131 0.0	0722 4.3	1352 0.1	1938 4.2
19	W	0053 0.5	0651 4.0	1317 0.5	1908 4.0
5	W	0212 0.2	0801 4.1	1432 0.3	2017 4.0
20	TH	0130 0.5	0725 4.0	1353 0.6	1943 4.0
6	TH	0253 0.4	0841 3.9	1512 0.6	2055 3.8
21	F	0209 0.6	0803 3.9	1432 0.7	2022 3.9
7	F	0335 0.6	0921 3.7	1554 0.8	2137 3.6
22	SA	0253 0.7	0846 3.8	1516 0.8	2108 3.8
8	SA	0421 0.9	1005 3.4	1642 1.1	◐ 2225 3.3
23	SU	0343 0.9	0936 3.6	1608 1.0	2203 3.6
9	SU	0516 1.2	1059 3.2	1743 1.3	2330 3.1
24	M	0442 1.0	1038 3.4	1715 1.1	◑ 2311 3.4
10	M	0623 1.3	1218 3.0	1857 1.4	
25	TU	0555 1.1	1152 3.3	1836 1.2	
11	TU	0105 3.1	0740 1.3	1346 3.1	2016 1.3
26	W	0034 3.4	0717 1.1	1317 3.3	1958 1.0
12	W	0224 3.2	0856 1.2	1452 3.3	2124 1.1
27	TH	0159 3.5	0837 0.8	1435 3.5	2111 0.7
13	TH	0321 3.5	0954 0.9	1544 3.5	2215 0.8
28	F	0309 3.8	0945 0.5	1539 3.8	2211 0.4
14	F	0407 3.7	1038 0.7	1627 3.7	2253 0.7
29	SA	0406 4.0	1039 0.3	1631 4.0	2302 0.2
15	SA	0447 3.9	1112 0.6	1704 3.9	2323 0.6
30	SU	0454 4.2	1128 0.1	1717 4.2	● 2347 0.0
31	M	0538 4.3	1209 0.0	1759 4.2	

APRIL

Day	DoW	Time m	Time m	Time m	Time m
1	TU	0028 0.0	0619 4.3	1249 0.1	1837 4.2
16	W	0554 4.0	1220 0.4	1814 4.0	
2	W	0109 0.1	0657 4.2	1328 0.2	1914 4.1
17	TH	0032 0.4	0628 4.0	1258 0.4	1849 4.0
3	TH	0147 0.2	0734 4.0	1406 0.4	1950 4.0
18	F	0112 0.4	0707 4.0	1337 0.5	1927 4.0
4	F	0226 0.4	0811 3.8	1444 0.6	2027 3.8
19	SA	0154 0.5	0748 4.0	1420 0.6	2010 3.9
5	SA	0306 0.7	0849 3.6	1524 0.8	2106 3.6
20	SU	0241 0.6	0835 3.8	1507 0.7	2059 3.8
6	SU	0350 0.9	0930 3.4	1609 1.0	2151 3.4
21	M	0333 0.7	0927 3.6	1601 0.8	2155 3.6
7	M	0441 1.1	1019 3.2	1705 1.2	2248 3.2
22	TU	0432 0.9	1028 3.4	1706 1.0	◑ 2302 3.5
8	TU	0543 1.3	1126 3.0	1814 1.3	
23	W	0542 1.0	1140 3.3	1821 1.0	
9	W	0010 3.1	0654 1.3	1256 3.0	1928 1.3
24	TH	0020 3.4	0659 0.9	1259 3.4	1939 0.9
10	TH	0139 3.2	0805 1.2	1411 3.2	2034 1.1
25	F	0140 3.5	0816 0.8	1414 3.5	2050 0.7
11	F	0241 3.4	0905 1.0	1506 3.4	2128 0.9
26	SA	0246 3.7	0922 0.5	1516 3.8	2150 0.4
12	SA	0329 3.6	0954 0.8	1551 3.6	2211 0.7
27	SU	0343 3.9	1017 0.4	1609 3.9	2241 0.3
13	SU	0410 3.8	1034 0.6	1630 3.8	2248 0.6
28	M	0432 4.1	1105 0.2	1656 4.1	2327 0.2
14	M	0447 3.9	1110 0.5	1706 3.9	2321 0.5
29	TU	0516 4.1	1147 0.2	1738 4.1	●
15	TU	0521 4.0	1145 0.5	1740 4.0	○ 2355 0.4
30	W	0008 0.2	0556 4.1	1228 0.2	1816 4.1

Chart Datum: 0·13 metres above Ordnance Datum (Dublin)
HAT is 4·5m above Chart Datum

TIDES

TIME ZONE (UT)
For Summer Time add ONE hour in **non-shaded areas**

IRELAND – COBH
LAT 51°51′N   LONG 8°18′W
TIMES AND HEIGHTS OF HIGH AND LOW WATERS

Dates in amber are **SPRINGS**
Dates in yellow are **NEAPS**

2014

MAY

Day	Time	m	Day	Time	m
1 TH	0047	0.3	16 F	0015	0.4
	0634	4.0		0611	4.0
	1305	0.3		1243	0.4
	1852	4.0		1834	4.1
2 F	0124	0.4	17 SA	0059	0.3
	0710	3.9		0654	4.0
	1342	0.5		1326	0.4
	1926	3.9		1917	4.1
3 SA	0201	0.6	18 SU	0145	0.4
	0745	3.8		0740	3.9
	1419	0.6		1412	0.4
	2002	3.8		2004	4.0
4 SU	0239	0.7	19 M	0234	0.5
	0822	3.6		0829	3.8
	1457	0.7		1502	0.5
	2041	3.6		2055	3.9
5 M	0320	0.9	20 TU	0326	0.6
	0902	3.5		0922	3.7
	1539	1.0		1556	0.6
	2123	3.5		2150	3.8
6 TU	0408	1.1	21 W	0424	0.7
	0947	3.3		1020	3.6
	1629	1.1		1656	0.8
	2213	3.3		2252	3.6
7 W	0504	1.2	22 TH	0528	0.8
	1043	3.2		1125	3.5
	1730	1.2		1804	0.9
	2315	3.2			
8 TH	0608	1.3	23 F	0002	3.5
	1152	3.1		0639	0.8
	1837	1.3		1236	3.5
				1916	0.8
9 F	0032	3.2	24 SA	0114	3.6
	0713	1.2		0751	0.8
	1309	3.2		1345	3.5
	1940	1.2		2025	0.7
10 SA	0143	3.3	25 SU	0219	3.7
	0812	1.1		0855	0.7
	1412	3.4		1448	3.7
	2036	1.0		2126	0.6
11 SU	0238	3.5	26 M	0316	3.8
	0904	0.9		0952	0.6
	1503	3.6		1544	3.8
	2125	0.8		2219	0.5
12 M	0325	3.7	27 TU	0408	3.9
	0952	0.7		1042	0.5
	1549	3.7		1633	3.9
	2210	0.7		2307	0.4
13 TU	0408	3.8	28 W	0454	3.9
	1037	0.6		1127	0.4
	1631	3.9		1717	4.0
	2252	0.5		2348	0.4
14 W	0449	3.9	29 TH	0536	4.0
	1119	0.5		1207	0.4
	1712	4.0		1756	4.0
	2334	0.4			
15 TH	0529	4.0	30 F	0026	0.5
	1200	0.4		0613	3.9
	1753	4.1		1244	0.5
				1832	4.0
			31 SA	0102	0.6
				0648	3.9
				1319	0.6
				1906	3.9

JUNE

Day	Time	m	Day	Time	m
1 SU	0136	0.7	16 M	0136	0.3
	0723	3.8		0731	4.0
	1354	0.7		1404	0.3
	1941	3.8		1956	4.1
2 M	0212	0.8	17 TU	0225	0.3
	0758	3.7		0821	4.0
	1430	0.9		1453	0.3
	2018	3.7		2047	4.0
3 TU	0251	0.9	18 W	0316	0.4
	0837	3.6		0912	3.8
	1508	0.9		1545	0.5
	2058	3.6		2139	3.9
4 W	0334	1.0	19 TH	0410	0.6
	0919	3.5		1005	3.7
	1552	1.1		1640	0.6
	2142	3.5		2234	3.7
5 TH	0423	1.1	20 F	0508	0.7
	1007	3.4		1102	3.6
	1644	1.2		1741	0.7
	2233	3.4		2335	3.6
6 F	0519	1.2	21 SA	0612	0.8
	1102	3.3		1205	3.5
	1743	1.2		1848	0.8
	2331	3.4			
7 SA	0621	1.2	22 SU	0041	3.5
	1205	3.3		0719	0.9
	1846	1.2		1313	3.5
				1955	0.8
8 SU	0035	3.4	23 M	0148	3.6
	0721	1.1		0825	0.8
	1310	3.4		1418	3.5
	1945	1.1		2059	0.8
9 M	0139	3.5	24 TU	0249	3.6
	0819	1.0		0926	0.8
	1411	3.5		1518	3.6
	2042	0.9		2157	0.7
10 TU	0236	3.6	25 W	0344	3.7
	0914	0.9		1021	0.7
	1506	3.7		1611	3.8
	2135	0.8		2247	0.6
11 W	0330	3.8	26 TH	0433	3.8
	1006	0.7		1108	0.6
	1558	3.9		1657	3.9
	2227	0.6		2330	0.6
12 TH	0420	3.9	27 F	0516	3.8
	1056	0.5		1148	0.6
	1648	4.0		1738	3.9
	2315	0.4			
13 F	0509	4.0	28 SA	0007	0.6
	1143	0.4		0554	3.9
	1735	4.1		1224	0.6
				1814	3.9
14 SA	0002	0.3	29 SU	0040	0.7
	0556	4.1		0629	3.9
	1230	0.3		1256	0.6
	1821	4.2		1848	3.9
15 SU	0049	0.3	30 M	0111	0.7
	0643	4.1		0703	3.8
	1316	0.3		1328	0.7
	1908	4.2		1921	3.9

JULY

Day	Time	m	Day	Time	m
1 TU	0144	0.8	16 W	0210	0.2
	0736	3.8		0805	4.1
	1401	0.8		1437	0.2
	1955	3.8		2030	4.1
2 W	0220	0.9	17 TH	0259	0.3
	0812	3.7		0853	4.0
	1436	0.9		1525	0.3
	2031	3.8		2118	4.0
3 TH	0300	1.0	18 F	0348	0.5
	0851	3.7		0941	3.8
	1516	1.0		1616	0.5
	2111	3.7		2208	3.8
4 F	0343	1.0	19 SA	0440	0.7
	0933	3.6		1033	3.6
	1600	1.0		1710	0.7
	2155	3.6		2302	3.6
5 SA	0431	1.1	20 SU	0537	0.8
	1021	3.5		1130	3.5
	1651	1.1		1811	0.9
	2245	3.5			
6 SU	0527	1.2	21 M	0005	3.4
	1115	3.5		0642	1.0
	1751	1.2		1237	3.4
	2343	3.5		1920	1.0
7 M	0631	1.2	22 TU	0114	3.4
	1218	3.5		0752	1.0
	1857	1.2		1349	3.4
				2030	1.0
8 TU	0048	3.5	23 W	0221	3.4
	0736	1.1		0901	1.0
	1325	3.5		1454	3.5
	2003	1.1		2135	0.9
9 W	0154	3.6	24 TH	0321	3.5
	0839	1.0		1001	0.9
	1430	3.6		1550	3.6
	2105	0.9		2229	0.8
10 TH	0258	3.7	25 F	0412	3.7
	0939	0.8		1050	0.7
	1531	3.8		1638	3.8
	2204	0.6		2312	0.7
11 F	0357	3.9	26 SA	0456	3.8
	1035	0.6		1130	0.6
	1627	4.0		1719	3.9
	2258	0.4		2348	0.7
12 SA	0451	4.0	27 SU	0535	3.9
	1127	0.3		1203	0.6
	1719	4.2		1755	4.0
	2348	0.3			
13 SU	0542	4.1	28 M	0017	0.7
	1215	0.2		0609	3.9
	1808	4.3		1232	0.6
				1827	4.0
14 M	0036	0.2	29 TU	0046	0.7
	0630	4.2		0642	3.9
	1302	0.1		1300	0.7
	1855	4.3		1858	3.9
15 TU	0123	0.1	30 W	0116	0.7
	0718	4.1		0713	3.9
	1349	0.1		1330	0.7
	1942	4.2		1929	3.9
			31 TH	0150	0.8
				0745	3.8
				1404	0.8
				2001	3.9

AUGUST

Day	Time	m	Day	Time	m
1 F	0226	0.9	16 SA	0321	0.4
	0820	3.8		0912	3.8
	1442	0.9		1546	0.5
	2038	3.8		2136	3.8
2 SA	0305	1.0	17 SU	0408	0.7
	0859	3.7		0959	3.6
	1523	1.0		1636	0.7
	2118	3.8		2225	3.5
3 SU	0348	1.1	18 M	0501	0.9
	0942	3.6		1053	3.4
	1609	1.1		1733	1.0
	2205	3.6		2324	3.3
4 M	0438	1.2	19 TU	0604	1.1
	1034	3.6		1200	3.2
	1705	1.2		1841	1.2
	2301	3.5			
5 TU	0542	1.2	20 W	0038	3.2
	1136	3.5		0717	1.2
	1813	1.2		1321	3.2
				1959	1.2
6 W	0007	3.4	21 TH	0155	3.2
	0656	1.2		0834	1.1
	1247	3.5		1432	3.3
	1927	1.2		2111	1.1
7 TH	0121	3.5	22 F	0258	3.4
	0809	1.1		0940	1.0
	1401	3.6		1529	3.5
	2039	1.0		2207	0.9
8 F	0233	3.6	23 SA	0350	3.5
	0916	0.8		1030	0.8
	1510	3.8		1616	3.6
	2144	0.7		2251	0.8
9 SA	0338	3.8	24 SU	0434	3.8
	1016	0.5		1109	0.7
	1610	4.0		1657	3.9
	2242	0.4		2325	0.7
10 SU	0435	4.0	25 M	0513	3.9
	1109	0.3		1140	0.6
	1703	4.2		1732	4.0
	2332	0.2		2353	0.6
11 M	0526	4.2	26 TU	0547	3.9
	1158	0.1		1205	0.6
	1751	4.3		1804	4.0
12 TU	0019	0.1	27 W	0019	0.6
	0613	4.3		0617	3.9
	1244	0.0		1231	0.6
	1836	4.4		1832	4.0
13 W	0105	0.0	28 TH	0048	0.7
	0658	4.2		0646	3.9
	1329	0.0		1300	0.6
	1921	4.3		1900	4.0
14 TH	0150	0.1	29 F	0120	0.7
	0743	4.2		0717	3.9
	1415	0.1		1334	0.7
	2006	4.2		1931	3.9
15 F	0235	0.2	30 SA	0155	0.8
	0828	4.0		0749	3.9
	1500	0.3		1411	0.8
	2050	4.0		2006	3.9
			31 SU	0233	0.9
				0826	3.8
				1451	0.9
				2045	3.8

Chart Datum: 0·13 metres above Ordnance Datum (Dublin)
HAT is 4·5m above Chart Datum

TIME ZONE (UT)
For Summer Time add ONE hour in **non-shaded areas**

IRELAND – COBH
LAT 51°51′N   LONG 8°18′W
TIMES AND HEIGHTS OF HIGH AND LOW WATERS

Dates in amber are **SPRINGS**
Dates in yellow are **NEAPS**

2014

SEPTEMBER

Day	Time m	Time m	Time m	Time m
1 M	0315 1.0	0909 3.7	1537 1.0	2131 3.7
16 TU	0428 1.0	1016 3.4	1657 1.1	(2242 3.3
2 TU	0403 1.1	1000 3.6	1631 1.1	(2228 3.5
17 W	0528 1.2	1121 3.2	1803 1.3	2356 3.1
3 W	0506 1.2	1104 3.5	1740 1.3	2337 3.4
18 TH	0641 1.3	1249 3.1	1922 1.3	
4 TH	0624 1.3	1219 3.4	1900 1.2	
19 F	0123 3.1	0801 1.2	1405 3.3	2038 1.2
5 F	0055 3.4	0744 1.1	1341 3.5	2017 1.0
20 SA	0231 3.3	0909 1.1	1502 3.5	2136 1.0
6 SA	0214 3.6	0855 0.8	1453 3.8	2126 0.7
21 SU	0323 3.6	1000 0.9	1549 3.7	2220 0.8
7 SU	0321 3.8	0957 0.5	1553 4.0	2224 0.4
22 M	0407 3.8	1039 0.7	1629 3.9	2255 0.7
8 M	0418 4.1	1051 0.2	1645 4.3	2314 0.2
23 TU	0446 3.9	1110 0.6	1705 4.0	2323 0.6
9 TU	0507 4.2	1139 0.0	1732 4.4	O
24 W	0520 4.0	1136 0.6	1736 4.0	● 2351 0.6
10 W	0000 0.0	0553 4.3	1224 0.0	1815 4.4
25 TH	0551 4.0	1203 0.6	1804 4.0	
11 TH	0044 0.0	0636 4.3	1308 0.0	1858 4.3
26 F	0020 0.6	0620 4.0	1234 0.6	1832 4.0
12 F	0126 0.1	0718 4.2	1350 0.1	1939 4.2
27 SA	0054 0.7	0650 4.0	1308 0.7	1903 4.0
13 SA	0209 0.3	0800 4.0	1433 0.3	2021 4.0
28 SU	0130 0.7	0724 3.9	1346 0.7	1939 4.0
14 SU	0252 0.5	0842 3.8	1517 0.6	2103 3.8
29 M	0208 0.8	0802 3.9	1428 0.8	2020 3.9
15 M	0338 0.7	0926 3.6	1604 0.9	2148 3.5
30 TU	0252 0.9	0846 3.8	1515 1.0	2108 3.7

OCTOBER

Day	Time m	Time m	Time m	Time m
1 W	0343 1.1	0939 3.6	1611 1.1	(2206 3.5
16 TH	0453 1.3	1040 3.2	1725 1.4	2307 3.1
2 TH	0446 1.2	1043 3.5	1719 1.2	2316 3.4
17 F	0601 1.4	1202 3.1	1838 1.4	
3 F	0603 1.2	1201 3.4	1839 1.2	
18 SA	0035 3.1	0716 1.3	1325 3.2	1950 1.3
4 SA	0036 3.4	0723 1.1	1324 3.6	1958 1.0
19 SU	0152 3.3	0823 1.2	1426 3.4	2050 1.1
5 SU	0157 3.6	0837 0.8	1436 3.8	2108 0.7
20 M	0247 3.5	0916 1.0	1514 3.7	2138 1.0
6 M	0304 3.8	0939 0.5	1535 4.1	2205 0.4
21 TU	0333 3.7	0959 0.8	1556 3.9	2217 0.8
7 TU	0359 4.1	1032 0.3	1626 4.3	2255 0.2
22 W	0413 3.9	1034 0.7	1632 4.0	2251 0.7
8 W	0448 4.3	1120 0.1	1712 4.4	O 2340 0.1
23 TH	0449 4.0	1106 0.6	1705 4.1	2324 0.6
9 TH	0533 4.3	1204 0.1	1755 4.4	
24 F	0523 4.1	1138 0.6	1736 4.1	2357 0.6
10 F	0022 0.1	0615 4.3	1247 0.1	1835 4.3
25 SA	0555 4.1	1212 0.6	1808 4.1	
11 SA	0104 0.2	0655 4.2	1327 0.3	1914 4.2
26 SU	0033 0.6	0629 4.1	1250 0.6	1843 4.1
12 SU	0144 0.4	0734 4.1	1408 0.5	1952 4.0
27 M	0111 0.7	0706 4.0	1330 0.7	1922 4.0
13 M	0226 0.6	0814 3.9	1450 0.7	2031 3.8
28 TU	0153 0.8	0747 4.0	1414 0.8	2005 3.9
14 TU	0309 0.8	0856 3.6	1534 1.0	2114 3.5
29 W	0239 0.9	0834 3.9	1504 0.9	2055 3.8
15 W	0356 1.1	0942 3.4	1624 1.2	(2202 3.3
30 TH	0332 1.0	0929 3.7	1600 1.1	2154 3.6
31 F	0434 1.1	1032 3.6	1705 1.2	(2301 3.5

NOVEMBER

Day	Time m	Time m	Time m	Time m
1 SA	0546 1.2	1146 3.6	1821 1.2	
16 SU	0622 1.4	1220 3.3	1856 1.4	
2 SU	0018 3.5	0704 1.1	1305 3.6	1939 1.0
17 M	0048 3.3	0727 1.3	1332 3.4	1957 1.3
3 M	0136 3.6	0817 0.9	1415 3.8	2048 0.8
18 TU	0156 3.5	0824 1.2	1427 3.6	2050 1.1
4 TU	0243 3.8	0919 0.6	1514 4.0	2145 0.6
19 W	0248 3.7	0909 1.0	1514 3.8	2137 0.9
5 W	0339 4.0	1014 0.4	1605 4.2	2236 0.4
20 TH	0334 3.8	0957 0.9	1555 3.9	2219 0.8
6 TH	0429 4.2	1102 0.3	1652 4.3	O 2321 0.3
21 F	0416 4.0	1038 0.7	1634 4.0	2259 0.7
7 F	0514 4.3	1146 0.3	1735 4.3	
22 SA	0456 4.1	1118 0.7	1712 4.1	● 2338 0.6
8 SA	0003 0.4	0556 4.3	1228 0.4	1814 4.2
23 SU	0535 4.2	1157 0.6	1750 4.2	
9 SU	0043 0.4	0635 4.2	1313 0.5	1851 4.1
24 M	0018 0.6	0614 4.2	1238 0.6	1829 4.1
10 M	0122 0.5	0712 4.1	1346 0.7	1928 4.0
25 TU	0100 0.6	0655 4.2	1321 0.6	1912 4.1
11 TU	0201 0.7	0750 3.9	1425 0.9	2004 3.8
26 W	0144 0.6	0740 4.1	1407 0.7	1958 4.0
12 W	0241 0.9	0830 3.7	1505 1.1	2044 3.6
27 TH	0232 0.7	0829 4.0	1456 0.8	2048 3.9
13 TH	0324 1.1	0913 3.6	1551 1.2	2129 3.5
28 F	0324 0.8	0922 3.8	1550 0.9	2144 3.7
14 F	0414 1.3	1003 3.4	1645 1.4	(2222 3.3
29 SA	0422 0.9	1021 3.7	1656 1.0	(2246 3.6
15 SA	0515 1.4	1104 3.3	1749 1.5	2329 3.2
30 SU	0527 1.0	1127 3.7	1800 1.1	2355 3.6

DECEMBER

Day	Time m	Time m	Time m	Time m
1 M	0640 1.0	1238 3.7	1914 1.1	
16 TU	0627 1.4	1217 3.4	1902 1.4	
2 TU	0108 3.6	0752 0.9	1348 3.8	2023 0.9
17 W	0048 3.4	0730 1.3	1323 3.5	2002 1.3
3 W	0217 3.7	0857 0.8	1449 3.9	2124 0.8
18 TH	0154 3.6	0828 1.2	1423 3.7	2058 1.1
4 TH	0317 3.9	0955 0.7	1544 4.0	2217 0.6
19 F	0252 3.7	0922 1.0	1517 3.8	2149 0.9
5 F	0410 4.1	1046 0.6	1634 4.1	2304 0.6
20 SA	0344 3.9	1013 0.8	1606 4.0	2238 0.7
6 SA	0458 4.2	1131 0.5	1718 4.1	O 2346 0.5
21 SU	0432 4.1	1100 0.7	1652 4.1	2323 0.6
7 SU	0540 4.2	1212 0.6	1757 4.1	
22 M	0518 4.2	1145 0.7	1736 4.2	●
8 M	0025 0.6	0618 4.2	1249 0.6	1833 4.1
23 TU	0006 0.5	0602 4.3	1229 0.5	1819 4.2
9 TU	0102 0.6	0655 4.1	1325 0.8	1907 4.0
24 W	0050 0.4	0647 4.3	1313 0.5	1904 4.2
10 W	0137 0.8	0730 4.0	1400 0.9	1942 3.9
25 TH	0135 0.4	0732 4.3	1359 0.5	1950 4.1
11 TH	0213 0.9	0807 3.9	1437 1.0	2019 3.8
26 F	0222 0.5	0820 4.2	1446 0.6	2039 4.0
12 F	0248 1.1	0846 3.8	1517 1.2	2059 3.7
27 SA	0312 0.6	0911 4.1	1537 0.7	2129 3.9
13 SA	0334 1.2	0929 3.6	1603 1.3	2145 3.5
28 SU	0404 0.7	1003 3.9	1631 0.9	(2224 3.7
14 SU	0424 1.3	1017 3.5	1656 1.4	2237 3.4
29 M	0503 0.9	1101 3.8	1731 1.0	2325 3.6
15 M	0522 1.4	1113 3.5	1758 1.4	2339 3.4
30 TU	0609 1.0	1205 3.6	1841 1.1	
31 W	0033 3.5	0721 1.0	1315 3.6	1953 1.1

Chart Datum: 0·13 metres above Ordnance Datum (Dublin)
HAT is 4·5m above Chart Datum

TIDES

GALWAY

MEAN SPRING
AND NEAP CURVES

MEAN RANGES
Springs 4.3m
Neaps   1.9m

Factor

0·9 0·8 0·7 0·6 0·5 0·4 0·3 0·2 0·1

L.W. +5ʰ +4ʰ +3ʰ +2ʰ +1ʰ H.W. -1ʰ -2ʰ -3ʰ -4ʰ -5ʰ L.W.

M. H. W. S.

M. H. W. N.

M. L. W. N.

M. L. W. S.

H.W.Hts. m.

L.W.Hts. m.

CHART DATUM

IRELAND – GALWAY
LAT 53°16′N   LONG 9°03′W
TIMES AND HEIGHTS OF HIGH AND LOW WATERS

Dates in amber are **SPRINGS**
Dates in yellow are **NEAPS**

2014

JANUARY

Time	m	Time	m
1 0429	5.5	**16** 0516	5.0
1036	0.6	1104	1.1
W 1659	5.4	TH 1739	4.9
● 2255	0.7	○ 2315	1.2
2 0518	5.7	**17** 0552	5.1
1121	0.4	1137	1.0
TH 1748	5.5	F 1815	4.9
2340	0.6	2349	1.1
3 0606	5.8	**18** 0628	5.1
1206	0.4	1211	1.0
F 1836	5.5	SA 1850	4.9
4 0025	0.7	**19** 0022	1.2
0654	5.7	0700	5.0
SA 1252	0.5	SU 1245	1.0
1924	5.4	1923	4.8
5 0111	0.8	**20** 0056	1.2
0742	5.5	0731	4.9
SU 1338	0.6	M 1319	1.1
2013	5.2	1956	4.7
6 0200	1.1	**21** 0131	1.3
0832	5.3	0801	4.8
M 1428	0.9	TU 1355	1.2
2104	4.9	2030	4.6
7 0253	1.4	**22** 0210	1.5
0924	4.9	0838	4.6
TU 1522	1.3	W 1435	1.4
2158	4.6	2111	4.4
8 0353	1.6	**23** 0254	1.6
1021	4.6	0926	4.4
W 1624	1.6	TH 1521	1.6
◑ 2300	4.3	2202	4.3
9 0505	1.9	**24** 0345	1.8
1129	4.3	1023	4.3
TH 1735	1.9	F 1614	1.8
		◐ 2300	4.2
10 0016	4.2	**25** 0444	2.0
0619	2.0	1127	4.2
F 1253	4.1	SA 1718	1.9
1846	2.0		
11 0133	4.2	**26** 0005	4.2
0730	1.9	0600	2.0
SA 1403	4.2	SU 1238	4.2
1951	1.9	1849	1.9
12 0233	4.3	**27** 0117	4.4
0832	1.6	0749	1.8
SU 1459	4.3	M 1355	4.4
2045	1.8	2021	1.6
13 0322	4.5	**28** 0227	4.7
0921	1.6	0852	1.4
M 1545	4.5	TU 1502	4.7
2128	1.7	2115	1.3
14 0403	4.7	**29** 0325	5.1
0959	1.4	0942	0.9
TU 1626	4.6	W 1557	5.1
2205	1.5	2202	0.9
15 0440	4.9	**30** 0417	5.5
1031	1.2	1027	0.6
W 1703	4.8	TH 1646	5.4
2240	1.3	● 2246	0.6
		31 0505	5.7
		1110	0.3
		F 1733	5.6
		2328	0.5

FEBRUARY

Time	m	Time	m
1 0552	5.9	**16** 0607	5.1
1152	0.2	1148	0.8
SA 1819	5.6	SU 1827	5.0
2 0010	0.5	**17** 0000	0.9
0637	5.8	0638	5.1
SU 1234	0.3	M 1220	0.8
1904	5.5	1857	5.0
3 0052	0.6	**18** 0033	0.9
0722	5.7	0705	5.0
M 1315	0.5	TU 1253	0.8
1948	5.3	1926	4.9
4 0135	0.8	**19** 0108	1.0
0807	5.4	0733	4.9
TU 1359	0.8	W 1329	0.9
2034	5.0	1957	4.8
5 0221	1.2	**20** 0146	1.1
0854	5.0	0809	4.7
W 1446	1.2	TH 1409	1.1
2120	4.7	2037	4.6
6 0314	1.5	**21** 0229	1.3
0943	4.6	0855	4.5
TH 1541	1.6	F 1453	1.4
◑ 2210	4.3	2126	4.4
7 0423	1.9	**22** 0317	1.6
1038	4.2	0952	4.3
F 1653	2.0	SA 1544	1.7
2308	4.1	◐ 2226	4.2
8 0541	2.1	**23** 0414	1.8
1159	3.9	1058	4.1
SA 1809	2.1	SU 1647	1.9
		2334	4.1
9 0055	4.0	**24** 0528	1.9
0652	2.1	1214	4.0
SU 1341	3.9	M 1817	2.0
1915	2.1		
10 0213	4.1	**25** 0053	4.2
0757	1.9	0735	1.7
M 1443	4.1	TU 1341	4.2
2014	2.0	2011	1.7
11 0306	4.3	**26** 0213	4.5
0852	1.7	0843	1.3
TU 1530	4.3	W 1452	4.6
2103	1.8	2106	1.3
12 0348	4.5	**27** 0314	5.0
0934	1.5	0932	0.8
W 1610	4.5	TH 1545	5.0
2144	1.5	2151	0.9
13 0425	4.7	**28** 0404	5.4
1010	1.2	1015	0.5
TH 1645	4.7	F 1632	5.4
2221	1.3	2232	0.5
14 0500	4.9		
1044	1.0		
F 1720	4.9		
○ 2256	1.1		
15 0534	5.0		
1116	0.9		
SA 1754	5.0		
2328	1.0		

MARCH

Time	m	Time	m
1 0450	5.7	**16** 0509	4.9
1055	0.2	1051	0.8
SA 1716	5.6	SU 1726	4.9
● 2312	0.4	○ 2304	0.8
2 0535	5.8	**17** 0541	5.0
1133	0.2	1121	0.7
SU 1759	5.6	M 1758	5.0
2350	0.3	2335	0.7
3 0618	5.8	**18** 0612	5.0
1210	0.2	1152	0.6
M 1841	5.5	TU 1828	5.0
4 0028	0.4	**19** 0008	0.7
0700	5.6	0640	5.0
TU 1248	0.5	W 1227	0.6
1921	5.3	1858	5.0
5 0108	0.7	**20** 0045	0.7
0742	5.3	0711	4.9
W 1327	0.8	TH 1304	0.8
2003	5.0	1931	4.9
6 0150	1.0	**21** 0125	0.8
0825	4.9	0750	4.8
TH 1410	1.2	F 1345	1.0
2045	4.7	2012	4.7
7 0237	1.4	**22** 0208	1.0
0911	4.5	0836	4.5
F 1459	1.6	SA 1430	1.3
2131	4.4	2102	4.5
8 0340	1.8	**23** 0257	1.3
1000	4.1	0933	4.3
SA 1610	2.0	SU 1523	1.6
◑ 2222	4.1	2201	4.2
9 0505	2.0	**24** 0356	1.6
1058	3.8	1041	4.0
SU 1735	2.2	M 1628	1.9
2322	3.8	◐ 2312	4.1
10 0617	2.1	**25** 0511	1.7
1311	3.7	1200	4.0
M 1843	2.2	TU 1801	1.9
11 0146	3.8	**26** 0035	4.1
0720	2.0	0721	1.6
TU 1421	3.9	W 1330	4.1
1942	2.0	1958	1.6
12 0243	4.1	**27** 0158	4.4
0816	1.7	0830	1.2
W 1508	4.1	TH 1438	4.5
2034	1.8	2052	1.2
13 0326	4.3	**28** 0258	4.8
0902	1.5	0917	0.8
TH 1547	4.4	F 1530	4.9
2118	1.5	2136	0.8
14 0402	4.6	**29** 0348	5.2
0942	1.2	0958	0.5
F 1622	4.6	SA 1614	5.3
2157	1.2	2215	0.5
15 0436	4.8	**30** 0433	5.5
1018	0.9	1035	0.3
SA 1654	4.8	SU 1657	5.4
2232	1.0	● 2252	0.4
		31 0516	5.6
		1110	0.3
		M 1737	5.5
		2328	0.3

APRIL

Time	m	Time	m
1 0557	5.5	**16** 0543	5.0
1145	0.4	1126	0.6
TU 1817	5.4	W 1759	5.1
		2345	0.5
2 0004	0.5	**17** 0617	5.0
0637	5.4	1202	0.6
W 1221	0.6	TH 1834	5.1
1855	5.3		
3 0043	0.7	**18** 0024	0.5
0718	5.1	0655	5.0
TH 1258	0.9	F 1243	0.7
1935	5.0	1913	5.0
4 0123	1.0	**19** 0107	0.7
0800	4.8	0736	4.8
F 1339	1.3	SA 1326	0.9
2016	4.7	1957	4.8
5 0208	1.3	**20** 0153	0.9
0844	4.5	0827	4.6
SA 1424	1.6	SU 1414	1.2
2101	4.4	2048	4.6
6 0302	1.7	**21** 0245	1.1
0931	4.1	0925	4.3
SU 1524	2.0	M 1510	1.5
2149	4.1	2148	4.4
7 0426	1.9	**22** 0345	1.4
1024	3.9	1030	4.1
M 1700	2.2	TU 1618	1.8
◑ 2243	3.9	◐ 2257	4.2
8 0541	2.0	**23** 0458	1.5
1126	3.7	1148	4.0
TU 1810	2.2	W 1746	1.8
2349	3.7		
9 0644	1.9	**24** 0018	4.2
1343	3.8	0646	1.5
W 1910	2.1	TH 1312	4.2
		1934	1.6
10 0205	3.9	**25** 0138	4.4
0740	1.7	0806	1.2
TH 1435	4.0	F 1418	4.5
2002	1.8	2032	1.2
11 0252	4.1	**26** 0238	4.7
0829	1.5	0856	0.9
F 1515	4.3	SA 1509	4.8
2048	1.5	2117	0.9
12 0331	4.3	**27** 0328	5.0
0912	1.2	0937	0.7
SA 1549	4.5	SU 1554	5.1
2129	1.2	2157	0.7
13 0405	4.6	**28** 0414	5.1
0949	1.0	1014	0.6
SU 1621	4.7	M 1635	5.2
2205	1.0	2233	0.6
14 0437	4.8	**29** 0456	5.2
1023	0.8	1047	0.6
M 1653	4.9	TU 1715	5.3
2237	0.8	● 2308	0.5
15 0510	4.9	**30** 0538	5.2
1053	0.7	1120	0.7
TU 1725	5.0	W 1754	5.2
○ 2309	0.6	2343	0.6

Chart Datum: 0·20 metres above Ordnance Datum (Dublin)
HAT is 5·9m above Chart Datum

TIDES

IRELAND – GALWAY
LAT 53°16′N   LONG 9°03′W
TIMES AND HEIGHTS OF HIGH AND LOW WATERS

Dates in amber are **SPRINGS**
Dates in yellow are **NEAPS**

2014

MAY

Day	Time m	Time m	Time m	Time m
1 TH	0618 5.1	1156 0.8	1832 5.1	
16 F	0557 5.1	1142 0.6	1815 5.2	
2 F	0020 0.8	0657 4.9	1234 1.0	1911 5.0
17 SA	0007 0.5	0642 5.0	1226 0.7	1859 5.2
3 SA	0101 1.0	0738 4.7	1314 1.3	1951 4.7
18 SU	0053 0.5	0729 4.9	1313 0.9	1947 5.0
4 SU	0143 1.2	0820 4.5	1356 1.6	2035 4.5
19 M	0142 0.7	0820 4.7	1404 1.1	2039 4.8
5 M	0231 1.5	0906 4.2	1444 1.9	2121 4.2
20 TU	0235 0.9	0916 4.5	1501 1.4	2137 4.6
6 TU	0332 1.8	0955 4.0	1602 2.1	2211 4.0
21 W	0334 1.2	1018 4.3	1606 1.6	2242 4.4
7 W	0456 1.9	1049 3.8	1730 2.2	2307 3.8
22 TH	0442 1.3	1129 4.2	1724 1.7	2356 4.3
8 TH	0603 1.9	1151 3.8	1833 2.1	
23 F	0603 1.4	1246 4.3	1855 1.6	
9 F	0012 3.8	0701 1.8	1331 3.9	1927 1.9
24 SA	0112 4.3	0729 1.3	1352 4.4	2004 1.4
10 SA	0154 3.9	0753 1.6	1426 4.1	2016 1.7
25 SU	0215 4.5	0829 1.2	1446 4.7	2055 1.2
11 SU	0244 4.2	0838 1.4	1504 4.4	2058 1.4
26 M	0308 4.7	0915 1.1	1533 4.9	2139 1.0
12 M	0322 4.6	0918 1.1	1539 4.7	2136 1.1
27 TU	0355 4.8	0953 1.0	1615 5.0	2217 0.9
13 TU	0359 4.7	0952 0.9	1615 4.9	2210 0.9
28 W	0439 4.9	1027 1.0	1655 5.1	2251 0.8
14 W	0436 4.9	1026 0.8	1652 5.1	2245 0.7
29 TH	0520 4.9	1100 1.0	1734 5.1	2325 0.8
15 TH	0515 5.0	1102 0.7	1732 5.2	2324 0.5
30 F	0600 4.9	1136 1.1	1812 5.0	
31 SA	0002 0.9	0639 4.8	1214 1.2	1850 4.9

JUNE

Day	Time m	Time m	Time m	Time m
1 SU	0041 1.0	0718 4.7	1253 1.3	1930 4.8
16 M	0041 0.4	0717 5.1	1302 0.8	1935 5.3
2 M	0121 1.2	0758 4.5	1332 1.5	2011 4.6
17 TU	0131 0.5	0808 5.0	1352 1.0	2026 5.1
3 TU	0202 1.4	0840 4.4	1412 1.7	2053 4.4
18 W	0222 0.7	0901 4.8	1446 1.2	2121 4.8
4 W	0245 1.6	0925 4.2	1455 1.9	2139 4.2
19 TH	0317 1.0	0959 4.6	1547 1.4	2221 4.6
5 TH	0334 1.8	1013 4.0	1551 2.1	2228 4.0
20 F	0419 1.3	1103 4.4	1657 1.6	2329 4.4
6 F	0442 1.9	1105 4.0	1732 2.2	2322 3.9
21 SA	0528 1.4	1215 4.3	1815 1.7	
7 SA	0608 1.9	1202 4.0	1843 2.1	
22 SU	0044 4.3	0645 1.5	1325 4.3	1931 1.6
8 SU	0021 4.0	0709 1.8	1305 4.1	1937 1.8
23 M	0153 4.4	0756 1.5	1424 4.5	2032 1.5
9 M	0127 4.1	0800 1.6	1405 4.3	2024 1.6
24 TU	0250 4.4	0851 1.4	1514 4.6	2122 1.3
10 TU	0229 4.3	0844 1.4	1455 4.6	2106 1.3
25 W	0339 4.5	0935 1.4	1559 4.8	2203 1.2
11 W	0319 4.6	0924 1.1	1540 4.9	2146 1.0
26 TH	0424 4.7	1010 1.3	1639 4.9	2237 1.1
12 TH	0406 4.9	1003 0.9	1625 5.2	2227 0.7
27 F	0505 4.7	1044 1.2	1718 5.0	2309 1.0
13 F	0453 5.1	1044 0.8	1711 5.3	2310 0.5
28 SA	0544 4.8	1118 1.2	1756 5.0	2343 1.0
14 SA	0540 5.2	1128 0.7	1758 5.4	2355 0.4
29 SU	0622 4.8	1154 1.2	1833 4.9	
15 SU	0628 5.2	1214 0.7	1846 5.4	
30 M	0020 1.0	0659 4.8	1231 1.2	1910 4.9

JULY

Day	Time m	Time m	Time m	Time m
1 TU	0057 1.1	0736 4.7	1307 1.4	1947 4.7
16 W	0115 0.4	0749 5.2	1335 0.8	2008 5.3
2 W	0133 1.2	0814 4.5	1343 1.5	2024 4.5
17 TH	0203 0.6	0839 5.0	1425 1.0	2059 5.0
3 TH	0210 1.4	0853 4.4	1421 1.7	2104 4.4
18 F	0254 0.9	0931 4.7	1521 1.3	2154 4.7
4 F	0250 1.5	0936 4.2	1505 1.8	2148 4.2
19 SA	0351 1.3	1029 4.4	1627 1.6	2257 4.4
5 SA	0336 1.7	1024 4.1	1557 2.0	2239 4.1
20 SU	0456 1.6	1138 4.2	1742 1.8	
6 SU	0428 1.8	1117 4.1	1658 2.0	2336 4.0
21 M	0609 1.8	1258 4.2	1857 1.8	
7 M	0533 1.9	1215 4.1	1825 2.0	
22 TU	0132 4.1	0722 1.8	1406 4.2	2007 1.7
8 TU	0038 4.0	0706 1.8	1317 4.3	1948 1.7
23 W	0235 4.2	0824 1.8	1500 4.4	2103 1.5
9 W	0145 4.3	0813 1.6	1419 4.6	2042 1.4
24 TH	0326 4.3	0914 1.6	1545 4.6	2146 1.3
10 TH	0249 4.5	0904 1.3	1514 4.9	2130 1.0
25 F	0410 4.5	0952 1.4	1626 4.8	2219 1.2
11 F	0344 4.8	0949 1.0	1605 5.2	2215 0.7
26 SA	0449 4.6	1026 1.3	1703 4.9	2250 1.0
12 SA	0435 5.1	1033 0.8	1654 5.5	2259 0.4
27 SU	0526 4.8	1100 1.2	1739 5.0	2323 0.9
13 SU	0524 5.3	1117 0.6	1742 5.6	2344 0.3
28 M	0602 4.8	1134 1.1	1815 5.0	2356 0.9
14 M	0613 5.4	1202 0.5	1831 5.7	
29 TU	0637 4.8	1208 1.1	1849 4.9	
15 TU	0029 0.3	0700 5.4	1248 0.6	1919 5.6
30 W	0030 0.9	0711 4.8	1242 1.1	1922 4.8
31 TH	0105 1.0	0744 4.7	1316 1.2	1952 4.7

AUGUST

Day	Time m	Time m	Time m	Time m
1 F	0140 1.1	0818 4.5	1353 1.4	2026 4.5
16 SA	0224 1.0	0859 4.8	1451 1.3	2123 4.7
2 SA	0218 1.3	0856 4.4	1434 1.6	2108 4.4
17 SU	0318 1.4	0950 4.4	1555 1.6	2220 4.3
3 SU	0301 1.5	0942 4.3	1521 1.7	2200 4.2
18 M	0425 1.7	1049 4.1	1713 1.9	2337 4.0
4 M	0350 1.7	1037 4.1	1617 1.9	2300 4.1
19 TU	0540 2.0	1227 4.0	1827 1.9	
5 TU	0447 1.9	1137 4.1	1724 2.0	
20 W	0114 3.9	0650 2.0	1349 4.1	1935 1.9
6 W	0005 4.0	0601 1.9	1244 4.2	1914 1.8
21 TH	0221 4.0	0754 1.9	1445 4.2	2036 1.7
7 TH	0117 4.2	0751 1.7	1353 4.5	2026 1.4
22 F	0312 4.2	0846 1.7	1530 4.5	2119 1.4
8 F	0229 4.5	0850 1.4	1456 4.9	2118 1.0
23 SA	0354 4.4	0928 1.5	1609 4.7	2154 1.2
9 SA	0329 4.8	0938 1.0	1550 5.3	2204 0.6
24 SU	0431 4.6	1004 1.3	1644 4.8	2226 1.0
10 SU	0420 5.2	1022 0.7	1639 5.6	2247 0.3
25 M	0505 4.8	1038 1.1	1719 4.9	2259 0.8
11 M	0508 5.4	1105 0.4	1726 5.8	2329 0.1
26 TU	0539 4.9	1111 1.0	1752 5.0	2331 0.8
12 TU	0555 5.5	1146 0.4	1813 5.8	
27 W	0612 4.9	1143 0.9	1825 5.0	
13 W	0011 0.1	0640 5.4	1229 0.4	1859 5.7
28 TH	0003 0.8	0643 4.9	1216 0.9	1854 4.9
14 TH	0054 0.3	0725 5.4	1313 0.6	1945 5.4
29 F	0036 0.8	0713 4.8	1250 1.0	1920 4.8
15 F	0137 0.6	0811 5.1	1359 0.9	2033 5.1
30 SA	0111 0.9	0743 4.7	1327 1.1	1952 4.6
31 SU	0149 1.1	0819 4.5	1408 1.3	2034 4.4

Chart Datum: 0·20 metres above Ordnance Datum (Dublin)
HAT is 5·9m above Chart Datum

IRELAND – GALWAY
LAT 53°16'N   LONG 9°03'W
TIMES AND HEIGHTS OF HIGH AND LOW WATERS

Dates in amber are **SPRINGS**
Dates in yellow are **NEAPS**

2014

SEPTEMBER

Day	Time m	Time m	Time m	Time m		Day	Time m	Time m	Time m	Time m
1 M	0232 1.4	0905 4.4	1454 1.5	2128 4.2		16 TU	0351 1.9	1005 4.1	1644 1.9	2246 3.9
2 TU	0320 1.6	1002 4.2	1548 1.8	2231 4.0		17 W	0512 2.1	1109 3.9	1757 2.0	
3 W	0417 1.9	1106 4.1	1655 1.9	2341 4.0		18 TH	0052 3.7	0620 2.2	1325 3.9	1900 1.9
4 TH	0533 2.0	1217 4.1	1853 1.8			19 F	0201 3.9	0721 2.0	1423 4.1	1958 1.7
5 F	0059 4.1	0738 1.8	1335 4.4	2014 1.4		20 SA	0251 4.1	0815 1.8	1508 4.3	2044 1.5
6 SA	0219 4.4	0838 1.4	1443 4.8	2105 0.9		21 SU	0331 4.3	0859 1.5	1546 4.6	2124 1.2
7 SU	0317 4.8	0925 0.9	1536 5.2	2149 0.5		22 M	0407 4.6	0938 1.3	1620 4.7	2159 1.0
8 M	0406 5.2	1007 0.6	1623 5.6	2230 0.2		23 TU	0439 4.7	1014 1.0	1653 4.9	2233 0.8
9 TU	0451 5.5	1048 0.3	1708 5.8	2310 0.1		24 W	0511 4.9	1047 0.9	1726 5.0	2304 0.7
10 W	0534 5.6	1127 0.3	1753 5.8	2348 0.1		25 TH	0543 4.9	1118 0.8	1757 5.0	2335 0.7
11 TH	0617 5.6	1207 0.3	1837 5.6			26 F	0614 5.0	1150 0.8	1827 4.9	
12 F	0027 0.3	0659 5.4	1248 0.6	1921 5.4		27 SA	0008 0.7	0642 4.9	1225 0.8	1854 4.8
13 SA	0109 0.6	0742 5.1	1331 0.9	2006 4.9		28 SU	0045 0.8	0713 4.8	1304 0.9	1928 4.7
14 SU	0153 1.0	0826 4.8	1420 1.3	2053 4.6		29 M	0124 1.0	0751 4.7	1345 1.1	2012 4.5
15 M	0243 1.5	0913 4.4	1522 1.7	2145 4.2		30 TU	0207 1.3	0838 4.5	1432 1.4	2106 4.2

OCTOBER

Day	Time m	Time m	Time m	Time m		Day	Time m	Time m	Time m	Time m
1 W	0257 1.6	0935 4.3	1528 1.6	2211 4.0		16 TH	0438 2.2	1027 4.0	1722 2.0	2319 3.7
2 TH	0357 1.9	1042 4.1	1637 1.8	2323 3.9		17 F	0548 2.2	1138 3.8	1825 1.9	
3 F	0517 2.0	1156 4.1	1830 1.7			18 SA	0126 3.8	0648 2.1	1348 4.0	1920 1.8
4 SA	0047 4.0	0723 1.8	1319 4.4	1959 1.3		19 SU	0220 4.0	0742 1.9	1436 4.2	2009 1.5
5 SU	0207 4.4	0823 1.4	1427 4.8	2049 0.9		20 M	0301 4.3	0829 1.6	1515 4.4	2052 1.3
6 M	0302 4.8	0909 0.9	1520 5.2	2131 0.5		21 TU	0336 4.5	0911 1.4	1550 4.6	2131 1.1
7 TU	0349 5.2	0950 0.6	1606 5.6	2210 0.3		22 W	0408 4.7	0948 1.1	1623 4.8	2206 0.9
8 W	0432 5.4	1029 0.4	1650 5.6	2247 0.2		23 TH	0439 4.9	1022 0.9	1655 4.9	2237 0.8
9 TH	0513 5.5	1106 0.3	1733 5.6	2324 0.3		24 F	0511 5.0	1053 0.8	1728 5.0	2309 0.7
10 F	0554 5.5	1144 0.4	1816 5.5			25 SA	0543 5.1	1126 0.7	1801 5.0	2343 0.7
11 SA	0001 0.5	0634 5.4	1224 0.6	1858 5.2		26 SU	0616 5.1	1203 0.7	1836 4.9	
12 SU	0041 0.8	0715 5.1	1306 0.9	1941 4.9		27 M	0022 0.8	0652 5.0	1245 0.8	1915 4.8
13 M	0123 1.2	0758 4.8	1352 1.3	2026 4.5		28 TU	0104 1.0	0733 4.9	1329 1.0	2001 4.6
14 TU	0211 1.6	0843 4.5	1449 1.6	2115 4.2		29 W	0150 1.3	0821 4.7	1418 1.2	2055 4.4
15 W	0313 2.0	0932 4.2	1609 1.9	2209 3.9		30 TH	0242 1.6	0918 4.5	1515 1.4	2158 4.2
						31 F	0344 1.8	1023 4.3	1623 1.6	2308 4.1

NOVEMBER

Day	Time m	Time m	Time m	Time m		Day	Time m	Time m	Time m	Time m
1 SA	0502 1.9	1136 4.2	1754 1.6			16 SU	0611 2.2	1157 3.9	1842 1.9	
2 SU	0031 4.1	0652 1.8	1259 4.4	1933 1.3		17 M	0123 3.9	0707 2.1	1343 4.0	1934 1.7
3 M	0147 4.4	0802 1.4	1407 4.7	2027 1.0		18 TU	0216 4.2	0757 1.8	1433 4.2	2020 1.5
4 TU	0242 4.8	0850 1.1	1501 5.0	2111 0.8		19 W	0255 4.4	0842 1.6	1512 4.5	2102 1.3
5 W	0329 5.1	0932 0.8	1548 5.2	2150 0.6		20 TH	0330 4.7	0922 1.3	1548 4.7	2139 1.1
6 TH	0412 5.3	1011 0.6	1632 5.4	2227 0.6		21 F	0404 4.9	0957 1.1	1623 4.9	2212 1.0
7 F	0453 5.4	1048 0.6	1715 5.4	2302 0.6		22 SA	0439 5.1	1031 0.9	1700 5.0	2246 0.9
8 SA	0533 5.4	1126 0.6	1755 5.3	2339 0.8		23 SU	0516 5.2	1107 0.8	1739 5.1	2323 0.8
9 SU	0613 5.3	1204 0.8	1839 5.1			24 M	0555 5.3	1147 0.7	1821 5.1	
10 M	0017 1.0	0652 5.1	1245 1.0	1920 4.9		25 TU	0005 0.9	0636 5.2	1230 0.7	1905 5.0
11 TU	0059 1.3	0733 4.9	1328 1.3	2003 4.6		26 W	0049 1.0	0721 5.1	1316 0.8	1953 4.8
12 W	0143 1.6	0817 4.6	1417 1.6	2049 4.3		27 TH	0137 1.2	0810 5.0	1406 1.0	2045 4.6
13 TH	0234 1.9	0903 4.4	1519 1.8	2138 4.1		28 F	0230 1.4	0904 4.7	1502 1.2	2143 4.4
14 F	0346 2.2	0953 4.1	1637 2.0	2232 3.9		29 SA	0331 1.6	1005 4.5	1605 1.4	2249 4.3
15 SA	0507 2.3	1049 4.0	1744 2.0	2337 3.8		30 SU	0441 1.8	1114 4.4	1719 1.5	

DECEMBER

Day	Time m	Time m	Time m	Time m		Day	Time m	Time m	Time m	Time m
1 M	0005 4.3	0605 1.8	1233 4.4	1850 1.5		16 TU	0625 2.2	1204 4.0	1854 2.0	
2 TU	0119 4.4	0732 1.6	1344 4.5	2000 1.3		17 W	0048 4.1	0722 2.1	1315 4.1	1947 1.8
3 W	0219 4.7	0830 1.3	1441 4.8	2050 1.2		18 TH	0154 4.3	0812 1.8	1420 4.3	2033 1.6
4 TH	0309 4.9	0917 1.1	1531 4.9	2133 1.1		19 F	0245 4.5	0856 1.6	1509 4.6	2115 1.4
5 F	0354 5.1	0959 1.0	1617 5.1	2211 1.0		20 SA	0328 4.8	0936 1.3	1553 4.8	2153 1.2
6 SA	0437 5.2	1036 0.9	1700 5.1	2246 1.0		21 SU	0410 5.1	1015 1.0	1636 5.0	2230 1.0
7 SU	0517 5.3	1112 0.9	1742 5.1	2322 1.1		22 M	0453 5.3	1054 0.8	1721 5.2	2310 0.8
8 M	0556 5.2	1148 0.9	1823 5.0	2359 1.2		23 TU	0538 5.4	1135 0.6	1806 5.3	2353 0.8
9 TU	0635 5.1	1226 1.0	1902 4.9			24 W	0623 5.5	1219 0.6	1852 5.2	
10 W	0038 1.3	0713 5.0	1306 1.2	1942 4.7		25 TH	0038 0.8	0709 5.4	1305 0.6	1940 5.1
11 TH	0119 1.5	0754 4.8	1347 1.4	2024 4.6		26 F	0125 1.0	0757 5.3	1353 0.8	2030 5.0
12 F	0200 1.7	0836 4.6	1431 1.6	2108 4.4		27 SA	0216 1.2	0849 5.1	1445 1.0	2124 4.7
13 SA	0244 2.0	0922 4.4	1521 1.8	2155 4.2		28 SU	0311 1.4	0945 4.8	1542 1.3	2223 4.5
14 SU	0339 2.2	1011 4.2	1631 2.0	2247 4.1		29 M	0414 1.6	1048 4.5	1647 1.5	2332 4.4
15 M	0512 2.3	1105 4.0	1752 2.1	2343 4.0		30 TU	0528 1.8	1202 4.4	1804 1.7	
						31 W	0048 4.3	0654 1.8	1319 4.4	1927 1.7

TIDES

Chart Datum: 0·20 metres above Ordnance Datum (Dublin)
HAT is 5·9m above Chart Datum

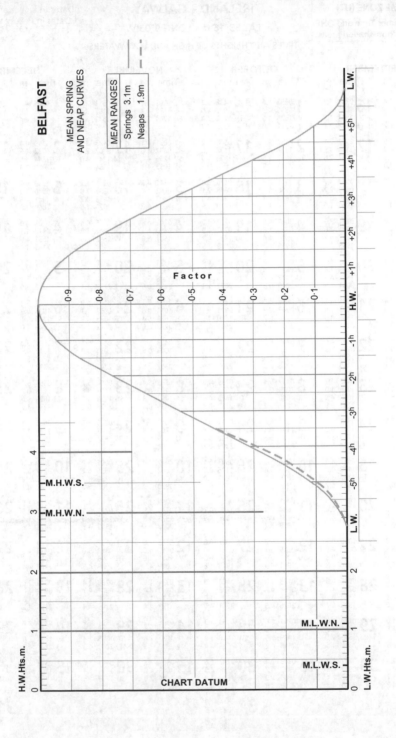

BELFAST

MEAN SPRING
AND NEAP CURVES

MEAN RANGES	
Springs	3.1m
Neaps	1.9m

Factor

CHART DATUM

NORTHERN IRELAND – BELFAST

LAT 54°36′N   LONG 5°55′W

TIMES AND HEIGHTS OF HIGH AND LOW WATERS

2014

JANUARY

Day	Time m		Day	Time m	
1 W ●	0413 0.5 / 1033 3.7 / 1650 0.4 / 2300 3.6		**16** TH ○	0459 0.8 / 1127 3.6 / 1720 0.7 / 2348 3.2	
2 TH	0500 0.5 / 1121 3.8 / 1736 0.3 / 2350 3.6		**17** F	0532 0.8 / 1200 3.6 / 1752 0.6	
3 F	0547 0.5 / 1211 3.9 / 1823 0.3		**18** SA	0018 3.2 / 0605 0.8 / 1231 3.6 / 1824 0.6	
4 SA	0042 3.6 / 0634 0.5 / 1302 3.9 / 1911 0.3		**19** SU	0043 3.2 / 0639 0.7 / 1258 3.6 / 1857 0.6	
5 SU	0136 3.5 / 0724 0.6 / 1353 3.9 / 2002 0.3		**20** M	0108 3.2 / 0714 0.8 / 1328 3.6 / 1932 0.6	
6 M	0229 3.4 / 0815 0.7 / 1445 3.8 / 2056 0.4		**21** TU	0142 3.2 / 0751 0.8 / 1404 3.5 / 2010 0.6	
7 TU	0323 3.4 / 0908 0.8 / 1538 3.6 / 2155 0.6		**22** W	0222 3.2 / 0831 0.8 / 1445 3.5 / 2052 0.7	
8 W ◐	0419 3.3 / 1007 0.9 / 1634 3.5 / 2300 0.7		**23** TH	0306 3.1 / 0916 0.9 / 1532 3.4 / 2140 0.8	
9 TH	0517 3.2 / 1113 1.0 / 1737 3.3		**24** F ◑	0358 3.1 / 1008 1.0 / 1627 3.3 / 2236 0.9	
10 F	0005 0.9 / 0622 3.1 / 1223 1.1 / 1851 3.2		**25** SA	0500 3.0 / 1111 1.1 / 1734 3.2 / 2342 1.0	
11 SA	0108 0.9 / 0729 3.1 / 1331 1.1 / 2002 3.1		**26** SU	0612 3.0 / 1237 1.1 / 1848 3.1	
12 SU	0207 1.0 / 0830 3.2 / 1434 1.0 / 2102 3.1		**27** M	0105 0.9 / 0724 3.1 / 1400 0.9 / 1957 3.2	
13 M	0301 0.9 / 0923 3.3 / 1529 0.9 / 2152 3.2		**28** TU	0218 0.8 / 0830 3.2 / 1500 0.7 / 2101 3.3	
14 TU	0347 0.9 / 1009 3.5 / 1612 0.8 / 2235 3.2		**29** W	0314 0.7 / 0928 3.4 / 1552 0.5 / 2156 3.5	
15 W	0425 0.8 / 1050 3.6 / 1647 0.7 / 2314 3.2		**30** TH ●	0403 0.5 / 1019 3.6 / 1640 0.3 / 2246 3.5	
			31 F	0449 0.4 / 1107 3.8 / 1725 0.1 / 2335 3.6	

FEBRUARY

Day	Time m		Day	Time m	
1 SA	0534 0.4 / 1156 3.8 / 1810 0.1		**16** SU	0542 0.6 / 1205 3.5 / 1800 0.5	
2 SU	0025 3.5 / 0618 0.4 / 1245 3.9 / 1855 0.1		**17** M	0012 3.2 / 0615 0.6 / 1226 3.5 / 1832 0.5	
3 M	0115 3.5 / 0704 0.4 / 1334 3.8 / 1941 0.2		**18** TU	0034 3.2 / 0649 0.6 / 1257 3.5 / 1905 0.5	
4 TU	0205 3.4 / 0750 0.5 / 1423 3.7 / 2028 0.4		**19** W	0110 3.2 / 0723 0.6 / 1335 3.5 / 1941 0.5	
5 W	0253 3.4 / 0839 0.6 / 1511 3.6 / 2119 0.6		**20** TH	0150 3.2 / 0801 0.6 / 1417 3.5 / 2021 0.5	
6 TH ◑	0341 3.3 / 0931 0.7 / 1600 3.4 / 2219 0.8		**21** F	0234 3.2 / 0844 0.7 / 1504 3.4 / 2108 0.6	
7 F	0431 3.2 / 1033 0.9 / 1653 3.2 / 2326 0.9		**22** SA ◐	0322 3.1 / 0935 0.8 / 1559 3.2 / 2202 0.8	
8 SA	0527 3.0 / 1147 1.0 / 1758 3.0		**23** SU	0421 3.0 / 1037 1.0 / 1707 3.1 / 2307 1.0	
9 SU	0032 1.1 / 0641 3.0 / 1259 1.1 / 1936 2.9		**24** M	0536 2.9 / 1210 1.0 / 1823 3.0	
10 M	0136 1.1 / 0803 3.0 / 1405 1.0 / 2043 2.9		**25** TU	0041 1.0 / 0656 3.0 / 1344 0.8 / 1939 3.0	
11 TU	0234 1.0 / 0901 3.2 / 1504 0.9 / 2134 3.0		**26** W	0204 0.9 / 0812 3.1 / 1445 0.6 / 2048 3.2	
12 W	0324 0.9 / 0948 3.3 / 1549 0.7 / 2217 3.1		**27** TH	0301 0.7 / 0914 3.4 / 1538 0.3 / 2143 3.3	
13 TH	0403 0.8 / 1029 3.4 / 1624 0.6 / 2254 3.1		**28** F	0351 0.5 / 1005 3.6 / 1625 0.1 / 2232 3.4	
14 F ○	0437 0.7 / 1106 3.5 / 1656 0.6 / 2328 3.2				
15 SA	0510 0.6 / 1139 3.5 / 1728 0.5 / 2357 3.1				

MARCH

Day	Time m		Day	Time m	
1 SA ●	0436 0.4 / 1052 3.7 / 1709 0.1 / 2319 3.5		**16** SU ○	0445 0.6 / 1108 3.4 / 1700 0.4 / 2326 3.2	
2 SU	0519 0.3 / 1139 3.8 / 1752 0.1		**17** M	0518 0.5 / 1131 3.4 / 1733 0.4 / 2340 3.2	
3 M	0005 3.5 / 0600 0.3 / 1226 3.8 / 1833 0.1		**18** TU	0551 0.5 / 1154 3.4 / 1805 0.4	
4 TU	0052 3.5 / 0642 0.3 / 1313 3.7 / 1915 0.2		**19** W	0006 3.3 / 0624 0.5 / 1229 3.5 / 1838 0.4	
5 W	0138 3.4 / 0725 0.4 / 1358 3.6 / 1958 0.4		**20** TH	0043 3.3 / 0659 0.5 / 1311 3.5 / 1915 0.4	
6 TH	0223 3.4 / 0809 0.5 / 1443 3.5 / 2043 0.6		**21** F	0125 3.3 / 0737 0.5 / 1356 3.4 / 1957 0.5	
7 F	0306 3.3 / 0856 0.6 / 1529 3.3 / 2134 0.8		**22** SA	0210 3.3 / 0821 0.5 / 1446 3.3 / 2044 0.6	
8 SA ◑	0352 3.2 / 0952 0.8 / 1618 3.0 / 2240 0.8		**23** SU	0259 3.2 / 0914 0.7 / 1543 3.2 / 2139 0.8	
9 SU	0443 3.0 / 1107 1.0 / 1714 2.8 / 2354 1.1		**24** M ◐	0358 3.1 / 1018 0.8 / 1652 3.0 / 2246 1.0	
10 M	0542 2.9 / 1224 1.0 / 1841 2.7		**25** TU	0512 3.0 / 1201 0.8 / 1809 2.9	
11 TU	0100 1.2 / 0712 2.9 / 1331 1.0 / 2019 2.7		**26** W	0023 1.0 / 0636 3.0 / 1326 0.7 / 1928 3.0	
12 W	0201 1.1 / 0831 3.0 / 1430 0.9 / 2110 2.9		**27** TH	0146 0.9 / 0757 3.1 / 1428 0.5 / 2035 3.1	
13 TH	0254 0.9 / 0920 3.2 / 1517 0.7 / 2129 3.3		**28** F	0245 0.7 / 0859 3.3 / 1520 0.2 / 2129 3.3	
14 F	0336 0.8 / 1001 3.3 / 1554 0.6 / 2227 3.1		**29** SA	0335 0.5 / 0950 3.5 / 1607 0.1 / 2216 3.4	
15 SA	0411 0.7 / 1037 3.4 / 1628 0.5 / 2259 3.1		**30** SU ●	0420 0.4 / 1036 3.6 / 1650 0.1 / 2300 3.4	
			31 M	0502 0.3 / 1121 3.6 / 1731 0.1 / 2344 3.5	

APRIL

Day	Time m		Day	Time m	
1 TU	0542 0.3 / 1205 3.6 / 1811 0.2		**16** W	0526 0.5 / 1129 3.5 / 1738 0.4 / 2343 3.4	
2 W	0028 3.5 / 0621 0.3 / 1250 3.6 / 1850 0.4		**17** TH	0602 0.4 / 1207 3.5 / 1815 0.4	
3 TH	0111 3.5 / 0701 0.4 / 1333 3.5 / 1929 0.5		**18** F	0022 3.4 / 0639 0.4 / 1252 3.5 / 1855 0.5	
4 F	0152 3.4 / 0742 0.4 / 1416 3.3 / 2010 0.7		**19** SA	0107 3.4 / 0721 0.4 / 1341 3.4 / 1940 0.5	
5 SA	0234 3.4 / 0826 0.6 / 1500 3.2 / 2055 0.8		**20** SU	0154 3.4 / 0809 0.5 / 1434 3.3 / 2030 0.7	
6 SU	0318 3.3 / 0915 0.7 / 1547 3.0 / 2151 1.0		**21** M	0246 3.3 / 0904 0.6 / 1534 3.2 / 2127 0.8	
7 M	0407 3.1 / 1022 0.9 / 1641 2.8 / 2309 1.2		**22** TU ◐	0346 3.2 / 1013 0.7 / 1643 3.0 / 2236 1.0	
8 TU	0503 3.0 / 1145 1.0 / 1743 2.7		**23** W	0457 3.1 / 1146 0.7 / 1800 3.0	
9 W	0021 1.2 / 0605 2.9 / 1252 0.9 / 1931 2.7		**24** TH	0003 1.0 / 0621 3.1 / 1304 0.6 / 1914 3.0	
10 TH	0123 1.1 / 0724 2.9 / 1350 0.8 / 2033 2.8		**25** F	0121 0.9 / 0739 3.2 / 1406 0.4 / 2017 3.2	
11 F	0217 1.0 / 0836 3.0 / 1439 0.7 / 2115 2.9		**26** SA	0223 0.7 / 0840 3.3 / 1459 0.3 / 2110 3.3	
12 SA	0303 0.8 / 0920 3.2 / 1520 0.6 / 2150 3.1		**27** SU	0316 0.6 / 0932 3.5 / 1546 0.2 / 2157 3.4	
13 SU	0342 0.7 / 0957 3.3 / 1555 0.5 / 2221 3.2		**28** M	0402 0.5 / 1018 3.5 / 1629 0.2 / 2241 3.4	
14 M	0417 0.6 / 1029 3.3 / 1629 0.4 / 2249 3.2		**29** TU ●	0445 0.4 / 1103 3.5 / 1709 0.3 / 2324 3.5	
15 TU	0451 0.5 / 1057 3.4 / 1703 0.4 / 2312 3.3		**30** W	0525 0.4 / 1146 3.5 / 1748 0.4	

Chart Datum: 2·01 metres below Ordnance Datum (Belfast)
HAT is 3·9m above Chart Datum

TIDES

TIME ZONE (UT)
For Summer Time add ONE hour in **non-shaded areas**

NORTHERN IRELAND – BELFAST
LAT 54°36′N   LONG 5°55′W
TIMES AND HEIGHTS OF HIGH AND LOW WATERS

Dates in amber are **SPRINGS**
Dates in yellow are **NEAPS**

2014

MAY

Day	Time m	Time m	Time m	Time m
1 TH	0005 3.5	0603 0.4	1228 3.4	1827 0.5
2 F	0045 3.5	0642 0.4	1308 3.3	1905 0.7
3 SA	0125 3.5	0720 0.5	1349 3.2	1943 0.8
4 SU	0206 3.5	0800 0.6	1432 3.1	2024 0.9
5 M	0249 3.4	0844 0.7	1519 3.0	2111 1.0
6 TU	0336 3.3	0937 0.8	1611 2.9	2211 1.1
7 W	0429 3.1	1047 0.9	1708 2.8	2328 1.2
8 TH	0526 3.0	1204 0.9	1809 2.8	
9 F	0036 1.2	0626 3.0	1305 0.9	1913 2.8
10 SA	0133 1.1	0728 3.0	1356 0.7	2012 2.9
11 SU	0224 1.0	0825 3.1	1441 0.6	2059 3.1
12 M	0307 0.8	0911 3.2	1520 0.5	2139 3.2
13 TU	0347 0.7	0952 3.4	1558 0.5	2214 3.3
14 W	0425 0.6	1030 3.4	1635 0.4	2248 3.4
15 TH	0504 0.5	1109 3.5	1714 0.4	2326 3.5
16 F	0543 0.4	1152 3.5	1756 0.4	
17 SA	0009 3.5	0625 0.3	1240 3.5	1840 0.5
18 SU	0056 3.6	0711 0.3	1332 3.4	1929 0.6
19 M	0145 3.5	0802 0.4	1427 3.3	2021 0.7
20 TU	0238 3.5	0859 0.4	1528 3.2	2119 0.8
21 W	0337 3.4	1005 0.5	1635 3.1	2224 0.9
22 TH	0444 3.3	1124 0.6	1746 3.1	2338 0.9
23 F	0602 3.2	1237 0.5	1853 3.1	
24 SA	0050 0.9	0716 3.2	1339 0.5	1953 3.2
25 SU	0156 0.8	0818 3.3	1434 0.4	2047 3.3
26 M	0254 0.7	0912 3.4	1523 0.4	2137 3.4
27 TU	0344 0.6	1001 3.4	1608 0.5	2223 3.4
28 W	0429 0.6	1047 3.4	1649 0.5	2305 3.5
29 TH	0510 0.5	1129 3.3	1728 0.6	2345 3.5
30 F	0548 0.5	1208 3.3	1806 0.7	
31 SA	0023 3.5	0624 0.5	1245 3.2	1842 0.8

JUNE

Day	Time m	Time m	Time m	Time m
1 SU	0101 3.5	0700 0.6	1323 3.2	1918 0.8
2 M	0140 3.5	0735 0.6	1405 3.1	1956 0.9
3 TU	0222 3.5	0815 0.6	1450 3.0	2038 0.9
4 W	0305 3.4	0859 0.7	1540 3.0	2126 1.0
5 TH	0353 3.3	0950 0.8	1633 2.9	2221 1.1
6 F	0445 3.1	1050 0.9	1728 2.9	2326 1.2
7 SA	0542 3.1	1159 0.9	1825 2.9	
8 SU	0035 1.1	0640 3.1	1304 0.8	1919 3.0
9 M	0137 1.1	0737 3.1	1358 0.7	2012 3.1
10 TU	0230 0.9	0831 3.2	1445 0.6	2100 3.2
11 W	0318 0.7	0920 3.3	1529 0.5	2144 3.4
12 TH	0402 0.6	1006 3.5	1612 0.5	2227 3.5
13 F	0446 0.4	1051 3.5	1655 0.4	2310 3.6
14 SA	0529 0.3	1138 3.5	1740 0.4	2356 3.6
15 SU	0614 0.3	1228 3.5	1827 0.5	
16 M	0045 3.7	0701 0.2	1321 3.4	1917 0.5
17 TU	0137 3.7	0752 0.3	1417 3.4	2009 0.6
18 W	0230 3.6	0847 0.3	1516 3.3	2105 0.7
19 TH	0325 3.5	0948 0.4	1618 3.2	2205 0.8
20 F	0426 3.4	1058 0.5	1722 3.2	2311 0.9
21 SA	0535 3.3	1207 0.6	1825 3.1	
22 SU	0020 0.9	0648 3.2	1310 0.6	1926 3.2
23 M	0128 0.9	0755 3.2	1409 0.6	2024 3.2
24 TU	0231 0.8	0854 3.2	1502 0.6	2117 3.3
25 W	0327 0.7	0946 3.3	1548 0.7	2205 3.4
26 TH	0414 0.7	1032 3.3	1630 0.7	2248 3.5
27 F	0455 0.6	1114 3.2	1708 0.7	2328 3.5
28 SA	0531 0.6	1151 3.2	1745 0.7	
29 SU	0004 3.5	0605 0.6	1225 3.2	1819 0.8
30 M	0039 3.5	0637 0.6	1258 3.2	1852 0.8

JULY

Day	Time m	Time m	Time m	Time m
1 TU	0115 3.5	0710 0.6	1336 3.1	1928 0.8
2 W	0152 3.5	0746 0.6	1416 3.1	2007 0.8
3 TH	0230 3.4	0825 0.6	1500 3.0	2050 0.9
4 F	0309 3.4	0908 0.7	1547 3.0	2136 1.0
5 SA	0353 3.3	0958 0.8	1640 3.0	2229 1.1
6 SU	0447 3.1	1054 0.8	1736 2.9	2331 1.1
7 M	0550 3.1	1200 0.9	1833 3.0	
8 TU	0046 1.1	0654 3.1	1313 0.8	1930 3.1
9 W	0157 1.0	0756 3.2	1414 0.7	2026 3.2
10 TH	0254 0.8	0853 3.3	1506 0.6	2118 3.4
11 F	0345 0.6	0945 3.4	1554 0.5	2206 3.5
12 SA	0431 0.4	1034 3.5	1640 0.4	2253 3.6
13 SU	0516 0.3	1123 3.5	1725 0.4	2342 3.7
14 M	0601 0.2	1213 3.5	1812 0.4	
15 TU	0032 3.8	0647 0.1	1306 3.5	1900 0.5
16 W	0123 3.8	0736 0.2	1400 3.4	1950 0.5
17 TH	0215 3.7	0827 0.3	1455 3.3	2043 0.6
18 F	0308 3.6	0923 0.4	1550 3.3	2139 0.7
19 SA	0402 3.5	1026 0.5	1648 3.2	2241 0.8
20 SU	0502 3.3	1135 0.7	1749 3.1	2351 0.9
21 M	0614 3.1	1240 0.8	1856 3.1	
22 TU	0101 1.0	0731 3.1	1342 0.8	2000 3.1
23 W	0208 0.9	0836 3.1	1440 0.8	2057 3.2
24 TH	0310 0.8	0931 3.1	1530 0.8	2147 3.4
25 F	0359 0.7	1017 3.1	1611 0.8	2230 3.4
26 SA	0438 0.6	1057 3.2	1647 0.7	2309 3.5
27 SU	0511 0.6	1133 3.1	1721 0.7	2344 3.5
28 M	0541 0.6	1205 3.1	1753 0.7	
29 TU	0016 3.5	0611 0.6	1233 3.1	1825 0.7
30 W	0046 3.5	0643 0.6	1300 3.1	1859 0.7
31 TH	0116 3.5	0716 0.6	1332 3.1	1936 0.8

AUGUST

Day	Time m	Time m	Time m	Time m
1 F	0149 3.5	0752 0.6	1409 3.1	2015 0.8
2 SA	0227 3.4	0831 0.6	1451 3.1	2057 0.9
3 SU	0310 3.3	0916 0.7	1539 3.1	2146 1.0
4 M	0401 3.2	1008 0.8	1638 3.0	2243 1.1
5 TU	0504 3.1	1109 0.9	1745 3.0	2356 1.1
6 W	0616 3.0	1226 1.0	1853 3.0	
7 TH	0131 1.0	0726 3.1	1350 0.9	1957 3.2
8 F	0236 0.8	0831 3.2	1449 0.7	2055 3.4
9 SA	0329 0.5	0927 3.4	1539 0.5	2147 3.5
10 SU	0417 0.3	1018 3.5	1624 0.4	2236 3.7
11 M	0501 0.1	1106 3.5	1708 0.4	2325 3.8
12 TU	0545 0.1	1155 3.5	1753 0.4	
13 W	0014 3.8	0629 0.1	1246 3.5	1838 0.4
14 TH	0105 3.8	0714 0.2	1337 3.5	1926 0.5
15 F	0155 3.7	0801 0.3	1428 3.4	2015 0.5
16 SA	0245 3.6	0851 0.5	1518 3.3	2108 0.7
17 SU	0335 3.4	0949 0.7	1610 3.2	2208 0.8
18 M	0428 3.2	1058 0.9	1706 3.1	2320 0.9
19 TU	0530 3.0	1208 1.0	1813 3.1	
20 W	0033 1.0	0705 2.9	1314 1.1	1933 3.1
21 TH	0143 1.0	0819 2.9	1415 1.0	2035 3.2
22 F	0247 0.9	0914 3.0	1507 0.9	2125 3.3
23 SA	0338 0.7	0958 3.1	1549 0.8	2208 3.4
24 SU	0414 0.7	1037 3.1	1624 0.8	2246 3.5
25 M	0444 0.6	1111 3.2	1655 0.7	2320 3.5
26 TU	0514 0.6	1142 3.2	1726 0.7	2349 3.5
27 W	0544 0.6	1204 3.2	1758 0.7	
28 TH	0010 3.5	0614 0.5	1221 3.2	1831 0.7
29 F	0039 3.5	0646 0.5	1253 3.2	1905 0.7
30 SA	0115 3.5	0720 0.5	1331 3.3	1942 0.7
31 SU	0155 3.5	0758 0.6	1413 3.2	2023 0.8

Chart Datum: 2·01 metres below Ordnance Datum (Belfast)
HAT is 3·9m above Chart Datum

NORTHERN IRELAND – BELFAST
LAT 54°36'N   LONG 5°55'W
TIMES AND HEIGHTS OF HIGH AND LOW WATERS

Dates in amber are **SPRINGS**
Dates in yellow are **NEAPS**

2014

SEPTEMBER

#	Time	m	Time	m	#	Time	m	Time	m
1 M	0239 0842 1500 2111	3.4 0.7 3.2 0.9			16	0357 1014 1625 2244	3.2 1.0 3.2 1.0		
2 TU	0330 0933 1556 2208	3.2 0.8 3.1 1.0			17	0453 1132 1724	2.9 1.2 3.1		
3 W	0434 1034 1707 2321	3.1 1.0 3.0 1.1			18	0002 0614 1240 1845	1.1 2.8 1.2 3.0		
4 TH	0549 1149 1822	3.0 1.1 3.0			19	0110 0756 1342 2005	1.1 2.8 1.2 3.1		
5 F	0111 0704 1331 1933	1.0 3.0 1.0 3.2			20	0213 0850 1437 2058	0.9 2.9 1.1 3.3		
6 SA	0218 0814 1433 2037	0.7 3.2 0.8 3.4			21	0304 0934 1521 2141	0.8 3.1 0.9 3.4		
7 SU	0312 0912 1523 2131	0.5 3.4 0.6 3.6			22	0342 1011 1556 2218	0.7 3.2 0.8 3.5		
8 M	0359 1002 1608 2220	0.2 3.5 0.5 3.7			23	0413 1043 1628 2250	0.6 3.2 0.8 3.5		
9 TU	0443 1049 1650 2307	0.1 3.6 0.4 3.8			24	0443 1112 1659 2316	0.6 3.3 0.7 3.5		
10 W	0525 1136 1732 2355	0.1 3.6 0.4 3.8			25	0514 1132 1731 2337	0.6 3.3 0.7 3.5		
11 TH	0607 1223 1815	0.2 3.6 0.4			26	0546 1150 1804	0.6 3.3 0.7		
12 F	0044 0648 1312 1900	3.8 0.3 3.5 0.5			27	0008 0617 1224 1838	3.5 0.6 3.4 0.7		
13 SA	0133 0732 1359 1946	3.7 0.4 3.5 0.6			28	0047 0652 1303 1915	3.6 0.6 3.4 0.7		
14 SU	0220 0818 1446 2036	3.6 0.6 3.4 0.7			29	0130 0731 1347 1957	3.5 0.6 3.4 0.7		
15 M	0307 0909 1534 2132	3.4 0.8 3.3 0.8			30	0217 0816 1434 2047	3.4 0.7 3.3 0.8		

OCTOBER

#	Time	m	Time	m	#	Time	m	Time	m
1 W	0311 0908 1530 2146	3.3 0.9 3.2 1.0			16	0421 1045 1645 2322	2.9 1.3 3.2 1.1		
2 TH	0416 1010 1640 2302	3.1 1.1 3.1 1.0			17	0522 1200 1747	2.8 1.4 3.1		
3 F	0531 1127 1758	3.0 1.2 3.1			18	0030 0708 1303 1903	1.1 2.8 1.3 3.1		
4 SA	0050 0648 1308 1915	0.9 3.0 1.1 3.2			19	0131 0815 1359 2015	1.0 2.9 1.2 3.2		
5 SU	0157 0759 1413 2022	0.7 3.2 0.9 3.4			20	0222 0900 1446 2103	0.9 3.1 1.0 3.3		
6 M	0251 0857 1505 2116	0.5 3.4 0.7 3.6			21	0304 0936 1525 2142	0.8 3.2 0.9 3.4		
7 TU	0339 0946 1550 2205	0.3 3.5 0.6 3.7			22	0339 1009 1600 2216	0.7 3.3 0.8 3.5		
8 W	0423 1032 1632 2251	0.2 3.6 0.5 3.8			23	0412 1039 1633 2245	0.6 3.4 0.8 3.5		
9 TH	0504 1117 1713 2337	0.3 3.7 0.6 3.8			24	0445 1103 1707 2312	0.6 3.4 0.7 3.6		
10 F	0544 1202 1755	0.3 3.7 0.5			25	0518 1127 1741 2346	0.6 3.5 0.7 3.6		
11 SA	0024 0624 1248 1837	3.7 0.5 3.6 0.5			26	0553 1202 1818	0.6 3.6 0.7		
12 SU	0110 0705 1332 1921	3.6 0.6 3.6 0.6			27	0027 0631 1243 1857	3.6 0.6 3.6 0.7		
13 M	0155 0748 1416 2007	3.5 0.8 3.6 0.7			28	0113 0713 1329 1942	3.5 0.7 3.6 0.7		
14 TU	0240 0835 1502 2058	3.3 1.0 3.5 0.9			29	0203 0800 1418 2033	3.4 0.8 3.5 0.8		
15 W	0328 0929 1551 2202	3.1 1.2 3.3 1.0			30	0259 0853 1515 2134	3.3 1.0 3.4 0.9		
					31 F	0403 0956 1621 2252	3.2 1.1 3.3 0.9		

NOVEMBER

#	Time	m	Time	m	#	Time	m	Time	m
1 SA	0517 1112 1738	3.1 1.2 3.2			16	0547 1214 1807	2.9 1.4 3.2		
2 SU	0023 0634 1239 1858	0.9 3.1 1.1 3.3			17	0042 0653 1314 1909	1.1 2.9 1.3 3.2		
3 M	0131 0742 1348 2005	0.7 3.3 1.0 3.5			18	0136 0758 1406 2009	1.0 3.1 1.2 3.3		
4 TU	0227 0840 1443 2101	0.6 3.4 0.8 3.5			19	0223 0848 1451 2059	0.9 3.2 1.0 3.4		
5 W	0317 0929 1532 2150	0.5 3.5 0.7 3.7			20	0303 0930 1530 2141	0.8 3.3 0.9 3.5		
6 TH	0401 1016 1616 2237	0.4 3.6 0.6 3.7			21	0341 1007 1608 2218	0.7 3.4 0.8 3.5		
7 F	0443 1100 1658 2322	0.5 3.7 0.6 3.7			22	0418 1039 1645 2253	0.7 3.5 0.7 3.6		
8 SA	0524 1143 1739	0.6 3.7 0.6			23	0456 1111 1724 2331	0.6 3.6 0.6 3.6		
9 SU	0006 0603 1226 1820	3.6 0.7 3.7 0.6			24	0535 1147 1804	0.6 3.7 0.6		
10 M	0049 0643 1307 1901	3.5 0.8 3.7 0.7			25	0014 0616 1230 1847	3.6 0.7 3.7 0.6		
11 TU	0131 0724 1349 1943	3.4 0.9 3.7 0.7			26	0102 0701 1317 1934	3.6 0.7 3.7 0.6		
12 W	0214 0806 1433 2028	3.3 1.0 3.6 0.8			27	0153 0750 1408 2026	3.5 0.8 3.6 0.6		
13 TH	0300 0852 1520 2119	3.2 1.2 3.5 1.0			28	0249 0844 1503 2125	3.4 0.9 3.6 0.7		
14 F	0351 0948 1611 2223	3.0 1.3 3.3 1.1			29	0352 0944 1605 2235	3.3 1.0 3.5 0.8		
15 SA	0446 1103 1707 2338	2.9 1.4 3.2 1.1			30	0503 1053 1718 2353	3.2 1.1 3.4 0.8		

DECEMBER

#	Time	m	Time	m	#	Time	m	Time	m
1 M	0615 1208 1837	3.2 1.1 3.4			16	0603 1213 1822	3.0 1.3 3.2		
2 TU	0101 0720 1319 1945	0.7 3.3 1.0 3.4			17	0040 0701 1318 1920	1.1 3.0 1.3 3.2		
3 W	0201 0819 1420 2044	0.7 3.4 0.9 3.5			18	0138 0758 1414 2017	1.0 3.1 1.1 3.3		
4 TH	0254 0912 1515 2136	0.6 3.5 0.8 3.6			19	0229 0851 1502 2108	0.9 3.3 1.0 3.4		
5 F	0342 1000 1603 2225	0.6 3.6 0.7 3.6			20	0314 0936 1546 2153	0.8 3.4 0.8 3.5		
6 SA	0426 1045 1647 2310	0.7 3.7 0.7 3.5			21	0356 1016 1628 2235	0.7 3.5 0.7 3.6		
7 SU	0507 1128 1728 2352	0.7 3.7 0.7 3.5			22	0438 1055 1710 2317	0.6 3.7 0.5 3.6		
8 M	0547 1208 1807	0.8 3.7 0.7			23	0520 1136 1753	0.6 3.7 0.5		
9 TU	0031 0625 1247 1844	3.4 0.9 3.7 0.7			24	0002 0603 1220 1837	3.6 0.6 3.8 0.4		
10 W	0110 0702 1326 1921	3.3 0.9 3.7 0.7			25	0051 0649 1308 1924	3.6 0.6 3.8 0.4		
11 TH	0150 0739 1407 2000	3.3 1.0 3.7 0.8			26	0143 0738 1358 2015	3.5 0.7 3.8 0.4		
12 F	0233 0820 1451 2042	3.2 1.1 3.6 0.9			27	0238 0830 1452 2110	3.4 0.8 3.7 0.5		
13 SA	0320 0905 1538 2130	3.1 1.1 3.4 0.9			28	0337 0926 1550 2213	3.3 0.8 3.6 0.6		
14 SU	0411 0957 1629 2226	3.0 1.2 3.3 1.0			29	0440 1028 1655 2323	3.2 0.9 3.5 0.7		
15 M	0506 1100 1724 2332	3.0 1.3 3.2 1.1			30	0547 1138 1809	3.1 1.0 3.4		
					31 W	0032 0635 1251 1922	0.8 3.2 1.0 3.3		

Chart Datum: 2·01 metres below Ordnance Datum (Belfast)
HAT is 3·9m above Chart Datum

TIDES

ESBJERG

MEAN SPRING AND NEAP CURVES

MEAN RANGES	
Springs	1.8m
Neaps	1.0m

TIME ZONE -0100
(Danish Standard Time)
Subtract 1 hour for UT
For Danish Summer Time add
ONE hour in **non-shaded areas**

DENMARK – ESBJERG
LAT 55°28'N   LONG 8°26'E
TIMES AND HEIGHTS OF HIGH AND LOW WATERS

Dates in amber are **SPRINGS**
Dates in yellow are **NEAPS**
2014

JANUARY

Time m	Time m
1 W 0211 1.9 / 0806 0.2 / ● 2028 0.3	**16** TH 0257 2.0 / 0900 0.3 / ○ 2108 0.3
2 TH 0302 2.0 / 0857 0.2 / 2116 0.2	**17** F 0335 1.9 / 0936 0.3 / 2141 0.3
3 F 0350 2.1 / 0946 0.1 / 2202 0.2	**18** SA 0406 1.9 / 1008 0.3 / 2211 0.3
4 SA 0436 2.1 / 1033 0.1 / 2248 0.2	**19** SU 0434 1.9 / 1037 0.3 / 2242 0.3
5 SU 0521 2.1 / 1121 0.1 / 2333 0.2	**20** M 0500 1.9 / 1108 0.3 / 2315 0.2
6 M 0606 2.1 / 1208 0.0 / 1841 1.8	**21** TU 0529 2.0 / 1142 0.2 / 2353 0.2
7 TU 0021 0.2 / 0655 2.1 / 1257 0.2 / 1930 1.8	**22** W 0603 2.0 / 1221 0.2 / 1828 1.8
8 W 0110 0.3 / 0748 2.0 / 1350 0.3 / ◐ 2024 1.7	**23** TH 0034 0.2 / 0644 2.0 / 1304 0.2 / 1912 1.8
9 TH 0205 0.3 / 0846 2.0 / 1448 0.3 / 2124 1.7	**24** F 0120 0.2 / 0732 1.9 / 1352 0.2 / ◑ 2003 1.7
10 F 0306 0.4 / 0951 1.9 / 1552 0.4 / 2228 1.8	**25** SA 0212 0.3 / 0828 1.9 / 1447 0.3 / 2103 1.7
11 SA 0417 0.4 / 1057 1.9 / 1701 0.4 / 2331 1.8	**26** SU 0312 0.3 / 0936 1.8 / 1550 0.4 / 2216 1.7
12 SU 0530 0.4 / 1201 1.9 / 1805 0.4	**27** M 0422 0.4 / 1057 1.7 / 1702 0.4 / 2336 1.7
13 M 0030 1.8 / 0634 0.3 / 1300 1.8 / 1900 0.4	**28** TU 0539 0.4 / 1218 1.7 / 1814 0.4
14 TU 0125 1.9 / 0730 0.3 / 1352 1.8 / 1949 0.3	**29** W 0048 1.8 / 0651 0.3 / 1327 1.8 / 1916 0.3
15 W 0214 1.9 / 0818 0.3 / 2031 0.3	**30** TH 0150 1.9 / 0750 0.2 / 1425 1.8 / ● 2010 0.2
	31 F 0245 1.9 / 0842 0.1 / 1518 1.8 / 2059 0.1

FEBRUARY

Time m	Time m
1 SA 0333 2.0 / 0931 0.0 / 1605 1.8 / 2145 0.1	**16** SU 0345 1.9 / 0943 0.2 / 1604 1.7 / 2148 0.2
2 SU 0420 2.0 / 1016 0.0 / 1649 1.8 / 2229 0.0	**17** M 0414 1.9 / 1012 0.1 / 1633 1.7 / 2220 0.1
3 M 0503 2.1 / 1101 0.0 / 1731 1.8 / 2313 0.0	**18** TU 0442 1.9 / 1043 0.1 / 1700 1.7 / 2254 0.1
4 TU 0547 2.0 / 1145 0.0 / 1813 1.8 / 2358 0.1	**19** W 0511 1.9 / 1118 0.1 / 1730 1.7 / 2330 0.0
5 W 0631 2.0 / 1230 0.1 / 1857 1.7	**20** TH 0544 1.9 / 1156 0.1 / 1804 1.7
6 TH 0044 0.1 / 0718 1.9 / 1317 0.2 / ◑ 1945 1.7	**21** F 0012 0.0 / 0623 1.9 / 1238 0.1 / 1845 1.7
7 F 0134 0.2 / 0812 1.8 / 1409 0.3 / 2039 1.7	**22** SA 0057 0.1 / 0709 1.8 / 1324 0.1 / ◑ 1932 1.7
8 SA 0230 0.3 / 0912 1.7 / 1509 0.4 / 2143 1.7	**23** SU 0147 0.1 / 0804 1.7 / 1418 0.2 / 2030 1.6
9 SU 0339 0.4 / 1021 1.7 / 1621 0.4 / 2251 1.7	**24** M 0246 0.2 / 0912 1.6 / 1520 0.3 / 2142 1.6
10 M 0501 0.4 / 1128 1.6 / 1734 0.4 / 2356 1.7	**25** TU 0358 0.3 / 1039 1.6 / 1635 0.4 / 2310 1.6
11 TU 0612 0.3 / 1230 1.7 / 1835 0.4	**26** W 0521 0.3 / 1202 1.6 / 1752 0.3
12 W 0054 1.8 / 0709 0.3 / 1325 1.7 / 1925 0.3	**27** TH 0027 1.7 / 0634 0.2 / 1310 1.7 / 1857 0.2
13 TH 0146 1.8 / 0757 0.2 / 1413 1.7 / 2009 0.3	**28** F 0130 1.8 / 0733 0.0 / 1409 1.7 / 1951 0.1
14 F 0232 1.9 / 0838 0.2 / 1456 1.7 / 2045 0.2	
15 SA 0311 1.9 / 0912 0.2 / ○ 2118 0.1	

MARCH

Time m	Time m
1 SA 0226 1.9 / 0825 -0.1 / ● 2040 0.0	**16** SU 0241 1.8 / 0842 0.1 / ○ 2050 0.1
2 SU 0315 1.9 / 0912 -0.1 / 1545 1.8 / 2125 -0.1	**17** M 0318 1.8 / 0914 0.0 / 1539 1.7 / 2123 0.0
3 M 0400 2.0 / 0955 -0.1 / 1626 1.8 / 2209 -0.1	**18** TU 0351 1.8 / 0945 0.0 / 1610 1.7 / 2157 0.0
4 TU 0443 2.0 / 1038 -0.1 / 1705 1.7 / 2251 -0.1	**19** W 0421 1.8 / 1018 0.0 / 1640 1.7 / 2232 0.0
5 W 0524 1.9 / 1119 0.0 / 1743 1.7 / 2333 -0.1	**20** TH 0454 1.8 / 1054 0.0 / 1711 1.7 / 2310 -0.1
6 TH 0605 1.8 / 1200 0.1 / 1822 1.7	**21** F 0528 1.8 / 1133 0.0 / 1745 1.7 / 2352 -0.1
7 F 0017 0.0 / 0648 1.8 / 1243 0.2 / ◑ 1904 1.7	**22** SA 0608 1.7 / 1215 0.0 / 1824 1.7
8 SA 0103 0.1 / 0735 1.7 / 1329 0.3 / ◑ 1952 1.6	**23** SU 0037 0.0 / 0654 1.7 / 1302 0.1 / 1911 1.6
9 SU 0155 0.2 / 0830 1.6 / 1421 0.4 / 2051 1.6	**24** M 0129 0.0 / 0751 1.6 / 1355 0.2 / ◑ 2009 1.6
10 M 0258 0.3 / 0937 1.5 / 1529 0.4 / 2203 1.6	**25** TU 0229 0.1 / 0902 1.5 / 1458 0.3 / 2124 1.6
11 TU 0423 0.4 / 1048 1.5 / 1652 0.4 / 2314 1.6	**26** W 0342 0.2 / 1028 1.5 / 1614 0.3 / 2251 1.6
12 W 0541 0.3 / 1154 1.5 / 1801 0.4	**27** TH 0505 0.2 / 1147 1.5 / 1732 0.3
13 TH 0017 1.6 / 0639 0.2 / 1251 1.6 / 1854 0.3	**28** F 0007 1.7 / 0616 0.1 / 1253 1.6 / 1836 0.2
14 F 0112 1.7 / 0727 0.2 / 1342 1.6 / 1938 0.2	**29** SA 0110 1.8 / 0714 0.0 / 1348 1.6 / 1930 0.0
15 SA 0159 1.7 / 0807 0.1 / 2016 0.1	**30** SU 0206 1.8 / 0804 -0.1 / 1438 1.7 / ● 2019 -0.1
	31 M 0255 1.9 / 0850 -0.2 / 1521 1.7 / 2105 -0.2

APRIL

Time m	Time m
1 TU 0340 1.9 / 0933 -0.2 / 2148 -0.2	**16** W 0325 1.7 / 0918 -0.1 / 1546 1.7 / 2133 -0.1
2 W 0421 1.8 / 1013 -0.1 / 1639 1.7 / 2230 -0.2	**17** TH 0402 1.7 / 0954 -0.1 / 1621 1.7 / 2212 -0.1
3 TH 0500 1.8 / 1053 0.0 / 1715 1.7 / 2311 -0.1	**18** F 0438 1.7 / 1032 -0.1 / 1654 1.7 / 2253 -0.1
4 F 0539 1.7 / 1131 0.0 / 1750 1.7 / 2351 0.0	**19** SA 0517 1.7 / 1113 0.0 / 1731 1.7 / 2336 -0.1
5 SA 0617 1.6 / 1210 0.1 / 1827 1.6	**20** SU 0559 1.6 / 1157 0.0 / 1812 1.7
6 SU 0034 0.1 / 0657 1.5 / 1251 0.2 / 1909 1.6	**21** M 0024 -0.1 / 0648 1.6 / 1245 0.1 / 1900 1.6
7 M 0121 0.2 / 0746 1.5 / 1337 0.3 / ◑ 2000 1.6	**22** TU 0116 0.0 / 0746 1.5 / 1338 0.2 / ◑ 1959 1.6
8 TU 0216 0.3 / 0846 1.4 / 1433 0.4 / 2104 1.5	**23** W 0218 0.1 / 0857 1.4 / 1441 0.2 / 2113 1.6
9 W 0328 0.3 / 0958 1.4 / 1548 0.4 / 2220 1.5	**24** TH 0329 0.1 / 1016 1.4 / 1554 0.3 / 2233 1.6
10 TH 0452 0.3 / 1108 1.4 / 1709 0.4 / 2329 1.6	**25** F 0446 0.1 / 1128 1.5 / 1709 0.2 / 2345 1.7
11 F 0557 0.2 / 1209 1.5 / 1810 0.3	**26** SA 0554 0.0 / 1231 1.5 / 1813 0.1
12 SA 0028 1.6 / 0647 0.1 / 1303 1.5 / 1859 0.2	**27** SU 0048 1.7 / 0651 -0.1 / 1326 1.6 / 1909 0.0
13 SU 0120 1.7 / 0729 0.1 / 1351 1.6 / 1941 0.1	**28** M 0144 1.8 / 0742 -0.1 / 1415 1.7 / 1959 -0.1
14 M 0206 1.7 / 0806 0.0 / 1433 1.6 / 2019 0.0	**29** TU 0234 1.8 / 0827 -0.1 / 1459 1.7 / ● 2045 -0.2
15 TU 0247 1.7 / 0842 0.0 / 1511 1.7 / ○ 2056 0.0	**30** W 0320 1.8 / 0910 -0.1 / 1539 1.7 / 2129 -0.2

Chart Datum: 0·69 metres below Dansk Normal Null
HAT is 2·2 metres above Chart Datum

TIDES

TIME ZONE -0100
(Danish Standard Time)
Subtract 1 hour for UT
For Danish Summer Time add
ONE hour in **non-shaded areas**

DENMARK – ESBJERG
LAT 55°28'N   LONG 8°26'E
TIMES AND HEIGHTS OF HIGH AND LOW WATERS

Dates in amber are SPRINGS
Dates in yellow are NEAPS
2014

MAY

Day	Time m	Time m	Time m	Time m		Day	Time m	Time m	Time m	Time m
1 TH	0401 1.7	0950 -0.1	1616 1.7	2210 -0.1		16 F	0343 1.7	0932 -0.1	1602 1.7	2154 -0.1
2 F	0439 1.6	1028 0.0	1651 1.7	2250 -0.1		17 SA	0425 1.7	1013 -0.1	1641 1.7	2238 -0.1
3 SA	0515 1.6	1105 0.1	1724 1.7	2329 0.0		18 SU	0509 1.6	1056 0.0	1721 1.7	2324 -0.1
4 SU	0548 1.5	1141 0.1	1756 1.6			19 M	0554 1.6	1142 0.0	1805 1.7	
5 M	0009 0.1	0624 1.4	1218 0.2	1832 1.6		20 TU	0012 -0.1	0644 1.5	1230 0.1	1854 1.7
6 TU	0051 0.1	0705 1.4	1300 0.2	1915 1.6		21 W	0106 0.0	0741 1.5	1324 0.1	1952 1.7
7 W	0137 0.2	0756 1.4	1348 0.3	2009 1.6		22 TH	0205 0.0	0845 1.4	1423 0.2	2100 1.7
8 TH	0233 0.3	0859 1.4	1446 0.3	2115 1.5		23 F	0311 0.1	0955 1.4	1531 0.2	2212 1.7
9 F	0340 0.3	1010 1.4	1557 0.3	2227 1.5		24 SA	0421 0.1	1103 1.5	1642 0.2	2322 1.7
10 SA	0451 0.2	1118 1.4	1708 0.3	2335 1.6		25 SU	0528 0.0	1205 1.6	1748 0.1	
11 SU	0552 0.2	1218 1.5	1809 0.4			26 M	0025 1.7	0627 0.0	1300 1.6	1847 0.1
12 M	0034 1.6	0643 0.1	1311 1.6	1900 0.4		27 TU	0122 1.8	0719 0.0	1351 1.7	1939 0.0
13 TU	0127 1.7	0728 0.0	1358 1.6	1946 0.4		28 W	0214 1.7	0806 0.0	1438 1.7	2028 -0.1
14 W	0215 1.7	0810 0.0	1442 1.7	2029 0.0		29 TH	0301 1.7	0850 0.0	1520 1.7	2113 -0.1
15 TH	0300 1.7	0851 -0.1	1523 1.7	2112 -0.1		30 F	0343 1.7	0930 0.0	1557 1.7	2154 0.0
						31 SA	0421 1.6	1007 0.1	1632 1.7	2233 0.0

JUNE

Day	Time m	Time m	Time m	Time m		Day	Time m	Time m	Time m	Time m
1 SU	0454 1.5	1042 0.1	1703 1.7	2309 0.1		16 M	0500 1.7	1042 0.0	1712 1.8	2312 -0.1
2 M	0525 1.5	1115 0.2	1732 1.7	2345 0.1		17 TU	0546 1.6	1127 0.0	1757 1.8	
3 TU	0556 1.4	1151 0.2	1803 1.7			18 W	0000 -0.1	0634 1.6	1215 0.0	1845 1.8
4 W	0022 0.1	0631 1.4	1229 0.2	1841 1.7		19 TH	0051 0.0	0727 1.5	1306 0.1	1940 1.8
5 TH	0103 0.2	0714 1.4	1312 0.2	1927 1.7		20 F	0146 0.0	0824 1.5	1402 0.1	2041 1.8
6 F	0150 0.2	0806 1.4	1402 0.3	2021 1.6		21 SA	0246 0.1	0927 1.5	1503 0.2	2148 1.7
7 SA	0243 0.2	0907 1.4	1500 0.3	2124 1.6		22 SU	0351 0.1	1032 1.5	1612 0.2	2256 1.7
8 SU	0345 0.2	1016 1.5	1606 0.3	2235 1.6		23 M	0459 0.1	1135 1.6	1722 0.2	
9 M	0450 0.2	1125 1.5	1714 0.3	2345 1.6		24 TU	0000 1.7	0602 0.1	1234 1.7	1826 0.1
10 TU	0553 0.2	1227 1.6	1817 0.2			25 W	0100 1.7	0657 0.1	1328 1.7	1923 0.1
11 W	0048 1.6	0649 0.1	1323 1.6	1913 0.1		26 TH	0154 1.7	0748 0.1	1417 1.8	2014 0.0
12 TH	0145 1.7	0739 0.1	1414 1.7	2004 0.0		27 F	0243 1.7	0833 0.0	1501 1.8	2100 0.0
13 F	0237 1.7	0827 0.0	1501 1.7	2053 0.0		28 SA	0326 1.7	0912 0.0	1541 1.8	2140 0.1
14 SA	0327 1.7	0912 0.0	1545 1.8	2139 -0.1		29 SU	0404 1.6	0949 0.1	1615 1.8	2217 0.1
15 SU	0413 1.7	0957 0.0	1629 1.8	2225 -0.1		30 M	0436 1.6	1022 0.2	1645 1.8	2250 0.2

JULY

Day	Time m	Time m	Time m	Time m		Day	Time m	Time m	Time m	Time m
1 TU	0505 1.5	1054 0.2	1712 1.8	2322 0.2		16 W	0530 1.7	1111 0.0	1744 2.0	2344 -0.1
2 W	0532 1.5	1127 0.2	1739 1.8	2355 0.2		17 TH	0615 1.7	1157 0.0	1830 1.9	
3 TH	0603 1.6	1202 0.2	1812 1.8			18 F	0031 0.0	0703 1.7	1245 0.1	1921 1.9
4 F	0032 0.2	0639 1.6	1242 0.2	1853 1.8		19 SA	0121 0.1	0754 1.6	1336 0.1	2016 1.9
5 SA	0114 0.2	0724 1.6	1327 0.2	1941 1.8		20 SU	0215 0.2	0851 1.6	1434 0.2	2119 1.8
6 SU	0201 0.2	0817 1.6	1419 0.2	2036 1.7		21 M	0317 0.3	0955 1.6	1541 0.3	2227 1.7
7 M	0256 0.2	0918 1.6	1518 0.3	2142 1.7		22 TU	0426 0.3	1102 1.7	1656 0.3	2334 1.7
8 TU	0357 0.3	1029 1.6	1625 0.3	2257 1.7		23 W	0536 0.3	1205 1.7	1807 0.3	
9 W	0506 0.3	1142 1.6	1737 0.3			24 TH	0036 1.7	0636 0.3	1303 1.8	1907 0.2
10 TH	0012 1.7	0613 0.2	1248 1.7	1845 0.2		25 F	0133 1.7	0729 0.2	1355 1.8	1959 0.1
11 F	0118 1.7	0712 0.2	1348 1.7	1943 0.1		26 SA	0223 1.7	0815 0.2	1442 1.9	2044 0.1
12 SA	0218 1.7	0806 0.1	1440 1.8	2036 0.0		27 SU	0306 1.7	0854 0.2	1522 1.9	2124 0.2
13 SU	0311 1.7	0854 0.1	1529 1.9	2124 0.0		28 M	0345 1.7	0930 0.2	1557 1.9	2157 0.2
14 M	0400 1.7	0940 0.0	1615 1.9	2212 -0.1		29 TU	0417 1.7	1002 0.2	1627 1.9	2228 0.2
15 TU	0445 1.7	1026 0.0	1659 2.0	2257 -0.1		30 W	0445 1.7	1032 0.2	1653 1.9	2257 0.2
						31 TH	0510 1.7	1103 0.2	1718 1.9	2328 0.2

AUGUST

Day	Time m	Time m	Time m	Time m		Day	Time m	Time m	Time m	Time m
1 F	0537 1.7	1137 0.2	1748 1.9			16 SA	0006 0.1	0634 1.8	1221 0.1	1856 2.0
2 SA	0003 0.2	0610 1.7	1215 0.2	1825 1.9		17 SU	0053 0.2	0720 1.8	1310 0.2	1948 2.0
3 SU	0043 0.2	0650 1.7	1259 0.2	1909 1.9		18 M	0142 0.3	0812 1.8	1404 0.3	2047 1.8
4 M	0127 0.2	0737 1.7	1347 0.2	2001 1.8		19 TU	0239 0.4	0915 1.7	1509 0.4	2154 1.8
5 TU	0218 0.3	0833 1.7	1442 0.3	2103 1.8		20 W	0348 0.5	1024 1.7	1629 0.5	2305 1.7
6 W	0318 0.3	0939 1.7	1548 0.4	2219 1.7		21 TH	0506 0.5	1132 1.8	1746 0.4	
7 TH	0427 0.4	1100 1.7	1705 0.4	2344 1.7		22 F	0009 1.8	0612 0.3	1233 1.9	1848 0.3
8 F	0542 0.4	1217 1.7	1821 0.3			23 SA	0107 1.8	0706 0.3	1328 1.9	1939 0.3
9 SA	0057 1.7	0649 0.3	1323 1.8	1924 0.2		24 SU	0157 1.8	0752 0.2	1416 2.0	2023 0.3
10 SU	0159 1.8	0745 0.2	1419 1.9	2018 0.1		25 M	0242 1.8	0833 0.2	1458 2.0	2100 0.2
11 M	0253 1.8	0836 0.2	1510 2.0	2107 0.0		26 TU	0321 1.8	0907 0.2	1534 2.0	2133 0.3
12 TU	0342 1.9	0922 0.1	1557 2.1	2154 0.0		27 W	0353 1.8	0938 0.2	1604 2.0	2201 0.3
13 W	0427 1.9	1007 0.0	1642 2.1	2238 0.0		28 TH	0422 1.8	1008 0.3	1631 2.0	2230 0.3
14 TH	0509 1.9	1051 0.0	1725 2.1	2322 0.0		29 F	0448 1.8	1039 0.2	1658 2.0	2302 0.2
15 F	0551 1.8	1136 0.0	1809 2.1			30 SA	0515 1.8	1114 0.2	1727 2.0	2336 0.2
						31 SU	0545 1.9	1151 0.2	1803 1.9	

Chart Datum: 0·69 metres below Dansk Normal Null
HAT is 2·2 metres above Chart Datum

TIME ZONE -0100
(Danish Standard Time)
Subtract 1 hour for UT
For Danish Summer Time add
ONE hour in **non-shaded areas**

DENMARK – ESBJERG
LAT 55°28'N   LONG 8°26'E
TIMES AND HEIGHTS OF HIGH AND LOW WATERS

Dates in amber are **SPRINGS**
Dates in yellow are **NEAPS**
2014

SEPTEMBER

#	Time m	#	Time m
1	0015 0.2 / 0623 1.9 / M 1234 0.2 / 1845 2.0	**16**	0109 0.4 / 0733 1.9 / TU 1335 0.4 / (2012 1.8
2	0100 0.3 / 0706 1.9 / TU 1321 0.3 / (1936 1.9	**17**	0200 0.5 / 0830 1.8 / W 1436 0.5 / 2117 1.8
3	0149 0.4 / 0759 1.8 / W 1416 0.3 / 2037 1.8	**18**	0304 0.6 / 0939 1.8 / TH 1555 0.6 / 2228 1.7
4	0247 0.5 / 0903 1.8 / TH 1522 0.4 / 2155 1.8	**19**	0425 0.7 / 1052 1.8 / F 1717 0.5 / 2335 1.8
5	0357 0.5 / 1026 1.8 / F 1642 0.4 / 2324 1.8	**20**	0539 0.6 / 1157 1.9 / SA 1820 0.5
6	0515 0.5 / 1151 1.8 / SA 1800 0.4	**21**	0033 1.8 / 0636 0.5 / SU 1254 2.0 / 1910 0.4
7	0038 1.8 / 0627 0.4 / SU 1300 1.9 / 1905 0.3	**22**	0126 1.9 / 0723 0.5 / M 1344 2.0 / 1954 0.4
8	0140 1.9 / 0725 0.3 / M 1358 2.0 / 1959 0.2	**23**	0211 1.9 / 0804 0.4 / TU 1427 2.0 / 2030 0.3
9	0233 1.9 / 0815 0.2 / TU 1450 2.1 / O 2047 0.1	**24**	0251 1.9 / 0839 0.4 / W 1505 2.0 / ● 2103 0.3
10	0321 2.0 / 0902 0.1 / W 1537 2.2 / 2133 0.1	**25**	0327 2.0 / 0912 0.3 / TH 1539 2.0 / 2133 0.3
11	0404 2.0 / 0947 0.1 / TH 1621 2.2 / 2215 0.1	**26**	0357 2.0 / 0943 0.3 / F 1609 2.0 / 2203 0.3
12	0445 2.0 / 1030 0.1 / F 1704 2.1 / 2257 0.1	**27**	0427 2.0 / 1016 0.3 / SA 1639 2.0 / 2236 0.3
13	0524 2.0 / 1113 0.1 / SA 1746 2.1 / 2340 0.2	**28**	0455 2.0 / 1052 0.3 / SU 1710 2.0 / 2312 0.3
14	0604 1.9 / 1157 0.2 / SU 1830 2.0	**29**	0526 2.0 / 1131 0.2 / M 1747 2.0 / 2353 0.3
15	0023 0.3 / 0646 1.9 / M 1244 0.3 / 1917 1.9	**30**	0602 2.0 / 1215 0.3 / TU 1829 2.0

OCTOBER

#	Time m	#	Time m
1	0036 0.4 / 0645 2.0 / W 1303 0.3 / (1920 1.9	**16**	0123 0.6 / 0746 1.9 / TH 1402 0.6 / 2033 1.7
2	0127 0.4 / 0736 1.8 / TH 1358 0.4 / 2023 1.8	**17**	0218 0.7 / 0848 1.9 / F 1511 0.6 / 2142 1.7
3	0224 0.5 / 0842 1.9 / F 1505 0.5 / 2142 1.8	**18**	0329 0.7 / 1001 1.9 / SA 1632 0.6 / 2251 1.8
4	0334 0.6 / 1004 1.9 / SA 1624 0.5 / 2307 1.8	**19**	0448 0.7 / 1110 1.9 / SU 1739 0.6 / 2352 1.8
5	0452 0.6 / 1127 1.9 / SU 1740 0.4	**20**	0553 0.6 / 1210 2.0 / M 1831 0.5
6	0018 1.9 / 0603 0.5 / M 1236 2.0 / 1843 0.3	**21**	0046 1.9 / 0645 0.6 / TU 1303 2.0 / 1915 0.4
7	0118 1.9 / 0702 0.4 / TU 1336 2.1 / 1937 0.2	**22**	0135 2.0 / 0728 0.5 / W 1351 2.0 / 1954 0.4
8	0211 2.0 / 0754 0.3 / W 1428 2.2 / O 2025 0.2	**23**	0218 2.0 / 0807 0.4 / TH 1433 2.1 / ● 2030 0.4
9	0258 2.0 / 0841 0.2 / TH 1516 2.2 / 2109 0.2	**24**	0257 2.0 / 0843 0.4 / F 1511 2.1 / 2103 0.3
10	0341 2.1 / 0926 0.1 / F 1600 2.2 / 2152 0.2	**25**	0333 2.0 / 0918 0.3 / SA 1547 2.1 / 2137 0.3
11	0421 2.1 / 1009 0.1 / SA 1642 2.1 / 2233 0.2	**26**	0406 2.0 / 0955 0.3 / SU 1621 2.0 / 2214 0.3
12	0459 2.0 / 1052 0.2 / SU 1723 2.1 / 2314 0.3	**27**	0438 2.0 / 1034 0.3 / M 1657 2.0 / 2252 0.3
13	0536 2.0 / 1135 0.3 / M 1803 2.0 / 2354 0.4	**28**	0512 2.0 / 1115 0.3 / TU 1737 2.0 / 2334 0.4
14	0614 2.0 / 1219 0.3 / TU 1846 1.9	**29**	0549 2.0 / 1200 0.3 / W 1821 1.9
15	0036 0.5 / 0657 2.0 / W 1307 0.4 / (1934 1.8	**30**	0019 0.4 / 0633 2.0 / TH 1250 0.3 / 1914 1.9
		31	0110 0.5 / 0725 2.0 / F 1346 0.4 / (2017 1.8

NOVEMBER

#	Time m	#	Time m
1	0207 0.6 / 0830 2.0 / SA 1451 0.4 / 2132 1.8	**16**	0231 0.7 / 0900 1.9 / SU 1524 0.6 / 2152 1.7
2	0315 0.6 / 0948 2.0 / SU 1604 0.5 / 2248 1.8	**17**	0338 0.7 / 1009 1.9 / M 1634 0.6 / 2258 1.8
3	0428 0.6 / 1106 2.0 / M 1717 0.4 / 2356 1.9	**18**	0450 0.7 / 1116 1.9 / TU 1736 0.6 / 2359 1.8
4	0538 0.5 / 1214 2.1 / TU 1819 0.3	**19**	0552 0.6 / 1216 2.0 / W 1828 0.5
5	0055 2.0 / 0639 0.4 / W 1314 2.1 / 1914 0.3	**20**	0053 1.9 / 0645 0.5 / TH 1309 2.0 / 1913 0.4
6	0148 2.0 / 0732 0.3 / TH 1407 2.2 / O 2003 0.2	**21**	0142 2.0 / 0731 0.5 / F 1358 2.0 / 1954 0.4
7	0235 2.1 / 0821 0.2 / F 1457 2.2 / 2048 0.2	**22**	0226 2.0 / 0814 0.4 / SA 1443 2.0 / ● 2034 0.4
8	0319 2.1 / 0907 0.2 / SA 1542 2.1 / 2130 0.3	**23**	0307 2.0 / 0855 0.3 / SU 1526 2.0 / 2114 0.3
9	0359 2.1 / 0951 0.2 / SU 1623 2.0 / 2211 0.3	**24**	0345 2.1 / 0936 0.3 / M 1607 2.0 / 2154 0.3
10	0436 2.1 / 1034 0.3 / M 1702 2.0 / 2250 0.4	**25**	0423 2.1 / 1018 0.3 / TU 1648 2.0 / 2236 0.3
11	0512 2.1 / 1115 0.3 / TU 1739 1.9 / 2328 0.5	**26**	0501 2.1 / 1103 0.2 / W 1731 1.9 / 2319 0.3
12	0548 2.0 / 1157 0.4 / W 1817 1.8	**27**	0542 2.1 / 1149 0.2 / TH 1817 1.9
13	0007 0.5 / 0624 2.0 / TH 1240 0.5 / 1858 1.8	**28**	0006 0.4 / 0627 2.1 / F 1239 0.3 / 1909 1.8
14	0049 0.6 / 0707 2.0 / F 1327 0.5 / (1946 1.7	**29**	0055 0.4 / 0719 2.0 / SA 1333 0.3 / (2008 1.8
15	0136 0.6 / 0758 1.9 / SA 1421 0.6 / 2045 1.7	**30**	0151 0.5 / 0821 2.0 / SU 1434 0.4 / 2114 1.8

DECEMBER

#	Time m	#	Time m
1	0253 0.5 / 0930 2.0 / M 1542 0.4 / 2224 1.8	**16**	0240 0.6 / 0904 1.9 / TU 1523 0.5 / 2153 1.7
2	0402 0.5 / 1042 2.0 / TU 1650 0.4 / 2330 1.9	**17**	0342 0.6 / 1012 1.9 / W 1627 0.5 / 2301 1.8
3	0512 0.5 / 1151 2.0 / W 1754 0.4	**18**	0450 0.6 / 1121 1.9 / TH 1731 0.5
4	0030 1.9 / 0615 0.4 / TH 1252 2.1 / 1851 0.3	**19**	0005 1.8 / 0556 0.5 / F 1226 1.9 / 1829 0.4
5	0124 2.0 / 0712 0.3 / F 1348 2.1 / 1942 0.3	**20**	0103 1.9 / 0654 0.5 / SA 1324 1.9 / 1921 0.4
6	0214 2.0 / 0804 0.3 / SA 1439 2.1 / O 2028 0.3	**21**	0155 1.9 / 0746 0.4 / SU 1418 1.9 / 2008 0.3
7	0300 2.1 / 0852 0.2 / SU 1525 2.0 / 2112 0.3	**22**	0242 2.0 / 0834 0.3 / M 1507 1.9 / ● 2053 0.3
8	0342 2.1 / 0937 0.3 / M 1606 1.9 / 2152 0.4	**23**	0327 2.0 / 0920 0.2 / TU 1553 1.9 / 2136 0.3
9	0419 2.0 / 1019 0.3 / TU 1644 1.9 / 2230 0.4	**24**	0409 2.1 / 1005 0.2 / W 1638 1.9 / 2221 0.3
10	0454 2.0 / 1058 0.3 / W 1718 1.8 / 2306 0.4	**25**	0451 2.1 / 1050 0.1 / TH 1722 1.9 / 2305 0.2
11	0526 2.0 / 1136 0.4 / TH 1751 1.8 / 2342 0.5	**26**	0534 2.1 / 1136 0.1 / F 1808 1.9 / 2351 0.3
12	0557 2.0 / 1214 0.4 / F 1824 1.7	**27**	0619 2.1 / 1225 0.2 / SA 1857 1.8
13	0018 0.5 / 0633 2.0 / SA 1253 0.5 / 1903 1.7	**28**	0039 0.3 / 0709 2.1 / SU 1316 0.2 / (1950 1.8
14	0100 0.5 / 0715 2.0 / SU 1336 0.5 / (1951 1.7	**29**	0132 0.3 / 0806 2.0 / M 1412 0.3 / 2049 1.8
15	0146 0.5 / 0805 1.9 / M 1426 0.5 / 2048 1.7	**30**	0229 0.4 / 0909 2.0 / TU 1514 0.3 / 2154 1.8
		31	0334 0.4 / 1018 2.0 / W 1621 0.4 / 2300 1.8

Chart Datum: 0·69 metres below Dansk Normal Null
HAT is 2·2 metres above Chart Datum

TIDES

TIME ZONE -0100	GERMANY – HELGOLAND	Dates in amber are SPRINGS
(German Standard Time)		Dates in yellow are NEAPS
Subtract 1 hour for UT	LAT 54°11′N LONG 7°53′E	
For German Summer Time add	TIMES AND HEIGHTS OF HIGH AND LOW WATERS	2014
ONE hour in non-shaded areas		

JANUARY

Time	m		Time	m		Time	m		Time	m
1 0547	0.5	**16**	0639	0.6						
1122	3.1		1215	2.9						
W 1808	0.5	TH	1850	0.6						
● 2345	3.2		○							

JANUARY

No	Time / m	No	Time / m
1	0547 0.5 / 1122 3.1 / W 1808 0.5 / ● 2345 3.2	**16**	0639 0.6 / 1215 2.9 / TH 1850 0.6 / ○
2	0640 0.4 / 1215 3.1 / TH 1900 0.5	**17**	0029 3.2 / 0715 0.6 / F 1250 3.0 / 1924 0.6
3	0035 3.3 / 0733 0.4 / F 1307 3.1 / 1952 0.5	**18**	0103 3.2 / 0748 0.6 / SA 1322 3.0 / 1956 0.6
4	0125 3.3 / 0826 0.3 / SA 1400 3.1 / 2042 0.5	**19**	0135 3.2 / 0819 0.6 / SU 1353 3.0 / 2026 0.6
5	0215 3.4 / 0915 0.4 / SU 1447 3.1 / 2127 0.5	**20**	0204 3.2 / 0848 0.6 / M 1423 3.0 / 2055 0.6
6	0300 3.3 / 0959 0.4 / M 1532 3.0 / 2209 0.5	**21**	0233 3.2 / 0919 0.6 / TU 1456 2.9 / 2128 0.6
7	0345 3.3 / 1043 0.5 / TU 1617 2.9 / 2253 0.6	**22**	0307 3.2 / 0953 0.6 / W 1533 2.9 / 2204 0.7
8	0434 3.2 / 1128 0.6 / W 1706 2.9 / ☽ 2340 0.7	**23**	0343 3.1 / 1027 0.7 / TH 1609 2.9 / 2239 0.7
9	0529 3.1 / 1217 0.8 / TH 1801 2.8	**24**	0419 3.1 / 1101 0.7 / F 1647 2.8 / ☽ 2321 0.8
10	0037 0.8 / 0629 3.0 / F 1315 0.8 / 1904 2.8	**25**	0505 2.9 / 1149 0.8 / SA 1740 2.8
11	0146 0.9 / 0739 2.9 / SA 1424 0.9 / 2015 2.8	**26**	0023 0.9 / 0610 2.8 / SU 1300 0.8 / 1853 2.8
12	0304 0.9 / 0851 2.9 / SU 1536 0.9 / 2124 2.9	**27**	0144 0.9 / 0732 2.8 / M 1424 0.8 / 2016 2.8
13	0415 0.8 / 0956 2.9 / M 1639 0.8 / 2223 3.0	**28**	0310 0.8 / 0855 2.9 / TU 1546 0.7 / 2132 2.9
14	0513 0.7 / 1050 2.9 / TU 1730 0.7 / 2312 3.0	**29**	0428 0.6 / 1010 2.9 / W 1657 0.6 / 2238 3.1
15	0559 0.6 / 1135 2.9 / W 1813 0.6 / 2353 3.1	**30**	0534 0.4 / 1112 3.0 / TH 1757 0.5 / ● 2334 3.2
		31	0631 0.3 / 1205 3.1 / F 1851 0.4

FEBRUARY

No	Time / m	No	Time / m
1	0024 3.3 / 0723 0.3 / SA 1255 3.1 / 1941 0.4	**16**	0041 3.2 / 0726 0.5 / SU 1300 3.0 / 1937 0.5
2	0112 3.3 / 0814 0.3 / SU 1345 3.1 / 2029 0.4	**17**	0112 3.2 / 0756 0.5 / M 1329 3.0 / 2006 0.4
3	0200 3.4 / 0901 0.3 / M 1431 3.1 / 2113 0.4	**18**	0142 3.1 / 0826 0.5 / TU 1400 3.0 / 2037 0.4
4	0244 3.3 / 0942 0.3 / TU 1512 3.0 / 2151 0.4	**19**	0213 3.1 / 0858 0.5 / W 1435 3.0 / 2112 0.4
5	0325 3.3 / 1019 0.5 / W 1551 3.0 / 2229 0.5	**20**	0248 3.1 / 0934 0.5 / TH 1511 3.0 / 2148 0.5
6	0408 3.2 / 1054 0.6 / TH 1631 2.9 / ☽ 2307 0.6	**21**	0324 3.1 / 1006 0.5 / F 1545 3.0 / 2220 0.5
7	0452 3.0 / 1132 0.7 / F 1714 2.9 / 2352 0.7	**22**	0356 3.0 / 1035 0.6 / SA 1617 2.9 / ☽ 2254 0.6
8	0543 2.9 / 1220 0.8 / SA 1809 2.8	**23**	0434 2.9 / 1115 0.7 / SU 1703 2.8 / 2349 0.7
9	0055 0.8 / 0648 2.7 / SU 1329 0.9 / 1922 2.7	**24**	0536 2.8 / 1224 0.8 / M 1816 2.7
10	0218 0.8 / 0808 2.7 / M 1452 0.9 / 2045 2.8	**25**	0113 0.8 / 0703 2.7 / TU 1355 0.8 / 1948 2.8
11	0343 0.8 / 0927 2.7 / TU 1610 0.8 / 2158 2.9	**26**	0249 0.7 / 0837 2.8 / W 1527 0.7 / 2114 2.9
12	0451 0.7 / 1031 2.8 / W 1710 0.7 / 2252 3.0	**27**	0415 0.5 / 0958 2.9 / TH 1644 0.6 / 2225 3.1
13	0540 0.6 / 1118 2.9 / TH 1754 0.6 / 2333 3.1	**28**	0523 0.4 / 1102 3.0 / F 1745 0.5 / 2320 3.2
14	0619 0.5 / 1156 2.9 / F 1831 0.6		
15	0008 3.2 / 0654 0.5 / SA 1229 3.0 / ○ 1905 0.5		

MARCH

No	Time / m	No	Time / m
1	0618 0.3 / 1153 3.0 / SA 1838 0.4 / ●	**16**	0623 0.4 / 1200 3.0 / SU 1839 0.5 / ○
2	0009 3.3 / 0708 0.2 / SU 1239 3.1 / 1925 0.3	**17**	0011 3.1 / 0656 0.4 / M 1232 3.0 / 1912 0.4
3	0054 3.3 / 0755 0.2 / M 1324 3.1 / 2010 0.3	**18**	0045 3.1 / 0728 0.4 / TU 1304 3.0 / 1944 0.4
4	0139 3.3 / 0838 0.3 / TU 1408 3.1 / 2052 0.3	**19**	0118 3.1 / 0802 0.4 / W 1337 3.0 / 2018 0.3
5	0222 3.3 / 0916 0.4 / W 1447 3.1 / 2129 0.3	**20**	0152 3.1 / 0837 0.4 / TH 1413 3.0 / 2055 0.3
6	0302 3.2 / 0950 0.5 / TH 1523 3.1 / 2204 0.4	**21**	0229 3.1 / 0914 0.4 / F 1450 3.0 / 2133 0.3
7	0340 3.1 / 1020 0.6 / F 1557 3.0 / 2237 0.5	**22**	0306 3.1 / 0948 0.4 / SA 1525 3.0 / 2207 0.4
8	0419 3.0 / 1051 0.7 / SA 1633 2.9 / ☽ 2315 0.6	**23**	0341 3.0 / 1018 0.5 / SU 1559 2.9 / 2242 0.5
9	0502 2.8 / 1132 0.8 / SU 1721 2.8	**24**	0422 2.9 / 1059 0.6 / M 1646 2.9 / ☽ 2336 0.7
10	0009 0.7 / 0601 2.6 / M 1236 0.9 / 1831 2.7	**25**	0523 2.7 / 1208 0.7 / TU 1759 2.8
11	0128 0.8 / 0722 2.5 / TU 1404 0.9 / 1959 2.7	**26**	0100 0.7 / 0650 2.7 / W 1341 0.8 / 1931 2.9
12	0259 0.8 / 0849 2.6 / W 1532 0.8 / 2121 2.8	**27**	0236 0.6 / 0825 2.7 / TH 1514 0.7 / 2059 3.0
13	0418 0.7 / 1001 2.7 / TH 1640 0.7 / 2222 3.0	**28**	0401 0.5 / 0945 2.9 / F 1628 0.6 / 2207 3.1
14	0511 0.5 / 1050 2.8 / F 1726 0.6 / 2303 3.0	**29**	0505 0.3 / 1045 2.9 / SA 1726 0.4 / 2301 3.2
15	0549 0.5 / 1127 2.9 / SA 1803 0.5 / 2338 3.1	**30**	0558 0.3 / 1134 3.0 / SU 1818 0.4 / ● 2349 3.2
		31	0646 0.3 / 1219 3.1 / M 1905 0.3

APRIL

No	Time / m	No	Time / m
1	0034 3.2 / 0731 0.3 / TU 1301 3.1 / 1948 0.3	**16**	0015 3.1 / 0659 0.2 / W 1236 3.1 / 1920 0.3
2	0117 3.2 / 0811 0.3 / W 1341 3.1 / 2028 0.3	**17**	0052 3.1 / 0737 0.3 / TH 1312 3.1 / 1959 0.3
3	0158 3.2 / 0847 0.4 / TH 1419 3.1 / 2105 0.3	**18**	0130 3.1 / 0816 0.3 / F 1350 3.1 / 2039 0.3
4	0237 3.1 / 0919 0.4 / F 1454 3.1 / 2139 0.4	**19**	0211 3.1 / 0855 0.3 / SA 1429 3.1 / 2118 0.3
5	0314 3.0 / 0949 0.5 / SA 1527 3.0 / 2211 0.4	**20**	0252 3.0 / 0932 0.4 / SU 1509 3.1 / 2158 0.3
6	0350 2.9 / 1019 0.6 / SU 1601 2.9 / 2245 0.6	**21**	0334 3.0 / 1011 0.5 / M 1551 3.1 / 2241 0.4
7	0430 2.7 / 1056 0.7 / M 1644 2.9 / ☽ 2330 0.7	**22**	0422 2.9 / 1058 0.6 / TU 1643 3.0 / ☽ 2338 0.5
8	0522 2.6 / 1151 0.9 / TU 1745 2.8	**23**	0525 2.8 / 1206 0.7 / W 1753 2.9
9	0039 0.8 / 0634 2.5 / W 1312 0.9 / 1906 2.7	**24**	0056 0.6 / 0646 2.7 / TH 1332 0.7 / 1918 3.0
10	0206 0.8 / 0759 2.6 / TH 1441 0.8 / 2029 2.8	**25**	0225 0.6 / 0812 2.8 / F 1457 0.7 / 2040 3.1
11	0328 0.7 / 0914 2.7 / F 1554 0.7 / 2135 2.9	**26**	0342 0.5 / 0925 2.9 / SA 1607 0.6 / 2145 3.1
12	0427 0.5 / 1008 2.8 / SA 1645 0.6 / 2222 3.0	**27**	0441 0.4 / 1021 2.9 / SU 1701 0.5 / 2237 3.1
13	0508 0.4 / 1048 2.9 / SU 1725 0.5 / 2300 3.0	**28**	0531 0.3 / 1109 3.0 / M 1753 0.4 / 2327 3.1
14	0545 0.4 / 1124 3.0 / M 1805 0.5 / 2338 3.1	**29**	0621 0.3 / 1156 3.0 / TU 1843 0.3 / ●
15	0622 0.4 / 1201 3.0 / TU 1843 0.4 / ○	**30**	0014 3.1 / 0706 0.3 / W 1238 3.1 / 1926 0.3

TIDES

Chart Datum: 1·68 metres below Normal Null (German reference level)
HAT is 3·0 metres above Chart Datum

TIDES

TIME ZONE -0100
(German Standard Time)
Subtract 1 hour for UT
For German Summer Time add ONE hour in **non-shaded areas**

GERMANY – HELGOLAND
LAT 54°11'N   LONG 7°53'E
TIMES AND HEIGHTS OF HIGH AND LOW WATERS

Dates in amber are **SPRINGS**
Dates in yellow are **NEAPS**

2014

MAY

Day	Time m	Time m	Time m	Time m		Day	Time m	Time m	Time m	Time m
1 TH	0056 3.1	0744 0.3	1315 3.1	2005 0.3		16 F	0026 3.1	0713 0.3	1248 3.1	1939 0.3
2 F	0135 3.1	0818 0.4	1351 3.1	2040 0.3		17 SA	0110 3.1	0757 0.4	1331 3.2	2024 0.3
3 SA	0212 3.0	0851 0.4	1427 3.1	2114 0.4		18 SU	0157 3.1	0841 0.4	1415 3.2	2108 0.3
4 SU	0250 2.9	0923 0.5	1502 3.1	2147 0.5		19 M	0243 3.0	0923 0.4	1459 3.2	2153 0.3
5 M	0326 2.9	0954 0.6	1538 3.0	2221 0.6		20 TU	0331 3.0	1008 0.5	1547 3.2	2243 0.4
6 TU	0405 2.8	1029 0.7	1616 3.0	2301 0.7		21 W	0424 2.9	1101 0.6	1643 3.1	2342 0.5
7 W	0450 2.7	1115 0.8	1706 2.9	(2356 0.8		22 TH	0525 2.8	1204 0.7	1748 3.1	
8 TH	0548 2.6	1220 0.9	1811 2.8			23 F	0050 0.5	0636 2.8	1317 0.7	1902 3.0
9 F	0108 0.7	0700 2.6	1339 0.8	1926 2.8		24 SA	0205 0.5	0751 2.8	1433 0.6	2015 3.1
10 SA	0225 0.7	0813 2.7	1453 0.7	2035 2.9		25 SU	0314 0.5	0858 2.8	1539 0.6	2119 3.1
11 SU	0329 0.5	0914 2.8	1552 0.7	2131 2.9		26 M	0412 0.4	0954 2.9	1636 0.5	2213 3.1
12 M	0419 2.9	1002 0.6	1641 0.6	2218 3.0		27 TU	0503 0.4	1043 3.0	1729 0.4	2304 3.1
13 TU	0503 0.4	1045 3.0	1728 0.5	2303 3.1		28 W	0554 0.4	1131 3.0	1821 0.4	2354 3.0
14 W	0547 0.4	1127 3.1	1813 0.5	○ 2345 3.1		29 TH	0641 0.4	1215 3.1	1905 0.3	
15 TH	0630 0.4	1207 3.1	1856 0.4			30 F	0036 3.0	0720 0.4	1253 3.1	1943 0.3
						31 SA	0114 3.0	0753 0.4	1328 3.2	2018 0.4

JUNE

Day	Time m	Time m	Time m	Time m		Day	Time m	Time m	Time m	Time m
1 SU	0151 3.0	0827 0.5	1405 3.2	2052 0.5		16 M	0147 3.1	0831 0.4	1404 3.3	2102 0.3
2 M	0228 2.9	0900 0.5	1440 3.2	2126 0.5		17 TU	0236 3.1	0917 0.4	1451 3.3	2150 0.3
3 TU	0304 2.9	0932 0.6	1515 3.1	2200 0.6		18 W	0325 3.0	1004 0.5	1540 3.3	2240 0.4
4 W	0341 2.9	1006 0.7	1551 3.1	(2236 0.7		19 TH	0417 2.9	1055 0.5	1634 3.2	(2334 0.5
5 TH	0420 2.8	1045 0.8	1631 3.0	(2319 0.7		20 F	0514 2.9	1150 0.6	1734 3.2	
6 F	0506 2.7	1134 0.8	1721 3.0			21 SA	0032 0.5	0615 2.8	1251 0.6	1837 3.1
7 SA	0013 0.7	0602 2.7	1236 0.8	1823 2.9		22 SU	0133 0.6	0719 2.8	1359 0.7	1945 3.0
8 SU	0117 0.7	0708 2.7	1347 0.8	1932 2.9		23 M	0238 0.6	0824 2.8	1508 0.7	2051 3.0
9 M	0225 0.6	0813 2.8	1454 0.8	2037 2.9		24 TU	0341 0.6	0925 2.9	1612 0.6	2151 3.0
10 TU	0326 0.6	0912 2.9	1555 0.7	2135 3.0		25 W	0438 0.5	1019 3.0	1709 0.5	2245 3.0
11 W	0422 0.5	1005 3.0	1652 0.6	2229 3.1		26 TH	0531 0.5	1110 3.0	1801 0.4	2335 3.0
12 TH	0515 0.5	1055 3.1	1745 0.5	2318 3.1		27 F	0618 0.5	1155 3.1	1845 0.4 ●	
13 F	0605 0.4	1142 3.1	1834 0.4 ○			28 SA	0019 3.0	0658 0.4	1234 3.1	1924 0.4 ○
14 SA	0006 3.1	0653 0.4	1228 3.2	1923 0.4		29 SU	0057 3.0	0733 0.5	1311 3.2	1959 0.5
15 SU	0055 3.1	0742 0.4	1316 3.3	2013 0.4		30 M	0132 3.0	0807 0.5	1346 3.3	2033 0.5

JULY

Day	Time m	Time m	Time m	Time m		Day	Time m	Time m	Time m	Time m
1 TU	0207 3.0	0840 0.6	1419 3.3	2104 0.6		16 W	0225 3.1	0908 0.4	1440 3.4	2140 0.3
2 W	0240 3.0	0910 0.6	1451 3.2	2136 0.6		17 TH	0311 3.0	0952 0.4	1526 3.3	2226 0.4
3 TH	0314 2.9	0943 0.7	1525 3.2	2211 0.7		18 F	0359 3.0	1038 0.5	1616 3.3	2313 0.5
4 F	0351 2.9	1019 0.8	1602 3.1	2248 0.7		19 SA	0450 2.9	1126 0.6	1709 3.2 (	
5 SA	0430 2.9	1058 0.8	1642 3.1	(2327 0.7		20 SU	0000 0.6	0542 2.9	1218 0.7	1805 3.1
6 SU	0513 2.8	1144 0.8	1731 3.0			21 M	0051 0.7	0639 2.9	1320 0.7	1909 3.0
7 M	0018 0.8	0608 2.8	1246 0.9	1833 2.9		22 TU	0155 0.8	0745 2.9	1434 0.8	2020 2.9
8 TU	0123 0.7	0714 2.8	1358 0.8	1944 2.9		23 W	0307 0.8	0855 2.9	1550 0.7	2130 2.9
9 W	0234 0.7	0823 2.9	1512 0.7	2055 2.9		24 TH	0416 0.7	1000 3.0	1653 0.6	2230 2.9
10 TH	0344 0.6	0929 2.9	1620 0.6	2201 3.0		25 F	0512 0.6	1053 3.0	1744 0.5	2319 2.9
11 F	0448 0.5	1028 3.1	1722 0.5	2259 3.0		26 SA	0559 0.6	1138 3.1	1826 0.5 ●	
12 SA	0546 0.5	1122 3.2	1818 0.4	○ 2352 3.1		27 SU	0001 3.0	0638 0.6	1217 3.2	1904 0.5
13 SU	0639 0.4	1213 3.3	1910 0.3			28 M	0039 3.0	0715 0.6	1252 3.2	1939 0.6
14 M	0044 3.1	0731 0.4	1303 3.3	2003 0.3		29 TU	0112 3.0	0748 0.6	1325 3.3	2011 0.6
15 TU	0136 3.1	0821 0.4	1353 3.4	2054 0.3		30 W	0143 3.1	0818 0.6	1355 3.3	2039 0.6
						31 TH	0213 3.0	0847 0.6	1425 3.2	2109 0.6

AUGUST

Day	Time m	Time m	Time m	Time m		Day	Time m	Time m	Time m	Time m
1 F	0245 3.0	0919 0.7	1459 3.2	2144 0.7		16 SA	0334 3.1	1014 0.5	1552 3.3	2241 0.7
2 SA	0323 3.0	0955 0.7	1536 3.2	2219 0.7		17 SU	0417 3.0	1056 0.6	1639 3.2	(2320 0.7
3 SU	0400 3.0	1030 0.7	1611 3.1	2251 0.7		18 M	0502 3.0	1141 0.7	1728 3.0	
4 M	0435 2.9	1106 0.8	1650 3.0	(2330 0.8		19 TU	0005 0.9	0554 2.9	1238 0.8	1829 2.9
5 TU	0518 2.8	1157 0.9	1744 2.9			20 W	0108 1.0	0702 2.8	1355 0.9	1945 2.8
6 W	0030 2.8	0622 2.8	1310 0.9	1859 2.8		21 TH	0229 1.0	0822 2.9	1521 0.9	2106 2.8
7 TH	0149 0.8	0741 2.8	1436 0.8	2023 2.8		22 F	0350 0.9	0939 3.0	1634 0.7	2214 2.9
8 F	0313 0.7	0900 2.9	1557 0.6	2141 2.9		23 SA	0454 0.7	1037 3.1	1726 0.6	2302 2.9
9 SA	0427 0.6	1009 3.1	1705 0.5	2246 3.0		24 SU	0539 0.7	1118 3.1	1804 0.6	2340 3.0
10 SU	0531 0.6	1107 3.2	1804 0.4	○ 2341 3.1		25 M	0616 0.6	1154 3.2	1839 0.6 ●	
11 M	0627 0.5	1158 3.3	1857 0.3			26 TU	0014 3.0	0651 0.6	1228 3.2	1913 0.6
12 TU	0031 3.2	0718 0.4	1247 3.4	1949 0.3		27 W	0046 3.1	0724 0.6	1300 3.2	1943 0.6
13 W	0120 3.2	0806 0.4	1335 3.4	2038 0.3		28 TH	0116 3.1	0754 0.6	1330 3.2	2012 0.6
14 TH	0207 3.1	0851 0.4	1422 3.4	2122 0.4		29 F	0146 3.1	0824 0.6	1400 3.2	2042 0.6
15 F	0251 3.1	0933 0.4	1506 3.4	2202 0.5		30 SA	0219 3.1	0857 0.6	1434 3.2	2117 0.6
						31 SU	0255 3.1	0933 0.6	1510 3.2	2152 0.7

Chart Datum: 1·68 metres below Normal Null (German reference level)
HAT is 3·0 metres above Chart Datum

TIME ZONE -0100
(German Standard Time)
Subtract 1 hour for UT
For German Summer Time add
ONE hour in **non-shaded areas**

GERMANY – HELGOLAND
LAT 54°11'N LONG 7°53'E
TIMES AND HEIGHTS OF HIGH AND LOW WATERS

Dates in amber are **SPRINGS**
Dates in yellow are **NEAPS**

2014

SEPTEMBER

Day	Time m	Time m	Day	Time m	Time m
1 M	0331 3.0 / 1007 0.7	1545 3.1 / 2221 0.7	**16** TU	0423 3.0 / 1105 0.8	1652 2.9 / ☽2322 1.0
2 TU	0403 3.0 / 1038 0.7	1620 3.0 / ☽2255 0.8	**17** W	0511 2.9 / 1156 0.9	1749 2.8
3 W	0443 2.9 / 1123 0.8	1711 2.8 / 2352 0.9	**18** TH	0021 1.1 / 0618 2.9	1310 1.0 / 1905 2.7
4 TH	0545 2.8 / 1237 0.9	1829 2.8	**19** F	0144 1.1 / 0742 2.9	1441 1.0 / 2031 2.7
5 F	0117 1.0 / 0711 2.9	1411 1.0 / 2002 2.8	**20** SA	0314 1.0 / 0906 2.9	1603 0.9 / 2146 2.8
6 SA	0251 0.9 / 0839 3.0	1539 0.7 / 2126 2.9	**21** SU	0425 0.9 / 1009 3.1	1658 0.7 / 2237 2.9
7 SU	0411 0.8 / 0953 3.1	1651 0.5 / 2233 3.0	**22** M	0512 0.8 / 1050 3.1	1735 0.6 / 2311 3.0
8 M	0516 0.6 / 1050 3.2	1748 0.4 / 2327 3.1	**23** TU	0546 0.7 / 1133 3.1	1806 0.6 / 2343 3.0
9 TU	0610 0.5 / 1140 3.3	1839 0.4 / ○	**24** W	0621 0.6 / 1157 3.2	1839 0.6 / ●
10 W	0014 3.2 / 0700 0.5	1227 3.4 / 1928 0.4	**25** TH	0016 3.1 / 0655 0.6	1231 3.2 / 1911 0.6
11 TH	0100 3.2 / 0746 0.4	1314 3.4 / 2014 0.4	**26** F	0048 3.1 / 0728 0.6	1304 3.2 / 1944 0.6
12 F	0144 3.2 / 0830 0.5	1400 3.4 / 2056 0.5	**27** SA	0120 3.1 / 0801 0.6	1336 3.2 / 2017 0.6
13 SA	0226 3.2 / 0910 0.5	1443 3.3 / 2132 0.6	**28** SU	0153 3.1 / 0835 0.6	1410 3.2 / 2052 0.6
14 SU	0305 3.2 / 0948 0.5	1524 3.2 / 2207 0.7	**29** M	0228 3.1 / 0911 0.6	1446 3.1 / 2125 0.7
15 M	0343 3.1 / 1025 0.6	1606 3.1 / 2241 0.8	**30** TU	0304 3.1 / 0946 0.6	1522 3.1 / 2157 0.8

OCTOBER

Day	Time m	Time m	Day	Time m	Time m
1 W	0339 3.1 / 1019 0.7	1601 3.0 / ☽2234 0.9	**16** TH	0435 3.0 / 1119 1.0	1712 2.7 / 2338 1.1
2 TH	0422 3.0 / 1106 0.8	1656 2.8 / 2333 1.0	**17** F	0534 2.9 / 1224 1.1	1820 2.7
3 F	0526 2.9 / 1220 0.9	1815 2.8	**18** SA	0054 1.2 / 0652 2.9	1347 1.1 / 1942 2.7
4 SA	0059 1.1 / 0652 3.0	1354 0.9 / 1948 2.8	**19** SU	0221 1.1 / 0814 2.9	1511 1.0 / 2059 2.8
5 SU	0234 1.0 / 0822 3.1	1524 0.8 / 2112 2.9	**20** M	0337 1.0 / 0922 3.0	1613 0.8 / 2155 2.9
6 M	0354 0.9 / 0934 3.2	1632 0.6 / 2216 3.0	**21** TU	0430 0.9 / 1009 3.1	1654 0.7 / 2234 3.0
7 TU	0455 0.7 / 1030 3.3	1727 0.6 / 2307 3.1	**22** W	0508 0.8 / 1046 3.1	1727 0.7 / 2308 3.1
8 W	0548 0.6 / 1119 3.3	1816 0.4 / ○2354 3.1	**23** TH	0546 0.7 / 1123 3.1	1803 0.7 / ●2345 3.1
9 TH	0638 0.5 / 1207 3.3	1904 0.4	**24** F	0624 0.7 / 1201 3.2	1840 0.6
10 F	0038 3.2 / 0724 0.5	1253 3.3 / 1947 0.5	**25** SA	0020 3.1 / 0702 0.6	1237 3.2 / 1917 0.6
11 SA	0119 3.2 / 0806 0.5	1336 3.3 / 2026 0.6	**26** SU	0054 3.2 / 0738 0.6	1313 3.2 / 1954 0.6
12 SU	0159 3.3 / 0846 0.5	1418 3.2 / 2102 0.7	**27** M	0130 3.2 / 0816 0.6	1349 3.1 / 2030 0.6
13 M	0236 3.2 / 0922 0.6	1458 3.1 / 2134 0.7	**28** TU	0206 3.2 / 0853 0.6	1427 3.1 / 2105 0.7
14 TU	0312 3.2 / 0957 0.6	1537 3.0 / 2207 0.8	**29** W	0243 3.2 / 0930 0.6	1507 3.1 / 2141 0.8
15 W	0350 3.1 / 1033 0.8	1620 2.9 / ☽2245 1.0	**30** TH	0324 3.2 / 1010 0.7	1553 3.0 / 2226 0.9
			31 F	0413 3.1 / 1102 0.9	1650 2.9 / ☽2326 1.0

NOVEMBER

Day	Time m	Time m	Day	Time m	Time m
1 SA	0516 3.1 / 1213 0.9	1805 2.8	**16** SU	0001 1.2 / 0554 3.0	1246 1.1 / 1841 2.7
2 SU	0046 1.1 / 0637 3.1	1339 0.9 / 1931 2.8	**17** M	0115 1.2 / 0707 2.9	1402 1.0 / 1954 2.7
3 M	0214 1.0 / 0801 3.1	1502 0.8 / 2051 2.9	**18** TU	0232 1.1 / 0819 2.9	1510 0.9 / 2058 2.9
4 TU	0330 0.9 / 0912 3.2	1608 0.7 / 2153 3.0	**19** W	0335 1.0 / 0918 3.0	1603 0.8 / 2148 3.0
5 W	0431 0.8 / 1008 3.2	1701 0.6 / 2244 3.1	**20** TH	0424 0.9 / 1005 3.1	1646 0.7 / 2231 3.1
6 TH	0524 0.7 / 1059 3.2	1752 0.6 / ○2331 3.1	**21** F	0510 0.8 / 1048 3.1	1729 0.7 / 2312 3.1
7 F	0616 0.6 / 1148 3.2	1840 0.5	**22** SA	0554 0.7 / 1130 3.2	1810 0.7 / ●2351 3.2
8 SA	0016 3.2 / 0703 0.5	1233 3.2 / 1921 0.5	**23** SU	0636 0.7 / 1210 3.2	1852 0.6
9 SU	0055 3.2 / 0744 0.5	1314 3.2 / 1958 0.6	**24** M	0030 3.2 / 0717 0.6	1252 3.1 / 1934 0.6
10 M	0133 3.2 / 0822 0.6	1354 3.1 / 2033 0.7	**25** TU	0110 3.2 / 0800 0.6	1335 3.1 / 2016 0.6
11 TU	0210 3.2 / 0858 0.6	1434 3.1 / 2107 0.7	**26** W	0151 3.3 / 0841 0.6	1418 3.1 / 2055 0.7
12 W	0247 3.2 / 0932 0.7	1513 3.0 / 2140 0.8	**27** TH	0232 3.3 / 0923 0.6	1500 3.1 / 2135 0.7
13 TH	0324 3.2 / 1007 0.8	1552 2.9 / 2216 1.0	**28** F	0315 3.3 / 1008 0.7	1548 3.0 / 2223 0.9
14 F	0404 3.1 / 1047 1.0	1637 2.8 / ☽2301 1.1	**29** SA	0406 3.2 / 1101 0.8	1645 2.9 / ☽2321 0.9
15 SA	0452 3.0 / 1139 1.1	1732 2.7	**30** SU	0507 3.2 / 1205 0.8	1752 2.9

DECEMBER

Day	Time m	Time m	Day	Time m	Time m
1 M	0030 0.9 / 0618 3.1	1318 0.8 / 1907 2.8	**16** TU	0010 1.1 / 0600 2.9	1249 1.0 / 1843 2.7
2 TU	0146 0.9 / 0734 3.1	1432 0.8 / 2021 2.9	**17** W	0119 1.1 / 0709 2.9	1359 1.0 / 1951 2.8
3 W	0300 0.9 / 0846 3.2	1539 0.8 / 2125 3.0	**18** TH	0231 1.1 / 0818 3.0	1505 0.9 / 2055 2.9
4 TH	0405 0.8 / 0947 3.2	1636 0.7 / 2220 3.0	**19** F	0335 1.0 / 0920 3.0	1603 0.8 / 2150 3.0
5 F	0503 0.7 / 1041 3.1	1730 0.6 / 2310 3.1	**20** SA	0433 0.9 / 1014 3.1	1656 0.7 / 2240 3.1
6 SA	0557 0.6 / 1131 3.1	1818 0.6 / ○2355 3.1	**21** SU	0525 0.8 / 1103 3.1	1745 0.7 / 2326 3.2
7 SU	0644 0.5 / 1216 3.1	1859 0.5	**22** M	0613 0.6 / 1149 3.1	1831 0.6 / ●
8 M	0035 3.2 / 0724 0.5	1256 3.0 / 1935 0.6	**23** TU	0009 3.2 / 0700 0.6	1236 3.1 / 1919 0.6
9 TU	0112 3.2 / 0801 0.6	1335 3.0 / 2010 0.7	**24** W	0054 3.3 / 0748 0.5	1324 3.1 / 2006 0.6
10 W	0150 3.3 / 0837 0.7	1414 3.0 / 2045 0.7	**25** TH	0140 3.3 / 0835 0.5	1411 3.1 / 2050 0.6
11 TH	0227 3.3 / 0912 0.7	1451 3.0 / 2118 0.8	**26** F	0224 3.3 / 0919 0.5	1454 3.1 / 2132 0.6
12 F	0301 3.3 / 0944 0.8	1526 2.9 / 2151 0.9	**27** SA	0308 3.3 / 1005 0.5	1540 3.0 / 2218 0.7
13 SA	0335 3.2 / 1019 0.9	1604 2.9 / 2228 1.0	**28** SU	0357 3.3 / 1055 0.6	1632 3.0 / ☽2309 0.7
14 SU	0414 3.1 / 1059 1.0	1647 2.8 / ☽2312 1.1	**29** M	0453 3.2 / 1149 0.7	1730 2.9
15 M	0500 3.0 / 1148 1.1	1739 2.7	**30** TU	0006 0.8 / 0554 3.1	1248 0.9 / 1834 2.8
			31 W	0112 0.8 / 0703 3.1	1355 0.9 / 1944 2.8

Chart Datum: 1·68 metres below Normal Null (German reference level)
HAT is 3·0 metres above Chart Datum

TIDES

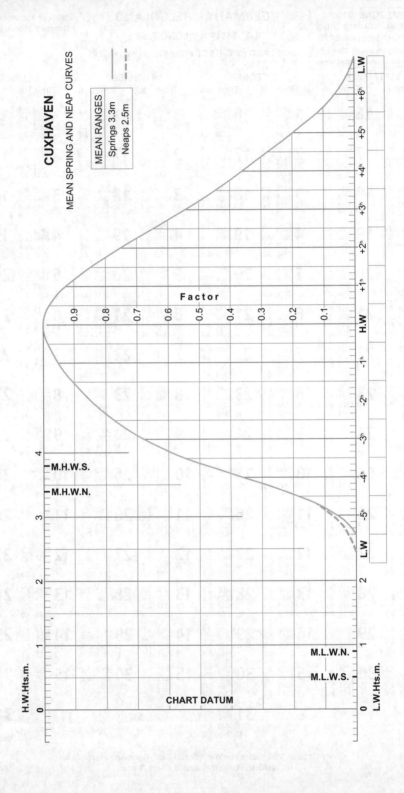

CUXHAVEN

MEAN SPRING AND NEAP CURVES

MEAN RANGES
Springs 3.3m
Neaps 2.5m

TIME ZONE -0100
(German Standard Time)
Subtract 1 hour for UT
For German Summer Time add ONE hour in **non-shaded areas**

GERMANY – CUXHAVEN

LAT 53°52′N   LONG 8°43′E

TIMES AND HEIGHTS OF HIGH AND LOW WATERS

Dates in amber are **SPRINGS**
Dates in yellow are **NEAPS**

2014

JANUARY

Time m / Time m

1 W 0009 3.6 / 0711 0.4 / 1237 3.5 / ● 1933 0.4
16 TH 0106 3.6 / 0803 0.5 / 1330 3.4 / ○ 2013 0.5
2 TH 0100 3.7 / 0805 0.3 / 1331 3.6 / 2025 0.4
17 F 0142 3.7 / 0840 0.5 / 1404 3.4 / 2047 0.5
3 F 0150 3.7 / 0858 0.3 / 1425 3.6 / 2118 0.4
18 SA 0216 3.7 / 0914 0.5 / 1437 3.5 / 2120 0.5
4 SA 0241 3.8 / 0951 0.3 / 1518 3.6 / 2209 0.4
19 SU 0247 3.8 / 0946 0.5 / 1507 3.5 / 2149 0.5
5 SU 0329 3.9 / 1041 0.4 / 1606 3.6 / 2253 0.4
20 M 0316 3.7 / 1013 0.5 / 1538 3.5 / 2217 0.5
6 M 0415 3.9 / 1125 0.4 / 1651 3.5 / 2333 0.4
21 TU 0346 3.7 / 1042 0.5 / 1611 3.4 / 2249 0.6
7 TU 0500 3.8 / 1207 0.4 / 1735 3.4
22 W 0420 3.7 / 1116 0.6 / 1646 3.4 / 2324 0.6
8 W 0013 0.5 / 0547 3.7 / 1251 0.4 / ◑ 1821 3.3
23 TH 0456 3.6 / 1148 0.6 / 1721 3.4 / 2358 0.6
9 TH 0058 0.6 / 0639 3.6 / 1336 0.6 / 1913 3.2
24 F 0531 3.5 / 1220 0.6 / 1800 3.3 ◐
10 F 0150 0.7 / 0738 3.4 / 1431 0.7 / 2014 3.2
25 SA 0037 0.7 / 0616 3.4 / 1304 0.7 / 1854 3.3
11 SA 0258 0.8 / 0848 3.3 / 1539 0.8 / 2125 3.2
26 SU 0136 0.8 / 0721 3.3 / 1412 0.8 / 2007 3.3
12 SU 0417 0.8 / 1002 3.3 / 1652 0.8 / 2235 3.3
27 M 0257 0.8 / 0842 3.3 / 1538 0.7 / 2128 3.3
13 M 0532 0.7 / 1109 3.3 / 1758 0.7 / 2335 3.4
28 TU 0426 0.7 / 1005 3.3 / 1703 0.6 / 2244 3.4
14 TU 0633 0.6 / 1204 3.3 / 1852 0.6
29 W 0548 0.5 / 1121 3.4 / 1819 0.5 / 2350 3.6
15 W 0025 3.5 / 0722 0.5 / 1250 3.4 / 1936 0.5
30 TH 0657 0.3 / 1226 3.5 / 1922 0.4 ●
31 F 0047 3.7 / 0755 0.3 / 1321 3.6 / 2016 0.3

FEBRUARY

Time m / Time m

1 SA 0137 3.8 / 0847 0.2 / 1412 3.6 / 2107 0.3
16 SU 0153 3.7 / 0851 0.4 / 1412 3.5 / 2059 0.4
2 SU 0225 3.8 / 0938 0.2 / 1502 3.6 / 2155 0.3
17 M 0223 3.7 / 0921 0.4 / 1441 3.5 / 2129 0.3
3 M 0312 3.9 / 1025 0.2 / 1547 3.6 / 2238 0.3
18 TU 0253 3.6 / 0950 0.4 / 1512 3.5 / 2158 0.3
4 TU 0357 3.9 / 1106 0.3 / 1628 3.5 / 2315 0.3
19 W 0324 3.6 / 1020 0.4 / 1547 3.5 / 2232 0.4
5 W 0439 3.8 / 1143 0.4 / 1707 3.4 / 2349 0.4
20 TH 0400 3.6 / 1055 0.4 / 1623 3.5 / 2308 0.4
6 TH 0521 3.7 / 1217 0.5 / 1745 3.4 ◑
21 F 0436 3.6 / 1128 0.4 / 1657 3.5 / 2339 0.4
7 F 0024 0.6 / 0603 3.5 / 1251 0.6 / 1826 3.3
22 SA 0508 3.5 / 1154 0.5 / 1730 3.4 ◐
8 SA 0104 0.6 / 0652 3.3 / 1333 0.7 / 1919 3.2
23 SU 0010 0.6 / 0546 3.4 / 1229 0.6 / 1816 3.3
9 SU 0202 0.7 / 0757 3.2 / 1438 0.8 / 2032 3.2
24 M 0101 0.6 / 0647 3.2 / 1333 0.7 / 1928 3.2
10 M 0324 0.7 / 0918 3.1 / 1602 0.8 / 2154 3.2
25 TU 0223 0.6 / 0813 3.2 / 1506 0.7 / 2058 3.3
11 TU 0453 0.7 / 1038 3.2 / 1724 0.7 / 2307 3.4
26 W 0401 0.6 / 0946 3.2 / 1642 0.6 / 2224 3.4
12 W 0607 0.6 / 1143 3.3 / 1828 0.6
27 TH 0532 0.4 / 1108 3.4 / 1805 0.5 / 2335 3.6
13 TH 0002 3.5 / 0701 0.5 / 1214 3.4 / 1915 0.5
28 F 0644 0.3 / 1214 3.5 / 1910 0.4
14 F 0045 3.6 / 0741 0.5 / 1309 3.4 / 1953 0.5
15 SA 0120 3.7 / 0817 0.4 / 1342 3.4 / ○ 2027 0.4

MARCH

Time m / Time m

1 SA 0032 3.7 / 0741 0.2 / 1308 3.6 / ● 2002 0.3
16 SU 0049 3.6 / 0744 0.3 / 1310 3.5 / ○ 1959 0.3
2 SU 0121 3.8 / 0831 0.2 / 1355 3.6 / 2049 0.3
17 M 0122 3.6 / 0818 0.3 / 1342 3.5 / 2033 0.3
3 M 0206 3.8 / 0917 0.2 / 1440 3.6 / 2133 0.2
18 TU 0155 3.6 / 0851 0.3 / 1414 3.5 / 2105 0.2
4 TU 0251 3.9 / 1000 0.2 / 1522 3.6 / 2215 0.3
19 W 0227 3.6 / 0923 0.3 / 1447 3.5 / 2139 0.2
5 W 0334 3.9 / 1038 0.3 / 1600 3.6 / 2251 0.3
20 TH 0302 3.6 / 0957 0.3 / 1524 3.5 / 2215 0.2
6 TH 0415 3.8 / 1112 0.3 / 1636 3.5 / 2324 0.3
21 F 0340 3.6 / 1033 0.3 / 1601 3.5 / 2252 0.2
7 F 0453 3.6 / 1142 0.4 / 1710 3.5 / 2353 0.4
22 SA 0419 3.6 / 1108 0.3 / 1637 3.5 / 2326 0.3
8 SA 0530 3.5 / 1209 0.6 / 1745 3.4 ◐
23 SU 0455 3.5 / 1137 0.4 / 1712 3.5 / 2358 0.3
9 SU 0024 0.5 / 0612 3.3 / 1243 0.7 / 1831 3.4 ◐
24 M 0535 3.3 / 1214 0.5 / 1759 3.4
10 M 0112 0.6 / 0710 3.0 / 1341 0.8 / 1940 3.2
25 TU 0048 0.5 / 0636 3.2 / 1318 0.6 / 1911 3.3
11 TU 0230 0.7 / 0830 3.0 / 1508 0.8 / 2107 3.2
26 W 0210 0.6 / 0802 3.2 / 1450 0.7 / 2041 3.4
12 W 0406 0.7 / 0958 3.0 / 1641 0.7 / 2229 3.3
27 TH 0349 0.5 / 0935 3.2 / 1628 0.6 / 2208 3.5
13 TH 0530 0.6 / 1111 3.2 / 1755 0.6 / 2330 3.5
28 F 0518 0.4 / 1055 3.3 / 1748 0.5 / 2317 3.6
14 F 0629 0.4 / 1201 3.3 / 1845 0.5
29 SA 0625 0.3 / 1157 3.4 / 1849 0.3
15 SA 0013 3.6 / 0709 0.4 / 1238 3.4 / 1924 0.4
30 SU 0012 3.7 / 0719 0.2 / 1248 3.5 / ○ 1940 0.3
31 M 0100 3.7 / 0807 0.2 / 1333 3.6 / 2026 0.2

APRIL

Time m / Time m

1 TU 0146 3.8 / 0851 0.2 / 1415 3.6 / 2109 0.2
16 W 0124 3.6 / 0819 0.2 / 1347 3.6 / 2040 0.2
2 W 0228 3.8 / 0931 0.2 / 1454 3.7 / 2149 0.2
17 TH 0202 3.6 / 0857 0.2 / 1423 3.6 / 2118 0.2
3 TH 0310 3.8 / 1007 0.3 / 1530 3.7 / 2225 0.3
18 F 0241 3.6 / 0935 0.2 / 1502 3.6 / 2158 0.2
4 F 0349 3.6 / 1039 0.3 / 1604 3.6 / 2257 0.3
19 SA 0323 3.6 / 1013 0.2 / 1542 3.6 / 2238 0.2
5 SA 0426 3.5 / 1108 0.4 / 1638 3.5 / 2326 0.3
20 SU 0406 3.5 / 1051 0.3 / 1622 3.6 / 2318 0.2
6 SU 0502 3.4 / 1135 0.5 / 1712 3.4 / 2355 0.5
21 M 0450 3.4 / 1129 0.4 / 1705 3.6 / 2359 0.3
7 M 0540 3.2 / 1206 0.6 / 1754 3.3 ◐
22 TU 0538 3.4 / 1214 0.5 / 1758 3.5 ◐
8 TU 0036 0.6 / 0631 3.0 / 1256 0.7 / 1855 3.2
23 W 0053 0.4 / 0640 3.3 / 1318 0.6 / 1907 3.4
9 W 0142 0.7 / 0743 2.9 / 1414 0.8 / 2016 3.2
24 TH 0209 0.5 / 0759 3.2 / 1443 0.6 / 2030 3.5
10 TH 0311 0.6 / 0907 3.0 / 1546 0.7 / 2138 3.3
25 F 0338 0.5 / 0924 3.2 / 1611 0.6 / 2150 3.6
11 F 0438 0.5 / 1023 3.1 / 1705 0.6 / 2244 3.4
26 SA 0459 0.3 / 1037 3.3 / 1723 0.5 / 2254 3.6
12 SA 0542 0.4 / 1118 3.2 / 1801 0.5 / 2331 3.5
27 SU 0600 0.3 / 1133 3.4 / 1820 0.4 / 2347 3.7
13 SU 0625 0.3 / 1158 3.4 / 1844 0.4
28 M 0650 0.2 / 1222 3.5 / 1913 0.3
14 M 0010 3.6 / 0704 0.3 / 1234 3.5 / 1924 0.4
29 TU 0037 3.7 / 0739 0.2 / 1309 3.6 / ● 2003 0.2
15 TU 0047 3.6 / 0742 0.3 / 1311 3.5 / ○ 2003 0.3
30 W 0125 3.7 / 0824 0.2 / 1351 3.6 / 2046 0.2

Chart Datum: 2·06 metres below Normal Null (German reference level)
HAT is 4·1 metres above Chart Datum

TIDES

GERMANY – CUXHAVEN

TIME ZONE -0100 (German Standard Time) **Subtract 1 hour for UT** — For German Summer Time add ONE hour in **non-shaded areas**

LAT 53°52'N LONG 8°43'E

TIMES AND HEIGHTS OF HIGH AND LOW WATERS

Dates in amber are **SPRINGS** — Dates in yellow are **NEAPS**

2014

MAY

Day					Day				
1 TH	0208 3.6	0902 0.3	1428 3.7	2124 0.2	**16** F	0138 3.6	0831 0.2	1401 3.7	2059 0.2
2 F	0247 3.6	0936 0.3	1503 3.7	2159 0.3	**17** SA	0224 3.6	0916 0.2	1444 3.7	2144 0.2
3 SA	0324 3.5	1008 0.3	1537 3.7	2232 0.3	**18** SU	0312 3.6	1000 0.3	1528 3.7	2229 0.2
4 SU	0401 3.4	1039 0.4	1611 3.6	2303 0.4	**19** M	0400 3.5	1042 0.3	1613 3.7	2315 0.3
5 M	0438 3.4	1109 0.5	1647 3.5	2335 0.5	**20** TU	0449 3.5	1127 0.4	1702 3.7	
6 TU	0516 3.3	1141 0.6	1726 3.5		**21** W	0003 0.4	0541 3.4	1218 0.5	1757 3.7
7 W	0012 0.6	0601 3.1	1223 0.7	1817 3.4	**22** TH	0059 0.4	0641 3.3	1319 0.6	1902 3.6
8 TH	0103 0.6	0659 3.0	1325 0.8	1923 3.3	**23** F	0205 0.4	0751 3.3	1430 0.6	2014 3.6
9 F	0214 0.6	0810 3.0	1444 0.7	2038 3.3	**24** SA	0320 0.4	0904 3.5	1546 0.5	2126 3.6
10 SA	0333 0.5	0923 3.1	1603 0.6	2146 3.4	**25** SU	0431 0.4	1011 3.3	1654 0.5	2229 3.6
11 SU	0441 0.4	1024 3.3	1706 0.5	2241 3.5	**26** M	0530 0.3	1106 3.4	1752 0.4	2323 3.6
12 M	0534 0.4	1113 3.4	1758 0.5	2328 3.6	**27** TU	0621 0.3	1156 3.5	1847 0.4	
13 TU	0620 0.3	1157 3.5	1847 0.4		**28** W	0015 3.6	0711 0.3	1244 3.6	1940 0.3
14 W	0012 3.6	0706 0.3	1240 3.6	1933 0.4	**29** TH	0105 3.6	0759 0.3	1328 3.6	2025 0.2
15 TH	0055 3.6	0749 0.3	1320 3.7	2015 0.3	**30** F	0150 3.5	0837 0.3	1406 3.7	2102 0.2
					31 SA	0227 3.5	0911 0.3	1441 3.7	2137 0.3

JUNE

Day					Day				
1 SU	0304 3.5	0944 0.4	1515 3.8	2212 0.4	**16** M	0304 3.7	0952 0.3	1519 3.9	2225 0.3
2 M	0340 3.5	1016 0.4	1549 3.7	2245 0.5	**17** TU	0354 3.6	1038 0.3	1606 3.9	2312 0.3
3 TU	0417 3.4	1048 0.5	1625 3.7	2318 0.5	**18** W	0444 3.5	1124 0.4	1655 3.8	
4 W	0454 3.4	1121 0.6	1702 3.6	2352 0.6	**19** TH	0002 0.4	0535 3.5	1214 0.5	1748 3.8
5 TH	0534 3.3	1158 0.7	1744 3.6		**20** F	0054 0.4	0630 3.4	1308 0.5	1847 3.7
6 F	0032 0.7	0619 3.2	1245 0.8	1835 3.5	**21** SA	0149 0.5	0729 3.3	1406 0.5	1949 3.6
7 SA	0123 0.6	0714 3.2	1346 0.8	1938 3.4	**22** SU	0249 0.5	0832 3.3	1512 0.6	2056 3.6
8 SU	0227 0.6	0820 3.2	1457 0.7	2045 3.4	**23** M	0354 0.5	0937 3.3	1621 0.6	2203 3.5
9 M	0336 0.5	0927 3.3	1607 0.6	2148 3.5	**24** TU	0457 0.5	1038 3.4	1727 0.5	2303 3.5
10 TU	0440 0.5	1027 3.4	1711 0.6	2245 3.6	**25** W	0555 0.5	1133 3.5	1826 0.4	2358 3.5
11 W	0538 0.4	1120 3.5	1810 0.5	2339 3.6	**26** TH	0649 0.5	1224 3.6	1920 0.4	
12 TH	0633 0.4	1209 3.6	1905 0.4		**27** F	0049 3.5	0737 0.4	1309 3.6	2006 0.3
13 F	0030 3.6	0723 0.3	1256 3.7	1954 0.3	**28** SA	0134 3.5	0817 0.4	1348 3.7	2045 0.3
14 SA	0120 3.7	0812 0.3	1342 3.8	2044 0.3	**29** SU	0212 3.5	0852 0.4	1424 3.8	2120 0.4
15 SU	0212 3.7	0902 0.3	1430 3.8	2135 0.3	**30** M	0247 3.5	0926 0.5	1458 3.8	2155 0.5

JULY

Day					Day				
1 TU	0321 3.6	0958 0.5	1530 3.8	2226 0.5	**16** W	0344 3.7	1031 0.3	1554 4.0	2304 0.3
2 W	0354 3.5	1028 0.6	1602 3.8	2256 0.6	**17** TH	0430 3.6	1114 0.3	1641 3.9	2349 0.4
3 TH	0429 3.5	1101 0.6	1637 3.7	2330 0.6	**18** F	0517 3.5	1158 0.4	1730 3.8	
4 F	0506 3.4	1137 0.7	1716 3.7		**19** SA	0035 0.5	0605 3.4	1245 0.5	1822 3.7
5 SA	0005 0.7	0544 3.4	1214 0.7	1756 3.6	**20** SU	0120 0.6	0655 3.4	1333 0.6	1918 3.6
6 SU	0043 0.7	0628 3.4	1258 0.8	1846 3.5	**21** M	0208 0.6	0751 3.3	1432 0.7	2021 3.5
7 M	0130 0.7	0723 3.3	1357 0.8	1947 3.4	**22** TU	0309 0.7	0858 3.3	1545 0.7	2134 3.4
8 TU	0234 0.7	0830 3.3	1509 0.7	2057 3.4	**23** W	0421 0.7	1009 3.4	1702 0.6	2244 3.4
9 W	0346 0.6	0939 3.4	1625 0.6	2206 3.5	**24** TH	0532 0.6	1114 3.5	1809 0.5	2345 3.4
10 TH	0458 0.5	1044 3.5	1737 0.5	2312 3.5	**25** F	0631 0.5	1208 3.6	1903 0.5	
11 F	0605 0.5	1143 3.6	1842 0.4		**26** SA	0035 3.4	0719 0.5	1253 3.7	1948 0.4
12 SA	0012 3.6	0705 0.4	1237 3.7	1939 0.3	**27** SU	0118 3.5	0759 0.5	1331 3.7	2027 0.4
13 SU	0108 3.7	0800 0.4	1328 3.8	2033 0.3	**28** M	0155 3.5	0835 0.5	1406 3.8	2103 0.5
14 M	0202 3.7	0853 0.4	1418 3.9	2126 0.3	**29** TU	0228 3.6	0909 0.5	1439 3.9	2135 0.5
15 TU	0255 3.7	0944 0.3	1507 4.0	2217 0.3	**30** W	0258 3.6	0939 0.5	1508 3.8	2203 0.6
					31 TH	0328 3.6	1007 0.5	1537 3.8	2231 0.6

AUGUST

Day					Day				
1 F	0401 3.5	1039 0.6	1612 3.8	2305 0.6	**16** SA	0451 3.6	1136 0.4	1707 3.8	
2 SA	0437 3.5	1116 0.7	1649 3.8	2340 0.7	**17** SU	0005 0.6	0533 3.5	1215 0.5	1753 3.7
3 SU	0514 3.5	1150 0.7	1725 3.6		**18** M	0042 0.7	0616 3.5	1256 0.7	1842 3.5
4 M	0011 0.7	0550 3.5	1223 0.7	1804 3.5	**19** TU	0123 0.8	0706 3.4	1348 0.8	1942 3.3
5 TU	0046 0.7	0634 3.4	1310 0.8	1859 3.4	**20** W	0220 0.9	0814 3.3	1503 0.8	2059 3.2
6 W	0142 0.7	0739 3.3	1421 0.8	2013 3.3	**21** TH	0340 0.9	0936 3.3	1631 0.8	2221 3.3
7 TH	0300 0.7	0857 3.3	1548 0.7	2136 3.4	**22** F	0504 0.7	1053 3.5	1750 0.5	2330 3.5
8 F	0427 0.7	1015 3.4	1713 0.5	2253 3.4	**23** SA	0612 0.7	1152 3.6	1846 0.6	
9 SA	0546 0.5	1123 3.6	1826 0.4		**24** SU	0019 3.4	0700 0.6	1234 3.7	1927 0.5
10 SU	0000 3.6	0653 0.5	1222 3.7	1927 0.3	**25** M	0057 3.7	0738 0.6	1309 3.7	2002 0.5
11 M	0058 3.7	0750 0.4	1314 3.9	2022 0.3	**26** TU	0131 3.5	0813 0.5	1342 3.7	2037 0.5
12 TU	0150 3.7	0841 0.4	1403 3.9	2113 0.3	**27** W	0202 3.6	0846 0.5	1414 3.7	2108 0.5
13 W	0240 3.7	0930 0.4	1450 4.0	2202 0.3	**28** TH	0232 3.6	0917 0.5	1443 3.7	2136 0.5
14 TH	0327 3.7	1016 0.3	1537 4.0	2245 0.3	**29** F	0301 3.6	0946 0.5	1513 3.7	2205 0.6
15 F	0410 3.6	1057 0.4	1622 3.9	2325 0.4	**30** SA	0334 3.6	1018 0.5	1546 3.7	2238 0.6
					31 SU	0410 3.6	1054 0.6	1624 3.7	2313 0.6

Chart Datum: 2·06 metres below Normal Null (German reference level)
HAT is 4·1 metres above Chart Datum

TIME ZONE -0100
(German Standard Time)
Subtract 1 hour for UT
For German Summer Time add
ONE hour in **non-shaded areas**

GERMANY – CUXHAVEN

LAT 53°52'N   LONG 8°43'E

TIMES AND HEIGHTS OF HIGH AND LOW WATERS

Dates in amber are **SPRINGS**
Dates in yellow are **NEAPS**

2014

SEPTEMBER

Day				
1 M	0445 3.6	1128 0.6	1658 3.6	2342 0.7
2 TU ☽	0518 3.5	1158 0.6	1734 3.4	
3 W	0013 0.7	0559 3.4	1239 0.7	1826 3.3
4 TH	0105 0.6	0702 3.3	1350 0.8	1945 3.2
5 F	0229 0.9	0827 3.3	1524 0.8	2117 3.3
6 SA	0406 0.8	0954 3.5	1657 0.6	2241 3.4
7 SU	0532 0.7	1108 3.6	1813 0.4	2349 3.5
8 M	0641 0.5	1206 3.7	1913 0.3	
9 TU ○	0045 3.6	0736 0.5	1257 3.8	2005 0.3
10 W	0134 3.7	0824 0.4	1344 3.9	2053 0.3
11 TH	0220 3.7	0910 0.4	1430 4.0	2138 0.4
12 F	0304 3.8	0954 0.4	1516 4.0	2220 0.4
13 SA	0344 3.7	1035 0.4	1600 3.9	2256 0.5
14 SU	0422 3.7	1111 0.5	1641 3.7	2330 0.6
15 M	0459 3.6	1145 0.6	1722 3.6	
16 TU	0003 0.8	0537 3.5	1220 0.7	◐ 1806 3.4
17 W	0038 0.9	0623 3.4	1306 0.8	1902 3.2
18 TH	0132 1.0	0729 3.3	1418 0.9	2019 3.1
19 F	0252 1.1	0855 3.3	1550 0.9	2147 3.2
20 SA	0425 1.0	1020 3.4	1718 0.8	2302 3.3
21 SU	0543 0.8	1124 3.5	1819 0.6	2353 3.4
22 M	0633 0.7	1206 3.6	1857 0.5	
23 TU	0027 3.5	0709 0.6	1239 3.6	1929 0.5
24 W ●	0059 3.5	0744 0.5	1311 3.6	2003 0.5
25 TH	0131 3.6	0819 0.5	1345 3.6	2037 0.5
26 F	0203 3.6	0852 0.5	1417 3.7	2109 0.5
27 SA	0236 3.6	0924 0.5	1449 3.7	2141 0.5
28 SU	0309 3.6	0958 0.5	1524 3.6	2213 0.5
29 M	0344 3.6	1034 0.5	1601 3.6	2247 0.6
30 TU	0419 3.6	1108 0.5	1638 3.5	2318 0.7

OCTOBER

Day				
1 W ☽	0454 3.6	1141 0.6	1717 3.4	2353 0.8
2 TH	0538 3.5	1225 0.7	1812 3.3	
3 F	0049 0.9	0642 3.4	1336 0.9	1931 3.2
4 SA	0214 1.0	0809 3.4	1511 0.8	2104 3.3
5 SU	0352 0.9	0938 3.5	1644 0.7	2228 3.4
6 M	0517 0.8	1051 3.6	1756 0.5	2334 3.5
7 TU	0621 0.6	1147 3.7	1852 0.4	
8 W ○	0026 3.6	0715 0.5	1236 3.8	1942 0.4
9 TH	0113 3.6	0803 0.5	1323 3.8	2029 0.4
10 F	0157 3.7	0849 0.4	1409 3.9	2112 0.4
11 SA	0238 3.8	0931 0.4	1453 3.8	2151 0.5
12 SU	0317 3.8	1011 0.5	1535 3.8	2225 0.6
13 M	0353 3.7	1046 0.5	1615 3.6	2257 0.6
14 TU	0427 3.6	1117 0.6	1653 3.5	2328 0.8
15 W ☽	0504 3.5	1150 0.7	1734 3.3	
16 TH	0002 0.9	0547 3.4	1232 0.9	1825 3.2
17 F	0049 1.1	0645 3.4	1333 1.0	1934 3.1
18 SA	0202 1.1	0803 3.3	1458 1.0	2056 3.1
19 SU	0331 1.1	0927 3.4	1626 0.9	2214 3.2
20 M	0453 0.9	1037 0.7	1733 0.7	2310 3.3
21 TU	0551 0.8	1125 3.5	1816 0.6	2349 3.4
22 W	0632 0.7	1202 3.6	1851 0.6	
23 TH ●	0024 3.5	0710 0.6	1238 3.6	1928 0.6
24 F	0100 3.6	0749 0.6	1314 3.6	2005 0.5
25 SA	0136 3.6	0826 0.5	1350 3.6	2042 0.5
26 SU	0211 3.7	0903 0.5	1427 3.6	2118 0.5
27 M	0247 3.7	0940 0.5	1505 3.6	2153 0.5
28 TU	0323 3.7	1017 0.5	1545 3.5	2227 0.6
29 W	0400 3.7	1055 0.5	1626 3.5	2303 0.7
30 TH	0440 3.7	1134 0.7	1711 3.4	2346 0.9
31 F ☽	0529 3.6	1224 0.8	1808 3.3	

NOVEMBER

Day				
1 SA	0045 1.0	0633 3.5	1332 0.9	1922 3.3
2 SU	0204 1.0	0753 3.5	1459 0.8	2048 3.3
3 M	0334 0.9	0916 3.6	1625 0.7	2207 3.3
4 TU	0454 0.8	1028 3.7	1733 0.6	2310 3.4
5 W	0556 0.7	1124 3.7	1827 0.5	2347 3.5
6 TH ○	0002 3.5	0650 0.6	1214 3.7	1916 0.5
7 F	0049 3.6	0742 0.5	1304 3.7	2004 0.4
8 SA	0133 3.7	0828 0.5	1349 3.7	2046 0.5
9 SU	0213 3.7	0909 0.5	1431 3.7	2122 0.5
10 M	0250 3.7	0946 0.5	1511 3.6	2156 0.6
11 TU	0326 3.7	1022 0.6	1550 3.5	2229 0.6
12 W	0401 3.7	1055 0.6	1629 3.4	2300 0.7
13 TH	0437 3.6	1128 0.7	1708 3.3	2334 0.9
14 F ☽	0516 3.6	1205 0.9	1752 3.2	
15 SA	0015 1.0	0604 3.5	1253 1.0	1846 3.1
16 SU	0112 1.1	0706 3.4	1359 1.0	1954 3.1
17 M	0226 1.1	0821 3.4	1517 0.9	2107 3.3
18 TU	0346 1.0	0933 3.5	1629 0.8	2213 3.3
19 W	0454 0.9	1032 3.5	1724 0.7	2304 3.4
20 TH	0547 0.8		1809 0.6	2347 3.5
21 F	0634 0.7	1203 3.6	1853 0.6	
22 SA ●	0028 3.6	0719 0.7	1244 3.6	1935 0.6
23 SU	0108 3.6	0801 0.6	1325 3.6	2017 0.5
24 M	0147 3.7	0843 0.5	1408 3.6	2059 0.5
25 TU	0227 3.7	0926 0.5	1453 3.6	2140 0.6
26 W	0308 3.8	1008 0.5	1537 3.5	2219 0.6
27 TH	0349 3.8	1049 0.5	1621 3.5	2259 0.7
28 F	0432 3.8	1134 0.6	1709 3.5	2345 0.8
29 SA ☽	0522 3.7	1225 0.7	1803 3.4	
30 SU	0041 0.9	0622 3.8	1326 0.8	1908 3.3

DECEMBER

Day				
1 M	0149 0.9	0732 3.6	1439 0.8	2022 3.3
2 TU	0306 0.9	0848 3.6	1554 0.7	2136 3.3
3 W	0422 0.8	0959 3.6	1702 0.7	2240 3.4
4 TH	0529 0.8	1101 3.6	1800 0.6	2335 3.5
5 F	0628 0.6	1155 3.6	1853 0.5	
6 SA ○	0026 3.6	0722 0.5	1246 3.6	1942 0.5
7 SU	0112 3.6	0810 0.5	1332 3.5	2023 0.5
8 M	0151 3.7	0849 0.4	1412 3.5	2059 0.5
9 TU	0228 3.7	0926 0.5	1451 3.5	2133 0.6
10 W	0304 3.8	1003 0.6	1529 3.5	2207 0.6
11 TH	0339 3.8	1037 0.7	1606 3.5	2239 0.7
12 F	0413 3.7	1109 0.7	1642 3.4	2311 0.8
13 SA	0449 3.7	1141 0.8	1720 3.3	2346 0.9
14 SU ☽	0527 3.6	1217 0.9	1801 3.2	
15 M	0028 1.0	0614 3.5	1303 0.9	1852 3.2
16 TU	0123 1.1	0713 3.4	1404 0.9	1956 3.2
17 W	0232 1.0	0821 3.4	1514 0.9	2105 3.3
18 TH	0346 1.0	0930 3.4	1623 0.8	2210 3.4
19 F	0454 0.9	1031 3.5	1724 0.7	2306 3.5
20 SA	0555 0.8		1819 0.6	2356 3.6
21 SU	0650 0.7	1217 3.6	1909 0.6	
22 M ●	0041 3.6	0739 0.6	1304 3.6	1956 0.6
23 TU	0125 3.7	0826 0.5	1352 3.6	2044 0.5
24 W	0210 3.8	0915 0.5	1442 3.6	2132 0.5
25 TH	0256 3.8	1003 0.4	1530 3.6	2216 0.5
26 F	0340 3.9	1047 0.6	1615 3.5	2257 0.5
27 SA	0423 3.8	1131 0.5	1701 3.5	2341 0.6
28 SU ☽	0512 3.8	1219 0.6	1751 3.4	
29 M	0031 0.7	0606 3.7	1311 0.6	1846 3.3
30 TU	0126 0.7	0706 3.6	1408 0.7	1947 3.3
31 W	0230 0.8	0814 3.5	1514 0.7	2056 3.3

Chart Datum: 2·06 metres below Normal Null (German reference level)
HAT is 4·1 metres above Chart Datum

TIDES

WILHELMSHAVEN

MEAN SPRING
AND NEAP CURVES

MEAN RANGES
Springs 4.3m
Neaps 3.1m

Factor

0.9 0.8 0.7 0.6 0.5 0.4 0.3 0.2 0.1

H.W. +1ʰ +2ʰ +3ʰ +4ʰ +5ʰ L.W.
-1ʰ -2ʰ -3ʰ -4ʰ -5ʰ -6ʰ L.W.

M.H.W.S.
M.H.W.N.

H.W.Hts.m.

CHART DATUM

M.L.W.N.
M.L.W.S.
L.W.Hts.m.

TIME ZONE -0100
(German Standard Time)
Subtract 1 hour for UT
For German Summer Time add ONE hour in **non-shaded areas**

GERMANY – WILHELMSHAVEN
LAT 53°31'N   LONG 8°09'E
TIMES AND HEIGHTS OF HIGH AND LOW WATERS

Dates in amber are **SPRINGS**
Dates in yellow are **NEAPS**

2014

JANUARY

Day	Time	m	Day	Time	m
1 W ●	0609 / 1223 / 1835	0.6 / 4.6 / 0.6	16 TH ○	0051 / 0705 / 1315 / 1916	4.6 / 0.6 / 4.4 / 0.7
2 TH	0048 / 0705 / 1318 / 1929	4.7 / 0.5 / 4.6 / 0.6	17 F	0128 / 0743 / 1351 / 1953	4.7 / 0.6 / 4.5 / 0.7
3 F	0139 / 0758 / 1413 / 2024	4.8 / 0.4 / 4.6 / 0.6	18 SA	0203 / 0819 / 1423 / 2027	4.8 / 0.6 / 4.5 / 0.7
4 SA	0230 / 0852 / 1506 / 2115	4.9 / 0.4 / 4.6 / 0.5	19 SU	0234 / 0852 / 1453 / 2057	4.8 / 0.7 / 4.5 / 0.7
5 SU	0319 / 0941 / 1555 / 2157	5.0 / 0.4 / 4.5 / 0.5	20 M	0303 / 0920 / 1521 / 2125	4.8 / 0.7 / 4.5 / 0.7
6 M	0405 / 1025 / 1638 / 2234	5.0 / 0.4 / 4.5 / 0.5	21 TU	0332 / 0949 / 1553 / 2156	4.7 / 0.7 / 4.4 / 0.7
7 TU	0449 / 1108 / 1711 / 2314	4.9 / 0.5 / 4.4 / 0.7	22 W	0406 / 1023 / 1628 / 2230	4.7 / 0.8 / 4.4 / 0.8
8 W ☽	0535 / 1152 / 1806 / 2358	4.7 / 0.7 / 4.3 / 0.8	23 TH	0441 / 1055 / 1703 / 2303	4.7 / 0.8 / 4.4 / 0.8
9 TH	0624 / 1238 / 1855	4.6 / 0.9 / 4.2	24 F ☾	0517 / 1126 / 1741 / 2340	4.6 / 0.8 / 4.3 / 0.9
10	0050 / 0722 / 1331 / 1955	0.9 / 4.4 / 1.0 / 4.2	25 SA	0601 / 1207 / 1834	4.4 / 0.9 / 4.2
11 SA	0106 / 0830 / 1437 / 2106	1.1 / 4.3 / 1.1 / 4.2	26 SU	0035 / 0705 / 1311 / 1948	1.1 / 4.3 / 1.0 / 4.2
12 SU	0313 / 0944 / 1550 / 2216	1.1 / 4.3 / 1.1 / 4.4	27 M	0154 / 0826 / 1433 / 2110	1.1 / 4.3 / 1.0 / 4.3
13 M	0428 / 1052 / 1657 / 2318	1.0 / 4.4 / 0.9 / 4.5	28 TU	0321 / 0950 / 1558 / 2229	1.0 / 4.3 / 0.9 / 4.4
14 TU	0531 / 1148 / 1751	0.8 / 4.4 / 0.8	29 W	0442 / 1108 / 1716 / 2338	0.7 / 4.4 / 0.7 / 4.6
15 W	0009 / 0620 / 1235 / 1837	4.6 / 0.7 / 4.4 / 0.7	30 TH ●	0552 / 1214 / 1823	0.5 / 4.5 / 0.6
			31 F	0036 / 0653 / 1310 / 1921	4.7 / 0.4 / 4.6 / 0.5

FEBRUARY

Day	Time	m	Day	Time	m
1 SA	0128 / 0747 / 1402 / 2013	4.8 / 0.3 / 4.6 / 0.4	16 SU	0142 / 0756 / 1401 / 2007	4.7 / 0.5 / 4.5 / 0.5
2 SU	0217 / 0839 / 1453 / 2101	5.0 / 0.3 / 4.6 / 0.4	17 M	0213 / 0828 / 1430 / 2037	4.7 / 0.5 / 4.5 / 0.5
3 M	0305 / 0926 / 1539 / 2142	5.0 / 0.3 / 4.6 / 0.3	18 TU	0243 / 0857 / 1500 / 2106	4.7 / 0.5 / 4.6 / 0.5
4 TU	0349 / 1008 / 1618 / 2217	5.0 / 0.3 / 4.5 / 0.4	19 W	0314 / 0928 / 1533 / 2139	4.7 / 0.5 / 4.5 / 0.5
5 W	0430 / 1046 / 1655 / 2251	4.9 / 0.4 / 4.5 / 0.5	20 TH	0349 / 1003 / 1609 / 2214	4.7 / 0.5 / 4.5 / 0.5
6 TH	0509 / 1122 / 1731 / 2326	4.7 / 0.6 / 4.4 / 0.7	21 F	0425 / 1035 / 1642 / 2244	4.7 / 0.6 / 4.5 / 0.6
7 F	0549 / 1157 / 1810	4.5 / 0.8 / 4.3	22 SA	0457 / 1101 / 1713 / 2313	4.6 / 0.6 / 4.4 / 0.7
8 SA	0006 / 0636 / 1238 / 1902	0.8 / 4.3 / 1.0 / 4.2	23 SU ☾	0533 / 1132 / 1759	4.4 / 0.8 / 4.2
9 SU	0102 / 0741 / 1340 / 2014	1.0 / 4.2 / 1.1 / 4.2	24 M	0000 / 0633 / 1232 / 1912	0.8 / 4.2 / 0.9 / 4.2
10 M	0222 / 0902 / 1502 / 2138	1.1 / 4.1 / 1.2 / 4.2	25 TU	0119 / 0759 / 1402 / 2043	0.9 / 4.2 / 1.0 / 4.3
11 TU	0351 / 1024 / 1624 / 2253	1.0 / 4.2 / 1.0 / 4.4	26 W	0256 / 0933 / 1538 / 2211	0.9 / 4.2 / 0.9 / 4.4
12 W	0506 / 1129 / 1729 / 2349	0.8 / 4.3 / 0.9 / 4.5	27 TH	0426 / 1057 / 1703 / 2324	0.7 / 4.4 / 0.7 / 4.6
13 TH	0601 / 1217 / 1817	0.7 / 4.4 / 0.7	28 F	0539 / 1205 / 1812	0.5 / 4.5 / 0.6
14 F	0032 / 0644 / 1256 / 1857	4.6 / 0.6 / 4.4 / 0.7			
15 SA	0108 / 0722 / 1330 / 1934	4.7 / 0.6 / 4.5 / 0.6			

MARCH

Day	Time	m	Day	Time	m
1 SA ●	0023 / 0640 / 1300 / 1908	4.7 / 0.3 / 4.6 / 0.4	16 SU ○	0039 / 0649 / 1301 / 1906	4.6 / 0.5 / 4.5 / 0.5
2 SU	0114 / 0732 / 1348 / 1956	4.9 / 0.3 / 4.6 / 0.3	17 M	0113 / 0725 / 1334 / 1941	4.7 / 0.4 / 4.5 / 0.4
3 M	0201 / 0820 / 1433 / 2040	4.9 / 0.2 / 4.6 / 0.3	18 TU	0147 / 0759 / 1406 / 2014	4.7 / 0.4 / 4.6 / 0.4
4 TU	0246 / 0904 / 1516 / 2120	5.0 / 0.2 / 4.6 / 0.3	19 W	0220 / 0832 / 1439 / 2047	4.7 / 0.4 / 4.6 / 0.4
5 W	0328 / 0944 / 1553 / 2156	4.9 / 0.3 / 4.6 / 0.3	20 TH	0255 / 0907 / 1514 / 2122	4.7 / 0.4 / 4.5 / 0.3
6 TH	0407 / 1019 / 1627 / 2227	4.8 / 0.4 / 4.6 / 0.4	21 F	0332 / 0942 / 1551 / 2158	4.7 / 0.4 / 4.5 / 0.3
7 F	0443 / 1050 / 1658 / 2257	4.7 / 0.6 / 4.5 / 0.5	22 SA	0410 / 1015 / 1625 / 2230	4.6 / 0.5 / 4.5 / 0.4
8 SA	0517 / 1119 / 1731 / 2329	4.5 / 0.7 / 4.4 / 0.7	23 SU	0445 / 1044 / 1659 / 2301	4.5 / 0.5 / 4.5 / 0.5
9 SU	0557 / 1152 / 1816	4.2 / 0.9 / 4.2	24 M ☾	0524 / 1119 / 1745 / 2349	4.3 / 0.7 / 4.3 / 0.7
10	0016 / 0654 / 1248 / 1924	0.9 / 4.0 / 1.1 / 4.1	25	0624 / 1219 / 1857	4.2 / 0.9 / 4.3
11 TU	0130 / 0816 / 1411 / 2053	1.0 / 3.9 / 1.2 / 4.2	26 W	0107 / 0750 / 1349 / 2029	0.8 / 4.1 / 1.0 / 4.3
12 W	0305 / 0945 / 1542 / 2217	1.0 / 4.2 / 1.1 / 4.3	27 TH	0244 / 0924 / 1527 / 2157	0.8 / 4.2 / 0.9 / 4.5
13 TH	0430 / 1059 / 1656 / 2320	0.8 / 4.2 / 0.9 / 4.5	28 F	0414 / 1046 / 1649 / 2308	0.6 / 4.3 / 0.7 / 4.6
14 F	0530 / 1149 / 1747	0.6 / 4.4 / 0.7	29 SA	0524 / 1149 / 1752	0.4 / 4.5 / 0.5
15 SA	0004 / 0613 / 1227 / 1828	4.6 / 0.5 / 4.5 / 0.6	30 SU ●	0005 / 0620 / 1241 / 1846	4.7 / 0.3 / 4.5 / 0.4
			31 M	0056 / 0710 / 1328 / 1934	4.8 / 0.3 / 4.6 / 0.3

APRIL

Day	Time	m	Day	Time	m
1 TU	0142 / 0756 / 1411 / 2016	4.8 / 0.2 / 4.7 / 0.3	16 W	0118 / 0728 / 1341 / 1949	4.7 / 0.3 / 4.6 / 0.4
2 W	0225 / 0837 / 1450 / 2055	4.9 / 0.3 / 4.7 / 0.3	17 TH	0156 / 0806 / 1417 / 2026	4.7 / 0.3 / 4.6 / 0.3
3 TH	0305 / 0914 / 1526 / 2131	4.8 / 0.3 / 4.7 / 0.3	18 F	0236 / 0845 / 1456 / 2105	4.7 / 0.3 / 4.6 / 0.3
4 F	0343 / 0948 / 1558 / 2202	4.7 / 0.4 / 4.6 / 0.3	19 SA	0317 / 0922 / 1535 / 2144	4.6 / 0.3 / 4.6 / 0.2
5 SA	0417 / 1018 / 1629 / 2231	0.5 / 0.5 / 4.5 / 0.4	20 SU	0359 / 0959 / 1614 / 2221	4.5 / 0.4 / 4.6 / 0.3
6 SU	0444 / 1045 / 1700 / 2301	0.4 / 0.6 / 4.4 / 0.6	21 M	0440 / 1037 / 1654 / 2301	0.5 / 0.5 / 4.6 / 0.4
7 M	0526 / 1117 / 1740 / 2342	4.2 / 0.8 / 4.3 / 0.8	22 TU ☾	0527 / 1120 / 1745 / 2354	4.3 / 0.7 / 4.5 / 0.6
8 TU	0616 / 1205 / 1840	4.0 / 1.0 / 4.2	23	0628 / 1222 / 1855	4.2 / 0.8 / 4.4
9 W	0046 / 0728 / 1320 / 2002	0.9 / 3.9 / 1.1 / 4.2	24 TH	0108 / 0748 / 1344 / 2019	0.7 / 4.2 / 0.9 / 4.4
10 TH	0213 / 0855 / 1449 / 2127	1.0 / 3.9 / 1.1 / 4.2	25 F	0237 / 0914 / 1512 / 2141	0.7 / 4.2 / 0.8 / 4.6
11 F	0339 / 1012 / 1607 / 2235	0.8 / 4.1 / 0.6 / 4.4	26 SA	0358 / 1028 / 1626 / 2247	0.5 / 4.3 / 0.7 / 4.7
12 SA	0443 / 1108 / 1703 / 2322	0.6 / 4.3 / 0.7 / 4.5	27 SU	0501 / 1126 / 1724 / 2341	0.4 / 4.4 / 0.5 / 4.7
13 SU	0529 / 1149 / 1748	0.5 / 4.4 / 0.6	28 M	0553 / 1216 / 1818	0.3 / 4.5 / 0.4
14 M	0001 / 0609 / 1227 / 1831	4.6 / 0.4 / 4.5 / 0.5	29 TU ●	0033 / 0643 / 1304 / 1908	4.7 / 0.3 / 4.6 / 0.3
15 TU	0039 / 0650 / 1304 / 1911	4.6 / 0.4 / 4.6 / 0.4	30 W	0122 / 0730 / 1347 / 1952	4.7 / 0.3 / 4.7 / 0.2

Chart Datum: 2·7 metres below Normal Null (German reference level)
HAT is 5·1 metres above Chart Datum

TIDES

| TIME ZONE -0100 (German Standard Time) **Subtract 1 hour for UT** For German Summer Time add ONE hour in **non-shaded areas** | **GERMANY – WILHELMSHAVEN** LAT 53°31′N   LONG 8°09′E TIMES AND HEIGHTS OF HIGH AND LOW WATERS | Dates in amber are **SPRINGS** Dates in yellow are **NEAPS** **2014** |

MAY

Date	Time m	Time m	Time m	Time m
1 TH	0205 4.7	0809 0.3	1425 4.7	2030 0.3
2 F	0243 4.6	0845 0.3	1459 4.7	2105 0.3
3 SA	0319 4.6	0918 0.4	1531 4.7	2137 0.4
4 SU	0354 4.5	0950 0.5	1603 4.6	2209 0.4
5 M	0427 4.3	1019 0.6	1636 4.6	2242 0.6
6 TU	0502 4.2	1052 0.8	1714 4.4	2320 0.7
7 W ◐	0545 4.1	1134 1.0	1803 4.3	
8 TH	0010 0.9	0643 4.0	1234 1.0	1909 4.3
9 F	0119 0.9	0756 4.0	1349 1.0	2026 4.3
10 SA	0236 0.8	0912 4.1	1505 0.9	2136 4.4
11 SU	0344 0.6	1014 4.3	1609 0.8	2232 4.5
12 M	0438 0.5	1104 4.4	1703 0.7	2320 4.6
13 TU	0527 0.5	1150 4.5	1753 0.6	
14 W ○	0005 4.6	0615 0.4	1234 4.6	1841 0.5
15 TH	0049 4.7	0659 0.4	1315 4.7	1924 0.4
16 F	0133 4.7	0741 0.3	1356 4.7	2007 0.3
17 SA	0219 4.7	0825 0.3	1439 4.7	2051 0.2
18 SU	0306 4.6	0909 0.4	1523 4.7	2135 0.2
19 M	0353 4.5	0951 0.4	1607 4.7	2219 0.3
20 TU	0440 4.4	1035 0.5	1654 4.7	2306 0.4
21 W ○	0532 4.3	1124 0.7	1748 4.7	
22 TH	0002 0.5	0631 4.3	1223 0.7	1851 4.6
23 F	0107 0.6	0740 4.2	1332 0.8	2005 4.6
24 SA	0221 0.6	0853 4.2	1448 0.8	2118 4.6
25 SU	0332 0.5	1001 4.3	1557 0.7	2222 4.7
26 M	0433 0.5	1057 4.4	1655 0.6	2317 4.7
27 TU	0525 0.4	1149 4.5	1750 0.6	
28 W ●	0011 4.6	0616 0.4	1239 4.6	1844 0.4
29 TH	0102 4.6	0704 0.4	1324 4.6	1930 0.3
30 F	0146 4.6	0744 0.3	1402 4.7	2008 0.3
31 SA	0223 4.5	0820 0.4	1436 4.8	2044 0.4

JUNE

Date	Time m	Time m	Time m	Time m
1 SU	0259 4.5	0854 0.5	1510 4.8	2119 0.5
2 M	0333 4.5	0928 0.5	1542 4.8	2153 0.5
3 TU	0406 4.4	1000 0.7	1615 4.7	2227 0.6
4 W	0440 4.3	1032 0.8	1651 4.6	2302 0.7
5 TH ◐	0517 4.2	1109 0.9	1731 4.5	2342 0.8
6 F ◐	0602 4.1	1155 1.0	1822 4.4	
7 SA	0031 0.8	0659 4.1	1253 1.0	1924 4.4
8 SU	0133 0.8	0807 4.2	1402 1.0	2033 4.4
9 M	0241 0.8	0915 4.3	1511 0.9	2137 4.5
10 TU	0345 0.6	1016 4.4	1616 0.8	2237 4.5
11 W	0444 0.6	1111 4.5	1716 0.7	2332 4.6
12 TH	0540 0.5	1203 4.6	1811 0.6	
13 F	0025 4.7	0632 0.4	1252 4.7	1902 0.4
14 SA	0115 4.7	0721 0.4	1339 4.8	1951 0.3
15 SU	0206 4.7	0812 0.4	1427 4.9	2041 0.3
16 M	0259 4.6	0903 0.4	1515 4.9	2131 0.3
17 TU	0349 4.6	0948 0.4	1601 4.9	2217 0.3
18 W	0437 4.5	1031 0.5	1649 4.9	2305 0.4
19 TH ◐	0527 4.4	1119 0.6	1742 4.8	2358 0.5
20 F	0620 4.4	1212 0.7	1838 4.7	
21 SA	0054 0.6	0717 4.3	1309 0.7	1940 4.6
22 SU	0153 0.6	0820 4.3	1415 0.8	2047 4.6
23 M	0257 0.7	0925 4.3	1524 0.8	2154 4.6
24 TU	0401 0.6	1027 4.4	1630 0.7	2256 4.6
25 W	0500 0.6	1124 4.5	1729 0.6	2352 4.5
26 TH	0554 0.5	1216 4.6	1823 0.5	
27 F ●	0043 4.5	0642 0.5	1303 4.6	1911 0.4
28 SA	0128 4.5	0725 0.4	1342 4.7	1952 0.4
29 SU	0206 4.5	0802 0.5	1418 4.8	2029 0.3
30 M	0241 4.6	0838 0.6	1452 4.9	2105 0.5

JULY

Date	Time m	Time m	Time m	Time m
1 TU	0314 4.6	0912 0.6	1523 4.9	2137 0.6
2 W	0344 4.5	0942 0.7	1553 4.8	2208 0.7
3 TH	0416 4.4	1013 0.8	1627 4.7	2242 0.8
4 F ◐	0451 4.4	1048 0.9	1704 4.7	2317 0.8
5 SA	0528 4.3	1125 0.9	1744 4.6	2354 0.8
6 SU	0612 4.3	1208 0.9	1832 4.5	
7 M	0039 0.8	0707 4.3	1305 1.0	1934 4.4
8 TU	0141 0.9	0815 4.3	1415 1.0	2044 4.4
9 W	0251 0.8	0927 4.3	1530 0.9	2156 4.4
10 TH	0402 0.7	1034 4.5	1641 0.7	2304 4.5
11 F ●	0509 0.6	1136 4.6	1746 0.5	1855 0.5
12 SA ○	0006 4.6	0612 0.5	1232 4.8	1844 0.4
13 SU	0102 4.7	0709 0.4	1324 4.9	1939 0.3
14 M	0156 4.7	0804 0.4	1415 5.0	2033 0.3
15 TU	0250 4.7	0856 0.4	1504 5.1	2124 0.2
16 W	0340 4.6	0941 0.3	1551 5.0	2210 0.3
17 TH	0425 4.6	1021 0.4	1637 5.0	2254 0.4
18 F	0510 4.5	1104 0.5	1725 4.9	2341 0.5
19 SA ◐	0556 4.4	1150 0.6	1814 4.8	
20 SU	0027 0.7	0643 4.4	1238 0.7	1907 4.6
21 M	0116 0.8	0737 4.3	1336 0.8	2009 4.5
22 TU	0215 0.9	0843 4.3	1448 0.9	2122 4.4
23 W	0327 0.9	0956 4.4	1605 0.9	2235 4.4
24 TH	0438 0.8	1103 4.5	1713 0.7	2337 4.4
25 F	0537 0.7	1158 4.6	1808 0.6	
26 SA ●	0027 4.5	0626 0.6	1244 4.7	1855 0.5
27 SU	0110 4.5	0708 0.6	1324 4.8	1936 0.5
28 M	0148 4.5	0747 0.6	1359 4.8	2013 0.5
29 TU	0221 4.6	0823 0.6	1432 4.9	2047 0.4
30 W	0251 4.7	0856 0.6	1501 4.9	2116 0.6
31 TH	0319 4.6	0922 0.6	1530 4.8	2144 0.7

AUGUST

Date	Time m	Time m	Time m	Time m
1 F	0350 4.5	0952 0.7	1603 4.8	2218 0.8
2 SA	0425 4.5	1027 0.8	1639 4.8	2253 0.8
3 SU	0459 4.5	1101 0.8	1714 4.7	2323 0.8
4 M ◐	0533 4.4	1133 0.9	1751 4.5	2356 0.8
5 TU	0617 4.3	1218 0.9	1844 4.4	
6 W	0048 0.9	0722 4.3	1327 1.0	1958 4.3
7 TH	0204 1.0	0843 4.3	1451 0.9	2122 4.3
8 F	0329 0.9	1003 4.4	1614 0.7	2242 4.4
9 SA	0449 0.7	1114 4.6	1727 0.5	2352 4.5
10 SU ○	0559 0.6	1216 4.8	1831 0.4	
11 M	0051 4.7	0700 0.5	1309 4.9	1927 0.3
12 TU	0144 4.7	0754 0.4	1359 5.0	2020 0.3
13 W	0235 4.7	0843 0.4	1448 5.1	2109 0.3
14 TH	0322 4.7	0927 0.3	1534 5.1	2153 0.3
15 F	0404 4.6	1005 0.4	1618 5.0	2235 0.4
16 SA	0444 4.6	1043 0.5	1700 4.9	2315 0.6
17 SU ◑	0524 4.5	1122 0.6	1743 4.7	2353 0.8
18 M	0604 4.5	1203 0.8	1828 4.5	
19 TU	0033 1.0	0651 4.4	1254 0.9	1927 4.3
20 W	0129 1.1	0757 4.3	1407 1.1	2045 4.2
21 TH	0247 1.2	0920 4.3	1535 1.0	2209 4.2
22 F	0411 1.1	1039 4.5	1655 0.9	2319 4.3
23 SA	0520 0.7	1140 4.7	1753 0.7	
24 SU	0008 4.4	0609 0.7	1223 4.9	1835 0.6
25 M ●	0047 4.5	0648 0.6	1259 4.8	1913 0.6
26 TU	0122 4.8	0726 0.7	1333 4.8	1948 0.6
27 W	0154 4.8	0800 0.7	1405 4.8	2020 0.6
28 TH	0224 4.6	0831 0.7	1435 4.8	2050 0.6
29 F	0252 4.6	0900 0.6	1505 4.8	2119 0.7
30 SA	0323 4.6	0931 0.7	1538 4.8	2152 0.7
31 SU	0358 4.6	1006 0.7	1615 4.7	2226 0.8

Chart Datum: 2·7 metres below Normal Null (German reference level)
HAT is 5·1 metres above Chart Datum

TIME ZONE -0100
(German Standard Time)
Subtract 1 hour for UT
For German Summer Time add
ONE hour in **non-shaded areas**

GERMANY – WILHELMSHAVEN
LAT 53°31'N LONG 8°09'E
TIMES AND HEIGHTS OF HIGH AND LOW WATERS

Dates in amber are **SPRINGS**
Dates in yellow are **NEAPS**

2014

SEPTEMBER

Time	m	Time	m
1 0432	4.6	**16** 0524	4.5
1038	0.7	1128	0.8
M 1648	4.7	TU 1750	4.4
2255	0.8	◗ 2351	1.1
2 0502	4.5	**17** 0607	4.4
1106	0.8	1213	1.0
TU 1716	4.5	W 1845	4.1
◗ 2323	0.9		
3 0541	4.4	**18** 0043	1.3
1145	0.9	0711	4.3
W 1810	4.3	TH 1322	1.2
		2001	4.0
4 0012	1.0	**19** 0201	1.4
0644	4.3	0836	4.3
TH 1253	1.0	F 1454	1.2
1927	4.2	2130	4.1
5 0132	1.1	**20** 0332	1.3
0810	4.3	1003	4.4
F 1425	1.0	SA 1622	1.1
2100	4.2	2247	4.3
6 0308	1.1	**21** 0449	1.1
0940	4.4	1109	4.5
SA 1557	0.8	SU 1725	0.8
2227	4.4	2339	4.4
7 0436	0.9	**22** 0541	0.9
1056	4.6	1152	4.6
SU 1714	0.6	M 1805	0.7
2338	4.5		
8 0547	0.7	**23** 0015	4.5
1157	4.8	0618	0.8
M 1816	0.4	TU 1226	4.7
		1838	0.6
9 0036	4.6	**24** 0047	4.5
0646	0.6	0655	0.7
TU 1251	4.9	W 1259	4.7
○ 1911	0.4	● 1914	0.6
10 0126	4.7	**25** 0121	4.6
0737	0.5	0731	0.6
W 1340	5.0	TH 1333	4.7
2001	0.3	1949	0.6
11 0213	4.7	**26** 0154	4.6
0823	0.4	0805	0.6
TH 1426	5.1	F 1407	4.7
2047	0.3	2022	0.6
12 0257	4.8	**27** 0225	4.7
0906	0.4	0837	0.6
F 1511	5.0	SA 1440	4.7
2130	0.4	2054	0.7
13 0338	4.7	**28** 0258	4.6
0945	0.4	0910	0.6
SA 1553	4.9	SU 1514	4.7
2209	0.5	2126	0.7
14 0414	4.7	**29** 0332	4.6
1019	0.5	0944	0.6
SU 1632	4.8	M 1550	4.7
2243	0.7	2158	0.7
15 0449	4.6	**30** 0406	4.6
1053	0.7	1016	0.7
M 1710	4.6	TU 1625	4.6
2316	0.9	2229	0.8

OCTOBER

Time	m	Time	m
1 0439	4.6	**16** 0529	4.4
1047	0.8	1139	1.1
W 1702	4.4	TH 1805	4.1
2302	1.0		
2 0520	4.4	**17** 0000	1.3
1129	0.9	0625	4.3
TH 1754	4.2	F 1239	1.3
2355	1.1	1913	4.0
3 0623	4.3	**18** 0110	1.5
1238	1.1	0743	4.3
F 1911	4.2	SA 1402	1.3
		2036	4.0
4 0117	1.3	**19** 0237	1.4
0749	4.4	0908	4.3
SA 1411	1.1	SU 1529	1.2
2044	4.2	2155	4.2
5 0254	1.2	**20** 0357	1.2
0920	4.5	1019	4.4
SU 1543	0.9	M 1636	0.9
2210	4.4	2253	4.3
6 0420	1.0	**21** 0456	1.0
1036	4.6	1108	4.5
M 1657	0.7	TU 1721	0.8
2318	4.5	2333	4.4
7 0527	0.8	**22** 0538	0.9
1135	4.8	1145	4.6
TU 1755	0.5	W 1758	0.7
8 0013	4.6	**23** 0009	4.5
0623	0.7	0618	0.8
W 1227	4.9	TH 1221	4.6
○ 1848	0.4	● 1837	0.7
9 0102	4.6	**24** 0046	4.6
0713	0.6	0659	0.7
TH 1317	4.9	F 1259	4.6
1936	0.4	1916	0.7
10 0147	4.7	**25** 0123	4.6
0759	0.5	0737	0.7
F 1403	4.9	SA 1337	4.7
2021	0.5	1953	0.6
11 0230	4.8	**26** 0158	4.7
0841	0.5	0814	0.6
SA 1446	4.9	SU 1415	4.7
2101	0.5	2030	0.7
12 0308	4.8	**27** 0234	4.7
0919	0.5	0850	0.6
SU 1526	4.8	M 1453	4.6
2138	0.6	2104	0.7
13 0343	4.7	**28** 0310	4.7
0953	0.5	0926	0.6
M 1603	4.6	TU 1531	4.6
2138	0.7	2210	0.7
14 0415	4.7	**29** 0346	4.7
1024	0.7	1001	0.6
TU 1639	4.4	W 1611	4.5
2240	0.9	2213	0.9
15 0449	4.5	**30** 0425	4.6
1057	0.9	1039	0.8
W 1717	4.3	TH 1654	4.4
2314	1.1	2254	1.0
		31 0511	4.6
		1127	1.0
		F 1749	4.3
		◗ 2350	1.2

NOVEMBER

Time	m	Time	m
1 0613	4.5	**16** 0020	1.4
1234	1.1	0645	4.3
SA 1902	4.2	SU 1303	1.3
		1931	4.0
2 0106	1.3	**17** 0131	1.5
0733	4.5	0800	4.3
SU 1358	1.1	M 1418	1.3
2027	4.2	2046	4.1
3 0235	1.2	**18** 0248	1.4
0858	4.6	0913	4.3
M 1523	0.9	TU 1530	1.1
2147	4.3	2153	4.3
4 0355	1.1	**19** 0355	1.2
1011	4.7	1012	4.5
TU 1633	0.8	W 1627	0.9
2251	4.4	2245	4.4
5 0459	0.9	**20** 0450	1.1
1109	4.7	1100	4.6
W 1729	0.6	TH 1715	0.8
2344	4.5	2329	4.5
6 0555	0.8	**21** 0540	1.0
1202	4.8	1144	4.6
TH 1821	0.6	F 1800	0.8
○			
7 0035	4.6	**22** 0012	4.6
0647	0.7	0626	0.8
F 1254	4.8	SA 1227	4.6
1910	0.6	● 1844	0.7
8 0121	4.7	**23** 0053	4.6
0735	0.6	0709	0.7
SA 1340	4.7	SU 1309	4.6
1953	0.5	1925	0.7
9 0202	4.7	**24** 0132	4.7
0815	0.5	0750	0.6
SU 1421	4.7	M 1353	4.6
2031	0.4	2007	0.7
10 0239	4.8	**25** 0213	4.8
0852	0.6	0832	0.6
M 1459	4.6	TU 1438	4.6
2107	0.7	2049	0.7
11 0313	4.8	**26** 0254	4.8
0927	0.6	0914	0.6
TU 1537	4.5	W 1521	4.6
2140	0.9	2128	0.7
12 0346	4.7	**27** 0335	4.8
1000	0.7	0954	0.6
W 1612	4.4	TH 1605	4.5
2212	0.9	2207	0.8
13 0420	4.6	**28** 0417	4.7
1034	0.9	1037	0.7
TH 1648	4.4	F 1652	4.4
2244	1.1	2251	1.0
14 0457	4.5	**29** 0507	4.7
1112	1.1	1127	0.9
F 1729	4.1	SA 1746	4.3
◗ 2325	1.3	◗ 2345	1.1
15 0544	4.4	**30** 0605	4.6
1200	1.2	1227	1.0
SA 1823	4.0	SU 1850	4.2

DECEMBER

Time	m	Time	m
1 0049	1.1	**16** 0027	1.4
0714	4.6	0652	4.4
M 1337	1.0	TU 1307	1.2
2002	4.2	1934	4.1
2 0205	1.2	**17** 0134	1.4
0830	4.6	0801	4.4
TU 1452	1.0	W 1416	1.2
2115	4.3	2044	4.2
3 0321	1.1	**18** 0247	1.3
0941	4.6	0910	4.4
W 1601	0.9	TH 1525	1.1
2220	4.4	2149	4.3
4 0428	1.0	**19** 0356	1.2
1044	4.7	1012	4.5
TH 1701	0.8	F 1626	0.9
2316	4.5	2247	4.4
5 0528	0.9	**20** 0458	1.0
1140	4.7	1108	4.5
F 1755	0.7	SA 1722	0.8
		2338	4.4
6 0009	4.6	**21** 0553	0.9
0623	0.7	1159	4.6
SA 1233	4.6	SU 1813	0.8
○ 1845	0.6		
7 0057	4.6	**22** 0026	4.6
0712	0.6	0642	0.7
SU 1320	4.6	M 1248	4.6
1928	0.6	● 1901	0.7
8 0138	4.7	**23** 0111	4.7
0752	0.5	0729	0.6
M 1400	4.5	TU 1337	4.6
2005	0.6	1950	0.7
9 0215	4.8	**24** 0157	4.8
0830	0.6	0818	0.6
TU 1437	4.5	W 1427	4.6
2042	0.7	2039	0.6
10 0250	4.8	**25** 0243	4.9
0907	0.7	0906	0.5
W 1514	4.5	TH 1516	4.6
2117	0.8	2123	0.6
11 0324	4.8	**26** 0327	4.9
0943	0.7	0949	0.5
TH 1549	4.5	F 1601	4.6
2150	0.9	2202	0.6
12 0356	4.7	**27** 0411	4.9
1015	0.8	1033	0.5
F 1622	4.4	SA 1646	4.5
2220	1.0	2244	0.7
13 0430	4.7	**28** 0459	4.8
1048	1.0	1121	0.7
SA 1657	4.3	SU 1736	4.5
2254	1.2	◗ 2332	0.8
14 0508	4.6	**29** 0552	4.7
1125	1.1	1212	0.8
SU 1738	4.1	M 1829	4.3
◗ 2335	1.3		
15 0554	4.4	**30** 0025	0.9
1209	1.2	0650	4.6
M 1829	4.1	TU 1308	0.9
		1929	4.3
		31 0128	1.0
		0756	4.5
		W 1412	1.0
		2036	4.3

Chart Datum: 2·7 metres below Normal Null (German reference level)
HAT is 5·1 metres above Chart Datum

TIDES

HOEK VAN HOLLAND
MEAN SPRING AND NEAP CURVES

MEAN RANGES
Springs 1.9m
Neaps 1.5m

Factor

Note - Double LWs often occur.
The predictions are for the lower
LW which is usually the first.

TIME ZONE -0100
(Dutch Standard Time)
Subtract 1 hour for UT
For Dutch Summer Time add
ONE hour in **non-shaded areas**

NETHERLANDS – HOEK VAN HOLLAND
LAT 51°59′N   LONG 4°07′E
TIMES AND HEIGHTS OF HIGH AND LOW WATERS

Dates in amber are **SPRINGS**
Dates in yellow are **NEAPS**

2014

JANUARY

Time m	Time m
1 0201 2.3 / 0719 0.3 / W 1420 2.3 / ● 1945 0.4	**16** 0304 2.1 / 0814 0.3 / TH 1516 2.2 / ○ 2035 0.5
2 0247 2.3 / 0759 0.3 / TH 1507 2.4 / 2021 0.5	**17** 0339 2.1 / 0845 0.3 / F 1548 2.3 / 2120 0.5
3 0335 2.2 / 0845 0.2 / F 1552 2.4 / 2105 0.5	**18** 0409 2.1 / 0909 0.2 / SA 1619 2.3 / 2330 0.5
4 0420 2.2 / 0928 0.1 / SA 1639 2.4	**19** 0446 2.1 / 0946 0.2 / SU 1655 2.3
5 0034 0.5 / 0508 2.0 / SU 1016 0.1 / 1728 2.4	**20** 0025 0.4 / 0516 2.1 / M 1020 0.2 / 1726 2.4
6 0136 0.5 / 0558 2.1 / M 1109 0.1 / 1821 2.3	**21** 0054 0.4 / 0538 2.1 / TU 1055 0.2 / 1756 2.2
7 0150 0.6 / 0651 2.1 / TU 1215 0.1 / 1915 2.2	**22** 0140 0.4 / 0615 2.0 / W 1130 0.2 / 1831 2.2
8 0115 0.5 / 0744 2.1 / W 1314 0.1 / ☾ 2025 2.1	**23** 0210 0.5 / 0656 2.0 / TH 1216 0.1 / 1914 2.2
9 0204 0.5 / 0850 2.0 / TH 1425 0.2 / 2136 2.0	**24** 0150 0.5 / 0745 2.0 / F 1304 0.2 / ☽ 2025 2.1
10 0304 0.5 / 1000 1.9 / F 1534 0.3 / 2245 1.9	**25** 0245 0.4 / 0900 1.9 / SA 1446 0.2 / 2146 2.0
11 0426 0.5 / 1116 1.9 / SA 1645 0.3	**26** 0336 0.4 / 1016 1.9 / SU 1544 0.3 / 2250 2.0
12 0000 2.0 / 0536 0.5 / SU 1220 2.0 / 1800 0.4	**27** 0435 0.4 / 1126 2.0 / M 1700 0.3
13 0100 2.0 / 0905 0.4 / M 1316 2.0 / 1844 0.4	**28** 0000 2.0 / 0525 0.4 / TU 1226 2.1 / 1754 0.4
14 0144 2.0 / 0955 0.4 / TU 1405 2.1 / 1924 0.5	**29** 0058 2.1 / 0614 0.3 / W 1319 2.2 / 1843 0.4
15 0235 2.1 / 0746 0.3 / W 1434 2.2 / 2015 0.5	**30** 0149 2.1 / 0705 0.3 / TH 1407 2.3 / ● 1925 0.4
	31 0237 2.2 / 0741 0.2 / F 1452 2.4 / 2010 0.5

FEBRUARY

Time m	Time m
1 0317 2.2 / 0826 0.1 / SA 1536 2.4 / 2050 0.5	**16** 0345 2.1 / 0846 0.2 / SU 1555 2.3 / 2316 0.4
2 0406 2.2 / 0908 0.1 / SU 1622 2.4	**17** 0416 2.1 / 0911 0.2 / M 1626 2.3 / 2354 0.4
3 0025 0.5 / 0451 2.2 / M 0956 0.1 / 1707 2.4	**18** 0445 2.1 / 1230 0.2 / TU 1655 2.3
4 0120 0.5 / 0535 2.2 / TU 1046 0.1 / 1755 2.3	**19** 0040 0.3 / 0515 2.1 / W 1019 0.2 / 1728 2.2
5 0215 0.5 / 0625 2.2 / W 1145 0.1 / 1849 2.2	**20** 0115 0.3 / 0548 2.1 / TH 1055 0.1 / 1805 2.2
6 0040 0.4 / 0716 2.1 / TH 1255 0.1 / ☽ 1945 2.1	**21** 0145 0.4 / 0625 2.1 / F 1139 0.1 / 1849 2.2
7 0124 0.4 / 0804 2.0 / F 1354 0.2 / 2046 1.9	**22** 0000 2.1 / 0712 2.1 / SA 1245 0.1 / ☽ 1945 2.1
8 0235 0.4 / 0904 1.9 / SA 1504 0.3 / 2154 1.8	**23** 0200 0.3 / 0809 2.0 / SU 1425 0.2 / 2055 1.9
9 0355 0.4 / 1046 1.8 / SU 1625 0.3 / 2346 1.8	**24** 0254 0.3 / 0946 1.9 / M 1530 0.3 / 2226 1.8
10 0504 0.4 / 1153 1.9 / M 1734 0.4	**25** 0405 0.3 / 1100 1.9 / TU 1634 0.4 / 2335 1.8
11 0034 1.8 / 0600 0.3 / TU 1300 2.0 / 1834 0.4	**26** 0505 0.3 / 1204 2.0 / W 2020 0.4
12 0136 1.9 / 0935 0.3 / W 1343 2.0 / 2145 0.4	**27** 0045 1.9 / 0554 0.3 / TH 1306 2.1 / 2120 0.4
13 0215 2.0 / 1015 0.3 / TH 1426 2.1 / 2230 0.4	**28** 0132 2.0 / 0646 0.2 / F 1351 2.3 / 2144 0.4
14 0256 2.0 / 0754 0.3 / F 1455 2.2 / 2030 0.5	
15 0315 2.1 / 0819 0.2 / SA 1525 2.2 / ○ 2054 0.5	

MARCH

Time m	Time m
1 0218 2.1 / 0718 0.1 / SA 1435 2.3 / ● 2224 0.5	**16** 0250 2.0 / 0749 0.3 / SU 1455 2.2 / ○ 2220 0.4
2 0300 2.2 / 0806 0.1 / SU 1516 2.4 / 2315 0.5	**17** 0315 2.1 / 0816 0.2 / M 1526 2.3 / 2245 0.3
3 0345 2.2 / 0846 0.1 / M 1605 2.4	**18** 0345 2.2 / 0845 0.2 / TU 1555 2.3 / 2346 0.3
4 0004 0.4 / 0425 2.3 / TU 0929 0.1 / 1646 2.3	**19** 0415 2.2 / 1215 0.2 / W 1629 2.3
5 0106 0.4 / 0511 2.3 / W 1015 0.1 / 1735 2.2	**20** 0014 0.3 / 0449 2.2 / TH 1235 0.2 / 1705 2.2
6 0156 0.4 / 0555 2.2 / TH 1115 0.1 / 1817 2.1	**21** 0106 0.2 / 0525 2.2 / F 1028 0.2 / 1745 2.2
7 0235 0.4 / 0639 2.2 / F 1225 0.2 / 1905 2.0	**22** 0134 0.3 / 0605 2.2 / SA 1119 0.2 / 1828 2.1
8 0045 0.3 / 0724 2.1 / SA 1340 0.2 / ☽ 2006 1.8	**23** 0200 0.3 / 0648 2.1 / SU 1219 0.2 / 1919 2.0
9 0145 0.3 / 0824 1.9 / SU 1450 0.3 / 2105 1.7	**24** 0144 0.2 / 0746 2.0 / M 1415 0.2 / ☽ 2036 1.8
10 0330 0.3 / 0944 1.7 / M 1604 0.3 / 2254 1.6	**25** 0246 0.2 / 0915 1.9 / TU 1514 0.3 / 2200 1.7
11 0456 0.3 / 1130 1.8 / TU 1720 0.4	**26** 0346 0.2 / 1040 1.9 / W 1625 0.4 / 2319 1.7
12 0016 1.7 / 0533 0.3 / W 1235 1.9 / 1805 0.4	**27** 0434 0.2 / 1155 2.0 / TH 1955 0.3
13 0110 1.9 / 0636 0.3 / TH 1314 2.0 / 2126 0.3	**28** 0025 1.8 / 0830 0.2 / F 1248 2.1 / 2100 0.3
14 0149 1.9 / 0951 0.2 / F 1355 2.1 / 2155 0.3	**29** 0115 1.9 / 0926 0.2 / SA 1336 2.2 / 2134 0.4
15 0226 2.0 / 1025 0.3 / SA 1426 2.1 / 2246 0.4	**30** 0158 2.0 / 0659 0.1 / SU 1417 2.3 / ● 2216 0.4
	31 0240 2.1 / 0745 0.1 / M 1456 2.3 / 2005 0.4

APRIL

Time m	Time m
1 0326 2.2 / 0821 0.1 / TU 1542 2.3 / 2345 0.4	**16** 0310 2.2 / 0814 0.2 / W 1529 2.3 / 2315 0.3
2 0405 2.3 / 0905 0.1 / W 1625 2.2	**17** 0347 2.2 / 0851 0.2 / TH 1607 2.3
3 0040 0.3 / 0446 2.3 / TH 1315 0.1 / 1708 2.1	**18** 0005 0.2 / 0425 2.2 / F 1220 0.2 / 1646 2.2
4 0135 0.3 / 0527 2.2 / F 1405 0.2 / 1756 2.0	**19** 0044 0.3 / 0502 2.2 / SA 1306 0.2 / 1725 2.1
5 0215 0.3 / 0612 2.2 / SA 1230 0.3 / 1836 1.9	**20** 0136 0.2 / 0545 2.2 / SU 1324 0.2 / 1811 2.0
6 0014 0.2 / 0700 2.0 / SU 1320 0.3 / 1926 1.8	**21** 0200 0.2 / 0631 2.1 / M 1345 0.2 / 1906 1.9
7 0105 0.2 / 0744 1.9 / M 1424 0.3 / ☽ 2020 1.6	**22** 0120 0.1 / 0736 2.0 / TU 1415 0.3 / ☽ 2026 1.7
8 0310 0.2 / 0855 1.8 / TU 1545 0.3 / 2124 1.5	**23** 0205 0.1 / 0900 1.9 / W 1516 0.3 / 2145 1.7
9 0415 0.2 / 1034 1.7 / W 1706 0.3 / 2335 1.5	**24** 0315 0.1 / 1025 1.9 / TH 1815 0.4 / 2254 1.7
10 0520 0.2 / 1149 1.8 / TH 1744 0.3	**25** 0415 0.2 / 1129 2.0 / F 1945 0.3
11 0036 1.7 / 0555 0.2 / F 1239 1.9 / 2017 0.3	**26** 0006 1.8 / 0754 0.1 / SA 1228 2.1 / 2040 0.3
12 0115 1.8 / 0650 0.2 / SA 1319 2.0 / 2131 0.3	**27** 0056 1.9 / 0900 0.1 / SU 1315 2.2 / 2105 0.3
13 0139 1.9 / 0946 0.2 / SU 1349 2.1 / 2216 0.3	**28** 0138 2.0 / 0645 0.2 / M 1357 2.2 / 2150 0.4
14 0209 2.0 / 0725 0.3 / M 1418 2.2 / 2240 0.3	**29** 0221 2.1 / 0725 0.2 / TU 1440 2.2 / ● 1944 0.4
15 0239 2.1 / 0745 0.2 / TU 1452 2.3 / ○ 2250 0.3	**30** 0306 2.2 / 0805 0.2 / W 1525 2.2 / 2325 0.3

Chart Datum: 0·92 metres below NAP Datum
HAT is 2·5 metres above Chart Datum

TIDES

TIME ZONE -0100
(Dutch Standard Time)
Subtract 1 hour for UT
For Dutch Summer Time add
ONE hour in **non-shaded areas**

NETHERLANDS – HOEK VAN HOLLAND
LAT 51°59'N   LONG 4°07'E
TIMES AND HEIGHTS OF HIGH AND LOW WATERS

Dates in amber are **SPRINGS**
Dates in yellow are **NEAPS**

2014

MAY

Day	Time m	Time m	Time m	Time m		Day	Time m	Time m	Time m	Time m
1 TH	0346 2.2	1150 0.2	1607 2.1			16 F	0325 2.2	0836 0.3	1545 2.2	
2 F	0026 0.2	0426 2.2	1245 0.2	1648 2.0		17 SA	0001 0.2	0405 2.3	1154 0.3	1627 2.1
3 SA	0100 0.2	0505 2.2	1336 0.3	1729 2.0		18 SU	0046 0.2	0446 2.2	1234 0.3	1711 2.0
4 SU	0146 0.2	0550 2.1	1405 0.3	1809 1.9		19 M	0125 0.1	0531 2.2	1315 0.3	1758 1.9
5 M	0000 0.1	0625 2.0	1320 0.3	1856 1.8		20 TU	0205 0.1	0625 2.2	1354 0.3	1859 1.8
6 TU	0034 0.1	0720 1.9	1410 0.4	1945 1.7		21 W	0050 0.1	0725 2.1	1420 0.3	◑ 2016 1.8
7 W	0124 0.2	0825 1.8	1524 0.4	◑ 2046 1.6		22 TH	0144 0.0	0846 2.0	1454 0.4	2114 1.7
8 TH	0400 0.2	0925 1.8	1635 0.3	2145 1.5		23 F	0250 0.1	0955 2.1	1804 0.4	2236 1.8
9 F	0450 0.2	1045 1.8	1715 0.3	2315 1.6		24 SA	0343 0.1	1105 2.0	1926 0.3	2335 1.8
10 SA	0535 0.2	1150 1.9	1840 0.3			25 SU	0746 0.1	1206 2.1	2025 0.3	
11 SU	0026 1.7	0630 0.2	1238 2.0	2055 0.3		26 M	0031 1.9	0830 0.2	1258 2.1	2105 0.3
12 M	0055 1.9	0855 0.2	1311 2.1	2135 0.2		27 TU	0119 2.0	0635 0.2	1345 2.1	1854 0.4
13 TU	0129 2.0	0645 0.3	1348 2.2	2226 0.3		28	0205 2.1	0714 0.3	● 1934 0.3	
14 W	0206 2.1	0715 0.3	1425 2.3	○ 2250 0.3		29 TH	0245 2.2	0804 0.3	1516 2.1	2019 0.2
15 TH	0246 2.2	0755 0.3	1506 2.3	2314 0.2		30 F	0327 2.2	0844 0.3	1556 2.1	2054 0.2
						31 SA	0405 2.2	1207 0.3	1635 2.0	2140 0.2

JUNE

Day	Time m	Time m	Time m	Time m		Day	Time m	Time m	Time m	Time m
1 SU	0449 2.2	1305 0.3	1716 2.0	2225 0.1		16 M	0432 2.3	1224 0.4	1706 2.0	2215 0.1
2 M	0525 2.1	1334 0.4	1749 1.9	2309 0.1		17 TU	0521 2.3	1320 0.4	1748 2.0	2305 0.1
3 TU	0605 2.1	1327 0.4	1830 1.8	2355 0.1		18 W	0615 2.2	1400 0.4	1849 1.9	
4 W	0649 2.0	1400 0.4	1905 1.8			19 TH	0005 0.0	0715 2.2	1430 0.4	◑ 1955 1.9
5 TH	0045 0.1	0745 1.9	1450 0.4	◑ 2005 1.7		20 F	0115 0.0	0814 2.1	1424 0.4	2056 1.9
6 F	0134 0.2	0845 1.9	1555 0.4	2111 1.7		21 SA	0215 0.0	0930 2.1	1734 0.4	2206 1.9
7 SA	0235 0.2	0946 1.9	1640 0.4	2205 1.7		22 SU	0324 0.1	1035 2.0	1840 0.4	2310 1.9
8 SU	0514 0.2	1045 1.9	1727 0.3	2316 1.8		23 M	0654 0.2	1146 2.0	1950 0.4	
9 M	0540 0.3	1145 2.0	1820 0.3			24 TU	0009 1.9	0535 0.2	1245 2.0	2055 0.4
10 TU	0005 1.9	0534 0.3	1236 2.1	2106 0.3		25 W	0106 2.0	0624 0.3	1336 2.0	1844 0.3
11 W	0056 2.0	0615 0.3	1320 2.2	2157 0.3		26 TH	0149 2.1	0714 0.3	1425 2.1	1935 0.3
12 TH	0137 2.1	0654 0.3	1358 2.2	1925 0.3		27 F	0235 2.1	0755 0.4	1505 2.0	● 2004 0.2
13 F	0221 2.2	0739 0.3	1445 2.2	○ 2006 0.2		28 SA	0315 2.2	0844 0.4	1545 2.0	2045 0.2
14 SA	0306 2.3	0819 0.3	1529 2.2	2039 0.2		29 SU	0355 2.2	0920 0.5	1619 2.0	2114 0.2
15 SU	0347 2.3	1156 0.4	1612 2.1	2125 0.1		30 M	0429 2.2	1227 0.4	1655 2.0	2153 0.2

JULY

Day	Time m	Time m	Time m	Time m		Day	Time m	Time m	Time m	Time m
1 TU	0505 2.2	1300 0.4	1724 2.0	2235 0.2		16 W	0505 2.3	1254 0.5	1736 2.1	2239 0.1
2 W	0545 2.1	1324 0.4	1754 1.9	2315 0.2		17 TH	0556 2.3	1350 0.5	1825 2.0	2339 0.1
3 TH	0620 2.1	1350 0.4	1846 1.9	2359 0.2		18 F	0649 2.2	1450 0.5	1919 2.0	
4 F	0655 2.0	1420 0.4	1926 1.8			19 SA	0055 0.1	0750 2.1	1406 0.4	◑ 2014 2.0
5 SA	0044 0.2	0734 2.0	1440 0.4	◑ 2027 1.8		20 SU	0154 0.1	0856 2.0	1445 0.4	2114 1.9
6 SU	0155 0.2	0855 2.0	1455 0.4	2126 1.8		21 M	0255 0.2	1006 1.9	1556 0.4	2235 1.9
7 M	0244 0.2	0956 2.0	1554 0.4	2231 1.8		22 TU	0414 0.3	1126 1.9	1645 0.4	2350 1.9
8 TU	0345 0.3	1100 2.0	1700 0.4	2325 1.9		23 W	0536 0.3	1229 1.9	1745 0.4	
9 W	0454 0.3	1200 2.1	1744 0.3			24 TH	0049 2.0	0614 0.4	1325 2.0	1835 0.3
10 TH	0028 2.0	0554 0.3	1256 2.1	1824 0.3		25 F	0139 2.1	0704 0.4	1415 2.0	1914 0.3
11 F	0115 2.1	0646 0.3	1341 2.1	1905 0.2		26 SA	0226 2.1	0749 0.5	1455 2.1	● 2000 0.2
12 SA	0202 2.2	0725 0.4	1427 2.2	○ 1946 0.2		27 SU	0254 2.2	0825 0.5	1529 2.1	2023 0.2
13 SU	0247 2.3	0806 0.4	1515 2.1	2026 0.1		28 M	0336 2.2	0854 0.5	1554 2.1	2055 0.2
14 M	0332 2.4	0846 0.5	1558 2.1	2106 0.1		29 TU	0405 2.2	1130 0.5	1629 2.1	2125 0.2
15 TU	0417 2.4	1220 0.5	1645 2.1	2149 0.1		30 W	0441 2.2	1205 0.5	1706 2.1	2159 0.2
						31 TH	0516 2.2	1245 0.4	1728 2.0	2235 0.2

AUGUST

Day	Time m	Time m	Time m	Time m		Day	Time m	Time m	Time m	Time m
1 F	0546 2.2	1336 0.4	1806 2.0	2309 0.2		16 SA	0621 2.2	1427 0.5	1846 2.2	
2 SA	0618 2.2	1355 0.4	1836 2.0	2356 0.2		17 SU	0014 0.2	0716 2.1	1305 0.5	◑ 1939 2.1
3 SU	0656 2.1	1400 0.4	1920 2.0			18 M	0124 0.2	0815 2.0	1355 0.4	2046 2.0
4 M	0034 0.2	0745 2.1	1420 0.4	◑ 2015 1.9		19 TU	0234 0.3	0925 1.8	1526 0.4	2155 1.9
5 TU	0210 0.2	0855 2.0	1516 0.4	2140 1.9		20 W	0406 0.4	1055 1.9	1634 0.4	2330 1.9
6 W	0325 0.3	1015 2.0	1605 0.4	2256 1.9		21 TH	0504 0.4	1216 1.9	1724 0.4	
7 TH	0435 0.4	1136 2.0	1705 0.4			22 F	0035 2.0	0610 0.5	1309 2.0	1814 0.3
8 F	0002 2.0	0534 0.4	1236 2.0	1806 0.3		23 SA	0130 2.1	0940 0.5	1355 2.0	2154 0.3
9 SA	0055 2.1	0624 0.4	1325 2.1	1839 0.3		24 SU	0204 2.2	1017 0.5	1435 2.1	1935 0.3
10 SU	0147 2.3	0705 0.5	1411 2.1	○ 1926 0.2		25 M	0239 2.2	0755 0.5	1505 2.1	● 2004 0.3
11 M	0229 2.4	0746 0.5	1455 2.2	2002 0.1		26 TU	0309 2.3	0829 0.5	1528 2.1	2024 0.3
12 TU	0316 2.4	0821 0.5	1541 2.2	2046 0.1		27 W	0346 2.3	0844 0.5	1605 2.2	2055 0.3
13 W	0359 2.4	0905 0.6	1625 2.2	2125 0.1		28 TH	0411 2.3	1135 0.5	1636 2.2	2125 0.3
14 TH	0446 2.4	1256 0.5	1709 2.2	2215 0.1		29 F	0445 2.3	1236 0.5	1702 2.1	2205 0.3
15 F	0530 2.3	1345 0.5	1755 2.2	2309 0.1		30 SA	0512 2.3	1316 0.4	1729 2.1	2235 0.3
						31 SU	0548 2.2	1345 0.5	1806 2.1	2315 0.2

Chart Datum: 0·92 metres below NAP Datum
HAT is 2·5 metres above Chart Datum

TIME ZONE -0100
(Dutch Standard Time)
Subtract 1 hour for UT
For Dutch Summer Time add
ONE hour in **non-shaded areas**

NETHERLANDS – HOEK VAN HOLLAND

LAT 51°59'N   LONG 4°07'E

TIMES AND HEIGHTS OF HIGH AND LOW WATERS

Dates in amber are **SPRINGS**
Dates in yellow are **NEAPS**

2014

SEPTEMBER

Time m		Time m	
1 0626 2.2 / 1136 0.4 / M 1845 2.2	**16** 0104 0.3 / 0735 1.9 / TU 1314 0.4 / ◐ 2006 2.0		
2 0000 0.2 / 0712 2.2 / TU 1225 0.4 / ◐ 1936 2.1	**17** 0205 0.4 / 0833 1.8 / W 1444 0.4 / 2125 1.9		
3 0114 0.3 / 0816 2.0 / W 1436 0.4 / 2045 2.0	**18** 0340 0.5 / 1030 1.7 / TH 1604 0.4 / 2255 1.9		
4 0255 0.4 / 0935 1.9 / TH 1535 0.4 / 2226 1.9	**19** 0444 0.5 / 1150 1.8 / F 1714 0.4		
5 0415 0.5 / 1106 1.9 / F 1634 0.4 / 2335 2.0	**20** 0015 2.0 / 0600 0.5 / SA 1245 1.9 / 1816 0.4		
6 0514 0.5 / 1216 1.9 / SA 1736 0.3	**21** 0106 2.1 / 0916 0.5 / SU 1336 2.0 / 2135 0.4		
7 0039 2.2 / 0845 0.5 / SU 1308 2.0 / 1815 0.3	**22** 0145 2.2 / 0945 0.5 / M 1409 2.1 / 2215 0.4		
8 0127 2.3 / 0925 0.5 / M 1355 2.1 / 1855 0.2	**23** 0216 2.2 / 1030 0.5 / TU 1435 2.1 / 1935 0.4		
9 0211 2.4 / 0725 0.6 / TU 1435 2.2 / ○ 1938 0.2	**24** 0241 2.3 / 0755 0.5 / W 1459 2.2 / ● 1954 0.4		
10 0255 2.5 / 0805 0.6 / W 1519 2.3 / 2020 0.1	**25** 0308 2.3 / 0824 0.5 / TH 1525 2.2 / 2030 0.3		
11 0336 2.5 / 0842 0.5 / TH 1602 2.3 / 2105 0.2	**26** 0341 2.4 / 1114 0.5 / F 1559 2.3 / 2059 0.3		
12 0422 2.4 / 0925 0.5 / F 1645 2.3 / 2149 0.2	**27** 0412 2.4 / 1205 0.5 / SA 1631 2.3 / 2132 0.3		
13 0507 2.3 / 1015 0.5 / SA 1728 2.3 / 2245 0.3	**28** 0447 2.3 / 1245 0.4 / SU 1705 2.3 / 2205 0.3		
14 0556 2.2 / 1105 0.5 / SU 1815 2.2 / 2344 0.3	**29** 0523 2.3 / 1030 0.4 / M 1740 2.3 / 2249 0.3		
15 0641 2.1 / 1204 0.4 / M 1906 2.2	**30** 0602 2.2 / 1105 0.4 / TU 1820 2.3 / 2334 0.4		

OCTOBER

Time m		Time m	
1 0648 2.1 / 1205 0.4 / W 1912 2.2	**16** 0135 0.5 / 0755 1.8 / TH 1350 0.4 / 2046 1.9		
2 0150 0.4 / 0745 2.0 / TH 1345 0.4 / 2019 2.0	**17** 0314 0.6 / 0904 1.7 / F 1545 0.4 / 2205 1.8		
3 0256 0.5 / 0925 1.8 / F 1505 0.4 / 2200 2.0	**18** 0425 0.6 / 1116 1.7 / SA 1655 0.4 / 2341 1.9		
4 0349 0.6 / 1040 1.8 / SA 1604 0.4 / 2320 2.1	**19** 0530 0.6 / 1215 1.8 / SU 1745 0.4		
5 0736 0.5 / 1149 1.9 / SU 2000 0.4	**20** 0030 2.1 / 0816 0.5 / M 1255 1.9 / 1830 0.4		
6 0015 2.2 / 0824 0.5 / M 1245 2.0 / 1744 0.3	**21** 0105 2.2 / 0915 0.5 / TU 1336 2.0 / 1904 0.4		
7 0105 2.3 / 0920 0.5 / TU 1335 2.1 / 1835 0.3	**22** 0139 2.2 / 1005 0.5 / W 1359 2.1 / 1920 0.4		
8 0151 2.4 / 0706 0.6 / W 1415 2.2 / ○ 1916 0.2	**23** 0209 2.3 / 1036 0.5 / TH 1425 2.2 / ● 1935 0.4		
9 0236 2.4 / 0739 0.5 / TH 1456 2.3 / 1955 0.2	**24** 0239 2.4 / 0754 0.5 / F 1456 2.3 / 2006 0.4		
10 0316 2.4 / 0819 0.5 / F 1538 2.4 / 2045 0.4	**25** 0311 2.4 / 0829 0.5 / SA 1531 2.3 / 2035 0.4		
11 0400 2.4 / 0906 0.5 / SA 1622 2.4 / 2125 0.3	**26** 0347 2.4 / 1145 0.4 / SU 1607 2.3 / 2115 0.4		
12 0446 2.3 / 0945 0.5 / SU 1706 2.4 / 2214 0.4	**27** 0425 2.3 / 1236 0.4 / M 1642 2.3 / 2155 0.4		
13 0528 2.2 / 1034 0.4 / M 1749 2.3 / 2314 0.5	**28** 0506 2.3 / 1016 0.4 / TU 1721 2.3 / 2240 0.5		
14 0615 2.0 / 1134 0.4 / TU 1835 2.3	**29** 0546 2.2 / 1054 0.3 / W 1805 2.3 / 2335 0.5		
15 0040 0.5 / 0706 1.9 / W 1235 0.4 / ◐ 1924 2.1	**30** 0631 2.1 / 1154 0.3 / TH 1855 2.2		
	31 0206 0.5 / 0731 2.0 / F 1330 0.3 / ◐ 2004 2.1		

NOVEMBER

Time m		Time m	
1 0234 0.6 / 0906 1.8 / SA 1435 0.3 / 2147 2.0	**16** 0354 0.6 / 0925 1.7 / SU 1614 0.4 / 2214 1.9		
2 0556 0.6 / 1016 1.8 / SU 1535 0.3 / 2256 2.1	**17** 0500 0.6 / 1054 1.7 / M 1726 0.4 / 2335 2.0		
3 0714 0.5 / 1125 1.9 / M 1935 0.3 / 2355 2.2	**18** 0550 0.5 / 1155 1.8 / TU 1805 0.4		
4 0805 0.5 / 1226 2.0 / TU 2024 0.3	**19** 0014 2.1 / 0825 0.5 / W 1239 1.9 / 2031 0.4		
5 0045 2.3 / 0906 0.6 / W 1312 2.1 / 1818 0.3	**20** 0059 2.2 / 0920 0.4 / TH 1315 2.0 / 1845 0.5		
6 0136 2.3 / 0927 0.6 / TH 1356 2.2 / ○ 1906 0.3	**21** 0136 2.3 / 0954 0.4 / F 1356 2.2 / 1909 0.4		
7 0217 2.3 / 0726 0.5 / F 1427 2.3 / 1946 0.3	**22** 0208 2.3 / 0740 0.4 / SA 1427 2.3 / ● 1945 0.4		
8 0301 2.4 / 0806 0.5 / SA 1519 2.4 / 2025 0.4	**23** 0247 2.4 / 0805 0.4 / SU 1505 2.3 / 2019 0.4		
9 0346 2.4 / 0845 0.4 / SU 1602 2.4 / 2115 0.4	**24** 0325 2.4 / 0839 0.4 / M 1547 2.4 / 2054 0.5		
10 0429 2.2 / 0935 0.4 / M 1646 2.4 / 2139 0.5	**25** 0407 2.3 / 0919 0.3 / TU 1627 2.4		
11 0110 0.5 / 0516 2.1 / TU 1020 0.3 / 1726 2.3	**26** 0448 2.2 / 1005 0.3 / W 1707 2.4		
12 0155 0.5 / 0555 2.0 / W 1105 0.3 / 1811 2.2	**27** 0106 0.5 / 0536 2.1 / TH 1055 0.3 / 1756 2.3		
13 0010 0.6 / 0640 1.9 / TH 1155 0.3 / 1855 2.1	**28** 0146 0.5 / 0620 2.0 / F 1143 0.2 / 1845 2.2		
14 0110 0.6 / 0736 1.8 / F 1255 0.3 / ◐ 2000 2.0	**29** 0200 0.5 / 0725 1.9 / SA 1254 0.2 / ◐ 1954 2.1		
15 0230 0.6 / 0815 1.8 / SA 1536 0.4 / 2105 1.9	**30** 0215 0.6 / 0840 1.9 / SU 1416 0.2 / 2116 2.1		

DECEMBER

Time m		Time m	
1 0515 0.6 / 0956 1.9 / M 1505 0.3 / 2226 2.1	**16** 0410 0.6 / 0945 1.8 / TU 1635 0.4 / 2226 1.9		
2 0650 0.6 / 1100 1.9 / TU 1855 0.3 / 2329 2.1	**17** 0510 0.5 / 1045 1.8 / W 1740 0.4 / 2314 2.0		
3 0800 0.5 / 1155 2.0 / W 2016 0.3	**18** 0600 0.5 / 1149 1.9 / TH 1810 0.4		
4 0025 2.2 / 0835 0.5 / TH 1251 2.1 / 1805 0.4	**19** 0026 2.1 / 0846 0.5 / F 1239 2.0 / 1820 0.4		
5 0115 2.2 / 0917 0.5 / F 1339 2.2 / 1853 0.4	**20** 0105 2.2 / 0924 0.4 / SA 1325 2.1 / 1855 0.4		
6 0206 2.2 / 0715 0.5 / SA 1425 2.3 / ○ 1939 0.4	**21** 0146 2.2 / 1016 0.4 / SU 1405 2.2 / 1929 0.4		
7 0251 2.2 / 0759 0.4 / SU 1506 2.3 / 2024 0.5	**22** 0227 2.3 / 0744 0.4 / M 1447 2.3 / ● 2005 0.5		
8 0336 2.2 / 0839 0.3 / M 1547 2.4 / 2110 0.5	**23** 0311 2.3 / 0825 0.4 / TU 1529 2.4 / 2045 0.5		
9 0415 2.2 / 0914 0.3 / TU 1628 2.4	**24** 0352 2.2 / 0901 0.2 / W 1610 2.4 / 2354 0.5		
10 0040 0.5 / 0454 2.1 / W 0959 0.3 / 1708 2.3	**25** 0437 2.2 / 0948 0.2 / TH 1656 2.4		
11 0136 0.6 / 0535 2.1 / TH 1050 0.2 / 1755 2.2	**26** 0055 0.5 / 0525 2.1 / F 1036 0.2 / 1742 2.3		
12 0000 0.6 / 0616 2.0 / F 1135 0.2 / 1836 2.1	**27** 0136 0.5 / 0615 2.1 / SA 1129 0.1 / 1836 2.3		
13 0040 0.6 / 0656 1.9 / SA 1219 0.2 / 1926 2.1	**28** 0200 0.5 / 0715 2.0 / SU 1234 0.1 / ◐ 1939 2.2		
14 0130 0.6 / 0740 1.9 / SU 1315 0.3 / ◐ 2015 2.0	**29** 0210 0.5 / 0816 2.0 / M 1345 0.1 / 2045 2.1		
15 0230 0.6 / 0840 1.8 / M 1410 0.3 / 2115 1.9	**30** 0234 0.6 / 0920 2.0 / TU 1456 0.2 / 2156 2.1		
	31 0325 0.6 / 1026 1.9 / W 1555 0.3 / 2305 2.0		

Chart Datum: 0·92 metres below NAP Datum
HAT is 2·5 metres above Chart Datum

TIDES

371

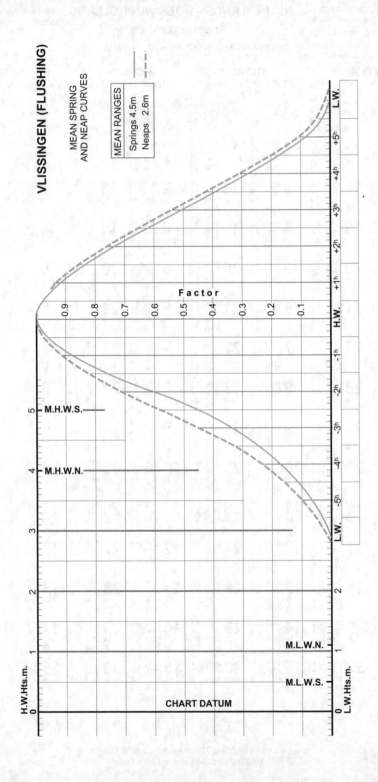

VLISSINGEN (FLUSHING)

MEAN SPRING
AND NEAP CURVES

MEAN RANGES

Springs 4.5m
Neaps 2.6m

TIME ZONE -0100
(Dutch Standard Time)
Subtract 1 hour for UT
For Dutch Summer Time add
ONE hour in **non-shaded areas**

NETHERLANDS – VLISSINGEN

LAT 51°27'N   LONG 3°36'E

TIMES AND HEIGHTS OF HIGH AND LOW WATERS

Dates in amber are **SPRINGS**
Dates in yellow are **NEAPS**

2014

JANUARY

Time	m	Time	m
1 0115	5.0	**16** 0215	4.7
0746	0.6	0828	0.7
W 1336	5.1	TH 1429	4.8
● 2006	0.6	○ 2036	0.9
2 0203	5.1	**17** 0245	4.7
0833	0.4	0901	0.6
TH 1423	5.2	F 1501	4.9
2052	0.6	2110	0.8
3 0249	5.1	**18** 0315	4.8
0923	0.3	0940	0.6
F 1508	5.3	SA 1535	4.9
2138	0.6	2146	0.8
4 0336	5.1	**19** 0349	4.8
1012	0.3	1015	0.6
SA 1557	5.2	SU 1606	4.9
2225	0.7	2216	0.8
5 0426	5.0	**20** 0421	4.8
1056	0.3	1050	0.6
SU 1646	5.1	M 1637	4.8
2308	0.7	2245	0.9
6 0512	5.0	**21** 0455	4.7
1145	0.3	1120	0.7
M 1739	5.0	TU 1707	4.8
2355	0.8	2319	0.9
7 0605	4.8	**22** 0526	4.6
1236	0.4	1156	0.7
TU 1835	4.8	W 1745	4.7
		2356	0.9
8 0046	0.9	**23** 0605	4.6
0702	4.7	1230	0.7
W 1326	0.6	TH 1829	4.6
◐ 1936	4.6		
9 0134	1.1	**24** 0046	1.0
0759	4.4	0656	4.4
TH 1425	0.8	F 1321	0.8
2039	4.4	◑ 1929	4.4
10 0250	1.2	**25** 0140	1.0
0905	4.3	0806	4.3
F 1535	1.0	SA 1419	0.9
2156	4.2	2048	4.3
11 0416	1.3	**26** 0256	1.1
1025	4.1	0920	4.3
SA 1706	1.0	SU 1538	1.0
2311	4.3	2201	4.3
12 0537	1.2	**27** 0415	1.1
1135	4.3	1036	4.3
SU 1800	1.0	M 1650	0.9
		2308	4.4
13 0005	4.4	**28** 0536	0.9
0630	1.0	1138	4.6
M 1232	4.5	TU 1800	0.8
1845	0.8		
14 0056	4.5	**29** 0012	4.6
0716	0.9	0632	0.7
TU 1320	4.6	W 1236	4.8
1925	0.7	1901	0.7
15 0139	4.6	**30** 0100	4.8
0749	0.8	0732	0.5
W 1358	4.7	TH 1325	5.0
2006	0.9	● 1948	0.6
		31 0146	5.0
		0822	0.3
		F 1409	5.2
		2037	0.6

FEBRUARY

Time	m	Time	m
1 0235	5.1	**16** 0256	4.8
0907	0.2	0919	0.5
SA 1453	5.3	SU 1507	4.9
2122	0.6	2119	0.7
2 0316	5.2	**17** 0325	4.9
0955	0.2	0952	0.5
SU 1540	5.3	M 1537	5.0
2205	0.6	2158	0.7
3 0405	5.2	**18** 0353	4.9
1040	0.2	1025	0.5
M 1626	5.2	TU 1609	4.9
2248	0.6	2230	0.7
4 0449	5.1	**19** 0425	4.9
1126	0.2	1055	0.5
TU 1715	5.0	W 1643	4.9
2329	0.7	2306	0.7
5 0537	5.0	**20** 0457	4.8
1206	0.4	1130	0.6
W 1806	4.8	TH 1716	4.8
		2338	0.8
6 0011	0.8	**21** 0536	4.8
0628	4.8	1208	0.6
TH 1245	0.6	F 1759	4.7
◑ 1858	4.6		
7 0102	0.9	**22** 0015	0.8
0726	4.5	0619	4.6
F 1340	0.8	SA 1256	0.7
1956	4.2	◑ 1851	4.5
8 0206	1.1	**23** 0116	0.9
0825	4.2	0721	4.4
SA 1445	1.0	SU 1350	0.9
2115	4.0	2005	4.3
9 0314	1.2	**24** 0226	1.0
0950	4.0	0848	4.2
SU 1604	1.2	M 1505	1.0
2240	3.9	2130	4.1
10 0450	1.2	**25** 0345	1.0
1115	4.1	1008	4.2
M 1725	1.2	TU 1625	1.0
2346	4.1	2248	4.2
11 0606	1.1	**26** 0510	0.9
1216	4.3	1119	4.4
TU 1826	1.1	W 1745	0.9
		2352	4.4
12 0039	4.3	**27** 0626	0.7
0655	0.9	1217	4.7
W 1259	4.5	TH 1845	0.8
1905	1.0		
13 0118	4.5	**28** 0045	4.7
0738	0.8	0721	0.5
TH 1335	4.8	F 1308	5.0
1939	0.9	1936	0.7
14 0156	4.6		
0810	0.7		
F 1410	4.9		
2016	0.9		
15 0226	4.7		
0842	0.6		
SA 1439	4.8		
○ 2046	0.8		

MARCH

Time	m	Time	m
1 0132	4.9	**16** 0156	4.7
0807	0.3	0816	0.6
SA 1353	5.1	SU 1408	4.9
● 2018	0.6	○ 2026	0.7
2 0215	5.1	**17** 0222	4.8
0852	0.2	0845	0.5
SU 1436	5.2	M 1438	5.0
2103	0.5	2055	0.6
3 0257	5.2	**18** 0253	5.0
0936	0.1	0925	0.4
M 1520	5.2	TU 1511	5.0
2146	0.5	2136	0.6
4 0342	5.2	**19** 0326	5.0
1016	0.2	1000	0.4
TU 1603	5.2	W 1546	5.0
2225	0.5	2210	0.6
5 0425	5.1	**20** 0359	5.0
1058	0.3	1035	0.4
W 1646	5.0	TH 1618	5.0
2305	0.6	2246	0.6
6 0507	5.0	**21** 0435	4.9
1135	0.4	1112	0.5
TH 1735	4.8	F 1655	4.9
2345	0.7	2326	0.6
7 0556	4.8	**22** 0514	4.9
1215	0.6	1150	0.6
F 1819	4.5	SA 1737	4.7
8 0030	0.8	**23** 0006	0.7
0639	4.5	0558	4.7
SA 1300	0.9	SU 1239	0.7
◑ 1909	4.2	1828	4.4
9 0125	1.0	**24** 0100	0.8
0740	4.2	0702	4.4
SU 1354	1.1	M 1336	0.9
2009	3.8	◑ 1949	4.2
10 0245	1.2	**25** 0210	0.9
0906	3.9	0831	4.2
M 1526	1.3	TU 1445	1.0
2200	3.7	2111	4.0
11 0416	1.2	**26** 0324	0.9
1040	3.9	0950	4.2
TU 1645	1.2	W 1610	1.1
2318	3.9	2230	4.1
12 0525	1.1	**27** 0500	0.8
1145	4.1	1101	4.4
W 1744	1.1	TH 1730	1.0
		2336	4.3
13 0015	4.2	**28** 0609	0.6
0630	0.9	1205	4.7
TH 1236	4.4	F 1835	0.8
1834	1.0		
14 0056	4.4	**29** 0027	4.6
0716	0.8	0705	0.4
F 1309	4.6	SA 1250	4.9
1915	0.9	1918	0.7
15 0126	4.5	**30** 0112	4.8
0745	0.7	0748	0.3
SA 1341	4.7	SU 1335	5.0
1950	0.8	● 2002	0.6
		31 0155	5.0
		0832	0.2
		M 1416	5.1
		2046	0.5

APRIL

Time	m	Time	m
1 0236	5.1	**16** 0226	5.0
0911	0.2	0856	0.4
TU 1459	5.1	W 1443	5.1
2125	0.5	2108	0.5
2 0318	5.2	**17** 0259	5.1
0956	0.3	0933	0.4
W 1543	5.1	TH 1519	5.1
2206	0.5	2148	0.5
3 0401	5.1	**18** 0335	5.1
1032	0.4	1012	0.4
TH 1623	4.9	F 1556	5.0
2245	0.5	2232	0.5
4 0442	5.0	**19** 0415	5.0
1106	0.5	1056	0.5
F 1705	4.7	SA 1636	4.8
2326	0.6	2312	0.5
5 0526	4.7	**20** 0458	4.9
1146	0.7	1136	0.6
SA 1750	4.4	SU 1726	4.6
6 0006	0.8	**21** 0000	0.5
0607	4.5	0547	4.7
SU 1226	0.9	M 1225	0.7
1836	4.2	1819	4.4
7 0056	0.9	**22** 0056	0.6
0706	4.2	0656	4.5
M 1326	1.2	TU 1319	0.9
1926	3.9	◑ 1935	4.2
8 0205	1.1	**23** 0159	0.7
0804	3.9	0816	4.3
TU 1450	1.3	W 1435	1.0
2040	3.6	2049	4.1
9 0325	1.1	**24** 0320	0.8
0945	3.8	0932	4.3
W 1554	1.3	TH 1555	1.1
2236	3.7	2206	4.1
10 0433	1.1	**25** 0446	0.7
1102	4.0	1041	4.5
TH 1705	1.1	F 1716	1.0
2336	4.0	2315	4.3
11 0539	0.9	**26** 0555	0.6
1157	4.3	1145	4.7
F 1754	1.0	SA 1817	0.8
12 0015	4.2	**27** 0007	4.6
0629	0.8	0646	0.4
SA 1236	4.5	SU 1232	4.8
1845	0.9	1900	0.7
13 0049	4.5	**28** 0052	4.7
0710	0.7	0728	0.4
SU 1305	4.7	M 1316	4.9
1916	0.8	1946	0.6
14 0118	4.7	**29** 0135	4.9
0739	0.6	0807	0.3
M 1336	4.9	TU 1359	5.0
1952	0.6	● 2026	0.5
15 0150	4.8	**30** 0216	5.0
0818	0.5	0847	0.3
TU 1409	5.0	W 1440	5.0
○ 2028	0.5	2105	0.5

Chart Datum: 2·56 metres below NAP Datum
HAT is 5·4 metres above Chart Datum

TIDES

TIME ZONE -0100
(Dutch Standard Time)
Subtract 1 hour for UT
For Dutch Summer Time add
ONE hour in **non-shaded areas**

NETHERLANDS – VLISSINGEN
LAT 51°27′N   LONG 3°36′E
TIMES AND HEIGHTS OF HIGH AND LOW WATERS

Dates in amber are **SPRINGS**
Dates in yellow are **NEAPS**

2014

MAY

Time	m		Time	m
1 TH 0259	5.1		**16** F 0236	5.1
0928	0.4		0908	0.4
1522	4.9		1458	5.1
2146	0.5		2132	0.4
2 F 0339	5.0		**17** SA 0317	5.1
1007	0.5		0952	0.5
1602	4.8		1540	5.0
2226	0.5		2215	0.4
3 SA 0421	4.9		**18** SU 0400	5.0
1046	0.7		1035	0.5
1645	4.6		1626	4.8
2302	0.6		2301	0.4
4 SU 0501	4.7		**19** M 0446	4.9
1118	0.8		1122	0.6
1721	4.4		1716	4.6
2339	0.7		2356	0.4
5 M 0541	4.5		**20** TU 0541	4.8
1155	1.0		1209	0.7
1806	4.2		1816	4.5
6 TU 0025	0.8		**21** W 0050	0.5
0636	4.3		0650	4.6
1234	1.1		1305	0.9
1856	4.0		1922	4.3
7 W 0135	1.0		**22** TH 0149	0.5
0724	4.0		0759	4.5
1405	1.3		1411	1.0
1956	3.8		2029	4.3
8 TH 0251	1.0		**23** F 0300	0.6
0835	3.9		0905	4.5
1520	1.2		1523	1.0
2105	3.8		2139	4.2
9 F 0356	1.0		**24** SA 0420	0.6
1006	4.0		1019	4.5
1626	1.2		1656	1.0
2236	3.9		2248	4.4
10 SA 0444	0.9		**25** SU 0530	0.6
1106	4.2		1121	4.6
1711	1.0		1756	0.9
2325	4.1		2345	4.5
11 SU 0535	0.8		**26** M 0622	0.5
1150	4.5		1215	4.7
1754	0.9		1846	0.8
12 M 0008	4.4		**27** TU 0036	4.7
0628	0.7		0708	0.5
1226	4.7		1301	4.8
1846	0.8		1925	0.7
13 TU 0042	4.6		**28** W 0117	4.8
0705	0.6		0748	0.5
1302	4.9		1346	4.8
1919	0.6		2005	0.6
14 W 0119	4.8		**29** TH 0202	4.9
0746	0.5		0825	0.5
1341	5.0		1427	4.8
2006	0.5		2045	0.5
15 TH 0156	5.0		**30** F 0246	4.9
0826	0.4		0905	0.6
1419	5.1		1507	4.8
2046	0.4		2128	0.5
			31 SA 0322	4.9
			0942	0.7
			1546	4.8
			2208	0.5

JUNE

Time	m		Time	m
1 SU 0402	4.9		**16** M 0348	5.1
1018	0.8		1022	0.6
1622	4.7		1616	4.9
2245	0.6		2255	0.3
2 M 0441	4.7		**17** TU 0436	5.0
1057	0.9		1108	0.6
1659	4.5		1705	4.8
2326	0.7		2346	0.3
3 TU 0521	4.6		**18** W 0530	4.9
1130	1.0		1158	0.7
1740	4.4		1758	4.7
4 W 0006	0.8		**19** TH 0038	0.3
0605	4.4		0636	4.8
1203	1.1		1249	0.8
1826	4.2		1902	4.6
5 TH 0045	0.9		**20** F 0136	0.4
0656	4.2		0735	4.7
1255	1.2		1350	0.9
1917	4.1		2006	4.5
6 F 0156	0.9		**21** SA 0235	0.5
0750	4.2		0839	4.5
1405	1.2		1456	1.0
2012	4.0		2110	4.4
7 SA 0256	1.0		**22** SU 0340	0.6
0852	4.1		0949	4.5
1536	1.2		1610	1.0
2120	4.0		2215	4.4
8 SU 0356	0.9		**23** M 0506	0.7
1000	4.2		1100	4.5
1625	1.1		1731	1.0
2225	4.1		2321	4.4
9 M 0445	0.8		**24** TU 0601	0.7
1100	4.4		1155	4.6
1716	0.9		1826	0.8
2319	4.4			
10 TU 0540	0.7		**25** W 0019	4.6
1148	4.7		0646	0.7
1805	0.8		1247	4.7
			1911	0.7
11 W 0007	4.6		**26** TH 0109	4.7
0625	0.6		0728	0.7
1236	4.8		1336	4.7
1856	0.7		1949	0.6
12 TH 0053	4.8		**27** F 0150	4.8
0718	0.6		0805	0.7
1317	5.0		1416	4.7
1940	0.5		2029	0.6
13 F 0136	5.0		**28** SA 0230	4.8
0802	0.5		0846	0.8
1359	5.0		1452	4.8
2028	0.4		2109	0.5
14 SA 0218	5.1		**29** SU 0308	4.9
0848	0.5		0920	0.8
1443	5.0		1527	4.8
2117	0.3		2148	0.5
15 SU 0303	5.1		**30** M 0346	4.9
0935	0.5		0956	0.8
1528	5.0		1605	4.7
2205	0.3		2231	0.5

JULY

Time	m		Time	m
1 TU 0421	4.8		**16** W 0423	5.2
1036	0.9		1050	0.6
1640	4.7		1648	5.0
2306	0.6		2325	0.2
2 W 0458	4.7		**17** TH 0516	5.0
1106	0.9		1138	0.7
1715	4.5		1737	4.9
2340	0.7			
3 TH 0536	4.6		**18** F 0015	0.3
1140	1.0		0609	4.9
1750	4.4		1226	0.8
			1835	4.8
4 F 0004	0.8		**19** SA 0106	0.4
0612	4.5		0708	4.7
1215	1.1		1318	0.9
1829	4.3		1936	4.6
5 SA 0043	0.8		**20** SU 0155	0.6
0654	4.4		0805	4.5
1300	1.1		1415	1.0
1926	4.2		2035	4.4
6 SU 0133	0.9		**21** M 0259	0.8
0800	4.3		0921	4.3
1355	1.1		1530	1.1
2031	4.2		2145	4.3
7 M 0256	0.9		**22** TU 0414	0.9
0909	4.3		1036	4.3
1526	1.1		1655	1.1
2136	4.2		2306	4.3
8 TU 0356	0.9		**23** W 0536	0.9
1009	4.4		1146	4.4
1636	1.0		1806	0.9
2240	4.3			
9 W 0455	0.8		**24** TH 0005	4.5
1111	4.6		0625	0.9
1730	0.9		1235	4.5
2336	4.5		1856	0.8
10 TH 0556	0.7		**25** F 0059	4.6
1207	4.7		0709	0.9
1826	0.7		1326	4.6
			1935	0.7
11 F 0029	4.8		**26** SA 0146	4.7
0652	0.7		0748	0.9
1257	4.9		1401	4.7
1926	0.6		2015	0.7
12 SA 0116	5.0		**27** SU 0219	4.8
0742	0.6		0825	0.9
1346	5.0		1436	4.8
2012	0.4		2052	0.6
13 SU 0203	5.1		**28** M 0251	4.9
0830	0.6		0858	0.9
1426	5.0		1506	4.8
2102	0.3		2131	0.6
14 M 0248	5.2		**29** TU 0326	4.9
0917	0.6		0935	0.8
1513	5.1		1538	4.8
2149	0.2		2205	0.5
15 TU 0333	5.2		**30** W 0358	4.9
1003	0.6		1011	0.8
1559	5.0		1611	4.8
2237	0.2		2240	0.6
			31 TH 0427	4.8
			1039	0.9
			1642	4.7
			2310	0.7

AUGUST

Time	m		Time	m
1 F 0458	4.7		**16** SA 0539	4.9
1109	0.9		1156	0.8
1716	4.6		1801	4.9
2340	0.7			
2 SA 0528	4.6		**17** SU 0029	0.5
1146	1.0		0636	4.7
1750	4.6		1246	0.9
			1856	4.7
3 SU 0009	0.8		**18** M 0120	0.7
0609	4.5		0732	4.4
1226	1.0		1339	1.0
1829	4.5		2000	4.4
4 M 0056	0.8		**19** TU 0214	1.0
0659	4.5		0846	4.2
1316	1.0		1455	1.2
1930	4.3		2115	4.2
5 TU 0156	0.9		**20** W 0334	1.1
0816	4.3		1005	4.1
1419	1.1		1625	1.2
2050	4.2		2242	4.2
6 W 0311	1.0		**21** TH 0505	1.1
0931	4.3		1126	4.2
1545	1.1		1746	1.0
2201	4.3		2349	4.4
7 TH 0419	1.0		**22** F 0610	1.1
1046	4.4		1219	4.4
1700	1.0		1846	0.9
2311	4.5			
8 F 0536	0.9		**23** SA 0045	4.6
1146	4.6		0655	1.0
1805	0.8		1308	4.6
			1925	0.8
9 SA 0011	4.7		**24** SU 0126	4.7
0636	0.8		0724	1.0
1237	4.8		1346	4.7
1906	0.6		1955	0.7
10 SU 0100	5.0		**25** M 0159	4.8
0726	0.7		0806	0.9
1326	5.0		1411	4.8
1958	0.4		2032	0.7
11 M 0146	5.2		**26** TU 0227	4.9
0812	0.6		0836	0.9
1410	5.1		1441	4.8
2046	0.3		2106	0.6
12 TU 0231	5.3		**27** W 0257	5.0
0858	0.6		0905	0.8
1455	5.2		1511	4.9
2133	0.2		2138	0.6
13 W 0316	5.3		**28** TH 0327	5.0
0946	0.6		0946	0.8
1539	5.2		1541	4.9
2218	0.2			
14 TH 0401	5.2		**29** F 0357	5.0
1028	0.7		1015	0.9
1626	5.2		1612	4.9
2302	0.2		2242	0.7
15 F 0449	5.1		**30** SA 0427	4.9
1112	0.7		1046	0.9
1710	5.1		1642	4.8
2345	0.4		2316	0.7
			31 SU 0500	4.8
			1116	0.9
			1716	4.8
			2346	0.8

Chart Datum: 2·56 metres below NAP Datum
HAT is 5·4 metres above Chart Datum

TIME ZONE -0100
(Dutch Standard Time)
Subtract 1 hour for UT
For Dutch Summer Time add
ONE hour in **non-shaded areas**

NETHERLANDS – VLISSINGEN

LAT 51°27′N   LONG 3°36′E

TIMES AND HEIGHTS OF HIGH AND LOW WATERS

Dates in amber are **SPRINGS**
Dates in yellow are **NEAPS**

2014

SEPTEMBER

Time	m		Time	m
1 0537 / 1157 / M 1755	4.7 / 0.9 / 4.7	**16** 0039 / 0656 / TU 1305 / ◐ 1919	0.9 / 4.3 / 1.1 / 4.4
2 0026 / 0621 / TU 1246 / ◐ 1848	0.8 / 4.6 / 1.0 / 4.5	**17** 0147 / 0756 / W 1419 / 2034	1.2 / 4.0 / 1.2 / 4.1
3 0120 / 0730 / W 1350 / 2010	1.0 / 4.3 / 1.1 / 4.3	**18** 0255 / 0935 / TH 1545 / 2215	1.3 / 3.9 / 1.3 / 4.1
4 0229 / 0855 / TH 1516 / 2137	1.1 / 4.2 / 1.1 / 4.3	**19** 0430 / 1056 / F 1704 / 2325	1.3 / 4.0 / 1.2 / 4.3
5 0356 / 1015 / F 1635 / 2249	1.1 / 4.2 / 1.0 / 4.4	**20** 0546 / 1156 / SA 1816	1.2 / 4.3 / 1.0
6 0510 / 1125 / SA 1756 / 2350	1.1 / 4.4 / 0.8 / 4.7	**21** 0015 / 0624 / SU 1239 / 1900	4.5 / 1.1 / 4.5 / 0.8
7 0615 / 1218 / SU 1849	0.9 / 4.7 / 0.6	**22** 0058 / 0706 / M 1315 / 1932	4.7 / 1.0 / 4.6 / 0.8
8 0042 / 0708 / M 1306 / 1942	5.0 / 0.8 / 4.6 / 0.4	**23** 0129 / 0736 / TU 1342 / 2002	4.8 / 1.0 / 4.8 / 0.7
9 0126 / 0756 / TU 1350 / ○ 2027	5.2 / 0.7 / 5.1 / 0.3	**24** 0159 / 0806 / W 1408 / ● 2035	4.9 / 0.9 / 4.9 / 0.7
10 0211 / 0840 / W 1433 / 2109	5.3 / 0.6 / 5.3 / 0.3	**25** 0228 / 0840 / TH 1439 / 2106	5.0 / 0.8 / 5.0 / 0.6
11 0255 / 0926 / TH 1516 / 2155	5.3 / 0.6 / 5.3 / 0.3	**26** 0257 / 0916 / F 1511 / 2140	5.1 / 0.7 / 5.0 / 0.6
12 0339 / 1007 / F 1559 / 2235	5.3 / 0.6 / 5.3 / 0.4	**27** 0327 / 0950 / SA 1543 / 2216	5.1 / 0.8 / 5.0 / 0.7
13 0426 / 1048 / SA 1645 / 2317	5.1 / 0.7 / 4.9 / 0.5	**28** 0359 / 1022 / SU 1615 / 2246	5.0 / 0.8 / 5.0 / 0.7
14 0511 / 1130 / SU 1729 / 2358	4.9 / 0.8 / 4.9 / 0.7	**29** 0435 / 1101 / M 1650 / 2322	4.9 / 0.8 / 4.9 / 0.8
15 0559 / 1216 / M 1818	4.6 / 0.9 / 4.7	**30** 0513 / 1141 / TU 1733	4.8 / 0.9 / 4.8

OCTOBER

Time	m		Time	m
1 0006 / 0557 / W 1226 / ◑ 1825	0.9 / 4.6 / 0.9 / 4.6	**16** 0100 / 0709 / TH 1355 / 1955	1.3 / 4.0 / 1.2 / 4.1
2 0055 / 0706 / TH 1330 / 1946	1.1 / 4.3 / 1.0 / 4.3	**17** 0215 / 0820 / F 1506 / 2125	1.5 / 3.8 / 1.3 / 3.9
3 0205 / 0831 / F 1456 / 2109	1.2 / 4.1 / 1.1 / 4.3	**18** 0333 / 1010 / SA 1620 / 2245	1.5 / 3.8 / 1.2 / 4.1
4 0330 / 0950 / SA 1613 / 2230	1.3 / 4.2 / 1.0 / 4.4	**19** 0445 / 1117 / SU 1730 / 2339	1.4 / 4.1 / 1.1 / 4.4
5 0444 / 1102 / SU 1746 / 2331	1.2 / 4.4 / 0.9 / 4.7	**20** 0545 / 1159 / M 1825	1.2 / 4.3 / 1.0
6 0606 / 1157 / M 1839	1.0 / 4.6 / 0.6	**21** 0026 / 0624 / TU 1236 / 1901	4.6 / 1.1 / 4.5 / 0.9
7 0026 / 0652 / TU 1245 / 1922	5.0 / 0.7 / 4.8 / 0.5	**22** 0055 / 0706 / W 1305 / 1928	4.8 / 1.0 / 4.7 / 0.8
8 0106 / 0736 / W 1328 / ○ 2007	5.1 / 0.6 / 5.1 / 0.4	**23** 0126 / 0738 / TH 1335 / ● 1955	4.9 / 0.9 / 4.9 / 0.7
9 0152 / 0817 / TH 1412 / 2048	5.2 / 0.6 / 5.2 / 0.4	**24** 0156 / 0809 / F 1408 / 2035	5.0 / 0.8 / 5.0 / 0.7
10 0235 / 0903 / F 1453 / 2130	5.3 / 0.6 / 5.3 / 0.4	**25** 0226 / 0851 / SA 1443 / 2110	5.1 / 0.7 / 5.1 / 0.6
11 0318 / 0946 / SA 1537 / 2210	5.2 / 0.6 / 5.3 / 0.5	**26** 0303 / 0928 / SU 1518 / 2148	5.1 / 0.7 / 5.1 / 0.7
12 0401 / 1026 / SU 1621 / 2248	5.1 / 0.7 / 5.1 / 0.7	**27** 0336 / 1007 / M 1555 / 2229	5.1 / 0.7 / 5.1 / 0.7
13 0447 / 1105 / M 1706 / 2325	4.8 / 0.8 / 5.0 / 0.9	**28** 0416 / 1046 / TU 1633 / 2309	5.0 / 0.7 / 5.0 / 0.8
14 0528 / 1146 / TU 1748	4.6 / 0.8 / 4.7	**29** 0456 / 1130 / W 1717 / 2350	4.8 / 0.8 / 4.9 / 0.9
15 0008 / 0618 / W 1236 / ◑ 1846	1.1 / 4.3 / 1.1 / 4.4	**30** 0545 / 1220 / TH 1816	4.6 / 0.8 / 4.6
		31 0045 / 0649 / F 1326 / ◐ 1929	1.1 / 4.3 / 0.9 / 4.4

NOVEMBER

Time	m		Time	m
1 0144 / 0810 / SA 1435 / 2049	1.2 / 4.2 / 1.0 / 4.4	**16** 0250 / 0835 / SU 1526 / 2136	1.5 / 3.8 / 1.2 / 4.0
2 0305 / 0925 / SU 1555 / 2201	1.3 / 4.2 / 1.0 / 4.5	**17** 0356 / 1005 / M 1630 / 2246	1.4 / 3.9 / 1.0 / 4.2
3 0430 / 1035 / M 1721 / 2309	1.3 / 4.3 / 0.8 / 4.7	**18** 0449 / 1105 / TU 1736 / 2336	1.3 / 4.1 / 1.1 / 4.4
4 0540 / 1132 / TU 1815	1.1 / 4.6 / 0.7	**19** 0545 / 1149 / W 1815	1.2 / 4.4 / 1.0
5 0002 / 0636 / W 1222 / 1902	4.6 / 1.0 / 4.8 / 0.6	**20** 0016 / 0626 / TH 1229 / 1845	4.6 / 1.0 / 4.6 / 0.9
6 0049 / 0716 / TH 1308 / ○ 1945	5.0 / 0.8 / 5.0 / 0.5	**21** 0052 / 0706 / F 1306 / 1925	4.8 / 0.9 / 4.8 / 0.8
7 0133 / 0802 / F 1353 / 2027	5.1 / 0.7 / 5.1 / 0.5	**22** 0125 / 0742 / SA 1341 / ● 2005	5.0 / 0.8 / 4.9 / 0.7
8 0216 / 0845 / SA 1436 / 2107	5.1 / 0.6 / 5.2 / 0.6	**23** 0202 / 0826 / SU 1419 / 2045	5.1 / 0.7 / 5.1 / 0.7
9 0300 / 0926 / SU 1516 / 2146	5.1 / 0.6 / 5.2 / 0.7	**24** 0241 / 0906 / M 1456 / 2129	5.1 / 0.6 / 5.1 / 0.7
10 0345 / 1006 / M 1600 / 2226	5.0 / 0.6 / 5.1 / 0.8	**25** 0319 / 0949 / TU 1538 / 2210	5.1 / 0.6 / 5.1 / 0.7
11 0425 / 1046 / TU 1642 / 2300	4.8 / 0.7 / 4.9 / 1.0	**26** 0403 / 1038 / W 1622 / 2256	5.0 / 0.6 / 5.0 / 0.8
12 0506 / 1126 / W 1727 / 2338	4.6 / 0.7 / 4.7 / 1.1	**27** 0446 / 1126 / TH 1711 / 2340	4.8 / 0.6 / 4.9 / 0.9
13 0550 / 1210 / TH 1815	4.4 / 0.9 / 4.4	**28** 0537 / 1215 / F 1806	4.6 / 0.7 / 4.7
14 0025 / 0636 / F 1305 / ◐ 1910	1.3 / 4.2 / 1.1 / 4.2	**29** 0036 / 0639 / SA 1315 / ◐ 1915	1.0 / 4.5 / 0.7 / 4.6
15 0135 / 0730 / SA 1415 / 2015	1.5 / 4.0 / 1.2 / 4.0	**30** 0136 / 0745 / SU 1415 / 2028	1.2 / 4.3 / 0.8 / 4.5

DECEMBER

Time	m		Time	m
1 0240 / 0858 / M 1525 / 2135	1.2 / 4.3 / 0.9 / 4.5	**16** 0256 / 0850 / TU 2130	1.4 / 4.0 / 1.2 / ...
2 0355 / 1005 / TU 1646 / 2246	1.3 / 4.2 / 0.9 / 4.5	**17** 0401 / 0955 / W 1626 / 2235	1.4 / 4.0 / 1.1 / 4.3
3 0504 / 1109 / W 1750 / 2342	1.2 / 4.5 / 0.8 / 4.7	**18** 0456 / 1100 / TH 1720 / 2332	1.2 / 4.2 / 1.0 / 4.5
4 0616 / 1206 / TH 1842	1.0 / 4.7 / 0.7	**19** 0546 / 1152 / F 1804	1.1 / 4.5 / 0.9
5 0036 / 0659 / F 1255 / 1925	4.8 / 0.9 / 4.8 / 0.7	**20** 0016 / 0632 / SA 1236 / 1857	4.7 / 0.9 / 4.7 / 0.8
6 0121 / 0743 / SA 1337 / ○ 2005	4.9 / 0.7 / 4.9 / 0.7	**21** 0102 / 0715 / SU 1318 / 1940	4.9 / 0.8 / 4.9 / 0.7
7 0207 / 0828 / SU 1422 / 2045	5.0 / 0.6 / 5.0 / 0.7	**22** 0143 / 0806 / M 1359 / ● 2025	5.0 / 0.6 / 5.1 / 0.7
8 0247 / 0908 / M 1506 / 2121	4.9 / 0.6 / 5.0 / 0.8	**23** 0226 / 0856 / TU 1442 / 2111	5.1 / 0.5 / 5.1 / 0.7
9 0329 / 0950 / TU 1545 / 2200	4.9 / 0.6 / 5.0 / 0.9	**24** 0306 / 0940 / W 1525 / 2155	5.1 / 0.5 / 5.1 / 0.7
10 0407 / 1025 / W 1625 / 2235	4.8 / 0.6 / 4.9 / 1.0	**25** 0350 / 1028 / TH 1613 / 2242	5.0 / 0.4 / 5.1 / 0.7
11 0446 / 1106 / TH 1705 / 2316	4.7 / 0.7 / 4.7 / 1.1	**26** 0436 / 1116 / F 1659 / 2326	4.9 / 0.4 / 5.0 / 0.7
12 0526 / 1146 / F 1748 / 2356	4.5 / 0.7 / 4.6 / 1.2	**27** 0527 / 1205 / SA 1756	4.8 / 0.4 / 4.9
13 0606 / 1226 / SA 1832	4.4 / 1.0 / 4.4	**28** 0015 / 0626 / SU 1258 / ◐ 1855	0.8 / 4.7 / 0.5 / 4.9
14 0030 / 0650 / SU 1305 / ◐ 1925	1.3 / 4.2 / 1.1 / 4.2	**29** 0110 / 0725 / M 1356 / 2002	1.0 / 4.5 / 0.6 / 4.6
15 0125 / 0745 / M 1414 / 2026	1.4 / 4.1 / 1.2 / 4.1	**30** 0204 / 0828 / TU 1455 / 2108	1.1 / 4.4 / 0.8 / 4.4
		31 0315 / 0936 / W 1605 / 2218	1.2 / 4.3 / 0.9 / 4.4

Chart Datum: 2·56 metres below NAP Datum
HAT is 5·4 metres above Chart Datum

TIDES

375

ZEEBRUGGE

MEAN SPRING
AND NEAP CURVES

MEAN RANGES
Springs 4.3m
Neaps 2.9m

TIME ZONE -0100
(Belgian Standard Time)
Subtract 1 hour for UT
For Belgian Summer Time add
ONE hour in non-shaded areas

BELGIUM – ZEEBRUGGE

LAT 51°21'N   LONG 3°12'E

TIMES AND HEIGHTS OF HIGH AND LOW WATERS

Dates in amber are SPRINGS
Dates in yellow are NEAPS

2014

JANUARY

Time	m	Time	m
1 0052	4.7	**16** 0147	4.5
0715	0.6	0803	0.7
W 1314	4.8	TH 1403	4.5
● 1935	0.6	○ 2007	1.0
2 0137	4.8	**17** 0218	4.5
0802	0.5	0830	0.7
TH 1400	5.0	F 1434	4.5
2021	0.6	2034	0.9
3 0222	4.8	**18** 0247	4.5
0848	0.4	0859	0.6
F 1445	5.0	SA 1504	4.6
2107	0.6	2103	0.8
4 0307	4.8	**19** 0316	4.6
0934	0.3	0930	0.6
SA 1532	5.0	SU 1534	4.6
2153	0.6	2137	0.8
5 0353	4.8	**20** 0346	4.6
1022	0.3	1004	0.5
SU 1621	4.9	M 1606	4.7
2241	0.7	2213	0.8
6 0442	4.8	**21** 0419	4.6
1112	0.3	1040	0.6
M 1712	4.8	TU 1642	4.7
2330	0.8	2251	0.8
7 0533	4.6	**22** 0457	4.6
1203	0.4	1119	0.6
TU 1808	4.6	W 1723	4.6
		2332	0.9
8 0023	0.9	**23** 0541	4.5
0631	4.5	1203	0.7
W 1300	0.6	TH 1811	4.5
1909	4.4		
9 0122	1.1	**24** 0020	1.0
0734	4.3	0633	4.4
TH 1403	0.8	F 1258	0.9
2016	4.2	◑ 1910	4.3
10 0232	1.2	**25** 0123	1.2
0845	4.1	0738	4.2
F 1512	0.9	SA 1412	1.0
2129	4.1	2021	4.2
11 0349	1.2	**26** 0249	1.2
1001	4.1	0853	4.1
SA 1624	1.0	SU 1530	1.0
2244	4.1	2136	4.1
12 0506	1.1	**27** 0407	1.2
1113	4.2	1008	4.1
SU 1732	1.0	M 1637	1.0
2346	4.3	2246	4.2
13 0607	1.0	**28** 0513	1.0
1209	4.3	1115	4.3
M 1827	1.0	TU 1738	0.9
		2347	4.3
14 0034	4.4	**29** 0611	0.8
0654	0.8	1212	4.5
TU 1253	4.4	W 1831	0.8
1908	1.0		
15 0113	4.4	**30** 0037	4.5
0732	0.8	0701	0.6
W 1330	4.5	TH 1300	4.7
1941	1.0	● 1920	0.7
		31 0122	4.7
		0748	0.4
		F 1345	4.9
		2005	0.6

FEBRUARY

Time	m	Time	m
1 0205	4.8	**16** 0221	4.6
0833	0.2	0834	0.5
SA 1429	5.0	SU 1438	4.7
2050	0.5	2041	0.7
2 0249	4.9	**17** 0250	4.7
0918	0.1	0907	0.4
SU 1515	5.1	M 1508	4.8
2135	0.5	2116	0.6
3 0334	5.0	**18** 0321	4.7
1004	0.1	0942	0.4
M 1601	5.0	TU 1541	4.8
2220	0.5	2153	0.6
4 0420	4.9	**19** 0355	4.8
1050	0.2	1018	0.4
TU 1649	4.9	W 1617	4.8
2306	0.6	2230	0.6
5 0508	4.8	**20** 0433	4.8
1137	0.3	1056	0.5
W 1739	4.7	TH 1657	4.7
2353	0.8	2309	0.7
6 0559	4.6	**21** 0515	4.7
1228	0.6	1137	0.6
TH 1833	4.4	F 1741	4.6
◐		2353	0.9
7 0046	1.0	**22** 0603	4.5
0656	4.3	1225	0.8
F 1327	0.8	SA 1834	4.3
1935	4.1	◐	
8 0155	1.2	**23** 0048	1.0
0805	4.0	0702	4.3
SA 1439	1.1	SU 1332	1.0
2049	3.9	1942	4.1
9 0318	1.3	**24** 0211	1.2
0926	3.9	0820	4.1
SU 1553	1.2	M 1500	1.1
2211	3.8	2106	3.9
10 0435	1.2	**25** 0341	1.2
1046	3.9	0945	4.0
M 1705	1.2	TU 1614	1.1
2320	4.0	2225	4.0
11 0543	1.1	**26** 0452	1.0
1147	4.1	1058	4.2
TU 1805	1.1	W 1719	1.0
		2329	4.2
12 0012	4.1	**27** 0553	0.8
0634	0.9	1157	4.5
W 1232	4.3	TH 1815	0.8
1850	1.1		
13 0051	4.3	**28** 0020	4.4
0713	0.8	0645	0.5
TH 1309	4.4	F 1245	4.7
1920	1.0	1903	0.7
14 0124	4.4		
0742	0.7		
F 1340	4.5		
1944	0.9		
15 0153	4.5		
0806	0.6		
SA 1409	4.6		
○ 2009	0.8		

MARCH

Time	m	Time	m
1 0104	4.7	**16** 0123	4.5
0730	0.3	0736	0.6
SA 1328	4.9	SU 1340	4.6
● 1947	0.6	○ 1943	0.7
2 0147	4.9	**17** 0152	4.6
0814	0.2	0807	0.4
SU 1411	5.0	M 1410	4.8
2031	0.5	2017	0.5
3 0229	5.0	**18** 0222	4.8
0858	0.1	0841	0.3
M 1454	5.1	TU 1442	4.9
2114	0.4	2054	0.5
4 0313	5.0	**19** 0256	4.8
0942	0.0	0918	0.3
TU 1539	5.0	W 1517	4.9
2157	0.4	2132	0.5
5 0357	5.0	**20** 0332	4.9
1026	0.1	0956	0.4
W 1624	4.9	TH 1554	4.8
2240	0.5	2211	0.5
6 0443	4.8	**21** 0411	4.8
1109	0.4	1035	0.5
TH 1710	4.6	F 1633	4.7
2323	0.7	2250	0.6
7 0529	4.6	**22** 0453	4.7
1155	0.6	1116	0.6
F 1758	4.3	SA 1717	4.5
		2333	0.8
8 0009	0.9	**23** 0540	4.5
0619	4.3	1203	0.8
SA 1247	1.0	SU 1808	4.3
◐ 1852	4.0		
9 0113	1.2	**24** 0027	1.0
0722	3.9	0639	4.3
SU 1402	1.3	M 1308	1.0
2004	3.7	◑ 1915	4.0
10 0243	1.3	**25** 0149	1.1
0844	3.7	0758	4.0
M 1518	1.4	TU 1435	1.2
2128	3.6	2043	3.8
11 0356	1.3	**26** 0317	1.1
1007	3.7	0926	4.0
TU 1626	1.4	W 1551	1.1
2242	3.7	2204	3.9
12 0503	1.2	**27** 0428	0.9
1113	3.9	1040	4.2
W 1729	1.3	TH 1658	1.0
2338	3.9	2309	4.1
13 0559	1.0	**28** 0531	0.7
1201	4.1	1139	4.5
TH 1817	1.1	F 1756	0.9
		2359	4.4
14 0020	4.1	**29** 0624	0.5
0640	0.8	1227	4.7
F 1238	4.3	SA 1845	0.7
1849	1.0		
15 0054	4.3	**30** 0045	4.6
0710	0.7	0711	0.3
SA 1310	4.5	SU 1310	4.9
● 1914	0.9	● 1928	0.6
		31 0127	4.8
		0754	0.2
		M 1352	5.0
		2011	0.4

APRIL

Time	m	Time	m
1 0209	5.0	**16** 0155	4.8
0836	0.1	0816	0.3
TU 1434	5.0	W 1416	4.9
2053	0.4	2032	0.4
2 0252	5.0	**17** 0232	4.9
0918	0.2	0855	0.3
W 1517	4.9	TH 1454	4.8
2134	0.4	2113	0.4
3 0335	4.9	**18** 0311	4.9
1000	0.3	0935	0.4
TH 1600	4.7	F 1533	4.8
2215	0.5	2153	0.5
4 0418	4.8	**19** 0351	4.8
1041	0.5	1016	0.5
F 1642	4.5	SA 1614	4.6
2255	0.6	2235	0.6
5 0501	4.5	**20** 0435	4.7
1121	0.7	1059	0.7
SA 1725	4.2	SU 1659	4.4
2336	0.9	2321	0.7
6 0546	4.2	**21** 0525	4.5
1202	1.1	1149	0.9
SU 1811	3.9	M 1752	4.2
7 0026	1.1	**22** 0017	0.8
0639	3.9	0625	4.3
M 1309	1.4	TU 1253	1.1
1913	3.7	◑ 1859	4.0
8 0203	1.3	**23** 0135	0.9
0755	3.7	0744	4.1
TU 1437	1.5	W 1413	1.2
2036	3.5	2023	3.9
9 0314	1.3	**24** 0253	0.9
0917	3.6	0906	4.1
W 1541	1.5	TH 1526	1.0
2151	3.6	2140	3.9
10 0415	1.2	**25** 0402	0.6
1025	3.8	1018	4.3
TH 1639	1.3	F 1633	1.0
2252	3.8	2245	4.2
11 0509	1.0	**26** 0506	0.6
1118	4.0	1118	4.5
F 1729	1.2	SA 1734	0.9
2338	4.0	2340	4.4
12 0554	0.9	**27** 0602	0.5
1200	4.3	1208	4.7
SA 1807	1.0	SU 1825	0.7
13 0016	4.3	**28** 0026	4.6
0630	0.7	0650	0.4
SU 1235	4.5	M 1252	4.8
1841	0.8	1910	0.6
14 0049	4.5	**29** 0109	4.8
0702	0.5	0733	0.3
M 1308	4.7	TU 1334	4.8
1915	0.6	● 1952	0.5
15 0121	4.7	**30** 0151	4.8
0738	0.4	0815	0.3
TU 1341	4.8	W 1415	4.8
1953	0.5	○ 2033	0.4

Chart Datum: 0·19 metres below TAW Datum
HAT is 5·6 metres above Chart Datum

TIDES

TIME ZONE -0100
(Belgian Standard Time)
Subtract 1 hour for UT
For Belgian Summer Time add
ONE hour in **non-shaded areas**

BELGIUM – ZEEBRUGGE
LAT 51°21′N   LONG 3°12′E
TIMES AND HEIGHTS OF HIGH AND LOW WATERS

Dates in amber are **SPRINGS**
Dates in yellow are **NEAPS**
2014

MAY

Time	m		Time	m
1 0233	4.8	**16**	0211	4.8
0856	0.4		0833	0.4
TH 1457	4.7	F	1433	4.8
2113	0.4		2054	0.4
2 0315	4.8	**17**	0253	4.8
0935	0.5		0916	0.5
F 1537	4.6	SA	1515	4.7
2152	0.5		2138	0.5
3 0356	4.6	**18**	0336	4.8
1012	0.7		1000	0.6
SA 1617	4.4	SU	1559	4.6
2230	0.6		2223	0.5
4 0436	4.4	**19**	0423	4.7
1048	0.9		1046	0.7
SU 1655	4.2	M	1646	4.4
2307	0.8		2313	0.6
5 0517	4.2	**20**	0515	4.6
1122	1.1		1138	0.9
M 1735	4.0	TU	1740	4.3
2348	1.0			
6 0601	4.0	**21**	0010	0.7
1204	1.3		0615	4.4
TU 1822	3.8	W	1239	1.0
			1845	4.1
7 0058	1.2	**22**	0118	0.7
0702	3.8		0727	4.3
W 1331	1.5	TH	1349	1.1
1934	3.6		1959	4.0
8 0225	1.2	**23**	0227	0.7
0819	3.7		0842	4.2
TH 1450	1.5	F	1457	1.1
2052	3.6		2112	4.1
9 0324	1.2	**24**	0333	0.7
0928	3.8		0952	4.3
F 1547	1.3	SA	1605	1.0
2155	3.7		2219	4.2
10 0417	1.0	**25**	0438	0.6
1026	4.0		1055	4.4
SA 1639	1.2	SU	1710	0.9
2248	4.0		2318	4.4
11 0505	0.9	**26**	0539	0.5
1115	4.2		1150	4.5
SU 1725	1.0	M	1807	0.8
2333	4.2			
12 0548	0.7	**27**	0009	4.5
1157	4.4		0631	0.5
M 1807	0.8	TU	1237	4.6
			1854	0.7
13 0013	4.4	**28**	0055	4.6
0629	0.5		0715	0.5
TU 1236	4.7	W	1319	4.6
1848	0.6		1936	0.6
14 0051	4.6	**29**	0137	4.7
0709	0.4		0756	0.6
W 1314	4.8	TH	1400	4.7
1929	0.5		2016	0.5
15 0130	4.8	**30**	0218	4.7
0751	0.4		0834	0.6
TH 1353	4.8	F	1439	4.6
2012	0.4		2054	0.5
		31	0257	4.6
			0910	0.7
		SA	1517	4.5
			2131	0.6

JUNE

Time	m		Time	m
1 0336	4.5	**16**	0323	4.9
0945	0.8		0945	0.6
SU 1554	4.4	M	1545	4.6
2207	0.6		2212	0.4
2 0413	4.4	**17**	0411	4.8
1017	0.9		1033	0.7
M 1629	4.3	TU	1633	4.4
2241	0.7		2303	0.4
3 0449	4.3	**18**	0503	4.7
1050	1.0		1124	0.8
TU 1704	4.2	W	1726	4.5
2318	0.8		2357	0.4
4 0528	4.2	**19**	0600	4.6
1128	1.1		1220	0.9
W 1743	4.0	TH	1825	4.4
2359	0.9			
5 0614	4.1	**20**	0056	0.5
1216	1.3		0705	4.5
TH 1834	3.9	F	1321	1.0
			1931	4.3
6 0111	1.0	**21**	0158	0.6
0716	4.0		0813	4.3
F 1331	1.3	SA	1426	1.0
1943	3.8		2040	4.2
7 0227	1.1	**22**	0303	0.7
0826	4.0		0922	4.3
SA 1451	1.3	SU	1535	1.0
2053	3.9		2150	4.2
8 0326	1.0	**23**	0411	0.7
0930	4.1		1031	4.3
SU 1551	1.2	M	1647	1.0
2155	4.0		2257	4.3
9 0419	0.9	**24**	0517	0.7
1027	4.2		1133	4.4
M 1645	1.0	TU	1750	0.9
2249	4.2		2355	4.4
10 0510	0.7	**25**	0613	0.7
1119	4.4		1224	4.5
TU 1735	0.8	W	1841	0.8
2339	4.4			
11 0557	0.6	**26**	0043	4.5
1206	4.6		0700	0.7
W 1823	0.7	TH	1307	4.5
			1923	0.7
12 0025	4.6	**27**	0125	4.5
0643	0.6		0739	0.8
TH 1250	4.7	F	1346	4.5
1908	0.6		2001	0.6
13 0109	4.7	**28**	0203	4.5
0728	0.6		0814	0.8
F 1332	4.7	SA	1422	4.5
1953	0.6		2036	0.6
14 0153	4.8	**29**	0240	4.5
0813	0.5		0846	0.9
SA 1415	4.7	SU	1457	4.5
2038	0.4		2110	0.6
15 0237	4.9	**30**	0315	4.5
0858	0.6		0918	0.9
SU 1459	4.7	M	1530	4.4
2124	0.4		2143	0.6

JULY

Time	m		Time	m
1 0349	4.5	**16**	0355	5.0
0950	0.9		1016	0.6
TU 1602	4.4	W	1616	4.8
2217	0.6		2246	0.2
2 0422	4.5	**17**	0445	4.9
1023	0.9		1105	0.7
W 1635	4.4	TH	1706	4.7
2252	0.7		2337	0.3
3 0457	4.4	**18**	0538	4.8
1100	1.0		1155	0.8
TH 1710	4.3	F	1800	4.6
2330	0.7			
4 0537	4.4	**19**	0030	0.4
1141	1.0		0636	4.6
F 1753	4.3	SA	1250	0.9
			1900	4.4
5 0016	0.8	**20**	0128	0.6
0625	4.3		0740	4.4
SA 1232	1.1	SU	1353	1.0
1846	4.2		2007	4.3
6 0115	0.9	**21**	0234	0.8
0725	4.2		0849	4.2
SU 1339	1.2	M	1507	1.1
1952	4.1		2120	4.1
7 0229	1.0	**22**	0344	0.9
0834	4.2		1004	4.1
M 1500	1.2	TU	1623	1.1
2103	4.1		2236	4.2
8 0336	0.9	**23**	0455	0.9
0941	4.2		1114	4.2
TU 1607	1.1	W	1733	1.0
2209	4.2		2341	4.3
9 0435	0.8	**24**	0557	0.9
1044	4.3		1209	4.3
W 1706	0.9	TH	1827	0.8
2309	4.3			
10 0530	0.7	**25**	0030	4.4
1139	4.4		0645	0.9
TH 1800	0.8	F	1252	4.4
2359	4.5		1910	0.8
11 0621	0.7	**26**	0110	4.5
1229	4.6		0722	0.9
F 1849	0.6	SA	1329	4.5
			1945	0.7
12 0051	4.7	**27**	0146	4.5
0709	0.6		0753	0.9
SA 1314	4.7	SU	1402	4.5
1936	0.5		2017	0.6
13 0136	4.8	**28**	0219	4.6
0755	0.6		0822	0.9
SU 1359	4.8	M	1434	4.5
2023	0.4		2047	0.6
14 0222	5.0	**29**	0251	4.6
0841	0.6		0851	0.8
M 1443	4.8	TU	1504	4.6
2110	0.3		2118	0.5
15 0308	5.0	**30**	0323	4.7
0928	0.6		0924	0.8
TU 1528	4.8	W	1535	4.6
2157	0.2		2151	0.5
		31	0354	4.7
			0959	0.8
		TH	1607	4.6
			2226	0.5

AUGUST

Time	m		Time	m
1 0428	4.7	**16**	0513	4.9
1035	0.8		1129	0.7
F 1641	4.6	SA	1733	4.8
2302	0.6		2359	0.4
2 0505	4.7	**17**	0605	4.6
1113	0.8		1219	0.9
SA 1721	4.6	SU	1828	4.5
2342	0.7			
3 0548	4.6	**18**	0056	0.7
1156	0.9		0704	4.3
SU 1808	4.5	M	1320	1.1
			1931	4.3
4 0029	0.8	**19**	0203	1.0
0640	4.4		0814	4.1
M 1250	1.1	TU	1438	1.2
1905	4.3		2049	4.0
5 0132	0.9	**20**	0318	1.1
0744	4.3		0934	3.9
TU 1406	1.2	W	1557	1.2
2016	4.2		2211	4.0
6 0254	1.0	**21**	0429	1.2
0900	4.1		1049	4.0
W 1533	1.2	TH	1708	1.1
2134	4.2		2319	4.2
7 0405	1.0	**22**	0534	1.1
1013	4.2		1146	4.2
TH 1641	1.0	F	1806	0.9
2244	4.3			
8 0506	0.9	**23**	0010	4.4
1117	4.3		0625	1.1
F 1739	0.8	SA	1230	4.4
2343	4.5		1850	0.8
9 0601	0.8	**24**	0049	4.5
1210	4.5		0701	1.0
SA 1832	0.6	SU	1306	4.5
			1924	0.7
10 0034	4.8	**25**	0123	4.6
0651	0.7		0729	0.9
SU 1257	4.7	M	1338	4.6
1920	0.4		1952	0.6
11 0120	5.0	**26**	0154	4.7
0738	0.6		0756	0.8
M 1340	4.9	TU	1407	4.7
2006	0.3		2020	0.5
12 0204	5.1	**27**	0225	4.8
0824	0.5		0826	0.7
TU 1424	5.0	W	1437	4.8
2052	0.2		2051	0.5
13 0249	5.2	**28**	0255	4.8
0910	0.5		0859	0.6
W 1509	5.1	TH	1507	4.8
2138	0.1		2125	0.4
14 0335	5.2	**29**	0326	4.9
0956	0.5		0935	0.6
TH 1555	5.1	F	1539	4.9
2225	0.1		2200	0.4
15 0423	5.1	**30**	0400	4.9
1042	0.5		1011	0.6
F 1643	5.0	SA	1614	4.9
2312	0.2		2236	0.5
		31	0437	4.8
			1049	0.7
		SU	1653	4.8
			2314	0.6

Chart Datum: 0·19 metres below TAW Datum
HAT is 5·6 metres above Chart Datum

TIME ZONE -0100
(Belgian Standard Time)
Subtract 1 hour for UT
For Belgian Summer Time add
ONE hour in **non-shaded areas**

BELGIUM – ZEEBRUGGE
LAT 51°21′N   LONG 3°12′E
TIMES AND HEIGHTS OF HIGH AND LOW WATERS

Dates in amber are **SPRINGS**
Dates in yellow are **NEAPS**

2014

SEPTEMBER				OCTOBER				NOVEMBER				DECEMBER			
Time	m	Time	m	Time	m	Time	m	Time	m	Time	m	Time	m	Time	m

SEPTEMBER

1 M — 0518 4.7, 1129 0.8, 1738 4.7, 2358 0.8
16 TU — 0022 0.9, 0628 4.3, 1245 1.1, ◗ 1856 4.2
2 TU — 0605 4.5, 1217 1.0, 1831 4.5 ◐
17 W — 0130 1.2, 0735 4.2, 1409 1.3, 2013 4.0
3 W — 0054 1.0, 0705 4.3, 1326 1.2, 1941 4.3
18 TH — 0248 1.4, 0856 3.8, 1526 1.3, 2137 3.9
4 TH — 0219 1.1, 0825 4.1, 1504 1.2, 2106 4.2
19 F — 0357 1.4, 1014 3.9, 1633 1.2, 2248 4.1
5 F — 0340 1.1, 0948 4.1, 1617 1.0, 2224 4.3
20 SA — 0501 1.3, 1115 4.1, 1733 1.0, 2340 4.3
6 SA — 0445 1.0, 1057 4.3, 1719 0.8, 2326 4.6
21 SU — 0555 1.1, 1201 4.3, 1819 0.8
7 SU — 0542 0.9, 1151 4.5, 1813 0.6
22 M — 0021 4.5, 0633 1.0, 1237 4.5, 1854 0.7
8 M — 0017 4.8, 0633 0.7, 1238 4.8, 1902 0.4
23 TU — 0055 4.7, 0701 0.9, 1309 4.6, 1922 0.6
9 TU — 0102 5.0, 0720 0.6, 1321 5.0, ○ 1947 0.2
24 W — 0126 4.8, 0729 0.8, 1339 4.8, ● 1951 0.5
10 W — 0145 5.2, 0805 0.5, 1404 5.1, 2032 0.1
25 TH — 0156 4.9, 0800 0.6, 1409 4.9, 2024 0.4
11 TH — 0229 5.1, 0849 0.4, 1448 5.2, 2117 0.1
26 F — 0227 5.0, 0836 0.5, 1440 5.0, 2059 0.4
12 F — 0314 5.2, 0934 0.4, 1533 5.2, 2202 0.2
27 SA — 0300 5.0, 0913 0.5, 1514 5.0, 2136 0.4
13 SA — 0400 5.1, 1018 0.5, 1619 5.1, 2246 0.3
28 SU — 0335 4.9, 0950 0.6, 1550 5.0, 2213 0.5
14 SU — 0446 4.9, 1102 0.6, 1706 4.8, 2332 0.6
29 M — 0412 4.9, 1028 0.7, 1630 4.9, 2251 0.7
15 M — 0535 4.6, 1149 0.8, 1757 4.6
30 TU — 0453 4.7, 1108 0.8, 1714 4.7, 2335 0.9

OCTOBER

1 W — 0540 4.5, 1156 1.0, 1807 4.5 ◐
16 TH — 0047 1.4, 0654 3.9, 1335 1.3, 1933 3.9
2 TH — 0030 1.1, 0638 4.2, 1305 1.1, 1917 4.3
17 F — 0212 1.5, 0812 3.7, 1450 1.3, 2053 3.8
3 F — 0153 1.2, 0800 4.0, 1440 1.2, 2046 4.2
18 SA — 0319 1.5, 0928 3.8, 1552 1.2, 2204 4.0
4 SA — 0316 1.2, 0926 4.0, 1554 1.0, 2204 4.3
19 SU — 0419 1.4, 1032 3.9, 1650 1.1, 2301 4.2
5 SU — 0423 1.1, 1035 4.3, 1657 0.8, 2307 4.6
20 M — 0513 1.2, 1122 4.2, 1739 0.9, 2346 4.4
6 M — 0522 0.9, 1131 4.5, 1753 0.6, 2358 4.9
21 TU — 0556 1.1, 1203 4.4, 1817 0.8
7 TU — 0615 0.8, 1218 4.8, 1842 0.4
22 W — 0023 4.6, 0629 0.9, 1237 4.6, 1849 0.7
8 W — 0044 5.1, 0702 0.6, 1302 5.0, ○ 1928 0.2
23 TH — 0056 4.8, 0701 0.7, 1309 4.8, ● 1922 0.5
9 TH — 0127 5.2, 0746 0.5, 1345 5.2, 2012 0.2
24 F — 0128 4.9, 0736 0.6, 1341 4.9, 1957 0.5
10 F — 0210 5.2, 0829 0.4, 1428 5.2, 2055 0.2
25 SA — 0201 5.0, 0813 0.5, 1416 5.0, 2035 0.4
11 SA — 0253 5.1, 0912 0.4, 1512 5.2, 2138 0.3
26 SU — 0236 5.0, 0852 0.5, 1452 5.0, 2113 0.5
12 SU — 0337 5.0, 0955 0.5, 1557 5.0, 2221 0.5
27 M — 0313 4.9, 0931 0.6, 1531 5.0, 2152 0.6
13 M — 0421 4.8, 1037 0.6, 1642 4.8, 2303 0.8
28 TU — 0352 4.8, 1011 0.7, 1612 4.9, 2233 0.8
14 TU — 0506 4.5, 1121 0.8, 1729 4.5, 2347 1.1
29 W — 0434 4.6, 1054 0.8, 1658 4.7, 2319 0.9
15 W — 0554 4.2, 1211 1.1, 1822 4.2 ◐
30 TH — 0522 4.4, 1145 0.9, 1753 4.5
31 F — 0016 1.1, 0622 4.2, 1254 1.0, ◗ 1903 4.3

NOVEMBER

1 SA — 0133 1.3, 0741 4.1, 1417 1.0, 2026 4.3
16 SU — 0232 1.6, 0833 3.8, 1507 1.2, 2110 3.9
2 SU — 0251 1.2, 0902 4.1, 1528 0.9, 2141 4.4
17 M — 0332 1.5, 0938 3.9, 1602 1.1, 2211 4.1
3 M — 0358 1.1, 1011 4.3, 1632 0.7, 2245 4.6
18 TU — 0426 1.3, 1035 4.0, 1653 1.0, 2302 4.3
4 TU — 0501 1.0, 1109 4.5, 1731 0.6, 2340 4.8
19 W — 0515 1.1, 1122 4.3, 1737 0.9, 2346 4.5
5 W — 0557 0.8, 1200 4.8, 1823 0.4
20 TH — 0556 1.0, 1202 4.5, 1816 0.7
6 TH — 0027 4.9, 0645 0.7, 1245 4.9, ○ 1909 0.4
21 F — 0025 4.7, 0635 0.8, 1240 4.7, 1854 0.6
7 F — 0111 5.0, 0729 0.6, 1329 5.0, 1953 0.4
22 SA — 0101 4.8, 0713 0.7, 1316 4.8, ● 1933 0.5
8 SA — 0153 5.0, 0812 0.5, 1412 5.1, 2035 0.4
23 SU — 0138 4.9, 0753 0.6, 1354 4.9, 2013 0.5
9 SU — 0236 5.0, 0854 0.5, 1455 5.0, 2116 0.5
24 M — 0215 4.9, 0834 0.5, 1433 4.9, 2054 0.6
10 M — 0318 4.8, 0935 0.5, 1538 4.9, 2156 0.7
25 TU — 0255 4.8, 0916 0.5, 1515 4.9, 2136 0.7
11 TU — 0400 4.7, 1016 0.6, 1620 4.7, 2235 0.9
26 W — 0336 4.7, 0959 0.6, 1559 4.9, 2220 0.8
12 W — 0441 4.5, 1056 0.8, 1704 4.5, 2313 1.1
27 TH — 0421 4.6, 1046 0.7, 1647 4.7, 2308 0.9
13 TH — 0524 4.2, 1141 1.0, 1751 4.2, 2357 1.4
28 F — 0510 4.5, 1139 0.7, 1742 4.6
14 F — 0613 4.0, 1246 1.2, 1849 4.0 ◐
29 SA — 0005 1.1, 0609 4.3, 1242 0.8, ◗ 1849 4.4
15 SA — 0113 1.5, 0718 3.8, 1406 1.1, 2001 3.9
30 SU — 0112 1.2, 0719 4.2, 1352 0.8, 2003 4.4

DECEMBER

1 M — 0222 1.2, 0834 4.2, 1500 0.8, 2115 4.4
16 TU — 0233 1.5, 0834 3.9, 1511 1.2, 2112 4.0
2 TU — 0331 1.1, 0944 4.3, 1606 0.7, 2222 4.5
17 W — 0337 1.4, 0938 3.9, 1606 1.1, 2212 4.2
3 W — 0438 1.0, 1048 4.4, 1710 0.7, 2323 4.6
18 TH — 0432 1.2, 1035 4.1, 1657 1.0, 2306 4.3
4 TH — 0540 0.9, 1144 4.6, 1806 0.6
19 F — 0523 1.1, 1126 4.3, 1744 0.8, 2354 4.5
5 F — 0014 4.7, 0632 0.8, 1233 4.7, 1855 0.6
20 SA — 0610 0.9, 1212 4.5, 1828 0.7
6 SA — 0100 4.8, 0717 0.7, 1318 4.8, ○ 1938 0.6
21 SU — 0036 4.6, 0653 0.7, 1254 4.7, 1911 0.7
7 SU — 0142 4.8, 0759 0.6, 1400 4.8, 2018 0.7
22 M — 0117 4.7, 0736 0.6, 1336 4.8, ● 1954 0.6
8 M — 0222 4.7, 0839 0.6, 1441 4.8, 2056 0.7
23 TU — 0158 4.8, 0819 0.5, 1418 4.9, 2037 0.6
9 TU — 0301 4.7, 0918 0.6, 1521 4.7, 2133 0.8
24 W — 0239 4.8, 0903 0.5, 1502 4.9, 2121 0.7
10 W — 0340 4.6, 0956 0.6, 1600 4.6, 2208 1.0
25 TH — 0323 4.8, 0949 0.6, 1547 4.9, 2208 0.7
11 TH — 0418 4.5, 1034 0.7, 1639 4.5, 2243 1.1
26 F — 0408 4.7, 1037 0.4, 1636 4.8, 2256 0.8
12 F — 0455 4.3, 1112 0.8, 1720 4.3, 2319 1.2
27 SA — 0457 4.6, 1128 0.5, 1729 4.7, 2349 0.9
13 SA — 0535 4.2, 1156 1.0, 1804 4.2
28 SU — 0552 4.5, 1224 0.6, 1829 4.6 ◐
14 SU — 0003 1.3, 0621 4.0, 1256 1.1, ◗ 1859 4.1
29 M — 0047 1.0, 0654 4.4, 1325 0.7, 1936 4.4
15 M — 0109 1.5, 0723 3.9, 1409 1.2, 2006 4.0
30 TU — 0151 1.1, 0803 4.3, 1430 0.7, 2046 4.3
31 W — 0301 1.2, 0915 4.2, 1539 0.8, 2158 4.3

Chart Datum: 0·19 metres below TAW Datum
HAT is 5·6 metres above Chart Datum

TIDES

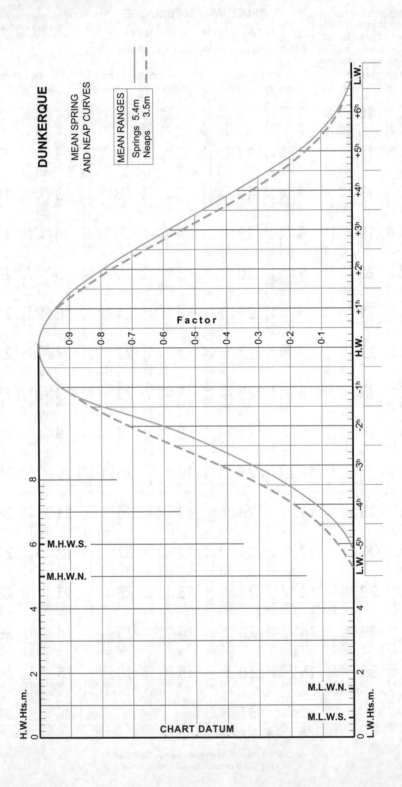

DUNKERQUE

MEAN SPRING
AND NEAP CURVES

MEAN RANGES
Springs 5.4m
Neaps 3.5m

TIME ZONE -0100
(French Standard Time)
Subtract 1 hour for UT
For French Summer Time add
ONE hour in **non-shaded areas**

FRANCE – DUNKERQUE

LAT 51°03'N   LONG 2°22'E

TIMES AND HEIGHTS OF HIGH AND LOW WATERS

Dates in amber are **SPRINGS**
Dates in yellow are **NEAPS**

2014

JANUARY

Day	Time m	Day	Time m
1	0658 0.7 / 1217 6.1 / W 1922 0.6 ●	**16**	0049 5.6 / 0742 0.8 / TH 1306 5.7 / ○ 1956 1.0
2	0041 6.1 / 0747 0.5 / TH 1305 6.3 / 2010 0.5	**17**	0121 5.7 / 0815 0.8 / F 1337 5.8 / 2029 0.9
3	0127 6.2 / 0835 0.3 / F 1353 6.4 / 2058 0.5	**18**	0150 5.8 / 0848 0.7 / SA 1407 5.8 / 2102 0.9
4	0214 6.2 / 0923 0.3 / SA 1442 6.3 / 2145 0.6	**19**	0220 5.8 / 0921 0.7 / SU 1439 5.8 / 2134 0.9
5	0302 6.2 / 1011 0.3 / SU 1532 6.2 / 2232 0.7	**20**	0252 5.8 / 0953 0.7 / M 1512 5.8 / 2204 1.0
6	0349 6.0 / 1059 0.5 / M 1622 6.0 / 2319 0.9	**21**	0323 5.7 / 1025 0.8 / TU 1544 5.7 / 2236 1.0
7	0437 5.8 / 1149 0.7 / TU 1714 5.7	**22**	0354 5.6 / 1059 0.9 / W 1617 5.5 / 2312 1.2
8	0009 1.1 / 0530 5.6 / W 1243 1.0 / ◐ 1813 5.4	**23**	0428 5.5 / 1138 1.0 / TH 1659 5.4 / 2354 1.3
9	0105 1.4 / 0633 5.3 / TH 1343 1.2 / 1924 5.1	**24**	0517 5.3 / 1225 1.2 / F 1759 5.2 ◑
10	0209 1.6 / 0750 5.1 / F 1451 1.4 / 2036 5.0	**25**	0048 1.5 / 0627 5.1 / SA 1327 1.3 / 1911 5.1
11	0320 1.6 / 0902 5.0 / SA 1606 1.5 / 2142 5.0	**26**	0200 1.6 / 0742 5.1 / SU 1448 1.4 / 2025 5.1
12	0437 1.5 / 1006 5.1 / SU 1715 1.4 / 2241 5.1	**27**	0326 1.5 / 0901 5.1 / M 1607 1.2 / 2145 5.2
13	0540 1.3 / 1101 5.3 / M 1807 1.1 / 2331 5.3	**28**	0443 1.2 / 1019 5.4 / TU 1718 1.0 / 2252 5.5
14	0628 1.1 / 1149 5.4 / TU 1849 1.1	**29**	0550 0.9 / 1119 5.8 / W 1819 0.7 / 2345 5.8
15	0013 5.5 / 0708 1.0 / W 1230 5.6 / 1924 1.0	**30**	0646 0.6 / 1209 6.1 / TH 1911 0.6 ●
		31	0031 6.1 / 0736 0.3 / F 1256 6.3 / 1958 0.4

FEBRUARY

Day	Time m	Day	Time m
1	0115 6.2 / 0823 0.2 / SA 1341 6.4 / 2043 0.4	**16**	0130 5.8 / 0825 0.6 / SU 1345 5.9 / 2038 0.7
2	0158 6.3 / 0908 0.1 / SU 1426 6.3 / 2127 0.4	**17**	0157 5.9 / 0858 0.6 / M 1414 5.9 / 2110 0.7
3	0242 6.2 / 0953 0.2 / M 1512 6.2 / 2210 0.6	**18**	0227 5.9 / 0930 0.5 / TU 1445 5.9 / 2141 0.7
4	0326 6.1 / 1037 0.3 / TU 1556 6.0 / 2253 0.7	**19**	0255 5.9 / 1002 0.6 / W 1514 5.8 / 2213 0.8
5	0409 5.9 / 1120 0.5 / W 1642 5.7 / 2335 1.0	**20**	0324 5.8 / 1034 0.7 / TH 1545 5.7 / 2247 0.9
6	0456 5.7 / 1205 0.9 / TH 1732 5.4	**21**	0358 5.7 / 1111 0.8 / F 1624 5.5 / 2326 1.1
7	0022 1.2 / 0550 5.3 / F 1257 1.3 / 1833 5.0	**22**	0443 5.5 / 1155 1.0 / SA 1719 5.3 ○
8	0120 1.5 / 0700 5.0 / SA 1401 1.6 / 1949 4.8	**23**	0016 1.3 / 0550 5.2 / SU 1254 1.3 / 1836 5.0
9	0231 1.7 / 0823 4.8 / SU 1520 1.7 / 2106 4.7	**24**	0126 1.5 / 0712 5.1 / M 1416 1.4 / 1958 4.9
10	0357 1.7 / 0939 4.8 / M 1644 1.6 / 2215 4.8	**25**	0257 1.5 / 0842 5.1 / TU 1543 1.3 / 2130 5.1
11	0514 1.5 / 1047 5.0 / TU 1744 1.4 / 2311 5.1	**26**	0423 1.2 / 1009 5.4 / W 1702 1.1 / 2241 5.4
12	0607 1.2 / 1138 5.3 / W 1829 1.2 / 2355 5.4	**27**	0536 0.9 / 1109 5.7 / TH 1805 0.8 / 2334 5.7
13	0648 1.0 / 1213 5.5 / TH 1904 1.0	**28**	0633 0.5 / 1158 6.0 / F 1856 0.5
14	0031 5.6 / 0721 0.8 / F 1248 5.7 / 1934 0.9		
15	0102 5.7 / 0752 0.7 / SA 1318 5.8 / ○ 2006 0.8		

MARCH

Day	Time m	Day	Time m
1	0017 6.0 / 0721 0.3 / SA 1242 6.2 / ● 1942 0.4	**16**	0037 5.7 / 0724 0.6 / SU 1252 5.8 / ○ 1938 0.7
2	0058 6.2 / 0806 0.1 / SU 1323 6.3 / 2024 0.4	**17**	0104 5.8 / 0757 0.5 / M 1319 5.9 / 2012 0.7
3	0138 6.2 / 0849 0.1 / M 1406 6.3 / 2105 0.4	**18**	0131 5.9 / 0831 0.5 / TU 1347 5.9 / 2045 0.6
4	0219 6.2 / 0930 0.2 / TU 1448 6.2 / 2146 0.5	**19**	0200 5.9 / 0905 0.4 / W 1418 6.0 / 2119 0.6
5	0301 6.2 / 1010 0.3 / W 1529 6.0 / 2225 0.6	**20**	0230 6.0 / 0939 0.5 / TH 1449 5.9 / 2152 0.6
6	0342 6.0 / 1049 0.6 / TH 1610 5.7 / 2304 0.8	**21**	0302 5.9 / 1014 0.6 / F 1523 5.8 / 2228 0.8
7	0425 5.7 / 1129 0.9 / F 1654 5.4 / 2345 1.1	**22**	0340 5.8 / 1051 0.7 / SA 1605 5.6 / 2308 0.9
8	0513 5.4 / 1214 1.3 / SA 1746 5.0 ◐	**23**	0428 5.6 / 1136 1.0 / SU 1703 5.3
9	0035 1.4 / 0614 5.0 / SU 1311 1.6 / 1858 4.6	**24**	0000 1.1 / 0537 5.3 / M 1236 1.2 / ◐ 1820 5.0
10	0142 1.7 / 0707 4.6 / M 1429 1.8 / 2024 4.5	**25**	0110 1.3 / 0659 5.1 / TU 1358 1.4 / 1942 4.9
11	0308 1.8 / 0904 4.6 / TU 1600 1.8 / 2141 4.6	**26**	0241 1.4 / 0832 5.1 / W 1527 1.3 / 2116 5.0
12	0435 1.6 / 1016 4.8 / W 1710 1.5 / 2241 4.9	**27**	0407 1.1 / 0955 5.4 / TH 1645 1.1 / 2226 5.4
13	0535 1.3 / 1110 5.1 / TH 1759 1.2 / 2327 5.2	**28**	0519 0.8 / 1054 5.7 / F 1747 0.8 / 2316 5.7
14	0618 1.0 / 1147 5.4 / F 1835 1.0	**29**	0615 0.5 / 1142 6.0 / SA 1838 0.6 / 2359 5.9
15	0005 5.5 / 0652 0.8 / SA 1222 5.6 / 1906 0.9	**30**	0702 0.3 / 1223 6.1 / SU 1921 0.5 ●
		31	0037 6.1 / 0746 0.2 / M 1303 6.2 / 2002 0.5

APRIL

Day	Time m	Day	Time m
1	0116 6.2 / 0826 0.2 / TU 1342 6.2 / 2042 0.4	**16**	0103 5.9 / 0804 0.5 / W 1320 5.9 / 2021 0.6
2	0156 6.2 / 0906 0.2 / W 1423 6.1 / 2121 0.5	**17**	0134 6.0 / 0841 0.4 / TH 1354 6.0 / 2058 0.5
3	0237 6.1 / 0944 0.5 / TH 1502 5.9 / 2159 0.6	**18**	0210 6.0 / 0919 0.5 / F 1431 5.9 / 2136 0.5
4	0317 5.9 / 1020 0.7 / F 1542 5.7 / 2236 0.8	**19**	0249 6.0 / 0958 0.6 / SA 1512 5.8 / 2216 0.6
5	0358 5.7 / 1057 1.0 / SA 1622 5.4 / 2315 1.0	**20**	0334 5.8 / 1040 0.7 / SU 1601 5.6 / 2301 0.8
6	0443 5.4 / 1138 1.3 / SU 1710 5.1	**21**	0430 5.6 / 1128 1.0 / M 1702 5.4 / 2355 1.0
7	0000 1.3 / 0537 5.0 / M 1228 1.6 / ◐ 1810 4.7	**22**	0537 5.4 / 1230 1.2 / TU 1811 5.1 ○
8	0057 1.6 / 0647 4.7 / TU 1337 1.8 / 1928 4.5	**23**	0106 1.2 / 0650 5.2 / W 1349 1.3 / 1928 5.0
9	0215 1.7 / 0812 4.5 / W 1506 1.8 / 2053 4.5	**24**	0229 1.2 / 0819 5.2 / TH 1510 1.3 / 2057 5.1
10	0342 1.6 / 0932 4.7 / TH 1621 1.6 / 2159 4.8	**25**	0348 1.0 / 0936 5.4 / F 1623 1.1 / 2203 5.4
11	0448 1.3 / 1028 5.0 / F 1716 1.3 / 2249 5.1	**26**	0457 0.8 / 1034 5.7 / SA 1725 0.9 / 2253 5.6
12	0537 1.0 / 1112 5.3 / SA 1758 1.1 / 2330 5.4	**27**	0553 0.6 / 1121 5.8 / SU 1816 0.7 / 2337 5.8
13	0616 0.8 / 1149 5.6 / SU 1833 0.9	**28**	0641 0.5 / 1203 5.9 / M 1900 0.6
14	0004 5.6 / 0651 0.7 / M 1221 5.7 / 1908 0.7	**29**	0016 5.9 / 0724 0.4 / TU 1241 6.0 / ● 1941 0.5
15	0034 5.8 / 0727 0.5 / TU 1250 5.9 / ○ 1944 0.6	**30**	0056 6.0 / 0804 0.5 / W 1321 6.0 / 2020 0.5

Chart Datum: 2·69 metres below IGN Datum
HAT is 6·4 metres above Chart Datum

TIDES

TIDES

TIME ZONE -0100
(French Standard Time)
Subtract 1 hour for UT
For French Summer Time add
ONE hour in **non-shaded areas**

FRANCE – DUNKERQUE

LAT 51°03'N LONG 2°22'E

TIMES AND HEIGHTS OF HIGH AND LOW WATERS

Dates in amber are **SPRINGS**
Dates in yellow are **NEAPS**

2014

MAY

Time	m	Time	m
1 0136	6.0	**16** 0114	6.0
0842	0.5	0820	0.5
TH 1401	5.9	F 1335	6.0
2059	0.5	2041	0.5
2 0217	6.0	**17** 0156	6.1
0904	0.6	0903	0.5
F 1440	5.8	SA 1419	6.0
2136	0.6	2125	0.4
3 0257	5.8	**18** 0243	6.0
0955	0.8	0947	0.6
SA 1519	5.7	SU 1507	5.9
2214	0.8	2210	0.5
4 0337	5.6	**19** 0334	5.9
1032	1.0	1034	0.7
SU 1558	5.4	M 1600	5.7
2251	1.0	2259	0.6
5 0419	5.4	**20** 0430	5.8
1110	1.3	1126	0.9
M 1641	5.2	TU 1657	5.5
2332	1.2	2355	0.8
6 0508	5.1	**21** 0530	5.6
1154	1.5	1226	1.1
TU 1733	4.9	W 1757	5.3
☽			
7 0020	1.4	**22** 0100	0.9
0605	4.9	0636	5.4
W 1249	1.7	TH 1335	1.2
☾ 1835	4.7	1908	5.2
8 0122	1.6	**23** 0212	1.0
0712	4.7	0757	5.3
TH 1403	1.8	F 1447	1.2
1947	4.6	2029	5.2
9 0241	1.6	**24** 0323	0.9
0826	4.7	0910	5.4
F 1523	1.7	SA 1556	1.1
2100	4.8	2135	5.3
10 0352	1.4	**25** 0431	0.8
0934	5.0	1009	5.5
SA 1625	1.4	SU 1700	1.0
2200	5.0	2228	5.5
11 0448	1.1	**26** 0531	0.7
1026	5.2	1059	5.6
SU 1714	1.2	M 1754	0.9
2248	5.3	2315	5.6
12 0535	0.9	**27** 0620	0.7
1109	5.5	1144	5.7
M 1757	1.0	TU 1840	0.8
2327	5.5	2359	5.7
13 0617	0.7	**28** 0704	0.7
1145	5.7	1224	5.8
TU 1837	0.8	W 1922	0.7
		●	
14 0001	5.7	**29** 0040	5.8
0657	0.6	0744	0.7
W 1219	5.8	TH 1304	5.8
○ 1917	0.7	2002	0.6
15 0036	5.9	**30** 0121	5.9
0738	0.5	0822	0.7
TH 1255	5.9	F 1344	5.8
1958	0.5	2040	0.6
		31 0201	5.8
		0858	0.8
		SA 1422	5.8
		2118	0.7

JUNE

Time	m	Time	m
1 0240	5.8	**16** 0235	6.2
0934	0.9	0937	0.5
SU 1459	5.7	M 1458	6.0
2154	0.7	2203	0.3
2 0318	5.6	**17** 0327	6.1
1010	1.0	1026	0.6
M 1536	5.5	TU 1549	5.9
2230	0.9	2253	0.4
3 0357	5.5	**18** 0420	6.0
1045	1.2	1116	0.8
TU 1616	5.3	W 1641	5.7
2307	1.0	2346	0.5
4 0440	5.3	**19** 0515	5.8
1124	1.3	1211	0.9
W 1702	5.1	TH 1737	5.6
2348	1.2	☽	
5 0530	5.1	**20** 0044	0.7
1208	1.5	0615	5.6
TH 1754	5.0	F 1312	1.1
☾		1840	5.4
6 0037	1.3	**21** 0148	0.9
0625	5.0	0727	5.4
F 1303	1.6	SA 1417	1.2
1852	4.8	1954	5.3
7 0137	1.4	**22** 0254	1.0
0725	4.9	0839	5.3
SA 1414	1.6	SU 1525	1.2
1955	4.8	2104	5.3
8 0250	1.4	**23** 0403	1.0
0828	5.0	0942	5.3
SU 1527	1.5	M 1633	1.2
2100	5.0	2203	5.3
9 0357	1.2	**24** 0508	1.0
0931	5.1	1038	5.4
M 1628	1.3	TU 1734	1.1
2158	5.2	2256	5.4
10 0453	1.0	**25** 0602	0.9
1025	5.4	1128	5.5
TU 1720	1.1	W 1824	0.9
2248	5.4	2344	5.6
11 0543	0.9	**26** 0648	0.9
1111	5.6	1212	5.6
W 1808	0.9	TH 1908	0.8
2332	5.7		
12 0630	0.7	**27** 0029	5.7
1154	5.8	0727	0.9
TH 1854	0.7	F 1252	5.7
		● 1947	0.7
13 0014	5.9	**28** 0110	5.7
0716	0.6	0804	0.9
F 1236	5.9	SA 1330	5.7
○ 1940	0.5	2024	0.7
14 0058	6.0	**29** 0148	5.8
0802	0.5	0839	0.9
SA 1321	5.6	SU 1405	5.7
2027	0.4	2100	0.7
15 0145	6.1	**30** 0223	5.7
0849	0.5	0914	0.9
SU 1408	6.0	M 1439	5.7
2114	0.3	2135	0.6

JULY

Time	m	Time	m
1 0257	5.7	**16** 0312	6.2
0948	1.0	1010	0.5
TU 1512	5.6	W 1530	6.1
2209	0.8	2237	0.2
2 0333	5.6	**17** 0401	6.1
1021	1.1	1058	0.7
W 1549	5.5	TH 1618	5.9
2242	0.9	2326	0.4
3 0411	5.5	**18** 0452	5.9
1055	1.2	1147	0.9
TH 1628	5.4	F 1710	5.8
2318	1.0		
4 0453	5.3	**19** 0018	0.6
1132	1.3	0547	5.6
F 1712	5.2	SA 1241	1.1
2358	1.1	☽ 1807	5.5
5 0541	5.2	**20** 0116	0.9
1217	1.4	0650	5.4
SA 1804	5.1	SU 1342	1.3
☾		1917	5.3
6 0047	1.2	**21** 0220	1.2
0635	5.1	0802	5.1
SU 1312	1.5	M 1450	1.4
1902	5.0	2032	5.1
7 0149	1.3	**22** 0332	1.3
0735	5.0	0913	5.1
M 1424	1.6	TU 1606	1.4
2005	5.0	2140	5.1
8 0304	1.3	**23** 0446	1.3
0839	5.1	1017	5.1
TU 1540	1.5	W 1715	1.2
2111	5.1	2242	5.3
9 0412	1.2	**24** 0545	1.2
0944	5.2	1113	5.3
W 1645	1.2	TH 1809	1.0
2215	5.3	2337	5.4
10 0513	1.0	**25** 0632	1.1
1044	5.5	1159	5.5
TH 1743	1.0	F 1853	0.9
2310	5.6		
11 0609	0.8	**26** 0016	5.6
1135	5.7	0711	1.0
F 1836	0.7	SA 1238	5.6
2359	5.9	● 1931	0.8
12 0700	0.6	**27** 0055	5.7
1222	5.9	0746	0.9
SA 1926	0.5	SU 1313	5.7
○		2005	0.7
13 0046	6.1	**28** 0130	5.8
0748	0.5	0819	0.9
SU 1308	6.1	M 1345	5.8
2014	0.3	2039	0.6
14 0133	6.3	**29** 0202	5.8
0836	0.4	0852	0.9
M 1354	6.1	TU 1415	5.8
2102	0.2	2112	0.6
15 0222	6.3	**30** 0232	5.8
0923	0.4	0924	0.9
TU 1442	6.1	W 1445	5.8
2150	0.2	2144	0.7
		31 0304	5.8
		0955	1.0
		TH 1518	5.7
		2215	0.8

AUGUST

Time	m	Time	m
1 0337	5.7	**16** 0423	5.9
1026	1.0	1118	0.8
F 1550	5.6	SA 1639	5.9
2248	0.8	2347	0.9
2 0411	5.5	**17** 0513	5.6
1059	1.1	1205	1.1
SA 1622	5.4	SU 1733	5.6
2324	1.0	☾	
3 0447	5.4	**18** 0038	1.1
1138	1.3	0611	5.3
SU 1703	5.3	M 1302	1.4
		1839	5.2
4 0007	1.1	**19** 0140	1.4
0539	5.2	0723	5.0
M 1227	1.4	TU 1411	1.6
☾ 1806	5.1	1958	5.0
5 0101	1.3	**20** 0256	1.6
0647	5.0	0842	4.8
TU 1331	1.6	W 1535	1.6
1919	5.0	2116	4.9
6 0215	1.4	**21** 0420	1.6
0757	5.0	0954	4.9
W 1456	1.6	TH 1653	1.4
2034	5.1	2227	5.1
7 0336	1.3	**22** 0524	1.4
0913	5.1	1054	5.2
TH 1615	1.3	F 1750	1.1
2152	5.3	2320	5.3
8 0448	1.1	**23** 0613	1.2
1025	5.4	1141	5.4
F 1724	1.0	SA 1833	0.9
2255	5.6		
9 0551	0.9	**24** 0004	5.6
1121	5.7	0651	1.1
SA 1822	0.7	SU 1218	5.6
2347	6.0	1910	0.8
10 0645	0.6	**25** 0035	5.7
1208	6.0	0723	1.0
SU 1912	0.4	M 1252	5.7
○		● 1941	0.7
11 0033	6.2	**26** 0108	5.8
0734	0.5	0753	0.9
M 1252	6.2	TU 1321	5.8
1959	0.2	2013	0.6
12 0118	6.4	**27** 0136	5.9
0819	0.4	0825	0.9
TU 1336	6.3	W 1347	5.9
2045	0.1	2045	0.6
13 0203	6.4	**28** 0203	5.9
0904	0.4	0857	0.9
W 1420	6.3	TH 1415	5.9
2131	0.1	2117	0.6
14 0250	6.3	**29** 0232	5.9
0949	0.5	0928	0.9
TH 1505	6.2	F 1444	5.8
2215	0.2	2148	0.7
15 0336	6.2	**30** 0302	5.6
1033	0.6	0958	1.0
F 1551	6.1	SA 1512	5.8
2300	0.4	2219	0.8
		31 0331	5.7
		1030	1.0
		SU 1542	5.6
		2253	0.9

Chart Datum: 2·69 metres below IGN Datum
HAT is 6·4 metres above Chart Datum

TIME ZONE -0100
(French Standard Time)
Subtract 1 hour for UT
For French Summer Time add
ONE hour in **non-shaded areas**

FRANCE – DUNKERQUE

LAT 51°03'N   LONG 2°22'E

TIMES AND HEIGHTS OF HIGH AND LOW WATERS

Dates in amber are SPRINGS
Dates in yellow are NEAPS

2014

SEPTEMBER

Day	Time m	Day	Time m
1 M	0404 5.5 / 1620 5.5 / 2334 1.1	**16** TU ◐	0532 5.2 / 1108 1.2 / 1801 5.2
2 TU ◐	0450 5.3 / 1718 5.2	**17** W	0056 1.6 / 0640 4.9 / 1328 1.7 / 1920 4.8
3 W	0026 1.3 / 0604 5.1 / 1256 1.6 / 1845 5.1	**18** TH	0213 1.9 / 0804 4.7 / 1455 1.8 / 2046 4.8
4 TH	0139 1.5 / 0726 5.0 / 1423 1.6 / 2009 5.0	**19** F	0343 1.8 / 0922 4.8 / 1620 1.6 / 2159 5.0
5 F	0308 1.5 / 0851 5.0 / 1551 1.4 / 2136 5.3	**20** SA	0454 1.6 / 1025 5.0 / 1721 1.3 / 2253 5.3
6 SA	0428 1.2 / 1010 5.4 / 1706 1.0 / 2242 5.7	**21** SU	0545 1.3 / 1112 5.4 / 1806 1.0 / 2337 5.5
7 SU	0535 0.9 / 1806 0.6 / 2333 6.1	**22** M	0623 1.1 / 1151 5.6 / 1841 0.8
8 M	0629 0.7 / 1153 6.0 / 1856 0.4	**23** TU	0009 5.7 / 0655 1.0 / 1224 5.8 / 1912 0.7
9 TU ○	0017 6.3 / 0716 0.5 / 1233 6.2 / 1941 0.2	**24** W ●	0041 5.9 / 0725 0.9 / 1253 5.9 / 1943 0.7
10 W	0058 6.4 / 0800 0.5 / 1314 6.3 / 2025 0.2	**25** TH	0107 5.9 / 0756 0.8 / 1318 5.9 / 2016 0.6
11 TH	0141 6.4 / 0842 0.5 / 1356 6.4 / 2108 0.2	**26** F	0133 6.0 / 0829 0.8 / 1345 6.0 / 2049 0.6
12 F	0224 6.3 / 0924 0.5 / 1439 6.3 / 2150 0.3	**27** SA	0202 6.0 / 0902 0.8 / 1414 6.0 / 2122 0.7
13 SA	0307 6.2 / 1006 0.7 / 1523 6.1 / 2232 0.6	**28** SU	0231 6.0 / 0934 0.9 / 1444 5.9 / 2154 0.8
14 SU	0352 5.9 / 1048 0.9 / 1608 5.9 / 2314 0.9	**29** M	0303 5.8 / 1008 1.0 / 1518 5.8 / 2230 0.9
15 M	0438 5.6 / 1131 1.1 / 1659 5.6 / 2359 1.3	**30** TU	0339 5.7 / 1046 1.1 / 1559 5.6 / 2311 1.2

OCTOBER

Day	Time m	Day	Time m
1 W	0427 5.4 / 1133 1.3 / 1659 5.3	**16** TH	0014 1.7 / 0554 4.9 / 1244 1.7 / 1834 4.8
2 TH	0004 1.4 / 0541 5.1 / 1236 1.5 / 1826 5.1	**17** F	0121 2.0 / 0711 4.7 / 1403 1.9 / 1958 4.7
3 F	0117 1.6 / 0705 5.0 / 1402 1.6 / 1951 5.1	**18** SA	0250 2.0 / 0837 4.7 / 1529 1.8 / 2117 4.9
4 SA	0248 1.6 / 0833 5.0 / 1532 1.4 / 2121 5.4	**19** SU	0407 1.8 / 0944 4.9 / 1636 1.5 / 2215 5.1
5 SU	0409 1.3 / 0953 5.4 / 1647 1.0 / 2226 5.8	**20** M	0504 1.5 / 1035 5.2 / 1727 1.2 / 2258 5.4
6 M	0516 1.0 / 1049 5.7 / 1747 0.6 / 2316 6.1	**21** TU	0547 1.3 / 1117 5.5 / 1806 1.0 / 2336 5.7
7 TU	0610 0.8 / 1133 6.0 / 1837 0.4 / 2358 6.3	**22** W	0622 1.1 / 1152 5.7 / 1839 0.8
8 W	0656 0.6 / 1213 6.2 / 1921 0.3	**23** TH ●	0009 5.8 / 0654 1.0 / 1222 5.8 / 1912 0.7
9 TH	0038 6.4 / 0739 0.6 / 1252 6.3 / 2003 0.3	**24** F	0036 5.9 / 0728 0.9 / 1248 6.0 / 1947 0.6
10 F	0118 6.4 / 0820 0.6 / 1333 6.4 / 2044 0.4	**25** SA	0104 6.0 / 0803 0.8 / 1318 6.0 / 2023 0.7
11 SA	0159 6.3 / 0900 0.6 / 1414 6.3 / 2125 0.5	**26** SU	0135 6.1 / 0839 0.8 / 1350 6.1 / 2059 0.7
12 SU	0240 6.1 / 0941 0.7 / 1458 6.1 / 2204 0.8	**27** M	0209 6.0 / 0915 0.8 / 1426 6.0 / 2136 0.8
13 M	0323 5.9 / 1020 0.9 / 1541 5.9 / 2243 1.1	**28** TU	0246 5.9 / 0953 0.9 / 1506 5.9 / 2215 1.0
14 TU	0406 5.6 / 1101 1.1 / 1628 5.5 / 2324 1.4	**29** W	0328 5.7 / 1034 1.0 / 1554 5.7 / 2259 1.2
15 W ◐	0454 5.2 / 1147 1.4 / 1724 5.2	**30** TH	0421 5.5 / 1124 1.2 / 1659 5.5 / 2353 1.4
		31 F	0531 5.2 / 1227 1.4 / 1813 5.3

NOVEMBER

Day	Time m	Day	Time m
1 SA	0104 1.6 / 0645 5.1 / 1348 1.4 / 1933 5.2	**16** SU	0141 2.0 / 0725 4.7 / 1423 1.8 / 2010 4.8
2 SU	0228 1.5 / 0810 5.1 / 1510 1.3 / 2100 5.4	**17** M	0304 1.9 / 0843 4.8 / 1537 1.6 / 2120 5.0
3 M	0346 1.4 / 0929 5.4 / 1623 1.0 / 2205 5.7	**18** TU	0409 1.7 / 0946 5.0 / 1635 1.4 / 2214 5.2
4 TU	0453 1.1 / 1026 5.7 / 1725 0.7 / 2256 6.0	**19** W	0501 1.4 / 1035 5.3 / 1723 1.1 / 2257 5.5
5 W	0549 0.9 / 1112 5.9 / 1816 0.6 / 2339 6.1	**20** TH	0544 1.2 / 1115 5.6 / 1804 1.0 / 2334 5.7
6 TH ○	0636 0.8 / 1153 6.1 / 1901 0.5	**21** F	0623 1.0 / 1150 5.7 / 1842 0.8
7 F	0018 6.2 / 0719 0.7 / 1232 6.2 / 1943 0.5	**22** SA ●	0006 5.9 / 0701 0.9 / 1222 5.9 / 1921 0.7
8 SA	0057 6.2 / 0800 0.6 / 1313 6.2 / 2023 0.6	**23** SU	0039 6.0 / 0740 0.8 / 1256 6.0 / 2000 0.7
9 SU	0138 6.1 / 0840 0.7 / 1355 6.2 / 2102 0.7	**24** M	0115 6.1 / 0820 0.7 / 1334 6.1 / 2041 0.7
10 M	0219 6.0 / 0919 0.7 / 1437 6.0 / 2140 0.9	**25** TU	0154 6.1 / 0902 0.6 / 1416 6.1 / 2123 0.7
11 TU	0259 5.8 / 0958 0.9 / 1519 5.8 / 2217 1.2	**26** W	0237 6.0 / 0945 0.7 / 1502 6.0 / 2207 0.9
12 W	0339 5.6 / 1037 1.1 / 1602 5.6 / 2255 1.4	**27** TH	0324 5.8 / 1030 0.8 / 1554 5.7 / 2253 1.0
13 TH	0422 5.3 / 1118 1.3 / 1650 5.3 / 2338 1.7	**28** F	0417 5.7 / 1120 1.0 / 1652 5.7 / 2346 1.2
14 F ◐	0512 5.1 / 1205 1.6 / 1746 5.0	**29** SA ◐	0517 5.5 / 1220 1.1 / 1756 5.5
15 SA	0030 1.9 / 0612 4.8 / 1304 1.7 / 1853 4.8	**30** SU	0050 1.4 / 0622 5.3 / 1331 1.2 / 1910 5.4

DECEMBER

Day	Time m	Day	Time m
1 M	0204 1.5 / 0739 5.2 / 1445 1.2 / 2032 5.4	**16** TU	0144 1.9 / 0729 4.8 / 1425 1.7 / 2006 4.9
2 TU	0317 1.4 / 0859 5.3 / 1556 1.0 / 2139 5.6	**17** W	0303 1.8 / 0838 4.9 / 1537 1.5 / 2113 5.0
3 W	0426 1.2 / 1001 5.5 / 1702 0.9 / 2234 5.7	**18** TH	0408 1.6 / 0942 5.1 / 1636 1.3 / 2211 5.3
4 TH	0527 1.1 / 1052 5.7 / 1757 0.8 / 2322 5.8	**19** F	0503 1.4 / 1035 5.3 / 1728 1.1 / 2259 5.5
5 F	0618 0.9 / 1137 5.9 / 1844 0.8	**20** SA	0552 1.2 / 1120 5.6 / 1814 0.9 / 2340 5.7
6 SA	0004 5.9 / 0703 0.8 / 1219 6.0 / 1927 0.8	**21** SU	0637 0.9 / 1200 5.8 / 1858 0.8
7 SU	0044 6.0 / 0745 0.8 / 1301 6.0 / 2006 0.8	**22** M ●	0019 5.9 / 0721 0.7 / 1240 6.0 / 1942 0.7
8 M	0124 6.0 / 0824 0.7 / 1342 6.0 / 2044 0.9	**23** TU	0100 6.1 / 0805 0.6 / 1322 6.2 / 2027 0.6
9 TU	0203 5.9 / 0903 0.7 / 1422 6.0 / 2120 1.0	**24** W	0143 6.1 / 0850 0.5 / 1407 6.2 / 2112 0.6
10 W	0240 5.8 / 0940 0.8 / 1501 5.8 / 2155 1.1	**25** TH	0227 6.1 / 0937 0.5 / 1455 6.2 / 2158 0.7
11 TH	0316 5.7 / 1016 1.0 / 1539 5.6 / 2230 1.3	**26** F	0314 6.0 / 1023 0.5 / 1544 6.1 / 2245 0.8
12 F	0354 5.5 / 1052 1.1 / 1619 5.4 / 2307 1.5	**27** SA	0403 5.9 / 1112 0.6 / 1637 5.9 / 2334 1.0
13 SA	0436 5.3 / 1130 1.3 / 1705 5.2 / 2348 1.6	**28** SU ◐	0456 5.7 / 1206 0.8 / 1734 5.7
14 SU ◐	0526 5.1 / 1215 1.5 / 1759 5.0	**29** M	0030 1.2 / 0555 5.5 / 1307 1.0 / 1840 5.4
15 M	0038 1.8 / 0624 4.9 / 1312 1.6 / 1900 4.9	**30** TU	0135 1.4 / 0704 5.3 / 1415 1.1 / 1957 5.3
		31 W	0244 1.2 / 0824 5.2 / 1526 1.2 / 2110 5.3

Chart Datum: 2·69 metres below IGN Datum
HAT is 6·4 metres above Chart Datum

TIDES

DIEPPE

MEAN SPRING
AND NEAP CURVES

MEAN RANGES
Springs 8.5m
Neaps 4.9m

Factor

0.9
0.8
0.7
0.6
0.5
0.4
0.3
0.2
0.1

M.H.W.S.
M.H.W.N.

H.W.Hts.m.

M.L.W.N.
M.L.W.S.

L.W.Hts.m.

CHART DATUM

H.W.
+1ʰ +2ʰ +3ʰ +4ʰ +5ʰ +6ʰ L.W.
-1ʰ -2ʰ -3ʰ -4ʰ L.W.

TIME ZONE -0100
(French Standard Time)
Subtract 1 hour for UT
For French Summer Time add
ONE hour in **non-shaded areas**

LAT 49°56'N   LONG 1°05'E

TIMES AND HEIGHTS OF HIGH AND LOW WATERS

Dates in amber are **SPRINGS**
Dates in yellow are **NEAPS**

2014

JANUARY

Time m — Time m

Day	Time m	Time m	Time m	Time m	Day	Time m	Time m	Time m	Time m
1 W ●	0552 1.0	1117 9.4	1822 0.7	2345 9.4	**16** TH ○	0629 1.5	1154 8.8	1852 1.2	
2 TH	0646 0.7	1207 9.7	1916 0.4		**17** F	0014 8.8	0705 1.3	1227 8.9	1927 1.2
3 F	0035 9.7	0739 0.6	1256 9.8	2006 0.3	**18** SA	0047 8.9	0739 1.3	1300 8.9	1959 1.1
4 SA	0123 9.7	0827 0.6	1344 9.8	2053 0.4	**19** SU	0120 8.9	0810 1.3	1333 8.9	2029 1.2
5 SU	0211 9.6	0913 0.7	1431 9.5	2138 0.6	**20** M	0152 8.8	0840 1.4	1404 8.8	2059 1.3
6 M	0257 9.3	0957 1.0	1518 9.2	2220 1.0	**21** TU	0224 8.7	0911 1.5	1437 8.6	2129 1.5
7 TU	0343 8.9	1041 1.4	1605 8.6	2302 1.5	**22** W	0257 8.5	0944 1.7	1511 8.3	2202 1.8
8 W ☽	0431 8.4	1127 1.9	1657 8.1	2349 2.0	**23** TH	0333 8.2	1022 2.0	1551 8.0	2242 2.0
9 TH	0526 7.9	1223 2.4	1758 7.6		**24** F ☽	0416 7.9	1108 2.2	1639 7.7	2332 2.3
10 F	0047 2.4	0632 7.5	1329 2.5	1912 7.3	**25** SA	0511 7.6	1207 2.4	1745 7.4	
11 SA	0158 2.6	0750 7.4	1443 2.5	2030 7.4	**26** SU	0038 2.5	0629 7.5	1321 2.5	1912 7.4
12 SU	0312 2.5	0902 7.6	1553 2.2	2134 7.7	**27** M	0202 2.4	0755 7.7	1448 2.2	2034 7.8
13 M	0417 2.2	0958 8.0	1649 1.9	2224 8.0	**28** TU	0325 2.0	0907 8.2	1604 1.6	2141 8.4
14 TU	0508 1.9	1042 8.3	1735 1.6	2305 8.4	**29** W	0434 1.5	1009 8.8	1709 1.1	2240 9.0
15 W	0551 1.7	1117 8.6	1815 1.4	2341 8.6	**30** TH ●	0537 1.0	1104 9.3	1810 0.6	2333 9.4
					31 F	0635 0.7	1156 9.7	1905 0.3	

FEBRUARY

Time m — Time m

Day	Time m	Time m	Time m	Time m	Day	Time m	Time m	Time m	Time m
1 SA	0023 9.7	0728 0.4	1244 9.9	1955 0.1	**16** SU	0026 9.0	0719 1.1	1240 9.1	1939 0.9
2 SU	0109 9.9	0816 0.3	1329 10.0	2040 0.1	**17** M	0058 9.1	0751 1.0	1311 9.1	2010 0.9
3 M	0153 9.8	0858 0.5	1413 9.8	2120 0.4	**18** TU	0129 9.1	0821 1.0	1343 9.1	2039 1.0
4 TU	0235 9.5	0937 0.8	1454 9.4	2155 0.8	**19** W	0201 9.0	0852 1.1	1415 8.9	2109 1.1
5 W	0315 9.1	1013 1.2	1536 8.8	2229 1.4	**20** TH	0233 8.8	0924 1.3	1449 8.7	2140 1.4
6 TH ☽	0356 8.5	1050 1.7	1620 8.2	2306 2.0	**21** F	0307 8.6	0958 1.6	1527 8.3	2216 1.8
7 F	0441 7.9	1135 2.3	1712 7.5	2355 2.5	**22** SA ☽	0347 8.2	1040 1.9	1612 7.9	2302 2.1
8 SA	0539 7.3	1236 2.7	1822 6.9		**23** SU	0438 7.8	1135 2.2	1713 7.5	
9 SU	0104 2.9	0700 6.9	1355 2.9	1953 6.8	**24** M	0006 2.5	0553 7.4	1249 2.4	1843 7.3
10 M	0229 3.0	0830 7.1	1518 2.6	2110 7.2	**25** TU	0132 2.5	0729 7.5	1423 2.2	2015 7.6
11 TU	0347 2.6	0935 7.5	1624 2.2	2203 7.7	**26** W	0304 2.1	0850 8.0	1546 1.7	2128 8.3
12 W	0445 2.1	1021 8.0	1714 1.7	2244 8.2	**27** TH	0418 1.5	0956 8.7	1655 1.1	2228 8.9
13 TH	0531 1.7	1059 8.4	1756 1.4	2320 8.5	**28** F	0523 1.0	1052 9.3	1756 0.6	2320 9.4
14 F	0610 1.4	1134 8.7	1833 1.2	2353 8.8					
15 SA ○	0646 1.2	1207 8.9	1907 1.0						

MARCH

Time m — Time m

Day	Time m	Time m	Time m	Time m	Day	Time m	Time m	Time m	Time m
1 SA ●	0621 0.6	1141 9.7	1850 0.2		**16** SU ○	0619 1.2	1142 8.9	1841 0.9	
2 SU	0006 9.7	0712 0.3	1227 9.9	1937 0.1	**17** M	0000 9.0	0654 1.0	1215 9.1	1914 0.8
3 M	0050 9.9	0757 0.3	1309 9.9	2018 0.2	**18** TU	0032 9.2	0727 0.9	1248 9.2	1947 0.8
4 TU	0130 9.8	0836 0.4	1350 9.6	2054 0.4	**19** W	0105 9.3	0800 0.8	1321 9.2	2019 0.8
5 W	0209 9.6	0911 0.7	1428 9.4	2126 0.8	**20** TH	0137 9.2	0833 0.8	1355 9.1	2050 1.0
6 TH	0246 9.1	0942 1.1	1506 8.9	2155 1.3	**21** F	0211 9.1	0906 1.0	1431 8.9	2123 1.2
7 F	0322 8.6	1014 1.6	1545 8.2	2228 1.9	**22** SA	0248 8.8	0942 1.3	1510 8.5	2159 1.6
8 SA ☽	0400 7.9	1053 2.2	1629 7.5	2311 2.6	**23** SU	0329 8.4	1024 1.7	1556 8.0	2246 2.0
9 SU	0449 7.2	1147 2.8	1732 6.8		**24** M ☽	0420 7.9	1119 2.1	1659 7.5	2350 2.4
10 M	0014 3.1	0604 6.7	1304 3.1	1904 6.6	**25** TU	0536 7.4	1232 2.3	1830 7.3	
11 TU	0141 3.2	0745 6.7	1433 2.9	2034 6.9	**26** W	0117 2.5	0712 7.5	1407 2.2	2001 7.7
12 W	0308 2.8	0901 7.2	1547 2.4	2131 7.5	**27** TH	0248 2.1	0834 8.0	1530 1.6	2113 8.3
13 TH	0412 2.3	0951 7.7	1642 1.9	2214 8.0	**28** F	0403 1.5	0941 8.6	1638 1.1	2211 8.9
14 F	0500 1.8	1031 8.3	1726 1.4	2251 8.5	**29** SA	0507 1.0	1035 9.2	1738 0.7	2301 9.3
15 SA	0542 1.4	1107 8.7	1805 1.2	2326 8.8	**30** SU ●	0603 0.7	1123 9.5	1829 0.4	2345 9.6
					31 M	0651 0.5	1206 9.7	1913 0.3	

APRIL

Time m — Time m

Day	Time m	Time m	Time m	Time m	Day	Time m	Time m	Time m	Time m
1 TU	0026 9.7	0733 0.4	1247 9.7	1951 0.4	**16** W	0005 9.2	0702 0.8	1223 9.2	1922 0.8
2 W	0105 9.6	0810 0.5	1325 9.6	2026 0.6	**17** TH	0040 9.3	0739 0.7	1259 9.3	1958 0.8
3 TH	0141 9.4	0843 0.7	1402 9.3	2056 1.0	**18** F	0116 9.3	0816 0.7	1337 9.3	2033 0.9
4 F	0217 9.1	0913 1.1	1438 8.8	2125 1.4	**19** SA	0154 9.2	0853 0.9	1417 9.0	2110 1.1
5 SA	0251 8.6	0944 1.6	1515 8.2	2157 1.9	**20** SU	0234 8.9	0933 1.1	1500 8.7	2151 1.5
6 SU	0327 8.0	1019 2.1	1556 7.6	2236 2.5	**21** M	0319 8.5	1017 1.5	1551 8.2	2241 1.9
7 M	0411 7.3	1106 2.6	1649 7.0	2331 3.0	**22** TU ☽	0414 8.0	1113 1.9	1656 7.7	2344 2.2
8 TU	0513 6.8	1212 3.0	1808 6.6		**23** W	0529 7.6	1225 2.1	1819 7.6	
9 W	0049 3.2	0643 6.6	1338 3.0	1939 6.8	**24** TH	0107 2.3	0656 7.6	1352 2.0	1941 7.8
10 TH	0215 3.0	0808 6.9	1456 2.6	2045 7.3	**25** F	0231 2.0	0814 8.0	1509 1.6	2051 8.3
11 F	0324 2.5	0907 7.5	1556 2.1	2134 7.9	**26** SA	0342 1.5	0920 8.5	1615 1.2	2149 8.8
12 SA	0417 1.9	0953 8.0	1645 1.6	2216 8.4	**27** SU	0445 1.2	1014 9.1	1713 0.9	2238 9.1
13 SU	0503 1.5	1034 8.5	1728 1.3	2254 8.8	**28** M	0539 0.9	1101 9.2	1803 0.8	2322 9.3
14 M	0545 1.2	1111 8.8	1808 1.0	2330 9.0	**29** TU ●	0625 0.8	1144 9.3	1845 0.7	
15 TU ○	0624 1.0	1148 9.1	1846 0.9		**30** W	0002 9.4	0706 0.7	1224 9.3	1922 0.8

TIDES

Chart Datum: 4·43 metres below IGN Datum
HAT is 10·1 metres above Chart Datum

TIME ZONE -0100
(French Standard Time)
Subtract 1 hour for UT
For French Summer Time add
ONE hour in **non-shaded areas**

FRANCE – DIEPPE
LAT 49°56'N   LONG 1°05'E
TIMES AND HEIGHTS OF HIGH AND LOW WATERS

Dates in amber are **SPRINGS**
Dates in yellow are **NEAPS**

2014

MAY

Day	Time m	Time m	Time m	Time m
1 TH / **16** F	0040 9.3 / 0742 0.8 / 1301 9.3 / 1957 0.9	0017 9.3 / 0719 0.7 / 1241 9.3 / 1940 0.8		
2 F / **17** SA	0116 9.2 / 0817 0.9 / 1338 9.1 / 2030 1.1	0059 9.4 / 0802 0.6 / 1324 9.3 / 2021 0.8		
3 SA / **18** SU	0151 8.9 / 0849 1.2 / 1414 8.7 / 2101 1.5	0141 9.3 / 0844 0.7 / 1409 9.2 / 2103 1.0		
4 SU / **19** M	0226 8.6 / 0920 1.5 / 1451 8.3 / 2133 1.9	0227 9.1 / 0929 0.9 / 1456 8.9 / 2148 1.3		
5 M / **20** TU	0302 8.1 / 0953 2.0 / 1529 7.8 / 2209 2.3	0316 8.7 / 1016 1.2 / 1549 8.5 / 2240 1.6		
6 TU / **21** W	0341 7.6 / 1034 2.4 / 1615 7.3 / 2256 2.7	0412 8.3 / 1111 1.5 / 1651 8.1 / 2341 1.9		
7 W / **22** TH	0432 7.1 / 1127 2.7 / 1716 7.0 / ☽ 2357 3.0	0519 8.0 / 1217 1.8 / 1800 7.9		
8 TH / **23** F	0542 6.8 / 1237 2.8 / 1833 6.9	0052 2.0 / 0632 7.8 / 1330 1.8 / 1913 8.0		
9 F / **24** SA	0111 2.9 / 0702 6.9 / 1352 2.7 / 1947 7.2	0206 1.9 / 0746 8.0 / 1441 1.7 / 2023 8.2		
10 SA / **25** SU	0223 2.6 / 0812 7.3 / 1459 2.3 / 2045 7.7	0315 1.7 / 0854 8.2 / 1546 1.5 / 2123 8.5		
11 SU / **26** M	0325 2.1 / 0908 7.8 / 1556 1.8 / 2134 8.2	0418 1.4 / 0951 8.5 / 1645 1.3 / 2215 8.7		
12 M / **27** TU	0418 1.7 / 0955 8.3 / 1646 1.5 / 2217 8.6	0512 1.2 / 1040 8.8 / 1734 1.2 / 2300 8.9		
13 TU / **28** W	0506 1.3 / 1038 8.6 / 1732 1.2 / 2258 8.9	0559 1.1 / 1124 8.9 / 1817 1.2 / ● 2340 9.0		
14 W / **29** TH	0552 1.1 / 1119 8.9 / 1816 1.0 / ○ 2338 9.2	0640 1.1 / 1203 8.9 / 1855 1.0		
15 TH / **30** F	0636 0.8 / 1200 9.2 / 1858 0.8	0017 9.0 / 0718 1.0 / 1241 8.9 / 1932 1.2		
31 SA		0053 8.9 / 0754 1.1 / 1317 8.9 / 2007 1.3		

JUNE

Day	Time m	Time m
1 SU / **16** M	0129 8.8 / 0828 1.2 / 1353 8.7 / 2041 1.5	0132 9.5 / 0840 0.5 / 1401 9.4 / 2059 0.8
2 M / **17** TU	0205 8.6 / 0901 1.5 / 1430 8.4 / 2112 1.8	0220 9.3 / 0927 0.6 / 1450 9.2 / 2146 1.0
3 TU / **18** W	0240 8.3 / 0932 1.7 / 1506 8.1 / 2146 2.0	0310 9.1 / 1013 0.8 / 1541 8.9 / 2235 1.3
4 W / **19** TH	0317 7.9 / 1007 2.0 / 1545 7.7 / 2225 2.3	0402 8.7 / 1103 1.2 / 1634 8.5 / ☽ 2328 1.6
5 TH / **20** F	0358 7.5 / 1050 2.3 / 1632 7.4 / ☽ 2314 2.6	0459 8.3 / 1157 1.5 / 1733 8.2
6 F / **21** SA	0449 7.2 / 1143 2.5 / 1730 7.2	0028 1.8 / 0603 8.0 / 1259 1.8 / 1839 8.0
7 SA / **22** SU	0013 2.7 / 0554 7.1 / 1247 2.6 / 1840 7.2	0134 2.0 / 0713 7.8 / 1406 1.9 / 1949 7.9
8 SU / **23** M	0119 2.6 / 0708 7.2 / 1356 2.4 / 1949 7.5	0243 1.9 / 0825 7.9 / 1513 1.9 / 2056 8.1
9 M / **24** TU	0227 2.3 / 0816 7.5 / 1503 2.1 / 2048 7.9	0348 1.8 / 0929 8.1 / 1615 1.8 / 2153 8.3
10 TU / **25** W	0330 1.9 / 0914 8.0 / 1602 1.7 / 2140 8.4	0447 1.6 / 1022 8.3 / 1709 1.6 / 2241 8.5
11 W / **26** TH	0428 1.5 / 1005 8.4 / 1657 1.4 / 2227 8.8	0536 1.4 / 1107 8.5 / 1753 1.5 / 2322 8.6
12 TH / **27** F	0521 1.2 / 1053 8.8 / 1748 1.1 / 2313 9.1	0618 1.3 / 1147 8.7 / 1833 1.4 / ● 2359 8.7
13 F / **28** SA	0613 0.9 / 1140 9.1 / 1837 0.9 / ○ 2359 9.3	0657 1.2 / 1223 8.7 / 1911 1.3
14 SA / **29** SU	0703 0.7 / 1226 9.3 / 1925 0.7	0035 8.8 / 0734 1.2 / 1259 8.8 / 1948 1.3
15 SU / **30** M	0045 9.5 / 0752 0.5 / 1314 9.4 / 2013 0.7	0110 8.8 / 0810 1.2 / 1334 8.7 / 2022 1.4

JULY

Day	Time m	Time m
1 TU / **16** W	0144 8.7 / 0842 1.3 / 1408 8.6 / 2053 1.5	0209 9.6 / 0918 0.3 / 1436 9.5 / 2137 0.7
2 W / **17** TH	0218 8.5 / 0912 1.5 / 1442 8.4 / 2123 1.7	0255 9.4 / 1002 0.6 / 1522 9.2 / 2220 1.0
3 TH / **18** F	0251 8.3 / 0943 1.7 / 1516 8.1 / 2157 1.9	0342 9.0 / 1044 1.0 / 1609 8.8 / 2305 1.4
4 F / **19** SA	0327 8.0 / 1018 2.0 / 1553 7.9 / 2238 2.2	0432 8.5 / 1129 1.5 / 1700 8.3 / ☽ 2356 1.8
5 SA / **20** SU	0408 7.7 / 1101 2.2 / 1638 7.6 / ☽ 2326 2.4	0528 7.9 / 1222 2.0 / 1800 7.8
6 SU / **21** M	0458 7.4 / 1154 2.4 / 1735 7.4	0057 2.2 / 0636 7.5 / 1327 2.3 / 1912 7.6
7 M / **22** TU	0024 2.5 / 0603 7.3 / 1257 2.5 / 1847 7.4	0208 2.3 / 0755 7.4 / 1440 2.4 / 2029 7.6
8 TU / **23** W	0132 2.4 / 0721 7.3 / 1411 2.4 / 2001 7.7	0320 2.2 / 0909 7.6 / 1549 2.2 / 2134 7.9
9 W / **24** TH	0246 2.1 / 0834 7.7 / 1523 2.0 / 2105 8.1	0424 1.9 / 1006 8.0 / 1648 1.9 / 2225 8.2
10 TH / **25** F	0355 1.7 / 0935 8.2 / 1627 1.5 / 2201 8.6	0517 1.6 / 1052 8.3 / 1735 1.7 / 2307 8.5
11 F / **26** SA	0456 1.2 / 1031 8.7 / 1725 1.2 / 2253 9.0	0601 1.4 / 1131 8.5 / 1816 1.5 / ● 2343 8.7
12 SA / **27** SU	0554 0.9 / 1123 9.1 / 1820 0.9 / ○ 2344 9.4	0640 1.3 / 1205 8.7 / 1853 1.3
13 SU / **28** M	0650 0.6 / 1213 9.4 / 1914 0.6	0016 8.8 / 0716 1.2 / 1239 8.8 / 1928 1.3
14 M / **29** TU	0033 9.6 / 0743 0.4 / 1302 9.6 / 2005 0.5	0049 8.9 / 0750 1.1 / 1311 8.9 / 2001 1.3
15 TU / **30** W	0122 9.7 / 0833 0.3 / 1350 9.7 / 2052 0.5	0122 8.9 / 0821 1.2 / 1344 8.8 / 2031 1.3
31 TH		0154 8.8 / 0849 1.3 / 1415 8.7 / 2100 1.5

AUGUST

Day	Time m	Time m
1 F / **16** SA	0225 8.6 / 0918 1.5 / 1446 8.5 / 2131 1.6	0317 9.1 / 1017 1.1 / 1540 8.9 / 2235 1.4
2 SA / **17** SU	0258 8.3 / 0949 1.7 / 1520 8.3 / 2206 1.9	0401 8.5 / 1055 1.7 / 1625 8.3 / ☽ 2319 2.0
3 SU / **18** M	0334 8.0 / 1026 2.0 / 1559 7.9 / 2248 2.2	0452 7.8 / 1142 2.2 / 1719 7.6
4 M / **19** TU	0418 7.7 / 1112 2.3 / 1648 7.6 / ☽ 2340 2.4	0016 2.5 / 0557 7.2 / 1246 2.5 / 1832 7.2
5 TU / **20** W	0514 7.4 / 1211 2.5 / 1754 7.4	0130 2.7 / 0723 7.0 / 1406 2.8 / 2001 7.2
6 W / **21** TH	0047 2.5 / 0633 7.3 / 1328 2.6 / 1919 7.5	0251 2.6 / 0848 7.3 / 1524 2.5 / 2114 7.5
7 TH / **22** F	0210 2.3 / 0801 7.5 / 1452 2.2 / 2036 7.9	0402 2.2 / 0947 7.8 / 1627 2.1 / 2206 8.0
8 F / **23** SA	0329 1.8 / 0912 8.1 / 1603 1.7 / 2140 8.5	0456 1.8 / 1032 8.2 / 1715 1.7 / 2246 8.4
9 SA / **24** SU	0436 1.3 / 1013 8.7 / 1706 1.2 / 2237 9.1	0540 1.5 / 1109 8.6 / 1755 1.5 / 2321 8.7
10 SU / **25** M	0538 0.8 / 1108 9.2 / 1806 0.8 / ○ 2330 9.5	0618 1.3 / 1142 8.8 / 1831 1.4 / ● 2354 8.9
11 M / **26** TU	0637 0.5 / 1159 9.6 / 1902 0.5	0653 1.1 / 1214 8.9 / 1905 1.2
12 TU / **27** W	0019 9.8 / 0730 0.2 / 1247 9.8 / 1952 0.4	0026 9.0 / 0726 1.1 / 1246 9.0 / 1937 1.2
13 W / **28** TH	0106 9.9 / 0818 0.1 / 1332 9.9 / 2037 0.4	0057 8.9 / 0756 1.1 / 1317 9.0 / 2007 1.2
14 TH / **29** F	0151 9.8 / 0901 0.2 / 1415 9.7 / 2119 0.6	0128 8.9 / 0825 1.1 / 1347 9.0 / 2036 1.3
15 F / **30** SA	0234 9.6 / 0940 0.6 / 1457 9.4 / 2157 0.9	0159 8.9 / 0853 1.3 / 1418 8.8 / 2107 1.4
31 SU		0231 8.6 / 0923 1.6 / 1451 8.5 / 2139 1.7

Chart Datum: 4·43 metres below IGN Datum
HAT is 10·1 metres above Chart Datum

TIME ZONE -0100
(French Standard Time)
Subtract 1 hour for UT
For French Summer Time add
ONE hour in **non-shaded areas**

FRANCE – DIEPPE

LAT 49°56'N   LONG 1°05'E

TIMES AND HEIGHTS OF HIGH AND LOW WATERS

Dates in amber are **SPRINGS**
Dates in yellow are **NEAPS**

2014

SEPTEMBER

Time m	Time m
1 M 0307 8.3 / 0957 1.9 / 1528 8.2 / 2218 2.0	**16** TU 0416 7.7 / 1103 2.5 / 1639 7.5 / ☽ 2335 2.7
2 TU 0348 7.9 / 1040 2.3 / 1614 8.2 / ☽ 2308 2.3	**17** W 0517 7.1 / 1204 3.0 / 1748 7.0
3 W 0443 7.5 / 1138 2.6 / 1718 7.4	**18** TH 0048 3.0 / 0643 6.8 / 1328 3.2 / 1922 6.8
4 TH 0015 2.6 / 0602 7.2 / 1257 2.7 / 1849 7.4	**19** F 0215 2.9 / 0816 7.0 / 1451 2.8 / 2043 7.2
5 F 0143 2.5 / 0739 7.5 / 1430 2.4 / 2015 7.8	**20** SA 0329 2.5 / 0918 7.6 / 1556 2.3 / 2136 7.8
6 SA 0310 1.9 / 0855 8.1 / 1546 1.7 / 2123 8.5	**21** SU 0425 2.0 / 1002 8.1 / 1645 1.8 / 2217 8.3
7 SU 0420 1.3 / 0958 8.8 / 1650 1.2 / 2222 9.1	**22** M 0510 1.6 / 1039 8.6 / 1726 1.5 / 2253 8.6
8 M 0522 0.8 / 1052 9.3 / 1750 0.7 / 2313 9.6	**23** TU 0549 1.3 / 1113 8.9 / 1803 1.3 / 2327 8.9
9 TU 0620 0.4 / 1141 9.7 / 1844 0.5 / ○	**24** W 0624 1.1 / 1146 9.0 / 1838 1.2 / ● 2359 9.0
10 W 0001 9.9 / 0711 0.2 / 1227 9.9 / 1933 0.3	**25** TH 0658 1.1 / 1218 9.1 / 1910 1.1
11 TH 0046 10.0 / 0756 0.2 / 1309 9.9 / 2016 0.4	**26** F 0031 9.1 / 0729 1.0 / 1249 9.2 / 1942 1.1
12 F 0128 9.9 / 0837 0.6 / 1350 9.7 / 2055 0.8	**27** SA 0102 9.1 / 0800 1.1 / 1320 9.1 / 2014 1.1
13 SA 0209 9.6 / 0913 0.8 / 1430 9.4 / 2129 1.0	**28** SU 0135 9.0 / 0830 1.2 / 1353 9.0 / 2046 1.3
14 SU 0249 9.1 / 0946 1.3 / 1509 8.8 / 2203 1.5	**29** M 0209 8.8 / 0902 1.5 / 1428 8.7 / 2119 1.5
15 M 0330 8.4 / 1020 1.9 / 1550 8.2 / 2242 2.1	**30** TU 0247 8.5 / 0937 1.8 / 1506 8.4 / 2158 1.9

OCTOBER

Time m	Time m
1 W 0329 8.1 / 1020 2.2 / 1553 7.9 / ☽ 2248 2.3	**16** TH 0437 7.2 / 1123 3.1 / 1703 7.0
2 TH 0425 7.6 / 1119 2.6 / 1658 7.5 / 2355 2.5	**17** F 0000 3.1 / 0552 6.8 / 1240 3.3 / 1826 6.7
3 F 0546 7.3 / 1239 2.7 / 1831 7.4	**18** SA 0124 3.1 / 0722 6.9 / 1404 3.1 / 1952 7.0
4 SA 0125 2.5 / 0722 7.5 / 1413 2.4 / 1957 7.8	**19** SU 0241 2.8 / 0832 7.3 / 1512 2.6 / 2053 7.5
5 SU 0253 1.9 / 0838 8.2 / 1529 1.7 / 2106 8.5	**20** M 0341 2.2 / 0922 7.9 / 1605 2.1 / 2139 8.0
6 M 0403 1.3 / 0940 8.8 / 1633 1.2 / 2204 9.1	**21** TU 0430 1.8 / 1003 8.4 / 1650 1.6 / 2219 8.5
7 TU 0504 0.8 / 1033 9.4 / 1731 0.8 / 2254 9.6	**22** W 0512 1.5 / 1040 8.8 / 1730 1.4 / 2256 8.8
8 W 0558 0.5 / 1120 9.7 / 1823 0.6 / ○ 2341 9.8	**23** TH 0551 1.2 / 1115 9.0 / 1808 1.2 / 2331 9.0
9 TH 0647 0.4 / 1204 9.8 / 1909 0.5	**24** F 0627 1.1 / 1149 9.2 / 1843 1.1
10 F 0024 9.8 / 0730 0.5 / 1245 9.8 / 1951 0.6	**25** SA 0005 9.1 / 0702 1.1 / 1222 9.3 / 1918 1.0
11 SA 0105 9.7 / 0809 0.7 / 1324 9.6 / 2028 0.8	**26** SU 0039 9.2 / 0736 1.1 / 1257 9.3 / 1954 1.0
12 SU 0144 9.4 / 0843 1.0 / 1402 9.3 / 2101 1.1	**27** M 0115 9.2 / 0811 1.2 / 1333 9.2 / 2030 1.1
13 M 0223 9.0 / 0915 1.5 / 1439 8.8 / 2134 1.6	**28** TU 0153 9.0 / 0847 1.4 / 1411 8.9 / 2107 1.4
14 TU 0302 8.4 / 0949 2.0 / 1518 8.2 / 2209 2.2	**29** W 0234 8.7 / 0926 1.7 / 1453 8.5 / 2149 1.7
15 W 0344 7.8 / 1028 2.6 / 1603 7.5 / ☽ 2255 2.7	**30** TH 0320 8.3 / 1012 2.1 / 1543 8.1 / 2240 2.1
	31 F 0418 7.8 / 1110 2.4 / 1650 7.7 / ☽ 2345 2.3

NOVEMBER

Time m	Time m
1 SA 0536 7.6 / 1227 2.6 / 1815 7.6	**16** SU 0018 3.1 / 0613 6.9 / 1258 3.2 / 1844 6.9
2 SU 0109 2.3 / 0702 7.7 / 1355 2.3 / 1936 7.9	**17** M 0135 3.0 / 0729 7.1 / 1412 2.9 / 1956 7.2
3 M 0233 1.9 / 0816 8.2 / 1509 1.8 / 2045 8.4	**18** TU 0245 2.6 / 0831 7.6 / 1514 2.4 / 2053 7.7
4 TU 0341 1.4 / 0918 8.8 / 1613 1.3 / 2143 8.9	**19** W 0342 2.2 / 0920 8.1 / 1606 1.9 / 2140 8.2
5 W 0441 1.1 / 1011 9.2 / 1709 1.0 / 2234 9.3	**20** TH 0431 1.8 / 1003 8.6 / 1653 1.6 / 2223 8.6
6 TH 0534 0.9 / 1058 9.5 / 1800 0.8 / ○ 2320 9.5	**21** F 0516 1.5 / 1043 8.9 / 1736 1.3 / 2302 8.9
7 F 0621 0.6 / 1141 9.6 / 1845 0.7	**22** SA 0557 1.3 / 1121 9.1 / 1818 1.1 / ● 2341 9.1
8 SA 0002 9.6 / 0703 0.8 / 1221 9.6 / 1925 0.8	**23** SU 0637 1.1 / 1159 9.3 / 1858 1.0
9 SU 0043 9.4 / 0741 1.0 / 1300 9.4 / 2002 0.9	**24** M 0020 9.2 / 0717 1.1 / 1238 9.4 / 1939 0.9
10 M 0121 9.2 / 0817 1.2 / 1337 9.2 / 2036 1.2	**25** TU 0100 9.3 / 0757 1.1 / 1319 9.3 / 2020 0.9
11 TU 0159 8.9 / 0850 1.5 / 1414 8.8 / 2109 1.6	**26** W 0143 9.2 / 0838 1.2 / 1402 9.1 / 2102 1.1
12 W 0237 8.5 / 0923 2.0 / 1452 8.3 / 2143 2.0	**27** TH 0227 8.9 / 0921 1.5 / 1448 8.8 / 2147 1.4
13 TH 0317 8.0 / 0959 2.4 / 1532 7.7 / 2221 2.5	**28** F 0317 8.6 / 1009 1.8 / 1540 8.4 / 2236 1.7
14 F 0402 7.5 / 1044 2.8 / 1621 7.2 / ☽ 2311 2.9	**29** SA 0413 8.2 / 1105 2.1 / 1641 8.1 / ☽ 2336 2.0
15 SA 0459 7.1 / 1144 3.1 / 1726 6.9	**30** SU 0520 8.0 / 1213 2.2 / 1753 7.9

DECEMBER

Time m	Time m
1 M 0048 2.1 / 0634 7.9 / 1330 2.2 / 1908 7.9	**16** TU 0019 2.9 / 0614 7.1 / 1256 2.9 / 1845 7.0
2 TU 0204 2.0 / 0747 8.1 / 1443 1.9 / 2019 8.2	**17** W 0130 2.8 / 0729 7.3 / 1409 2.7 / 1958 7.3
3 W 0314 1.7 / 0852 8.5 / 1549 1.6 / 2121 8.5	**18** TH 0242 2.6 / 0832 7.7 / 1516 2.3 / 2058 7.7
4 TH 0416 1.5 / 0949 8.8 / 1647 1.3 / 2215 8.8	**19** F 0345 2.1 / 0925 8.2 / 1614 1.9 / 2149 8.2
5 F 0511 1.3 / 1038 9.1 / 1738 1.1 / 2302 9.0	**20** SA 0440 1.7 / 1012 8.6 / 1706 1.4 / 2236 8.6
6 SA 0558 1.2 / 1122 9.2 / 1823 1.0 / ○ 2345 9.1	**21** SU 0529 1.4 / 1056 9.0 / 1754 1.1 / 2320 9.0
7 SU 0639 1.2 / 1202 9.2 / 1903 1.0	**22** M 0616 1.1 / 1140 9.3 / 1842 0.9 / ●
8 M 0024 9.1 / 0718 1.2 / 1240 9.2 / 1940 1.0	**23** TU 0004 9.3 / 0703 0.9 / 1224 9.5 / 1928 0.7
9 TU 0102 9.1 / 0754 1.3 / 1317 9.1 / 2016 1.2	**24** W 0049 9.4 / 0749 0.9 / 1309 9.6 / 2014 0.6
10 W 0139 8.9 / 0830 1.5 / 1353 8.8 / 2050 1.4	**25** TH 0135 9.4 / 0834 0.9 / 1355 9.5 / 2059 0.7
11 TH 0215 8.6 / 0902 1.8 / 1429 8.5 / 2121 1.8	**26** F 0221 9.3 / 0919 1.0 / 1442 9.3 / 2144 0.9
12 F 0252 8.3 / 0934 2.1 / 1505 8.1 / 2153 2.1	**27** SA 0309 9.0 / 1005 1.3 / 1531 8.9 / 2230 1.2
13 SA 0329 7.9 / 1010 2.4 / 1544 7.7 / 2231 2.4	**28** SU 0400 8.7 / 1054 1.6 / 1624 8.5 / ☽ 2320 1.6
14 SU 0412 7.6 / 1055 2.7 / 1630 7.3 / 2319 2.7	**29** M 0456 8.3 / 1151 1.9 / 1725 8.1
15 M 0505 7.2 / 1150 2.9 / 1730 7.0	**30** TU 0018 1.9 / 0600 8.0 / 1257 2.1 / 1835 7.8
	31 W 0128 2.1 / 0713 7.9 / 1411 2.1 / 1950 7.8

Chart Datum: 4·43 metres below IGN Datum
HAT is 10·1 metres above Chart Datum

TIDES

LE HAVRE

MEAN SPRING
AND NEAP CURVES

MEAN RANGES
Springs 6.7m
Neaps 3.8m

Factor

0.9 0.8 0.7 0.6 0.5 0.4 0.3 0.2 0.1

L.W +6ʰ +5ʰ +4ʰ +3ʰ +2ʰ +1ʰ H.W. -1ʰ -2ʰ -3ʰ -4ʰ L.W

M.H.W.S.
M.H.W.N.

M.L.W.N.
M.L.W.S.

H.W.Hts.m.
L.W.Hts.m.

CHART DATUM

JANUARY

#	Time	m	#	Time	m
1 W ●	0502 / 1020 / 1732 / 2250	1.4 / 8.1 / 1.1 / 8.1	16 TH ○	0540 / 1053 / 1804 / 2318	1.9 / 7.7 / 1.6 / 7.6
2 TH	0557 / 1109 / 1827 / 2338	1.1 / 8.3 / 0.8 / 8.2	17 F	0617 / 1125 / 1839 / 2350	1.8 / 7.7 / 1.5 / 7.6
3 F	0650 / 1156 / 1918	1.0 / 8.4 / 0.7	18 SA	0651 / 1157 / 1911	1.7 / 7.8 / 1.5
4 SA	0026 / 0740 / 1244 / 2006	8.3 / 1.0 / 8.4 / 0.7	19 SU	0022 / 0723 / 1229 / 1942	7.6 / 1.7 / 7.8 / 1.6
5 SU	0113 / 0826 / 1330 / 2050	8.2 / 1.1 / 8.2 / 1.0	20 M	0055 / 0754 / 1302 / 2012	7.6 / 1.8 / 7.7 / 1.7
6 M	0200 / 0910 / 1417 / 2132	8.0 / 1.4 / 7.9 / 1.4	21 TU	0128 / 0826 / 1337 / 2043	7.5 / 1.9 / 7.5 / 1.9
7 TU	0248 / 0953 / 1505 / 2214	7.7 / 1.9 / 7.5 / 1.9	22 W	0204 / 0858 / 1414 / 2116	7.4 / 2.1 / 7.3 / 2.1
8 W ◐	0338 / 1038 / 1559 / 2300	7.3 / 2.3 / 7.1 / 2.4	23 TH	0243 / 0935 / 1456 / 2154	7.1 / 2.4 / 7.0 / 2.4
9 TH	0436 / 1131 / 1705 / 2356	7.0 / 2.7 / 6.8 / 2.8	24 F ◑	0327 / 1019 / 1547 / 2242	6.9 / 2.7 / 6.8 / 2.7
10 F	0545 / 1114 / 1820 / 2345	6.8 / 2.8 / 6.7 / 2.9	25 SA	0425 / 1118 / 1655	6.8 / 2.8 / 6.7
11 SA	0104 / 0658 / 1349 / 1937	2.9 / 6.8 / 2.9 / 6.7	26 SU	0542 / 1226 / 1821	6.7 / 2.9 / 6.7
12 SU	0217 / 0807 / 1458 / 2042	2.9 / 6.9 / 2.6 / 6.9	27 M	0112 / 0705 / 1402 / 1946	2.8 / 6.9 / 2.6 / 7.0
13 M	0322 / 0901 / 1557 / 2131	2.6 / 7.1 / 2.3 / 7.2	28 TU	0241 / 0817 / 1517 / 2052	2.4 / 7.3 / 2.0 / 7.4
14 TU	0416 / 0944 / 1644 / 2211	2.3 / 7.4 / 2.0 / 7.4	29 W	0347 / 0916 / 1620 / 2147	1.9 / 7.7 / 1.5 / 7.8
15 W	0500 / 1020 / 1726 / 2245	2.1 / 7.5 / 1.6 / 7.5	30 TH ●	0449 / 1007 / 1722 / 2237	1.4 / 8.1 / 1.0 / 8.1
			31 F	0550 / 1055 / 1819 / 2324	1.0 / 8.3 / 0.7 / 8.3

FEBRUARY

#	Time	m	#	Time	m
1 SA	0643 / 1142 / 1909	0.8 / 8.4 / 0.5	16 SU	0633 / 1137 / 1852	1.5 / 7.8 / 1.3
2 SU	0010 / 0730 / 1227 / 1954	8.3 / 0.7 / 8.4 / 0.5	17 M	0000 / 0704 / 1210 / 1922	7.7 / 1.5 / 7.8 / 1.3
3 M	0055 / 0812 / 1312 / 2033	8.3 / 0.8 / 8.3 / 0.7	18 TU	0033 / 0734 / 1243 / 1952	7.8 / 1.4 / 7.8 / 1.4
4 TU	0138 / 0850 / 1354 / 2109	8.1 / 1.1 / 8.0 / 1.2	19 W	0106 / 0806 / 1318 / 2024	7.7 / 1.5 / 7.7 / 1.6
5 W	0220 / 0926 / 1436 / 2143	7.8 / 1.6 / 7.6 / 1.8	20 TH	0141 / 0839 / 1355 / 2056	7.6 / 1.7 / 7.5 / 1.9
6 TH ◑	0301 / 1002 / 1521 / 2219	7.4 / 2.1 / 7.1 / 2.4	21 F	0217 / 0913 / 1434 / 2131	7.3 / 2.0 / 7.2 / 2.2
7 F	0348 / 1045 / 1618 / 2306	7.0 / 2.7 / 6.7 / 2.9	22 SA ◑	0258 / 0953 / 1521 / 2214	7.0 / 2.4 / 6.9 / 2.6
8 SA	0451 / 1143 / 1737	6.6 / 3.1 / 6.4	23 SU	0351 / 1043 / 1627 / 2314	6.8 / 2.7 / 6.6 / 2.9
9 SU	0013 / 0613 / 1301 / 1907	3.3 / 6.5 / 3.2 / 6.4	24 M	0509 / 1154 / 1759	6.6 / 2.9 / 6.6
10 M	0136 / 0710 / 1424 / 2024	3.3 / 6.5 / 3.0 / 6.6	25 TU	0045 / 0643 / 1339 / 1932	2.9 / 6.8 / 2.6 / 6.9
11 TU	0254 / 0843 / 1532 / 2115	3.0 / 6.8 / 2.6 / 6.9	26 W	0221 / 0802 / 1458 / 2040	2.5 / 7.2 / 2.1 / 7.3
12 W	0355 / 0927 / 1625 / 2153	2.5 / 7.1 / 2.1 / 7.2	27 TH	0332 / 0901 / 1606 / 2134	1.9 / 7.6 / 1.5 / 7.8
13 TH	0443 / 1002 / 1708 / 2226	2.1 / 7.4 / 1.8 / 7.5	28 F	0438 / 0952 / 1711 / 2222	1.4 / 8.0 / 1.0 / 8.0
14 F	0524 / 1034 / 1746 / 2257	1.8 / 7.6 / 1.5 / 7.6			
15 SA ○	0600 / 1105 / 1821 / 2328	1.6 / 7.7 / 1.4 / 7.7			

MARCH

#	Time	m	#	Time	m
1 SA ●	0539 / 1039 / 1806 / 2307	1.0 / 8.2 / 0.6 / 8.2	16 SU ○	0535 / 1041 / 1755 / 2302	1.6 / 7.7 / 1.4 / 7.7
2 SU	0629 / 1124 / 1852 / 2350	0.7 / 8.3 / 0.4 / 8.3	17 M	0609 / 1114 / 1827 / 2335	1.4 / 7.8 / 1.3 / 7.8
3 M	0712 / 1207 / 1933	0.6 / 8.4 / 0.5	18 TU	0640 / 1148 / 1858	1.3 / 7.8 / 1.2
4 TU	0032 / 0750 / 1249 / 2009	8.2 / 0.7 / 8.2 / 0.8	19 W	0009 / 0712 / 1223 / 1930	7.9 / 1.2 / 7.9 / 1.2
5 W	0112 / 0825 / 1329 / 2041	8.1 / 1.0 / 8.0 / 1.2	20 TH	0043 / 0746 / 1259 / 2003	7.8 / 1.3 / 7.8 / 1.4
6 TH	0149 / 0857 / 1407 / 2111	7.8 / 1.5 / 7.6 / 1.8	21 F	0119 / 0820 / 1338 / 2037	7.7 / 1.5 / 7.6 / 1.7
7 F	0226 / 0928 / 1447 / 2141	7.4 / 2.1 / 7.1 / 2.4	22 SA	0157 / 0855 / 1419 / 2112	7.5 / 1.8 / 7.3 / 2.1
8 SA ◑	0305 / 1003 / 1536 / 2222	7.0 / 2.6 / 6.6 / 3.0	23 SU	0239 / 0934 / 1508 / 2156	7.2 / 2.2 / 7.0 / 2.5
9 SU	0359 / 1053 / 1652 / 2325	6.5 / 3.1 / 6.3 / 3.4	24 M ◑	0333 / 1023 / 1614 / 2256	6.9 / 2.5 / 6.7 / 2.9
10 M	0523 / 1210 / 1825	6.2 / 3.4 / 6.1	25 TU	0450 / 1136 / 1748	6.7 / 2.8 / 6.6
11 TU	0048 / 0654 / 1339 / 1952	3.5 / 6.3 / 3.2 / 6.4	26 W	0033 / 0627 / 1322 / 1918	2.9 / 6.8 / 2.6 / 6.9
12 W	0218 / 0811 / 1457 / 2047	3.2 / 6.5 / 2.8 / 6.8	27 TH	0204 / 0744 / 1440 / 2023	2.5 / 7.1 / 2.1 / 7.3
13 TH	0325 / 0859 / 1554 / 2125	2.7 / 6.9 / 2.3 / 7.1	28 F	0315 / 0843 / 1550 / 2115	1.9 / 7.5 / 1.5 / 7.7
14 F	0415 / 0935 / 1640 / 2158	2.2 / 7.2 / 1.9 / 7.4	29 SA	0423 / 0933 / 1654 / 2202	1.4 / 7.8 / 1.1 / 7.9
15 SA	0458 / 1008 / 1720 / 2230	1.9 / 7.5 / 1.6 / 7.6	30 SU ●	0520 / 1019 / 1746 / 2245	1.1 / 8.0 / 0.8 / 8.1
			31 M	0608 / 1103 / 1829 / 2327	0.8 / 8.1 / 0.7 / 8.1

APRIL

#	Time	m	#	Time	m
1 TU	0648 / 1145 / 1907	0.8 / 8.1 / 0.8	16 W	0614 / 1124 / 1832 / 2344	1.3 / 7.8 / 1.2 / 7.9
2 W	0006 / 0724 / 1225 / 1940	8.1 / 0.9 / 8.0 / 1.0	17 TH	0650 / 1202 / 1908	1.2 / 7.9 / 1.2
3 TH	0044 / 0757 / 1303 / 2011	7.9 / 1.0 / 7.8 / 1.4	18 F	0021 / 0727 / 1242 / 1945	7.9 / 1.2 / 7.8 / 1.4
4 F	0119 / 0827 / 1340 / 2040	7.7 / 1.5 / 7.5 / 1.9	19 SA	0101 / 0804 / 1324 / 2021	7.8 / 1.3 / 7.7 / 1.6
5 SA	0154 / 0857 / 1418 / 2110	7.4 / 2.0 / 7.1 / 2.4	20 SU	0142 / 0841 / 1410 / 2059	7.6 / 1.6 / 7.4 / 2.0
6 SU	0229 / 0929 / 1501 / 2147	7.0 / 2.5 / 6.7 / 2.9	21 M	0228 / 0921 / 1501 / 2145	7.3 / 2.0 / 7.1 / 2.4
7 M ◑	0314 / 1014 / 1605 / 2244	6.6 / 3.0 / 6.3 / 3.4	22 TU ◑	0323 / 1013 / 1607 / 2249	7.0 / 2.3 / 6.9 / 2.7
8 TU	0427 / 1122 / 1734 / 2359	6.2 / 3.3 / 6.2 / 3.6	23 W	0438 / 1129 / 1735	6.8 / 2.6 / 6.8
9 W	0558 / 1242 / 1854	6.1 / 3.3 / 6.3	24 TH	0023 / 0606 / 1303 / 1856	2.8 / 6.8 / 2.4 / 7.0
10 TH	0123 / 0714 / 1404 / 1959	3.4 / 6.3 / 3.0 / 6.6	25 F	0144 / 0720 / 1417 / 2000	2.4 / 7.1 / 2.1 / 7.3
11 F	0237 / 0813 / 1508 / 2044	2.9 / 6.7 / 2.5 / 7.0	26 SA	0253 / 0820 / 1525 / 2053	2.0 / 7.4 / 1.7 / 7.6
12 SA	0333 / 0857 / 1559 / 2122	2.4 / 7.0 / 2.1 / 7.3	27 SU	0359 / 0912 / 1627 / 2139	1.6 / 7.6 / 1.4 / 7.8
13 SU	0420 / 0935 / 1643 / 2157	2.0 / 7.3 / 1.8 / 7.6	28 M	0455 / 0958 / 1719 / 2222	1.3 / 7.8 / 1.2 / 7.9
14 M	0501 / 1011 / 1721 / 2232	1.7 / 7.6 / 1.5 / 7.7	29 TU ●	0542 / 1041 / 1801 / 2302	1.2 / 7.8 / 1.2 / 7.9
15 TU ○	0538 / 1048 / 1757 / 2308	1.5 / 7.7 / 1.3 / 7.8	30 W	0621 / 1122 / 1837 / 2340	1.1 / 7.9 / 1.2 / 7.9

TIDES

Chart Datum: 4·38 metres below IGN Datum
HAT is 8·4 metres above Chart Datum

TIME ZONE -0100
(French Standard Time)
Subtract 1 hour for UT
For French Summer Time add
ONE hour in **non-shaded areas**

FRANCE – LE HAVRE
LAT 49°29'N   LONG 0°07'E
TIMES AND HEIGHTS OF HIGH AND LOW WATERS

Dates in amber are **SPRINGS**
Dates in yellow are **NEAPS**

2014

MAY

Day	Time m	Time m	Time m	Time m
1 TH	0656 1.2	1202 7.8	1911 1.4	
2 F	0016 7.8	0729 1.3	1239 7.6	1943 1.6
3 SA	0051 7.6	0801 1.6	1316 7.4	2014 2.0
4 SU	0126 7.4	0831 2.0	1353 7.1	2045 2.4
5 M	0201 7.1	0903 2.4	1432 6.8	2119 2.8
6 TU	0239 6.8	0941 2.8	1521 6.5	2207 3.2
7 W	0331 6.4	1037 3.1	1635 6.3	◑ 2310 3.4
8 TH	0452 6.2	1144 3.2	1752 6.3	
9 F	0021 3.3	0611 6.3	1255 3.1	1856 6.5
10 SA	0132 3.1	0714 6.5	1405 2.8	1952 6.9
11 SU	0236 2.6	0808 6.8	1505 2.4	2039 7.2
12 M	0331 2.2	0855 7.2	1556 2.0	2121 7.5
13 TU	0419 1.9	0938 7.4	1642 1.7	2201 7.7
14 W	0504 1.6	1020 7.6	1725 1.5	○ 2240 7.8
15 TH	0547 1.3	1101 7.8	1807 1.3	2320 7.9
16 F	0629 1.1	1144 7.9	1849 1.3	
17 SA	0002 8.0	0711 1.1	1228 7.9	1930 1.3
18 SU	0046 7.9	0752 1.2	1314 7.8	2012 1.5
19 M	0132 7.8	0834 1.4	1402 7.6	2054 1.8
20 TU	0220 7.6	0918 1.7	1454 7.3	2144 2.2
21 W	0315 7.3	1011 2.0	1557 7.1	◐ 2248 2.4
22 TH	0421 7.0	1122 2.3	1712 7.0	
23 F	0005 2.5	0538 7.0	1238 2.3	1826 7.1
24 SA	0116 2.4	0650 7.0	1347 2.2	1930 7.2
25 SU	0222 2.2	0753 7.2	1452 2.0	2026 7.4
26 M	0327 1.9	0849 7.4	1554 1.8	2115 7.5
27 TU	0425 1.7	0938 7.5	1647 1.7	2159 7.6
28 W	0513 1.6	1022 7.6	● 1730 1.7	2239 7.7
29 TH	0553 1.5	1103 7.6	1808 1.6	2317 7.7
30 F	0630 1.5	1141 7.6	1844 1.7	2352 7.7
31 SA	0704 1.5	1218 7.5	1918 1.8	

JUNE

Day	Time m	Time m	Time m	Time m
1 SU	0027 7.6	0738 1.7	1304 7.9	1952 2.0
2 M	0101 7.4	0810 1.9	1330 7.2	2023 2.3
3 TU	0135 7.2	0841 2.2	1406 7.0	2057 2.5
4 W	0211 7.0	0915 2.5	1445 6.8	2134 2.8
5 TH	0252 6.8	0955 2.7	1533 6.6	◐ 2223 3.0
6 F	0345 6.5	1048 2.9	1638 6.5	2321 3.1
7 SA	0455 6.4	1149 3.0	1749 6.6	
8 SU	0024 3.1	0608 6.5	1255 2.9	1852 6.8
9 M	0132 2.8	0713 6.7	1404 2.6	1950 7.0
10 TU	0239 2.4	0812 7.0	1509 2.3	2042 7.3
11 W	0338 2.0	0905 7.3	1605 1.9	2130 7.6
12 TH	0431 1.7	0954 7.5	1656 1.6	2215 7.8
13 F	0522 1.4	1042 7.8	1746 1.4	○ 2301 8.0
14 SA	0611 1.1	1129 7.9	1834 1.3	2347 8.1
15 SU	0700 1.0	1216 8.0	1922 1.2	
16 M	0034 8.1	0748 1.0	1304 7.9	2009 1.3
17 TU	0121 8.0	0834 1.1	1352 7.8	2056 1.5
18 W	0210 7.8	0921 1.4	1443 7.6	2145 1.8
19 TH	0301 7.5	1010 1.7	1537 7.3	◐ 2238 2.1
20 F	0358 7.2	1104 2.1	1639 7.1	2338 2.4
21 SA	0504 7.0	1206 2.3	1748 7.0	
22 SU	0043 2.5	0616 6.9	1311 2.4	1857 7.0
23 M	0148 2.4	0725 6.9	1416 2.4	1959 7.1
24 TU	0253 2.3	0828 7.1	1519 2.3	2053 7.3
25 W	0353 2.1	0921 7.2	1615 2.2	2140 7.4
26 TH	0445 1.9	1006 7.3	1702 2.0	2221 7.5
27 F	0528 1.8	1047 7.4	1743 1.9	● 2257 7.6
28 SA	0607 1.7	1123 7.5	1821 1.8	2331 7.6
29 SU	0644 1.6	1158 7.5	1858 1.8	
30 M	0005 7.6	0718 1.6	1232 7.4	1931 1.9

JULY

Day	Time m	Time m	Time m	Time m
1 TU	0039 7.6	0751 1.8	1306 7.4	2003 2.0
2 W	0112 7.5	0821 1.9	1340 7.3	2034 2.2
3 TH	0145 7.3	0851 2.1	1414 7.1	2106 2.4
4 F	0222 7.1	0923 2.4	1453 7.0	2144 2.6
5 SA	0305 6.9	1003 2.6	1541 6.8	◐ 2230 2.8
6 SU	0358 6.7	1053 2.8	1640 6.7	2327 2.9
7 M	0504 6.6	1155 2.9	1750 6.7	
8 TU	0034 2.9	0618 6.6	1309 2.8	1900 6.9
9 W	0153 2.6	0730 6.8	1429 2.5	2006 7.2
10 TH	0305 2.2	0837 7.2	1535 2.1	2104 7.5
11 F	0405 1.7	0934 7.5	1633 1.7	2156 7.8
12 SA	0502 1.3	1025 7.8	1729 1.4	○ 2245 8.1
13 SU	0558 1.0	1114 8.0	1824 1.2	2333 8.2
14 M	0652 0.8	1202 8.1	1916 1.0	
15 TU	0020 8.3	0742 0.7	1250 8.1	2004 1.0
16 W	0107 8.2	0828 0.8	1337 8.0	2049 1.2
17 TH	0153 8.0	0911 1.1	1423 7.8	2132 1.5
18 F	0240 7.7	0953 1.5	1510 7.5	2215 1.9
19 SA	0329 7.4	1036 2.0	1602 7.2	◐ 2305 2.3
20 SU	0427 7.0	1128 2.5	1705 6.9	
21 M	0005 2.6	0539 6.7	1232 2.8	1819 6.8
22 TU	0113 2.8	0658 6.7	1342 2.8	1932 6.9
23 W	0221 2.6	0810 6.8	1449 2.7	2035 7.0
24 TH	0325 2.4	0908 7.0	1549 2.5	2124 7.2
25 F	0422 2.1	0953 7.2	1641 2.2	2204 7.4
26 SA	0508 1.9	1031 7.4	1724 2.0	● 2239 7.6
27 SU	0548 1.7	1104 7.5	1803 1.9	2311 7.7
28 M	0625 1.6	1136 7.5	1838 1.8	2343 7.7
29 TU	0658 1.6	1209 7.6	1911 1.8	
30 W	0016 7.7	0729 1.6	1241 7.5	1941 1.8
31 TH	0048 7.7	0758 1.7	1313 7.5	2011 1.9

AUGUST

Day	Time m	Time m	Time m	Time m
1 F	0121 7.5	0827 1.9	1346 7.4	2042 2.1
2 SA	0156 7.3	0857 2.1	1422 7.2	2115 2.3
3 SU	0235 7.1	0931 2.4	1503 7.0	2154 2.6
4 M	0321 6.9	1014 2.7	1554 6.8	2244 2.8
5 TU	0420 6.7	1110 2.9	1701 6.7	2348 2.9
6 W	0537 6.6	1224 3.0	1822 6.8	
7 TH	0115 2.8	0701 6.7	1401 2.7	1939 7.1
8 F	0241 2.3	0817 7.1	1513 2.2	2045 7.5
9 SA	0345 1.7	0918 7.6	1615 1.7	2139 7.9
10 SU	0446 1.3	1010 7.9	1716 1.3	○ 2229 8.2
11 M	0546 0.9	1058 8.1	1814 1.0	2316 8.4
12 TU	0641 0.6	1145 8.3	1905 0.8	
13 W	0002 8.4	0729 0.6	1231 8.3	1949 0.8
14 TH	0048 8.4	0812 0.7	1315 8.2	2030 1.0
15 F	0132 8.2	0850 1.0	1358 7.9	2109 1.4
16 SA	0215 7.8	0926 1.5	1440 7.6	2146 1.9
17 SU	0259 7.4	1002 2.1	1524 7.2	◐ 2227 2.4
18 M	0351 6.9	1046 2.7	1621 6.8	2323 2.9
19 TU	0502 6.5	1149 3.1	1739 6.6	
20 W	0035 3.1	0629 6.4	1307 3.2	1904 6.6
21 TH	0152 3.0	0753 6.6	1423 3.0	2016 6.8
22 F	0301 2.6	0852 6.9	1528 2.7	2107 7.1
23 SA	0400 2.3	0935 7.2	1621 2.3	2145 7.4
24 SU	0447 1.9	1010 7.4	1704 2.0	2218 7.6
25 M	0527 1.7	1041 7.6	● 1742 1.8	2248 7.7
26 TU	0603 1.6	1111 7.7	1817 1.7	2320 7.8
27 W	0635 1.5	1143 7.7	1847 1.6	2352 7.8
28 TH	0704 1.5	1214 7.7	1917 1.6	
29 F	0024 7.8	0733 1.5	1246 7.7	1947 1.7
30 SA	0057 7.7	0803 1.7	1320 7.6	2019 1.8
31 SU	0133 7.5	0834 1.9	1355 7.4	2052 2.1

Chart Datum: 4·38 metres below IGN Datum
HAT is 8·4 metres above Chart Datum

TIME ZONE -0100
(French Standard Time)
Subtract 1 hour for UT
For French Summer Time add
ONE hour in **non-shaded areas**

FRANCE – LE HAVRE

LAT 49°29'N LONG 0°07'E

TIMES AND HEIGHTS OF HIGH AND LOW WATERS

Dates in amber are **SPRINGS**
Dates in yellow are **NEAPS**

2014

SEPTEMBER

Day	Time m	Time m	Time m	Time m
1 M	0211 7.2	1434 7.1	2128 2.4	
16 TU	0317 6.9	1539 6.8	2240 3.0	
2 TU	0255 7.0	0947 2.6	1522 6.9	2214 2.7
17 W	0425 6.5	1106 3.4	1657 6.4	2352 3.3
3 W	0353 6.7	1039 2.9	1629 6.7	2316 2.9
18 TH	0555 6.3	1228 3.5	1826 6.4	
4 TH	0513 6.6	1154 3.1	1756 6.7	
19 F	0116 3.2	0722 6.5	1352 3.3	1946 6.6
5 F	0050 2.9	0646 6.8	1342 2.8	1922 7.1
20 SA	0231 2.9	0826 6.8	1500 2.8	2040 7.0
6 SA	0222 2.3	0804 7.2	1456 2.2	2029 7.5
21 SU	0330 2.4	0908 7.2	1553 2.4	2118 7.3
7 SU	0328 1.7	0902 7.2	1559 1.6	2123 7.9
22	0417 2.0	0941 7.5	1637 2.0	2151 7.6
8 M	0430 1.2	0953 8.0	1701 1.2	2211 8.2
23 TU	0458 1.7	1012 7.6	1716 1.8	2222 7.8
9 TU	0531 0.8	1039 8.2	1757 0.9	2257 8.4
24 W	0535 1.6	1043 7.8	1750 1.6	2255 7.9
10 W	0623 0.6	1124 8.3	1845 0.7	2342 8.5
25 TH	0607 1.5	1115 7.8	1821 1.5	2327 7.9
11 TH	0708 0.6	1208 8.3	1928 0.8	
26 F	0637 1.4	1147 7.8	1852 1.5	
12 F	0025 8.4	0748 0.8	1250 8.2	2006 1.0
27 SA	0000 7.9	0708 1.5	1220 7.8	1924 1.5
13 SA	0108 8.1	0823 1.2	1330 7.9	2041 1.4
28 SU	0036 7.8	0741 1.6	1255 7.7	1958 1.7
14 SU	0148 7.8	0856 1.7	1408 7.6	2114 2.0
29 M	0113 7.6	1333 7.5	2033 1.9	
15 M	0230 7.4	0927 2.0	1448 7.2	2150 2.5
30 TU	0154 7.4	1414 7.3	2110 2.3	

OCTOBER

Day	Time m	Time m	Time m	Time m
1 W	0240 7.1	0928 2.6	1503 7.0	2154 2.6
16	0348 6.5	1027 3.4	1611 6.4	2307 3.4
2 TH	0339 6.8	1021 2.9	1611 6.8	2255 2.9
17 F	0512 6.3	1142 3.6	1738 6.3	
3 F	0500 6.7	1138 3.1	1740 6.8	
18 SA	0025 3.4	0630 6.4	1305 3.5	1854 6.5
4 SA	0034 2.8	0634 6.9	1327 2.8	1906 7.1
19 SU	0145 3.1	0738 6.7	1419 3.0	1956 6.8
5 SU	0205 2.3	0747 7.3	1439 2.2	2010 7.5
20 M	0249 2.6	0827 7.1	1515 2.6	2041 7.1
6 M	0310 1.7	0844 7.7	1542 1.6	2104 7.9
21 TU	0340 2.2	0905 7.4	1602 2.2	2118 7.4
7 TU	0412 1.3	0933 8.1	1643 1.2	2152 8.2
22 W	0423 1.9	0939 7.6	1643 1.9	2154 7.7
8 W	0510 1.0	1018 8.2	1736 1.0	2237 8.3
23 TH	0501 1.7	1013 7.8	1719 1.7	2229 7.8
9 TH	0600 0.8	1101 8.3	1823 0.9	2320 8.3
24 F	0537 1.6	1047 7.9	1754 1.5	2304 7.9
10 F	0642 0.9	1143 8.3	1903 0.9	
25 SA	0610 1.5	1122 7.9	1828 1.4	2340 7.9
11 SA	0003 8.3	0720 1.1	1223 8.1	1939 1.2
26 SU	0645 1.5	1157 7.9	1904 1.4	
12 SU	0044 8.0	0755 1.4	1301 7.9	2013 1.5
27 M	0017 7.9	0721 1.6	1235 7.9	1941 1.5
13 M	0123 7.7	0826 1.9	1339 7.6	2045 2.0
28 TU	0058 7.7	0758 1.8	1316 7.7	2018 1.8
14 TU	0203 7.3	0857 2.4	1416 7.2	2118 2.5
29 W	0143 7.5	0835 2.1	1401 7.5	2057 2.1
15 W	0247 6.9	0917 2.9	1502 6.8	2202 3.0
30 TH	0232 7.3	0917 2.5	1453 7.2	2142 2.4
31 F	0331 7.0	1010 2.8	1559 7.0	2244 2.7

NOVEMBER

Day	Time m	Time m	Time m	Time m
1 SA	0449 6.9	1130 3.0	1722 6.9	
16 SU	0533 6.5	1201 3.5	1755 6.4	
2 SU	0019 2.7	0615 7.0	1307 2.7	1843 7.1
17 M	0037 3.3	0638 6.6	1315 3.3	1859 6.6
3 M	0142 2.3	0725 7.4	1418 2.2	1948 7.5
18 TU	0150 3.0	0735 6.6	1424 2.9	1955 6.9
4 TU	0248 1.8	0822 7.7	1521 1.8	2043 7.8
19 W	0252 2.6	0822 7.2	1519 2.4	2041 7.2
5 W	0349 1.5	0911 8.0	1620 1.4	2132 8.0
20 TH	0342 2.2	0904 7.5	1605 2.1	2123 7.5
6 TH	0445 1.3	0956 8.1	1713 1.2	2217 8.1
21 F	0425 1.9	0943 7.7	1647 1.8	2203 7.7
7 F	0534 1.2	1039 8.1	1758 1.1	2301 8.1
22 SA	0506 1.7	1021 7.9	1727 1.5	2242 7.8
8 SA	0615 1.2	1120 8.1	1837 1.2	2342 8.1
23 SU	0546 1.5	1059 8.0	1808 1.4	2322 7.9
9 SU	0653 1.4	1158 8.0	1914 1.3	
24 M	0626 1.5	1139 8.0	1848 1.3	
10 M	0022 7.9	0727 1.6	1236 7.8	1947 1.6
25 TU	0004 7.9	0707 1.5	1221 8.0	1929 1.3
11 TU	0101 7.7	0800 2.0	1312 7.6	2021 2.0
26 W	0048 7.9	0747 1.6	1305 7.9	2010 1.6
12 W	0139 7.4	0833 2.4	1349 7.3	2054 2.4
27 TH	0135 7.7	0828 1.9	1353 7.7	2051 1.8
13 TH	0220 7.0	0908 2.8	1429 7.0	2132 2.8
28 F	0225 7.5	0913 2.2	1444 7.5	2138 2.1
14 F	0309 6.7	0953 3.2	1520 6.6	2223 3.2
29 SA	0321 7.3	1006 2.5	1545 7.2	2237 2.3
15 SA	0419 6.5	1053 3.5	1639 6.4	2326 3.3
30 SU	0430 7.1	1118 2.7	1658 7.1	2356 2.5

DECEMBER

Day	Time m	Time m	Time m	Time m
1 M	0547 7.1	1239 2.6	1815 7.1	
16 TU	0532 6.6	1200 3.3	1754 6.5	
2 TU	0113 2.4	0657 7.3	1351 2.3	1923 7.3
17 W	0032 3.2	0636 6.7	1309 3.1	1900 6.6
3 W	0221 2.1	0757 7.5	1456 2.0	2022 7.5
18 TH	0144 2.9	0735 7.0	1424 2.8	2000 6.9
4 TH	0323 1.9	0850 7.7	1557 1.8	2114 7.7
19 F	0254 2.6	0827 7.3	1525 2.3	2052 7.2
5 F	0420 1.7	0937 7.8	1650 1.6	2201 7.8
20 SA	0349 2.2	0914 7.6	1617 1.9	2139 7.5
6 SA	0509 1.6	1020 7.9	1735 1.4	2245 7.9
21 SU	0438 1.8	0958 7.8	1704 1.6	2224 7.8
7 SU	0551 1.6	1100 7.9	1815 1.4	2325 7.9
22 M	0525 1.4	1041 8.0	1751 1.3	2308 8.0
8 M	0629 1.6	1138 7.9	1852 1.4	
23 TU	0612 1.4	1125 8.1	1838 1.1	2353 8.1
9 TU	0004 7.8	0705 1.7	1214 7.8	1927 1.6
24	0658 1.3	1210 8.2	1923 1.0	
10 W	0041 7.7	0740 1.9	1249 7.7	2001 1.8
25 TH	0039 8.1	0744 1.3	1256 8.1	2008 1.1
11 TH	0118 7.5	0813 2.2	1325 7.5	2034 2.1
26 F	0126 8.0	0828 1.5	1344 8.0	2052 1.3
12 F	0154 7.2	0847 2.5	1400 7.2	2107 2.5
27 SA	0214 7.8	0913 1.7	1432 7.8	2137 1.6
13 SA	0233 7.0	0923 2.8	1438 6.9	2144 2.8
28 SU	0305 7.5	1001 2.1	1525 7.5	2226 2.0
14 SU	0318 6.7	1006 3.1	1527 6.6	2231 3.0
29 M	0403 7.3	1057 2.4	1627 7.2	2326 2.3
15 M	0421 6.6	1059 3.3	1637 6.5	2328 3.2
30 TU	0511 7.1	1205 2.6	1741 7.0	
31 W	0037 2.5	0624 7.0	1318 2.6	1856 7.0

Chart Datum: 4·38 metres below IGN Datum
HAT is 8·4 metres above Chart Datum

TIDES

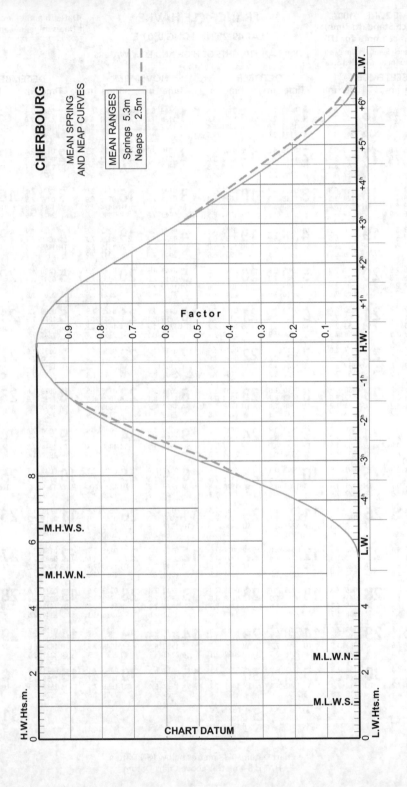

CHERBOURG

MEAN SPRING
AND NEAP CURVES

MEAN RANGES
Springs 5.3m
Neaps 2.5m

TIME ZONE -0100
(French Standard Time)
Subtract 1 hour for UT
For French Summer Time add
ONE hour in **non-shaded areas**

FRANCE – CHERBOURG

LAT 49°39'N   LONG 1°38'W

TIMES AND HEIGHTS OF HIGH AND LOW WATERS

Dates in amber are **SPRINGS**
Dates in yellow are **NEAPS**

2014

JANUARY

Day	Time m	Day	Time m
1	0246 1.3 / 0821 6.6 / W 1516 1.0 / ● 2052 6.5	16	0326 1.7 / 0857 6.1 / TH 1551 1.5 / ○ 2123 6.0
2	0338 1.1 / 0912 6.8 / TH 1608 0.8 / 2143 6.7	17	0401 1.6 / 0931 6.2 / F 1624 1.4 / 2155 6.1
3	0429 1.0 / 1001 6.9 / F 1657 0.7 / 2233 6.7	18	0434 1.6 / 1002 6.3 / SA 1656 1.4 / 2226 6.1
4	0518 1.0 / 1050 6.9 / SA 1745 0.7 / 2321 6.6	19	0506 1.6 / 1033 6.2 / SU 1728 1.4 / 2258 6.0
5	0605 1.1 / 1137 6.7 / SU 1831 0.9	20	0538 1.7 / 1106 6.2 / M 1759 1.5 / 2330 5.9
6	0007 6.3 / 0651 1.4 / M 1222 6.4 / 1916 1.3	21	0610 1.8 / 1139 6.0 / TU 1830 1.7
7	0052 6.0 / 0738 1.7 / TU 1309 6.0 / 2003 1.7	22	0004 5.8 / 0644 2.0 / W 1214 5.8 / 1906 1.9
8	0139 5.7 / 0829 2.1 / W 1359 5.6 / ◐ 2054 2.1	23	0040 5.6 / 0719 2.2 / TH 1252 5.5 / 1947 2.1
9	0233 5.4 / 0929 2.4 / TH 1500 5.3 / 2156 2.4	24	0123 5.4 / 0813 2.4 / F 1340 5.3 / ◐ 2041 2.4
10	0340 5.2 / 1041 2.6 / F 1615 5.1 / 2310 2.6	25	0219 5.2 / 0917 2.6 / SA 1447 5.1 / 2152 2.5
11	0455 5.2 / 1155 2.5 / SA 1732 5.1	26	0336 5.1 / 1036 2.5 / SU 1616 5.1 / 2316 2.4
12	0020 2.5 / 0603 5.3 / SU 1259 2.3 / 1837 5.3	27	0507 5.3 / 1158 2.3 / M 1745 5.3
13	0119 2.3 / 0658 5.6 / M 1352 2.1 / 1928 5.5	28	0032 2.1 / 0618 5.7 / TU 1307 1.8 / 1851 5.7
14	0207 2.1 / 0743 5.8 / TU 1437 1.8 / 2011 5.8	29	0137 1.7 / 0716 6.1 / W 1409 1.3 / 1949 6.1
15	0249 1.9 / 0822 6.0 / W 1515 1.6 / 2048 5.9	30	0236 1.3 / 0810 6.5 / TH 1506 0.9 / ● 2043 6.5
		31	0330 1.0 / 0902 6.8 / F 1558 0.6 / 2134 6.7

FEBRUARY

Day	Time m	Day	Time m
1	0420 0.8 / 0952 7.0 / SA 1646 0.5 / 2221 6.8	16	0414 1.4 / 0944 6.3 / SU 1635 1.2 / 2206 6.2
2	0506 0.7 / 1038 7.0 / SU 1730 0.5 / 2305 6.7	17	0446 1.3 / 1015 6.3 / M 1706 1.2 / 2236 6.2
3	0549 0.8 / 1121 6.8 / M 1812 0.7 / 2346 6.5	18	0517 1.4 / 1046 6.3 / TU 1736 1.3 / 2307 6.1
4	0630 1.1 / 1202 6.5 / TU 1851 1.1	19	0548 1.4 / 1119 6.2 / W 1807 1.4 / 2340 6.0
5	0024 6.1 / 0711 1.5 / W 1241 6.1 / 1931 1.6	20	0621 1.6 / 1152 6.0 / TH 1840 1.7
6	0102 5.8 / 0753 2.0 / TH 1322 5.6 / ◑ 2013 2.1	21	0013 5.8 / 0658 1.8 / F 1228 5.7 / 1918 2.0
7	0145 5.4 / 0842 2.4 / F 1413 5.1 / 2105 2.5	22	0051 5.5 / 0744 2.1 / SA 1312 5.4 / ◑ 2008 2.3
8	0244 5.0 / 0949 2.7 / SA 1527 4.8 / 2219 2.8	23	0142 5.3 / 0844 2.4 / SU 1415 5.1 / 2119 2.5
9	0406 4.9 / 1114 2.7 / SU 1701 4.8 / 2344 2.8	24	0259 5.1 / 1006 2.5 / M 1553 5.0 / 2251 2.6
10	0533 5.0 / 1230 2.5 / M 1818 5.0	25	0445 5.1 / 1136 2.3 / TU 1733 5.2
11	0054 2.5 / 0637 5.3 / TU 1330 2.2 / 1911 5.3	26	0016 2.2 / 0603 5.5 / W 1253 1.8 / 1841 5.6
12	0148 2.2 / 0724 5.6 / W 1417 1.9 / 1953 5.6	27	0125 1.8 / 0703 6.0 / TH 1357 1.3 / 1938 6.1
13	0231 1.9 / 0803 5.8 / TH 1456 1.6 / 2029 5.8	28	0225 1.3 / 0758 6.4 / F 1453 0.9 / 2030 6.4
14	0308 1.7 / 0839 6.1 / F 1531 1.4 / 2103 6.0		
15	0342 1.5 / 0913 6.2 / SA 1604 1.3 / ○ 2135 6.1		

MARCH

Day	Time m	Day	Time m
1	0317 0.9 / 0849 6.8 / SA 1543 0.6 / ● 2118 6.7	16	0316 1.5 / 0848 6.2 / SU 1536 1.3 / ○ 2110 6.2
2	0405 0.7 / 0936 6.9 / SU 1628 0.4 / 2202 6.8	17	0349 1.3 / 0921 6.3 / M 1608 1.1 / 2141 6.3
3	0448 0.6 / 1019 6.9 / M 1709 0.5 / 2242 6.7	18	0422 1.2 / 0953 6.4 / TU 1641 1.1 / 2212 6.3
4	0528 0.7 / 1059 6.8 / TU 1747 0.7 / 2319 6.5	19	0455 1.2 / 1025 6.4 / W 1712 1.2 / 2244 6.3
5	0605 1.0 / 1136 6.5 / W 1823 1.1 / 2353 6.2	20	0528 1.2 / 1059 6.3 / TH 1745 1.3 / 2317 6.2
6	0641 1.4 / 1211 6.0 / TH 1858 1.6	21	0602 1.4 / 1135 6.1 / F 1819 1.6 / 2353 6.0
7	0026 5.8 / 0719 1.8 / F 1248 5.5 / 1935 2.1	22	0640 1.6 / 1213 5.8 / SA 1900 1.9
8	0103 5.4 / 0801 2.3 / SU 1332 5.1 / ◑ 2020 2.6	23	0032 5.7 / 0726 1.9 / SU 1259 5.4 / 1951 2.3
9	0153 5.0 / 0858 2.7 / SU 1440 4.7 / 2127 2.9	24	0124 5.3 / 0826 2.2 / M 1403 5.1 / ◑ 2103 2.5
10	0311 4.7 / 1024 2.9 / M 1620 4.6 / 2302 3.0	25	0241 5.1 / 0948 2.4 / TU 1545 5.0 / 2236 2.6
11	0451 4.7 / 1152 2.7 / TU 1750 4.8	26	0428 5.1 / 1120 2.2 / W 1721 5.2
12	0022 2.7 / 0606 5.0 / W 1258 2.4 / 1844 5.1	27	0002 2.3 / 0546 5.5 / TH 1237 1.8 / 1827 5.6
13	0120 2.4 / 0656 5.3 / TH 1347 2.0 / 1925 5.5	28	0111 1.8 / 0647 5.9 / F 1340 1.3 / 1922 6.0
14	0205 2.0 / 0736 5.7 / F 1428 1.7 / 2002 5.8	29	0209 1.4 / 0740 6.3 / SA 1434 1.0 / 2012 6.4
15	0242 1.7 / 0814 6.0 / SA 1503 1.5 / 2037 6.0	30	0259 1.0 / 0831 6.6 / SU 1522 0.7 / ● 2057 6.6
		31	0344 0.8 / 0914 6.7 / M 1605 0.7 / 2137 6.6

APRIL

Day	Time m	Day	Time m
1	0426 0.8 / 0955 6.7 / TU 1644 0.7 / 2215 6.6	16	0356 1.2 / 0928 6.3 / W 1614 1.1 / 2146 6.4
2	0503 0.8 / 1033 6.6 / W 1720 1.0 / 2249 6.4	17	0432 1.1 / 1004 6.4 / TH 1650 1.2 / 2222 6.4
3	0539 1.1 / 1109 6.3 / TH 1753 1.3 / 2322 6.2	18	0509 1.1 / 1042 6.3 / F 1726 1.3 / 2259 6.3
4	0613 1.4 / 1144 5.9 / F 1827 1.7 / 2355 5.8	19	0547 1.2 / 1121 6.1 / SA 1805 1.5 / 2338 6.1
5	0648 1.8 / 1219 5.5 / SA 1902 2.1	20	0629 1.5 / 1204 5.9 / SU 1850 1.8
6	0029 5.5 / 0727 2.2 / SU 1300 5.5 / 1944 2.6	21	0023 5.8 / 0719 1.7 / M 1254 5.5 / 1945 2.2
7	0112 5.1 / 0816 2.6 / M 1357 4.8 / ◑ 2042 2.9	22	0118 5.5 / 0820 2.0 / TU 1400 5.2 / ◑ 2056 2.4
8	0217 4.8 / 0927 2.8 / TU 1525 4.6 / 2208 3.0	23	0233 5.2 / 0936 2.2 / W 1534 5.1 / 2222 2.5
9	0348 4.6 / 1059 2.8 / W 1700 4.7 / 2335 2.9	24	0406 5.3 / 1101 2.1 / TH 1700 5.3 / 2343 2.2
10	0515 4.8 / 1210 2.5 / TH 1802 5.0	25	0522 5.5 / 1215 1.8 / F 1804 5.6
11	0037 2.5 / 0613 5.1 / F 1304 2.2 / 1846 5.4	26	0050 1.9 / 0623 5.8 / SA 1317 1.5 / 1859 5.9
12	0125 2.2 / 0659 5.5 / SA 1348 1.9 / 1926 5.7	27	0147 1.5 / 0717 6.1 / SU 1410 1.2 / 1947 6.2
13	0206 1.8 / 0739 5.8 / SU 1426 1.6 / 2003 6.0	28	0237 1.2 / 0806 6.3 / M 1457 1.1 / 2031 6.4
14	0243 1.6 / 0817 6.1 / M 1502 1.4 / 2039 6.2	29	0321 1.1 / 0850 6.4 / TU 1539 1.0 / ● 2110 6.4
15	0319 1.3 / 0853 6.2 / TU 1538 1.2 / ○ 2113 6.3	30	0401 1.0 / 0931 6.4 / W 1617 1.1 / 2146 6.4

TIDES

Chart Datum: 3·33 metres below IGN Datum
HAT is 7·0 metres above Chart Datum

FRANCE – CHERBOURG

LAT 49°39'N LONG 1°38'W

TIMES AND HEIGHTS OF HIGH AND LOW WATERS

TIME ZONE -0100
(French Standard Time)
Subtract 1 hour for UT
For French Summer Time add
ONE hour in non-shaded areas

Dates in amber are SPRINGS
Dates in yellow are NEAPS

2014

MAY

Day	Time m	Day	Time m
1 TH	0438 1.1 / 1008 6.3 / 1652 1.3 / 2221 6.3	**16** F	0412 1.1 / 0945 6.3 / 1630 1.2 / 2203 6.5
2 F	0513 1.2 / 1044 6.1 / 1726 1.5 / 2254 6.1	**17** SA	0454 1.0 / 1028 6.3 / 1713 1.3 / 2245 6.4
3 SA	0547 1.5 / 1119 5.9 / 1759 1.8 / 2328 5.9	**18** SU	0538 1.1 / 1112 6.2 / 1757 1.4 / 2329 6.3
4 SU	0622 1.8 / 1155 5.6 / 1835 2.1	**19** M	0624 1.3 / 1159 6.0 / 1846 1.7
5 M	0002 5.6 / 0659 2.1 / 1233 5.2 / 1914 2.5	**20** TU	0018 6.0 / 0715 1.5 / 1251 5.7 / 1942 2.0
6 TU	0041 5.2 / 0742 2.4 / 1321 4.9 / 2004 2.8	**21** W	0113 5.7 / 0813 1.8 / 1354 5.4 / 2047 2.2
7 W	0132 5.0 / 0837 2.6 / 1426 4.8 / ◑ 2109 2.9	**22** TH	0220 5.5 / 0920 2.0 / 1511 5.3 / 2201 2.3
8 TH	0242 4.8 / 0950 2.7 / 1545 4.7 / 2229 2.9	**23** F	0338 5.4 / 1035 2.0 / 1628 5.3 / 2316 2.2
9 F	0402 4.8 / 1107 2.6 / 1700 4.9 / 2340 2.7	**24** SA	0451 5.5 / 1146 1.9 / 1733 5.5
10 SA	0513 5.0 / 1208 2.4 / 1756 5.2	**25** SU	0023 2.0 / 0554 5.6 / 1248 1.8 / 1830 5.8
11 SU	0035 2.4 / 0610 5.3 / 1259 2.1 / 1842 5.6	**26** M	0121 1.8 / 0651 5.8 / 1343 1.6 / 1920 6.0
12 M	0122 2.0 / 0657 5.6 / 1343 1.8 / 1924 5.9	**27** TU	0212 1.6 / 0742 6.0 / 1431 1.5 / 2005 6.1
13 TU	0206 1.7 / 0741 5.9 / 1426 1.5 / 2004 6.1	**28** W	0257 1.4 / 0828 6.1 / 1513 1.5 / 2045 6.2
14 W	0248 1.4 / 0823 6.1 / 1507 1.3 / ○ 2043 6.3	**29** TH	0338 1.3 / 0908 6.1 / 1551 1.5 / 2121 6.2
15 TH	0330 1.2 / 0904 6.3 / 1549 1.2 / 2123 6.4	**30** F	0415 1.3 / 0946 6.0 / 1628 1.5 / 2156 6.2
		31 SA	0451 1.4 / 1022 6.0 / 1702 1.6 / 2231 6.1

JUNE

Day	Time m	Day	Time m
1 SU	0525 1.5 / 1058 5.8 / 1736 1.8 / 2305 5.9	**16** M	0530 0.9 / 1105 6.4 / 1751 1.3 / 2323 6.5
2 M	0559 1.7 / 1133 5.7 / 1811 2.0 / 2339 5.7	**17** TU	0618 1.0 / 1154 6.2 / 1841 1.4
3 TU	0634 1.9 / 1209 5.4 / 1848 2.3	**18** W	0011 6.3 / 0708 1.2 / 1244 6.0 / 1933 1.7
4 W	0015 5.5 / 0712 2.1 / 1248 5.2 / 1930 2.5	**19** TH	0103 6.0 / 0800 1.5 / 1338 5.7 / ◑ 2029 2.0
5 TH	0057 5.2 / 0756 2.4 / 1336 5.0 / ◑ 2021 2.7	**20** F	0159 5.7 / 0857 1.8 / 1439 5.5 / 2133 2.2
6 F	0149 5.0 / 0849 2.5 / 1435 4.9 / 2122 2.8	**21** SA	0304 5.5 / 1002 2.1 / 1547 5.3 / 2243 2.3
7 SA	0252 4.9 / 0954 2.6 / 1543 5.0 / 2232 2.7	**22** SU	0414 5.3 / 1111 2.2 / 1656 5.4 / 2352 2.2
8 SU	0401 5.0 / 1104 2.5 / 1651 5.1 / 2339 2.5	**23** M	0523 5.4 / 1217 2.1 / 1759 5.5
9 M	0510 5.1 / 1206 2.3 / 1751 5.4	**24** TU	0054 2.1 / 0626 5.5 / 1315 2.0 / 1854 5.7
10 TU	0037 2.2 / 0611 5.4 / 1301 2.0 / 1843 5.7	**25** W	0148 1.9 / 0722 5.6 / 1406 1.9 / 1942 5.9
11 W	0128 1.8 / 0705 5.7 / 1351 1.7 / 1931 6.0	**26** TH	0236 1.7 / 0809 5.8 / 1451 1.8 / 2024 6.0
12 TH	0218 1.5 / 0755 6.0 / 1440 1.5 / 2017 6.3	**27** F	0318 1.6 / 0850 5.9 / 1531 1.7 / ○ 2101 6.1
13 F	0306 1.2 / 0843 6.2 / 1528 1.3 / ○ 2103 6.5	**28** SA	0356 1.5 / 0928 5.9 / 1607 1.7 / 2136 6.1
14 SA	0355 1.0 / 0930 6.4 / 1615 1.2 / 2149 6.6	**29** SU	0431 1.5 / 1003 5.9 / 1642 1.7 / 2210 6.1
15 SU	0442 0.9 / 1018 6.4 / 1703 1.2 / 2235 6.6	**30** M	0505 1.5 / 1037 5.9 / 1716 1.8 / 2244 6.0

JULY

Day	Time m	Day	Time m
1 TU	0538 1.6 / 1110 5.8 / 1748 1.9 / 2317 5.9	**16** W	0607 0.7 / 1143 6.4 / 1828 1.2
2 W	0610 1.7 / 1143 5.7 / 1822 2.0 / 2351 5.8	**17** TH	0000 6.5 / 0652 1.0 / 1228 6.2 / 1915 1.4
3 TH	0643 1.9 / 1218 5.5 / 1858 2.2	**18** F	0045 6.2 / 0738 1.4 / 1313 5.9 / 2004 1.8
4 F	0027 5.5 / 0720 2.1 / 1257 5.4 / 1939 2.4	**19** SA	0132 5.8 / 0827 1.8 / 1402 5.6 / ◑ 2059 2.2
5 SA	0108 5.3 / 0803 2.3 / 1343 5.2 / ◑ 2030 2.6	**20** SU	0227 5.4 / 0923 2.2 / 1502 5.3 / 2205 2.4
6 SU	0159 5.2 / 0856 2.5 / 1439 5.1 / 2132 2.6	**21** M	0335 5.2 / 1032 2.4 / 1615 5.2 / 2319 2.5
7 M	0301 5.0 / 1002 2.5 / 1546 5.1 / 2244 2.6	**22** TU	0452 5.1 / 1146 2.5 / 1729 5.2
8 TU	0414 5.1 / 1116 2.4 / 1701 5.3 / 2355 2.3	**23** W	0028 2.3 / 0605 5.2 / 1251 2.4 / 1832 5.4
9 W	0530 5.3 / 1224 2.2 / 1808 5.6	**24** TH	0127 2.1 / 0705 5.4 / 1346 2.2 / 1923 5.7
10 TH	0057 2.0 / 0636 5.6 / 1323 1.9 / 1904 5.9	**25** F	0217 1.9 / 0753 5.6 / 1432 2.0 / 2006 5.9
11 F	0154 1.6 / 0733 5.9 / 1419 1.5 / ● 1956 6.3	**26** SA	0259 1.7 / 0833 5.8 / 1512 1.8 / ● 2043 6.0
12 SA	0248 1.2 / 0826 6.2 / 1512 1.3 / ○ 2047 6.6	**27** SU	0336 1.5 / 0909 5.9 / 1548 1.7 / 2118 6.1
13 SU	0341 0.9 / 0918 6.4 / 1604 1.1 / 2137 6.7	**28** M	0411 1.4 / 0942 6.0 / 1622 1.6 / 2150 6.2
14 M	0431 0.7 / 1008 6.6 / 1654 1.0 / 2226 6.8	**29** TU	0443 1.4 / 1014 6.0 / 1654 1.6 / 2222 6.2
15 TU	0520 0.7 / 1057 6.6 / 1741 1.0 / 2313 6.8	**30** W	0514 1.4 / 1045 6.0 / 1725 1.7 / 2253 6.1
		31 TH	0544 1.5 / 1116 5.9 / 1756 1.8 / 2325 6.0

AUGUST

Day	Time m	Day	Time m
1 F	0615 1.7 / 1149 5.8 / 1828 1.9 / 2359 5.8	**16** SA	0021 6.3 / 0711 1.4 / 1242 6.0 / 1934 1.8
2 SA	0647 1.9 / 1223 5.6 / 1904 2.1	**17** SU	0102 5.8 / 0753 1.9 / 1324 5.6 / ◑ 2023 2.2
3 SU	0035 5.6 / 0724 2.1 / 1301 5.4 / 1948 2.3	**18** M	0151 5.4 / 0843 2.4 / 1417 5.2 / 2125 2.6
4 M	0118 5.3 / 0810 2.4 / 1350 5.2 / 2045 2.5	**19** TU	0256 5.0 / 0951 2.8 / 1531 5.0 / 2245 2.7
5 TU	0215 5.1 / 0914 2.6 / 1455 5.1 / 2159 2.6	**20** W	0423 4.9 / 1115 2.8 / 1659 5.0
6 W	0331 5.0 / 1035 2.6 / 1621 5.2 / 2322 2.4	**21** TH	0003 2.6 / 0547 5.0 / 1228 2.6 / 1811 5.2
7 TH	0502 5.2 / 1156 2.4 / 1742 5.5	**22** F	0105 2.3 / 0648 5.3 / 1326 2.3 / 1904 5.6
8 F	0034 2.1 / 0617 5.5 / 1304 2.0 / 1845 5.9	**23** SA	0156 2.0 / 0733 5.6 / 1412 2.1 / 1945 5.8
9 SA	0136 1.6 / 0717 5.9 / 1404 1.6 / 1940 6.3	**24** SU	0237 1.7 / 0811 5.8 / 1451 1.8 / 2022 6.1
10 SU	0233 1.1 / 0812 6.3 / 1459 1.2 / ○ 2033 6.7	**25** M	0314 1.5 / 0846 6.0 / 1526 1.7 / ● 2056 6.2
11 M	0327 0.8 / 0904 6.6 / 1551 0.9 / 2123 6.9	**26** TU	0347 1.4 / 0919 6.1 / 1558 1.6 / 2128 6.3
12 TU	0417 0.6 / 0954 6.7 / 1640 0.8 / 2212 7.0	**27** W	0418 1.3 / 0949 6.2 / 1629 1.5 / 2158 6.3
13 W	0504 0.5 / 1040 6.7 / 1725 0.8 / 2257 6.9	**28** TH	0448 1.5 / 1018 6.2 / 1700 1.5 / 2228 6.3
14 TH	0548 0.6 / 1123 6.6 / 1808 1.0 / 2340 6.7	**29** F	0518 1.4 / 1048 6.1 / 1730 1.6 / 2300 6.2
15 F	0630 0.9 / 1204 6.4 / 1851 1.3	**30** SA	0547 1.5 / 1120 6.1 / 1801 1.7 / 2333 6.0
		31 SU	0618 1.7 / 1153 5.9 / 1836 1.9

Chart Datum: 3·33 metres below IGN Datum
HAT is 7·0 metres above Chart Datum

TIME ZONE -0100
(French Standard Time)
Subtract 1 hour for UT
For French Summer Time add
ONE hour in **non-shaded areas**

FRANCE – CHERBOURG

LAT 49°39′N   LONG 1°38′W

TIMES AND HEIGHTS OF HIGH AND LOW WATERS

Dates in amber are **SPRINGS**
Dates in yellow are **NEAPS**

2014

SEPTEMBER

Time	m	Time	m
1 M 0008	5.8	**16** 0117	5.3
0653	2.0	0805	2.5
1229	5.6	TU 1336	5.2
1917	2.2	☽ 2042	2.7
2 0049	5.5	**17** 0219	4.9
0737	2.3	0908	2.9
TU 1314	5.4	W 1447	4.9
☽ 2011	2.5	2204	2.9
3 0144	5.2	**18** 0349	4.7
0840	2.6	1039	3.0
W 1420	5.1	TH 1621	4.9
2126	2.6	2331	2.8
4 0305	5.0	**19** 0522	4.9
1007	2.7	1200	2.8
TH 1555	5.1	F 1743	5.1
2258	2.5		
5 0448	5.1	**20** 0036	2.5
1138	2.5	0622	5.2
F 1726	5.4	SA 1259	2.5
		1837	5.4
6 0016	2.1	**21** 0126	2.1
0604	5.5	0705	5.6
SA 1249	2.0	SU 1345	2.2
1830	5.9	1918	5.8
7 0121	1.6	**22** 0208	1.8
0703	6.0	0742	5.9
SU 1350	1.6	M 1424	1.9
1925	6.4	1955	6.0
8 0218	1.1	**23** 0244	1.6
0756	6.4	0817	6.1
M 1445	1.2	TU 1459	1.7
2017	6.8	2030	6.2
9 0310	0.7	**24** 0317	1.4
0847	6.7	0850	6.2
TU 1535	0.9	W 1531	1.5
○ 2106	7.0	● 2103	6.4
10 0358	0.6	**25** 0349	1.3
0934	6.8	0921	6.3
W 1621	0.7	TH 1603	1.4
2152	7.1	2133	6.4
11 0443	0.6	**26** 0420	1.3
1017	6.8	0951	6.3
TH 1704	0.8	F 1635	1.4
2235	7.0	2204	6.4
12 0524	0.7	**27** 0451	1.4
1057	6.7	1021	6.3
F 1744	1.0	SA 1707	1.4
2315	6.7	2236	6.3
13 0603	1.1	**28** 0522	1.5
1134	6.4	1054	6.2
SA 1823	1.3	SU 1739	1.6
2354	6.3	2311	6.1
14 0640	1.5	**29** 0555	1.7
1210	6.0	1129	6.0
SU 1903	1.8	M 1815	1.8
		2348	5.9
15 0032	5.8	**30** 0632	2.0
0719	2.1	1207	5.8
M 1248	5.6	TU 1857	2.1
1946	2.3		

OCTOBER

Time	m	Time	m
1 0032	5.6	**16** 0144	5.0
0717	2.3	0826	3.0
W 1255	5.5	TH 1404	5.0
☽ 1952	2.4	2113	2.9
2 0130	5.3	**17** 0304	4.8
0823	2.6	0949	3.1
TH 1402	5.2	F 1529	4.8
2107	2.5	2242	2.9
3 0254	5.1	**18** 0435	4.9
0951	2.8	1117	3.0
F 1540	5.2	SA 1656	5.0
2239	2.4	2354	2.7
4 0438	5.2	**19** 0542	5.1
1123	2.5	1220	2.7
SA 1709	5.5	SU 1757	5.3
5 0000	2.1	**20** 0047	2.3
0550	5.6	0628	5.5
SU 1234	2.1	M 1309	2.3
1813	6.0	1843	5.6
6 0104	1.6	**21** 0131	2.0
0647	6.1	0707	5.8
M 1334	1.6	TU 1350	2.0
1907	6.4	1923	5.9
7 0159	1.2	**22** 0209	1.8
0738	6.5	0744	6.1
TU 1421	1.2	W 1427	1.8
1958	6.7	2000	6.2
8 0250	0.9	**23** 0244	1.6
0825	6.7	0819	6.3
W 1515	0.9	TH 1501	1.5
○ 2045	6.9	2035	6.3
9 0336	0.7	**24** 0319	1.4
0909	6.8	0852	6.4
TH 1559	0.8	F 1536	1.4
2130	6.9	2108	6.4
10 0419	0.8	**25** 0353	1.4
0950	6.8	0924	6.5
F 1640	0.9	SA 1611	1.3
2211	6.8	2142	6.4
11 0458	1.0	**26** 0427	1.4
1028	6.7	0958	6.5
SA 1719	1.1	SU 1647	1.3
2250	6.6	2217	6.4
12 0535	1.3	**27** 0503	1.5
1104	6.4	1033	6.4
SU 1756	1.4	M 1723	1.4
2327	6.2	2255	6.2
13 0611	1.7	**28** 0539	1.7
1140	6.1	1112	6.2
M 1833	1.8	TU 1803	1.6
		2337	6.0
14 0005	5.8	**29** 0621	2.0
0648	2.2	1155	6.0
TU 1217	5.7	W 1848	1.9
1914	2.2		
15 0048	5.4	**30** 0025	5.7
0730	2.6	0711	2.3
W 1301	5.3	TH 1246	5.7
☽ 2003	2.6	1944	2.2
		31 0124	5.4
		0816	2.6
		F 1353	5.4
		☽ 2055	2.4

NOVEMBER

Time	m	Time	m
1 0246	5.2	**16** 0327	4.9
0938	2.7	1011	3.1
SA 1523	5.4	SU 1546	4.9
2219	2.3	2251	2.8
2 0419	5.4	**17** 0442	5.0
1103	2.5	1126	2.9
SU 1647	5.6	M 1700	5.1
2338	2.0	2355	2.6
3 0529	5.7	**18** 0540	5.3
1215	2.1	1223	2.6
M 1751	5.9	TU 1757	5.4
4 0042	1.7	**19** 0046	2.3
0625	6.0	0626	5.6
TU 1314	1.7	W 1310	2.2
1846	6.3	1844	5.7
5 0138	1.4	**20** 0130	2.0
0716	6.4	0708	5.9
W 1407	1.4	TH 1352	1.9
1937	6.5	1927	6.0
6 0228	1.2	**21** 0210	1.7
0802	6.6	0747	6.2
TH 1454	1.2	F 1432	1.6
○ 2024	6.7	2007	6.2
7 0313	1.1	**22** 0249	1.5
0845	6.7	0825	6.4
F 1538	1.1	SA 1511	1.4
2108	6.7	2045	6.3
8 0355	1.1	**23** 0329	1.3
0925	6.7	0902	6.5
SA 1618	1.1	SU 1551	1.3
2148	6.6	2124	6.4
9 0433	1.3	**24** 0408	1.4
1002	6.6	0940	6.6
SU 1656	1.2	M 1632	1.2
2226	6.4	2204	6.4
10 0510	1.5	**25** 0449	1.4
1038	6.4	1020	6.5
M 1733	1.5	TU 1713	1.3
2304	6.1	2246	6.3
11 0545	1.8	**26** 0531	1.6
1114	6.1	1102	6.4
TU 1809	1.8	W 1757	1.4
2342	5.8	2331	6.2
12 0621	2.2	**27** 0616	1.8
1150	5.9	1149	6.2
W 1847	2.1	TH 1845	1.7
13 0022	5.5	**28** 0020	5.9
0701	2.5	0708	2.0
TH 1230	5.5	F 1240	6.0
1929	2.5	1939	1.8
14 0110	5.2	**29** 0117	5.7
0749	2.8	0808	2.3
F 1320	5.2	SA 1342	5.7
☽ 2023	2.7	☽ 2041	2.1
15 0211	4.9	**30** 0229	5.5
0851	3.0	0918	2.4
SA 1428	4.9	SU 1458	5.5
2133	2.9	2154	2.2

DECEMBER

Time	m	Time	m
1 0349	5.4	**16** 0323	5.0
1036	2.4	1009	2.9
M 1616	5.5	TU 1543	4.9
2310	2.1	2245	2.7
2 0500	5.6	**17** 0434	5.1
1149	2.2	1122	2.8
TU 1724	5.7	W 1656	5.1
		2352	2.5
3 0017	1.9	**18** 0538	5.4
0600	5.8	1224	2.5
W 1252	1.9	TH 1800	5.4
1824	5.9		
4 0115	1.7	**19** 0047	2.2
0653	6.1	0630	5.7
TH 1347	1.6	F 1316	2.1
1918	6.1	1853	5.7
5 0207	1.5	**20** 0137	1.9
0741	6.3	0717	6.0
F 1436	1.5	SA 1403	1.8
2007	6.3	1941	6.0
6 0253	1.4	**21** 0223	1.7
0825	6.4	0801	6.2
SA 1520	1.3	SU 1450	1.4
2051	6.3	2026	6.2
7 0334	1.4	**22** 0309	1.4
0904	6.5	0844	6.5
SU 1600	1.3	M 1535	1.2
2130	6.3	2110	6.4
8 0413	1.5	**23** 0354	1.2
0941	6.4	0927	6.6
M 1638	1.3	TU 1621	1.0
2208	6.2	2154	6.5
9 0449	1.8	**24** 0439	1.2
1017	6.3	1011	6.7
TU 1714	1.5	W 1706	1.0
2245	6.1	2239	6.5
10 0524	1.8	**25** 0525	1.3
1053	6.2	1056	6.7
W 1748	1.6	TH 1752	1.0
2321	5.9	2326	6.4
11 0559	2.0	**26** 0612	1.4
1128	6.0	1143	6.5
TH 1823	1.9	F 1839	1.2
2358	5.7		
12 0635	2.3	**27** 0014	6.2
1204	5.7	0701	1.6
F 1900	2.2	SA 1232	6.3
		1928	1.4
13 0036	5.4	**28** 0105	5.9
0715	2.5	0754	1.9
SA 1242	5.4	SU 1325	5.9
1941	2.4	☽ 2022	1.8
14 0120	5.2	**29** 0202	5.6
0801	2.7	0853	2.2
SU 1331	5.2	M 1427	5.6
☽ 2031	2.6	2123	2.1
15 0216	5.0	**30** 0311	5.4
0859	2.9	1003	2.3
M 1432	5.0	TU 1540	5.4
2133	2.8	2235	2.2
		31 0424	5.4
		1119	2.3
		W 1655	5.4
		2348	2.2

Chart Datum: 3·33 metres below IGN Datum
HAT is 7·0 metres above Chart Datum

TIDES

ST MALO

MEAN SPRING
AND
NEAP CURVE

MEAN RANGES
Springs 10.7m
Neaps 5.1m

Factor

| TIME ZONE -0100
(French Standard Time)
Subtract 1 hour for UT
For French Summer Time add
ONE hour in **non-shaded areas** | **FRANCE – ST MALO**
LAT 48°38′N   LONG 2°02′W
TIMES AND HEIGHTS OF HIGH AND LOW WATERS | Dates in amber are **SPRINGS**
Dates in yellow are **NEAPS**

2014 |

JANUARY

Time m	Time m
1 0108 1.7 0635 12.2 W 1337 1.3 ● 1903 12.2	**16** 0142 2.4 0711 11.4 TH 1405 2.3 ○ 1935 11.3
2 0203 1.3 0726 12.7 TH 1432 0.9 1953 12.6	**17** 0218 2.2 0745 11.6 F 1440 2.1 2007 11.4
3 0255 1.0 0814 13.0 F 1523 0.6 2041 12.7	**18** 0253 2.1 0817 11.7 SA 1514 2.1 2039 11.4
4 0343 0.9 0901 13.0 SA 1610 0.7 2127 12.5	**19** 0325 2.1 0848 11.7 SU 1545 2.2 2109 11.4
5 0427 1.1 0946 12.6 SU 1654 1.1 2210 12.0	**20** 0355 2.3 0919 11.6 M 1614 2.3 2140 11.1
6 0511 1.7 1029 12.0 M 1735 1.7 2253 11.4	**21** 0424 2.5 0950 11.3 TU 1643 2.6 2210 10.8
7 0551 2.4 1113 11.2 TU 1816 2.6 2337 10.6	**22** 0455 2.9 1022 10.8 W 1714 3.0 2243 10.3
8 0633 3.2 1200 10.3 W 1901 3.4 ☽	**23** 0530 3.3 1057 10.3 TH 1751 3.5 2322 9.8
9 0027 9.8 0724 3.9 TH 1259 9.6 1955 4.0	**24** 0612 3.8 1143 9.8 F 1838 3.9 ☽
10 0133 9.3 0819 4.4 F 1418 9.1 2103 4.3	**25** 0017 9.4 0710 4.2 SA 1249 9.4 1944 4.2
11 0256 9.2 0947 4.3 SA 1539 9.2 2219 4.1	**26** 0137 9.2 0829 4.2 SU 1417 9.3 2113 4.1
12 0410 9.6 1059 3.9 SU 1645 9.7 2324 3.7	**27** 0307 9.5 0959 3.8 M 1544 9.7 2241 3.5
13 0507 10.1 1157 3.4 M 1737 10.2	**28** 0424 10.3 1115 2.9 TU 1657 10.5 2350 2.6
14 0017 3.2 0554 10.7 TU 1245 2.9 1821 10.7	**29** 0529 11.2 1224 2.0 W 1759 11.4
15 0102 2.8 0635 11.1 W 1327 2.5 1859 11.0	**30** 0055 1.8 0625 12.1 TH 1326 1.2 ● 1854 12.1
	31 0154 1.1 0716 12.8 F 1423 0.6 1944 12.7

FEBRUARY

Time m	Time m
1 0246 0.6 0804 13.2 SA 1513 0.3 2030 12.9	**16** 0235 1.9 0758 11.9 SU 1456 1.8 2019 11.7
2 0332 0.5 0848 13.3 SU 1557 0.3 2112 12.9	**17** 0307 1.8 0830 12.0 M 1528 1.8 2049 11.8
3 0414 0.7 0930 13.0 M 1637 0.7 2152 12.4	**18** 0338 1.8 0900 12.0 TU 1557 1.9 2119 11.6
4 0451 1.2 1009 12.3 TU 1713 1.4 2228 11.7	**19** 0408 2.0 0930 11.7 W 1625 2.1 2148 11.3
5 0526 2.0 1046 11.4 W 1747 2.4 2305 10.9	**20** 0437 2.3 1001 11.3 TH 1654 2.6 2219 10.8
6 0600 3.0 1124 10.4 TH 1821 3.3 ☾ 2344 10.0	**21** 0509 2.8 1034 10.7 F 1727 3.1 2254 10.3
7 0639 3.8 1211 9.4 F 1904 4.2	**22** 0547 3.4 1115 10.0 SA 1809 3.7 ☾ 2342 9.7
8 0037 9.2 0745 4.5 SA 1324 8.7 2009 4.7	**23** 0639 4.0 1215 9.4 SU 1910 4.2
9 0205 8.7 0900 4.8 SU 1507 8.6 2137 4.7	**24** 0059 9.2 0757 4.2 M 1348 9.1 2044 4.3
10 0341 8.9 1028 4.5 M 1624 9.1 2257 4.2	**25** 0243 9.3 0936 3.9 TU 1529 9.4 2222 3.7
11 0446 9.5 1134 3.8 TU 1718 9.8 2355 3.5	**26** 0410 10.0 1100 3.1 W 1647 10.3 2337 2.8
12 0534 10.3 1225 3.1 W 1801 10.4	**27** 0517 11.1 1212 2.1 TH 1748 11.3
13 0042 2.9 0615 10.9 TH 1308 2.6 1839 10.9	**28** 0043 1.8 0613 12.0 F 1314 1.2 1841 12.2
14 0123 2.5 0652 11.4 F 1347 2.2 1915 11.3	
15 0201 2.1 0726 11.7 SA 1423 2.0 ○ 1948 11.6	

MARCH

Time m	Time m
1 0141 1.0 0702 12.8 SA 1408 0.5 ● 1928 12.7	**16** 0135 2.1 0700 11.7 SU 1357 1.9 ○ 1922 11.7
2 0231 0.5 0748 13.2 SU 1456 0.2 2011 13.0	**17** 0211 1.8 0734 12.0 M 1432 1.7 1954 12.0
3 0315 0.4 0830 13.3 M 1537 0.3 2051 12.9	**18** 0245 1.6 0807 12.1 TU 1506 1.6 2025 12.1
4 0353 0.6 0909 13.0 TU 1613 0.9 2127 12.5	**19** 0318 1.5 0838 12.2 W 1536 1.6 2056 12.0
5 0426 1.1 0944 12.3 W 1645 1.5 2200 11.9	**20** 0350 1.6 0910 12.0 TH 1607 1.9 2127 11.7
6 0458 2.0 1018 11.4 TH 1714 2.4 2232 11.0	**21** 0421 2.0 0942 11.6 F 1637 2.3 2200 11.2
7 0527 2.9 1051 10.4 F 1742 3.4 2306 10.1	**22** 0453 2.5 1018 11.0 SA 1711 2.9 2237 10.6
8 0558 3.8 1130 9.4 SA 1818 4.2 ☾ 2349 9.2	**23** 0532 3.1 1101 10.2 SU 1753 3.6 2327 9.9
9 0643 4.6 1230 8.6 SU 1916 4.9	**24** 0624 3.7 1202 9.5 M 1855 4.2 ☾
10 0106 8.5 0801 5.1 M 1425 8.2 2051 5.1	**25** 0043 9.3 0742 4.1 TU 1337 9.1 2029 4.3
11 0301 8.5 0948 4.9 TU 1555 8.7 2223 4.7	**26** 0227 9.3 0921 3.9 W 1517 9.4 2208 3.8
12 0415 9.1 1102 4.2 W 1650 9.4 2325 3.9	**27** 0354 10.0 1046 3.1 TH 1633 10.3 2322 2.8
13 0505 9.9 1155 3.4 TH 1733 10.2	**28** 0500 11.0 1156 2.1 F 1731 11.3
14 0014 3.2 0546 10.6 F 1239 2.8 1812 10.9	**29** 0026 1.9 0554 11.9 SA 1255 1.3 1821 12.0
15 0056 2.6 0624 11.2 SA 1320 2.3 1848 11.4	**30** 0121 1.2 0642 12.5 SU 1347 0.8 ● 1906 12.5
	31 0209 0.8 0726 12.8 M 1432 0.6 1947 12.7

APRIL

Time m	Time m
1 0251 0.7 0807 12.9 TU 1510 0.7 2025 12.7	**16** 0219 1.6 0741 12.1 W 1441 1.5 2000 12.2
2 0328 0.9 0844 12.6 W 1544 1.1 2059 12.4	**17** 0257 1.4 0816 12.2 TH 1515 1.5 2034 12.2
3 0359 1.4 0918 12.0 TH 1614 1.7 2132 11.8	**18** 0332 1.5 0852 12.1 F 1550 1.7 2109 12.0
4 0428 2.0 0951 11.3 F 1642 2.5 2203 11.1	**19** 0408 1.7 0929 11.7 SA 1625 2.1 2147 11.6
5 0457 2.8 1023 10.4 SA 1709 3.3 2235 10.3	**20** 0445 2.2 1010 11.1 SU 1702 2.7 2230 10.9
6 0526 3.6 1059 9.5 SU 1742 4.2 2314 9.4	**21** 0528 2.8 1058 10.4 M 1749 3.4 2324 10.2
7 0604 4.4 1148 8.7 M 1831 4.9 ☾	**22** 0622 3.4 1201 9.7 TU 1852 4.0 ☾
8 0014 8.6 0707 5.0 TU 1322 8.2 1953 5.2	**23** 0037 9.6 0737 3.8 W 1326 9.4 2020 4.1
9 0158 8.4 0849 5.0 W 1504 8.5 2131 5.0	**24** 0208 9.6 0904 3.6 TH 1455 9.6 2146 3.7
10 0324 8.8 1013 4.5 TH 1607 9.1 2240 4.3	**25** 0329 10.1 1023 3.0 F 1608 10.3 2259 2.9
11 0422 9.5 1111 3.8 F 1654 9.9 2332 3.5	**26** 0435 10.8 1131 2.4 SA 1706 11.1
12 0507 10.3 1159 3.1 SA 1735 10.6	**27** 0001 2.0 0530 11.5 SU 1229 1.8 1756 11.7
13 0018 2.8 0549 10.9 SU 1242 2.5 1813 11.2	**28** 0056 1.7 0618 11.9 M 1320 1.5 1840 12.1
14 0100 2.3 0628 11.5 M 1323 2.0 1850 11.7	**29** 0143 1.5 0702 12.2 TU 1403 1.4 ● 1921 12.2
15 0141 1.9 0705 11.9 TU 1402 1.7 1926 12.0	**30** 0223 1.4 0743 12.2 W 1441 1.4 1958 12.2

Chart Datum: 6·29 metres below IGN Datum
HAT is 13·6 metres above Chart Datum

TIDES

TIME ZONE -0100
(French Standard Time)
Subtract 1 hour for UT
For French Summer Time add
ONE hour in **non-shaded areas**

FRANCE – ST MALO
LAT 48°38′N LONG 2°02′W
TIMES AND HEIGHTS OF HIGH AND LOW WATERS

Dates in amber are **SPRINGS**
Dates in yellow are **NEAPS**

2014

MAY

Day	Time m	Time m	Time m	Time m
1 TH	0259 1.5	0819 12.0	1513 1.7	2032 12.0
2 F	0331 1.8	0854 11.7	1544 2.0	2105 11.7
3 SA	0402 2.2	0926 11.1	1614 2.6	2137 11.1
4 SU	0432 2.8	0959 10.5	1643 3.2	2210 10.5
5 M	0501 3.4	1035 9.8	1715 3.9	2247 9.8
6 TU	0536 4.1	1118 9.1	1756 4.5	2336 9.1
7 W	0624 4.6	1221 8.6	1856 5.0	
8 TH	0047 8.7	0733 4.8	1347 8.5	2018 5.0
9 F	0212 8.7	0903 4.7	1504 8.9	2137 4.6
10 SA	0322 9.2	1012 4.1	1602 9.6	2238 3.9
11 SU	0417 9.9	1107 3.5	1650 10.3	2330 3.0
12 M	0506 10.6	1157 2.8	1734 11.0	
13 TU	0019 2.6	0551 11.1	1245 2.3	1815 11.5
14 W	0106 2.1	0634 11.6	1331 1.9	1856 11.9
15 TH	0152 1.7	0715 11.9	1415 1.6	1935 12.2
16 F	0235 1.4	0756 12.1	1457 1.5	2015 12.3
17 SA	0318 1.4	0837 12.1	1537 1.6	2056 12.2
18 SU	0400 1.5	0921 11.9	1618 1.9	2140 11.9
19 M	0443 1.8	1006 11.4	1701 2.4	2227 11.3
20 TU	0529 2.4	1057 10.8	1750 3.0	2321 10.7
21 W	0622 2.9	1155 10.2	1849 3.5	
22 TH	0025 10.2	0726 3.3	1305 9.8	2001 3.7
23 F	0140 9.9	0838 3.4	1422 9.8	2116 3.6
24 SA	0257 10.1	0951 3.2	1535 10.1	2227 3.2
25 SU	0404 10.4	1058 2.9	1636 10.6	2330 2.8
26 M	0502 10.9	1158 2.5	1728 11.1	
27 TU	0026 2.4	0553 11.2	1249 2.3	1815 11.5
28 W	0114 2.2	0639 11.4	1333 2.1	1856 11.7
29 TH	0155 2.0	0720 11.5	1411 2.1	1934 11.7
30 F	0232 2.0	0758 11.5	1446 2.1	2009 11.7
31 SA	0306 2.1	0833 11.3	1519 2.3	2043 11.5

JUNE

Day	Time m	Time m	Time m	Time m
1 SU	0340 2.3	0906 11.1	1551 2.6	2116 11.2
2 M	0411 2.7	0939 10.7	1622 3.0	2149 10.8
3 TU	0441 3.1	1014 10.2	1653 3.5	2224 10.3
4 W	0513 3.6	1051 9.7	1728 4.0	2304 9.7
5 TH	0551 4.0	1136 9.3	1813 4.4	2354 9.3
6 F	0640 4.4	1235 9.0	1911 4.6	
7 SA	0059 9.1	0743 4.5	1348 9.0	2023 4.6
8 SU	0213 9.2	0858 4.3	1458 9.3	2136 4.2
9 M	0320 9.6	1011 3.8	1559 9.9	2241 3.6
10 TU	0419 10.2	1113 3.2	1652 10.6	2339 2.9
11 W	0513 10.8	1208 2.6	1742 11.2	
12 TH	0034 2.3	0604 11.3	1302 2.1	1829 11.8
13 F	0127 1.8	0653 11.8	1353 1.7	1915 12.2
14 SA	0218 1.4	0740 12.1	1442 1.5	2001 12.5
15 SU	0307 1.2	0827 12.3	1529 1.4	2047 12.6
16 M	0354 1.1	0914 12.2	1614 1.5	2134 12.4
17 TU	0440 1.4	1001 11.9	1659 1.9	2221 11.9
18 W	0526 1.8	1049 11.4	1745 2.4	2310 11.3
19 TH	0614 2.4	1139 10.8	1835 3.0	
20 F	0004 10.6	0706 2.9	1235 10.2	1932 3.5
21 SA	0106 10.1	0805 3.4	1341 9.8	2039 3.7
22 SU	0218 9.8	0912 3.6	1455 9.8	2150 3.7
23 M	0332 9.9	1021 3.5	1604 10.1	2258 3.4
24 TU	0436 10.2	1125 3.2	1702 10.5	2357 3.0
25 W	0531 10.5	1220 2.9	1752 10.9	
26 TH	0048 2.7	0619 10.8	1306 2.7	1836 11.2
27 F	0131 2.5	0702 11.1	1347 2.5	1915 11.4
28 SA	0210 2.3	0740 11.2	1424 2.4	1951 11.5
29 SU	0246 2.3	0815 11.2	1458 2.3	2024 11.5
30 M	0320 2.3	0847 11.2	1532 2.4	2056 11.4

JULY

Day	Time m	Time m	Time m	Time m
1 TU	0352 2.5	0919 11.0	1602 2.7	2129 11.2
2 W	0422 2.7	0952 10.7	1632 3.0	2201 10.8
3 TH	0451 3.1	1024 10.4	1703 3.4	2235 10.4
4 F	0522 3.5	1100 9.9	1738 3.8	2313 9.9
5 SA	0600 3.8	1142 9.5	1824 4.2	
6 SU	0002 9.5	0650 4.2	1240 9.3	1922 4.4
7 M	0108 9.3	0754 4.4	1353 9.3	2037 4.3
8 TU	0224 9.4	0914 4.1	1508 9.6	2156 3.9
9 W	0337 9.8	1031 3.6	1615 10.2	2304 3.2
10 TH	0442 10.4	1137 2.9	1715 11.0	
11 F	0007 2.5	0542 11.1	1237 2.3	1809 11.7
12 SA	0107 1.8	0637 11.7	1335 1.7	1901 12.3
13 SU	0204 1.3	0728 12.2	1429 1.3	1950 12.8
14 M	0257 0.9	0817 12.5	1519 1.0	2038 13.0
15 TU	0347 0.7	0904 12.6	1605 1.0	2123 12.9
16 W	0432 0.9	0949 12.4	1649 1.3	2208 12.5
17 TH	0514 1.3	1035 12.1	1731 1.9	2251 11.8
18 F	0555 2.0	1115 11.2	1811 2.7	2336 10.9
19 SA	0638 2.9	1201 10.4	1858 3.4	
20 SU	0029 10.1	0726 3.6	1258 9.8	1956 4.0
21 M	0137 9.4	0829 4.1	1413 9.4	2111 4.2
22 TU	0300 9.3	0943 4.2	1534 9.5	2228 4.0
23 W	0415 9.5	1055 3.9	1641 10.0	2333 3.5
24 TH	0514 10.0	1155 3.4	1733 10.5	
25 F	0026 3.1	0602 10.5	1245 3.0	1818 11.0
26 SA	0111 2.7	0644 10.9	1327 2.6	1857 11.3
27 SU	0151 2.4	0721 11.2	1405 2.4	1932 11.6
28 M	0227 2.3	0755 11.3	1440 2.3	2005 11.7
29 TU	0301 2.2	0827 11.4	1512 2.3	2036 11.7
30 W	0333 2.2	0857 11.4	1542 2.3	2106 11.6
31 TH	0400 2.4	0927 11.2	1610 2.6	2136 11.3

AUGUST

Day	Time m	Time m	Time m	Time m
1 F	0428 2.7	0957 10.9	1639 2.9	2207 10.9
2 SA	0456 3.0	1027 10.5	1710 3.3	2239 10.4
3 SU	0529 3.5	1102 10.0	1748 3.8	2319 9.9
4 M	0610 3.9	1148 9.6	1838 4.2	
5 TU	0015 9.4	0707 4.3	1257 9.3	1948 4.4
6 W	0136 9.2	0827 4.4	1425 9.4	2118 4.1
7 TH	0305 9.5	0958 3.9	1548 9.9	2239 3.4
8 F	0422 10.2	1115 3.2	1656 10.8	2348 2.5
9 SA	0527 11.0	1220 2.3	1755 11.7	
10 SU	0052 1.7	0624 11.8	1322 1.6	1848 12.5
11 M	0152 1.0	0716 12.5	1417 1.0	1937 13.1
12 TU	0245 0.5	0804 12.9	1507 0.7	2023 13.3
13 W	0333 0.4	0848 13.0	1552 0.7	2107 13.2
14 TH	0416 0.6	0930 12.8	1631 1.0	2148 12.7
15 F	0454 1.2	1009 12.2	1709 1.4	2227 11.9
16 SA	0529 2.0	1047 11.4	1743 2.6	2306 10.9
17 SU	0604 3.0	1126 10.5	1822 3.5	2351 9.9
18 M	0645 3.9	1215 9.6	1912 4.3	
19 TU	0054 9.1	0743 4.5	1329 9.0	2030 4.3
20 W	0230 8.7	0906 4.7	1506 9.0	2200 4.5
21 TH	0356 9.1	1030 4.5	1620 9.5	2312 3.9
22 F	0456 9.7	1134 3.7	1713 10.2	
23 SA	0005 3.3	0542 10.4	1223 3.1	1756 10.9
24 SU	0050 2.7	0622 10.9	1306 2.7	1835 11.4
25 M	0130 2.4	0658 11.3	1344 2.3	1909 11.7
26 TU	0206 2.2	0731 11.6	1418 2.2	1942 11.9
27 W	0238 2.0	0803 11.7	1450 2.1	2013 12.0
28 TH	0310 2.0	0832 11.7	1520 2.1	2042 11.9
29 F	0337 2.1	0901 11.6	1548 2.2	2111 11.7
30 SA	0405 2.3	0929 11.4	1616 2.5	2141 11.3
31 SU	0432 2.7	0958 11.0	1646 2.9	2212 10.8

Chart Datum: 6·29 metres below IGN Datum
HAT is 13·6 metres above Chart Datum

TIME ZONE -0100

TIME ZONE -0100
(French Standard Time)
Subtract 1 hour for UT
For French Summer Time add
ONE hour in **non-shaded areas**

FRANCE – ST MALO

LAT 48°38′N   LONG 2°02′W

TIMES AND HEIGHTS OF HIGH AND LOW WATERS

Dates in amber are **SPRINGS**
Dates in yellow are **NEAPS**

2014

SEPTEMBER

Time m	Time m
1 0503 3.2 / 1031 10.4 / M 1721 3.5 / 2249 10.2 ◑	**16** 0605 4.1 / 1135 9.6 / TU 1829 4.5
2 0542 3.8 / 1114 9.8 / TU 1808 4.0 / ◐ 2341 9.5	**17** 0012 8.9 / 0658 4.8 / W 1244 8.8 / 1941 5.0
3 0635 4.3 / 1219 9.3 / W 1915 4.4	**18** 0154 8.4 / 0826 5.2 / TH 1431 8.7 / 2126 4.9
4 0104 9.1 / 0756 4.5 / TH 1357 9.2 / 2053 4.3	**19** 0329 8.8 / 1000 4.8 / F 1552 9.2 / 2243 4.3
5 0247 9.3 / 0939 4.1 / F 1531 9.8 / 2222 3.8	**20** 0430 9.5 / 1105 4.0 / SA 1646 10.0 / 2337 3.5
6 0410 10.1 / 1059 3.2 / SA 1642 10.8 / 2334 2.5	**21** 0514 10.2 / 1154 3.3 / SU 1728 10.7
7 0514 11.1 / 1206 2.3 / SU 1740 11.8	**22** 0021 2.9 / 0553 10.9 / M 1237 2.7 / 1806 11.3
8 0038 1.6 / 0609 12.0 / M 1307 1.4 / 1832 12.7	**23** 0101 2.4 / 0629 11.4 / TU 1316 2.3 / 1842 11.7
9 0136 0.9 / 0659 12.7 / TU 1401 0.9 / ○ 1920 13.2	**24** 0137 2.1 / 0703 11.7 / W 1351 2.1 / ● 1915 12.0
10 0227 0.4 / 0744 13.1 / W 1449 0.6 / 2004 13.4	**25** 0211 2.0 / 0735 11.9 / TH 1425 1.9 / 1947 12.1
11 0312 0.4 / 0827 13.1 / TH 1531 0.6 / 2046 13.2	**26** 0244 1.9 / 0805 12.0 / F 1456 1.9 / 2018 12.1
12 0352 0.7 / 0906 12.8 / F 1608 1.1 / 2124 12.7	**27** 0314 2.0 / 0835 11.9 / SA 1527 2.0 / 2048 11.9
13 0428 1.3 / 0942 12.2 / SA 1643 1.8 / 2200 11.9	**28** 0343 2.2 / 0905 11.7 / SU 1557 2.2 / 2119 11.6
14 0459 2.2 / 1017 11.4 / SU 1713 2.7 / 2236 10.9	**29** 0413 2.5 / 0936 11.3 / M 1629 2.7 / 2152 11.1
15 0529 3.2 / 1052 10.5 / M 1746 3.6 / 2316 9.8	**30** 0445 3.0 / 1011 10.7 / TU 1705 3.2 / 2231 10.4

OCTOBER

Time m	Time m
1 0524 3.7 / 1055 10.1 / W 1752 3.8 / ◐ 2325 9.6	**16** 0618 4.8 / 1159 8.9 / TH 1853 5.0
2 0618 4.2 / 1202 9.4 / TH 1859 4.3	**17** 0100 8.4 / 0734 5.3 / F 1336 8.5 / 2031 5.1
3 0050 9.1 / 0741 4.5 / F 1342 9.3 / 2036 4.2	**18** 0243 8.5 / 0912 5.1 / SA 1506 8.9 / 2157 4.6
4 0235 9.3 / 0926 4.1 / SA 1515 9.9 / 2206 3.5	**19** 0350 9.2 / 1023 4.4 / SU 1605 9.6 / 2255 3.9
5 0355 10.1 / 1043 3.2 / SU 1625 10.8 / 2318 2.5	**20** 0437 9.9 / 1115 3.7 / M 1651 10.3 / 2342 3.2
6 0457 11.1 / 1149 2.3 / M 1722 11.8	**21** 0518 10.7 / 1200 3.0 / TU 1732 11.0
7 0020 1.6 / 0550 12.0 / TU 1247 1.5 / 1813 12.6	**22** 0024 2.7 / 0555 11.3 / W 1241 2.5 / 1810 11.5
8 0115 1.0 / 0637 12.6 / W 1340 1.0 / ○ 1859 13.0	**23** 0104 2.3 / 0631 11.7 / TH 1320 2.1 / ● 1846 11.8
9 0204 0.7 / 0721 12.9 / TH 1426 0.8 / 1942 13.1	**24** 0141 2.0 / 0706 12.0 / F 1358 1.9 / 1921 12.0
10 0247 0.7 / 0802 12.9 / F 1507 0.9 / 2022 12.9	**25** 0218 1.9 / 0739 12.1 / SA 1434 1.8 / 1954 12.1
11 0325 1.1 / 0839 12.6 / SA 1542 1.3 / 2059 12.4	**26** 0252 1.9 / 0811 12.1 / SU 1509 1.8 / 2028 12.0
12 0358 1.6 / 0914 12.1 / SU 1616 2.0 / 2134 11.7	**27** 0326 2.0 / 0845 12.0 / M 1543 2.0 / 2103 11.8
13 0429 2.4 / 0948 11.4 / M 1645 2.7 / 2209 10.8	**28** 0359 2.3 / 0921 11.6 / TU 1619 2.4 / 2142 11.3
14 0458 3.3 / 1022 10.6 / TU 1716 3.6 / 2246 9.8	**29** 0436 2.8 / 1001 11.1 / W 1659 2.9 / 2226 10.6
15 0531 4.1 / 1102 9.7 / W 1754 4.4 / ◐ 2335 9.0	**30** 0518 3.4 / 1050 10.4 / TH 1748 3.5 / 2323 9.9
	31 0614 4.0 / 1157 9.8 / F 1855 3.9 / ◐

NOVEMBER

Time m	Time m
1 0042 9.4 / 0733 4.3 / SA 1325 9.6 / 2021 3.9	**16** 0126 8.6 / 0758 5.1 / SU 1353 8.7 / 2045 4.9
2 0214 9.5 / 0904 4.0 / SU 1451 10.0 / 2144 3.4	**17** 0248 8.8 / 0920 4.8 / M 1507 9.1 / 2158 4.4
3 0332 10.2 / 1020 3.3 / M 1601 10.7 / 2255 2.6	**18** 0348 9.5 / 1018 3.9 / TU 1604 9.7 / 2253 3.7
4 0424 11.0 / 1126 2.5 / TU 1659 11.5 / 2356 1.9	**19** 0435 10.2 / 1115 3.5 / W 1651 10.4 / 2341 3.1
5 0527 11.7 / 1224 1.9 / W 1750 12.1	**20** 0518 10.9 / 1202 2.8 / TH 1735 11.0
6 0051 1.5 / 0614 12.2 / TH 1316 1.5 / ○ 1837 12.4	**21** 0026 2.6 / 0558 11.4 / F 1247 2.3 / 1816 11.5
7 0138 1.3 / 0658 12.5 / F 1401 1.3 / 1920 12.5	**22** 0110 2.2 / 0637 11.8 / SA 1330 2.0 / ● 1856 11.8
8 0220 1.1 / 0738 12.5 / SA 1441 1.4 / 2000 12.3	**23** 0153 1.9 / 0715 12.1 / SU 1413 1.7 / 1935 12.0
9 0257 1.5 / 0815 12.3 / SU 1516 1.7 / 2037 12.0	**24** 0234 1.8 / 0753 12.2 / M 1454 1.6 / 2014 12.1
10 0330 1.9 / 0850 12.0 / M 1550 2.1 / 2112 11.5	**25** 0313 1.8 / 0832 12.2 / TU 1535 1.7 / 2055 11.9
11 0402 2.5 / 0924 11.4 / TU 1621 2.7 / 2147 10.8	**26** 0353 2.0 / 0914 12.0 / W 1617 1.9 / 2139 11.6
12 0433 3.1 / 0958 10.7 / W 1653 3.4 / 2223 10.1	**27** 0435 2.4 / 0959 11.5 / TH 1701 2.4 / 2226 11.0
13 0506 3.9 / 1035 10.0 / TH 1727 4.0 / 2304 9.4	**28** 0520 2.9 / 1049 10.9 / F 1750 2.9 / 2320 10.4
14 0545 4.5 / 1121 9.3 / F 1812 4.6 / ◐	**29** 0614 3.4 / 1148 10.3 / SA 1849 3.3 / ◐
15 0002 8.8 / 0640 5.0 / SA 1227 8.8 / 1916 5.0	**30** 0025 9.9 / 0719 3.8 / SU 1300 10.0 / 1958 3.5

DECEMBER

Time m	Time m
1 0142 9.8 / 0836 3.8 / M 1418 10.0 / 2113 3.4	**16** 0123 8.8 / 0757 4.8 / TU 1350 8.9 / 2034 4.7
2 0259 10.0 / 0950 3.6 / TU 1532 10.3 / 2225 3.0	**17** 0240 9.0 / 0915 4.6 / W 1504 9.2 / 2155 4.2
3 0405 10.5 / 1059 2.9 / W 1635 10.8 / 2329 2.6	**18** 0345 9.6 / 1023 4.0 / TH 1605 9.8 / 2256 3.6
4 0502 11.1 / 1159 2.4 / TH 1729 11.3	**19** 0438 10.3 / 1122 3.3 / F 1659 10.5 / 2350 3.0
5 0025 2.2 / 0552 11.6 / F 1252 2.1 / 1818 11.6	**20** 0527 11.0 / 1215 2.6 / SA 1748 11.1
6 0113 2.0 / 0637 11.9 / SA 1338 1.9 / ○ 1902 11.8	**21** 0041 2.4 / 0612 11.6 / SU 1306 2.0 / 1835 11.6
7 0156 1.9 / 0718 12.0 / SU 1419 1.8 / 1943 11.8	**22** 0131 1.9 / 0656 12.0 / M 1356 1.6 / ● 1920 12.0
8 0233 1.9 / 0756 12.0 / M 1455 1.9 / 2020 11.7	**23** 0219 1.6 / 0740 12.4 / TU 1444 1.3 / 2005 12.2
9 0308 2.1 / 0831 11.8 / TU 1529 2.1 / 2055 11.4	**24** 0306 1.4 / 0825 12.6 / W 1531 1.2 / 2050 12.3
10 0341 2.4 / 0905 11.5 / W 1603 2.5 / 2128 11.0	**25** 0351 1.4 / 0909 12.5 / TH 1616 1.3 / 2135 12.1
11 0414 2.8 / 0939 11.1 / TH 1634 3.0 / 2202 10.5	**26** 0434 1.7 / 0955 12.2 / F 1701 1.6 / 2221 11.7
12 0445 3.3 / 1013 10.5 / F 1705 3.5 / 2243 10.1	**27** 0519 2.1 / 1042 11.6 / SA 1746 2.1 / 2309 11.1
13 0517 3.9 / 1049 9.9 / SA 1738 4.0 / 2318 9.4	**28** 0605 2.7 / 1132 11.0 / SU 1834 2.7 / ◐
14 0557 4.4 / 1133 9.4 / SU 1821 4.4	**29** 0001 10.4 / 0658 3.3 / M 1230 10.3 / 1930 3.3
15 0011 9.0 / 0649 4.7 / M 1233 9.0 / 1920 4.7	**30** 0104 9.9 / 0801 3.7 / TU 1340 9.9 / 2036 3.6
	31 0219 9.7 / 0914 3.8 / W 1459 9.8 / 2150 3.6

Chart Datum: 6·29 metres below IGN Datum
HAT is 13·6 metres above Chart Datum

TIDES

ST PETER PORT

MEAN SPRING
AND NEAP CURVES

MEAN RANGES
Springs 7.9m
Neaps 3.4m

CHANNEL ISLES – ST PETER PORT

LAT 49°27'N   LONG 2°31'W

TIMES AND HEIGHTS OF HIGH AND LOW WATERS

2014

JANUARY

Day	Time m	Time m	Time m	Time m
1 W ●	0004 1.6	0603 9.4	1233 1.1	1831 9.3
16 TH ○	0039 2.1	0635 8.8	1304 2.0	1859 8.6
2 TH	0056 1.2	0653 9.7	1324 0.8	1920 9.6
17 F	0114 2.0	0710 8.9	1338 1.8	1934 8.7
3 F	0144 0.9	0741 10.0	1412 0.6	2008 9.7
18 SA	0147 1.9	0744 9.0	1410 1.8	2006 8.7
4 SA	0231 0.9	0827 10.0	1458 0.7	2053 9.6
19 SU	0218 1.9	0816 8.9	1440 1.9	2037 8.6
5 SU	0315 1.1	0912 9.7	1542 1.0	2136 9.2
20 M	0248 2.1	0846 8.7	1509 2.1	2106 8.4
6 M	0359 1.5	0956 9.3	1626 1.5	2220 8.7
21 TU	0318 2.3	0917 8.5	1538 2.3	2137 8.1
7 TU	0443 2.1	1042 8.6	1711 2.1	2307 8.1
22 W	0350 2.6	0950 8.2	1611 2.6	2211 7.9
8 W ☽	0531 2.7	1133 8.0	1801 2.8	
23 TH	0426 2.9	1030 7.9	1650 2.9	2254 7.6
9 TH	0000 7.6	0628 3.3	1234 7.4	1901 3.3
24 F ☽	0512 3.2	1119 7.5	1741 3.2	2351 7.3
10 F	0108 7.2	0728 3.6	1351 7.1	2014 3.6
25 SA	0615 3.4	1225 7.3	1850 3.4	
11 SA	0230 7.1	0904 3.6	1508 7.1	2130 3.5
26 SU	0107 7.2	0741 3.5	1349 7.2	2021 3.4
12 SU	0339 7.3	1011 3.3	1610 7.4	2230 3.2
27 M	0237 7.4	0910 3.1	1516 7.5	2145 2.9
13 M	0432 7.7	1103 2.9	1659 7.7	2319 2.8
28 TU	0354 7.9	1024 2.5	1627 8.1	2254 2.3
14 TU	0517 8.2	1147 2.5	1743 8.1	
29 W	0457 8.6	1126 1.8	1727 8.7	2352 1.6
15 W	0001 2.4	0557 8.5	1228 2.2	1822 8.4
30 TH	0552 9.3	1222 1.1	1821 9.3	
31 F	0045 1.0	0642 9.8	1312 0.6	1909 9.7

FEBRUARY

Day	Time m	Time m	Time m	Time m
1 SA	0133 0.6	0729 10.1	1359 0.3	1954 9.9
16 SU	0128 1.6	0725 9.1	1350 1.5	1946 8.9
2 SU	0218 0.5	0813 10.2	1442 0.3	2036 9.9
17 M	0200 1.5	0757 9.1	1419 1.5	2016 8.9
3 M	0300 0.6	0855 10.0	1523 0.6	2116 9.5
18 TU	0230 1.6	0827 9.0	1448 1.7	2045 8.7
4 TU	0339 1.0	0935 9.5	1602 1.1	2154 9.0
19 W	0259 1.8	0856 8.8	1516 1.9	2114 8.5
5 W	0417 1.6	1013 8.8	1639 1.9	2231 8.3
20 TH	0329 2.1	0928 8.5	1547 2.2	2146 8.2
6 TH	0455 2.4	1054 8.0	1719 2.4	2312 7.6
21 F	0402 2.4	1005 8.1	1623 2.6	2226 7.9
7 F	0539 3.1	1141 7.3	1807 3.4	
22 SA	0444 2.8	1051 7.7	1709 3.0	2318 7.5
8 SA	0004 7.0	0639 3.7	1251 6.7	1912 3.9
23 SU	0542 3.2	1154 7.2	1815 3.4	
9 SU	0128 6.7	0806 4.0	1430 6.6	2042 4.0
24 M	0031 7.1	0707 3.4	1321 7.0	1951 3.5
10 M	0305 6.8	0941 3.7	1546 6.9	2203 3.6
25 TU	0210 7.2	0850 3.2	1500 7.3	2129 3.1
11 TU	0409 7.3	1041 3.2	1639 7.4	2257 3.1
26 W	0338 7.2	1011 2.5	1616 7.9	2242 2.4
12 W	0456 7.8	1126 2.7	1722 7.8	2340 2.6
27 TH	0444 8.5	1113 1.7	1715 8.6	2339 1.6
13 TH	0537 8.3	1206 2.3	1801 8.3	
28 F	0538 9.2	1206 1.0	1806 9.3	
14 F	0019 2.1	0615 8.7	1243 1.9	1838 8.6
15 SA	0055 1.8	0651 8.9	1318 1.6	1913 8.8

MARCH

Day	Time m	Time m	Time m	Time m
1 SA ●	0030 0.9	0626 9.8	1255 0.5	1852 9.7
16 SU	0027 1.8	0625 8.9	1250 1.5	1847 8.9
2 SU	0116 0.5	0711 10.1	1340 0.2	1935 10.0
17 M	0103 1.5	0700 9.1	1323 1.3	1921 9.1
3 M	0159 0.3	0754 10.2	1421 0.2	2015 9.9
18 TU	0137 1.3	0733 9.2	1355 1.3	1952 9.1
4 TU	0239 0.4	0833 10.0	1459 0.5	2051 9.6
19 W	0208 1.3	0805 9.2	1425 1.4	2022 9.0
5 W	0315 0.8	0910 9.5	1534 1.1	2125 9.1
20 TH	0239 1.4	0836 9.0	1455 1.6	2053 8.8
6 TH	0349 1.5	0944 8.8	1607 1.8	2157 8.4
21 F	0310 1.7	0910 8.7	1527 1.9	2127 8.5
7 F	0422 2.2	1018 8.0	1640 2.6	2231 7.7
22 SA	0345 2.1	0948 8.3	1604 2.4	2207 8.1
8 SA	0458 3.0	1058 7.3	1719 3.4	2313 7.1
23 SU	0428 2.5	1035 7.8	1651 2.9	2300 7.6
9 SU	0549 3.7	1153 6.6	1818 4.0	
24 M ☽	0526 3.0	1138 7.3	1757 3.4	
10 M	0019 6.6	0707 4.1	1332 6.3	1943 4.2
25 TU	0013 7.2	0651 3.3	1307 7.0	1935 3.5
11 TU	0211 6.5	0852 4.0	1512 6.6	2121 3.9
26 W	0152 7.2	0835 3.1	1446 7.3	2115 3.1
12 W	0335 6.9	1008 3.5	1610 7.1	2225 3.3
27 TH	0321 7.7	0954 2.4	1600 7.9	2224 2.3
13 TH	0427 7.5	1056 2.9	1654 7.7	2311 2.7
28 F	0425 8.4	1054 1.7	1656 8.6	2320 1.6
14 F	0509 8.0	1136 2.3	1734 8.2	2350 2.2
29 SA	0518 9.1	1145 1.1	1745 9.2	
15 SA	0548 8.5	1214 1.9	1812 8.6	
30 SU	0009 1.0	0605 9.6	1233 0.6	1829 9.6
31 M	0055 0.6	0650 9.9	1316 0.4	1911 9.8

APRIL

Day	Time m	Time m	Time m	Time m
1 TU	0136 0.5	0731 9.9	1356 0.5	1950 9.8
16 W	0110 1.3	0707 9.2	1329 1.2	1926 9.2
2 W	0215 0.6	0809 9.7	1433 0.8	2025 9.5
17 TH	0146 1.2	0743 9.2	1403 1.3	2000 9.2
3 TH	0250 1.0	0845 9.3	1506 1.3	2057 9.0
18 F	0221 1.2	0819 9.1	1438 1.4	2036 9.1
4 F	0322 1.6	0917 8.7	1537 2.0	2128 8.5
19 SA	0257 1.4	0857 8.8	1514 1.8	2114 8.8
5 SA	0353 2.2	0950 8.0	1607 2.7	2200 7.8
20 SU	0336 1.8	0939 8.4	1554 2.2	2158 8.3
6 SU	0426 2.9	1026 7.3	1642 3.3	2238 7.2
21 M	0422 2.3	1029 7.9	1644 2.8	2253 7.8
7 M	0510 3.5	1115 6.7	1733 3.9	2332 6.7
22 TU ☽	0523 2.8	1132 7.4	1752 3.2	
8 TU	0621 3.9	1233 6.4	1853 4.1	
23 W	0004 7.5	0644 3.0	1255 7.2	1923 3.3
9 W	0102 6.5	0749 4.0	1415 6.5	2020 4.0
24 TH	0133 7.4	0815 2.9	1424 7.4	2053 3.0
10 TH	0239 6.7	0912 3.6	1525 6.9	2135 3.5
25 F	0256 7.8	0930 2.4	1535 7.9	2201 2.4
11 F	0343 7.2	1011 3.1	1615 7.5	2229 2.9
26 SA	0400 8.3	1029 1.9	1631 8.5	2256 1.8
12 SA	0431 7.8	1056 2.5	1658 8.0	2313 2.4
27 SU	0454 8.8	1120 1.4	1720 9.0	2345 1.4
13 SU	0513 8.3	1137 2.0	1738 8.5	2354 1.9
28 M	0542 9.2	1207 1.1	1805 9.3	
14 M	0553 8.7	1216 1.6	1816 8.9	
29 TU ●	0030 1.1	0626 9.4	1251 1.0	1846 9.5
15 TU	0032 1.5	0631 9.0	1253 1.4	1851 9.1
30 W	0112 1.0	0708 9.4	1330 1.0	1924 9.4

Chart Datum: 5·06 metres below Ordnance Datum (Local)
HAT is 10·3 metres above Chart Datum

TIDES

CHANNEL ISLES – ST PETER PORT

LAT 49°27'N LONG 2°31'W

TIMES AND HEIGHTS OF HIGH AND LOW WATERS

TIME ZONE (UT)
For Summer Time add ONE hour in **non-shaded areas**

Dates in amber are **SPRINGS**
Dates in yellow are **NEAPS**

2014

MAY

Day	Time m	Time m	Time m	Time m
1 TH	0151 1.1	0746 9.3	1407 1.2	2000 9.2
2 F	0226 1.3	0821 8.9	1440 1.6	2032 8.9
3 SA	0258 1.7	0854 8.5	1511 2.1	2103 8.5
4 SU	0329 2.2	0927 8.0	1541 2.6	2136 8.0
5 M	0402 2.8	1003 7.5	1615 3.2	2213 7.5
6 TU	0442 3.3	1047 7.0	1659 3.6	2259 7.1
7 W	0538 3.6	1147 6.7	1805 3.9	
8 TH	0005 6.8	0653 3.8	1307 6.6	1923 3.9
9 F	0129 6.8	0808 3.6	1423 6.9	2035 3.6
10 SA	0243 7.1	0913 3.2	1524 7.3	2137 3.2
11 SU	0341 7.5	1007 2.8	1614 7.8	2229 2.6
12 M	0431 8.0	1055 2.3	1659 8.3	2316 2.1
13 TU	0516 8.4	1139 1.9	1741 8.7	
14 W	0000 1.7	0559 8.8	1223 1.5	1822 9.1
15 TH	0044 1.3	0642 9.1	1304 1.3	1902 9.3
16 F	0126 1.1	0724 9.2	1345 1.2	1943 9.4
17 SA	0207 1.1	0806 9.2	1425 1.3	2024 9.3
18 SU	0249 1.2	0849 9.0	1507 1.6	2107 9.0
19 M	0333 1.5	0935 8.6	1552 2.0	2154 8.7
20 TU	0423 1.9	1026 8.2	1644 2.4	2248 8.2
21 W	0521 2.4	1125 7.8	1747 2.9	2352 7.8
22 TH	0631 2.7	1236 7.6	1903 3.0	
23 F	0108 7.7	0747 2.7	1353 7.6	2023 2.9
24 SA	0225 7.8	0859 2.5	1504 7.8	2132 2.6
25 SU	0332 8.0	1000 2.2	1603 8.2	2230 2.2
26 M	0428 8.3	1054 2.0	1653 8.5	2320 1.9
27 TU	0518 8.6	1141 1.7	1739 8.8	
28 W	0007 1.7	0604 8.8	1226 1.6	1821 9.0
29 TH	0050 1.5	0646 8.9	1307 1.6	1901 9.1
30 F	0129 1.5	0725 8.8	1344 1.7	1937 9.0
31 SA	0205 1.7	0801 8.7	1417 1.9	2011 8.8

JUNE

Day	Time m	Time m	Time m	Time m
1 SU	0238 1.9	0835 8.4	1449 2.2	2044 8.5
2 M	0310 2.2	0909 8.1	1520 2.5	2116 8.2
3 TU	0342 2.6	0943 7.7	1553 2.9	2151 7.8
4 W	0417 2.9	1021 7.4	1631 3.3	2231 7.4
5 TH	0500 3.3	1107 7.1	1720 3.6	2321 7.2
6 F	0556 3.5	1204 6.9	1824 3.7	
7 SA	0023 7.0	0704 3.5	1314 6.9	1935 3.6
8 SU	0135 7.1	0813 3.4	1423 7.2	2043 3.3
9 M	0245 7.3	0916 3.0	1524 7.6	2144 2.9
10 TU	0346 7.7	1013 2.6	1618 8.1	2239 2.4
11 W	0440 8.2	1106 2.2	1708 8.5	2331 1.9
12 TH	0532 8.6	1156 1.7	1757 9.0	
13 F	0021 1.4	0621 9.0	1245 1.4	1843 9.3
14 SA	0110 1.1	0709 9.2	1332 1.2	1929 9.5
15 SU	0157 0.9	0756 9.3	1417 1.1	2015 9.6
16 M	0243 0.9	0842 9.3	1503 1.3	2101 9.4
17 TU	0330 1.1	0928 9.0	1549 1.6	2148 9.1
18 W	0418 1.5	1017 8.7	1638 2.0	2238 8.7
19 TH	0510 1.9	1110 8.2	1732 2.4	2333 8.2
20 F	0607 2.4	1209 7.8	1834 2.8	
21 SA	0037 7.8	0712 2.7	1317 7.6	1946 3.0
22 SU	0150 7.6	0823 2.9	1429 7.6	2100 3.0
23 M	0302 7.6	0930 2.8	1534 7.7	2204 2.8
24 TU	0404 7.8	1028 2.6	1629 8.0	2258 2.5
25 W	0457 8.0	1119 2.4	1717 8.3	2346 2.2
26 TH	0544 8.3	1204 2.1	1801 8.6	
27 F	0029 2.0	0627 8.5	1246 2.0	1840 8.8
28 SA	0110 1.8	0706 8.6	1324 1.9	1918 8.8
29 SU	0146 1.8	0743 8.6	1358 2.0	1953 8.8
30 M	0219 1.9	0817 8.5	1430 2.1	2026 8.6

JULY

Day	Time m	Time m	Time m	Time m
1 TU	0251 2.1	0850 8.3	1501 2.3	2057 8.4
2 W	0321 2.3	0922 8.1	1532 2.6	2129 8.1
3 TH	0352 2.6	0955 7.8	1605 2.9	2203 7.8
4 F	0426 2.9	1031 7.5	1642 3.2	2243 7.6
5 SA	0507 3.2	1115 7.3	1730 3.4	2333 7.3
6 SU	0601 3.4	1211 7.1	1833 3.5	
7 M	0036 7.2	0711 3.4	1321 7.2	1949 3.4
8 TU	0150 7.2	0827 3.3	1436 7.4	2103 3.1
9 W	0305 7.5	0936 2.9	1543 7.8	2209 2.6
10 TH	0411 8.0	1039 2.4	1643 8.4	2309 2.0
11 F	0511 8.4	1136 1.9	1737 8.9	
12 SA	0004 1.4	0605 8.9	1230 1.4	1828 9.4
13 SU	0058 1.0	0657 9.3	1321 1.0	1918 9.7
14 M	0147 0.6	0745 9.6	1409 0.8	2005 9.9
15 TU	0234 0.5	0832 9.6	1454 0.8	2050 9.8
16 W	0319 0.7	0916 9.5	1538 1.1	2134 9.5
17 TH	0404 1.0	1001 9.1	1622 1.5	2219 9.0
18 F	0449 1.6	1046 8.5	1708 2.1	2307 8.4
19 SA	0537 2.3	1136 7.9	1800 2.8	
20 SU	0002 7.7	0633 2.9	1236 7.4	1904 3.3
21 M	0112 7.2	0741 3.3	1350 7.2	2024 3.5
22 TU	0233 7.1	0859 3.4	1507 7.3	2141 3.3
23 W	0344 7.3	1006 3.2	1608 7.6	2240 3.0
24 TH	0440 7.6	1100 2.8	1658 8.0	2329 2.6
25 F	0527 8.0	1146 2.5	1742 8.3	
26 SA	0012 2.2	0608 8.3	1227 2.2	1821 8.6
27 SU	0051 2.0	0647 8.5	1304 2.0	1858 8.8
28 M	0126 1.8	0723 8.7	1339 1.9	1933 8.9
29 TU	0159 1.8	0757 8.7	1410 1.9	2006 8.8
30 W	0229 1.8	0828 8.6	1440 2.0	2036 8.7
31 TH	0258 2.0	0858 8.4	1509 2.2	2105 8.5

AUGUST

Day	Time m	Time m	Time m	Time m
1 F	0325 2.3	0926 8.2	1538 2.5	2136 8.2
2 SA	0355 2.6	0958 7.9	1611 2.8	2211 7.9
3 SU	0430 2.9	1036 7.6	1650 3.1	2254 7.6
4 M	0515 3.2	1125 7.3	1744 3.4	2351 7.3
5 TU	0617 3.5	1231 7.2	1900 3.5	
6 W	0107 7.1	0743 3.5	1356 7.2	2030 3.3
7 TH	0235 7.3	0909 3.2	1517 7.7	2148 2.8
8 F	0353 7.8	1021 2.6	1625 8.3	2253 2.1
9 SA	0457 8.4	1122 1.9	1723 9.0	2351 1.4
10 SU	0553 9.0	1217 1.3	1815 9.6	
11 M	0044 0.8	0643 9.5	1308 0.8	1903 10.0
12 TU	0133 0.4	0730 9.8	1355 0.5	1949 10.2
13 W	0218 0.3	0815 9.9	1439 0.5	2033 10.1
14 TH	0301 0.4	0857 9.8	1520 0.8	2114 9.8
15 F	0342 0.9	0937 9.3	1600 1.4	2155 9.2
16 SA	0422 1.6	1017 8.7	1640 2.0	2236 8.4
17 SU	0503 2.4	1059 8.0	1724 2.9	2323 7.6
18 M	0552 3.1	1150 7.3	1821 3.6	
19 TU	0027 6.9	0656 3.7	1306 6.9	1941 3.9
20 W	0203 6.7	0823 3.9	1439 6.9	2117 3.7
21 TH	0326 6.9	0944 3.6	1548 7.2	2222 3.3
22 F	0422 7.3	1040 3.2	1638 7.7	2310 2.8
23 SA	0506 7.8	1125 2.7	1720 8.2	2350 2.4
24 SU	0546 8.3	1205 2.3	1759 8.6	
25 M	0027 2.0	0623 8.6	1241 1.9	1835 8.9
26 TU	0102 1.7	0658 8.8	1315 1.7	1910 9.1
27 W	0134 1.6	0732 8.9	1347 1.7	1942 9.1
28 TH	0204 1.5	0803 8.9	1417 1.7	2012 9.0
29 F	0232 1.6	0831 8.7	1445 1.9	2041 8.8
30 SA	0259 2.0	0859 8.5	1513 2.2	2110 8.5
31 SU	0327 2.3	0929 8.2	1544 2.5	2143 8.2

Chart Datum: 5·06 metres below Ordnance Datum (Local)
HAT is 10·3 metres above Chart Datum

CHANNEL ISLES – ST PETER PORT

LAT 49°27'N   LONG 2°31'W

TIMES AND HEIGHTS OF HIGH AND LOW WATERS

Dates in amber are **SPRINGS**
Dates in yellow are **NEAPS**

2014

SEPTEMBER

Day	Time m	Time m	Time m	Time m		Day	Time m	Time m	Time m	Time m
1 M	0400 2.7	1005 7.9	1621 2.9	2225 7.8		**16** TU	0511 3.3	1106 7.3	1739 3.6	2340 6.8 ☽
2 TU	0442 3.1	1052 7.5	1712 3.3	2320 7.3 ☽		**17** W	0611 4.0	1214 6.7	1855 4.1	
3 W	0542 3.5	1158 7.2	1826 3.6			**18** TH	0119 6.5	0738 4.2	1401 6.6	2041 4.1
4 TH	0039 7.1	0712 3.7	1329 7.2	2008 3.4		**19** F	0259 6.7	0914 4.0	1519 7.0	2154 3.6
5 F	0218 7.2	0852 3.3	1501 7.6	2134 2.8		**20** SA	0356 7.2	1013 3.4	1611 7.6	2242 3.0
6 SA	0341 7.8	1008 2.7	1611 8.3	2240 2.1		**21** SU	0439 7.8	1057 2.9	1653 8.1	2321 2.5
7 SU	0444 8.5	1108 1.9	1708 9.0	2336 1.3		**22** M	0518 8.3	1136 2.4	1731 8.6	2358 2.1
8 M	0537 9.2	1201 1.2	1759 9.7			**23** TU	0554 8.7	1212 2.0	1808 8.9	
9 TU	0026 0.7	0625 9.7	1250 0.7	1845 10.1 ○		**24** W	0032 1.8	0629 8.9	1247 1.7	1843 9.1 ●
10 W	0114 0.3	0710 10.0	1336 0.4	1930 10.3		**25** TH	0105 1.6	0703 9.1	1320 1.6	1916 9.2
11 TH	0157 0.3	0753 10.1	1418 0.4	2012 10.2		**26** F	0136 1.6	0735 9.1	1351 1.6	1947 9.2
12 F	0238 0.5	0832 9.9	1457 0.8	2051 9.8		**27** SA	0206 1.7	0804 9.0	1422 1.7	2017 9.0
13 SA	0316 1.0	0910 9.4	1534 1.3	2128 9.1		**28** SU	0235 1.9	0834 8.8	1452 2.0	2048 8.7
14 SU	0352 1.7	0946 8.7	1611 2.1	2205 8.3		**29** M	0305 2.2	0906 8.5	1524 2.3	2123 8.4
15 M	0429 2.5	1022 8.9	1649 2.9	2245 7.5		**30** TU	0339 2.6	0943 8.1	1603 2.7	2206 7.9

OCTOBER

Day	Time m	Time m	Time m	Time m		Day	Time m	Time m	Time m	Time m
1 W	0422 3.1	1032 7.7	1654 3.2	2303 7.4 ☽		**16** TH	0526 4.0	1126 6.9	1810 4.1	
2 TH	0523 3.5	1139 7.3	1810 3.5			**17** F	0020 6.5	0645 4.3	1259 6.6	1938 4.2
3 F	0023 7.1	0656 3.7	1312 7.2	1953 3.4		**18** SA	0207 6.6	0818 4.2	1431 6.9	2105 3.8
4 SA	0205 7.3	0839 3.4	1445 7.7	2119 2.8		**19** SU	0316 7.0	0930 3.7	1531 7.3	2200 3.3
5 SU	0326 7.9	0953 2.7	1553 8.4	2223 2.1		**20** M	0403 7.6	1019 3.1	1617 7.9	2244 2.8
6 M	0426 8.6	1051 1.9	1649 9.1	2317 1.4		**21** TU	0443 8.1	1100 2.6	1657 8.4	2322 2.3
7 TU	0517 9.2	1142 1.3	1738 9.6			**22** W	0521 8.6	1139 2.2	1736 8.8	2359 1.9
8 W	0005 0.9	0603 9.7	1229 0.8	1824 10.0 ○		**23** TH	0558 8.9	1216 1.8	1813 9.0 ●	
9 TH	0051 0.6	0647 10.0	1314 0.7	1908 10.1		**24** F	0034 1.7	0633 9.1	1252 1.6	1848 9.2
10 F	0134 0.6	0728 10.0	1355 0.7	1949 10.0		**25** SA	0109 1.6	0707 9.2	1327 1.5	1923 9.2
11 SA	0213 0.8	0807 9.8	1434 1.0	2027 9.6		**26** SU	0142 1.6	0740 9.2	1402 1.6	1957 9.1
12 SU	0250 1.2	0843 9.3	1509 1.5	2102 9.0		**27** M	0215 1.8	0814 9.1	1436 1.8	2033 8.9
13 M	0324 1.9	0916 8.7	1544 2.2	2137 8.3		**28** TU	0250 2.1	0850 8.8	1513 2.1	2112 8.5
14 TU	0357 2.7	0951 8.1	1619 2.9	2214 7.6		**29** W	0328 2.5	0932 8.4	1555 2.5	2158 8.1
15 W	0434 3.4	1030 7.4	1703 3.6	2301 6.9 ☽		**30** TH	0414 2.9	1023 8.0	1649 3.0	2255 7.6
						31 F	0515 3.4	1129 7.6	1802 3.3 ☽	

NOVEMBER

Day	Time m	Time m	Time m	Time m		Day	Time m	Time m	Time m	Time m
1 SA	0012 7.3	0642 3.6	1255 7.5	1934 3.2		**16** SU	0049 6.7	0709 4.2	1319 6.8	1951 3.9
2 SU	0145 7.4	0818 3.3	1421 7.8	2056 2.8		**17** M	0211 6.9	0825 3.9	1432 7.1	2100 3.6
3 M	0303 7.9	0931 2.8	1530 8.3	2200 2.2		**18** TU	0313 7.3	0927 3.5	1529 7.5	2154 3.1
4 TU	0403 8.5	1029 2.1	1626 8.8	2254 1.7		**19** W	0401 7.8	1017 3.0	1617 8.0	2241 2.7
5 W	0454 9.0	1120 1.6	1716 9.3	2342 1.3		**20** TH	0444 8.3	1102 2.5	1701 8.4	2323 2.2
6 TH	0541 9.4	1207 1.2	1803 9.6 ○			**21** F	0525 8.7	1144 2.0	1743 8.8	
7 F	0028 1.1	0624 9.7	1247 1.1	1846 9.6		**22** SA	0004 1.9	0604 9.1	1226 1.7	1823 9.0 ●
8 SA	0110 1.1	0705 9.7	1333 1.1	1927 9.5		**23** SU	0044 1.7	0643 9.2	1307 1.5	1903 9.2
9 SU	0149 1.3	0743 9.5	1412 1.3	2005 9.2		**24** M	0123 1.6	0721 9.4	1347 1.4	1943 9.2
10 M	0226 1.6	0819 9.2	1448 1.7	2041 8.8		**25** TU	0202 1.6	0801 9.3	1427 1.5	2024 9.1
11 TU	0259 2.1	0852 8.7	1521 2.3	2114 8.3		**26** W	0242 1.8	0842 9.1	1509 1.7	2107 8.8
12 W	0331 2.7	0926 8.2	1555 2.8	2150 7.7		**27** TH	0324 2.1	0927 8.8	1554 2.1	2154 8.4
13 TH	0405 3.2	1003 7.7	1634 3.4	2231 7.2		**28** F	0412 2.5	1018 8.4	1647 2.5	2249 8.0
14 F	0448 3.8	1049 7.2	1725 3.8	2328 6.8		**29** SA	0510 3.0	1118 8.0	1751 2.8	2355 7.7
15 SA	0551 4.1	1156 6.9	1835 4.0			**30** SU	0623 3.2	1231 7.8	1906 3.0	

DECEMBER

Day	Time m	Time m	Time m	Time m		Day	Time m	Time m	Time m	Time m
1 M	0113 7.6	0746 3.2	1350 7.8	2024 2.9		**16** TU	0050 6.9	0715 4.0	1319 7.0	1950 3.8
2 TU	0232 7.8	0903 2.9	1502 8.0	2132 2.6		**17** W	0207 7.0	0826 3.7	1431 7.2	2057 3.5
3 W	0337 8.2	1005 2.5	1603 8.4	2230 2.2		**18** TH	0311 7.4	0929 3.3	1532 7.6	2156 3.0
4 TH	0431 8.6	1059 2.1	1656 8.7	2321 1.9		**19** F	0405 7.9	1025 2.8	1626 8.0	2249 2.6
5 F	0519 9.0	1148 1.8	1744 9.0			**20** SA	0454 8.4	1115 2.3	1715 8.5	2338 2.1
6 SA	0007 1.7	0603 9.2	1233 1.6	1828 9.1		**21** SU	0539 8.9	1203 1.8	1802 8.8 ○	
7 SU	0050 1.6	0645 9.3	1315 1.5	1909 9.1		**22** M	0024 1.7	0624 9.2	1251 1.4	1848 9.1 ●
8 M	0130 1.6	0724 9.3	1354 1.6	1948 9.0		**23** TU	0110 1.4	0708 9.5	1336 1.2	1933 9.3
9 TU	0206 1.8	0759 9.1	1429 1.8	2023 8.7		**24** W	0154 1.3	0752 9.6	1421 1.1	2017 9.3
10 W	0239 2.1	0833 8.8	1502 2.2	2056 8.4		**25** TH	0238 1.3	0836 9.6	1506 1.2	2102 9.2
11 TH	0310 2.5	0906 8.4	1534 2.5	2130 8.0		**26** F	0322 1.5	0921 9.5	1551 1.4	2147 8.9
12 F	0342 2.9	0940 8.0	1607 3.0	2205 7.6		**27** SA	0407 1.9	1009 8.9	1638 1.8	2236 8.5
13 SA	0417 3.3	1018 7.6	1645 3.3	2247 7.2		**28** SU	0457 2.4	1101 8.4	1731 2.3	2331 8.0 ☽
14 SU	0501 3.7	1104 7.2	1734 3.7	2340 7.0		**29** M	0556 2.8	1201 8.0	1832 2.8	
15 M	0601 3.9	1204 7.0	1839 3.8			**30** TU	0036 7.6	0707 3.2	1314 7.6	1944 3.0
						31 W	0154 7.5	0828 3.2	1432 7.6	2100 3.0

Chart Datum: 5·06 metres below Ordnance Datum (Local)
HAT is 10·3 metres above Chart Datum

TIDES

ST. HELIER

MEAN SPRING
AND NEAP CURVES

MEAN RANGES
Springs 9.6m
Neaps 4.1m

Factor

0.9 0.8 0.7 0.6 0.5 0.4 0.3 0.2 0.1

L.W. +6ʰ +5ʰ +4ʰ +3ʰ +2ʰ +1ʰ H.W. -1ʰ -2ʰ -3ʰ -4ʰ L.W.

M.H.W.S.
M.H.W.N.

H.W.Hts.m.

CHART DATUM

L.W.Hts.m.

M.L.W.N.
M.L.W.S.

TIME ZONE (UT)	CHANNEL ISLES – ST HELIER	Dates in amber are SPRINGS
For Summer Time add ONE hour in **non-shaded areas**	LAT 49°11′N LONG 2°07′W	Dates in yellow are NEAPS
	TIMES AND HEIGHTS OF HIGH AND LOW WATERS	**2014**

JANUARY

Time m	Time m
1 0011 1.6 / 0553 11.0 / W 1239 1.2 / ● 1821 11.1	**16** 0046 2.3 / 0626 10.2 / TH 1310 2.1 / ○ 1850 10.1
2 0104 1.2 / 0644 11.5 / TH 1333 0.8 / 1911 11.4	**17** 0121 2.1 / 0700 10.4 / F 1343 2.0 / 1922 10.2
3 0155 1.0 / 0733 11.7 / F 1423 0.6 / 1959 11.5	**18** 0154 2.0 / 0732 10.5 / SA 1415 1.9 / 1954 10.3
4 0243 0.9 / 0820 11.7 / SA 1509 0.7 / 2045 11.3	**19** 0225 2.0 / 0803 10.5 / SU 1445 2.0 / 2024 10.2
5 0328 1.1 / 0904 11.4 / SU 1554 1.0 / 2128 10.9	**20** 0256 2.1 / 0834 10.4 / M 1515 2.1 / 2054 10.0
6 0411 1.6 / 0947 10.9 / M 1636 1.6 / 2211 10.2	**21** 0326 2.3 / 0904 10.1 / TU 1545 2.4 / 2125 9.7
7 0453 2.2 / 1031 10.1 / TU 1719 2.3 / 2254 9.5	**22** 0358 2.7 / 0936 9.7 / W 1617 2.8 / 2157 9.3
8 0538 2.9 / 1118 9.3 / W 1805 3.0 / ◑ 2344 8.9	**23** 0433 3.1 / 1012 9.3 / TH 1653 3.2 / 2237 8.8
9 0631 3.5 / 1215 8.7 / TH 1903 3.6	**24** 0516 3.5 / 1058 8.8 / F 1740 3.6 / ◑ 2332 8.4
10 0049 8.4 / 0740 3.9 / F 1331 8.3 / 2015 3.9	**25** 0615 3.9 / 1204 8.4 / SA 1850 3.9
11 0209 8.3 / 0858 3.9 / SA 1452 8.3 / 2129 3.7	**26** 0050 8.3 / 0738 3.9 / SU 1331 8.3 / 2020 3.8
12 0323 8.6 / 1009 3.6 / SU 1559 8.7 / 2233 3.4	**27** 0221 8.6 / 0906 3.4 / M 1459 8.8 / 2145 3.2
13 0422 9.1 / 1107 3.1 / M 1652 9.1 / 2325 2.9	**28** 0340 9.3 / 1022 2.7 / TU 1614 9.5 / 2255 2.4
14 0509 9.6 / 1153 2.7 / TU 1736 9.6	**29** 0445 10.1 / 1128 1.8 / W 1716 10.3 / 2357 1.7
15 0008 2.6 / 0550 10.0 / W 1234 2.4 / 1815 9.9	**30** 0542 10.9 / 1228 1.1 / TH 1811 11.0 / ●
	31 0053 1.1 / 0633 11.6 / F 1322 0.6 / 1900 11.5

FEBRUARY

Time m	Time m
1 0145 0.7 / 0721 11.9 / SA 1411 0.3 / 1946 11.7	**16** 0137 1.8 / 0713 10.7 / SU 1357 1.6 / 1933 10.5
2 0231 0.5 / 0805 12.0 / SU 1456 0.3 / 2028 11.6	**17** 0208 1.6 / 0744 10.8 / M 1427 1.6 / 2003 10.6
3 0313 0.7 / 0847 11.7 / M 1536 0.6 / 2107 11.2	**18** 0239 1.6 / 0814 10.7 / TU 1456 1.7 / 2033 10.5
4 0352 1.1 / 0926 11.1 / TU 1613 1.3 / 2144 10.6	**19** 0309 1.8 / 0845 10.5 / W 1525 1.9 / 2103 10.2
5 0427 1.8 / 1003 10.3 / W 1647 2.1 / 2220 9.8	**20** 0339 2.1 / 0915 10.2 / TH 1555 2.3 / 2133 9.8
6 0503 2.6 / 1041 9.4 / TH 1723 3.0 / ◐ 2259 9.0	**21** 0412 2.6 / 0949 9.6 / F 1628 2.8 / 2209 9.2
7 0543 3.5 / 1127 8.5 / F 1807 3.7 / 2352 8.2	**22** 0450 3.1 / 1031 9.0 / SA 1710 3.4 / ◐ 2258 8.7
8 0640 4.1 / 1235 7.9 / SA 1916 4.3	**23** 0544 3.6 / 1131 8.4 / SU 1814 3.8
9 0114 7.8 / 0808 4.4 / SU 1413 7.7 / 2047 4.3	**24** 0014 8.3 / 0704 3.8 / M 1302 8.2 / 1950 3.9
10 0249 8.0 / 0937 4.1 / M 1535 8.1 / 2205 3.9	**25** 0155 8.3 / 0843 3.5 / TU 1443 8.5 / 2126 3.4
11 0358 8.5 / 1043 3.5 / TU 1632 8.7 / 2302 3.2	**26** 0325 9.0 / 1006 2.7 / W 1603 9.3 / 2241 2.5
12 0449 9.2 / 1132 2.9 / W 1717 9.3 / 2347 2.7	**27** 0433 10.0 / 1115 1.8 / TH 1705 10.2 / 2344 1.6
13 0530 9.7 / 1213 2.4 / TH 1756 9.8	**28** 0529 10.9 / 1214 1.0 / F 1757 11.0
14 0027 2.3 / 0607 10.1 / F 1251 2.0 / ○ 1830 10.1	
15 0103 2.0 / 0641 10.4 / SA 1325 1.8 / 1902 10.4	

MARCH

Time m	Time m
1 0039 1.0 / 0618 11.5 / SA 1307 0.5 / ● 1844 11.5	**16** 0038 1.9 / 0615 10.4 / SU 1300 1.7 / ○ 1836 10.5
2 0129 0.5 / 0704 11.9 / SU 1353 0.2 / 1926 11.8	**17** 0114 1.6 / 0648 10.7 / M 1334 1.5 / 1908 10.7
3 0213 0.4 / 0746 12.0 / M 1435 0.3 / 2006 11.7	**18** 0147 1.4 / 0721 10.9 / TU 1406 1.4 / 1940 10.8
4 0252 0.5 / 0825 11.7 / TU 1511 0.6 / 2042 11.3	**19** 0219 1.3 / 0753 10.9 / W 1436 1.4 / 2011 10.8
5 0328 0.9 / 0901 11.1 / W 1544 1.3 / 2115 10.7	**20** 0251 1.4 / 0825 10.8 / TH 1506 1.6 / 2043 10.6
6 0359 1.7 / 0934 10.3 / TH 1614 2.1 / 2147 9.9	**21** 0323 1.7 / 0859 10.4 / F 1538 2.0 / 2116 10.1
7 0429 2.5 / 1007 9.4 / F 1644 3.0 / 2220 9.1	**22** 0357 2.2 / 0934 9.8 / SA 1613 2.6 / 2153 9.5
8 0501 3.4 / 1045 8.5 / SA 1720 3.8 / ◐ 2303 8.3	**23** 0437 2.8 / 1018 9.1 / SU 1656 3.2 / 2243 8.9
9 0547 4.1 / 1143 7.7 / SU 1817 4.4	**24** 0530 3.3 / 1115 8.4 / M 1800 3.7 / ◐ 2358 8.4
10 0016 7.6 / 0706 4.6 / M 1329 7.4 / 1954 4.6	**25** 0650 3.6 / 1250 8.2 / TU 1935 3.9
11 0207 7.6 / 0854 4.4 / TU 1503 7.8 / 2128 4.2	**26** 0140 8.4 / 0827 3.4 / W 1431 8.5 / 2110 3.3
12 0326 8.2 / 1009 3.8 / W 1604 8.4 / 2231 3.5	**27** 0310 9.0 / 0949 2.7 / TH 1548 9.3 / 2224 2.5
13 0420 8.9 / 1101 3.1 / TH 1649 9.1 / 2318 2.8	**28** 0416 9.9 / 1056 1.8 / F 1647 10.0 / 2326 1.7
14 0503 9.5 / 1143 2.5 / F 1728 9.7 / 2359 2.3	**29** 0511 10.7 / 1154 1.2 / SA 1737 10.9
15 0541 10.0 / 1223 2.0 / SA 1804 10.1	**30** 0019 1.1 / 0558 11.3 / SU 1245 0.7 / ● 1822 11.3
	31 0107 0.7 / 0642 11.6 / M 1330 0.6 / 1903 11.5

APRIL

Time m	Time m
1 0149 0.6 / 0723 11.6 / TU 1409 0.6 / 1941 11.5	**16** 0122 1.4 / 0655 10.9 / W 1341 1.3 / 1915 11.0
2 0227 0.8 / 0800 11.4 / W 1444 1.0 / 2015 11.2	**17** 0158 1.2 / 0732 11.0 / TH 1416 1.3 / 1951 11.0
3 0300 1.2 / 0835 10.9 / TH 1515 1.5 / 2047 10.6	**18** 0233 1.3 / 0809 10.9 / F 1450 1.5 / 2027 10.8
4 0330 1.8 / 0907 10.2 / F 1543 2.2 / 2117 9.9	**19** 0309 1.5 / 0847 10.5 / SA 1526 1.9 / 2105 10.4
5 0359 2.5 / 0939 9.3 / SA 1612 3.0 / 2148 9.2	**20** 0348 1.9 / 0929 10.0 / SU 1605 2.4 / 2148 9.8
6 0429 3.3 / 1014 8.5 / SU 1645 3.7 / 2226 8.4	**21** 0432 2.5 / 1017 9.3 / M 1653 3.0 / 2242 9.1
7 0510 3.9 / 1104 7.8 / M 1734 4.3 / ◐ 2327 7.8	**22** 0528 3.0 / 1120 8.7 / TU 1758 3.5 / ◐ 2354 8.7
8 0614 4.4 / 1234 7.4 / TU 1854 4.7	**23** 0643 3.3 / 1242 8.4 / W 1923 3.6
9 0109 7.5 / 0750 4.5 / W 1415 7.6 / 2033 4.4	**24** 0124 8.7 / 0800 3.1 / TH 1411 8.7 / 2049 3.2
10 0239 7.9 / 0917 4.0 / TH 1522 8.2 / 2145 3.8	**25** 0246 9.1 / 0918 2.6 / F 1524 9.3 / 2200 2.6
11 0339 8.6 / 1016 3.3 / F 1610 8.9 / 2238 3.1	**26** 0352 9.8 / 1031 2.0 / SA 1623 10.0 / 2301 1.9
12 0425 9.2 / 1103 2.7 / SA 1652 9.5 / 2323 2.5	**27** 0447 10.4 / 1128 1.5 / SU 1713 10.6 / 2354 1.5
13 0505 9.8 / 1146 2.2 / SU 1729 10.0	**28** 0535 10.8 / 1218 1.3 / M 1757 10.9
14 0005 2.0 / 0542 10.3 / M 1227 1.8 / 1805 10.5	**29** 0042 1.2 / 0619 11.0 / TU 1302 1.2 / ● 1837 11.1
15 0045 1.6 / 0619 10.6 / TU 1305 1.5 / 1840 10.8	**30** 0124 1.2 / 0659 11.0 / W 1341 1.2 / 1914 11.1

Chart Datum: 5·88 metres below Ordnance Datum (Local)
HAT is 12·2 metres above Chart Datum

TIDES

TIME ZONE (UT)
For Summer Time add ONE hour in **non-shaded areas**

CHANNEL ISLES – ST HELIER
LAT 49°11'N   LONG 2°07'W
TIMES AND HEIGHTS OF HIGH AND LOW WATERS

Dates in amber are **SPRINGS**
Dates in yellow are **NEAPS**

2014

MAY

Time m	Time m
1 0201 1.3 / 0736 10.9 / TH 1415 1.5 / 1949 10.9	**16** 0138 1.2 / 0713 11.0 / F 1357 1.3 / 1934 11.1
2 0234 1.6 / 0811 10.5 / F 1447 1.8 / 2021 10.5	**17** 0219 1.2 / 0756 10.9 / SA 1438 1.4 / 2016 11.0
3 0305 2.0 / 0844 10.0 / SA 1516 2.3 / 2052 10.0	**18** 0301 1.3 / 0841 10.7 / SU 1519 1.7 / 2101 10.7
4 0334 2.5 / 0916 9.4 / SU 1546 2.9 / 2124 9.4	**19** 0345 1.6 / 0927 10.2 / M 1604 2.1 / 2148 10.2
5 0406 3.1 / 0951 8.7 / M 1620 3.5 / 2201 8.7	**20** 0433 2.0 / 1018 9.7 / TU 1654 2.6 / 2241 9.6
6 0444 3.6 / 1035 8.2 / TU 1703 4.0 / 2250 8.2	**21** 0527 2.5 / 1115 9.2 / W 1753 3.0 / 2344 9.2
7 0535 4.1 / 1139 7.7 / W 1805 4.4	**22** 0631 2.9 / 1223 8.9 / TH 1904 3.3
8 0004 7.8 / 0645 4.3 / TH 1308 7.7 / 1924 4.4	**23** 0058 9.0 / 0743 2.9 / F 1340 8.9 / 2020 3.2
9 0133 7.9 / 0807 4.1 / F 1423 8.0 / 2043 4.1	**24** 0214 9.1 / 0855 2.8 / SA 1451 9.2 / 2130 2.8
10 0243 8.3 / 0917 3.6 / SA 1520 8.6 / 2146 3.5	**25** 0322 9.4 / 1000 2.4 / SU 1553 9.6 / 2232 2.4
11 0336 8.9 / 1014 3.1 / SU 1607 9.2 / 2238 2.8	**26** 0420 9.8 / 1058 2.1 / M 1645 10.0 / 2328 2.1
12 0422 9.5 / 1103 2.5 / M 1649 9.8 / 2326 2.3	**27** 0511 10.2 / 1150 1.9 / TU 1732 10.4
13 0506 10.0 / 1150 2.0 / TU 1731 10.3	**28** 0017 1.9 / 0555 10.4 / W 1235 1.8 / 1813 10.6
14 0012 1.8 / 0548 10.5 / W 1235 1.7 / 1811 10.8	**29** 0100 1.8 / 0636 10.4 / TH 1315 1.8 / 1851 10.6
15 0056 1.4 / 0630 10.8 / TH 1317 1.4 / 1852 11.0	**30** 0137 1.8 / 0714 10.4 / F 1350 1.9 / 1926 10.6
	31 0211 1.9 / 0750 10.2 / SA 1423 2.1 / 2000 10.4

JUNE

Time m	Time m
1 0243 2.1 / 0824 9.9 / SU 1454 2.4 / 2032 10.0	**16** 0256 1.0 / 0835 11.0 / M 1515 1.3 / 2055 11.1
2 0314 2.4 / 0857 9.6 / M 1526 2.7 / 2105 9.6	**17** 0342 1.1 / 0922 10.7 / TU 1601 1.6 / 2142 10.7
3 0346 2.8 / 0931 9.1 / TU 1559 3.1 / 2140 9.2	**18** 0429 1.5 / 1009 10.2 / W 1649 2.1 / 2231 10.2
4 0421 3.2 / 1008 8.7 / W 1637 3.6 / 2220 8.7	**19** 0518 2.0 / 1059 9.7 / TH 1740 2.6 / 2324 9.6
5 0503 3.6 / 1055 8.3 / TH 1725 3.9 / 2311 8.3	**20** 0611 2.5 / 1155 9.2 / F 1838 3.0
6 0555 3.9 / 1155 8.0 / F 1825 4.1	**21** 0025 9.1 / 0711 2.9 / SA 1301 8.9 / 1945 3.3
7 0018 8.1 / 0659 4.0 / SA 1309 8.0 / 1936 4.1	**22** 0136 8.9 / 0819 3.1 / SU 1413 8.8 / 2056 3.2
8 0133 8.2 / 0811 3.8 / SU 1418 8.4 / 2047 3.7	**23** 0248 8.9 / 0927 3.0 / M 1520 9.1 / 2203 3.0
9 0239 8.6 / 0919 3.4 / M 1516 8.9 / 2150 3.2	**24** 0353 9.2 / 1030 2.8 / TU 1619 9.5 / 2303 2.7
10 0337 9.2 / 1019 2.9 / TU 1608 9.5 / 2247 2.6	**25** 0448 9.5 / 1125 2.6 / W 1709 9.8 / 2354 2.4
11 0430 9.8 / 1113 2.3 / W 1658 10.2 / 2340 2.0	**26** 0536 9.8 / 1212 2.4 / TH 1752 10.1
12 0521 10.3 / 1205 1.8 / TH 1746 10.7	**27** 0038 2.2 / 0618 10.0 / F 1253 2.2 / 1831 10.3
13 0031 1.5 / 0610 10.7 / F 1255 1.5 / 1834 11.1	**28** 0117 2.1 / 0656 10.1 / SA 1329 2.2 / 1907 10.4
14 0121 1.2 / 0659 11.0 / SA 1343 1.3 / 1921 11.3	**29** 0152 2.0 / 0731 10.1 / SU 1403 2.2 / 1941 10.4
15 0209 1.0 / 0747 11.1 / SU 1430 1.2 / 2008 11.3	**30** 0224 2.1 / 0805 10.0 / M 1435 2.2 / 2013 10.2

JULY

Time m	Time m
1 0255 2.2 / 0837 9.9 / TU 1506 2.4 / 2045 10.0	**16** 0333 0.7 / 0908 11.2 / W 1552 1.1 / 2128 11.2
2 0326 2.4 / 0908 9.6 / W 1538 2.7 / 2117 9.7	**17** 0416 1.1 / 0952 10.7 / TH 1634 1.6 / 2212 10.6
3 0358 2.7 / 0941 9.2 / TH 1612 3.0 / 2151 9.3	**18** 0459 1.7 / 1035 10.0 / F 1718 2.3 / 2257 9.8
4 0433 3.1 / 1017 8.8 / F 1651 3.4 / 2230 8.8	**19** 0543 2.4 / 1121 9.3 / SA 1806 3.0 / 2348 9.1
5 0513 3.5 / 1100 8.5 / SA 1737 3.8 / 2319 8.5	**20** 0634 3.1 / 1218 8.7 / SU 1907 3.5
6 0604 3.8 / 1158 8.2 / SU 1837 4.0	**21** 0055 8.5 / 0739 3.6 / M 1331 8.4 / 2021 3.7
7 0025 8.3 / 0709 3.9 / M 1311 8.2 / 1950 3.9	**22** 0215 8.3 / 0854 3.7 / TU 1450 8.5 / 2137 3.6
8 0141 8.4 / 0825 3.7 / TU 1426 8.6 / 2105 3.5	**23** 0330 8.5 / 1005 3.4 / W 1556 8.9 / 2243 3.2
9 0255 8.8 / 0939 3.2 / W 1532 9.2 / 2213 2.8	**24** 0430 9.0 / 1103 3.0 / TH 1649 9.4 / 2335 2.7
10 0400 9.4 / 1043 2.6 / TH 1632 9.9 / 2314 2.1	**25** 0519 9.4 / 1152 2.6 / F 1734 9.8
11 0500 10.1 / 1142 2.0 / F 1727 10.6	**26** 0020 2.4 / 0600 9.8 / SA 1233 2.4 / 1812 10.2
12 0012 1.5 / 0555 10.7 / SA 1239 1.5 / 1820 11.2	**27** 0058 2.2 / 0637 10.0 / SU 1310 2.2 / 1848 10.4
13 0108 1.0 / 0647 11.1 / SU 1331 1.1 / 1910 11.5	**28** 0133 2.0 / 0711 10.2 / M 1344 2.1 / 1921 10.5
14 0159 0.7 / 0737 11.4 / M 1421 0.9 / 1958 11.7	**29** 0205 1.9 / 0743 10.3 / TU 1415 2.0 / 1953 10.5
15 0248 0.6 / 0824 11.4 / TU 1507 0.9 / 2044 11.6	**30** 0235 1.9 / 0814 10.2 / W 1446 2.1 / 2023 10.4
	31 0305 2.1 / 0844 10.1 / TH 1517 2.2 / 2053 10.1

AUGUST

Time m	Time m
1 0335 2.3 / 0913 9.8 / F 1548 2.6 / 2124 9.8	**16** 0433 1.7 / 1005 10.2 / SA 1650 2.3 / 2226 9.8
2 0405 2.7 / 0944 9.4 / SA 1621 3.0 / 2156 9.3	**17** 0511 2.6 / 1044 9.3 / SU 1731 3.1 / 2310 8.9
3 0439 3.1 / 1018 8.9 / SU 1700 3.4 / 2236 8.8	**18** 0554 3.4 / 1133 8.5 / M 1824 3.9
4 0520 3.6 / 1105 8.5 / M 1751 3.8 / 2333 8.4	**19** 0012 8.1 / 0655 4.1 / TU 1247 8.0 / 1943 4.2
5 0619 3.9 / 1215 8.2 / TU 1903 4.0	**20** 0144 7.8 / 0820 4.3 / W 1421 8.0 / 2112 4.1
6 0053 8.2 / 0741 3.9 / W 1344 8.4 / 2029 3.7	**21** 0311 8.1 / 0941 3.9 / TH 1536 8.5 / 2222 3.5
7 0223 8.5 / 0908 3.5 / TH 1506 9.0 / 2148 3.0	**22** 0412 8.7 / 1043 3.3 / F 1630 9.2 / 2314 2.9
8 0341 9.2 / 1022 2.8 / F 1614 9.8 / 2255 2.2	**23** 0500 9.3 / 1130 2.8 / SA 1714 9.7 / 2357 2.5
9 0446 10.0 / 1126 2.0 / SA 1713 10.6 / 2357 1.4	**24** 0540 9.8 / 1211 2.4 / SU 1752 10.2
10 0543 10.7 / 1224 1.3 / SU 1807 11.3	**25** 0035 2.1 / 0615 10.1 / M 1248 2.1 / 1826 10.5
11 0054 0.8 / 0634 11.3 / M 1318 0.9 / 1856 11.8	**26** 0110 1.9 / 0648 10.4 / TU 1322 1.9 / 1858 10.6
12 0146 0.4 / 0722 11.7 / TU 1407 0.6 / 1942 12.0	**27** 0142 1.8 / 0719 10.5 / W 1353 1.8 / 1929 10.7
13 0233 0.3 / 0806 11.7 / W 1452 0.6 / 2026 11.9	**28** 0213 1.7 / 0749 10.5 / TH 1424 1.8 / 1959 10.7
14 0316 0.4 / 0848 11.5 / TH 1534 0.9 / 2107 11.5	**29** 0242 1.8 / 0818 10.4 / F 1454 1.9 / 2029 10.5
15 0356 0.9 / 0927 10.9 / F 1613 1.5 / 2147 10.7	**30** 0311 2.0 / 0846 10.2 / SA 1524 2.2 / 2058 10.1
	31 0340 2.4 / 0915 9.8 / SU 1556 2.6 / 2129 9.6

Chart Datum: 5·88 metres below Ordnance Datum (Local)
HAT is 12·2 metres above Chart Datum

TIMES AND HEIGHTS OF HIGH AND LOW WATERS

2014

SEPTEMBER

Time	m		Time	m
1 0411	2.9	**16**	0513	3.7
0947	9.3		1051	8.5
M 1632	3.2	TU 1741	4.1
2206	9.1	◗ 2329	7.9
2 0449	3.5	**17**	0609	4.4
1030	8.7		1159	7.8
TU 1720	3.7	W 1858	4.6
◗ 2259	8.5			
3 0546	3.9	**18**	0107	7.5
1137	8.3		0739	4.7
W 1832	4.0	TH 1347	7.7
		2039	4.4
4 0023	8.1	**19**	0245	7.8
0711	4.1		0911	4.3
TH 1316	8.2	F 1509	8.2
2006	3.8	2153	3.8
5 0205	8.3	**20**	0347	8.5
0849	3.7		1014	3.6
F 1451	8.8	SA 1604	9.0
2131	3.1	2245	3.2
6 0329	9.1	**21**	0433	9.2
1006	2.8		1102	3.0
SA 1601	9.8	SU 1647	9.6
2240	2.2	2327	2.6
7 0434	10.0	**22**	0513	9.8
1111	2.0		1142	2.4
SU 1659	10.7	M 1725	10.1
2341	1.3			
8 0528	10.9	**23**	0005	2.2
1208	1.2		0547	10.2
M 1751	11.5	TU 1220	2.1
		1759	10.5
9 0036	0.7	**24**	0042	1.9
0617	11.5		0620	10.5
TU 1300	0.7	W 1255	1.8
○ 1838	11.9	● 1832	10.7
10 0127	0.4	**25**	0116	1.7
0702	11.8		0651	10.7
W 1348	0.5	TH 1329	1.7
1922	12.1	1903	10.9
11 0212	0.3	**26**	0147	1.6
0744	11.8		0722	10.8
TH 1431	0.6	F 1400	1.6
2004	11.9	1934	10.9
12 0252	0.6	**27**	0218	1.7
0823	11.6		0752	10.8
F 1510	0.9	SA 1432	1.7
2043	11.4	2005	10.7
13 0329	1.1	**28**	0247	1.9
0859	11.0		0822	10.5
SA 1546	1.6	SU 1503	2.0
2119	10.6	2037	10.4
14 0403	1.9	**29**	0318	2.2
0934	10.2		0853	10.1
SU 1620	2.4	M 1536	2.4
2155	9.7	2110	9.9
15 0436	2.8	**30**	0351	2.8
1008	9.3		0928	9.6
M 1655	3.3	TU 1614	3.0
2234	8.7	2150	9.2

OCTOBER

Time	m		Time	m
1 0431	3.4	**16**	0526	4.4
1012	9.0		1113	7.9
W 1703	3.5	TH 1807	4.6
◗ 2245	8.6			
2 0529	3.9	**17**	0016	7.5
1120	8.4		0644	4.8
TH 1816	3.9	F 1253	7.6
		1943	4.6
3 0009	8.2	**18**	0200	7.7
0656	4.1		0822	4.6
F 1300	8.3	SA 1426	8.0
1950	3.7	2106	4.2
4 0153	8.4	**19**	0309	8.3
0833	3.7		0932	4.0
SA 1435	8.9	SU 1526	8.6
2115	3.0	2204	3.5
5 0315	9.1	**20**	0358	9.0
0950	2.9		1023	3.3
SU 1545	9.8	M 1612	9.3
2223	2.2	2249	2.9
6 0417	10.1	**21**	0438	9.6
1052	2.0		1106	2.7
M 1641	10.7	TU 1651	9.9
2321	1.4	2329	2.4
7 0509	10.8	**22**	0515	10.1
1148	1.3		1146	2.2
TU 1732	11.3	W 1728	10.3
8 0014	0.9	**23**	0008	2.0
0556	11.4		0549	10.5
W 1238	0.9	TH 1225	1.9
○ 1817	11.7	● 1802	10.6
9 0103	0.7	**24**	0046	1.8
0639	11.7		0622	10.7
TH 1324	0.7	F 1302	1.7
1900	11.8	1836	10.8
10 0146	0.7	**25**	0121	1.7
0719	11.7		0655	10.9
F 1406	0.8	SA 1337	1.6
1940	11.6	1911	10.9
11 0225	1.0	**26**	0155	1.7
0757	11.4		0729	11.0
SA 1444	1.2	SU 1412	1.6
2018	11.2	1946	10.8
12 0300	1.5	**27**	0228	1.8
0832	10.9		0804	10.8
SU 1518	1.8	M 1446	1.8
2053	10.5	2023	10.6
13 0332	2.2	**28**	0302	2.1
0904	10.2		0840	10.4
M 1550	2.5	TU 1523	2.2
2127	9.6	2102	10.1
14 0404	3.0	**29**	0340	2.6
0937	9.4		0920	9.9
TU 1623	3.3	W 1605	2.7
2203	8.7	2146	9.5
15 0438	3.8	**30**	0424	3.1
1015	8.6		1009	9.3
W 1704	4.1	TH 1657	3.2
◗ 2252	8.0	2244	8.8
		31	0523	3.6
		1115	8.8
		F 1807	3.5
		◗		

NOVEMBER

Time	m		Time	m
1 0001	8.5	**16**	0048	7.7
0643	3.9		0709	4.6
SA 1243	8.6	SU 1317	7.8
1931	3.5	1955	4.4
2 0132	8.6	**17**	0211	8.0
0812	3.6		0830	4.3
SU 1411	9.0	M 1432	8.2
2052	3.0	2107	4.0
3 0251	9.2	**18**	0310	8.5
0927	2.9		0934	3.8
M 1521	9.7	TU 1526	8.8
2159	2.4	2202	3.4
4 0353	9.9	**19**	0356	9.1
1029	2.2		1024	3.2
TU 1619	10.4	W 1611	9.4
2257	1.8	2249	2.8
5 0446	10.6	**20**	0437	9.6
1125	1.7		1110	2.6
W 1710	10.9	TH 1652	9.9
2350	1.4	2333	2.4
6 0533	11.0	**21**	0516	10.2
1215	1.3		1153	2.1
TH 1756	11.2	F 1732	10.4
○				
7 0037	1.2	**22**	0015	2.0
0615	11.3		0553	10.7
F 1301	1.2	SA 1236	1.8
1838	11.3	● 1811	10.7
8 0120	1.2	**23**	0056	1.7
0655	11.3		0632	10.9
SA 1342	1.3	SU 1316	1.6
1918	11.2	1851	10.9
9 0159	1.4	**24**	0135	1.6
0732	11.1		0711	11.1
SU 1419	1.5	M 1356	1.5
1955	10.8	1932	10.9
10 0233	1.8	**25**	0214	1.7
0807	10.8		0752	11.0
M 1453	2.0	TU 1436	1.5
2030	10.3	2015	10.8
11 0305	2.3	**26**	0253	1.9
0840	10.2		0834	10.8
TU 1525	2.5	W 1518	1.8
2104	9.7	2059	10.4
12 0337	2.9	**27**	0336	2.2
0913	9.6		0919	10.4
W 1557	3.1	TH 1603	2.2
2139	9.0	2147	9.9
13 0410	3.6	**28**	0423	2.7
0949	8.9		1009	9.8
TH 1633	3.7	F 1655	2.6
2221	8.3	2240	9.4
14 0451	4.1	**29**	0518	3.1
1035	8.3		1107	9.3
F 1722	4.2	SA 1755	3.0
◗ 2320	7.9	◗ 2344	9.0
15 0550	4.5	**30**	0626	3.4
1144	7.9		1217	9.0
SA 1832	4.5	SU 1906	3.2

DECEMBER

Time	m		Time	m
1 0059	8.8	**16**	0044	7.9
0742	3.4		0713	4.4
M 1336	9.0	TU 1311	8.0
2021	3.1	1952	4.2
2 0217	9.0	**17**	0202	8.1
0857	3.1		0830	4.2
TU 1450	9.3	W 1425	8.3
2130	2.7	2104	3.9
3 0324	9.5	**18**	0304	8.6
1003	2.7		0936	3.7
W 1553	9.8	TH 1523	8.8
2231	2.3	2204	3.3
4 0421	10.0	**19**	0355	9.2
1102	2.2		1032	3.0
TH 1648	10.2	F 1615	9.4
2326	2.0	2257	2.7
5 0511	10.4	**20**	0442	9.9
1154	1.9		1123	2.4
F 1736	10.5	SA 1703	10.0
		2347	2.2
6 0015	1.8	**21**	0528	10.4
0555	10.7		1212	1.9
SA 1241	1.7	SU 1750	10.5
○ 1819	10.7			
7 0059	1.8	**22**	0034	1.8
0635	10.9		0613	10.9
SU 1322	1.7	M 1259	1.5
1900	10.7	● 1837	10.9
8 0137	1.8	**23**	0120	1.5
0713	10.8		0658	11.2
M 1359	1.8	TU 1345	1.2
1937	10.5	1923	11.1
9 0212	2.0	**24**	0205	1.4
0748	10.7		0744	11.4
TU 1433	2.0	W 1430	1.1
2012	10.2	2009	11.1
10 0244	2.3	**25**	0249	1.4
0821	10.3		0829	11.3
W 1505	2.4	TH 1515	1.2
2045	9.8	2055	10.9
11 0315	2.7	**26**	0333	1.6
0854	9.9		0915	11.0
TH 1536	2.8	F 1600	1.5
2119	9.4	2140	10.5
12 0347	3.1	**27**	0418	2.0
0927	9.4		1001	10.5
F 1608	3.2	SA 1646	1.9
2154	8.9	2228	10.0
13 0422	3.6	**28**	0506	2.5
1004	8.9		1050	9.9
SA 1646	3.7	SU 1737	2.5
2235	8.4	◗ 2319	9.4
14 0505	4.0	**29**	0601	3.0
1050	8.4		1147	9.3
SU 1734	4.1	M 1835	2.9
◗ 2330	8.0			
15 0602	4.3	**30**	0020	8.9
1152	8.0		0706	3.4
M 1837	4.3	TU 1256	8.9
		1943	3.3
		31	0134	8.7
		0821	3.5
		W 1414	8.8
		2056	3.3

Chart Datum: 5·88 metres below Ordnance Datum (Local)
HAT is 12·2 metres above Chart Datum

TIDES

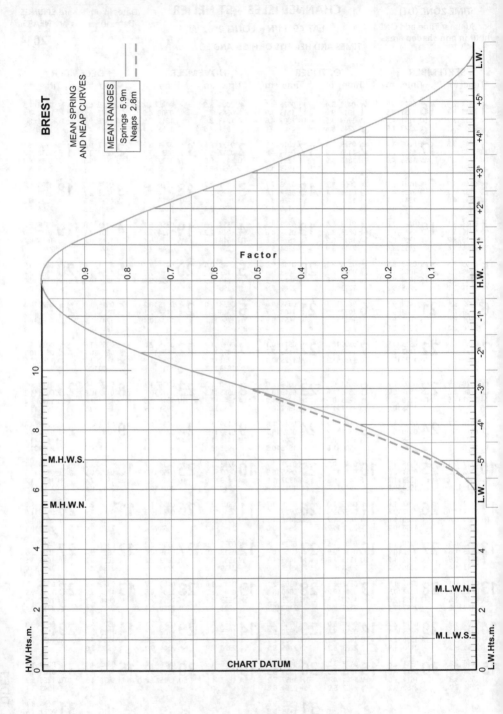

BREST

MEAN SPRING
AND NEAP CURVES

MEAN RANGES	
Springs	5.9m
Neaps	2.8m

TIME ZONE -0100
(French Standard Time)
Subtract 1 hour for UT
For French Summer Time add
ONE hour in **non-shaded areas**

FRANCE – BREST

LAT 48°23'N   LONG 4°30'W

TIMES AND HEIGHTS OF HIGH AND LOW WATERS

Dates in amber are **SPRINGS**
Dates in yellow are **NEAPS**

2014

JANUARY

Time	m		Time	m
1 0429	7.2	**16**	0505	6.7
1050	0.9		1129	1.6
W 1654	7.2		TH 1723	6.6
● 2313	1.0		○ 2339	1.6
2 0518	7.5	**17**	0538	6.8
1140	0.7		1202	1.5
TH 1743	7.4		F 1755	6.6
3 0002	0.8	**18**	0012	1.6
0606	7.7		0610	6.8
F 1228	0.6		SA 1234	1.5
1831	7.4		1827	6.6
4 0051	0.8	**19**	0044	1.6
0654	7.6		0641	6.8
SA 1316	0.7		SU 1306	1.6
1918	7.2		1859	6.6
5 0139	1.0	**20**	0117	1.7
0741	7.4		0713	6.7
SU 1404	0.9		M 1338	1.7
2005	6.9		1931	6.4
6 0227	1.3	**21**	0150	1.8
0828	7.1		0745	6.5
M 1453	1.3		TU 1412	1.9
2053	6.5		2006	6.2
7 0317	1.7	**22**	0227	2.0
0918	6.6		0821	6.3
TU 1544	1.8		W 1450	2.1
2145	6.1		2046	6.0
8 0411	2.1	**23**	0308	2.2
1012	6.1		0903	6.0
W 1640	2.2		TH 1534	2.3
◖ 2244	5.8		2135	5.8
9 0511	2.4	**24**	0357	2.5
1115	5.8		0957	5.8
TH 1743	2.5		F 1628	2.5
2352	5.6		◗ 2237	5.6
10 0619	2.7	**25**	0458	2.6
1227	5.6		1106	5.6
F 1853	2.7		SA 1736	2.7
			2350	5.6
11 0105	5.6	**26**	0612	2.6
0732	2.6		1225	5.6
SA 1341	5.6		SU 1853	2.6
2002	2.6			
12 0213	5.8	**27**	0108	5.8
0838	2.5		0731	2.4
SU 1442	5.8		M 1345	5.9
2100	2.4		2008	2.2
13 0307	6.0	**28**	0220	6.2
0932	2.2		0843	1.9
M 1532	6.1		TU 1454	6.3
2148	2.1		2113	1.7
14 0352	6.3	**29**	0322	6.7
1016	2.0		0944	1.4
TU 1613	6.3		W 1551	6.8
2228	1.8		2209	1.3
15 0430	6.5	**30**	0416	7.2
1054	1.8		1037	0.9
W 1649	6.5		TH 1643	7.2
2305	1.8		● 2301	0.9
		31	0506	7.6
			1127	0.5
			F 1731	7.5
			2349	0.6

FEBRUARY

Time	m		Time	m
1 0553	7.8	**16**	0549	6.9
1215	0.4		1211	1.3
SA 1816	7.5		SU 1805	6.8
2 0036	0.6	**17**	0022	1.4
0638	7.8		0620	6.9
SU 1300	0.5		M 1242	1.3
1900	7.4		1835	6.8
3 0121	0.7	**18**	0054	1.4
0721	7.6		0650	6.9
M 1344	0.7		TU 1314	1.4
1942	7.1		1907	6.7
4 0205	1.0	**19**	0127	1.5
0804	7.2		0722	6.8
TU 1427	1.2		W 1346	1.6
2024	6.7		1940	6.5
5 0250	1.5	**20**	0203	1.7
0846	6.6		0757	6.5
W 1512	1.7		TH 1423	1.8
2108	6.2		2017	6.3
6 0337	2.0	**21**	0243	1.9
0932	6.1		0837	6.2
TH 1600	2.2		F 1505	2.1
◗ 2158	5.8		2103	6.0
7 0429	2.4	**22**	0330	2.2
1027	5.6		0926	5.9
F 1657	2.7		SA 1557	2.4
2302	5.4		◗ 2202	5.7
8 0534	2.8	**23**	0428	2.5
1140	5.3		1033	5.6
SA 1808	2.9		SU 1703	2.7
			2318	5.6
9 0021	5.3	**24**	0542	2.6
0653	2.9		1157	5.5
SU 1307	5.3		M 1826	2.7
1928	2.9			
10 0143	5.4	**25**	0044	5.7
0812	2.7		0708	2.4
M 1421	5.5		TU 1328	5.7
2036	2.6		1950	2.3
11 0245	5.7	**26**	0204	6.1
0911	2.4		0827	2.0
TU 1513	5.8		W 1441	6.2
2127	2.3		2059	1.8
12 0332	6.1	**27**	0308	6.7
0956	2.1		0929	1.4
W 1554	6.1		TH 1538	6.7
2208	2.0		2155	1.3
13 0411	6.4	**28**	0402	7.2
1034	1.8		1023	0.9
TH 1630	6.4		F 1628	7.2
2244	1.8		2246	0.8
14 0445	6.6			
1108	1.6			
F 1702	6.6			
2317	1.6			
15 0517	6.8			
1140	1.4			
SA 1734	6.7			
○ 2350	1.4			

MARCH

Time	m		Time	m
1 0450	7.6	**16**	0451	6.7
1111	0.5		1113	1.4
SA 1714	7.5		SU 1708	6.8
● 2333	0.6		○ 2324	1.3
2 0536	7.8	**17**	0523	6.9
1156	0.4		1145	1.2
SU 1757	7.5		M 1739	6.9
			2357	1.2
3 0017	0.5	**18**	0555	7.0
0618	7.8		1217	1.2
M 1239	0.5		TU 1811	7.0
1837	7.4			
4 0100	0.6	**19**	0030	1.2
0658	7.5		0627	7.0
TU 1319	0.8		W 1249	1.2
1915	7.1		1843	6.9
5 0141	1.0	**20**	0105	1.3
0736	7.1		0701	6.9
W 1359	1.2		TH 1324	1.4
1953	6.8		1918	6.8
6 0221	1.4	**21**	0142	1.4
0814	6.6		0737	6.7
TH 1439	1.7		F 1401	1.6
2031	6.3		1957	6.5
7 0303	1.9	**22**	0224	1.7
0855	6.1		0819	6.3
F 1521	2.3		SA 1445	2.0
2115	5.8		2043	6.2
8 0351	2.4	**23**	0313	2.0
0944	5.6		0909	5.9
SA 1612	2.7		SU 1537	2.3
◗ 2212	5.4		2143	5.8
9 0449	2.8	**24**	0412	2.3
1052	5.2		1016	5.6
SU 1720	3.1		M 1644	2.6
2331	5.1		◗ 2300	5.6
10 0606	3.1	**25**	0526	2.5
1222	5.0		1142	5.5
M 1844	3.1		TU 1809	2.7
11 0101	5.2	**26**	0028	5.7
0733	2.9		0652	2.4
TU 1348	5.2		W 1314	5.7
2002	2.9		1935	2.4
12 0213	5.5	**27**	0148	6.1
0840	2.6		0811	1.9
W 1445	5.6		TH 1426	6.2
2057	2.5		2043	1.8
13 0303	5.8	**28**	0251	6.6
0926	2.2		0912	1.4
TH 1527	6.0		F 1522	6.7
2139	2.1		2138	1.3
14 0342	6.2	**29**	0343	7.1
1005	1.9		1004	1.0
F 1602	6.3		SA 1610	7.1
2216	1.8		2228	0.9
15 0417	6.5	**30**	0430	7.4
1040	1.6		1051	0.7
SA 1636	6.6		SU 1653	7.3
2250	1.5		● 2313	0.7
31 0514	7.5			
1135	0.6			
M 1734	7.4			
2355	0.7			

APRIL

Time	m		Time	m
1 0554	7.5	**16**	0530	7.0
1215	0.7		1151	1.2
TU 1812	7.3		W 1746	7.1
2 0036	0.8	**17**	0007	1.1
0633	7.3		0605	7.0
W 1253	1.0		TH 1227	1.2
1848	7.1		1822	7.1
3 0115	1.1	**18**	0046	1.1
0709	6.9		0643	6.9
TH 1330	1.3		F 1305	1.3
1923	6.8		1901	6.9
4 0153	1.5	**19**	0127	1.3
0745	6.5		0723	6.7
F 1408	1.8		SA 1346	1.5
1959	6.3		1944	6.7
5 0233	1.9	**20**	0212	1.5
0823	6.1		0809	6.4
SA 1448	2.3		SU 1433	1.9
2039	5.9		2034	6.3
6 0317	2.4	**21**	0303	1.8
0908	5.6		0903	6.0
SU 1533	2.7		M 1528	2.2
2129	5.5		2136	6.0
7 0409	2.8	**22**	0403	2.1
1008	5.2		1010	5.7
M 1632	3.0		TU 1635	2.5
◗ 2239	5.2		◗ 2250	5.8
8 0516	3.0	**23**	0515	2.3
1129	5.0		1131	5.6
TU 1749	3.2		W 1756	2.5
9 0004	5.1	**24**	0011	5.9
0637	3.0		0635	2.2
W 1254	5.1		TH 1255	5.8
1909	3.0		1916	2.3
10 0120	5.3	**25**	0126	6.1
0750	2.8		0749	1.9
TH 1400	5.4		F 1404	6.1
2012	2.7		2022	1.9
11 0218	5.6	**26**	0228	6.5
0843	2.4		0850	1.5
F 1447	5.8		SA 1500	6.5
2059	2.3		2118	1.5
12 0303	6.0	**27**	0321	6.8
0926	2.0		0942	1.3
SA 1526	6.2		SU 1548	6.8
2140	1.9		2207	1.2
13 0342	6.4	**28**	0408	7.0
1004	1.7		1029	1.1
SU 1603	6.5		M 1631	7.0
2218	1.6		2251	1.0
14 0419	6.6	**29**	0451	7.1
1040	1.4		1111	1.0
M 1638	6.8		TU 1710	7.1
2255	1.4		● 2333	1.0
15 0454	6.9	**30**	0531	7.1
1116	1.3		1151	1.1
TU 1712	7.0		W 1747	7.1
○ 2331	1.2			

TIDES

Chart Datum: 3·64 metres below IGN Datum
HAT is 7·9 metres above Chart Datum

TIME ZONE -0100
(French Standard Time)
Subtract 1 hour for UT
For French Summer Time add
ONE hour in non-shaded areas

FRANCE – BREST

LAT 48°23'N   LONG 4°30'W

TIMES AND HEIGHTS OF HIGH AND LOW WATERS

Dates in amber are **SPRINGS**
Dates in yellow are NEAPS

2014

MAY

	Time	m		Time	m
1 TH	0012 0608 1228 1823	1.1 6.9 1.3 6.9	**16** F	0546 1207 1806	7.0 1.1 7.1
2 F	0050 0644 1304 1857	1.3 6.7 1.5 6.7	**17** SA	0030 0629 1250 1850	1.0 7.0 1.2 7.1
3 SA	0128 0720 1341 1933	1.6 6.4 1.8 6.4	**18** SU	0115 0715 1336 1937	1.1 6.8 1.4 6.9
4 SU	0206 0758 1419 2011	1.9 6.0 2.2 6.0	**19** M	0203 0804 1426 2030	1.3 6.5 1.7 6.6
5 M	0247 0839 1500 2055	2.3 5.7 2.6 5.7	**20** TU	0256 0859 1521 2129	1.6 6.2 2.0 6.3
6 TU	0333 0929 1550 2151	2.6 5.4 2.8 5.4	**21** W	0355 1001 1625 2235	1.9 5.9 2.2 6.1
7 W	0429 1034 1653 2302	2.8 5.2 3.0 5.2	**22** TH	0501 1112 1737 2347	2.1 5.8 2.3 6.0
8 TH	0536 1148 1805	2.9 5.1 3.0	**23** F	0612 1227 1850	2.1 5.8 2.2
9 F	0016 0646 1257 1913	5.3 2.8 5.3 2.8	**24** SA	0058 0721 1335 1956	6.1 2.4 6.0 2.0
10 SA	0120 0747 1355 2010	5.5 2.5 5.7 2.5	**25** SU	0201 0824 1434 2054	6.2 1.8 6.3 1.8
11 SU	0214 0838 1443 2058	5.8 2.2 6.0 2.1	**26** M	0257 0918 1524 2145	6.4 1.7 6.5 1.6
12 M	0301 0923 1525 2142	6.1 1.9 6.4 1.7	**27** TU	0345 1006 1608 2231	6.6 1.7 6.7 1.4
13 TU	0344 1005 1606 2224	6.5 1.6 6.7 1.4	**28** W	0429 1049 1649 2313	6.7 1.5 6.8 1.4
14 W	0425 1046 1645 2305	6.7 1.3 6.9 1.2	**29** TH	0509 1128 1726 2352	6.7 1.5 6.8 1.4
15 TH	0505 1126 1725 2347	6.9 1.2 7.1 1.1	**30** F	0547 1205 1801	6.6 1.5 6.7
			31 SA	0029 0623 1241 1836	1.5 6.5 1.7 6.6

JUNE

	Time	m		Time	m
1 SU	0105 0658 1317 1911	1.6 6.3 1.8 6.4	**16** M	0104 0706 1326 1929	0.9 7.0 1.1 7.1
2 M	0142 0734 1353 1946	1.9 6.1 2.1 6.2	**17** TU	0154 0756 1416 2020	1.0 6.8 1.3 6.9
3 TU	0220 0812 1431 2025	2.1 5.9 2.3 5.9	**18** W	0245 0848 1510 2114	1.3 6.5 1.6 6.6
4 W	0300 0855 1513 2110	2.3 5.6 2.6 5.7	**19** TH	0339 0944 1607 2213	1.6 6.2 1.9 6.3
5 TH	0345 0945 1603 2206	2.6 5.4 2.8 5.5	**20** F	0439 1045 1710 2317	1.9 5.9 2.2 6.0
6 F	0439 1046 1703 2311	2.7 5.3 2.9 5.4	**21** SA	0543 1153 1818	2.1 5.8 2.3
7 SA	0542 1153 1811	2.7 5.3 2.9	**22** SU	0025 0650 1302 1926	5.9 2.2 5.8 2.3
8 SU	0019 0647 1257 1916	5.4 2.6 5.5 2.6	**23** M	0132 0755 1406 2030	5.9 2.2 6.0 2.1
9 M	0121 0747 1355 2014	5.7 2.4 5.8 2.3	**24** TU	0233 0854 1501 2125	6.0 2.1 6.1 1.9
10 TU	0218 0841 1447 2106	6.0 2.1 6.2 1.9	**25** W	0326 0945 1549 2213	6.2 1.9 6.3 1.8
11 W	0309 0931 1535 2156	6.3 1.7 6.6 1.5	**26** TH	0411 1029 1630 2255	6.3 1.8 6.5 1.7
12 TH	0357 1019 1621 2243	6.6 1.4 6.9 1.2	**27** F	0451 1109 1708 2333	6.4 1.7 6.6 1.6
13 F	0445 1105 1707 2330	6.8 1.2 7.1 1.0	**28** SA	0528 1145 1743	6.5 1.7 6.6
14 SA	0531 1151 1754	7.0 1.1 7.3	**29** SU	0009 0603 1220 1816	1.6 6.4 1.8 6.6
15 SU	0017 0618 1238 1841	0.9 7.1 1.0 7.3	**30** M	0044 0637 1254 1850	1.6 6.4 1.7 6.5

JULY

	Time	m		Time	m
1 TU	0118 0711 1328 1923	1.7 6.3 1.9 6.4	**16** W	0139 0740 1402 2003	0.7 7.0 1.0 7.2
2 W	0152 0745 1403 1957	1.9 6.1 2.0 6.2	**17** TH	0227 0828 1451 2052	1.0 6.7 1.3 6.8
3 TH	0227 0821 1440 2035	2.1 5.9 2.2 6.0	**18** F	0317 0918 1543 2144	1.4 6.3 1.7 6.4
4 F	0306 0902 1522 2119	2.3 5.7 2.4 5.7	**19** SA	0410 1012 1640 2242	1.9 6.0 2.1 5.9
5 SA	0350 0952 1612 2214	2.5 5.5 2.6 5.6	**20** SU	0509 1115 1744 2350	2.3 5.7 2.4 5.6
6 SU	0444 1053 1713 2320	2.6 5.4 2.7 5.5	**21** M	0615 1227 1856	2.5 5.6 2.5
7 M	0548 1201 1822	2.6 5.5 2.7	**22** TU	0104 0726 1339 2007	5.6 2.5 5.7 2.4
8 TU	0030 0657 1308 1931	5.5 2.5 5.7 2.4	**23** W	0212 0832 1441 2107	5.7 2.4 5.9 2.2
9 W	0138 0803 1412 2034	5.8 2.2 6.0 2.0	**24** TH	0309 0926 1532 2157	5.9 2.2 6.1 2.0
10 TH	0240 0902 1509 2131	6.1 1.9 6.4 1.6	**25** F	0355 1011 1614 2238	6.1 2.0 6.3 1.8
11 F	0336 0957 1602 2224	6.5 1.5 6.9 1.2	**26** SA	0434 1050 1650 2315	6.3 1.8 6.5 1.6
12 SA	0428 1048 1653 2315	6.8 1.1 7.2 0.8	**27** SU	0509 1125 1724 2349	6.4 1.7 6.6 1.6
13 SU	0518 1137 1741	7.1 0.9 7.4	**28** M	0542 1158 1756	6.5 1.6 6.7
14 M	0003 0606 1226 1829	0.6 7.2 0.8 7.5	**29** TU	0021 0614 1230 1827	1.5 6.5 1.6 6.7
15 TU	0051 0653 1314 1916	0.6 7.2 0.8 7.4	**30** W	0053 0645 1303 1858	1.6 6.5 1.6 6.6
			31 TH	0124 0716 1335 1929	1.7 6.4 1.8 6.4

AUGUST

	Time	m		Time	m
1 F	0156 0749 1409 2003	1.8 6.2 2.0 6.2	**16** SA	0250 0846 1514 2111	1.4 6.4 1.7 6.3
2 SA	0231 0825 1447 2042	2.0 6.0 2.2 6.0	**17** SU	0338 0936 1607 2205	2.0 6.0 2.3 5.8
3 SU	0311 0909 1533 2130	2.2 5.8 2.4 5.7	**18** M	0433 1036 1709 2313	2.4 5.6 2.6 5.4
4 M	0400 1005 1628 2232	2.5 5.6 2.6 5.5	**19** TU	0539 1151 1824	2.8 5.4 2.8
5 TU	0501 1115 1738 2348	2.6 5.5 2.7 5.5	**20** W	0034 0657 1313 1943	5.3 2.8 5.4 2.7
6 W	0615 1231 1855	2.6 5.5 2.5	**21** TH	0152 0810 1421 2048	5.4 2.6 5.7 2.4
7 TH	0106 0732 1345 2009	5.6 2.4 5.9 2.1	**22** F	0251 0906 1512 2137	5.7 2.4 6.0 2.1
8 F	0219 0840 1450 2113	6.0 2.0 6.4 1.6	**23** SA	0336 0950 1553 2217	6.0 2.1 6.3 1.8
9 SA	0320 0939 1547 2208	6.5 1.5 6.9 1.1	**24** SU	0413 1028 1629 2252	6.3 1.8 6.5 1.6
10 SU	0414 1032 1638 2259	6.9 1.1 7.4 0.7	**25** M	0447 1102 1701 2325	6.5 1.7 6.7 1.5
11 M	0503 1122 1726 2348	7.2 0.7 7.6 0.5	**26** TU	0518 1134 1732 2356	6.6 1.5 6.8 1.4
12 TU	0550 1210 1812	7.4 0.6 7.7	**27** W	0548 1205 1802	6.7 1.5 6.8
13 W	0034 0635 1256 1857	0.4 7.4 0.6 7.6	**28** TH	0026 0618 1237 1832	1.4 6.7 1.5 6.8
14 TH	0120 0719 1341 1941	0.6 7.2 0.8 7.3	**29** F	0057 0649 1308 1903	1.6 6.6 1.6 6.7
15 F	0204 0802 1427 2025	0.9 6.9 1.2 6.9	**30** SA	0128 0720 1342 1935	1.6 6.5 1.8 6.5
			31 SU	0202 0755 1420 2012	1.8 6.3 2.0 6.2

Chart Datum: 3·64 metres below IGN Datum
HAT is 7·9 metres above Chart Datum

TIME ZONE -0100
(French Standard Time)
Subtract 1 hour for UT
For French Summer Time add
ONE hour in **non-shaded areas**

FRANCE – BREST

LAT 48°23'N   LONG 4°30'W

TIMES AND HEIGHTS OF HIGH AND LOW WATERS

Dates in amber are **SPRINGS**
Dates in yellow are **NEAPS**

2014

SEPTEMBER

Day	Time m	Day	Time m
1 M	0241 2.1 / 0837 6.0 / 1504 2.3 / 2058 5.9	**16** TU	0356 2.6 / 0955 5.6 / 1633 2.8 / ☽ 2235 5.3
2 TU	0328 2.4 / 0930 5.7 / 1559 2.5 / ☾ 2159 5.6	**17** W	0500 3.0 / 1112 5.3 / 1748 3.0
3 W	0428 2.7 / 1042 5.5 / 1708 2.7 / 2319 5.4	**18** TH	0000 5.1 / 0621 3.1 / 1239 5.3 / 1912 2.9
4 TH	0546 2.7 / 1206 5.6 / 1830 2.6	**19** F	0124 5.3 / 0740 2.9 / 1353 5.6 / 2020 2.6
5 F	0046 5.6 / 0711 2.5 / 1327 5.9 / 1950 2.2	**20** SA	0224 5.6 / 0838 2.5 / 1445 5.9 / 2109 2.3
6 SA	0204 6.0 / 0824 2.0 / 1434 6.5 / 2056 1.6	**21** SU	0309 6.0 / 0922 2.2 / 1525 6.2 / 2148 1.9
7 SU	0306 6.5 / 0924 1.5 / 1531 7.0 / 2152 1.1	**22** M	0346 6.3 / 1000 1.9 / 1601 6.5 / 2223 1.7
8 M	0358 7.0 / 1016 1.0 / 1621 7.5 / 2242 0.7	**23** TU	0419 6.6 / 1034 1.7 / 1634 6.7 / 2256 1.5
9 TU	0446 7.4 / 1105 0.7 / 1708 7.7 / ○ 2329 0.4	**24** W	0451 6.7 / 1107 1.5 / 1705 6.9 / ● 2328 1.4
10 W	0531 7.5 / 1151 0.5 / 1752 7.8	**25** TH	0522 6.9 / 1139 1.4 / 1736 6.9 / 2359 1.4
11 TH	0014 0.4 / 0613 7.5 / 1235 0.6 / 1834 7.6	**26** F	0552 6.9 / 1212 1.4 / 1807 6.9
12 F	0057 0.7 / 0654 7.3 / 1318 0.9 / 1915 7.3	**27** SA	0030 1.4 / 0623 6.9 / 1245 1.5 / 1839 6.8
13 SA	0138 1.1 / 0734 7.0 / 1401 1.3 / 1956 6.8	**28** SU	0103 1.5 / 0656 6.7 / 1320 1.6 / 1913 6.6
14 SU	0220 1.6 / 0814 6.5 / 1445 1.8 / 2039 6.3	**29** M	0138 1.8 / 0732 6.5 / 1359 1.9 / 1952 6.3
15 M	0305 2.1 / 0859 6.0 / 1534 2.3 / 2128 5.7	**30** TU	0219 2.1 / 0815 6.2 / 1445 2.2 / 2039 6.0

OCTOBER

Day	Time m	Day	Time m
1 W	0308 2.4 / 0910 5.9 / 1540 2.4 / 2141 5.6	**16** TH	0419 3.0 / 1026 5.3 / 1705 3.0 / 2315 5.1
2 TH	0409 2.7 / 1023 5.7 / 1650 2.6 / 2303 5.5	**17** F	0533 3.2 / 1150 5.2 / 1825 3.0
3 F	0528 2.8 / 1149 5.7 / 1813 2.5	**18** SA	0037 5.2 / 0653 3.1 / 1307 5.4 / 1936 2.8
4 SA	0032 5.6 / 0655 2.5 / 1311 6.0 / 1934 2.1	**19** SU	0143 5.5 / 0757 2.8 / 1405 5.7 / 2029 2.5
5 SU	0150 6.1 / 0808 2.1 / 1417 6.5 / 2039 1.6	**20** M	0232 5.9 / 0845 2.4 / 1449 6.1 / 2112 2.1
6 M	0249 6.6 / 0907 1.5 / 1512 7.0 / 2133 1.1	**21** TU	0311 6.2 / 0926 2.1 / 1527 6.4 / 2149 1.8
7 TU	0340 7.0 / 0958 1.1 / 1601 7.4 / 2223 0.8	**22** W	0347 6.5 / 1003 1.8 / 1603 6.7 / 2225 1.6
8 W	0426 7.4 / 1045 0.8 / 1647 7.6 / ○ 2308 0.6	**23** TH	0422 6.8 / 1039 1.6 / 1637 6.9 / ● 2259 1.4
9 TH	0509 7.5 / 1130 0.7 / 1730 7.7 / 2352 0.7	**24** F	0455 6.9 / 1114 1.4 / 1711 7.0 / 2333 1.4
10 F	0550 7.5 / 1213 0.8 / 1811 7.5	**25** SA	0528 7.0 / 1149 1.3 / 1745 7.0
11 SA	0033 0.9 / 0629 7.3 / 1255 1.0 / 1850 7.1	**26** SU	0007 1.4 / 0602 7.0 / 1225 1.4 / 1820 6.9
12 SU	0112 1.3 / 0707 7.0 / 1336 1.4 / 1929 6.7	**27** M	0043 1.5 / 0638 6.9 / 1303 1.5 / 1858 6.7
13 M	0152 1.7 / 0745 6.5 / 1418 1.7 / 2009 6.2	**28** TU	0122 1.7 / 0718 6.7 / 1346 1.7 / 1941 6.5
14 TU	0234 2.2 / 0826 6.1 / 1503 2.4 / 2056 5.7	**29** W	0206 2.0 / 0805 6.4 / 1434 2.0 / 2031 6.1
15 W	0321 2.7 / 0916 5.7 / 1557 2.8 / ☽ 2156 5.3	**30** TH	0257 2.3 / 0901 6.1 / 1530 2.3 / 2134 5.8
		31 F	0358 2.6 / 1012 5.9 / 1638 2.4 / ☾ 2251 5.6

NOVEMBER

Day	Time m	Day	Time m
1 SA	0514 2.7 / 1132 5.9 / 1757 2.4	**16** SU	0550 3.1 / 1203 5.3 / 1835 3.0
2 SU	0015 5.8 / 0637 2.5 / 1250 6.1 / 1913 2.1	**17** M	0044 5.4 / 0700 3.0 / 1309 5.5 / 1936 2.7
3 M	0129 6.1 / 0748 2.1 / 1356 6.5 / 2018 1.7	**18** TU	0142 5.7 / 0758 2.7 / 1404 5.8 / 2027 2.4
4 TU	0229 6.5 / 0847 1.7 / 1452 6.9 / 2113 1.4	**19** W	0230 6.0 / 0846 2.3 / 1449 6.2 / 2111 2.1
5 W	0320 6.9 / 0939 1.3 / 1541 7.2 / 2202 1.1	**20** TH	0312 6.4 / 0930 2.0 / 1530 6.5 / 2151 1.8
6 TH	0406 7.2 / 1026 1.1 / 1627 7.3 / ○ 2248 1.0	**21** F	0352 6.7 / 1010 1.7 / 1610 6.7 / 2230 1.5
7 F	0449 7.3 / 1111 1.0 / 1709 7.3 / 2330 1.0	**22** SA	0430 6.9 / 1049 1.4 / 1648 6.9 / ● 2309 1.4
8 SA	0529 7.3 / 1153 1.0 / 1750 7.2	**23** SU	0508 7.1 / 1129 1.3 / 1727 7.0 / 2348 1.3
9 SU	0010 1.2 / 0607 7.2 / 1233 1.2 / 1828 6.9	**24** M	0547 7.1 / 1209 1.2 / 1807 7.0
10 M	0049 1.5 / 0644 6.9 / 1313 1.5 / 1906 6.6	**25** TU	0029 1.4 / 0628 7.1 / 1252 1.3 / 1849 6.9
11 TU	0127 1.8 / 0721 6.6 / 1353 1.9 / 1945 6.2	**26** W	0112 1.5 / 0712 7.0 / 1337 1.4 / 1936 6.7
12 W	0207 2.2 / 0759 6.2 / 1435 2.3 / 2027 5.9	**27** TH	0158 1.7 / 0800 6.7 / 1426 1.6 / 2027 6.4
13 TH	0249 2.5 / 0843 5.8 / 1521 2.6 / 2117 5.5	**28** F	0250 2.0 / 0855 6.5 / 1521 1.9 / 2126 6.1
14 F	0338 2.9 / 0937 5.5 / 1617 2.9 / ☽ 2221 5.3	**29** SA	0349 2.2 / 0958 6.2 / 1624 2.2 / ☾ 2234 5.9
15 SA	0438 3.1 / 1048 5.3 / 1734 3.0 / 2334 5.2	**30** SU	0457 2.4 / 1109 6.1 / 1735 2.3 / 2349 5.9

DECEMBER

Day	Time m	Day	Time m
1 M	0611 2.4 / 1223 6.1 / 1847 2.2	**16** TU	0551 3.0 / 1202 5.4 / 1832 2.9
2 TU	0102 6.0 / 0722 2.2 / 1331 6.3 / 1953 2.0	**17** W	0042 5.5 / 0659 2.9 / 1308 5.6 / 1934 2.6
3 W	0205 6.3 / 0825 1.9 / 1431 6.5 / 2051 1.7	**18** TH	0142 5.7 / 0801 2.6 / 1407 5.9 / 2029 2.3
4 TH	0259 6.6 / 0920 1.6 / 1523 6.8 / 2143 1.5	**19** F	0235 6.1 / 0854 2.2 / 1457 6.2 / 2118 2.0
5 F	0347 6.8 / 1009 1.4 / 1610 6.9 / 2229 1.4	**20** SA	0322 6.5 / 0942 1.8 / 1544 6.5 / 2204 1.7
6 SA	0431 7.0 / 1054 1.3 / 1652 6.9 / ○ 2311 1.4	**21** SU	0407 6.8 / 1027 1.5 / 1628 6.8 / 2248 1.4
7 SU	0511 7.0 / 1136 1.3 / 1732 6.9 / 2351 1.4	**22** M	0451 7.1 / 1112 1.2 / 1712 7.0 / ● 2332 1.2
8 M	0549 7.0 / 1215 1.4 / 1810 6.8	**23** TU	0534 7.3 / 1156 1.0 / 1756 7.1
9 TU	0029 1.6 / 0625 6.9 / 1253 1.6 / 1846 6.6	**24** W	0017 1.1 / 0619 7.4 / 1241 0.9 / 1841 7.1
10 W	0106 1.7 / 0701 6.7 / 1330 1.8 / 1923 6.3	**25** TH	0102 1.1 / 0705 7.3 / 1328 1.0 / 1928 7.0
11 TH	0142 2.0 / 0736 6.4 / 1408 2.1 / 2000 6.1	**26** F	0150 1.3 / 0752 7.1 / 1416 1.2 / 2018 6.7
12 F	0220 2.3 / 0813 6.1 / 1447 2.4 / 2041 5.8	**27** SA	0240 1.5 / 0843 6.7 / 1508 1.5 / 2111 6.4
13 SA	0301 2.6 / 0855 5.8 / 1531 2.6 / 2128 5.5	**28** SU	0333 1.8 / 0938 6.5 / 1604 1.9 / ☽ 2209 6.1
14 SU	0347 2.8 / 0946 5.6 / 1623 2.8 / ☾ 2227 5.3	**29** M	0433 2.1 / 1040 6.2 / 1707 2.2 / 2316 5.9
15 M	0444 3.0 / 1051 5.4 / 1725 2.9 / 2335 5.3	**30** TU	0541 2.3 / 1150 6.0 / 1816 2.3
		31 W	0029 5.8 / 0653 2.4 / 1303 5.9 / 1926 2.3

Chart Datum: 3·64 metres below IGN Datum
HAT is 7·9 metres above Chart Datum

TIDES

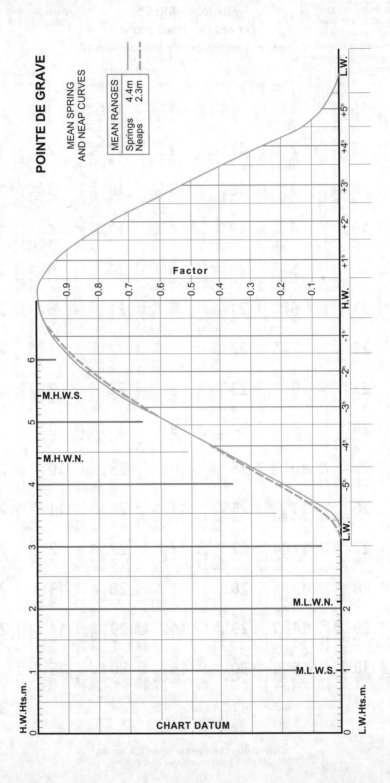

POINTE DE GRAVE

MEAN SPRING
AND NEAP CURVES

MEAN RANGES
Springs 4.4m
Neaps 2.3m

Factor

Chart Datum

TIME ZONE -0100
(French Standard Time)
Subtract 1 hour for UT
For French Summer Time add
ONE hour in **non-shaded areas**

FRANCE – POINTE DE GRAVE

LAT 45°34'N   LONG 1°04'W

TIMES AND HEIGHTS OF HIGH AND LOW WATERS

Dates in amber are **SPRINGS**
Dates in yellow are **NEAPS**

2014

JANUARY

Day	Time m	Time m	Time m	Time m	Day	Time m	Time m	Time m	Time m
1 W	0440 5.5	1038 1.0	1710 5.4	●2301 1.0	16 TH	0514 5.1	1117 1.4	1734 5.0	○2325 1.4
2 TH	0530 5.7	1129 0.8	1758 5.5	2350 0.9	17 F	0546 5.1	1150 1.4	1806 5.0	2358 1.4
3 F	0619 5.8	1217 0.8	1847 5.5		18 SA	0618 5.1	1223 1.4	1837 5.0	
4 SA	0038 0.9	0708 5.7	1304 0.8	1936 5.3	19 SU	0031 1.4	0649 5.1	1255 1.4	1907 5.0
5 SU	0124 1.0	0757 5.6	1350 1.0	2026 5.1	20 M	0103 1.4	0720 5.0	1327 1.5	1940 4.9
6 M	0211 1.2	0848 5.3	1437 1.2	2118 4.9	21 TU	0137 1.5	0754 4.9	1400 1.6	2016 4.7
7 TU	0300 1.4	0942 5.0	1526 1.5	2217 4.6	22 W	0212 1.6	0833 4.8	1437 1.7	2100 4.6
8 W	0354 1.7	1042 4.7	1623 1.8	☾2324 4.4	23 TH	0253 1.8	0920 4.6	1520 1.9	2154 4.4
9 TH	0456 1.9	1150 4.5	1729 2.0		24 F	0343 1.9	1020 4.5	1615 2.0	☽2301 4.4
10 F	0037 4.3	0608 2.0	1304 4.4	1843 2.1	25 SA	0448 2.1	1132 4.4	1727 2.1	
11 SA	0145 4.4	0721 2.0	1412 4.4	1952 2.0	26 SU	0019 4.4	0604 2.0	1256 4.4	1844 2.0
12 SU	0241 4.5	0825 1.9	1506 4.5	2049 1.9	27 M	0136 4.6	0718 1.9	1412 4.6	1956 1.8
13 M	0327 4.7	0918 1.8	1550 4.7	2135 1.7	28 TU	0241 4.9	0828 1.6	1514 4.9	2100 1.5
14 TU	0406 4.9	1003 1.6	1628 4.8	2215 1.6	29 W	0337 5.2	0931 1.3	1608 5.2	2158 1.2
15 W	0441 5.0	1042 1.5	1702 4.9	2251 1.5	30 TH	0428 5.5	1026 1.0	1658 5.4	●2250 0.9
					31 F	0517 5.7	1117 0.7	1746 5.5	2338 0.8

FEBRUARY

Day	Time m	Time m	Time m	Time m	Day	Time m	Time m	Time m	Time m
1 SA	0605 5.8	1204 0.7	1832 5.5		16 SU	0556 5.2	1201 1.3	1813 5.1	
2 SU	0024 0.7	0651 5.8	1248 0.7	1917 5.4	17 M	0010 1.2	0626 5.2	1232 1.3	1843 5.1
3 M	0108 0.8	0736 5.6	1331 0.9	2000 5.2	18 TU	0041 1.3	0657 5.2	1303 1.3	1914 5.0
4 TU	0150 1.0	0820 5.3	1412 1.1	2043 4.9	19 W	0113 1.3	0730 5.1	1334 1.4	1948 4.9
5 W	0234 1.2	0905 5.0	1456 1.4	2129 4.6	20 TH	0147 1.4	0807 4.9	1409 1.5	2029 4.8
6 TH	0321 1.6	0955 4.6	1545 1.8	☾2225 4.4	21 F	0226 1.6	0851 4.7	1449 1.7	2119 4.6
7 F	0416 1.9	1059 4.3	1645 2.1	2342 4.2	22 SA	0313 1.7	0948 4.5	1540 1.9	☽2224 4.4
8 SA	0527 2.1	1223 4.1	1801 2.3		23 SU	0414 1.9	1101 4.3	1651 2.1	2347 4.4
9 SU	0108 4.2	0648 2.2	1345 4.2	1921 2.2	24 M	0534 2.0	1235 4.3	1816 2.1	
10 M	0216 4.3	0802 2.0	1446 4.3	2026 2.0	25 TU	0115 4.5	0657 1.9	1358 4.5	1937 1.9
11 TU	0307 4.5	0858 1.6	1532 4.5	2115 1.8	26 W	0225 4.8	0814 1.6	1502 4.9	2047 1.5
12 W	0348 4.7	0943 1.7	1609 4.7	2155 1.6	27 TH	0322 5.2	0918 1.2	1555 5.2	2145 1.2
13 TH	0423 4.9	1021 1.5	1642 4.9	2231 1.5	28 F	0414 5.5	1012 0.9	1644 5.4	2235 0.9
14 F	0455 5.0	1056 1.4	1713 5.0	2305 1.4					
15 SA	0526 5.2	1129 1.3	1743 5.1	○2338 1.3					

MARCH

Day	Time m	Time m	Time m	Time m	Day	Time m	Time m	Time m	Time m
1 SA	0501 5.7	1101 0.7	1729 5.5	●2322 0.7	16 SU	0459 5.1	1101 1.3	1715 5.1	○2312 1.2
2 SU	0546 5.8	1145 0.7	1812 5.5		17 M	0530 5.2	1133 1.2	1746 5.2	2345 1.2
3 M	0006 0.7	0629 5.7	1227 0.7	1852 5.4	18 TU	0602 5.3	1206 1.2	1818 5.2	
4 TU	0047 0.7	0711 5.6	1307 0.9	1930 5.3	19 W	0018 1.1	0634 5.3	1238 1.2	1851 5.2
5 W	0126 0.9	0750 5.3	1345 1.1	2007 5.0	20 TH	0052 1.2	0709 5.2	1311 1.3	1927 5.1
6 TH	0206 1.2	0828 4.9	1424 1.4	2044 4.7	21 F	0127 1.2	0747 5.0	1347 1.4	2008 4.9
7 F	0248 1.5	0910 4.6	1507 1.8	2129 4.4	22 SA	0207 1.4	0833 4.8	1428 1.6	2059 4.7
8 SA	0337 1.9	1007 4.2	1600 2.1	☾2237 4.2	23 SU	0254 1.6	0930 4.5	1520 1.8	2204 4.5
9 SU	0442 2.2	1131 4.0	1714 2.4		24 M	0356 1.8	1045 4.3	1630 2.0	☽2328 4.4
10 M	0012 4.1	0607 2.3	1305 4.0	1840 2.4	25 TU	0515 1.9	1223 4.3	1758 2.1	
11 TU	0137 4.2	0728 2.2	1414 4.2	1952 2.2	26 W	0058 4.6	0641 1.8	1344 4.5	1921 1.9
12 W	0236 4.4	0828 2.0	1502 4.4	2044 2.0	27 TH	0207 4.9	0758 1.6	1446 4.8	2030 1.6
13 TH	0319 4.6	0913 1.8	1540 4.6	2126 1.7	28 F	0305 5.2	0900 1.3	1538 5.1	2127 1.2
14 F	0355 4.8	0952 1.6	1613 4.8	2204 1.5	29 SA	0356 5.4	0953 1.0	1625 5.3	2216 1.0
15 SA	0428 5.0	1027 1.4	1645 5.0	2238 1.4	30 SU	0442 5.6	1039 0.8	1707 5.4	●2301 0.8
					31 M	0524 5.6	1123 0.8	1747 5.5	2344 0.8

APRIL

Day	Time m	Time m	Time m	Time m	Day	Time m	Time m	Time m	Time m
1 TU	0605 5.6	1202 0.9	1825 5.4		16 W	0538 5.3	1138 1.1	1755 5.3	2356 1.1
2 W	0023 0.8	0644 5.4	1240 1.0	1901 5.2	17 TH	0614 5.3	1214 1.1	1832 5.3	
3 TH	0101 1.0	0720 5.1	1316 1.2	1934 5.0	18 F	0033 1.1	0653 5.2	1251 1.2	1912 5.2
4 F	0138 1.2	0755 4.9	1353 1.5	2008 4.8	19 SA	0113 1.1	0736 5.0	1331 1.3	1958 5.1
5 SA	0217 1.5	0835 4.5	1432 1.8	2050 4.5	20 SU	0156 1.3	0824 4.8	1416 1.5	2051 4.9
6 SU	0301 1.8	0926 4.3	1520 2.1	2146 4.3	21 M	0245 1.5	0923 4.6	1511 1.7	2154 4.7
7 M	0357 2.1	1039 4.0	1624 2.3	☾2307 4.1	22 TU	0346 1.7	1039 4.4	1620 1.9	☾2315 4.6
8 TU	0515 2.3	1206 4.0	1745 2.4		23 W	0501 1.8	1210 4.4	1741 2.0	
9 W	0034 4.1	0636 2.3	1322 4.1	1900 2.3	24 TH	0037 4.7	0622 1.7	1325 4.6	1859 1.8
10 TH	0145 4.2	0742 2.1	1418 4.3	1959 2.1	25 F	0146 4.8	0735 1.6	1425 4.8	2007 1.6
11 F	0237 4.5	0832 1.9	1500 4.6	2047 1.9	26 SA	0244 5.0	0837 1.4	1517 5.0	2104 1.3
12 SA	0318 4.7	0914 1.6	1537 4.8	2128 1.6	27 SU	0334 5.2	0929 1.2	1602 5.2	2153 1.1
13 SU	0354 4.9	0952 1.4	1611 5.0	2206 1.4	28 M	0420 5.3	1015 1.0	1643 5.3	2238 1.0
14 M	0428 5.1	1028 1.3	1645 5.2	2243 1.2	29 TU	0502 5.3	1057 1.0	1722 5.3	●2320 1.0
15 TU	0503 5.2	1103 1.2	1720 5.3	○2319 1.1	30 W	0541 5.2	1137 1.1	1759 5.3	2359 1.0

Chart Datum: 2·83 metres below IGN Datum
HAT is 6·1 metres above Chart Datum

TIDES

TIME ZONE -0100
(French Standard Time)
Subtract 1 hour for UT
For French Summer Time add
ONE hour in **non-shaded areas**

FRANCE – POINTE DE GRAVE
LAT 45°34'N   LONG 1°04'W
TIMES AND HEIGHTS OF HIGH AND LOW WATERS

Dates in amber are **SPRINGS**
Dates in yellow are **NEAPS**

2014

MAY

Time	m	Time	m
1 TH 0619/1213/1834	5.2/1.2/5.2	**16** F 0558/1155/1818	5.3/1.1/5.4
2 F 0036/0654/1249/1908	1.1/5.0/1.3/5.0	**17** SA 0018/0642/1237/1903	1.0/5.2/1.1/5.3
3 SA 0113/0730/1325/1942	1.3/4.8/1.5/4.8	**18** SU 0102/0729/1321/1952	1.0/5.1/1.2/5.2
4 SU 0150/0808/1403/2021	1.5/4.6/1.7/4.6	**19** M 0148/0820/1409/2046	1.1/4.9/1.4/5.0
5 M 0231/0853/1446/2109	1.7/4.3/2.0/4.4	**20** TU 0239/0918/1504/2147	1.3/4.7/1.6/4.9
6 TU 0318/0952/1538/2212	2.0/4.2/2.2/4.2	**21** W 0336/1030/1607/2259	1.5/4.5/1.7/4.7
7 W 0420/1104/1646/2326	2.2/4.1/2.3/4.1	**22** TH 0443/1149/1719	1.6/4.5/1.8
8 TH 0533/1216/1759	2.2/4.1/2.3	**23** F 0013/0555/1259/1832	4.7/1.7/4.6/1.7
9 F 0037/0641/1318/1902	4.2/2.1/4.2/2.2	**24** SA 0120/0707/1400/1939	4.8/1.6/4.7/1.6
10 SA 0139/0739/1410/1957	4.4/1.9/4.5/1.9	**25** SU 0220/0810/1453/2038	4.8/1.5/4.8/1.5
11 SU 0230/0828/1454/2045	4.6/1.7/4.7/1.7	**26** M 0312/0904/1539/2130	4.9/1.4/4.9/1.3
12 M 0314/0911/1535/2129	4.8/1.5/4.9/1.5	**27** TU 0359/0951/1620/2216	5.0/1.3/5.0/1.2
13 TU 0356/0952/1614/2211	5.0/1.3/5.1/1.3	**28** W 0441/1034/1659/2259	5.0/1.2/5.1/1.2
14 W 0436/1033/1654/2253	5.1/1.2/5.3/1.1	**29** TH 0521/1113/1736/2338	5.0/1.2/5.1/1.2
15 TH 0517/1113/1735/2335	5.2/1.1/5.3/1.0	**30** F 0558/1150/1812	5.0/1.3/5.1
		31 SA 0015/0634/1225/1846	1.2/4.9/1.4/5.0

JUNE

Time	m	Time	m
1 SU 0051/0708/1301/1920	1.3/4.8/1.5/4.9	**16** M 0052/0721/1312/1944	0.8/5.2/1.0/5.4
2 M 0127/0744/1337/1957	1.5/4.6/1.6/4.7	**17** TU 0139/0812/1400/2037	0.9/5.0/1.1/5.2
3 TU 0204/0824/1416/2039	1.6/4.5/1.8/4.6	**18** W 0228/0907/1452/2133	1.1/4.8/1.3/5.0
4 W 0245/0910/1500/2127	1.8/4.3/1.9/4.4	**19** TH 0320/0959/1548/2236	1.3/4.5/1.5/4.8
5 TH 0333/1006/1553/2226	1.9/4.2/2.1/4.3	**20** F 0419/1119/1652/2343	1.5/4.5/1.6/4.7
6 F 0431/1110/1657/2331	2.1/4.2/2.2/4.2	**21** SA 0524/1229/1801	1.7/4.5/1.7
7 SA 0537/1215/1803	2.1/4.2/2.1	**22** SU 0051/0635/1334/1911	4.6/1.7/4.5/1.7
8 SU 0036/0640/1316/1904	4.3/2.0/4.4/2.0	**23** M 0155/0742/1430/2014	4.6/1.7/4.6/1.6
9 M 0137/0737/1410/1959	4.4/1.8/4.6/1.8	**24** TU 0253/0841/1519/2110	4.6/1.6/4.7/1.5
10 TU 0233/0829/1459/2052	4.6/1.6/4.8/1.5	**25** W 0342/0931/1602/2158	4.7/1.5/4.8/1.4
11 W 0324/0918/1546/2142	4.8/1.4/5.0/1.3	**26** TH 0424/1014/1640/2241	4.8/1.4/4.9/1.3
12 TH 0412/1006/1632/2230	5.0/1.2/5.2/1.1	**27** F 0503/1054/1717/2320	4.8/1.4/5.0/1.3
13 F 0459/1053/1718/2318	5.2/1.1/5.4/0.9	**28** SA 0539/1130/1752/2356	4.9/1.3/5.0/1.3
14 SA 0545/1139/1805	5.3/1.0/5.5	**29** SU 0614/1205/1825	4.9/1.3/5.0
15 SU 0005/0632/1225/1854	0.8/5.3/1.0/5.5	**30** M 0031/0646/1239/1858	1.3/4.8/1.4/4.9

JULY

Time	m	Time	m
1 TU 0105/0719/1313/1932	1.4/4.7/1.5/4.8	**16** W 0126/0757/1346/2020	0.7/5.2/0.9/5.4
2 W 0140/0748/1348/2008	1.5/4.6/1.6/4.7	**17** TH 0212/0847/1433/2111	0.9/4.9/1.1/5.1
3 TH 0215/0832/1426/2049	1.6/4.5/1.7/4.6	**18** F 0259/0941/1524/2207	1.2/4.7/1.4/4.8
4 F 0254/0917/1509/2137	1.7/4.4/1.8/4.4	**19** SA 0351/1042/1622/2310	1.4/4.5/1.6/4.5
5 SA 0339/1011/1601/2234	1.9/4.3/2.0/4.3	**20** SU 0451/1153/1729	1.7/4.3/1.8
6 SU 0434/1115/1704/2340	2.0/4.2/2.0/4.3	**21** M 0021/0601/1306/1843	4.3/1.9/4.3/1.9
7 M 0541/1223/1813	2.0/4.3/2.0	**22** TU 0133/0715/1410/1953	4.3/1.9/4.4/1.8
8 TU 0049/0648/1330/1918	4.3/1.9/4.5/1.8	**23** W 0236/0820/1503/2053	4.4/1.8/4.5/1.7
9 W 0157/0751/1429/2019	4.5/1.7/4.7/1.6	**24** TH 0327/0913/1546/2142	4.5/1.7/4.7/1.5
10 TH 0258/0849/1523/2117	4.7/1.5/5.0/1.3	**25** F 0409/0957/1624/2225	4.6/1.5/4.8/1.4
11 F 0352/0944/1614/2212	5.0/1.2/5.2/1.1	**26** SA 0445/1036/1658/2302	4.7/1.4/4.9/1.3
12 SA 0443/1036/1703/2304	5.2/1.0/5.5/0.8	**27** SU 0519/1112/1731/2337	4.8/1.3/5.0/1.3
13 SU 0532/1126/1752/2353	5.3/0.9/5.6/0.7	**28** M 0551/1145/1803	4.9/1.3/5.0
14 M 0621/1214/1841	5.4/0.8/5.6	**29** TU 0010/0622/1218/1834	1.3/4.9/1.3/5.0
15 TU 0040/0709/1300/1930	0.7/5.3/0.8/5.5	**30** W 0042/0652/1250/1905	1.3/4.9/1.4/5.0
		31 TH 0114/0723/1322/1937	1.4/4.8/1.4/4.9

AUGUST

Time	m	Time	m
1 F 0145/0757/1355/2013	1.4/4.7/1.5/4.7	**16** SA 0233/0906/1457/2133	1.2/4.7/1.3/4.7
2 SA 0219/0836/1433/2056	1.6/4.6/1.7/4.6	**17** SU 0320/0959/1550/2233	1.5/4.4/1.7/4.4
3 SU 0258/0924/1518/2149	1.7/4.4/1.8/4.4	**18** M 0416/1110/1656/2349	1.8/4.2/1.9/4.2
4 M 0346/1025/1615/2255	1.9/4.3/2.0/4.3	**19** TU 0526/1235/1816	2.1/4.2/2.1
5 TU 0449/1139/1729	2.0/4.3/2.0	**20** W 0111/0646/1349/1933	4.1/2.1/4.2/2.0
6 W 0012/0606/1257/1844	4.3/2.0/4.4/1.9	**21** TH 0218/0758/1445/2034	4.2/2.0/4.5/1.8
7 TH 0131/0720/1407/1954	4.4/1.8/4.7/1.6	**22** F 0309/0853/1528/2123	4.6/1.8/4.6/1.6
8 F 0239/0827/1505/2059	4.7/1.6/5.0/1.3	**23** SA 0349/0937/1604/2204	4.6/1.6/4.8/1.5
9 SA 0336/0927/1558/2157	5.0/1.3/5.3/1.0	**24** SU 0423/1015/1637/2240	4.8/1.5/5.0/1.4
10 SU 0428/1022/1648/2249	5.2/1.0/5.6/0.8	**25** M 0454/1049/1707/2313	4.9/1.4/5.1/1.4
11 M 0517/1112/1736/2338	5.4/0.8/5.7/0.6	**26** TU 0525/1122/1738/2345	5.0/1.3/5.1/1.2
12 TU 0604/1159/1823	5.5/0.7/5.7	**27** W 0554/1154/1807	5.0/1.3/5.1
13 W 0024/0650/1244/1910	0.6/5.4/0.7/5.6	**28** TH 0016/0624/1225/1837	1.3/5.0/1.3/5.1
14 TH 0107/0735/1327/1956	0.7/5.3/0.8/5.4	**29** F 0046/0654/1256/1909	1.3/5.0/1.3/5.0
15 F 0150/0819/1411/2043	0.9/5.0/1.0/5.1	**30** SA 0117/0726/1328/1943	1.4/4.9/1.4/4.9
		31 SU 0149/0803/1404/2024	1.5/4.7/1.6/4.7

Chart Datum: 2·83 metres below IGN Datum
HAT is 6·1 metres above Chart Datum

TIME ZONE -0100
(French Standard Time)
Subtract 1 hour for UT
For French Summer Time add
ONE hour in **non-shaded areas**

FRANCE – POINTE DE GRAVE

LAT 45°34'N   LONG 1°04'W

TIMES AND HEIGHTS OF HIGH AND LOW WATERS

Dates in amber are **SPRINGS**
Dates in yellow are **NEAPS**

2014

SEPTEMBER

Day	Time m	Time m	Time m	Time m
1 M	0226 1.6	0850 4.6	1447 1.7	2117 4.5
2 TU	0312 1.8	0950 4.4	1542 1.9	2225 4.3 ◐
3 W	0413 2.0	1107 4.3	1656 2.0	2349 4.3
4 TH	0534 2.1	1235 4.4	1820 1.9	
5 F	0116 4.4	0657 1.9	1350 4.4	1936 1.7
6 SA	0225 4.7	0810 1.6	1449 5.1	2043 1.3
7 SU	0321 5.0	0912 1.3	1542 5.4	2140 1.0
8 M	0412 5.3	1005 1.0	1630 5.7	2232 0.8
9 TU	0459 5.5	1054 0.8	1717 5.8	2319 0.6 ○
10 W	0544 5.5	1140 0.7	1802 5.8	
11 TH	0003 0.7	0627 5.5	1223 0.7	1846 5.6
12 F	0044 0.8	0709 5.3	1305 0.9	1929 5.4
13 SA	0125 1.0	0749 5.1	1346 1.1	2011 5.0
14 SU	0205 1.3	0829 4.8	1428 1.4	2057 4.7
15 M	0248 1.6	0916 4.6	1517 1.8	2154 4.3
16 TU	0340 2.0	1022 4.2	1620 2.1	2313 4.1 ◐
17 W	0447 2.2	1048 4.4	1743 2.3	
18 TH	0041 4.0	0611 2.3	1317 4.2	1905 2.2
19 F	0151 4.2	0727 2.2	1418 4.4	2008 2.0
20 SA	0241 4.4	0824 2.0	1502 4.6	2055 1.8
21 SU	0321 4.6	0909 1.8	1538 4.8	2135 1.6
22 M	0354 4.8	0947 1.6	1610 5.0	2211 1.4
23 TU	0425 5.0	1022 1.4	1641 5.1	2244 1.3
24 W	0456 5.1	1055 1.3	1711 5.2	2316 1.3 ●
25 TH	0527 5.1	1128 1.3	1742 5.2	2348 1.2
26 F	0557 5.2	1200 1.2	1813 5.2	
27 SA	0019 1.3	0629 5.1	1232 1.3	1845 5.1
28 SU	0051 1.4	0703 5.0	1306 1.4	1921 5.0
29 M	0125 1.5	0742 4.9	1344 1.5	2004 4.8
30 TU	0204 1.7	0829 4.7	1427 1.7	2058 4.5

OCTOBER

Day	Time m	Time m	Time m	Time m
1 W	0251 1.9	0930 4.5	1523 1.9	2208 4.4 ◐
2 TH	0353 2.1	1048 4.4	1637 2.0	2338 4.3
3 F	0515 2.1	1218 4.5	1802 2.0	
4 SA	0105 4.5	0639 2.0	1333 4.8	1920 1.7
5 SU	0210 4.8	0752 1.7	1432 5.1	2025 1.4
6 M	0305 5.1	0853 1.4	1524 5.4	2121 1.1
7 TU	0353 5.3	0946 1.1	1612 5.6	2211 0.9
8 W	0438 5.5	1034 0.9	1657 5.7	2256 0.8 ○
9 TH	0521 5.5	1119 0.8	1740 5.7	2339 0.8
10 F	0603 5.5	1201 0.8	1822 5.5	
11 SA	0020 1.0	0642 5.4	1241 1.0	1903 5.3
12 SU	0058 1.2	0720 5.1	1321 1.2	1943 5.0
13 M	0137 1.4	0757 4.9	1401 1.5	2025 4.6
14 TU	0218 1.7	0839 4.6	1446 1.8	2117 4.3
15 W	0305 2.0	0936 4.3	1542 2.1	2229 4.1 ◐
16 TH	0406 2.3	1058 4.2	1658 2.3	2353 4.1
17 F	0524 2.4	1225 4.2	1820 2.3	
18 SA	0107 4.2	0641 2.4	1334 4.3	1927 2.1
19 SU	0202 4.4	0743 2.2	1425 4.5	2017 1.9
20 M	0245 4.6	0831 1.9	1505 4.8	2059 1.7
21 TU	0321 4.8	0912 1.7	1539 5.0	2136 1.5
22 W	0354 5.0	0950 1.5	1612 5.1	2211 1.4
23 TH	0427 5.1	1026 1.4	1645 5.2	2246 1.3 ●
24 F	0500 5.2	1101 1.3	1718 5.3	2320 1.3
25 SA	0534 5.3	1137 1.2	1753 5.3	2355 1.3
26 SU	0609 5.3	1213 1.2	1829 5.2	
27 M	0031 1.3	0648 5.2	1251 1.3	1909 5.1
28 TU	0109 1.5	0731 5.1	1331 1.4	1955 4.9
29 W	0151 1.6	0821 4.9	1417 1.6	2051 4.6
30 TH	0241 1.8	0921 4.6	1513 1.8	2201 4.5
31 F	0343 2.0	1036 4.6	1624 1.9	2329 4.4 ◐

NOVEMBER

Day	Time m	Time m	Time m	Time m
1 SA	0500 2.1	1200 4.7	1743 1.9	
2 SU	0049 4.6	0619 2.0	1313 4.9	1859 1.7
3 M	0152 4.8	0731 1.7	1413 5.1	2004 1.5
4 TU	0246 5.1	0832 1.5	1506 5.3	2100 1.3
5 W	0334 5.3	0925 1.2	1554 5.5	2149 1.1
6 TH	0418 5.4	1013 1.1	1638 5.5	2234 1.0 ○
7 F	0500 5.4	1101 1.0	1721 5.5	2316 1.1
8 SA	0540 5.4	1140 1.0	1802 5.4	2356 1.1
9 SU	0619 5.3	1220 1.1	1841 5.2	
10 M	0034 1.3	0656 5.2	1259 1.3	1919 5.0
11 TU	0112 1.5	0732 5.0	1338 1.6	1958 4.7
12 W	0151 1.7	0812 4.7	1419 1.8	2044 4.5
13 TH	0234 2.0	0859 4.5	1507 2.1	2142 4.3
14 F	0325 2.2	1002 4.3	1607 2.3	2253 4.1 ◐
15 SA	0430 2.4	1117 4.2	1719 2.3	
16 SU	0005 4.2	0542 2.4	1230 4.3	1829 2.3
17 M	0108 4.3	0648 2.3	1333 4.4	1927 2.1
18 TU	0200 4.5	0743 2.1	1423 4.6	2015 1.9
19 W	0243 4.7	0831 1.9	1505 4.8	2058 1.7
20 TH	0322 4.9	0915 1.7	1543 5.0	2138 1.5
21 F	0359 5.1	0956 1.5	1621 5.2	2216 1.4
22 SA	0437 5.3	1036 1.3	1659 5.3	2255 1.3 ●
23 SU	0516 5.4	1116 1.2	1738 5.3	2335 1.2
24 M	0556 5.4	1157 1.2	1819 5.3	
25 TU	0016 1.3	0639 5.4	1240 1.2	1903 5.2
26 W	0058 1.3	0725 5.3	1324 1.3	1951 5.0
27 TH	0144 1.5	0816 5.1	1412 1.4	2046 4.8
28 F	0235 1.7	0914 5.0	1505 1.6	2152 4.6
29 SA	0333 1.8	1022 4.8	1608 1.7	2311 4.6 ◐
30 SU	0441 1.9	1138 4.6	1719 1.8	

DECEMBER

Day	Time m	Time m	Time m	Time m
1 M	0026 4.6	0554 1.9	1249 4.8	1832 1.8
2 TU	0130 4.8	0705 1.8	1353 5.0	1940 1.6
3 W	0227 4.9	0809 1.6	1449 5.1	2038 1.5
4 TH	0317 5.1	0905 1.4	1539 5.2	2129 1.4
5 F	0401 5.2	0955 1.3	1624 5.2	2215 1.3
6 SA	0443 5.3	1041 1.2	1706 5.2	2257 1.3
7 SU	0522 5.3	1123 1.2	1745 5.2	2336 1.3
8 M	0600 5.3	1202 1.3	1823 5.1	
9 TU	0014 1.4	0637 5.2	1240 1.4	1859 5.0
10 W	0050 1.5	0712 5.0	1317 1.5	1934 4.8
11 TH	0127 1.6	0747 4.9	1355 1.7	2013 4.6
12 F	0206 1.8	0827 4.7	1435 1.9	2057 4.4
13 SA	0248 2.0	0914 4.5	1521 2.1	2152 4.3
14 SU	0338 2.2	1012 4.4	1616 2.2	2256 4.2
15 M	0439 2.3	1119 4.3	1722 2.3	
16 TU	0003 4.2	0546 2.3	1228 4.3	1828 2.2
17 W	0106 4.4	0650 2.2	1332 4.4	1926 2.1
18 TH	0201 4.6	0747 2.0	1427 4.6	2018 1.9
19 F	0249 4.8	0839 1.8	1515 4.8	2105 1.7
20 SA	0334 5.0	0927 1.6	1559 5.0	2151 1.5
21 SU	0417 5.2	1014 1.3	1642 5.2	2235 1.3
22 M	0500 5.4	1059 1.2	1726 5.3	2320 1.2 ●
23 TU	0545 5.5	1145 1.0	1810 5.4	
24 W	0005 1.1	0630 5.6	1230 1.0	1856 5.3
25 TH	0050 1.1	0718 5.5	1316 1.0	1944 5.2
26 F	0136 1.2	0808 5.4	1402 1.1	2036 5.0
27 SA	0225 1.4	0901 5.2	1452 1.3	2135 4.8
28 SU	0318 1.5	1001 5.0	1547 1.5	2242 4.6 ◐
29 M	0418 1.7	1110 4.8	1651 1.7	2356 4.6
30 TU	0526 1.8	1222 4.7	1802 1.9	
31 W	0106 4.6	0638 1.8	1332 4.7	1914 1.8

Chart Datum: 2·83 metres below IGN Datum
HAT is 6·1 metres above Chart Datum

TIDES

Practical Boat Owner

Subscribe to Britain's best-selling boating magazine today!

From just £19.99

Practical Boat Owner is packed with expert advice to help you make the most of your boating. Every four weeks PBO is crammed with: Tests on the latest boats and gear • Great money-saving ideas • Tips and techniques for better boating • Inspiring cruising experiences.

Don't miss your copy – subscribe today!

2 easy ways to subscribe
Visit: www.pbo.co.uk/subs
Call: +44 (0)844 848 0848 and quote code: 15Y
Lines open 7 days a week from 8am to 9pm (UK time)

Practical Boat Owner digital edition available from **www.pbo.co.uk/digital**

PBO IS ALSO AVAILABLE ON THESE DIGITAL PLATFORMS

   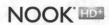